ROUTLEDGE ENCYCLOPEDIA
OF INTERPRETING STUDIES

The *Routledge Encyclopedia of Interpreting Studies* is the authoritative reference for anyone with an academic or professional interest in interpreting.

Drawing on the expertise of an international team of specialist contributors, this single-volume reference presents the state of the art in interpreting studies in a much more fine-grained matrix of entries than has ever been seen before.

For the first time, all key issues and concepts in interpreting studies are brought together and covered systematically and in a structured and accessible format.

With entries alphabetically arranged and extensively cross-referenced, this text combines clarity with scholarly accuracy and depth, defining and discussing key terms in context to ensure maximum understanding and ease of use.

Practical and unique, the *Encyclopedia of Interpreting Studies* presents a genuinely comprehensive overview of the fast growing and increasingly diverse field of interpreting studies.

Franz Pöchhacker is Associate Professor of Interpreting Studies in the Center for Translation Studies at the University of Vienna. His professional background is in conference interpreting, and he has worked freelance in conference and media settings since the late 1980s. He has lectured widely and published some 100 papers and reviews. He is the author of the textbook *Introducing Interpreting Studies* (Routledge 2004/2016), Associate Editor of the 'Benjamins Translation Library' series and co-editor of *Interpreting: International Journal of Research and Practice in Interpreting* (John Benjamins).

ROUTLEDGE ENCYCLOPEDIA OF INTERPRETING STUDIES

Edited by
Franz Pöchhacker

Associate Editor:
Nadja Grbić

Consultant Editors:
Peter Mead and Robin Setton

LONDON AND NEW YORK

First published 2015 by Routledge

2 Park Square, Milton Park, Abingdon, Oxfordshire OX14 4RN
52 Vanderbilt Avenue, New York, NY 10017

Routledge is an imprint of the Taylor & Francis Group, an informa business

First issuedinpaperback2019

Copyright© 2015 Franz Pöchhacker

British Library Cataloguing in Publication Data
A catalogue record for this book is available from the British Library

Library of Congress Cataloging in Publication Data
A catalog record for this book has been requested

ISBN: 978-0-415-63432-8 (hbk)
ISBN: 978-0-367-86726-3 (pbk)

Typeset in Times New Roman
by Taylor & Francis Books

To Miriam Shlesinger
who would have loved
to live to see this book

TABLE OF CONTENTS

ACKNOWLEDGEMENTS

This Encyclopedia is first and foremost a collective endeavor, and my sincere thanks go to all 139 colleagues in the interpreting studies community and specialists in related disciplines who agreed to contribute, supplied their drafts on time, and then patiently waited for and graciously responded to the editor's requests for revision. For most of the entries, the load of the editorial review process was shared by Nadja Grbić, whose deep involvement as Associate Editor has, in many ways, been crucial to bringing this project to fruition. Critical input also came from Robin Setton, who agreed to support me as Consultant Editor even when he was overwhelmed with work on a magnum opus of his own. Very special thanks are due to Peter Mead, whose role as Consultant Editor went far beyond providing input on entries in his fields of expertise. His thorough review of every single article from a style editor's point of view, while accommodating the linguistic diversity which is so appropriate to a volume like this, resolved countless problems of expression to the authors' (and the reader's) advantage.

A perfect complement to the editorial team was Samantha Vale Noya, the Associate Editor in charge of the project at Routledge, whose competent support throughout the genesis of this project is gratefully acknowledged. I am also grateful to Isja Conen, her counterpart at John Benjamins, for lending a hand with software for compiling the index.

A warm word of thanks also to all those friends and colleagues whose company I consciously neglected during more than a year of intense editing work. I hope we can pick up where we left off.

Much more than I can express here and say thank you for has come from Doris, who has given me encouragement and strength throughout, and has brightened my life with her love.

FRANZ PÖCHHACKER
3 March 2015

INTRODUCTION

On what we know about interpreting, and how

As often happens with invited speakers, who are introduced by well-briefed chairpersons as needing no introduction, and then lengthily introduced after all, it could be said that this book needs no introduction. Most people would expect a volume with the title "Encyclopedia of Interpreting Studies" simply to give access to the knowledge available about interpreting, as developed in the academic field of study which gives the book its name. Indeed, the less familiar prospective readers are with this discipline, the more likely they are to skip this Introduction. With little need to take an interest in "The Making of...", they will assume that this Encyclopedia contains articles on the most relevant topics, written by those who know the subject best, and presented in the most appropriate form. Readers with more knowledge about the field, in contrast, may well have a greater interest in the rationale underlying this particular presentation of the state of the art in interpreting studies. The questions they might be asking about how this volume has been put together will be addressed here under a number of why-questions about the book and its contents, contributors, features and structure. This will not so much make the volume more usable (by offering guidance in a "how to use this book" format), as enhance its value for the scholarly community by making explicit some of the main choices and principles shaping its content, allowing fellow scholars to understand – and question – authorial and, in particular, editorial decisions, and thus reflect on how this account of their field of study might possibly be improved.

Why this book?

This Encyclopedia goes back to an idea in one of the relevant departments at Routledge to publish a reference volume similar to that edited for translation studies by Mona Baker (Baker 1998; Baker & Saldanha 2009). An invitation to take interest in such a project reached me on 1 July 2011, and drew considerable skepticism. Admittedly, the idea of a 'companion volume' had worked very well twice before, and given our field both *The Interpreting Studies Reader* (Pöchhacker & Shlesinger 2002) and the 2004 textbook analogous to Jeremy Munday's (2001) *Introducing Translation Studies*, now in its third edition. The idea of a parallel encyclopedia project seemed more problematic, however, given the coverage of interpreting in the *Routledge Encyclopedia of Translation Studies*, under such headwords as 'community interpreting', 'conference interpreting', 'court interpreting', 'dialogue interpreting', 'interpretive approach', 'relay' and 'signed language interpreting'. Moreover, comprehensive reference volumes on translation and interpreting studies had been prepared by other publishers, including, first and foremost, the Benjamins *Handbook of Translation Studies* (Gambier & van Doorslaer 2010, 2011, 2012, 2013), the Wiley *Encyclopedia of Applied Linguistics* (Chapelle 2013), with a section on translation and interpreting coordinated by

Claudia Angelelli, Brian Baer and Nadja Grbić, and the more compact *Oxford Handbook of Translation Studies* (Malmkjær & Windle 2011) – not to mention Routledge's own *Handbook of Translation Studies* (Millán & Bartrina 2013), in preparation at the time. With interpreting types and topics broadly represented in these volumes, usually by leading authors in the field of interpreting studies, it seemed doubtful, at best, whether there would be room, or need, for yet another reference volume on interpreting (studies).

The aim of offering added value was therefore the principal motivation behind my proposal for this book, submitted to the publisher, not without hesitation, in late 2011. Based on favorable responses from four reviewers, the project went ahead and a contract was signed – before I learned of parallel plans for *The Routledge Handbook of Interpreting* (Mikkelson & Jourdenais 2015). All the more reason to make this Encyclopedia a unique resource, with qualities not found in other reference volumes in the field of translation and interpreting studies.

The rationale for this volume, shared by most of the titles mentioned above, is to take stock of existing knowledge about interpreting. Efforts to do so were made on other occasions, and in other forms, in the past; examples include the 1994 Turku Conference on "Interpreting: What Do We Know, and How?", alluded to in the title of this Introduction, and the 2006 volume of *Linguistica Antverpiensia* entitled *Taking Stock: Research and Methodology in Community Interpreting* (Hertog & van der Veer 2006). The shift of emphasis toward community interpreting, and the fact that the proceedings volume of the Turku Conference (Gambier et al. 1997) ended up with 'conference interpreting' in its title, despite other types of interpreting being in evidence at that event, point to the fundamental objective of the present volume – that is, to achieve a single, detailed survey of the field that would include the various domains and research traditions of interpreting not only side by side, but in an *integrated* manner. This has major implications for the structure of the book as a whole, and for the content of individual articles. What it essentially means is that every article reflects an effort by its author to cover the headword, where applicable, *across domains, modes and settings*. Notwithstanding the often uneven pattern of research on any given topic, contributors have been asked to look beyond the type and modality of interpreting they may be specialized in, and consider the relevance of their topic in other areas of work.

The aim of making this volume *comprehensive* would be a more evident aspiration for an encyclopedia. In practical terms, comprehensive coverage is attempted in this book not only by ensuring breadth (e.g. by including less familiar topics) but also, and especially, by achieving depth. This depth of coverage relates to the choice of headwords, as explained in greater detail below. Rather than make do with the basic typological points of reference found in comparable publications (e.g. Baker & Saldanha 2009), the present volume has a *fine-grained* conceptual structure that allows the reader to zoom in and out, as it were, from familiar central categories. It is thus the goal of providing an integrated – that is, coherent and detailed – account of the topic, through a multi-layered arrangement of headwords in a differentiated conceptual structure, that made this Encyclopedia a project worth undertaking. If the volume meets its intended purpose of providing a coherent *web of knowledge* (or a 'hypertext', in the original sense of the term), the rationale for this Encyclopedia will have been fully achieved.

Why this structure?

The *macro-structure* of this volume corresponds to its underlying design, as well as the conventions of the genre. Unlike a handbook, an encyclopedia could be expected to be structured around headwords in *alphabetical* order. This is in fact the case for this Encyclopedia, though recent examples in the field of translation and interpreting studies include not only handbooks with contents in alphabetical order (e.g. Angelelli & Baer 2015) but also encyclopedias with a thematic arrangement of contents (e.g. Chan 2015).

If the basic structure of this Encyclopedia is more conventional, with a single main section containing all entries from A to Z, so is its medium of presentation in the form of a printed book – for the time being. This makes it somewhat more difficult for readers to take advantage of the hypertext design and quickly jump to related entries by following the *embedded cross-references* in the text, which appear in SMALL CAPITALS – once, when the headword referred to first occurs in a given article.

A future online version of the Encyclopedia would eliminate this inconvenience and make all content available as the web of interrelated knowledge as which this book has been designed. In either format, though, readers without a thorough understanding of the field will benefit from an account of the thematic and conceptual structure that is lacking in any alphabetical arrangement. This is provided in the book in two ways. First, the alphabetical list of contents is followed by a 'thematic outline of entries', in which an attempt has been made to assign the headwords to a set of broad thematic categories, such as 'History', 'Profession', 'Settings' and 'Methodology'. Admittedly, many headwords might well be placed into more than one category, so that the thematic outline must clearly fall short of a taxonomy, or a definitive 'mapping' (van Doorslaer 2009) of knowledge components in interpreting studies. This is addressed by a second feature, in the *micro-structure* of the Encyclopedia: the indication of key *conceptual links* underneath the headword. Rather than a list of related topics for 'further reading', these links to other articles at the 'head' of the entry represent the most immediate conceptual relations for a given headword, at three different levels: an upward arrow ($\uparrow$) points to a closely related article on a headword that represents a superordinate concept, such as '$\uparrow$ Strategies' in the entry on 'Anticipation'; a horizontal arrow ($\rightarrow$) indicates a closely related conceptual link, such as '$\rightarrow$ Quality' in the entry on 'Competence'; and a downward arrow ($\downarrow$) points to key subordinate concepts, such as '$\downarrow$ Video relay service' in the entry on 'Remote interpreting'. Conceptual relations are indicated only for the level immediately above or below. For instance, the upward link from 'Simultaneous with text' is only to 'Simultaneous interpreting' and not to the superordinate concept of 'Modes'; and the downward link from 'Quality' is only to 'Quality criteria' (among others), and not to subordinate concepts like 'Accuracy', 'Cohesion', 'Fluency', 'Intonation' or 'Voice quality'. In this case, in particular, but also in many others, the conceptual links provided may well be questioned; the complexity of many key concepts and the nature of categorization processes do not allow a more Cartesian formalization. Nevertheless, the reader should find it possible, in many cases, to develop a sense of conceptual relations even before beginning to read the article itself, which will then of course make the conceptual status of the headword more explicit in the form of definitions and theoretical analysis.

A more conventional, if not standard, micro-structural feature found in this book, apart from the embedded cross-references mentioned earlier, is the use of in-text references pointing to relevant sources. These are listed in a single collective bibliography at the end of the volume – a part of the macro-structure of this Encyclopedia which should prove highly valuable, in its own right, as a bibliography of reference in interpreting studies.

A feature that some readers will find missing is illustrations. The editorial decision not to include figures, tables or photographs may, indeed, be regretted. However, remedying this lack of graphic information would have required incommensurate effort to resolve issues of rights and reproduction, quite apart from questions of balance and epistemological needs. A larger editorial team may well be able to produce an 'illustrated encyclopedia' of interpreting studies in the future; the present text should serve well as a foundation.

Why these headwords?

Over and above issues of design and structure, the choice of headwords to be covered in the articles of the Encyclopedia is undoubtedly crucial. The procedure adopted for compiling the list of headwords can be characterized as a pragmatic data-driven ('bottom-up') approach. The original book proposal included a list of some 300 headwords, identified on the basis of the subject index in *Introducing Interpreting Studies* (Pöchhacker 2004a). Once the project was under way and Nadja Grbić had been recruited as Consultant Editor, the draft list was reviewed and checked against lists of entries in comparable reference publications and other bibliographic resources, with additional input from Consultant Editor Robin Setton.

The crucial next step of deciding which of the headwords should be treated in the form of full articles, and which by way of referral to other entries, was accomplished by screening the LIDOC bibliographic database maintained at the University of Graz for relevant publications, using titles and keyword information. (It was in this painstaking process that Nadja Grbić, with her mastery in querying that database, 'earned' her status of Associate Editor early on.) Thus, the decision to have a full entry on a given topic was not based on top-down mapping, as described by van Doorslaer (2009) for the keyword scheme in the Benjamins *Translation Studies Bibliography*; rather, it was based on the joint assessment of the published research output on the headword in question. While the Benjamins *Translation Studies Bibliography* also proved highly instrumental in this process, reliance on the LIDOC database was deemed advisable because of its particularly thorough coverage of publications on signed language interpreting. The goal was to establish whether there was a 'critical mass' of publications on a given topic, in the sense of a more or less coherent line of work, with studies building on one another, or creating new insights in a dialectical fashion. Even so, decisions were not based on purely quantitative parameters; a number of qualitative considerations (such as the type and medium of publication) were also taken into account in deciding whether to include a topic as a headword treated in a full article.

Editorial choices regarding the headwords concern form as well as content, and it proved unavoidable in some cases to impose one preference or another. Examples include opting for a full entry on 'Community interpreting' and listing its synonym 'public service interpreting' as a 'blind' (referring) entry, or preferring 'Dialogue interpreting' over 'liaison interpreting' and 'Time lag' over 'ear–voice span'. Similar choices concern lexical alternatives such as 'Signed language interpreting' vs. 'sign language interpreting' and 'Courtroom interpreting' vs. 'court interpreting', with the terminological rationale in the latter case being explained in the article.

This process led to a 'headword list' envisaging 297 entries (213 with full articles and 84 blind entries) at the start of the project. This served as the basis for recruiting contributors, who received the headword list as well as a description of the Encyclopedia's design. The ensuing collaborative process produced a small number of changes to the headword list. Some of these were due to preferences on the part of the contributing authors, and others were additions, often in the form of 'spin-offs' from larger entries by the same author – for example, in the case of 'Neutrality' as a separate subordinate entry relating to 'Ethics', or 'Footing' as a separate entry under 'Participation framework'. The final headword count thus comes to an even 300, 221 of which are entries in the form of full articles.

Why these authors?

Compared to the process of choosing headwords for inclusion and full coverage, deciding whom to invite as contributors proved relatively easy. As a collective effort by and for the interpreting studies community, this Encyclopedia is written primarily by authors who would indicate 'interpreting studies' as their main area of research interest or disciplinary affiliation. The fact that the interpreting studies community is not excessively large, and that research areas tend to be increasingly specialized, implied many rather obvious choices, and practically everyone I approached responded favorably, and often even with enthusiasm. It can thus be noted with some pride that the 139 contributors from some 30 different countries include most of the *leading scholars* in this field, from its most senior representatives to colleagues who have only recently completed their doctoral research.

Nevertheless, the list of contributors goes beyond interpreting scholars in the strict sense and includes authors doing research on interpreting in other disciplinary frameworks. This includes, in particular, experts in fields like history (such as Rachel Mairs and Natalie Rothman), cognitive psychology and psycholinguistics (such as Teresa Bajo and Annette de Groot) and qualitative social research (such as Ros Edwards).

With either type of contributor, the aim was to have topics covered by authors particularly well placed to do so on the basis of their specialist knowledge and experience. In most cases, this status is based on major contributions made to the state of the art by the authors concerned. The fact that these contributors thus describe, in large measure, their own work, or at least the line of work to which they have contributed, should ensure that the various entries in the Encyclopedia offer an authoritative treatment of the topics covered. A potential drawback could be seen in the possible lack of detachment or critical perspective, but this is, most crucially perhaps, where the role of the editor comes in, and every effort has indeed been made throughout the painstaking editing process to ensure that the knowledge (re)presented in every article of this Encyclopedia is as balanced and comprehensive as possible.

Why these sources?

The goals of balance and comprehensiveness, as well as integration across professional domains, language modalities and institutional settings, are reflected in the choice of sources referred to in the individual articles. As with some of the issues of content alluded to above, decisions regarding references were shaped by often considerable editorial 'bullying'. Many authors would have preferred to give more references, but agreed to accept editorial suggestions that mainly related to the requirement for the bibliography to be as *relevant* and *accessible* as possible.

The assumption underlying this referencing approach is that the sources given in the text of the article are of particular relevance to a full understanding of the topic, in ways that become clear from how the in-text references are presented. This also implies that there is no need for a separate indication of references 'for further reading'. Moreover, the multiple embedded cross-references often obviate the need for further explicit in-text references (which are also omitted where the reference would be to the author who contributed the article on the cross-referenced headword). Compared to the more extensive referencing common in research articles and papers, the use of sources – or even literal quotations – in the Encyclopedia articles may thus, in most cases, appear relatively sparse. The fact that the collective bibliography at the end of the book nevertheless runs to over 2,100 entries should be sufficient proof that the knowledge presented in this volume is adequately documented, aside from vindicating the editor's plea for economy in the list of references.

The principle that references should be as accessible as possible was even more difficult to implement. The issues here relate to the language and the type of publication. With English as the language of this Encyclopedia, and the most common lingua franca of the field it covers, preference has been given, wherever possible, to published sources in that language. Aside from the vexed issue of linguistic hegemony, which is by no means specific to interpreting studies, opting for English also clashes, in part, with the goal of balanced and comprehensive coverage. Certain topics are treated more extensively in works published in one language or another, and yet, giving greater attention to such sources would make access difficult for many readers. Publications in German or Spanish, as well as in the major Asian languages, are obvious cases in point. This quandary has been hard to resolve in a principled manner, and much must be put down to the editor's discretion. The same applies to accessibility in terms of the type or medium of publication. The aim of making this Encyclopedia a reliable source of research-based knowledge would suggest giving preference to publications in peer-reviewed international journals, and this has in fact been done wherever possible. Nevertheless, publications in the relatively young discipline of interpreting studies, with its close links to concerns of the interpreting profession, are highly diverse, and relevant sources include documents on websites of professional associations and university journals, as well as unpublished theses and dissertations (often in languages other than English). Though the declared preference is for works published (in print, if possible) in 'mainstream' scientific media, numerous exceptions can be found.

With regard to references, as with other aspects of this Encyclopedia, absolute consistency has been impossible to achieve, if it is feasible at all in a project of this scope. What has been achieved, though, is the first ever comprehensive presentation of the state of the art in interpreting studies. This is above all a collective task, and it has been a privilege to steer this undertaking in the role of editor. No less vital has been the intensive collaboration with the other three members of the editorial team – Consultant Editors Peter Mead and Robin Setton and, in particular, Associate Editor Nadja Grbić. Their input and support provides the answer to the final why-question in this Introduction – that is, why the interpreting studies community and interested readers in other fields and walks of life now have access, in a single volume, to an impressive range of knowledge and insights about the multifaceted phenomenon of interpreting.

FRANZ PÖCHHACKER
3 March 2015

LIST OF ARTICLES AND AUTHORS

LIST OF CONTRIBUTORS

Barbara Ahrens Cologne University of Applied Sciences, Germany

Michaela Albl-Mikasa Zurich University of Applied Sciences, Winterthur, Switzerland

Dörte Andres University of Mainz, Germersheim, Germany

Claudia V. Angelelli Heriot-Watt University, Edinburgh, UK

Rachele Antonini Università di Bologna a Forlì, Italy

Jesús Baigorri-Jalón Universidad de Salamanca, Spain

María Teresa Bajo Universidad de Granada, Spain

Mária Bakti University of Szeged, Hungary

Claudio Baraldi Università di Modena e Reggio Emilia, Italy

Magdalena Bartłomiejczyk University of Silesia, Sosnowiec, Poland

Morven Beaton Cologne University of Applied Sciences, Germany

Martina Behr University of Mainz, Germersheim, Germany

Claudio Bendazzoli Università di Torino, Italy

Julie Boéri Universitat Pompeu Fabra, Barcelona, Spain

Hanneke Bot Utrecht, Netherlands

Sabine Braun University of Surrey, Guildford, UK

Jeremy L. Brunson Gallaudet University, Washington, DC, USA

Alev Bulut Istanbul University, Turkey

Svetlana Burlyay Moscow State Linguistic University, Russian Federation

Ivana Čeňková Charles University in Prague, Czech Republic

Catherine Chabasse University of Mainz, Germersheim, Germany

Andrew K. F. Cheung Hong Kong Polytechnic University, China

Ingrid K. Christoffels Leiden University, Netherlands

Libby Clark Charles Sturt University, Australia

Ángela Collados Aís Universidad de Granada, Spain

Eugenia Dal Fovo Università degli Studi di Trieste, Italy

Helle V. Dam Aarhus University, Denmark

Elena Davitti University of Surrey, Guildford, UK

Annette M. B. de Groot University of Amsterdam, Netherlands

Robyn Dean University of Rochester Medical Center, USA

Jean Delisle University of Ottawa, Canada

Ebru Diriker Boğaziçi University, Istanbul, Turkey

Rosalind Edwards University of Southampton, UK

Caterina Falbo Università degli Studi di Trieste, Italy

Isabel Galhano Rodrigues Universidade do Porto, Portugal

Nikolay Garbovskiy Lomonosov Moscow State University, Russian Federation

Olalla García Becerra Universidad de Granada, Spain

Giuliana Garzone Università degli Studi di Milano, Italy

Laura Gavioli Università di Modena e Reggio Emilia, Italy

Adolfo Gentile University of Queensland, Brisbane, Australia

Daniel Gile Université Sorbonne Nouvelle – Paris 3, France

Nadja Grbić University of Graz, Austria

Patrice Guex Université de Lausanne, Switzerland

Ewa Gumul University of Silesia, Sosnowiec, Poland

Sandra B. Hale University of New South Wales, Sydney, Australia

Erik Hertog KU Leuven, Belgium

Adelina Hild University of Leicester, UK

Ildikó Horváth Eötvös Loránd University, Budapest, Hungary

Elaine Hsieh University of Oklahoma, USA

Emilia Iglesias Fernández Universidad de Granada, Spain

Moira Inghilleri University of Massachusetts, Amherst, USA

Susanne Jekat Zurich University of Applied Sciences, Winterthur, Switzerland

Mira Kadrić University of Vienna, Austria

Sylvia Kalina Cologne University of Applied Sciences, Germany

Frances Karttunen University of Texas at Austin, USA

Francine Kaufmann Bar-Ilan University, Ramat Gan, Israel

Nataly Kelly Nashua, NH, USA

Kim Nam Hui Kyungpook National University, South Korea

Leong Ko University of Queensland, Brisbane, Australia

Turgay Kurultay Istanbul University, Turkey

Pauline Lane Anglia Ruskin University, Chelmsford, UK

Eike Lauterbach Leipzig, Germany

Yvan Leanza Université Laval, Québec, Canada

Marianne Lederer Université Sorbonne Nouvelle – Paris 3, France

Lorraine Leeson Trinity College Dublin, Ireland

Konstantina Liontou Ioannina, Greece

Minhua Liu Middlebury Institute of International Studies at Monterey, USA

Rachel Lung Lingnan University, Hong Kong, China

Rachel Mairs University of Reading, UK

Karen Malcolm Vancouver, BC, Canada

Aída Martínez-Gómez City University of New York, USA

Katrijn Maryns Ghent University, Belgium

Carlo Marzocchi General Secretariat of the Council of the EU, Brussels, Belgium

Ian Mason Heriot-Watt University, Edinburgh, UK

Igor Matyushin Moscow State Linguistic University, Russian Federation

Peter Mead NATO Defense College, Rome, Italy

Raffaela Merlini Università di Macerata, Italy

Claudia Monacelli Università degli Studi Internazionali di Roma, Italy

Ruth Morris Bar-Ilan University, Ramat Gan, Israel

Barbara Moser-Mercer Université de Genève, Switzerland

Ricardo Muñoz Martín Universidad de Las Palmas de Gran Canaria, Spain

Jemina Napier Heriot-Watt University, Edinburgh, UK

Natacha S. A. Niemants Università di Modena e Reggio Emilia, Italy

Uldis Ozolins University of Western Sydney, Australia

Presentación Padilla Universidad de Granada, Spain

Carol J. Patrie Annapolis, MD, USA

Gracie Peng Tunghai University, Taichung, Taiwan

Isabelle Perez Heriot-Watt University, Edinburgh, UK

Jessica Pérez-Luzardo Universidad de Las Palmas de Gran Canaria, Spain

Franz Pöchhacker University of Vienna, Austria

Nike K. Pokorn University of Ljubljana, Slovenia

Sonja Pöllabauer University of Graz, Austria

Macarena Pradas Macías Universidad de Granada, Spain

Erich Prunč University of Graz, Austria

Karin Reithofer University of Vienna, Austria

Sylvi Rennert University of Vienna, Austria

Alessandra Riccardi Università degli Studi di Trieste, Italy

Roda P. Roberts University of Ottawa, Canada

Siobhán Rocks University of Leeds, UK

Rhéa Rocque Université Laval, Québec, Canada

Pablo Romero-Fresco University of Roehampton, UK

E. Natalie Rothman University of Toronto Scarborough, Canada

Cynthia B. Roy Gallaudet University, Washington, DC, USA

Mariachiara Russo Università di Bologna a Forlì, Italy

Anja Rütten Cologne University of Applied Sciences, Germany

Heidemarie Salevsky Berlin, Germany

Annalisa Sandrelli Università degli Studi Internazionali di Roma, Italy

David B. Sawyer University of Maryland, College Park, MD, USA

Tomina Schwenke Emory University School of Medicine, Atlanta, GA, USA

Kilian G. Seeber Université de Genève, Switzerland

Robin Setton Paris, France

Sherry Shaw University of North Florida, Jacksonville, FL, USA

Yael Shlesinger Levinsky College of Education, Tel Aviv, Israel

Pascal Singy Université de Lausanne, Switzerland

Helen Slatyer Macquarie University, Sydney, Australia

Michael Stinson National Technical Institute for the Deaf, Rochester, NY, USA

Christopher Stone Gallaudet University, Washington, DC, USA

Daniel B. Swartz Cherry Hill, NJ, USA

Kayoko Takeda Rikkyo University, Tokyo, Japan

Masato Takimoto Ryukoku University, Kyoto, Japan

Christopher Thiéry Université Sorbonne Nouvelle – Paris 3, France

Anna C. Ticca University of Bern, Switzerland

Liisa Tiittula University of Helsinki, Finland

Šárka Timarová Leuven, Belgium

Rebecca Tipton University of Manchester, UK

Elisabet Tiselius Stockholm University, Sweden

Rachel Tribe University of East London, UK

Małgorzata Tryuk University of Warsaw, Poland

Chikako Tsuruta Tokyo University of Foreign Studies, Japan

Anna-Riitta Vuorikoski Tampere, Finland

Cecilia Wadensjö Stockholm University, Sweden

Kim Wallmach University of the Witwatersrand, Johannesburg, South Africa

Anne-Marie Widlund-Fantini Paris, France

Elizabeth A. Winston TIEM Center, Loveland, CO, USA

Michaela Wolf University of Graz, Austria

Dmitry Yermolovich Moscow State Linguistic University, Russian Federation

Elena Zagar Galvão Universidade de Coimbra, Portugal

Klaus Ziegler SDI Munich, Germany

Cornelia Zwischenberger University of Vienna, Austria

THEMATIC OUTLINE OF ENTRIES

Theoretical Concepts and Approaches

Activist approach
Bilingualism
Bilingualism (societal)
Child language brokering
Cognitive approaches
Demand control schema
Discourse analytical approaches
Effort Models
Expertise
Face
Fidelity
Footing
Gender
Habitus
Interdisciplinarity
Interpreting
Interpretive Theory

Language policy
Linguistic/pragmatic approaches
Mediation
Models
Modes
Natural translation/interpreting
Neuroscience approaches
Norms
Paradigms
Participation framework
Psycholinguistic approaches
Relevance theory
Settings
Sociolinguistic approaches
Sociological approaches
Transcoding

History

Africa
Australia
Canada
China
Concentration camps
Dostert
Dragomans
Egypt
Habsburg Monarchy
Herbert
History
Japan

Jeunes de langues
Jewish tradition
Korea
Malinche
Mantoux
Nuremberg Trial
Rome
Russia
Sacajawea
Spain
Velleman

Modes

Consecutive interpreting
Dialogue interpreting
Directionality
Fingerspelling
Interpreting for deafblind persons
Note-taking
Relay interpreting

Respeaking
Sight interpreting/translation
Signed language interpreting
Simultaneous interpreting
Simultaneous with text
Speech-to-text interpreting
Transliteration

Settings

Asylum settings
Business interpreting
Community interpreting
Conference interpreting
Conflict zones
Courtroom interpreting
Diplomatic interpreting
Disaster relief interpreting
Educational interpreting
Film interpreting
Healthcare interpreting
Legal interpreting
Media interpreting
Mental health settings

Military interpreting
News interpreting
Parliamentary settings
Pediatric settings
Police settings
Prison settings
Psychotherapy
Religious settings
Speech pathology
Talk show interpreting
Theater interpreting
Tribunal interpreting
Truth and reconciliation commission

Process

Anticipation
Cognitive load
Competence
Comprehension
Compression
Explicitation
Inferencing
Input variables

Memory
Mental representation
Numbers
Segmentation
Strategies
Time lag
Working memory

Product and Performance

Accent
Accuracy
Body language
Coherence
Cohesion
Communicative effect
Discourse management

Error analysis
Fluency
Gaze
Gesture
Hypertext
Interference
Intonation

Expert–novice paradigm
Eye tracking
Interviews
Methodology

Mixed methods research
Retrospective protocols
Survey research
Transcription

Interpreting Studies as a Discipline

Chernov
CIRIN Bulletin
Critical Link
Gerver
International Journal of Interpreter Education
Interpreters' Newsletter
Interpreting
Interpreting studies

Journal of Interpretation
Paris School
Seleskovitch
Shlesinger
Soviet School
Trieste Symposium
Venice Symposium

ACCENT

↑ INPUT VARIABLES, ↑ QUALITY CRITERIA

Accent is defined in (socio)linguistics as a manner of pronunciation specific to a given region, or to an ethnic or social group. Speakers using an acquired (foreign) language may carry over the phonetic patterns of their native language, giving rise to a non-native or 'foreign' accent, which is often understood to involve not only pronunciation (i.e. phonetic substitutions, deletions and distortions) but also non-native stress, rhythm and INTONATION. While both unfamiliar native accents and non-native accents may pose challenges in interpreter-mediated communication, most research attention is focused on non-native speech – mainly on the part of original speakers, but also on the part of interpreters themselves. In the former case, non-native accent is discussed as one of the INPUT VARIABLES in the interpreting process, while in the latter it relates to the QUALITY of the interpreter's output or performance.

Accent as an input variable

Among the input variables likely to affect an interpreter's performance, a speaker's unfamiliar accent is generally rated as one of the potentially most problematic factors, in both CONFERENCE INTERPRETING (Mackintosh 2002) and COMMUNITY INTERPRETING settings (Valero-Garcés 2003). The assumption is that non-native accents may increase the processing resources required for COMPREHENSION. Particularly in SIMULTANEOUS INTERPRETING (SI), where Gile's (2009) EFFORT MODEL indicates that the interpreter is usually working at – or near – the limit of available processing capacity, the demand for additional effort in listening to heavily accented input is likely to affect output quality (Gile 2011). Even so, there is little conclusive evidence of the link between unfamiliar accents and substandard interpreting performance. In studies with student subjects, Sabatini (2000) and Kurz (2008) found that output quality in SI deteriorated when the source language was heavily accented, and Lin, Chang and Kuo (2013) observed that accented speech led to information loss in SI.

The potential risk posed by non-native accents to the COMMUNICATIVE EFFECT of (simultaneous) interpreting is particularly relevant in relation to the widespread use of ENGLISH AS A LINGUA FRANCA in international conferences. An interview-based study by Chang and Wu (2014) among conference interpreters in Taiwan confirms that non-native speakers of English have become a normal part of professional reality. The survey indicates that accents are considered the major challenge in interpreting non-native speakers, with some accents perceived to be more difficult than others, and that experienced professionals have developed a number of STRATEGIES for coping with the difficulties arising from non-native English.

The way interpreters cope with accents also depends on DIRECTIONALITY. Understanding a B language when that language is 'clouded' by an unfamiliar accent is clearly more difficult than understanding one's A language in the same situation (McAllister 2000), and interpreters are known to perform better when the accented source language is their A language (Mazzetti 1999). It is thus possible that the difficulties of a speaker's non-native accent may be more readily overcome when an interpreter works from A into B. However, interpreters themselves may have a non-native accent when working into their B languages, which raises the issue of a non-native accent as a feature of the interpreter's performance quality.

Accent as a feature of output quality

An interpreter's strong accent would be likely to make listeners' comprehension more difficult. Since it is the interpreter's professional task to facilitate understanding, it seems safe to assume that a professional interpreter's non-native accent in the B language will not be so marked as to detract from intelligibility. Indeed, the results of SURVEY RESEARCH on USER EXPECTATIONS indicate that both conference interpreters and delegates rate a native accent as less important than such QUALITY CRITERIA as ACCURACY and faithfulness (FIDELITY) to the source message.

However, there may be variations in non-native accent tolerance among linguistic groups. For instance, it has been suggested that English and Russian listeners may be more tolerant of an interpreter's non-native accent than French listeners (Bartło-miejczyk 2004; Kalina 2005a; Martin 2005). Moreover, the location in which SI takes place may also determine the degree of importance placed upon an interpreter's native accent. For instance, a native German accent is a clear prerequisite when interpreters work for German TV stations (Kurz & Pöchhacker 1995) and for conferences that take place in Germany (Kalina 2005a). In addition, preferences for regional accents also vary. Although Taiwan and China both have Mandarin Chinese as their official language, the Taiwanese participants in Chang's (2009) study gave the highest rating of professionalism to a Mandarin interpreter perceived to be from Taiwan, whereas the participants from China gave the highest such rating to the interpreter perceived to be from that country.

How users evaluate the quality of SI with a non-native accent is therefore elusive. Cheung (2003) and Stévaux (2007), for instance, show that non-native accents can have a negative influence on SI listeners' quality perceptions, whereas research done in the context of various MA theses has yielded contradictory findings. However, all of these studies were conducted in an experimental setting, and the participants may have behaved differently from genuine conference attendees listening to SI.

In an effort to enhance validity, Cheung (2013) incorporated the "need for SI" into his experimental study of how native Cantonese speakers in Hong Kong rate SI into Cantonese by one native and two non-native interpreters: the requirement that participants take a comprehension test before filling in an evaluation questionnaire ensured that they would follow the interpretation attentively. The native Cantonese-speaking participants rated the two non-native interpreters (a native Mandarin speaker and a native English speaker) significantly lower than the native interpreter. The slightly higher rating given to the interpreter with a Mandarin non-native accent than to her counterpart with an English non-native accent may be attributed to participants' familiarity with Mandarin-accented Cantonese, as China is Hong Kong's major source of migrants.

Although most studies on non-native accents focus on simultaneous conference interpreting, interpreters with non-native accents also operate in other MODES and SETTINGS. Hale, Bond and Sutton (2011), in a study of CONSECUTIVE INTERPRETING in a mock courtroom setting, found that interpreters' non-native accents did not affect how source speakers were perceived.

ANDREW K. F. CHEUNG

ACCREDITATION

see under CERTIFICATION

ACCURACY

↑ ASSESSMENT → FIDELITY,
→ QUALITY CRITERIA, → USER EXPECTATIONS
↓ ERROR ANALYSIS

The requirement of accuracy is specified in many codes of conduct for interpreters around the world. There are, however, few explicit definitions of the concept of accuracy, or consolidated descriptions of what accuracy in interpreting actually consists of. According to SELESKOVITCH (1968, 1978a), 'total accuracy' (or *fidélité absolue*, as it was labeled in French) is achieved when an interpretation ensures a COMMUNICATIVE EFFECT equivalent to the understanding achieved by the original listeners. In the literature on ASSESSMENT in interpreting, there seems to be a consensus both among interpreters and among interpreting scholars as to what accurate interpreting consists of. In this respect, Pöchhacker (2004a) refers to accuracy as a widely accepted yardstick that many researchers have sought to apply. Similarly, Setton and Motta (2007) describe assessors in one of their experiments as being "interpreters familiar with quality norms for accuracy, style etc. as applied in training institutions and by professional consensus". Jacobson (2009) stresses that accuracy is a vital part of a comprehensive instrument for assessing the construct of interpreter COMPETENCE.

Measuring accuracy

The interpreting product can be assessed in two ways: componentially, when the sum of different parts, such as accuracy, OMISSIONS, additions and FLUENCY, is used to measure the product; and holistically, when the product is measured as an intrinsic whole. There are many examples of different types of measurement in the literature on interpreting. Barik (1975) measured both accuracy, as gauged by omissions, additions, substitutions ('errors of translation'), and translation disruptions; Mackintosh (1983) measured the 'semantic equivalence' of 'meaning units'; Gile (1999a, 2011) investigated his 'tightrope hypothesis' through errors, omissions and infelicities; and when Kurz (1993a) followed up on Bühler's (1986) study on QUALITY CRITERIA, her surveys of different user groups included the expectation of "sense consistency with the original". These dissimilar conceptual approaches seem to indicate that accuracy has been used as an evaluation criterion without a uniform definition of what it consists of or how it is actually measured.

Déjean le Féal (1990) contends that there is a shared standard of what interpreters consider to be a professional interpretation. However, such a standard seems so far to have eluded a common definition. Gile (1999b), for example, noting that measurements of QUALITY rely heavily on the frequency of errors and omissions (Gile 2003), has demonstrated that users show highly variable results when evaluating interpreting, while Collados Aís et al. (2011) have shown that componential evaluations are affected by raters' variable and dissimilar understanding of the components to be assessed.

For measurements of the interpreting product in professional situations, such as CERTIFICATION tests, Turner, Lai and Huang (2010) claim that most such tests for interpreters use the following methods: (1) error analysis/deduction systems; (2) criterion-referencing (the use of scales of descriptors to describe test performance), with no system of error analysis/deduction; or (3) a combination of the two.

Accuracy seems to be fuzzily defined in certification tests, and perhaps deliberately so. The oral component of the US Federal Court Interpreter Certification Examination (FCICE) uses so-called scoring units (i.e. selected words and phrases deemed to represent features of language that must be rendered 'accurately and completely without altering any of the meaning or style of speech'); in order to pass, 80% of these scoring units have to be transferred correctly (FCICE 2014). In Britain, the candidate handbook for the Diploma in Public Service Interpreting (DIPSI) gives the following description for the highest performance level regarding 'accuracy' (as opposed to 'delivery' and 'language use') in the interpreting units: "The candidate [.] conveys sense of original message with complete accuracy; transfers all information without omissions, additions, distortions; demonstrates complete competence in conveying verbal content and familiarity with subject matter" (IoLET 2010: 10). And in Sweden, the regulations for state certification include the following instructions for assessment: "Semantic/terminological rendering: The interpreter must provide the central information from both parties. During the test this is calculated from the number of transferred meaning-bearing elements. The interpreting is unacceptable if key information is omitted" (Kammarkollegiet 2014, my translation). The US FCICE is rare among accreditation tests in publically quantifying a passing score (80%).

Defining accuracy

Although it may seem obvious to strive for complete accuracy, defining it may prove challenging. Gile (2009), Hale (1997a) and others have pointed out that omissions may be necessary in interpreting in order to ensure accuracy, and that an acceptable target speech may in fact require deviations from linguistic equivalence. Donovan-Cagigos (1990) also underscores that accuracy is relative to a communicative situation. To date there are few definitions of total accuracy and few, if any, research constructs of accuracy to be tested.

Seleskovitch's (1978a: 102) definition of accuracy as dependent on the communicative effect of the interpretation is compelling, as it seems to encompass all types of interpreters and all types of interpreting. It is also hard to pin down, however, since there are as yet no measurements of how much information needs to be transferred in order for that understanding to take place. Information is by no means an ethically, culturally or linguistically unbiased unit. It can be argued that Seleskovitch's definition is monolingual and biased towards the concept of a standard, indivisible national language. Even listeners who share a language may understand information differently, depending on their social, cultural and economic background. Furthermore, accuracy in interpreting also differs according to whether the perspective is monologic or dialogic (Wadensjö 1998). If meaning is co-constructed in a dialogic interpreting context, then at least part of the accuracy is too.

There is arguably a least common denominator of what accurate interpreting consists of. Although many researchers have studied which elements both interpreters and their clients consider to be essential for good interpreting, few have investigated accuracy as a construct in its own right or ventured evidence-based definitions. It remains largely unclear what type of information, and how much of it, needs to be conveyed in order for communication to occur. Gile's (2009: 35) proposal to view accuracy, or FIDELITY, in interpreting as a variably weighted combination of 'content' (information transfer) and 'packaging' provides some conceptual foundation. It remains to be tested, however, how much information is 'enough' and what makes it 'understandable' in a given situation of interaction.

ELISABET TISELIUS

4

ACTION RESEARCH

↑ METHODOLOGY

Action research is a form of inquiry that aims to translate research outcomes into social gains by way of participatory and collaborative projects. Rather than a METHODOLOGY, action research is best described as an *orientation* to the research process (Reason & Bradbury 2008), since action research projects may reflect differences in EPISTEMOLOGY and employ a variety of research methods.

The origins of action research lie in philosophical explorations into the relationship between knowledge acquisition and experience, and into the interrelation between knowledge and action (see Kemmis & McTaggart 1988; Kemmis et al. 2014). These philosophical influences have engendered two main, but distinct, epistemological approaches to action research: reflective practice and critical theory, respectively. The former could encompass research to improve professional practice at the local, or perhaps the classroom or community of practice level, within the capacities of individuals and the situations in which they are working; for the latter, action research is part of a broader agenda of changing practice, changing systems, and changing society.

Social psychologist Kurt Lewin is most often credited with being the founder of action research. In a series of change experiments undertaken in workplaces in America in the 1940s, Lewin sought to change the attitudes and social conditions of participants through their active involvement in decision-making during the research process (Lewin 1947). He held that stakeholders who would be affected by change should be involved in the processes leading up to it, and that such participation was crucial to the success of the research.

The action research process is conceived of as a spiral or series of cycles, with reflexivity embedded in every step. Each turn in the spiral comprises the stages of analysis, reconnaissance, reconceptualization of the problem, planning the intervention, implementation of the plan and evaluation of the effectiveness of the intervention. Subsequent cycles relate to revised planning and implementation, until outcomes are satisfactory in terms of resolution of the problem. More than one cycle must be undertaken for the reflective processes to be completed, though many published reports fail to clearly articulate the different cycles in relation to the procedures and methods followed.

Action research is typically undertaken *with* participants rather than *on* participants (Reason & Bradbury 2008), which tends to blur the traditional roles of researchers and research participants. However, reflective practitioners contest the necessity of collaboration, arguing that action research can also be implemented for individualistic applications.

In INTERPRETING STUDIES, action research has been applied primarily in the context of interpreter EDUCATION and training. Projects range from large-scale CURRICULUM evaluations and more focused projects on designing and implementing curricular innovation (e.g. Napier 2005a; Slatyer 2006) to evaluations of an intervention in the interpreting classroom (Boéri & de Manuel Jeréz 2011; Gorm Hansen & Shlesinger 2007; Krouse 2010; Napier et al. 2013; Pierce & Napier 2010). These projects are all observational case studies for which data was collected using one or more of the following methods: pre-/post-intervention surveys and INTERVIEWS, learning journals, focus groups, and collection and analysis of learning tasks and assessments.

The introduction of an innovation into an educational program requires careful monitoring of the strengths and weaknesses of the intervention. An action research orientation allows for the adjustment of the conditions of the intervention to ensure that it meets the needs of the participants. Typical of this type of action research is the project by Gorm Hansen and Shlesinger (2007), which was motivated by an economic and social imperative to reduce the number of face-to-face teaching hours and make learning less stressful in a course in CONSECUTIVE INTERPRETING. The PEDAGOGY was changed to a more self-directed learning approach, and new TECHNOLOGY introduced to enable students to work independently in the lab. With a similar goal of improving students' consecutive interpreting performance, Napier, Song and Ye (2013) explored the use of iPads and dedicated software in the interpreting classroom. The action research orientation allowed for ongoing monitoring and reappraisal of the methods and technology that were used.

Action research projects drawing on critical theory, where the aim is to implement a change in perceptions, cultures or systems, are rare in interpreting studies. Noteworthy exceptions include the Marius Project at the University of Granada (Boéri & de Manuel Jerez 2011), which sought to fundamentally change the social profile of conference interpreters by applying a social-critical stance to interpreter education in a series of dynamic change cycles, and the work of Weber, Singy and Guex (2005) in Lausanne. With the aim of increasing the use of interpreters in the health system, the researchers held focus groups with key stakeholders (patients, healthcare providers and interpreters) before and after an intervention aimed at enhancing the skills of medical interpreters. Divergent views about GENDER emerged as a major issue in relation to the ROLE of medical interpreters.

Individual reflective projects are less commonly reported. These are small-scale case studies of personal relevance that focus on aspects of practice as professional development. A notable exception is the special issue of *Deaf Worlds* reported by Hale and Napier (2013, Ch. 4), which was devoted to a series of interpreter case studies.

There is clearly much potential for greater implementation of action research in interpreting studies, in the educational sphere, but also beyond, so as to exploit the inherent reflexivity for interpreting practice and also to apply it in the broader context of social systems in which interpreters work.

HELEN SLATYER

ACTIVIST APPROACH

↑ ETHICS, ↑ IDEOLOGY

Activist practices of interpreting constitute a fairly recent object of enquiry in interpreting studies. It is in the area of CONFERENCE INTERPRETING that the activist approach emerged and developed, (a) as a result of the conference-like format of international activist gatherings and (b) as a reaction against the tendency of mainstream conference interpreting scholarship and professional practice to focus on providing a service for the most powerful players in society.

The scope of the literature on activist interpreting revolves around case studies of networks and associations of volunteer interpreters positioned outside the classic interpreting labour market and catering for the communicative needs of civil society and the social movements sector. These include ECOS – Translators and Interpreters for Solidarity – an association of volunteers based at the University of Granada, Spain, and Babels, an international network of volunteer translators and interpreters. Both support grassroots initiatives, broadly subsumed within the Alter-globalization and Global Justice movements. Another group is International Conference Volunteers (ICV), which works for the non-governmental sector, closely linked to UN agencies.

While activist interpreter groups give voice to resistant rather than dominant ideologies and to global political agendas, they may take different stances on activism – ranging from a charitable, humanitarian activism which responds to a need not covered by mainstream society, to political activism which seeks to bring about a transformation of society. Along the spectrum between the two, activist interpreting ranges from a free-of-charge conventional interpreting service (with an emphasis on efficiency, QUALITY and professionalism) to the launching of an alternative organizational policy for interpreting which prefigures the desired social change (with an emphasis on the empowerment of minoritized communities). Structures may vary accordingly, from strong institutionalization, typical of the non-governmental sector, to lack of formalization, typical of the large grassroots networks.

Even though activist interpreter communities take a clear stance within this spectrum of possibilities – ICV as an institutionalized group which offers a free but conventional interpreting service, and ECOS and Babels as participative networks which propose an alternative inter-preting policy – they are pressured both to provide quality interpreting and to practise the political principles they advocate, as a result of their "hybrid interpreter-activist profile" (Boéri 2008: 31) and of the liminal space they occupy "between the service economy and activism" (Baker 2013). This inclines them to seek innovative ways of addressing issues related to quality and participation, as in the case of Babels and ECOS, which have professionals and novices teaming up in the booth and launching ad hoc training sessions (Lampropoulou 2010; Sánchez Balsalobre et al. 2010).

The uneven successes achieved by these groups in implementing political principles against logistical constraints make their relationships with the communities they serve (Boéri 2012), and with the professional conference interpreting community, particularly contentious. Boéri's (2008) analysis of the conflict between Babels and the professional conference interpreting community in the International Association of Conference Interpreters (AIIC) electronic forum accounts for a broad spectrum of attitudes, within professional circles, to activist interpreting: fierce opposition to volunteer work from a commercial standpoint; fierce opposition to activism per se, based on a professional ethos of NEUTRALITY; acceptance of a volunteer interpreting service subject to strict respect for professional standards; active support of Babels' alternative interpreting policy.

Privileging ethnographic fieldwork methodology, scholars have primarily focused on the collective identity, the collective action and the structure of these activist communities (an approach typical of Social Movement Theory), rather than on the actual interpreting. Apart from Gambier's (2007) descriptivist approach to activist groups of (translators and) interpreters, research has largely been carried out from a socio-critical perspective by scholars who are sup-portive (but at the same time critical) of the activist initiatives concerned. Such studies have been extended beyond civil society, in an attempt to examine the crucial role of researchers, educators and professionals in supporting and redressing the power asymmetries in the field and in society. This broad research agenda gave rise to the First International Forum on Translation/Interpreting and Social Activism (Boéri & Maier 2010). Beyond conference interpreting, it has led to the challenging of prescriptive codes of conduct that limit interpreters' capacity to pro-mote "mutually effective dialogue oriented toward just outcomes" (Inghilleri 2010: 154), to calls for educators to educate citizens for society and not only to train interpreters for the labour market, and to appeals for a more inclusive and mutually supportive professional community of interpreters (de Manuel Jerez 2010; Kahane 2008; Boéri & de Manuel Jerez 2011).

JULIE BOÉRI

ADDITIONS

see under ERROR ANALYSIS

ADVOCACY

see under ROLE

AFRICA

↑ HISTORY

Though written records on the subject are scanty and interpreters have hardly ever occupied the limelight through the ages, it is reasonable to hypothesise that the practice of interpreting from one natural language to another on the African continent, as elsewhere, goes back thousands of years. For most of human history, communication has been based essentially on speech, and ORALITY and oral tradition are indeed of particular relevance in the African context.

In the ancient African kingdoms, such as those found in present-day Ghana, Mali and Zimbabwe, the professional linguist was considered the official spokesperson and the repository of the memory and knowledge of his people, with a special talent for narrating their history and culture (Bandia 2009). A case in point are the Ashanti 'linguists', whose functions are described as "repeating the words of their patron after him, acting as herald to make it clear to all his audience and to add to his utterances the extra authority of remoteness" (Danquah 1928: 42). On this account, the 'linguist' was also entrusted with perfecting the speech of a chief who was not sufficiently eloquent.

In many African societies, the professional linguist – also known as a *griot* ('bard') in Francophone Africa (Bandia 2009), or as an *imbongi* or traditional praise singer in Southern Africa (Stuart 1968) – belonged to a long line of gifted orators and tribal historians who devised praise songs to celebrate the 'praise names', victories and glorious qualities of the chief and his ancestors, and recited these on important public occasions. Professional linguists often enjoyed a privileged position in society, and wielded a great deal of political power due to their proximity to the king. Their interventions took many forms, from respeaking the king's words in more accessible or more poetic forms (intralingual interpreting) to interpreting into other languages. They were known for their mastery of several languages (Bandia 2010), and in fact the oral art of West African *griots* and Southern African *iimbongi* largely continues today, with praise singers acting as modern political commentators on post-independence leaders such as Senghor and Mandela (Kaschula 1999).

The history of interpreting in Africa can broadly be divided into three periods (Bandia 2009): the pre-colonial, the colonial and the post-colonial era.

The pre-colonial period

In West Africa, there was commerce with the Arab world as early as the seventh and eighth centuries, always involving locals who acted as intermediaries and interpreters. The Portuguese explored the eastern and southern coasts and traded with the locals from the fifteenth century, but beyond the trading posts on the coast, and strategically important areas such as Algeria and South Africa, the rulers of African land were African, and Europe saw no reason to intervene (Pakenham 1991).

Two famous interpreters from Southern Africa stand out as legendary figures: Autshumato and Eva. Autshumato ('Chief Harry'), seen as the embodiment of the interpreter as traitor, was a Khoikhoi leader. He became an interpreter for Jan Van Riebeeck, who wished to establish a refreshment station at the Cape of Good Hope at the southern tip of Africa on behalf of the Dutch East India Company in 1652. Although the situation looked promising, the Company's need for cattle meant barter with the local inhabitants or *strandlopers* (lit. 'beach walkers'), who spoke an incomprehensible tongue. Chief Autshumato, who had learned to speak English after being taken to the East on an English ship, helped to facilitate trade. However, Autshumato rightly saw the Dutch as a threat to the existence of his tribe, and in 1658 was accused of misinterpretation and lack of loyalty to the Dutch. He was imprisoned on Robben Island, but was one of the very few political prisoners there who managed to escape.

Krotoa, also known as Eva, was Autshumato's niece, born around 1642, and was the embodiment of the interpreter as collaborator or 'slave'. Eva's story parallels that of MALINCHE. In return for cattle (to be secured by Autshumato), housekeeping and interpreting services, Van Riebeeck offered Krotoa a Christian home. She quickly learned Dutch, donned Western attire, converted to Christianity, and soon acted as both interpreter and mistress to Van Riebeeck. It is clear from a jubilant entry in Van Riebeeck's journal ("Eva says she has a Dutch heart") that the Dutch commander's interest in her was crucial to relations at the Cape. Much like the Mexicans' distrust of La Malinche, Khoi descendants saw Eva as 'the woman between', both collaborator and traitor. Dan Sleigh's book *Eilande*, written originally in Afrikaans and translated into English as *Islands* (2004), traces the stories of the early settlers in the Cape, with examples of FICTIONAL INTERPRETERS.

The colonial period: explorers, evangelists and their interpreters

By the mid-1800s, explorers such as David Livingstone had opened up the interior for discovery, and the 'Scramble for Africa' had begun. Within half a generation, Europe had annexed almost the entire continent, with six nations in particular – France, Britain, Portugal, Germany, Italy and Belgium – changing Africa's linguistic landscape forever. Journalist-explorers such as Henry Stanley, sailor-explorers like Pierre de Brazza, soldier-explorers like Frederick Lugard and gold and diamond tycoons like Cecil Rhodes all rushed to heed Livingstone's call in 1857 for a worldwide crusade to open up Africa to 'commerce and Christianity' and to combat the slave trade organised by Swahili and Arabs in East Africa (Pakenham 1991). There were hardly any exploratory expeditions into the African hinterland that did not include interpreters, some of whom no doubt saved their leaders from disaster, and others whose linguistic skills were doubtful in the extreme.

As time went by, interpreters were increasingly needed not only to facilitate trade and exploration, but also to assist in the negotiation of often one-sided treaties with colonial powers. When the colonisers proceeded to effective occupation, interpreters also became involved in the inevitable armed conflicts that ensued.

African interpreters proved indispensable to the operation of the colonial system. In courtrooms, district offices and health clinics, African colonial employees enabled communication, provided information, and oversaw the implementation – and reinterpretation – of colonial policies (Lawrance et al. 2006). Interpreters were crucial to the effective functioning of the colonial administration, because few Europeans learned African languages, but also because budgetary constraints prevented the hiring of European interpreters. The colonial period saw the STATUS of the African interpreter being raised and made official, bolstering his rank in the social and administrative hierarchy (Niang 1990). However, there were numerous issues with interpreters' NEUTRALITY, particularly in COURTROOM INTERPRETING, and many may have taken advantage of their privileged positions, as described by Amadou Hampâté Bâ (1973) in *L'étrange destin de Wangrin*.

Interpreters (and translators) have also played an important role in the evangelisation of Africa, assisting missionaries from Europe and America to spread the word of God and, at the same time, to codify the languages of Africa for the first time. This tradition continues today, with interpreting in RELIGIOUS SETTINGS being performed to assist multilingual congregations all over Africa.

In the South African colonial context, after British rule had made way for descendants of Dutch settlers known as Afrikaners to take power, the influence of the ideology of *apartheid* or 'separate development' (i.e. enforced racial separation and the entrenching of white supremacy) from 1948 to 1994 was intimately entwined with the politics of language, and therefore also with translation and interpreting. After Afrikaans (derived originally from seventeenth-century Dutch) was declared an official language alongside English in 1925, the National Party government began a development programme aimed at ensuring that Afrikaans would become established at a level comparable with English, the powerful language of imperialism. The nine African languages of South Africa also underwent a government-sponsored surge of translation and interpreting activity in the courts, the media and in education, but only as far as this served the policy of separate development (Ntuli & Swanepoel 1993).

The post-colonial period

It was only after independence, achieved mainly between the 1950s and 1970s, that the modern interpreter appeared on the African continent. With the acquisition of national sovereignty, some African countries adopted the languages of the coloniser (e.g. French in Senegal), while others adopted local languages as the official language, such as Ethiopia (Amharic) and Tanzania (Swahili) (Niang 1990). Interpreters were needed to assist in communicating with local populations during campaigns for independence, since many African leaders, having been educated in Europe, no longer spoke the local languages. Their services were also required in the courts and in various government organisations.

A particularly complex example of multilingualism in Africa is post-apartheid South Africa, under whose 1996 constitution eleven languages (Afrikaans, English, Zulu, Xhosa, Swati, Ndebele, Pedi, Sotho, Tswana, Tsonga and Venda) have equal status as official languages. (All eleven are languages of limited diffusion, and seven of them fall into two cognate groups.) South African Sign Language, the Khoi, Nama and San languages, as well as other 'heritage languages', such as German, Greek, Gujarati, Hindi, Portuguese, Tamil, Telegu, Urdu, Arabic, Hebrew and Sanskrit, are also recognised constitutionally (Kamwangamalu 2013). Such a complex linguistic landscape clearly has ramifications for the use of interpreting. For example, several South African universities make university lectures in English and Afrikaans available to speakers of other (national) languages through the use of SIMULTANEOUS INTERPRETING. This form of EDUCATIONAL INTERPRETING is unique to South Africa (Verhoef & du Plessis 2008).

The hearings of the South African TRC (1996–1998), arguably the best-known example of TRUTH AND RECONCILIATION COMMISSIONS, marked the first opportunity for many South Africans to become acquainted with the marvels of simultaneous interpreting in the eleven official languages. Since then, simultaneous interpreting has become the norm at national and provincial legislatures, municipal council meetings and conferences. The conspicuous use of sign language interpreters on these occasions as well as on television news (Wehrmeyer 2015) has assisted considerably with the development and promotion of South African Sign Language, a move which has yet to take hold for other signed languages on the continent. However, the entrenchment and institutionalisation of multilingualism does have its downside for translators and interpreters: in South Africa, this has led to a tendency to value political correctness over QUALITY (Wallmach 2014).

Public service interpreting (COMMUNITY INTERPRETING) is widespread, particularly in legal contexts. In most countries throughout the world, the language of the court is the language of the majority of citizens, but South African court cases are conducted in the languages of the minority, namely English and/or Afrikaans, with interpreting services provided for speakers of the INDIGENOUS LANGUAGES, who form the majority of the population. English is the language of record. South Africa's apartheid legacy has therefore meant that the majority of court cases require interpreting. In some magistrates' courts, especially in the province of Gauteng, about 90 percent of court cases require interpreting (Moeketsi & Wallmach 2005). To address this need, the Department of Justice employs several thousand full-time court interpreters to provide services in the official languages of South Africa, and also funds interpreter training. Foreign language interpreters for the languages of immigrants to South Africa (including Chinese, Portuguese, French, Swahili, Igbo, Yoruba and Bemba) are generally not employed full-time, not well paid, and have few training opportunities. As a result, the quality of interpreting service provision is low. In other African countries, COURTROOM INTERPRETING between indigenous languages and past colonial languages such as French, English or Portuguese is also widespread, with a similar lack of trained professionals.

The same complex linguistic profile as in legal settings applies to health contexts and social services, with the difference that there are few, if any, formal arrangements for interpreting in these SETTINGS. Lack of access to medical care as a result of linguistic and cultural barriers is a major problem, but African states do not generally make provision for HEALTHCARE INTERPRETING. The overwhelming majority of healthcare professionals, with the exception of nurses, cannot speak any of the indigenous African languages (Levin 2006). In South African public hospitals in particular, the language barrier has been shown to cause frustration for both medical staff and patients, as well as errors in diagnosis and treatment (e.g. Schlemmer & Mash 2006). Untrained ad hoc interpreters (such as relatives, fellow doctors, nurses, cleaners, porters and other patients) are used to overcome communication barriers, since there is no statutory interpreting service in South Africa. However, the use of NON-PROFESSIONAL INTERPRETING has been shown to lead to more complications, including breach of patient confidentiality, distortion and/or omission of information (Penn et al. 2011; Wallmach 2013).

At the international level, the participation of various African countries in international organisations has provided increasing opportunities for conference interpreters at institutions such as the African Union, the United Nations in Nairobi, the World Health Organisation, and the African Development Bank, as well as for regional organisations such as the Economic Community of West African States (ECOWAS), the East African Community (EAC) and the Southern African Development Community (SADC), amongst others. Recent initiatives in the field of conference interpreter EDUCATION include the establishment of the Pan-African Masters Consortium in Interpretation and Translation (PAMCIT) in 2012, following the Second Pan-African Conference on Training of Translators, Conference Interpreters and Public Service Interpreters in Addis Ababa. This initiative was born out of a United Nations Report from Nairobi in 2008 which pointed out that, with only a few exceptions, no fully fledged training for translators, conference interpreters and public service interpreters was available at master's level in African universities, despite the huge potential of the continent's multilingualism. The report also stressed the importance of using local languages in business, courts, hospitals and the public service. Supported by the European Commission and the European Parliament, and following a CURRICULUM similar to that of the European Masters in Conference Interpreting (EMCI), the consortium unites five core regional training institutions representing the five linguistic regions of the African continent: the universities of Nairobi (Kenya), Buea (Cameroon), Maputo (Mozambique), Legon (Ghana) and Cairo (Egypt). These universities have signed a Memorandum of Understanding, aimed at strengthening inter-institutional collaboration to make way for quality higher education collaboration. The consortium has been expanded further, to include two potential partners in the south and the north: the University of the Witwatersrand in Johannesburg, and the University of Ouagadougou (Burkina Faso).

KIM WALLMACH

AGENCIES

↑ PROFESSION

Agencies, or interpreter brokers, are central to the organisation of language services of any size or complexity. While they are of relatively limited importance in CONFERENCE INTER-PRETING, where interpreters can often advertise themselves or have long-standing contracts with clients, agencies have become crucial for DIALOGUE INTERPRETING in institutional settings, particularly where clients require interpreters in a multiplicity of languages.

Indeed, it has been the rise of interpreting in community-based settings, mostly referred to as public service or COMMUNITY INTERPRETING, that has led to the increasing importance of agencies. Such agencies cover a spectrum of organisational types: small family operators, fully commercial companies, NGOs or not-for-profit organisations, and government agencies. While the NGOs and government agencies will concentrate almost exclusively on public sector interpreting, commercial agencies have increased in prominence, building market share by forging close links with government bodies or NGOs needing their services and finding interpreters through community connections; they may also try to gain a reputation for providing interpreters for commercially rewarding assignments, such as compensation suits, conference and BUSINESS INTERPRETING.

Interpreting agencies typically work in a constrained environment. Unlike translation agencies, which may have an international field of operation, interpreting agencies will be largely concerned with the local market, only occasionally extending to work internationally through the use of TECHNOLOGY, as in the case of TELEPHONE INTERPRETING and (video) REMOTE INTERPRETING. Furthermore, agencies work subject to two overriding constraints. First, to the extent that they concentrate on public sector work, they are currently subject to ever-tightening government budgets. Second (and equally challenging), they are faced with rapidly growing multilingualism in virtually all areas of service, meaning that issues of recruitment, professional socialisation, reliability and quality of practitioners become key problems in supply and performance standards (Ozolins 2010). One agency for African language interpreters in the US (Jones 1996) identified an increase in such problems since the 1980s and 1990s, pointing to the scarcity of freelance interpreters for unofficial African languages and the difficulty of quality control for particular language varieties.

Agencies can also become important, however, when sophisticated language services and necessary infrastructure (including training and CERTIFICATION) have been specified in public policy for equity of access and to ensure standards. In some cases, such as AUSTRALIA, governments use private agencies alongside state-run language services: these agencies strive to provide accredited interpreters, and also to source interpreters in non-accredited languages by whatever means possible (Ozolins 2007). In other cases, there is a desire to outsource or to remove government from direct service delivery and to provide more work directly to private agencies – a broader political agenda, as seen in Sweden and the UK, that is by no means limited to interpreting alone.

Despite their significance, agencies' commercial nature and lack of public documentation has made them difficult to research, and available literature is scant (Ozolins 2007). A Swedish report (see Norström et al. 2012) provides a comprehensive overview of the issues surrounding the use of agencies, and identifies the poor STATUS of interpreting, low remuneration, and insufficient supervision of procurement as the main reasons for agencies' poor performance. Other problems of ensuring quality services include: the diversity of languages (often more than 100), with an insufficient number of interpreters; procurers (government officials) failing to understand issues in interpreting, and seeing procurement largely in terms of price; diverse practices regarding briefing and recruitment standards; agencies' unwillingness to train uncertified interpreters; and a 'drive to the bottom', with agencies offering interpreters low fees after a successful tender bid. Such issues persist despite quality accreditation (ISO or similar standards) of the major agencies.

The danger of outsourcing to one provider has been shown in the UK, where the Department of Justice awarded the contract for all court interpreting to one relatively small agency (Applied Language Solutions), which soon after was taken over by a very large outsourcing company (Capita). The contract was announced as saving millions of pounds in taxpayer money, and replacing a previous system where courts themselves could seek interpreters. However, the rates and conditions offered under the new contract were below what had previously been offered to interpreters, leading to a prolonged boycott of the agency by many of the best-qualified interpreters – those of the National Register of Public Service Interpreters, who had previously serviced the courts. Complaints were manifest about the quality of the interpreters the agency was sending, leading to many courts going back to finding their own better-qualified interpreters (see ITI 2014).

Criticism of such moves can also come in situations where, despite limited availability of organised language services, private agencies with their profit motive seemingly go against ideals of equitable service provision and social utility (see Valero-Garcés 2010). One promising development has been the formation of interpreting industry bodies in some countries, where agencies can adopt codes of practice or act as identifiable parties in policy discussions. More problematic are attempts to introduce ISO standards for inter-preting services in general, and community interpreting in particular, for such initiatives are not likely to solve the intersecting problems of supply, remuneration, training and pro-fessional socialisation that characterise the field as a whole and directly affect the working of agencies.

ULDIS OZOLINS

AGENCY

see under ROLE

AIIC

↑ PROFESSION

After the first systematic use of SIMULTANEOUS INTERPRETING at the NUREMBERG TRIAL and the United Nations, the number of professional interpreters, mainly in Europe, increased con-siderably, and the need was felt to introduce some sort of organisation. Following several local attempts to organise freelancers, in Geneva and London in particular (see Keiser 2004), the International Association of Conference Interpreters, known by the French acronym, AIIC, was founded in Paris on November 11, 1953, by a handful of professionals led by Constantin Andronikof, chief interpreter of the Organisation for European Economic Cooperation (OEEC). He enlisted the support of André Kaminker, chief interpreter of the

Council of Europe, and Hans Jacob, UNESCO chief interpreter; both had formerly worked in consecutive interpreting at the League of Nations.

Andronikof's vision was original and ambitious. AIIC was to be a central organisation to which professional conference interpreters all over the world, both freelance and staff, would belong directly (i.e. not via national organisations), and which would define the ethical and material conditions under which conference interpreters would operate, as members of a new profession. Many doubted whether such far-reaching aims could be attained – only 33 interpreters were present at the constituent assembly in 1953. In 2013, however, with around 3000 members on all five continents, one can say that the pessimists have been proved wrong. The AIIC Code of Ethics and Professional Standards was formally adopted in 1957; the principle of strict and total confidentiality was established at the outset, alongside commitments to integrity and professionalism.

Membership is open to all professional conference interpreters, including (since 2012) sign language interpreters, who undertake to abide by AIIC rules and regulations. Applicants need at least 150 days of working experience and at least three sponsors who are active AIIC members with five years of seniority in the working language they are sponsoring, and who have listened to the applicant work at a meeting. Working languages are classified as A, B or C languages: A = a native language, or another language which is strictly equivalent; B = another language of which the interpreter has a perfect command; C = a language of which the interpreter has a complete understanding. While AIIC does not consider its peer-based admissions procedure a CERTIFICATION in the strict sense of the word, it seeks to ensure that all its members, listed in the annual Directory, are fully competent professionals.

One of AIIC's roles from the very outset was to improve WORKING CONDITIONS, which also meant better interpreting booths and sound equipment. In the early days booths were often an afterthought, with no space, no view of the meeting room, no air and poor sound transmission. In 1971 the AIIC Technical Committee drafted the first standard for interpreting booths for the French standards organisation, AFNOR, which was to form the basis of ISO 2603 (1974) for fixed booths and ISO 4043 (1998) for mobile booths. Sound quality standards followed. The Technical Committee has tracked developments in TECHNOLOGY, such as REMOTE INTERPRETING, that may impact quality and working conditions, and AIIC continues to work closely with ISO, inter alia on the definition of the CONFERENCE INTERPRETING profession.

AIIC has always devoted considerable attention to the training of interpreters, with the adoption of criteria for interpreting schools in 1959, and over the years has sponsored or organised a succession of publications, surveys, seminars, etc., culminating in 2012 in the fully searchable online Schools Directory.

AIIC has also set up an extensive programme of Training of Trainers seminars. Following an initial two-day seminar in Porto in 2003, by the end of 2013 more than 300 interpreter trainers had attended AIIC courses around the world, with 20 (out of a total of 50 applicants) being sponsored by the Association to attend.

Through its Research Committee, AIIC has commissioned a number of research projects, including a user expectation survey (Moser 1996) and the Workload Study (Mackintosh 2002). It has also served as the primary target population for survey research on such topics as true BILINGUALISM (Thiéry 1978) and QUALITY CRITERIA (Bühler 1986; Zwischenberger 2010).

One of AIIC's major achievements was the signing, in 1969, of the first five-year agreements with the three groups of large intergovernmental organisations: the United Nations and Specialised Agencies, the Coordinated Organisations (Council of Europe, NATO, etc.), and the European Union. The agreements are generally renegotiated every five years, and still define the working conditions, remuneration and pension provisions for freelance interpreters employed by those organisations, members and non-members alike.

An important development was "deregulation" in the 1990s. Initially, AIIC had enforced a schedule of minimum fees, on the principle that competition should bear on quality, not cost. The United States Federal Trade Commission (FTC) decided however that AIIC was composed not of persons, but of business enterprises, and that any form of price-fixing was illegal. The European Union authorities followed suit. AIIC challenged the decision and, after a long (and expensive) legal battle, managed to salvage most of the working conditions (team manning strengths, etc.) but had to remove any reference to remuneration from its rules.

AIIC maintains two websites: a public site (www.aiic.net), which provides abundant information on the profession, how to become an interpreter and how to find an interpreter, with a list of members and their linguistic qualifications, etc., and gives access to AIIC publications; and a "members only" extranet for internal affairs.

Since December 1999 AIIC has published *Communicate!*, a webzine which appears on the public website twice a year. It aims at a broad audience, with articles on the profession, including varied opinions on controversial issues.

Until 2012 AIIC was run by a 23-member Council, representing all regions but elected by the tri-annual Assembly, and a Bureau consisting of the president, three vice-presidents and the treasurer. In 2012 a new structure was adopted, effective as of 2015: the Association is now run by a decision-making body of seven members elected by the Assembly, while a larger body representing the regions, committees, etc. meets once a year and has an advisory and coordinating role.

The regional assemblies were instituted in 1979, when it became apparent that in different parts of the world interpreters needed a forum for discussing matters of purely local interest, while adhering strictly to the principle of a single organisation to which all members would belong directly.

AIIC is registered under the French law on Associations of 1901. The Secretariat was moved from Paris to Geneva in 1969. On the occasion of its 60th anniversary, AIIC published a history of the organisation, and of the profession (AIIC History Group 2013).

CHRISTOPHER THIÉRY

ANIMATOR

see under FOOTING

ANTICIPATION

↑ STRATEGIES

Anticipation is one of the most widely discussed STRATEGIES in SIMULTANEOUS INTERPRETING (SI). Viewed as a way of overcoming the challenge posed by syntactic asymmetry, mostly in SI from languages with an SOV (subject–object–verb) sentence structure into languages with a more rigid subject–verb–object order, anticipation refers to the prediction of source-text constituents not yet available for the interpreter's output planning. It thus tends to be considered not only as specific to the simultaneous mode of interpreting, but also as a language-pair-specific phenomenon.

Aside from this understanding of anticipation in its narrow sense as a form of strategic prediction, described in greater detail below, the concept of anticipation has also been discussed in a much wider sense in research on interpreting. Ghelly CHERNOV (1978, 2004), in his seminal work on the process of SI, made anticipatory processes the core of his theoretical model of COMPREHENSION in SI. He drew on work from the 1960s by Soviet psychologist Josef Feigenberg, who saw 'probabilistic prognosis' as a fundamental mechanism underlying human actions in response to changes in the environment. Such prediction of likely future events, by relying on experience stored in MEMORY, was assumed to facilitate the 'presetting for action' in any human activity. Chernov applied the principle of probability prediction mainly to comprehension in SI, and Kalina (1998) lists anticipation as a comprehension-oriented strategy in interpreting, but anticipation in the broader sense must be assumed to be part of any process of understanding based on prior experience and knowledge. In this universal sense, anticipating a speaker's meaning in discourse comprehension is difficult to detect, or to regard as strategic; however, evidence of this process can be found in SI when the interpreter expresses an element of source speech meaning before the corresponding word or phrase is uttered by the original speaker. It is in this specific sense that anticipation has been an object of study in a considerable body of empirical research.

Strategic anticipation in SI

Most studies of anticipation have involved SI from languages such as German (e.g. Wilss 1978; Lederer 1981; Jörg 1997; Riccardi 1996; Setton 1999; Liontou 2012) and Dutch (Bevilacqua 2009), which can have verb constituents in clause-final position, but there have also been contributions on SI from other languages with left-branching word order, such as Chinese (Setton 1999) and Japanese (Gile 1992). The choice of METHODOLOGY has included qualitative observational studies (e.g. Lederer 1981) and quantitative CORPUS-BASED RESEARCH (e.g. Liontou 2012), as well as EXPERIMENTAL RESEARCH (e.g. Jörg 1997; Donato 2003; Bevilacqua 2009).

The very first systematic study, on anticipation in German–English SI, was done by Mattern (1974), whose findings are commented on by Wilss (1978). Mattern's focus on the 'cues' in the source text that appear to act as triggers of anticipation gave rise to a widely used distinction between two basic types of anticipation: linguistic and extralinguistic anticipation (e.g. Gile 1995a). Lederer (1978) characterizes the former as 'language prediction' (based on collocations, etc.) and the latter as based on 'sense expectation' (relying on contextual, situational and world knowledge).

Another important distinction, especially in quantitative studies, relates to the correctness of anticipation. Jörg (1997), for example, classifies instances of anticipation in his experimentally generated corpus as either 'successful' or 'incorrect', with the former category further subdivided into 'exact' and 'more general'. Empirical findings for this analytical criterion have invariably shown a majority of successful anticipation, with only a few instances of incorrect or erroneous anticipation, which are often corrected by REPAIRS. Liontou (2012), for example, in her authentic corpus of Greek simultaneous interpretations of German speeches from the European Parliament (totaling 5.5 hours), found that anticipation was successful in 93% of all (187) cases. These and other findings suggest that anticipation is used as a relatively safe strategy, in cases where interpreters are reasonably certain about the way the source text will continue. Alternative strategies include SEGMENTATION (chunking) as well as waiting or 'stalling', but these have different implications for the interpreter's memory load. Liontou (2011) found very frequent use of stalling (i.e. the production of generic filler utterances to 'buy time'), which imposes a higher load on the interpreter's memory.

The assumption that strategic anticipation in the face of syntactic asymmetry is largely language-specific has been corroborated in several studies comparing SI from typologically different languages. Donato (2003), for instance, found that the student interpreters in her experiment used anticipation nearly ten times more often when working from German into Italian than when working from English. The direction of interpreting, or DIRECTIONALITY, can also be assumed to play a role in this respect. In Jörg's (1997) experimental study of German-to-English simultaneous interpreting by students and professional interpreters, in both cases with German as either the A or the B language, there was a tendency for German A-language participants to achieve a higher percentage of exact anticipation.

The research-based finding that strategic anticipation in SI is largely a language-specific phenomenon and mostly involves clause-final verb constituents also has implications for training. While there is some skepticism regarding the degree to which strategies such as anticipation can be practiced and taught, the fundamental role of anticipation can certainly be impressed upon students. One way in which this can be done is through PRE-INTERPRETING EXERCISES such as auditory CLOZE, serving to enhance prediction skills in comprehension in general, and prepare the ground for strategic anticipation in SI.

KONSTANTINA LIONTOU

APTITUDE TESTING

↑ EDUCATION

→ CLOZE, → PSYCHOMETRIC TESTS, → SHADOWING

Unlike other types of testing, especially ASSESSMENT, aptitude tests appraise current abilities and traits which are assumed or known to *predict* whether someone will be able to acquire a particular skill in the future. Such prerequisites may include general cognitive abilities, previously acquired knowledge, PERSONALITY traits, physical abilities, etc. An additional factor is the time needed for acquiring the skill: even if everyone is capable of acquiring it, some individuals may need a very long time to reach a satisfactory level of performance.

In interpreting, aptitude testing is primarily used in admission procedures to select candidates for training in interpreter EDUCATION. Interest in aptitude for interpreting arose very early in the process of establishing (conference) interpreter training at university level – a landmark event being the AIIC colloquium on interpreter training in 1965 (see Russo 2011). In the face of growing demand for trained interpreters, it was not clear whether anyone was capable of acquiring the required proficiency, especially the fairly new and highly complex skill of SIMULTANEOUS INTERPRETING, or whether the ability to interpret was a talent that could not be taught. It was not until the late 1980s that the 'born or made' debate inclined towards the latter (Mackintosh 1999). With more sophisticated training methods and systematic training programmes, interpreting is now considered a complex skill which can be acquired, but only after a substantial amount of practice. Interpreter training remains very costly, the size of interpreting programmes is limited, and demand often remains high, all of which necessitates that most interpreting schools apply a selection process as part of their admission procedures.

Prerequisites and admission tests

There is a substantial body of (profession-oriented) literature on the topic of abilities and skills underlying successful interpreting. The most commonly mentioned core skills and characteristics required of an aspiring interpreter are excellent knowledge of working languages (which includes mother tongue proficiency beyond the level of a common native speaker, such as sensitivity to REGISTER and the ability to use various styles, understand regional varieties and accents, etc.), general world knowledge and a wide range of interests, COMPREHENSION and analytical skills, MEMORY, verbal FLUENCY and expressive ability, language transfer and communication skills, STRESS resistance and stamina, good VOICE QUALITY and confident delivery, and team spirit (see Russo 2011). Moreover, specific skills are needed for particular interpreting MODES and SETTINGS, for example psychomotor skills in SIGNED LANGUAGE INTERPRETING or interpersonal interaction skills in DIALOGUE INTERPRETING.

The list of skills and abilities is extensive and mostly formulated on the basis of their face value in the light of practical interpreting experience. It would not be feasible and practical to deal with all of them in the context of admission testing, and many of them do not lend themselves to a straightforward test. For example, there is no ready-made standard test of interactional skills or the kind of stress resistance required in interpreting. To satisfy the practical need for screening and/or selection of candidates, schools usually test knowledge of languages, general or world knowledge, comprehension and analysis, and communication skills. The tests most commonly used to tap these abilities are basic CONSECUTIVE INTERPRETING (usually without notes), translation, summarising, short speeches made by the candidate, and interviews (Timarová & Ungoed-Thomas 2008). Most of the tests are quite complex and there is not always a clear link between the test used and the ability tested. For example, summaries are used as a complex test of comprehension, analysis, language knowledge and communication skills. There are also some concerns about the predictive validity of such tests. Gringiani (1990) showed that 36% of those who 'failed' a diagnostic aptitude test went on to successfully complete training, while 45% of those who 'passed' did not. This suggests that the predictive component of admission testing is rather weak and may in fact screen out potentially successful students. More recent survey data from 18 interpreting schools indicate that, despite careful selection, fewer than 60% of admitted students successfully complete the training programme (i.e. qualify as interpreters) (Timarová & Ungoed-Thomas 2008). It seems that most of the admission tests seek to ascertain whether a candidate is ready to start interpreter training, rather than predicting future acquisition of fully fledged skills. Russo (2011) discusses the distinction in the literature between a focus on current abilities (already acquired) and on future abilities, noting the tendency to concentrate more on the former and thus prioritise readiness to undertake interpreter training. Admission tests remain a practical need, but there are doubts whether they deserve to be called aptitude tests.

Research into aptitude

Research into aptitude in interpreting addresses the shortcomings of current admission tests by (1) searching for components of interpreting aptitude, and (2) aiming to develop reliable and valid tests for each component. The search for components of interpreting aptitude is still largely based on observations from practice, and the components are generally similar or identical to those used in admission testing. To a lesser extent, researchers define new constructs which may potentially prove to be predictive. Some of the inspiration comes from more general interpreting research with student populations (aspects related to learning and skill acquisition) or with professional interpreters. The biggest contribution has come from the area of test development and, crucially, the investigation of test properties, primarily their predictive validity. An effective (multi-component) aptitude test should predict with reasonable accuracy whether a candidate for an interpreter training programme will successfully complete it. Importantly, research also focuses on many of the aptitude components which are not easily implemented on a practical level or for which no intuitive test exists.

Two major classes of tests are used in research into aptitude: (a) those borrowed from, or inspired by, work in other disciplines; (b) those developed by interpreting researchers specifically for testing in the context of interpreting. Tests of the first type often focus on underlying cognitive abilities and personality traits. Examples include tests of verbal fluency (e.g. Carroll 1978), speed stress (Gerver et al. 1989) and PSYCHOMETRIC TESTS measuring anxiety (Jiménez

Ivars & Pinazo Calatayud 2001). The majority of these tests focus on a single component. However, since interpreting is considered to be a very complex skill, the contribution of any single element tested in this way is presumably quite limited. A comprehensive aptitude test would have to be composed of a whole battery of such tests, tapping a range of different aptitude components. Such tests would provide a much more accurate understanding of the structure of aptitude for interpreting, and allow for a more fine-tuned profile of the individual concerned. A practical difficulty with incorporating such tests into admission testing is that they often require the use of specialist instruments and (psychological) training for their use.

Tests developed within interpreting studies are often more ecological, that is, they bear closer resemblance to the actual interpreting task. These tests include a variety of text-based tasks, such as summarising a text or speech (e.g. Gerver et al. 1989), paraphrasing (e.g. Russo & Pippa 2004), CLOZE tests (e.g. Pöchhacker 2011a) or SHADOWING (e.g. Lambert 1992). The tests are typically administered before any training has taken place, and test scores can later be compared to performance on an interpreting task, often to exam results at the end of the training programme.

Several studies report a battery of tests which have proved reasonably effective at predicting final interpreting exam performance (Gerver et al. 1989; Moser-Mercer 1985), and other authors report good results with individual tests. There are, however, some problems with implementation in admission testing. Promising results from a successful study are not always followed up by further validation and, where follow-up research is done, results do not always confirm the original findings (see e.g. Shaw et al. 2008). An exception in this respect is the work of Russo (e.g. 2011, 2014), who has been active in aptitude research for more than 20 years, developing, validating and refining her testing tools on several generations of students. Moreover, not all tests with good predictive properties are feasible in the fairly time-constrained context of admission testing, where large numbers of candidates need to be tested in an efficient manner. The issue of choosing among predictive tests on the basis of their usability in practice is discussed by Chabasse and Kader (2014).

Apart from the traditional focus on skills and abilities directly related to interpreting, recent trends in research focus on learners' characteristics and suggest that these too be considered as part of aptitude or admission tests (Shaw & Hughes 2006). With regard to aptitude, the time needed to achieve the standard of performance required for successful completion of training is an important determinant. Students' confidence and motivation, and the type of learning support they need, are some of the factors that are thought to influence successful programme completion. This approach recognises that aptitude may need to be supported by an appropriate learning environment, in order to be fully expressed in the acquisition of interpreting skill. Viewing skill development as a function of complex external and internal factors, as discussed in greater detail by Moser-Mercer (2008), allows for better discrimination between (a) true aptitude, i.e. abilities which the candidate must have and which cannot be taught, (b) abilities expected to have been acquired before interpreter training, and (c) abilities which will be acquired during training (Bontempo & Napier 2009). Different training programmes may offer a different balance between (b) and (c). For example, many sign language interpreter training programmes provide language training as well.

Aptitude testing is improving in terms of its validity and a sharper focus on the predictive aspect of the tests. Several candidates have emerged which may prove to be useful for selection purposes (see the Special Issue of *INTERPRETING* (13:1, 2013) or its expanded reprint, Pöchhacker & Liu 2014). These tests focus on linguistic flexibility (Russo 2014; Pöchhacker 2011a) as well as general cognitive flexibility (Macnamara et al. 2011), including aspects of attention management (Chabasse & Kader 2014) and WORKING MEMORY. Nevertheless, more research is needed before available findings can be turned into a feasible and reliable admission test.

ŠÁRKA TIMAROVÁ

ASSESSMENT

↑ QUALITY → COMPETENCE,
→ QUALITY CRITERIA
↓ ACCURACY, ↓ ERROR ANALYSIS, ↓ FLUENCY

The term 'assessment' generally refers to a "systematic method of obtaining information from tests and other sources, used to draw inferences about characteristics of people, objects, or programs" (AERA et al. 1999: 172). Evaluation, a term that is often associated with assessment, can be better understood as one possible use of assessment which involves making judgments and decisions (Bachman 2004).

In the field of interpreting, assessment has been a topic in professional and academic discussions for as long as the interpreting community has been concerned about quality. Aside from its role in professional CERTIFICATION, assessment is an integral component of interpreter EDUCATION and is used for a wide array of purposes, including student selection, progress monitoring, and degree or certificate conferral (Sawyer 2004). Nevertheless, assessment in interpreting continues to be characterized by a lack of systematic methods and consistent standards and practices, as manifested in the arbitrary selection of test content, inconsistent test administration, and a failure to establish and respect objective scoring criteria (Sawyer 2004).

Assessment in interpreting mainly targets interpreting output. However, since interpreting quality as a concept is considered "essentially relative and multi-dimensional" (Pöchhacker 2004a: 153), it is generally believed that assessment should not only include the interpreter's output but also consider the context, situation and WORKING CONDITIONS as well as the user perspective (see Kalina 2005a). Conceptually justified as it may be to view quality in relation to variable contexts, the practical drawback of this perspective is that it does not offer useful guidance for assessment, which, in its essence, is about measurement. To make the concept of quality measurable, it first needs to be defined in terms of observable and distinguishable constructs.

Measurable constructs and rating

Among the constructs that have been used to describe the different dimensions of interpreting quality, FIDELITY (including ACCURACY and completeness) and FLUENCY (of language use and delivery) are generally considered the most important, and are widely used as the main QUALITY CRITERIA in the assessment practices of interpreter training institutions (Liu et al. 2008). Even so, these two constructs largely remain 'fuzzy' and are often not operationalized to make them measurable in actual assessment practice. These criteria tend to be merely labeled, but not described, and raters are left to use their own judgment as to what the criteria mean, and to make a rating decision that represents no more than an overall impression of a performance (Liu 2013). Rater bias is inevitable in this situation. As Wu (2013) shows in his study on rater behavior, raters may be very inconsistent in their assessment of an interpreting performance, possibly as a result of the difficulty of differentiating between the various rating criteria.

The problem of rater bias is conventionally addressed by resorting to group decisions. Rating may be done independently, but the final decision on 'pass' or 'fail' is often based on a joint agreement among raters, most often a small group of professional interpreters and/or interpreter trainers. Using expert judgment may seem like an ideal way for performance assessment. However, it has been observed that raters' professional EXPERTISE does not lead to a high degree of agreement in professional judgment (Sawyer 2004). The approach of collective judgment by experts may work well if rater training is in place, to ensure that consensus is based on agreed-upon standards. However, rater training is rarely an integral component of assessment practices in interpreting.

One way to operationalize rating criteria such as accuracy is by taking into account the severity of errors when an error deduction approach is used. This is based on source–target informational correspondence and ERROR ANALYSIS. If an error of meaning is considered *major*, more points are deducted from the total score than for a *minor* error. However, as the errors are seldom predefined, which error is considered major or minor is often up to each rater to decide, so that there is a strong tendency for rater bias.

In addition to the highly subjective nature of judging the severity of an error, it is difficult to determine whether an error is a single word, a complete sentence or an inferred link between two sentences. One (albeit uncommon) way of addressing this is to determine the rating units in the source material before the assessment starts (e.g. Liu et al. 2004; Mackintosh 1983). For this purpose, the source text may be decomposed into propositions, conceived to represent basic units of structurally related concepts. Accuracy is then rated according to the number of propositions correctly rendered in the target language (e.g. Chang & Schallert 2007; Liu & Chiu 2009).

The advantage of using meaning units in rating is that a decision on accuracy can no longer rely on an impression of the whole interpretation, but has to be based on how meaning is created in each defined unit in a text. As not all meaning units are equally important, there is an attempt to assign different values to the rating units based on their contribution to the overall meaning of the test material (Liu 2013). A disadvantage of using rating units is the potential tendency to overlook intersentential COHESION and textual COHERENCE in an interpreting output.

While error deduction is one of the most widely used assessment methods for accuracy, criterion-referenced, rubric-based assessment has also been a popular option for interpreting assessment, particularly in certification testing. Carroll's (1966) scoring rubric, originally developed for judging the quality of machine-translated texts, has been adopted in several studies on interpreting assessment, often with modifications (e.g. Anderson 1994; Clifford 2005; Gerver 1974a; Liu 2013; Tiselius 2009). As interpreting is typically judged on multiple criteria, an analytic scoring rubric is often used, each criterion being scored on a separate scale with different levels and corresponding descriptors.

Since scoring rubrics are predefined, subjectivity in rating can be reduced. The descriptor used to characterize the assessed performance at each level also increases the likelihood of consistency among scores assigned by independent raters (Moskal 2000). This can help achieve higher rater reliability – an issue that is rarely addressed in interpreting assessment. Another advantage of using scoring rubrics is that the descriptors can serve as a source of feedback on an interpreting performance for the person being assessed (e.g. interpreting students). This is particularly true for analytic scoring, where the descriptors for the different criteria have the potential to provide more detailed and more extensive information about the ability being assessed than is the case with holistic scoring, where different dimensions of the assessed performance are judged on one single scale.

Notwithstanding the advantages of analytic scoring, which allows raters to focus attention on specific rubrics, rating criteria for interpreting such as accuracy and fluency can remain difficult to distinguish at the operational level. This may be because language competence (i.e. listening and speaking) permeates all assessment criteria for interpreting (Wu 2013). Several studies (e.g. Clifford 2005; Yeh & Liu 2008) have explored the extent to which rating criteria like accuracy and fluency can be treated as separate constructs, and found correlations ranging between .67 and .75. Clifford (2005) suggests that it is not appropriate to treat these moderately but significantly correlated constructs as separate criteria, and that performance tests assessed this way cannot be considered multidimensional, but are unidimensional (i.e. only one construct is measured).

The possibility that the judgment of one criterion affects that of another was tested in a study on the so-called halo effect, an overall impression resulting in a biased view of a particular property. Results showed that no such effect existed in the group of raters who judged fidelity and delivery at the same time, using the analytic scoring scales of the two criteria (Wu et al. 2013). The fact that rater training had been given before the assessment task suggests that this, or other preliminary steps, may help prevent a halo or a reverse halo effect.

Reliability

The state of the art in the assessment of interpreting performance reflects a general lack of adherence to an essential element of quality in test design – test reliability, which is a prerequisite for test validity. In addition to problems with inter-rater reliability as discussed above, there is evidence that ratings by the same individual of the same interpreting performance may differ from one rating to another – a violation of intra-rater reliability (see Gile 1999b). Moreover, inconsistency regarding the INPUT VARIABLES (e.g. the information density of the test materials, or the SPEECH RATE at which a source speech is delivered) and the conditions under which the tests are administered can pose a threat to test reliability. If a test taker's chance of success depends on the rater or on the situation, one cannot be confident that a test predicts the actual COMPETENCE of the individual assessed. This lack of reliability may not be considered serious in *formative* assessments conducted by instructors in training programs, but insufficient justification of scores in high-stakes *summative* assessments, such as exit examinations of training institutions or national certification examinations, can cause distrust and give grounds for outcomes to be challenged.

There have been efforts to improve the consistency of assessment practices and outcomes by moving toward PSYCHOMETRIC TESTS (e.g. Clifford 2005). In translation testing, Eyckmans, Anckaert and Segers (2009) adopted an approach similar to what is known in modern testing theory as item response. In a Dutch text to be translated into French, the researchers selected individual segments for their discriminating power and had the translations of these units rated as 'dichotomous items' (i.e. either correct or incorrect). The authors compared the rating results obtained with this approach to those achieved with holistic scoring and analytic scoring, and demonstrated that assessment based on dichotomous items yielded much higher test reliability and discriminating power than the other two methods.

The idea of developing more objective tests seems to be generally welcomed in the field of interpreting, but efforts to implement psychometrically sound assessment procedures have met with considerable resistance. Aside from the emphasis on the diverse real-life contexts in which an interpreter's output is produced, a certain diffidence regarding the use of statistics to capture quality (Eyckmans et al. 2009) may also help explain this unwillingness to base assessment on systematically quantifiable measures.

MINHUA LIU

ASYLUM SETTINGS

↑ LEGAL INTERPRETING

Asylum seekers and refugees usually do not speak the language of the host country. They will express themselves either in an international LINGUA FRANCA or through an interpreter. Research on interpreting in asylum settings has concentrated on those encounters that matter most to the people seeking asylum, that is, settings where they interact with the host government authorities responsible for the granting of rights (asylum and protection) and resources (counselling and medical support). Basically, these institutional encounters directly or indirectly relate to the asylum application process, a legal–administrative procedure by which a country's authorities assess asylum claims on the basis of the 1951 United Nations Geneva Convention and the 1967 Protocol. This is an interview-based procedure in which asylum seekers have to submit personal documents and explain their motivation for seeking protection in the country to which they are applying.

National legislation for refugee status determination may vary. According to EU minimum standards, for example, asylum seekers have the right to an interpreter, either provided by the authorities or of their own choice. Considering the essentially asymmetrical nature of these encounters, the asylum status determination interview is a very intricate interpreting setting where a diversity of linguistic, socio-cultural and institutional resources and expectations meet.

Given the diversity of perspectives (from legal and linguistic to socio-cultural and sociological), research into interpreter-mediated communication in asylum settings has drawn on a range of disciplines and extended far beyond interpreting studies as such. This entry first reviews the various methods and approaches before providing an overview of the main themes and concerns, on a micro-interactional and a macro-ideological level, in the domain of asylum interpreting.

Methods and approaches

Pioneering research on asylum interviews in legal analysis (Kälin 1986) and migration studies (Monnier 1995) touches upon some critical aspects of the interpreter's ROLE and responsibilities in the asylum process. From the mid-1990s onwards, there was a parallel development towards a more exhaustive examination of the interactional dynamics of asylum interviews in the fields of linguistics and interpreting studies alike. Barsky (1994) was the first to conduct an in-depth field study of immigration service encounters. In his critical analysis of the written records of Canadian Convention refugee hearings, he identified a tendency among applicants, in their attempt to meet institutional requirements, to fill discursive and procedural gaps between their personal accounts and the bureaucratically recognized reports by discursively constructing the identity of a 'productive' Convention refugee. He suggested a "performative turn" in interpreting, identifying interpreters as involved performers in the asylum hearing who "should be legally recognized as active intermediaries between the claimant and the adjudicating body, rather than as innocuous translating devices" (1996: 46). However, his idea that interpreters can make up for institutional limitations and inadequate processing of asylum cases has been criticized for representing the intercultural space occupied by the interpreter as an "ideological void", disregarding the "inherently heterogeneous and hybrid places where cultures/meanings overlap" (Inghilleri 2005a: 77).

The empirical base for both micro- and macro-level research mainly consists in field studies within particular national contexts, mostly inspired by Wadensjö's (1998) study of DIALOGUE

INTERPRETING in institutional encounters. Such work has been done, for instance, in Austria (Pöllabauer 2004; Kolb & Pöchhacker 2008), Belgium (Blommaert 2001; Maryns 2006, 2013a), the UK (Inghilleri 2003, 2005a, 2012; Williams 2005), Sweden (Keselman et al. 2010), Italy (Merlini 2009a; Jacquemet 2011), Albania (Jacquemet 2010) and SPAIN (Gómez Díez 2010). These field studies draw from a set of data-collection methods: participant observation, ETHNOGRAPHIC METHODS (fieldwork), SURVEY RESESARCH, INTERVIEWS with applicants, asylum officers and interpreters, and audio/video recordings of authentic asylum interviews. What renders data collection particularly difficult in this domain is a general reluctance to allow asylum interviews to be recorded. The main problem, however, is not to obtain permission from the asylum seekers themselves, despite issues of privacy and the often very sensitive information they have to convey, but rather to be 'allowed in' by the institutional representatives. Still, notwithstanding the difficulty in accessing data, intensive fieldwork throughout the different tiers of the asylum process has yielded useful research material.

Researchers examining language in context in this field use an amalgam of discourse analytical methods, with an emphasis on linguistic-anthropological and SOCIOLOGICAL APPROACHES. In the former orientation, various studies adopt an interaction- and discourse-centred approach to examine how identities are constructed in micro-sequences of talk (e.g. Gómez Díez 2010; Jacquemet 2011; Kolb & Pöchhacker 2008; Merlini 2009a; Pöllabauer 2004). From a more sociological perspective, several studies have used Goffman's concepts of PARTICIPATION FRAMEWORK, 'footing' and FACE in examining the interpreter's role (e.g. Merlini 2009a; Pöllabauer 2007). Substantial research contributions by Inghilleri (2003, 2005a, 2012) apply Bourdieu's concepts of HABITUS, 'capital' and 'field' to theorize the social positioning of interpreters in the asylum process. Tipton (2008a) has used Giddens' concept of 'reflexivity' in analyzing how asylum seekers position themselves as "knowledgeable agents" and advance their "authentic voice" in the narrative process.

Alongside this considerable amount of research on interpreting in asylum interviews, the role of the interpreter in communication with asylum seekers is also discussed in studies on PSYCHOTHERAPY, and on interpreting in MENTAL HEALTH SETTINGS in general.

Micro-interactional research

From this range of multidisciplinary methods and approaches, a wide spectrum of interacting and partially overlapping research themes has emerged. A recurring topic in empirical research on asylum interpreting is the gap between deontology (normative standards and expectations) and professional practice. The professional STATUS of interpreters in the asylum system has been laid down in deontological guidelines and accredited training programmes, both at national and international levels (EU, UNHCR). As a rule, these normative standards assert 'objective neutrality' on the part of the interpreter: apart from "a competent command of the relevant languages", interpreters should have "adequate interpreting skills" such as "the ability to accurately and faithfully interpret what is said by the interviewer and applicant without omission, addition, comment, summarizing or embellishing" (UNHCR 2010: 33). On the assumption of absolute equivalence of meaning between languages, interpreters are placed in a position of INVISIBILITY in the triadic exchange.

Although the asylum process generally prioritizes the conduit function of the interpreter, empirical research has demonstrated that recommended practice is not necessarily matched by the actual conduct of interpreters in asylum settings. The ambiguity inherent in the interpreter's role recurs as a leitmotiv in asylum interpreting research. Conflicting role perceptions are manifest in different facets of practice, ranging from the availability of competent interpreters to the POSITIONING of the interpreter in the interaction and the replicability of the interpreter's rendition.

Availability of competent interpreters: lay versus professional

Although certified interpreters are generally preferred, they are often not available in certain refugee languages. In these situations, freelance interpreters without any specific qualification are used. Empirical research has identified some recurring problems with the employment of such interpreters in asylum settings, including issues of language variation (Maryns 2006; Bögner et al. 2010), proficiency (Merlini 2009a; Keselman et al. 2010), ACCURACY (Pöllabauer 2004; Maryns 2006; Gómez Díez 2010) and NEUTRALITY (Kälin 1986; Bögner et al. 2010). It goes without saying that lack of accuracy and detail may cause great damage in asylum determination contexts, where every piece of information can be used as factual evidence in the assessment of the case.

Positioning of the interpreter in the interaction: experiential versus institutional

One of the greatest challenges for interpreters in the asylum process is that they constantly have to navigate between the informal–experiential event perspective of asylum seekers and the formal–institutional perspective of the examining agencies. Bearing enormous responsibilities in achieving the best possible compromise between the primary participants' conflicting concerns, interpreters have to aim for comprehensibility in a space where 'ontological' and 'public' narratives meet (Inghilleri 2012). Despite deontological requirements of impartiality, research on interpreting in asylum adjudication and mental health settings has found a tendency for asylum interpreters to align themselves with the institutions they are working for, either by facilitating the bureaucratic process or, more controversially, by assuming the role of institutional gatekeeper. Increased emphasis on the adversarial dimension in current asylum procedures – establishing the credibility of the asylum seeker's account – is not insignificant here: in their rendition of the primary speakers' turns, interpreters tend to anticipate what is perceived as a bureaucratically valid account, that is, an account that meets particular formal genre characteristics – "coherent, plausible, consistent" (UNHCR 2005: 124) – which serve as a guiding principle for the assessment of the speaker's credibility. In this way, interpreters become "agents of institutional efficiency" (Kolb & Pöchhacker 2008) in the interviewing process itself, either as co-interviewers eliciting more institutionally appropriate answers (Keselman et al. 2010), or in the subsequent 'entextualization' process, as co-producers of the written record (Maryns 2006; Pöchhacker & Kolb 2009). The issue of interpreter intervention is even more problematic when interpreters become actively engaged in the determination of the national origin of applicants, where they take on the role of "auxiliary police officers" (Pöllabauer 2004) or "communicative detectives" (Jacquemet 2010) by assessing the characteristics of their speech.

Replicability of the interpreter's rendition: transient (oral) versus replicable (written)

The ambivalence inherent in the interpreter's role is particularly tangible in the multimodality characterizing the asylum interpreter's performance. While the interpreter is generally defined as an "oral translator" in the asylum process (UNHCR 2009: 18), the written word keeps pervading the interpreter's performance: (a) in the way particular criteria of scripted texts – COHERENCE, consistency, FLUENCY – are anticipated in the interpreter's rendition; (b) in the routine of interpreting "directly for the record", offering asylum officers all the necessary and 'ready-made' oral input for the written record (Pöchhacker & Kolb 2009); and (c) in the practice of interpreters conducting the interview and passing on their written translations of the applicant's answers to the asylum officer (Maryns 2006). This tension between ORALITY and written text in asylum interpreting also involves varying degrees of immediacy and replicability of the rendering: the interpreter's oral renditions go on record in written reports, meaning that they are no longer transient in nature but become replicable discourses in the text's subsequent trajectory. The implications of these ambivalences can be observed particularly when dealing with vulnerable groups such as children (Keselman et al. 2010) or rape victims (Bögner et al. 2010; Maryns 2013a).

Macro-ideological research

Interpreting in asylum interviews has been further theorized in relation to the macro-ideological structures that directly or indirectly condition the interpreting activity. Inghilleri (2003, 2005a, 2012) has made significant research contributions in this area, discussing the ways in which the interpreting HABITUS is consistently attuned to reproducing target culture standards and ideologies. The work of Blommaert (2001, 2009) and Maryns (2006, 2013a) has theorized the inequality of linguistic resources in asylum interaction, focusing on the ways in which linguistic minority speakers are severely constrained in using their multilingual resources in the monolingual institutional space. In the context of language use and interpreter allocation in the asylum process, the multilingual repertoires of asylum seekers have been shown to challenge the "myth of equilingualism" (Hlavac 2010) – the prototypical form of interpreting as mediated interaction between two monolingual codes – that is still potent in the institutional space. Ongoing research on language shifting in interpreted asylum interaction (Maryns 2006; Hlavac 2010; Angermeyer 2013) shows how issues of mobility and displacement complicate the process of determining the minority speaker's 'dominant language'. The multiplicity of socio-discursive parameters at play in asylum interaction confirms the need for more latitude in negotiating language, including the possibility of 'stand-by interpreting' (Cooke 1996; Angermeyer 2013) as a means to integrate the benefits of direct and interpreter-mediated communication with the authorities.

KATRIJN MARYNS

ATTENTION MANAGEMENT

see under WORKING MEMORY

AUSTRALIA

↑ HISTORY

Interpreting in Australia can be considered as being constituted by four manifestations of the PROFESSION: interpreting in INDIGENOUS LANGUAGES, SIGNED LANGUAGE INTERPRETING, CONFERENCE INTERPRETING and what came to be called COMMUNITY INTERPRETING. Each of these strands has its own history, and for a time the strands developed in their separate ways, each barely acknowledging the existence of the others. Over the past decades, these strands have come together in a unified accreditation system, with professional associations accepting members from across the spectrum. In terms of practitioners, there is a great degree of overlap between conference interpreting and community interpreting, given the nature of the market and the availability of qualified professionals in the relevant language combinations. Though some prefer to be known as 'health interpreters' and others as 'legal interpreters', such nomenclature is rarely justified, given the difficulty of specialising in the Australian market. The only exception perhaps lies in one of the types of interpreting pioneered in Australia, that of TELEPHONE INTERPRETING.

The interpreting landscape in Australia has been shaped by two main developments – the migration program and the National Accreditation Authority for Translators and Interpreters (NAATI). The discussion here subsumes the domains of interpreting in indigenous languages and signed language interpreting. The conference interpreting sector has developed more slowly, in terms of both training (with only a few programs offered) and employment, though there has been a modest increase in demand – particularly in languages of growing geopolitical significance. As regards community interpreting (a term not widely used in Australia until its adoption internationally), this was pioneered in Australia from the mid-seventies and produced innovations in CURRICULUM, research, practice and accreditation which have been emulated by a number of countries (see Ozolins 1998).

Immigration and interpreting

The arrival of the British to colonise the country in the late eighteenth century was simply the beginning of successive waves of immigration – some forced, as with the penal settlement, others motivated by a number of personal or world events, such as the discovery of gold, flight from famine or war, or by a sense of adventure. As far as interpreting is concerned, the connection with migration began in earnest following the Second World War, where, for the first time, large numbers of speakers of languages other than English (LOTE) were coming to Australia at the invitation – and sometimes with the support – of the government, either as political refugees or as assisted migrants to satisfy the great demand for labour.

The assumption made by successive government policies on migration was that the new arrivals would undergo *assimilation* into the hegemonic culture and become indistinguishable from the local population. When this assumption was proved by the facts on the ground to be a false one, the policies were modified, firstly to espouse the ideas of *integration* and finally, from the late 1970s, of *multiculturalism* (see Jupp 1998; Martin 1978). A great deal of store was placed in the belief that people would learn English in the course of the process of adaptation to the new culture. However, in the late 1960s and early 1970s the government was becoming aware, mainly through a number of welfare organisations, that this was not the case and that the inability to communicate adequately in the English language was causing grave difficulties and at times putting people's lives and well-being at risk. The areas of concern were not only the law and health; there was also a position which espoused the rights of permanent residents to participate in the political and social life of the nation in which they lived, and this participation required interpreters.

The provision of organised language services (a term encompassing both interpreting and translating) began when a 'translation unit' was created, within the then Department of Immigration, in 1960. In 1973 the Emergency Telephone Interpreter Service was set up within the same department – a world first. This enabled a person whose English was not adequate to call someone in their own language, be connected to a desired service, and to have an interpreter for that interaction free of charge. The government (in late 1973) commissioned the Committee on Overseas Professional Qualifications (COPQ) to provide a report on establishing standards for interpreting and translating, helping interpreters and translators to gain recognition as a professional group, and improving the level of interpreting and translating services available to the community. The COPQ formed a working party which reported in

August 1974. Its main recommendation was to base the classification of standards for interpreters and translators in Australia on five levels of skill, and to implement this by establishing a National Council on Interpreting and Translating (see Ozolins 1998).

The COPQ Report was well received and, following the inevitable political and bureaucratic machinations, the National Accreditation Authority for Translators and Interpreters was created in 1977. It adopted the levels system recommended by the COPQ, with some minor modifications.

Indigenous languages

Indigenous languages have been spoken in Australia for some 40,000 years. Their number is said to have been more than 500, but has decreased over time. Very little is known about interpreting practices in Australia before colonisation. Initial attempts by the British to communicate with the Aborigines with the help of kidnapped or orphaned natives, such as Arabanoo, Nanbaree and Boorong, were largely unsuccessful (Wakabayashi 2011). The person who has often been referred to as the first interpreter between English and an indigenous language was Bennelong (1764?–1813). He was thought to have been captured and brought to Sydney Cove in 1789 by order of the then governor, Arthur Phillip, who took him to England in 1792. Bennelong returned to Australia with the new governor, John Hunter, in 1795 and died in 1813 (Dark 1966).

In more recent times interpreting in indigenous languages has come to the fore in the area of law, understood in broad terms as relating not simply to courts but also to POLICE SETTINGS and PRISON SETTINGS. The most pronounced difficulties relate to the supply of qualified and trained interpreters for a large number of languages over vast areas, areas where the cultural traditions are often at odds with the notion of interpreters and their ROLE. In addition, the mainstream institutions display a reluctance to engage interpreters; recurrent linguistic/cultural problems remain unresolved despite the work of interpreters, due to differences which are little understood by the majority of non-indigenous participants in the interactions (e.g. Cooke 2009a; Goldflam 1997).

There was initial reluctance to incorporate indigenous languages in the overall scheme of national interpreter accreditation because this system was seen to be associated with 'migrant languages', and this was anathema to indigenous Australians. This issue was overcome, and indigenous languages are now an integral part of the accreditation system.

Signed language interpreting

Australian Sign Language (Auslan) is said to have developed from varieties of British Sign Language introduced by deaf immigrants, teachers of the deaf (both deaf and hearing) and others concerned with the welfare of the deaf from the early period of colonisation (Johnston & Schembri 2007). In the late 1980s, major policy developments included the acknowledgement by the Federal Government of Auslan as the language of the Australian Deaf community in the National Policy on Languages (1987) and the enactment of the Disability Discrimination Act (1992).

Signed language interpreting was incorporated in the national interpreter accreditation scheme in 1982, with an initial testing program for 'Deaf Sign language' and other test components influenced by the tradition of oralism (Napier et al. 2010; Ozolins & Bridge 1999). In 2013 the credential of 'recognition' as a DEAF INTERPRETER was added to the national system, to provide for an interpreter who is deaf and fluent in Auslan and written English and who may have familiarity with a foreign sign language or pidgin.

Accreditation

Originally set up under the auspices of the Department of Immigration, NAATI was changed in 1983 into a company limited by guarantee, owned by the Federal, State and Territory Governments and administered by a Board appointed by the governments.

The system of five levels of accreditation, with separate designations for translators and interpreters, has undergone some modification, and the current system for interpreting comprises the Conference Interpreter (Senior) level (formerly known as Level 5); the Conference Interpreter level (formerly known as Level 4); the Professional Interpreter level (formerly known as Level 3); the Paraprofessional Interpreter level (formerly known as Level 2); and the Language Aide qualification (NAATI 2010).

Depending on the level, NAATI accreditation may be obtained in five ways: passing a NAATI accreditation test; completing a NAATI-approved course of studies in translation and/or interpreting at an Australian institution; providing evidence of a specialised tertiary qualification in translation and/or interpreting obtained from an educational institution overseas; providing evidence of membership of a recognised international professional association of translators or interpreters; and providing evidence of advanced standing in the translating or interpreting profession.

The available NAATI-approved training courses cater for the bulk of the languages in demand but problems are ever present in languages of recently arrived groups, where there are difficulties meeting service demands because of unavailability of courses or testing, in part due to the lack of suitably qualified and experienced personnel to take on the roles of trainers or testers.

NAATI testing is conducted in nearly 100 languages, including 37 indigenous languages and Auslan. By 2012 it had issued accreditations in 115 languages. Most of the accreditations (some 70%) are based on completion of NAATI-approved courses in Australia; 28% on the testing program; and 2% on completion of courses overseas.

In Australia there is no legislated requirement for practising interpreters to be accredited by NAATI. However, most government policies on the employment of interpreters (and translators) stipulate NAATI accreditation as a requirement (see Hale 2011a). NAATI has introduced a system of revalidation, such that accreditations have a finite duration and their continuation depends on the holder undertaking a certain amount of practice and participating in professional development activities during the relevant period.

Before 1987 there were separate professional associations in each state of Australia. Under the auspices of NAATI, the Australian Institute of Interpreters and Translators (AUSIT) was created in that year. The tensions created by the different expectations of the Institute to operate as a professional body as well as a trade union were resolved in 2012, when Professionals Australia (a trade union encompassing a number of professional fields) created a section for interpreters and translators, where industrial issues related to the work of interpreters can be properly represented.

ADOLFO GENTILE

AUTHOR

see under FOOTING

AUTOMATIC INTERPRETING

see MACHINE INTERPRETING

BIBLIOMETRIC RESEARCH

↑ METHODOLOGY

Scientific disciplines are complex entities composed of individual researchers, groups and institutions. They operate with ideas, methods, equipment and, most importantly, with other people; resources available to them are finite, their activities are subject to certain norms, and their performance is variable. It therefore makes sense to scrutinize the disciplines themselves as an object of study, both in theoretical and in empirical terms. Bibliometrics is the statistical analysis of patterns of publication and citation within (mostly) academic fields, where publications are a tangible and reliable manifestation of research activity. Besides reporting on the content and results of scientific studies, publications also include their authors' affiliations, abstracts, keywords, and systematic references (citations) to other authors and their works used in preparing the citing study. This information lends itself to quantification for the purpose of assessing productivity (by individual authors and/or institutions, as well as for different periods, types of publication, journal ranks, etc.); the influence, or 'impact', of authors and their works can be measured by citation analysis, although the 'impact factors' developed for this purpose are controversial (Franco Aixelá 2013). Bibliometric analyses are used by authorities, national or otherwise, when deciding to allocate research funds and when granting or refusing promotion to academics. They are also used by sociologists of science, who investigate the social fabric and dynamics within academic fields.

In the field of translation studies, interest in bibliometrics is fairly recent (see Grbić 2013). In INTERPRETING STUDIES, Gile systematically used quantitative bibliometric data, compiled since the late 1980s and subsequently reported in the *CIRIN BULLETIN*, in his analyses of research into CONFERENCE INTERPRETING (e.g. Gile 1995b, 2000). In the first bibliometric papers in the field, Pöchhacker (1995a, 1995b) quantified publications by authors and institutions as well as publication types and topics to identify centers and focal points of activity. Grbić (2007) and Grbić and Pöllabauer (2008a, 2008b, 2009) were the first to use larger databases and specialized software for their analyses. Grbić (2007) investigated the development of research into SIGNED LANGUAGE INTERPRETING from 1970 to 2005, focusing on the distribution of themes and disciplinary affiliations. Grbić and Pöllabauer (2008a) used a set of bibliometric, network analytical and textlinguistic (keyword analysis, title word analysis, co-occurrence analysis) methodological tools to investigate research into spoken and signed COMMUNITY INTERPRETING in German-speaking countries between 1979 and 2006. Other bibliometric studies have been conducted in CHINA, where the growth of interpreting studies offers ample scope for quantitative analyses. Tang (2010), for instance, analyzed EXPERIMENTAL RESEARCH on interpreting published over the course of 50 years in 16 of China's 'core journals' and identified such characteristics as a concern with training and growing interdisciplinary relations as well as methodological shortcomings.

The case of China points to some of the problems inherent in bibliometric research, which essentially have to do with the nature and scope of the underlying bibliographic databases. In (translation and) interpreting studies, there are many publications in Japanese, Korean and especially Chinese that may not be covered in comprehensive databases. Moreover, unpublished theses and dissertations, which may have relatively more weight in a young discipline, remain untapped by accessible databases, such as BITRA, a bibliography of translation and interpreting compiled by Javier Franco Aixelá (2013) at the University of Alicante, Spain, or the online *Translation Studies Bibliography* by John Benjamins (see van Doorslaer 2011). Another limitation of scientometrics in interpreting studies at this point is the relatively small number of publications in the field, making it hazardous to apply the statistical laws that have proved useful in more established disciplines (where the volume of research output is larger by several orders of magnitude).

Aside from its use in assessing productivity and influence/impact, citation analysis can serve other purposes, such as analyzing INTERDISCIPLINARITY by categorizing citations depending on the disciplines to which cited authors and works belong (Gile 2006). It is also possible to identify the relative weight of different types of research in a discipline by categorizing publications as referring to concepts, ideas and opinions versus research methodology and findings from empirical research (Gile 2005a).

DANIEL GILE

BILINGUALISM

→ BILINGUALISM, SOCIETAL

Bilingualism refers to the co-existence of two languages within an individual (implying that a person speaks two languages) or within a society. Studies on individual bilingualism and societal bilingualism tend, on the whole, to fall within two distinct domains: psycholinguistics and sociolinguistics, respectively. However, the two phenomena are closely interrelated, and both are of obvious relevance to INTERPRETING, albeit in different ways. Whereas bilingualism in the individual (as discussed below) is the sine qua non for the act of interpreting, the co-existence of two (or more) language groups in a society both generates interpreting needs and variously shapes the acquisition and use of one or more additional languages.

The study of individual bilingualism, viewed as a subfield of psycholinguistics, focuses on the cognitive and neural mechanisms, processes and knowledge structures that enable the acquisition and use of two (or more) languages. As there are many factors influencing second-language (L2) acquisition, and different parameters of proficiency, bilinguals are not a homogeneous group. Rather, they can be classified according to multiple dimensions, such as their relative FLUENCY in the two languages, their functional ability in the two languages, and the age at which L2 was acquired (see Butler 2013). These dimensions lead, respectively, to a differentiation between 'balanced' and 'dominant' (or 'unbalanced') bilinguals (with equal proficiency in L1 and L2 vs. lower proficiency in L2 than in L1); between receptive and productive bilinguals (with the ability to understand L2 but not to produce it vs. the ability to both understand and produce L2); and between 'simultaneous', 'early sequential', and 'late' bilinguals (exposed to both languages from birth vs. not from birth but still at an early age, after some L1 acquisition has already taken place vs. first exposed to L2 later in life, after having completed L1 acquisition). To meet the requirements of interpreting, interpreters must be productive and (close to) balanced bilinguals, but they may be simultaneous, early sequential, or late bilinguals, because all ages of first exposure to two languages may ultimately lead to balanced bilingualism with a high level of proficiency in both languages. Though there is widespread consensus in INTERPRETING STUDIES that bilingualism is a necessary, but not a sufficient condition for performing as an interpreter, the notion of NATURAL TRANSLATION/ INTERPRETING points to the fact that all bilinguals, without any special training, have some ability to translate (Harris 1976).

A persistent finding in bilingualism research is that both languages are always activated to at least some extent, not only when bilinguals perform some translational task but also when they are communicating in a monolingual setting and intend to use only one language. A substantial part of the relevant evidence comes from studies in which word recognition and word production in bilinguals is examined. These have shown that during word recognition the presented word activates in MEMORY not only the corresponding lexical representation, but also the representations of words with similar forms in both the selected and the non-selected language (e.g. Grainger & Dijkstra 1992). Similarly, during word production an activated lexical concept triggers the associated lexical representations in both languages (e.g. Hermans et al. 1998). This phenomenon raises the question of how bilinguals manage language control – that is, how they make sure that, when one language has been selected for use in production, the other language does not constantly interfere in the form of unintentional code-switches. This issue constitutes a focus of bilingualism research that is especially relevant to SIMULTANEOUS INTERPRETING (SI), where both languages must continuously be available at the same time. Several theoretical proposals have been advanced (see de Groot 2011, Ch. 6), three of which have considered the special case of language control in SI.

Theories of language control

The language-mode theory proposed by Grosjean (1997, 2001) includes the assumption that activation of the two language subsystems (briefly called 'languages' by Grosjean) in bilingual memory can be adapted to the specific characteristics of the communicative context, so that the two languages become activated to different degrees. Grosjean assumes that the selected language (the 'base language') is always as highly activated as possible, but that the level of activation of the other language (the 'guest language') varies with the contextual circumstances. For instance, when conversing with monolingual speakers, bilinguals will be in a 'monolingual mode', wherein the guest language is deactivated as far as possible. In contrast, when their interlocutors are bilingual speakers of the same two languages, bilinguals may be in a 'bilingual mode', wherein the guest language too is highly activated (though less so than the base language). Intermediate language-mode states (i.e. in-between states of activation of the guest language) may also arise, depending upon various factors such as the conversational topic and the interlocutors' knowledge about one another's level of fluency in the two languages and language use preferences. According to these ideas, language maintenance in mono-lingual settings is secured by the monolingual mode in which the bilingual participants are operating in these situations.

Grosjean (2001) extended his language-mode theory to account for language control in SI. To the two language subsystems in the original model (which can be viewed as stores of linguistic units) he added two processing mechanisms per language, one dealing with input and the other with output. He assumed that during SI the two language subsystems are both highly, and equally, activated (in other words, they are in a bilingual mode), whereas activation across the four processing mechanisms varies. He supposed the two mechanisms for output processing to be in a monolingual mode, with maximal activation of the one for output in the target language and the highest possible degree of deactivation of the mechanism for processing source-language output. This set-up enables target-language production while preventing source-language production. In addition, Grosjean hypothesized that during SI the two mechanisms for input processing are in a bilingual mode. This enables processing of input not only in the source language (for purposes of COMPREHENSION) but also, at the same time, in the target language (for self-monitoring by the interpreter).

Grosjean's original idea of two language subsystems that can be activated and deactivated independently of one another and to varying degrees, depending on the language user's current needs and goals, is also central to the neurolinguistic theory of bilingualism developed by Paradis (1994, 2004). Paradis focuses on the individual linguistic items in the language sub-systems and on what happens to them during language use, using neural terminology to describe the processes involved. In this account, a word is recognized or produced the moment the amount of activation in its neural substrate surpasses a critical threshold. During language use the representation of a targeted item (e.g. a specific word) is activated by positive neural impulses, while at the same time the activation thresholds of competing items are raised so that these items become less available. Paradis furthermore assumes that neural impulses are less easily generated from an internal (mental) source than from an external stimulus. To enable not only comprehension (which results from external stimulation and is thus relatively easy) but also production (which comes from internally generated neural impulses and is thus more difficult), he additionally assumes that production requires lower threshold settings than comprehension. In other words, at a certain, relatively high, threshold setting, comprehension is still possible whereas production is not. Finally, Paradis assumes that a bilingual's intention to use one language but not the other has the effect that positive neural impulses are sent to all elements of the targeted language, while the activation thresholds of the elements of the other language are automatically raised to a high level.

To account for SI, where both the source and the target language must be readily available (to enable comprehension and production, respectively), Paradis (1994) assumes that the activation thresholds for both languages are set at a relatively low, though not equal, level. To prevent source-language elements from being output, the activation threshold of the source language is set higher than that of the target language. This relatively high threshold for the source language is thought to nevertheless allow comprehension, because external stimulation generates neural impulses relatively easily so that the critical threshold level will still be reached.

A third idea for explaining language control in SI divides each of a bilingual's two sub-lexicons (one for each language), into an input lexicon and an output lexicon. Christoffels and de Groot (2005) propose that during SI the resulting four subcomponents of the bilingual mental lexicon are activated to different degrees. Thus, the output lexicon of the source language is deactivated as far as possible (to prevent output in this language), while the source-language input lexicon and the target-language output lexicon are both highly activated, to enable comprehension and production, respectively. Finally, to enable output monitoring, the input lexicon of the target language is also activated, though presumably at less than the maximum level, given the assumption of greater excitability of elements in the input lexicons (see Paradis 2004).

Language control as executive control

Several sources of evidence suggest that (a subset of) the mental devices regulating language control are not specific to language processing, but are domain-general mechanisms involved in the regulation of behavior of all sorts (often called 'executive control' or 'cognitive control'). One indication of this derives from bilingual studies that address a form of language control that is involved in all forms of translation: language switching. These studies have shown that when unbalanced bilinguals are forced to switch between their languages at unpredictable moments in word production tasks (e.g. picture naming), the switch cost (the difference in naming time between switch and no-switch trials) is larger for switching from the weaker to the dominant language than vice versa (e.g. Meuter & Allport 1999). This asymmetrical switch cost has been attributed to the workings of a control system that suppresses the elements of the language subsystem not requested on the current trial and does so proportionally to the strength of the two languages: a stronger language is suppressed to a greater extent than a weaker one. When a language switch is requested on the next trial, the previously suppressed language must be reactivated. The more strongly it was suppressed, the greater the effort required for its reactivation. That the control system in question is not specific to language processing, but domain-general, is suggested by the finding that similar asymmetrical switch costs arise for switching between tasks (rather than languages) of unequal difficulty (e.g. between word reading and color naming).

Other evidence to suggest that language control is effected by a domain-general mental control system is the finding that bilinguals who speak both their languages daily outperform monolinguals on various nonverbal tasks that are known to involve the executive-control system – that is, the system regulating the planning and execution of behavior by means of various processes such as attending to relevant information, suppressing irrelevant information, monitoring and adjusting behavior (e.g. Bialystok 2009). If bilinguals exert control over their languages by involving their executive-control system, the implication is that they appeal to this system more often than monolinguals do, and consequently become particularly skilled in executive control.

A third body of evidence comes from neuropsychological studies showing that lesions in brain areas known to be involved in executive control result in failures to maintain a selected language. Depending upon the site of the lesion, this specific problem may manifest itself in alternating involuntarily between the languages in successive utterances, or in mixing languages within utterances. It appears that in the former case the afflicted brain areas are a frontal region in the left hemisphere called the dorsolateral prefrontal cortex and a region known as the anterior cingulate cortex, the frontal part of the cingulate cortex that encircles the corpus callosum (Fabbro et al. 2000). The lesion site associated with within-utterance mixing is the left caudate nucleus, a component of the basal ganglia that are located within the forebrain just below the white matter of the cortex (Abutalebi et al. 2000). Neuroimaging studies using hemodynamic signals (e.g. fMRI studies) have shown that these brain areas are core components of the domain-general executive-control network (e.g. Egner & Hirsch 2005). The fact that lesions in these areas are associated with involuntary language switching in bilinguals indicates that language maintenance is controlled by these same structures.

Finally, neuroimaging studies aimed at identifying brain activation patterns in healthy bilinguals performing tasks that require language control have shown that the activated areas are largely the same as those involved in executive-control tasks that do not probe bilingualism (see Hervais-Adelman et al. 2011).

Executive control and SI

Language control in SI, requiring the fine-tuning of activation levels of multiple input and output lexicons or multiple language processing systems, is likely to tax the executive-control system more than language control in more mundane language use. At the same time, other task components of SI also appeal to the limited resources of the executive-control system. Components of SI that take up their share of the control system's limited capacity are (short-term) memory and coordination, responsible for the temporary storage of information and the coordination of all the separate components of SI, respectively. But because comprehension and production are not fully automatized, they will also draw on the executive-control system's limited resources. The consequence of all these competing demands on the interpreter's limited mental resources is that capacity 'saturation' may arise, and this may lead to breakdowns in performance, as hypothesized by Gile (1995a) in the framework of his EFFORT MODELS. To avoid this, sub-processes must be automatized and perhaps modified as compared with these same processes executed by non-interpreters; executive-control operations must run smoothly, and interpreting-specific processing routines that circumvent possible mental bottlenecks may be developed. In PSYCHOLINGUISTIC APPROACHES to studying SI, word recognition, word retrieval and memory processes are compared in simultaneous interpreters, non-interpreter bilinguals and monolinguals to identify differences between these groups and to see how SI modifies its sub-processes. The awareness that language control may largely be handled by a domain-general executive-control system, and that the pressure on this system is extremely high in SI, has led some researchers to test whether simultaneous interpreters excel, even more than non-interpreter bilinguals by comparison with monolinguals, in nonverbal tasks known to involve executive control. Among the executive-control operations simultaneous interpreters have been found to be particularly good at are activities requiring mental flexibility, task switching, and psychomotor speed (Macnamara et al. 2011; Yudes et al. 2011), the neural foundations of which are being investigated in NEUROSCIENCE APPROACHES to research on SI.

ANNETTE M. B. DE GROOT

BILINGUALISM, SOCIETAL

Unlike BILINGUALISM in the individual, as studied from cognitive and neurolinguistic vantage points, the co-existence of two languages within a society is approached from a broadly sociolinguistic perspective, with special regard for diverse relationships between different language communities as well as the use of more than one language in various social contexts. The relationship between individual and societal bilingualism (including situations of 'diglossia') is not causal or even necessary; rather, one can exist without the other (see Fishman 1967). Typically, though, the two dimensions of bilingualism are closely interrelated, and in turn there is a multifaceted relationship between bilingualism and interpreting as a social practice.

Societal bilingualism (or multilingualism) may arise in a number of ways when two (or more) distinct language communities come into contact. Throughout history, this would have been the case for different linguistic groups living in neighboring areas, or sharing a border, which facilitated the emergence of bilingual individuals able to serve as interpreters and enable interlingual communication. On a broader scale, social bilingualism has resulted from territorial conquest and colonization, with AFRICA as an egregious case in point. Often as a consequence, numerous countries, including AUSTRALIA and many states in the Americas, have linguistic minorities using INDIGENOUS LANGUAGES, with variable needs for interpreting (and translation). Where different language groups have formed a political union, they may co-exist more or less on an equal footing, as in the case of Belgium and CANADA or, on a supranational level, the European Union. It is in this type of constellation, as well as in the case of nations with indigenous language communities, that a national LANGUAGE POLICY is most likely to mandate the provision of interpreting (and translation) services, at least in such public domains as PARLIAMENTARY SETTINGS and legal institutions.

Aside from such historical and geopolitical developments, the most powerful drive toward bi- and multi-lingualism in modern societies has come from migration flows, with immigrants forming sub-communities often defined by language and culture. In this context, as in the case of indigenous and deaf communities, one of the languages involved can be defined as the dominant/societal language and the other as the minority language. A given language can be classified as dominant in one national context and as a minority language in another, minority languages being those that are used by subaltern or non-elite groups within a society (Niño-Murcia & Rothman 2009). Societies consequently assign different values to the various languages co-existing within them, which impacts on what is known as language choice by bilinguals. These values also influence policy decisions, and thus the type and extent of interpreting services offered. Such interpreting to meet intra-social communication needs, commonly referred to as COMMUNITY INTERPRETING or public service interpreting, is crucial to ensuring access to public services for minority-language users who do not speak the societal language. In many cases, public institutions resort to bilinguals acting as ad hoc interpreters, but they may also use the professional services of qualified interpreters (who by definition are also bi-/multi-lingual).

The distinction between professional and NON-PROFESSIONAL INTERPRETING also relates to assumptions regarding the type of bilingualism required. The discussion of bilingualism in interpreting studies typically narrows the focus to 'balanced' bilinguals, who demonstrate high proficiency in both languages. The assumption is that a bilingual individual should exhibit virtually equal proficiency in both the first and second language, in order to acquire interpreting skills or perform competently as an interpreter. However, interpreting SETTINGS vary in terms of social expectations regarding the bilingual ability of interpreters (Valdés & Angelelli 2003). In CONFERENCE INTERPRETING, a bilingual may be perceived as performing best in both directions if s/he has two A languages, which Thiéry (1978) referred to as 'true bilingualism'. In other settings, by contrast, criteria of bilingualism are less stringent, and LEGAL INTERPRETING and HEALTHCARE INTERPRETING may be performed by bilinguals of varying abilities.

A relevant distinction here is the notion of elective versus circumstantial bilingualism (Valdés & Figueroa 1994). Circumstantial bilinguals are individuals who are forced to learn another language due to circumstances beyond their control. Aside from immigrants and their children, this includes children born into mixed marriages in which two languages are spoken, and children of deaf parents, who grow up using sign language and the societal language. Often children of immigrant parents, who learn the societal language at school, perform CHILD LANGUAGE BROKERING for their families and communities as well as for members of the host society (Angelelli 2010; Antonini 2010; Valdés et al. 2000). An awareness of the difference between elective and circumstantial bilingualism not only helps in understanding the rationale for language choice and for provision of interpreting, but also implies the need to examine how the PEDAGOGY of interpreting might best respond to differences in the acquisition of interpreting skills and in trainees' bilingual profiles (Angelelli 2010).

Another phenomenon of bilingualism with a bearing on interpreting is code-switching, that is, a speaker's use of more than one language or linguistic variety within the same speech situation, alternating either within or between complete sentences (see Wei 2007). While DIALOGUE INTERPRETING may require the interpreter to switch rapidly between the languages used by the interacting parties, code-switching as such is discouraged as a deviation from monolingual renditions. Code-switching in interpreting may nevertheless occur, depending on the languages (or varieties) shared in a given interaction (e.g. Anderson 2012; Angermeyer 2010; Martinez 2007), and thus constitutes one of many issues highlighting the interrelation between bilingualism and interpreting.

CLAUDIA V. ANGELELLI

BODY LANGUAGE

↑ NONVERBAL COMMUNICATION
↓ GAZE, ↓ GESTURE

Nonverbal visual elements of communication, which are referred to as kinesics or body motion communication (Birdwhistell 1970) and are frequently grouped under the term 'body language', are considered an inseparable part of the verbal communication process. These elements of NONVERBAL COMMUNICATION include gestures and other kinesic elements, such as facial expression, eye contact and posture, as well as proxemics, that is, the interlocutors' spatial constellation in a certain situation. In their entirety, they can limit, accompany and complement, but also replace or even contradict, the verbal components of interaction, either wholly or in part (Kendon 2004). Used effectively, body language can support and optimize the communication of what is said, and therefore make a significant contribution towards the constitution of the meaning of the spoken word. As body language partly eludes a speaker's conscious control, inadvertent kinesic elements can also have a negative and disruptive impact on communication (Argyle 1988).

In addition to its relevance for the constitution of meaning in spoken languages, body language belongs to the inventory for constituting meaning in sign languages. Sign languages are natural languages that are perceived visually and produced by body movements. Signing relies not only on manual but also on non-manual articulators such as facial expression, head movements and, in many European sign languages, mouthing of spoken words. Individual signs are defined by their major formational parameters: handshape, orientation, movement and place of articulation. Sign languages also have prosodic components, which are encoded by both manual and non-manual articulators (Pfau et al. 2012). Body language is thus a vital component of the communication process, not only for sign languages in general but also with specific reference to SIGNED LANGUAGE INTERPRETING.

Even though the significance of body language is undisputed for communication in general, its role is rarely discussed in the literature on interpreting. For interpreters, visually perceived nonverbal elements are important in two ways. On the one hand, interpreters must understand these elements in the source text, because they make an essential contribution towards its meaning; on the other hand, interpreters must be able to express such elements in the target language in a way that is appropriate to the situation. Moreover, interpreters also receive the nonverbal reactions of listeners and may need to react to these, if necessary, while interpreting. For these reasons, interpreters insist on having VISUAL ACCESS to both the speaker and the audience (AIIC 2012; Viaggio 1997; Weale 1997).

The complex flow of verbal and nonverbal information in interpreting, as outlined by Poyatos (1987/2002: 237, 1997: 251), largely depends on the mode of interpreting (i.e. simultaneous or consecutive). Verbal and nonverbal signals may come from different interlocutors, or may be superimposed on one another. Particularly in SIMULTANEOUS INTERPRETING, the nonverbal and verbal channels of communication are intertwined for the target-language audience (see Ahrens 2004): target-language listeners perceive the body language of the source-language speaker in combination with the verbal signals received from the interpreter. In this context, there is a risk of irritation and misunderstandings on the part of the audience due to the cultural specificity of nonverbal elements and the time delay between source-language and target-language texts (Weale 1997). The simultaneous interpreter working in the booth is restricted to the acoustic channel; his or her use of kinesic elements cannot be intended for target-language listeners, but may serve to support meaning processing and to accentuate target-language production (see Zagar Galvão 2009).

In the case of CONSECUTIVE INTERPRETING, it is primarily the kinesic elements – gestures, facial movements, eye contact and posture – that have an impact on the audience, as both the speaker and the interpreter are present (and visible to the listeners). Therefore, the interpreter's body language may have a major influence on the COMMUNICATIVE EFFECT of the interpretation. It is unclear, however, to what extent the interpreter's gestures and facial expressions should emulate the speaker's. Herbert's (1952) recommendation that interpreters should avoid reproducing any emphatic gesturing which might have accompanied the source speech implies that they should, on the whole, opt for less visible body language; another possible argument in favour of such a position is that the audience has already perceived the source-language speaker's body language, so that the interpreter's serves only as a complement.

BARBARA AHRENS

BROADCAST INTERPRETING

see MEDIA INTERPRETING

BURNOUT

↑ PROFESSION

Burnout is a syndrome defined by increased emotional exhaustion and depersonalization as well as reduced feelings of personal accomplishment (Maslach 1982). Research on burnout suggests that professionals who work with other people in emotionally challenging situations experience ongoing pressure that renders them vulnerable to negative outcomes such as deterioration in the quality of the service they provide, increased job turnover, absenteeism, low morale, substance abuse, marital problems and fatigue (Maslach & Jackson 1981). Interpreters may suffer from burnout in part due to competing or excessive physical and cognitive demands (AIIC 2002), and the syndrome is identified as a primary factor associated with early departure, or reduction in work hours, within the PROFESSION of SIGNED LANGUAGE INTERPRETING (Dean & Pollard 2001; Qin et al. 2008; Schwenke et al. 2014).

Burnout affects the mental health of human service professionals, including interpreters, as it is associated with numerous psychophysiological arousal symptoms, including insomnia, emotional numbing, psychosomatic complaints, and difficulty concentrating. Its symptomatology overlaps with such clinical disorders as anxiety and depression. In combination with secondary traumatization, or VICARIOUS TRAUMA, burnout is conceptualized as compassion fatigue (Figley 1995), a condition known to affect interpreters, with symptoms that approximate posttraumatic stress disorder.

Within the field of interpreting, researchers have identified several environmental and personal antecedents to burnout. These include role conflict and ambiguity, perception of one's work as underappreciated, unsatisfactory supervision, low levels of satisfaction with one's job performance, perceptions of high performance expectations, limited support outlets, and perceived skill inadequacies (Schwenke et al. 2014; Y. Shlesinger 2007). In research related to sign language interpreters, those working in VIDEO RELAY SERVICE environments reported particularly high levels of burnout, with documented rates in one sample as high as seventy-five percent (Bower 2013). In a study of spoken-language interpreters working with trauma survivors, significantly higher levels of burnout were exhibited when interpreters had personal trauma histories (Y. Shlesinger 2007). In MENTAL HEALTH SETTINGS, in particular, protective coping measures against the effects of burnout include peer support (Anderson 2012), debriefing and structured supervision.

TOMINA SCHWENKE

BUSINESS INTERPRETING

↑ SETTINGS → DIALOGUE INTERPRETING

Business interpreting involves interpreter-assisted cross-linguistic interactions in the private sector, including business negotiations, discussions, site visits, presentations, and so on. It can therefore be situated somewhere in the middle of the spectrum between inter-social and intra-social SETTINGS. Topics in business cover a wide range, and the physical environment where interpreting takes place also varies greatly: from a factory shop floor to a meeting room, or from a dinner party to a more formal banquet. In such settings, all kinds of MODES of interpreting can be utilised – from short-consecutive DIALOGUE INTERPRETING in bilateral talks, to SIMULTANEOUS INTERPRETING for more formal, conference-like settings with multiple participants. Despite this remarkable diversity, very little attention has been directed toward business interpreting within the field of interpreting studies to date, and research output has been extremely limited. Among the reasons for this lack of research is the obvious difficulty of obtaining natural data due to confidentiality and other constraints.

Business interpreting in conference-like settings, in consecutive or simultaneous mode, is not considered to be much different from CONFERENCE INTERPRETING in other settings. By contrast, in face-to-face dialogue situations interpreters often play a crucial ROLE for purposes of liaison between the two parties who do not share the same language. Research investigating dialogue (or short-consecutive) interpreting has expanded greatly, predominantly in the area of COMMUNITY INTERPRETING. In interpreting in public-sector institutions, issues of POWER and distance or sensitivity and tension are regularly involved (e.g. Mason 1999a). While these issues may also be relevant in many instances in business interpreting, they tend to take different forms, since interpreting in business is not typically conceptualised in terms of powerless newcomers and an institutional authority. Power in business settings is generally based on the relative positions of the participants in a given communicative interaction with regard to the business relationship in question (e.g. Garzone 2002a). In addition, institutional requirements concerning the interpreter's behaviour or linguistic output (such as a code of ETHICS) do not usually exist. Furthermore, business interactions often involve discussions and negotiations which may be characterised by culturally specific styles. This multitude of factors, which may influence the interpreter's behaviour as well as the nature of the task, make interpreting in business settings highly complex.

Makarová (1995) briefly discusses the role of English and Slovak interpreters in the business setting, and states that cultural PREPARATION is crucial since the interpreter must play the role of a cultural mediator. Nocella (1995: 30), on the other hand, holds that interpreters in the business setting are not expected to be neutral, but that they are required to be loyal to their own clients, because they are seen to belong to one of the two sides. Ko (1996) also argues that USER EXPECTATIONS include not only matters relating to interpreting but also various other requests, which directly links to the issue of impartiality. He also points out that the interpreter in this setting is even used as a scapegoat when things go wrong. Although these claims are prescriptive in nature and are not based on empirical data, they do reflect clear expectations that the interpreter in this setting should play a more active and extended role than in other settings. Such a view is perfectly understandable when the so-called "in-house" interpreter (who belongs to the same company as the person(s) for whom s/he provides interpreting) takes on an interpreting assignment. There are also cases where both sides employ their own interpreter independently, especially when there is a significant or potential conflict of interests between the parties concerned. In these instances, it is logical that the interpreter's task should be to maximize the business objectives of the party to which s/he belongs. Based on INTERVIEWS with several accredited professional freelance interpreters in AUSTRALIA, Takimoto (2006) found that some interpreters were in fact ready to take on a much more proactive role in the business setting, while still using the requirements set down in the NAATI code of ethics as a professional benchmark. Interestingly, the interpreters in the study reported that they would be prepared to adjust their role in response to the perceived expectations of clients, while they strove to deliver accurate interpreting and maintain NEUTRALITY when and if they were able to do so. Takimoto (2008) pursued this further on the basis of audio recordings of authentic business interpreting situations, and stimulated-recall interviews immediately after the interpreting assignments. Detailed analysis of the RETROSPECTIVE PROTOCOLS confirmed that the interpreters in the study in fact engaged in intensive monitoring of the clients, in an attempt to understand and respond to their expectations. In other words, the interpreters were ready to accommodate their function and the nature of their task to the needs of clients.

MASATO TAKIMOTO

CANADA

↑ HISTORY

Since its exploration in 1534 by French navigator Jacques Cartier, Canada has seen an impressively long succession of interpreters in all spheres of activity. Governor de La Barre of New France wrote in 1682 that among those indispensable to the service of the King were interpreters. Until the mid-nineteenth century, these "*truchements*" or spokespersons orchestrated diplomatic and trade relations between the French, the English, and the First Nations.

In the twentieth century, SIMULTANEOUS INTERPRETING first appeared in Montreal in the late 1940s at the headquarters of the International Civil Aviation Organization (ICAO). Soon thereafter it was introduced in the House of Commons, the seat of democracy in Canada. That was all it took for interpreting to acquire the prestige and distinction of a liberal PROFESSION, which has since expanded rapidly and evolved in various domains.

The first interpreters

In 1534, Jacques Cartier took back to France the sons of the Iroquois chief of Stadacona (present-day Québec City), Domagaya and Taignoagny, to teach them the basics of French and thus go beyond communication through signs. On his second voyage, the explorer was able to learn about the geography, resources, and inhabitants of the land from his interpreters. They even saved his crew from certain death by scurvy. However, when Cartier came to suspect them of being untrustworthy and plotting against him, he had them kidnapped and took them back to France, where they died shortly thereafter. Such was the fate of Canada's first two known interpreters.

Before the arrival of the white man, the aboriginal peoples had interpreters to facilitate intertribal trade and other types of negotiations. These interpreters were mostly prisoners of war who were kept as slaves. Kidnapping and slavery are therefore inseparable from the early beginnings of interpreting in Canada.

The founder of Québec City, Samuel de Champlain, initiated the institution of resident interpreters in the new colony in 1610 by sending young Étienne Brûlé to live among the Algonquians (Cranston 1969). The adventurers that Champlain placed in the allied tribes lived harmoniously with the indigenous peoples and fully adopted their ways of thinking and worldviews. Indeed, the nickname given by the Algonquians to one of these interpreters (François Marguerie) was *Abe nijin*, meaning 'double man'; two others (Jean Nicolet and Guillaume Couture) were known by the Mohawks as *Achirra*, or 'two times a man'. Such names were considered highly complimentary, reflecting the influence which these intermediaries had over the aboriginals – an influence from which the merchants and civil authorities would benefit.

Even though the many languages spoken in the territory belonged to only two large language families (Algonquian or Algic and Huron-Iroquois), a different interpreter was required for specific languages such as Abenakis, Algonquian, Micmac, Montagnais, and so on. Concerned about maintaining their monopoly over communication with the indigenous peoples, interpreters rarely worked with missionaries and produced no dictionaries or grammars. "King's interpreter" was the title of the official interpreters, whose ranks included Joseph Godin, Thomas Lefebvre, Pierre Gamelin Maugras, Maurice Ménard, and Nicolas Perrot ("the man with the iron legs").

The courts required interpreters for INDIGENOUS LANGUAGES, as well as for English and Dutch, languages used by merchants in the colonies to the south. Most of the court interpreters worked on a freelance basis. Also serving as interpreters were two women, one of whom was Élizabeth Couc. Born in 1667 of a French father and an Algonquian mother, she was abducted by an Ottawa chief at the age of 26 while detained and awaiting trial in Québec City for her life as a woman of ill repute. Under the name of Isabelle Montour, she became a celebrated interpreter and diplomat for the English. She spoke at least four languages (Vincens 2011).

Military interpreters were members of the regular forces and often held command posts. During the siege of Québec City by General Wolfe's army in 1759, the troops of the Marquis de Montcalm included over 1,700 aboriginals and 10 or so interpreters.

The earliest interpreters formed a sort of buffer that helped to ease culture shock. The resulting encounter between Europeans and aboriginal peoples did not have the same genocidal brutality of conquest that it had elsewhere. Of course, this is not to say that the French were never guilty of massacring aboriginals. However, generally speaking, the interpreters demonstrated through their approach that true communication hinges less on words than on an understanding of the cultural, religious, and other significant symbols of a society.

The fur trade

After the British Conquest (1760), interpreters were most in demand in the western regions. In the fur trade, the main contingent was still made up of French-Canadians, who were more skilled than their English-speaking compatriots at forging ties with the indigenous peoples and gaining their trust. The number of *voyageurs* transporting goods to aboriginal territory and bringing back pelts jumped significantly following the creation in 1783 of the North-West Company, a fierce competitor of the Hudson's Bay Company, and reached 3,000 in 1821, at the height of the fur trade.

Within the structure of this bourgeoning trade, the interpreters occupied the middle ranks between the *engagés* (hired labourers) and the *bourgeois* (shareholders or associates holding the executive positions). They constituted a sort of aristocracy, enjoying more privileges and higher pay than other employees in the trade. In 1804, the North-West Company alone had 68 interpreters, 12 of whom were English-speaking and 56 French-speaking (Podruchny 2006).

Serving missionaries

The competition that Catholic and Protestant missionaries engaged in among the aboriginal peoples also required the participation of many interpreters, as did the colonisation of the western plains. Jean L'Heureux is certainly one of the most representative of these nineteenth-century interpreters. Even though he had never been ordained, he passed himself off as a secular priest at a Jesuit mission, and, wearing a cassock, he not only preached but also performed baptisms and marriages.

This false priest accompanied Father Albert Lacombe in his proselytising work among the Blackfoot. The missionary Oblates made extensive use of his services as a guide, a recruiter and, when they went to administer the sacraments, an interpreter. A cultured man of deeply held humanist beliefs, L'Heureux wrote ethnological notes on Blackfoot mores, customs and handmade goods in order to increase awareness of them.

During the famines that periodically struck his adopted people, the interpreter petitioned the civil authorities or the mounted police for provisions. Playing Robin Hood, he even resorted to stealing horses and livestock, which he then distributed to the most destitute. He felt deep compassion for his hosts in their suffering (Delisle 2012).

Peter Erasmus, nicknamed the "prince of interpreters," is another legendary figure of Western Canada. This Métis, born of a Cree mother and a Danish father, spoke Cree, Sauteux, Blackfoot, and Assiniboin in addition to English, and could even read Greek. He interpreted hundreds of sermons and translated excerpts from the Bible (Erasmus 1976).

Treaty negotiators

Through various treaties, the government acquired land for settlement and provided for the creation of reserves for the aboriginal peoples. At those negotiations, the interpreters were key players.

Peter Erasmus acted as interpreter-negotiator at the treaty talks with the Woodland Cree and the Plains Cree. Hired by the federal government, this accomplished polyglot received an annual salary of $600, a staggering sum at the time.

James McKay took part in the talks for five treaties. He acted as both an interpreter and a negotiator, as did many other interpreters. Respected by the aboriginals, he wielded great influence over them to the benefit of the government.

John C. McDougall, who took part in the treaty negotiations with the Blackfoot, in addition to working with Methodist missionaries, tried to protect the aboriginals of the West from the loss of their ancestral way of life and prepared them for the arrival of the North-West Mounted Police, created in 1873.

For twenty-two years, Jerry Potts was the official interpreter of this police force (now the Royal Canadian Mounted Police). He dressed like a white man but lived among aboriginals and was an exceptional guide who knew the land like the back of his hand. In 1885, during the North-West Rebellion (a Métis uprising organised by Louis Riel in Saskatchewan), Potts succeeded, thanks to his power of persuasion, in obtaining the neutrality of the Blackfoot and thus avoiding a bloodbath. He was known for his brevity, his fondness for alcohol, and the swear words that were littered throughout his interpretations (Fardy 1984).

During this transitional period, the aboriginal peoples saw their nomadic way of life as hunters and fur traders transform, with the arrival of the settlers, into an increasingly sedentary existence. At the crossroads of these two civilisations, the interpreters, who were rarely neutral, sometimes defended the interests of the aboriginal peoples, sometimes those of the government. They signed treaties as advisors, interpreters, and witnesses.

In addition to the interpreters referred to above, mention should be made of Nicolas Chatelain (described as "one of nature's noblemen"), Henry Cochrane (who did much to prevent the aboriginals from supporting Louis Riel), and James Bird (who was fluent in five aboriginal languages in addition to English and French).

Explorers' companions

There were hardly any expeditions to explore Canada's vast territory that did not include daring interpreters. There is no lack of examples of expeditions saved from disaster by the intelligence, tact, and know-how of interpreters.

From Alexander Mackenzie to Simon Fraser, after both of whom a major Canadian river has been named, every explorer was accompanied by interpreters. Métis Jean-Baptiste Boucher, Fraser's travel companion, was the most influential man west of the Rockies.

The longer the distances to be travelled, the greater the number of interpreters required, given the tremendous diversity of languages spoken. In 1858, for example, James McKay, Peter Erasmus, and Felix Monroe, who were all Métis, took part in the scientific expedition of Irish-born explorer John Palliser. Both Arctic expeditions led by John Franklin and George Back also required the participation of many interpreters, including Thomas Hassall (a Chipewyan killed accidentally by a rifle bullet), Pierre Saint-Germain (a Franco-Déné), Tattannoeuck (an Inuit nicknamed Augustus, who saved one of the expeditions) and Ooligbuck (an Inuit whose presence in a hostile environment was reassuring). Métis François Maurice interpreted for James Williams Tyrrell, who in 1893 crossed 5,200 kilometres of the subarctic desert regions by boat and with snowshoes.

These long expeditions demanded extraordinary physical endurance from the interpreters and cost several of them their life. The interpreter and guide for Samuel Hearne's Arctic expedition, Matonabbee, committed suicide. In their voyage journals, explorers would refer to their interpreters as guides and interpreters interchangeably, given that these two roles often went hand in hand.

The excellent reputation of Canada's interpreters was also known across the border. To lead their scientific expedition to the Pacific coast, American explorers Lewis and Clark hired several French-Canadian interpreters, including Toussaint Charbonneau, Pierre Cruzatte, René Jussaume, and Georges Drouillard, who was massacred by the Gros Ventre (Skarsten 1964).

After the Conquest, British institutions were gradually introduced in Canada, beginning with the courts. Given that the judges were English-speaking while the population spoke only French, the services of bilingual English speakers were used. This practice continued after 1867, during which time the "bilingual" jurisdictions outside Québec, namely Manitoba (until 1889) and the Northwest Territories (until 1892), hired court interpreters who often served as translators as well. These interpreters helped to shape – albeit imperfectly, it should be noted – the French legal terminology used in Canada.

The cradle of conference interpreting

After the Second World War, the area of activity for interpreters expanded, owing in particular to the creation by the United Nations of special agencies such as the ICAO, which established its headquarters in Montreal. Given that the ICAO's working languages were English, Spanish, and French, the need for a team of interpreters was obvious from the start.

When the ICAO was officially born in April 1947, the type of interpreting practised there was essentially consecutive. Earlier that year, Harold W. Mandefield, the right-hand man of the head of language services, was sent to New York City with Québec engineer Tony Pilon to familiarise himself with Léon DOSTERT's simultaneous interpreting system. Upon his return, he had a booth set up for testing and training purposes in the Dominion Square Building, on Sainte-Catherine Street.

The future interpreters trained there under his direction. Some would read speeches aloud while others would interpret them and others still would listen and criticise the interpretations. In this way, the first conference interpreters in the country, totalling a dozen or so, trained each other without the help of experienced practitioners.

By June 5, the ICAO Council had decided to purchase the IBM simultaneous interpreting equipment that it had borrowed from the UN and installed for testing purposes in the Council

Chamber, in the Sun Life Building. In light of the positive test results, the Council had decided that all of its debates would be held from then on in the ICAO's three official languages.

In addition to Harold W. Mandefield (Canada's Léon Dostert), the first conference interpreters in Canada included master-interpreter Fernand Cordier, who delivered the French interpretation of Neil Armstrong's famous words: "That's one small step for [a] man, one giant leap for mankind."

As for Tony Pilon, a Quebecer of aboriginal origin, he had helped, along with the Royal Corps of Signals, to set up the IBM equipment used at the NUREMBERG TRIAL. He put this experience to use in New York and Montreal (Delisle 1990).

Official language interpreting

Beginning in the 1950s, governments, unions, and businesses across the country began to use the services of interpreters here and there at conventions and assemblies that had been dominated by English until then. Simultaneous interpreting, which was taught at the Université de Montréal by Jean-Paul Vinay, was increasingly replacing CONSECUTIVE INTERPRETING. The profession was spreading its wings both at home and abroad. Bit by bit, a market for freelance interpreters was taking shape.

In January 1958, a significant event greatly increased the young profession's visibility. Three graduates of the Université de Montréal – Andrée Francœur, André d'Allemagne, and Blake T. Hanna – were invited by the CBC to provide simultaneous interpreting of the speeches given in English and French at the Liberal Party Convention, in Ottawa. This first attempt was a great success and made all Canadians aware of the profession and its advantages.

It would be several years, however, before groups of interpreters set out to regulate the profession. In the 1950s and 1960s, it was still more or less the Wild West.

Parliamentary interpreting

In January 1959, Canada introduced parliamentary interpreting, an institution of linguistic, political, and symbolic importance. During his election campaign in 1958, John Diefenbaker, then Leader of the Opposition, promised French-Canadians bilingual cheques and "instantaneous translation" of Commons debates. The idea to provide this service had been around for six years already. On election day, March 31, 1958, Diefenbaker's party won a resounding victory. True to his word, the Prime Minister had a motion passed on August 11, 1958, providing for simultaneous interpreting in the Lower House.

A competition was organised by the only person in the federal government who had experience in simultaneous interpreting, Henriot Mayer, then head of the Debates Division of the Bureau for Translations. He had dabbled in simultaneous interpreting after the war. The three-member panel selected seven candidates, including four experienced Debates translators – Raymond Aupy, Ernest Plante, Raymond Robichaud, and Maurice Roy – nicknamed "the dictators" because they dictated their translations on a dictaphone.

As a result, since January 15, 1959, not a single word has been spoken on the floor of the House of Commons that has not been echoed in the other official language. This service has not been seen simply as a support to communication, but as a constitutional necessity that supports BILINGUALISM in Parliament, the cornerstone of Canadian institutions. In 1961, the Senate in turn acquired interpreting booths. Without interpreters in the booths, the Houses of Parliament are paralysed and cannot sit (Delisle 1984, 2009).

Evolution

The first interpreters made their knowledge of aboriginal languages and ways of thinking available to fur traders, explorers, scientists, missionaries, politicians, and law-enforcement officers. Thanks to their diplomatic skills, they played a strategic and peace-making role, even though many of them were illiterate. The fact that their efforts to seek peace and compromise prevented conflict on many occasions is among their greatest achievements.

From their booths, the first conference interpreters and the pioneers in parliamentary interpreting helped to gain visibility and recognition for the PROFESSION. The profession has since been evolving and diversifying according to the changing needs of society, including interpreting services in courts, healthcare institutions, aboriginal communities, and provincial legislatures, as well as SIGNED LANGUAGE INTERPRETING, the use of new technologies, training programs, and professional CERTIFICATION.

Interpreters form, indeed, an integral part of Canada's linguistic, cultural, and historical landscape. They have not simply played bit parts, and this is undoubtedly why they are not all unsung heroes lost to history. The memory of many of them is preserved in paintings, postage stamps, historical novels, biographies, commemorative plaques, literary prizes, and statues. Many streets, schools, parks, lakes and rivers have also been named after them, from coast to coast.

JEAN DELISLE
TRANSLATED FROM FRENCH BY EMMA HARRIES

CERTIFICATION

↑ PROFESSION
→ PSYCHOMETRIC TESTING, → STATUS

Certification is the process by which a person's COMPETENCE, knowledge, or skills in a particular field of activity are assessed against predetermined standards. The term 'accreditation', often used interchangeably with certification, refers more specifically to a third-party evaluation process applied to a program or an institution (see Browning et al. 1996). Like EDUCATION, certification is often considered an integral part of the professionalization of an occupation, as it contributes to assuring and enhancing the quality of practice in that occupation (Shanahan et al. 1994).

Formal certification in the field of interpreting did not exist until the 1970s, despite the fact that professional associations and training institutions – both considered critical to the STATUS of a PROFESSION – were established decades earlier. Thus, for a long time, membership of the International Association of Conference Interpreters (AIIC), which requires endorsement of applicants' qualification by active members ('sponsors'), represented the only affirmation of QUALITY for conference interpreters, functioning similarly to certification.

The end-of-training ASSESSMENT performed by many interpreter training institutions in the form of exit examinations also serves as a type of certification for students, though with limited influence due to its program-based scope. In a plea for certification as a way to boost the professional standing of community interpreters, Roberts (1994) pointed to the limitations of the evaluation performed at the end of training, and emphasized that community interpreters' skills should be assessed and their competency guaranteed by a professional body in order to achieve national recognition. Along these lines, the US Registry of Interpreters for the Deaf (RID) has operated a certification system in the field of signed language interpreting since 1972.

Certification administered by professional associations of interpreters has recently become an important driving force in the professionalization of interpreting, particularly for COMMUNITY INTERPRETING. The certification of medical interpreters in the US is a case in point. Based on efforts by the National Council on Interpreting in Health Care since 2006, a first certification scheme (Certified Medical Interpreter) was launched in 2009 by the International Medical Interpreters Association in collaboration with LanguageLine Solutions, a commercial language service provider. This was followed by the Certified Healthcare Interpreter certification program developed by the Certification Commission for Healthcare Interpreters (Youdelman 2015). These developments, founded on twenty years of stakeholder collaboration, clearly represent a major step in the professionalization of HEALTHCARE INTERPRETING.

In some countries, the government is involved in the certification of interpreters. In AUSTRALIA, NAATI, the National Accreditation Authority for Translators and Interpreters, set up in 1977, is jointly owned by the Commonwealth, State and Territory governments. In CHINA, the China Accreditation Test for Translators and Interpreters (CATTI) is authorized by the Ministry of Human Resources and Social Security (TAC 2015). The impetus for creating such certification programs has often come from legal provisions. In the US, for instance, the Federal Court Interpreter Certification Examination (FCICE) was created after the passing of the Court Interpreters Act of 1978 (Feuerle 2013). Similar momentum has been generated for LEGAL INTERPRETING in Europe by Directive 2010/64/EU, which requires interpreters in criminal proceedings to be 'appropriately qualified'.

State-authorized certification generally enjoys high status, as obtaining credentials from these certification programs is often required for government-related work or employment. For example, what sets CATTI apart from other certification programs for translators and interpreters in China is that it constitutes a mandatory requirement for translation-related positions within the Chinese government. Nevertheless, programs of this sort do not preclude work by non-certified practitioners on the freelance market. Rarely is there a certification program so comprehensive as to grant all interpreters the legal recognition and professional protection of licensure, the final step in the professionalization process according to the model by Tseng (1992).

Common to many certification programs for interpreters is the existence of different levels of credentials. For example, NAATI's interpreter credentials include conference interpreter (senior), conference interpreter, professional interpreter, paraprofessional interpreter, and language aide (NAATI 2010). In most cases, the various categories represent the different levels of skills that a certification program recognizes. In other cases, a category is established due to irregular or low demand for certification in the languages concerned, or in relation to a lack of formal certification instruments (e.g. tests). One such case arose when the category of Professionally Qualified Interpreter was created for the FCICE, because accreditation as a Certified Interpreter is currently available only for Spanish.

The most common method for obtaining certification is qualification by testing (Hlavac 2013a), provided that the test for a specific category or language is available. Since many instruments employed must meet the requirements for PSYCHOMETRIC TESTS, developing and administering them requires considerable know-how and resources (see Clifford 2005). Some certification programs, such as NAATI, also recognize training received at approved educational institutions, membership of an approved professional association, or advanced standing in the profession, including credentials obtained in other countries. However, mutual recognition of interpreter certification from different countries or regions in the world remains rare. This is a particular challenge for the European Union (see Pym et al. 2012), where efforts to ensure cross-border recognition of interpreter qualifications and certification remain on the agenda.

MINHUA LIU

CHERNOV

Ghelly Vassilievich Chernov (1929–2000) was a Russian conference interpreter, translator, linguist and teacher, and an early and seminal contributor to interpreting studies.

Ghelly Chernov grew up in the Urals, where his father worked as a chemical engineer. He did very well in secondary school, studying German and learning English from an American-born Finnish woman living in exile. Finishing school with the highest distinction should have given him entry to the university of his choice, but his application to study international relations and become a diplomat was turned down, and he opted for translation instead. He attended the Maurice Thorez Institute of Foreign Languages in Moscow, where he graduated in 1952 and defended his dissertation in 1955. After teaching at the Thorez Institute (1955–1961), he worked at the UN in New York (1961–1967) as the first Soviet (i.e. non-emigré) interpreter and then returned to teach again at his alma mater (1967–1976). From 1976 to 1982 Chernov headed the Russian Section of the UN Interpretation Service in New York, and also completed his post-doctoral thesis on SIMULTANEOUS INTERPRETING (SI) during that time. In 1986 he became Professor, then Chair, of Interpreting and Interpreting Studies at the Thorez Institute (later to become the Moscow State Linguistic University – MGLU), one of the first chairs in the world for this discipline. Chernov worked at different private universities in Moscow, and from 1995 until his death in 2000 he was Professor at MGLU.

Chernov is the author of two monographs on SI (Chernov 1978, 1987) and more than sixty articles. A revised English edition of his 1987 monograph, edited by R. Setton and A. Hild, was published posthumously (Chernov 2004). Chernov was also the editor of an English/Russian pocket dictionary and of the English–Russian encyclopedic dictionary *Americana*.

In the early 1970s his scientific curiosity drove him to build an experimental device for measuring the simultaneity of original and interpretation in SI, on the basis of synchronized magnetic tape recordings. The device, patented in 1976, allowed him to prove that the interpreter spoke simultaneously with the original speaker about 70 percent of the time (Chernov 1978).

Chernov's 1978 monograph was probably the first ever in-depth investigation of the SI process on both an experimental and corpus-analytic basis. For his corpus, Chernov used about 40 hours of tape-recorded UN debates (recorded in 1968) with parallel transcripts of SI into four official UN languages, namely English, French, Spanish and Russian, and transcripts of the 1978 UN remote (satellite) interpretation experiment in Buenos Aires, as well as observations of the performance of SI students on the UN training course at the Thorez Institute in Moscow between 1968 and 1975.

Chernov's ideas developed out of his practical work as a conference interpreter and the experimental studies he conducted around 1970 with the psychologist Irina A. Zimnyaya – a rare and early example of interdisciplinary collaboration. However, as befitted a pioneer, his theoretical sources were multi-disciplinary; he declared a theoretical debt to the Russian anthropologists, psychologists and philosophers (notably the proponents of 'Activity Theory'), such as Vygotsky, A. N. Leont'ev, A. A. Leont'ev, Luria and Feigenberg, and above all Zimnyaya (1973), but also to functional (Prague School) linguistics and Western psycholinguistics. In his later work, Chernov also took a strong interest in post-Gricean pragmatics in the form of RELEVANCE THEORY.

For Chernov, the very possibility of SI depends crucially on a sufficient level of redundancy in the input, coupled with background knowledge in the interpreter, to enable some degree of ANTICIPATION or 'probability prediction'. He saw this not as probabilistic in any mathematical sense, but as a constant process of predictive INFERENCING which, while not peculiar to SI, is the central cognitive process making it possible. In making these successive anticipatory hypotheses, which must be confirmed or rejected before production, the inter-preter can exploit both subjective redundancy (information in the discourse already known to him or her) and the objective redundancies that are built into all speech at multiple levels. These range from the phonetic, syntactic and semantic (with reference to Chafe's description of 'semantic agreement') through to – most importantly – the salient cyclical patterns of new and old information, or theme and rheme, described by the functional linguists, to which the interpreter can become attuned, focusing heightened attention on the newer, rheme component while using the potential for compression in the relatively redundant theme. These patterns vary according to speech genre – political speeches, for example, are rich in a highly redundant 'evaluative' component – and between formal and 'communicative' word order.

Chernov was the leading representative of the SOVIET SCHOOL of interpreting studies, and one of the first to apply empirical methods to the study of interpreting. While his theoretical sources, constructs and terminology may seem somewhat obscure to the modern reader, his pioneering works remain as landmarks of research into simultaneous interpreting that uniquely combine theoretical, didactic and practical perspectives.

HEIDEMARIE SALEVSKY

CHILD LANGUAGE BROKERING

↑ NATURAL TRANSLATION/INTERPRETING, ↑ NON-PROFESSIONAL INTERPRETING

Child language brokering (CLB) denotes interpreting and translation activities carried out by bilingual children who mediate linguistically and culturally in formal and informal contexts and domains for their family and friends as well as members of the linguistic community to which they belong. Since children, through schooling, tend to become pro-ficient in a new language and to adapt to the new culture more quickly than their parents, they are often asked to take on the role of the linguistic and cultural mediator. While CLB is generally perceived and studied as a phenomenon involving members of immigrant groups and communities, it is important to note that it is also a practice performed by chil-dren who belong to specific minority language groups, such as children of deaf adults (CODAs), who have grown up learning and using a signed and a spoken language (Preston 1996; Napier 2008).

The term 'language brokering' was first introduced by Shannon (1990) and soon became commonly used to refer to interpreting and translation activities carried out by children, as it best captures the complexity of the role these children play. This role encompasses not only the ability to transfer a message into another language, but also adult decision-making and sociolinguistic skills (Tse 1995).

Despite the significant contribution that child language brokers make to the economic and social life of their families as well as to the institutions that avail themselves of the language service these children provide (Hall & Sham 2007), CLB is still an unacknowledged aspect of migration in many countries. It remains 'invisible' to most of the parties that are usually involved in it – primarily family members and public service providers – but also to the children themselves (e.g. Ahamer 2013). In the past two decades it has become a topic of study within disciplines such as anthropology, educational studies, psychology and sociolinguistics, but, until quite recently, it was a disregarded area of research within interpreting and translation studies. One of the main reasons for this neglect can be ascribed to the opposition to this practice expressed by professional interpreters and translators and scholars of interpreting and translation alike.

Following the introduction of the notion of NATURAL TRANSLATION/INTERPRETING (Harris 1977), research on CLB has contributed to accurately describing the beneficiaries of these interactions, as well as the subject matter and the situations in which they take place. Researchers have noted that CLB takes place in a wide variety of settings, and that the primary beneficiaries of CLB are the children's families and service providers such as teachers, doctors and public service operators. Language brokers are also required to do SIGHT TRANSLATION/INTERPRETING of texts that involve the use of sophisticated vocabulary and concepts, such as bank statements, medical prescriptions, immigration forms and utility bills.

Since the mid-1990s, research has shifted to other aspects of CLB and related issues, namely the effects of this practice on the cognitive, educational and psychological development of language brokers. This includes parentification and adultification issues that emerge when children assume the role of the decision-maker in the family and that may have a significant impact on family relationships, on the children's acculturation and learning process, as well as their attitudes towards their native and/or second language and culture (Weisskirch 2007).

As Orellana (2010) points out in her review of the literature on CLB, research is mostly based on qualitative and ETHNOGRAPHIC METHODS, ranging from observational studies to in-depth INTERVIEWS and small-scale SURVEY RESEARCH. In its early stages, it was primarily US-based and centred mainly on Latino immigrant communities (Orellana 2009). CLB among other language groups (e.g. Asian and Russian communities) has since been researched more consistently. The study of CLB in Europe was introduced in the late 1990s and was initially almost exclusively UK-based. More recently, it has developed in other European countries too, focussing on the communities that represent the largest migrant groups present in each country, like Moroccan communities in Spain, North African and Italian immigrants in Germany, and a variety of immigrant groups in Italy.

This being such a young field of research, there are still many aspects of this phenomenon that have so far been neglected or underresearched, and investigation of which would contribute to elucidating the phenomenon of CLB in all its complexity. They include GENDER- and family-related dynamics, identity construction, attitudes towards this practice held by all the parties involved, the STRATEGIES that language brokers adopt and implement when translating, and culture brokering.

RACHELE ANTONINI

CHINA

↑ HISTORY

China's first documented account of interpreting, dating back around 3000 years, makes reference to designations for interpreters working in the four directions, namely, *ji* 寄 for the East, *xiang* 象 for the South, *Didi* 狄鞮 for the West, and *yi* 譯 for the North. These designations are commonly understood in the literature as functionary titles of interpreters (Cheung 2005). Some authors have argued, however, that these terms might simply be transliterations of the word for interpreter as phonologically represented in the indigenous vernaculars of various regions with which Zhou China (1100–221 BCE) had diplomatic contacts (Oyung 2001; Lung 2009a). This is supported first by the existence of another written variant 羈 (*The Annals of Lü Buwei*), also transcribed and pronounced as *ji*, though in a different tone, to refer to interpreters in the East; and second, by the bi-syllabic composition of *Didi*, which violates the monosyllabic pattern of classical Chinese.

China's imperial records, in which most accounts of interpreting up to the end of its dynastic tradition in 1911 were archived, feature interpreters in diplomatic encounters with its vassal states. A distinction is made between interpreting officials (functionaries) and 'foreign interpreters', recruited in the absence of 'autonomous' provision for the required languages.

Interpreting officials

Interpreting officials, referred to as *xiangxu* 象胥 (interpreting-functionaries) and *sheren* 舌人 (tongue-men), were first recorded as early as the Zhou dynasty (Li 2006). These officials were subordinates of *daxingren* 大行人 (senior messengers) in the official hierarchy, entrusted to communicate with – and interpret for – foreign envoys. DIPLOMATIC INTERPRETING officials in these categories were later described as *yiguanling* 譯官令 (interpreting prefects for envoys from vassal states) and *jiuyiling* 九譯令 (interpreting prefects for envoys from surrendered states) in Han China (206 BCE–220 CE), where they were placed within the court of diplomatic receptions, *dahonglu* 大鴻臚, or *honglusi* 鴻臚寺 as it was retitled in subsequent dynasties. This court was further developed in the Sui (581–618) and Tang (618–907) dynasties, as a result of China's growing diplomatic ties and cosmopolitan attraction, and it was more often mentioned in connection with the increased interpreting needs generated by exchanges with non-Chinese-speaking envoys. The court in Tang times normally recruited twenty interpreters, who ranked no higher than seventh in the traditional hierarchy of nine tiers. Known as *yiyuren* 譯語人 in Tang China, the court's interpreters primarily interpreted for officials and foreign guests. When it came to imperial audiences, these interpreters were also charged with ushering the guests in and coaching them in proper etiquette. Sometimes they were deployed to chaperon foreign envoys to visit scenic sites of interest outside the official premises (Lung 2008a). In addition, one of the required duties of the court's interpreters was to mediate in interviews with foreign envoys, providing crucial opportunities to collect intelligence about foreign countries, their geography, cultures, and peoples.

Apart from their interpreting duties in the court, interpreters were sometimes deployed as envoys, or to accompany envoys, within diplomatic missions. The possible rationale for the physical presence of these envoys-cum-interpreters in the presentation of China's letters to foreign states – regularly written in Chinese, the written LINGUA FRANCA in North Asia and East Asia in the first millennium – was their ability to give a sight translation of the contents in the foreign vernacular. The interpreter was often mentioned at the end of the missives, as a record of his mandate to interpret in diplomatic encounters. He was entrusted by the throne to convey China's intent and feelings to the foreign recipient (Lung 2011).

As mentioned above, interpreting officials were traditionally confined to the lower ranks of officialdom. This may have been because of their frequent contacts with foreigners, who were perceived as inferior and as lacking a sense of propriety and etiquette (Hung 2005). Arguably, though, their persistently inferior rank was also related to the essentially supporting role they played in diplomatic exchanges. Moreover, the Chinese intellectual tradition placed a premium on literary creation rather than translation, and on written work rather than oratory skills. This was arguably yet another reason for placing interpreting officials in the inferior ranks.

Foreign interpreters

In the Chinese imperial tradition, the learning of foreign languages was rarely encouraged, probably because of China's pride in its own culture and language. China's deep-rooted preconceptions of foreign countries as uncouth, and of foreigners as barbarians who should look up to China for acculturation, only served to reinforce this Sino-centric mentality. In view of China's perceived superiority, the learning of other languages and cultures was not deemed necessary. It was, in this light, the foreign countries' responsibility to resolve the language problems attendant on their tributary visits.

There was little incentive for the mastery of a foreign language until the first half of the nineteenth century, when Qing China (1644–1911) could not avoid dealing with Western nations after the Opium Wars (1839–1842 and 1856–1860). Nevertheless, there was a constant need for interpreters in diplomatic contacts, which was met by using foreign interpreters.

Sogdians were noted in Tang records to have served as the court's interpreters. Originating from Samarkand and Tashkent, they were multilinguals of ancient Iranian ethnicity, mostly active in the first millennium. Dien (1965) highlights the dominant status of the Sogdians, whose language became the commercial lingua franca across Central and Northern Asia, in the Silk Road caravan trade. It was their intimate knowledge of nomadic peoples which rendered the Sogdians indispensable in diplomatic exchanges with the Turkic-speaking nomads in northern Asia. However, there is archival evidence that Sogdian interpreters were suspected of biased translations in Tang China's dealings with the Uyghur empire (744–839) and that their integrity in inter-state politics was called into doubt.

Much later, in the seventeenth and eighteenth centuries, China used European missionaries who spoke Latin in its dealings with RUSSIA. Being the only source of Latin mediators who could converse with the Russian envoys, these Jesuit missionaries had sole discretion in the negotiations and were believed to have compromised China's territorial interests in the process in order to advance the influence of the Catholic Church in Russia. China's paranoia over this suspected betrayal as a result of its linguistic disadvantage triggered its decision to start a Russian language school to train Manchu Chinese. While the far earlier setting up of foreign language schools in the Yuan dynasty (1271–1368) had been intended to satisfy the practical requirements of Mongol rule, the Qing attempt to educate young people with a specific emphasis on Russian language skills was politically motivated.

The lack of foreign language experts continued to be a growing concern during the eighteenth and nineteenth centuries in China's encounters with the British, who were eager to market their industrial goods. When the Macartney (1792–1794) and Amherst (1816–1817) embassies from Britain approached China, MEDIATION was conducted lopsidedly through interpreters working for the British. On occasion, China deployed Latin-speaking Jesuit missionaries as linguistic go-betweens, but these missionaries did not have a sufficient command of English to establish communication. In fact, in the Macartney mission, two young Chinese Catholic converts with knowledge of Latin and Italian were recruited in Naples for the trip to China. For the Amherst mission, Robert Morrison (1782–1834), a protestant missionary, was hired as the only interpreter between the British and the Chinese. China was equally uncomfortable about the service of foreign interpreters in the treaty negotiations at the time of the two Opium Wars, as no Chinese officials were sufficiently competent to convey the terms of the treaties.

In the civilian sphere, three multilingual peoples were active throughout the first millennium in different regions of China as entrepreneurial interpreters serving the linguistic and logistic needs of China-bound envoys or traders. They were the Sogdians along the Silk Road, the Tuyuhuns in western China, and the Sillans (ancient Koreans) in eastern coastal China. The Sogdians, as a diasporic people with a talent in cross-border trade and a mastery of major languages such as Chinese and Turkic, were active as interpreters and commercial agents, usually working for magnates stationed in Central Asia. The Tuyuhun state was multi-ethnic, and parts of its population well versed in Chinese, Tibetan, Turkic, Sogdian and other northeastern Asian vernaculars. This enhanced its role as a service provider for distant travelers heading for China, either to pay tribute or for trade. The Sillans, active in the second half of the first millennium, were important mediators in marine transport between China, Japan and unified Silla (668–935), using their maritime skills and language proficiency to good advantage. With a strong Sillan settlement on the eastern coast of China, Sillans, who spoke Chinese and Japanese as well as Sillan (Old Korean), were popular linguistic mediators for East Asian commercial and political exchanges at the time.

Civilian interpreters are hardly mentioned in China's imperial archives, as standard histories attended almost exclusively to the activities of official mediators. Known as *tongshi* 通事 in Qing China, such interpreters nevertheless played an important part in mediating between Chinese and Western merchants who traded in Canton during the eighteenth and nineteenth centuries. Usually of modest social background and questionable integrity, they were notorious for their limited English, interpreting incompetence, and reported tendency to make deliberate mistranslations for personal material gains. This perception of interpreters did not change until the fall of the Qing dynasty.

Historiography and translation

In Chinese archives, interpreters are rarely identified by name, unless they were considered patriotic martyrs in diplomatic missions. Even so, a provincial clerk, Tian Gong, who served as an interpreter to collect information about – and mediate for – some non-Han-Chinese minority peoples in Latter Han China (25–220), was unusually complimented in his superior's memorial to the throne (Lung 2008b). Sometimes there is a direct record of interaction with foreign language speakers, as in phrases like 'the interpreter said' or 'the throne asked the interpreter to inquire' (Lung 2011: 162). Most often, however, interpreters are absent from written archives, as if the interlingual exchanges had been conducted without any language barrier. Despite such textual INVISIBILITY, generic references to interpreters or interpreting in imperial archives carry symbolic and ideological value. When foreign envoys are described as 'earnestly' hoping to pay tribute to the Chinese throne despite the arduous use of multiple relay interpreters, such rhetoric serves to brag about China's imposing appeal for foreign countries and peoples.

In addition to their interpreting function as such, interpreters were assigned specific roles in China's historiography of diplomatic encounters. They were entrusted to contribute to the making of archival records documenting China's interlingual and intercultural exchanges. In research on this subject, Li (2002) first identified the recurrent use of dialogue in the narrative style in which interpreter-mediated exchanges are recorded in standard archives. Lung (2009a) then traced the workflow from the interpreter-mediated interviews with foreign envoys in the court to the reporting of the exchanges in writing. Reports were based on a list of question cues and had to be submitted to the History Bureau within a month after the interview. This link between the court's interpreters and the archives about foreign countries and peoples is illustrated by a flow chart that spells out the connection between a mediated interview with the Kirzhiz in 843 and a compilation of the Kirzhiz account in the *Xintangshu*, a new history of Tang China, in 1061 (Lung 2011: 120).

Another feature of the Chinese interpreting tradition is the prominent role of 'oral translators'. Oral translators are deemed interpreters because, even though the source text is in written form, the target text is delivered orally. Given imperial China's general neglect of foreign language training throughout much of its educational tradition, oral translators served to give a spoken rendition of source texts written in other languages so as to facilitate COMPREHENSION and communication. Such SIGHT INTERPRETING/TRANSLATION of non-Chinese written texts, which would otherwise not have been translated into Chinese, was practiced in the early rendition of sutras by monks from Central Asia in the second and third centuries. The initial, piecemeal introduction of Buddhism to China was undoubtedly compromised by these monks' limited knowledge of Chinese. Again with religious motives, Jesuit missionaries in the sixteenth century undertook to interpret into spoken Chinese a large number of scientific works, before their collaborators – Chinese literati or scholar-officials – reformulated these interpretations in elegant Chinese prose (Hung & Pollard 1998). Science was thus deployed to attract converts and promote the image of the missionaries. A similar approach was taken in the second half of the nineteenth century, when Christianity was promoted by protestant missionaries. With limited spoken Chinese, these missionaries again served as oral translators in the Chinese rendition of major scientific and technical publications of the time. Many of them, such as John Fryer (1839–1928) and Young John Allen (1836–1907), were hired by the Translation Bureau (1868–1913) to co-translate, with Chinese stylists, science and technology publications with a view to facilitating the arms production of the Jiangnan Arsenal (1865–1913).

With the growth of Western-style colleges in major cities in late nineteenth century, a small number of Chinese intellectuals with good English or French proficiency emerged. The most distinguished figures among these newly groomed bilinguals were Wei Yi (1880–1932) and Wang Shouchang (1864–1926), the first oral translators to introduce Western literature to China, in collaboration with renowned Chinese classical stylists.

Interpreter training since the 1980s

Mainland China has witnessed rapid changes in interpreter training since the 1980s. These changes resulted from the opening of China after 1978, and the explosive economic development with which this has so far been associated. The opening of China created a huge demand for interpreting talent to cope with increased political, cultural, and economic exchanges with the international community. Most notably, it kick-started the UN training program for interpreters and translators at Beijing University of Foreign Studies (1979–1995), which produced some 100 interpreters, most of whom went on to work at the UN (Wang & Mu 2009). The year 1979 is therefore considered a watershed in the professional training of interpreters (Zhan 2010). Before that, interpreting courses were simply perceived as tools for improving foreign language skills, and constituted a subsidiary part of degree programs in languages and literature. In 2000, interpreting was made a compulsory subject in foreign language and literature departments in all universities, and is now offered as a two-semester course in the final years of most BA programs (Wang & Mu 2009). Even so, the concern with improving students' foreign language competence, rather than with nurturing professional interpreters, is still present among interpreting instructors, most of whom graduated from such programs.

Amid growing awareness, in higher education as well as in government, that someone with foreign language competence does not necessarily make a professional interpreter, the nature of interpreter training was quickly transformed in the new millennium to meet the escalating demand for professional interpreters in China's increasingly complex global exchanges. Since then, about one hundred BA programs in translation and interpreting have been created on the mainland, and some 150 universities have been given the mandate to launch MA programs in translation and interpreting (MTI). Some of these have been authorized to offer a master's degree in interpreting (MI), with a focus on professional training. Six universities offer doctoral programs in interpreting studies. The postgraduate CURRICULUM for interpreting typically includes four components, namely skills-based modules, subject-knowledge modules, language-specific modules, and professional internships or practicum modules. This structure represents a shift from the conventional theme-based training mode to a skills-based orientation, in a more modern design.

RACHEL LUNG

CHUCHOTAGE

see under SIMULTANEOUS INTERPRETING

CHUNKING

see SEGMENTATION

CHURCH INTERPRETING

see under RELIGIOUS SETTINGS

CIRIN BULLETIN

In the 1980s, research into CONFERENCE INTERPRETING was scattered, with a few productive centers, a rather small number of individual researchers (see Pöchhacker 1995a), and little exchange of information between them. As a step towards better dissemination of information, the Interpretation Research and Theory Information Network (IRTIN) was set up as an individual initiative by Daniel Gile in 1990. It was originally structured as a network with headquarters in Paris and 'nodes' in eight other countries (five European countries as well as Australia, Canada and the US). The nodes' role was to promote the network in their respective countries and serve as a relay for information between individual participants and Paris. From the start, the main activity of the network has been the pub-lication, twice a year, of an information bulletin. This *IRTIN Bulletin*, later renamed *IRN Bulletin*, became the *CIRIN Bulletin* when the network changed its name to Conference Interpreting Research Information Network (CIRIN). Its purpose, as stated in *Bulletin* no. 1, published in February 1991, has remained unchanged – that is, to disseminate short pieces of information on interpreting research not easily (or not yet) found in the major translation and interpreting journals, for the benefit of interpreting researchers scattered around the world and often unaware of each other's work.

In the course of the 1990s, the number of national nodes grew rapidly to more than 30, and the *Bulletin* went online in 1998 (www.cirinandgile.com). CIRIN operates at very low cost, essentially limited to web-hosting and domain-name fees.

The *Bulletin*, written in English, features an editorial and various sections with biblio-graphical references, generally including abstracts or brief summaries. Most of the CIRIN material on articles and books is collected by Gile throughout the year, and valuable input on Master's theses and doctoral dissertations is provided by colleagues around the globe.

Many comments in the literature (e.g. Pöchhacker 2004a) suggest that CIRIN is widely viewed as having contributed significantly to the dissemination of information on research into interpreting. It has served as a database for BIBLIOMETRIC RESEARCH in interpreting studies (e.g. Pöchhacker 1995a; Gile 2000, 2005a), and was a key source for the "Bibliography on inter-pretation" published in the late 1990s by AIIC. There are now other convenient information channels for mainstream publications on conference interpreting research in Western languages, such as online journals, but CIRIN may be more efficient in providing information about unpublished theses and dissertations and about publications from Far-Eastern countries.

As indicated by the network's name, CIRIN specializes in conference interpreting (though MEDIA INTERPRETING is included), and information about publications on other types of interpreting is marginal in the *Bulletin*. While Gile has encouraged colleagues to develop a similar tool for other branches of interpreting, this idea has not taken shape.

DANIEL GILE

CLOZE

↑ APTITUDE TESTING, ↑ PRE-INTERPRETING EXERCISES
→ ANTICIPATION, → CREATIVITY

The cloze test was devised by W. L. Taylor in 1953 to assess language proficiency. Essentially a gap-filling exercise, the cloze task is based on the assumption that texts are redundant in that they contain more information than is required for them to be understood. Due to this redundancy, which is reflected in words, sentence and textual structures, recipients are even able to understand a message if it is incomplete or grammatically incorrect. Native speakers 'reconstruct' the message automatically and practically effortlessly, whereas non-native speakers require significantly more cognitive resources for this task.

Cloze exercises are created using authentic texts from which certain words are removed, either randomly or according to predetermined rules. For example, every fifth word could be omitted, or words belonging to a certain grammatical category (connectors, adjectives or verbs). The first two or three sentences remain unchanged, to provide contextual knowledge. Students are asked to fill in the blanks by drawing on their language skills, grasping the text's inherent structure, anticipating information and, ultimately, coming to conclusions (closure). Cloze tests therefore serve the purpose of assessing language proficiency in terms of vocabulary, listening and reading comprehension as well as ANTICIPATION skills (Oller & Conrad 1971), short-term and long-term MEMORY capacity as well as CREATIVITY (Anaya & Lopez 1990).

Cloze exercises are well suited to train key skills in preparation for interpreting, as students are required to apply their knowledge and intuitively understand the underlying meaning of texts even if they are not familiar with every single word (Lambert 1989a; Anaya & Lopez 1990). Cloze exercises also lend themselves to interpreting admission exams (Gerver et al. 1989; Chabasse & Kader 2014).

Cloze tests can be conducted in written and oral form. When conducted orally, the missing passages are completed either by stating the answer out loud or by writing it down.

There are two evaluation techniques for cloze exercises. In the case of *closed cloze*, only the exact words that were originally deleted are accepted, whereas in the case of *open cloze*, all grammatically correct solutions are permissible.

Pöchhacker (2011a) developed the *SynCloze* task to assess aptitude for interpreting. *SynCloze* combines anticipation and vocabulary exercises (synonyms, paraphrase). Using a headset and microphone, students listen to a speech and, at the sound of a beep, fill in the gap and give as many synonyms as possible.

Another variation of the cloze test is *personalized cloze* (Timarová & Ungoed-Thomas 2009): students hear a text containing biographical references to the speaker, and are asked to shadow most of it, but substitute references to the speaker with references to their own life. The exercise therefore combines elements of SHADOWING and paraphrasing.

CATHERINE CHABASSE

COGNITIVE APPROACHES

Cognitive approaches to the study of interpreting follow the tradition of cognitive psychology, a concept introduced by Ulric Neisser (1967) to define the branch of psychology attempting to describe how humans take in and process information. Whilst influenced by other branches of psychology, cognitive approaches differ from biological, behaviorist, psychodynamic, humanistic, evolutionary and sociocultural approaches. In line with the original meaning of the term, derived from the Latin *cognoscere*, 'to know', scholars following cognitive approaches are interested in the processes by which humans acquire knowledge of the world around them. When it comes to the study of interpreting, they are interested in the mental activities underlying the interpreting task, proposing theories predicting certain outcomes, and MODELS describing the processes involved in producing these outcomes. While the so-called information-processing paradigm of the seventies has dominated cognitive approaches in various fields of research, including INTERPRETING STUDIES, for decades, the connectionist paradigm (Rumelhart & McClelland 1986) has gained traction as a viable alternative to explain many cognitive processes.

The basic assumption underlying the information-processing paradigm is that the human processor, the brain, interprets discrete symbol systems based on algorithms (Neisser 1967). It can therefore be compared to a central processor, a computer: it can input, store, retrieve, combine and output data, and it is limited in the amount of data it can process at any given time. In spite of these apparent similarities, the computer metaphor has a major shortcoming: it suggests that the human processor, much like a computer, in principle executes one operation at a time, making processes predominantly (although not exclusively) serial in nature. Unlike a computer, however, which has only one processor, the human brain comprises several billion neurons, each of which can be conceived of as a processor in its own right.

The basic assumption of the connectionist paradigm, therefore, is that the human brain works like a network of interconnected processors. Processing in this system is intrinsically distributed and parallel, with many neurons contributing to task execution. Unlike a computer that relies on its program to execute tasks, a connectionist network has the ability to learn and, consequently, process unknown stimuli. It does so by spreading information through networks of neurons, based on the excitatory and inhibitory connections among them (Bechtel & Abrahamsen 2002).

Another recent extension of the scientific approach to cognition is known as 'situated cognition', or 'embodied cognition'. Scholars in this domain foreground the role of our experience in the physical world in the execution of cognitive tasks, including translation (e.g. Risku 2013), but there is little work on situated cognition in interpreting to date.

Methods

Notwithstanding the difference between the two main cognitive paradigms, interpreting scholars adopting a cognitive approach typically investigate behavior and use the results to make inferences about the underlying mental processes, as the latter cannot be observed directly. Many proponents of cognitive approaches thus apply the 'classic' scientific method and conduct EXPERIMENTAL RESEARCH, involving careful control and manipulation of variables and precise measurement of (indicators of) cognitive performance. There is, however, a considerably broader range of methods and techniques known from cognitive psychology: introspective, observational, behavioral, psychophysiological and neurological methods. While each has inherent advantages and disadvantages, the unique characteristics of a complex object of study like interpreting may attenuate some of these and accentuate others. A careful look at each method's potential and limitations is therefore essential to understand the implications of the results it can deliver.

Introspection, sometimes also referred to as subjective observation, is one of the earliest methods used in psychology. It is also the only method allowing humans to observe their mental processes directly as they unfold – based on the vocalization of processes in real time. Given that interpreting, in the simultaneous and note-based consecutive modes, requires the concurrent processing of input and output, yet another stream of concurrent auditory output is not practicable. Consequently, interpreting has been explored principally by using backward or delayed introspection, yielding RETROSPECTIVE PROTOCOLS. This type of backward introspection obviously does not allow the actual observation of mental processes but is tantamount to recalling and analyzing memorized experiences, which inevitably introduces 'noise'. Moreover, the observer's dual role constitutes a twofold limitation of this method. Not only are interpreters expected to perform a cognitively demanding task and, in addition, analyze their performance, but they are also expected to disclose experiences that potentially reveal inadequacies in their performance. Pressure to conform to a QUALITY ideal might therefore distort retrospective reports by professional interpreters and students alike. Lastly, unconscious processes cannot be observed by introspection or retrospection. This means that an unquantifiable part of the process might escape scrutiny through this method, and interpreters may retroactively explain certain strategic choices they never made in the first place.

Observational methods have been used by psychologists for decades to systematically and objectively observe and record human behavior. In interpreting studies, direct observation (with or without active participation of the observer) and indirect observation (based on recorded events) are widely used. The main strength of observational methods for the study of interpreting is their ecological validity. By observing interpreters or studying naturalistic corpora (both recordings and transcripts), researchers can analyze the product resulting from the task performed in its natural environment: the interpreters are hired for a genuine assignment, with material for PREPARATION and realistic WORKING CONDITIONS, and with a clear sense of communicative purpose (see Pöchhacker 1994a, 1995c) and a rich, true-to-life context (see Monacelli 2009). The main limitation of observational methods is the researcher's inability to isolate or manipulate a specific independent variable. While correlations between events may be identified, it is impossible to establish cause-and-effect relationships, as co-occurrence does not imply causation.

Behavioral methods attempt to shed light on human cognition by analyzing recordable human reactions to overt stimuli. This is done by means of experimental setups, which, thanks to the meticulous control of variables, allow for cause-and-effect relationships to be tested. However, the complexity of the interpreting task, associated with a range of potential confounds, rarely allows researchers to study it holistically using behavioral methods. When the focus is on component tasks, on the other hand, the extent to which these actually sub-serve the interpreting task is often unknown. Thus, while the quantitative nature of the events measured in behavioral studies all but eliminates the danger of researcher bias in the data collection process, the artificial nature of experimental tasks and the low ecological validity this implies are often identified as the principal weaknesses of behavioral approaches.

Psychophysiological methods try to measure the interaction between physiological and psychological phenomena. Cognitive psychophysiology, in particular, focuses on cognitive task performance and psychological events. For the study of the interpreting process this means that parts of the cognitive task will be measured through physiological responses, such as heart rate, skin conductance, stress hormones, or eye movements, to particular stimuli. Unlike many behavioral methods, psychophysiological methods are implicit, meaning that they do not require the measurement of overt performance. This is particularly relevant when researching an already complex task like interpreting that often makes it impossible to perform other cognitive tasks at the same time. The main advantage of psychophysiological methods, therefore, is their potential to provide continuous and objective data without interfering with the task at hand: as they usually measure responses of the autonomic nervous system, they are not subject to participants' control. The varying latency of different psychophysiological methods makes some of them (e.g. EYE TRACKING and pupillometry) more suitable for the analysis of local phenomena, and others (e.g. galvanic skin response and hormones in the study of STRESS) more appropriate for the exploration of general phenomena. The many-to-one mapping inherent to most of these methods, however, means that the measures derived from them are compounds, the individual component factors of which can often not be discerned.

Neurological methods are the most direct way of measuring activity in the human cortex in real time. Electroencephalography (EEG), for example, records the brain's electrophysiological response to a stimulus with impressive temporal resolution (less than 1 ms). Its sampling rates of over 500 Hz match the rate of receptive language processing, and its multidimensional nature allows the distinction between syntactic and semantic phenomena (Kaan 2007). Whilst EEG is an ideal method to time-lock cognitive phenomena related to language processing, its vulnerability to noise generated by articulatory movements severely restricts its usefulness for the study of interpreting. The use of EEG is in effect limited to a covert-articulation paradigm, in which interpreters only mentally articulate their output.

Functional neuroimaging techniques (fMRI), on the other hand, enable researchers to quantify the brain's metabolic response to particular stimuli, in other words, the blood flow to a certain area of the brain. This method determines the network of brain areas engaged in the performance of certain tasks with extremely high spatial resolution (in the range of 1 to 5 mm). However, hemodynamic-based modalities of identifying brain activity measure a surrogate signal (i.e. changes in blood flow) rather than its source (i.e. neural activity). This means that they cannot distinguish between the activities resulting from the increase in the amount of signal sent (excitation) and attempts to decrease that signal (inhibition). Furthermore, for tasks like SIMULTANEOUS INTERPRETING (SI) that require complex processing with response times of 2 to 3 seconds, the latency of the hemodynamic response (about 1 to 4 seconds) makes it impossible to relate specific events in the input or output to a particular activation pattern, so that the application of these methods is limited to such material as single words or sentences.

Topics

Scholars from within and from outside the field of interpreting studies have used the methods reviewed above to make substantial contributions to the body of scientific literature on interpreting. Although these address a great variety of topics, some of the main recurrent themes include MEMORY (especially the constructs of WORKING MEMORY and processing capacity), COMPREHENSION (particularly the notion of phonological interference), STRATEGIES (such as ANTICIPATION) and aspects of bilingual processing such as DIRECTIONALITY.

The idea that conference interpreters need outstanding MEMORY was first introduced by HERBERT (1952), who, applying an introspective approach, drew attention to such feats as the storage of an exceptionally large vocabulary, technical terms and accurate and detailed representation of propositions. The first model of the (simultaneous) interpreting process was put forward by GERVER (1975), who carried out experiments to investigate recall after different types of input processing (Gerver 1974b) in a traditional behaviorist paradigm. An account of the cognitive processing capacity requirements inherent to interpreting was subsequently provided by MODELS of the task such as the EFFORT MODELS and Seeber's (2011) model of COGNITIVE LOAD. Both models are based on an analytical approach and find empirical support in observational and empirical studies. When it comes to interpreters' ability to keep information in working memory, results gathered from behaviorist experiments are as yet inconclusive: while some evidence points to superior working memory storage capacity in interpreters as compared to non-interpreters (Christoffels et al. 2006; Signorelli et al. 2012), results reported in other studies suggest no difference between the two groups (Köpke & Signorelli 2012; Liu et al. 2004). Even so, some breakthroughs have been achieved in identifying particular brain areas involved in the SI task thanks to neurophysiological approaches. A comparison of the cerebral networks engaged during SHADOWING and SI shows increased task-contingent activity in a network of brain regions associated with cognitive control (involving action selection and inhibition, and error-monitoring), as well as regions associated with speech comprehension (Hervais-Adelman et al. 2014). Corroborating behavioral evidence suggests a relationship between interpreting EXPERTISE and the ability to inhibit distractors (Timarová et al. 2014). The same kind of relationship was not found, however, between interpreting expertise and response inhibition (the suppression of automated but inappropriate responses), 'updating' (the continuous comparison of incoming and stored information) or attention switching (the constant shifting of attention among different sub-tasks).

Whether, and how, COMPREHENSION might be affected by the need in SI to speak and listen at the same time is a prominent research question that has been explored by various scholars using cognitive approaches. Studies using behavioral measures in classic experimental designs have established, for instance, that recall of prose after listening is superior to recall after SI and after shadowing (Gerver 1974b; Lambert 1988a). Although the allegedly deeper processing of the original during interpreting leads to better recall than the more mechanical shadowing task (Gerver 1974b), the assumed additional cognitive load generated by the complex concurrent operations involved in SI reduces recall as compared to a simple listening comprehension task (Lambert 1988a). Additional behavioral evidence showing that SI affects the recall of digits more than a concurrent articulation task (Darò & Fabbro 1994) suggests that concurrent listening and speaking may not be the only source of interference with memory tasks during SI. Interestingly, while recall is negatively affected after spoken-language interpreting, the same is not true for SIGNED LANGUAGE INTERPRETING (Isham 1995). This implies that the comprehension process during spoken-language SI is indeed affected by phonological interference – a result that was corroborated in more recent research (Christoffels 2006; Christoffels & de Groot 2004).

The notion of STRATEGIES is a pervasive topic among advocates of cognitive approaches to the study of interpreting. Over the years, much of what interpreters do has been characterized as being the instantiation of a strategy, such as omitting, deleting, compressing, adding, completing, expanding, attenuating, substituting, approximating, generalizing, chunking, anticipating, waiting, stalling, monitoring, and correcting (see Gile 1995a; Kohn & Kalina 1996; Riccardi 1996; Setton 1999), with much of the evidence based on introspective, retrospective and observational data. In addition, the theoretical distinction between skill-based and knowledge-based strategies (Riccardi 2005) maps onto the well-known psychological concepts of automatic and controlled processing (Schneider & Chein 2003). The discussion of anticipation, the phenomenon whereby interpreters produce constituents before they are uttered in the original (e.g. Van Besien 1999), provides a good example to illustrate the contributions to the topic made by scholars using cognitive approaches. Early studies identifying anticipation as a defining feature of SI (Chernov 1978; Moser 1978; Wilss 1978) were largely based on observational evidence. But while some see this phenomenon as a natural part of language comprehension (Lederer 1981; Seleskovitch 1976/2014), others see in it a strategy specifically deployed by simultaneous interpreters to overcome task-inherent constraints such as syntactic differences between source and target languages. Behavioral evidence collected for SI from languages with verb-final structures (e.g. German) into languages with verb-initial structures (e.g. English) shows that sentence-final verbs are anticipated correctly in 50% of cases (Jörg 1997; Seeber 2001). Interestingly, Van Besien's (1999) re-analysis of Lederer's (1981) data reveals an even higher incidence of (verb-final to verb-initial) verb anticipation in SI, suggesting that it might indeed be a language-specific phenomenon. As for the cues enabling anticipation, the current consensus is that both top-down and bottom-up processes guide this kind of processing. Recent psychophysiological evidence suggests that top-down processes do not offset the load generated by bottom-up (e.g. syntactic) constraints (Seeber & Kerzel 2012); rather, it is contextual constraints (i.e. semantic and syntactic cues in context) and not transitional probability (i.e. the statistical likelihood of a verb occurring with the rest of the sentence) that guide interpreters in verb anticipation (Hodzik 2013).

Among the many aspects of BILINGUALISM that have a bearing on interpreting, the issue of DIRECTIONALITY, that is, whether conference interpreters (should) work into their 'A' language (mother tongue) or from their A into a so-called B language (second/acquired language), was once the dividing line between two opposing ideological camps (Gile 2005b). Informed mainly by theoretical argument, the debate still shows considerable discord. Greater strides towards understanding the implications of directionality in interpreting have become possible thanks to neurophysiological insights into the cognitive processes involved during SI: increased activation in the right hemisphere is found when interpreters work into a foreign language (Petsche et al. 1993). Additional evidence (Rinne et al. 2000) shows that SI into a foreign language (and in certain language combinations) engenders more extensive fronto-temporal activation increases, and is thus conceivably more demanding of neural resources than SI into the mother tongue.

KILIAN G. SEEBER

COGNITIVE LOAD

↑ COGNITIVE APPROACHES
→ WORKING MEMORY
↓ INPUT VARIABLES

Cognitive load is a multidimensional construct used in the field of psychology. It is based on the assumption that the human processor, the brain, is limited in the number of operations it can carry out and in the amount of information it can keep available for processing at a given time (Miller 1956). Cognitive load can refer to the processing load imposed on the performer by a particular task (Paas & van Merriënboer 1993), or the perceived mental effort the performer invests in a task (Yin et al. 2008). This load can be further distinguished as follows: 'instantaneous load' is the load at a given moment in time, which fluctuates throughout the performance of a task; 'peak load' reflects the maximum value of instantaneous load reached; 'accumulated load' is the total amount of load experienced; and 'average load' is the mean intensity of load (Xie & Salvendy 2000). Whether the cognitive resources that are depleted by this load, or that fuel this effort, are unitary or multiple is a matter of debate, as is the very need for a concept that may simply reflect processing structures.

The explanatory potential of this concept for the interpreting process, which combines language COMPREHENSION and language production in real time and is generally accepted as one of the most difficult linguistic skills, is manifest. The notion of cognitive load was first introduced to the field of interpreting studies by Gile (1985), in an attempt to explain information loss observed in professional interpreters. His EFFORT MODELS, which describe interpreting in terms of listening and analysis, production and MEMORY, were originally devised as a pedagogical tool but have long evolved beyond their initial purpose and are among the most widely used theoretical frameworks to explain cognitive processes in interpreting. However, the conceptual framework of the Effort Models has yet to find unequivocal empirical support (Seeber 2011). Similarly, the notion that interpreters work at a level close to cognitive saturation most of the time, reflected in Gile's (1999a) 'tightrope hypothesis', is yet to be empirically corroborated. Indeed, one of the major challenges in applying the construct of cognitive load to research in interpreting has been the difficulty of measuring the phenomenon. For example, performance measures, particularly error scores during a secondary task, are often used to quantify cognitive load in psychology (e.g. Power 1986), but are ill suited to assess cognitive load in interpreting: as both CONSECUTIVE INTERPRETING and SIMULTANEOUS INTERPRETING already involve multiple concurrent tasks (comprehension and note-taking in consecutive interpreting; comprehension and production in simultaneous interpreting), combining them with further tasks is impracticable. Moreover, individual differences in TIME LAG and regulatory focus make it impossible to establish a clear cause-and-effect relationship between cognitive load, performance speed and performance ACCURACY (Seeber 2013). On the other hand, psychophysiological measures, like cognitive pupillometry using EYE TRACKING, albeit more costly and arguably more complex, appear to be better suited for the measurement of cognitive load during the interpreting process (Seeber & Kerzel 2012) and hold considerable potential for future research.

KILIAN G. SEEBER

COHERENCE

↑ LINGUISTIC/PRAGMATIC APPROACHES
→ COHESION, → QUALITY CRITERIA

In simple terms, 'to cohere' means 'to hang together'; it stems from the Latin *cohaerere*, literally 'stick' (*haerere*) 'together' (*co-*). The word 'text' has its origins in a similar metaphor, the Latin *textus*, literally 'something woven'. For linguists, what distinguishes a passage of speech or writing as a text rather than a random sequence of utterances or sentences is precisely its coherence as a unified whole (Halliday & Hasan 1976).

Coherence is generally seen as having two dimensions. The first is semantic and concerns the relationship of a text with the 'real' world. From this perspective, a text is a unified discourse that relates consistently to a picture of the extra-linguistic universe. In this respect, some researchers stress the role of mental schemata – expectations about common situations and events – in achieving coherence in both the production and COMPREHENSION of texts (e.g. Gernsbacher & Givón 1995). Thus, coherence can also be seen as the result of the interaction between a text and the text users, for whom the concepts and relations underlying the text must be 'mutually accessible and relevant' (Beaugrande & Dressler 1981). In other words, understanding a text requires INFERENCING based on an individual's knowledge and expectations.

The second dimension of coherence concerns the lexical and grammatical features of the surface text that signal the underlying concepts and relations. This is usually referred to as

COHESION, and treated separately, though the two dimensions of textuality are inseparably intertwined. For a text to 'make sense' to the listener or reader, it has to display a 'continuity of senses' that takes into account the receiver's prior knowledge of the world (Beaugrande & Dressler 1981). One way to judge the quality of a text is therefore to see how easy it is for readers or listeners to comprehend the intended message. To promote ease of understanding, the speaker or writer can employ cohesive devices to explicitly signal cognitive relationships between text parts, such as contrast, equivalence, cause, consequence, and temporal sequence. Corresponding rhetorical links are 'although', 'similarly', 'because', 'thus' and 'then'. These cues help to present, organise and interpret information coherently.

In interpreting, coherence plays a crucial role both in the source text and in the target text. It is important both at the point where the interpreter hears and tries to make sense of what has been said in the source language, and at the point where the audience hears and tries to make sense of the interpreter's rendition in the target language. The more coherent a text, the easier it will be for its users (the interpreter or the listeners) to comprehend, and the better it will fulfil its intended communicative function. The schemata and expectations which the original speaker assumes in the source language audience may not be shared by those listening to the interpretation in the target language, and a major element of the interpreter's challenge is to compensate in real time for any such 'mismatches', which could otherwise increase the COGNITIVE LOAD on the receiver and impede understanding.

Coherence as a benchmark

In professional settings, 'making sense' is held to be one of the most important criteria for judging the success of a given rendition, in CONSECUTIVE INTERPRETING as well as SIMULTA-NEOUS INTERPRETING. Hatim and Mason (1997) maintain that in consecutive interpreting an effective performance should make apparent a clear outline of the way the target text is structured, and that structure is the best indicator of the quality of a consecutive interpretation. In simultaneous interpreting, the simultaneity constraint can result *de facto* in a reduction of coherence, increasing the load on the listener.

For an interpreted text to 'make sense' to the target audience, it needs to be clearly sign-posted with cohesive links, and its underlying structure must be logical. This is clearly reflected in the results of a number of survey studies on interpreters' and users' QUALITY CRITERIA for judging an interpreter's performance (e.g. Bühler 1986; Kurz 1993a; Moser 1996; Zwischenberger 2010), in which the criterion 'logical cohesion of utterance' has consistently ranked near the top. Coherence is therefore widely accepted as one of the most important criteria for judging interpreting performance, whether in recruitment tests by institutional employers or in the ASSESSMENT of trainees' progress in interpreter EDUCATION programs.

Coherence, however, is not an attribute that can be easily analysed or measured. Peng (2011) used Rhetorical Structure Theory to describe and compare coherence profiles of renditions of the same speeches by professional and novice interpreters. Each rendition was visualised as a tree-like structure with the cohesive devices as nodes and the related text spans as branches. The analysis confirmed that interpretations, like translated texts, are more explicitly marked with cohesive devices than the source speech, and that, when comprehension of the source speech is not a concern, interpretations into the A language exhibit better coherence. Last but not least, the difference between professional and novice interpreters was shown to lie in differences in the degree of coherence achieved in the interpreted rendition. Performances by professional interpreters reflected better global coherence in so far as multiple branches could be traced back to a common root. By contrast, the visualisations of trainees' renditions showed only local coherence, looking more like a series of 'bushes' with no single root.

Drawing on narrative theory, Baker (2006) adds to the notions of structural coherence (cohesion and internal logic) and material coherence (consistency and completeness of the narrative in relation to the outside world) the concept of characterological coherence, which refers to the credibility and reliability of the narrator. Interpreters, especially in DIALOGUE INTERPRETING, play an active and highly visible part in the interaction between two parties, and the credibility of the interpreter as narrator can impact on the clients' perceptions of one another.

GRACIE PENG

COHESION

↑ LINGUISTIC/PRAGMATIC APPROACHES
→ COHERENCE, → QUALITY CRITERIA

Cohesion is an essential aspect of text organisation as studied in discourse analysis or text linguistics. The two major models that have provided the theoretical underpinning for most work on cohesion in translation and interpreting studies are those of Halliday and Hasan (1976) and Beaugrande and Dressler (1981). In their account of 'texture', Halliday and Hasan analyse the relationships among items in a text. These relations, established by grammatical or lexical means, are referred to as 'cohesive ties', and further divided into six broad categories: reference, substitution, ellipsis, conjunction, reiteration and collocation. While using the term 'cohesion' with reference to Halliday and Hasan, Beaugrande and Dressler's understanding of cohesion is considerably broader, and includes all means of signaling text surface dependencies, ranging from pro-forms, ellipsis, junction, paraphrase and (partial) recurrence to syntactic parallelism, such as the consistent use of tense and aspect. With regard to 'spoken texts', Beaugrande and Dressler mention INTONATION as a subsidiary cohesive system that gives a text its audible contours. Unlike Halliday and Hasan, Beaugrande and Dressler (1981) draw a distinction between cohesion (relying on grammatical dependencies) and COHERENCE, which is based on the concepts and relations underlying the surface text. This dual focus on cohesion and coherence, which many authors view as closely interdependent, is also applied in PSYCHOLINGUISTIC APPROACHES to text COMPREHENSION (e.g. Graesser et al. 2007).

In translation and interpreting studies, a major impetus for the investigation of cohesion came from the work of Blum-Kulka (1986), whose EXPLICITATION hypothesis centres on shifts of cohesion that are not language-specific and therefore result from the translation process as such. This was applied to interpreting by SHLESINGER (1995a) in her pioneering study on shifts of cohesion in SIMULTANEOUS INTERPRETING. Shlesinger analysed shifts in the number and type of cohesive ties of an impromptu conference speech rendered from English into Hebrew by thirteen advanced interpreting students. She postulates three interpreting-specific constraints – time constraint, linearity constraint and (un)shared knowledge constraint – assumed to influence the recognition and rendering of cohesive ties by simultaneous interpreters. Examining her data for the six types of devices identified by Halliday and Hasan (1976), Shlesinger finds shifts across all categories of cohesive markers. The most common type of shift is complete omission, which is especially frequent in the case of sentence-final elements. The cohesive pattern may also be altered by the interpreter because a given cohesive device is perceived as not essential for rendering the sense of the message, or because its recognition depends on specialised knowledge that is not available. On the other hand, the rate of OMISSIONS tends to decrease considerably when the interpreter has had prior access to the source text, or when s/he is familiar with the subject matter.

Shlesinger's experiment was replicated by Mizuno (1999), who had ten advanced students interpret the English speech used in Shlesinger's experiment into Japanese. His findings confirmed those for English–Hebrew only to a certain extent, partly as a result of language-specific differences (such as zero-pronouns in Japanese). The retention rates for lexical cohesion and causal conjunctions, on the other hand, were found to be high in both language pairs.

Other work on the topic includes Gallina's (1992) analysis of cohesion in English and Italian political speeches delivered in the European Parliament, and studies by Gumul (2006a, 2012), including an experimental comparison of cohesive patterns in consecutive and simultaneous interpreting. In line with Blum-Kulka's (1986) hypothesis, Gumul found shifts of cohesion in both MODES of interpreting, but observed a greater prevalence in the consecutive mode, with higher rates of category change and omission. In a study of cohesion in SIGNED LANGUAGE INTERPRETING (English–American Sign Language), McDermid (2014), working in an EXPERT-NOVICE PARADIGM, examines why the signed target texts of the experienced professionals in his sample were rated as more fluent than those of the novice interpreters (recent graduates of an interpreter training program). Finding that experts used significantly more conjunctive devices, McDermid identifies a significant correlation between target text FLUENCY and the employment of (additional) cohesive ties in the interpretation.

The focus on fluency also points to the role attributed to 'cohesion' as one of the most important QUALITY CRITERIA for judging an interpreter's performance. However, the way the item was formulated in Bühler's (1986) original questionnaire (and used in subsequent work on USER EXPECTATIONS) – that is, 'logical cohesion of utterance' – appears to go beyond grammatical relations on the text surface and to encompass conceptual relations more frequently discussed under the heading of coherence.

EWA GUMUL

COMMUNICATIVE EFFECT

↑ QUALITY
→ COMPREHENSION

Communication always has some effect – i.e. outcome, consequence or result – on the individuals involved in communicative interaction. These effects may be cognitive, affective or psychomotor, meaning they may cause a change in knowledge (cognitive), attitudes, beliefs or feelings (affective), or behaviour (psychomotor) (DeVito 1997). In the field of interpreting, it is axiomatic that the target text should, as far as possible, produce the same effect and have the same cognitive content as the source speech (e.g. Déjean le Féal 1990; Hale 2004). The main question is how to measure effect in general, and 'sameness' (equivalence) of effect in particular.

Measuring (cognitive) effect

In DIALOGUE INTERPRETING, the effect of an utterance on the interlocutor may be gleaned from some immediate response that can be given in face-to-face interaction. In CONFERENCE INTERPRETING, on the other hand, where the source text is typically monologic and interpreters are at a distance from their audience, communicative effect is more difficult to gauge. While it would be hard to measure a change in attitudes or beliefs, at least the cognitive effect – i.e. changes in knowledge – in the listeners might be assessed by checking for comprehension of what has been communicated. Surprisingly, only a few empirical studies have adopted this approach.

In his ground-breaking work, GERVER (1976) used COMPREHENSION testing to measure the cognitive effects of consecutive vs. simultaneous interpretations of the same source text. His findings showed no significant difference in the audience's understanding of the simultaneous vs. the consecutive rendition. SHLESINGER (1994) used comprehension testing to find out whether 'interpretational INTONATION' affected listeners' comprehension. In her experiment, participants had to answer questions on the content of two versions of a speech, one being an authentic simultaneous interpretation and the other a read transcript of the same. The results showed that the group listening to the read text scored considerably better than those listening to the interpretation.

Comprehension testing has been used in SIGNED LANGUAGE INTERPRETING since the mid-1970s to find out which mode of signing – sign language proper, TRANSLITERATION or other forms – was more effective for its users (e.g. Livingston et al. 1994). However, these studies only looked at the effect of different target-text versions.

Testing the equivalence of effect of an original speech and its interpretation was advocated by various interpreting scholars (e.g. Déjean le Féal 1990; Shlesinger 1997), who suggested comparing comprehension among source-text and target-text listeners as a means of assessing interpreting QUALITY. Once again, this was first taken up in research on signed language interpreting, where several studies used comprehension testing to compare the cognitive effect of a speech in a source-text versus a target-text audience. Steiner (1998), who compared a deaf audience's understanding of different forms of signed news on TV with a hearing control group, found that the hearing subjects – the source-text audience – scored far better than the deaf group, meaning that the interpreting users did not draw as much cognitive benefit from the programme. Similar results were reported in a study comparing deaf and hearing students' comprehension of lectures (Marschark et al. 2004). Again, the hearing audience achieved a significantly higher score than the deaf students relying on either interpreting into sign language or TRANSLITERATION. In contrast, no significant differences were found by Napier and Spencer (2008) between the comprehension test scores of deaf and hearing jurors in a courtroom setting, which suggests that deaf persons should be allowed to serve on juries as they can effectively follow court proceedings through an interpretation.

Applying the comprehension-testing approach to SIMULTANEOUS INTERPRETING between spoken languages, Reithofer (2013) compared the cognitive effect of a speech delivered by an Italian speaker using ENGLISH AS A LINGUA FRANCA to that of its simultaneous interpretation into German. Using a thoroughly tested questionnaire and carefully controlled experimental design with large groups of participants, she found that the interpretation led to a significantly better cognitive effect in the audience than the original speech.

All of these studies show that comprehension testing as a means of measuring the communicative or, more specifically, cognitive effect of a speech can serve as a valid method for measuring what is believed to be a central component of quality in interpreting, as expressed in the standard of equivalent effect.

KARIN REITHOFER

COMMUNITY INTERPRETING

↓ EDUCATIONAL INTERPRETING, ↓ HEALTHCARE INTERPRETING, ↓ LEGAL INTERPRETING, ↓ RELIGIOUS SETTINGS

Community interpreting is the type of interpreting that takes place between people who live in the same 'community', society or country but who do not share a common language. It has been said that it is the most common type of interpreting in the world (Wadensjö 2009). Unlike CONFERENCE INTERPRETING, which mostly takes place in international gatherings or meetings, community interpreting takes place in intra-national contexts, such as a doctor's surgery, a court or a parent–teacher interview at a school. The two major domains that fall under the umbrella term 'community interpreting' are medical or HEALTHCARE INTERPRETING and LEGAL INTERPRETING (Hale 2007).

Community interpreters are generally required to interpret between migrant, refugee, indigenous or deaf populations who are unable to speak, understand or hear the mainstream language, and public service officials or private practitioners with whom they come into contact. The need for interpreters in these SETTINGS is often more real than in international conferences, where the participants can often speak a LINGUA FRANCA but choose to speak their national language for political reasons. In community settings, those who require the services of interpreters rely on them to access or to deliver the most fundamental community services. Thus, interpreters in these settings interpret for both the minority language speakers and the service providers or relevant institutions. The interpreter therefore represents a crucial link on which both parties depend equally in order to receive or provide professional services.

Controversies over its name

There has been some controversy over the term 'community interpreting' (e.g. Gentile 1997), and different countries have adopted different labels to refer to this type of interpreting. The expression most widely accepted as a synonym is 'public service interpreting', whereas 'cultural interpreting' and 'social interpreting' are far less common. 'Bilateral interpreting' and 'liaison interpreting' (Gentile et al. 1996) are broader, and not linked to a particular setting. This applies also to DIALOGUE INTERPRETING, which has become established as the most comprehensive designation for interpreting in non-conference settings. With reference to social institutional settings, community interpreting seems to be the most widely used label, notwithstanding the slightly different connotations and scope of the term depending on who uses it.

The overarching label of community interpreting includes specialised areas, such as legal, medical, mental health, welfare, religious or educational settings, which are sometimes seen as separate types of interpreting. Court interpreting, in particular, has been treated as a separate field in countries such as the United States and Canada (Bancroft et al. 2013).

The controversy over the label is partly explained by the social status of community interpreting. While interpreting in community settings is a recognised professional activity in some countries, in others it is still an unpaid activity performed by untrained bilingual volunteers, some of whom are friends, family or neighbours of the minority language speaker (Wadensjö 2009). As analysed by Ozolins (2000), countries differ widely along several dimensions in their policies on meeting multilingual communication needs – from neglect and ad hoc measures to comprehensive language service provision. Even where there is formal EDUCATION and CERTIFICATION for interpreters, pre-service training may only be optional, and the remuneration for interpreting in community settings is well below that for conference interpreting, even when the same interpreter is employed. The status of the activity seems to be linked to the status of the minority language speaker, rather than to the complexity of the task and the EXPERTISE required of the community interpreter. Some professional interpreters therefore resist the label and would rather call themselves 'interpreters' who work in different settings. The label, however, is useful for research and training purposes. Once an activity is identified as being distinct from others, it becomes an object of systematic study, the results of which can inform the practice, which can in turn inform the CURRICULUM. Such cross-fertilisation between research, training and practice will serve to elevate the status of community interpreting as a professional activity.

Modes used in community interpreting

In community settings, all modes of interpreting are regularly used. In interview situations, dialogue interpreting is commonly practised by spoken language interpreters in the consecutive mode, working into both languages. Sign language interpreters use the simultaneous as well as the consecutive mode, the former being the default option. The opposite is true for spoken language interpreters, who tend to use the simultaneous mode only in some settings, such as the courtroom or mental health consultations. This can be done either with or without equipment. In a court, SIMULTANEOUS INTERPRETING in whispering mode (*chuchotage*) is carried out by having the interpreter sit either behind or next to the person who needs to hear the interpretation. This tends to take place while people other than the accused/defendant are speaking, and the interpreting is provided for the benefit of the accused/defendant in order to make him/her linguistically present. The short consecutive mode is commonly used while the accused/defendant is the one giving evidence. In MENTAL HEALTH SETTINGS, this mode is employed so as to avoid interrupting the flow of the patient's talk. Some interpreters also use a hybrid mode between consecutive and simultaneous.

The classic mode of CONSECUTIVE INTERPRETING can also be used in community settings. This can happen in court when the judge or magistrate is delivering a ruling and the interpreter is not in a position to interpret simultaneously, or at a community information session where one speaker is interpreted for the benefit of many but no simultaneous interpreting equipment is available.

Another mode of interpreting that falls in between interpreting and translation is SIGHT INTERPRETING/TRANSLATION, for the benefit of those who cannot read the text in the original language.

Community interpreting is also done remotely, either by telephone or via video-conferencing. Such REMOTE INTERPRETING has been considered a less desirable option, used only where interpreters are unavailable to assist in person (Ozolins 2011). More recently, however, videoconference-based remote interpreting is being explored as a viable and even a preferred option, particularly in court and POLICE SETTINGS (Braun & Taylor 2012a).

Community interpreting as a profession

The state of community interpreting as a PROFESSION differs according to country. Generally, in countries that have a long history of immigration, such as Australia, Canada and Sweden, the profession is better established, with university degrees and other training courses, accreditation or CERTIFICATION examinations, professional associations and industrial unions promoting the interests of their members. In some of these countries there is even training for those who use interpreting services, to guide them in working collaboratively with interpreters (Tebble 2012). In countries that have only recently begun to receive large numbers of migrants and refugees (e.g. some European countries like SPAIN, or some Asian countries like JAPAN), the profession is less established (see e.g. Ortega Herráez et al. 2009). Overall, the professionalisation of community interpreting tends to be hampered by a number of factors that will be discussed below.

One factor, which is probably the most difficult to control, is the frequent change in the languages required, depending on the migration waves of the time. This impacts the availability of formal training and fuels a disparity in competence levels among practising interpreters (Townsley 2007). Another major factor has been the lack of a universal requirement for all community interpreters to undergo compulsory pre-service training, even in countries where certification systems have been in place. This results in highly diverse behaviour by interpreters who are paid the same rates and afforded the same status, but who have very different educational backgrounds and levels of technical and ethical competence.

The requirement for all would-be practitioners to undergo formal training and be certified before being admitted into the profession has not been met for community interpreting anywhere in the world (Hlavac 2013a). One reason for this has been the lack of training programs in all the required languages. Another reason is the considerable investment of time and money required to become qualified, with no incentive in the form of higher pay or volume of work for those who have the necessary qualifications.

Some solutions to these problems have been suggested. One is the recommendation that all aspiring interpreters complete non-language-specific training, as offered by some universities around the world, before sitting language-specific accreditation examinations. Another is to move towards a virtual community of practice (D'Hayer 2012), where educational institutions share training resources, especially in different languages, with access to distance and E-LEARNING methods.

A repercussion of the inconsistent educational backgrounds of practising interpreters is a lack of professional identity and a tendency to undermine the work of the interpreter (Hale 2005). This is sometimes evident in the tendency of some untrained bilinguals to use interpreting as a part-time job while they are studying to become professionals in another field. Their assumption that speaking two languages automatically makes them interpreters is often shared by users of interpreting services.

Role and ethics in community interpreting

One of the consequences of working with a mixed pool of trained and untrained, professional and ad hoc interpreters is the confusion over their ROLE and their degree of participation or involvement in the interaction (Tebble 2012). Bilingual friends or family members of the service recipient who help out as ad hoc interpreters are under no obligation to interpret, let alone do so accurately and impartially. These helpers normally are not paid, have not been trained and do not abide by a professional code of ETHICS. They are what Harris and Sherwood (1978) have called "natural translators", and most likely do what comes naturally, that is, summarise what they hear, provide their own commentary, ask their own questions and provide their own answers according to their knowledge and understanding of the situation. Professional interpreters, on the other hand, if trained and certified, are expected to abide by a professional code of ethics that requires them to interpret everything accurately and impartially.

Nevertheless, there is some controversy and confusion over the interpreter's ROLE as prescribed by professional codes of ethics. The requirement for ACCURACY is at times misunderstood to mean a literal, word-for-word translation. But rather than literal translation, some will argue that accurate interpreting requires a "pragmatic approach" (Hale 2004, 2007), with due consideration for such factors as the purpose of the encounter, the discourse practices and goals of the professional setting, the cross-cultural differences of the speakers, and the grammatical and pragmatic differences of the language pair, to name just a few. Whereas USER EXPECTATIONS and role perceptions may differ from one institutional setting to another, the aim of the interpreter should always be to match the intention of the original, to achieve as similar a COMMUNICATIVE EFFECT as possible in the target language listener to that experienced by a source language listener, and to empower both speakers to communicate with each other in spite of the language barrier. Such a task is very complex and will often require different STRATEGIES from the interpreter to ensure accuracy. When this cannot be achieved implicitly, interpreters may need to intervene explicitly to explain a translation difficulty or cultural difference and highlight any potential misunderstandings (Hale 2013).

Beyond ensuring accuracy, such NON-RENDITIONS, in which interpreters speak for themselves rather than on behalf of others (Wadensjö 1998), focus on the organisation of the interaction (coordination) and can also include introductions and closings, requests for breaks and other forms of interaction and DISCOURSE MANAGEMENT, all of which fall within the role prescribed by professional codes of ethics (Gentile et al. 1996; Tebble 2012).

Some, however, have argued for the interpreter to go beyond interpreting accurately and become an active advocate for the minority language speaker. The work of Barsky (1996) on interpreters in ASYLUM SETTINGS is a case in point. Others have discussed the way some interpreters (often paid but untrained) go beyond the normative role to become an "involved participant", or even "gatekeeper", deciding what should be interpreted and what not (Angelelli 2004a; Bolden 2000; Davidson 2000). Such positions and observations have made the interpreter's role (and ethics) a prominent concern in the research literature on community interpreting (Hale 2007). Given the great diversity of community settings and interpreting practices, and the growth and diversification of research in this broad domain, the debate is likely to continue.

SANDRA B. HALE

COMPETENCE

→ EDUCATION, → QUALITY

The notion of competence is used in a number of different disciplines, and it is difficult to find a precise or commonly agreed definition. In linguistics it goes back to Chomsky's distinction between 'competence', as the unconscious knowledge of the grammar of a language, and 'performance', as actual language use in a given situation. Psychologists, on the other hand, have proposed a continuum ranging from abilities to competences to EXPERTISE. Interest is then focused on how competence, defined as a set of skills needed for high performance in a certain field, is acquired and how it can be developed to the level of expertise (Sternberg 2005). In education, fostering competences is the stated objective of every course or program, and hence also a key concern in international exchange in education and professional development. Thus, the *European Qualifications Framework* distinguishes between knowledge, skills and competences, and other projects in Europe, often associated with the Bologna process, regard competences as a dynamic combination of knowledge, understanding, skills and abilities that can be subdivided into instrumental, interpersonal, and systemic competence (Kennedy et al. 2009).

With or without a clear definition, the notion of competence has been applied in various areas of translation and interpreting studies, most notably in research on cognitive processes, in EDUCATION (including CURRICULUM design, APTITUDE TESTING and PEDAGOGY) and in CERTIFICATION programs. In a linguistic sense, competence is fundamental to the concept of NATURAL TRANSLATION/INTERPRETING, as Harris and Sherwood (1978) view the natural ability of bilinguals to translate in relation to Chomskyan linguistic competence.

Much effort has been expended in translation studies on developing deductive models of translation competence and its components. Earlier models tended to enumerate sub-competences like language, subject matter, cultural and transfer competence, while multi-dimensional models of competence envision competences on various levels. These may include strategic, interpersonal or psycho-physiological sub-competences, that is, different types of cognitive and attitudinal components of translation competence. In some cases, these models have been submitted to empirical testing (see Hurtado Albir 2010; Lesznyák 2007). A common framework of professional competences has also been developed by the European university consortium responsible for the European Master's of Translation (EMT 2009).

In interpreting studies, the construct of competence has been of somewhat limited importance to date, if only because most authors have preferred to speak of abilities and skills, pre-sumably as a result of influential COGNITIVE APPROACHES to the study of interpreting processes. A few MODELS of interpreting competence have nevertheless been put forward, mostly by authors in German-speaking countries. Pöchhacker (2000a) summarized the widespread consensus on the skills required for interpreting (i.e. language and cultural skills, translational skills, subject-matter knowledge) in a multidimensional model, with linguistic transfer compe-tence as a core element, complemented by cultural competence and interaction management skills, all these elements being 'encased' by professional role performance skills and ethical behavior. Using Kalina's (2002) comprehensive process model of interpreting as her point of departure, Albl-Mikasa (2013a) draws up a detailed model comprising five skill areas, each with its respective subskills: pre-process (e.g. language proficiency, TERMINOLOGY management, PREPARATION); in-process (e.g. comprehension, transfer, production); peri-process (teamwork, resistance to pressure); post-process (terminology work, quality control); and para-process (e.g. business know-how, customer relations, meta-reflection). Albl-Mikasa also makes reference to Kutz (2010), the author of yet another detailed model of (sub)competences assumed to play a role in professional interpreters' successful task performance.

Whereas most of these competence models have been developed with a view to CON-FERENCE INTERPRETING, recent proposals also focus explicitly on competence in COMMUNITY INTERPRETING. An example is the proposal by Kaczmarek (2010) for a model of community interpreter competence built on a model of intercultural communication. Central assump-tions of the model, which characterizes the community interpreter and his or her clients in terms of knowledge, skills and motivation, include the interdependence between community interpreter competence and context, an important variable being participants' individual perception of the dynamics of interpersonal communication.

NADJA GRBIĆ AND FRANZ PÖCHHACKER

COMPLETENESS

see under QUALITY CRITERIA

COMPREHENSION

↑ COGNITIVE APPROACHES, ↑ PSYCHOLINGUISTIC APPROACHES
→ MEMORY, → MENTAL REPRESENTATION
↓ INFERENCING

Comprehension is the fundamental prerequisite in the process of interpreting, conceived as re-expressing in another language what one has understood. In MODELS of the interpreting process, from the INTERPRETIVE THEORY and the EFFORT MODELS to complex conceptualizations drawing on insights from PSYCHOLINGUISTIC APPROACHES, source message comprehension features as one of the main components. However natural its accomplishment is in everyday communication, language comprehension has been found to be a highly complex phenomenon – so much so that unraveling its intricacies becomes indispensable for a fuller understanding of the interpreting process.

Language comprehension has been an object of study in various disciplines, including linguistics, psychology and neuroscience. There is therefore a variety of analytical models to represent the process of comprehension. Even so, there is consensus that it is a 'constructive' cognitive process taking place at (and through) several levels, from the phonological, lexical and syntactic to the levels of text and discourse in their situational context. Among the most influential accounts of discourse comprehension is the Construction-Integration Model developed by Walter Kintsch (1988). He posits lexical/semantic processing (word recognition, etc.) and syntactic parsing leading to the construction of a 'propositional textbase', which is further enriched through knowledge-based INFERENCING and the strategic application of 'macro-structures' (van Dijk & Kintsch 1983), and stored in MEMORY as some form of MENTAL REPRESENTATION. Beyond propositions, Kintsch posits the level of a 'situation model', conceived of as a type of mental model that includes 'analogue' features such as visualizations. In general, currently accepted models of comprehension, such as the Construction-Integration Model (Kintsch 1988, 2004), the Structure Building Framework (Gernsbacher 1990) and the Landscape Model (van den Broek et al. 1999, 2005), describe it as a dynamic process that encompasses micro- and macro-processing operations aiming at the construction of an internal (linguistic or abstract) representation of a particular event. Micro-processing includes low-level operations allowing the recognition and decoding of linguistic information explicitly provided in the text, while macro-processing entails high-level strategies to integrate textual information with prior knowledge and with details of the communicative situation (Ericsson & Kintsch 1995; Kintsch 1988, 2004; van Dijk & Kintsch 1983).

The account developed from the field of interpreting by CHERNOV (1978, 2004) equally envisages comprehension as a multi-layered process and foregrounds the role of prior knowledge in comprehending new (text-based) information, placing special emphasis on expectation-based ('top-down') processing to accelerate comprehension under the time constraints of SIMULTANEOUS INTERPRETING (SI). Mackintosh (1985) suggested applying van Dijk and Kintsch's (1983) model of comprehension to consecutive and simultaneous interpreting. She argues that many errors in interpreting can be attributed to failures in operations such as deletion of irrelevant propositions or the construction of macro-propositions from the source speech. This points to one of the specific research issues regarding the interpreter's achievement of comprehension, that is, the extent to which it depends on different processes from those occurring in language processing tasks other than interpreting. These differences may be found at all levels of representation that are combined in the creation of a mental model of what is being communicated.

Levels of representation and mental model

At a *lexical and semantic level*, the interpreter can recognize the perceived unit(s) and access all possible meanings. Experimental research has shown that interpreters become very efficient at retrieving lexical and semantic information (Bajo et al. 2000; Christoffels & de Groot 2005). This skill may be especially relevant since experimental evidence also suggests that when interpreters recognize words, information from both languages is activated in parallel. This activation of both languages in bilingual comprehension, depending on the translation context, has been demonstrated with behavioural (Macizo & Bajo 2009) as well as with electrophysiological measures (Yudes et al. 2010). However, parallel lexical access to both the source language and the target language during comprehension in interpreting imposes a heavy COGNITIVE LOAD on the interpreter. This problem can be resolved only through efficient lexical processing.

At a *meaning or propositional level*, research on SEGMENTATION in interpreting has shown that interpreters work with larger units of information than non-interpreters, and that these units are adapted to the syntactic features of the target language (Meuleman & Van Besien 2009). A study comparing error monitoring in interpreters and untrained bilinguals (Yudes et al. 2013) showed that professional interpreters detected more inconsistencies and had more accurate recall of the stimulus texts. This superior performance was more evident for syntactic and semantic errors which involved larger units of information and deeper linguistic analyses, as opposed to lexical/ orthographic inconsistencies. This pattern is consistent with previous results suggesting that interpreters devote more effort in the interpreting process to monitoring the meaning of the discourse than to lexical analysis (Christoffels & de Groot 2005; Fabbro et al. 1991).

At the higher level of representation, the *macrostructure and situation model* are built through a series of macro-processes such as tracking references, inferencing, resolving ambiguities, and suppressing irrelevant information. Research at the discourse level is scarce and shows mixed results. For example, Dillinger (1994) provided evidence that experienced interpreters and untrained bilinguals responded similarly to narrativity and text structure, suggesting that the two groups relied on similar processes to comprehend the texts used in the experiment. In contrast, Macizo and Bajo (2009) found that previous access to a summary of the source text had different effects depending on whether the goal of reading was (consecutive/simultaneous) interpreting or mere comprehension.

Nevertheless, what is extremely important for interpreting is for the situation model to reflect contextual communicative factors, such as (i) the way in which the interpreter listens to and analyses the discourse, which is conditioned by his/her previous knowledge of the subject, the addressees of the interpreted message, and the circumstances that give rise to or motivate the discourse ('orienting conditions'); and (ii) the final function of the message, which also determines the manner in which the comprehension task is approached, since emphasis is placed on the most important or relevant factors in the discourse (Danks & Griffin 1997).

For the construction of this mental model, two types of cognitive processing are particularly important: *bottom-up* and *top-down* processes.

Bottom-up processes progress from the input to the representation of discourse meaning. In this sense, the interpreting process should not be seen as limited to a language-bound opera- tion to transmit information regarding something understood, but rather as an intellectual task related to what is being expressed through languages. This view is compatible with the nature of the interpreting task itself, and with the use of strategic behaviour in certain communicative situations.

Top-down processes go from the conceptual representation to the analysis of the input. The construction of the mental model requires the interpreter to go beyond a representation of the surface characteristics of the discourse, and incorporate world knowledge from long- term memory (Zwaan & Radvansky 1998). Such knowledge helps the interpreter to predict what comes next, and allows a richer understanding of the context even with less attention allo- cated to bottom-up information. It also enables the interpreter to automatically activate some of the commonly used related information, and thus devote more attention to other processes.

The interaction between bottom-up and top-down processes is itself a dynamic process. Accordingly, as each new piece of information is processed, it must be integrated into the mental representation that is being constructed. This might involve both the activation of additional knowledge from long-term memory and the ongoing modification of the current situation model.

There is a great deal of empirical evidence supporting the key role of prior topic-specific knowledge in discourse processing and related measures of performance (McNamara et al. 2007). These include, at the micro-processing level, interaction with text structure and verbal ability, and, at the macro-processing level, the management of meta-cognitive inferencing strategies (McNamara & O'Reilly 2010; Ozuru et al. 2009). In this sense, comprehension is a repetitive process of anticipation, confirmation/falsification, re-anticipation, and re-confirmation. From this perspective, and as corroborated in experimental studies (Díaz Galaz et al. 2015), world knowledge must be constantly updated and prior knowledge acquisition is a basic skill for interpreters.

Comprehension and working memory

WORKING MEMORY plays a crucial role in facilitating comprehension during interpreting, particularly in the simultaneous mode (see Gile 1997, 2009; Padilla et al. 1999). In order to integrate new information with previously processed information, it is necessary to have access to the results of previous processes. Thus, the efficient use of working memory and the processes related to comprehension are especially significant. Empirical research indicates that interpreters develop specific STRATEGIES to extend their memory capacity and efficiency, and that training and experience in interpreting foster the development of a set of cognitive skills involved in comprehension (Christoffels & de Groot 2005; Padilla et al. 2005; Yudes et al. 2012). Thus, interpreters can perform a series of mental tasks without the support of a rehearsal component in working memory, and are therefore able to read faster and more accurately. This ability is combined with quicker access to lexical and semantic information. Furthermore, interpreters not only have more working memory capacity available, but they are also able to use these cognitive resources more efficiently. As a result, their ability to understand and memorize in SI is not impaired by articulatory suppression in the phonological component of working memory.

As reflected by the specific role of working memory in SI, there are obviously relevant differences in the way comprehension is accomplished in different MODES of interpreting (Padilla et al. 2007). With regard to *temporal parameters*, SI demands immediate input processing, constrained not only by the speaker's pace but also by the need for real-time re-expression. In CONSECUTIVE INTERPRETING, on the other hand, where comprehension overlaps with NOTE-TAKING rather than with target text production, the interpreter is arguably more flexible in allocating resources and time to receptive processes. The *processing unit* is in effect conditioned by the position of breaks in the speaker's discourse, or by turn-taking among the participants. The interpreter thus has time to create a micro- and a macro-structure of the discourse. The macro-structural processes are especially relevant in consecutive interpreting of longer speeches, since the interpreter is often asked to give a summarized rendering. In SI, by contrast, the unit of processing never exceeds a few propositions (Christoffels & de Groot 2005), which makes the creation of the macrostructure considerably more difficult.

PRESENTACIÓN PADILLA AND MARÍA TERESA BAJO

COMPRESSION

↑ STRATEGIES
→ OMISSIONS

Compression in interpreting refers to a strategy used in the production of the target text. It can range from lexical and semantic compression at the level of the 'text surface' to information reduction through selection (Kirchhoff 1976a, 1976/2002) and to rendering only the main ideas or macrostructure of the source text, dispensing with less relevant details. Generally speaking, compression is easier when the source speech is impromptu (Déjean le Féal 1982) and contains features characteristic of ORALITY.

CHERNOV, who emphasizes the role of redundancy in speech as a fundamental prerequisite to the interpreting process, describes lexico-semantic compression as a reduction in the number of syllables, words and semantic elements. This results in a shorter target text with higher information density (Chernov 1969, 1994). Linguistic compression is also achieved when PROSODY is used to replace verbal information, for instance when qualifiers are expressed in the target language by means of prosodic stress.

Compression is often considered a recommended strategy for CONSECUTIVE INTERPRETING. In his *Interpreter's Handbook*, HERBERT goes as far as to recommend that 'full consecutive' should never take more than 75% of the time used by the original speaker, which is to be achieved by a slightly more rapid pace and by not rendering unintentional repetitions and the hesitation phenomena typical of spontaneous speech (1952: 67). Though there is not much empirical evidence of such compression in the consecutive mode, Dam (1993), in a study on consecutive conference interpreting in which she identifies mainly pronominal and lexical substitutions as ways of making the target text shorter, reaffirms the value of 'text condensing' as a necessary and usually good strategy. Albl-Mikasa (2006) draws on RELEVANCE THEORY (Sperber & Wilson 1986/1995) to describe reduction processes during NOTE-TAKING: ellipsis, restructuring, and high condensation.

In SIMULTANEOUS INTERPRETING, most authors, including Chernov, have focused on compression as a way of coping with particularly fast and dense source texts. In his early experimental study, GERVER (1969/2002) found that simultaneous interpreters omitted more phrases and longer passages as the input SPEECH RATE increased. Kalina (1998) foregrounds the use of compression as an emergency strategy in the consecutive as well as the simultaneous mode when the source speech rate is excessively high, noting, however, that considerable cognitive effort is required to identify those elements that can be either left out or rendered with less detail.

In general, compression can be achieved by selecting source-text elements that include others; by generalization (e.g. finding a hyperonym); by simplifying segments with complex wording; or by 'construction', that is, replacing several propositions by a single higher-order proposition in the target text (see Alexieva 1983; Gile 1995a; Kalina 1998; Bartłomiejczyk 2006). Since all of these compression techniques are adopted deliberately, this type of strategic target-text production must be distinguished from non-strategic or even unintentional OMISSIONS (i.e. leaving out elements at random), often as a result of cognitive overload (see Gile 1995a). It is, however, hard to draw the line between intentional information reduction by strategic compression and more or less conscious omission, or 'reduced' or 'zero' renditions in Wadensjö's (1998) terms.

Compression has been discussed as an acceptable or even necessary strategy, mainly for monologic speeches in conference-like SETTINGS. It is generally not considered admissible in LEGAL INTERPRETING, at least when rendering utterances by suspects, defendants or witnesses for the legal professionals. By contrast, summarized renditions may be required, for instance in COURTROOM INTERPRETING, when the legal proceedings are conveyed in whispering mode for participants who do not understand the language of the court. In a study of ACCURACY in simulated healthcare consultations with SIGNED LANGUAGE INTERPRETING for a deaf patient, Major and Napier (2012) found that one-fifth of all renditions analyzed included some form of reduction in comparison with the original utterances, but that only a small proportion of these reduced renditions negatively affected the message.

As compression is used for different purposes and in different settings, it has to be part of interpreter training (e.g. Cheung 2007). Various PRE-INTERPRETING EXERCISES have been proposed (e.g. Viaggio 1989; Gillies 2013) to teach trainees how to identify the most relevant parts of a speech and sum up its main arguments and macrostructure.

SYLVIA KALINA

COMPUTER ASSISTED INTERPRETER TRAINING

↑ PEDAGOGY, ↑ TECHNOLOGY
→ E-LEARNING
↓ PRE-INTERPRETING EXERCISES

In simple terms, Computer Assisted Interpreter Training (CAIT) is the idea that computer TECHNOLOGY can be used to enhance interpreter training. It comes from the well-established Computer Assisted Language Learning (CALL) paradigm in language teaching. The PEDAGOGY of interpreting relies heavily on deliberate (and sometimes repetitive) practice, especially in the initial stages of training (Sandrelli 2007, 2015). Thus, in the mid-1990s a few interpreter trainers in various countries began to think that dedicated computer-based materials could be used to support students' autonomous learning and provide the necessary individual focus (Sandrelli 2007). Over the years, this idea has evolved under the influence of pedagogical trends and of technological innovation and related changes in the interpreting PROFESSION. On the one hand, technological progress has made distance teaching possible, albeit still complex. On the other hand, technology plays a growing role in professional interpreting, with various forms of computer-aided interpreting, VIDEOCONFERENCE INTERPRETING and REMOTE INTERPRETING becoming more and more common. As a result, today the term CAIT has acquired a much wider meaning to embrace all kinds of E-LEARNING activities (Sandrelli 2015). A tentative periodization sees three stages in the history of CAIT.

Early period

In the early years, computers had limited multimedia capability and the Internet was in its infancy. The first CAIT experiences involved the digitization of interpreter training materials, meant for off-line use by single users. Two main paradigms emerged: the *repository approach* and the *authoring tool* or *courseware approach*. The former refers to the creation of digital speech banks, such as IRIS and Marius (Carabelli 1999; Gran et al. 2002; de Manuel Jerez 2003; Sandrelli & de Manuel Jerez 2007). The latter consisted in developing interpreting courseware, that is, computer-based teaching packages which students used by following a pre-established learning path (i.e. with materials and activities arranged in a specific order by teachers). This approach was first introduced by *Interpr-It*, a dialogue-interpreting package with a pilot consecutive interpreting module (Merlini 1996; Gran et al. 2002). A few years later, Melissi Multimedia Ltd. developed the *Black Box* authoring tool, an empty "shell" with ready-made and custom templates to create a range of PRE-INTERPRETING EXERCISES and a wide variety of interpreting exercises, including SIMULTANEOUS INTERPRETING, DIALOGUE INTERPRETING/CONSECUTIVE INTERPRETING, SI WITH TEXT and SIGHT INTERPRETING/TRANSLATION. Trainers with no specific software development skills could create CAIT materials on their own, by easily assembling audio, video and textual resources into exercises, modules and courses (Sandrelli 2007; Sandrelli & de Manuel Jerez 2007).

Middle period

As the technical specifications of PCs improved and Internet connections became more widely available and faster, the range of possible CAIT applications expanded. Of particular relevance are computer mediated communication (CMC) tools, both asynchronous (email, discussion forums, etc.) and synchronous (text-based chat tools and VoIP systems for online voice communication). These tools have made it possible to devise online collaborative activities, thus shifting the focus from single to multiple users.

CAIT continued to develop and improve on the previous paradigms, but also took steps towards encouraging user interaction and collaborative learning. *Interpreter training websites* are the online version of the earlier interpreting courseware (e.g. the ORCIT training package for beginners in interpreting). Similarly, *online speech banks* are the web-based development of speech repositories, the best-known example being the Speech Repository of SCIC (DG Interpretation). At the same time, a new paradigm emerged which envisaged the use of Course Management Systems (CMS) or Virtual Learning Environments (VLE). These are online learning platforms used in education to deliver all kinds of courses. The best known of them is *Moodle*, an open source environment that enables teachers to publish course schedules and materials, and students to engage in discussions and carry out collaborative work online. In interpreter training, CMS are often used in combination with traditional interpreter training labs (e.g. Gorm Hansen & Shlesinger 2007). A further step was taken by the University of Geneva, which developed the first dedicated VLE specifically for interpreter training purposes. The 'Virtual Institute' is used to deliver 'training the trainers' courses and to support Conference Interpreting MA students as well, in line with blended learning principles, that is, face-to-face classes complemented by an online component (e.g. Moser Mercer et al. 2005).

Current developments

Today computer technology is also used to take interpreter training beyond the classroom. The availability of web-streaming and videoconferencing technology has made it possible to have real-time distance interaction. An example is the collaboration between SCIC and the EMCI (European Master's in Conference Interpreting) Consortium universities, which has led to the organization of live multilingual virtual classes involving universities in different countries.

Distance learning and blended learning experiences have also been taking place in various countries outside the EU, including Australia, Canada, Norway, South Africa and the US. These solutions seem especially suitable when the required language combinations or geographical distance make traditional face-to-face courses unviable, as may be the case with training for COMMUNITY INTERPRETING (e.g. Skaaden & Wattne 2009; Sandrelli 2011a), BUSINESS INTERPRETING (e.g. Ko 2006a; Sandrelli 2011b) and also SIGNED LANGUAGE INTERPRETING.

Current CAIT projects are also trying to simulate professional SETTINGS in order to make learning more immersive and realistic. An example of this is IVY (Interpreting in Virtual Reality), which uses an avatar-based multi-user 3D virtual environment (*Second Life*) to create a virtual reality conference centre, business meeting room, courtroom, and so on. Students in different physical locations can 'meet' in this environment via their avatars and practise interpreting. Finally, Scene Cinema Ltd (formerly Melissi Multimedia Ltd.) is redeveloping its interpreting software for compatibility with wireless and mobile broadband connections (via dedicated apps). The idea is to enable students and teachers to access training materials, wherever they are, by using their PCs, notebooks, tablets and smartphones, thus overcoming cross-platform restrictions.

ANNALISA SANDRELLI

CONCENTRATION CAMPS

↑ HISTORY, ↑ SETTINGS
→ PRISON SETTINGS

Concentration camps are among the most violent SETTINGS of linguistic and other mediation activities (Levi 1988). In Nazi death camps and concentration camps, prisoners with the necessary language skills served as (non-professional) interpreters, also as a survival strategy in inhuman circumstances. Violence was exercised even through language – by means of interpreters, and often without: with cruel irony, the bludgeon used by Nazi guards was called a *Dolmetscher*, meaning an 'interpreter' whose brutal language was only too readily understood.

Despite the massive amount of material about Nazi concentration camps during the Second World War (archival material, survivor accounts, interviews with survivors, etc.), there is hardly any literature on interpreting in the camps; by contrast, translation scholars have explored various issues, examples being the metaphorical dimension of translation as violence (e.g. Insana 2009) and the translation of Holocaust survivor memoirs (e.g. Kuhiwczak 2011). Tryuk (e.g. 2010) has analyzed archival material from the Auschwitz-Birkenau Memorial and Museum Archives in Oświęcim, while Wolf (2013a) has investigated accounts of survivors. However, references to interpreting and interpreters are scant, and when they do occur they tend to be random, brief and laconic.

Interpreting needs

In many of the hundreds of Nazi concentration camps the inmates represented between 35 and 40 different national or ethnic groups, each with their own language. As in other multilingual social situations, interpreters were needed. Like all the paperwork, oral communication with the camp guards, who were mostly members of the SS (*Schutzstaffel*, 'Protection Squadron'), had to be in German. In the barracks and work blocks, all rules, orders, and instructions were delivered in German. In essence, two languages were used: German and a specific camp language called *lagerszpracha*, a mixture of German, Yiddish, Polish or other languages used by the inmates in the camps.

Interpreters

In most Nazi camps, three groups of persons acting as interpreters can be distinguished. The first group consisted of SS staff, often *Volksdeutsche* fluent in Polish or Czech, or other staff members with a knowledge of languages. A separate group were the *ex officio* interpreters (*Lagerdolmetscher*). They were so-called prisoner functionaries, whose tasks often included policing duties. The large majority of 'interpreters' were self-proclaimed ad hoc language mediators who facilitated communication between their fellow prisoners, and in most cases tried to ease their suffering.

Interpreting work generally was not linked to any privileges (for example, in terms of additional food rations), nor did it guarantee survival. Like the other prisoner functionaries, in some camps, interpreters wore an armband on their striped prison uniforms.

Camp interpreters' duties

The *Lagerdolmetscher* had to interpret the 'welcome speech' given to the newly arrived deportees by the camp commandant. Furthermore, they had to interpret when punishment was inflicted and in various other situations of conflict. In addition to their interpreting duties, they often served as camp or barrack registrars.

Survivor accounts often mention interpreters giving a helping hand – both to prisoners and to the SS staff, which testifies to the ambiguous ROLE of many camp interpreters. They were not simply an instrument used to convey petrifying information about life and death in the camp, degrading insults and humiliating orders; rather, they could also use their knowledge, and hence a certain amount of POWER, for the benefit of their own condition as well as that of others. This deeply human, ethically fraught, and dangerous role has no parallel in the history of interpreting. What camp interpreters had to translate impacted on their lives. Survival was the ultimate goal, and any sort of interpreting in whatever circumstances was subordinate to it.

MAŁGORZATA TRYUK AND MICHAELA WOLF

CONDUIT

see under ROLE

CONFERENCE INTERPRETING

→ DIPLOMATIC INTERPRETING
↓ PARLIAMENTARY SETTINGS

Since its beginnings in the early twentieth century, conference interpreting has become the most professionalised type of interpreting in history and, thanks to the high-profile SETTINGS in which it takes place, it may also be the most salient and prestigious. The evolution of conference interpreting has played a major role in bringing interpreting into the limelight, facilitating the development of professional standards, and ultimately allowing interpreting studies to carve out a place in academia.

In its broadest sense, conference interpreting can be defined as the rendering of speeches delivered in one language into another at formal and informal conferences and in conference-like settings, in either the simultaneous or the consecutive mode (AIIC 1984; Pöchhacker 2013a). As this definition suggests, the term 'conference interpreting' actually refers to a setting where various MODES of interpreting may be used. These settings typically include international conferences, multilateral meetings (particularly in institutions such as the EU and the UN), and workshops, but they also extend to official dinners, press conferences, parliamentary sessions, international tribunals, and even university lecture halls and church services.

Conference interpreting has traditionally been closely associated with spoken languages, but, of course, interpreting in conference-like settings is also, and increasingly, done in signed languages – mostly 'spoken to signed', but also vice versa, between signed languages, or from written text or captions into a signed language (Turner 2007). The recent opening up of

AIIC, the International Association of Conference Interpreters, to sign language interpreters reflects this growing recognition. Not only are sign language interpreters increasingly present in conference settings, but they also work primarily in the simultaneous mode, as do most conference interpreters today. Indeed, the prevalent – and often exclusive – use of SIMULTANEOUS INTERPRETING (SI) in conferences has made this mode all but synonymous with conference interpreting. It is, however, useful to distinguish between SI as a mode of interpreting (which has been a primary object of research, particularly in the framework of COGNITIVE APPROACHES), and conference interpreting as a professional domain.

Professionalisation

The beginnings of conference interpreting date back to the multilateral negotiations that took place at the end of World War I and conferences held by the League of Nations and ILO, where interpreters worked consecutively. CONSECUTIVE INTERPRETING remained the predominant mode of conference interpreting until the mid-twentieth century, although SI had been successfully developed and tested in the late 1920s (see Baigorri-Jalón 2014). The use of SI at the NUREMBERG TRIAL (Gaiba 1998) and the proliferation of international organisations and conferences in the aftermath of World War II led to the most rapid and robust institutionalisation process in history for interpreting.

As conference interpreting flourished, there was a growing need for trained professionals, and this gave rise to the founding of schools for interpreter EDUCATION. Over time, these developed from professionally oriented training schools into full-fledged departments and faculties, combining university-level teaching and academic research. The founding, in 1953, of AIIC as a global professional organisation dedicated to conference interpreting proved crucial to the institutionalisation of the PROFESSION. AIIC became a driving force in establishing WORKING CONDITIONS and professional standards in the field, negotiating collective bargaining agreements with major international organisations. Research on occupational STRESS (Cooper et al. 1982) and conference interpreters' workload (AIIC 2002), commissioned by AIIC, provided evidence of the stressful nature of the job and served as a scientific basis for developing and defending professional and technical arrangements in the field. Moreover, AIIC's 'school policy', which recommended training at postgraduate level with the active involvement of practicing professionals (Mackintosh 1999), also reinforced the academic standing of this professional domain, as did the development of a theoretical framework that ultimately became the most influential in the discipline. The key figure in this was Danica SELESKOVITCH, whose combination of professional experience as a practicing conference interpreter, active involvement in AIIC (e.g. as Secretary-General), leading educator of conference interpreters at the *École Supérieure d'Interprètes et de Traducteurs* (ESIT) in Paris, and author of seminal publications that served as the cornerstone of what later became known as the PARIS SCHOOL, made her the foremost representative of conference interpreting as a field of professional practice and object of academic research.

Initial research interest in the work of conference interpreters on the part of psychologists had focused on the cognitive and psycholinguistic aspects of SI, whereas the consecutive mode was largely neglected. As a practitioner of both modes, Seleskovitch placed the emphasis on consecutive interpreting to highlight the essence of her INTERPRETIVE THEORY, also known as *théorie du sens*, whose basic tenet is that interpreting entails the transfer of the 'sense' of a message and not the words. This theoretical framework, and the training approach associated with it (Seleskovitch & Lederer 1989), was readily adopted by many interpreters, professional organisations, interpreter trainers, and scholars of interpreting, empowering the profession and shaping the field of INTERPRETING STUDIES in its formative stage.

Conferences as a setting

Research on conferences as a setting has centred on conference typologies and studies of specific conference settings. Conference typologies attempt to classify the features that specific meeting types are likely to possess, for instance regarding the homogeneity of participants, the structure of the event or the use of visual aids (see Gile 1989; Snelling 1989; Pöchhacker 1994a). Accordingly, technical conferences can be expected to have a rather homogeneous participant group and a fairly high degree of structural complexity, and to involve frequent use of visual support material, whereas press conferences tend to have less homogeneity and structural complexity. Naturally, these typologies only give a general indication of what to expect, and real-life situations will often be more diverse and unpredictable.

There has been relatively little systematic observational research on the diversity of more or less formalized or ritualized communicative situations in which conference interpreting takes place. These include PARLIAMENTARY SETTINGS, international tribunals, university lecture halls (e.g. Verhoef & du Plessis 2008) and RELIGIOUS SETTINGS. A number of studies have targeted institutions such as the EU and the UN, which are among the most important employers of conference interpreters and which have exerted considerable influence on professional practice, not so much out of interest in the institutional setting as such, but because simultaneously interpreted proceedings may be routinely recorded and, in the case of the European Parliament (EP), accessible online in two dozen official languages. While some of the literature describes the main features of international organisations as a setting (e.g. Marzocchi 1998; Apostolou 2011), other studies explore the interplay between interpreting and the institutional settings themselves. An interesting finding from a study of the EP using ETHNOGRAPHIC METHODS is the conviction among interpreters that speakers' insistence on using poor (non-native) English leads to communication and representation problems, whereas parliamentarians are not always equally cognizant of the inherent challenges of monolingual communication (Kent 2009). A key finding from another study on conference interpreters' performance in institutional settings is the tendency to make speakers' implicit or vague formulations more explicit and consistent with the discourse of the institution, suggesting that interpreters may be identifying with the IDEOLOGY of the institution in which they work (Beaton 2007; Beaton-Thome 2010). There is also evidence that 'self-preservation' might supersede all other concerns, even in institutional contexts, when interpreters have to interpret face-threatening communication (Monacelli 2009).

Professional standards and status

In response to SHLESINGER's (1989a) call for an exploration of NORMS in interpreting, a number of studies have found that 'identifying with the speaker by adopting his/her first person' and 'being an impartial and loyal intermediary' are the strongest professional norms in conference interpreting (Harris 1990; Schjoldager 1995). It would appear that these norms are quite prevalent among both insiders and outsiders to the profession. Despite their prevalence at a discursive level, sociological studies on interpreting behaviour suggest that putting these norms into practice is highly challenging, and that actual situations generally require a case-based negotiation of the interpreters' presence and performance (Pöchhacker 1994a; Diriker 2004; Monacelli 2009).

Recent discussions on standards of professional ETHICS further reinforce awareness regarding the gap between idealised ROLE definitions of conference interpreters and the complexity of real-life interpreting situations. Initially triggered by studies on interpreters working in CONFLICT ZONES and wars, differences of opinion on what constitutes 'ethical behaviour' in conference interpreting have emerged most vividly in the debate surrounding voluntary interpreting networks, such as Babels, and other ACTIVIST APPROACHES in interpreting (e.g. Boéri 2008). These discussions openly challenge the assumption of interpreters as 'detached' and 'impartial' intermediaries.

In research on professional standards a prominent issue has been QUALITY in conference interpreting, and what constitutes quality for whom. One major line of research has sought to elicit the views of various stakeholders regarding the importance of different aspects of quality in an interpreter's performance. SURVEY RESEARCH on QUALITY CRITERIA has shown that users of interpreting services as well as interpreters themselves consistently give the highest importance to 'sense consistency with the original message' (Bühler 1986; Kurz 1993a; Moser 1996; Zwischenberger 2010). Ethnographic studies, however, show considerable variation in the way these criteria are defined and assessed in actual situations. Accordingly, the definition of what constitutes 'quality' differs greatly, not only among members of the same audience, but also for the same person in different contexts, and many users seem to view and judge interpreting quality according to their immediate needs (Mack & Cattaruzza 1995; Vuorikoski 1998; Collados Aís et al. 2007, 2011).

Professional standards regarding such issues as quality and ethical behaviour play an important part in shaping the image and STATUS attributed to a profession in society. Among translational professions, conference interpreting is generally assumed to enjoy the highest status, as indicated by frequent references to superior working conditions, higher remuneration and more advanced professionalisation. However, studies exploring interpreters' self-perception of their roles and occupational status bear out this belief only in part, and suggest that interpreters see themselves in a more modest light. Among EU staff interpreters and translators, for instance, interpreters tend to rate their job prestige higher than translators, but the difference seems not nearly as marked as one would expect (Dam & Zethsen 2013). Comparable results emerge from a study in CHINA (Setton & Guo 2011). Both translators and interpreters emphasize that their work demands a high degree of EXPERTISE, but feel that this is not sufficiently appreciated. The somewhat higher ratings interpreters give to their job prestige seem to be directly related to the slightly better external recognition they feel they receive in comparison to translators. Interestingly, these studies also point to a connection between interpreting mode and perceived status: conference interpreters associate the shift from consecutive interpreting to SI with a loss of visibility and a decline in their status, and those who work more in the consecutive mode tend to rate their work as more important than those doing mainly SI (Zwischenberger 2011).

Despite the relatively modest levels of self-perceived status found among conference interpreters, and the feeling that they receive insufficient recognition for their expertise, 82% of interpreters in a survey by AIIC (2002) report being satisfied with their jobs. Similar findings from studies carried out in China suggest that high levels of JOB SATISFACTION are also enjoyed by conference interpreters in emerging markets (Setton & Guo 2011).

Research on the social image of conference interpreting as a profession provides further insights into why conference interpreters feel insufficiently appreciated. According to these studies, outsiders to the profession judge conference interpreters by the rather subjective criterion of 'FIDELITY to the original word'. In the media, interpreters are similarly judged by this yardstick and applauded when 'complete fidelity' is attained, but they are also harshly criticised when they allegedly fall short of this goal (Diriker 2011). Insiders to the profession, including interpreters and their professional associations, emphasize that the task of the interpreter is to render the speakers' intended 'meanings' rather than their words. Anecdotal accounts by interpreters go even a step further, and analyses of real-life interpreting performances confirm that interpreters shape their delivery not only with regard to the linguistic or even semantic aspects of the original speech, but also with regard to situational, psychological, political and other relevant factors (Pöchhacker 1994a; Setton 1999; Diriker 2004; Monacelli 2009).

Future challenges

Some of the trends that have the potential to impact conference interpreting are the spread of ENGLISH AS A LINGUA FRANCA (ELF), advances in the area of REMOTE INTERPRETING and efforts made towards national and worldwide standardisation.

The spread of ELF is clearly a challenge to conference interpreters, and a number of studies have demonstrated a considerable level of awareness and concern. In one study, a majority of interpreters reported a decrease in the number of their professional assignments due to an increase in English-only events, and 40% of respondents voiced fears that there would be a further decline in interpreting jobs in the future (Albl-Mikasa 2010). Interpreters have also noted that 'simpler' conferences are increasingly held using only English, while more technical and challenging meetings will still use interpreting. Interpreters also feel challenged by the increasing use of non-native English on the floor and have had to develop ways of coping with this challenge (Albl-Mikasa 2010; Chang & Wu 2014). And while conference participants may be unaware of the situation, even expert listeners with good English skills seem to understand a speech significantly better when they listen to its interpretation in their mother tongue than when they listen to the speaker's non-native English (Reithofer 2013).

There is no doubt that the emergence of new technologies is having a major impact on conference interpreting, in ways that are still difficult to gauge. Most attention to date has focused on REMOTE INTERPRETING, which has been the subject of experiments in several major international institutions. While such arrangements, in which interpreters are no longer present at the site of the conference, have become increasingly feasible from a technical point of view (Mouzourakis 2006), interpreters have seen them as posing a further threat to their visibility (Moser-Mercer 2005a), even though the quality of performance achieved in remote mode may not be significantly lower than when working on site (Roziner & Shlesinger 2010).

Another development that will affect conference interpreting as a profession is the establishment of national and international standards. Such efforts have been undertaken in several European countries, as well as on the international (ISO) level. Much of this work focuses on working conditions and technical equipment and facilities, thus continuing a development that has characterized the profession of conference interpreting for many decades – that is, the evolution of a professional service in response to socio-political and technological change.

EBRU DIRIKER

CONFIDENTIALITY

see under ETHICS

CONFLICT ZONES

↑ SETTINGS
→ MILITARY INTERPRETING

Interpreting in conflict zones comprises both MILITARY INTERPRETING and interpreting in humanitarian settings and is emerging as a new area of specialization in research and practice, positioned at the cross-roads of international relations, diplomacy, humanitarian action, international law and humanitarian ethics. Wallensteen (2007) recognizes three general forms of conflict: interstate, internal, and state-formation conflicts. Interstate conflicts are disputes between nation-states or violations of the state system. Examples of internal and state-formation conflicts include civil and ethnic wars, anti-colonial struggles, secessionist and autonomous movements, territorial conflicts, and battles over control of government. Some conflicts are country-wide, such as in Rwanda, while others are localized in specific parts of a country, such as in the Darfur region of Sudan.

Most conflicts involve some form of national and/or international intervention, whether military or humanitarian, and during almost all types of intervention, language barriers need to be overcome, not only in disputes between nation-states, but also in internal conflicts, and during civil and ethnic wars. Overcoming language barriers in conflict zones may involve different kinds of personnel: 'military linguists' are for the most part embedded in the military; humanitarian interpreters are civilians and are engaged by humanitarian actors to facilitate a variety of relief operations, including efforts to get access to disputed zones in negotiations that sometimes take place under military cover.

All actors in an armed conflict come under the provisions of International Humanitarian Law, which seeks to strengthen the protection of civilians, defined by the Fourth Geneva Convention as any person not belonging to the armed forces, including non-nationals and refugees. The distinction between military and civilian interpreting is a vital element in securing protection (Moser-Mercer 2015), as the responsibility to protect ('R2P') lies with states, whether on their own territory or in their military operations in other contexts. The concept of protection in turn has far-reaching consequences for the QUALITY of interpreting in conflict zones, as NEUTRALITY and impartiality, two fundamental humanitarian principles that also resonate with interpreters, can be seriously jeopardized if personal risk has to be factored into the interpreter's decisions about how to convey the message. With few exceptions, notably the International Committee of the Red Cross, humanitarian organizations and non-governmental organizations active in conflict zones engage interpreters locally and do not offer them regular work contracts. This compromises protection, as interpreters are often considered traitors, and find themselves outside the framework of labor law and persecuted by members of their own community.

Additional pressures arise for those humanitarian interpreters who work in contexts of human rights violations, implementation of refugee law and detention/prisons. As locals they may themselves have experienced the narratives of beatings, torture, rape and mass murder that they are asked to interpret on a regular basis; male interpreters outnumber female interpreters in the field, whereas many victims are women, and considering the topics covered in interpreted encounters, this GENDER mismatch may further compromise the faithful transmission of messages from one language and culture to another. Fundamental challenges also arise from lack of training and experience, low levels of language proficiency, cultural and religious barriers, and a lack of awareness regarding the interpreter's professional ROLE. The role of translators and interpreters in conflict has been the subject of a growing body of research (e.g. Stahuljak 1999; Dragovic-Drouet 2007; Inghilleri & Harding 2010). The British *Languages at War* project has highlighted the role of languages in war and the policies and practices that shape language contacts in conflict. Moser-Mercer, Kherbiche and Class (2014) describe the multiple challenges that humanitarian interpreters must contend with on a daily basis in terms of ethics, emotional trauma and protection. Interpreters working for the United Nations High Commissioner for Refugees (UNHCR), for instance, are themselves refugees interpreting for other refugee-applicants the experiences they themselves have had to endure; they are displaced persons who have suffered emotional and physical trauma, with no home community to support them.

The issue of protection of interpreters working in conflict zones has been highlighted in the media, with a focus on local interpreters embedded in the military rather than on humanitarian interpreters. Organizations such as Red T have been set up to establish translators and interpreters as a global, protected community. In collaboration with AIIC and FIT, they published the *Conflict Zone Field Guide for Civilian Translators/Interpreters and Users of Their Services* (Red T 2012). It must be remembered, however, that not even the most authoritative piece of international law developed for these contexts, the Geneva Conventions, is consistently respected in times of conflict and war. For interpreters working in these contexts, the most effective protection will be a regulated employment status moving them out of the informal economy (Bartolini 2009; Moser-Mercer 2015), and professionalization through training. Such initiatives are most effective when they are offered in the field, where awareness-raising with users of interpreting services must become an integral part of humanitarian action, and where training is embedded in a context in which interpreters can benefit immediately from enhanced skills. An example is the InZone project, coordinated by the University of Geneva. It offers a basic course for humanitarian field interpreters, in a blended format, with on-site training in the field followed by virtual training that covers basic interpreting skills and professional ethics. Most research efforts in this domain are seriously hampered by the lack of physical access to conflict zones, the difficulty of identifying research resources, including field interpreters, and the degree of anonymity and confidentiality that is required to ensure maximum protection for interpreters participating in research. What is more, researchers must understand and respect the legal framework of International Humanitarian Law, International Human Rights Law and Refugee Law when planning to conduct a study of interpreting in conflict zones.

BARBARA MOSER-MERCER

CONSECUTIVE INTERPRETING

↑ MODES
→ DIALOGUE INTERPRETING
↓ NOTE-TAKING

Interpreters, whose presence was attested in ancient EGYPT, have for centuries served rulers, conquerors, military and religious leaders, as well as traders and explorers. They would typically have worked between two parties in consecutive mode, speaking after someone had spoken in another language. However, no special label was used for this age-old practice before the twentieth century, when it came to be referred to as liaison interpreting or, more commonly now, DIALOGUE INTERPRETING. The term 'consecutive interpreting', used as a broad label for the 'default' mode of interpreting, came into use after the 1920s, to mark the difference between traditional interpreting and what was then the newly tested 'telephonic' (i.e. simultaneous) mode (Baigorri-Jalón 2014). It was in the League of Nations, the first international organisation to employ its own staff interpreters, that 'classic' consecutive interpreting flourished. Gustave Camerlynck, André Kaminker and Paul MANTOUX are famous examples of interpreters who worked professionally but without any special training, as did all interpreters at the time. Comments on their work are found in MEMOIRS by interpreters (e.g. Schmidt 1949; Jacob 1962) and politicians (e.g. Lansing 1921; Madariaga 1974), and interpreters themselves also provided an account of their work in an early study by Sanz (1930).

Following the successful use of SIMULTANEOUS INTERPRETING (SI) at the NUREMBERG TRIAL and its subsequent adoption by the United Nations (Baigorri-Jalón 2004), consecutive interpreting was gradually displaced by the new mode of CONFERENCE INTERPRETING. Indeed, consecutive interpreting is the exception rather than the rule in the work of most conference interpreters today.

Since consecutive interpreting, broadly defined, may involve the rendering of source-language utterances lasting anywhere from a few seconds to several minutes or more (e.g. González et al. 1991/2012), there is no hard and fast distinction between 'classic consecutive' and 'short consecutive'. Prototypically, the former implies (monologic) speeches with a duration of five or six – or sometimes even as long as twenty – minutes; the latter usually deals with utterances as short as a single phrase or sentence. In practice, these two extremes can be said to be increasingly converging, though there is a lack of systematic empirical data in this regard (as is, indeed, the case for many other aspects of consecutive interpreting).

Major topics

The literature on consecutive interpreting is dominated by publications with a didactic orientation, often with NOTE-TAKING forming the core of the guidance provided. Jean HERBERT's (1952) classic *Interpreter's Handbook* is a case in point. Much of it is devoted to the consecutive mode, the emphasis being mainly on note-taking, but it also includes reflections on text analysis and COMPREHENSION, speech production and presentation, as well as discussion of the traditional view that consecutive is a prerequisite skill for SI training. This last point is still the subject of much debate (e.g. Seleskovitch & Lederer 1989; Gile 2001a; Russell et al. 2010).

A didactic focus is also present in Seleskovitch's (1975) study on note-taking, which was fundamental for theorizing the process by postulating that the process of understanding is based not on words, but on their meaning (*sens*). Her *théorie du sens*, or INTERPRETIVE THEORY, led to the well-known sense-based triangular 'process' model of interpreting. A useful overview of other influential ideas in the PEDAGOGY and practice of consecutive interpreting can be found in Ilg & Lambert (1996).

Prominent topics in publications on consecutive interpreting include STRATEGIES in text comprehension and analysis, memory storage and re-expression (e.g. Jones 1998; Kautz 2000). Gile (1995a) focuses on processing capacity and coping tactics, Dam (1993) on text 'condensing', and Kalina (1998) on these and other processing strategies, such as identifying macrostructures and prioritising information.

Various authors have dealt with the development of MODELS for consecutive interpreting, amongst other things for teaching purposes, to help identify and practice the different skills required. One of the first researchers to introduce a model for consecutive interpreting was Kade (1963), who divided the process into six stages and illustrated the links between the different stages as well as between MEMORY capacity and note-taking. Most authors simply posit two or three phases in the process of consecutive interpreting (e.g. Bowen & Bowen 1984; Żmudzki 2008); more elaborate models are few and far between. Two models that offer a different approach were put forward by Kirchhoff (1979) and Gile (1995a, 2009). Kirchhoff (1979) describes the processing of information in consecutive interpreting as a division of labour between two storage systems that differ from, and complement, each other – storage in memory and storage aided by a note-taking system. Gile (1995a), in the framework of his teaching-oriented EFFORT MODELS, outlines two main stages in consecutive interpreting (referred to as the "listening" and the "reformulation" phase); he uses this perspective to address the issue of the limited cognitive resources the interpreter has available for processing information, thus necessitating process capacity management, which needs to be taught.

More recent efforts to conceptualise the consecutive interpreting process (see Andres et al. 2013) apply the SI models of GERVER (1976), Moser (1978) and Setton (1999) to consecutive interpreting, giving particular attention to the role of memory. Unlike the cognitive aspects, nonverbal and non-translational features of consecutive interpreting as a communicative activity in situated interaction have received little attention. Among the few exceptions is Poyatos (1987), who modeled the paraverbal and kinesic sign systems produced and received by the speaker, listener and interpreter, including such components as eye contact, INTONATION and GESTURE. Andres (2002) investigated these in an EXPERT–NOVICE PARADIGM and found that professionals used eye contact to gloss over hesitation and doubt, and gestures to emphasise words, whereas students displayed insecurity by shaking their heads, looking at their notes at the expense of eye contact with the audience, and making gestures such as putting their hand to their mouth and scratching their head or nose.

Considering the crucial dependence of consecutive interpreting on memory storage, as emphasised by authors such as Minyar-Beloruchev (1969a), Seleskovitch (1975), González et al. (1991/2012) and Kautz (2000), there has been surprisingly little empirical (experimental) work on the consecutive mode in COGNITIVE APPROACHES to the study of interpreting. Among the few exceptions are the study by Gerver (1976), comparing reception of consecutive and SI in difficult listening conditions, and the work of Lambert (1988a, 1989b) on recall and recognition after consecutive interpreting compared to SI, SHADOWING and listening. In the conceptual framework of the depth-of-processing hypothesis, Lambert concludes that there is evidence of deeper processing in the listening-only condition and in the consecutive mode.

More recent empirical research focuses on EXPERTISE in consecutive interpreting. Mead (2002a) concentrates on language production, comparing professional and student subjects with regard to their FLUENCY of delivery. Examining hesitation phenomena as an index of fluency, he explored the use of RETROSPECTIVE PROTOCOLS to study interpreters' views on the reasons for their hesitations, mostly attributed to difficulties with lexical retrieval (i.e. finding the right word or expression) in the target language and uncertainties in deciphering notes. With a similar focus, Yin (2011) investigated the frequency of PAUSES, fillers and repetitions in 28 consecutive interpretations by Chinese undergraduates, in an attempt to identify causes and offer solutions. Abuín González (2007) classified problems in consecutive interpreting and proposed strategies for dealing with these in training.

A number of studies on consecutive interpreting have addressed the issues of QUALITY and ASSESSMENT (e.g. Marrone 1993; Viezzi 1993; Gile 1995c; Kutz 1997), and the extensive empirical study of note-taking by Andres (2002) also included an evaluation of the 28 interpretations by experts and novices as 'good', 'average' or 'poor'. Quality also features in the debate on whether greater ACCURACY is achieved in consecutive or in SI. Gile (2001b) investigated how simultaneous and consecutive interpreters coped with potential problem triggers in the source text, such as false starts, digressions and incomplete or particularly challenging speech segments, and found the consecutive interpretations to be inferior in terms of overall accuracy. The opposite emerged from a broader-based study by Russell (2002) on SIGNED LANGUAGE INTERPRETING in a courtroom setting. Two teams of two ASL/English interpreters worked one mock trial each in consecutive and simultaneous mode, and higher accuracy rates were found for consecutive interpreting in each of the two simulated cases. Comparative analyses have also been carried out for the technology-assisted mode known as SIMULTANEOUS CON-SECUTIVE, in which the interpreter's rendering, in simultaneous mode, of the recorded source speech generally achieves greater accuracy (Hamidi & Pöchhacker 2007; Orlando 2014).

Technological tools have come to be used, in particular to enhance training practices in consecutive interpreting. Orlando (2010) proposed using digital pen technology for note-taking. As the 'Smartpen' can capture the notes being taken at the same time as audio-recording the speech, students can be given better feedback and advice based on the synchronised record of their note-taking behaviour.

Outlook

According to AIIC statistics, the consecutive mode nowadays accounts on average for only some six or seven percent of assignments, with relatively higher demand in the Asia-Pacific region – partly due to the market in China – as well as in northern and southern Europe. If dialogue interpreting, much of which is done in consecutive mode, is taken into account, estimated demand for consecutive interpreting is considerably greater. Thus the question arises as to whether consecutive interpreting in its 'classic' form (i.e. for monologic speeches) will in the long term fade from the international conference market, only to resurface as dialogue interpreting. Such a shift must also be viewed in relation to the increasing use of REMOTE INTERPRETING in community-based SETTINGS, which, for the time being, is done mainly in consecutive mode. All of this is likely to impact future training and testing practices. Stakeholders in the (inter-)national political arena have traditionally attached great value to (classic) consecutive, which remains part of the accreditation tests for international institutions. As long as their expectations regarding content accuracy and performance skills remain as high as at present, consecutive interpreting – and note-taking – will continue to play a major role in the interpreter training CURRICULUM.

DÖRTE ANDRES

CONVERSATION ANALYSIS

see under DISCOURSE ANALYTICAL APPROACHES

COPING TACTICS

see under STRATEGIES

CORPUS-BASED RESEARCH

↑ METHODOLOGY
↓ TRANSCRIPTION

The use of corpora in interpreting research has been increasingly advocated since the late 1990s, in the wake of the insights afforded by studies based on corpora of translated texts (e.g. Baker 1993) and promising applications to both translator training and professional practice (e.g. Beeby et al. 2009, Bernardini & Castagnoli 2008; Zanettin et al. 2003). Miriam SHLESINGER (1998) first referred to 'Corpus-based Interpreting Studies' (CIS) as an 'offshoot' of Corpus-based Translation Studies (CTS) in the title of her pioneering paper in a special issue of *Meta* devoted to the so-called corpus-based approach. The much greater maturity of CTS compared to CIS is due to a number of intrinsic challenges in the development of interpreting corpora, ranging from access to large amounts of authentic data (and speech communities, i.e. interpreters and users of interpreting services) to TRAN-SCRIPTION of spoken language features (Cencini 2002; Niemants 2012), multilingualism and so on. Despite this, an overview of CIS projects (Setton 2011) shows that interpreting corpora have been growing in number, size and accessibility across MODES and SETTINGS over the last two decades and have become increasingly common resources in research (Straniero Sergio & Falbo 2012) and, to a lesser extent, in interpreter training (Sandrelli 2010; Bale 2013).

Within corpus linguistics a corpus is generally defined as "a large collection of authentic texts that have been gathered in electronic form according to a specific set of criteria" (Bowker & Pearson 2002: 9), thus implying that some kind of automatic or semi-automatic analysis can be carried out. However, this is not always the case in CIS, as there are many examples of studies that are classed as corpus-based but in which the occurrences under analysis are extracted manually, without relying on any corpus-linguistic tool. Neither are there many significantly large interpreting corpora compared to the greater size of general reference corpora (now reaching millions, if not billions, of words) or even translation corpora and other types of spoken and signed language corpora. Nevertheless, the field of CIS has evolved dramatically, from principled samples of data collected on the basis of inclusion/ exclusion criteria, with transcripts suitable for manual analysis, and tape-recorded or digitally recorded samples partially available online or from the researchers in charge (some pioneering examples are Pöchhacker 1994a; Kalina 1998; Setton 1999; more recent studies are van Besien & Meuleman 2004; Diriker 2004; Vuorikoski 2004; Petite 2005; Straniero Sergio 2007; Monacelli 2009; Falbo 2012), to fully computerized corpora with annotated transcripts in electronic form and digital recordings (Cencini & Aston 2002; Kajzer-Wietrzny 2013; Monti et al. 2005), to open-access, online resources with fully machine-readable transcripts aligned with audio/video files and possibly enriched with a variety of linguistic and extralinguistic annotations (Angermeyer et al. 2012; Bendazzoli 2012; Bührig et al. 2012; House et al. 2012).

Regardless of how stringently the definition of corpus is applied, a common distinguishing feature of any CIS project is the attempt to overcome one of the main limitations associated more particularly with early studies of interpreting: as Shlesinger (1998) noted, these were based on sparse and often anecdotal data, while a key aim of CIS is to deliver results on the basis of a representative and authentic sample, making use of systematic observations.

Corpus types and designs

Interpreting corpora are spoken/signed language corpora based on transcripts of audio or video recordings from interpreter-mediated communicative events. Typically, a researcher records and transcribes an interpreter-mediated communicative event, thus creating a multimedia archive and a database from which corpus material can be selected. Recordings may be aligned with the transcripts, as in multimedia corpora, or made available as separate files. At least two languages (the source speaker's and the interpreter's output, i.e. a source and target language respectively) are generally involved. In fact, depending on how a corpus is designed, there can be many different kinds of interpreting corpora: monolingual, bilingual or multilingual corpora (with only one, two, or more languages represented); parallel corpora, including both source and target speeches; comparable corpora, in which one language is represented both as a source language and as a target language (from one or more source languages); and intermodal corpora, which feature the output obtained in one or more target languages from the same source text, using different translation and interpreting modes without altering the language combination and direction (e.g. Shlesinger 2008).

Interpreting corpora must follow the same development stages entailed in the creation of any spoken corpus, namely data collection, transcription, mark-up and annotation, and access (see Thompson 2004). In addition, two further stages complete the development process of an interpreting corpus: an initial stage of corpus design (since a number of features depend on the interpreting mode and setting under consideration, and on whether the data are produced in experimental or real-life conditions), together with the alignment of source and target texts, as well as text and sound/video (Bendazzoli 2010a). In fact both annotation and alignment are optional, but they certainly give greater added value to a corpus in terms of research potential (e.g. part-of-speech or POS tagging, but also annotation of nonverbal or pragmatic features). The annotation of meta-data to classify each speech event is linked to the fundamental issue of representativeness and needs to be based on a clear definition of the object under study (Biber 1993; Halverson 1998). Notwithstanding many technological advances and the availability of more user-friendly tools (e.g. speech recognition software to transcribe spoken language and automatic taggers), developing and building a DIY (i.e. do it yourself) interpreting corpus is still a laborious, time-consuming and challenging endeavour. This points to the need for greater accessibility of existing resources and the design of internationally shared standards for transcribing and encoding spoken language features. Access to real-life events may be increasingly possible, but open access and distribution (at the end of the corpus compilation process) may not be granted due to the confidential nature of many situations, especially in COMMUNITY INTERPRETING.

CIS resources

One of the main factors that has strongly influenced the development of resources for corpus-based research is the degree of access to the settings where interpreting is performed. The European Parliament (EP) is a case in point: its intensive translational activity, the increasing number of official languages in use, and easy access to its data (e.g. plenary sittings are broadcast by the EbS satellite TV channel, and the EP website contains the full video archive of part-sessions from April 2006) have attracted the attention of several scholars (Bendazzoli 2010b). Indeed, one of the first fully computerized, POS-tagged and publicly available SIMULTANEOUS INTERPRETING corpora is EPIC, the European Parliament Interpreting Corpus (Monti et al. 2005; Russo et al. 2012; Sandrelli et al. 2010), a trilingual corpus (English, Italian, Spanish) compiled from plenary sittings of the EP.

External access to interpreter-mediated communicative situations, in particular through TV broadcasts, has also led to the creation of interpreting corpora encompassing other modes (including short and standard CONSECUTIVE INTERPRETING), such as the Italian Television Interpreting Corpus or CorIT (Straniero Sergio 2007) and the corpus of Chinese–English interpreting at the Chinese Premier's annual press conferences (Wang 2012).

Simulations and experimental research have always been a convenient (albeit more questionable) alternative to fieldwork for the harvesting of larger data sets. For instance, simulated lectures and conversations (in English and Japanese) interpreted by multiple teams of professional simultaneous interpreters are recorded and transcribed in the Simultaneous Interpretation Database (SIDB) of Nagoya University (Matsubara et al. 2002; Ono et al. 2008; Tohyama et al. 2005), which is reportedly the first machine-readable simultaneous interpreting corpus of substantial size (one million words).

Notwithstanding the greater difficulties entailed by fieldwork, interpreting corpora have also been created from data collected in the interpreting market, especially by practising professionals who also work in academia. Examples from CONFERENCE INTERPRETING include the Directionality in Simultaneous Interpreting Corpus or DIRSI-C (Bendazzoli 2012) from English/Italian medical conferences held in Italy (the DIRSI Multimedia Archive contains further data from other international conferences on different topics); the FOOTIE Corpus (Sandrelli 2012) from football press conferences; and the CoSi corpus (House et al. 2012), which includes both simultaneous and consecutive interpreting.

Surprisingly, there are fewer (monologic) consecutive interpreting corpora, though source and target text alignment would be less challenging in this mode. By contrast, additional obstacles are to be faced in the creation of SIGNED LANGUAGE INTERPRETING corpora (e.g. Kellett Bidoli

2004; Metzger & Roy 2011). Corpus-based studies of short consecutive interpreting (in dialogic interactions) are embedded in a variety of institutional contexts, such as healthcare, legal, business and school settings (see Baraldi & Gavioli 2012a; Bührig et al. 2012). Most of these data, however, are not in the public domain in the form of machine-readable corpora and have thus far been analyzed above all using DISCOURSE ANALYTICAL APPROACHES (Gavioli & Baraldi 2011). This also applies to one of the rare examples of interpreting learner corpora (Niemants 2013), which comprises audio recordings and transcripts from doctor–patient encounters in real-life and training settings (ROLE PLAY used in a training programme and the relevant final exam).

Research focus and prospects

Corpus-based research has been fruitful in many respects, first and foremost for the creation of language resources (i.e. corpora) to be exploited by the research community, interpreter trainers and trainees alike. Corpora have proved instrumental to investigating both the product and the process of interpreting (e.g. STRATEGIES), opening up descriptive studies in quantitative and qualitative terms (Shlesinger & Ordan 2012). Moreover, since the creation of a corpus requires a systematic classification of the data collected so as to establish their representativeness, corpora provide a sound basis for replication, which is much needed to compare results from different studies and possibly gain a better understanding of the so-called universals of interpreting, as well as interpreting NORMS and styles (see Laviosa 2003 for a discussion in CTS). Yet corpus size is still a critical factor: many corpora are analyzed manually and do not take advantage of automatic feature extraction (which is in itself a symptom of the limited size of a corpus, as manual analysis would not be practical in very large corpora). This can be illustrated with reference to two corpus-based studies on the same subject, i.e. disfluencies in simultaneous interpreting, where the occurrences are detected manually (Petite 2005) and automatically (Bendazzoli et al. 2011). On the other hand, lexical patterns, such as lexical density and lexical variety, can be investigated systematically only by employing corpus-linguistic tools (see Kajzer-Wietrzny 2013; Russo et al. 2006).

Finally, corpus-based research has also had a profound impact on interpreter training, not so much in terms of building learner corpora (i.e. corpora based on trainees' performances) or tapping existing corpora as pedagogical tools (e.g. Sandrelli 2010; Tohyama & Matsubara 2006), but more in terms of exploitation of language resources for educational purposes. The increasing number of undergraduate and postgraduate theses based on wider CIS projects is clear evidence of this (Dal Fovo 2011; Russo 2010); similarly, multimedia archives of corpora in the form of speech repositories are now widespread. Examples include the pioneering corpus of consecutive interpreting by Dollerup and Ceelen (1996), with audio recordings and transcripts of a training programme in the European Commission; the dataset of speeches from EP plenary sittings and the World Social Forum event series compiled by de Manuel Jerez (2003); and other corpora for pedagogical applications (e.g. Bale 2013; Leeson 2008; Schembri et al. 2013). Whereas CTS has provided translators with useful tools at different levels, corpus use in interpreters' professional practice is virtually non-existent and remains to be explored.

Considering how corpus-based research has evolved so far, with the modest data samples of early studies now superseded by fully computerized corpora on a far greater scale, CIS is likely to continue to expand in scope thanks to the increasing availability of very large corpora and more user-friendly tools. Such resources, provided that they are devised with basic annotation (at least initially) and flexible formats, can speed up the corpus development process and allow for greater exploitation (and systematic subsequent annotation) by different scholars to cover the entire spectrum of interpreter-mediated interaction, contributing to empirical research, theory-building and training as a fully-fledged research paradigm.

CLAUDIO BENDAZZOLI

CORPUS-LINGUISTIC METHODS

see under CORPUS-BASED RESEARCH

COURT INTERPRETING

see LEGAL INTERPRETING; TRIBUNAL INTERPRETING

COURTROOM INTERPRETING

↑ LEGAL INTERPRETING
↓ TRIBUNAL INTERPRETING

Courtroom interpreting, as a particular domain of LEGAL INTERPRETING, refers to situations where, due to one or more participants' limited (or complete lack of) proficiency in the language of the court, or to speech and/or hearing impairments, interpreting services are required in oral judicial proceedings in order to overcome difficulties in communication. Other-language speakers may include witnesses, defendants, legal counsel, jurors and judges, who need such services so that the legal procedure – pre-trial hearings, trial, sentencing – can take place.

Whereas the term 'court interpreting' is often used more broadly as a synonym of 'legal interpreting', the reference here is to the courtroom (or 'court') as a specific setting within the legal process, typically characterised by complex ritualized interaction and power hierarchies, where the judge is the most powerful figure in the courtroom (Napier et al. 2010; Stern 2011). Judges' attitudes to interpreters in their courts are therefore crucial (Morris 2007). Most research into courtroom interpreting focuses on its provision in criminal proceedings, although increasingly the no less crucial civil sector is also being studied (Abel 2009). Some parties may be denied due process, in other words not receive a fair and impartial trial, because judges are either insensitive to the necessity of using qualified court interpreters to protect the rights of a limited-language-proficient individual, or act as if they have no control over the interpreter, and hence over the proceedings (Shlesinger 1991; Morris 2007, 2008).

Judicial systems

Courtroom interpreting practices are significantly shaped by the respective legal tradition. In adversarial (common-law) systems, interpreters are involved at all stages of what is essentially an oral process. The inquisitorial (continental) system makes more use of written material, and hence interpreters may be required to do SIGHT INTERPRETING/TRANSLATION. The all-important cross-examination does not exist in the continental trial, although the parties and their counsel are generally permitted to ask questions. When Japan, in 2009, introduced the lay judge system, for example, there was also a shift from written to oral evidence, which affected the importance of court interpreters and their renderings. There are also hybrid legal systems. In Belgium, for example, pre-trial proceedings are mainly inquisitorial, while the trial itself is usually considered as accusatorial. Anglo-American-style juries, or variations on this format (as in Japan), may be involved in legal proceedings, with significant implications for the interpreting process.

In jury trials, judges must provide specific instructions to both counsel and jurors as to the procedure to follow when interpreter renderings are challenged. Because of what is called the 'same evidence' rule, jurors should be instructed that they must listen and relate only to the interpreter's version, even when they can understand the original language. In some jurisdictions, particularly in the United States, signed-language interpreters can be used for Deaf jurors for all stages of the trial process, including jury deliberations, although elsewhere – notably in CANADA, Great Britain and AUSTRALIA – this is not allowed, on the grounds that a thirteenth person cannot legally be allowed in the jury room (Lucas 2003).

The impact on court interpreters of the legal tradition and of systemic changes has been the subject of some research. In the case of JAPAN, lay judges were initially found to be suspicious of interpreters' performance but subsequently came to regard the interpreter's words as 'what the defendant said', and court interpreters' renderings consequently came to play a pivotal role in their decision-making (Mizuno et al. 2013), as they do in the case of jurors in common-law systems (Kida 2013). Venezuela, in 1999, changed from the inquisitorial to the adversarial system. Not atypically, its new Criminal Procedure Code protects the language rights of those who do not speak Spanish and entitles them to court interpreting, but makes no reference to the ROLE, rights or duties of court interpreters (Vilela Biasi 2003). Similarly, Lebese (2011) notes the absence of legislation in South Africa that clearly defines the role of court interpreters; consequently, the latter find themselves performing tasks which should be the responsibility of other officers of the court. A similar situation, albeit in a totally different setting, is described in Lipkin's (2010) account of the duties other than interpreting performed by Hebrew/Arabic servicemen working as interpreters at the Yehuda Military Court near Jerusalem. Beyond such specific institutional and systemic constraints, the interpreter's role in the courtroom stands out as a much-discussed issue and the subject of a considerable body of research (e.g. Kadric 2000; Hale 2008; Lee 2009a; Mikkelson 2008).

Regulations, codes and practices

Among community-based institutional SETTINGS, interpreting practices in the courtroom tend to be the most explicitly – and most strictly – regulated. Although legislation, like codes of professional ETHICS, will not solve all problems, regulatory provisions can make a major contribution to best practice. In the US, the seminal 1970 'Negrón' case (of a Spanish-speaking farm worker convicted of murder without having been able to understand his trial) inspired Congress to pass the Federal Court Interpreters Act of 1978, with subsequent Amendments of 1988 (see Berk-Seligson 1990; Morris 1999a). The Negrón case (United States ex rel. Negrón v. the State of New York 434 F 2d 386 1970) determined that a litigant's linguistic, and not just physical, presence in the courtroom is the sine qua non for due process. This was also the issue in the 1998 Australian appellate case of Gradidge (Gradidge v. Grace Bros. Pty. Ltd. (1988) 93 FLR 414): If a Deaf litigant was entitled to a fair trial, then this required the provision of a signed version of all exchanges in open court.

One important consequence of the US Court Interpreters Act was the creation of the Spanish/English Federal Court Interpreter Certification Examination (FCICE) in 1980, introducing to the court interpreting environment the concept of performance-based interpreter testing, based on rigorous testing practices (see FCICE 2014).

Unlike their counterparts in non-legal settings, judicial interpreters generally take an oath to translate accurately and completely to the best of their ability (Morris 1999a). Nevertheless, actual performance is often unsatisfactory, with serious implications for due process. Even within the same country, differences in conditions of employment, particularly financial aspects, often directly influence the level of COMPETENCE of those who interpret in court-rooms, and the quality of their output, as well as the total number of interpreters available for particular language combinations. In one and the same courtroom, spoken-language and signed-language interpreters often face different WORKING CONDITIONS, attitudes and treatment (Napier et al. 2010), for example with regard to team interpreting, which is more likely to be allowed for signed-language interpreters than for their spoken-language peers.

Among other things, interpreters' working conditions are crucial to achieving QUALITY in courtroom interpreting (see Hale & Stern 2011). In adversarial courtrooms, in particular, this relates not only to such criteria as ACCURACY and completeness, but also to the pragmatic effects of a court interpreter's renderings, not least on jury members. This fundamental issue has been addressed using ETHNOGRAPHIC METHODS as well as EXPERIMENTAL RESEARCH in the landmark studies by Berk-Seligson (1990) and, more recently, by Hale (2004), who investigated, among other things, how changes in speech style can affect mock jurors' impressions of a witness.

Different stages in proceedings require interpreters to use different working MODES (e.g. Jacobsen 2012; Gallez & Maryns 2014). Where rules or judges allow the use of wireless equipment, interpreters can sit anywhere in the courtroom when providing SIMULTANEOUS INTERPRETING. Signed-language interpreters must stand where they can be clearly seen by their Deaf clients and vice versa. Appropriate decisions about POSITIONING must also be made for spoken-language CONSECUTIVE INTERPRETING, which is practically always used for witness testimony in national/domestic courts.

Profound changes in working conditions for court interpreters as a result of organisational pressures have been discussed under the heading of 'de-professionalisation' (García-Beyaert 2015), with the outsourcing of interpreting services for the entire court system in Great Britain to a single commercial agency as a striking case in point. On the whole, academic research rarely addresses such down-to-earth matters, so that interested parties must pri-marily rely on administrative, legal, press and professional association reports. One of many examples is an extreme case of maladministration of court interpreting in Ontario, Canada, where failure to provide competent interpreting led to a $35-million class-action lawsuit alleging that incompetent government-appointed court interpreters had brought about miscarriages of justice and even wrongful convictions (Sadava 2010).

Freelance interpreters in both domestic and international courts who suffer VICARIOUS TRAUMA are generally not offered institutional psychological support or counselling. In some TRIBUNAL INTERPRETING settings there is awareness of these situations and help may be available, in part because of the existence of interpreting teams and the long-term nature of interpreting engagements.

RUTH MORRIS

CREATIVITY

→ PERSONALITY

Interpreting (and translation in general) can be characterised as 're-creation' – a secondary form of creation based on a source text in a different language (Kussmaul 1995). It is therefore moot, even among professionals, whether interpreting should be considered a creative activity (Horváth 2010). The answer depends largely on the way the concept is defined. Creativity is a multifaceted construct and can be studied from various angles. The most common view links creativity to genius and uniqueness. The psychometric approach, in contrast, sees creativity as an innate capacity or PERSONALITY trait of any individual and seeks to measure individual differences. Underlying this view is a focus on the mental processes and structures involved in creative thinking. This is based on the distinction by J. P. Guilford, the 'father of creativity research', between convergent and divergent thinking, the latter involving novel approaches to solving problems, and such abilities as flexibility, originality and fluency. Thus, in a wider sense, creativity can also be seen as the capacity to adapt to new situations and environments, for which prior knowledge and flexibility in perception play a major role (Sternberg 1988).

Creativity in interpreting can be studied on three levels. In a *product*-centred view, the solutions an interpreter manages to find for unexpected challenges in the source speech reflect creative performance. MacRae (1989) suggests that creating something new in interpreting is not restricted to the target language form of the original message and would also extend to interpreters creating their own working techniques, such as a system and set of symbols for NOTE-TAKING.

The second level is that of the creative mental *processes*, based on strategic decision-making, in the interpreter's problem-solving. One of the basic STRATEGIES in interpreting is the ANTICIPATION of message development, which implies the use of creative imagination based on what has been said and done to predict what is going to happen next in an interpreted communication situation. Riccardi's (1998) 'strategy of least commitment' is a good example of divergent thinking during SIMULTANEOUS INTERPRETING. It consists in envisioning a variety of possible linguistic solutions for an interpreting problem while the source language message is still unfolding.

On a third level, creativity can be investigated in interpreters' overall *behaviour* in engaging with a particular communicative situation in a given SETTING. While much of this may become automatised with EXPERTISE, the place, situational characteristics, participants and subject matter change with every assignment. Creativity in this sense is closely linked to spontaneity and flexibility, which enable the interpreter to respond to new situations in a constructive and efficient way.

ILDIKÓ HORVÁTH

CRITICAL LINK

↑ COMMUNITY INTERPRETING

COMMUNITY INTERPRETING, like CONFERENCE INTERPRETING before it, owes its development and recognition as a PROFESSION to the birth and growth of professional associations. One of the oldest community interpreting associations, and probably the best known, is Critical Link, an international, non-profit organization committed to the advancement of the field of interpreting in the social, legal and healthcare sectors. While its primary focus is spoken language interpreting, it works closely with those in the area of sign language interpreting and has served to bring spoken and sign language interpreters together.

The Critical Link network began in 1992 in Canada when Brian Harris of the University of Ottawa, with the support of Geoffrey Kingscott of *Language International* magazine, gathered together a group of people working in the field to organize the first international conference on community interpreting. In December 2000, after the organization of two such conferences in Canada, Critical Link became incorporated as Critical Link Canada: National Council for the Development of Community Interpreting. In June 2010 Critical

Link Canada became Critical Link International, to better reflect the international community that Critical Link had become.

Although the name of the association has changed somewhat over time, its objectives have remained the same: (1) promoting the establishment of standards which guide the practice of community interpreters; (2) encouraging and sharing research in the field of community interpreting; (3) adding to the discussion about the educational and training requirements for community interpreters; (4) advocating for the provision of professional community interpreting services by social, legal and healthcare institutions; and (5) raising awareness about community interpreting as a profession.

Critical Link conferences

The primary means used to achieve these objectives has been the organization of international conferences on community interpreting every three years, starting in 1995 with the very first international conference in this field. Over the years, Critical Link has been held in a number of different locations: Critical Link 1 (1995) – Geneva Park, Canada; Critical Link 2 (1998) – Vancouver, Canada; Critical Link 3 (2001) – Montreal, Canada; Critical Link 4 (2004) – Stockholm, Sweden; Critical Link 5 (2007) – Sydney, Australia; Critical Link 6 (2010) – Birmingham, UK; Critical Link 7 (2013) – Toronto, Canada. At the time of writing, the next in the series will be Critical Link 8 (2016), in Edinburgh, UK. From the very beginning, these conferences have attracted well-known professionals and researchers from many countries as speakers and participants. The conferences have addressed a wide variety of aspects (e.g. the role of the community interpreter, theoretical aspects of community interpreting, issues and challenges, practice, training, evaluation and accreditation), from different perspectives (e.g. by country, by approach, by discipline, service provider vs. client). The sharing of ideas, problems and solutions among the conference participants has been extended to a wider audience by the publication in the Benjamins Translation Library book series of selected proceedings from these conferences (e.g. Carr et al. 1997).

Other Critical Link activities

Although Critical Link is best known for its conferences, it has undertaken a number of other activities or participated in them with other organizations.

An early initiative was the publication by the National Committee of Critical Link of a newsletter entitled *The Critical Link/Un Maillon Essentiel.* The newsletter became a journal in 2003: *The Critical Link – a quarterly journal dedicated to interpreting in the social, health care and legal sectors.* However, despite its worthy aim to connect community interpreters throughout Canada and the world, the journal ceased publication in 2004 after only a couple of issues. It was replaced in 2009 by a quarterly e-bulletin – *The Link* – available to members only.

In 2003, Critical Link Canada joined forces with the Healthcare Interpretation Network of Toronto in a major project, funded by Health Canada, entitled Health Care Interpreter Services: Strengthening Access to Primary Care (Hoen et al. 2006). The research aimed at assessing the language barriers to primary healthcare within the Canadian public health system, by investigating current approaches and models of primary healthcare delivery in Canada's three largest cities. The study documented what was long suspected: practices were not standardized across the country, and there were only a few instances where healthcare providers had been able to implement systematic mechanisms to work with trained healthcare interpreters.

Critical Link Canada was also an instrumental partner in the development and dissemination of the National Standard Guide for Community Interpreting Services (HIN 2007). The Guide, the first of its kind in Canada, aims to provide clear and consistent definitions of the characteristics and competencies of qualified spoken language interpreters working in the social, legal and healthcare fields, and to serve as an educational tool for clients, service providers and interpreters.

More recently, together with over 50 stakeholders, Critical Link International joined a newly-formed pan-Canadian alliance, called Canadian Coalition on Community Interpreting, which hopes to promote a national approach to professionalizing the field. But while encouraging the growth of new organizations in the field and even participating in them, Critical Link continues to maintain its own identity, with planning for the next Critical Link conference always underway.

RODA P. ROBERTS

CULTURAL BROKER

see under ROLE

CULTURAL INTERPRETING

see under COMMUNITY INTERPRETING

CULTURAL MEDIATOR

see under ROLE

CURRICULUM

↑ EDUCATION
→ ASSESSMENT, → COMPETENCE
↓ PEDAGOGY

The discussion of curriculum in interpreting studies focuses on the design, development, implementation, and evaluation of programs preparing bilingual or multilingual individuals to serve as interpreters in a wide variety of SETTINGS and institutions. Curriculum considerations are thus distinct from broader considerations of interpreter EDUCATION and narrower aspects of interpreting PEDAGOGY, or teaching methodology specific to the interpretation classroom. Much of the INTERPRETING STUDIES literature that informs curricular decision-making continues to be published on topics that may not mention curriculum explicitly, but are grounded in the research themes of education and pedagogy, including APTITUDE TESTING, ASSESSMENT, and E-LEARNING, among others.

Curricular frameworks emerge and evolve through a consensus-building process among all stakeholders, both internal and external to the educational institution. This process can be traced through the interpreting studies literature, following the professionalization of CONFERENCE INTERPRETING and its institutionalization in academia. In addition to those directly involved in curriculum implementation – educational administrators, instructors, and students – stakeholders include employer organizations, professional associations, and other standard-setting bodies that provide guidelines. For example, CIUTI (Conférence Internationale Permanente d'Instituts Universitaires de Traducteurs et Interprètes) unites university-level translator and interpreter education programs around a common set of curriculum guidelines established to ensure QUALITY, while concurrently allowing for highly diverse educational and cultural settings. The US-based

Conference of Interpreter Trainers (CIT), with the Commission on Collegiate Interpreter Education (CCIE) as its accrediting body, and the European Forum of Sign Language Interpreters (EFSLI) publish standards serving as guidelines for curricula, assessment, and program evaluation in the signed language communities, and the proceedings of their annual conferences provide important curriculum resources. Such guidelines reflect a general consensus emerging from high-level stakeholder deliberations; on the program level, some educators have adopted an evidence-based approach to the consensus-building process by pursuing ACTION RESEARCH to develop and/or review their programs (see Roy 2006).

Definition

Curriculum can generally be defined as a "course", in particular a regular course of study or training, as at a school or university. It refers to a planned program of instruction designed to create an organizational structure and thus bring order to a course of study (Jackson 1992). Considered by some to be synonymous with the British usage of *syllabus*, curriculum subsumes two aspects of a plan of action: (1) curriculum as a process, which can be seen as the sequencing of the content of instruction; and (2) curriculum as a form of interaction and exchange, which includes the structuring of the learning environment in a specific cultural context (Sawyer 2004). In interpreter education, curriculum design and development thus address the progression of skill and knowledge acquisition at the program level, en route to professional levels of COMPETENCE and EXPERTISE, and the creation of communicative exchanges that promote skill and knowledge attainment, most notably through lesson planning that considers aspects of feedback provided through formal and informal ASSESSMENT.

As noted by Freihoff (1995), the curriculum design process clarifies the goals and functions of the curriculum internally and externally to the educational institution. This information is ideally captured in *primary sources* that create an orientation framework for the implementation of the official or explicit curriculum and have a public relations function. Such primary sources may include statements of aims and goals, plans of study, test specifications, and even course descriptions. Despite their program-internal nature, these documents are increasingly provided online and can be easily referenced by external stakeholders, such as prospective students and employers, thus making comparative analyses across programs feasible. *Secondary sources* have a fundamentally different character and may include research-oriented articles and essays. Discussions in secondary sources tend to transcend specific programs and include national or international reports and surveys of programs and their structure (e.g. Park 1998; Napier 2009; Wang & Mu 2009; Rico 2010).

Evolution

University curricula tailored to the needs of the interpreter were first formalized during the institutionalization of conference interpreter training in higher education around the time of the Second World War. Although curriculum documents from this period are not widely available, it may be assumed that curriculum designers had a new structure in mind, one that was fundamentally different from foreign language study. Arjona (1984), for example, begins her discussion of curriculum with the model that VELLEMAN introduced at the University of Geneva in 1941. This course of study included five components: area studies, multidisciplinary studies, applied language arts and linguistic studies, practicum courses, and deontology.

While the number of university programs grew steadily in the latter half of the twentieth century, most contributions to the literature did not address issues of curriculum as distinct from pedagogy until the 1970s and after, as translation and interpreting studies emerged as distinct areas of inquiry. These discussions focusing on conference interpreting in the spoken languages touched upon any number of topics beyond curriculum, including entrance examinations, employment prospects, and desirable traits of applicants. It was also around this time that the first curricula for signed language interpreting programs began to appear (e.g. Sternberg et al. 1973), but interaction between the spoken and signed language communities on curriculum topics was limited.

In the 1980s, a new focus on higher order aims and goals in conference interpreting curricula and discussion of the most common models in place in university settings would lead to a shift in how university programs were seen. Rather than interpreter training in the strict vocational sense, dedicated perhaps even to the requirements of one or a few select institutional employers, programs assumed a comprehensive educational purpose. With this in mind, Arjona (1984) discusses content and task analysis as design criteria for developing curricula for interpreter (and translator) education, which she views as a form of integrated professional studies extending beyond ancillary skills training, clearly distinguishing interpreter training from the study of foreign languages and cultures. In describing established curriculum models, Arjona focuses on relationships between translation and interpreting instruction and describes five types of sequencing: linear, modified linear, Y or forked-track, modified Y track, and parallel track. By this time, the skill sequence of translation, CONSECUTIVE INTERPRETING, and SIMULTANEOUS INTERPRETING had become a widely recognized organizing principle in conference interpreter education (e.g. Renfer 1992), and Cokely (2005a) describes the exchanges between spoken language and signed language interpreter educators that had a substantial impact on skill sequencing and course structure in signed language programs in the United States.

In the late 1980s, a project-oriented approach to developing consensus-driven model curricula was being pursued in the sign language community (Baker-Shenk et al. 1988; Baker-Shenk 1990). By the mid-1990s, Mackintosh (1995) saw a consensus emerging around best practices in conference interpreter training, which would include structuring the curriculum according to a progression of teaching and learning objectives. Revisiting these common principles in interpreter education in an article returning to HERBERT's assertion that "interpreters are made not born", Mackintosh (1999) discusses the relationships between curriculum, interpreting theory, employer requirements, activities aimed at training interpreter trainers, and contributions of employer institutions and professional associations to interpreter education programs over the years.

Freihoff (e.g. 1995) was also among the early authors to draw directly from the field of curriculum studies for the purposes of interpreter (and translator) education. He points to the impact of the cultural (institutional) context and stakeholders' values, while introducing concepts such as open vs. closed curriculum models and the official and hidden curriculum. As researchers explore attitudes and beliefs among educators in sign language programs (Winston 2005), theoretical constructs such as the explicit, implied, and null curriculum are utilized as discussion frameworks (McDermid 2009).

The curriculum models for conference interpreting converged further through the establishment of a European Masters in Conference Interpreting (EMCI) in 2001. The EMCI Consortium of European universities, collaborating under the auspices of the European Union institutions, lays out a general curricular framework consisting of the following components: theory of interpreting, practice of interpreting, consecutive interpreting, simultaneous interpreting, and the EU and international organizations. Members agree upon a common policy on student recruitment and assessment, based on the aims of the program and quality assurance criteria. The curriculum model follows the widely accepted sequence of instruction that begins with consecutive interpreting and SIGHT INTERPRETING/TRANSLATION in an initial phase and continues with an introduction to simultaneous interpreting, which occurs before SIMULTANEOUS WITH TEXT and interpreting of specialized texts are taught. Courses in professional ETHICS complete the final stages of the curriculum.

The principles of the EMCI model, well established in conference interpreting, have been questioned as an organizational structure for programs focused on other settings. Educators in signed language and spoken language (community) interpreting programs (e.g. Cokely 2005a; Shaw et al. 2006; Slatyer 2006; Merlini 2007) advance orientation frameworks based upon type of (dialogic) discourse and the role of the interpreter in the interaction, rather than the temporal synchrony seen as a key driver of the translation and (monologic) consecutive and simultaneous interpreting skill sets in the EMCI model.

By definition, curriculum evolves to adjust to new needs and requirements, and discussions of curriculum reform have given impetus to the literature. In the late 1990s, the Bologna Process and Accords initiated the harmonization of the architecture of the European higher education system through the introduction of Bachelor and Master of Arts degrees throughout a new European Higher Education Area, resulting in a renewed discussion and the comparison of (translator and) interpreter education curricula across Europe (Rico 2010). The rise of CHINA on the world stage has heightened the importance of interpreter (and translator) education and led to the wide-scale introduction, early in the new millennium, of Bachelor and Master of Arts degrees in interpreting (and translation) as well as PhD programs. Wang and Mu (2009) describe a range of curriculum models following the centralized guidelines of the Chinese Ministry of Education. Among other developments, there has been a distinction between more academically oriented Master of Arts degrees and the professionally oriented Master of Translation and Interpreting (MTI), with some programs focusing on either interpreting or translation.

As recognition of the PROFESSION of interpreting has spread across settings and domains and the number of programs around the world has rapidly grown, so too has the scope of curriculum goals. Programs for signed languages flourished at the Associate and BA level in the United States and other countries in the seventies and eighties, and Master's-level programs soon emerged (see Shaw et al. 2006; Napier 2009). Some curriculum models have integrated components for LEGAL INTERPRETING and HEALTHCARE INTERPRETING, or COMMUNITY INTERPRETING, or may even focus exclusively on one of these domains, which continue to be served primarily by short courses in non-academic workshop formats in many countries around the world (see Ertl & Pöllabauer 2010).

Although there may now be a consensus regarding the constituent elements to be included in curriculum models, fundamental tensions still exist. In addition to broadening the scope of practice to include a range of settings, a balance must be struck between the role of language-specific and general instruction as well as monologism vs. dialogism as organizing principles. Most curricula focusing on professional practice include a theory component, as recommended by AIIC, EMCI, CIT/CCIE and EFSLI, and the roles of theory and practice must be reconciled, if not integrated. Similarly, technological innovation has led to a boom in online and blended instruction, which in turn are reshaping some curricula, as the barriers of geographical distance are overcome and regular collaboration between institutions even on opposite sides of the globe becomes possible. With these competing trends towards convergence and diversification, it stands to reason that the curriculum in place at any given institution will continue to be fundamentally shaped by that institution's educational philosophy, which is governed by specific political, cultural, legislative, and market-specific constellations and traditions in its country and region of the world.

DAVID B. SAWYER

DEAF INTERPRETER

↑ SIGNED LANGUAGE INTERPRETING
→ RELAY INTERPRETING

Although it might appear that people who cannot hear would not be able to interpret, deaf people have probably been undertaking non-professional translating and NON-PROFESSIONAL INTERPRETING ever since they first came (or were brought) together to form communities. The earliest reference to deaf translators/interpreters is from the seventeenth century, when a deaf man 'worked' alongside two hearing 'sign language interpreters' for a deaf woman being examined to gain full participation in a Puritan church in Massachusetts.

Many deaf interpreters first experience language brokering within the educational environment, interpreting for their deaf peers when misunderstanding occurs with teachers (Adam et al. 2011). They also perform SIGHT INTERPRETING/TRANSLATION, in this case working between a written language and sign language (that has no written form), both in the classroom and for home correspondence within residential SETTINGS. Another traditional starting point is INTERPRETING FOR DEAFBLIND PERSONS (Adam et al. 2014). Thanks to the increasing availability of training, some of these individuals develop their knowledge and experience to a professional level and are also able to access CERTIFICATION.

Deaf people work with vulnerable/disadvantaged children and adults, including migrants, in a variety of COMMUNITY INTERPRETING settings (e.g. Morgan & Adam 2013). Deaf interpreters are often engaged in relay interpreting (Bienvenu & Colonomos 1992) or work as co-interpreters in interpreting teams (Stone & Russell 2014), drawing on their lived experience of being deaf for subtle interpreting decisions that their non-deaf colleagues are less able to incorporate. In conference settings deaf interpreters work from subtitles/captions produced live by way of RESPEAKING or other types of SPEECH-TO-TEXT INTERPRETING, or serve as relay interpreters/co-interpreters, either intralingually or interlingually (Boudreault 2005). In MEDIA INTERPRETING, deaf translators/interpreters work from scripts via autocue/teleprompter, not only for television (Allsop & Kyle 2008; Stone 2009) but also, increasingly, on the web and in other settings.

CHRISTOPHER STONE

DÉCALAGE

see TIME LAG

DEMAND CONTROL SCHEMA

→ COMMUNITY INTERPRETING, → PEDAGOGY, → SIGNED LANGUAGE INTERPRETING

The demand control schema (DC-S) refers to a series of theoretical constructs and educational approaches developed by Robyn Dean and Robert Pollard. Originally conceived in regard to SIGNED LANGUAGE INTERPRETING, DC-S addresses the importance of contextual factors and the interactional nature of COMMUNITY INTERPRETING. The highly interpersonal nature of interpreting in community SETTINGS makes it similar to other practice professions (e.g. medicine, social work, education), standing in contrast to technical professions, such as laboratory science and engineering, which are less dependent on an interactive social context.

Dean and Pollard (2001) analysed the work of sign language interpreters in community settings through the framework of demand control theory (Karasek 1979). Research based on Karasek's theory demonstrates that work effectiveness and occupational well-being are a function of the dynamic interplay between the demands (requirements) of a job and the controls (e.g. skills, resources, knowledge, authority) of the worker (Karasek & Theorell 1990). These demand control interactions yield outcomes ranging from active and engaging to stressful and ineffective. Dean and Pollard (2001) conclude that inherent in signed language interpreting is a mismatch between the demands of the job and the controls often afforded to interpreters through interpreter education and ethical codes – a mismatch that impacts the effectiveness of the work and the health of the interpreter.

In their adaptation of Karasek's work, Dean and Pollard propose that interpreters in community settings face four types of demands: *environmental, interpersonal, paralinguistic,* and *intrapersonal* (EIPI). These demands comprise the interpreting *context* and must form the basis for interpreters' decisions – how they should optimally respond or behave in varying contexts (e.g. medical, legal). Effective control decisions, or responses to demands, can be employed before, during and/or after the assignment and fall along a liberal (action-oriented) to conservative (reserving action) spectrum (Dean & Pollard 2005, 2013). These elements of DC-S (EIPI demands and control opportunities) make up the theoretical framework that is often used for predicting and analysing types of work settings (i.e. PREPARATION for the job) and the suitability of an interpreter for a certain job, as well as for setting-specific teaching.

Using the DC-S theoretical constructs, Dean and Pollard have developed a decision-making model that emphasises the importance of a socially constructed and negotiated approach to decision-making. An interpreter begins the analysis with an appreciation for the broad EIPI demands of the job, including the overarching goal of the environment (Dean & Pollard 2013). When a job demand arises, s/he entertains effective control decisions from along the liberal to conservative spectrum, mentally predicting the consequences likely to arise from particular demand–control interactions, making a final control choice. This corresponds to the DC-S emphasis on teleological (outcomes-focused) ETHICS, as opposed to the deontological or rule-based approach evident in many interpreting codes of ethics. The interpreter is further prepared to respond to any demands resulting from that control choice, and it is this back-and-forth interplay of outcomes and the willingness to respond to resulting demands that Dean and Pollard (2011) frame as the "response-ability", or responsiveness, of any practice professional.

The third aspect of DC-S is comprised of the many learning and teaching methods built upon the DC-S theoretical constructs and decision-making model. Many of these methods are based on experiential learning paradigms, which have become increasingly prominent in the PEDAGOGY of signed language interpreting (e.g. Bentley-Sassaman 2009; Monikowski & Peterson 2005). This includes the authors' approach to 'supervision' (Dean & Pollard 2011, 2013), a form of reflective practice that frequently employs case conferencing as a technique for developing critical thinking and judgement skills.

ROBYN K. DEAN

DEVERBALIZATION

see under INTERPRETIVE THEORY

DIALOGUE INTERPRETING

→ DISCOURSE ANALYTICAL APPROACHES
↓ DISCOURSE MANAGEMENT, ↓ TURN-TAKING

As a comprehensive designation for a broad and diversified range of non-conference interpreting practices, 'dialogue interpreting' has gained increased currency since the late 1990s, particularly in the wake of two seminal publications with this title edited by Ian Mason (1999b, 2001). Evidence of this lately acquired popularity is the inclusion of an entry on dialogue interpreting in the second edition of the *Routledge Encyclopedia of Translation Studies* (Baker & Saldanha 2009) – in addition to the one on COMMUNITY INTERPRETING which had already appeared in the first edition. Although the two expressions have been used as synonyms, the prevailing approach is to view dialogue interpreting as the overarching category, comprising interpreting activities in a broad variety of SETTINGS, particularly 'in the community'. Leaving aside geographically more circumscribed denominations, such as bilateral, contact and cultural interpreting, the only other label with comparable potential for inclusiveness is 'liaison interpreting' (Gentile et al. 1996; Erasmus et al. 1999). The ascendance of 'dialogue interpreting' in scholarly publications to the detriment of the latter expression is the result of a theoretical turn in INTERPRETING STUDIES, which has brought to the fore the dialogic nature of many interpreter-mediated encounters, and has come to be known as the "dialogic discourse-based interaction (DI) paradigm" (Pöchhacker 2004a).

Definition

What, then, is the defining trait of dialogue interpreting that underlies such strikingly diverse situations as medical consultations, welfare and police interviews, immigration hearings, courtroom trials, parent–teacher meetings, business and diplomatic encounters, broadcast interviews, and TV talk shows? In Mason's ground-breaking definition, dialogue interpreting is described as "interpreter-mediated communication in spontaneous face-to-face interaction" (1999a: 147). In his later review of the concept, Mason (2009a) lists four fundamental characteristics: dialogue, entailing bi-directional translation; spontaneous speech; face-to-face exchange; and CONSECUTIVE INTERPRETING mode. If this set of features were to be strictly complied with (though Mason himself presents cases of deviation), interpreting events which are now widely held to fall within the domain of dialogue interpreting would not qualify. TELEPHONE INTERPRETING, for instance, would have to be excluded as the face-to-face condition does not usually obtain (with the exception of more technologically advanced, yet still rarely used, video-calls). Being normally conducted in the simultaneous mode, SIGNED LANGUAGE INTERPRETING – the very field where the DI paradigm was born (Roy 1996, 2000a) – would equally fall outside the boundaries of dialogue interpreting, as would TALK SHOW INTERPRETING, where mixing consecutive and *chuchotage* is a very common practice (the latter mode being used for the benefit of the foreign guests on the show). More quintessentially than the face-to-face dimension or the mode, it is therefore the *discourse format* that constitutes the unifying element among a vast array of interpreter-mediated social activities, setting these apart from the monologue-based communication of most conference interpreting events.

Highlighting the core notion of dialogue entails a number of significant shifts in perspective. Whereas the 'liaison interpreting' label places emphasis on the connecting function performed by the interpreter, and consequently on the centrality – both physical and metaphorical – of 'the person in the middle', what is foregrounded in dialogue interpreting is interaction itself (see Merlini 2007). More specifically, the type of interaction is one which involves all the participants in the joint definition of meanings, mutual alignments, roles and identities. The first shift in perspective is thus that interpreters are revealed as full-fledged social agents on a par with primary interlocutors, with whom they co-construct the communicative event. Secondly, the interpreter's clients, on their part, are seen to play a crucial role as co-determiners of communicative success or failure. Thirdly, though bilingual communication remains largely dependent on the interpreter's verbal contributions to the exchange, increased emphasis is placed on directly accessible features, such as eye contact, facial expressions, GESTURES, postures and PROSODY, which may offer primary interlocutors complementary or even alternative cues for sense-making and rapport-building.

This novel outlook on interpreting has been consolidated by a growing number of studies resting on sociolinguistic and sociological underpinnings, and on real-life data analysis. The ensuing body of research based on DISCOURSE ANALYTICAL APPROACHES has given dialogue interpreting a clearly defined identity of its own within the field of interpreting studies, and is thus to be considered as its other distinctive and unifying trait. Quite significantly, in the earliest scholarly publications which deal explicitly with dialogue interpreting, the rationale for this terminological choice is instantly clear. Though working independently of each other, Cecilia Wadensjö (1993) and Helen Tebble (1993), two pioneers of research on spoken-language dialogue interpreting, raised the same focal points, namely: whatever is attained or unattained in communication is a *collective activity* requiring the efforts of all participants; interlocutors' *turn-by-turn contributions* to the exchange need close scrutiny at a micro-analytical level through recording and TRANSCRIPTION; and the *interpersonal and socio-institutional dimensions* also require investigation at a macro-analytical level – all of which was taken to call for a new *discourse-based approach* to the study of dialogue interpreting.

In light of these considerations, the following account of the state of the art in dialogue interpreting is divided into two sections. The first provides a comparative overview of a few domains of dialogue interpreting practice, which have been selected on account of their stark contextual dissimilarities. The aim here is to show that, underneath such diversity, the salience of interactionally negotiated interpersonal dynamics is a constant throughout. The second section looks into the core concepts of dialogue interpreting, and presents the main research topics.

Domain-specific challenges

All communicative events involving dialogue interpreting are instances of institutional talk, whereby the activities being performed are in some way subject to ritualised conversational behaviours, i.e. norms and rules about what topics are selected and how, who is expected to talk at any one time and for how long, and how contributions are assessed (Drew & Heritage 1992). This implies that at least one participant in the encounter is in charge of monitoring compliance with pre-established routines. The POWER associated with this gate-keeping function is usually exerted by institutional representatives, who are likely to orient the transaction towards a given institution's goals and expectations. Yet, in bilingual encounters, responsibility for the way in which interactions unfold is necessarily shared with interpreters. The following paragraphs illustrate some of the decisions with which the latter are therefore faced.

A markedly asymmetrical configuration is found in ASYLUM SETTINGS. As is the case for LEGAL INTERPRETING in general, in asylum interviews patterns of interaction are rigidly set; the power to police the agenda is firmly in the hands of adjudicating authorities, who are called upon to enforce the law by establishing the credibility of an applicant's claim. Within an intrinsically adversarial framework, the asylum seekers' accounts are thoroughly examined for inconsistencies and contradictions. Life narratives are thus depersonalised to fit in with the discursive practices and IDEOLOGY of the legal institution (Barsky 1994; Maryns 2006). In this context, interpreters are seen to play a pivotal role, in that they may either contribute to the maintenance of existing policies of exclusion (which tend to limit the right of claimants to be appropriately heard) or become agents of change. By challenging the NORMS both of their own PROFESSION and of the socio-institutional system, they may create a new space for inclusion and dialogue (Inghilleri 2005a). Non-negligible factors in this choice are the interpreter's personal background, closeness to the claimant's experience, and perception of her/his own identity (Merlini 2009a).

In medical consultations, notwithstanding the built-in asymmetry of knowledge and topic (it is the patient's condition which is under examination and not the doctor's), the trajectory is more open to local negotiation between participants, since in this case a common goal is being pursued, i.e. the wellbeing of the patient. For HEALTHCARE INTERPRETING this means that the medical practitioner's adoption of a given discourse model as the most effective means (in her/his view) for successful provision of medical care may be shared, but may also be countered by patient and interpreter alike. When the approach is a doctor-centred one, priority is given to the "voice of medicine" with its scientific objectivity and emotional detachment (Mishler 1984). By affiliating with the patient's expressions of concern or embarrassment, the interpreter can make up for the doctor's lack of involvement – though not always and not necessarily in such a way as to favour a successful outcome (Merlini 2009b; Baraldi & Gavioli 2007). In a patient-centred medical approach, on the other hand, the interpreter can opt either for further reinforcing the doctor's displays of affectivity towards the patient (Merlini & Favaron 2005) or, conversely, for blocking out altogether the patient's "voice of the lifeworld" as medically irrelevant, through reduced and discursively reframed renditions (Bolden 2000).

Even more open to negotiation are power relations in talk show interpreting. Here the gate-keeping function is naturally vested in the talk show host, who exerts all types of conversational dominance – *quantitative*, by taking the floor for longer turns, and more often than the other participants; *qualitative*, by asking questions; and *semantic*, by imposing a viewpoint through topic control. In the artificially intimate atmosphere of talk shows, however, the focus is not so much on propositional content, but rather on relational moves (flattering, provoking a polemical reaction, embarrassing, etc.), as talk becomes 'play'. Given the overarching goal of entertainment, roles are therefore often hybrid and interchangeable. Hosts may step into the interpreter's shoes, more or less playfully offering alternative versions, or straightforwardly acting as interpreters themselves. Interpreters, on their part, are required to play along, abandoning the normative low-profile role for a more telegenic one (Straniero Sergio 1999, 2007). Responding with the assertiveness of the language expert, manifesting empathic involvement, making unsolicited remarks and even extemporaneous jokes are some of the ways in which interpreters on the show construct their televised identities as well as a new, unorthodox image for their professional category.

Unlike these asymmetrical situations, the setting of business negotiations is typically symmetrical – on three grounds: primary interlocutors generally have comparable institutional status; they share specialist knowledge of their commercial sector; and the predominant orientation in international business relations is founded on the idea of an equal partnership between negotiating parties (Smirnov 1997). The absence of power or status disparities, however, is not tantamount to a less problematic POSITIONING of the interpreter, considering that to clinch a deal a compromise between divergent needs, expectations and stances has to be reached. A first challenge in BUSINESS INTERPRETING arises from the frequent reluctance of business people to hire external professionals, who tend to be seen as untrustworthy intruders with little understanding of corporate goals. When hired, interpreters thus feel under constant pressure to establish their EXPERTISE, preserve their NEUTRALITY or, on the contrary, prove their allegiance to the party that pays them (Rudvin & Tomassini 2011). Added to this is interpreters' sensitivity towards cultural differences in negotiating behaviours, which may lead them to take autonomous initiatives (e.g. prompting unasked-for explanations, interrupting and re-allocating the floor, offering advice) for the benefit of the less assertive party (Takimoto 2006). A specific activity performed by interpreters in this context is mitigation. As Merlino (2009) demonstrates, in contrast to monolingual business encounters where negotiating parties tend to minimize disagreement, in linguistically mediated ones the expression of criticism, conflict, and even offense is much less inhibited. Interpreters are thus often found to take upon themselves the task of steering the conversation away from problematic sequences, thereby restoring rapport between the parties and allowing the encounter to reach its objectives.

Core concepts and research topics

In his comprehensive discussion of the opposite epistemologies of monologism and dialogism, Per Linell (1998) points out that ideas about information being conveyed, distorted or lost change radically according to which of the two perspectives is being adopted. A monologic view of communication presupposes that meanings are the products of individual speakers and exist as pre-determined and complete entities in their minds. Successful communication takes place if, on its way from the speaker's to the listener's mind, the message has not been distorted by any kind of 'noise'. Whereas monologism construes communication as a 'from–to' process, *dialogism* sees it as a 'between' process, where the speaker's sense-making activity depends on the listener as co-author, as well as on the relevant contextual elements. Meanings grow out of vague thoughts and are gradually developed as utterances are formulated, becoming shared knowledge only when all parties to the interaction mutually provide evidence that they have established a shared understanding. In this theoretical framework, Linell argues, the Gricean cooperative principle – which invokes an idealised speech situation characterised by consensus between complicitous interlocutors – should be replaced by the more practical concept of *coordination*, defined as the "co-accomplishment of concerted activities by conversational partners" (1998: 74).

This very notion of coordination is one of the key concepts in Cecilia Wadensjö's (1998) seminal *Interpreting as Interaction*, where she demonstrates that interpreting in real face-to-face talk goes well beyond the activity of translating texts and includes the simultaneously performed function of coordinating primary parties' utterances. The most basic form of coordination is implicit in the linguistic bi-directionality of dialogue interpreting events and in the principle that the interpreter's "renditions" occupy every second turn at talk; when working in the consecutive mode it is simply by speaking in either language that interpreters select the next speaker, thus managing the flow of conversation. The turn-taking routine of Speaker 1 – Interpreter – Speaker 2 – Interpreter – Speaker 1 – Interpreter – etc. is, however, a rare occurrence. Primary parties may, for instance, have some knowledge of their interlocutors' language(s) or simply grasp the gist of an utterance and reply directly, making the interpreter's turn superfluous. Or they may address the interpreter as the 'responder' (intending the utterance for the interpreter's use only), thereby initiating radical changes in 'footing' (see Wadensjö 1998; Merlini & Favaron 2005). Interpreters themselves may carry out explicit coordination moves through NON-RENDITIONS – such as requests for clarifications, comments on their own translations, invitations to start or continue talking, interruptions of overlapping turns, etc. – which alter the turn-taking order. Investigations of authentic dialogue interpreting data have revealed, in particular, the high frequency of monolingual dyadic sequences, which may or may not be subsequently summarised by the interpreter into the other language for the benefit of the excluded primary party. Depending on this decision, interlocutors are either empowered or disempowered, and cross-cultural adaptation encouraged or discouraged (Baraldi & Gavioli 2007).

Compelling insights into how the concept of coordination connects with those of intercultural MEDIATION, participation, agency and empowerment have been brought together by Baraldi and Gavioli (2012a). Drawing on both conversation analysis and social systems theory, they suggest reconsidering Wadensjö's implicit vs. explicit coordination in terms of a "basic" vs. "reflexive" perspective, thereby overcoming the rigidities of a sharp distinction between renditions and non-renditions. Basic coordination indicates the intrinsic mechanism by which participants in talk shape their actions and react to others' actions in ways that allow them to make sense of such actions. *Reflexive coordination*, on the other hand, is a meta-communicative activity, whose aim is to resolve communication problems by, for instance, clarifying, expanding, repairing, questioning, or formulating understanding of the meaning of conversational actions. As it facilitates the achievement of a shared perspective, reflexive coordination largely coincides with intercultural mediation; the lack of fit to be remedied in this case being a distinctly cultural one. The outcome of successful mediation is the appearance of new cross-cultural dimensions built on the perception of diversity as mutually enriching rather than disconnecting. Mediation, in turn, entails active participation from a double angle; on the one hand, interpreters become fully involved in the interaction as social actors in their own right; on the other hand, interpreters' involvement may foster – or thwart – agency by primary participants.

Since the very beginning, the recognition of coordination as a fundamental feature of dialogue interpreting has fuelled debate on the potential repercussions for professional ETHICS. Despite Wadensjö's (2004) warning that professional ideology must be distinguished from professional practice, the normative requirement of neutrality has appeared to be incompatible with the complexity of dialogically organised encounters. In their introduction to a volume on the interpreter's role in community settings, Valero-Garcés and Martin (2008) raise a number of relevant questions. For example, how do practitioners shape their role in light of wide cultural gaps, power imbalances, urgency of communication needs, dramatic life situations and, not least, lack of adequate training? Is there only one role or may there be several? Who defines what is normative vs. non-normative behaviour? Is interpreting called upon to empower individuals? In other words, is interpreting mediation? Assessing the implications of equating the two (above all the risk of hampering professionalization), Pöchhacker (2008a) concludes that a distinction should be drawn between contractual mediation, with its incumbent task of resolving conflicts at the level of social relations, and professional interpreting, with its inherent function of enabling communication by mediating at the linguistic, cognitive and cultural levels. Clearly, discussion of role in the various fields in which dialogue interpreting is practised remains highly topical (e.g. Schäffner et al. 2013).

Alongside the research perspectives mentioned so far, two more avenues of investigation, which have attracted relatively less attention and may offer scope for further development, are worth taking into account. Though issues of FACE are pivotal in dialogue interpreting (witness Berk-Seligson's 1988 cornerstone study on court interpreting), infrequent use has been made of *politeness* as a model of strategic message construction. Existing studies of dialogue interpreting are mostly concerned with adversarial contexts (e.g. Hale 1997b; Mason & Stewart 2001), with a few recent exceptions where face-threatening, face-saving and face-enhancing behaviour has been looked at in the somewhat unusual environment of supportive (healthcare, educational, and welfare) interactions entailing a variety of PARTICIPATION FRAMEWORKS (Merlini & Falbo 2011; Merlini 2013).

The second under-researched area is BODY LANGUAGE, an even more constitutive interactional element in the majority of dialogue interpreting settings. Probably owing to the difficulty of obtaining permission to video-record encounters of a delicate nature, studies focusing on participants' positioning in space (Wadensjö 2001a), posture, GESTURE, facial expression and GAZE are rather rare (though there is also a striking deficit in the case of publicly broadcast interpreter-mediated interactions). Years after Lang's (1976) work on interpreting in Papua New Guinea showed how gaze can signal involvement or exclusion, this point has been taken up again. Thus, Bot (2005), Davitti (2013) and Mason (2012) analyse the interplay between gaze shifts, attention-giving and attention-seeking, turn-taking coordination, conversational alignments, and ultimately reciprocal perceptions of status, power, role and identity.

RAFFAELA MERLINI

DIPLOMATIC INTERPRETING

↑ SETTINGS
→ CONFERENCE INTERPRETING

The term 'diplomatic interpreting' is often taken to refer to the manner in which language barriers have been overcome in meetings of heads of state and dignitaries over the centuries and up to the present day. Much information about diplomatic interpreters in the course of HISTORY can be found in Roland (1999), and there are also studies focusing on (diplomatic) interpreting in particular regions and periods, such as early Imperial CHINA (Lung 2011) and the Ottoman Empire.

History

Diplomacy is one of the oldest SETTINGS in which interpreting has been practised. Even so, throughout history, diplomatic contacts have also involved the use of a common language, or LINGUA FRANCA, obviating the need for interpreters. In Europe, Latin was the common diplomatic language from the Middle Ages, to be replaced later by French until the end of World War I, and the twenty-first century has seen the emergence of ENGLISH AS A LINGUA FRANCA on a global scale. Nevertheless, there have always been diplomatic encounters requiring linguistic intermediaries. We know very little, however, about who these may have been, and how they performed their task. Among the few interpreters to have left their mark in history is La MALINCHE, who acted for Cortés during the conquest of the Aztec Empire. Mention should also be made of the DRAGOMANS officiating in contacts at the Sublime Porte of the Ottoman Empire.

The STATUS of the interpreter in diplomatic encounters has varied. In some African countries, as he spoke immediately after the King, the interpreter traditionally had a privileged position in society and wielded considerable POWER (Bandia 2009). The interpreters trained by the European powers (France and the HABSBURG MONARCHY in particular) for dealing with the Ottoman Empire could gradually move to ambassadorial rank (Bowen 2012), and even today diplomatic staff in many countries (such as China) begin their careers as interpreters.

However, with the rise of multilateralism, and particularly since World War II, communication in international meetings has been enabled by professional conference interpreters, in multilateral conferences as well as bilateral talks. Indeed, similar skills are required in both SETTINGS, and it could be said that modern-day diplomatic interpreting is in fact conference interpreting in a diplomatic setting.

Modern practice

Interpreting for heads of state and government and high-ranking national representatives is usually organised by the ministries of foreign affairs, which recruit freelance interpreters as required and may also maintain a staff of permanent interpreters.

When two dignitaries meet, quite frequently only one of them will have an interpreter. The interpreter will work both ways, often in consecutive, or in a sort of semi-simultaneous 'voice-over' mode: The interpreter speaks almost at the same time as the person being interpreted, loudly enough to be heard by the listener and those accompanying him, but not too loud so as not to distract the person speaking. The latter must be consulted beforehand, because it is not easy to follow one's train of thought with someone else (the interpreter) speaking at the same time.

When two interpreters are present, each is normally responsible for rendering his or her principal's message in the other language. For example, a US State Department interpreter will render the US President's remarks in French for the President of France, whose reply will then be interpreted into English by his own interpreter. In practice, however, they will often switch language direction, with each side's interpreter whispering for his principal. This saves time, although there can be problems for the aides, since it is hard to 'whisper' to several people at once. Such an arrangement evidently implies that either side has full confidence in the other interpreter's professionalism and reliability.

When an interpreter accompanies a dignitary on a foreign visit, s/he will be expected to officiate in a multitude of situations: speeches, impromptu or otherwise, press conferences (along with a host interpreter if it is a joint press conference held in simultaneous, for instance), informal press briefings, TV interviews, after-dinner speeches, etc., requiring full mastery of all the facets of professional conference interpreting.

The constraints that apply to all conference interpreting also apply in a diplomatic setting – with some additional considerations, such as the need to be as inconspicuous as possible. Strict confidentiality is an obvious requirement, but the question may be raised whether an interpreter can be expected to be impartial when s/he is a member of an official delegation. For professional conference interpreters (members of AIIC, for instance), the question does not arise: the interpreter's allegiance is towards the persons for whom s/he is interpreting, whoever they may be and regardless of who the interpreter's employer may be. If, on the other hand, the interpreter's allegiance is primarily towards the employer, as in the case of diplomats acting as interpreters, the situation may be different.

The principle of confidentiality, which is firmly enshrined in the AIIC code of professional ETHICS, would imply that diplomatic/conference interpreters cannot publish their MEMOIRS. Quite a few interpreters, though not AIIC members, have nevertheless done so. Examples include Hitler's interpreter, Paul-Otto Schmidt (1949); Gomulka's interpreter for German, Erwin Weit (1973); and Soviet interpreters such as Berezhkov (1993), Korchilov (1999) and Palazchenko (1997).

CHRISTOPHER THIÉRY

DIRECTIONALITY

Interpreters who are bilingual from childhood and therefore can mediate between two native languages are relatively rare; a great majority have a few working languages, only one of which is native, referred to as an A language in the classification by AIIC. Directionality contrasts interpreting into one's native or A language (from another active working language, or B language, or from a so-called passive, or C language) with interpreting out of one's native language into a B language (into-B interpreting, retour interpreting). It is discussed mainly in connection with CONFERENCE INTERPRETING and in particular with SIMULTANEOUS INTERPRETING, as this mode often involves working in one direction only for a given speech or at a given event. This applies also to SIGNED LANGUAGE INTERPRETING, particularly in educational settings. In DIALOGUE INTERPRETING, in contrast, the interpreter normally has to work in two directions due to the inherently bilateral nature of the interaction.

Directionality is one of the oldest and the most contentious issues in conference interpreting research, which is reflected by a large body of literature, including a few collective volumes (Kelly et al. 2003; Godijns & Hinderdael 2005; EMCI 2002). Underlying the debate about directionality is the assumption that the QUALITY of into-B interpreting is inferior – or, if one takes the opposite view, superior – to that of working into A. Opinions were long based on "a mix of personal experience, ideology and tradition" (Gile 2005b: 10), before findings generated by empirical studies emerged. Research into directionality seems to have reached its peak in the first decade of the twenty-first century, although interest in the topic continues. Historically, the dominant view that interpreting should preferably be done into the interpreter's native language was expressed most insistently by the PARIS SCHOOL, while it was mainly scholars from what was then the communist bloc who claimed the opposite. The positions of the two sides are perhaps best illustrated by SELESKOVITCH (1968) and Denissenko (1989).

While not condemning CONSECUTIVE INTERPRETING into the B language, Seleskovitch presents a strongly negative view on the quality of simultaneous interpreting in this direction, believing that it should actually not be done or taught at all. The only exception she makes, very reluctantly, concerns "technical material that includes a great many words which can be translated literally" (1978a: 100). Her belief is that interpretation into B inherently suffers from severe source language INTERFERENCE, even if the interpreter is a very fluent speaker of his or her B language. She does not concede that listening to a source text in one's native language might constitute an advantage, believing that COMPREHENSION in the B language occurs spontaneously provided the interpreter's knowledge of it is good enough. Another frequent argument against retour interpreting is the higher COGNITIVE LOAD and excessive STRESS that the interpreter is exposed to (e.g. Seleskovitch & Lederer 1989).

Denissenko's view on the superiority of into-B interpreting, on the other hand, is based on the belief that comprehension is always significantly better when listening to a speech in one's native language, especially under difficult conditions such as a high SPEECH RATE or heavy ACCENT of the original speaker. Good comprehension is seen as a prerequisite for the other stages of the interpreting process, as "the losses at input cannot be repaired" (1989: 157). Moreover, when producing an utterance in a foreign language the interpreter is faced with a smaller number of possible target language renditions, which facilitates quick decision-making and control processes. Considering USER EXPECTATIONS, Denissenko believes that listeners are willing to excuse the interpreter for "somewhat stiff, less idiomatic or slightly accented language" (1989: 157).

The Paris School's position on directionality has become dominant, and the popular expression 'retour interpreting' also seems to imply into-A interpreting as the default option. Nevertheless, into-B interpreting is often a practical necessity in conference interpreting due to genuine market needs. This is especially visible in the European Union, where some of the newer official languages (e.g. Finnish, Hungarian, Romanian) are very rare as interpreters' B or C languages. This has caused the Paris School to soften its position, and now into-B interpreting is increasingly tolerated, though only as a necessary evil, and provided that it is not taught too early in an interpreting course, i.e. before students have mastered interpreting into A (e.g. Déjean le Féal 2003).

Interestingly, empirical research has provided evidence for either position in the directionality debate, though not many studies have investigated the actual quality of interpretations. In studies evaluating the output of professional interpreters by means of propositional ACCURACY scores, Chang and Schallert (2007) report higher scores for interpreting from English B into Chinese A, whereas van Dijk et al. (2011) report higher scores for interpreting from Dutch A into Sign Language of the Netherlands, the interpreters' B language. The results based on accuracy scores are confirmed by a count of lexical and grammatical errors in the former study and by subjective evaluations by independent assessors in the latter.

Other studies do not address interpreting quality directly but are used to draw conclusions on directionality. The superiority of one or the other direction may be extrapolated, for example, from interpreters' declared preferences. Surveys by Donovan (2004) and Nicodemus and Emmorey (2013) confirm a preference for into-A among spoken-language interpreters and the opposite among sign language interpreters. Another indication is faster lexical access for A-language counterparts of B-language words (de Bot 2000). On the other hand, the superiority of into-B interpreting may be supported by better ANTICIPATION scores (Kurz & Färber 2003), more efficient strategic processing (Al-Salman & Al-Khanji 2002) or better working memory for A-language input (Opdenhoff 2012).

Several authors have suggested that the importance of directionality *per se* has been overrated. Kalina (2005b), for example, emphasizes that directionality should not be considered separately from such factors as the working languages involved, the type of conference, the nationality of speakers and listeners, and the numbers of delegates using each language. Likewise, Gile (2005b) highlights a number of language-specific and language-pair specific factors which may facilitate or hinder interpreting from one language to another, quite independently of the source or the target language being the interpreter's A. According to the findings of a survey conducted by Donovan (2004), directionality does not seem to play an important role for conference delegates, who do not notice quality differences between B–A and A–B interpreting and sometimes even have difficulty in determining whether the interpreter is working into his or her native language.

MAGDALENA BARTŁOMIEJCZYK

DISASTER RELIEF INTERPRETING

↑ SETTINGS

Disaster relief interpreting (DRI) refers to the interpreting services provided in disaster relief contexts as part of an emergency management plan. DRI settings can be described as emergency situations, characterized primarily by the field tasks required for the operation and flow of international disaster assistance. Disaster relief interpreters are intermediaries between local people and authorities, and foreign search and rescue (SAR), relief and logistic support workers. Basically provided by volunteers with some level of training, DRI mainly uses the consecutive mode and can be viewed as a special type of 'interpreting in the community'. In contrast to typical COMMUNITY INTERPRETING (CI) situations, however, the foreign language speakers involved are service providers from abroad. DRI is also peculiar in its role, before, during and after disaster relief and emergency response operations.

As an indispensable requirement for international SAR, relief, medical and logistic work at disasters, DRI requires due consideration of the physical and psychological conditions which characterize emergency situations. At the disaster preparedness stage, the interpreters involved are registered or affiliated with public or private institutions and their task is largely similar to pre-planned CI. By contrast, field tasks like interpreting for international SAR, medical response and relief assistance are undertaken by trained DRI volunteers, or newcomers guided by them (e.g. Powell & Pagliara-Miller 2012), and are closer in nature to emergency settings such as war and CONFLICT ZONES or refugee camps. In Turkey, for instance, the Gulf conflicts of 1990 and 2003 and the Syrian conflict of 2011 resulted in a massive influx of refugees, which led to contingency CI plans involving *bilingual Turkish citizens of Arab origin.*

As part of a national plan for disaster relief assistance, DRI is needed when there is a lack of self-operating international structures. It operates within a country's emergency management plan throughout its different stages (i.e. preparedness, pre-operation calls, operation and post-operation debriefing), ensuring communication with international relief assistance structures such as the Virtual On-site Operations Coordination Centre of the UN Office for the Coordination of Human Affairs.

A well-described example of DRI is Afette Rehber Çevirmenlik (ARÇ, meaning 'Disaster Relief Interpreting Volunteers'), which emerged in the Turkish context after the devastating earthquakes of 1999. ARÇ, previously referred to in English as Interpreters-in-Aid at Disasters, is an initiative of volunteers in the Turkish Association of Translation. It was designed as a triangular model of emergency response collaboration between the state, civil society and universities. Based on a protocol signed in 2001 with the national disaster and emergency management authority (AFAD), ARÇ has a structural basis for taking further professionalisation measures if and when necessary.

Training for ARÇ volunteers is offered in two formats: 100-hour basic training and one-day seminars. Basic training includes 30 hours of official SAR certificate training administered by AFAD, 15 hours of first-aid training seminars given by professional emergency medicine teams, and some 50 hours of technical seminars (geomorphology, architecture, psychology, radio communication, disaster management, international disaster assistance, interpreting techniques and practice) given by ARÇ trainers and field experts. A written exam and a drill are then required for CERTIFICATION by the collaborating universities. Some 120 volunteers in several cities have completed this basic training, and hundreds more have participated in one-day seminars. Trained ARÇ volunteers may be joined by 'newcomers' on the site of a disaster, to form a DRI task force.

Research on DRI was introduced by scholars who took part in the Turkish initiative as the first volunteers and trainers of ARÇ (e.g. Bulut & Kurultay 2001), with articles and presentations on ARÇ in Turkish and English (e.g. Doğan 2012; Doğan & Kahraman 2011) as well as undergraduate and Master's theses on such topics as training, structural weaknesses and issues of sustainability. In particular, research has analysed contingent DRI issues so as to develop sustainable responses that can be incorporated into practical DRI training scenarios and simulations. DRI practice, training and research will be tested by whatever difficulties future disasters may bring.

TURGAY KURULTAY AND ALEV BULUT

DISCOURSE ANALYTICAL APPROACHES

Broadly conceived, discourse analysis is the investigation of how people use language to communicate for a given purpose in particular contexts (Brown & Yule 1983: ix). Thus, 'discourse' in this sense is to be understood as the process of communication (with text as its product – see Widdowson 2004: 8). From its beginnings in the 1970s, discourse analysis and text linguistics moved linguistic analysis beyond sentence level to focus on the ways in which language users achieve their communicative goals over a whole text or sequence of talk. (In the early days, 'discourse analysis' tended to focus on speech rather than written texts, but this distinction was later abandoned.) This new perspective was of obvious relevance to translation and interpreting, and studies using it began to appear from the 1980s onwards. Discourse analysis is a diverse and interdisciplinary field, variously involving sociolinguistics, psycholinguistics, corpus linguistics, pragmatics, ethnography and sociology. In studies of interpreting we can distinguish three methodological approaches: a broad mainstream sometimes drawing on other fields; Conversation Analysis (CA); and Critical Discourse Analysis (CDA).

Discourse analysis

Discourse analysis offered descriptive interpreting studies a means of discovering regularities of interpreter behaviour. Moving away from the focus on COGNITIVE APPROACHES, it focussed on the product of language use (text, talk) as evidence of the process (discourse) and of interpreter decision-making and STRATEGIES.

In an early beyond-the-sentence analysis of SIMULTANEOUS INTERPRETING, SHLESINGER (1995a) analysed the treatment of cohesive markers by comparing the output of eleven advanced-level trainee interpreters with the input speech. She found that shifts of COHESION were more common towards the start of an interpreted speech than later in the output (relating this to the fact that co-textual clues to context become more available to interpreters as the speech unfolds), and that omission of cohesive devices occurred more frequently when they were not seen as essential to the transmission of informational content.

Working within the framework of Systemic Functional Linguistics, Tebble (1999, see also 2013) analysed the discourse structure of medical interpreting encounters with a focus on interpersonal meaning and REGISTER shifts. Noting the distinct linguistic character of each stage of the medical consultation genre (e.g. introductions, stating the problem, ascertaining facts, resolution/exposition, patient's decision), Tebble was able to show the importance of translating interpersonal meaning in ensuring the establishment of rapport between patient and physician. She highlighted the frequent use by doctors of vectors of affect (euphemism, downtoning of bad news, hesitation, repetition), and the fact that interpreters focussing on information content sometimes overlook these. Hale (1997c, 2004) also investigated shifts of register (in COURTROOM INTERPRETING), finding that interpreters addressing the court tend to increase the formality of witness speech but translate speech addressed to witnesses more informally, thus accommodating to the perceived communicative style of addressees.

The most thorough and most influential study using discourse analysis has been the interactional approach to face-to-face interpreting propounded by Wadensjö (1998), who goes well beyond mainstream discourse analysis in order to achieve a more socially grounded account. Drawing on Bakhtin's theory of dialogism, she insists on the triadic nature of the event, in which each participant, including the interpreter, negotiates the progression of talk and the exchange of meanings. Goffman's notions of PARTICIPATION FRAMEWORK and FOOTING (the alignment each participant takes towards an utterance) are central to Wadensjö's detailed analyses of sequences from her corpus, showing the importance of the interpreter's coordinating ROLE, the interdependence of each participant in a three-way exchange, and the way in which meaning is negotiated among participants. Crucially, shifts of footing (e.g. an interviewer addressing the interpreter instead of the interviewee, or the interpreter's use of 'I' to mean the person she is translating or to mean herself) have a bearing on the meanings that are communicated and the direction in which talk proceeds. In this way, the choice of particular moves may affect the outcomes of the interpreted event.

Wadensjö's pioneering framework has encouraged many scholars to pursue interactional discourse studies of interpreted encounters. The studies brought together by Pöchhacker and Shlesinger (2007) in the field of HEALTHCARE INTERPRETING are a case in point. Collectively, they offer a wealth of data, both quantitative and qualitative, documenting shifts of footing, as reflected for example in pronoun use and styles of address. These studies, some of which use conversation analysis (see below), contribute to our understanding of the ROLE interpreters actually adopt (as opposed to prescriptive statements of role).

Angelelli (2004a) uses ETHNOGRAPHIC METHODS in a comprehensive investigation into interpreting at a large hospital. The study includes discourse analysis of a corpus of interpreted medical encounters but also involves long-term (22-month) observation of the encounters and of the environment in which these take place, field notes, extensive INTERVIEWS with stakeholders, SURVEY RESEARCH of interpreters' beliefs about their role, and the collection of relevant artifacts (guidelines, person-to-person messages, pamphlets, etc.). Thus triangulation is achieved and the findings of discourse analysis are set in their social context. Comparison of what interpreters say about themselves and their role with their actual behaviour in interaction shows how they attempt to resolve the tension between their institutionally prescribed role and the visibility they actually adopt – and are sometimes encouraged to adopt by healthcare providers.

What all of these accounts share is a descriptive concern to discover patterned behaviour in the interests of a better understanding of the interpreting process. Within this broad perspective, the trend in discourse analysis over the years has been towards a more socially situated account of interpreters at work and towards the study not just of the interpreter but of all participants and their interaction: each participant's moves affect the others', in a constant process of negotiation of meaning.

Conversation Analysis (CA)

CA is grounded in ethnomethodology, which focuses on the experience of participants themselves – not through interviews or surveys, but by a fine-grained examination of meanings actually received. Participants' take-up, that is, the way in which conversationalists' responses show the sense in which they have understood what they have heard and how they seek to move the interaction forwards, constitutes the conversation analyst's primary evidence.

In strict CA, context (extralinguistic, situational) is not to be posited in advance (via the analyst's subjective selection of what counts as relevant context) but should be allowed to emerge from the evidence of interactants' conversational moves. Otherwise there is the risk of pre-determining the nature of an interaction and perhaps overlooking important cues in the talk itself that re-contextualize the event or provide evidence of something else going on (cf. Schegloff 1992, 1997). All this of course limits what can be said in advance of analysis but it allows the analyst to understand far more about the organization of interaction (TURN-TAKING, sequence organization, the function of PAUSES, dealing with problems in talk) and to search for the clues that point towards the meanings that are projected, received and negotiated among participants.

The most salient application of CA to interpreting is perhaps Roy (2000a). In this study, the author makes a detailed examination of the turn exchange system (Sacks et al. 1974) in an interpreted interview between a student using American Sign Language and a university professor. The analysis explores such features as silences, PAUSES, overlaps and the interpreter's intervention in order to offer or control turns. Roy finds that the interpreter's ROLE is both created and defined in his performance – his discourse decisions, turn management, and knowledge of social factors such as the relative status of participants. In a similar way,

Russell (2002) analyses turn-taking and overlapping talk in POLICE SETTINGS, finding that the interpreter's coordination of turn-taking is both problematic (e.g. open to challenge) and crucial in its potential for affecting outcomes. Bolden (2000) also uses CA to investigate the history-taking phase of medical consultations, showing how the interpreter's goal-orientedness leads to the filtering of patients' accounts to exclude their subjective descriptions and transfer their discourse into that of the 'voice of medicine' preferred by physicians.

Using the institutional interaction framework of CA (Drew & Heritage 1992), Valero-Garcés (2005) compares transcripts of direct (dyadic) and interpreted (triadic) doctor/patient consultations, the latter case subdivided into instances of trained and untrained interpreter performance. Her analysis examines conversational features such as accommodation, distribution of roles and turn-taking. She also provides quantitative evidence of the percentage of questions that are actually translated during the sequences examined (only 14% in the case of the untrained interpreter, 100% in the case of the trained interpreters). Taken together, the quantitative and qualitative data show both interactional similarities and differences between the various types of encounters and offer evidence that enables an assessment to be made of the QUALITY of communication achieved in each case.

Gavioli and Baraldi (2011) seek to combine CA with an account of intercultural MEDIATION, a combination that relates the social context to interactional moves in an insightful way. They show how, in a legal setting, interpreters may from time to time suspend the normal turn-taking sequence by exchanging successive turns with a judge or with a defendant but quickly revert to direct and immediate translation of what is said. Conversely there is a tendency in their corpus of healthcare encounters for interpreters to suspend translation as, in response to a doctor's turn, they give minimal responses that function as a prompt to the doctor to continue speaking. The result is a long series of turns given to the doctor, a summary of which is then translated for the patient. Although interpreters in the healthcare context are seen as cultural mediators and the task of the mediator is to empower other participants, the interpreters' strategy in these encounters is in fact disempowering as the suspended summary translations "risk reducing the relevance of third participants' contributions" (2011: 224). In other words, they tend to deprive patients of their own voice. In this analysis the perspective of CA is broadened to ensure that the institutional and intercultural framework within which interaction takes place is related to the findings of the micro-analysis of transcripts, thus overcoming the objection that pure CA takes small samples of speech and isolates them from their context of occurrence.

Critical Discourse Analysis (CDA)

Whereas most scholars within the discourse analysis framework adopt a scrupulously descriptive stance, it is the goal of CDA to go beyond description and to introduce social critique into analyses by revealing the agendas behind talk, the consequences of POWER differentials and the uneven distribution of communication rights in interaction. For example, while Wadensjö (1992, 1998) uses Bakhtin's account of dialogism in order to enhance her descriptive category of dialogue, Barsky's (1994) use of the same concept contributes to his notion of the "construction of the Other". In his analysis it is only by constructing a productive Other (that is, projecting an image of oneself that conforms not to one's own identity but to the norms of the prospective host country) that an asylum seeker can be successful in having his or her narrative heard and accepted in a refugee hearing.

In Barsky's account it is clear that "constructed Otherness" is a starting point, rather than an outcome, of the analysis. This provides an example of the way in which CDA typically proceeds: an initial assessment of social structures involving power and control often provides the motivation for a discourse analysis which, in its selection of material and choice of parameters, seeks to reveal how power structures are instantiated in discourse and how discourse concurrently reinforces power. Barsky's (1994, 1996) studies, drawing on Bourdieu and Foucault as well as Bakhtin, show the centrality and instrumentality of the interpreter in ASYLUM SETTINGS. By filling in cultural gaps, compensating for incoherence in a claimant's narrative, and shifting register to assist in the construction of the Other that is acceptable to adjudicators, the interpreter can reduce the cultural and linguistic deficit of the displaced person. Conversely, an interpreter who translates only the words uttered inevitably reproduces the discourse in a way that is alien and inadequate in its host environment, thus contributing to the likelihood of rejection of the claim.

In a similar study using the kind of CDA pioneered by Fairclough (e.g. 1995), Pöllabauer (2004) investigates the behaviour of interpreters in asylum cases in Austria, striving for "a descriptive reconstruction of the motives underlying the speakers' statements" (2004: 153). Her focus is on the highly visible nature of interpreters' moves, role expectations and role conflicts, and the asymmetrical distribution of power. She finds that in the field of asylum interviews there appears to be no consensus as to the role and responsibilities of the interpreter. Nevertheless her analysis reveals the interpreters to be highly interventionist and, contrary to Barsky's notion of compensation for disadvantage, to be seeking at times to meet or even to anticipate the expectations of the immigration officers conducting the interviews. At the same time, there is also evidence of interpreters' willingness to be cooperative towards the interviewees and to protect the FACE of all parties involved.

Angelelli (2011a) asks whether the interpreter affects power differentials by mitigating or reinforcing expected behaviours and if so, in what ways. She examines a sequence in which the medical interpreter exercises considerable agency, adjusts questions and pursues questioning on his own account, and re-adjusts register in an effort to improve comprehension. She notes that whereas the practitioner, a nurse, takes the initiative in relinquishing control of the interview, the interpreter both accepts and reinforces this, thus denying the patient direct dialogue with the practitioner. In this study, once again, the institutional power differentials between participants are a starting assumption; what is examined is how these are mitigated or re-negotiated during the interaction.

One problem involved in all such studies arises from the tenets of CDA itself. Precisely because CDA posits that power relations in society control discourse and discourse shapes power relations in society, there is a danger of circularity in analysis: talk is explained by pre-existing power relations and the power relations are explained by talk. In many cases of CDA no independent evidence is presented, although it is important to note that Barsky's (1994) and Angelelli's (2011a) INTERVIEWS with interpreter informants do offer triangulation of the findings and a source of evidence external to the analyst.

Perspectives

Given the increasing openness of interpreting studies to SOCIOLOGICAL APPROACHES, the future of discourse analytical approaches lies in the direction of both social critique and inter-culturality. Blommaert (2005) criticizes CDA for, among other things, allowing the stentorian voice of the analyst to impose interpretations on text, thus drowning out the voice of actual participants or of alternative 'readings' of texts. In analysing interpreted encounters, self-reflection by the analyst is called for, as is recognition of the power wielded by analysts in attributing meanings or intentions to participants. At the same time, there is a risk that 'cultures' come to be treated in a monolithic, top-down way, attributing national characteristics to individuals. In many studies of interpreting, behaviours are linked to speakers' cultures of origin, located in particular countries or regions. As Piller (2012) observes, such character-izations (English culture, Chinese culture, etc.) not only risk gross over-generalization but also obscure inequalities of power and access to resources among participants. The concept of communities of practice (Wenger 1998) offers a rather more focused way of analysing difference among participants in interpreter-mediated encounters.

Meanwhile, some have argued that discourse analytical approaches simply cannot capture the macro-social forces that shape or determine interpreter activity. In this view, interpreters need to be seen "as active agents in wider social and political processes" (Inghilleri 2006: 58), and sociological or ethnographic accounts that draw on interviews with stakeholders, relevant institutional documentation and observation of institutional practices are to be preferred over analysis of corpora of transcribed talk. In reality, both approaches may be necessary – in order first to widen the perspective of narrow discourse analysis, and second to appreciate the effects of social and political forces on actual decision-making by interpreters.

IAN MASON

DISCOURSE MANAGEMENT

↑ DIALOGUE INTERPRETING
→ MEDIATION, → TURN-TAKING

Discourse management is a term used for the activity of (dialogue) interpreters geared toward organizing interaction in bi- or multi-lingual encounters. Many discussions about how to define the interpreter's ideal/appropriate ROLE, and the scope of the dialogue inter-preter's task, can be seen as resulting from the fact that participants in interpreter-mediated face-to-face interaction tend to ascribe a certain responsibility for the organization of inter-action to the interpreter, while interpreters tend to take on a certain responsibility not just for promoting the participants' understanding of each other's talk, but also for managing the talking, that is the discourse flow of the exchange.

Interpreters' discourse management is occasionally mentioned in literature on INTERPRETING from the 1970s and 1980s. For instance, in a study exploring an authentic court session in Papua New Guinea, Lang (1978) finds that the realization of the interpreter's role "depends on the active co-operation of his clients and the extent to which they wish to include him as an active participant not only linguistically but also gesturally, posturally, and gaze-wise" (1978: 241). In an article discussing how to prepare students for various interpreter assignments, Keith (1984) states that the liaison interpreter's job, unlike that of translators and conference interpreters, consists of both translating texts and organizing discourse.

During the 1990s, amid growing interest in interpreting in community settings, discourse management was increasingly seen as an inherent feature of DIALOGUE INTERPRETING. Wadensjö (1992, 1998) discusses the interpreter's twofold task in terms of 'interpreting/translating' and 'coordinating', describing these activities as mutually compatible. In order to capture the complex character of dialogue interpreters' performance, Wadensjö suggests two parallel typologies: viewed as target-text production, interpreting may be seen as resulting in various kinds of 'renditions'; viewed as activities to meet participants' needs for coordinating their turn-taking in an interpreted encounter, the interpreter's contributions can be analysed as 'coordinating moves', which may be either 'implicit' or 'explicit'.

In Wadensjö's (1998) model, interpreters implicitly coordinate a conversation simply by taking, in principle, every second turn at talk, with the substance and progression of talk partly determined by whatever the interpreter contributes, or refrains from contributing.

Some of the interpreter's utterances are manifestly designed to coordinate talk. Such 'explicit coordinating moves' have no corresponding counterpart in preceding primary participants' talk (see NON-RENDITION).

Explicit coordinating moves can be either 'text-oriented' or 'interaction-oriented', and include various kinds of request (e.g. for clarification, for time to translate, for orderly turn-taking, for information solicited but not yet provided), meta-comments on linguistic and other matters, as well as invitations to start or continue talking.

Wadensjö's work, which constitutes one of the most influential DISCOURSE ANALYTICAL APPROACHES in INTERPRETING STUDIES, demonstrates the discourse management of dialogue interpreters on the basis of naturally occurring data from a range of settings, including medical encounters, immigration hearings, police interviews and broadcast interviews. For instance, in a study of interaction in TALK SHOW INTERPRETING, Wadensjö (2008a) shows how the interpreter-mediated BBC interview with former Soviet Head of State Mikhail Gorbachev helped portray the interviewee as a witty and adequate performer, even though he did not speak English, the language of the broadcast and the viewers. Thanks in part to Gorbachev's skill in adapting to the specific communicative conditions of the interpreter-mediated format, the interpreter effectively coordinated the discourse flow exclusively by implicit coordinating moves.

The term 'discourse management' was suggested by Roy (2000a), in an extensive study of a student–professor conference involving interpreting between English and American Sign Language. Roy describes the interpreter's role performance, looking in particular at issues of feedback, overlapping talk and turn-taking. These features were also studied by Apfelbaum (2004), drawing on data from interpreter-mediated specialist education sessions at a German car factory, and by Englund Dimitrova (1997) in a Swedish–Spanish interpreter-mediated medical interview. With special regard for the communicative feedback signals typical of spoken-language interaction, Englund Dimitrova raises questions about what the involvement of the other parties may imply for the interpreter's responsibility in interaction.

Davidson (2000) uses the notion of 'gate-keeping' to highlight interpreters' discourse management and its effect on the participants' possibility of communicating in interpreter-mediated medical encounters in a Californian hospital. Also in the HEALTHCARE INTERPRETING context, Bolden (2000) focuses on the history-taking phase in a medical interview to tease out the discursive mechanisms behind the interpreter's management of the discourse flow. Using three video-recorded parent–teacher meetings, Davitti (2013) shows how interpreters can coordinate turns not just verbally but also through GAZE. This aspect is also mentioned in Bot's (2005) study of interpreter-mediated PSYCHOTHERAPY sessions with traumatised refugees, part of which examines the interpreter's varied use of the first and third person singular and its possible effects on the dynamics of the encounter, that is, the proximity between the primary parties and the middle (or central) position of the interpreter. Interpreters' use of reported or direct speech is a central theme in discussions about the interpreter's ideal/appropriate role.

Data drawn from bilingual and multilingual constellations where participants volunteer as ad hoc interpreters or language mediators have also underpinned studies on discourse management in dialogue interpreting, for instance in early papers by Knapp-Potthoff and Knapp (1987) and Müller (1989). Valero-Garcés (2005) explores encounters between Spanish-speaking doctors and non-Spanish-speaking patients involving ad hoc interpreters, trained interpreters, or no interpreters at all. She demonstrates that doctors and patients accommodate to each other less when a trained interpreter is present, possibly trusting that competent interpreters will manage regardless, and viewing smooth turn-taking as confirmation of that assumption. In a collective volume on *Coordinating Participation in*

Dialogue Interpreting (Baraldi & Gavioli 2012a), two articles deal specifically with discourse management in NON-PROFESSIONAL INTERPRETING: Meyer (2012) describes standard practices of communication with migrant patients in German hospitals, demonstrating how transparent language constellations shape the PARTICIPATION FRAMEWORK, while Traverso (2012) studies multilingual workplace meetings and describes how ad hoc interpreting occurs, how it can develop into collaborative translation, and how problems related to managing the participation framework may arise.

CECILIA WADENSJÖ

DOSTERT

Léon É. Dostert (1904–1971) was born in Longwy, France, a border town close to Germany, Luxembourg and Belgium. The German army invaded the area when World War I broke out in 1914 and German became a compulsory subject for all schoolchildren in the town. Dostert learned it so well that after elementary school, when he was hired to unload supplies for the German army, he was assigned to act as interpreter between the occupying soldiers and his French co-workers. At the end of the war, in 1918, the Americans liberated the area, and Dostert began to study English. After a few months he was able to serve as interpreter between the American troops and the local population (MacDonald 1967). These activities as a go-between across languages and cultures were destined to mark the course of his entire life.

In 1920 Dostert migrated to the United States, sponsored by a US soldier who had befriended him during the liberation of Longwy. He lived with the soldier's family in Pasadena, California, and worked at a grocer's to pay his expenses while finishing high school. He then went to Occidental College in Los Angeles and, from there, to Georgetown University, where he earned two bachelor's degrees (in foreign service and in philosophy) and an MA in languages (1931). He obtained his doctorate at Johns Hopkins University in 1935. Throughout these years he taught French at Georgetown, starting as instructor and ending up as full professor (Vasconcellos 2000).

Dostert was still a French citizen in 1939, so when World War II began he took up duty as a military attaché at the French Embassy in Washington, a post he kept until he became an American citizen in August 1941 (MacDonald 1967). During the war Dostert was the official interpreter to General Giraud and to General Eisenhower (Tucker & Zarechnak 1989). After the war he became Chief of the Translation Division of the NUREMBERG TRIAL, where he set up the SIMULTANEOUS INTERPRETING system that would thus come to the world's attention (Gaiba 1998).

Dostert's scientific curiosity and his 'modern' mentality explain his involvement in simultaneous interpreting, first at Nuremberg and then at the United Nations (UN). The revolution he caused meant a sea change in the profession at the UN, where a real battle took place between him, as an enthusiast of the new system, and the team of consecutive interpreters led, among others, by Jean HERBERT, staunch champion of the *modus operandi* that had prevailed at the League of Nations and in other international conference settings. Eventually Dostert prevailed and simultaneous interpreting was adopted as the main interpreting mode at the UN (Baigorri-Jalón 2004).

Dostert's penchant for teaching and for technical innovation found full expression at Georgetown, where he pursued his passion and priority – "mechanical translation" (Vasconcellos 2000). He introduced tape recorders as a teaching aid at the Institute of Languages and Linguistics, which he had helped establish in 1949 and coordinated for ten years. His mission was "to train American students to achieve adequate communication with people of different cultures in various areas of the world, in order to meet the increasing needs of America's international responsibilities" (Dostert 1953: 3). The Institute's major innovations were the multilingual room and the language laboratory, which allowed simultaneous interpreting in five languages (Tucker & Zarechnak 1989).

Dostert coordinated with IBM the 1954 experiment in Russian–English machine translation, supported by the CIA, as the level of threat perception in the early Cold War years and the US' increasingly tense relations with the Soviet Union stimulated large-scale funding for projects of this sort. He left Georgetown in 1959, but he continued with machine translation (MT) research and with other projects, such as training the blind in different language skills (MacDonald 1967). He was head of the department of languages and linguistics at Occidental College when he died unexpectedly in September 1971, while attending a conference in Bucharest.

JESÚS BAIGORRI-JALÓN

DRAGOMANS

↑ DIPLOMATIC INTERPRETING
→ HABSBURG MONARCHY
↓ JEUNES DE LANGUES

The institution of dragoman (Italian: *dragomanno*; Greek: dragoumanos; French: *drogman/truchement*; Spanish: *trujamán/dragomán*), an official state or diplomatic interpreter, developed in the context of polyglot premodern Mediterranean societies from Antiquity onwards. A staple of diplomatic practice (and of statecraft more generally), DRAGOMANS were crucial actors in many of the political and commercial arenas of the region's empires, where their ROLE far exceeded that of rendering a speaker's message in another language. Dragomans' social background, as well as the institutional parameters of their work, evolved over the centuries thanks to their sustained interactions across linguistic and juridical boundaries.

The etymology of the word 'dragoman', a foreignizing loanword, betrays its Mediterranean roots, and can be traced to the words *targuman, turgeman, tarjuman* and *tercuman* in Aramaic, Hebrew, Arabic and Turkish, respectively (Bosworth 2000). References to dragomans can be found in Italian sources as early as the thirteenth century, mostly in the context of negotiations with the Fatimids and Mamluks in EGYPT and with Turkic principalities in the Black Sea region. Similar etymologies can be traced for the word's several European cognates. Whereas in the medieval Mediterranean basin dragomans served a range of political, commercial, and diplomatic functions as essential intermediaries between the rulers and the ruled, in the following centuries, and especially outside that region, dragomans – often attached to chanceries and boards of trade – increasingly came to be associated almost exclusively with interpreting and translation to and from 'Oriental' languages, such as Arabic, Turkish, and Persian.

The scholarship on dragomans mostly follows this sharp divide between studies of dragomans of the Ottoman imperial *divan* (*Divân-ı* Hümâyûn Tercümanı) on the one hand, and studies of dragomans employed by European powers in their own capitals as well as in Istanbul, on the other. However, dragomans of the two 'types' not only were heirs to a largely shared, circum-Mediterranean body of diplomatic and chancery practices (Wansbrough 1996), but often sustained strong and enduring ties with one another. In more than one case they were actually one and the same person, whose career trajectory led to work with multiple employers and across several empires (e.g. Ali Ufki, né Wojciech Bobowski; see Neudecker 2005). The following discussion thus emphasizes the ways in which dragomans' recruitment and employment patterns as well as interpretive practices (and, indeed, their very concepts of interpreting and translation) circulated across linguistic, juridical and confessional boundaries and at the same time helped articulate these very boundaries.

Mediating in polyglot medieval polities

There are several ancient precedents for the use of official diplomatic and state interpreters. Especially noteworthy are the empires of Pharaonic Egypt and ROME (Hermann 1956/2002; Mairs 2012a), which already featured many of the characteristics of later dragomans, such as their role in the MEDIATION of relationships between a sovereign and various subject populations, construed along lines of linguistic difference; the merging of diplomatic, commercial, proto-ethnographic, and juridical roles; the blending of written and oral communicative techniques; the effort to train cadres at the imperial centre drawn from youth recruited in the provinces; and, more broadly, the discursive emphasis on polyglottism as the hallmark of imperial governmentality. These features came into full bloom in the premodern Mediterranean and Indian Ocean. Dragomans' translingual disposition and multi-perspectival HABITUS, extended social ties, and flexible patronage relations proved highly desirable, whether in the context of flourishing courtly societies interested in facilitating literary and theological translations (Pym 2000; Hagen 2003; Alam & Subrahmanyam 2010; Paker 2011; Truschke 2012), or in pilgrimage sites, port cities and other commercial hubs that attracted large numbers of foreign sojourners. Thus, we find Mamluk, Ottoman, Safavid and Mughal dragomans serving as diplomatic emissaries (Zele 1990; Pedani 1994; Conley 2002; Touzard 2005) as well as commercial brokers (Grenet 2013), pilgrim guides (Williams 2002; Borromeo 2007; Lonni 2009), and even spies (Alam & Subrahmanyam 2004; Gürkan 2012). Ottoman dragomans especially were ubiquitous in a variety of state institutions, ranging from provincial chanceries, customs houses, and court houses (Veinstein 2000; Çiçek 2002; Ergene 2004) to ministers' *divans* (Janos 2006; Balcı 2013). Indeed, in their role as intermediaries between the sultan and his polyglot subjects as well as (inevitably lesser) rulers, Ottoman dragomans performed as ritual figurations of sovereignty itself, of which mediated – rather than direct – communication increasingly became an essential aspect (Perocco 2010). Similarly, in the sprawling colonial administration of late medieval and early modern Venice, interpreters, while not always bearing the title of 'dragoman', are well documented as having performed an equally broad range of functions, both in its Dalmatian and Aegean colonial territories (Eufe 2003) and in metropolitan settings (Rothman 2011a; 2011b).

From medieval chancery to early modern diplomacy

The ubiquity of dragomans across diverse sociopolitical spaces speaks to the centrality of linguistic plurality to premodern conceptions of imperial power (Dakhlia 2008; Peirce 2010). In the context of the Ottoman Empire, dragomans' importance continued to grow with the massive territorial expansion of the fifteenth and sixteenth centuries, which brought into the imperial orbit large numbers of Greek, Slavic and Arabic speakers. Throughout Ottoman lands, dragomans continued to serve as important, though by no means exclusive, intermediaries between the sultan's representatives and non-Turkish-speaking subjects well into the nineteenth century (Philliou 2001). At the same time, Mehmet II's conquest of Constantinople in 1453 transformed that city, already richly multilingual, into a veritable polyglot metropolis, with sizeable populations of slaves from Sub-Saharan Africa and the Black Sea regions; elite soldiery and government bureaucrats drawn largely from Slavic Southeastern Europe; Arabic and Persianate scholars from the Arab provinces and Central

Asia; and, of course, Greek-, Judeo-Spanish- and Armenian-speaking merchant communities. By the late sixteenth century, the city's suburb of Pera also boasted a significant number of foreign consulates and resident embassies. With Ottoman Turkish now the exclusive language of court ceremonial, but the sultan himself increasingly inaccessible to all but his innermost circle, dragomans came to embody Ottoman alterity, at least to their foreign employers. For unlike other capitals, where command of the local courtly language(s) would grant a resident ambassador direct access to the sovereign, dragomans were *de rigueur* in Ottoman diplomatic practice, precluding the possibility of direct communication. Thus, ironically, dragomans' ubiquity may have provided a further disincentive for diplomats sent to the Porte to acquire Ottoman Turkish themselves. This, in turn, exacerbated perceptions of the Ottoman language as inaccessible, and of the Ottoman political system as particularly arcane and impenetrable (Höfert 2003). By obviating the need for foreign diplomats to master the Ottoman language prior to assuming a position in Istanbul, dragomans therefore ultimately contributed to the sense of Ottoman alterity among European elites – an alterity which dragomans themselves sometimes helped accentuate and which in any case ensured their continued relevance.

Recruitment

Dragomans' careers were characterized by spatial dislocation from their inception, as a large proportion of both Ottoman imperial dragomans and diplomatic interpreters serving foreign powers, at least up to the late seventeenth century, hailed from regions beyond the Ottoman capital. For example, of the dozen or so known Ottoman imperial dragomans in the sixteenth century, at least five were foreign-born: two (Murad Bey and Zülfikar) were Hungarian, one (Ahmed, né Heinz Tulman) was German, another (Mahmud Bey) was Austrian, and yet another (Ibrahim Bey né Joachim Strasz) was a Pole. Another dragoman, Yunus Bey, was of Greek origin and reputedly a Muslim convert's son (Ács 2000; Krstić 2011).

Foreign diplomatic dragomans, while rarely converts themselves, often underwent comparable types of dislocation upon recruitment. Indeed, many of them either moved to the Ottoman capital for training, or experienced significant spatial and social mobility as part of their training in various commercial outposts in the Adriatic and Eastern Mediterranean. While efforts to recruit *jeunes de langues* and systematically train them *in situ* were only partially successful, they led to the eventual consolidation of a veritable dragoman caste by the late seventeenth century, largely thanks to intensive and repeated intermarriage between foreign-born and local dragoman families (Rothman 2009a; Miović 2013). Descendants of these 'dragoman dynasties' could still be found on the payrolls of virtually all major foreign embassies in Istanbul in the nineteenth century (e.g. de Groot 1997).

Employment

Perhaps the most distinctive feature of the dragomans' PROFESSION was their spatial mobility and circulation among a range of offices and locales, often spanning multiple jurisdictions. Far from being limited to interpreting during audiences with Ottoman ministers in consecutive and in whispering mode, embassy dragomans' daily activities encompassed a wide range of diplomatic, consular and commercial duties, and entailed the development of a dense network of alignments and loyalties in Istanbul, in their employers' capital cities, and, as importantly, in other Ottoman commercial hubs. Indeed, both *divan* and embassy dragomans' careers involved diplomatic, commercial, and juridical missions across political boundaries, whether as emissaries to foreign courts or as top political functionaries in the tributary states of Ragusa, Moldavia, and Wallachia (Miović 2001; Luca 2003). Venetian dragomans were similarly appointed on several occasions as official emissaries. They recorded their delicate diplomatic missions (to Persia in 1574, to North Africa in 1624, and to the Gates of Vienna following the Ottoman army in 1683) in extensive reports, or *Relazioni*, presented to the Venetian Senate upon their return, much like patrician ambassadors (e.g. Rothman 2009b).

Over time, an elaborate hierarchy emerged to distinguish between several specific types of embassy dragomans. In the case of Venice, dragoman ranks included the *giovane di lingua* or apprentice dragoman, the *protogero*, a low-level clerk in charge of naval and commercial affairs, the *dragomanno di strada* (road dragoman), entrusted with accompanying Venetian representatives to and from Istanbul, and, of course, the Grand Dragoman, the most senior of the corps, who appeared in audiences in front of the grand vizier (alongside the Ottoman Grand Dragoman) and served as the mission's 'eyes and ears' – an oft-repeated trope in several senior diplomats' reports from their missions. In addition, at least one dragoman was regularly assigned to the Venetian colonial headquarters in Zadar (now in Croatia), and several others were appointed to Venetian consulates in Alexandria, Aleppo, and later Izmir. Finally, from the early sixteenth century on, a 'Public Dragoman' was also attached to the Venetian Board of Trade, where he helped translate incoming documents from Ottoman lands, assisted sojourning Ottoman merchants and dignitaries while on Venetian soil, and produced reports and memoranda concerning Ottoman and Safavid affairs. With few exceptions, all dragomans appointed to this prestigious and lucrative post were Venetian citizens with significant prior history of consular service in the Ottoman capital. Although far less stringent in its citizenship requirements, the HABSBURG MONARCHY also tended to elect as dragomans at the court in Vienna persons who had long sojourned in Ottoman lands, either on private business or as formal dragoman apprentices in the Habsburg legation in Istanbul (e.g. Wolf 2005).

The Venetian dragoman corps in early modern Istanbul was probably the largest and most diversified, but by the seventeenth century virtually all foreign embassies in the Ottoman capital sought to keep at least one, and often several, dragomans exclusively on their payroll. While generally following the Venetian division of dragomans' labor, the seniority and power of individual dragomans could not always be immediately gleaned from their titles, as there was no necessary correlation between linguistic qualifications and career trajectories. Some dragomans were even kept on embassy payrolls for years while essentially not performing any work, simply due to their family connections to dragomans serving other embassies, and therefore out of fear that, if dismissed, they might reveal state secrets to a rival power.

Dragomans' legal status has been the subject of some scholarly debate. Indeed, under Ottoman law dragomans serving foreign powers enjoyed a special status as *berath*, that is, the holders of a patent. The imperial charters granted by the sultan to friendly foreign powers often included several clauses concerning dragomans, where their numbers, privileges, and responsibilities were enumerated. And whereas the majority of *berath* were bona fide dragomans, by the nineteenth century a certain number of them enjoyed this status without performing any actual diplomatic duties, contributing in no small measure to the reputation of the system as corrupt and unsustainable. The Ottoman authorities themselves sought to limit the number of dragomans allocated to each embassy for precisely this reason. The fact that dragomans enjoyed certain legal immunities and were considered subjects of their employers (even as the vast majority of them were Ottoman subjects) exacerbated an already complex situation (Heywood 2000; Van den Boogert 2005; Castiglione 2014). The ambiguity of dragomans' legal status was made more acute by the shifting borders of central Europe, and by several dragoman families' successful bids for aristocratic status in Venetian, Habsburg and Polish realms (e.g. Marković 2005; Pippidi 2006).

Enlightenment Phanariots and the rise of linguistic nationalisms

Patterns of dragoman recruitment for the Ottoman *divan* initially paralleled those of foreign embassies in significant ways, privileging bilingual subjects of either foreign extraction (war captives and renegades) or provincial background (child-levy recruits), many of whom were graduates of the palace school. These patterns changed decisively in the second half of the seventeenth century, with the rise of the so-called 'Phanariot' dragomans. These were members of elite Greek-speaking, Christian Orthodox families, so named after the district of Phanar in Istanbul where many of them resided and where the Orthodox Patriarchate was located (Patrinelis 2001; Philliou 2011). Phanariot dragomans certainly differed from their predecessors not only in religion, but in their educational background, understanding of the Ottoman enterprise and their place therein. Yet they shared two important features: BILINGUALISM due to provenance in another language community, and foreign contacts (in the latter case, due to university education abroad and/or prior service as a diplomatic dragoman for a foreign power). These features were exemplified by the first Phanariot Grand Dragoman, Panagiotis Nikoussios (1613–1673), who occupied that position from 1669 until his death, but who had previously served as the dragoman for the Habsburg resident in Istanbul, and who had an extensive manuscript library which was the envy of France's Minister Colbert. By the eighteenth century Phanariot dragomans received the title of *hospodar* of Moldavia and Wallachia, effectively ruling the Danubian principalities and turning them into centres of Greek learning, where they played a significant role in advancing particular political theories and language ideologies in close conjunction with migrant Greek-speaking communities elsewhere (Păun 2008; Mackridge 2010: 40–44).

Dragomans and the genealogies of Orientalism

Dragomans were well placed to serve as influential intermediaries in the development of several fields of knowledge, including Ottoman history, Oriental philology, and Islamic studies, which ultimately came to constitute the core of Orientalism as a discipline and a set of methodological and epistemological dispositions (Rothman 2012, 2013). The dragomans' scholarly contributions extended from the sixteenth century to the twentieth. Indeed, the dragomans' impact ranges from their obvious role as the translators (and key negotiators) of major diplomatic treaties between the Ottomans and virtually all their political and military rivals (with the exception of the Safavids) (e.g. Keenan 1967; Theunissen 1998; Kołodziejczyk 2011) to their position as vital nodes in the circulation of (often oral) news from Istanbul to other capitals (Gürkan 2012; Ghobrial 2014). But their impact went far beyond diplomacy. Dragomans authored some of the earliest, most authoritative, and most widely circulating works on the Ottoman-Turkish language. Some of their linguistic and lexicographic works even circulated back to Ottoman territories (Kappler 1999; Święcicka 2000). They were important interlocutors in the religious polemics of the Age of Confessionalization (Krstić 2009; Koutzakiotis 2011), and played a decisive role in the circulation of scientific knowledge as well (Şeşen 1992; Günergun 2007; Krstić 2011). Even more pronounced was their contribution to proto-ethnographic writings about Ottoman society and culture and to the philological study of early Ottoman texts (Ménage 1971; Schmidt 2000; Van den Boogert 2009). They also translated several extended Ottoman chronicles and were key nodes in the bibliophile networks that sought to identify, acquire, and annotate 'Oriental manuscripts' for various Oriental libraries, whether royal, university, or privately owned (Elgohary 1979; Hamilton & Richard 2004; Dew 2009).

Importantly, dragomans' contributions to nascent Orientalism were based not only (or even primarily) on their linguistic competence and professionally cultivated philological sensibilities, but rather on their structural position at the heart of the Ottoman Empire, their deep familiarity with both Ottoman and foreign governmental procedures and documentary practices, strong ties with a range of political elites across the region, and access to valuable knowledge of various kinds by virtue of their association with foreign diplomats and merchants. Such a position, coupled with their acquaintance with sojourning European artists and opportunities to relocate to other capitals, allowed several dragomans to author and even commercially publish foundational works related to Ottoman language, history, arts and sciences, theology, music, and botany, to name but a few.

Dragomans' prolific and varied textual output speaks to an important aspect of this group's habitus: not only were they adept at employing multiple perspectives and genres to appeal to several publics at once, but they were also quite keen to cultivate their own (at times contradictory) self-representations (e.g. Findley 2003; Fraser 2010). Indeed, dragomans' ego-documents (e.g. Miović 2002) allow us to probe their own understandings of their complex trans-imperial positionality. Attending to dragomans' textual production may broaden the scope of conventional INTERPRETING STUDIES and offer a more comprehensive model of mediation, which could, indeed, be applicable to other types of interpreters as well. Perhaps most significantly, dragomans' writings give us access to the minute textual STRATEGIES through which interpreters help articulate boundaries and calibrate categories rather than bridge immutable, a-priori distinct cultural-cum-linguistic codes (see e.g. Rothman 2011b; Pym 2000; Tymoczko 2003). Dragomans' textual output calls attention to the interaction between dimensions of ORALITY, literacy, and performance in interpreters' work, to the important role of interpreters' communities of practice in shaping their translational strategies, and to the potential insights gained by combining social history and semiotic analysis in their exploration.

E. NATALIE ROTHMAN

DUAL-TASK EXERCISES

see under PRE-INTERPRETING EXERCISES

EAR–VOICE SPAN

see TIME LAG

EDUCATION

↓ ASSESSMENT, ↓ CURRICULUM, ↓ PEDAGOGY

Interpreter education has been understood in recent decades to encompass preparatory and professional development programs and courses for spoken and signed language interpreters working in highly diverse SETTINGS and domains. The term 'education' implies comprehensive learning through academic and professional studies in pursuit of higher-order CURRICULUM aims and goals, which are often deontological in nature and in part define a PROFESSION. At the same time, the term is traditionally contrasted with the skills-based training that is most aptly pursued through PEDAGOGY grounded in deliberate and reflective practice and that culminates in the automaticity and case-based reasoning processes characteristic of high levels of EXPERTISE. Given this duality, interpreter education programs incorporate elements of apprenticeships that are specific to professional workplace settings and require the inculcation of NORMS, ETHICS, and codes of conduct through an extended socialization process. Most interpreter educators, including those represented in the Conférence Internationale Permanente d'Instituts Universitaires de Traducteurs et Interprètes (CIUTI), now insist on the independence and autonomy of interpreter education in the academy. Many programs are housed in Departments of Translation and/or Interpreting, which may be regarded as a sign of their maturity and self-sufficiency, but many are also found in academic units devoted primarily to the study of languages, literatures and cultures, applied linguistics, or (intercultural) communication. Education for SIGNED LANGUAGE INTERPRETING (SLI) can also be found in departments of disability studies, signed language or deaf studies, welfare or social sciences.

Educational infrastructure, which includes academic programs, educational associations and research conferences and publications, developed in the decades of the mid-to-late twentieth century, as interpreting became increasingly professionalized across domains and settings. Separate roots can be found in diplomatic and CONFERENCE INTERPRETING in spoken languages and in public service interpreting in signed languages, with spoken-language COMMUNITY INTERPRETING emerging through processes more similar to those of SLI than spoken-language conference interpreting. Conference interpreter education has often been treated in the broader context of translator education, and programs for spoken and signed languages have been discussed in separate publications and conferences, sometimes with a regional focus (e.g. Caminade & Pym 1998; Park 1998; Hagemann 2004; Napier 2004a, 2009; Wang & Mu 2009).

Towards the end of the twentieth century, these separate strands began to integrate, creating considerable momentum, measured in terms of the number of programs, activities of professional associations, and research publications and conferences devoted to educational and pedagogical issues. Online directories maintained by the many international and national associations of interpreters list anywhere from several dozen to hundreds of training programs and courses, depending on the criteria for inclusion.

History and development

A watershed moment in interpreter education was the establishment of postgraduate programs in spoken-language conference interpreting during and after the Second World War. A similar juncture was reached when regulatory frameworks began to prescribe the use of interpreters as a human rights and language access issue in the 1970s, which in turn brought about additional vocational training opportunities and CERTIFICATION programs. However, by most accounts, institutional efforts to educate interpreters began in the mid-sixteenth century and focused on the grooming of diplomatic interpreters from a young age. The so-called *giovani di lingua*, or JEUNES DE LANGUES, were to serve as DRAGOMANS in dealings with the Ottoman Empire, and their training took place in embassies and legations there, and increasingly in special language schools established for this purpose, such as the *École des jeunes de langues* founded by Jean-Baptiste Colbert in 1669. Schools were established in Constantinople, Smyrna, and in 1721 in Paris, where French-born boys studied to become interpreters for Turkish, Arabic, and Persian (Bowen 2012). Further examples of language schools for (future) diplomats who would begin their careers as interpreters include the Oriental Academy of the HABSBURG MONARCHY, founded in Vienna in 1754 (Bowen 2012), and the Department of Oriental Languages at the University of Berlin, established in 1887 (Wilss 1999). Such training inevitably focused on language and background knowledge acquisition through formal studies in the home country and through immersion experiences abroad, rather than interpreting technique per se. In the early twentieth century, the US Department of State's Corps of Student-Interpreters (1902–1924) followed these examples, and the tradition of ministries of foreign affairs training interpreters to provide language support in diplomatic settings continues to this day (Feldweg 2003; Sawyer 2008).

Conference interpreter education

Despite such precursors, a distinct interpreting pedagogy addressing teaching methodology in the classroom, and hence interpreter education in the modern sense, did not emerge until conference interpreting programs were institutionalized in universities in the mid-twentieth century. The rise of the conference industry in the early part of the twentieth century, the shift away from French as the LINGUA FRANCA of diplomacy and business, and the introduction of technical equipment to facilitate SIMULTANEOUS INTERPRETING in the 1920s created the preconditions for the establishment of conference interpreting programs in European and North American universities (Gaiba 1998; Wilss 1999). These programs generally offered conference interpreting (and translation) in spoken languages and were often situated from the outset at the postgraduate level. Three early groupings have been identified (Caminade & Pym 1998; Kelly & Martin 2008; Bowen 2012). The first includes programs predating the end of the Second World War and the introduction of instruction in simultaneous interpreting: Moscow (where a first but short-lived translator/interpreter training program from 1930 to 1933 was reopened in 1942), Heidelberg (1933), Geneva (1941) and Vienna (1943). The second group includes programs founded directly after 1945 in association with the Allied peace efforts: Innsbruck (1945), Graz (1946), Mainz/Germersheim (1947), Saarbrücken (1948), Paris (1948) and Washington (1949). The third includes two programs founded in Paris in 1957, which continue to operate today.

In the following decades, the number of university-level conference interpreting programs rose rapidly, as postgraduate programs were established throughout Europe and beyond. Educators soon formed their own associations, with roots dating back to 1960, when the universities of Geneva, Heidelberg, Mainz/Germersheim, Paris-Sorbonne, Saarbrücken and Trieste formed a quality circle that in turn led to the founding of CIUTI (Conférence Internationale Permanente d'Instituts Universitaires de Traducteurs et Interprètes) in 1964. Originally a western European association, this global network listed 45 members in 2014. Similarly, in 2014, the International Association of Conference Interpreters (AIIC), founded in 1953, listed 63 programs in a schools directory maintained by its training committee. As an example of the exponential growth of interpreter education programs, in CHINA alone, the number of programs officially approved to offer a Master of Translation and Interpreting (MTI) had reached 158 by 2010.

Signed language interpreter education

The path leading to university programs for interpreter education in signed languages was separate from that of conference interpreting. Rather than being created with little prior preparation at the postgraduate level in universities, signed language programs emerged from vocational training, with short programs, courses, and curriculum development projects paving the way. Interpreters emerged from within Deaf communities, where Deaf members select and 'teach' interpreters. Soon, local Deaf associations, welfare or social services, churches, or educational institutions housing Deaf education programs offered courses in a signed language and one or two courses in SLI. As Deaf people fought for access to communication with the wider world and persuaded governments to provide needed services, the most frequently requested service was interpreting.

While the United States, the United Kingdom, and Sweden led the way in organizing and then teaching SLI, other countries took longer to follow suit (Ozolins & Bridge 1999), but the pathways to formal education are quite similar. The UK and AUSTRALIA, for example, began providing in-service training and proficiency testing as early as 1928 and 1929 to missioner/welfare officers to the Deaf (Simpson 1991). In the US, vocational rehabilitation services provided financial support for workshops to develop a curriculum and write a handbook, *Interpreting for Deaf People* (Quigley 1972), which was used as a training manual for over 20 years. Japan, in the 1970s, trained and placed sign language volunteers in social welfare offices to interpret for deaf people who came for services (Takada & Koide 2009). Over time and in most countries, Deaf associations and interpreters themselves would begin to advocate for a professional ROLE unencumbered by other duties, with adherence to a professional code of conduct.

Training in SLI progresses from short courses of several weeks, to longer programs lasting a year, such as those at Finnish and Swedish 'folk high schools', to two-year collegiate programs, as has been the case in Finland and the Netherlands in the 1980s and in Ireland, Japan and Sweden in the 1990s (see Napier 2009). These first post-secondary programs and courses were often located in departments of education, deaf education, speech and hearing sciences, or communication sciences, and were taught by experienced practitioners who had little or no post-secondary education themselves.

As two-year collegiate programs prospered, educators took account of student struggles to become fluent while simultaneously learning to interpret, as well as their inadequate mastery of the commonly spoken language, and the lack of a general liberal arts knowledge base. As national membership associations developed standards and qualifications for work (increasingly requiring a four-year degree), and universities began to recognize signed languages, SLI programs began to thrive in universities or polytechnic universities, and sometimes came to be associated with spoken-language programs (Napier 2005b; Grbić 2009). In the countries of Western Europe, and in Australia and the United States, bachelor's and master's degree programs are flourishing, and Europe currently has over 50 educational programs for SLI, varying from two-year to five-year programs.

Spoken-language community interpreter education

Generally speaking, the development of spoken-language programs focusing on legal, healthcare and other community settings has followed paths similar to signed language interpreter training, with Australia, Sweden, and the United States leading the way (see Hale 2007, Ch. 6). Where national certification programs were established, short training courses followed in the 1980s and 1990s. A milestone in the professionalization of community interpreting (Mikkelson 1996) was the founding of the CRITICAL LINK conference series and network to promote interpreting in these settings. Increasingly, university programs offer postgraduate degrees with specializations in public service interpreting, and entities that have traditionally focused on conference interpreting are integrating community interpreting into their activities.

Stakeholders and guidelines

Interpreter education is governed by political and regulatory frameworks that are shaped by diverse stakeholders, such as government policymakers, university decision-makers, direct (curriculum) participants, and language industry participants, including employer organizations and educational and professional associations, some of which issue specific guidelines driven by operational requirements (e.g. Durand 2005). LANGUAGE POLICY mandates apply in specific international, national, and regional contexts where fundamental rights of language access, multilingualism, and equity are overriding concerns. At the same time, interpreting studies research has informed educators' decision-making processes through conference series, academic journals, and edited research volumes and monographs.

In the 1960s, a theoretical discussion of the interpreter's skill set and how to teach it began to take place in conferences and research publications. Key issues were (and continue to be) the organization and implementation of curriculum and ASSESSMENT at the program and course levels, including APTITUDE TESTING. As the status of interpreting as an activity evolved from an ad hoc service to a recognized professional occupation, the aims and goals of teaching and learning were conceptualized and later informed by educational philosophies rooted in systematic reflection and research grounded in the various strands of INTERPRETING STUDIES, in which educational matters have traditionally been a chief concern (e.g. Arjona 1984; Freihoff 1995; Mackintosh 1999; Roy 2000b, 2005, 2006; Sawyer 2004; Winston & Monikowski 2013). After roughly a half century of experience with university programs, the first comprehensive retrospective descriptions of the development of (conference) interpreter education appeared (Mackintosh 1995, 1999; Ilg & Lambert 1996; Moser-Mercer 2005b; Seleskovitch 1999). A transition was thus completed from a view of the preparation of interpreters as a narrow form of vocational, skills-based training to a view of interpreter education as a comprehensive undertaking grounded in academic and professional studies (Pöchhacker 2010a).

Beginning in the 1970s, legal provisions began to mandate language access through interpreting (and translation) services. Notable examples include the Education for All Handicapped Children Act (1975), the Court Interpreters Act (1978), and Executive Order 13166 on Improving Access to Services for Persons with Limited English Proficiency (2000) in the United States; Directive 2010/64/EU of the European Parliament and of the Council on the Right to Interpretation and Translation in Criminal Proceedings; and the Multicultural Access and Equity Policy of the Department of Immigration and Border Protection of the Australian government. Although such provisions normally do not spell out educational requirements, mandatory services create demand for training and certification programs.

Today, associations and employers shape the educational infrastructure by defining QUALITY CRITERIA, providing guidelines, and supporting programs independently and through consortia. In addition to professional bodies such as AIIC and WASLI, the World Association of Sign Language Interpreters, scholarly societies such as the European Society for Translation Studies (EST) and the International Association of Translation and Intercultural Studies (IATIS) devote considerable attention to educational issues, as do many national associations around the globe. Some programs have been established at the behest of representatives of organizations such as the United Nations, European Union institutions, and other entities represented in the Heads of Interpretation Services (HINTS), an informal network of individuals serving in influential chief interpreter positions. These employers have founded consortia, such as the United Nations MOU Network and the European Union's Masters in Conference Interpreting (EMCI), which influence educational policy by issuing quality assurance criteria and guidelines.

Another approach to quality assurance is program accreditation, as has developed or become well established in many countries, specifically the US, the UK and Australia, as well as some European countries. The UK has national occupational standards for both spoken and signed language interpreting, while Australia has the National Accreditation Authority for Translators and Interpreters (NAATI), both of which influence how training is delivered within educational programs so that graduates can achieve professional status (Napier 2004a). The European Forum of Sign Language Interpreters (efsli), a professional body formally established in 1993, has published standards for educational programs in Europe, including learning outcomes and assessment guidelines. Some ten years earlier, the Conference of Interpreter Trainers (CIT), a US-based professional organization of interpreter educators established in 1979, endorsed national standards for interpreter education detailing the key skills and competences that students should develop through their education or training. In 2006, the CIT set up an independent body, the Commission on Collegiate Interpreter Education (CCIE), that accredits professional preparation programs in interpreting. In conference interpreter (and translator) education, CIUTI's membership application procedure requires a review process that is widely seen as a quality assurance measure.

While many countries in Western Europe and North America have well-established Deaf associations and professional interpreting organizations to promote the training and education of signed language interpreters, countries in AFRICA, Asia – with the exception of Japan (Takada & Koide 2009) – and South America are just beginning to develop such associations and training programs. Kenya, for example, began with ad hoc training workshops offered through the national Deaf association in the 1990s, conducted by the Kenya Sign Language Research Project at the University of Nairobi (Okombo et al. 2009), but there are still no formal, university-level interpreter education programs. Uganda started its first university training in 2002 (Michael 2011). Brazil, on the other hand, did not officially start formal SLI education until 2008, but jumped from short-term courses in the 1990s to a four-year university-level program at the Federal University of Santa Catarina, which offers distance learning via the web incorporating principles of visual learning (de Quadros & Stumpf 2009).

Instructor training and educational research

Once training becomes an academic endeavor, the focus turns towards the educators themselves, and the requirement to teach and do research, typically in the form of a PhD. An important step in this regard was the founding, by Danica SELESKOVITCH, of the first doctoral studies program devoted to translation and interpreting studies at ESIT (Paris-Sorbonne III) in the mid-1970s. By the early 2000s, many universities housing translation and interpreting programs had followed suit, and a PhD program in SLI was created at Gallaudet University in 2010. By 2014, EST had identified over 40 PhD programs and 40 research groups devoted to interpreting (and translation) studies.

With a more immediate educational orientation, instructor training programs and publications devoted specifically to interpreter (and translator) education have flourished. A book series on "Interpreter Education" was started in 2000 by Gallaudet University Press with the goal of promoting evidence-based teaching (see e.g. Roy 2000b, 2005, 2006; Napier 2009; Winston & Monikowski 2013). *The Interpreter and Translator Trainer*, a journal devoted entirely to research on education and training, was launched in 2007, and CIT began publishing the INTERNATIONAL JOURNAL OF INTERPRETER EDUCATION in 2009.

Among instructor training programs, the certificate course leading to the University of Geneva's Master of Advanced Studies in Interpreter Training was a pioneer, and other institutions, including AIIC, efsli and other international and national associations, now offer instructor training seminars and workshops regularly.

Distance education

Many programs now offer alternative paths to degrees, in particular through E-LEARNING. Institutional employers also increasingly make use of distance education technology to promote collaboration and exchange within their university consortia, in particular by offering master classes via videoconference. For example, in the US, universities offer bachelor's degrees in ASL/English interpreting that are fully online. In Brazil, Australia and the US, some signed language interpreting programs offer traditional classes which are also webcast to students who live far away from the campus. There is also blended learning, where some courses are offered online while others are offered face-to-face and students come to a campus for a few weeks, either during an academic term, or during a break. In Europe, an innovative master's degree program (EUMASLI) is a collaboration among three universities in three different countries (Finland, Germany and the UK), where students spend time on each university campus and also participate in online courses and study on their own. In spoken-language conference interpreting, the University of Geneva's Interpreting Department pioneered online instruction through a Virtual Institute and has extended its reach to include programs providing introductory-level instruction for interpreters working in CONFLICT ZONES and areas of natural disasters. Distance education programs for spoken-language interpreting have also been launched at North American universities, some with the option or requirement to attend at least part of the course of study on campus.

Part of a wider trend in higher education, the decision to use distance learning technology entails weighing the advantages and disadvantages of classroom communication, interaction, and feedback in face-to-face vs. distance or remote settings, as well as the dynamics of synchronous vs. asynchronous instruction. One clear advantage of the emerging use of educational technology is a broadening of the educational community to include instructors and students whose participation would otherwise be unlikely, if not impossible, due to geographical constraints.

DAVID B. SAWYER AND CYNTHIA B. ROY

EDUCATIONAL INTERPRETING

↑ SETTINGS
→ SIGNED LANGUAGE INTERPRETING

Interpreting in educational settings can be described from a variety of perspectives. Many define it simply by the setting, as a means of providing access to educational services. Within this broad context, it occurs in almost every environment where people want to learn and where an interpreter is provided. Education can take the form of workshops for professionals, ongoing training for business clients, and academic courses and programs. The more common definition, and the topic discussed here, is interpreting that occurs specifically within educational institutions such as universities, colleges, institutes, and schools (both primary and secondary).

Educational interpreting has been most widely researched in the educational placements of deaf and hard-of-hearing students from primary through post-secondary settings. Since this educational practice is particularly widespread in the US, most of the discussion focuses on this national context. Given the crucial role of government policy in this field, special attention must be given to pertinent legislation and subsequent implementation measures.

Societal implementation

The practice of educational interpreting is generally perceived as a means of conveying information between teacher and student, with minimal psycho-social impact or consequence.

However, educational interpreting, or interpreted education, is better understood when defined by the educational purposes it is intended to serve, the people for whom it is provided, and the impact it has upon those services and consumers. These purposes are conditioned by societal factors and implemented through government policy by administrators, consumers and service providers. Underlying this type of LANGUAGE POLICY are ideals of language equality and rights to accessible education.

In some national contexts, educational interpreting occurs as the result of a societal desire to promote multilingualism for various cultures and language groups. In others, educational interpreting occurs because education is only available in a single majority language, and all non-users must access it either directly or through interpretation. Two extreme examples are the educational interpreting policies of South Africa and the US. In South Africa, interpreters are provided at university in order to promote and encourage multilingual access to education, assuring speakers of other official languages their right to use these as their medium of learning. Educational interpreters are provided to adult students who choose to pursue courses possibly not available in their languages (Verhoef & du Plessis 2008).

In contrast to the South African practice, the US, like many other countries, provides educational interpreting as a means to support individuals with disabilities, e.g. deaf and hard-of-hearing students, in gaining access to the mainstream educational system. Policy in the US is the result of a series of laws implemented from 1954 to 1990, to promote the inclusion of people with disabilities in mainstream learning opportunities. These include, in particular, the Vocational Rehabilitation Act of 1954; the Education for All Handicapped Children Act (EHA) of 1975, which marked a major shift in the education of deaf children, both in terms of physical placement and linguistic access; the Individuals with Disabilities Education Act (IDEA) of 1990, which amended and superseded the EHA; and the Americans with Disabilities Act (ADA) of the same year. The various laws created an immediate demand for educational interpreting, and an urgent need for educational interpreters, in a vacuum of knowledge and experience, with little existing information, data or understanding of the impact of interpreted education on deaf students, and with inadequate funding to develop any of these resources. The result has been that many who provide educational interpreting do not meet the basic qualification requirements and therefore have a low status in the system.

Interpreters

There are no definitive statistics on the number of deaf students receiving interpreter-mediated education in the US, or on the number of interpreters practicing such MEDIATION. Individual states are required to report numbers of educational interpreters, but often do not, or do it poorly, by conflating the position with other personnel providing support services. The lack of data about interpreters and interpreting is exacerbated by the uncertain ROLE and qualifications of those performing in the settings concerned.

Interpreter roles

The current roles of educational interpreters have been established primarily by school systems and educators, and only occasionally by interpreters themselves. Definitions have been based largely on perceived gaps in mainstream schools. Such shortcomings include the need for someone who can communicate directly with the deaf student; who is expected to bridge the gap between the deaf student's language abilities and world knowledge and those required to succeed in the age-based grade level s/he is placed in; who serves as a language model for purposes of acquisition; and who can directly monitor the deaf student's behavior. As the only adult in the setting who can communicate directly via signing, the interpreter is often assigned all of these roles, with often limited consideration of the possibilities of success or of the interpreter's qualifications. These roles have become the de facto current practice, as described in various studies (e.g. Jones 2004; Winston 2004; Marschark & Spencer 2009). There exists little to no evidence that this arrangement is effective.

Interpreter qualifications

The Commission on Education of the Deaf noted that deaf students were required by law to "be integrated into regular classrooms to the maximum extent possible, but if quality interpreting services are not provided, that goal becomes a mockery" (1988: 103). The information available about the quality of services, based primarily on legal requirements for qualifications rather than evidence-based research about interpreted educations, must be evaluated within the context of this statement. Those school systems in the US that did report actual numbers of educational interpreters indicate considerable variation in their skill, training, and experience.

Again using the US as an example, due to the relative amount of available research and information, the educational system allows each state, and sometimes each school, to regulate the hiring and qualifications of educational interpreters for deaf children. Many rely on a test called the Educational Interpreter Performance Assessment. This ASSESSMENT instrument evaluates both educational interpreting knowledge and performance, using a rating scale ranging between 0 and 5 (0 = none, 5 = advanced). Due to legal requirements, almost all states have established minimum requirements for educational interpreters, but the standard accepted score continues to average 3.5 for most. This score represents an interpretation that conveys basic, but not complex, content, and that can be expected to exhibit mistakes, mis-understandings, and deleted information (Classroom Interpreting 2014). Further, most states have some type of 'backdoor' policy that allows schools to hire unqualified educational interpreters if no others can be found. This enables unqualified interpreters to continue working without even minimal qualifications in educational interpreting. In a 2004 study, some 50% of educational interpreters in several states had not been evaluated for interpreting skills. Of those evaluated in several western US states, 83% had no national certification (Jones 2004). In 2009, the Registry of Interpreters for the Deaf (RID) Educational Interpreter Committee conducted two surveys of RID members. Less than 40% of the 955 educational interpreters responding held any type of certification for educational work, while some 67% reported having worked in 'K–12' (kindergarten to twelfth grade) for more than five years, and 43% had more than ten years' experience in education (RID-EIC 2009).

Thus, students can generally expect to rely on interpreters who may at best be able to convey some simple classroom content, but may have difficulty with more advanced topics and interactions. Yet complex topics and rapid TURN-TAKING abound in education, and these descriptors do not reflect the social and cognitive levels and needs of students in such settings.

In addition to this low level of legal requirements and the very limited monitoring of educational interpreters' qualifications, another significant factor is the system of interpreter EDUCATION itself. Most basic programs relegate educational interpreting to the more advanced courses, because it requires advanced skills; meanwhile school systems often pay educational interpreters poorly, assuming they need fewer skills and qualifications than teachers, nurses, or coaches. Jones (2004) reported that in 1991, two thirds of interpreter training program graduates entered educational interpreting, yet by 2004 only one in 74 interpreter preparation programs included some type of training in educational interpreting. In addition, anecdotal evidence indicates that many students leave interpreter preparation programs without graduating to accept work in educational settings.

A further factor contributing to the current state of interpreted education is the preparation of educators of the deaf, whose curricula and textbooks show minimal attention to the processes of interpreting or interpreted education. What little research about interpreter-mediated education is available rarely finds its way into the preparation of deaf educators.

Interpreter-mediated education

Some ten years after the EHA, 68% of deaf children in the US were placed in special classrooms in public schools or in mainstreamed classrooms with some support personnel, usually an interpreter or teacher of the deaf (Marschark et al. 2002). This reflects an abrupt shift from the former prevalence of placements in residential schools for the deaf, where students received direct educational access. The resulting change in educational approach was informed by virtually no prior information on interpreter-mediated education, which was little known or understood.

Access to language

The concept of accessing education via interpretation is complex and multi-faceted. Students, especially at the primary and secondary levels, receive not only facts and information in school, they are also socialized into interactional norms and mores of society, all through direct interaction with others in the society's language (Cazden 2001). Language is the cornerstone of education and socialization.

Most students, entering an educational system where the medium of instruction is not their native language, do at least have a native or first language. They also have access to the language of instruction in many ways – through friends, the media and daily interaction in a home environment where that non-native language is used constantly. This is usually not the case for deaf students, who are most frequently born into families where spoken rather than visual language is used. Many deaf children therefore arrive in the classroom without age-appropriate natively acquired language. This language deficit has a detrimental impact on their background knowledge and understanding of the world, and leaves them at a disadvantage in the system (Marschark & Spencer 2009).

Interpreting assumes that both parties have a language that can be interpreted to and from. When one participant has little or no language, and minimal world knowledge, interpreting cannot occur. Monikowski (2004) describes the fundamental requirement for deaf children to be competent in a language prior to being able to learn through interpretation. Yet interpreters continue to be placed with these children, and the interpreter often becomes the sole individual (adult or peer) from whom the deaf student receives visual language input. Many educators and parents have also promoted the practice of coded signing and the use of various systems for visually representing some aspects of the majority spoken language. However, few such codes can fully represent the spoken source language. Schick (2003) suggests that attempts at visual presentation of auditory language features may conflict with the structure of visual languages. Wilbur (2003) observes that there is comparable scope in all natural languages for layering of natural articulatory features in order to produce multiple components or aspects of meaning simultaneously. An example of this would be the possibility, in spoken languages, of overlaying tone with lexical units; or, in signed languages, the formation of a verb with a co-occurring movement to indicate direction. Such layering takes advantage of the language modality. Coded systems, which attempt to represent auditory features visually, do not adequately layer such features.

Even those students who enter the system with an intact primary language (e.g. the small minority of deaf children born to deaf parents) have only a limited number of ways to access the language of education, and to learn the speech habits and daily jargon of the classroom as well as the content. Winston (2004) describes several specific discourse styles of classroom teachers that add another dimension to the situational requirements of educational interpreting. The classroom teacher must actively practice accommodation at every level in order to provide visual access to all information, materials, and resources during class. These adaptations include presenting sequentially rather than simultaneously; adapting the pace of teaching, turn-taking, and interactions to allow for time and language constraints; and including explicit and redundant wording in classroom discussions that are mediated by interpreting. Further, the teacher must render all audio-based input into a visually accessible form. These teaching styles, which are closely related to discourse patterns such as pacing, explicitness, redundancy and turn-taking, are different for each teacher; some patterns are more compatible with interpreting than others, and some teachers are more willing and able to adapt than others. Given the constraints and limitations which interpreting places on language acquisition and educational development, the issue of acquiring competence in academic language persists for deaf students throughout the educational process.

Access to socialization

The purpose of education extends far beyond simple language and content learning. Socialization is a major goal for students. As with language, this too is often mediated by the interpreter. Interacting with peers at the age of twelve, through the mediation of an adult, possibly of a different gender, race, and/or ethnicity than oneself, can be awkward at best, and oppressive at worst when students are aware that interpreters may report bad behavior as part of their responsibilities. Oliva (2004) shares findings from the perspective of a deaf adult who survived the system of interpreter-mediated education. For deaf students, who face the presence of an interpreter throughout the educational experience, the prospect can be daunting. They are often unaware of, or confused about, the roles of interpreters, and thus have little idea of how they can effectively interact with others. Brown Kurz and Caldwell Langer (2004) report deaf students' perceptions of limited social interaction and even isolation. Winston (1992) characterizes the experiences of deaf students in mainstreaming as fundamentally different in every aspect of their education, and socialization is one such aspect. Of the existing research, much focuses on the element of socialization, highlighting the differences in deaf students' experience of interpreted education (e.g. Oliva & Lytle 2014; Ramsey 1997).

Effectiveness

There is little research that explores the effectiveness of interpreter-mediated education as an educational approach. Marschark and Spencer (2009) report that, in general, direct teaching methods are more effective for deaf students' learning than indirect or interpreter-mediated methods. Many consider that deaf and hard-of-hearing students most often have only illusionary access to a system that is fundamentally biased toward auditory rather than visual learning needs. The limited research on access to education via interpreting reports findings primarily about adults at the post-secondary level. More than 20 years after educational interpreting became widely implemented in 1974, Stewart and Kluwin (1996) summarized the many challenges that educational interpreting poses, and encouraged more research.

Reiterating the same need years later, Ramsey (2004) continues to question whether even skilled interpreting can be an effective medium for the instruction of deaf children. Despite ongoing concerns, educational interpreting as a means of providing access for the majority of deaf students continues. Organizations and individuals alike question the implementation and effectiveness of interpreted education. Individual interpreters and researchers share these concerns, and calls for evidence continue to be more common than relevant and reliable research.

ELIZABETH A. WINSTON

EFFORT MODELS

↑ COGNITIVE APPROACHES

The Effort Models are a set of MODELS of interpreting that center on cognitive effort and were designed to help students and practitioners understand recurring difficulties that could not be explained by lack of linguistic or extralinguistic knowledge alone. Their purpose was not to describe the interpreting process, but to highlight the theoretical and practical consequences of the limited availability of processing capacity (attentional resources) on the process.

The Effort Models were developed by Daniel Gile, initially for SIMULTANEOUS INTERPRETING (Gile 1983), on the basis of observation and introspection. Gile saw the main cause of difficulties encountered regularly by students and professionals in the limited availability of some kind of 'mental energy' required to perform the cognitive operations underlying interpreting. He posited three 'Efforts', one relating to COMPREHENSION of the source speech, one to the production of the target speech and one to the MEMORY storage and retrieval of information over short periods. He further assumed that requirements often exceeded the available 'energy' and that at other times they did not in absolute terms, but 'energy' management errors (such as devoting too much attention to production) led to an 'energy' deficit in one or several Efforts, resulting in errors, OMISSIONS and/or infelicities (EOIs).

Gile found support for his intuitive idea of a limited 'energy' in the cognitive psychology literature, which distinguished between automatic and controlled operations, the latter drawing on a limited supply of available processing capacity (also referred to as attentional resources). He also saw the need to add a 'Coordination Effort' to the three core Efforts to account for the management of attentional resources, in particular the allocation of attention to the various Efforts. Recent advances (Timarová et al. 2014) suggest that this Coordination Effort is particularly important.

Models

The original Effort Model for simultaneous interpreting (SI) between spoken languages comprised three Efforts – Listening and Analysis (L), Memory (M) and Production (P), later complemented by the Coordination Effort (C). The model was typically represented as: SI = L + M + P + C (Gile 1995a).

In order to accommodate SI from a signed language into a spoken language, the receptive Effort (in this case watching and analyzing the source speech) can be represented more broadly as 'R' (Reception): SI = R + M + P + C. The model for SI in the opposite direction, from a spoken language into a signed language, includes two additional components: 'Self-Management in Space', which refers to the interpreter's physical positioning and use of space to optimize source speech reception and visibility to the Deaf audience, and 'Online

Interaction with Deaf persons': SI = L + M + P + SMS + OID + C. The latter Effort (OID) corresponds to the need for the interpreter to attend to any signing by Deaf audience members, to each other or to the interpreter, while s/he is interpreting the spoken speech (see Pointurier-Pournin 2014).

The model for SIGHT INTERPRETING/TRANSLATION is similar to the one for SI into spoken languages (R + M + P + C). The Reception Effort in this case refers to the reading of the written source text. Production is assumed to require more conscious resistance against INTERFERENCE than in SI. In the model for SIMULTANEOUS WITH TEXT, the receptive component comprises both a Listening Effort and a Reading Effort: L + R + M + P + C.

The Effort Model for CONSECUTIVE INTERPRETING is divided into two parts, reflecting the two main phases of the process. Each includes a specific Effort relating to NOTE-TAKING: a Note Production Effort in the comprehension phase (L + M + NP + C) and a Note Reading Effort in the reformulation phase, which also comprises an Effort for speech reconstruction (SR) from memory (NR + SR + P + C).

In all the models, the receptive (L/R) and productive (P) Efforts are assumed to depend crucially on the interpreter's cognitive ability to access linguistic knowledge in long-term memory. This is captured in Gile's (1995a, 2009) Gravitational Model of Language Availability, which represents the cognitive availability of linguistic knowledge units (words, spelling, rules of grammar, stylistic rules, etc.) in terms of time and processing capacity requirements.

In cognitive terms, aside from the requirement of linguistic and extralinguistic knowledge, Gile (1995a, 2009) posits two necessary conditions for smooth interpreting: (1) at any time, the total required processing capacity for all active Efforts must not exceed the interpreter's total available capacity, and (2) at any time, the processing capacity available for any active Effort should be sufficient for performing the corresponding task.

Application

The relationships conceptualized in the Effort Models and the frequent EOIs observed in the field and reported in the literature led Gile (1999a) to the assumption that interpreters tend to work near the limit of their processing capacity, that is, close to 'saturation' ('close' meaning that any sudden increase in processing capacity requirements and any coordination error can disrupt the smooth operation of the process). This so-called 'Tightrope Hypothesis' accounts for EOIs presumably caused by 'problem triggers', that is, factors and conditions which increase processing capacity requirements or make the interpreter more vulnerable to attention lapses and attention management errors. Problem triggers include speeches with high information density and SPEECH RATE, enumerations, compound names, unfamiliar accents, poor voice quality, singular logic, non-standard lexical usage, syntactic complexity, interpreting between syntactically very different languages, lexical gaps and short words with little redundancy such as names and NUMBERS, as their information content can be difficult to recover in the case of any momentary lapse of attention in the Listening Effort.

Gile (1995a, 2009) also uses the Effort Models to analyze tactics used by interpreters to cope with the various problem triggers, in terms of their cognitive cost (in time and/or processing capacity), with implications for risks of saturation, including delayed saturation affecting a later segment. Such coping tactics include paraphrasing, generalization, deliberate omission, borrowing of the source-language term, consultation with a colleague in the booth, consultation of glossaries or other documents, referring the listeners to the information on a screen, etc. He also relates the selection of coping tactics to general priorities, referred to as 'laws': (1) the law of maximum information restitution; (2) the law of minimum cognitive interference with the restitution of segments other than the one being processed; (3) the law of maximum impact of the speech in the direction assumed to be desired by the speaker (under the speaker loyalty condition); (4) the law of least effort (assumed to be a natural tendency to save on effort, but not a desirable law, and in contradiction with the first three); and (5) the law of self-protection (face-saving), which, like the law of least effort, is deemed undesirable in terms of professional ETHICS.

The Effort Models have been used and referred to extensively by interpreters in both spoken and signed languages and by some psychologists (e.g. de Groot 2000; Bajo et al. 2001; Christoffels et al. 2003; Shreve & Diamond 1997). In line with their initial intended purpose, they have served as an explanatory conceptual framework, especially in a didactic environment, and as an analytical tool in empirical studies on interpreter training (e.g. Mead 2002b; Soler Caamaño 2006; Zhou 2010; Ersöz Demirdağ 2013). Moreover, they have been used to generate research hypotheses – mostly about problem triggers – for subsequent empirical testing (e.g. Mazza 2001; Cattaneo 2004; Puková 2006; Chen 2010). However, the Effort Models are not a theory in the strict sense of the word; they were designed as a conceptual framework to be intuitively comprehensible to non-specialists who could relate them to their personal experience, rather than for the purpose of exploring interpreting cognition. Nevertheless, if the COGNITIVE LOAD associated with comprehension, production and memory can be quantified online, for instance with pupillometric techniques, even a conceptual framework as simple as the Effort Models may have some potential for providing direct answers to research questions about problem triggers, the relative merit of interpreting tactics, and DIRECTIONALITY.

DANIEL GILE

EGYPT

↑ HISTORY

Interpreters feature very infrequently in the literature or epigraphic and documentary record of Egypt at any period, despite intensive contact with foreign states and populations, and, in later periods at least, considerable linguistic diversity within Egypt itself. As well as terminological problems in identifying individuals specifically as linguistic mediators, interpreters in Ancient Egypt seem to have experienced the same INVISIBILITY as those in many other historical contexts. Although some attention has been paid to Egyptian material by scholars in interpreting studies, some misconceptions require to be corrected, and some comparatively neglected evidence deserves to be given new prominence.

Egyptian literary and autobiographical texts describe many scenarios in which interpreting must have taken place, but without further information on the personnel and practices involved. (For English translations of the Egyptian texts cited here, see Lichtheim 1973–1980.) The tomb biographies of Weni and Harkhuf (Old Kingdom, c. 2649–2051 BCE) and Ahmose son of Abana (New Kingdom, c. 1550–1070 BCE), all of whom were active in Nubia or the Levant, contain no mention of foreign languages. In the Middle Kingdom *Tale of Sinuhe*, Sinuhe finds refuge after fleeing Egypt with the nomadic Retjenu chief Ammunenshi, who reassures him that he will "hear the language of Egypt." In the Late Egyptian *Report of Wenamun*, a fictional tale, Wenamun arrives at the island of Alasiya (Cyprus) and asks the assembled crowd whether any of them speaks Egyptian. An Egyptian-speaking bystander then acts as interpreter for Wenamun's conversation with the Princess of Alasiya. This interpreter is not referred to as such, and indeed is not mentioned again, with the remaining conversation being presented as unmediated speech.

Documentary sources, on the other hand, and in particular the Amarna Letters (diplomatic correspondence with Near Eastern kingdoms of the mid-fourteenth century BCE), make it clear that interpreters of foreign languages existed and were necessary in diplomacy, but appear not to have been accorded any well-defined or elevated STATUS as interpreters per se. This indeterminate position, in accordance with the common requirement that interpreters be 'invisible' in a transaction, is one of the reasons for the imprecision and semantic overlap of three Egyptian words with the root meanings of 'repeat', 'unravel' and 'be/speak foreign' (*whm*, *wh3* and ' or *3"*), which may be used in certain contexts to refer to interpreting of foreign languages. Given the reception of many outdated discussions of these terms in the interpreting studies literature, it should be emphasised that these expressions offer only an illusion of sociolinguistic precision, although their use does draw attention to wider questions of cultural and linguistic contact. Earlier linguistically informed studies of Egyptian interpreters (e.g. Hermann 1956; Kurz 1985) should be read in this light.

The only work to treat the subject of Egyptian terms for 'interpreter' at length is Bell (1976, see also 1973), which deals for the most part with individuals described as '(plural '.w) or *3"* in relations between Pharaonic Egypt, Nubia and Western Asia. The role of '.w is often ambiguous, difficult to separate from generic 'foreigners' or 'speakers of foreign languages', although earlier scholars, such as Gardiner (1915), translated the term fairly confidently as 'dragoman', and identified individuals such as Harkhuf, whose tomb biography was referred to above, as involved in language MEDIATION or its management. On reliefs from the Old Kingdom pyramid temple of Sahure at Abusir (c. 2480 BCE) depicting the arrival of boatloads of Asiatics, for example, some men on the boats, clean-shaven and wearing Egyptian wigs, have the caption '.w. Interpretations of this scene vary (Goedicke 1966), although the suggestion that these men were mediators, linguistic or otherwise, seems probable. A more clear-cut example is the depiction of foreigners on reliefs in the tomb of Horemheb at Saqqara (c. 1350 BCE), in which individuals in Egyptian dress are shown spatially in between the king and the assembled Asiatics, evidently relaying information. Linguistic mediation may be inferred, but cannot definitively be proven.

The Amarna Letters, New Kingdom records of diplomatic exchanges between the Egyptian court and various kingdoms of the Near East (Cohen & Westbrook 2000; Moran 1992), contain few references to interpreters and no direct references to written translation. The vast majority of the letters found at Amarna are from foreign powers, and are in Akkadian. (On interpreters in the languages of the Near East, see Gelb 1968.) There are, however, a couple of references in the Amarna Letters to interpreters who accompanied messengers between foreign rulers. Kind treatment of such messengers and interpreters showed respect for the kings whose representatives they were. In a friendly letter to Amenhotep IV, Tushratta of Mitanni makes a point of mentioning that "Mane, [my brother's] messenger, and Hane, my brother's interpre[ter], I have ex[alted] like gods. I have given [them] many presents and treated them very kindly, for their report was excellent" (*EA* 11, ll. 5–6, 9–20, trans. Moran 1992). The implication seems to be that messengers themselves did not speak the necessary foreign languages. Certainly, diplomacy in the Amarna period was facilitated by the use of Akkadian as a written LINGUA FRANCA and evidently, from the references to interpreters in the Amarna Letters, by the use of oral mediators rather than by widespread multilingualism among messenger-diplomats themselves.

In the fifth century BCE, the Greek historian Herodotos visited Egypt and recorded how an interpreter (*hermēneus*) had read for him hieroglyphs at the Great Pyramid at Giza. He also provides an insight into the near-contemporary training of interpreters between Greeks and Egyptians, in his account of how king Psammetichos (663–610 BCE) sent Egyptian boys to the Greek city of Naukratis in the Nile Delta to learn Greek and form the nucleus of a new professional class. There is no further evidence of Herodotos' corps of interpreters elsewhere, but the tale suggests an awareness, on the part of some in Egypt, that good interpreters required a long period of language immersion to prepare them for their role.

After the conquest of Egypt by Alexander the Great in 332 BCE, connections with the rest of the Mediterranean world intensified. Egypt was ruled first by a Greek dynasty, the Ptolemies, who encouraged large-scale Greek immigration, and then by ROME. References to interpreters in historical and documentary source material, however, continue to be few and far between. Cleopatra VII, the last Ptolemaic ruler of Egypt, is said to have been able to converse in the languages of her subjects without the need for an interpreter (Plutarch, *Life of Antony*). Although this implies that her predecessors did make use of interpreters, these are invisible in our extant sources.

RACHEL MAIRS

E-LEARNING

↑ PEDAGOGY, ↑ TECHNOLOGY

In the context of interpreter EDUCATION, e-learning refers to teaching and learning interpreting using electronic devices. Such devices include computers (notebooks, tablets) and smartphones, with Internet and intranet connections; television may also be involved through a telecommunications network, a satellite connection, or even a telephone link. This form of PEDAGOGY is often used in situations where the teacher and students are not in the same physical location. It can also be used as a means of supplementing face-to-face teaching and learning, referred to as blended learning.

Teaching interpreting – in any of its MODES – usually comprises two major components, namely, conveying and fostering knowledge, and interpreting practice. In any attempt to teach interpreting online, the biggest challenge usually lies in teaching interpreting *per se*, due to its interactive nature. Interpreting can be taught in synchronous or asynchronous modes. In the former, teaching and learning take place instantaneously as if the teacher and students were in the same location; in the latter, they do not take place at the same time. In addition, teaching and learning can involve either visual contact, where the teacher and students can see each other (e.g. videoconferencing), or sound only (e.g. teleconferencing). There are also other ways of teaching interpreting online, such as self-study or guided self-study, supplemented by certain forms of face-to-face and/or online teaching and/or tutoring (e.g. Moeketsi & Wallmach 2005; Blasco Mayor & Jiménez Ivars 2007).

E-learning is feasible and can be as effective as face-to-face learning. However, it usually takes time for both the teacher and students to adapt to this new pedagogical mode. In particular, it may take students more time to improve their interpreting skills to a level comparable with those acquired in face-to-face contact. However, the more time students spend learning online, the more resilient they will become. An empirical study on training interpreters via teleconferencing and telephone found that online students could eventually perform as well as those learning through a face-to-face mode, after a sufficient period of training (Ko 2008).

An e-learning scenario often involves a combination of a variety of devices and software – for instance, the use of computers and Internet as the main media, supplemented by mobile phones; the use of teleconferencing and telephone, supplemented by email communication; or the use of television, together with other means of communication. Also, depending on teaching and training needs, an e-learning scenario can involve different interpreting practice set-ups, such as live DIALOGUE INTERPRETING in small groups, CONSECUTIVE INTERPRETING, SIGHT TRANSLATION/INTERPRETING in which interpreters are provided with a written text for perusal, and SIMULTANEOUS INTERPRETING. Different combinations of devices used in diversified interpreting SETTINGS will have their respective advantages, constraints and challenges.

Using modern computers with video cameras and the Internet can enable the teacher and students to see and hear each other. For instance, in an online teaching experiment using computers and Internet (Chen & Ko 2010; Ko & Chen 2011), a virtual lecture theatre and separate classroom or booths, equipped with the necessary instruction and communication tools such as a whiteboard and instant text message facility, were created to achieve synchronous teaching and learning. In such an environment, the teacher and students are able to see and hear each other as if in a physical classroom or language lab; the teacher can arrange for students to practise interpreting individually, in pairs, in groups or as a class, without interfering with each other; the teacher can visit a particular group of students; lectures and students' practice can be recorded; and the teacher can assess students' practice online. However, such a setting poses a number of constraints. For example, it is impossible to write brief notes on the written text on the normal computer screen for sight translation purposes; when monitoring students' interpreting practice in small groups, it takes time for the teacher to switch from one group to another because of delays in network connection; visual interaction is limited due to the size of the computer screen; and, depending on the technologies used, some delays in communication may be experienced.

The basic technology of teleconferencing and telephone has the advantage of being accessible to most people, including those in remote areas, but it often precludes the option of visual interaction, which is usually considered important for interpreting and interpreter training. Students learning in an environment without visual interaction tend to perform less satisfactorily in terms of paralinguistic skills than those who learn face-to-face (Ko 2008). Television is a readily available medium that provides a visual image, but it is almost impossible to arrange interactive interpreting practice using TV.

In any case, the use of e-learning in interpreter training requires special consideration of specific training needs, the technical devices and software to be used, and possible constraints and challenges.

LEONG KO

ENGLISH AS A LINGUA FRANCA

↑ LINGUA FRANCA

English is the first language that has been used as a LINGUA FRANCA on a global scale across continents, domains, and social strata. As a means of cross-lingual and cross-cultural communication, it has come to be used in global business, international politics, science, technology, the media, and so forth. As a consequence, native speakers of English are far outnumbered by non-native speakers. Carrying forward his 2003 analysis of "English as a Global Language" in a 2012 lecture, David Crystal estimated that one third of the world's population speaks English; since native speakers account for a total of 400 million, there are now five non-native speakers for every native speaker.

Although the use of English as a lingua franca (ELF) dates back centuries, its unparalleled expansion is a recent phenomenon spurred on by the rise in popularity of the Internet in the mid-1990s. The *study* of ELF started in the 1980s with a few small-scale exploratory studies, then picked up rapidly in the 1990s, growing into a full-blown research discipline with annual conferences since 2008, the establishment of the de Gruyter *Journal of English as a Lingua Franca* in 2012, as well as monographs and doctoral studies. Research topics include the phonology of ELF, attitudes and ideologies, conceptual issues and general processes, academic English, Asian Englishes, and implications for the teaching and learning of English as a foreign language (EFL).

The study of interpreting (and translation) in relation to ELF is even younger. Initial research focused on the effect of non-native speakers' ACCENT on the interpreter's task (e.g. McAllister 2000; Kurz 2008). More recent work has considered the wider impact of ELF on interpreting and interpreter-mediated communication (e.g. Albl-Mikasa 2010, 2013b). Reithofer (2010, 2013) compared source-speech comprehension among conference participants listening to the non-native English original or to a simultaneous interpretation into their mother tongue, and found a significant benefit of SI even when listeners shared the same technical background as the non-native speaker.

Based on different aims and assumptions, ELF researchers and interpreting scholars have approached the topic of ELF from different angles. Against the backdrop of the deficit view of the EFL paradigm, a major driving force of research into ELF (sometimes also called Global English or International English) is an emancipatory effort to liberate the majority of the world's English speakers from the unattainable target model of the native speaker gold standard upheld by vested ELT (English Language Teaching) interests, and to shift the focus from correctness to appropriateness. A conceptual reorientation, reflecting the realities of globalized communication in the twenty-first century, has brought recognition of ELF as a legitimate use of English in its own right, independent of native speaker norms, and as an asset to international communication, with corpus-based studies of spoken ELF to substantiate the argument (Mauranen 2012; Seidlhofer 2011).

ELF researchers thus stress the successful nature of ELF communication on the basis of creative appropriation of linguistic resources, co-constructive meaning negotiation, and effective interactional strategies. By contrast, interpreting analysts take a more critical stance towards ELF, with most attention focusing on interpreting in international conference settings. Issues of concern relate to both the *macro* level of professional markets and the *micro* level of the interpreter's processing task.

At the macro level, the increasing use of ELF in conferences impacts the demand for professional interpreting services. The use of 'English only' obviously makes ELF and interpreting mutually exclusive. More importantly, the multilingual conferencing typical of the twentieth century, with interpreting provided into and out of a range of languages, is giving way to events with only one booth for retour interpreting between English and the language of the host country or of political choice.

At the micro level, the use of ELF tends to add to interpreters' COGNITIVE LOAD, mainly in the COMPREHENSION phase. The ever-increasing variety of foreign accents, with features transferred from source speakers' first languages and highly uneven levels of proficiency, can make heavy demands on the interpreters' processing and impede fundamental processes such as INFERENCING and ANTICIPATION as well as the retrieval of translation equivalents and transfer routines (Albl-Mikasa 2013b). Interpreters may consequently experience ELF as disruptive, insufficient, and counter-productive to communication, and speak disparagingly of 'BSE' (bad simple English), and 'Globish'. Even so, they are developing strategies for coping with the various challenges arising from the use of ELF (e.g. Chang & Wu 2014).

A number of ELF-induced problems can be put down to the specific processing conditions in interpreter-mediated communicative events. Most importantly, SIMULTANEOUS INTERPRETING of monologic speech does not allow for the co-constructive, interactional strategies typically employed in conversational ELF encounters. But even in DIALOGUE INTERPRETING, pragmatic moves like 'let-it-pass' (i.e. treating incomprehensible elements of the speaker's discourse as inconsequential) are not a viable option for interpreters, whereas resorting to interruption and clarification questions can impact the interpreter's credibility and the dynamics of the interaction. Thus, what is described by ELF scholars as supporting successful ELF communication often renders the interpreter's task more difficult.

MICHAELA ALBL-MIKASA

EPIC

see under CORPUS-BASED RESEARCH

EPISTEMOLOGY

→ METHODOLOGY, → PARADIGMS

Largely an empirical discipline, INTERPRETING STUDIES is positioned within the social ('human') sciences (Pöchhacker 2011b), since the activity of interpreting lies in a linguistic-cognitive domain and is essentially social in nature (Monacelli 2009). The various PARADIGMS of interpreting studies are, for the most part, shaped by frameworks that existed before the discipline charted its own scientific territory, and by cross-fertilization from other disciplines, as reflected in particular in COGNITIVE APPROACHES, DISCOURSE ANALYTICAL APPROACHES and SOCIOLOGICAL APPROACHES. These multiple disciplinary perspectives on interpreting, and the multi-faceted nature of the object of study, with its different MODES and SETTINGS, have given rise to a vast array of MODELS as well as diverse theoretical perspectives and methodological approaches. Though questions of epistemology (i.e. the nature of knowledge and ways of acquiring it) have received little explicit attention in interpreting studies, the discipline's epistemological basis has also been constructed by the way the research community has valued different types of METHODOLOGY.

After initial research efforts in the paradigm of experimental psychology, the study of interpreting was first positioned within a socio-cognitive framework by the PARIS SCHOOL (Seleskovitch 1975; García-Landa 1995), whose INTERPRETIVE THEORY (IT) dominated the discipline for nearly two decades.

Criticism leveled at the IT paradigm concerned its introspection and speculative theorizing (Gile 1990) and led to a neo-positivist reorientation advocated by champions of empirical research. Moser-Mercer (1994a) called for productive interaction between these two distinct research perspectives, which she labeled as the "liberal arts community" and the "natural science paradigm", but there has been little or no such interaction, even after similar appeals from interpreting scholars (e.g. Gile 2001c; Shlesinger 2001) in answer to the initiative by Chesterman and Arrojo (2000) to find "shared ground in Translation Studies".

The neo-positivist trend was ultimately called into question by a post-positivist research perspective which problematized an objective reality and the notion of natural data. This postmodern orientation, and constructivist and phenomenological epistemologies, in particular, hold that data are not a 'given' but are 'taken' by the analyst (Chesterman & Arrojo 2000) with a specific research stance.

On this basis, interpreting scholars further explored the social domain by examining systemic aspects of how interpreting is effected in relation to the social context in which it takes place, but also of how the social context is affected by the provision of interpreting (e.g. Diriker 2004; Inghilleri 2003). More recently, Pöchhacker (2011b) reviewed some basic ontological issues and suggested that interpreting studies may be best served by a constructivist epistemology, given the multiple interpretive ('sense-making') procedures involved in its object of study. Several scholars have notably drawn on various schools of constructivist thought: Monacelli (2000) uses it to formulate an approach to research, Rudvin (2006) describes interpreters constructing meaning in COMMUNITY INTERPRETING, and Grbić (2008) explores QUALITY as a social construct.

Overall, changes in the epistemological stance taken within interpreting studies, from introspective to empiricist to constructivist, have mirrored the paradigm shift under way in several branches of science that are concerned with socially situated human intellectual activity.

CLAUDIA MONACELLI

EQUIVALENT EFFECT

see under COMMUNICATIVE EFFECT

ERROR ANALYSIS

↑ ASSESSMENT
→ ACCURACY
↓ OMISSIONS

Error analysis can be considered a tool for the ASSESSMENT of an interpreter's performance with regard to the standard of ACCURACY and completeness. It is used in both PEDAGOGY and research, and focuses on the interpreted text as the product of the interpreting process. There is considerable conceptual overlap between such error categories as OMISSIONS and additions and interpreting STRATEGIES, and several authors have sought to distinguish between intentional and unintentional deviations from the source text (e.g. Napier 2002, 2004b).

The first and perhaps best-known attempt at classifying 'departures' from the source text was made by Henri Barik in his pioneering PhD thesis in 1969. As suggested in the title of one of his publications, "A description of various types of omissions, additions and errors of translation encountered in simultaneous interpretation" (Barik 1971), Barik suggests a distinction between omissions and additions on the one hand and errors on the other. In fact, according to Barik's taxonomy, some cases of omission and addition seem to fall under the umbrella of errors, since some types of omission are said to cause "loss of meaning", while some types of addition introduce "some new meaning or relationship to what is being said". Moreover, Barik's taxonomy of "substitutions and errors" comprises five categories of "combination of omission and addition" (Barik 1971: 201–204). This clearly shows that category boundaries are loose and permeable, indicating a lack of precise definition and thus a degree of methodological uncertainty.

In a study investigating student performances, Altman (1994) identifies four categories of error: omission, addition, inaccurate rendition of individual lexical items and inaccurate rendition of longer phrases. Each of these categories includes various types of error, whose seriousness is determined by measuring – or speculating on – "the extent to which they affect the communicative impact of the speaker's message" (1994: 30). Altman focuses on the communication process, stressing the importance of considering contextual and situational factors when identifying interpreter errors. This represents a great advance in error analysis, as it enables the researcher to distinguish between omissions involving complete or partial loss of an idea and those which simply eliminate redundancies.

Falbo (2002) highlights methodological problems deriving from the lack of a clear-cut distinction between the three phases of error analysis, namely error detection and classification, error evaluation – that is, degree of criticality – and identification of the cause. She argues that this methodological fuzziness leads to significant confusion and an unnecessary proliferation of error categories/subcategories, with researchers often relying on their own subjective evaluation to classify and assess errors. Limiting her focus to the identification and classification of errors, Falbo offers a new, two-level model of analysis in which the original and the interpreted text are considered products of a given communicative event. In line with the target orientation of functionalist translation theory (e.g. Pöchhacker 1994b), the interpretation is investigated, on a first level of analysis, as an independent text addressed to a given group of users, and analysed in terms of COHERENCE and target-language COHESION. On the second level, the analysis focuses on the relationship between the original and the interpreted text in terms of information content. Analysis at this level is deliberately not concerned with the target-language formulation, which is part of the first level of analysis. In the case of addition, for instance, its identification is based not on linguistic categories but on the presence of information in the interpreted text for which no trace can be found in the original. Cross-checking the results of the first and second levels of analysis can help shed light on certain errors, for which it would otherwise be difficult to see any apparent reason: it may become clear, for instance, that an error of coherence identified at the first level of analysis is caused by even slight divergence from the content of the original text, corresponding to an error of translation such as a *faux ami* or to some other type of INTERFERENCE.

A step forward in error analysis is represented by Wadensjö's (1998) work on DIALOGUE INTERPRETING, which explicitly factors in various aspects of interaction. Interpreter utterances, viewed as reformulations of prior original utterances, are categorized as different types of rendition (e.g. close, expanded, reduced, substituted).

Error analysis has been applied to research on interpreting in various SETTINGS. In HEALTHCARE INTERPRETING, the analysis often consists in more traditional "error coding" (e.g. Flores et al. 2003; Gany et al. 2007), with some of the "linguistic errors" (additions, omissions or substitutions) categorized more specifically as "medical errors", that is, linguistic errors involving medical information. The latter are assessed in terms of their clinical relevance, that is, the extent to which they are likely to affect clinical decision-making and outcomes.

CATERINA FALBO

ETHICS

↑ PROFESSION
→ ROLE
↓ FIDELITY, ↓NEUTRALITY

Ethics is a branch of moral philosophy that seeks to establish principles of fairness or justice (or right and wrong behaviour). Professional ethics, expressed in rules guiding the exercise of a particular occupation, are considered a hallmark of its professional status, alongside mastery of the relevant skills and knowledge and the ability to apply them in real-life situations. Principles of professional ethics are typically set out in codes of ethics, or conduct, and/or standards of practice to which members of a PROFESSION are bound. The moral tenets prevailing in codes of ethics can be expected to vary according to the *ethos* (customs, habits) of different periods and cultures, and especially in interpretations of how they should apply to specific dilemmas and situations. Some ethical principles, such as attorney–client privilege or patient–doctor confidentiality, are upheld by law or by the conventions of employing institutions. In self-regulated professions like translation and interpreting, standards of ethics and conduct depend on a consensus among members but may contribute to enhancing the profession's STATUS and the TRUST placed in it by its users.

Proposals in the literature for an ethics of translation, as well as the already numerous published codes, reflect a fairly consistent set of principles. Aside from general moral values such as truthfulness, honesty and trustworthiness, these include precepts such as FIDELITY (or faithfulness), NEUTRALITY, impartiality, loyalty, clarity and transparency. Chesterman (2001) proposes a 'Hieronymic oath' (from Saint Jerome, the patron of translation) based on key values such as truth, clarity, and trust, all subservient to understanding, to guide the value judgments that generate appropriate translation decisions. A common theme in countering pressures to reduce translation to a mechanistic function is the recognition of the translator/ interpreter as a decision-making agent, who must commit to strive for excellence or fairness in applying precepts like fidelity or loyalty in practice. Accordingly, leading theorists have placed loyalty to the profession, or to oneself (i.e. the translator's own ethical judgment and responsibility), above loyalty to the immediate demands of the client or audience. Prunč (1997, 2008) goes further by justifying withdrawal or termination of service when clients seek to deny the interpreter's autonomy to make ethical judgments, and calls on translators to work actively towards establishing a 'democratic translation culture' that would recognise the equal rights of all participants to exchanges, including interpreters. Interestingly, having insisted on the agency of the translator or interpreter, some authors lean toward a preventive rather than interventionist approach, aimed at minimising mis-communication or avoiding the collapse of trust (Chesterman 1997a), or providing enough coordination to ensure that communication is on track, rather than seeking to guarantee it (Wadensjö 1998).

The most complex and widely debated aspects of ethics in interpreting concern the inter-related issues of the nature, boundaries and flexibility of the interpreter's ROLE; the question of his or her neutrality (impartiality); possible hierarchies of interpreter 'loyalty' (e.g. to speaker vs. listener vs. paying client, patient vs. doctor, court vs. defendant, welfare or asylum applicant vs. authorities, etc.); the nature of the fidelity to speakers' messages that users may expect (e.g. to what extent the interpreter should aim to reproduce the tone, style, word choice and mood of the source speech – and even the content); the commitment to provide a quality service (implying justifiable demands for appropriate WORKING CONDITIONS and access to relevant information for PREPARATION); the obligations of access to privileged information (confidentiality vs. potentially overriding moral imperatives); the interpreter's 'visibility' and the extent and nature of the MEDIATION and/or related service s/he may or should provide; and of course, perhaps most controversially, the interpreter's neutrality, impartiality or 'loyalty' in offering the same or different services, or quality of service, to different stakeholders (e.g. clients and/or participants in the exchange). On the whole, positions on ethics in interpreting have ranged from a more universalist statement of a few general principles deemed capable of straightforward application (as in CONFERENCE INTERPRETING), through the recognition of possible variations according to setting, situation, or the needs of participants (as in COMMUNITY INTERPRETING) to more open-ended and relativistic attitudes.

Available knowledge on the HISTORY of interpreting suggests that, in most times and places, interpreters have probably lacked either an external framework to ratify their neutrality or independent guidelines on how to negotiate and explain their role. Explicit prescriptions seem to take shape when the function gains in importance, as at times of suddenly increased international contacts. In the sixteenth century, SPAIN enacted strict rules on interpreter neutrality for its colonial administration (Giambruno 2008); the rise of multilateralism in the mid-twentieth century saw the birth of a conference interpreting profession, represented globally by AIIC, with its own code of ethics and professional conduct (AIIC 2012); and more recently, at national level, the growing recognition of linguistic rights in healthcare and the judicial system has led to the emergence of a range of detailed codes in several countries. A pioneering role was played in this regard by the US Registry of Interpreters for the Deaf (RID) and its influential code of ethics for sign language interpreters, subsequently reissued as the NAD-RID Code of Professional Conduct (RID 2005). In HEALTHCARE INTERPRETING, a noteworthy example is the formulation of ethical principles by the California Healthcare Interpreting Association (CHIA 2002), which have also been the subject of empirical research (Angelelli 2007).

Common and near-universal principles

There is no one governing body or unified code of ethics for all interpreters across all sectors, but certain commonalities can be found. In the largest survey of existing codes yet conducted, Bancroft (2005) identifies five (near-)universal or widespread ethical principles. Of these, three – COMPETENCE, integrity and confidentiality – are fairly clear-cut, while two others – neutrality and fidelity – are more complex and controversial. Finally, *transparency* has been put forward as a key principle in recent literature, although it appears only obliquely in the wording of existing codes.

All professions aspire to *competence* and *integrity*, and they apply across all sectors and SETTINGS of interpreting. Competence entails a commitment to maintaining high standards of performance, and requires the interpreter to ensure that s/he has the requisite skills and knowledge (which entails preparing assignments, and declining any assignment for which s/he is not qualified, or will not have time to prepare) and adequate working conditions, including access to relevant information and documentation. Integrity includes honesty (avoiding or declaring conflicts of interest, and deriving no personal gain from information obtained in the exercise of the profession); responsibility (e.g. not cancelling bookings without cause); solidarity (cooperating and sharing knowledge with colleagues, supporting beginners, affording colleagues moral assistance and collegiality); and refusing any job or situation which might detract from the dignity of the profession or bring it into disrepute.

Confidentiality is universally recognised as a cornerstone of professional ethics for interpreters across all sectors and settings, albeit subject as elsewhere to legal constraints (such as the obligation to report criminal activity) or to a higher moral imperative, such as the duty to save lives. The emphasis placed on confidentiality in many codes reflects its vulnerability to pressure – for example, from the media, but also potentially from the interpreter's employers.

Surveys of published codes have found some variation in the degree of emphasis on the interpreter's responsibility to the speaker (ACCURACY, impartiality, confidentiality), to themselves (in defining their own role, for example), or to the profession (conduct, solidarity) (Hale 2007). In particular, there are significant differences in this respect across the main settings and branches of interpreting (Bancroft 2005). The strictest prescriptions on impartiality, especially with regard to fidelity (sometimes rather narrowly defined), are found in codes for legal interpreters, while the debate on neutrality is liveliest in community interpreting. The AIIC Code of Professional Ethics for conference interpreters stresses competence and confidentiality, but does not specifically address neutrality or fidelity. Detailed regulations in the area of working conditions (information, access, equipment, team composition and strength, working hours, user cooperation, autonomy, dignity, privacy, copyright) are laid down in a separate document – the AIIC Professional Standards.

As in any prescriptive project, the difficulty of formulating ethical rules of conduct for interpreters stems, firstly, from the wide variety of situations in which the profession is practised – from highly regulated and codified settings such as an intergovernmental organisation or a court of law, through less structured events like business negotiations or counselling sessions, to the urgency and chaos of crisis and conflict situations – and secondly, from the wide variation in the status, needs and POWER of participants.

Accordingly, the liveliest debate over such principles is focused on community interpreting, which is currently at the cusp of an effort towards greater codification of interpreting practice, but is also a locus of wide variation in the nature and structure of mediated encounters and the situations and status of their participants. In a survey of community interpreters, Hale (2007) found support in principle for guidelines, but widespread indifference or scepticism towards codes, which some respondents dismissed as too general or simplistic, or useless in solving ethical dilemmas in practice. Because of this variation, the debate has come to focus on the freedom of the interpreter to exercise judgment and take initiatives. Tate and Turner (1997/2002) found that sign language interpreters in the UK often override the literal prescriptions of their code of practice, using their own judgment and 'intervening' in different ways (e.g. to clarify or correct misunderstandings). To meet these practitioners' need for articulated guidelines, Tate and Turner propose an evolving 'case law' annex that would codify good new solutions found to dilemmas not adequately covered by the Code. Cokely (2000) goes further by advocating a 'rights-based' approach, focusing on interpreters' decision-making freedom rather than on prescriptions and limitations. Other authors have called for greater empowerment of public service interpreters, notably in legal settings (Mikkelson 1998), while Hale (2007) concludes that codes can only offer general guidance, and that ethical practice must be instilled chiefly through training.

Morality, conscience and individual preference

It is generally accepted that, like other professionals, interpreters may decline assignments not only for 'craft' reasons (inadequate conditions or qualification) but also on moral and ethical grounds – for example, refusing or terminating service that might benefit criminal activities or contribute directly to suffering or endangering life (Prunč 2012a). However, conflicting positions are possible on the morality of interpreting objectionable content. Refusing to interpret a speaker who denies the Holocaust or another documented genocide, or whose remarks may be deemed to incite racial hatred, would be vindicated by law in some countries. Prunč even justifies subversion of the message in extreme cases (totalitarianism). On the other hand, it can be argued that transparency requires exposing such views. To resolve this, Setton and Dawrant (2016) propose that such material may and sometimes should be interpreted in a context that publicises these views and allows counter-argument (as, for instance, in properly constituted legal proceedings), but not a political rally with only supporters present. Finally, some adversarial situations, such as interrogations in CONFLICT ZONES, may severely constrain the interpreter's ability to work ethically.

Some authors have highlighted the difficulty of interpreter neutrality vis-à-vis a broader ambient bias such as dominant IDEOLOGY, and a growing trend questions the possibility of the interpreter's full neutrality in any setting (e.g. Angelelli 2004b). Pöchhacker (2006a) provides historical examples of the ideological instrumentalisation of interpreters that have been downplayed or ignored. Buck (2002) observes that in the modern, globalised world, most interpreting in international settings is done from English, and that users of that language are thus favoured in representing and articulating their belief systems and goals, posing the risk of interpreters being "relegated to mere localisers of dominant ideologies." Similarly, in an era of competing models of globalisation, conference interpreters have been described as working mostly in the service of the First World and of geopolitically powerful industrialized nations (Cronin 2002; Pöchhacker 2006a).

If it is acknowledged that, given the wide variety of interpreting situations and settings, a few generic principles are inadequate to guide ethical practice, and that the interpreter must often exercise judgment, the focus shifts to possible checks on the interpreter's agency The attention given to USER EXPECTATIONS, conventions of service provision, and the requirement for 'ratification' are all consistent with upholding a principle of transparency, requiring the interpreter to do his/her best to ensure that all parties to the communication understand the interpreter's role and status as well as the service expected. This addresses the minimal duty of 'not deceiving' the user. A proactive transparency, however, defined by Prunč (2008) as openness and clarity about the translator's premises, strategies and choices, can contribute to meeting all the key ethical precepts. More generally, transparency has the potential to serve the higher-level values of clarity, truth, trust and understanding identified by Chesterman (1997a) as underlying a professional ethics of translation and interpreting.

ROBIN SETTON AND ERICH PRUNČ

ETHNOGRAPHIC METHODS

↑ METHODOLOGY
↓ INTERVIEWS

Ethnography is defined as "the art and science of describing a group or a culture" (Fetterman 1998), with the aim of identifying typical patterns of behavior that can be observed over time. For this purpose ethnographers use specific research designs, data collection techniques, tools for analysis and writing styles (LeCompte & Schensul 1999), with fieldwork as the core of the methodological approach. In interpreting studies, the term 'ethnographic methods' is often employed in a broader sense to refer to qualitative methods used in the social sciences, such as INTERVIEWS and participant or non-participant observation. When 'ethnography' is used in interpreting research, it generally refers to the ethnography of communication (Saville-Troike 2003), which is considered as a branch of sociolinguistics closely related to ethnomethodology (an approach from sociology dealing with questions of social order, organization and interactions mediated through language).

Within interpreting studies, loose conceptions of ethnography/ethnographic methods tend to confuse these with other research approaches such as case studies (Hale & Napier 2013, Ch. 4). Originating in the social sciences, case study is designed to answer a research question on one specific phenomenon, typically using qualitative techniques. The aim of ethnographies, whose origins are in anthropology, is in fact very different, the aim being to learn about the ways of being and doing of cultural groups or discourse communities. Ethnography does not begin with a question, but is triggered by a problem, a theory or a model.

Ethnographic fieldwork and data analysis

The most important part of ethnographic fieldwork is being present, to observe and absorb, and to ask what may, on the surface, appear to be naïve questions that are nevertheless apt to yield insightful responses. Ethnographers endeavor to have an open mind about their object of study (group or culture) and to keep their research designs flexible enough to accommodate and pursue lines of inquiry that may open up as fieldwork evolves, while still being rigorous in their work. They begin their journey by acknowledging biases and preconceived notions about the object of study, and guard against their negative effects by adopting control mechanisms such as triangulation, contextualization and non-judgmental orientation. Data collection from members of the group/culture being studied may involve such methods as participant/non-participant observation, ethnographic interviews and documentary/artifact analysis.

Gaining trust is an important part of ethnography, as it is the ticket to entering the community of participants on whom the study will be based. This is also referred to as 'gaining entry'. Once entry is gained, fieldwork varies in length. Shorter ethnographic studies average around six months, while the longest last up to two years (Fetterman 1998). Given the vast amount of data ethnographers collect in a variety of forms, such as field notes, recordings, transcripts and artifacts, the task of analyzing them and reporting on results is no less challenging than the fieldwork. In addition, data analysis and writing do not begin only after data collection has been completed; rather, reflection and meta-analysis are a constant part of the ethnographic method. Using structural or constitutive analysis, often with the help of software for cataloguing, organizing and coding data, ethnographers link together and find consistent relationships among components and structures. They may assemble constituents deductively (top-down), inductively (bottom-up) or in some combination of both, moving back and forth. The perspective researchers use to interpret and present data lies along a continuum between 'etic' (outsider) and 'emic' (insider) (Van Maanen 2011).

Examples

In interpreting studies, qualitative methods of data collection (e.g. observation, INTERVIEWS, focus groups) and data analysis (using mainly DISCOURSE ANALYTICAL APPROACHES) have become increasingly widespread and are sometimes referred to as ethnographic methods. However, ethnographies which look beyond the level of interaction are rare. Angelelli (2004a) stands out as a full-fledged ethnography of HEALTHCARE INTERPRETING, expanding on the work of researchers such as Metzger (1999), Davidson (2000) and Bolden (2000), who used mainly discourse analytical methods to study the interpreter's ROLE in medical settings. Angelelli's ethnography includes data from the community, the hospital and the language service unit of a public health institution in California, her key informants being ten interpreters and their manager. The study provides insight into the complexities of medical interpreting and draws on concepts from social theory, sociology and linguistic anthropology. The data, collected over a period of 22 months, comprise artifacts, field notes, participant and non-participant observations, semi-structured interviews, surveys and naturalistic data related to 392 interpreted communicative events (interpreter-mediated provider–patient interactions), and recursive analysis was carried out over a period of three years. Close attention was also paid to negative evidence, meaning behaviors or occurrences apparently inconsistent with the construct of a visible interpreter that emerged from the data.

Among the earliest ethnographic work on COMMUNITY INTERPRETING is the study by Kaufert and Koolage (1984) on role conflicts among native Canadian interpreters, for which the researchers collected data in two hospitals over a period of eighteen months. Using participant observation and analysis of videotaped clinical consultations, they saw interpreters under pressure to serve as language interpreters and culture brokers as well as patient advocates. The fieldwork underlying the discourse analytical study by Davidson (2000) included a 'linguistic ethnography' of a Californian hospital, for which the researcher used ethnographic methods such as participant observation, interviews and audio-recording of 50 clinical interactions. Davidson also carried out a language survey and identified the types of interpreter (professional, family, staff member) used in some 70 interpreted encounters during a given week.

A paradigm case of ethnographic work in legal settings is the pioneering study by Berk-Seligson (1990) on COURTROOM INTERPRETING. The researcher conducted daily non-participant observations in nine different courthouses over a seven-month period. This resulted in over 100 hours of audio-recorded judicial proceedings, complemented by interviews with the 18 interpreters and the lawyers involved.

Another large-scale ethnographic study which focuses on interpreting while crossing over from educational linguistics is the work of Valdés, Chávez, Angelelli et al. (2000) on young Spanish/English bilinguals and their ability to translate and interpret for their families and immediate communities. For five years the research team followed 25 youngsters as they brokered communication (face-to-face, on the phone as well as performing SIGHT INTERPRETING/ TRANSLATION) in their homes, schools, community centers, playgroups, etc. Aside from non-participant observations of such CHILD LANGUAGE BROKERING in the various contexts, researchers interviewed family and community members about their communicative needs, and bilingual youngsters about their experiences and perceptions.

Ethnographic research is not abundant, and interpreting studies is no exception. The likely reasons for this scarcity include the complexity of the task (gaining entry, finding a speech community that will remain stable over time, etc.), the methodological skills required, and the necessary commitment of time and funding. As a unique way to study inter-linguistic/cultural phenomena within bilingual communities or communities of practice, ethnographic fieldwork nevertheless holds great potential for gaining deeper insight into the ways of speaking of interpreters and the communities in and for which they work.

CLAUDIA V. ANGELELLI

EXPERIMENTAL RESEARCH

↑ METHODOLOGY

→ COGNITIVE APPROACHES

Among scientific methods, experiments are the most powerful means of establishing a causal relationship. This approach to explanation is based on isolating one factor or construct (the 'independent variable') and measuring its effect on another (the 'dependent variable'), while controlling for the influence of so-called 'confounds'. An experiment in the strict sense, or 'true experiment', requires a manipulation of the independent variable as well as randomization – that is, the random assignment of participants to different conditions or groups (Creswell 2003). More loosely defined, an experiment – as opposed to 'naturalistic' inquiry – means that the researcher makes something happen in order to observe the consequences. Experimental designs used in research on interpreting tend to fall between the strict and wide definitions, and would most commonly be labeled as 'pre-experiments' or 'quasi-experiments' (see Liu 2011).

Experimental research has long been part of the methodological tradition of INTERPRETING STUDIES. During what Gile (1994) calls the 'experimental psychology period' in the 1960s and early 1970s, when scholars of cognitive psychology and psycholinguistics showed interest in SIMULTANEOUS INTERPRETING (SI), experiments were often their method of choice. As their main interest was in the structures and processes underlying interpreting as a cognitive task, SI was often examined in the same way language processing was studied in a laboratory. This generated considerable controversy over issues of experimental research design in interpreting, many of which continue to plague the field today.

Typical of the experimental method, the objects of study chosen (e.g. noise, SPEECH RATE, text types) were operationalized into quantifiable independent variables to be manipulated in controlled conditions. For example, GERVER (1969) manipulated the speed of a source language speech to be delivered at five distinct speech rates so as to observe the effects of higher input rates on a group of professional interpreters' performance in SI. Such designs have been questioned for being artificial, and thus deemed to lack ecological validity. Moreover, some of the dependent variables used in these studies (e.g. TIME LAG, types of OMISSIONS or errors) have been criticized for not reflecting the QUALITY of the interpreter's output and use of STRATEGIES. Barik's (1975) categorization of what he observed as 'translation departures' (i.e. omissions, additions and substitutions) is a case in point.

Another criticism that experiments on interpreting often receive is the use of interpreting students or non-interpreter bilinguals instead of professional interpreters as participants. Although the concerns raised are often considered to be about ecological validity, the issue is actually one of population validity, that is, the generalizability of research findings to the target population (e.g. professional interpreters).

Attaining population validity requires random selection of the sample from the population, which is rarely achieved in research on interpreters. Added to the lack of random sampling is the problem of small sample sizes, as researchers find it difficult to recruit professionals willing to make themselves available and have their performance scrutinized under controlled conditions.

With small samples, usually drawn as convenience samples from available volunteers, it is helpful to have as homogeneous a group as possible. This too, however, is almost impossible to achieve. Participants in experiments on interpreting often differ in age, language combination, professional experience, and training background, etc., making it difficult to generalize the findings. Replications of experimental studies can be an effective way to enhance population validity, but such efforts have been rare in interpreting studies to date.

Ecological validity and population validity are part of external validity – the extent to which research results can be generalized to individuals and situations beyond the participants in the study. In interpreting research, sampling variability makes it no less difficult to achieve high internal validity – the extent to which extraneous variables other than the independent variable are controlled, so that any change observed in a dependent variable can be attributed with a high degree of likelihood to the effect of the independent variable (Gall et al. 1996). Studies on DIRECTIONALITY, for instance, may involve interpreters with different language combinations as participants, resulting in low internal validity and unreliable research findings. Likewise, the results of experiments on the effect of particular INPUT VARIABLES, such as speech rate, may be difficult to interpret when potential confounding variables, such as the syntactic complexity of the source speech, are not controlled.

Random assignment to different conditions or groups, which is fundamental to achieving internal validity, is rare in experimental studies on interpreting. One natural constraint is the fact that participants may belong to different intact groups. For example, Peng (2011) compared textual COHERENCE in the CONSECUTIVE INTERPRETING performances of students in two different courses, one of which included instruction on the topic of textual structures while the other did not. As the participants were not (and could not be) randomly assigned to the treatment and control groups, the study in question would be considered a quasi-experiment. In such cases, the researcher will try to select groups that are as similar as possible, or explain how the two groups can be considered similar.

However, the most common constraint limiting random assignment, or any group assignment, in studies on interpreting is probably small sample size. It is difficult to randomize an already small sample into groups with enough members to achieve statistical power. This may explain why one of the most widely used experimental designs in interpreting studies is to expose participants to all conditions. For example, each participant is asked to do a simultaneous interpretation not only from B to A but also from A to B (Bartłomiejczyk 2006), or to interpret both a fast speech and a complex speech (Meuleman & Van Besien 2009). This type of design could be referred to as a pre-experiment, or a one-shot case study (Gall et al. 1996).

Like most case studies, pre-experiments are a form of descriptive research. Despite their lack of internal validity, they allow the researcher to observe the individuals or phenomena of interest and often lead to the emergence of new research questions. As described by Bickman and Rog (2009), this design informs the 'what' and is often the approach of choice before the 'why' and 'how' are explored in an experiment.

MINHUA LIU

EXPERTISE

↑ COGNITIVE APPROACHES
→ COMPETENCE
↓ EXPERT–NOVICE PARADIGM

Expertise, defined from a cognitive perspective, is the outstanding work of an expert, exhibited at consistently high levels in different contexts within the same field. This is reflected in reliable knowledge about the domain, refined techniques for skill execution and authoritative judgment, as recognized by peers (Ericsson 2006). Expertise in interpreting comprises both the interpreting product (or output) and the interpreter's processing, and is achieved through countless hours of deliberate, goal-focused practice. From a sociological perspective, expertise also includes how each single community perceives the expert.

An experienced performer most certainly has interpreting COMPETENCE, but is not automatically an expert as defined in cognitive psychology (Ericsson et al. 2006). There are other definitions of expertise within translation studies (e.g. Hurtado Albir 2010; Muñoz Martín 2014), though these have yet to be explored by researchers in interpreting studies.

Theoretical context

The theory of expertise, as outlined in cognitive psychology by Ericsson, Charness, Feltovich and Hoffman (2006), did not enter the field of interpreting studies until the seminal articles by Hoffman (1997), Moser-Mercer (1997) and Ericsson (2000) that emanated from the interdisciplinary Ascona workshops organized by Barbara Moser-Mercer. Nevertheless, the dichotomy of expert vs. novice interpreters' performance can be traced to some of the earliest empirical studies (e.g. Barik 1973; Gerver 1976). Different aspects of the interpreter's product and performance, such as ACCURACY, COMPREHENSION, PAUSES, QUALITY and TIME LAG, have been studied with the aim of identifying differences between experienced and inexperienced interpreters. Most of this research has therefore been on *relative expertise* (i.e. novice vs. experienced interpreters), whereas there have been few if any studies of outstanding performers in their own right (*absolute expertise*). Since interpreting is a field without official rankings, the reason for this imbalance is quite obvious; it is, indeed, a far from straightforward task to identify the outstanding performer.

The study of expertise has become well established within COGNITIVE APPROACHES to research on interpreting. Expertise is differentiated from competence, in that it constitutes only a part of it: not all who have interpreting competence are experts in interpreting, but it can be assumed that any expert interpreter is competent (cf. Englund Dimitrova 2005). This restrictive definition of expertise means that the experienced interpreters studied in early interpreting research did not necessarily possess absolute expertise.

Expertise studies of interpreters have mostly been done with conference interpreters or students of CONFERENCE INTERPRETING (e.g. Ivanova 1999; Moser-Mercer 2000a; Liu et al. 2004; Vik-Tuovinen 2006; Köpke & Nespoulous 2006; Tiselius 2013). The approach is, presumably, just as applicable to COMMUNITY INTERPRETING (public service interpreting) and to SIGNED LANGUAGE INTERPRETING, although the methodology, variables and parameters for studying expertise in these domains may differ from those outlined below.

Research methods

Expertise should not be seen as one single construct, but as the sum of several different constructs studied through a variety of methods. According to Ericsson (2006: 9), experts' accumulated knowledge and skills are likely to reflect similarities in structure that depend on biological, psychological and cultural factors. Ericsson also contends that such an all-encompassing perspective gives rise to many challenging problems for the methodologies used to describe the organization of knowledge and related mechanisms. In interpreting studies, most (if not all) studies on expertise have been done within the professional domain of conference interpreting and used quantitative methods. Earlier studies of professional or very experienced simultaneous interpreters and their performance have been thoroughly covered by Liu's (2008) meta-analysis of experienced interpreters and their performance.

The concept of expert knowledge would presumably benefit from being investigated both quantitatively and qualitatively, from a cognitive perspective as well as from a sociological perspective. However, the methodological approaches used in research on expertise in conference interpreting have been experimental. Thus, studies investigating the difference between assumed experts and novices in terms of WORKING MEMORY have used listening and reading span tests or reading span tests as well as free recall tests (Liu et al. 2004; Köpke & Nespoulous 2006; Timarová et al. 2014). As SIMULTANEOUS INTERPRETING requires the ability to listen and speak at the same time, experienced interpreters' ability to repress auditory feedback has been studied by a variety of methods: temporal delay in SHADOWING, interpreting with delayed auditory feedback, and measures of verbal fluency (Moser-Mercer et al. 2000).

Other experimental methods include investigation of lag (ear–voice span) and pause length in the interpretation, linked to differentiation in the speech rate or linguistic complexity of the source speech (Barik 1973; Gerver 1976). ERROR ANALYSIS, holistic rating scales and componential scoring have all been used to investigate the quality of the product, in order to determine differences between experienced interpreters and novices (Barik 1973; Gerver 1976; Anderson 1994; Liu et al. 2004; Setton & Motta 2007; Tiselius 2013). A more intrusive method, which is also used (though rarely) in such research, is brain imaging through EEG (Hervais-Adelman et al. 2011).

Introspective methods, though not purely experimental, are rarely applied to authentic tasks. In interpreting studies they are used to investigate expertise and include RETROSPECTIVE

PROTOCOLS, with either the original speech or the interpreting as a cue (Ivanova 1999; Vik-Tuovinen 2006; Tiselius 2013). The rare qualitative and sociological studies of expertise studies in interpreting are based on in-depth interviews and focus groups (Tiselius 2010, 2013).

Studies on expertise in interpreting have so far been mainly of an exploratory and hypothesis-generating character. This may be because conference interpreters, who have until now been the primary object of study, constitute a small population, and studies with larger groups of informants may be difficult to design. Furthermore, since the nature of expert performance in interpreting has proved rather elusive, it is also difficult to design studies investigating absolute expertise.

Issues studied

Expertise in interpreting has been approached from different thematic angles. The question of whether there is any difference in working memory has not been clearly answered. Findings have indicated no difference in working memory between professional interpreters and students of interpreting (Liu et al. 2004), and students outperformed experienced interpreters in various working memory tests (Köpke & Nespoulous 2006). However, more recent research has shown that certain, though not all, working memory functions develop with interpreting expertise (Timarová et al. 2014). This finding could explain contradictory earlier results on the relationship between working memory and experience, or the presumed expertise associated with experience.

Whether experienced interpreters manage the interpreting process differently than inexperienced interpreters is another issue studied from an expertise perspective. Findings in this field show that experienced interpreters use a variety of explicit cognitive STRATEGIES to execute the interpreting task, and that they run into processing problems less frequently. Novices, on the other hand, resort to omission of information (Ivanova 1999; Tiselius 2013). Experienced interpreters focus on content and the final product, whereas novices focus more on understanding words and transferring meaning. Furthermore, experienced interpreters use a more efficient and goal-focused type of PREPARATION, while novices spend more time preparing (Vik-Tuovinen 2006).

Most research has focused on expertise in simultaneous interpreting, characterised as the result of well-practiced strategies in the comprehension, translation, and production processes specific to the needs of the task (Liu 2008). Experts in simultaneous interpreting produce fewer errors, have faster responses and use less effort; furthermore, they are more accurate and have quicker access to lexical information. They are also better at semantic processing, which means that they are better at judging the importance of the input, and better at monitoring the output. The main underlying factor in their superior performance is their ability to manage and shift attention between different tasks (Liu 2008).

Quality as an indicator of expertise, both alone and combined with other factors, is a recurring theme. Research has shown that experienced interpreters perform better than novice interpreters when interpreting under increased COGNITIVE LOAD. Furthermore, when judged by users, experienced interpreters seem to score better for quality than less experienced interpreters (Setton & Motta 2007). However, findings for differences in interpreting performance related to level of experience may also depend on whether the comparison is done inter- or intra-individually (Tiselius 2013).

In terms of experience-dependent plasticity of the interpreter's brain, the volume of gray matter in regions involved in semantic processing, executive function and error monitoring increases over time for students of interpreting (Hervais-Adelman et al. 2011).

On the whole, there are few studies within the expertise paradigm in interpreting studies, and the results so far do not indicate clear-cut trends regarding the characteristics of expertise in interpreting. Nevertheless, they do seem to support the notion that expertise in interpreting consists at least of the interpreter's ability to handle the different interpretational processes, and to manage and shift attention between the different tasks.

ELISABET TISELIUS

EXPERT–NOVICE PARADIGM

↑ EXPERTISE

EXPERTISE can be measured in an abstract way by studying exceptional individuals in different domains in order to identify global cognitive skills that underpin their performance, such as the quality of their analytical processing, generation of best solutions, detection and recognition of salient features and the deep structure of situations, the ability to consistently self-monitor performance, powerful task execution strategies and cognitive efficiency (Chi 2006; Hoffman et al. 1995; Patel & Groen 1991). Alternatively, expertise can be measured in relative terms by comparing expert to novice performance. This approach offers more latitude, as no absolute definition of expertise is required in order to establish the relationship between more or less proficient performers and a whole range of novice-like performers, from naïve to journeyman (Hoffman 1997), with whom they can be contrasted. Both approaches rely on fundamental theoretical assumptions regarding the level of domain knowledge, the sophistication of MEMORY structures and knowledge representation, the capacity for swift reasoning and speeded performance.

Interpreting is a performance skill whose acquisition has been of central interest in interpreter EDUCATION. Contrasting novices to experts provides insights into the skills and skill levels needed to become an accomplished expert; a more fine-grained comparison across different levels of novice-like performers on their way to becoming experts offers even more powerful insights regarding progression in skill acquisition and can make important contributions to interpreting PEDAGOGY, providing a better understanding of the stages experts need to go through on their way to highly professional performance. The expert–novice paradigm can also provide important insights into cognitive adaptability, brain plasticity and general capacity, and create research synergies with the field of performance psychology, which concerns itself with the theoretical description of human performance, the integration of formal models of cognitive psychology, and the influence of STRESS and individual difference factors on performance (Matthews 1997).

A number of studies in interpreting and in disciplines using interpreting as a research paradigm have employed the expert–novice paradigm. However, the definition of levels of expertise in interpreting continues to compromise the reliability of many of these studies and constitutes an obstacle to replication with a view to validating their results.

Research using variations of the expert–novice paradigm has addressed a range of topics in the broad domain of COGNITIVE APPROACHES to interpreting, including COMPREHENSION (Dillinger 1994; Bajo et al. 2000; Yudes et al. 2013), MEMORY and bilingual processing skills (Darò & Fabbro 1994; Chincotta & Underwood 1998; Christoffels et al. 2006; Hervais-Adelman et al. 2011), STRATEGIES (Sunnari 1995a), STRESS (Kurz 2003) and WORKING MEMORY performance (Köpke & Nespoulous 2006; Liu et al. 2004; Tzou et al. 2011).

BARBARA MOSER-MERCER

EXPLICITATION

Explicitation, understood as increased explicitness of a target text as compared to a source text, is one of the most thoroughly studied phenomena in translation studies. Almost universally hailed as one of translation's universals, explicitation has attracted considerable interest among translation scholars ever since Blum-Kulka (1986) hypothesised that a translation will be more explicit than a corresponding non-translation (see also e.g. Englund Dimitrova 2005).

In contrast, the scale of research on explicitation in interpreting is much smaller. Obviously, given the fundamental differences between written and oral translation as well as the inherent constraints of the interpreting process (e.g. severe limitation of time, the linearity constraint, and limited short-term memory capacity), explicitation tends to acquire a different dimension in interpreting. The potential for explicitation would seem most obvious in CONSECUTIVE INTERPRETING, where target text production is based on retrieval from MEMORY and notes. However, these intervening processes may also be seen as a complicating factor in studying this topic. Wadensjö (1998) posits 'expanded renditions' as including 'more explicitly expressed information than the preceding original utterance', but little work on DIALOGUE INTERPRETING has addressed the explicitation hypothesis as such. For SIMULTANEOUS INTERPRETING (SI), the initial assumption was that the constraints intrinsic to SI might preclude extensive and recurrent explicitation. However, the studies conducted so far supply evidence that this phenomenon does exist in SI and is by no means a marginal occurrence.

SHLESINGER's (1995a) study, aiming to investigate changes in cohesive patterns, revealed that interpreters tend to explicitate implicit links by inserting additional cohesive devices. In a larger study involving 28 advanced interpreting students working between Polish and English, Gumul (2007) identified and analysed various forms of explicitation, ranging from the lexical and syntactic levels to the pragmatic level. The results of this product-based study indicate that explicitation in SI is mainly related to COHESION. The six most common changes include the addition of connectives; shifts from referential cohesion to lexical cohesion, i.e. lexicalisation of pro-forms; replacement of nominalisations with verb phrases; reiteration of lexical items; expansion of elliptical constructions; and shifts from reiteration in the form of paraphrase to reiteration in the form of identical or partial repetition.

Data from another study (Gumul 2006b), both process- and product-oriented, show that explicitation in interpreting is in most cases an unconscious, i.e. non-strategic procedure. The analysis of both interpreting outputs and RETROSPECTIVE PROTOCOLS indicates that unconscious explicitation accounts for over 90% of all cases of explicitating shifts detected in the outputs. The vast majority of these are cohesion-related, whereas a large proportion of such operations as meaning specification, metaphor disambiguation, and explanation are fully conscious strategic choices of the interpreters.

However, most of the explicitating shifts are not strategic, indicating that explicitation in SI appears to be prevalently non-conscious. Further large-scale product- and process-oriented research, with professional interpreters as subjects, will be needed to determine whether the remaining cases of explicitation can be attributed, for instance, to the fully automated use of interpreting STRATEGIES, to automated norm-governed behaviour, to the occurrence of deverbalisation during the process of COMPREHENSION, or else to the translation process itself, as a by-product of language MEDIATION.

EWA GUMUL

EYE TRACKING

↑ METHODOLOGY
→ COGNITIVE LOAD

Eye tracking refers to the process of measuring the position and the movement of the human eye with devices known as eye trackers. It has its theoretical grounding in the eye–mind hypothesis (Just & Carpenter 1980), according to which the mind processes what the eye is looking at. Since the invention of the first prototypes in 1898 (Richardson & Spivey 2004), eye trackers have become very accurate and, in the case of remote systems, virtually non-invasive. Today's eye trackers can collect real-time data on the pupil's size and movements every .5 ms with tracking errors under .5°, giving researchers access to well over 100 different measures – capturing eye movements through space, determining their properties at spatial locations, quantifying eye-movement events and measuring their duration (Holmqvist et al. 2011). This makes eye tracking suitable for the study of the interpreting process.

While eye-tracking research into the translation process (see Göpferich et al. 2008; Grucza et al. 2013) has harnessed several of the robust measures used in reading studies (e.g. first fixation, first pass time, total reading times and regression paths), eye-tracking research into the interpreting process has had to rely on measures usually used in other paradigms (see Rayner 1998), given the absence of visual input in the form of written text. Early eye-tracking studies of SIMULTANEOUS INTERPRETING (SI) used pupil dilation to measure COGNITIVE LOAD (see Seeber 2013), recording for the first time physiological evidence of changes in load as a function of DIRECTIONALITY (Tommola & Niemi 1986), task modality (Hyönä et al. 1995) and syntactic structure (Seeber & Kerzel 2012). More recently, attempts have been made to explore the multimodal nature of the interpreting process using eye-tracking data to compare reading to SIGHT INTERPRETING/TRANSLATION (Huang 2011), to compare reading *for* SI and reading *during* SIMULTANEOUS WITH TEXT (Kumcu 2011), and to explore the use of visual-verbal and visual-spatial information during SI (Seeber 2012).

The main strengths of eye tracking as a research method in interpreting studies are its objective and online nature along with its limited invasiveness (allowing real-time measurements during an ongoing task such as SI), as well as its high temporal resolution (making it possible to time-lock ocular phenomena and cognitive processes down to the level of phonemes). The method has also been applied to the study of receptive processes in SIGNED LANGUAGE INTERPRETING (e.g. Wehrmeyer 2014), with promising results. Among the limitations of the method are phenomena like covert attention (Wright & Ward 2008) that detract from the eye–mind hypothesis, and the need for a visual input component for many measures – with noteworthy exceptions, such as pupil dilation.

KILIAN G. SEEBER

FACE

↑ DISCOURSE ANALYTICAL APPROACHES, ↑ LINGUISTIC/PRAGMATIC APPROACHES

Face, an apparently simple term, on closer examination turns out to be an "intoxicating metaphor" (Ting-Toomey & Cocroft 1994: 307). It addresses abstract qualities such as honor, respect, the self, or identity that are pivotal to human interaction. Though face is an everyday language concept, a precise definition has proven difficult. The concept has been debated in different disciplines (e.g. anthropology, sociology, linguistics) and is pivotal to politeness research, though politeness theory cannot be equated with face theory (Watts 2003). Originating with Asian notions of face, current conceptualizations are often based on the socio-anthropological perspective of Erving Goffman, who viewed face-work as part of the "rituals" of human interaction. Goffman (1967: 5) defined face as "the positive social value a person effectively claims for himself by the line others assume he has taken during a particular contact."

Whereas Goffman views face as an unstable entity that is "only on loan from society", it appears as a more fixed possession of the individual in the most influential theory based on the Goffmanian notion of face – the theory of politeness and universals in language usage by Brown and Levinson (1987), first put forward in the late 1970s. Brown and Levinson introduce a dualistic construct of face, defined as "the public self-image that every member [of a society] wants to claim for himself" (1987: 61). That construct consists of two opposing "wants": a "negative face" (the desire that one's actions are unimpeded by others), and a "positive face" (the desire that one's wants are approved by the other interactants). The variables of a given speech act – power, social distance and degree of imposition – determine which of various strategies is applied to counter face threats.

Whereas an array of other politeness and/or face theories have been proposed, issues of face have received scant attention in interpreting studies to date, though the concept has surfaced in works on other topics. Aside from Goffman's seminal work, only three different face constructs have been applied: Brown and Levinson's (1987) politeness theory, Spencer-Oatey's (2008) theory of rapport management, and Scollon and Scollon's (1995) politeness model.

Face has been discussed across a range of domains and MODES of interpreting, though references to spoken language COMMUNITY INTERPRETING predominate. Most authors have adopted qualitative DISCOURSE ANALYTICAL APPROACHES, with Brown and Levinson's (1987) politeness theory as the preferred theoretical framework.

In CONFERENCE INTERPRETING, Müller (1998) was one of the first to apply the Goffmanian concept of face to the analysis of a political speech interpreted simultaneously by student interpreters. Concentrating on mitigation STRATEGIES, he concludes that clarity is given priority at the expense of subtle nuances and hedging expressions. Monacelli (2009) focuses on face in her study of authentic interpreted conference speeches, which combines qualitative and quantitative elements as well as Brown and Levinson's (1987) and Spencer-Oatey's (2008) theoretical frameworks. She points to a trend towards distancing, indirectness, and mitigation of illocutionary force among conference interpreters, who seem to aim for "self-preservation" if their professional face is in danger. A study on CONSECUTIVE INTERPRETING of (simulated) formal speeches by Polish trainee interpreters, on the other hand, revealed deictic shifts that appeared to be motivated by efforts to protect "group face" (Warchal et al. 2011).

In an investigation of SIGNED LANGUAGE INTERPRETING in media settings, Savvalidou (2011) examines interpreter additions, substitutions, OMISSIONS and paraphrases in a TV debate before the Greek general elections and concludes that the interpreter's renditions may undermine the politicians' (im)politeness strategies and thus the perception of their public face. In an earlier study, Hoza (1999) tackled sign language interpreters' strategies for dealing with face-work, also taking up Scollon and Scollon's (1995) third type of politeness, or hierarchical politeness system, in which face strategies depend on the interactants' relative position in an encounter.

Face has been discussed in particular in LEGAL INTERPRETING settings. Using transcripts from a TV broadcast of the O.J. Simpson trial in the US and a televised UK immigration interview, Mason and Stewart (2001), applying Brown and Levinson's (1987) face theory, find that in both instances the interpreters' strategies may endanger the positive face – and thus the credibility – of the individuals being questioned. In a similar vein, Jacobsen (2008a, 2008b) and Lee (2013), investigating audio-recorded interpreter-mediated court trials, conclude that interpreters alter statements and avoid self-initiated REPAIRS so as not to threaten their own face. With a focus on ASYLUM SETTINGS, Barsky (1994) critically discusses Goffman's construct of face and complements it with a Bourdieusian view of discourse as a commodity, and Pöllabauer (2007) addresses face-work in a corpus of interpreted asylum hearings in Austria.

In research on interpreting in community settings, Knapp-Potthoff and Knapp (1987) were among the first to take up Brown and Levinson's (1987) construct of face in their pioneering work on non-professional MEDIATION, focusing on down-toning particles and strategies for claiming common ground. Wadensjö (1998) takes up Goffman's concept of face-work in her groundbreaking study of DIALOGUE INTERPRETING, using examples from authentic interpreter-mediated interactions to illustrate the complexity of attending to face.

SONJA PÖLLABAUER

FALSE STARTS

see under FLUENCY

FICTIONAL INTERPRETERS

Until the beginning of the twentieth century, interpreters only rarely figured in literary texts and, when they did, it was mainly in the context of war. Among the earliest works featuring interpreters as literary figures is Johann Wolfgang von Goethe's autobiography *Aus meinem Leben. Dichtung und Wahrheit* [*From My Life: Poetry and Truth*] (1811), which includes accounts of an interpreter staying with the nine-year-old Goethe and his family. In the mid-nineteenth century, George J. Whyte-Melville's *The Interpreter* (1856–1858), a story centering around Vere Egerton and his experiences as an interpreter in the Turkish and British armies during the Crimean War, was published in the American magazine *Littell's Living Age*. In the early twentieth century, André Maurois published four works set during the First World War, in which the author portrays himself as the interpreter Aurelle: *Le Général Bramble* [*General Bramble*] (1920), *Les silences du colonel Bramble* [*The Silence of Colonel Bramble*] (1950), *Les discours du Docteur O'Grady* [*The Discourses of Doctor O'Grady*] (1950) and *Nouveaux discours du Docteur O'Grady* [*The New Discourses of Doctor O'Grady*] (1950). Kurt Vonnegut's short story and play *Der arme Dolmetscher* (1955) also explore the narrative of interpreters in times of war, the protagonist being an American soldier appointed as a battalion interpreter during the Second World War despite his totally inadequate language proficiency.

Between 1960 and 1990, the number of works of fiction featuring interpreters increased considerably, and many were published in the course of the 1990s. Since the beginning of the twenty-first century, there has been an 'inflationary' surge in such publications. As stated in a review of John le Carré's thriller *The Mission Song* (2006) in a German newspaper, the interpreter appears to have become a key figure of modern-day global society. Increasingly, s/he is portrayed as a protagonist rather than a secondary character, with writers 'discovering' the interpreter as an ideal character through whom to explore a number of particularly contemporary topics such as: migration; hybrid (or in-between) cultures, characters and identities; restlessness; clashing cultures; self-identification; the power of language; language games; understanding and misunderstanding; and the nature of communication. The depiction of interpreters in literature is not only strongly influenced by authors' differing social, political and historical backgrounds, it also shows a variety of perspectives on the interpreter's experience, not merely as a professional occupation but as an allegory or metaphor. The image of the interpreter is deliberately moulded to meet the authors' own literary requirements – stereotypes and prejudices are propagated if they help to enforce the author's message.

These developments in literary production have attracted the attention of translation and interpreting scholars, and numerous works have been discussed and analyzed in articles, monographs and collective volumes (e.g. Delabastita & Grutman 2005; Kurz & Kaindl 2005; Kurz 2007; Lavric 2007; Andres 2008, 2014; Kaindl & Kurz 2008, 2010; Kaindl & Spitzl 2014). In the remainder of this entry, key examples of fictional interpreters will be reviewed with respect to some dominant themes. Overall, the impression emerges that authors draw on fictional interpreters to explore issues relating to identity, hybridity and migration. Interpreters are often represented as eternal wanderers struggling to straddle the divide between two different worlds and living in a permanent state of 'not belonging'. Due to their nomadic and multilingual nature, interpreters are depicted as lacking orientation and emotional bonds; they are shown as empty within, divided and torn apart by their different '(life)worlds'.

Language, power and truth

Fictional interpreters are used to exemplify a variety of topics, including language as a game, as a means of escaping, of bringing about change, of (ab)using POWER, of finding the truth and ultimately the protagonist finding him/herself – in some cases, even language as the expression of speechlessness. In 1893, Arthur C. Doyle's short story *The Greek Interpreter* described a Sherlock Holmes case in which a court and liaison interpreter becomes entangled in a criminal investigation. He 'duplicates' the role of the investigator, acts on his own authority, adds, distorts and omits meaning, taking full advantage of the licence he enjoys by virtue of no one having the necessary language skills to monitor his interpreting. This lack of control over the interpreter and the resulting scope for engaging in language games are also addressed in Michael Frayn's *The Russian Interpreter* (1966), Ronald Harwood's *Interpreters* (1986) and Javier Marías' *Corazón tan blanco* [*A Heart So White*] (1996). David Mitchell's *The Thousand Autumns of Jacob de Zoet* (2011) again deals with the theme of power as a result of exclusive access to language skills and the related cultures. *Native Tongue* (1984) by Suzette H. Elgin and *L'interprete* (2004) by Diego Marani examine the power of language in general, and artificial language in particular. Speechlessness and the (im)possibilities of communication are discussed in Ann Patchett's *Bel Canto* and Jonathan S. Foer's *Everything is Illuminated*, both published in 2002.

Identity

Identity, disintegrating identities and the quest for identity are common topoi in literary texts. It is particularly striking that many works convey a very questionable concept of identity, according to which encounters with other cultures and languages are a detrimental influence and result in a feeling of rootlessness. Relatively few authors seem to see identities-in-between, being rooted in two or more cultures and languages, as an opportunity and a source of great personal benefits.

The following works explore the individual's possession of coexisting cultures and their impact on identity, interpreters as bi- or multi-cultural individuals, and the search for one's own language and identity: Amadou H. Bâ, *L'étrange destin de Wangrin ou Les roueries d'un interprète africain* [*The Fortunes of Wangrin: the life and times of an African confidence man*] (1973); Ágnes Gergely, *A tolmács* [*Interpreter*] (1973); Natascha Wodin, *Die gläserne Stadt* (1983); Ivo Andrić, *Travnička hronika* [*The Days of the Consuls*] (1945); Robert Moss,

The Interpreter (1997); Eminde S. Özdamar, *Die Brücke vom goldenen Horn* [*The Bridge of the Golden Horn*] (1998); Jhumpa Lahiri, *Interpreter of Maladies* (1999); Jesús Díaz, *Siberiana* (2000); Jean-Christoph Rufin, *Rouge Brésil* [*Brazil Red*] (2001); Suki Kim, *The Interpreter* (2003); Liselotte Marshall, *Tongue-tied* (2004); John le Carré, *The Mission Song* (2006); Mario Vargas Llosa, *Travesuras de la niña mala* [*The Bad Girl*] (2006); Arnaldur Indriðason, *Vetrarborgin* [*Arctic Chill*] (2005); Jean Kwok, *Girl in Translation* (2010); Michael Schischkin, *Venerin volos* [*Maidenhair*] (2011). The last three examples are particularly topical, as their main focus is on migration, living in-between cultures and COMMUNITY INTERPRETING.

Néstor Ponce's *El Intérprete* (1998) and Brian Friel's play *Translations* (1981) revolve around the force of language. The following works discuss speechlessness, disintegrating identities and language devoid of meaning, through the example of fictional interpreters: Doris Lessing, *The Summer Before the Dark* (1973); Ingeborg Bachmann, *Simultan* [*Word for Word*] (1978); Christine Brooke-Rose, *Between* (1986); Max Davidson, *The Greek Interpreter* (1990); Abdelkebir Khatibi, *Un été à Stockholm* (1990); György Dalos, *Der Versteckspieler* (1994); Isabelle Maréchal, *Le poids du silence* (1996); Suzanne Glass, *The Interpreter* (1999); Alain Fleischer, *Prolongations* (2008); Kathrin Röggla, *Die Unvermeidlichen* (2011) (a play, which premiered in Mannheim on 6 February 2010). The recurrent idea is that the interpreter, whose profession it is to work with language, cannot escape its clutches. S/he is appropriated by language, particularly in SIMULTANEOUS INTERPRETING – turned into a machine which, at the flick of a switch, automatically spouts words stored in the brain. Speaking other languages relieves interpreters of having to grapple with themselves, of confronting the meaninglessness surrounding them. The interpreting profession is a means of filling the void within. They are nobodies, their inner selves are submerged, they are speechless.

Psychologically sound interpreters who are passionate about their profession and strictly adhere to the principles of professional ETHICS are quite few and far between in fiction. Examples of works featuring such interpreters are Elfriede Brüning's *Wie andere Leute auch* (1983), Hermann Kant's *Die Summe – Eine Begebenheit* (1987), Thomas C. Boyle's *Water Music* (1982) and Maggie Helwig's *Between Mountains* (2004).

Interpreting and war

Fictional interpreters have gained a new dimension in the twenty-first century. They embody political and human conflict in literary works set in a war context, epitomising the state of being 'in-between' languages, emotions and frontlines typically encountered in times of war. The following works of fiction explore this liminal space of 'in-between': Louis Guilloux, *O.K., Joe!* (2003); Ha Jin, *War Trash* (2004); Michael Goldfarb, *Ahmad's War, Ahmad's Peace. Surviving under Saddam, Dying in the new Iraq* (2005); Michael Wallner, *April in Paris* (2007); George Packer, *Betrayed* (2008); and Inaam Kachachi, *Al-Hafida al-amirikiyya* [*The American Granddaughter*] (2009).

DÖRTE ANDRES

FIDELITY

↑ ETHICS, ↑ QUALITY
→ ACCURACY, → TRUST

Fidelity or 'faithfulness' has been a key meme of discourse on translation and interpreting since earliest times, and has traditionally been seen as the primary criterion of QUALITY.

Fidelity and its equivalent terms in various languages are associated with notions of TRUST and integrity, and thus also engage the interpreter's professional ETHICS. ·Fidelity' is less commonly used in English-language translation studies than *fidélité* in French writing, and tends to connote ACCURACY of reproduction (as in 'high fidelity'). However, its Latin origin (*fides*: 'reliance, trust') also suggests COMPETENCE and integrity. In a similar vein, the Chinese translation theorist Yan Fu (1854–1921) identified *xin* 信 (also meaning 'trust' and 'reliability') as one of the three primary challenges of translation.

In contemporary usage, the 'faithfulness' of a translation is sometimes more narrowly understood to refer to its accuracy and completeness. But the semantic elements of trust and reliability in 'fidelity' make it a much broader challenge – reflected in sceptical phrases like '*traduttore traditore*' or '*les belles infidèles*' – to render not only the content but also the intent of a communication, achieved through linguistic and paralinguistic choices made for their impact in a particular context and situation. This multidimensional character of fidelity is reflected in the definition of faithfulness in the (bilingual French/English) Canadian Code of Ethics of the Association of Visual Language Interpreters of Canada (AVLIC 2000): "The fidelity of an interpretation includes an adaptation to make the form, the tone, and the deeper meaning of the source text felt in the target language and culture." Fidelity, faithfulness or faithful rendering appear as a key requirement of professional interpreting in 14 out of a random sub-sample of 16 codes of professional standards, from 9 countries, surveyed by Hale (2007). For 95% of interpreters responding to an accompanying survey, fidelity is not a goal pursued at word or sentence level, but refers to "a translation which takes into account the whole discourse and reproduces the intention and impact of the original" (Hale 2007: 116).

Any attempt to circumscribe fidelity in a prescriptive sense must consider what criterion is possible or desirable – faithfulness to the letter or the spirit, to the speaker's words or to his or her (intended) meaning. The non-isomorphism of languages clearly makes surface-linguistic equivalence incompatible with fidelity to ideas and sense. However, the need for ASSESSMENT naturally creates pressure for some consistent and verifiable yardstick for correspondence between elements of source and target texts.

It can be argued that fidelity in the wider sense should take into account the conditions of production and reception of messages, and in particular the immediacy of the process and the media of transmission (different combinations of text, speech and sign). The ORALITY of interpreting implies a shared live context of the unfolding exchange, in which the interpreter typically has both auditory and VISUAL ACCESS to evidence of speakers' intended meaning and the conditions of reception. While the translator of written texts must typically make the author's meaning transparent to future readers, an interpreter assumes responsibility only for listeners' immediate perception and understanding. It is also widely recognised that NORMS regarding fidelity may vary with the interpreter's ROLE, which in turn may vary significantly between, for example, the SETTINGS of an international conference, a courtroom or a medical consultation. Thus Gile (2009: 62) suggests that "in determining principles of fidelity for interpreting and translation, it seems appropriate to start not with the finished linguistic product, but with the communication setting."

Authors writing on CONFERENCE INTERPRETING have also been at pains to show how fidelity commonly entails active choices by the interpreter and significant departures from linguistic equivalence. According to Gile (2009), interpreters working in 'neutral mode' pursue a norm of 'minimum fidelity' that requires the message the speaker is trying to convey in an utterance to be re-expressed in the target language text, and may justify some deletions or additions of 'framing information'. In Setton and Dawrant (2016), 'basic fidelity' is the minimum required to convey a speaker's basic communicative intent, without misrepresentation or distortion, when severe constraints (such as poor acoustic conditions, or pressure to tone down or summarise) prevent a fuller rendering. This is contrasted with 'optimal' fidelity, embracing every aspect of the intent, content, expression, tone and style of the communication, that can be pursued in choices to optimise form (style, COHERENCE, concision, packaging, recapping, PROSODY and BODY LANGUAGE), content (adding, explicating, clarifying, 'localising' cultural references, filtering, toning down, correcting errors, etc.), or process (e.g. intervening in the exchange to correct misunderstandings). Authors in the INTERPRETIVE THEORY tradition stress that choices aimed at optimal fidelity are typically not conscious, but are generated by capturing the speaker's 'attitude' (Seleskovitch 1975). However, Donovan-Cagigos (1990) extends the theory to analyse fidelity in two dimensions that do require analysis by the interpreter: stylistic, achieved by distinguishing the effects in the source speech that are deliberate stylistic choices, and terminological, through PREPARATION of the subject matter.

A common theme of these various treatments is that fidelity may not be served, and indeed may be destroyed, by 'just translating' on the basis of strict linguistic equivalence. On the other hand, different forms of 'optimisation' are controversial to varying degrees. Concision or clarification is widely accepted in many circumstances. Using a target-language idiom where none exists in the source text may also be accepted if the meaning is preserved, even if the result is rhetorical enhancement. Conversely, the published consensus is probably against toning down aggressive language. Kondo (1990: 62) argues that by watering down politicians' statements, conference interpreters "might inflict long-term harm to genuine mutual understanding by acting too much like diplomats." In practice, however, interpreters may often soften such language spontaneously. Deliberate OMISSIONS, even when aimed at smoothing understanding or avoiding conflict, are clearly more controversial when only the interpreter understands the speaker.

Improving on a speaker's presentation or eloquence might be forbidden in LEGAL INTERPRETING, expected for one's own side only in DIPLOMATIC INTERPRETING or BUSINESS INTERPRETING, or voluntarily done in COMMUNITY INTERPRETING to level the communicative playing field between more or less powerful participants. However, these are generalisations: it seems clear that fidelity is in the spirit as much as the letter, and depends on context and situation. Light editing or explicating cultural references might be indispensable for making sense to some listeners, or may constitute welcome intercultural MEDIATION, but may also result in dilution or even censorship.

ROBIN SETTON

FIELDWORK

see under ETHNOGRAPHIC METHODS

FILM INTERPRETING

↑ SETTINGS
→ MEDIA INTERPRETING, → SIMULTANEOUS INTERPRETING, → THEATER INTERPRETING

Film interpreting is an oral mode of audiovisual translation used when films are neither dubbed nor subtitled (or when foreign language subtitles are shown), as is often the case at film festivals. The interpretation is provided in simultaneous mode, either as a 'voice-over', covering the original audio and involving just one interpreter, or via headphones, with interpreters working in teams from a booth. The former mode was common in Eastern

European countries when dubbing was of poor quality or not available. Film interpreting may be provided directly from the soundtrack, or as SIGHT TRANSLATION/INTERPRETING of subtitles or of a script. In the latter case, the interpreter must nevertheless rely on the audio to ensure suitable timing and to deal with any inconsistencies or gaps in the text. As a rule, there is no voice-matching for gender, and the same interpreter has to do all the characters.

Film interpreting differs from SIMULTANEOUS INTERPRETING in conference settings, not only in obvious features like topic and REGISTER. Thus, film interpreters do not have time to adjust to different speakers, to whom they have no direct access, and must cope with unique challenges, such as high SPEECH RATE, voice overlap, the need for minimal TIME LAG to ensure synchronisation with the characters' speaking turns, and the "feigned" fresh-talk nature of scripted dialogue (Taylor 1999). This may force interpreters – who are not actors or dubbers, and rarely have an already translated script – to make judicious cuts.

The relatively few publications about film interpreting, often by Italian scholars, mostly fall into two categories: (1) those by "practisearching" academics; and (2) unpublished empirical research in MA theses. Authors in the first group have covered topics such as the "minimalist" approach (Snelling 1990), quality prerequisites, strategies for sight-translating subtitles (Viezzi 1992), and film typologies and related interpreting strategies (Russo 1997). They have also analysed student performances and training experiences under experimental and real-life conditions, thereby assessing the teaching potential of film interpreting.

Theses on film interpreting, in some cases examining features like culture-bound terms and puns, are extensively discussed in Russo (2005). They include two surveys of USER EXPECTATIONS and response, based on questionnaires completed by about 200 spectators at two film festivals (with English–Italian and Spanish–Italian interpreting). While reflecting the specificities of film interpreting in certain quality parameters (word/image synchronisa-tion, dialogue completeness, adequate style, expressiveness/acting, explanation of nonverbal elements), the questionnaires were designed to allow comparison with published surveys on USER EXPECTATIONS and preferences in CONFERENCE INTERPRETING. Using a five-point scale to rate a set of QUALITY CRITERIA, respondents gave priority to general content, FLUENCY, syn-chronisation and style. VOICE QUALITY, expressiveness/acting and explanation of nonverbal elements ranked relatively low. User group-related differences in priorities emerged in one survey, where synchronisation and a "minimalist" style of interpreting were particularly valued by film critics (Guardini 2000).

Children as a special user group in film interpreting are discussed by Jüngst (2012), who reviews the specific needs of young audiences and also offers a thorough analysis of working methods and modes of presentation.

MARIACHIARA RUSSO

FINGERSPELLING

↑ SIGNED LANGUAGE INTERPRETING

Fingerspelling as a mode of signing operates on the alphabetic level and represents indivi-dual letters of the Roman alphabet (Stokoe et al. 1965). Fingerspelled tokens, each of which is a sign (a sequence of handshapes, locations, orientations, and movements), represent a graphic character of the alphabet and are used in sequences to create lexical items.

Fingerspelling systems differ by country and by the signed language with which they are associated, and the use of fingerspelling also depends on setting-related needs and language user preferences. American Sign Language (ASL) uses fingerspelling more often and more prominently than many other signed languages (Padden 2006). Research on fingerspelling in ASL is therefore relatively abundant, but not all of it may be generalizable to fingerspelling in other signed languages.

Fingerspelling in ASL is used to represent words with various grammatical functions such as proper nouns, adjectives, verbs, nouns, expletives, English function words, and transplanted English function words and phrases (Padden 1998). COMPREHENSION of fingerspelling is difficult for many hearing interpreters and is a source of errors in interpretations. Many interpreters report experiencing anxiety that interferes with fingerspelled word recognition.

Depending on the signed language and the way it uses fingerspelling, there may be at least three types of fingerspelling that interpreters must learn to recognize and produce: *careful* fingerspelling typically shows one fingerspelled token for each character in the corresponding printed word, and is characterized by a relatively slow speed and even rate of presentation; *rapid* fingerspelling, used for non-initial presentations of the word, has constituent signs of a shorter duration that tend to blend together or to be eliminated; and *lexicalized* fingerspelling tends not to vary much in speed or form from one presentation to the next. This type of fingerspelling has also been described as lexical borrowing, as it tends to have the rhythm and characteristics of a single sign rather than those of fingerspelling (Patrie & Johnson 2011).

Comprehending fingerspelling requires complex cognitive processes. The fingerspelled sequence must be processed, serially connected to an existing template (a pattern that is created and stored in the brain for that word if one exists), and converted by the receiver to a mental image of a written word with which they are familiar. Practice with rapid serial visual presentation (RSVP) and template building (Patrie & Johnson 2011) shows promise in addressing the pervasive difficulty associated with fingerspelled word recognition, and in reducing the corresponding effort related to comprehension.

CAROL J. PATRIE

FLUENCY

↑ QUALITY CRITERIA
→ PROSODY
↓ PAUSES, ↓ SPEECH RATE

Fluency in language production has a twofold meaning. In a broad sense, 'expressional' fluency refers to a speaker's oral (or signed) proficiency in a given language, which depends heavily on his or her agility in vocabulary activation and the availability of alternative turns of phrase and is an essential goal in public speaking and in foreign language acquisition. Interpreters are expected to be fluent bilinguals, though their fluency may differ from one language to another in relation to DIRECTIONALITY. The importance of interpreters' fluency in their working languages has been acknowledged in APTITUDE TESTING of prospective interpreting students.

In a more specific sense, fluency refers to 'delivery', that is, the physical characteristics of the acoustic signal produced by the speaker that go beyond the verbal component of speech and are often subsumed under the heading of PROSODY, with SPEECH RATE and PAUSES as central parameters. Since it is difficult to formulate standards or even rules for these 'temporal variables' of speech (Raupach 1980), much research on fluency focuses on perceived deviations from implicit NORMS, examining various types of hesitations or disfluency. These encompass such paralinguistic phenomena as drawled phonemes, voiced hesitation and anomalous pauses in terms of position or length, and also linguistic phenomena like false starts, REPAIRS and SLIPS. Such occurrences are quite frequent in everyday speech (and may tend to pass largely unnoticed by listeners); however, the lack of consensus among researchers regarding the definition and choice of fluency-related parameters hampers their systematic study on the basis of comparable empirical findings (Pradas Macías 2006). Furthermore, it is difficult to isolate fluency from related features of speech such as INTONATION and prosodic accent.

Fluency being a characteristic of individual speech behaviour, there is little correspondence between the occurrence of disfluencies in the source speech and in the interpreter's delivery – even in SIMULTANEOUS INTERPRETING, with its associated time constraints (Tissi 2000). As with intonation, interpreters will adopt a fluency pattern of their own, in particular with regard to pauses, due to psycholinguistic constraints.

In CONFERENCE INTERPRETING, fluency of delivery is one of the main QUALITY CRITERIA for the ASSESSMENT of an interpreter's performance. In SURVEY RESEARCH on USER EXPECTATIONS and professional interpreters' own performance standards, this criterion ranks below the main content-related criteria but far above other delivery-related features, which may reflect its special position at the interface of the linguistic and paralinguistic dimensions (Bühler 1986). Moreover, when users are asked to judge an actual interpreting performance in EXPERIMENTAL RESEARCH, the presence of disfluencies seems to impact on the assessment of various other quality criteria (Pradas Macías 2006; Rennert 2010).

In studies on fluency in interpreting, particular attention has been given to the identification and measurement of PAUSES, which raises a number of methodological issues. While the availability of audio editing software has made it easier to distinguish silence from sound, it remains difficult to differentiate very short pauses from mere breaks in articulation between distinct sounds. Researchers have attempted to overcome this problem by setting thresholds for pause duration, usually ranging from 100 to 250 ms. But this choice is tricky, because pauses can have varying communicative functions, and listeners' perception of them may vary. Indeed, there is imperfect correspondence between measured pauses and perceived pauses, especially in the case of practically inaudible breaks in articulation between distinct sounds.

When used as an independent variable in experimental studies, the effect of pauses on users' judgment of a simultaneous interpreting performance seems weaker and less consistent than the effect of features like ACCENT, exposure to which is continuous rather than only intermittent (Cheung 2013). Regardless of users' ability to identify quantifiable features of speech, a lack of fluency in the interpreter's delivery will tend to strain COMPREHENSION (Ahrens 2005a) and is likely to affect listeners' judgment of ACCURACY.

E. MACARENA PRADAS MACÍAS

FOCUS GROUPS

see under INTERVIEWS

FOOTING

↑ PARTICIPATION FRAMEWORK

The notion of footing is an analytical concept proposed by the sociologist Erving Goffman (1981) for the study of 'participation' in interaction. It must be understood in the context of Goffman's analysis of the PARTICIPATION FRAMEWORK and 'production format', two constructs affording a detailed theoretical perspective on the participation status of listeners and speakers.

In his essay "Footing", Goffman (1981) dissects the notion of 'hearer' by identifying the roles of ratified participants (the *addressed,* the *unaddressed* and the *bystander*) and non-ratified participants (*overhearers* and *eavesdroppers*). The notion of 'speaker' is teased apart in a different way. Goffman distinguishes between three ways of displaying aspects of self through talk: as *animator, author* and *principal* of an utterance. Discussing an earlier version of this typology, which he subsequently reworked into the threefold distinction summarized here, Goffman (1974) referred to the various ways in which a speaker can relate to an utterance as its 'production format'. This concept, enlarging on the various categories such as animator and principal, is also dealt with in his essay "Radio Talk" (Goffman 1981). When speaking as an *animator,* an individual acts as "a sounding box from which utterances come" (Goffman 1981: 226). However, a speaker can also be the *author* of the spoken words, that is, "the agent who puts together, composes, or scripts the lines that are uttered". A third possible role of the speaker in an utterance is that of *principal* – "the party to whose position, stand and belief the words attest". Thus, rather than simply attribute the ownership of any given utterance to the person who articulated it, Goffman recognizes participants' changes of footing as an ever-present feature of natural talk, highlighting the inherently dialogic organization of human language.

Change of footing is further explained as "change in the alignment we take up to ourselves and to others present as expressed in the way we manage the production or reception of an utterance" (Goffman 1981: 128). In his essay "The Lecture", Goffman mentions 'footing' as a notion referring to the alignment between speaker and listener that different ways of producing talk can help establish: "Memorization, aloud reading, and fresh talk are different production modes. Each presupposes its own special relation between speaker and listener, establishing the speaker on a characteristic 'footing' in regard to the audience" (Goffman 1981: 172).

In the literature on interpreting, Keith (1984) was one of the first to argue that insights from analyses of natural conversations can help devise strategies to teach interpreters. He borrows the Goffmanian notion of footing to distinguish what he calls "two distinct footings" in liaison interpreting, "one where the interpreter is, as it were, macro-conversationally oriented, translating the statements of one of the two interlocutors, the other where he is text-oriented, functioning as himself and dealing with matters of clarification, explanation, repetition, etc. related to one of the interlocutor's utterances" (Keith 1984: 314). More recently, Monacelli (2006, 2009) observed similar phenomena in natural discourse data drawn from samples of SIMULTANEOUS INTERPRETING and referred to these as changes of footing or of alignment.

Several authors also refer to the concept of footing in discussing interpreters' use of the first and third person when rendering a primary party's utterances: in this perspective, a switch of person by the interpreter can be seen both as a change of footing and as an indicator of the interpreter's shifting alignment with one party or another (e.g. Keselman et al. 2010; Merlini 2009a). In her study of a 'cultural mediator' interpreting at a Foreigners Advice Bureau in Italy, Merlini (2009a) notes that the mediator's change of footing via pronoun shifts not only indicates a change of alignment but also underscores cultural MEDIATION as an area of instability, where competing identities are interactively (re)constructed. Obviously, the inherent lack of mutual linguistic accessibility characteristic of interpreter-mediated encounters adds to this instability. Primary participants may not understand whether the interpreter uses the first or third person in the 'other' language, so their access to this way of signalling changes of footing is limited.

Goffman's analytical framework was adopted most prominently by Wadensjö (1992, 1998), who complemented his construct of the production format with a breakdown of the hearer's 'reception format' into three modes of listening: as *reporter, recapitulator,* and *responder.*

As pointed out by Linell (2005), Goffman's notion of footing is closely related to that of POSITIONING as developed by Mühlhäusler and Harré (1990) and others, and applied to the analysis of DIALOGUE INTERPRETING by Mason (2009b).

CECILIA WADENSJÖ

GAZE

↑ BODY LANGUAGE
→ EYE TRACKING, → VISUAL ACCESS

Interpreting as an interactional process is influenced by a number of variables belonging to the sphere of NONVERBAL COMMUNICATION. Gaze, that is the orientation displayed by people through the movement and direction of their eyes in relation to their environment, is one such resource, alongside facial expressions (whose compositionality is strongly affected by gaze), head movements, GESTURE, body posture and orientation, proxemics, object manipulation and spatial arrangement. The range of situated (para)linguistic, visual, aural, spatial and embodied resources contributing to social interaction can be subsumed under the super-ordinate term 'multimodal resources'. These have been studied alongside talk by scholars from different backgrounds and with a view to investigating different interactional phenomena (e.g. Norris 2004; Stivers & Sidnell 2005; Jewitt 2009).

Since the 1960s and 1970s, studies on monolingual (dyadic and multiparty) interaction from various perspectives have explored gaze in relation to ongoing talk as an important vector of meaning and coordination, performing three main, interconnected functions (see Kendon 1967; Argyle & Cook 1976; Goodwin 1981; Rossano 2012). The *expressive* function of gaze conveys affiliation, threat or hostility, usually accompanied by facial expressions, posture and gesture, thus acting as an indicator of participants' positioning within the exchange. The *regulatory* function of gaze serves to coordinate the initiation, maintenance and closure of social encounters; TURN-TAKING and sequential organization of talk; co-construction of meaning; and patterns of participation. In its *monitoring* function, gaze signals special states of recipiency, e.g. the display of attention and engagement (or lack thereof), a demand for feedback, or can be used to pursue a response that is perceived as missing.

Except for SIGNED LANGUAGE INTERPRETING, where gaze not only fulfils its interactional functions but is also part of grammar and plays a key role in action formation (Metzger 1995; Roy 2000a), very little research on interpreting has systematically examined gaze (and other embodied resources) alongside verbal behaviour. One reason for the scarcity of studies combining both dimensions may be that early research on (spoken-language) interpreting focused mainly on CONFERENCE INTERPRETING, particularly in the simultaneous mode, where the interactional dimension is limited by the largely monologic format. Poyatos (1997, 2002) provides a comprehensive semiotic account of paralinguistic and kinesic traits, showing that their cross-cultural manifestation has the potential to give rise to miscommunication and impact on QUALITY. More recent work on SIMULTANEOUS INTERPRETING (e.g. Seeber 2012) has employed EYE TRACKING to analyse how interpreters attend to multimodal input (e.g. speakers' facial expression and gesture or use of visual aid to complement talk) and its effect on the interpreting process.

Research focusing on the social and regulatory function of gaze in interpreting stems mainly from micro-analytical approaches to the study of authentic, mediated face-to-face encounters, where the issue of whether interpreters and participants 'should' gaze at each other while speaking/listening is closely linked to questions of INVISIBILITY and ROLE. Lang's (1978) pioneering work, based on video recordings of CONSECUTIVE INTERPRETING in a Papua New Guinea court, shows that the interpreter's preference for averting gaze to signal detachment and NEUTRALITY may interfere with smooth turn-taking due to reduced monitoring of other people's behaviour. It was only several decades later that Wadensjö (2001a), exploring interpreters' proxemics during therapeutic interviews, examined the influence of spatial POSITIONING and seating arrangements on opportunities for eye contact, and showed the positive impact of the interpreter's inclusion within a "shared communicative radius" on the outcome of the exchange. In a similar vein, Bot (2005) and Mason (2012) focus on how gaze patterns affect the PARTICIPATION FRAMEWORK in interpreter-mediated PSYCHOTHERAPY and in interviews in ASYLUM SETTINGS, respectively. Further studies on gaze in HEALTHCARE INTERPRETING include Ticca's (2008) investigation of the monitoring function as displayed by ad hoc interpreters, and Pasquandrea's (2011) exploration of gaze as a crucial component in the multimodal co-construction of courses of actions and participation frameworks. Davitti (2013) examines gaze in relation to talk in pedagogical settings (parent–teacher meetings), showing different gaze dynamics with respect to previous studies encompassing this dimension, and discussing the implications of her findings for participants' (dis)engagement, empowerment and intercultural MEDIATION.

Integrating the complex role of visual cues and gaze in interpreter-mediated interaction represents an important interface between interpreting research and a broadly semiotic approach to communication studies. Indeed, research into gaze in interpreting in (mainly) dialogic settings has yielded interesting insights into the interactional dynamics of triadic exchanges and provided further evidence that gaze behaviour in human communication is affected by, and at the same time shapes, the interactional environment in which it is produced. Most current research remains qualitative in nature, mainly due to the difficulties involved in gathering naturally occurring data from sensitive settings and the lack of a well-established conceptual and methodological framework to analyse data of such complexity. The interplay of these multiple levels in interaction, alongside cross-cultural differences in gaze behaviour and the relationship between gaze, affect and facial expressions, are among the topics requiring further research.

ELENA DAVITTI

GENDER

↑ SOCIOLINGUISTIC APPROACHES

Consistent with what sociolinguistic research has amply demonstrated since the 1960s about face-to-face interactions, interpreter-mediated encounters obviously do not occur in a social vacuum. They should therefore be investigated not only with regard to their socio-historical and socio-cultural contexts, but also with particular attention to the usually combined impact of the 'social distances' (Trudgill 2000) that separate the protagonists. Among these social distances at the basis of individuals' social identities, gender is certainly one of those that have generated most interest in the field of face-to-face communication. If a growing number of studies, mainly carried out in various Western societies, have demonstrated many similarities in the language practices of men and women, they also point to some clear differences. Most frequently described is the existence of two distinct communicative styles: masculine style is associated with assertiveness, competitiveness or directivity, reflected in discourse as interruptions, verbal dominance or transgression of etiquette; feminine style, by contrast, exhibits qualities such as empathy, cooperation and avoidance of conflict, and is linked to pragmatic strategies such as hedges, indirect questions or euphemisms. There is general agreement that such gender differences are not to be understood in absolute terms, but that certain clusters of linguistic features are more characteristic of the way men or women talk (Talbot 2010). Exactly why this should be so is the subject of some controversy. Whatever reason(s) one may wish to foreground, gender differences in language use are clearly relevant to interpreting, with regard both to the profession and to the analysis of interactions. Thus, it has been observed that CONFERENCE INTERPRETING, a male-dominated profession when it emerged in the early twentieth century, is now practised mainly by women, and that this might be associated with the shift from on-stage CONSECUTIVE INTER-PRETING to SIMULTANEOUS INTERPRETING in a booth. More generally, interpreting in most countries is predominantly a female occupation, which raises issues of language, identity and social STATUS (e.g. Shlesinger & Voinova 2012). Even so, the gender issue has not received much attention in interpreting studies to date, save the occasional mention of gender matching in MEDIA INTERPRETING contexts.

Even in SOCIOLINGUISTIC APPROACHES to interpreting, and in particular DIALOGUE INTERPRETING, efforts at theorizing gender issues are still the exception. However, there are at least three good reasons to envisage a greater focus on the relationship between gender and interpreting in face-to-face dialogue. First, interpreter-mediated encounters involve the presence of at least three participants, with the interpreter being seen as a 'whole' person with his/her own subjectivity (Wadensjö 1998; Davidson 2000). The interpreter's gender identity, like that of the primary participants, may thus affect the communication process. Second, the interpreter is required not only to provide an accurate rendition of utterances but also to take into consideration, among other things, gendered communicative styles adopted by the participants in the dialogue – styles which can, in addition, present cross-cultural differences to varying degrees. And third, any interpreter must cope with the fact that language systems reflect human experience in different ways, including issues of maleness and femaleness (Weber et al. 2005). The interpreter must therefore make choices regarding women's visibility in linguistic forms.

It would seem obvious that dealing with such complex issues of gender and identity in interpreter-mediated dialogue requires a certain level of professional COMPETENCE, especially in SETTINGS where people's safety and welfare are at stake. This applies in particular to HEALTHCARE INTERPRETING, even though several studies have shown that many clinicians would rather see the interpreter as an instrument – a machine capable of translating word for word – than as a full-fledged participant (e.g. Singy & Guex 2005). Numerous studies have clearly demonstrated the health benefits of using a professional interpreter, and it seems that these benefits may be even more pronounced when there is gender concordance between interpreter and patient. Thus, it has been found that in specific interpreted consultations, patients of the same gender as the interpreter are more confident and can therefore discuss their health problems more easily with the clinician (e.g. Binder et al. 2012). This is particularly salient in medical examinations relating, for example, to physical and psychological abuse and to intimacy: pregnancy for women and reproductive capability for men (Hadziabdic & Hjelm 2013). All of these findings clearly challenge a 'disembodied' conception of interpreting that does not make allowance for such aspects of the interpreter's identity as gender.

PASCAL SINGY AND PATRICE GUEX

GENEVA PARK CONFERENCE

see under CRITICAL LINK

GERVER

David Gerver (1932–1981) was a British psychologist whose pioneering experimental and theoretical work gave a major impetus to COGNITIVE APPROACHES in interpreting research.

Though Gerver can be considered a central figure in the formative years of INTERPRETING STUDIES, his interests as a psychologist were much broader, ranging from the clinical to the cognitive. Languages, however, played a role in his life long before his career in psychology. Born in London, Gerver spent most of the war years in the United States, with his mother and sister, but attended secondary school in Switzerland, which allowed him to acquire near-native proficiency in both French and German – languages to which he later added some knowledge of Italian, Russian and Hebrew. His fascination with multilingual, cross-cultural experiences remained with him throughout his life.

Having obtained his degree in psychology from the University of Hull and a Postgraduate Diploma in Abnormal Psychology from the University of London at age 30, he spent a year as a research assistant at the University of California, Berkeley before going to Oxford University, as a research student and also teacher of psychology at Oriel College. From 1966 to 1971 he was Lecturer in Psychology at the University of Durham, and it was during those years that he conducted his groundbreaking experimental work on SIMULTANEOUS INTERPRET-ING, supported by a three-year grant from the Social Science Research Council. Gerver reported most of this research in his doctoral thesis on *Aspects of Simultaneous Interpretation and Human Information Processing*, submitted to the University of Oxford in 1971. As stated in his Introduction, his main interest was in mechanisms of MEMORY and attention in human information processing activities, of which simultaneous interpreting served as a particularly complex example. His dissertation reports his classic experiment on the effect of input SPEECH RATE (Gerver 1969/2002) and his studies on the impact of degraded source-speech PROSODY and input-channel noise (Gerver 1974a), as chapters 2, 3 and 4 respectively; it also presents Gerver's psycholinguistic experiments on the effects of language, list length and strategy on bilingual subjects' recall of auditorily presented words from short-term memory. In his concluding chapter, Gerver proposes the very first cognitive process model of simultaneous interpreting, which subsequently gained widespread attention through an article in *Meta* (Gerver 1975) and his much-cited chapter (Gerver 1976) in the collective volume edited by Richard Brislin (1976). That book brought Gerver's work alongside that of some leading authors in the budding field of translation studies, including Eugene Nida, Wolfram Wilss – and Danica SELESKOVITCH, whom he would host, together with Jean HERBERT and some 100 other participants, at the 1977 VENICE SYMPOSIUM co-organized with Wallace Sinaiko (Gerver & Sinaiko 1978).

Judging on the sole basis of his academic affiliations during his regrettably short career, the key role which Gerver had come to play in international and interdisciplinary networking by the late 1970s was by no means a foregone conclusion. According to a curriculum vitae provided by his wife Elisabeth, he spent two years as a visiting professor at Queen's University, Canada, in the early 1970s before taking up the post of Senior Lecturer in Psychology at the University of Stirling, which he held until his untimely death from an asthma attack in 1981.

Interpreting remained one of Gerver's main research interests in the later stages of his career. In 1977 he spent a sabbatical term at the University of Ottawa, working on simultaneous interpreting, and participated in the FIT Congress in Warsaw (Gerver 1981). In the late 1970s, he worked on an APTITUDE TESTING project at the Polytechnic of Central London (Longley 1989), the results of which were published posthumously in the 1980s (Gerver et al.

1984, 1989) and continued to inspire research on aptitude until well into the twenty-first century (see Pöchhacker & Liu 2014). Nevertheless, Gerver also maintained a keen interest in clinical psychology, developing training programs in anger management for female prisoners and fear-of-flying courses for British Airways as well as co-founding a community psychology service in the town of Bridge of Allan near Stirling.

Even in the 1960s, the breadth of Gerver's interests had been impressive. A 1965 paper co-authored with Fay Fransella, who went on to become a leading figure in Personal Construct Therapy, dealt with statistics for predicting children's reading age from chronological age and verbal IQ, and Gerver's affinity towards computer science is illustrated by the Automatic Speech-Pause Analyzer he programmed for the analysis of dual-track audio recordings during his time at Queen's University (Gerver & Dineley 1972). In 1969 (the year he got married), he not only presented his input rate paper at the Second Louisville Conference on Rate and/or Frequency Controlled Speech, but also researched and presented two BBC programs on the human relationship between the conductor and the orchestra.

In a post to his "Unprofessional Translation" blog (dated May 30, 2010), Brian Harris cites David Gerver as asking him, presumably three or four decades earlier, "Why do universities insist that their older staff go on publishing? By the time they're 50, they've usually done their best work anyway." Gerver's death at age 49 did not give him a chance to put this claim to the test. Judging from his energy and ideas in so many different domains, however, it is quite likely that on this count he could have proved himself wrong.

FRANZ PÖCHHACKER

GESTURE

↑ BODY LANGUAGE

Gesture is the general term used to designate a variety of phenomena whose common denominator is their realization through visible bodily movements called gestures. The concept is best explained through 'Kendon's Continuum', comprising, from left to right, gesticulation, pantomime, emblems, and sign languages (McNeill 1992). Moving from gesticulation to sign language, there are two interrelated changes: the obligatory presence of speech linked to gesture fades and disappears as the linguistic systems used by deaf communities emerge; at the same time, the cultural markedness of gestures and the level of awareness of gesture use increase. Emblems (Ekman & Friesen 1969), like the 'thumbs up' or the 'OK' gesture, are culturally codified movements mostly involving the hands, which have specific shared configurations and meanings and can be used instead of the word(s) they stand for. As they are the most easily recognized type of gesture, they have been widely studied and documented in anthropology and ethnography. Indeed, in everyday language, the word 'gesture' is often used as a synonym for 'emblem'. Conversely, interest in the spontaneous gestures accompanying human speech has waxed and waned over the years. In the 1950s, these gestures became the primary object of investigation in kinesics (Birdwhistell 1970) and came to be regarded as a communicative modality in human interaction. At the same time, they were studied within the wider domain of NONVERBAL COMMUNICATION, but mostly as independent from other modalities. Research in the interdisciplinary field of Gesture Studies, however, has demonstrated that body movements are closely related to speech production at the phonological, semantic and pragmatic levels, as well as from a temporal viewpoint (Kendon 2004; McNeill 1992). Gestures, studied not in isolation but as an integral part of language and thought, are thus seen as having multiple functions in meaning building, cognition, discourse organization, and interaction regulation (Müller et al. 2013).

The importance of gesture for a full understanding of the communicative situation in which the interpreter operates was intuitively recognized very early on, and is reflected in the requirement for VISUAL ACCESS to the speaker and the audience in professional associations' codes on WORKING CONDITIONS. In interpreting research, gesture and BODY LANGUAGE have been marginally addressed as part of the visual input processed by conference interpreters (e.g. Alonso Bacigalupe 1999; Balzani 1990; Poyatos 1997) and as elements contributing to thought organization and natural INTONATION in SIMULTANEOUS INTERPRETING (SI) (Viaggio 1997). The probable reason for this lack of interest in interpreters' gesture production (an exception is Sineiro de Saa 2003) was that research in interpreting studies was long dominated by information processing models and a view of CONFERENCE INTERPRETING as a decontextualised, essentially cognitive activity.

More recently, some of the theoretical and methodological frameworks developed in Gesture Studies have been adapted to the study of gesture production by simultaneous interpreters. Galhano Rodrigues (2007) applies her model of holistic qualitative micro-analysis of speech and body movements in face-to-face interaction to investigate the gestural behaviour of a simultaneous interpreter in an authentic setting, concluding that gestures serve both cognitive and discursive functions. Zagar Galvão (2009, 2013) investigates the role of co-speech gestures in SI through a mixed approach, based on open experimenting, field observation and INTERVIEWS with professional conference interpreters. Findings reveal that gestures in SI have multiple interrelated functions and dimensions (pragmatic, discursive, interactional, modal, cognitive) and that interpreters' gestural behaviour crucially depends on contextual factors, such as booth position, type of meeting, empathy (or lack of it) with the speaker, personal interest in the speech, and DIRECTIONALITY, as well as on interpreters' personal and cultural traits and their perception of their own ROLE and professional identity. Applying McNeill's theoretical model and methods, Adam (Adam & Castro 2013) conducted an experimental study on SI students' co-speech gestures, showing that beats (i.e. biphasic gestures that accompany the rhythm of speech) are by far the most frequent and serve mostly cognitive and discourse-structuring functions.

Though a fully-fledged investigation of the multiple modalities that contribute to the co-construction of meaning and context in the different MODES of interpreting is still lacking, recent efforts point to possible developments, particularly in the study of DIALOGUE INTERPRETING, with potential implications for interpreter training and professional practice.

ELENA ZAGAR GALVÃO

GHOST ROLE

see under ROLE

HABITUS

↑ SOCIOLOGICAL APPROACHES

Habitus is a key concept in Pierre Bourdieu's theory of social construction and reproduction (e.g. Bourdieu 1977), and this and other Bourdieusian concepts have been applied within interpreting studies in order to observe and articulate the higher-level features of translational activity embedded within particular social structures and social institutions, and situated in specific cultural, historical and political contexts.

According to Bourdieu, social structure is conceived as comprised of inter-locking 'fields' and their accompanying habitus. Habitus refers to the internalized dispositions, or ways of perceiving the world, that are generated within specific fields in interaction with the social and biological trajectory (the embodiment of habitus over time) of individual agents. Fields are viewed as relatively autonomous structures in social space, each with its own particular set of values and regulative principles. Examples include the economic, political, legal, cultural, scientific, military and literary fields. All of these are understood to be structurally similar to the wider socio-cultural order; they are subordinate to the larger forces of symbolic and economic power, and are key sites for the ongoing struggle of social agents over access to both knowledge and power. In Bourdieu's theory of social reproduction, habitus and field are further linked to the notion of 'capital' – the social 'goods' that become associated with material or symbolic wealth and power in a given period. The possession of different forms of capital bestows status and prestige on its owners; capital positions agents within fields in specific ways, and confers legitimacy on particular ways of constructing and constituting social reality. Bourdieu understands competition and conflict over different forms of capital to be central to the 'game' of social life. He draws on the notion of *illusio* (from Latin *ludus*, game) to account for the tacit recognition amongst 'players' of the value and stakes of the game, and for the practical mastery of its rules. Habitus is understood to operate at the unconscious level in situated social experiences; the different ways that individuals construct and evaluate 'objective reality' are acquired through the inculcation of a set of social practices, initially in the family (primary habitus) and subsequently through participation in other social institutions, such as schools and professional organizations (specific habitus). Importantly, the formation of habitus is understood not as an abstracted form of consciousness but as "constituted in practice and always oriented to practical functions" (Bourdieu 1990: 52).

Translation scholar Daniel Simeoni (1998) brought the concept of habitus to prominence with his article, "The pivotal status of the translator's habitus", in which he characterized the field of translation as a 'pseudo- or would-be- field' in contrast to, for example, the literary, scientific, technical or legal fields in which translational activity takes place. This distinction between field and pseudo-field led him to conclude that translators (and presumably interpreters) brought only a 'social' or generalized habitus rather than a 'specific' or professional habitus to their work. This, he suggested, supported the continuation of an ingrained subservience and passivity on the part of translators in accordance with the normative practices of their PROFESSION.

The concept of habitus has been considered in relation to interpreters and the multiple fields in which they work. Much of this work, part of a larger body of empirical research that falls under the category of SOCIOLOGICAL APPROACHES, implicitly or explicitly takes Simeoni's claim of the translator's subservience as a starting point in considering the interaction of interpreter agency and the social and institutional structures in which they work in constructing the interpreting habitus. The interpreter's habitus or the interaction of different habitus within a particular field are examined across a range of diverse contexts, revealing both constancy and shifts in the ROLE of interpreters and in the expectations and experiences of their interlocutors in relation to this role, at both the macro-structural and local, interactional levels.

MOIRA INGHILLERI

HABSBURG MONARCHY

↑ HISTORY

→ DRAGOMANS, → JEUNES DE LANGUES

The 'Habsburg Monarchy', or Empire, is an unofficial designation by historians of the countries and provinces ruled by the Austrian branch of the House of Habsburg (which dates back to the late thirteenth century) and by the successor branch of Habsburg-Lorraine (until 1918). Like any multi-ethnic empire, the Habsburg Monarchy required differentiated communication strategies in order to guarantee the functioning of administration and daily life. According to the census of 1910, its more than 51 million inhabitants included 24% German speakers, 20% Hungarians, 13% Czechs, 10% Poles and 8% Ukrainians, followed by Romanians, Croats, Slovaks, Slovenes, Serbs, Bosniaks and Italians (Wolf 2015). Interpreters were instrumental in establishing a consensus in a highly intricate system of political, confessional, legal, ceremonial and, increasingly, national interests and differences. 'Interpreting' (German *Dolmetschen*), in those times, did not always correspond to the present-day understanding of the term, but could also involve cultural brokering as well as written translation (see Reiter 2013a).

Mediators between empires

Interpreting activities changed over the centuries and in accordance with political, economic and social developments. The Habsburg Court in Vienna was the Empire's political core and for centuries served as a hub between the East and the West, which made cross-cultural contacts in diplomacy and commerce a frequent occurrence. Between 1541 and 1884 the Court employed interpreters for Turkish/Oriental languages, Russian, Polish, Spanish, Hungarian, Swedish and English (Reiter 2013a). The activity of Spanish-speaking interpreters gained momentum in the first half of the sixteenth century. Russian interpreters, on the other hand, became important after the Treaty of Moscow in 1686, which fostered common interests of Russia and the Habsburgs and entailed the visit of numerous delegations to the Vienna Court. Lorenz von Churelitz (c. 1621–1681), Sebastian Glavinich and Adam Sty(l)la (died 1704) were interpreters for Russian and Polish in the second half of the seventeenth century (Reiter 2013b). Styla was also appointed Court Interpreter (*Hofdolmetsch*), a prestigious post in the hierarchy of the Court's civil servants between the sixteenth and nineteenth centuries.

Interpreters' main field of activity was communication with the Ottoman Empire, especially between the fifteenth and eighteenth centuries. As the Habsburg and Ottoman empires shared centuries of animosity and a history of mutual conflict, it is not surprising that historical data on interpreting mainly focus on these antagonisms. Even when they were not in (armed) conflict, the two powers and their respective satellites paid close attention to one another, conducting trade, receiving diplomatic delegations, and dealing with confessional questions, thus being constantly confronted with the image of the 'other', and contributing to shape it with continuous propaganda activities. Interpreters and DRAGOMANS were indispensable for communication between the two worlds (Kurz et al. 2005). Their interpreting activities were shaped by two main characteristics: loyalty and status. Loyalty towards the Habsburg family was the foremost principle. Far from the NEUTRALITY that in later centuries came to be seen as a key prerequisite of interpreters, they were expected to be loyal to the Monarchy at all times, not least as a result of negative experiences with Levantine interpreters 'borrowed' from the Ottoman Empire in the early sixteenth century. Status and ceremony also played a decisive role: Court Interpreters' duties included receiving diplomatic visitors from Constantinople; they not only interpreted between the persons involved, but often took an active part in the negotiations.

In such situations it was vital for them to strictly observe the position they were accorded in the Court's hierarchy. (For their visual representation, see Gürçağlar 2004.)

Training and institutionalization

From 1547, the Austrian Habsburgs were represented at the Sublime Porte in Constantinople by an ambassador (*Internuntius*); the Ottomans did not send a representative, but periodically dispatched delegations to Vienna. At that time there were hardly any available teachers of the Ottoman-Turkish language, and the interpreters who took part in diplomatic visits had often learned the language in years of wartime captivity, as was the case with Johann Gaudier (Petritsch 1987). To make up for the lack of Turkish-speaking interpreters, the Habsburgs adopted the Venetian (and French) idea of JEUNES DE LANGUES. The first 'language boys' (*Sprachknaben*), aged between ten and sixteen, were sent to the Sublime Porte in 1578. Under the official guidance of the *Internuntius*, whose educational commitment was admittedly often found wanting, they learned the language with Ottoman teachers and from their own local contacts. Upon their return to Vienna, they acted as teachers of Turkish and worked as Court Interpreters.

Not least due to the poor management of the language boys' education, the Academy for Oriental Languages was founded in Vienna in 1754 by Empress Maria Theresa. It was run for nearly 100 years by the Jesuits, who put great emphasis on morality, devotion and obedience. In addition to the Turkish language, geography, history, law, literature, Catholic religion and natural sciences were taught. The syllabus was then expanded to include French, Italian, Modern Greek, Arabic and Persian, and the students also learned to distinguish between the various dialects (Petritsch 2004). Teaching methods sought to transmit enthusiasm for the language, which was considered a prerequisite to being a good interpreter (Joukova 2004). Most graduates were employed in the service of the state, whether as translators, diplomats or academics. One of the first, Franz de Paula Thugut, became Minster of Foreign Affairs, while Joseph von Hammer-Purgstall was founder and first president of the Academy of Sciences and an important Austrian orientalist. By the end of the nineteenth century, the Ottoman Empire no longer posed any threat to the Austro-Hungarian Monarchy. Economic and trading issues now came to the fore, also affecting the syllabus of the Academy (Wolf 2005).

Improvements in the interpreters' training resulted in the broadening of their fields of activity: while initially they were primarily charged with ministering to diplomatic missions and translating the correspondence between the Habsburg and the Ottoman Empires, later on many of them became diplomats themselves. The Court's organizational structure provided for a gradual integration of interpreters into the civil service. In order to hold the office of Court Interpreter, each individual interpreter had to be appointed by imperial decree. The remuneration of Court Interpreters is well documented (Reiter 2013a; Wolf 2015). They received the average salary of a senior civil servant and were occasionally granted additional benefits, ranging from valuable gifts to a living allowance; sometimes they were even conferred with nobility.

In addition to Court Interpreters, linguistic MEDIATION was accomplished by other interpreters who received more or less the same remuneration, among them a woman, Johanna Brunetto, who worked as an interpreter for three years and died in 1682 (Sienell 2001).

In the field of LEGAL INTERPRETING, as early as 1803 the penal code stipulated the use of sworn interpreters. In the last 70 years of the Monarchy, 29 different languages were offered in Vienna by hundreds of sworn interpreters (Wolf 2015). After 1848, the institutionalization of interpreting (and especially translating) activity was enhanced by the creation of special administrative sections in various ministries, including the 'Editorial Office' of the *Reichsgesetzblatt* (imperial legal gazette), the 'Section for Ciphers and Translating', and the

Evidenzbureau, which provided – particularly during wars – for the training of military interpreters (Wolf 2015). Generally speaking, however, the level of institutionalization was relatively low when judged against the gigantic administrative apparatus of the pluricultural empire. On the other hand, the commercial translation sector, which developed in the late nineteenth century through the creation of an increasing number of translation and inter-preting bureaus, experienced an explicit process of professionalization (Wolf 2013b), mostly driven by the struggle for recognition in this field.

The intricate communication system of the Habsburg Monarchy was constituted mostly by multilingual civil servants, whose work would have required not only linguistic skills but also quick wits in adapting to countless different permutations of language needs. Given the enormous need for linguistic and cultural mediation activities, large parts of the population in need of such services tacitly agreed to get by in everyday situations without the help of translators or interpreters, although the call for such professional help became louder over the years.

MICHAELA WOLF

HEALTHCARE INTERPRETING

↑ COMMUNITY INTERPRETING
→ DIALOGUE INTERPRETING
↓ MENTAL HEALTH SETTINGS, ↓ PEDIATRIC SETTINGS, ↓ SPEECH PATHOLOGY

Healthcare interpreting, also known as medical interpreting, refers to interpreting activities that take place in healthcare contexts, with interpreters serving a larger communicative activity, namely, provider–patient communication in cross-cultural healthcare. Since the mid-1990s, healthcare interpreting has seen tremendous growth, both in its legal regulation and professional development as a field of practice and in its theoretical development as a field of research.

The literature has provided conclusive evidence of health disparities experienced by patients who do not share the same language, whether spoken or signed, as their providers (Jacobs et al. 2006). They often receive less preventive care, fewer referrals, follow-ups and public health services, but show more resource utilization (e.g. more diagnostic tests and longer hospital stays) when they do visit healthcare institutions. At an interpersonal level, they and their family members also tend to receive lower quality of care when judged by such measures as inter-personal support, patient-centered communication, and patient satisfaction, even in areas unrelated to language. Although researchers are uncertain about the exact processes and pathways by which language barriers create health disparities, interpreters have been viewed as the standard solution to improve language-discordant patients' access to and quality of care.

In various multi-ethnic societies, countries that receive many immigrants, and regions where international travelers are common (e.g. metropolitan areas for international commerce and destinations for medical tourism), efforts have been made by healthcare institutions, local governments, professional organizations, and academic institutions to develop appropriate guidelines and/or CERTIFICATION processes to ensure the quality of care.

Policy and regulation

The literature on healthcare interpreting has been dominated by countries that have strong sociopolitical support for language access in healthcare settings. For example, the increase of research publications in the UK coincided with a new policy, introduced in the late 1990s, that allowed non-English speakers to use their own language when using public services. In

Canada, one of the objectives of the 1985 Canada Health Act was to facilitate reasonable access to health services without language barriers.

Several reviews have identified the US as the most productive country in research publications on healthcare interpreting, due to its extensive federal and state legislative efforts to ensure language access in healthcare settings (Youdelman 2008). At the federal level, Title VI of the 1964 Civil Rights Act prohibits discrimination on the basis of race, color, or national origin by any recipient of federal funding. In 2000, the White House issued an Executive Order on 'Improving Access to Services for Persons with Limited English', which gave rise to written guidelines by the Department of Health and Human Services. Although there are no federal requirements for the quality of interpreters in healthcare settings, many states have legislation to clarify or broaden federal guidelines, providing language access for specific clinical contexts. In 2009, California became the first state in the US to require health insurance organizations to pay for interpreting and translating services.

Healthcare facilities in many countries often struggle to locate sufficient resources to fund interpreting services. In some cases, such as Belgium, the Netherlands, and some Scandinavian countries, previously high levels of public policy support for interpreter services have suffered a decline, making it increasingly difficult to take positive action at the national or local levels (Phelan 2012).

Types of healthcare interpreters

Healthcare interpreting includes a wide variety of interpreters and interpreting modalities, though researchers did not systematically examine the differences between various types of interpreters until the early 2000s (Hsieh 2006a). Topics examined in studies comparing professional and NON-PROFESSIONAL INTERPRETING in healthcare settings include differences in communicative patterns, participant dynamics, interpreting errors, patient/provider satisfaction, clinical impact, and ethical concerns.

Several reviews have found that *professional interpreters* can improve patients' quality of care. In healthcare settings, professional interpreting typically involves *on-site interpreters*, who are hospital-based or contracted through interpreting AGENCIES, and *technology-based services* such as TELEPHONE INTERPRETING and videoconference-based REMOTE INTERPRETING. This use of technology has gained popularity in the healthcare industry in recent years, thanks to its cost-effectiveness (e.g. by-minute rate) and high availability.

The core competencies of professional interpreters working in healthcare settings include (a) maintaining accuracy and completeness; (b) understanding medical terminology and the human body; (c) behaving ethically and making ethical decisions; (d) possessing non-verbal communication skills; and (e) possessing cross-cultural communication skills (Ono et al. 2013). Training for professional interpreters varies considerably, ranging from 40-hour courses to Master's degrees in interpreting. Interpreters' health-related expertise also varies significantly because some interpreters work exclusively in healthcare settings (e.g. hospital interpreters), while others (e.g. telephone interpreters) often work with a wider pool of clients.

Aside from recourse to *chance interpreters* (i.e. untrained persons used on a random basis, such as bilingual bystanders) and other ad hoc arrangements, it is not uncommon for healthcare facilities in many countries to rely on *family interpreters* (i.e. patients' family members and friends). For both these categories of interpreter, concerns have been raised about misinterpretation, patient privacy, disrupted social roles, and litigation risks. In particular when bilingual children serve as interpreters (also referred to as CHILD LANGUAGE BROKERING), they may not have adequate medical knowledge or emotional maturity to ensure the patient's quality of care or their own personal well-being. Nevertheless, family interpreters constitute a unique category due to their knowledge of the patients and special relationship of TRUST, which providers can draw on in certain circumstances, such as history taking and patient advocacy. Some researchers have argued that family interpreters can be valuable resources when providers are properly trained to utilize them appropriately and effectively. Others argue that a universal rejection of the use of family interpreters may be unrealistic, not least in clinical emergencies. It can also be viewed as an imposition of Western values on minority/marginalized populations, especially when patients feel strongly about relying on family interpreters for reasons of social obligation and established cultural practices.

Many healthcare facilities also purposefully recruit *bilingual staff* (both medical and administrative) who can not only interact with patients directly but also serve as in-house interpreters. Because of the importance attached to language concordance, bilingual providers serving patients directly are often viewed as the gold standard in cross-cultural care and have been used as a reference group in many comparative studies of healthcare interpreting. When they serve their colleagues as interpreters, their medical expertise, availability, and institutional roles set them apart as a distinct category of interpreters. However, a bilingual healthcare provider interpreting for another may pose challenges to the primary provider's authority and control over the encounter. A bilingual nurse may feel obligated to align herself with the physician's therapeutic objectives, rather than to advocate for the patient's needs. In addition, such dual-role interpreters do not always have sufficient language fluency or cultural competency, and often struggle to balance their additional workload as interpreters with their primary duties. Their communicative patterns also tend to focus on their own clinical needs and fail to address patients' concerns. Studies have found that bilingual providers and their patients often differ in their perceptions about patient satisfaction and quality of care. Thus, appropriate training, organizational assessments, and institutional guidelines are critical to ensure providers' appropriate and effective use of their language skills for clinical purposes (Diamond et al. 2012).

Research approaches and themes in theoretical development

Because healthcare interpreting is uniquely situated at the intersection of medicine, language, and culture, this interdisciplinary field has attracted researchers from various disciplines, including medicine, applied linguistics, and communication, as well as INTERPRETING STUDIES. While some of the earliest publications by healthcare practitioners date back to the 1960s, most studies until the late 1980s provided anecdotal observations and often focused on working with informal interpreters. The emergence of professional interpreters in the 1990s facilitated the development of systematic and evidence-based studies, with findings highlighting the authors' discipline-specific interests, such as clinical impacts for medical researchers, discourse pragmatics for applied linguists, and interpreter performance/visibility for researchers of interpreting studies. By the 2000s, a wide variety of interdisciplinary publications and reviews, including studies with sophisticated research designs and large samples, were beginning to address both the clinical/medical and the sociopolitical/sociocultural dimensions of healthcare interpreting (Bischoff 2012). Against this background, the themes and findings described below have shaped the recent theoretical development and practice of healthcare interpreting.

Utilization patterns and barriers

Patterns in use of interpreters by providers are central to assessing language access in healthcare settings. Studies on this topic typically rely on quantitative and/or qualitative

SURVEY RESEARCH as the primary data collection method. Various authors have found that providers consistently underutilize professional interpreters, who are involved in contacts with less than 20% of language-discordant patients, even where interpreter services are legally required and telephone interpreting is made accessible (Schenker et al. 2011). Although time pressure, lack of availability/accessibility, and cost concerns are often cited as providers' reasons for not using professional interpreters, research has pointed to a wide variety of issues involved in providers' choice of interpreters. Providers strategically utilize different types of interpreter depending on their communicative goals, including discussion of therapeutic objectives, interpersonal support, clinical urgency, clinical complexity, and legal considerations (Diamond et al. 2009; Hsieh & Hong 2010). For example, some providers would not consider using technology-based interpreting to disclose bad news, even when the interpreters are highly trained and easily accessible; telephone interpreters' anonymity may pose challenges for mental health providers, as their patients may be paranoid or distrustful; on-site interpreters may pose risks to patient privacy if the local immigrant community is small; bilingual nurses may choose to use a professional interpreter for discharge instructions, but use their own bilingual skills when administering medication. Thus, the different types of interpreter and the various interpreting modalities are not interchangeable, and may have unique clinical consequences in bilingual healthcare. Rather than focus on providers' utilization patterns, researchers have underlined the need to examine and regulate the providers' decision-making process in choosing the appropriate interpreting modalities.

Interpreter roles and functions

Interpreters' roles and functions have been studied extensively, facilitating the paradigm shift from a blind preference for the conduit model in healthcare settings to recognizing the interpreter as an active participant. Traditionally, studies on this topic use data from INTERVIEWS and focus groups to explore interpreters' and their clients' attitudes to, and expectations of, interpreters' possible roles. Several researchers have also juxtaposed interviews with actual interpreter-mediated medical encounters, examining the discrepancies between participants' attitudes and practices.

The conduit model has been influential in shaping the early development of healthcare interpreting. Interpreters are trained to adopt a neutral, faithful, and passive presence in provider–patient interactions, casting themselves as invisible linguistic machines that transfer information from one language to another. Various codes of ETHICS have conceptualized healthcare interpreters' default role as that of a conduit, reflecting institutional efforts to minimize interpreters' control and influence over the medical encounter. However, due to the differences in provider–patient health literacy, communicative norms, and illness ideologies, a conduit role can reinforce the POWER hierarchy, social injustice, and miscommunication in cross-cultural healthcare. Many researchers and interpreters have thus argued that a conduit-only model is unrealistic and impractical in healthcare settings (Hsieh & Kramer 2012).

Numerous typologies of interpreter roles have been proposed for training purposes (e.g. Roat 1996) and/or through evidence-based research (e.g. Kaufert & Koolage 1984; Leanza 2005). Many of the typologies share similar roles. For example, a *cultural broker/specialist* provides the necessary cultural framework to facilitate understanding. An *advocate* works on behalf of patients, to ensure their quality of care in addition to the quality of communication. By noting a continuum of interpreter roles in practice, from the passive conduit role to active advocacy roles, researchers have found that interpreters strategically shift between various levels of visibility to ensure quality of care and to facilitate other speakers' identity performances, communicative competence, and communicative goals (Angelelli 2004a; Brisset et al. 2013). While some roles (e.g. conduit and cultural broker) are primarily enacted during the medical encounters, others (e.g. patient advocate and system agent) may be adopted both inside and outside of medical appointments. In some role constructs (e.g. institutional gate-keeper), interpreters also appear to adopt organizational goals in monitoring resource utilization and institutional ethics (Davidson 2000; Hsieh 2008). By strategically constructing their relationships with others, interpreters define the communicative context, and thus shape what is appropriate behavior by others.

Communicative characteristics

Many studies have examined actual medical encounters, using various DISCOURSE ANALYTICAL APPROACHES to study interpreters' and providers' communicative patterns and collaboration (e.g. Pöchhacker & Shlesinger 2007). Professional interpreters have been found to adopt a physician-centered *and* biomedical approach in managing provider–patient interactions, favoring providers' biomedical perspectives and often ignoring other speakers' non-medical talk (e.g. rapport-building talk) and the changing dynamics in medical encounters (Butow et al. 2011). Because professional interpreters are trained to assume a neutral role, they often experience conflict and frustration in situations in which emotional or advocacy work is necessary. In contrast, family interpreters are typically found to assume a third interlocutor role in provider–patient interactions, interjecting their agenda, providing background information, advocating for patients, and actively controlling the content and process of communication (Rosenberg et al. 2008).

Finally, the QUALITY of healthcare interpreting (and cross-cultural healthcare) is not solely dependent on interpreters' performance but a result of successful collaboration among all parties involved (Jacobs et al. 2010). For example, when providers are unwilling to incorporate interpreters' cultural expertise, are unfamiliar with interpreters' communicative styles, adopt complicated or ambiguous discursive structures, or have conflicting communicative goals and expectations, interpreters may face greater difficulties in managing the content and process of bilingual health communication. From this perspective, provider training for bilingual healthcare should include not only knowledge about access to interpreters and the associated benefits, but also the specific communicative skills necessary to work effectively with healthcare interpreters.

Clinical consequences and specialty needs

The clinical impacts of healthcare interpreting have been investigated extensively by medical researchers. Recent reviews confirm that professional interpreters have a positive impact on patient satisfaction, clinical outcomes, and communicative processes. Though the assumption from earlier studies is that different types of interpreter may have distinct clinical impacts, the number of comparative studies and systematic investigations is too limited to provide conclusive findings.

Using content analysis to investigate actual medical encounters, researchers have confirmed that interpreter alterations (e.g. omission, substitution, and editorializing) are frequent. Whereas the earlier literature tends to see all interpreter alterations as errors or mistakes, several researchers have now argued that alterations introduced by the interpreter can actually be strategic acts to manage contextual demands in medical encounters. The findings about the clinical impacts of interpreter alterations have varied drastically, from nearly all interpreter alterations having a negative impact to most of them being inconsequential or having positive impacts. There have been mixed findings about whether professional inter-preters and family interpreters differ in the frequency and types of alteration they make, as well as the positive/negative consequences related to any such differences (Butow et al. 2011).

Different clinical specialties may also be associated with distinct expectations for interpreters' behaviors (Hsieh et al. 2013). Primary care, emergencies, mental health and PEDIATRIC SETTINGS are some of the most widely studied clinical specialties for bilingual healthcare. However, the number of comparative studies is limited and few studies highlight the impact of a given clinical setting on the findings. Recent evidence suggests that, while provi-ders share some universal expectations for interpreters' role performances (e.g. professionalism), different clinical specialties have their own particular expectations and demands regarding interpreters' behavior. For example, a seemingly casual remark for rapport-building (e.g. "Where are you from?") in a mental health encounter may trigger problematic episodes in patients who recently experienced traumatic events. In contrast, interpreters' rapport with patients is a valuable resource for oncologists who need to disclose bad news.

Tensions in provider–interpreter collaboration

The interplay between trust, control and power has been identified as a major theme in bilingual healthcare. The resulting dynamics can exist at the micro, interpersonal level of provider–patient–interpreter interaction and at the macro, system/cultural level of healthcare institutions and society at large (Brisset et al. 2013). By recognizing interpreters' active role in bilingual healthcare, recent studies have highlighted the importance of *relational contexts* (e.g. interpersonal trust and therapeutic alliances) in shaping providers' and interpreters' collaboration with each other. In addition, providers and interpreters often compete for control over the communicative process by monitoring others' performance, setting boundaries of time, space, and content in provider–patient interactions, and adopting specific verbal and nonverbal strategies to control others' behaviors.

Interpreter self-care

Starting from the early 1990s, researchers have examined factors contributing to physical injuries (e.g. upper extremity cumulative trauma disorders) experienced by signed language interpreters, noting that one in four interpreters may experience symptoms severe enough to modify their activities. Because those experiencing distress are often viewed as broken tools rather than professionals who suffer from job-related hazards, interpreters' psychological well-being was not systematically investigated until the mid to late 2000s. By identifying interpreters' experiences of BURNOUT, post-traumatic stress, and depression due to VICARIOUS TRAUMA as a result of working with torture victims, refugees, and asylum seekers (Splevins et al. 2010), researchers are now recognizing interpreters as active, engaging participants in provider–patient interaction.

ELAINE HSIEH

HERBERT

Jean Herbert (1897–1980) grew up bilingual (French/English), the son of a Frenchman who taught English at the School of Political Science in Paris. Herbert studied at the universities of Paris and Edinburgh. He was a conference interpreter for over sixty years, and he parti-cipated in the founding conferences of the League of Nations (Paris 1919) and the United

Nations (San Francisco 1945), two milestones in the history of interpreting. He was chief interpreter at UN headquarters in New York during the Organization's early years, and president of AIIC, the International Association of Conference Interpreters (1966–1969).

His long career allowed him to witness the birth and evolution of CONFERENCE INTERPRETING (see Herbert 1978), a PROFESSION he helped consolidate in the academic, social and professional domains. He had started as a bilingual French soldier, soon recruited to interpret for Anglo-American troops in World War I, and his first experience at a high diplomatic level was in June 1917 at Lloyd George's house, where he replaced Paul MANTOUX, who was not available.

Aware of the importance of mastering subject matter and TERMINOLOGY to ensure high-quality interpreting, Herbert published a *Lexique français-anglais-américain d'artillerie et de ballistique* in 1919, a much-needed aid in the multilingual context of World War I, where more than 3,000 French rank soldiers were involved in interpreting tasks with their British and American allies (Heimburger 2012a). His interest in terminology led him to coordinate specialized dictionaries for interpreters throughout his life (e.g. Herbert 1976).

A dozen interpreters were at work during the preliminaries to the 1919 Paris Peace Conference, where they developed "for the first time in history a technique of consecutive interpretation, with taking of notes, etc., as we now know it" (Herbert 1978: 6). Over the next 50 years Herbert was to witness a thousandfold increase in the number of interpreters, thanks to the development of specialized university-level programs for interpreter EDUCATION, which proved that interpreters were made, not born. Herbert himself was actively involved in interpreter training at the *École d'interprètes* at the University of Geneva; his 1952 *Interpreter's Handbook* on "how to become a conference interpreter" became a seminal resource not only for his students, but for the newly emerging PROFESSION worldwide.

A bitter controversy at the UN between consecutive interpreters, led by Herbert, and pioneers of SIMULTANEOUS INTERPRETING, led by DOSTERT, was echoed by diplomatic delegations and the New York press (see Baigorri-Jalón 2004). Although less than enthusiastic about the new system, Herbert practiced it for many years. Even so, he remained a staunch believer in the superiority of CONSECUTIVE INTERPRETING, maintaining that simultaneous interpreting, while "considerably easier to learn and to practice" (Herbert 1952: 91), was generally of a QUALITY far below that allowed by consecutive.

Herbert was also an expert in Oriental religions, particularly Hinduism and Shinto, after becoming interested in them in the 1930s. He translated the work of many Hindu sages, including those of Sri Aurobindo, his own guru, and wrote some 25 books on Indian philosophy. He found a certain parallelism between Hinduism and interpreting, given his belief that they both facilitate peaceful understanding and require self-effacement.

When Herbert died in Geneva in 1980 at the age of 83, he was in full command of his mental and physical faculties. Having worked with him at a very difficult meeting a few weeks earlier, his colleague Wadi Keiser (2005) remembered, "He was as brilliant as ever."

JESÚS BAIGORRI-JALÓN

HESITATION

see under FLUENCY

HISTORY

The term 'history' is used in different senses with reference to the study of translation and interpreting through the ages. For scholarly purposes, a useful distinction can be made between history in the sense of an account of past events in narrative form, and history as *historiography*, that is, the discourse on historical data based on certain principles, including, in particular, the methodology of writing history (Woodsworth 1998). With regard to metho-dological and epistemological issues, D'hulst (2010) adds the concept of metahistoriography, which serves well to indicate the main focus of this article.

Research on the history of interpreting, for which records date back around four thousand years, has been relatively limited, probably for a number of reasons. Chief among these is the shortage (or, sometimes, absence) of historical records, attributable to the few traces left by what is essentially an oral exercise. While this limitation undoubtedly applies, Cronin (2006) suggests that its importance may to a certain extent have been exaggerated as a form of justification for ignoring interpreting altogether. Indeed, Vermeer (1992) similarly argues that in most contexts and periods in history, the practice of interpreting appears to have been considered of too little importance to merit special attention, mention or documentation. In this light it is not surprising that interest in the topic comes more from interpreters themselves than from professional historians. Since interpreters generally do not have training in historiographic methods, and since INTERPRETING STUDIES is a young and rather small academic (sub)discipline, the paucity of research on history in interpreting studies thus seems understandable.

Nevertheless, the above considerations can be qualified with reference to the existence of a proto-historiography of interpreting in the early twentieth century in various disciplines. Thus, interpreters were a topic of research in such fields as classical studies (e.g. Gehman 1914), archaeology (Gardiner 1915), diplomacy (Corbett 1927), anthropology (Blom 1928), history (Danquah 1928) and theology (Gaechter 1936). Even so, these publications remained largely unknown in the emerging community of professional interpreters and have had little impact up to now. Practically the only exception is the study by Alfred Hermann (1956/ 2002) on "Interpreting in Antiquity". Hermann's seminal essay, based on a lecture delivered at the School of Foreign Studies and Interpreting at Germersheim, became the main source for follow-up studies by interpreters (e.g. Kurz 1985; Bowen 1995).

While still a relatively small area of work in interpreting studies, the volume of historical research on interpreting has increased considerably in recent times. History-minded scholars of interpreting have begun to draw on an increasing range of sources and methods of investigation, and covered, at least in part, some of the lines of research identified in Baigorri-Jalón (2006).

Methods and sources

Most research on interpreting and interpreters in history takes the form of case studies and is based on standard historical methods and sources. The main idea behind them is to provide a credible historical account, based on records of various types, which can establish a degree of causality in actions and intentions attributable to interpreters. Such descriptive and explanatory accounts may center on individuals, such as MALINCHE and SACAJAWEA, or pioneer conference interpreters in the twentieth century, such as MANTOUX, VELLEMAN, HERBERT and DOSTERT, or on interpreters as a social or institutional group, such as DRAGOMANS or inter-preters at the United Nations. Invariably, though, interpreters in these studies are treated as agents of history, however subaltern, or as major actors in the evolution of the PROFESSION or its technical conditions.

Authors have approached their subjects using a variety of records, giving preference to written or graphic archival sources, as professional historians would. In addition, there are studies based on oral testimonies (e.g. Baigorri-Jalón 2004; Gaiba 1998; Torikai 2009) or on MEMOIRS, where the issue of memory blends with history.

It is safe to assume that there is still a lot of undiscovered or unused material for further research. Repositories are located, inter alia, in public and private archives, some of which contain not only conventional written records, but also sound, video or photographic materials (see Fernández-Ocampo & Wolf 2014); in works by historians or other researchers, where interpreters are mentioned; in memoirs, written by participants in interpreted events or by the interpreters themselves; and in the memory of numerous interpreters or persons who worked with them, many of whom have not told their personal narrative yet. Researchers will often have to 'create' their own sources, for example with oral history techniques.

Themes and scope

An overview of themes and general lines of research, though far from exhaustive, must cover a wide variety of studies. These range from general histories and comprehensive accounts delimited by geography, periods or institutions to microstudies of particular events or individual interpreters, including biographies and even FICTIONAL INTERPRETERS.

A general history of interpreting, which would obviously require a collective endeavor, remains to be compiled. Summary accounts with a 'comprehensive' scope include the book chapters by Bowen (1995) and Andres (2012). The monograph by Roland (1999), though covering interpreters through the ages and throughout the world, foregrounds diplomacy and world affairs.

Most typically, histories of interpreting focus on a given country or territory, or even continent, as covered in a number of entries in this volume. Examples include AFRICA (see also Lawrance et al. 2006), AUSTRALIA, CANADA, CHINA, Germany (Wilss 1999), JAPAN, KOREA, RUSSIA and SPAIN. Along these lines, historians of interpreting have zoomed in on given periods and covered particular civilizations and empires, such as Ancient EGYPT and ROME or the HABSBURG MONARCHY. In this regard, the Spanish colonial empire has yielded a particularly rich line of inquiry (see Alonso-Araguás 2016; Valdeón 2014; Yannakakis 2008; Zavala 2000).

More specific still are histories of particular institutions in a given socio-political context. Noteworthy examples include studies on the JEUNES DE LANGUES of France (Balliu 2005) and Spain (Cáceres-Würsig 2012), or on the Spanish Inquisition (Sarmiento-Pérez 2016). An institutional focus is also applied in studies of relevant organizations, such as the United Nations (Baigorri-Jalón 2004) and the International Association of Conference Interpreters (AIIC) (AIIC History Group 2013).

Another significant object of inquiry consists of particular events in a given national or institutional context. On a broader scale, this encompasses many cases of interpreter involvement in wartime and peacemaking (e.g. Bowen 1994; Footitt & Kelly 2012a; Takeda 2016; Guo 2015; Lan 2016); more specifically, it relates to events like international conferences (e.g. Baigorri-Jalón 2005) or trials, such as the NUREMBERG TRIAL and other cases of TRIBUNAL INTERPRETING (see also Morris 1998).

On the most individual level, the history of interpreters is presented in the form of biographies, such as those of SELESKOVITCH or Thiéry (Balliu 2008), and memoirs (e.g. Berezhkov 1994; Korchilov 1999; Ji 2008). The historiographical value of the latter admittedly needs to be placed in perspective, since they do not always refer to conventional sources but rather to (selective) memory, incorporating elements of self-justification and very often not dwelling on interpreting as such. Similar considerations obviously apply to fictional historical studies based on films (Cronin 2009) or literature (e.g. Andres 2008; Kaindl & Spitzl 2014).

There is clearly a lot of further research to be done on the history of interpreting, and the lines of work enumerated here will continue to fill gaps in different domains, periods or geographical areas. Other paradigms or historiographical approaches, including those with postmodern, deconstructionist underpinnings, may yield further insights when applied to old and new topics or fields of specialization.

JESÚS BAIGORRI-JALÓN

HOSPITAL INTERPRETING

see under HEALTHCARE INTERPRETING

HYPERTEXT

→ CONFERENCE INTERPRETING

The term 'hypertext', coined in the early 1960s by information technologist Ted Nelson, is commonly used to refer to the branching and interlinked presentation of text in an electronic medium. The underlying idea is to connect texts by means of embedded references (hyperlinks) and thus create a more comprehensive web of information.

In the early 1990s, when this idea began to be implemented in the World Wide Web, the notion of hypertext was applied by Pöchhacker (1992) to the conceptual analysis of inter-related speeches ('texts') in conferences with SIMULTANEOUS INTERPRETING. A proposal along these lines had previously been made by Alexieva (1985), who saw the conference as a 'macro-text' and went on to identify its content relationships with individual 'micro-texts' (e.g. a 'parent–daughter text' relation). Pöchhacker's (1992, 1994a) account goes beyond viewing the conference as a higher-order text, and posits the hypertext as one dimension in a multi-level analytical framework that ranges from the contractual conditions for the assignment to specific situational constraints at a given moment during the proceedings. In line with the functionalist theoretical approach, the communicative purpose (*skopos*) of the conference is determined with reference to the contractual specifications for the hypertext, defined – on the basis of Beaugrande and Dressler's (1981) broad definition of text – as a 'communicative event'. The overall communicative function of the event may be, for instance, to exchange or present information, negotiate an agreement, reach a verdict (as in TRIBUNAL INTERPRETING) or foster learning (as in a workshop or seminar, or in a classroom setting in EDUCATIONAL INTERPRETING). The conference as a hypertext with a particular function can then be further analyzed with regard to distinctive 'textual' features such as its structural complexity, the degree of informational density, the extent of visual media use, and the dynamics of information flow. Using these features of interpreter-mediated conference-like events, Pöchhacker (1992, 1994a) proposes seven conference (proto)types. These include: assemblies of international organizations; technical conferences; training seminars; negotiations; press conferences and presentations; forums on current topics; and invited lectures.

From a professional point of view, the various hypertext types correspond to types of assignments for which an interpreter is recruited, with different structural and functional characteristics. Knowledge about these assignment types can be assumed to be part of a conference interpreter's EXPERTISE and serve as a basis for building relevant expectations. GERVER (1981) discussed these as knowledge 'frames', and Kalina (2005b) has linked the interpreter's awareness of situational and contextual variables in an assignment to the need for PREPARATION and other quality assurance measures.

Communicative analysis at the hypertext level foregrounds the role of the conference in CONFERENCE INTERPRETING, which has long been treated with surprising neglect. Even so, the notion of an overarching communicative event can also be applied to DIALOGUE INTERPRETING (e.g. Pöchhacker 2012a), where the types of interaction under study include such complex discourse genres as diagnostic and therapeutic sessions in SPEECH PATHOLOGY and entire judicial proceedings.

FRANZ PÖCHHACKER

ICTY

see under TRIBUNAL INTERPRETING

IDEOLOGY

The relationship between interpreting and ideology is a small but growing area of study, triggered in part by Cronin's (2002) plea for a 'cultural turn' in interpreting studies which would enable the discipline to more explicitly address issues of POWER, class, GENDER and race in interpreting situations.

The impetus for research into the relationship between ideology and interpreting came from work on ROLE issues in POLICE SETTINGS and COURTROOM INTERPRETING (Berk-Seligson 1990; Hale 2004; Wadensjö 1998). However, the topic of ideology now bridges the traditional divide between CONFERENCE INTERPRETING and COMMUNITY INTERPRETING, with studies involving data from SIMULTANEOUS INTERPRETING at international institutions such as TRUTH AND RECONCILIATION COMMISSIONS as well as conferences on the freelance market (e.g. Diriker 2004; Monacelli 2009).

The wealth of research approaches and methodologies is partly explained by the range of definitions and understandings of the term 'ideology' itself, which is of key importance in investigating the means of its (de-/re)construction in interpreted interaction or via interpreter behaviour.

Generally speaking, ideology in relation to interpreting has so far been examined in two distinct ways. One strand of research views ideology in the more traditional sense, as a belief system used as a tool by those wielding political and institutional power, i.e. as an instrument of domination, focusing particularly on historical case studies of interpreters acting to serve particular political ideologies. Examples include Pöchhacker's (2006a) discussion of German interpreters in the Third Reich and the Cold War, and Takeda's (2010a, 2010b) analysis of the distinction between types of interpreters according to ethnic origin at the post-war Tokyo Tribunal.

A second, more neutral, understanding of ideology as a kind of worldview or 'understanding of the way the world works' informs research which focuses on the interplay of multiple ideologies in interpreted and interpreter discourse. In this strand of work Diriker (2004), for instance, studies the contradictory discourses surrounding the role of the 'professional' conference interpreter; Beaton-Thome (2013) discusses the positioning and visibility of simultaneous interpreters when faced with competing ideologies on Guantánamo; and SHLE-SINGER (2011) likewise highlights the dilemmas facing interpreters forced to choose between ideologically marked terms in in the Arab–Israeli conflict.

Both understandings of ideology have informed work focusing on two dimensions that were also identified by Hatim and Mason (1997) for translation in general: (1) the interpreting of ideology, that is, how the interpreter reacts to specific ideological stimuli in the source text when producing the target text; and (2) the ideology of interpreting as an activity, i.e. what ideological effects the very provision of interpreting has on the specific interaction or even (historical) context, via the collective or individual choices made by interpreters.

A particular area of investigation in this context is the attempt to explore the agency and ideological positioning of individual interpreters (see Beaton-Thome 2013; Inghilleri 2012; Monacelli 2009), including an ACTIVIST APPROACH to interpreting. Such work aims to move towards an understanding of the interpreter as an agent who occupies an ideological space of his/her own, thus challenging the traditional view of the role of the interpreter as a 'conduit' that merely identifies and 'decodes' the (reified) ideology of the speaker or interlocutor, before 'encoding' it and rendering it 'unchanged' in the target language.

Methodologically, research into the relationship between interpreting/interpreters and ideology has mainly relied on DISCOURSE ANALYTICAL APPROACHES and ETHNOGRAPHIC METHODS. With a Foucauldian understanding of discourse at its base, and an explicit acknowledgement that ideologies are manifest in discourse, the tools of Critical Discourse Analysis (CDA), focusing on issues such as lexicalisation, transitivity and in-group/out-group positioning, have been employed to investigate the role of interpreters in creating in-/out-groups in asylum hearings in Austria (Pöllabauer 2004) or the lexicalisation of Guantánamo detainees in the European Parliament (Beaton-Thome 2013). Studies adopting an ethnographic approach, in contrast, are mostly based on INTERVIEWS (at times of a retrospective nature) or, less commonly, on limited participant observation (see Inghilleri 2012). The sole use of either set of methods is open to criticism, however, and a case should be made for MIXED METHODS RESEARCH (as exemplified by Diriker 2004) that allows scholars to address ideological motivations on a broader social level at the same time as studying actual interpreter behaviour through the (micro-level) analysis of discourse data.

MORVEN BEATON-THOME

IMPARTIALITY

see under NEUTRALITY

INDIGENOUS LANGUAGES

→ COMMUNITY INTERPRETING, → NON-PROFESSIONAL INTERPRETING

The expression 'indigenous languages' refers to languages spoken by peoples in independent countries who are regarded as indigenous on account of their descent from the populations which inhabited the country, or its geographical region, at the time of conquest or colonisation or the establishment of present state boundaries. Irrespective of their legal status, indigenous populations retain some or all of their own social, economic, cultural and political institutions and enjoy some linguistic rights (Pérez Fernández 2011). Indigenous languages include minority languages referred to as aboriginal, ancestral, or native, by virtue of their identification with indigenous peoples.

At the time of the European explorations and discoveries of new lands, as undertaken in particular by sixteenth-century SPAIN, communication between indigenous people and newcomers was often accomplished with the aid of speakers displaying a certain degree of knowledge of the foreign language, or at least a predisposition to learn and/or understand it. NATURAL TRANSLATION/INTERPRETING of this type has therefore been essential for allowing unilateral or mutual understanding between local, indigenous inhabitants and foreign visitors and conquerors.

The constitutions of some nations in which indigenous languages are spoken, such as AUSTRALIA, CANADA, and countries in Latin America, grant minority languages official status, or at least guarantee their protection as an integral part of the state's cultural heritage (e.g. Berk-Seligson 2008). This often implies the right to use the native language in certain spheres of social life (e.g. education, justice, public services), including the right to speak with the aid of interpreters. Professional interpreting for speakers of indigenous languages tends to be guaranteed in courts in Australia, Canada, and some Latin American countries, whereas this is not the case in many other parts of the world, such as AFRICA, with its over 2000 indigenous languages, where NON-PROFESSIONAL INTERPRETING (and translation) for indigenous languages prevails. Aside from COURTROOM INTERPRETING provided in this way, language differences, particularly in healthcare settings, are usually addressed with the aid of ad hoc interpreters, as is typical in HEALTHCARE INTERPRETING and in COMMUNITY INTERPRETING in general.

Although these non-professional practices are widespread in countries where indigenous languages are spoken, they have rarely been investigated. Studies using ETHNOGRAPHIC METHODS to analyse video-recordings of naturally occurring medical interactions have examined ad hoc interpreting in rural clinics in the Mayan area of Mexico, focusing on the emergence and management of conflicts and misunderstandings in interaction. Although these problems arise within the TURN-TAKING system, their emergence depends in part on the background of these social encounters and on the differences in implicit knowledge (e.g. basic healthcare notions and practices) that doctors and patients mobilise in interaction. When misunderstanding occurs in direct, dyadic exchanges drawing on existing second-language knowledge as well as on gestures and other nonverbal modalities, the activity of the interpreter becomes crucial in identifying and addressing any such problems (Ticca 2013).

There is clearly a great need for research on both language and cultural brokering in interactions involving indigenous people. Some indication of the complexity of these practices and the related needs emerges even when more professionalised interpreting services are involved, as illustrated in early ethnography-based studies with Canadian medical interpreters (Kaufert & Koolage 1984) and research on Aboriginal language interpreters in Australia (Cooke 2009b).

Despite efforts to train indigenous language speakers as professional interpreters, the scarcity of interpreters for indigenous languages persists, both in their home countries and in countries such as the United States when speakers of these languages migrate. One anomaly which thus remains unaddressed is the fact that courts often conduct trials in languages not mastered by the migrants participating in the proceedings. An important factor which accentuates this tendency to limit the use of native languages in the courtroom is the widespread official preference for adoption of any language which is widely available in the country concerned, and of which the migrant is generally presumed to have some knowledge (e.g. Spanish in the US), with potentially unfortunate consequences for the defendants (Haviland 2003).

In a broader linguistic perspective, interpreting activities in indigenous languages have also been associated with language revitalisation. Interpreting is viewed as a medium and a resource to support and reinforce the use, and therefore the vitality, of minority languages.

ANNA C. TICCA

INFERENCING

↑ COMPREHENSION

Inference is a step in reasoning that is not formally defined, though the term is widely used to denote inference relying on probabilistic and intuitive processes ('non-demonstrative' inference), in contrast to formal deductive inference that follows strict logical rules. In human communication, inferencing is now widely recognized as an indispensable component of COMPREHENSION, as listeners or readers spontaneously search for meaning to complement the under-determinacy of the linguistic signal. This process has been modelled in various frameworks that have been influential in INTERPRETING STUDIES. The Construction-Integration model of Kintsch and van Dijk (van Dijk & Kintsch 1983; Kintsch 1988) distinguishes between the surface code, the 'textbase' and a still more inferentially-enriched 'situation model' as bases for recall. In post-Gricean cognitive pragmatics, RELEVANCE THEORY (Sperber & Wilson 1986/1995) explains how listeners must make sense of utterances by processing the decoded linguistic signal in all available contexts, which may include beliefs, immediate perceptions and familiarity with sociocultural norms of communication.

Translation and interpreting provide particularly clear evidence of the need for inference in comprehension, since ambiguities in the linguistic code may *force* a choice of output when no equivalent ambiguous word exists in the target language (for example, in deciding to render 'sanction' as 'punish' or 'approve'). Inference in written translation and interpreting differs only in processing constraints (e.g. speed) and the contexts used. For interpreters, contextual knowledge is derived more from immediate visual perception and temporal co-presence than for a translator, who may have to rely more on client-provided documentation.

Linguistic utterances vary in the degree of explicitness and transparency with which they encode the speaker's intended meaning, raising the issue of whether an interpreter can (or should) 'just translate' or use inference to derive the most plausible intended sense. This debate is naturally bound up with NORMS concerning FIDELITY ('freer' vs. more 'literal'), and therefore also with the interpreter's ROLE, as passive transcoder vs. communicative mediator. Controversial positions on this issue are taken particularly in COMMUNITY INTERPRETING, and especially in COURTROOM INTERPRETING. (A related question is whether a meaning derived by inference is communicated only 'implicitly', and if the same degree of implicitness or explicitness should be preserved in the translation.)

With or without explicit recognition of the role granted by linguists to inference in utterance comprehension, several authors on CONFERENCE INTERPRETING have echoed its central importance in interpreting, notably for the strategy of ANTICIPATION. First and foremost, CHERNOV (2004) discusses the role of inference in interpreting at length, distinguishing four different kinds of inference (linguistic, cognitive, situational and pragmatic, only the first of which is language-specific) that support comprehension and assist the derivation of implicit sense, but also facilitate the interpreting process (notably, enabling anticipation) by increasing the 'subjective redundancy' of the discourse for the interpreter (see also Setton 1999). More specific examples include the resolution of synecdoche, a kind of metonymy where inference is from the general to the particular or vice versa (Lederer 1976/2014), and the inference of plausible meanings from elliptical, ill-formed, unclear, vague or ambiguous remarks, or from irony, humour, metaphor, etc. In production, too, an interpreter may rely on listeners' natural use of inference.

Much of the inferencing that underlies natural language comprehension depends on often banal subconscious and quasi-automatic processes, from filling inaudible micro-gaps in the phonetic stream to matching anaphoric pronouns like 'it' and 'this' with referents for which no explicit grammatical pointers are provided (Graesser et al. 1994). Where 'inferencing' has been listed among the STRATEGIES of interpreting (e.g. Gile 1995a, 2009; Kohn & Kalina 1996), it can therefore be taken to indicate a more conscious reliance on extratextual knowledge or context to resolve some difficulty in comprehending the source speech.

Some unconscious or habitual processes can presumably be brought to consciousness and actively resisted or suppressed, to respond to different externally imposed or prevailing norms and conventions. In adversarial (i.e. less 'cooperative') communication, as is typical in LEGAL INTERPRETING, a court may require interpreters to minimise the amount of inference they apply to understanding and rendering testimony, for example by translating as literally as possible and preserving ambiguity or vagueness. Elsewhere, and especially where wide cultural gaps must be bridged, users commonly rely on the interpreter to use cultural knowledge to infer both the speaker's intended sense and the form of rendition that will best convey the sense to the interlocutor.

ROBIN SETTON

INPUT VARIABLES

↓ NUMBERS, ↓ SPEECH RATE, ↓ TERMINOLOGY, ↓ VISUAL ACCESS

QUALITY in interpreting depends to a considerable extent on the source language input that the interpreter must process. This input not only comprises the content and form of the original speech or turn, but is also subject to the WORKING CONDITIONS affecting its reception by the interpreter.

The effects of source text features on the interpreting process have been extensively researched, particularly in SIMULTANEOUS INTERPRETING. This interest dates back to early empirical studies of interpreting, when psychologists and psycholinguists recognised SI as a form of highly constrained 'real-time' language processing and thus as a potential object of EXPERIMENTAL RESEARCH in relation to controlled source text variables, such as text type (Barik 1971) and input rate (Gerver 1969/2002).

In terms of message *content*, an important variable in all forms of interpreting is the information density of the original – not an easily defined feature, since the interpreter's response to it will partly depend on how familiar s/he is with the topic. Also variously referred to as 'semantic density' or 'propositional density', information density has been modelled and studied empirically in relation to COMPREHENSION in simultaneous interpreting (e.g. Alexieva 1999; Dillinger 1990).

Not only the content, but also the *form* of the source text has been analysed from various perspectives in relation to its impact on interpreting: formal features identified as relevant to the interpreter include lexical density, calculated as the number of lexical items per clause, and syntactic complexity, measured on the basis of features like cleft sentences and subordinate clauses (e.g. Messina 2000). Sentence length has also been examined as a possible predictor of difficulty for the interpreter (Liu & Chiu 2009).

Other important variables in source text form include TERMINOLOGY and low-redundancy speech segments such as names, acronyms and NUMBERS. Gile (1995a, 2009) identifies these as potential "problem triggers" and, in the theoretical perspective of the EFFORT MODELS, explains the resulting vulnerability of these input features to information loss.

The form of a speech or utterance is, of course, not simply a combination of lexical and syntactic features such as those above: it is also important to consider factors such as the speed, clarity and continuity of the speaker's delivery. A key variable in this regard is SPEECH RATE, an important component of FLUENCY and a major determinant of how much information the interpreter has to process in a given time – though this will also depend on other source text features like PAUSES (whether planned or unintentional), disfluencies, fillers or REPAIRS, as well as repetitions and redundancies.

Many key facets of the interpreter's input have to do with the ORALITY of real-time communication in interpreting from a spoken language. Distinctions regarding the

191

mode of source text delivery and its degree of orality are by no means limited to a simple binary opposition of improvised speech vs. reading aloud from a script (Kopczyński 1982), and include numerous features subsumed under the headings of PROSODY and BODY LANGUAGE.

Beyond the content, form and delivery of the source speech as such, a number of major input variables determine how it is received by the interpreter. In simultaneous CONFERENCE INTERPRETING, in particular, one fundamental requirement addressed in standards for interpreting equipment and TECHNOLOGY is sound quality. As early as the 1970s, an experimental study by GERVER (1974a) demonstrated that the simultaneous interpreter's processing of the source speech is delayed and disrupted by acoustic disturbance in the input. Of similar importance, not least in various forms of REMOTE INTERPRETING, is VISUAL ACCESS to speakers and to any material presented.

While there is a strong case that all these input variables impact the interpreting process and product, their exact role and effects, individually or in combination, are difficult to gauge. One methodological option for studying whether problems have actually been triggered by input variables (rather than, for example, by difficulties with target language expression) is research based on RETROSPECTIVE PROTOCOLS, as used in Napier's (2002) study of sign language interpreters' coping STRATEGIES in the face of informationally dense input.

PETER MEAD

INTERDISCIPLINARITY

↑ INTERPRETING STUDIES

→ PARADIGMS

In general terms, 'interdisciplinarity' refers to any form of dialogue or interaction between two or more disciplines (Moran 2010) and hence presupposes an established system of academic disciplines as platforms for generating and imparting knowledge (Repko 2012). The nature of interdisciplinary relations has however been controversial, and views range from a mere importing of concepts, theories and methods from other fields, to an insistence on integration as the goal of interdisciplinary work. Aspects of both can be discerned for INTERPRETING STUDIES.

The academic study of translation and interpreting began to be institutionalized as disciplinary entities in the 1970s (Gile 2012). Until then, some research on interpreting had been carried out within linguistics, cognitive psychology and psycholinguistics, with a more cognitive orientation in the case of spoken-language (conference) interpreting and a more linguistic one for SIGNED LANGUAGE INTERPRETING. Alongside the emergence of 'translation studies' as a distinct 'interdisciplinary' entity, promoted mainly by scholars of literature (e.g. Holmes 1972/2000), the push to develop INTERPRETING STUDIES came essentially from CONFERENCE INTERPRETING practitioners and trainers. Two strong personalities led this movement – Danica SELESKOVITCH of ESIT (Paris) in the 'West' and Ghelly CHERNOV of the Maurice Thorez Institute (Moscow) in the USSR and Eastern Europe. While Chernov cooperated with psychologists and psycholinguists, Seleskovitch and her followers preferred to develop interpreting research with practitioners of interpreting rather than with outsiders, despite some contacts and even initiatives in favor of INTERDISCIPLINARITY by the latter (as epitomized by the VENICE SYMPOSIUM organized by David GERVER). For close to two decades, there was little interdisciplinarity within interpreting studies in the West, in spite of the interest of some research-minded interpreters ('practisearchers') such as Ingrid Kurz,

Barbara Moser, Jennifer Mackintosh and Daniel Gile in working with scientists from other disciplines.

The tide eventually turned, as a larger number of practisearchers openly expressed the wish to bring into research on interpreting more theories and methods from disciplines they considered relevant. One example of this development was research with neurolinguists conducted at the interpreter and translator training school (SSLMIT) of the University of Trieste. The active involvement and guidance of neurophysiologist Franco Fabbro, who supervised many graduation theses of interpreting students, gave rise to innovative interdisciplinary research in cooperation with Laura Gran and others at the SSLMIT. This work was also featured at the TRIESTE SYMPOSIUM (Gran & Dodds 1989), a milestone conference that marked the beginning of a new era in research into conference interpreting. In parallel, research into other forms of interpreting began to develop in other parts of the world.

From the 1990s, interdisciplinarity has been a leitmotiv in interpreting studies, with practisearchers systematically seeking input from disciplines such as cognitive psychology and psycholinguistics (e.g. Minhua Liu, Presentación Padilla, Miriam SHLESINGER), linguistics (e.g. Claudio Bendazzoli, Robin Setton), sociology (e.g. Ebru Diriker, Claudia Monacelli) and education science (e.g. David Sawyer), to name only a few in relation to conference interpreting (Gile 2006). Several attempts were made to bring together practisearchers and researchers from such disciplines, especially linguistics and cognitive science, as reflected in conference proceedings (e.g. Danks et al. 1997; Englund Dimitrova & Hyltenstam 2000) and two issues of *INTERPRETING* with papers from the Ascona Workshops convened by Moser-Mercer (1997) for the same purpose. Nevertheless, actual collaboration on research projects between members of the relevant communities has essentially been limited to doctoral supervision and a relatively small number of isolated studies. In other words, in research into conference interpreting, there is mostly 'import interdisciplinarity' and little two-way interdisciplinarity, at least in the West. In JAPAN, there is more involvement from outsiders to the practice of interpreting, as reflected in papers published (mostly in Japanese) in *Interpreting and Translation Studies*, the journal of the Japan Association for Interpreting and Translation Studies.

In research into other branches of interpreting there is significant involvement of neighboring disciplines, in particular linguistics, with no history of rejection on the part of interpreting practitioners. In the domain of COURTROOM INTERPRETING, for example, the work of sociolinguist Susan Berk-Seligson (1990) is widely appreciated as seminal, and much of the research on HEALTHCARE INTERPRETING, from PEDIATRIC SETTINGS to MENTAL HEALTH SETTINGS, including PSYCHOTHERAPY, has in fact been conducted by linguists and medical professionals (Pöchhacker 2006b). In signed language interpreting, the role of linguistics and linguists has been particularly strong, perhaps to the detriment of research into signed language interpreting per se (see Pointurier-Pournin 2014 for a critical assessment of the situation in France).

The main challenges faced by researchers from cognate disciplines who wish to undertake interdisciplinary projects on interpreting, especially conference interpreting, have been the small number of available participants, limited access to interpreter-mediated events due to confidentiality issues, a lack of interest among interpreters in basic research, and communication difficulties with practisearchers lacking research training. The situation regarding the last-mentioned issue is improving, as more interpreters are being trained in research methods as part of their EDUCATION, and a number of those supervising the work of the younger generation have themselves received guidance from advisors in relevant disciplines.

While 'interdisciplinarity' generally implies relations between distinct academic disciplines, in translation studies in general, and in interpreting studies in particular, the spectrum of translation environments and research topics and methods is wide enough to also view cooperation between researchers from various branches of translation and/or interpreting as a form of interdisciplinarity, which could be called 'internal interdisciplinarity' (Gile 2006) or 'inter-subdisciplinarity' (Shlesinger 2004). Such cooperation was rare until the late 1990s, but is becoming increasingly common, with numerous contacts and exchanges between scholars of conference interpreting, LEGAL INTERPRETING and other domains of COMMUNITY INTERPRETING, as well as signed language interpreting. This trend is associated with the increasing prominence of social and psychosocial issues in research into interpreting, which Pöchhacker (2006c) has called the 'social turn' in interpreting studies.

DANIEL GILE

INTERFERENCE

The term interference is used in physics to denote interaction between overlapping waves. Linguists have used it since the 1950s to refer to the influence of one language system on another in situations of language contact. Also known as L1 interference or language transfer, this phenomenon manifests itself both in the individual speaker and in the language community or system. In the latter domain it includes various forms of positive (e.g. loan words) as well as negative transfer, whereas interference in individual language use is generally regarded as undesirable (i.e. as negative transfer). In either case, linguistic interference consists in a deviation from the norms of the target language on the lexical, morphological, syntactic, stylistic, phonological or prosodic levels. Typical examples include meaning-distorting false cognates (e.g. French *contrôler* often means 'monitor' in English, not 'control'), but unwanted intrusions from a source language are also common – though perhaps less obvious – on the structural level.

Translation, as a special form of bilingual language use, can be assumed to be subject to this phenomenon, and interference has indeed been discussed as a law (Toury 1995) or a universal of translation (e.g. Mauranen 2004) and investigated as a prominent feature of 'translationese' (Volansky et al. 2013). Interpreting is considered to be especially prone to interference due to the exceptional COGNITIVE LOAD of processing under severe time pressure, and the high level of neural activation of two languages, especially in SIMULTANEOUS INTERPRETING (SI) and in SIGHT INTERPRETING/TRANSLATION, where the source text remains visually present. Indeed, language control during bilingual processing in SI has been a focus of research in NEUROSCIENCE APPROACHES to interpreting and in the psycholinguistic study of BILINGUALISM.

Despite its assumed prevalence, the phenomenon of interference has not attracted much systematic scholarly attention in interpreting studies. Authors of small-scale case studies have proposed various typologies, but little is known about the factors influencing the frequency and the different types of interference in interpreters' output. In an experimental study comparing the performances of six professional interpreters in different MODES (sight translation, SI and CONSECUTIVE INTERPRETING), Agrifoglio (2004) found greater source-language interference in sight translation but fewer problems related to expression (e.g. calques and inappropriate collocations) in the consecutive mode, presumably due to the temporal separation of the COMPREHENSION and production stages.

In studies on interference in SI, data have often been taken from classroom and exam situations. Examples include the qualitative analysis by Simonetto (2002) of student performances in Spanish–Italian SI exams and the work of Lauterbach (2009) on German/English and German/Russian exam performances. Such studies have generally highlighted the more salient lexical types of interference, such as 'false friends' between cognate (e.g. Romance) languages, more than stylistic, syntactic or prosodic effects. Interestingly, they have also provided evidence that a third language may be involved in interference between source and target languages in the interpreting process (e.g. the Italian 'ghost calque' *disrispetto*, presumably influenced by English *disrespect*, for *desprestigio* in the Spanish source text).

Lamberger-Felber and Schneider (2008) conducted an elaborate quantitative study of interference in SI by twelve experienced professionals in an experimentally generated corpus from a larger study (Lamberger-Felber 2001). Using a typology comprising three basic types of interference (phonological, lexical, morphosyntactic) as well as two SI-specific interference phenomena ('simultaneous short-circuit' and grammatical agreement with source-text elements), these authors found a high degree of variability between participants as well as speeches, with the maximum number of interferences per interpreter and speech varying by a factor of up to seven. The vast majority of these were lexical and morpho-syntactic, with only one percent classified as phonological. However, in a study of English–Hungarian SI Bakti and Bóna (2014) have shown that professional interpreters may also experience interference at the suprasegmental (prosodic) level, such as erroneous stress placement.

Not surprisingly, resisting interference has been a focus of attention in training, particularly in SI, where students are often cautioned to beware of (false) cognates and to distance themselves as much as possible from the words and structures of the original speech. This is epitomized in the PARIS SCHOOL'S teaching of 'deverbalization' rather than linguistic TRANS-CODING, whereas in the framework of the EFFORT MODELS the emphasis is on managing attentional resources so as to keep enough processing capacity for the conscious effort to resist source-language interference.

EIKE LAUTERBACH AND FRANZ PÖCHHACKER

INTERNATIONAL JOURNAL OF INTERPRETER EDUCATION

↑ INTERPRETING STUDIES

The *International Journal of Interpreter Education* (*IJIE*) is a peer-reviewed scholarly journal, published by the Conference of Interpreter Trainers (CIT) in the United States. CIT was established in 1979, initially for the purpose of facilitating the exchange of information among signed language interpreter educators in the United States through a biennial convention. Over the years, the membership of CIT grew to include an international body of signed and spoken language interpreter educators, so the organisation identified a need for a scholarly publication featuring evidence-based discussions of issues in interpreter EDUCA-TION. Based on a competitive application procedure, Jemina Napier was appointed as the journal's inaugural editor, assisted by an editorial board composed of prominent interpreter educators and researchers who represent a variety of international perspectives and languages, both spoken and signed. The first volume of *IJIE* appeared in 2009, and the journal was published on an annual basis until 2012, when it moved to two issues per year due to an increasing number of submissions.

IJIE is the first journal to focus solely on interpreter education. In response to repeated calls for greater dialogue between research, education and practice in spoken and SIGNED LANGUAGE INTERPRETING, it serves to disseminate, and therefore indirectly encourage, empirical evidence of how to educate, train and assess interpreters. *IJIE* aims to address issues and principles surrounding effective development and delivery of interpreter education and training, including topics relating to second language learning, interpreting practice, program administration, interpreting research and educational theory.

The journal is divided into several sections, including research articles, commentary, the 'open forum', a student work section, and dissertation abstracts. The research articles section features submissions based on evidence-based, empirical research on interpreter education informed by a variety of disciplines (e.g. linguistics, education, anthropology) and methodologies, and particularly ACTION RESEARCH. In the commentary section, interpreter educators can share their reflections on classroom teaching activities with regard to preparing future interpreters, maintaining the skills of practicing professionals, or promoting the professional development of interpreter educators. The open forum section features reviews of books, curricula or resources that may be of interest to interpreter researchers, educators and trainers, and publishable interviews with leading interpreter educators and scholars. The student section allows authors of Master's dissertations on interpreter education to share their work, without undergoing the same level of stringent double-blind peer review as applied to other contributors.

Aside from the impressive diversity of topics in the field of interpreter education, the articles published in *IJIE* over the years reflect an ongoing process of convergence and increased interaction among spoken and signed language interpreter educators. As noted by Napier (2014) in her last editorial before handing over the editorship to her successors, George Major and Ineke Crezee, the journal's evolution has reflected the way interpreter education research has developed into a subdiscipline in its own right within the field of INTERPRETING STUDIES.

JEMINA NAPIER

INTERPRETERS' NEWSLETTER

↑ INTERPRETING STUDIES

The Interpreters' Newsletter was first published in 1988. It was conceived as a follow-up publication to keep contact among the participants of the TRIESTE SYMPOSIUM, held in 1986 as a forum for the exchange of information on interpreting research. The name 'Newsletter' was chosen to provide a vehicle for publishing letters, articles and announcements. In the words of the first editors, the *Newsletter* was to serve as "a channel of open dialogue between contributors and readers for an exchange of information from all over the world" (Gran & Dodds 1988: 2), welcoming the contribution of anyone interested in the study of interpreting.

As it happened, *The Interpreters' Newsletter* became the first international journal devoted entirely to interpreting research. Special attention was paid to interdisciplinary and empirical research projects on different aspects of both the product and the process of interpreting. The first issue was the result of joint efforts by scholars and researchers from the University of Trieste and other institutions, with contributions from Daniel Gile, Jennifer Mackintosh and Heidemarie Salevsky.

The first five issues, from 1988 to 1993, were in-house publications, put out by the Scuola Superiore di Lingue Moderne per Interpreti e Traduttori (SSLMIT) of the University of Trieste. While the list of contributors was highly international, the journal included a number of papers by SSLMIT teaching staff and by graduates reporting on their thesis research. There was also one Special Issue, in 1992, on the specific aspects of translation and interpreting from and into Japanese.

Subsequent years witnessed a change in publishing policy, although the editorial philosophy at the heart of *The Interpreters' Newsletter* remained unchanged. In particular, the journal remained accessible to Trieste students publishing the often impressive empirical research done for their graduation theses. At the same time, the *Newsletter* reflected the widening scope of INTERPRETING STUDIES from the late 1990s, and the ten issues published between 1995 (No. 6) and 2010 (No. 15) comprise a broad range of different research topics and approaches.

A change in editorial policy was introduced in 2011 with the decision to publish thematic issues. The first of these, No. 16 (2011), was devoted to "Television Interpreting", followed by No. 17 (2012) on "Public Service Interpreting", No. 18 (2013) on "Expertise in Interpreting", No. 19 (2014) on "Sign Language Interpreting" and No. 20 (2015) on "Dialogue Interpreting". All issues of *The Interpreters' Newsletter* are also available online through OpenstarTs (www.openstarts.units.it), the institutional repository of the University of Trieste.

ALESSANDRA RICCARDI

INTERPRETING

↑ INTERPRETING STUDIES
→ SHLESINGER

Interpreting: International Journal of Research and Practice in Interpreting was launched in the mid-1990s, as the first peer-reviewed scientific journal by an international publisher (John Benjamins) to focus solely on INTERPRETING. Founded at the initiative of Barbara Moser-Mercer together with cognitive psychologist Dominic Massaro, the first of its bi-annual issues was published in early 1996. The founding editors aspired to high academic standards, in line with those established for the cognitive sciences, and the five 'associate editors' on the original editorial team (Fabbro, Flores d'Arcais, Frauenfelder, Kurz, Lambert) all had a background in psychology. Even so, the scope of the journal, as printed on the inside front cover, explicitly included "all areas of interpreting: simultaneous, consecutive, media, conference, court, community, teleconferencing, sign language and computer-assisted interpreting". The journal's inaugural issue (1:1, 1996) aptly reflected this broad scope, with papers on MACHINE INTERPRETING, VIDEOCONFERENCE INTERPRETING, SIGNED LANGUAGE INTERPRETING and COMMUNITY INTERPRETING.

Emphasizing the journal's commitment to interdisciplinary and cross-disciplinary research, the founding editors foregrounded two thematic approaches: (1) the ecology of interpreting, including its various situational requirements; and (2) processes related to interpreting skills. The latter reflected a concern with COGNITIVE APPROACHES, as seen most clearly in the 1997 double issue devoted to papers from Barbara Moser-Mercer's interdisciplinary Ascona workshops.

The first special issue of the journal (4:1, 1999) was devoted to the HISTORY of interpreting in the twentieth century and included papers on the NUREMBERG TRIAL, on the emergence of SIMULTANEOUS INTERPRETING and of the interpreting PROFESSION, as well as on the PEDAGOGY of interpreting.

When publication lapsed after 2000, Miriam SHLESINGER, together with Franz Pöchhacker, took over the editorship and helped relaunch the journal in 2004 with a renewed advisory board and a team of associate editors representing major domains of INTERPRETING STUDIES, including Gile, Morris, Roberts, Roy and Setton. The journal's scope has been as extensive as ever, broadly characterized as comprising all aspects of interpreting in its various MODES, modalities and SETTINGS. Special issues have been devoted to HEALTHCARE INTERPRETING (7:2, 2005), court interpreting (10:1, 2008), CHINA and Chinese (11:2, 2009) and aptitude for interpreting (13:1, 2011). Thus, the journal has become established as the prime source of new research on a fast-developing object of study, playing its part in shaping the field while also being shaped by it (Shlesinger & Voinova 2013).

Following the untimely death of Miriam Shlesinger in late 2012, Minhua Liu joined Franz Pöchhacker as co-editor, as proposed by her predecessor, with Peter Mead as style editor. She had earlier written a methodological review of papers published in the twelve issues of *Interpreting* from 2004 to 2009 (Liu 2011), identifying trends in the recent evolution of interpreting research, and at the same time highlighting the journal's role as a key medium of publication in the field of interpreting studies.

FRANZ PÖCHHACKER

INTERPRETING

↑ INTERPRETING STUDIES
↓ MODES, ↓ SETTINGS

The concept of interpreting as the act of rendering something comprehensible has presumably been rooted in human thought since ancient times, and long before writing in one language was translated into another. Unlike written translation, which attracts attention to the materiality of the text(s), the ephemeral act of interpreting foregrounds the human agent performing it. Thus, some of the oldest expressions used to refer to the concept of interpreting have through the ages also served as designations for the figure of the interpreter. This is well attested for the Assyro-Babylonian root *targumânu/turgumânu*, which dates back as far as 1900 BCE. Though the etymology of the expression remains unclear, its corresponding Aramaic form *targmānā/turgmānā* (meaning 'explain') is the origin of the Arabic term *tarjumān* (ترجمان) and its descendants in various languages (Vermeer 1992), including the Byzantine Greek word *dragomános*, which came to designate the DRAGOMANS during the time of the Ottoman Empire. Moreover, the Turkish form *tercüman* led to the Hungarian *tolmács*, which in turn shaped the Middle High German word *tolmetsche*.

The central semantic component of 'explaining' is also found in the Greek word *hermeneus*, which, though of uncertain etymology, is the origin of the term 'hermeneutics', the theory of the exegesis (interpretation) of texts, later developed into a theory of human understanding. The fact that *hermeneus* denoted a translator or interpreter, like its Latin counterpart *interpres* (Hermann 1956/2002), points to the various ways in which linguistic choices available in particular languages have shaped the concept of interpreting and its status in relation to the concept of translation. Thus, modern Russian and other Slavic languages do not have a separate term for interpreting, which is therefore denoted by qualifying the generic term for translation, in this case *perevod*, as 'oral'. Similarly, *yi* (譯) was used in classical Chinese to refer to translation and interpreting as well as translators and interpreters, and the term *kouyi* (口譯), denoting 'oral translation', was coined only in twentieth-century Modern Standard Chinese (Lung 2009b). The same applies to terms used in medieval times in KOREA, where the lexical element *yŏk* meant 'interpreting'/'translating'. However, there were also expressions such as *sŏl-in*, literally meaning 'tongue person'.

The conceptual linkage between language and 'tongue', which is also found in the way interpreters were designated as *lenguas* in colonial SPAIN, points to ORALITY as a crucial aspect of interpreting. More than its obvious link with speech, orality highlights the production of utterances as a dynamic process of situated action, and hence need not exclude utterances in signed language. In either language modality, interpreting relies on features of NONVERBAL

COMMUNICATION and is characterized, in particular, by the need for communicative performance in real time. This conceptualization of interpreting also informs the proposal by Otto
Kade (1968) to distinguish interpreting from translation not by the use of spoken versus
written language, but based on the immediacy of the process. Thus, Kade views interpreting
as a form of translational activity in which a first and final rendition in another language is
produced on the basis of a one-time presentation of an utterance in a source language.
Kade's definition, which relies on the specification that the source message in interpreting
cannot be repeated (replayed, reviewed) and that the interpretation (target text) is produced
under time pressure, with little opportunity for correction and revision, naturally accom-
modates SIGNED LANGUAGE INTERPRETING as well as SIGHT INTERPRETING/TRANSLATION. However, some challenges to this definitional approach come from recent manifestations of
interpreting that involve a previewing or replaying of the source, such as delayed-broadcast
NEWS INTERPRETING and recorder-assisted SIMULTANEOUS CONSECUTIVE.

As indicated above, the extent to which the conceptual boundary between interpreting and
(written) translation is reflected in distinct lexical expressions depends on the linguistic
resources available and, much more so, on categorization needs and preferences shaped by
the experiential context: whereas an oral culture might focus on oral performance skills (as
in the case of 'professional linguists' or *griots* in AFRICA), a civilization that prizes literacy
may have no special regard (nor special term) for interpreting, and simply include it, as a
marginal phenomenon, within its dominant notion of translation. Dynamics of this nature
can be discerned even in the HISTORY of interpreting in recent centuries, and have also had an
influence on the evolution of INTERPRETING STUDIES as a discipline.

Conceptual distinctions

Notwithstanding the impact of linguistic and sociocultural factors on the feasibility and
acceptance of conceptual distinctions, defining the relationship between the concepts of
interpreting and translation is arguably fundamental to a thorough conceptual analysis. On
the whole, this relationship can be summarized, for present purposes, as both hyponymous
and 'antonymous'. Given the widespread use of the term 'translation' in a wider sense that
encompasses any translational activity, interpreting can be viewed as a hyponym of the
superordinate term 'translation', and interpreting hence considered as a form of translation.
At the same time, interpreting and translation can be defined (e.g. with reference to Kade 1968)
as distinct from each other, and positioned at opposite ends of the oral–literate continuum.

Once this basic distinction has been made, the concept of interpreting can be differentiated
further by applying a number of relevant criteria. Aside from the *modality* of the language(s)
involved, which serves to contrast spoken language with signed language interpreting, the
most common distinction is made in terms of the temporal relationship between the interpretation (target text) and the source text, which yields CONSECUTIVE INTERPRETING and
SIMULTANEOUS INTERPRETING as the two main MODES of interpreting. In a looser sense, different
'modes' can also be identified with reference to the directness of the interpreting process
(RELAY INTERPRETING) and the use of TECHNOLOGY to deliver the interpretation, as in the case
of REMOTE INTERPRETING provided in 'distance mode'. Much more relevant, however, are
conceptual distinctions with reference to the SETTINGS in which interpreter-mediated social
contacts take place. On the broadest level, *inter*-social (or inter-national) scenarios, involving
diplomats, politicians, scientists, business leaders or other types of representatives of comparable standing, can be viewed as different from *intra*-social (community-based) ones, in
which one of the interacting parties is an individual speaking on his or her own behalf. The
latter, subsumed under the broad heading of COMMUNITY INTERPRETING, allow multiple

subdivisions in terms of different institutional contexts, including LEGAL INTERPRETING, HEALTHCARE INTERPRETING and EDUCATIONAL INTERPRETING, with numerous institution-related subtypes. Yet another conceptual dimension that yields an important distinction is the type or format of interaction: interpersonal face-to-face dialogue, as the most natural form of communicative encounter, can be contrasted with the more ritualized format of a conference, yielding DIALOGUE INTERPRETING and CONFERENCE INTERPRETING respectively as major subtypes of interpreting.

A number of additional criteria can be brought to bear on the analysis of interpreting as a concept, all of which serve to highlight its complex and multifaceted nature. Two examples are the STATUS of interpreting as a PROFESSION (and of interpreters as professionals) and, most fundamentally perhaps, the extent to which interpreting is seen as a human performance or a feat of computer hardware and software. Here again, social and technological changes are making their mark on the concept of interpreting, as increasing attention is given to NON-PROFESSIONAL INTERPRETING, and technological progress requires MACHINE INTERPRETING to be taken more seriously as an option for service delivery. Such fundamental shifts have momentous implications not only for the concept of interpreting, but also for the way interpreting is conceptualized in theoretical terms (see Pöchhacker 2004a) – as a form of 'verbal transfer', 'cognitive information processing', 'text production', DISCOURSE MANAGEMENT or MEDIATION.

FRANZ PÖCHHACKER

INTERPRETING FOR DEAFBLIND PERSONS

→ SIGNED LANGUAGE INTERPRETING

DeafBlindness is a condition that manifests itself differently for each person along a spectrum of combined vision and hearing loss. Time of onset and residual vision or hearing are factors affecting language choice (signed or spoken), use of technological supports (cochlear implants, assistive listening devices, computer applications), receptive and expressive communication, employment, quality of life, leisure, relationships, independence, and education (RID 2007). This heterogeneity is also reflected in preferred terms and notations. 'Deaf-Blind', 'Deafblind' and 'deafblind' (without a hyphen, and with or without upper case) are preferred notations in the international community, and represent a single condition more complex than the combination of vision and hearing loss. The hyphenated term 'Deaf-Blind' is widely accepted by individuals with congenital deafness and acquired vision loss (usually after language development). Users of signed language who maintain cultural-linguistic ties to the Deaf community may also prefer the hyphenated designation. When referring to people with vision and hearing loss from birth or early childhood, 'deafblind' is commonly used.

Interpreting for the heterogeneous DeafBlind population is a complex specialty, requiring competence in communication methods beyond those required for SIGNED LANGUAGE INTE-RPRETING with the general Deaf population. Many interpreters begin their training as a Support Service Provider (SSP), a role characterized by independent living assistance that includes providing human guide services, environmental orientation, and supplementation of the interpreted message with visual information. Ethically, interpreters whose roles are expanded to include SSP responsibilities must take particular care not to encroach upon the service user's independence.

Interpreters working for DeafBlind persons need great flexibility in adjusting to personal communication preferences and varying degrees of independence of consumers, and they must be comfortable with close interaction and touch. As a consequence of physical proximity and contact, special attire and grooming are required, including a skin color-contrasting, plain shirt with three-quarter-length sleeves and a high neckline, manicured hands, and avoidance of colognes and shiny objects.

Interpreting for people who are DeafBlind requires use of tactile or non-tactile techniques that depend upon consumer preference, lighting and other contextual factors. A consumer who can access visual information in certain lighting or at a certain distance or angle might prefer the interpreter to work within a restricted field where signs can be seen more easily. This consumer may place his or her hands on the interpreter's forearms to follow signs in a limited area, using a method called tracking. When lighting is too dim for tracking, or the Deaf consumer has no functional vision, tactile interpreting allows the consumer's hands to maintain contact with the interpreter's for reading the message by touch. The tactile interpreting scenario presents options for POSITIONING (e.g. side-by-side, interlocking knees), sign adaptations, and use of one-handed and two-handed methods, all of which are highly contextual and negotiated by interpreters and consumers. Tactile interpreting can also be accomplished through methods other than a formal signed language, such as Lorm (more prevalent outside North America), print-on-palm, tactile braille, and FINGERSPELLING. Children or late-deafened consumers who use spoken language may communicate with the Tadoma Method, a seldom-utilized form of tactile lipreading which originated in the US (NCCC 2001).

Interpreters follow behavioral guidelines unique to the DeafBlind population, such as always self-identifying upon approach and anchoring a person to a tangible object before stepping away. They must also seek to incorporate relevant visual as well as auditory information about the environment, such as the room configuration, other persons present and their actions, the location of exits, and other items of interest. These interpreter-generated utterances ensure that the consumer is better informed and facilitate independent communication management (Metzger et al. 2004). In addition to interpreting signed or spoken messages, interpreters provide signals (also called haptic signals or haptics), which enhance a DeafBlind person's contextual awareness about the facial expression, responses, actions and emotions of others and allow the consumer to employ strategies for TURN-TAKING (Berge & Raanes 2013; Frankel 2002). Response signals are placed on a person's hands, wrist, elbow, arm, upper back, and knees, and their purpose is to promote social connectedness and active participation in interpreted communication events as well as private and group conversations (e.g. Berge 2014; Palmer & Lahtinen 2005). Pro-Tactile, a signaling method in the US derived from haptics, is a vibrant social movement with a philosophy and attitude of empowerment and autonomy within a DeafBlind cultural framework.

Interpreting techniques are unique to each DeafBlind individual and can vary from day to day with the same person, depending upon the stability of the condition as well as contextual factors. Interpreters work as partners with consumers, to identify the most efficient methods needed for full participatory access to an event. Some contexts necessitate team interpreting, particularly when an interpreter is working tactilely over a long period of time. All approaches to interpreting, teaming, communicating, and socializing with people who are DeafBlind incorporate collaboration and a concerted focus on the person rather than the condition.

SHERRY SHAW

INTERPRETING STUDIES

↓ INTERPRETING, ↓ INTERDISCIPLINARITY, ↓ METHODOLOGY, ↓ PARADIGMS

Interpreting studies as an academic discipline has its origins in the late twentieth century. A handful of individual research efforts devoted to aspects of interpreting were made in various fields in the first few decades of the last century, but it was not until the 1970s that a community of like-minded scholars with a primary interest in interpreting emerged. The name used to designate this area of academic study is younger still: 'interpreting studies' as a disciplinary label, analogous to translation studies, was probably used for the first time during the TRIESTE SYMPOSIUM, and first appeared in a scholarly paper in the early 1990s (Salevsky 1993). While the name of the field has thus been settled, its nature remains an issue of debate, and it is the purpose of the present article to address this issue, also providing an overview of the field's evolution (see also Pöchhacker 2004a, 2016), with particular attention to the various theoretical and methodological approaches within interpreting studies.

The nature of the discipline

A fundamental question regarding the nature of interpreting studies concerns its relationship with the field of translation studies. The latter, as mapped out by Holmes (1972/2000) and developed by Toury (1995), is now commonly understood in a comprehensive sense that includes all and any forms of translational activity, from Bible translation to software localization, and from advertising translation to COMMUNITY INTERPRETING (see Gambier & van Doorslaer 2014). In the mid-1990s, Miriam SHLESINGER had characterized interpreting studies as "a (sub)discipline in the making within a discipline in the making" (1995b: 9), elegantly hinting at its subordinate status as well as emphasizing its potential for further autonomous development. Both translation studies and interpreting studies have since experienced impressive growth and development, and achieved a degree of consolidation and institutional maturity. The issue of their (sub)disciplinary relationship, however, remains: while it is widely accepted that interpreting studies has a place, or 'position', within translation studies (e.g. Pöchhacker 2013b), the more explicit labeling of the field(s) as 'translation and interpreting studies' (e.g. in the names of journals and scholarly associations) gives an impression of distinct identities. Moreover, many indicators of disciplinary status, such as professorships, textbooks, anthologies, doctoral summer schools – and encyclopedias – reinforce a sense of autonomous disciplinary identity for interpreting studies. Much of this can be seen as a result of the relentless specialization characterizing the development of modern science. In the case of translation studies, it is becoming increasingly difficult for an author or program organizer to cover interpreting as well as translation in their endeavors.

A major force that is acting to defuse the issue of disciplinary boundaries, at least at the level of research as such, is INTERDISCIPLINARITY. Not only has the field of translation studies been viewed as an 'interdiscipline' (Snell-Hornby et al. 1994), but research in interpreting studies has also explored so many interdisciplinary boundary areas that the question of working within or between disciplines has lost much of its importance in either field. Many of these interdisciplinary alignments, often for a specific aspect of the object of study, are different for the two fields, and often even unique to one or the other. This weakens the case for pursuing a vision of disciplinary unity in translation studies as a whole, at the same time as it fuels the process of differentiation within either subdiscipline. Exemplary scenarios from the domain of interpreting might include: legal scholars investigating the role of COURTROOM INTERPRETING in ensuring due process in criminal proceedings; police officers studying ways of adjusting their interviewing techniques to the employment of VIDEOCONFERENCE INTERPRETING; medical researchers assessing the advantages of different forms of REMOTE INTERPRETING in doctor–patient communication; nursing specialists measuring patient satisfaction in mediated encounters involving ad hoc vs. professional HEALTHCARE INTERPRETING; cognitive psychologists determining WORKING MEMORY capacity in interpreters compared to non-interpreter bilinguals; or neuroscientists identifying the neural substrates of executive control processes used in SIMULTANEOUS INTERPRETING. In all of these cases, interpreting scholars involved in collaborative research would find few points of interface with translation research, or even interdisciplinary research (under such headings as 'translation & law' or 'translation & medicine') in translation studies.

This illustration of the multi-faceted nature of interpreting studies reflects great prospects for further growth and development, but also a considerable risk of fragmentation and of destabilization as a disciplinary entity. The viability of interpreting studies as a recognized field of academic study therefore depends on a core area that has its basis in interpreting as a PROFESSION. Although current definitions of the concept of INTERPRETING do not feature the professional STATUS of the activity as a necessary condition, the evolution of the discipline, and the make-up of the scholarly community sustaining it, highlight the essential role of the profession of interpreting in the discipline of interpreting studies. Conceived of as a socially recognized occupation, the exercise of which requires specialized knowledge and skills, the profession has as its crucial component the EDUCATION of future practitioners. This in turn gives educators a pivotal role in sustaining the field, by developing its PEDAGOGY and, more importantly, by cultivating and extending the scientific knowledge underlying it. The evolution of interpreting studies to date reflects these internal relationships, while also testifying to the significance of interdisciplinary enrichment.

Evolution

The earliest twentieth-century publications on interpreting and interpreters, dating from the 1910s to the 1930s, illustrate the state of affairs when there is no scientific community that has agreed to define a certain phenomenon, such as interpreting, as its object of study. A handful of authors chose to write about different aspects of interpreting from a variety of disciplinary vantage points, ranging from classical studies (Gehman 1914) and archeology (Gardiner 1915) to diplomacy (Corbett 1927) and theology (Gaechter 1936). This includes the study by Jesús Sanz (1930), a Spanish educator whose focus was on contemporary practices rather than examples from the past. Unlike those concerned with the HISTORY of interpreting, or with interpreters in their broadly historical domains, Sanz was keenly aware of the professional nature of the task he was studying among the *interprètes parlementaires* at the League of Nations and the ILO in Geneva. This focus on task demands applies even more to the efforts by psychologists in the 1960s (e.g. Oléron & Nanpon 1965) to understand the mechanisms underlying the intriguing new professional skill of simultaneous interpreting.

Pierre Oléron and fellow researchers such as Henri Barik and David GERVER approached simultaneous interpreting within the paradigm of experimental psychology, using EXPERIMENTAL RESEARCH in the 'laboratory' to generate empirical findings. Linguistics at the time offered little in the way of an alternative (e.g. Kade 1967; Kade & Cartellieri 1971), and both psychology and linguistics were in fact rejected as appropriate disciplinary frameworks by the emerging community of practitioner-researchers led by Danica SELESKOVITCH at the *École Supérieure d'Interprètes et de Traducteurs* (ESIT) in Paris. Firmly rooted in the fast-growing profession of CONFERENCE INTERPRETING as represented and promoted by AIIC, Seleskovitch and her associates in what came to be referred to as the PARIS SCHOOL endeavored to forge a disciplinary framework of their own, based on the INTERPRETIVE THEORY of Translation, and relying on introspection and on the qualitative analysis of authentic data from the field. Building on these theoretical and methodological foundations and on available institutional resources and support, Seleskovitch managed, in 1974, to launch a doctoral studies program in *Science et technique de l'interprétation et de la traduction* at the University of Paris (*Université Sorbonne Nouvelle*). Putting what came to be known more succinctly as *traductologie* on a fully academic footing represents a crucial milestone in the development of interpreting studies, or arguably even its beginning. It is nevertheless worth noting that, as much as Seleskovitch's special interest and experience was in interpreting, the academic program she promoted was not envisioned as separate from the study of translation. On the contrary: the short label for the new disciplinary entity privileged translation over interpreting, much like its current English-language counterpart 'translation studies'.

In 1977, the milestone VENICE SYMPOSIUM organized by Gerver and Sinaiko (1978) gave professionals and psychologists an opportunity to meet (and also interact with representatives from various other disciplines). In terms of the two main strands of research on interpreting that had emerged by the mid-1970s, it was an encounter between cognitive psychology and *traductologie*, with champions of the latter representing the most prestigious domain of the profession. (Participants also included practitioners and scholars of SIGNED LANGUAGE INTERPRETING.) The interdisciplinary perspective on interpreting did not prevail on that occasion, but foundations for it were laid. Pioneering work along those lines had meanwhile been done in the Soviet Union, where UN staff interpreter Ghelly CHERNOV, the principal representative of the SOVIET SCHOOL of interpreting research, conducted experimental studies in collaboration with a psychologist (Chernov 1978), highlighting the potential of an interdisciplinary approach.

The Paris School's pioneering efforts were taken further in a dialectic relationship between the newly established disciplinary foundations and an interdisciplinary scientific perspective. A group of research-minded conference interpreters, all members of AIIC, were ready to question and to go beyond the theoretical and methodological consensus at the time, taking inspiration from advances in cognitive science, and vindicating experiments, as modeled in particular by Gerver, as a legitimate method. Daniel Gile, an ESIT-trained conference interpreter who started out in Seleskovitch's doctoral seminar with prior training in mathematics, emerged as the leading figure of this group, which also included practitioner-researchers such as Jennifer Mackintosh (who later served as President of AIIC) and Barbara Moser-Mercer. Given their professional training, they did not differ from the group around Seleskovitch in the value they placed on the conference interpreting profession, nor in their interest in the cognitive processes underlying the task; rather, the fundamental disagreement was over the theoretical and methodological approach to be taken in studying the interpreting process, and hence in the choice of scientific paradigm.

Some ten years after the Venice Symposium, the interdisciplinary outlook prevailed, as highlighted by the TRIESTE SYMPOSIUM and developments around 1990, which Snell-Hornby (2006) characterized as an 'empirical turn'. Far beyond issues of METHODOLOGY, however, the (re)orientation that Gile (1994) called the 'Renaissance' in interpreting studies involved major efforts, not least by Gile himself, to promote scholarly exchange and networking. THE INTERPRETERS' NEWSLETTER, founded after the Trieste Symposium as a medium for continued information exchange among the conference participants, soon developed into the field's first international journal, and Daniel Gile's *IRTIN Bulletin* (now CIRIN BULLETIN) served to disseminate information about scholarly publications and events in the field of conference interpreting throughout the world. These community-building activities in the early 1990s also included Asian countries, with JAPAN leading the way. Pioneer conference interpreter Masaomi Kondo had spearheaded efforts to set up an Interpreting Research Association (later established officially as JAIS, the Japan Association for Interpretation Studies) that also publishes its own journal, *Tsuuyaku kenkyuu*.

The newly emerging and increasingly global scientific community of interpreting scholars was largely united in its high regard for empirical research as promoted by Gile (e.g. 1990).

Based on this methodological consensus, individual researchers adopted a variety of COGNI-TIVE APPROACHES to study aspects of the interpreting process, giving rise to a cognitive process (CP) paradigm that set itself apart from the Paris School. Following initial rivalry between the two PARADIGMS, the CP paradigm quickly assumed a dominant role, on the strength of its international networking, its information-sharing resources (in English rather than French) and its productivity: increasingly coherent lines of research developed around such issues as QUALITY and STRATEGIES, with special emphasis on the impact of various INPUT VARIABLES on the interpreter's performance. The impressive range of topics and approaches was very much in evidence at the 1994 Turku Conference, conceived as a stock-taking of progress in interpreting studies in the 'Trieste era' (Gambier et al. 1997). As a more sustained effort to reflect and develop the state of the art in the field, *INTERPRETING*, the first international peer-reviewed journal devoted solely to interpreting, was launched in 1996, co-founded by Barbara Moser-Mercer and cognitive psychologist Dominic Massaro.

The main obstacle to progress in the field's scientific aspirations was widely perceived to be a lack of methodological rigor, and a number of research training initiatives were undertaken around the mid-1990s to remedy this weakness (e.g. Gile et al. 2001). The growing number of doctoral theses with well-developed research designs may be seen as a reflection of this trend (Gile 2000). In parallel with these efforts to reach greater scientific depth, an altogether different development was under way that was to radically expand the discipline's breadth.

If the Trieste Symposium is seen as the starting point for the rise and dominance of the CP paradigm in interpreting studies, the First CRITICAL LINK Conference on "Interpreters in the Community" (Carr et al. 1997) marks the beginning of the emergence of COMMUNITY INTERPRETING as an internationally recognized field of professional practice and scholarly research. Rather than diplomats and international experts, users of this kind of interpreting included members of migrant communities on the one hand and representatives of social institutions (including legal, healthcare and social services) on the other. Instead of the cognitive processes and output quality of interpreters in international conferences, the focus in this new orientation was on the ROLE and qualifications of interpreters working in a variety of community-based SETTINGS, each with their specific institutional constraints. Since signed language interpreting is mostly practiced in community settings, the Critical Link forum joined together signed and spoken language interpreters whose task in dialogic settings was perceived to differ in fundamental ways from that of international conference interpreters.

Major theoretical and methodological momentum for the study of DIALOGUE INTERPRETING in community settings was generated in particular by the work of Cecilia Wadensjö (1992). Her dialogic discourse-based approach to the analysis of interpreter-mediated interaction, which draws on concepts from sociology (e.g. Goffman 1967, 1981), found a strong complement in Cynthia Roy's (2000a) use of SOCIOLINGUISTIC APPROACHES to analyze the interactional performance of sign language interpreters. Together they formed the core of a genuinely new approach to the study of interpreting, focused on dialogic discourse-based interaction (DI). This DI paradigm quickly gained ground, as community interpreting, or public service interpreting, attracted increasing attention among social stakeholders and researchers in various domains. Given its reliance on DISCOURSE ANALYTICAL APPROACHES, this paradigm has proved particularly open to contributions by scholars in branches of linguistics and sociology concerned with the study of discourse and interaction. The DI paradigm can thus avail itself of broad interdisciplinary foundations for the study of communicative interaction. On the other hand, its grounding in the profession is more tenuous, given the widespread lack of professionalization in fields like HEALTHCARE INTERPRETING and even LEGAL INTERPRETING. Indeed, the DI paradigm's largely descriptive orientation, as modeled by the work of Wadensjö (1998), has made it easier for researchers to include various forms of NON-PROFESSIONAL

INTERPRETING, from CHILD LANGUAGE BROKERING to volunteer interpreting in RELIGIOUS SETTINGS, in their purview.

Within a decade after the Turku Conference, interpreting studies had thus seen considerable expansion, in terms of its object of study as well as the theoretical and methodological approaches adopted to study it. If the discipline could be described early in the new millennium as a "remarkably heterogeneous series of loosely connected paradigms" (Pöchhacker & Shlesinger 2002: 4), heterogeneity and diversity have clearly become even more pronounced. The same applies to translation studies, however, and judging from steady progress in academic institutionalization, there seems little risk of disintegration for either field. Interpreting studies has thus come into its own as a distinct branch of science. With its largely uncontested claim to interpreting as its object of study, the quickening pace of social and technological change affecting interpreting as a profession, and an ever widening range of theories, models and methods applied to the systematic study of interpreting practices and practitioners, its evolution as an academic discipline seems set to continue.

FRANZ PÖCHHACKER

INTERPRETIVE THEORY

↑ PARIS SCHOOL
→ SELESKOVITCH
↓ TRANSCODING

The Interpretive Theory (IT) of Translation (*Théorie Interprétative de la Traduction*) was first developed by Danica SELESKOVITCH and her disciples at the *École Supérieure d'Interprètes et de Traducteurs* (ESIT) of *Université Sorbonne Nouvelle – Paris 3* (see Laplace 2005). It is a holistic theory developed by practicing interpreters, not by linguists or language teachers, nor is it based on any prior linguistic or psychological theory. Experience convinced those early scholars that interpreting was not just a matter of languages in contact, or of translating words, as was the prevalent view in the 1960s. They posited that interpreting (oral translation) is a cognitive operation based on (nonverbal) sense, the purpose of which is to convey speakers' messages to listeners who do not understand the original language.

IT, sometimes called the '*théorie du sens*' (García-Landa 1981), focuses on the ideal interpreting process in which well-trained professional interpreters with a thorough mastery of their languages work with adequate PREPARATION under proper WORKING CONDITIONS. It breaks down this process into three stages, with some overlap: (1) COMPREHENSION: construction by the interpreter of the sense to be transmitted; (2) deverbalization: once the sense, in its notional and emotional dimensions, is understood, its initial linguistic shell is discarded and it becomes language-free; (3) reformulation: deverbalized sense is re-expressed by the interpreter in the target language, as it would be expressed in intralingual communication (i.e. putting ideas into words).

Experience-based intuition was the starting point for this description of the ideal interpreting process (Seleskovitch 1968). This rough outline was then elaborated on in greater detail. Observation confirmed that successful interpreting followed this pattern, but Seleskovitch sought to give some scientific basis to her descriptions of the cognitive dimensions of interpreting and started looking for relevant literature. In the early 1960s there was no theoretical research on interpreting, and only a few publications on translation, such as the *Stylistique comparée* (Vinay & Darbelnet 1958), which she rejected as too linguistic, while work in structural and generative linguistics seemed even less relevant.

Seleskovitch then turned to other disciplines, and was disappointed by her first contacts with experimental psychologists: Oléron & Nanpon (1965) were willing to conduct experiments on SIMULTANEOUS INTERPRETING (SI), but unwilling to listen to methodological warnings from an expert interpreter. More support for Seleskovitch's ideas came from cognitive science research that was being developed in the 1970s and 1980s: cognitive psychologists and psycho-linguists (e.g. Levelt & Florès d'Arcais 1978; van Dijk & Kintsch 1983) were demonstrating that comprehension is based not only on language knowledge but also on prior knowledge and context, something that IT had been stressing since the early 1970s and that has since become universally accepted. Developmental psychologist Jean Piaget (1967) describes how mental schemata 'assimilate' new knowledge into prior knowledge and 'accommodate' to it, a process that is very similar to the way comprehension works according to IT. Neuropsychological research on aphasia and brain damage (e.g. Barbizet 1968) provided proof that language and thought were located in different areas in the brain, which gave support to the IT postulate of deverbalization.

Understanding sense

IT research first of all dealt with the comprehension side of the process, exploring how the speaker's intended meaning becomes the interpreter's sense.

Broken down schematically, understanding requires a double interpretive activity: the interpreting of sounds into mental concepts, then the addition of 'cognitive complements' to such concepts in order to access the sense of the speech. When interpreters possess an adequate knowledge of both languages and the topic under discussion, these two processes merge into a single act of interpretation immersed in context, and sounds are interpreted directly into sense. This sense remains present as awareness, while the sounds fall into oblivion.

IT questioned repeated assertions by translation scholars, inspired by research in machine translation, that word polysemy and speech ambiguity were central features of human language and communication. Problems of this kind arise only if no distinction is made between language as a system and language in use. Understanding is not just a question of word meanings. When words are used in their verbal and situational context, only one of their meanings makes sense and the sense of an utterance becomes clear. The feeling of inter-preters that a speech or part of a speech is ambiguous is usually due either to their lack of knowledge of the subject, or to a lack of clarity in the speaker's formulation, especially if s/he is using a foreign language.

As sense is based on the cognitive inputs of individual listeners or interpreters, it is to some degree an individual matter; its depth will vary according to the knowledge and the world experience of each person. Whatever its individual features, however, the sense intended and understood by each of the communication partners overlaps to a great extent, so that com-munication usually proceeds fairly smoothly. Interpreters, acting as mediators between speakers who want to communicate and listeners who want to understand them, operate in this area of overlap. Those who listen to them bring their own cognitive complements to the interpreted speech. The interpreters' rendering enables them to discover the speech according to their own relevant knowledge and motivations, superficially or deeply, in the same way as listeners following the original speech. Understanding speech is a universal phenomenon; the interpreter's understanding is only a specific example thereof. The difference between inter-preters and ordinary listeners is that the latter are free to interpret the sense of the speech any way they like, whereas interpreters, using all relevant contextual knowledge, must elicit the speaker's intended meaning (*vouloir dire*), their aim being to allow their own listeners as many interpretations as are available to those listening to the original speech.

Speech sounds reach interpreters' ears linearly, word by word, but interpreters do not understand word by word. The study of simultaneous interpreting (Lederer 1978, 1981) reveals that they understand *units of sense* as a few words coalesce with prior knowledge. Units of sense are conscious mental states caused by the simultaneous action of linguistic and extralinguistic knowledge on aural (or visual) discourse segments. As the speech develops, they overlap and merge into one another to form broader sense.

Deverbalization

IT is known for its assertion that deverbalization accompanies speech comprehension: as soon as it is understood, sense is processed in MEMORY, becoming part of prior knowledge – and most of the words which conveyed it disappear. This does not mean that interpreters' renderings are completely free of TRANSCODING (see below).

Empirical studies of both CONSECUTIVE INTERPRETING (Seleskovitch 1975) and simultaneous interpreting (Lederer 1981) clearly showed that understanding a segment of speech means deverbalizing it. Looking beyond interpreting, IT scholars became aware that deverbalization is not only a natural feature of interpreting, it is also a natural feature of human communication, recognized by writers, pragmatic linguists and cognitive psychologists.

Reformulation

One objection raised by translation scholars against IT was that it mainly dealt with the understanding stage of interpreting and neglected the production side, but the theory does address aspects of reformulation as well.

Deverbalization, the fact that verbal signs fade as notional and affective sense is grasped, is a great help to interpreters in avoiding transcoding and expressing sense idiomatically in the target language (Donovan-Cagigos 1990), but IT describes at least two more aspects of reformulation – the distinction between 'correspondences' and 'equivalences', and the balance between EXPLICITATION and implicitation.

IT makes a distinction between (a) *correspondences*, established between some words or set phrases (i.e. transcoding) and (b), since languages are not isomorphic, the creation of *equivalences* between utterances (Lederer 2002). Seleskovitch (1975) used the frequently quoted metaphor of the currant bun to explain the difference: in translation, NUMBERS, proper names and technical terms, which have context-independent meanings, emerge in the target language in recognizable form, like the raisins when a bun is taken out of the oven, while the ingredients making up the 'dough' – the bulk of the speech – are thoroughly transformed (see Setton 2002a).

IT scholars soon realized that communication always consists of both an explicit part (language) and an implicit part (speakers' and listeners' shared knowledge), which explains why interpreters have to infer sense not only from the words expressed but also from their own prior knowledge. Observation of numerous authentic speeches and their interpretations also showed that the *explicit/implicit balance* of either individual words or strings of words differs according to the language (as well as the characteristics of the speech and the speaker). The 'synecdochic principle' (a part for the whole), as Lederer (1976/2014) called it, derives directly from the fact that sense is built up by linguistic signs merging with listeners' inferences of what remains unsaid in speakers' output. This principle goes a long way towards justifying the statement that transcoding one language into another will not convey the message. Only the notional and emotional effects of the original wording must be taken into account: the actual words of the source language must be discarded, and a new idiomatic wording created in the target language.

Accordingly, the IT view of interpreting is *functionalist*: successful interpreting requires interpreters not only to use their background knowledge to understand the speaker, but also to ensure that their rendering is adapted to their listeners' background. Communication being the *raison d'être* of interpreting, in order to communicate speakers' meanings, it is sometimes necessary to alter the balance between the explicit and implicit parts of sense in moving from the source language to the target language: information that is implicit in one language may have to be made explicit in the other or vice versa. More generally, the way sense is understood is universal; the way it is expressed is language-specific.

Methodology and terminology

Seleskovitch was not specifically interested in empirical interpreting research (e.g. Seleskovitch 1976/2014); she saw the process of interpreting impromptu speeches as the most basic and transparent type of translation that could serve as the foundation for a general theory of translation, a theory of discourse and the study of the interrelationships between language and thought.

The IT-based research that has been carried out by the PARIS SCHOOL favors observational studies, with recordings and TRANSCRIPTIONS of authentic conference speeches and interpretations. IT scholars are wary of EXPERIMENTAL RESEARCH, which they feel entails the risk of misleading conclusions about the 'natural' interpreting process. Replication of experiments is also viewed as difficult, due to the numerous differences in variables from one study to another (Lederer 2008).

As the use of consecutive interpreting has receded, simultaneous interpreting has become the norm, and conference participants increasingly read out written texts. As a result, interpreting practices have changed. The IT model, however, remains valid and a number of developments in interpreting have yet to be analyzed according to the IT model.

Moreover, the scope of IT soon came to be extended beyond interpreting to written translation, where IT-oriented research has been carried out on a broad range of texts: 'pragmatic' (technical, legal, scientific), but also literary. A large number of doctoral theses have vindicated the IT model of translation (Israël 2005).

Over the years, an effort has been made to clarify and standardize the terminology used (Laplace 2005): 'discourse' replaces the Saussurean 'parole', and is used as a synonym of 'text'; 'sense' (*sens*) is the result of interpreters' comprehension of discourse (or chunks thereof), whereas 'meaning' (*signification*) applies to words and decontextualized sentences. A great many misunderstandings in the translation studies literature could be avoided if scholars made this distinction between 'sense' and 'meaning'. The same holds true for the distinction made by IT between 'correspondences' and 'equivalences'.

IT makes a point of using plain language that is accessible to students, practicing interpreters and translators; this may be a reason why scholars sometimes feel it is too simple, although the ideas developed were quite new at the time of its inception, and have been vindicated by a number of scientific studies.

MARIANNE LEDERER

INTERVIEWS

↑ METHODOLOGY

Interviews are a common method employed in qualitative research generally, and thus in the interpreting studies field specifically (Hale & Napier 2013). A key purpose and strength of the method is to elicit the experiences, perceptions and feelings of research participants in their own words and to highlight their concerns, rather than predetermining the features of interest to the research. Findings from qualitative interviews are not generalisable in the way that quantitative research hopes to be; rather, their 'generalisability' lies in the analysis and cogency of the theoretical reasoning that underpins them (Edwards & Holland 2013).

Interviews enable researchers to explore the texture and weave of everyday life; the understandings, experiences and imaginings of research participants; how social processes, institutions, discourses or relationships work; and the significance of the meanings that they generate. INTERPRETING STUDIES researchers have used them to address the delivery, process and/or receipt of interpreting services, variously exploring the perspectives of interpreters (formal and informal) and of people who use interpreters (professional and/or lay). As part of this, but also in research on other topics unrelated to interpreting, researchers may need to work with interpreters where they do not share a spoken or signed language.

Whether interviews are being conducted as part of research looking at the provision and use of interpreting services and/or with interpreters as part of the research process itself, they involve a sort of conversation or dialogue. Interviewers ask interviewees questions related to the topic of their research, which can range from broad 'tell me about … ' type enquiries to more specific questions concerning the what, when, how and why of an experience (Edwards & Holland 2013). Both semi-structured and unstructured interviews are used in interpreting studies. In a typical semi-structured interview, the interviewer has an interview schedule with a list of questions or series of topics they want to cover, but there is flexibility in how and when the questions are put and how the interviewee can respond. These interviews allow space for interviewees to answer on their own terms, but provide some structure for comparison across interviewees in a study. In an unstructured interview, the interviewer has a topic of study and research aims, but the importance of the method is to allow the interviewee to talk from their own perspective using their own frame of reference, and ideas and meanings that are familiar to them. The interviewer relies on the flow of interaction with the interviewee to steer the interview process. Whatever the variations in the style of interviews, they involve certain core features: (i) an exchange of dialogue between two or more participants, either face-to-face or by remote means; (ii) a thematic and topic-centred approach; and (iii) an understanding of the importance of context (Edwards & Holland 2013).

Epistemological approaches

The underpinnings of the core features of interviews can vary according to the philosophy or EPISTEMOLOGY adopted by the researchers. These have been described as two different approaches to research: metaphorically, the interviewer as a miner, or as a traveller (Kvale 1996). The interviewer-as-miner seeks to uncover nuggets of truth through interviews and thus access a seam of knowledge that is 'out there', ready to be gathered up. In contrast, the interviewer-as-traveller embarks upon an interactive and reflective interpretation of how they came to 'see' and transform particular 'sights' into knowledge.

Where research projects adopt a positivistic approach to the METHODOLOGY of qualitative interviews, the interviewer-as-miner is to the fore. Interviewers may attempt to ensure that all interviewees are asked the same questions in the same ways for example. The elimination (or, at the very least, minimisation) of any influence from the interviewer is regarded as crucial, based on concerns that semi-structured and unstructured interviews can lack objectivity and be subject to bias. For example, Hale and Napier (2013: 21) draw on this epistemological framework when they note that, where researchers use interpreters in cross-language contexts, the research may be jeopardised if they are not trained to be impartial. Further, because they are seen as reflecting an independent reality, interviewees' accounts of behaviour or events are regarded as being either truthful and reliable, or misleading and distorted. Hence the practice of checking interview material against other sources of data, often referred to as triangulation. In her study of hospital interpreters, Angelelli (2004a) triangulated data from semi-structured interviews with various stakeholders, a ROLE survey with interpreters, recordings of inter-preting interludes, and her own observation notes, in order to contrast interpreters' perceptions of their role boundaries with the data on their actual practice.

In interpretivist approaches, the interviewer-as-traveller is to the fore. Human interaction and negotiation is regarded as the basis for the creation and understanding of social life, so it is the interaction between interviewer and interviewee – or between interviewer, interpreter and interviewee – in the interview situation that creates meaning and knowledge. Thus, in their study of vicarious post-traumatic growth among interpreters working alongside trauma victims, Splevins et al. (2010) kept diaries reflecting on their interviews and the research process to inform their interpretive analysis.

An emancipatory perspective goes further, to make POWER visible as part of both society and interview interactions. The emphasis is on working collaboratively with, and placing control in the hands of, the people who are 'living' the research topic. For example, Springer et al. (2010) worked with community interpreters and community members as partners to develop the interview questions for their participatory research with Somali Bantu refugees on meeting their health needs. An additional way of realising emancipatory and social justice perspectives is to work with 'peer' or community interviewers as research colleagues. For example, Alexander et al. employed community members as research assistants in their study of the experiences of people who need interpreters to gain access to services, involving them in the broader research process and not just in interviews (discussed in Edwards & Alexander 2011).

Interviews, then, are not in themselves inherently biased or unbiased, oppressive or progressive, and so on; rather, it is the epistemological approach underpinning them that in large part creates such debates.

Group interviews

As noted earlier, interviews can involve two or more participants. Group interviews, often referred to as focus group research, involve people engaging in collective discussion of a topic set by the researcher. Often researchers will convene a number of group interviews involving different sets of people. For example, Napier (2011a) conducted interviews with separate groups of deaf people, of signed language interpreters and of hearing professionals, in a project seeking to compare their experiences of interpreting services. The interviewer puts questions to the group but may also act as a moderator (e.g. attempting to ensure everyone gets a chance to speak). Some researchers regard group interviews as a quick way of collecting a number of individual points of view, but others see their strength as lying in the interaction taking place between the participants, the group dynamics, and the insight and data that this interaction can produce.

Interviews in mixed designs

Interviews with groups and individuals can be combined in a single study, as well as with other methods of data generation, both qualitative and quantitative, usually referred to as MIXED METHODS RESEARCH. They can be used with other qualitative methods – for example, as an inte-gral part of a broader set of ETHNOGRAPHIC METHODS, where the researcher spends time in the field participating in and observing social groups or cultures under study. Lipkin's ethnographic study of interpreters in a military court setting (2010), for instance, involved participant observation and in-depth interviews. And interview material can also provide depth and detail to the more general picture offered by quantitative social data on interpreting.

Interpreters in interviewing

In addition to interpreting studies' focus on the topic itself, interpreters can be involved as part of the research process, enabling the interviewer to carry out interviews. Researchers taking an interpretive approach often stress the importance of acknowledging the 'three-way co-construction of data', with interpreters acting as key informants, gatekeepers and 'cultural brokers'. They may also highlight the interplay of TRUST and power in the researcher–interpreter relationship (Björk Brämberg & Dahlberg 2013; Edwards 1998, 2013; Edwards & Alexander 2011). In addition to taking this into account in analysis, researchers working with interpreters recommend investing time in inducting interpreters into the research topic and aims, in familiarising them with research process conventions and in agreeing working processes before undertaking interviews with them, as well as in debriefing after the interviews. There is, however, less consensus about the use of first- or third-person translation by interpreters in research interviews: for example, Björk Brämberg and Dahlberg (2013) assert that the interpreter should translate first person verbatim, while Edwards (1998) prefers third-person translation that clearly signals the involvement of an interpreter in the interview.

Quantity of qualitative interviews

Finally, there is the interesting question of how many interviews are enough. The number of interviewees in interpreting studies can range, for example, from five to over fifty. The concept of saturation is often mooted as a way of deciding how many interviews to undertake in a research study. This means that researchers should continue interviewing until their interviewees are not telling them anything that they have not heard before. In other words, it is the range of meanings that determines the number of interviewees in a study. A collection and review of advice from noted qualitative interview methodologists on how many interviews are enough finds the recurring answer 'it depends' (discussed in Edwards & Holland 2013). What it depends on includes: (i) epistemological and methodological questions about the nature and purpose of the research, whether the focus is on commonality or difference, on uniqueness or complexity, or on comparison or instances; (ii) practical issues, such as time and finances and institutional committee requirements; and (iii) the judgment of the epistemic community in which the researcher is located.

ROSALIND EDWARDS

INTO-B INTERPRETING

see under DIRECTIONALITY

INTONATION

↑ PROSODY, ↑ QUALITY CRITERIA

Intonation is a component of PROSODY and is defined as the pitch movement of an utterance (Cruttenden 1997). The acoustic correlate to auditorily perceived pitch is fundamental frequency (F_0), which averages 120 Hz for men and 220 Hz for women. While these values are indicative of speaker variables such as GENDER and age, an even more interesting parameter is the overall frequency range. Women not only have a higher mean F_0 value, but also a broader range within which they vary the pitch while speaking.

Pitch comprises two descriptive parameters: pitch *range* is the range of frequency within which changes in pitch occur; pitch *movement* describes whether the pitch is rising or falling. The pitch movement of an utterance displays *global* and *local* changes. A prosodic universal with regard to intonation is that the global F_0 contour falls during the course of an utterance. This global drop of F_0 is referred to as 'declination' and reinforces the auditory impression of falling final pitch movements, such as occur at the end of statements (Vaissière 1983).

Global pitch movement can be overlaid by local changes in pitch that result from tonal accents, leading to pitch 'peaks' or 'troughs' in the F_0 curve that are perceived as prominent. In addition, the final contours at the end of intonation units are of particular interest. Three basic contours are distinguished: fall, rise and level (or continuation) (Halliday 1966). Using pitch movements, speakers segment their utterances into shorter units (chunks), clarifying the underlying information structure of the utterance. Listeners in turn use the speaker's intonation and prosodic cues to segment the acoustic continuum during COMPREHENSION. The intonation-based structural units are referred to as intonation units or tone groups (Halliday 1966). They feature a coherent F_0 contour and at least one pitch movement that is perceived as prominent (Ahrens 2005a).

Intonation has several functions. In addition to its role in SEGMENTATION, it supports syntactic and semantic disambiguation, helps control TURN-TAKING, and provides clues to the speaker's mental and physical condition. Moreover, intonation has a social identifying function, as members of certain occupational groups exhibit specific intonational features that are characteristic of their work. Examples include auctioneers and preachers, but also simultaneous interpreters (Shlesinger 1994).

Investigations of the way simultaneous interpreters speak while interpreting have shown that interpretations sound "less smooth than 'natural' speech" (Barik 1975: 294), presumably because of the high COGNITIVE LOAD and the constraints of segment-by-segment processing at the original speaker's pace (see Ahrens 2005a; Nafá Waasaf 2007; Williams 1995). In the first study on simultaneous interpreters' intonation that used authentic (English–Hebrew) speech material, SHLESINGER (1994) described a *sui generis* intonation which she labeled 'interpretational intonation'. Drawing, inter alia, on Halliday's (1966) categories of segmentation into intonation units (*tonality*) and of pitch movement (*tone*), she found a higher number of progredient or slightly rising final pitch contours in her corpus than in monolingual speech production. As these contours also occurred where other final contours (e.g. fall) would be expected, Shlesinger hypothesized that this might make listeners' comprehension of the text more difficult, as was indeed seen to be the case in a small-scale experiment (Shlesinger 1994). More recent studies (e.g. Holub 2010) similarly document the influence of intonation on text comprehension.

Further evidence of simultaneous interpreters' deviation from normal intonation patterns was collected by Ahrens (2004, 2005a), in a descriptive study involving six professional interpreters working from English into German. Whereas the final pitch movement in the source speech was predominantly of the falling type, the three interpretations exhibited a predominance of rising, level and rise-level contours. Ahrens suggests that this may be because interpreters do not know how the source text will continue and therefore avoid intonational closure, in favour of a final pitch movement that indicates continuation.

In another line of research, the focus has been on intonation as a criterion for judging the QUALITY of a simultaneous interpreter's performance. In an innovative EXPERIMENTAL RESEARCH design, Collados Aís (1998) examined the influence of monotonous intonation in the interpretation on users' quality judgments. Whereas surveys on USER EXPECTATIONS had found intonation to be among the least important QUALITY CRITERIA, the experimental study demonstrated that intonation can actually have a significant impact on listeners' judgments of an interpreter's performance (see also Collados Aís et al. 2007). The negative effect of poor (i.e. flat) intonation on the evaluation of an interpretation was also demonstrated by Zwischenberger (2013), in a web-based rating experiment among members of AIIC, showing that two otherwise identical performances will be judged differently depending on the interpreter's intonation.

BARBARA AHRENS

INVISIBILITY

→ ROLE

The term 'invisibility' was first used in translation studies by Venuti (1995), to refer to the situation and activity of translators in contemporary Anglo-American culture. In his opening chapter of *The Translator's Invisibility*, Venuti cites US translator Norman Shapiro's influential 'pane of glass' metaphor, according to which a translation should be completely transparent and never call attention to itself. Though the meaning and subsequent understanding of invisibility have changed and evolved as the term traveled through time and fields of specialization, the ideology behind it has permeated every aspect of INTERPRETING STUDIES, from research and theory to pedagogical and professional practices in both signed and spoken languages.

The origin and justification of the ideology of invisibility for interpreters has been studied by such scholars as Angelelli (2004b), Roy (1993/2002) and Torikai (2009). While the term 'invisibility' was used in translation studies to indicate a preference for 'FLUENCY' of the translation in the target language and for the 'domestication' of texts (Venuti 1995), its use in interpreting studies relates to the alleged lack of agency or POWER of interpreters (Angelelli 2004b). Thus, descriptors such as 'window', 'channel', 'conduit', 'machine' or 'telephone' are frequently used to characterize the interpreter's ROLE, both by professionals using interpreting services and by interpreters themselves (Roy 1993/2002). While descriptions have evolved over time, they still tend to reflect the 'conduit model', in spoken language interpreting as well as SIGNED LANGUAGE INTERPRETING.

One possible justification for the notion of invisibility in interpreting can be found in SELESKOVITCH'S INTERPRETIVE THEORY, which implies that meaning can be grasped and transferred by the interpreter independently of linguistic form. Based on this claim, the interpreter can leave the language-independent meaning, or 'sense', intact and can thus be thought of as a conduit or channel through which the message may pass from one party to another rather than as someone involved in the co-construction of meaning by exercising his/her agency in the interaction (Angelelli 2004b). The conceptualization of the interpreter as a conduit or channel foregrounds ACCURACY as the most salient feature of performance, over and above such considerations as effectively working with participants' intentions and taking account of the objective of the exchange and of the context in which it takes place. In addition, invisibility overlooks social and cultural considerations that may be introduced by the different parties, as well as by the interpreter.

The idea of invisibility tends to inform the regulation of interpreters' activity and has been described (or prescribed) in various professional codes of ETHICS for conference, healthcare and legal SETTINGS. A noteworthy exception is the empirically-driven Code of Ethics and Standards of Practice, developed by the California Healthcare Interpreting Association (CHIA

2002). The CHIA Standards was the first document to openly discuss the full spectrum of interpreters' activities along a continuum of invisibility/visibility, from the interpreter as message converter, message clarifier and cultural clarifier to the role of patient advocate. When the interpreter participates in an exchange, the Code requires 'transparency', that is, keeping both parties fully informed of what is happening and what the interpreter is doing (see Angelelli 2007; Angelelli et al. 2007). If necessary, interpreters may contribute their own input to the interaction as long as they ensure that all parties are informed that the interpreter is the source of this input and that this message has been relayed to all parties involved.

In an attempt to measure interpreters' perceptions and beliefs about their agency (visibility), Angelelli (2004b) developed and administered a valid and reliable instrument called the Interpreter Interpersonal Role Inventory. In this first quantitative study to compare conference, court and medical interpreters, she found that perceptions of (in)visibility are not uniform, with healthcare interpreters showing a significantly greater sense of visibility than conference and court interpreters.

Whereas codes of ethics typically produce statements of a prescriptive nature, descriptive research has demonstrated the effects that interpreters have on an interpreted exchange. Since the 1990s, research based on SOCIOLINGUISTIC APPROACHES, DISCOURSE ANALYTICAL APPROACHES and SOCIOLOGICAL APPROACHES to the study of interpreting has explored the various participatory roles that interpreters play, and examined visibility as interpreters engage in activities of MEDIATION, advocacy, gatekeeping, and communication facilitation in medical (Angelelli 2004b; Davidson 2000; Metzger 1999) and legal settings (Berk-Seligson 1990, 2011; Inghilleri 2012). The construct of (in)visibility has also been explored among interpreters during wars (e.g. Torikai 2009; Fernández Sánchez 2012). As highlighted in the work of Angelelli (2004b, 2011a), Metzger (1999), Roy (2000a) and Wadensjö (1998), there are important differences between degrees of visibility and invisibility that are largely shaped by the nature of the interpreted communicative event.

Even if the myth of invisibility is still prevalent, reality (and research) shows that interpreters – and, by extension, translators – actually assume a very active and visible role as agents in interlingual/intercultural communication.

CLAUDIA V. ANGELELLI

JAPAN

↑ HISTORY

According to Yuzawa (2010), the first references in Japanese history texts to interpreting as a professional function date from the early seventh century. *Nihon Shoki* (The Chronicles of Japan) indicates that Kuratsukuri no Fukuri, an interpreter of Chinese descent, accompanied Ono no Imoko, an envoy appointed by the emperor to the imperial court of the Chinese Sui dynasty, in 607. It is believed that *toraijin* (people of Chinese and Korean origin, naturalized in Japan in the fourth to seventh centuries) and their descendants acted as interpreters in Japan's dealings with neighboring states in early times. Those originally from Silla, one of the three kingdoms in KOREA, also functioned as guides for Japanese missions to CHINA, because of their geographical knowledge as well as their proficiency in both Sillan and Chinese. History books and records written in seventh- to tenth-century Japan refer to interpreters as *osa*, with descriptions of their duties, status and backgrounds. In 730, the Japanese imperial court officially acknowledged the need to train Chinese interpreters. It also issued an order, dated 817, to train interpreters by setting up conversational Chinese classes at Daigaku-ryo (the highest academy for state officials). This effort was eventually abandoned, and government interpreting was mostly done by foreigners living in Japan and state clerks with relevant experience living in China (Mori 1998). A directive was also issued in 761 to teach young males Sillan as interpreter training in preparation for invading Silla.

The first Japanese interpreter of a European language is believed to have been Anjiro, who fled Japan as a criminal in 1546 (Kishino 2001). He was picked up by a Portuguese ship and taken to Malacca and Goa. After learning Portuguese and being baptized, Anjiro accompanied Francis Xavier and other Jesuits as an interpreter for their mission to Japan in 1549.

During the Edo Period (1603–1867), there were interpreters of Portuguese (until the start of the seclusion policy in 1633), Chinese and Dutch called *tsuji*, stationed mainly in Nagasaki. These hereditary interpreters were government officials with hierarchical titles, and engaged in trade-related administrative matters as well. *Oranda tsuji* (Dutch interpreters) also functioned as informants to the central government, gleaning knowledge of world affairs both through contacts with Dutch traders and through scholarly interest in European textual sources. It was they who introduced Western science and technology to Japan. In addition, Korean interpreters were stationed in Tsushima (islands located between the Japanese mainland and the Korean Peninsula), and a school for training young Japanese in Korean was established by Amenomori Hoshu in 1727. Towards the end of the Edo era, when Western nations started demanding that Japan open its door to the world, John Manjiro, who had returned to Japan after being shipwrecked and receiving education in the United States, played an important role as an interpreter and advisor to the Japanese government. It was *Oranda tsuji*, however, who worked in most negotiations with Western delegates, through RELAY INTERPRETING with Dutch as the pivot language and with the aid of notes in Chinese. At the same time, *Oranda tsuji* were directed to learn English and Russian in order to address new language needs.

Practice and training after World War II

During the occupation period after World War II, a great deal of interpreting was required in relation to the activities of the allied forces. This included TRIBUNAL INTERPRETING. The Tokyo War Crimes Tribunal (1946–1948) was a major event, in which a handful of Japanese nationals interpreted the court proceedings against Japanese war criminals. Although consecutive was the predominant mode, Takeda (2010a) regards interpreting at the Tribunal as a precursor of CONFERENCE INTERPRETING in Japan owing to its use of dedicated interpreters, an interpreting booth and equipment for SIMULTANEOUS INTERPRETING.

According to Torikai (2009), in 1950 Sen Nishiyama and Yukika Soma became the first Japanese to engage in simultaneous interpreting at an international conference. Other pioneers in conference interpreting were student volunteers who performed simultaneous interpreting at anti-nuclear conferences in Hiroshima, and interpreters who accompanied the Japan Productivity Center's missions to the United States from the 1950s to the early 1960s. They interpreted with virtually no formal training.

Amid increasing interest in interpreting as a PROFESSION, a book by interpreters on interpreter aptitude and recommended practice was published in 1961 (Fukui & Asano 1961). In preparation for the 1964 Tokyo Olympics, the International Christian University provided interpreter training for its students. This was the first time interpreters had been trained at university level in Japan.

In response to the increased demand for interpreters during the period of high economic growth, interpreting AGENCIES started operating in the mid-1960s. The first simultaneous interpreting class was launched at a private English school in 1965. Simultaneous interpreting became highly visible and attracted great attention during the interpreted live broadcast of the Apollo moon landing in 1969 (Torikai 2009). With the 1970 Osaka Expo and the increasing frequency of international conferences in Japan, the demand for interpreting expanded rapidly. Interpreting agencies started opening interpreter training schools in order to seek business opportunities and secure their own interpreters. This created an industry structure still prevalent today, where most interpreters are trained by, and work through, agencies. Indeed, the dominant role of interpreting agencies is the most salient feature of professional practice and interpreter training in Japan.

Interpreting-related courses are taught in higher education as well. Although a 2005 survey indicates that 105 undergraduate and graduate programs in Japan offer such courses, most of them are treated as part of English classes and very few universities offer professional training for interpreters (Someya et al. 2005). It was Daito Bunka University that launched an interpreting program at graduate level for the first time in Japan, in 1995. In 2000 the National Language Council acknowledged the desirability of training interpreters and interpreting researchers in higher education, which resulted in the establishment of a few more interpreting-related graduate programs.

Long before this rise in academization, a small group of research-minded Japanese interpreters, led by Masaomi Kondo of Daito Bunka University, had formed a group that became formally established in 2000 as the Japan Association for Interpretation Studies (Kondo 2009). With increasing momentum in the study of translation, the Association subsequently expanded its scope and name to include translation studies (Takeda 2012).

There is no national CERTIFICATION of interpreters in Japan, aside from government exams for licensed tour guides. With the rising number of foreign defendants and witnesses in Japanese courts, and following the introduction of a lay judge system in 2009, various issues in COURTROOM INTERPRETING have attracted increasing attention, especially with regard to interpreting QUALITY and interpreters' WORKING CONDITIONS (e.g. Mizuno & Nakamura 2010). In HEALTHCARE INTERPRETING and SIGNED LANGUAGE INTERPRETING, low levels of remuneration have been an obstacle to professionalization (Mizuno 2012), hence the widespread reliance on volunteers. Nevertheless, as the need for interpreting in all areas is likely to expand, community-based interpreting in Japan can be expected to receive greater attention in professional practice and in research.

KAYOKO TAKEDA

JEUNES DE LANGUES

↑ DRAGOMANS, ↑ EDUCATION

The French term *jeunes de langues*, calqued on the Italian *giovani di lingua* ('language youth'), refers to apprentice DRAGOMANS who trained in foreign embassies in Istanbul and who were destined for diplomatic service there or in other Eastern Mediterranean consular posts from the sixteenth through nineteenth centuries. The institution of dragoman apprenticeship was developed in a parallel and often connected fashion by several European embassies and consulates in Istanbul (and, at least in the eighteenth century, was adopted by the Ottoman court as well). It aimed to train its charges to become qualified diplomatic interpreters with strong attachment to their employers. While employers usually sought to recruit apprentices from among their country's own subjects and citizens, in reality many of them hailed from local Ottoman Catholic (and to a lesser degree Jewish, Greek, and Armenian) families. Recruits ranged in age from children as young as nine or ten years old to middle-aged apprentices by title only, but were typically young men in their late teens.

In recruiting apprentice dragomans for their embassies in Istanbul, all early modern foreign powers were faced with the same problem: the dearth of their own citizens and subjects willing to undergo such rigorous training in a faraway land. While the problem seemed perennial, and would endure well into the nineteenth century, each power sought to overcome it by different means. In particular, the solutions developed by Venice and by France – the two main 'trend setters' for diplomacy in Istanbul in the sixteenth and seventeenth centuries – reflected divergent visions of Ottoman 'Otherness' and how to overcome it.

From its inception in 1551 onwards, the Venetian dragoman apprenticeship program centered on the residence of the *bailo* (ambassador) in Istanbul. Initially, the plan was to recruit as apprentices only Venetian citizens (largely the sons of secretaries and other government functionaries). But starting in the early seventeenth century members of the Venetian colonial nobility in the Adriatic and Aegean, as well as sons of Istanbulite Catholic families, were admitted to the program in growing numbers (Rothman 2009b). Perhaps especially given these diverse sources of recruitment, the Venetians emphasized from early on the pragmatics of diplomatic interaction – rather than the mastery of languages per se – as the key component in dragomans' training. Accordingly, they came to value apprenticeship *in situ* over formal language instruction in Venice. Thus, regardless of their Venetian or Ottoman provenance, all apprentices were expected to reside in the *bailo*'s house in Istanbul away from their familial environment, with ample opportunities to shadow more seasoned dragomans in their daily activities and to interact with larger Ottoman society (Lucchetta 1989; Palumbo Fossati Casa 1997).

The French program of *Jeunes de langues* started in fits and bouts in 1669, when a royal decree established a college for French apprentices in Istanbul. According to the plan, six boys were to be sent to Istanbul annually, to be schooled in a local Capuchin monastery. After the program met with significant financial difficulties and very mixed results, in 1700 twelve scholarships were established for 'Oriental children' to study at the Jesuit College-Louis-le-Grand in Paris. By 1721, all boys destined for dragoman apprenticeships (whether of French or Ottoman-Christian families) were to be trained at the Parisian Jesuit college first, for about eight years, and only then travel to Istanbul. Although this program underwent various modifications over the years (and eventually admitted an equal number of 'Levantine' and French students), the basic model of extensive formal linguistic training in Latin, Turkish, and Arabic in the French metropole prior to going to Istanbul was kept intact (Degros 1984; Hitzel 1995; Hossain 1993; Testa & Gautier 2003).

Similar, if less systematic, efforts based on the Venetian model of sending young subjects to train as dragoman apprentices in Istanbul were made in the early seventeenth century by the Polish crown and by the HABSBURG MONARCHY. In both cases this proved relatively ineffective: the Polish crown continued to rely primarily on dragomans from a few Polish Tatar families, whereas the Habsburgs ultimately came to adopt the French model with the establishment of the Oriental Academy in Vienna in 1754, likewise with Jesuit involvement (Rathkolb 2004; Petritsch 2005; Wolf 2005). The French model was also the explicit template for a Spanish program to create a School of Oriental Languages in 1781 (Cáceres-Würsig 2012). In the absence of systematic apprenticeship programs either on their own soil or in Istanbul, other embassies continued to regularly recruit Greek, Armenian, and Jewish dragomans, as well as Catholic graduates of the Venetian and French apprenticeship programs (de Groot 1978; Bashan 1993; Berridge 2004). Their dragoman cadres, as a result, lacked the strong endogamy and confessional cohesion that characterized the Venetian cadre, but perhaps offered ties to a wider range of Ottoman commercial and political networks.

The enduring reliance on local Istanbulite families as a source for dragoman apprentices had important implications for the nature of Venetian apprenticeship. Formally, an apprentice dragoman's training began upon entry into the *bailo*'s household. In reality, however, many apprentices had started their training long before. As the sons, younger brothers, or nephews of acting dragomans, boys destined for the dragomanate often received language instruction at home in preparation for and in anticipation of their formal admission to the rank of apprentices. This was deemed necessary because the home language of local-born future dragomans was often demotic Greek (and, less frequently, Slavic, Armenian, or Judeo-Spanish). Even among Catholic families who traced their roots to Venetian and Genoese settlers in Constantinople in the wake of the Fourth Crusade, by the early modern period Italian was rarely spoken, let alone English, French, or German. Early language instruction also proved advantageous given the limited pedagogical resources available for formal training programs within ambassadorial households. Venetian consular reports repeatedly decry the inability of the Ottoman language instructor hired by the *bailo* to communicate with his charges, the absence of textbooks and other instructional materials, and young apprentices' tendency to run into trouble. Indeed, concern over apprentices' sexual impropriety, gambling, debts, and even potential conversion to Islam runs through these reports. Protracted dragoman apprenticeships thus served not simply to develop linguistic competence (in both Ottoman Turkish, the employers' written language, and less frequently Arabic, Persian, or Slavic). They also – perhaps primarily – were intended to socialize young men of widely diverse backgrounds into heteronormative masculinity and to carefully cultivate in them a command of diplomatic protocol premised on a more-or-less shared, circum-Mediterranean elite courtly culture.

The Venetian apprenticeship program proved relatively successful and enduring not simply thanks to its endogamous elements, but likely because it facilitated the development of a community of practice. Membership in this community, cultivated inter alia through prolonged cohabitation in the *bailo*'s house, underscored the practical and performative aspects of dragomans' HABITUS. It also fostered greater awareness of the intricacies of elite domestic social hierarchies (which in several fundamental ways were comparable across Ottoman and Venetian elite households) that helped young apprentices navigate the maze of political intrigue and competing interests at the Porte. Here again, apprentices hailing from local, long-established dragoman dynasties were at a clear advantage over recruits from either provincial or other metropolitan settings, as from a very early age they could acquire the performative dimensions of the craft from their dragoman fathers, uncles, and older siblings. Being part of familial information networks that crossed juridical boundaries (as siblings were sometimes apprenticed and worked for several different embassies) and having access to family archives of textual artifacts containing translations and other essential diplomatic text were also important, if rarely discussed, resources in their training. Unattached apprentices from far away had to rely on the good will of senior dragomans who were understandably less willing to share the secrets of their trade, especially if they felt threatened by younger competitors, or if they sought to secure apprenticeships for their own kinsmen.

What characterized a successful dragoman's apprenticeship more than anything, then, was the ability to integrate into a community of practice in order to master different aspects of courtly habitus, to learn by emulation how to perform measured deference to a carefully scalar range of local officials and diplomatic representatives, to show to advantage one's familiarity with Istanbulite elite culture, and to move across spaces, genres, linguistic registers and social groups with 'effortless' ease and confidence. These social skills also proved essential for dragoman apprentices' literary pursuits, as they allowed several among them to obtain Ottoman manuscripts from their associates in courtly and scholarly circles and to translate them for various patrons, whether their direct employers or the many bibliophile European sojourners in Istanbul (Dew 2009). Indeed, from the late seventeenth century onwards,

Venetian, French, and Austrian dragoman apprentices played a vital role in copying and translating Ottoman literary, historical, and diplomatic texts into a range of European languages (Ménage 1971; Elgohary 1979; Berthier 1997; Rothman 2013), thus making them available to a growing reading public beyond the Ottoman Empire.

E. NATALIE ROTHMAN

JEWISH TRADITION

↑ HISTORY
→ RELIGIOUS SETTINGS

The authors of the written translations of the Hebrew Old Testament, known as Targumists, have received scholarly attention since the nineteenth century, mainly in religious studies, Oriental studies, Bible studies, etc. A much more recent research topic is the professional practice of the oral interpreter, the *meturgeman*, working in Ancient times in the Jewish world (from the Second Temple era, beginning around 530 BCE). Insights into the interpreters' functions and STATUS are derived from rabbinic literature, an initially oral corpus put into writing from 200 CE: the two Talmuds and the Midrash, biblical commentaries and also the Responsa collections and Halakhic books. Despite the heterogeneity of this corpus (hundreds of thousands of pages written in various countries, mainly in Hebrew and Aramaic) and the presence of mythical and recomposed elements, these texts give a rather detailed idea of the way the PROFESSION of the Jewish interpreter evolved and was perceived over a period of more than 1500 years (between the fifth century BCE and the tenth and, in some places, twelfth century CE).

The predecessors of the *meturgeman* are mentioned in the Bible: the *melits* (the one who speaks well, and 'in favor of') worked in the Pharaoh's court in Egypt, interpreting between Joseph and his brothers (Genesis 42:23). Later on, Aaron acted as the 'mouth', the spokesman of his brother Moses, before Pharaoh or before the children of Israel (Exodus 4:10–16). The Jewish exegetes considered him to be the first *meturgeman*: translating, re-expressing and developing the ideas of his brother, and giving him added prestige by his mere presence and mediation. During the First Temple period, roughly between the 10th and 6th centuries BCE, there was a *balshane* (*baal lashon*, a language master and a polyglot) working in the Temple. Then, in the time of Ezra, when Israel came back from Babylon, speaking Aramaic after the long exile, there were *mevinim* ('those making understand'; Nehemiah 8:2–3, 9), translating orally and explaining the Hebrew text of the Torah when read in public in Jerusalem (538 BCE). The Talmud asserts that this is the source and the basis for synagogal readings of the Bible with consecutive interpretation (see Kaufmann 2005).

These interpreters (who were all men) are direct ancestors of the Targumists. They worked in synagogues, during services on Sabbaths and holidays, interpreting and chanting in the vernacular the segments of the Hebrew Bible chanted by a reader. In order to be sure that the interpreter, working from memory, would stay faithful (neither omitting nor adding anything) and would not mistranslate, the reading–translation process took place verse by verse from the scroll of the Pentateuch, or in sets of three verses for the prophetic books (Smelik 2003). There were, conspicuously, two different men, embodying the different status and role of the written Torah (*Torah shebikhtav*) and the oral Torah (*Torah shebe'al pe*): one reading from the scroll (the reader, who was forbidden to help the *meturgeman*), the other interpreting by heart, without looking at the scroll, each waiting for the other to finish before he went on, each harmonizing his voice to the level of the other, so that the original

Bible and its translation (pertaining to the oral Torah) were co-present and distinctly audible.

During the synagogal service, a *Darshan*, or preacher and teacher, gave a public sermon and the *meturgeman* translated it (mainly from Hebrew into Aramaic) and delivered it with musical intonation. Standing near the *Darshan*, who sat on a kind of throne and whispered to him, the *meturgeman* acted as a 'living loudspeaker', addressing the congregation with great rhetorical flourish and enhancing the dignity of the *Darshan* (Bregman 1982). The same could be said about the *Amora* (the alternative Babylonian term for *meturgeman*) working in a Talmudic academy (*beyt hamidrach*); the Rabbi sat and whispered his teachings briefly in a restrained voice to the *Amora*, who stood bending toward him; the *Amora* then translated and expanded the message in a strong, clear and convincing voice to the students sitting in circles in front of them. When the number of students was very large, several *meturgemanim* worked together (e.g. 13 for the 800 students listening to Rav Huna in the academy of Sura, Babylonia, in the third century CE).

Besides these liturgical and pedagogical functions, there were also *meturgemanim* in legal settings, assisting the Sanhedrin (rabbinic tribunal), mainly in civil suits, but not when the death penalty could be pronounced; in these cases, the judges were expected at least to understand the foreign language. Others worked 'freelance' at official events, such as the enthronement of a new judge or mourning ceremonies. Some interpreters were personally attached to a well-known Rabbi. Examples from the second century CE include Hutzpith, a famous martyr from Hadrian's reign, *meturgeman* of Rabban Gamliel II; Hananiah ben Akabya, *meturgeman* of Rabbi Judah bar Ilaï, and Abdon, who interpreted for Rabbi Judah the Prince. Later on, Rav (Abba Arikha) was appointed by Rabbi Hiyya bar Abbah and, upon his return from Palestine, deputized on one occasion for the regular *Amora* in the Babylonian academy of R. Shila. Yehudah bar Nahmani, whose personal teachings are cited in the Talmud, was the interpreter of Rabbi Shimon ben Lakish (third century CE).

If the appointment of an interpreter to a Rabbi was an honour and enhanced his status, the removal of his *meturgeman* was a mark of degradation. Some rabbis were bilingual, but used interpreters for reasons of protocol. Moreover, the function of the *meturgeman* was not always interlingual. He was more of a communication and rhetorical expert, sometimes respeaking the message, eloquently, in the same language. Some interpreters were trained as members of a well-recognized profession and received a salary. They were seen as mediators, knowing much more than common people but much less than the specialists. Their work was supervised and monitored, and they could be interrupted and corrected during interpretation. They knew which texts or locutions were to be read by the reader in the original but not translated, and which others had to be translated even if they seemed offensive (Alexander 1976).

In synagogues Jewish interpreters could be laymen and volunteers: *Targum* (the received way of interpreting each verse of the Bible) was indeed part of the curriculum of the elementary Hebrew schools, and each boy of around five or six, after learning *Mikra* (the written Bible) and before learning *Mishna* (oral law), learnt *Targum* (translating *Mikra* orally word by word) (York 1979). A child could be a *meturgeman* in the synagogue, but the *meturgemanim* were mainly schoolteachers (Levy 1963). They were trained to understand the text according to the traditional exegesis. They could probably adapt their language to the target audience, taking into account their listeners' knowledge of the Bible, the Hebrew language and the local dialect. Their fidelity was toward the text and the tradition, not toward a man or client. With time, the received translations were put into writing (e.g. the written Aramaic translation known as *Targum Onkelos* from the second century CE), memorized and then read in synagogues and pedagogical settings, so that gradually *meturgemanim* were no longer needed. Nowadays, only

Yemenite communities keep up the tradition: for pedagogical reasons, children serve as *meturgemanim* from Hebrew into Aramaic (and sometimes Arabic).

FRANCINE KAUFMANN

JOB SATISFACTION

↑ PROFESSION
→ BURNOUT, → STRESS, → WORKING CONDITIONS

Job satisfaction includes many connecting factors related to working life. EDUCATION, environment, salary, promotion, recognition, and ability are just a few of the variables that contribute to the larger whole that is job satisfaction. A multidimensional construct, job satisfaction includes the facets of satisfaction with communication, growth and promotion, organizational structure, pay, benefits, and security (Spector 1997).

Earlier research on job satisfaction in the general population found that the individual's degree of contentment depends on the actual or perceived gap between work performance and expectations (e.g. Locke 1976; Straw & Ross 1985): the closer to the desired level of performance, the higher the satisfaction. Early studies on job satisfaction among (conference) interpreters were mostly general and descriptive, showing a high level of satisfaction (e.g. Kurz 1991).

In the first in-depth examination of interpreter job satisfaction, Swartz (1999, 2006) surveyed sign language interpreters in the United States and Canada and found that autonomy, workload, ROLE conflict, supervision, and likelihood and/or possibility of promotion emerged as significant correlates of job satisfaction, with all but workload and role conflict showing a positive correlation. Interpreters were found to lack a connection with their work environment, perceive prospects for advancement as dismal, feel overwhelmed and underappreciated, and deplore a lack of understanding by others of the interpreter's role.

For organizations employing interpreters, ignoring the factors that lead to lower satisfaction can have costly consequences. When interpreters suffer a loss in vocational satisfaction and BURNOUT, they may leave the PROFESSION for an occupation involving less STRESS.

In the AIIC Workload Study (Mackintosh 2002), which examined psychological, physiological, physical, and performance factors in CONFERENCE INTERPRETING, 88% of the 607 respondents were satisfied with their profession, but less than half were satisfied with the travel involved and the prestige of the profession, which they saw as waning. Two thirds of the interpreters experienced high or very high levels of work-related stress (booth environment, fast speakers, lack of PREPARATION time, textual complexity, etc.), as confirmed by physiological measures (blood pressure, heart rate and cortisol levels). Choi (2007) surveyed conference interpreters in Korea, showing that more well-rounded training was needed to further the profession and maintain higher levels of work satisfaction.

Burnout, an important component in decreased job satisfaction, has been examined with perfectionism as a contributing factor (Bontempo & Napier 2011; Schwenke et al. 2014), and in relation to stress caused by maladaptive traits of work product satisfaction (Qin et al. 2008). Research supports the concept of setting realistic goals and of reflective practice – a thorough collective reflection on one's work, lessening the isolation interpreters typically face.

In COMMUNITY INTERPRETING settings, interpreters immersed in two cultures and positioned between two parties also experience stress from the need for MEDIATION of differences while meeting the needs of both sides. Harvey (2003) found that sign language interpreters often empathize with the Deaf participants in an interpreted encounter, mostly due to witnessing oppression (intentional and unintentional) at the hands of the hearing participants. Interpreters as compassionate participants are therefore at risk for VICARIOUS TRAUMA, with their physical, psychological, emotional and spiritual health responding and reacting to someone else's traumatic history (Bontempo & Malcolm 2012). Pressure also results from the fact that interpreters rarely enjoy the satisfaction that they have been involved in resolving any problems that have arisen during the interpreted encounter, often feeling worthless, and never recognized for their hard work. In their DEMAND CONTROL SCHEMA Dean and Pollard (2001) also suggest that the more interpreters are able to control the variables impacting any interpreting situation, the more effective the outcome and, by inference, the greater their satisfaction.

While burnout, vicarious trauma and job constraints are considered the psychological and emotional causes of decreased satisfaction, physical injury is obviously detrimental to an interpreter's overall well-being and satisfaction. Here, sign language interpreters are particularly at risk from repetitive motion injury, or repetitive strain injury, and occupational overuse syndrome. As shown in a survey by Fischer and Woodcock (2012) among Canadian sign language interpreters, 38% of the 314 respondents had been medically diagnosed with work-induced pain and musculoskeletal disorders, including carpal tunnel syndrome, arthritis, bursitis or tendonitis.

DANIEL B. SWARTZ

JOURNAL OF INTERPRETATION

↑ INTERPRETING STUDIES

The *Journal of Interpretation* (*JOI*) is the scholarly publication of the Registry of Interpreters for the Deaf, Inc. (RID), headquartered in Alexandria, Virginia (USA). While it testifies to the commitment of the American SIGNED LANGUAGE INTERPRETING community to developing its professional knowledge base through systematic inquiry, the journal has had a somewhat uneven history of publication. RID published the first *JOI*, edited by Edgar Shroyer, as Volume 1, Number 1 in September 1981; this was followed by Volume 1, Number 2 in March 1982. Volumes 2 to 4 were published from 1985 to 1987. The *JOI* did not appear between 1988 and 1992, and Volumes 5 and 6 were published respectively in 1992 and 1993. Beginning in 1995, the *JOI* was published biennially in 1995, 1997 and 1999, and the journal dropped volume numbers after the 1997 issue. The *JOI* has been published annually from 2000 to the present, except for the 2008/2009 volume (which covered two years) and the 2013 volume (actually published in 2014). Editors and co-editors over the years have included Marina McIntire, Sherman Wilcox, Douglas Watson and Anthony Aramburo as well as Len Roberson and Sherry Shaw, who have co-edited the *JOI* since 2010.

RID mailed the journal to all of its members until 2012, when the *JOI* became available in digital format. Currently, the journal is housed by Digital Commons at the University of North Florida as an open-access, online publication. As of 2013, RID began offering the *JOI* as a free community resource, regardless of membership status in the organization. Although initially developed to target signed language interpreters, the *JOI* has expanded to include original research, research application, and innovative practice manuscripts relating to all interpreters and translators, regardless of language pairs. According to RID (2014), the "JOI expressly aims to serve as an international forum for the cross-fertilization of ideas from diverse theoretical and applied fields, examining signed or spoken language interpreting and relationships between the two modalities."

The *JOI* uses a double-blind, peer-review process to evaluate submissions. The Editorial Board that reviews submissions is comprised of experts in interpreting, translating, interpreter education, linguistics, curriculum development, and research methods. To be considered for publication, manuscripts reporting research on human subjects must include documentation that the project was approved by a monitoring body, such as an institutional review board or research ethics committee. In addition, the *JOI* emphasizes that human-subjects research must use an informed consent process for enlisting participants.

The *JOI* is available at http://digitalcommons.unf.edu/joi/.

SHERRY SHAW

JUDICIAL INTERPRETING

see under LEGAL INTERPRETING

KINESICS

see under BODY LANGUAGE

KOREA

↑ HISTORY
→ CHINA

Several Sino-Korean terms appear in Korean history to refer to interpreting officials, mostly starting from the Koryŏ period (918–1392): *sŏl-in, t'ong-sa, t'ong-pyŏn, yŏk-kwan, yŏk-ŏ, yŏk-cha* and *yŏk-in*. In most cases, these contain the lexical elements 'go through' or 'communicate' (*t'ong*) and 'interpreting'/'translating' (*yŏk*). Lexemes such as *in* and *cha* mark 'human'; *kwan* stands for an 'office' or 'official'; *ŏ* originally refers to words, but here to a person who is involved with languages. *Sŏl* means 'tongue', so *sŏl-in* means 'tongue person'. *Yŏkhak*, a term used during the Chosŏn period (1392–1910), is the study of interpreting, but also covers learning, teaching and research in 'foreign languages', that is, the Four Languages (Chinese, Mongolian, Japanese and Jurchen, later called Manchu) (Kang 1966: 326).

T'ong-sa first appears in 667 CE in the History of Three Kingdoms, *Samguk Sagi* (Ch. 22). Both *T'ong-sa* and, to a lesser extent, *sŏl-in* were often used to refer to interpreters during the Koryŏ period. The former was also used in the Chosŏn period for interpreters who accompanied delegations to CHINA or JAPAN, or for interpreters who served visiting envoys, while *yŏkkwan* was used in the Chosŏn kingdom. Terms such as *yŏk-sang, sang-yŏk,* and *yŏksang-pae* (*sang* meaning 'commerce') tended to take on a derogatory connotation, mostly in the seventeenth and eighteenth centuries, when the private trading activities of interpreting officials were prominent.

It should be noted that the historical texts used as sources were all written in Classical Chinese. They are cited here on the basis of translations into Korean that are collected in the Annals of the Chosŏn Dynasty (http://sillok.history.go.kr/main/main.jsp), the Database of Korean History (http://db.history.go.kr) (*Samguk Sagi, Samguk Yusa*) and the Korean Classics Database (http://db.itkc.or.kr) (*Tongsagangmok, Koryŏsajŏllyo, Yŏllyŏshilgisul*), using McCune–Reischauer romanization.

Foreign relations before the twentieth century

It is difficult to find historical documents or research on interpreting before the Three Kingdoms period (i.e. before ~57 BCE). Sources like *Samguk Sagi* and the Memorabilia of the Three Kingdoms (*Samguk Yusa*) record the existence of several offices to receive Japanese and Chinese envoys, implying the presence of official interpreters. According to *Tongsagangmok*, there was a royal institution with trainees who were later put in charge of foreign affairs. Princes and high-ranking officials called *sugwi* were sent to China. They learned Chinese and played the role of messengers between China's Tang (618–907 CE) and Korea's Shilla (57 BCE–935 CE) dynasties, probably including duty as interpreters. There were also active exchanges with other ethnic groups such as the Khitan, the Mongolians and the Japanese, which would imply the existence of interpreting activities in royal courts during the Three Kingdoms era (57 BCE–668 CE).

Samguk Sagi and *Yŏllyŏshilgisul* contain the first explicit mention of an institution named *sadae* in T'aebong state (901–918 CE), which was in charge of teaching and interpreting. Similar institutions mentioned in historical sources are *t'ongmun'gwan* (established in 1276) in the Koryŏ period, and *sayŏgwŏn,* first established in 1389 in the Koryŏ dynasty and then again in 1393 in the Chosŏn period.

The Korean dynasties – especially Koryŏ and Chosŏn – adopted many customs and rites from China. Their texts were almost always written in Chinese, in acceptance of the Sinitic world order. Following Mongolian dominance in the late Koryŏ period, Chinese regained importance with the emergence of the Ming dynasty (1368–1644). The newly founded Chosŏn dynasty proclaimed a pro-Ming policy and proudly regarded itself as "little China". After the Manchu invasions (1636/1637) and the subsequent founding of the Qing Dynasty (1644), Chosŏn even regarded itself as the authentic successor of the Han-Chinese (Chŏng 1993). Chosŏn foreign policy fundamentally aimed to serve Great (Han) China and to maintain amicable relations with neighbours, meaning Japanese, Mongolians and Jurchen. The Chosŏn court sent tributes to China via delegations, and also exchanged delegations with Japan.

The Sino-centric worldview in Korea began to decline in the seventeenth century, as Chosŏn literati and interpreting officials came into contact with geographic and technical books and items brought by Western missionaries to China. International trade, which already flourished in the sixteenth century between Koreans, Chinese and Japanese (Ryukyu), as well as the Portuguese, was banned by the Qing in the seventeenth century due to Chinese and Japanese pirates. This enabled Koreans to do three-way trade with China and Japan. Facilitating trade was the official task of the *t'ong-sa*, who were also allowed to trade in private, since they had to partly bear their travel costs and were rarely paid for their work.

With the emergence of a modern, pro-Western Japan in the late nineteenth century as a new power in East Asia, the Chosŏn dynasty progressively reoriented itself towards Japan and the West. The defeat of the Qing in the First Sino-Japanese War (1894) finally marked the end of Korean allegiance to the Sinitic world order. The Chosŏn dynasty started to establish a new administrative and educational structure (1894) and proclaimed the Korean Empire (1897), which declined when the Japanese colonial era (1910–1945) began.

Education and social status of official interpreters

In general, only members of the freeborn class could become interpreters at the court in the Koryŏ period, but historical documents also mention interpreting by slaves (servants). Interpreters started from a low military rank and were rarely promoted. Over time, especially in the Koryŏ military regime (1170–1270), interpreters achieved higher positions thanks to their language skills (Lee 2006). During the Mongolian intervention in the thirteenth century, the *t'ongmun'gwan* was established to teach languages such as Mongolian, Chinese, Jurchen and Japanese. Of the 41 identified court interpreters, nearly 30 were active during the years when the kings cultivated close relationships with the Yuan court in China and actively engaged in cultural exchange and trade (Lee, M. 2009). With the growing importance of Chinese in the Ming period, the newly founded *sayŏgwŏn* replaced the *t'ongmun'gwan*, reflecting the shift in power from the Mongols to the Han-Chinese.

One way to become a *yŏkkwan* was through the *sayŏgwŏn* institute. The *sayŏgwŏn* was not only a training institute for interpreting officials, but also the office of interpreting and diplomatic affairs. It was located in the capital city of Seoul, but there were sub-offices near the Chinese frontier and at harbours in the south. Established one year after the founding of the dynasty in 1393, the *sayŏgwŏn* started to teach aspiring interpreting officials Chinese, Mongolian, Japanese and Jurchen, and had about 600 interpreting officials and general staff at any given time. Most of the candidates and later officials were the sons of concubines, low-ranking local officers and common people from the *jungin* middle class in the second half of the Chosŏn period. The education in the *sayŏgwŏn* lasted around three years, and the age limit for admission was fifteen (Baek 2003). Trainees could become interpreting officials after undergoing a complex procedure of screening and testing. They had to pass examinations in order to retain their position and be paid, as well as to be promoted or selected as interpreting officials for delegations (*T'ongmun'gwanji*, hereafter *TMGJ*, 1998: I, 73–99). Candidates were tested for spoken and written proficiency in languages, in addition to conversational and communication skills, along with knowledge of classical canons like the 'Four Books' and the 'Code of Governance'. The order of significance was Chinese, Mongolian, Japanese and Jurchen (Manchu), which was changed in 1765 by advancing Manchu directly behind Chinese (Song 2001; *TMGJ* 1998: I, 44).

The assured track to becoming an official was by passing the *yŏkkwa* civil service examination. The state examination for interpreters belonged to the 'miscellaneous' category. Candidates' family background and social position were screened. *Yŏkkwa* tested candidates' skills in reading, reciting, commenting and translating canonical classical Chinese texts, practical conversation and familiarity with the *Code of Governance* (*TMGJ* 1998: I, 75–80). The inclusion of the spoken language during the civil service examination is noteworthy, since it reflects the detailed practical aspects of the job in a society that relied overall more on written texts than oral communication.

In the same context, various measures were introduced to enhance foreign language competence: King Sejong (whose reign spanned the years 1418–1450) tried to send interpreting trainees to China in 1433, which was not permitted by the Chinese court. A regulation requiring that only foreign languages be spoken within *sayŏgwŏn* was introduced in 1442. In 1682, a department staffed by native speakers was established for conversation in the four foreign languages (*TMGJ* 1998: I, 58).

Following the Manchu invasions in the seventeenth century, war returnees were recruited as interpreting officials due to the language skills they had acquired in Manchu captivity (*TMGJ* 1998: I, 49), which did not necessarily help to elevate their social status. *Yŏkkwan* were not highly educated, were involved in trade and commerce, and did not belong to the *yangban* elite. They ranked last in the idealized Confucian classification of the 'four occupations' – scholar, farmer, artisan and merchant. The highest position *yŏkkwan* could normally reach was the third sub-rank. Even when, in some cases, interpreting officials attained the third upper rank of the ruling class, they still were not treated as such (Baek 2003). Historical records contain critical remarks about official interpreters and their extensive, often illegal, trading practices. From the seventeenth century, the middle class, especially interpreting and medical officials, progressively gained economic power. They constituted prominent clans, and marriage alliances among prominent *yŏkkwan* groups reinforced their networks.

In the list of 6115 successful applicants for the civil service examination in the 'miscellaneous' category from 1498–1773, there were 2976 successful applicants for interpreting (Annotation in *Chapkwabangmok*). Based on historical data, a prototype of the seventeenth-century interpreting official can be constructed as follows: he came from a middle-class family clan where other clan members were already working as interpreters, and passed the state examination for Chinese at the age of about 22. About one in seven officials might go on to become a teacher – not a high-ranking post, but a paid one. The *sayŏgwŏn*, with a staff of 600, could afford to pay only about one tenth of them for a maximum of 90 months (Kim 2003). The rest could hope to be selected as members of delegations to China or Japan.

Functions and influence of interpreting officials

The functions of interpreters during the Koryŏ period were not limited to rendering Korean into other languages, but also covered diplomatic tasks. Records from *Koryŏsajŏllyo* (year 1206: Ch. 14; year 1308: Ch. 23) and *Tongsagangmok* (year 1308: Ch. 13a) show that interpreters accompanied delegations to and from China and were put in charge of receiving delegations and of limiting Yuan cultural influence in the Koryŏ court. They were also sometimes entrusted with resolving diplomatic conflicts. Interpreters were rewarded for their achievements, though some were criticized for exploiting the poor and illegally accumulating a fortune. There were also Japanese interpreters, but historical information about them is much scarcer than that on Chinese and Mongolian interpreters. Especially during the Yuan period, Mongolian–Korean interpreters of the Koryŏ kingdom had very close links to the Yuan imperial court and were able to gather great political power.

Writing diplomatic documents was no longer an official task of interpreting officials during the Chosŏn period. However, the tasks of *yŏkkwan* were manifold compared with the Koryŏ period. They included interpreting in various situations (e.g. royal receptions, negotiations), accompanying and receiving envoys to and from foreign countries, handling practical affairs for delegations, taking care of foreign guests, collecting information – legally and illegally – by using their language skills and knowledge of visited countries, selecting ladies in waiting and boys to be sent as eunuchs to China for tribute, as well as bringing in, interrogating and sending back captives or displaced people. They were also aware of the need to train interpreters. Though not an official task, many officials were engaged in editing and publishing textbooks for the four foreign languages. However, one of their main tasks was to oversee official trade with the Chinese and Japanese, and the extent of their private trade increased considerably in the second half of the Chosŏn period.

Envoys to the Ming court were both politically and economically vital and were dispatched regularly – four times a year. The Chosŏn court was eager to send regular tributes, since it was virtually the only way to trade officially with the Ming, while for the delegation members it was a personal honour. Many delegations were also sent on an irregular basis for various tasks. A 70- to 80-strong delegation included many interpreting officials, who also took charge of trading in different fields. The number and frequency of delegations to China decreased in the Qing period (*TMGJ* 1998: I, 100–213); for the *yangban* delegation members it was no longer an honourable task, which encouraged more active participation by the interpreting officials.

Diplomatic relations with the Japanese were established around the beginning of the fifteenth century. After a brief freeze during the Japanese invasion (1592–1598), official ties were revived in 1607 and lasted until the Meiji restoration in Japan (Lee 1986). Although delegations to Japan were fewer and less frequent than to China, Japan was given a special privilege called *waegwan*, a place where Japanese people could stay and trade for longer periods. By modern standards, the *waegwan*, which was also used to accommodate delegations from Japan, could be thought of as a forerunner of the consulate. Issues relating to *waegwan* and controlling official trade were also tasks of interpreters.

Even though *yŏkkwan* did not gain real political power in the court, they accumulated wealth by means of trade and commerce which helped them to strengthen their networks. They were active in literary societies in the seventeenth and eighteenth centuries. The *yŏkkwan* – especially for Chinese and Manchu – played a significant role in disseminating ideas, knowledge, technology and skills from the West and from the once-despised Qing in the Chosŏn kingdom, and also developed their own (Jin 2011). In the nineteenth century, their activities and networking helped them to embrace new ideas as they progressed towards modernization, and to assume an active political role. The *yŏkkwan* readily abandoned the old order in favour of new ideas. They were actively engaged in the founding of a society (*kaehwadang*) to promote modernization during the Chosŏn era (Chŏng 2003).

When contacts with Western powers began in the nineteenth century, the Chosŏn court could communicate with them only via RELAY INTERPRETING through Chinese or Japanese. A first modern school for English was therefore established in 1883, aimed, among other things, at training interpreters. Schools were also established subsequently for Japanese, French, Russian, Chinese and German, but they were abolished in 1911 during the Japanese colonial era (Yu 2011; Park 2003). The training and work of official interpreters during the Japanese colonial era, the period of the United States Army Military Government in Korea (1945–1948) and subsequently until the end of the 1970s when the first graduate school of interpreting and translation was founded in Seoul (1979) still remain to be researched.

The infrastructure for such research certainly exists: aside from some 25 universities in Korea offering interpreter EDUCATION at the BA and MA levels, there are PhD programs in translation studies, academic journals, and scholarly societies, with a sizeable number of scholars specializing in the study of interpreting.

KIM NAM HUI

LANGUAGE POLICY

Every state requires a language policy. While it may leave some other matters to choice (religion for example), a state must determine a language (or small number of languages) for official use. And it must be able in some way to communicate with other states. Language policy is thus co-extensive with the history of organised governments, but an explicit link between interpreting and language policy was generally made only in the twentieth century, and even then in a patchy way: from a language policy perspective, the provision or otherwise of interpreting unerringly indexes the attitudes of a state towards speakers of other languages.

Historically, language policy related to interpreting has clearly differentiated between external and internal affairs. Externally, interpreters were usually closely tied to diplomatic or plenipotentiary work (Niang 1990; Lung 2011), but DIPLOMATIC INTERPRETING was often made unnecessary by the employment of a LINGUA FRANCA, which enabled widespread communication without interpreters. Internally, too, official languages did not necessarily reflect popular linguistic usage. While a modern view is that a government speaks in the language(s) of its people, this was not necessarily the case historically, particularly for multilingual empires. Interpreting was largely ignored when government was at a great distance from its subjects, but in some cases, as in the Ottoman Empire and the HABSBURG MONARCHY, DRAGOMANS, as a minority group that crossed linguistic boundaries, were employed for both external and internal communication.

The colonial period saw numerous individual cases of using natives as interpreters, MALINCHE being the most outstanding example. However, the rules for recruiting interpreters in the sixteenth-century colonial empire of SPAIN can be regarded as the first explicit language policy recognising interpreters, and one which may be read even today as providing a positive working environment for interpreters and confidence in their abilities as a result of monitoring processes (Giambruno 2008).

It took almost another four centuries for the next significant language policy related to interpreting to emerge in the Versailles peace talks after World War I (Baigorri-Jalón 2014). The initial arrangements invented there for interpreting in the major European languages continued in interwar international organisations such as the League of Nations. Concerns for efficiency led to experiments with SIMULTANEOUS INTERPRETING, first at the International Labour Organisation and after World War II famously at the NUREMBERG TRIAL. The subsequent growth of CONFERENCE INTERPRETING arose from high incentives for such work (paid out of international affairs budgets) and a corresponding EDUCATION policy whereby some major European universities provided simultaneous interpreting courses.

On the international level also, the explicit policy of the European Union to have all its members' languages recognised and used as official languages of EU institutions has highlighted interpreting needs, often with a scramble to provide interpreting into and out of the newer members' languages, partially allayed by some use of RELAY INTERPRETING and by a general, informal practice of often keeping to a smaller range of more widely known languages (Forrest 1998; Gazzola 2006). Finally, a more grim international issue has been the problematic policy of recruiting native interpreters for international forces in CONFLICT ZONES.

Perhaps the greatest challenge to governments in terms of language has been the post-World War II movement of multilingual populations of immigrants, not only in the New World but nowadays practically everywhere. This poses novel challenges for countries that saw settlement of immigrants and any language implications as a matter for the individual, with few language services – a path generally followed in many European and Asian countries. In AUSTRALIA and Sweden, on the other hand, early belief in assimilation was belied by continuing language maintenance of immigrants, and slowly systems of COMMUNITY INTERPRETING emerged for the most essential public services, usually led by law enforcement and health institutions, but becoming part of broader policy initiatives: accreditation systems, training, and state-sponsored language services developed from the 1970s, and have become part of the very fabric of government and social activity (Hale 2007). Great Britain, the Netherlands, Norway and some other countries have also moved in this direction. Unlike conference interpreting, however, remuneration for interpreters in community spheres has been poor and professionalism difficult to achieve, particularly in the light of increasingly diversified language needs (Ozolins 2010). One significant development in this regard at the European level is Directive 2010/64/EU, on the right to interpreting (and translation) in criminal proceedings.

Local political ideologies have often determined language policy responses. In the US, for example, despite initial lack of enthusiasm for providing interpreting services, rights-driven imperatives forced the state to respond in two areas on constitutional grounds: first, the Federal Court Interpreters Act of 1978 established a system of CERTIFICATION for federal court interpreters, though the number of languages covered has been limited (Schweda Nicholson 1986); second, the 1964 Civil Rights Act has been used to mandate interpreting services across a wide range of institutions, and state initiatives have in many cases developed strongly, particularly in LEGAL INTERPRETING and HEALTHCARE INTERPRETING (González et al. 1991/2012; Youdelman 2008).

Meanwhile, in a number of countries in Asia and the Mediterranean, interpreting services have barely emerged from being voluntary activities, reflecting an essentialist view of the host language, and a marked lack of language policy towards immigrants and other groups (e.g. Valero-Garcés & Martin 2008).

Interpreting needs have also been recognised in policy towards two other internal groups in many countries in response to their growing political and public presence. Interpreting in INDIGENOUS LANGUAGES has steadily – if unevenly – grown in the US, Australia and CANADA, though the question still calls for urgent attention in South America, AFRICA and elsewhere (Cooke 2009b). Meanwhile, provision of SIGNED LANGUAGE INTERPRETING has grown as a language policy initiative in relation to the needs of the Deaf, but sometimes quite outside the development of spoken-language interpreting, with policy mechanisms such as disability legislation and anti-discrimination measures increasingly mandating interpreting services.

ULDIS OZOLINS

LATERALIZATION

see under NEUROSCIENCE APPROACHES

LEGAL INTERPRETING

↑ COMMUNITY INTERPRETING
↓ ASYLUM SETTINGS, ↓ COURTROOM INTERPRETING, ↓ POLICE SETTINGS, ↓ PRISON SETTINGS

The legal process comprises a series of interdependent procedures involving a range of legal services. Legal interpreting takes place in the many different stages of criminal law procedures, from the discovery of the offence through various investigations and hearings to the decision and possible sentencing stage. It is also needed in a lawyer's or legal aid office, when an interpreter is required to accompany a search warrant party or police raid, in a police interviewing room, at an asylum hearing, in a civil law or juvenile courtroom, a probation office, a prison, etc. (Benmaman 1997; Bancroft et al. 2013; Hertog 2013). Legal interpreting thus encompasses a broad variety of SETTINGS, from COURTROOM INTERPRETING as the traditional focal point to POLICE SETTINGS, PRISON SETTINGS and ASYLUM SETTINGS. The other-language speakers involved may include victims, defendants, witnesses or inmates. Increasingly, legal interpreters also assist in communication between legal services across national borders, as in judicial collaboration to prevent terrorism or trafficking in drugs or people. While this extends the conceptual scope of legal interpreting beyond the intra-societal sphere, the overriding concern here is with legal settings 'in the community'.

As a result of the range and diversity of legal interpreting, the term has gained currency with respect to 'judicial interpreting' (Driesen 1985), 'forensic interpreting' (Roberts-Smith 2009) and 'court interpreting', which was until recently the most common term used to refer to interpreting in the legal domain (Mikkelson 2000). While it is true that different assignments – police interviews, depositions, asylum hearings, telephone taps, video links – will require additional specific skills, labelling legal interpreters by such descriptors may trigger uninformed perceptions of their status in the legal system. It may also have the disadvantage of establishing a potential hierarchy of competencies and pose the risk of fragmenting the process of professionalization. As the evidence heard in court relies on the evidence gathered during the investigative phase, the QUALITY of interpreting must be consistent and reliable throughout. Moreover, few legal interpreters can limit their activities to only one sector of the legal system.

Within the domain of justice attention has long been centred on courtroom interpreting. This includes TRIBUNAL INTERPRETING in the international sphere, such as the ground-breaking NUREMBERG TRIAL, but also high-profile court cases like the Demjanjuk, Lockerbie, O. J. Simpson or Madrid bombing trials. Research on the history of legal interpreting also tends to focus on courts (e.g. Morris 1999a, 2007, 2008; Roberts-Smith 2009), even as far back as the early code of conduct in the *Leyes de las Indias* (Giambruno 2008). All this accounts for the prominence of 'court interpreting' within the wider field of legal interpreting, as reflected in most entries on the topic in reference volumes (e.g. Stern 2011; Russell 2012).

Legal foundations and professional guidance

There has been increased awareness, since World War II, of fundamental rights enshrined in such documents as the 1950 *European Convention for the Protection of Human Rights and Fundamental Freedoms* – articles 5.2 and 6.3 on the right to a fair trial being crucial in this respect – and also a growing need for national legislation to guarantee the civil rights of more and more other-language speakers who are involved in the legal system in one way or another. The 1978 US Court Interpreters Act, the 1973 Australian Department of Immigration recommendations on legal interpreter training or the 1976 standards for legal interpreters in Sweden are early examples of development in the field. In the European Union this process has culminated in a number of 'directives' – legislation legally binding on the Member States – on the right to information, on access to a lawyer and on victims' rights, all of which include the provision of interpreting. The most fundamental is *Directive 2010/64/EU on the right to interpretation and translation in criminal proceedings*, requiring Member States to have a system in place that ensures quality of interpreting, whether face to face, over the telephone or in videoconference mode, in communications between suspected or accused persons and their legal counsel, during police questioning, in all court and interim hearings, and in proceedings for the execution of a European arrest warrant.

The fact remains, however, that adequate training and quality in legal interpreting are far from ensured in many countries around the world. As a result, a considerable number of publications strive to equip interpreters to work in the courts (e.g. González et al. 1991/2012; de Jongh 2012) or in the wider remits of police work, probation and prisons (e.g. Laster & Taylor 1994; Colin & Morris 1996). Guidance documents such as the London Metropolitan Police Guidelines on working with interpreters, the RID *Standard Practice Paper* on legal interpreting and the Finnish Refugee Advice Centre guide for interpreters working in the asylum process complement this 'good practice' literature.

Even with the benefit of training and guidance, interpreting in community-based legal settings holds many difficult challenges. In contrast to professional interpreters in international courts, who benefit from quality management measures (e.g. paid preparation time), abide by professional (e.g. AIIC) or institutional (e.g. ICTY) codes, and predominantly work in unidirectional simultaneous mode from a booth, community interpreters in legal settings work both ways, for as long as the event lasts, wherever and whenever they are needed, without significant preparation time. They interpret for people who may only speak local or non-standard language varieties and who may be anxious, vulnerable or uncooperative. They often have to deal with antagonistic relations among the participants, working alone and therefore without support in reconciling situational challenges with the precepts of their code of ETHICS. Much of the professional literature therefore focuses on language and knowledge competences, interpreting techniques and skills (e.g. NOTE-TAKING, SIGHT TRANSLATION/INTERPRETING), and ethics.

The legal interpreter's role

The one issue that, more than any other, has launched critical reflection and debate is that of the legal interpreter's ROLE. Judicial contexts generally have special characteristics, such as hierarchical role distribution, procedural conventions, strict legalistic interpretation of facts and statements, and the discourse strategies used to achieve certain objectives. One particular requirement for interpreters is legal professionals' insistence that, because justice is at stake and the interpreted rendition becomes the official record, the exchanges between the parties are translated 'verbatim' and that legal interpreters are absolutely accurate and impartial. As a result, and in the interests of self-preservation, some authors recommend that interpreters be unobtrusive, invisible 'ciphers' or 'machines', accurately rewording in language B what is said in language A and vice versa (Knapp-Potthoff & Knapp 1987; Schweda Nicholson 1994). This overriding demand for ACCURACY and impartiality also explains why virtually all codes tend to be highly prescriptive and deontologically normative: the interpreter must, shall, must not.

But statements do not flow 'literally' from one language into another in equal number and sequence; 'verbatim' is not synonymous with accuracy and impartiality does not entail INVISIBILITY. Close scrutiny of legal interpreting in action, and the insight that meaning and intent are necessarily construed as a joint activity by all parties together in an institutional communication situation, have led to the recognition and description of the complexity of the legal interpreter's role (Wadensjö 1998). Once the inherent subjectivity of interpreting 'talk in action' is acknowledged, a continuum opens up: at one end is a certain degree of pragmatic "latitude" (Shlesinger 1991), where the interpreter acts as "an independent persona" intervening to clarify or rectify out of a desire to be precise; in a more teleological view, the interpreter adopts an outcome-oriented ethical stance which hinges on an ongoing analysis of the dynamic context of each situation and is grounded in a professional responsibility for the needs and objectives of all primary speakers (Dean & Pollard 2011). Such an approach to the interpreter's role, articulated in a number of scholarly publications (e.g. Morris 1995; Cokely 2000; Turner & Brown 2001; Hale 2008; Martin & Ortega Herráez 2013), is obviously conditional upon training, great sensitivity and professional behaviour. At the very opposite end of the continuum some authors argue that, because of the strongly asymmetrical constellation and POWER imbalance in some settings, legal interpreters should position themselves as 'advocates' of the disadvantaged, disempowered party (e.g. Barsky 1994; Inghilleri 2005a) or indeed of the PROFESSION, as Berk-Seligson (2009) concludes in her study of "coerced confessions" and "linguistic police misconduct" in bilingual police interrogations that result from a failure to provide qualified legal interpreters.

This complexity of the interpreter's role is further compounded by conflicting conceptions and USER EXPECTATIONS. The role-related perceptions of legal professionals, individual clients and interpreters themselves have been investigated, often on the basis of SURVEY RESEARCH, in a number of studies, including: Angelelli (2004b) and Martin & Ortega Herráez (2009) on interpreters' self-perceptions; Fowler (1997), Kadrić (2001), Foley (2006), Ibrahim (2007) and Morris (2007) on judges' and lawyers' views; Lee (2009a) on legal professionals and interpreters; Ortega Herráez & Foulquié Rubio (2008) on police officers and interpreters; Hale & Luzardo (1997) on other-language speakers and interpreters; and Brennan (1999) on deaf clients. All of these testify to the challenging and divergent expectations to which legal interpreters must respond, often forcing them to act outside the normative code.

Discourse-based and pragmatic research

The issue of role is also related to another main body of research – the discourse-based analysis of dialogic question-and-answer sequences between legal professionals and witnesses or defendants. This line of research adopting DISCOURSE ANALYTICAL APPROACHES has again been dominated by courtroom evidence, mainly due to the public nature of the setting, which is less difficult to access than other, more confidential legal venues.

The landmark study here is Berk-Seligson's (1990) linguistic–ethnographic analysis of English/Spanish dialogues in various US courts, which showed that interpreters were often unaware of the strategic use of attorneys' and judges' questions and often altered the pragmatic effect of questions and answers by the primary speakers. For example, interpreters were found to add features of powerless speech to their renditions, thus affecting the impression of a witness's trustworthiness upon a jury. A follow-up study of leading questions (Berk-Seligson 1999) revealed that the force of such questions was systematically weakened. Interestingly, both the mode (consecutive vs. simultaneous) and the setting (trial vs. hearing or deposition) seemed to be significant predictors of this effect. A similar study by Hale (2004), on question-and-answer witness testimony in penal court cases in New South Wales, also shows interpreters struggling to render the propositional content accurately because they do not always understand the purpose or form of the attorney's questions being put to the witness. In trying to come up with a pragmatic equivalent, they are often found to change the strength and pragmatic intent of the statement, which in turn may affect the efficacy of the legal professional's strategy as well as the convincingness of the witness. While these studies are descriptive and quantitative, they are closely linked to upholding the norm of accuracy. Other studies have shown interpreters making inappropriate changes to COHERENCE and COHESION markers; omitting what they consider irrelevant and adding or clarifying what they think relevant; changing REGISTER and discourse markers and manipulating direct and indirect style (Hale 1997c,1999; Krouglov 1999; Rigney 1999; Dubslaff & Martinsen 2007; Lee 2009b, 2010; Wadensjö 2010; Cheung 2012; Ng 2013).

This predominantly micro-analytical discourse-based approach can be extended to the ostensive-inferential process in a relevance-theoretic account (Sperber & Wilson 1986/1995), and by analysing the ways in which interpreters engage in INFERENCING while operating on contextual assumptions. By taking into account the sociocultural institutional context into which the different speakers bring their pre-textual dispositions, assumptions and roles, more light has been shed on the pragmatic decisions and choices legal interpreters make (e.g. Mason 2005a, 2006). Interpreters try to infer what speakers intend to communicate from ostensive cues – institutional and contextual, as well as linguistic and nonverbal – in a pragmatic process of negotiation of meaning, ensuring that a speaker's communicative intention and not merely his or her words are available, trying to render the original utterance with the same illocutionary force and perlocutionary effect (Jacobsen 2003; Hale 2006, 2010). They will resort to the various STRATEGIES mentioned above, but also to shifts of 'footing' and FACE-saving strategies (Mason & Stewart 2001; Pöllabauer 2007; Jacobsen 2008a, 2008b) and may occasionally have in mind a meta-relevance beyond the semantic-pragmatic discourse level, such as the procedural conventions or expected objective of the event, and adapt their interpreting decisions accordingly. However, the inherent risk is that interpreters may attribute meanings and intentions to primary speakers which have not been said or intended. This is crucial because, for the purpose of the legal process, the 'originals' spoken by primary speakers in another language are in fact authored by the interpreter. The interpreter's choices in transferring the propositional content and illocutionary effect may thus entail a (re-)projection of identities of primary speakers without this being known. If, as a result, participants attribute 'ownership' of meaning and intent to primary speakers, this clash between pro-jected and re-projected identities may have serious repercussions on later talk in a judicial context (e.g. an interpreted defendant's statement taken up in the prosecutor's summing up) or on the perceived identity of a primary speaker (Hale & Gibbons 1999; Pym 1999; Matoesian 2001; Cotterill 2003; Mason 2005b; Heffer 2010; Gallez & Maryns 2014). The interpreter's wording may in fact be what a judge or jury eventually base their decisions on.

This more longitudinal approach – from police interrogation to court or from asylum interview to decision – highlights another important aspect, that is, the prominence of inter-textuality in many legal procedures, and the change from ORALITY to the written medium and back. In asylum hearings or in trials, for example, documents, interviews, depositions, testimonies, expert reports etc. are carried over from one context to another and are thus de- and re-contextualized. This 'entextualization' brings about pragmatic, meta-pragmatic and ultimately judicial consequences. Suspects are confronted with written versions of their oral statements to the police or the investigating judge which are supposed to be written down as far as possible in the suspect's own (interpreted) words, but which are in fact the legal professional's written version of what was said. They are the summary record of pre-vious talk (the interrogation) and, at the same time, part of the interaction in court, despite the fact that both speech events and their resultant texts occurred for different purposes (Komter 2002, 2006; Haworth 2013). As it is fashioned into an institutionally relevant nar-rative, the written record of an interpreted asylum interview or a suspect's statement may prioritize the agenda of the interviewer and shape the ultimate decision accordingly. Exam-ples of this can be found, for instance, in the studies by Fowler (2003) on witness statements; Cotterill (2002) on the O. J. Simpson trial; Maryns (2013b) on the intertextual construction of legal cases; and Pöchhacker and Kolb (2009) on the interpreter's role as co-producer of the written record in Austrian asylum review hearings.

Recent developments

Noteworthy developments in the field of legal interpreting include the *rapprochement* between the semantic-pragmatic approaches typical of interpreting research and the situational legal-forensic issues at stake. Fundamental insights in forensic linguistics (epitomized in Coulthard & Johnson 2010) show that language, whether interpreted or not, is the medium through which evidence and identity are forged into legal significance. In various legal settings such as police work (e.g. Krouglov 1999; Perez & Wilson 2007; Kredens & Morris 2010), asylum hearings (Pöllabauer 2004; Maryns 2006, 2013a), prisons (Kredens & Morris 2010; Martínez-Gómez 2014a; Baixauli-Olmos 2013), lawyer–client consultations (Foley 2006) or in particular settings of interpreting for the deaf (Brennan & Brown 1997; Turner 2005; Russell & Hale 2008; Roberson et al. 2011), there appears to be a greater alignment of the discourse-pragmatic approach with the legal-institutional context. There is thus increasing evidence of how, on the one hand, the setting impacts on the COGNITIVE LOAD, STRESS and responsibility of the legal interpreter, and how, on the other, the interpreter's decisions can have significant legal consequences.

Another ongoing development with major repercussions for legal interpreting is TECHNOLOGY: aside from TELEPHONE INTERPRETING (e.g. Wadensjö 1999; Ko 2006b; Lee 2007; Kelly 2008; Ozolins 2011), current interest focuses on VIDEOCONFERENCE INTERPRETING and REMOTE INTERPRETING (e.g. Federman 2006; Napier & Leneham 2011; Braun & Taylor 2012a; Fowler 2013; Licoppe & Vernier 2013). Videoconference interpreting is increasingly becoming common practice in many areas of criminal proceedings, owing to the search for cost-effective access to interpreting, efficiency and speed of communication, and security issues. High standards of quality for the audiovisual environment (lighting, seating, sound, etc.) and good inter-disciplinary guidelines seem to play an important role in interpreters' acceptance of, and adaptation to, the medium. More research is needed, however, to assess the effect of technology on the nature of the interaction and on the quality of interpreting in the legal process. More fundamentally, there is a need to understand the differences between audiovisually mediated and non-mediated events, and to identify potential disadvantages of audiovisual mediation for the other-language-speaking party, for instance reduction of mutual TRUST and under-standing, exacerbation of cultural differences and accentuation of the inherent power imbalance when professional legal users become acclimatized to the use of technology.

ERIK HERTOG

LIAISON INTERPRETING

see DIALOGUE INTERPRETING

LINGUA FRANCA

↓ ENGLISH AS A LINGUA FRANCA

A lingua franca is an auxiliary language adopted as a common means of communication between people with native languages that are mutually unintelligible. It is, thus, a vehicular language as opposed to a native or vernacular one. Lingua francas have always existed along-side interpreting and bilingual communication to cope with situations of multilingualism and language contact.

The term *lingua franca* is a historical reference to the Frankish kingdom which covered much of Western Europe in the first millennium AD, and was first applied in medie-val times to a trade language in the Mediterranean region – a *pidgin* (that is, a simplified language developed spontaneously among traveling people, mainly traders and labor migrants) that was based on Italian dialects and included elements from other languages (Vikør 2004).

Over different periods of time and across smaller and larger geographical areas, lingua francas have been used to varying degrees, in conjunction with – or as an alternative to – the use of interpreters: Aramaic in Southwest Asia from the seventh century BCE to about 650 CE; Latin throughout the Roman Empire, and among European scholars until the eighteenth century; Dutch, Spanish, Portuguese, English, and French as imperial languages in the Americas, Africa, and the Far East; and Swahili, a lingua franca for traders in East Africa over the centuries (Crystal 2003; Vikør 2004).

Historically, trade and diplomacy have been the most important domains for the use of a lingua franca. From the seventeenth until the early twentieth century, French was recognized as the dominant language of diplomacy across the whole of Europe, which largely restricted the need for DIPLOMATIC INTERPRETING. (The DRAGOMANS used in contacts with the Ottoman Empire constituted a noteworthy exception.) After World War I, the exclusive use of French was superseded by the principle of 'one nation – one language'. As a result, the rest of the twentieth century saw the heyday of interpreting in an era of multilingual international conferences. The twenty-first century, in turn, is marked by the global spread of ENGLISH AS A LINGUA FRANCA, with major implications for the interpreting profession.

MICHAELA ALBL-MIKASA

LINGUISTIC/PRAGMATIC APPROACHES

↓ FACE, ↓ INFERENCING, ↓ RELEVANCE THEORY

The advent in the mid-twentieth century of modern linguistics gave rise to many applications in related fields. The study of language acquisition, for example, and second-language pedagogy drew inspiration from structural linguistics and then from Chomsky's transformational-generative grammar. The latter was applied to the study of written translation by Nida (1964), who advanced the notion that transfer took place at the level of deep structure. Unlike in the study of written translation, however, the impact of linguistics on early research in interpreting was limited. Apart from the work of Kade and his colleagues at the University of Leipzig, who worked within a linguistics paradigm, early studies of CONFERENCE INTERPRETING drew inspiration from elsewhere, especially cognitive psychology. This relative neglect of linguistics is attributable to various factors.

First, the dominant linguistics of the time focused on the word group or at most the sentence as a unit of analysis (whereas interpreters work with a continuous flow of speech that is not always analysable into discrete sentences); second, the focus was on competence (the human language capacity) rather than performance (as experienced by interpreters and users of interpreting), and on virtual systems (sets of rules for generating sentences) rather than the actual processes that were of interest to scholars of interpreting. In this context it is hardly surprising that one of the most influential early theories of interpreting – the INTERPRETIVE THEORY, or *théorie du sens*, of the Paris-based scholars Danica SELESKOVITCH and Marianne Lederer – entirely rejected linguistics as a mode of enquiry.

However, this rejection appeared to overlook the contemporaneous evolution of linguistics towards a more communicative perspective. Beginning with the sociolinguist Dell Hymes (e.g. 1968), speech and language began to be viewed as situated communication involving people (speakers, hearers, bystanders) in purposeful activity. With text linguistics and discourse analysis in the 1970s and 1980s, the focus was widened from isolated sentences to the structure of whole utterances and texts, seen as responding to speakers' intentions. Pragmatics introduced the notion of language as action (the speech act) and sought to formalise the ways in which ordinary language users are able to communicate more than what they actually say: the processes of implicature and inference (Grice 1975).

From code to cooperation

Early studies of interpreting as a process relied on a code model of communication that assumed that what speakers say carries a quantifiable meaning that hearers are able to retrieve *in toto*. These assumptions appear to underlie studies (e.g. Barik 1975/2002) that evaluate interpreter output in terms of OMISSIONS, additions or substitutions of source text material (often individual items). The interpreter's goal was deemed to be complete semantic, if not grammatical, equivalence between a source-language 'message' and a corresponding target-language version. On this basis, a narrow, linguistic conception of ACCURACY served as the primary yardstick for evaluating an interpreter's performance (which survives to this day as a criterion for ASSESSMENT when interpreting is construed as a recoding operation).

The Russian interpreter and theorist Ghelly CHERNOV was one of the first to move beyond this narrow conception, invoking speech acts and implicatures as part of his semantic-pragmatic model of SIMULTANEOUS INTERPRETING. His account (e.g. Chernov 1979/2002, 2004) is based on the insight that redundancy (both semantic and 'situational') guides interpreters' "probability prediction" as a key element of their translational processing. He also speaks of "bridging the sense gap" by a process of decomposing and rearranging sense structures. In modern pragmatic parlance this is the process of INFERENCING, that is, deriving additional intended meaning from linguistic and contextual cues available to the hearer/ interpreter.

The Interpretive Theory (e.g. Seleskovitch 1976) also rejected the notion of equivalence at word or sentence level. Its insistence on *vouloir-dire* or intended meaning, via a process of deverbalisation and re-expression in the target language (TL), points towards pragmatics. Nevertheless the theory appeared to assume that the entire "sense" of a speech could be grasped and re-expressed exactly as intended, suggesting that speech is fully determinate.

It is not until Setton (1999) that a book-length study of simultaneous interpreting using RELEVANCE THEORY (Sperber & Wilson 1986/1995) and speech act theory stressed the fundamental under-determinacy of linguistic encoding: meaning is to be derived not only from what is encoded in words and grammar, but also from inferences drawn in processing. For Sperber and Wilson, communication is an ostensive-inferential process: speakers provide clues to their communicative intentions (ostension) that are then used by hearers to draw inferences about the intended cognitive effects (new or changed assumptions) of the communication. The principle of relevance (achieving maximum cognitive effects in exchange for the expenditure of minimum processing effort) applies particularly well to the real-time performance of the simultaneous interpreter, as shown by Setton with a wealth of empirical evidence of interpreters' performance.

Concurrently, studies of DIALOGUE INTERPRETING were drawing on speech act theory and Grice's Cooperative Principle. Berk-Seligson (1990: 197) was perhaps the first to call for the inclusion of pragmatics in court interpreter training programs as a means of sensitizing trainees to the potential effect on juries of the translational choices they make. Specifically, she showed the difficulties involved in handling hedging and politeness features in COURTROOM INTERPRETING – politeness, in the sense of management of relations among participants, being a key element of pragmatics. Following this, other scholars (e.g. Rigney 1999; Hale 2001) have investigated equivalence of illocutionary force in the translation of speech acts. Hale investigated the interpreting of questions in examination-in-chief and cross-examination in adversarial courtrooms, finding that the illocutionary force (particularly) of coercive questions is sometimes lost, partly due to the different form of such questions in Spanish and in English – with tag questions, for example, posing particular difficulties.

Meanwhile, others (Knapp-Potthoff & Knapp 1987; Berk-Seligson 1988; Mason & Stewart 2001) have documented politeness moves in interpreter-mediated exchanges, finding that, while all participants do facework, the interpreter attends not only to projecting other parties' FACE management but also to the protection of his or her own face.

Beyond cooperation and relevance

Useful as the Cooperative Principle and relevance theory have proven to be in enhancing our understanding of the complexities of the interpreter's task, both theories have been criticised for their reliance on an ideal speaker and hearer in an imagined context, devoid of cultural or social difference. All participants in real interpreter-mediated exchanges have their own cultural and social history, predispositions, personal narratives, etc. These predispositions, collectively termed "pre-text" by Widdowson (2004), heavily affect participants' processing of what they hear. In an ostensive/inferential model, ostension may be verifiable (from clues present in what is said), but inference is performed by hearers within their own context, to which the analyst does not have access. For Sperber and Wilson, context is to be understood as "a subset of the hearer's assumptions about the world" (1986: 15). However, the only reliable evidence of assumptions actually used by participants (including interpreters) is to be found in their response (uptake).

Two examples from the field of interpreting will serve to illustrate the point. Setton (1999: 259) comments on a sequence originally cited by Gile (1995a: 83) to show how processing load can induce multiple errors in the performance of even professional interpreters. Gile had identified eleven errors in a 70-second segment of interpreter output. Part of the source sequence is reproduced here:

> Before I dissertate on some of my ideas, first of all Bob Kearney says to me he says "I would much rather you have said your piece before lunch so we could have a good laugh and enjoy our lunch" And I took that as a compliment (…)

The sequence is obviously elliptical and Setton (1999: 259) provides an account of the pragmatic inferences necessary to make sense of it. But the inferences supplied by the analyst are not necessarily those actually made by receivers of the original utterance. The relevance-theoretic tendency to spell out the inferences (those that are consistent with the principle of relevance) leaves little room for genuine ambiguity. For example, it is suggested that "have a good laugh" offers the implicature that the speaker's views are laughable and therefore he should be offended. Thus, "I took that as a compliment" seeks to cancel that implicature. But in this context "have a good laugh" can equally implicate "we can be relaxed" (it being understood that conference speakers are nervous until they have finished their speech). In this case, "I took that as a compliment" could implicate: "he enjoys my company". The interpreter's perplexity may not be a case of pragmatic incompetence, but of genuine ambiguity.

Gutt (1991/2000: 123) cites an interpreting example of a different kind offered by Claude Namy (1978: 27). A French technocrat, addressing his American counterpart with the assistance of an interpreter, says:

> Quelle est la proportion de main d'oeuvre indirecte que vous appliquez à l'entretien du capital installé?

Namy offers two translations, preferring the second to the first (literal) one on the grounds that it "makes the message more clear":

1 What is the proportion of indirect labour you apply to the maintenance of the fixed capital?
2 How many people do you employ to keep the place clean and maintain the equipment?

Gutt's relevance-theoretic account of this is that (2) is preferred because it requires less processing effort in exchange for "adequately relevant aspects of the original" (1991/2000: 123). This seems both reasonable and elegant as an account of the decision-making process. But if the interpreter drew on the assumption that the French speaker was seeking a percentage figure, or that previous co-text had evoked the concepts "fixed capital" or "indirect labour", then a different version might be preferred. The relevance principle (greatest cognitive effect in exchange for least processing effort) no doubt obtains, but other factors are at play as well. As Namy suggests, there is a strong intercultural element here (French abstraction versus American informality) that professional interpreters are aware of, but such considerations have not been given much attention from a relevance-theoretic perspective.

Perspectives

In studies of both conference and COMMUNITY INTERPRETING, the case has been cogently made for the centrality of pragmatics to the understanding of the interpreting process. But pragmatics-based research in interpreting studies has far from exhausted its field of enquiry. Radical pragmatic approaches suggest that *all* communication is under-determinate. Rather than seeking logical mechanisms whereby hearers select the first interpretation consistent with the principle of relevance as being what the speaker intended, it would then have to be accepted that all actual participants have pre-textual assumptions of their own and that these are heavily constrained by issues of cultural background, identity, POWER differentials and so on. And it is on the basis of these that meanings are heard. Many scholars (e.g. Inghilleri 2012) have pointed towards a fully social and intercultural pragmatics of interpreting, but the integration of linguistic pragmatics and social and intercultural studies of interpreting still awaits large-scale investigation.

IAN MASON

LIVE SUBTITLING

see under RESPEAKING

LOYALTY

see under ETHICS

MACHINE INTERPRETING

↑ TECHNOLOGY

The development of machine interpreting, which came to the fore in the 1990s, is closely bound up with, and indeed dependent on, machine translation (MT). Whereas the first generation of MT systems suffered from linguistic ambiguities and general translation problems, considerable progress has been made, particularly in statistics-based (corpus-based) MT, thanks to improved access to data and data processing (Jekat & Volk 2010).

Large-scale research in machine interpreting (MI), also known as automatic speech-to-speech translation, started in the 1980s, when the Advanced Telecommunications Research Institute International (ATR), founded in Japan in 1986, started a speech translation research project linking various research institutes around the world (Nakamura 2009). Subsequently, more research projects were launched: Verbmobil in Germany, TC-Star and others in the European Union, and various military research projects in the United States. In recent years, some commercial systems suitable for use in the domain of travel have become available to consumers.

The typical architectures of MI systems combine automatic speech recognition and text-to-speech modules with MT; each of these elements is described in more detail below. This architecture could be considered inadequate for the construction of a complete system for MI, because it fails to account for the paraverbal and nonverbal features of spoken language (such as PROSODY, emphasis and gestures). However, many projects are still designed this way, but with additional components such as processing of context, noise reduction (important for mobile devices) and dialogue semantics.

Automatic speech recognition (ASR) systems

Recent progress in MI is the result of improved speech analysis technology (Somers 2003) and advances in processing several languages within one system (even dialectal or L2 variants of a given language and tonal languages). For such systems, the current challenges are automatic speech identification, multilingual acoustic models and multilingual language models.

State-of-the-art ASR systems are stochastic in nature and typically based on Hidden Markov Models. Automatic speech recognition itself is divided into several steps, as described by Bourlard et al. (2011) and Haiber (2004): (1) feature extraction: extracting relevant features from the signal and delivering a set of feature vectors; (2) unit matching: matching feature vectors to sound forms; (3) lexical decoding: comparing a sequence of sounds or syllables with entries in the lexicon; (4) syntax analysis: checking whether the recognised sequence of words maps to grammatical constraints of the language model or data in the language model.

Unit matching uses acoustic models, while lexical decoding and/or syntax analysis require language models. Both these types of models should be multilingual to cover several languages within one system. Whereas Bourlard et al. (2011) find that multilingual acoustic models have already been constructed successfully (e.g. Schultz 2006), multilingual language models still pose difficulties because formal grammars as well as n-grams (here meaning strings of n words that are used to predict the probability that a certain word will be the next to follow in a sequence already recognised) are not capable of handling the freer word order that is typical of spoken language, and because they have to cover the syntax (word order) of several languages in parallel. On the other hand, constructing different acoustic and language models for every language to be processed may not be feasible in terms of system memory or portability to languages with few R&D resources. As a consequence, research is focusing on building models that are shared across languages (Bourlard et al. 2011).

Text-to-text (machine translation) systems

The architectures of early MT systems were based either on *transfer* (rule-based translation) or on an *interlingua* (i.e. a language-independent representation of the source text). Interlingua-based systems suffer from the lack of a truly language-independent representation, but a quasi-interlingua mechanism can be added to a transfer-based system, for example by mapping domain-dependent concepts (e.g. 'GREET') to language-specific expressions (e.g. '*How do you do?*', '*Guten Tag*', etc.) (Schmitz & Jekat-Rommel 1994). While rule-based translation addresses some of the problems mentioned above, its dependency on pre-established linguistic rules makes it less reliable for processing variations of spoken language including performance phenomena.

Access to abundant data on the World Wide Web has made new approaches possible, of which statistics-based MT seems the most promising (Jekat & Volk 2010). A statistics-based system can be built automatically. The starting point is a parallel corpus, that is, a large corpus of texts and their human translations covering a certain domain. The system determines first which target language sentence corresponds to which source language sentence, by comparing the sentence lengths, and then which word of the target text is the translation of which word in the source text (alignment). It then uses these alignments to create a syntactic lexicon. During the phase in which the system is trained, the language model of the source text is supplemented by a language model of the target text, which describes typical word order patterns in the target language. (Unlike the language models of speech-to-text systems, mentioned above, which are based on acoustic analysis, these models are based on the analysis of text in the corpus.) While a purely statistics-based system works only with calculated probabilities, a purely example-based approach only processes parallel corpora, i.e. source texts and their translations (Somers 2003), but in practice, methods may also be combined in a hybrid system.

Text-to-speech systems

The output of the MT component is syntactically and semantically correct target text, which is then processed by the text-to-speech module (TTS). Like the ASR module, the TTS module is trained on a corpus of spoken utterances and their respective transcriptions. Both rely on a lexicon which stores word pronunciations. Bourlard et al. (2011) suggest the possibility of using a common framework for ASR and TTS and developing unified approaches to modelling speech for recognition and synthesis, as in the EMIME project described below.

Speech synthesis can be described as a two-phase process (Möbius & Haiber 2010): (1) linguistic analysis of the text and (2) translation of the linguistic representation into a synthetic speech signal. In TTS systems that use a full-form lexicon, the pronunciation of a word is established by its transcription in the lexicon and unknown words are transcribed with pronunciation rules.

Special challenges for TTS systems include the transformation of abbreviations or symbols into regular words, and elements of another language where pronunciation has to be changed within a given utterance. TTS systems are thus based on linguistic and prosodic models as well as an acoustic inventory, whereas concept-to-speech (CTS) systems generate synthetic speech on the basis of pragmatic and semantic knowledge.

Machine interpreting projects

One of the first European MI projects, and an important milestone, was Verbmobil (1993–2000), a speech-to-speech translation system for face-to-face dialogue (Wahlster 2000) in which large databases of spontaneous and semi-structured dialogues were compiled (Jekat & v. Hahn 2000). Featuring a multi-engine approach based on dialogue act recognition, its target domain was business, covering German, English and Japanese. More recent MI projects in Europe include TC-Star (2004–2007) with English, Spanish and Mandarin Chinese, focused on European Parliament speeches, and EuroMatrix (2006–2009) and its follow-up EuroMatrixPlus (2009–2012), which aimed to cover all European language pairs, used n-gram language models and focused on EU documents and communication (Stüker et al. 2012).

A recent European MI project is EMIME (English, Finnish, Japanese and Mandarin Chinese). Its goal is to develop techniques that allow TTS systems to be personalized (Bourlard et al. 2011). Another European project is EU-BRIDGE, which is designed to contribute to the development of multimedia captioning and translation services for audiovisual documents between European and non-European languages in the domains of TV broadcasts, lectures and speeches.

In Japan, a team of researchers from ATR and NICT, the national ICT research agency, have developed a speech-to-speech translation system for Chinese, Japanese and English which includes a hand-held device that can be used in the domain of travel and even in noisy environments (Shimizu et al. 2008). In the United States, the Defense Advanced Research Projects Agency (DARPA) has carried out various non-public projects for MT and MI from Arabic and Mandarin Chinese into English, including GALE, for formal news, TRANSTAC, a portable MI system for soldiers, and BOLT for informal speech and text (DARPA 2008).

The first commercial mobile MI device was developed by NEC in 2006, offering Japanese–English translation; in 2007, ATR developed the first system using a mobile phone (Nakamura 2009). In 2009, Jibbigo was released as the first offline MI application for mobile phones.

The system is suitable for use in the areas of tourism, military, hospitals and humanitarian missions, and its range of languages is being continuously expanded (Eck et al. 2010).

Outlook

Although much progress has been made in recent years, the scope of MI is still limited to specific domains and linguistic contexts and to a narrow range of highly standardised natural speech inputs. MI therefore still has a long way to go to replace human interpreting services and still offers a broad range of perspectives for research (Stüker et al. 2012). However, computer-based support to human interpreting, or computer-aided interpreting, is already feasible and useful.

SUSANNE JEKAT

MALINCHE

↑ HISTORY

→ SPAIN

The woman known as Malinche served Hernán Cortés in Mexico in the early sixteenth century.

From contemporary reports, and as could be inferred from her command of the subtleties of elite rhetoric, she had been born into a Nahuatl-speaking noble family in the borderlands between Central Mexico and the Yucatan peninsula. As a child she had passed into the hands of nearby Maya-speaking people and become bilingual – a rare circumstance for daughters of Mesoamerican nobility, who normally lived enclosed and closely guarded lives.

Upon landing on the mainland in 1519, Cortés rescued a Spaniard who had been shipwrecked several years previously and had learned the Maya language of Yucatan. This man, Jerónimo de Aguilar, was to become Cortés' interpreter between Spanish and Maya.

Shortly thereafter, the Chontal Maya presented Cortés with twenty women as part of a bribe. The women were given Spanish baptismal names, and one was baptized as Marina. The Nahuatl honorific form of this name is Malintzin, which the Spaniards heard and wrote as 'Malinche.' There is no reason to believe that this derived from any previous name she had borne.

Shortly after Marina began traveling with the Spaniards, Cortés discovered her bilingualism and set her to work in the chain of RELAY INTERPRETING: Aguilar from Spanish to Maya, and Marina from Maya to Nahuatl, and back. In the coastal area where unrelated languages were spoken, indigenous interpreters were on hand to work with Marina in translating from Nahuatl to the local language.

Once Cortés moved into the interior, where Nahuatl (literally 'intelligible speech') was the first language of the Aztecs and their neighbors and a lingua franca for others, the interpreting chain was shortened. Marina apparently learned serviceable Spanish quickly, and Aguilar ceased to be an intermediary.

Cortés and his young woman interpreter were so inseparable that local peoples referred to both of them as Malinche, the Hispanized form of a foreign and otherwise meaningless name.

Marina's skill in 'lordly speech' made it possible for her to effectively communicate the demands of Cortés to Moteuczoma ('Montezuma'), the ruler of the Aztec city-state of Tenochtitlan. During the conquest, both sides preferred her to Spaniards who had acquired some proficiency in Nahuatl.

Nahuatl has an honorific system, encompassing lexicon, morpho-syntax and changes in forms of address according to the direction of expression. Moreover, there is geographical variation of the language. None of this appears to have caused Marina difficulties in understanding and communicating. After the fall of Tenochtitlan, when Cortés undertook an expedition across the base of the Yucatan peninsula, Marina interpreted directly between Spanish and several Mayan languages. Her ability to find commonality behind superficial variation in language forms seems extraordinary.

Cortés mentions Marina only twice in his letters to SPAIN. In the second letter (October 30, 1520) he refers to "my interpreter, who is an Indian woman" and, in the fifth letter (September 3, 1526), he writes that if the Maya lord Canec "wished to learn the truth, he had only to ask the interpreter, Marina, who traveled always in my company" (Cortés 1986).

His biographer, Francisco López de Gómara (1964), describes Marina as one of the first to be baptized in New Spain, as "secretary" to Cortés, and – together with Aguilar – as "the only trusted interpreters between our men and those of the country." In the very next sentence López de Gómara refers to Marina as "the slave girl."

In his *Historia Verdadera de la Conquista de la Nueva España* (True History of the Conquest of Mexico), written decades after the event, Bernal Díaz del Castillo (2012) portrays Marina in heroic terms. According to his account, she was held in esteem by Spaniards and indigenous peoples alike. Spaniards referred to her as doña Marina, the literal equivalent of the Nahuatl honorific Malintzin.

In a marginal note to his copy of the work of López de Gómara, Nahua historian Chimalpahin states that her full name was Marina or Malintzin "Tenepal." Tenepal can be read as teneh-pal "by means of having lips." The sixteenth century lexicographer Alonso de Molina gives the meaning of the similar construction "tene, tlatole" (literally "one who possesses lips, one who possesses speech") as a metaphor for someone who speaks vigorously. In this interpretation, Tenepal would be the direct Nahuatl translation of "la lengua," a frequent Spanish sobriquet for Marina.

She is repeatedly portrayed at work in the text and illustrations of Book 12 of the *Florentine Codex*, an encyclopedic work created by Nahuatl-speaking assistants of Bernardino de Sahagún (1577), also dating from many decades after the events concerned. In the illustrations of the *Florentine Codex* and in other pictorial sources of the time, she is represented as an indigenous noblewoman. Standing with Cortés and his forces, she addresses Central Mexican nobles, pointing her index fingers as, in some of the illustrations, a speech scroll issues from her lips.

In other indigenous sources, Malintzin is represented as a powerful figure in her own right. In local pageants such as the "Dance of the Conquest," which survive to the present in indigenous communities, she is celebrated for bringing the Christian faith to the people; in Nahuatl folk tales, she is a sometimes a rescuer and guardian.

Stories of a long and comfortable life and of travel to Spain, on the other hand, have no basis. She participated in an unprecedented adventure for which she received recognition and reward, but she survived her association with the Spaniards in Mexico by less than a decade.

Cortés fathered children by several indigenous women, including a daughter of Moteuczoma. In 1522 Marina also gave birth to a child fathered by Cortés, a son he named after his father and succeeded in having legitimatized. After this birth, Cortés married Marina to one of his lieutenants, providing a handsome dowry. Marina bore a daughter to her husband in 1526. Twenty-one years later, in 1547, this daughter, raised by a Spanish stepmother, testified that her own mother, doña Marina, had been dead for twenty years.

When Mexico achieved independence from Spain in 1821, a scapegoat for the centuries of colonialism was needed, and this gave rise to the notion of 'malinchismo,' betrayal of one's race in pursuit of the foreign. Doña Marina became sexualized as "the mistress of Cortés" and vilified for her role in the conquest of Mexico. Authorities are in minor disagreement over the extent to which she had ever been free to make choices about loyalty (Karttunen 1994a, 1997; Townsend 2006).

FRANCES KARTTUNEN

MANTOUX

Paul Joseph Mantoux (1877–1956) was born in Paris, into a reasonably well-off family. His father instilled in him his love for the English language, and his command of French and English (and other languages acquired later) was the first major asset which stood him in good stead when he became an interpreter. Mantoux considered joining the navy, but decided to study history. He became a teacher in France at the age of twenty, and after one year of military service he went to teach in England, where he wrote a doctoral thesis on the Industrial Revolution in England and another on the proceedings of the British Parliament in the eighteenth century. This outstanding background in political affairs, his scientific mind and research experience, and his familiarity with political discourse and protocol provide the second major factor underpinning his superb interpreting skills.

After teaching at various French educational institutions, he became Professor of Modern French History and Institutions at the University of London in 1913 (Salomon 1993). His public speaking skills, acquired while lecturing, would represent a third key element in his proficiency as an interpreter. Mobilized in August 1914 as a private second class, he was soon recruited to interpret for the general staff of a British division in Flanders. This 'hands-on' experience effectively completed his credentials as an interpreter.

While he was recovering from serious wounds suffered in March 1915, he was called by his friend Albert Thomas, then French Minister of Armament, to interpret at a Franco-British meeting on munitions with Lloyd George in London in November 1915 (Salomon 1993). From then on, he interpreted at all of the inter-Allied conferences in Paris, London, Boulogne and Calais, and was Chief Interpreter at the 1919 Paris Peace Conference. His professional involvement with the Council of Four (Wilson, Lloyd George, Clemenceau, Orlando), where his linguistic services (and those of other colleagues such as Gustave Camerlynck) were needed, put the profession in the spotlight. Mantoux's name appeared often in the press, identified as the fifth personage with whom Orlando, the Italian Prime Minister, maintained a "mysterious dialogue in whispers", as the *Manchester Guardian* put it on April 7, 1919.

In 1920 Mantoux was appointed Director of the Political Section at the recently created League of Nations. Seven years later, together with William Rappard, he established the Graduate Institute of International and Development Studies, an institution that developed the spirit of conference diplomacy inaugurated after World War I. In 1935 Mantoux took a chair in industrial and commercial geography at the Conservatoire National des Arts et Métiers in Paris, and held that position until he was forced to resign by the Vichy government's anti-Semitic laws in 1940.

Based on the notes he had taken or dictated thirty-six years earlier, he wrote *Les Délibérations du Conseil des Quatre (24 Mars – 28 Juin 1919). Notes de l'Officier Interprète Paul Mantoux*. In these two-volume MEMOIRS, completed one year before he died in Paris in 1956, Mantoux reflects briefly on the different types of interpreting he had practiced during the Paris Peace Conference (short consecutive, long consecutive and sight translation), and on the essence of the interpreter's task (Mantoux 1955: 9): "It consisted of reproducing as faithfully as possible what I had just heard, and in such a way as to communicate the same impression I had received."

JESÚS BAIGORRI-JALÓN

MEDIA INTERPRETING

↑ SETTINGS
↓ NEWS INTERPRETING, ↓ TALK SHOW INTERPRETING

Media interpreting refers to a very broad and diversified category of mediated cross-language communication, within the wider field of audiovisual translation. In early contributions to the literature, the terms 'media interpreting', 'broadcast interpreting' and 'TV interpreting' are equally common, seemingly designating the same concept, although 'TV interpreting' specifies the medium more restrictively and is thus the least inclusive of the three. Less frequently used alternatives are 'live voice-over' and 'telecast simultaneous interpreting'. Media interpreting and TV interpreting have now become established as the most common terms, with the former encompassing all interpreting activities (in spoken or signed languages) performed in broadcast mass media, such as radio and TV, as well as newer types of electronic media transmission, such as webcasting.

Development and modes

The origins of media interpreting can be traced back to the 1930s, when André Kaminker reportedly interpreted Hitler's first speech at Nuremberg for the national French radio network (Baigorri-Jalón 2004). The history of SIMULTANEOUS INTERPRETING (SI) on television is closely linked to American space missions, culminating in the Apollo 11 moon landing in 1969 (e.g. Nishiyama 1988; Kurz 1997a). Today, media interpreting as a professional domain is more conspicuous and broadly established in some countries than others. Examples include the Franco-German channel ARTE (Andres & Fünfer 2011) in particular, and Japanese television in general, where NEWS INTERPRETING for channels such as BBC World or CNN, as well as the national public broadcaster NHK, has been practiced regularly for decades (see Mizuno 1997; Tsuruta 2011). A variety of interpreting arrangements in the mass media have also been described for the Spanish context (see Castillo 2015). There and in other countries, such as Italy, interpreting on television (public and commercial alike) has evolved rapidly in recent decades and is now often found in sports and entertainment programs, especially in the form of TALK SHOW INTERPRETING.

No less uneven than the situation of media interpreting in spoken languages is the use of SIGNED LANGUAGE INTERPRETING in TV broadcasts. Important work in this domain has been done in the UK (e.g. Steiner 1998), with similar efforts being made also by Chinese interpreting scholars (e.g. Xiao et al. 2015). Other ways of making broadcast content accessible to deaf viewers, such as closed-captioning, live subtitling and programs with deaf presenters or a DEAF INTERPRETER also remain important alternatives.

Most interpreting on television is performed in simultaneous mode, to the extent that media interpreting is typically understood to mean live 'voice-over' SI. CONSECUTIVE INTERPRETING is usually performed as 'short consecutive' without taking notes, most notably in talk shows, where the interpreter sits next to the guest, simultaneously whispering the translation of the host's questions in his/her ear, and subsequently interpreting the guest's answer aloud in consecutive mode. As regards SI, an important distinction can be made between SI on site, or *in praesentia*, and SI *in absentia* (Falbo 2012). The former entails the physical presence of the interpreter (or at least of his/her voice) together with the primary interlocutors. The latter refers to all those instances in which interpreters do not share the same physical and contextual location – or even time zone – with the primary participants (see also Pöchhacker 2010b). The choice of interpreting mode therefore depends on the type of interaction and TV genre, which have a direct impact on interpreters' WORKING CONDITIONS.

Special challenges

Early contributions to the literature date back to the 1980s and are mostly descriptive and anecdotal in nature, focusing on special challenges specifically related to particular events, tasks and SETTINGS (e.g. Daly 1985; Nishiyama 1988; Kurz 1990, 1993b). Various authors have characterized the media interpreter's job as extremely difficult and stressful, usually by comparison with SI in conference settings (e.g. Mack 2001; Kurz 2002a).

Physical and physiological STRESS factors include late-night (or early morning) assignments, lack of time for PREPARATION, speed of delivery and information density (e.g. Kurz 1993b). The latter constitute elements of the range of INPUT VARIABLES deriving from the source speech, which in many cases also include the speech's high status and significance (in the case of political and diplomatic events), its carefully crafted wording (including culture-specific items such as idioms), and/or delivery from a script (e.g. Pöchhacker 2007).

Additional specific constraints relate to such aspects as TIME LAG and TURN-TAKING. One of the key demands on interpreters performing SI in the media setting is to finish their inter-pretation at the same time as the speaker, and interpreters may even be asked to finish a few seconds before the speaker, so that the audience may hear part of the original.

Kurz (2002a) also draws attention to psycho-emotional pressure as a further category of stress factors. Working under difficult conditions, the TV interpreter is exposed to a very large audience with high expectations shaped by well-rehearsed and scripted media talk. On TV, where form is preferred over content, media interpreters' output is frequently evaluated against the high standards of voice and diction applied to moderators' or newsreaders' talk (Kurz 2002a). Indeed, just like the latter, media interpreters are required to have good diction and VOICE QUALITY, and preferably a native ACCENT (at least in some countries), and are mostly expected to produce a fluent, aesthetically pleasing output, even at the expense of com-pleteness (e.g. Daly 1985; Kurz 1990; Kurz & Pöchhacker 1995; Mizuno 1997; Steiner 1998; Straniero Sergio 2003).

Furthermore, emerging hybrid forms of language mediation – where leading journalists and talk show hosts, for instance, also act as interpreters, and professional interpreters (also) become primary interaction participants (e.g. Straniero Sergio 1999, 2011; Chiaro 2002; Katan & Straniero Sergio 2003) – have resulted in a discussion about redefining professional roles and NORMS in media interpreting. Indeed, interpreting scholars are attempting to strike a new balance between TV interpreters' INVISIBILITY and their role as "consummate med-iator" and "seasoned communicator" (Viaggio 2001), which requires them to manipulate the original message in order to adapt it to the target-language audience, especially in talk show interpreting. By contrast, Kurz (1993b) suggests that interpreters working for television simply do not have time to 'manipulate' – that is to say, to introduce comments or explanations, and should not even attempt to do so.

Given these special challenges with which TV interpreters have to cope in a condition of high public exposure, media interpreting is widely assumed to require special qualities and skills.

Research perspectives

Admittedly, the volume of media interpreting work still accounts for only a marginal share of interpreting assignments when compared to interpreting in international organizations, such as the EU or the UN. However, interpreting performed for the media lends itself particularly well to empirical research because of the accessibility of public broadcasting content for the purpose of recording and analysis. Empirical research on media interpreting has indeed been thriving in the past decades, with both established scholars and MA students contributing studies on recordings of various types of broadcast (e.g. Dal Fovo 2011; Pöchhacker 2011c). Considerable momentum has also come from the cross-fertilization with CORPUS-BASED RESEARCH, starting with case studies on (rather limited) recorded material and culminating in the design and creation of TV interpreting corpora, such as TIC (Cencini 2002) and CorIT (Straniero Sergio & Falbo 2012).

Research on media interpreting was initially based on a CONFERENCE INTERPRETING paradigm, for instance with comparative analyses of USER EXPECTATIONS (Kurz & Pöchhacker 1995). Thanks to advances in the study of DIALOGUE INTERPRETING, the intrinsically interactional nature of many types of media interpreting has been recognized as a key aspect of media settings. Discourse-based studies on interpreters' performances on TV have highlighted the multifaceted nature of possible interaction constellations of interpreter-mediated communication in the media, ranging from dialogue-like situations, such as interviews and talk shows (e.g. Straniero Sergio 1999; Alexieva 2001; Wadensjö 2008b), to SI coverage of various kinds of independently occurring media events (e.g. Kurz 1993b; Pöchhacker 1997; Amato 2002; Dal Fovo 2013).

With the increasing emphasis on interaction, the TV audience has become an acknowledged active participant – albeit mostly *off-screen* – in media communication, wielding its power by remote control. Many TV programmes must first and foremost be entertaining, that is to say, they must please the audience and satisfy their expectations – including when they involve interpreting. The audience's response is what the survival of the medium and its message depends on. Differences in NORMS and expectations therefore arise not only between the domains of professional interpreting and media communication, but also between various types of language mediation within the media setting itself. Indeed, media professionals and viewers are often accustomed to other forms of screen language transfer, such as subtitling or dubbing, that may shape their expectations and perception of interpreters' performance. This is reflected in some studies on quality expectations, in which special importance is attributed to aspects of TV interpreters' delivery such as voice, INTONATION, rhythm, and FLUENCY.

Overall, the increasing awareness of the importance of the medium has led to a reconsideration of professional and ideological issues in media interpreting. As noted by Katan and Straniero Sergio (2003: 144), "the force of TV's submerged ideology is producing media interpreters who can no longer feel comfortable in their traditional habitus, and are no longer being valued according to current accepted interpreting norms: the mere production of an invisible and neutral link between two languages". Hence the identification of new kinds of strategies, and possibly norms, to guide interpreters working within the unique media environment.

EUGENIA DAL FOVO

MEDIATION

→ DIALOGUE INTERPRETING

Although the idea of the 'interpreter as mediator' or 'the man (or woman) in the middle' was first introduced in the 1980s (Knapp-Potthoff & Knapp 1987), it was not until well into the 1990s that the upsurge of interest in COMMUNITY INTERPRETING, or public service interpreting, in most Western countries made the importance of mediation clear (e.g. Wadensjö 1998). The concept of mediation is highly complex. Pöchhacker (2008a) distinguishes three dimensions of mediation in interpreting: the linguistic/cultural, the cognitive and the contractual dimension. Linguistic/cultural mediation is based on the inextricability of the linguistic and the cultural components in interpreting. Along this dimension, interpreting in bilingual interaction is seen as a form of mediation in that it makes participants' talk mutually accessible and helps them make sense of each other's contributions (Wadensjö 1998). Linguistic mediation thus involves management and facilitation of interlocutors' active participation, including the linguistic and cultural meanings that are construed in the interaction (see Davidson 2001; Merlini 2009a).

Three issues stand out in the analysis of linguistic/cultural mediation in the context of interaction. First, meaning construction is rarely simple and straightforward; in order to clarify any differences that emerge in the interaction, interpreters may reformulate primary participants' turns by such means as expansions and linguistic adaptations (see Baraldi 2012; Van De Mieroop et al. 2012), minimal responses (Gavioli 2012) and even GAZE (Mason 2012; Davitti 2013). Second, reciprocity needs to be established (Davidson 2002). This means that, in order for participants to make sense of talk through an interpreter, interpreting needs to act on the communication process as such, re-establishing relevance and addressing problems as they become apparent in the interaction. In (interpreted) interaction, 'communication acts on communication' in accomplishing what Baraldi and Gavioli (2012b) have called 'reflexive coordination'. Third, participants' perspectives need to be represented. Baker (2006) observes that communications display participants' ideas of actions and events. By portraying and situating actions and events, participants create their 'narratives', their ways of seeing and constructing the meaning of reality. By displaying sensitivity to participants' narratives, interpreters contribute to the social construction of narrated events and the (re)construction of participants' perspectives.

The array of actions involved in linguistic/cultural mediation has inevitable consequences for the dimension that Pöchhacker (2008a) calls cognitive mediation. By mediating understanding, participation and narratives, interpreters are unavoidably involved in 'interpreting' the complexity of communication. For example, many utterances are not translatable without considering the contextual assumptions they entail. Interpreters must therefore first have, and then give, access to those contextual assumptions that 'make meaning' in talk (Mason 2006), which may lead them to go beyond 'faithful transmission' of utterances. This is a dilemma for interpreting ETHICS, as codes of conduct require direct, accurate and complete rendition of what is said. In accepting the need to account for contextual assumptions, it may be necessary to revisit normative pronouncements and allow for at least some pragmatic functions and constraints (see e.g. Hale 2007; Tebble 2012).

Besides affecting the linguistic and cognitive components of mediation, the cultural component has also been understood as a way of giving meaning to 'intercultural' bridging of values and beliefs, enhancing positive transformation of differences between cultural and speech communities (Cronin 2006). Intercultural mediation is thus achieved through language adaptation to participants' knowledge and cultural values. In doctor–patient communication, for instance, interpreters may adapt Western medical language to the cultural conditions of participation of Latin American patients (Angelelli 2004a, 2012) or Zulu patients (Penn & Watermeyer 2012).

The ROLE of intercultural mediator, as described above, implies a particular sensitivity toward the development of positive intercultural relationships in social encounters. In some countries, such as Italy and Spain, this has led to a differentiation in terms of role and training between interpreters and cultural mediators (e.g. Pittarello 2009). While interpreters are trained (by attending university courses) and employed as linguistic mediators, cultural mediators are primarily trained (in the vocational system) to deal with cultural differences and resolve misunderstandings and problems or conflicts arising in intercultural contacts.

The idea that mediation arises from conflictual situations is clear in studies of role conflict (e.g. Hsieh 2006b) and POWER relations (Inghilleri 2007; Mason & Ren 2012). They show that interactional constraints, depending on participants' potentially different expectations about the interpreter's position, may challenge interpreters' role and action, creating 'zones of uncertainty', where the distinction between adapting renditions to interactional constraints and mediating asymmetries may not be so clear-cut. This is what Pöchhacker (2008a) refers to as contractual mediation, which involves facilitation of communication as management of conflict and power imbalance. Studies that have looked at linguistic/cultural mediation, though, show that mediation involves much more than is entailed in contractual mediation, and that management of conflicts and asymmetries is not in itself sufficient to explain the complexity of the interpreters' mediating activity.

What is more, some analyses show that management of power relations often takes the form of gatekeeping by the interpreter, which reduces interlocutors' participation. In HEALTHCARE INTERPRETING, for example, interpreters may select patients' details and adjust them in renditions for doctors (Bolden 2000; Davidson 2000); assume the role of co-diagnostician (Hsieh 2007); or neglect to provide renditions following dyadic sequences with one interlocutor. Interpreters can sometimes 'story' weak parties' discourse in negative ways: for example, they can assimilate migrant parents to the dominant educational culture, promoting a unidirectional flow of talk in parent–teacher interactions (Davitti 2013), or they may discredit young asylum seekers in their interactions with the institutions (Keselman et al. 2010).

Overall, studies on interpreter-mediated interaction highlight two main aspects of mediation in interpreting. First, in order to achieve linguistic/cultural understanding, mediation focuses on communication facilitation, promoting primary participants' participation. This implies a shift away from looking at renditions as text-oriented, in favour of seeing them as communication-oriented. Second, mediation can sometimes involve management of power relations. This aspect goes far beyond linguistic/cultural mediation, and research shows it may reduce interlocutors' opportunities to participate. Both aspects highlight that mediation in interpreting is subject to multiple constraints of different types, and that a high degree of professionalism, skill and EXPERTISE is required to ensure effective interpreter-mediated communication.

CLAUDIO BARALDI AND LAURA GAVIOLI

MEDICAL INTERPRETING

see HEALTHCARE INTERPRETING

MEMOIRS

↑ HISTORY
→ DIPLOMATIC INTERPRETING

In literary studies, a distinction is made between memoirs and autobiographies as separate genres. Memoirs focus on depicting chronological events, and by this depiction the author attempts to portray reality objectively and confirm it historically. By contrast, autobiographies share a personal narrative: someone's life, encounters, experiences and feelings. It is often difficult to establish a clear boundary between the two, and the term 'memoirs' is used here in a broader sense which also includes interpreters' autobiographies.

Memoirs are a vital source of insights into events, value systems and mentalities. However, such narratives may also contain fictionalised moments, subjective truths or even false information, since authors may have an incomplete or incorrect recollection of events, or may have embellished or repressed facts out of vanity. Consequently, it is often difficult to verify a memoir's authenticity.

Interpreters' memoirs deal with current affairs and describe the interpreter's PROFESSION and responsibility; they also deal with self-depiction and the individual's ego. They are written by people who want to speak their mind and be heard, to provide an 'independent' contribution, to express their own sentiments and thoughts, sympathies and antipathies, and to decide for themselves what they will and will not say. Opinions are divided as to whether interpreters are free to do so. Thiéry (1985) states that memoirs violate interpreters' ethical obligation of confidentiality. By contrast, Kusterer (1995) sees writing memoirs as a thoroughly justified endeavour, since interpreters also have a duty toward history. Nevertheless, he regards discretion and maintaining confidentiality as the utmost priority, one which not all memoirists honour.

To date there have been few studies on the topic of interpreters' memoirs. Examples include Bowen (1995), Roland (1999) and, in particular, Andres (2002, 2008, 2012). These works show that memoirs – even if they sometimes serve as apologetics – contain important information for research on the HISTORY of interpreting and on interpreters' self-image and personal responsibility.

The vast majority of memoirs by interpreters have to do with their work in diplomacy and world affairs. For the purpose of a succinct review, they can roughly be subsumed under two broad (and interrelated) themes: (1) interpreters under communism, and (2) interpreters in conflicts, trials, diplomacy and camps.

Interpreters under communism

Interpreters in totalitarian systems must endure the pressure of surveillance, face the threat of terror and fear for their lives. They risk falling out of favour at any time. The memoirs of interpreters under Stalin confirm this, as illustrated in the following works: Tamara Solonewitsch in *Hinter den Kulissen der Sowjetpropaganda. Erlebnisse einer Sowjetdolmetscherin* (1938); Valentin M. Berezhkov in *Ich war Stalins Dolmetscher – Hinter den Kulissen der Politischen Weltbühne* (1991) [*At Stalin's Side: His Interpreter's Memoirs from the October Revolution to the Fall of the Dictator's Empire* (1994)]] and *Kak ja stal perevodtschikom Stalina* (1993); as well as Inez C. Jeffery in *Inside Russia. The Life and Times of Zoya Zarubina. Former Soviet Intelligence Officer and Interpreter during the Stalin Years* (1999). These authors see themselves as eyewitnesses, and interpreting does not feature prominently in their stories. Igor Korchilov (1999) and Pavel Palazhchenko (1997) also consider themselves as witnesses of events: both were interpreters at the United Nations in New York and the Soviet Ministry of Foreign Affairs, and both were active during the Gorbachev era. Korchilov discusses interpreting in more depth, providing extensive insight into problems interpreters face concerning the delivery of political speeches or when working from Russian into English. With Palazhchenko, the focus is more on historical events. The East-West dichotomy is a key issue for both authors.

Interpreters in Soviet satellite states were under great pressure, as can be seen in Wolfgang Ghantus' *Ein Diener vieler Herren. Als Dolmetscher bei den Mächtigen der Welt* (2011). Ghantus interpreted in the German Democratic Republic, from 1949 onwards, for leading GDR party officials such as Ulbricht und Honecker (see Andres 2012), as well as for prominent academics and artists. Erwin Weit worked as a German interpreter for Polish party leaders and members of government for thirteen years and published his memoirs, *Ostblock intern*, in 1970 (Weit 1973). Later he criticised the regime and had to leave Poland because of increasing anti-Semitism (see Andres 2012). Zsuzsanna Gedényi, the author of *Két pályám emlékezete* [*Recollections of My Two Professions*] (2000), was an interpreter for French, English and German in Hungary from 1948. Ivan Ivanji interpreted for Tito and other leading politicians in Yugoslavia and German-speaking countries. His memoirs, *Titos Dolmetscher. Als Literat am Pulsschlag der Politik*, date from 2007.

In CHINA, interpreters serve the state and communist IDEOLOGY. Zhou Chun became Party Chairman Mao Zedong's interpreter in 1949 and went on to publish *Ach, was für ein Leben!* (2001) [*China in My Heart!* (2012)]. His rejection of party ideology cost him dearly – as a consequence, he spent 22 years of his life in imprisonment. Ji Chaozhu was an English interpreter in China from 1954 to 1976, most notably working for Premier Zhou Enlai and Party Chairman Mao Zedong. In his memoirs *The Man on Mao's Right: From Harvard Yard to Tiananmen Square, My Life inside China's Foreign Ministry* (2008), he recounts his attempt to bridge the cultural gap between China and the Western world (and America in particular).

Interpreters in conflicts, trials, diplomacy and camps

Stephen Bonsal worked as an interpreter for Colonel House and President Wilson and discussed interpreting at the Paris Peace Conference in 1918 in his memoirs *Unfinished Business* (1944) and *Suitors and Suppliants – The Little Nations at Versailles* (1949). The NUREMBERG TRIAL is described by Richard Sonnenfeldt (2006), who was chief interpreter for the American prosecution, and by Siegfried Ramler (2009), who writes about interpreting during pre-trial interrogations as well as problems arising when interpreting from German into English during the International Military Tribunal and the subsequent Nuremberg proceedings. Tatjana Stupnikova (2003, 2013), a German–Russian interpreter for the USSR during the Nuremberg trials, offers haunting insights into the atrocities committed by both the Soviet Union and Germany during the Second World War. Like all Russian interpreters in Nuremberg, she was under constant surveillance by agents and informants. All these interpreters address the technical and interpreting-related challenges as well as the emotional strain of addressing the crimes of National Socialism day after day. Robert Ekvall (1960) provides an in-depth analysis of the interpreting PROFESSION, describing in great detail his experiences as an interpreter in the Chinese–Korean–American cease-fire negotiations (1951–53) in Panmunjom.

In *Mein Weg nach Halle* (1988), the memoirs of Wladimir Gall, and in *Zapiski voennogo perevodčika* [*Carnets de l'Interprète de Guerre*] (2007), the memoirs of Elena Rjevskaïa, two Russian military interpreters report on their work on the Eastern Front in the Second World War, questioning prisoners of war and contributing to propaganda campaigns among German troops. In *Als Dolmetscher im Osten* (1965), Siegfried von Vegesack writes of his time as a voluntary (non-national-socialist) interpreter/cultural mediator in the German-occupied eastern zones.

Arthur H. Birse, the British military interpreter in Moscow who served during Churchill's 1942 meeting with Stalin, offers eyewitness accounts rather than insights into interpreting in *Memoirs of an Interpreter* (1967). The same holds true for *Silent Missions* (1978) by Vernon A. Walters, an American intelligence officer and military interpreter who questioned POWs in French Morocco in 1942 and worked for top-level representatives of the American government. Another such example is Gottlieb Fuchs, a Swiss émigré to France who interpreted for Nazi war criminal Klaus Barbie and the Gestapo, worked with the Swiss intelligence agency and the French resistance, and was also an interpreter at Buchenwald, one of the most infamous

Nazi CONCENTRATION CAMPS, in 1944. In his memoirs *Le Renard. 30 Ans Après, l'Interprète de Barbie Parle* (1973), he mainly writes of his wartime contacts with Klaus Barbie.

Numerous interpreters who worked for the German Foreign Office have published their memoirs: Eugen Dollmann, a historian by profession, worked from 1937 to 1945 as an interpreter for Hitler and Mussolini and was exposed as a double agent after the war. His four memoirs, *Roma Nazista* (1949), *Call Me Coward* (1956), *Dolmetscher der Diktatoren* (1963) and *The Interpreter. Memoirs of Doktor Eugen Dollmann* (1967), contain inconsistencies. Paul Schmidt (1949) was chief interpreter at the Foreign Office from 1923 to 1945, interpreting for Foreign Minister Ribbentrop, Reichsmarschall Göring (Commander in Chief of the Luftwaffe) and Propaganda Minister Goebbels, as well as for Hitler. He seeks primarily to pass on his first-hand knowledge of historic events. Descriptions of his work as an interpreter are embedded in his narrative, thus permitting insights into his methods and strategies. Hans Jacob (1962), one of the co-founders of AIIC, worked as a freelance French interpreter for the Foreign Office from 1926 to 1932, only to subsequently leave Germany because of Nazi anti-Semitism. His written work contains a small number of references to interpreting at the League of Nations, as well as to his interpreter colleagues. As from 1930, his work centres around ethical and moral aspects of interpreting. Hermann Kusterer (1995) was chief interpreter for English and French at the Foreign Office from 1951 to 1971. His book describes the encounters between Adenauer and de Gaulle to which he was privy as an interpreter. However, he also describes the process of interpreting, his notes, the requirements he had to meet, and his feelings. Rolf-Dietrich Keil was a Russian interpreter in Soviet prison camps from 1945 to 1950 and worked as an interpreter for Chancellor Adenauer during his official visit to Moscow in 1955, which is described in *Mit Adenauer in Moskau* (1997). Ghazi Twal was a translator/interpreter for Arabic from 1976 to 1986 and worked at different embassies until 2010. His memoirs *Auf Posten. Bonn – Kairo – Riad* (2011) contain details about interpreting for top-level politicians.

Harry Obst (2010), a diplomatic interpreter at the US State Department, worked for seven US presidents from 1965 to 1984. His memoirs include remarks on ETHICS, training, interpreting techniques and NOTE-TAKING, as well as on fellow interpreters and on the presidents he worked for.

Interpreters have also been active in war and CONFLICT ZONES in the twenty-first century: Erik Saar worked as a linguist for military intelligence and as an interpreter in the detainee camp at Guantánamo Bay, interpreting for detainees undergoing torture (Saar & Novak 2005). Saima Wahab (2012) is a Pashtun American immigrant who worked as an interpreter and adviser for the US Army in Afghanistan. As an interpreter, she is on a mission to forge new bonds between the extremely different cultures of Afghanistan and the US. In a humanitarian context, Daoud Hari (2008) worked as a Sudanese interpreter for Western journalists in Darfur and for international observers and organizations in refugee camps. He spoke to hundreds of people in refugee camps and translated their stories.

DÖRTE ANDRES

MEMORY

↑ COGNITIVE APPROACHES, ↑ PSYCHOLINGUISTIC APPROACHES
→ COMPREHENSION
↓ WORKING MEMORY

Memory, a major determinant of efficiency in interpreting, comprises processes involved in acquiring information, retaining it for a period of time and subsequently retrieving it when needed. These processes of encoding, storage, and retrieval of information involve the interaction of several memory systems and their underlying brain circuits. Classical models of memory (Atkinson & Shiffrin 1968) divide it into three basic categories: *sensory* memory, *short-term* memory, and *long-term* memory.

A person can keep information in sensory memory for less than a second before this information moves to short-term memory, which retains it for about 20 to 30 seconds. With rehearsal or repetition, a piece of information can move to long-term memory (LTM), which stores the information indefinitely. More recent research has shown that these memory systems are somewhat more complex and that there is further differentiation (Schacter et al. 2000).

Accordingly, the concept of short-term memory has evolved and is now conceived as part of a more complex system that consciously maintains, processes and manipulates information needed for the task at hand, usually called WORKING MEMORY (Baddeley 2003): this is composed of two modality-specific storage systems (phonological and visual, with the phonological component being similar to short-term memory) and an executive component. Neuroimaging studies during SIMULTANEOUS INTERPRETING have shown that interactions between the neural networks underlying working memory (the prefrontal cortex, parietal cortex, and anterior cingulate) allow interpreters to maintain verbal information while continuously performing language and modality switches (Hervais-Adelman et al. 2011).

On the other hand, long-term memory is subdivided into *declarative* and *procedural* memory. Declarative memory is memory of facts and events that can be consciously recalled. Because this memory contains not only all of our conceptual knowledge (facts and concepts), but also knowledge about the episodes of our lives, it has been further subdivided into *semantic* and *episodic* memory (Tulving 2002). In contrast, procedural memory is the unconscious memory of how to perform automatized tasks and skills.

Since working memory is severely time-limited, declarative memory provides abundant background knowledge to facilitate the retrieval of relevant information and the rapid identification of incoming messages during interpreting. Studies by Ericsson and colleagues (Ericsson & Kintsch 1995; Hu & Ericsson 2012) suggest that expert performance relies upon the availability of well-organized declarative knowledge structures to working memory. These structures, referred to as 'long-term working memory' (LTWM), are developed over years of deliberate practice and allow fast and automatic retrieval of information from declarative memory.

Evidence supporting the use of LTWM processes by interpreters was provided by Padilla, Bajo and Macizo (2005), who explored how simultaneous overt verbalization affected the recall of words and pseudowords in a group of expert interpreters. The results showed that overt verbalization did not influence the recall of meaningful words, while it did reduce the number of pseudowords recalled. This seems to indicate that the interpreters efficiently used lexical and semantic information from LTM to encode information while successfully producing irrelevant speech. When support from LTWM was not possible (e.g. in the case of novel pseudowords), concurrent verbalization impaired recall. Similarly, Christoffels, de Groot and Waldorp (2003) found a significant association between speed of lexical access and QUALITY of interpreting in a group of untrained bilinguals.

During the interpreting process, declarative memory also interacts with working memory to help the interpreter make effective use of prior knowledge and conceptual information and predict what comes next. The advance PREPARATION which is part of interpreters' workflow includes the acquisition of assignment-related knowledge through the study of relevant concepts and TERMINOLOGY. Díaz-Galaz, Padilla and Bajo (2015) have shown that advance preparation efficiently supports the simultaneous interpreting process: even in difficult discourse segments with specialized terminology and non-redundant information, ear–voice span was shorter and interpreting ACCURACY was better than in similar segments produced without preparation. These results indicate that, for both experienced and inexperienced interpreters, the acquisition of declarative knowledge made the interpreting process faster and more efficient.

In addition, automatically activated reformulation procedures and STRATEGIES probably help the interpreter to automatize certain less demanding input processing tasks, thereby making more attention available for storage and production (Padilla et al. 2007, Ch. VI). Although the role of procedural memory in interpreting has not been studied in depth, research on the strategic knowledge of interpreters reveals that they tend to automatize procedures with a view to facilitating both production (e.g. repertoire of expressions) and COMPREHENSION (e.g. enhanced chunking abilities) (Moser-Mercer 2000b).

Although interpreting relies heavily upon the retrieval of information from memory, the encoding processes involved during interpreting do not lead to more effective consolidation of information in LTM. Memory consolidation, meaning the cognitive and biological processes that lead to stable long-term memory traces after initial learning, is usually better if encoding involves organization, integration, and deeper processing (Craik & Tulving 1975; Schott et al. 2013). Interestingly, CONSECUTIVE INTERPRETING involves the deepest form of processing for the interpreter because it demands a considerable amount of sustained effort in terms of memory and attention. It entails complicated processes of decoding, comprehension, and reformulation, which should arguably lead to better recall of the interpreted message. However, comparisons of recall after simultaneous interpreting, consecutive interpreting, listening, and SHADOWING showed similar results after consecutive interpreting and listening, with better scores in both cases than after SHADOWING (Lambert 1988a). The lack of effect of deeper processing in interpreting can likely be explained by the heavy COGNITIVE LOAD imposed by the task.

MARÍA TERESA BAJO AND PRESENTACIÓN PADILLA

MENTAL HEALTH SETTINGS

↑ HEALTHCARE INTERPRETING
↓ PSYCHOTHERAPY

Mental health consultations take many forms, including psychiatric assessments, medication reviews, psychometric tests, as well as family, couple and individual PSYCHOTHERAPY. In most of these, language plays an essential role as one of the clinician's most important tools. Therefore, when clinician and service user do not share a language, working effectively in partnership with an interpreter is vital. Ideally, health professionals should be trained in working with interpreters and vice versa. However, interaction between the fields of mental health and INTERPRETING STUDIES, in training as well as research, has largely been lacking. Most of the literature, which dates back to the 1970s (e.g. Marcos 1979; Price 1975), is by mental health professionals, often written with the aim of describing 'good practice' and providing guidance on working with interpreters (e.g. Farooq & Fear 2003; Tribe & Raval 2003; Tribe & Lane 2009), whereas there is little (discourse-based) empirical research on interpreting practices as such.

The specific challenges of interpreter-mediated mental health consultations are generally described with reference to important issues in various phases of the interaction, from PREPARATION to debriefing; the dynamics of working in a triad; and transcultural issues.

As the service user may be psychologically distressed, the interpreter should be briefed prior to the consultation so as to be prepared for this. During the encounter, service users may want to discuss taboo or sensitive topics, or experiences of trauma, and this can impact on the interpreter, to the point of producing VICARIOUS TRAUMA (Miller et al. 2005). Since interpreters are bound to respect the principle of confidentiality, they have little opportunity for coping with distressing content by talking about it. A debriefing session with the clinician after the consultation is therefore of great value, as it allows for clarification and feedback, and enables the interpreter to process any emotional reactions to the session's content.

The precise ROLE of the interpreter – invariably a major challenge in HEALTHCARE INTER-PRETING – will depend on the context and the particular case. The clinician is likely to be interested in the emotions of the patient, as well as in their behaviour and in precisely what they say. An added level of complexity is that when service users have mental health issues or distortions in their thought processes, they may make statements that do not make sense to others. Consequently, there is a risk that an interpreter may attempt to make sense of what is said before passing it on, rather than rendering what was said, and how.

On occasions, service users may be apprehensive, which highlights the fundamental issue of TRUST in the communicative relationship. When the interpreter is of the same ethnic background or from the same small community, patients may be suspicious about stigmatising personal information not being kept confidential. On the other hand, they may expect interpreters to advocate for them. This makes it important for the two professionals to openly discuss, and agree on, their respective roles and responsibilities.

Four models of interpreting are commonly used within mental health (Tribe & Thompson 2015): (1) In the *linguistic* mode, the interpreter tries to interpret (as far as is linguistically possible) on a word-for-word basis, and adopts a neutral and detached stance. (2) In the *psychotherapeutic* (or 'constructionist') mode, the feelings of what is being expressed are centre stage, and the interpreter is principally concerned with the emotional meaning to be communicated rather than a word-for-word interpretation. (3) In the role of *advocate*, the interpreter actively promotes the interests of the service user(s) at the individual, group or community level, going beyond the interpreting function as such. (This does not apply where the roles of advocate and interpreter have been developed as separate professional speciali-sations, as is the case for British Sign Language interpreters and advocates for deaf service users in the UK.) (4) As a *cultural broker* or *bicultural worker*, the interpreter explains relevant cultural and contextual variables in addition to the words spoken.

As culture is known to inform health beliefs, as well as influence preference for any therapy (Flynn et al. 2013), service users, clinicians and interpreters may hold differing explanatory health models and views about treatment. Mental health concerns may be expressed by referring to cultural idioms of distress, for example somatic symptoms (such as headaches, fatigue etc.). Research suggests that, occasionally, interpreters may withhold information from the clinician because of what they believe to be the 'client's best interest', and may actively dissuade patients from giving important information that might be seen as stigmatising in their culture or religion (Westermeyer 1990). Thus, while interpreters can helpfully act as bicultural brokers, this requires experience on the part of both the interpreter and the clin-ician, to ensure that any information is treated appropriately within the mental health setting and for the ultimate benefit of the service user.

A number of studies have emphasized the benefits of using interpreters in mental health. These include preliminary evidence, in a study with asylum-seekers (Bischoff et al. 2003), that the use of qualified interpreters in the early stages of mental health problems may be cost-effective, as the costs of poor diagnosis and referral can be higher than those of employing qualified interpreters. In a similar vein, Farooq and Fear (2003) claim that the use of qualified and experienced interpreters will minimize qualitative distortions in psychiatric interviews.

RACHEL TRIBE AND PAULINE LANE

MENTAL REPRESENTATION

→ COMPREHENSION, → MEMORY
↓ INFERENCING

The notion of a 'mental representation' is a core theoretical construct of mainstream cognitive science, part of the 'computational-representational understanding of mind' (CRUM). This assumes that 'thinking can best be understood in terms of representational structures in the mind and computational procedures that operate on these structures' (Thagard 2005: 19). While this hypothesis is broad enough to fit with a range of current approaches in cognitive science, including connectionist ones, there is much disagreement about the nature of such representations.

Like other constructs adopted by cognitive science to help model and understand thinking and break with the 'black box' approach of behaviourism, mental representations have not been robustly matched to any neural correlate (i.e. a place or process physiologically observable in the brain). The term can refer to any of a wide variety of possible mental entities, capturing visual, perceptual, logical, semantic or affective properties of experience or understanding, variously durable, to be manipulated in WORKING MEMORY, for example.

Interpreting could be modelled as a rapid sequence of source language decoding, word matching, and target language recoding, all involving multiple successive intermediate phonological, syntactic and semantic representations. However, examples of spontaneous idiomatic renditions which bear little formal resemblance to the original make it seem more economical and plausible – in the absence of neurological evidence one way or the other – to hypothesize that larger intermediate representations are formed/evoked, such as concepts, gestalts or remembered schemas, which would then in turn evoke expression in the target language directly.

Perhaps surprisingly, given its prominence in cognitive science, the idea of a mental representation (in any of these senses) has not been widely taken up by theorists of inter-preting who otherwise embrace COGNITIVE APPROACHES. This applies even to the INTERPRETIVE THEORY (or PARIS SCHOOL), which famously posits an intermediate 'deverbalization' stage. Exceptions include Setton (1999), who ventures the somewhat stronger hypothesis of a Language of Thought (Fodor 1975).

This contrast between the widespread acceptance of the idea of mental representations in cognitive science and its relative absence from interpreting studies may reflect mere episte-mological caution in some authors, pending more empirical evidence from neuroscience; and in others, perhaps reluctance to acknowledge a 'deverbalization'-like stage. However, accepting the very general idea of mental representation by no means entails accepting more specified proposals such as mental models, schemas, a language of thought, etc., or indeed the 'deverbalization' hypothesis, which seems to make the much more specific claim that in the interpreting process *some* representations, specifically those of linguistic properties of the source language input, are or should be suppressed, retaining only or chiefly 'sense'.

ROBIN SETTON

METHODOLOGY

→ EPISTEMOLOGY

↓ CORPUS-BASED RESEARCH, ↓ ETHNOGRAPHIC METHODS, ↓ EXPERIMENTAL RESEARCH, ↓ INTERVIEWS, ↓ MIXED METHODS RESEARCH, ↓ SURVEY RESEARCH

The investigation of interpreting as a situated social activity is by its very nature multi-disciplinary and interdisciplinary. Interpreters interpret for speakers of different backgrounds and professions, in different SETTINGS and using different MODES. This professional dimension of interpreting distinguishes the field of INTERPRETING STUDIES from other fields in the humanities, and has generated a great variety of research questions, ranging from those that have purely practical applications (applied research) to those that may be more theoretical (pure research). This multifaceted activity inevitably leads to similarly multifaceted and multidisciplinary modes of enquiry, or research methodologies. The term methodology refers to the overall approaches to the research process as a whole and is concerned with why certain data are collected, what, where and how data are collected, and how these data are analysed. The methodology chosen will depend on the underlying EPISTEMOLOGY, the disciplinary background and the expertise and theoretical orientation of the researcher or research team.

Interpreting studies has witnessed various shifts in research PARADIGMS, and therefore methodologies (Pöchhacker 2004a). Earlier work that predominantly examined the interpreting process using COGNITIVE APPROACHES or PSYCHOLINGUISTIC APPROACHES tended to rely on quantitative methodologies; this has shifted toward also considering interpreting as a situated practice, using various qualitative methods in the framework of SOCIOLINGUISTIC APPROACHES and SOCIOLOGICAL APPROACHES. This multiplicity of perspectives has caused much debate about the independence of an interpreting studies paradigm (Pöchhacker 2004b), or a translation studies paradigm in general. According to Gile (2001c: 150), "[t]he wide scope of TS and its exploratory function are associated with a diversity of relevant paradigms: literary, historical, cognitive, neurophysiological, linguistic, philosophical, etc.", and the list could go on almost indefinitely, with linguistics, discourse analysis, social sciences and psychology having had the greatest influence on interpreting research so far. In this connection Gile (2001c) also mentions that interpreting scholars tend to conduct research using methodologies for which they have not been trained, especially when practitioners embark on ACTION RESEARCH. This issue, although still true in some cases, is beginning to diminish, due mainly to two factors: (1) the increasing number of research training programs leading to doctorates in the field, supervised by teams with expertise in different disciplines; and (2) the increase in multi-disciplinary research teams, where researchers from diverse areas, such as psychology, sociology, law, medicine and technology, work together with interpreting researchers to investigate aspects of interpreting from different perspectives (see e.g. Hale et al. 2011; Napier 2011b). Therefore, a methodology for an interpreting research project can strictly follow a specific single paradigm or it can be less rigid and combine different ones in the form of a mixed-methods approach (Pöchhacker 2011b). Different methodologies will involve different research methods – that is, various specific tools or ways data can be collected and analysed, such as observations, recordings, questionnaires, INTERVIEWS and focus groups, to name a few (see Hale & Napier 2013). Most of these are becoming increasingly sophisticated thanks to the use of digital technologies, from hand-held video equipment and web-based survey tools to software for statistics and for the transcription and analysis of discourse data.

Basic orientations

Research is understood differently by different disciplines, and it is a challenge to position interpreting studies in this respect, given its multiple interdisciplinary perspectives. Placed in the broad context of the humanities and social sciences, interpreting studies is both a distinctly empirical discipline and a field open to theoretical inquiry. Unlike the study of translation, though, investigations of a more theoretical, philosophical nature (e.g. on such topics as ETHICS and IDEOLOGY) have not been prominent in interpreting studies; rather, most research on interpreting has been data-based, using both quantitative and qualitative approaches.

Gile (1990) possibly set the trend for a more empirical approach to the study of interpreting in his classic discussion of interpreting research, stating that there was an imperative need to be more scientific in our explorations of interpreting, rather than relying solely or principally on 'personal theorising'. In a volume dedicated to empirical research, Moser-Mercer (1994a) identified two distinct 'paradigms' in interpreting research – one being more closely aligned with the natural sciences (using more quantitative approaches) and the other showing greater affinity with the liberal arts and humanities (using more qualitative approaches). Such a distinction reflects different philosophies of research, which can be described as positivist vs. phenomenological approaches. The positivist approach generally aims to study a question from a detached, objective perspective, using mostly quantitative methods to collect data that can be analysed using descriptive and inferential statistics. The phenomenological approach is generally associated with qualitative methods, which aim at interpreting data subjectively and in depth, and does not seek to be representative of a whole population, nor replicable by other researchers. Generally speaking, quantitative studies operate within a hypothetico-deductive paradigm, where hypotheses are deduced from the existing theories, which are based on previous research studies. Qualitative studies, on the other hand, generally operate in what is known as an inductive paradigm, where more general questions will elicit much more complex answers that provide descriptions and interpretations of problems, and new findings or theories will be induced from the data.

Various types of research are valid for different reasons, and researchers need to be aware of the limitations of any research methodology or design. Interpreting researchers have tended to use relatively small data sets, which is not a problem in and of itself as long as care is taken not to claim generalisation when reporting the results of such research (see Gile 1990; Hale 2006). Indeed, given that the multitude of variables involved ranges from setting, situation, mode and modality to language pair, speech type, experience and WORKING CONDI-TIONS, the findings of a given empirical study could hardly be representative of all interpreters, or interpreting. The use of random sampling, where possible, helps address this issue, as does the detailed reporting of the research methods used so as to allow others to replicate the study.

Examples of quantitative approaches

While interpreting research has drawn on a range of established research methods and approaches, many scholars have also introduced variations and combinations to suit their purposes (see Hale 2007). In (mainly) quantitative SURVEY RESEARCH, samples are usually not randomised and not very large, for obvious reasons: questionnaires need to be targeted to small specialist populations that fit the relevant criteria. Some examples are Tate and Turner's (1997/2002) survey of signed language interpreters' perceptions of their role in relation to the code of ethics, Albl-Mikasa's (2010) survey on the impact of the globalisation of the English language on CONFERENCE INTERPRETING work, and Hale's (2011a) survey of Australian judicial officers, tribunal members and legal interpreters about interpreting practices, guidelines and protocols.

EXPERIMENTAL RESEARCH draws predominantly on the psychological or psycholinguistic paradigms, and has been popular in SIMULTANEOUS INTERPRETING research as well as some studies of LEGAL INTERPRETING. However, the experimental research conducted in interpreting studies has not always been experimental in the strict sense. Rather than designs involving the random assignment of participants to different groups, and comparison between a control group and an experimental group, many studies would be more appropriately described as 'one-shot case studies' (Liu 2011) – pre-experiments with selected participants who are matched on a range of variables, but without a control group. Similarly, there are many examples of quasi-experiments, in which there is no random assignment of subjects (see Hale & Napier 2013).

Experimental research designs are well suited to analysing process, product and expertise in interpreting (e.g. Alvstad et al. 2011), and to testing hypotheses generated by authentic qualitative data, such as recordings of interpreted interactions. A variety of mostly adapted experimental designs has been used to analyse such aspects of spoken and signed simultaneous interpreting as bilingual information processing (e.g. Isham & Lane 1994; Massaro & Shlesinger 1997), the relationship between WORKING MEMORY, short-term memory, long-term memory and/or attentional resources (e.g. Christoffels et al. 2006; van Dijk et al. 2012), and STRATEGIES or tactics (e.g. Bartłomiejczyk 2006; Van Besien 1999). Quasi-experimental designs in court interpreting have analysed the effects of interpreter interventions on witness answers and juror perceptions (Berk-Seligson 1990; Hale 2004).

CORPUS-BASED RESEARCH is becoming more prevalent in interpreting studies (Shlesinger 1998), with corpus-linguistic methods bringing a quantitative element to discourse analysis. Approaches include the search for patterns through the use of quantitative methods, but also the validation or refutation of discourse analytical findings through ETHNOGRAPHIC METHODS. Examples of corpus-based interpreting research are Krystallidou's (2012) analysis of agents' moves in video-recorded interpreted medical consultations and audio-recorded interviews, Dal Fovo's (2012) exploration of topical coherence in a corpus of Italian television interpreting, and Wang's (2013) examination of the working memory capacity of a sample of Australian Sign Language interpreters.

Examples of qualitative approaches

Research that examines interpreting within its social context tends to adopt ethnographic principles. Traditional ethnographic research requires prolonged engagement within a specific community, where people's behaviour is studied in everyday rather than experimental contexts, and data are gathered from a range of sources, chiefly by observation (either participant or non-participant observation) and/or relatively informal conversation as well as by interviews and focus group discussions. Examples of ethnographic studies, which are typically small in scale and focused on a single setting or group, include Angelelli's (2004a) exploration of HEALTHCARE INTERPRETING in a California hospital, Berk-Seligson's (1990) observations of Spanish/English LEGAL INTERPRETING in the United States, and Brennan and Brown's (1997) examination of deaf people's access to justice through SIGNED LANGUAGE INTERPRETING in Britain.

DISCOURSE ANALYTICAL APPROACHES can form a part of ethnographic research where, in addition to observing interpreters in action, the researcher also records and analyses linguistic elements of the interpreting process. Discourse analysis can also be used as a stand-alone method and is a popular method in DIALOGUE INTERPRETING research, drawing on relevant disciplines such as critical discourse analysis, conversation analysis or interactional sociolinguistics. Alternatively, an eclectic approach can be adopted to examine discourse features in interpreter-mediated interaction, including communicative elements such as the use of politeness, discourse markers, co-construction of meaning, TURN-TAKING, and DISCOURSE MANAGEMENT. Well-known examples are the studies by Wadensjö (1998) on Swedish/Russian interpreters, Roy (2000a) on an American Sign Language/English interpreter and Hale (2004) on Spanish/English court interpreting in AUSTRALIA.

Another type of qualitative research can be characterised as desk-top research. This refers to a way of collecting and analysing biographical, demographic and historical information through archives, databases and other (often electronic) sources of documents. Research of this type can sometimes also be classified as discourse analysis, as it analyses the way a phenomenon is represented or perceived in written form. For example, Phelan (2011) analysed newspaper archives to examine the representation of legal interpreters in Ireland. BIBLIOMETRIC RESEARCH is also a desk-top approach, relying on the collection of documentation, and consists in the analysis of publications over a period of time. For example, Gile (2000) offers a scientometric account of the history of research into conference interpreting, and Metzger (2006) and Grbić (2007) discuss the evolution of signed language interpreting research through a bibliometric review of publications.

Examples of research using mixed methods

Interpreting studies has tended to borrow and adapt from different research methods to suit its purposes. A number of research designs have incorporated triangulation of research data, using a combination of different methods in order to test or explore the same phenomena from different perspectives. The use of MIXED METHODS RESEARCH designs in interpreting studies helps account for the complexity of interpreting processes and practices (Pöchhacker 2011b). An example of a mixed methods study is Napier's (2002) examination of sign language interpreters' linguistic coping strategies, which combines a questionnaire-based survey of interpreters, a pre-experimental comparison of ten interpreters' renditions of the same text, RETROSPECTIVE PROTOCOLS eliciting information about the interpreters' choices, and a focus group with deaf users about their expectations.

JEMINA NAPIER AND SANDRA B. HALE

MILITARY INTERPRETING

↑ SETTINGS
→ CONFLICT ZONES

Documentation of the presence and participation of interpreters in military contexts is relatively scant before the twentieth century. Interpreters are mentioned in passing, often nameless and in the form of scattered accounts, in the retelling of a certain moment or event in a particular conflict. Since the First and the Second World Wars, more publications and archived material have become available, including oral histories, written MEMOIRS and military histories in which interpreters feature.

The specific ROLE of military interpreters has varied, given the different types of warfare and the different motivations and rationales for the employment of the instruments of war in specific conflicts. Each war is driven by different historical conditions and thus engenders different kinds of relationships between combatants, communities and national (or nationalist) agencies. The Second World War stands out by many measures of scale, not least the number of countries and languages – and interpreters – involved. Subsequent decades saw the proxy wars of the Cold War, such as Korea and Vietnam. The recent asymmetric wars in Iraq and Afghanistan have been characterized under the rubrics of insurgency/counter-insurgency and terrorism/counter-terrorism, and the intervening conflicts in Bosnia and Rwanda have variously been called territorial conflicts, genocide or campaigns of ethnic cleansing. In the twenty-first century, the growth of information technologies has made intelligence a more fundamental element in warfare than was ever previously the case. This has inevitably enhanced the importance of interpreters, situating them at the heart not only of critical intelligence mining but also of much expanded print and on-line news and related media.

Despite important differences, three interrelated issues with respect to the task(s) of the interpreter in CONFLICT ZONES may be said to remain constant across time and space: the instability of interpreters' identity and positionality (allegiance) in the conduct of war; the role of institutional affiliations in the expression of interpreters' agency; and the protection of interpreters' security. Each of these factors discloses further issues of relevance to the underlying ethical, social and political concerns of interpreters and the military alike.

Research on military interpreting examines these concerns and the challenges interpreters face when working in violent conflict situations. Over the past two decades in particular, studies from a number of different disciplinary vantage points, including historical, cultural, sociological, discursive, and geopolitical perspectives, have revealed the complex demands on interpreters in theatres of war and the multi-faceted role they must be prepared to play.

Research from a *historical* perspective, drawing on case studies, oral histories and archive material, has sought to understand the historical and geopolitical context of particular conflicts involving interpreted communication (e.g. C. Baker 2010; Footitt & Kelly 2012a; Heimburger 2012b; Footitt & Tobia 2013; Kelly & Baker 2013). Studies adopting a more *sociological* approach examine the structures of hierarchy and POWER of the relevant social institutions and the strategic and symbolic allegiances that interpreters form in the context of a particular conflict (e.g. Inghilleri 2008, 2009). Such research also explores the interaction of interpreter agency with structures of local and global power in the context of war. Questions of interpreter agency, allegiance and POWER are also explored through *textual/discursive* approaches by considering, for example, how interpreters exercise their agency against the range of public, politically inflected narratives that materialize in the context of war to attempt to define their identities (e.g. Stahuljak 2000; Baker 2006; Rafael 2007) or how, in the context of counter-insurgency operations and the US military's attempt to control language in its totality, interpreted utterances can serve not only as weapons for waging war, but as acts of resistance (e.g. Rafael 2012).

Despite these different theoretical and methodological approaches, the main points of interest in military interpreting research overlap in many respects, extending well beyond the translation of spoken utterances and local cultural knowledge and practices. Most studies tend to highlight issues of ETHICS (e.g. Monacelli & Punzo 2001).

In addition to scholarly studies, many insights into the challenges of military interpreting can be gained from first-hand accounts of interpreters and 'military linguists', covering, for example, the Second World War (Dingman 2009; Meehl 2012), Iraq (Williams & Staub 2005), Guantánamo Bay (Saar & Novak 2005) and Darfur (Hari 2008).

Taken as a whole, the expanding literature on military interpreting (see, in particular, Footitt & Kelly 2012b; Inghilleri & Harding 2010; Salama-Carr 2007) provides a detailed picture of the critical role that interpreters play in influencing both the conduct and the course of a war, irrespective of the historical period or the geopolitical nature of the conflict.

MOIRA INGHILLERI

MIXED METHODS RESEARCH

↑ METHODOLOGY

Mixed methods (or mixed method) research is an integrative form of inquiry in which the researcher collects and analyses data and integrates the findings using both qualitative and quantitative approaches or methods in a single study or project (Tashakkori & Creswell 2007). Consequently, this research tradition is often referred to as the 'third' research community or paradigm (Johnson & Onwuegbuzie 2004; Teddlie & Tashakkori 2009) and is seen by mixed methodologists as an alternative to pure qualitative or quantitative approaches. The advocates of mixed methods research challenge the epistemological dualism of the qualitative-vs.-quantitative opposition and believe that research designs can be situated along a continuum extending between the two 'purist' methodologies. These scholars embrace a philosophical stance of dialectical pragmatism, choosing 'what works' in answering a given research question, and moving between perspectives and research logics in an inductive-deductive cycle (Teddlie & Tashakkori 2009).

Mixed methods research has gained increasing acceptance and recognition among investigators in psychology, linguistics and social sciences, reflecting the growth of qualitative research, together with the proliferation of elaborate qualitative analytical techniques (Denzin & Lincoln 2011) and of triangulation strategies (Patton 2002). Although relatively new in interpreting studies, the number of publications reporting research with mixed method designs has been rising (see Liu 2011). The mixed method approach has been considered ideally suited to addressing the inherent complexity of interpreting processes and practices (Pöchhacker 2011b), viewed as a way of enhancing legitimacy in the METHODOLOGY of interpreting research (Hild 2007) and commended for its potential to allow for innovation in research designs (Hale & Napier 2013).

Designs

There is a large nomenclature of designs used in mixed methods research, but not all of these are deployed in interpreting studies, where there is a clear preference for a few combinations of methods. The most prevalent type appears to be the mixed method monostrand design (Teddlie & Tashakkori 2009), which involves converting verbal data (interpretations or RETROSPECTIVE PROTOCOLS) into numerical codes that can be statistically analysed. For example, Bartłomiejczyk (2006) quantified retrospective protocols and presented the data entirely in the form of frequency counts; Abuín González (2012) analysed the content of consecutive interpreters' notes and presented the results as counts of specific linguistic and non-linguistic signs. Although some mixing of qualitative and quantitative components occurs in these designs, they are also called quasi-mixed because they include only one type of data and one type of inference.

An example of a sequential mixed design is the research published by Shaw and Hughes (2006), which combines two strands chronologically. The data collected in focus groups in an earlier study (Shaw et al. 2004) were subsequently used to generate survey items for an investigation of how success in interpreter training is perceived by students and teachers. Similarly, Hale (2004) used the qualitative component in her study – an analysis of a corpus of LEGAL INTERPRETING – to generate hypotheses about the perception of witness testimonies, which were subsequently tested in EXPERIMENTAL RESEARCH using a quantitative matched-guise design.

Parallel mixed designs encompass two relatively independent strands which are implemented side by side to answer related aspects of one research question. For example, in assessing the efficacy of self-study sessions in interpreter training, Gorm Hansen and Shlesinger (2007) triangulated students' course evaluations, questionnaire data on student preferences and final test scores. Ivanova (1999) combined analysis of interpreting performance data, quantitative results from a recall task, and retrospection in generating meta-inferences about the effect of EXPERTISE on the processing of the source language discourse.

Evaluation

Mixed methods researchers tend to operate with their own nomenclature and standards when making judgments about the quality of the design and the rigor demonstrated in generating inferences from the data. While these issues have been widely discussed in relevant publications, few of the insights have reverberated in INTERPRETING STUDIES.

One challenge mixed methods research on interpreting faces lies in demonstrating how the mixture of methodological perspectives is achieved, and how it contributes to a deeper understanding of the investigated question in a way which is not impressionistic and vague. Another lies in achieving transparency about key aspects of the research process, that is, demonstrating convincingly that no distortions occur in the process of handling and analysing the data (see Liu 2011), specifically in demonstrating the credibility and reliability of verbal data coding (e.g. accuracy estimates, deriving codes for protocol analysis). Such concerns have been sporadically addressed (e.g. Hild 2007; Shaw et al. 2004), but many research papers still lack transparency and explicitness in reporting this phase of the research process.

ADELINA HILD

MODELS

A model can be seen as a snapshot or crystallization of a theory that aims to describe or explain a complex phenomenon or process in terms of components, sub-processes or relations. Like any theoretical proposal, a model is perfectible and, if explicit enough, falsifiable, but can still serve as a helpful thinking tool in an ongoing research process, an aid to teaching, or as a blueprint for an operational technology. Models of interpreting have typically been presented as diagrams or flowcharts representing processing components and operations.

Interpreting is a complex process in which cognitive, linguistic and social constraints interact variably depending on the type and situation of the mediated event and the intentions, competence and dispositions of participants. Alongside intuition, observation and experiment, researchers have drawn on the social and cognitive sciences for concepts and component processes, but all such models remain highly tentative due to the complexity of performance data, small samples, high inter-subject variability, and the challenge of ensuring ecological validity. Models of interpreting have not generally been 'designed' specifically for research or training, but some have been highly influential in one or both of these uses.

Two broad modelling perspectives can be distinguished. Social or relational models highlight the dynamics of the communicative relationship between participants in the mediated event (including the interpreter), and as such are particularly well suited to the study of DIALOGUE INTERPRETING. Cognitive process models, on the other hand, focus more on the interpreter's mental operations, and are the favoured approach for modelling CONFERENCE INTERPRETING, especially SIMULTANEOUS INTERPRETING (SI). The distinction is not watertight, however: many models have features of both types, or seek to link the interpreter's mental states and the unfolding situation, notably through the impact of context. Finally, models for MACHINE INTERPRETING do not necessarily aim to simulate human processes in the evolved brain, but must be highly specified to enable operational implementation.

Wider and narrower perspectives have also been presented, ranging from models of professionalization (e.g. Tseng 1992) to models of neural activation in bilingual processing (Paradis 2004).

Social or relational models

Relational models highlight the interaction between interpreters and their principals, which is shaped by established or implicit NORMS defining the interpreter's ROLE. These may vary according to socio-cultural context, setting, and the agreed or implicit function or purpose (*skopos*) of the interpretation (e.g. Kirchhoff 1976b; Salevsky 1994; Pöchhacker 1994a; Kalina 1998). Alexieva (1997) presents a model comprising multiple parameters on which an interpreter's ROLE can vary in different situations: distance vs. proximity (between speakers, addressees and interpreters); formality of setting and conventions (TURN-TAKING, rules of order); cooperativeness or initiative for negotiation; or the interactants' relative status ('power gradients') and the convergence between their goals (from cooperative to adversarial, as in legal proceedings).

The interpreter's role and status in the interaction is more variable and 'negotiated' in the face-to-face encounters of COMMUNITY INTERPRETING (public service interpreting) and MEDIA INTERPRETING than in international conferences. To account for such shifts in triadic inter-action, Wadensjö (1998) develops Goffman's (1981) model of the PARTICIPATION FRAMEWORK, complementing the three speaker roles of 'animator', 'author' and 'principal' with the three possible 'receiver roles' of 'reporter', 'recapitulator' and 'responder'.

The line between social/relational and cognitive process models is not a hard and fast one, since context or situation can be seen as both external reality and psychological construct. Pöchhacker's (1994a, 2005) 'interactant model' seeks to link the cognitive and social levels by relating each interpretation of a speech to the wider HYPERTEXT of the conference and the interpreter–client relationship. Stenzl's (1983) 'communicative information flow' model con-trasts the communicative *intention* of the sender, the communicative *function* for the receiver, and the different contexts in which the message is formulated – by the speaker against his or her socio-cultural and situational background, and by the interpreter based on his or her situational and textual knowledge, in both cases presupposing some knowledge and background in the receiver(s).

In some models context is mentioned only in passing, with the main focus on a more or less complex (or 'multichannel') characterization of the message as code. Examples include Ingram's (1985) semiotic model of communication, originally developed for SIGNED LANGUAGE INTERPRETING; Kirchhoff's (1976b) 'three-party model', in which speaker and receiver are con-nected by a coded message (including feedback and nonverbal channels) against a 'sociocultural background'; and the elaborations by Feldweg (1996) and Kondo (2003). The most complex of these multichannel models, with a focus on NONVERBAL COMMUNICATION, was developed by Poyatos (1997) as a matrix of the verbal, paraverbal and kinesic sign systems produced and received by the speaker, listener and interpreter in the two main modes of conference interpreting.

Cognitive process models

In conference interpreting, where the dominant mode is simultaneous, the interpreter's role is more standardized, with fewer expectations of relational management or advocacy but higher demands on speed and REGISTER. Accordingly, models of SI in particular focus more on the interpreter's mental processes. These models typically draw on cognitive psychology to model component processes like speech COMPREHENSION and production, MEMORY, attention/ resource allocation and coordination. Understanding how these interact or overlap in the complex task of deriving meaning from one linguistic form and expressing it in another, live and under time constraints, is a central challenge for modelling interpreting.

Early attempts took their cue from information-processing theories of communication as a single-channel, limited-capacity (noise-sensitive) system (Shannon & Weaver 1949) – a paradigm that inspired flowchart-type models of SI as a speech-processing and/or problem-solving task, with decision points, memory buffers and feedback loops (e.g. Gerver 1976). Such models did not easily accommodate a human interpreter's significant use of contextual and other knowledge to meet the challenges of translation under the constraints of simultaneity and 'linear' reception, though the process model proposed by Moser (1978) made allowance for the use of top-down knowledge and a predictive mechanism. The single-channel information-processing hypothesis was soon recognized as too rigid, and GERVER (1976: 193) hypothesized 'control processes' to "determine the distribution of attention to the different components of the task".

Gerver's model already includes the notion of alternate processing routes, variously referred to in the literature as TRANSCODING vs. reformulation, or form-based vs. meaning-based, sign-oriented vs. sense-oriented and 'horizontal' vs. 'vertical' processing. This is reminiscent of the timeless debate over 'literal' vs. 'free' translation, and indeed, more recently, of the choice between 'transfer' and 'interlingua' approaches in machine translation. Gerver cites Nida (1969) to acknowledge that the source language message must first be translated into some abstract form before it can be restructured in the target language, but that "experienced simultaneous interpreters may often short circuit the deeper level of analysis by selecting frequently occurring surface structure correspondences" (Gerver 1976: 198).

The challenges of re-expressing a speaker's message in a different language and doing so under the constraints of time and mental processing capacity are foregrounded in the two best-known models developed by 'practitioner–researchers', one of which focuses more on the translation process, the other more on COGNITIVE LOAD.

The PARIS SCHOOL's well-known triangular model developed by SELESKOVITCH sees the central mental process for successful interpreting (and translation) as an act of 'deverbalization' by which the interpreter captures the speaker's intended sense and then reformulates it in the target language rather than relying on a linguistic conversion of words and phrases. Applying this INTERPRETIVE THEORY to SI, Lederer (1981) observed an alternation – said to explain the variations in TIME LAG – between deverbalized reformulation of cognitively processed material and some rapid transcoding of self-contained or context-independent items in immediate (echoic) memory. Lederer posited an interplay between multiple operations: conceptualization overlapping with hearing, linguistic comprehension and enunciation; occasional transcoding of fixed terms or of the first few words of a new utterance before the speaker's meaning (a 'sense unit') is clear; and continuous 'awareness of the situation' and self-monitoring. The Paris School model has been widely used in interpreter and translator training (Seleskovich & Lederer 1989, 2002) and further glossed and developed by authors such as Déjean le Féal (1978), Donovan-Cagigos (1990), or Laplace (1994), who broadens the scheme to model production and reception processes in the other participants to the exchange.

The EFFORT MODELS developed by Daniel Gile (1985, 1997, 2009) explain variations in interpreting performance directly in terms of the fluctuating demand on processing capacity from four 'non-automatic' processes or 'efforts' – listening/analysis (L), memory (M), production (P) and coordination (C) – which compete for attentional resources. Problems can arise when either overall or effort-specific capacity is exceeded.

The difference in emphasis between Interpretive Theory and the Effort Models is illustrated in their account of the key resources needed to render an item like "surface diamond drilling program" (Lederer 1990: 55) into French in SI: Gile stresses the scanning, reordering and retrieval processes this entails, Lederer the external knowledge needed to render it correctly into French as *programme de forage au diamant en surface* ('program of drilling with diamond on surface').

Among models that have drawn more directly on discourse-oriented linguistics, CHERNOV's 'Probability Prediction Model' of SI (1978, 2004) focuses on the role of redundancy as a key property of discourse that facilitates ANTICIPATION and thus enhances the feasibility of SI. Redundancy is inherent in language at various levels, but is further enhanced by the interpreter's prior knowledge, INFERENCING during comprehension, and gradual attunement to the pattern of new and old information in the discourse, which is typically carried in the 'rheme' of each sentence, while the more redundant 'theme' offers opportunities for COMPRESSION. The model helps to understand why SI is not suited to particularly dense forms of communication like poetry or tightly drafted legal documents.

In a cognitive-pragmatic model that aims to reconcile cognitive and communicative aspects, Setton (1999) uses RELEVANCE THEORY (Sperber & Wilson 1986/1995) to describe a process in which linguistic decoding interacts with inference using both extratextual knowledge and pragmatic clues in the discourse, generating a continuously updated mental model of the speaker's communicative intent, against which the interpreter must reformulate successive segments to meet target language constraints. Processing capacity is seen as more elastic than in the Effort Models: with increasing EXPERTISE, knowledge schemas and a 'bilingual phrase-book' of more or less directly transcodable items free up attention, and problems arise mainly when the process is forced back onto low-level, 'bottom-up' operations (Setton 1998, 1999).

In terms of evidence, the process models described above have sought grounding in the analysis of authentic performance data. However, discovering the link between mental processes and interpreters' textual output is far from straightforward. Human interpreting displays complex patterns of STRATEGIES – compression, paraphrase, postponement, etc. – that are individually highly variable and thus pose a severe challenge to performance analysis and process modelling. In transcripts, predictable language processing operations may be scrambled and obscured by strategic and expertise effects, such as more restructuring and processing in larger chunks (Moser-Mercer et al. 2000). A realistic model must therefore allow for individual strategic choices.

Some theorists have pushed the cognitive modelling enterprise further, attempting to determine the neural correlates of interpreting. Based on double dissociation evidence from language pathologies, Paradis (1994, 2004) infers the existence of at least four neuro-functionally independent systems (for L1, L2, L1–L2 translation and L2–L1 translation), and ascribes the difficulty of SI to the effort of activating two languages at the same time but not to the same extent, production also requiring the voluntary self-activation of memory traces. The assumption is that interpreting engages both brain hemispheres, but to different degrees at different times: the left for primary linguistic (phonological, morphological, syntactic, lexical) decoding, the right for determining implicit meaning inference from knowledge, situation, affective PROSODY, and other paralinguistic features. On this neurolinguistic foundation, Paradis (1994) presents a dynamic model of SI showing eight successive overlapping operations on different segments, and specifying the cognitive steps through which each incoming chunk must pass: echoic memory, linguistic decoding, meaning ('a non-linguistic mental representation'), target language encoding, output, own output in echoic memory, linguistic decoding of own output, and comparison of meanings of input and own output. Four such steps may be going on simultaneously, and may take different times.

Taking their cue from Paradis' suggestion that interpreters rely on either a form-based or a sense-based approach depending on the syntactic or pragmatic characteristics of the utterance, the model by Darò and Fabbro (1994) shows two alternative routes for the interpreting process: chunks from WORKING MEMORY are passed either directly to one of the translation modules (e.g. L1-to-L2) or to long-term memory, which provides the translation systems with the necessary information for production of the target language speech.

The increasing convergence and cross-fertilization of neurolinguistic and COGNITIVE APPROACHES to the study of interpreting is reflected in recent models of the interpreting process inspired by the cognitive sciences. Parallel, distributed processing is accepted as the norm for complex tasks, with attention shared between processes at different levels. Working memory is seen as less partitioned than in the classic model (Baddeley & Hitch 1974) and as more flexible, both in format (visual and conceptual as well as verbal) and in capacity, which can be 'expanded' with increasing expertise by automating certain procedures and mobilizing cognitive and linguistic schemas stored in long-term memory (Shreve & Diamond 1997; Liu et al. 2004). Mizuno's (2005) dynamic SI model, for instance, follows Cowan's (1988) view of working memory as a temporarily active part of long-term memory, and Massaro and Shlesinger (1997) describe a connectionist system that integrates linguistic knowledge ('bottom-up' from the stimulus) and other top-down knowledge, with pattern recognition as the fundamental mechanism. Shreve and Diamond (1997) dispense with any 'Central Executive', suggesting instead that speech automatically triggers higher-order processes in the frontal lobes and selective activation in long-term memory of a 'working substrate' of lexical forms, word order patterns, conceptual/functional representations and communicative intentions, as well as tactics, strategies, textual schemata and possibly also 'integrated conceptual representations'.

Models developed for machine interpreting had moved as of the 1980s towards 'interlingua' rather than 'transfer' systems (cf. 'deverbalization' vs 'transcoding'), and hybrid architectures combining a bottom-up component for rule-based operations (like sentence parsing) with a connectionist network that is trained to recognize and match patterns against a database of past input and translation solutions (for a symbolic, i.e. non-connectionist design, see Lonsdale 1997). In the latest systems, statistical matching seems to have become overwhelmingly dominant.

Despite the difference in emphasis, cognitive process models of interpreting broadly share several points, such as recognizing the need for analysis and extratextual and situational knowledge, an intermediate stage between comprehension and formulation, and the constraints of memory and attentional capacity. However, a reliable detailed model of the (human) cognitive process of interpreting is not within reach. Inference from performance data can be supported by cognitive and linguistic theory, but as elsewhere in the humanities, source data cannot be exactly replicated, ruling out controlled experiments as a primary basis for building falsifiable models.

Application to teaching

The 'Paris Triangle' and, more recently, the 'Effort Models' have both been widely used In interpreter training, alongside a number of other models that have gained influence in specific regions or domains. In China, for example, the 'Xiada' model (Lin et al. 1999), named for Xiamen University, places more emphasis on language and thematic knowledge, less on pedagogical processes. Teaching models used in sign language and community interpreter training focus strongly on message analysis and the importance of context, situational awareness, imagination and anticipation, and have generally accepted a central role for the Paris principle of deverbalization. The pedagogical model developed by Colonomos (1992) stresses the need for attention and analysis, and lists the skills needed for this and for 'constructing' the message using 'context', which includes setting, participants, and the speaker's personality, culture, affiliations, ideas and style, with the speaker's goals at the centre.

The relative influence of current models of interpreting depends largely on such factors as their neatness, persuasiveness, exposure, or appeal to students. A good pedagogical model, for example, should show critical or vulnerable points for performance that can be highlighted and targeted by special exercises; it will be heuristically useful if it can demonstrate the need to use context, show how strategic choices must be weighed against constraints of time and coordination, illustrate the feasibility or difficulty of providing QUALITY in different conditions, or help anticipate the complexities of the interpreter's role.

ROBIN SETTON

MODES

↑ INTERPRETING
↓ CONSECUTIVE INTERPRETING, ↓ SIMULTANEOUS CONSECUTIVE, ↓ SIMULTANEOUS
INTERPRETING

Among the conceptual distinctions that can be made for INTERPRETING, that between different modes has long been of primary importance. Though the term 'mode' can be used more loosely to denote different ways or forms of doing something, modes of interpreting are generally defined with reference to the *temporal* relationship between the interpretation and the source text. This distinction is in fact of relatively recent origin: throughout most of the HISTORY of interpreting, the default mode was 'consecutive', that is, following after (the end of) the original speech, or parts of it. No word was needed to label interpreting as consecutive until the new, TECHNOLOGY-assisted mode of SIMULTANEOUS INTERPRETING became so prominent in the first half of the twentieth century as to require an explicit distinction from what in the late 1920s was still referred to as 'ordinary' interpreting (Sanz 1930).

After World War II and the successful use of simultaneous interpreting at the NUREMBERG TRIAL, it became customary to distinguish between simultaneous and CONSECUTIVE INTERPRETING. The fact that professional interpreting was at that time mainly performed in international conferences and meetings gave rise to the view that consecutive and simultaneous interpreting are the two modes in which CONFERENCE INTERPRETING is performed. With an exclusive focus on spoken-language interpreting, this conceptual relationship is sometimes misconstrued in a taxonomic sense, with consecutive and simultaneous interpreting being viewed as 'sub-forms' of conference interpreting. The need to separate modes from other conceptual distinctions, such as SETTINGS, becomes clear, however, when SIGNED LANGUAGE INTERPRETING – defined by the *modality* of the language(s) involved – is taken into account: most interpreting involving signed languages is done in community-based rather than in conference settings, and yet is mainly done in simultaneous mode.

A more intricate conceptual issue arises when such terms as liaison interpreting and DIALOGUE INTERPRETING, whose definitions are based on a particular form of interaction, are viewed as distinct from consecutive interpreting. Underlying this choice is the assumption that consecutive interpreting (as used traditionally in conference settings) involves long speeches and the use of NOTE-TAKING. Here again, a strict terminological view requires keeping the mode of interaction separate from the mode of interpreting. This means that interpreting in a dialogic setting could be conceived of as using the consecutive as well as the simultaneous mode, with or without technical equipment (see Jacobsen 2012 for an analysis of modes in COURTROOM INTERPRETING). Though it is customary to associate dialogue inter-preting with the use of 'short consecutive' (without notes), there are no firm grounds for a clear-cut distinction between 'short' versus 'long' (note-based) consecutive interpreting, or for equating dialogue interpreting with the short consecutive mode.

As indicated here with regard to consecutive interpreting, the main modes of interpreting can be further differentiated. For consecutive interpreting, the criterion may be the length of the source speech and the extent to which the interpreter relies on note-taking, but these criteria yield a conceptual continuum rather than a binary distinction. The simultaneous mode, on the other hand, can be further specified with reference to equipment use and the nature of the source text, which gives whispered interpreting ('whispering mode') and SIGHT INTERPRETING/TRANSLATION as sub-forms of the simultaneous mode (see Herbert 1952).

Some authors prefer to view sight interpreting/translation as a hybrid mode, given the combination of the written and the spoken (or signed) medium of expression. Hybrid modes in the stricter sense include the semi-simultaneous 'voice-over' mode used in bilateral DIPLOMATIC INTERPRETING, and SIMULTANEOUS CONSECUTIVE, a technology-assisted mode in which the interpreting process is simultaneous but the interpretation is delivered consecutively, after the original speech.

Distinct modes of interpreting can also be identified with reference to the directness of interpreting and to DIRECTIONALITY. Thus, one can speak of RELAY INTERPRETING as interpreting in 'relay mode', and also view interpreting 'into B' or *retour* as particular working modes. However, such distinctions are rarely made in a strict terminological sense, and this applies also to newer forms of interpreting made possible by the use of teleconferencing technology: while one may loosely speak of interpreting in 'remote mode', practices such as REMOTE INTERPRETING and VIDEOCONFERENCE INTERPRETING are best viewed as methods for delivering interpreting (Braun 2015), since they can in turn involve either of the main modes.

Comparative studies of interpreting in different modes are rare. Aside from experimental research on the hybrid simultaneous consecutive mode (Hamidi & Pöchhacker 2007; Hawel 2010; Sienkiewicz 2010), mode-based analyses have been carried out in particular by Gile (2001b) and, for signed-language court interpreting, by Russell (2002). Though the largely contradictory findings may in part be due to differences in study design and setting, they clearly point to a need for further research on the role of working modes in interpreting.

FRANZ PÖCHHACKER

MONITORING

see under REPAIRS

NATURAL TRANSLATION/INTERPRETING

→ BILINGUALISM, → COMPETENCE, → NON-PROFESSIONAL INTERPRETING
↓ CHILD LANGUAGE BROKERING

Natural translation (NT) is defined as "the translation done by bilinguals in everyday circumstances and without special training for it" (Harris 1976: 5). Harris argued that all bilinguals can translate (i.e., that translating is coextensive with bilingualism), and that their products should be evaluated in terms of information, and not of the quality of linguistic expression. Harris proposed that "translatology" should accommodate and prioritize the study of NT, which entailed a paradigm shift in the study of translation.

Harris' approach was first understood as blurring the difference between professional and unprofessional translation and interpreting. Krings (1986) welcomed the proposed enlargement of the field to NT as helpful in devising a (training-oriented) notion of translation competence, but was against giving it priority, because focusing on NT would render translation training (institutions) superfluous. Lörscher (1991) agreed with Harris that bilinguals have a rudimentary ability to mediate, but adopted a profession-oriented view, describing bilinguals' translations as "imperfect" or "restricted." Harris, however, in his first mention of NT, in 1972, had explicitly opposed it to professional translation. He was mainly pointing to translating as a (basic) universal ability, where "*natural* refers to the cognitive skills involved, not to the translation situation, per se" (Malakoff 1992: 518).

Contending views on NT vs. professional translation and interpreting have experienced a revival in recent research on COMMUNITY INTERPRETING and CHILD LANGUAGE BROKERING. In this realm, one side argues that resorting to non-professionals, especially children, is unethical and may be a dangerous practice with a potentially negative impact on the parties involved, including the children acting as mediators. The other side insists that children will translate even when laws provide that public services and institutions are to employ professionals (e.g. Angelelli 2011b; Antonini 2010). Increasingly, however, these positions are considered less contradictory. Harris, for one, never stated that bilingual children *should* translate in formal settings, but only that they often do.

Today, the existence of a natural ability to translate is not controversial within COGNITIVE APPROACHES and PSYCHOLINGUISTIC APPROACHES to translation and interpreting, where NT is often considered the starting point in the development of professional skills and abilities. Nevertheless, how such development takes place remains an issue. Harris and Sherwood (1978) suggested that the ability to translate was different from mastering two languages – a third competence for which humans have an innate predisposition that unfolds in parallel to their degree of bilingualism, through several age-related stages. Toury (1995) challenged the direct connection between NT development and biological age. He also argued that bilingualism was a necessary but not a sufficient condition to become socially recognized as a translator, and criticized NT for disregarding both situational and personal factors in the development of translation as a human skill. Toury (1995) coined the notion of "native translator" – referring to untrained bilinguals who develop translation skills by socialization, by apprehending informal, environmental feedback – that Harris would later incorporate in his approach.

Shreve (2012: 2) suggests that "different bilinguals will develop different translating skills along a spectrum from natural translation to highly specialized professional translation", depending on their communicative and task experiences. In other words, professional interpreting and translating seem to demand further cognitive adaptations that natural translators may not have developed (Muñoz Martín 2011), so that it is professionalism, not translating, which is not coextensive with bilingualism.

RICARDO MUÑOZ MARTÍN

NEUROSCIENCE APPROACHES

↑ COGNITIVE APPROACHES
→ PSYCHOLINGUISTIC APPROACHES

Neuroscience specializes in the study of the brain and the nervous system. The field of cognitive neuroscience, a branch of neuroscience, concerns itself with the scientific study of the neural substrates and mechanisms underlying cognition and its behavioral manifestations. It is one of the major domains of modern neuroscience, which lies at the interface of cognitive psychology (as the study of human behavior in the areas of perception, learning, memory, thought and language) and the brain sciences. Cognitive neuroscience is concerned with how the brain supports thought, perception, affection, action, social processes and other aspects of cognition and behavior, including how such processes evolve and change in the brain over time (see Mildner 2008). Through interactions among the psychological, medical and neuro-sciences, cognitive neuroscience has achieved considerable advances in the understanding of brain function and brain plasticity. This has been possible through the application of new methods for in-vivo functional neuroimaging of subjects performing behavioral tasks, such as positron emission tomography (PET), functional magnetic resonance imaging (fMRI), magneto-encephalography (MEG), optical imaging (functional near infra-red spectroscopy or fNIRS), electrophysiological approaches (EEG) including event-related potentials (ERP), and diffusion tensor imaging (DTI). In order to interpret the wealth of data acquired using these methods, theoretical models are needed that are usually the result of research in cognitive psychology and cognitive neuropsychology, using methods such as introspection, psychological experimentation, mathematical modeling and philosophical argumentation.

Cognitive neuroscience evidently holds great potential for studying how the human brain masters the complex cognitive process of interpreting. This involves studying the neural systems associated with language and communication within the framework of interacting brain systems that mediate interpreting performance between two languages. PSYCHOLINGUIS-TIC APPROACHES have explored the way in which two or more languages are represented and controlled, without yet arriving at a unified theory. Cognitive neuroscience proposes that representation and control of two or more languages are intimately connected, and explores this relationship on the basis of data from functional neuroimaging studies.

Language COMPREHENSION and production in bilinguals is a dynamic process involving cortical and subcortical structures that make use of inhibition to resolve lexical competition and to select the intended language (Abutalebi & Green 2007) through successful resolution of conflict between competing languages. SIMULTANEOUS INTERPRETING (SI) has emerged as a challenging paradigm in which to test theories of extreme language control in bilinguals. This approach to the study of BILINGUALISM continues to dominate cognitive neuroscience research on interpreting. Other major areas of interest are the temporal overlap between comprehension and production processes in SI and experience-dependent changes in the interpreting brain's architecture.

Neurolinguistic approaches to the study of interpreting were first used by researchers at the University of Trieste in the late 1980s (e.g. Fabbro et al. 1990, 1991). With a focus on cerebral lateralization for language (i.e. the fact that the left hemisphere tends to be specialized for language functions in right-handed monolinguals), they used mainly behavioral tasks, such as dichotic listening, or finger-tapping to measure verbal–manual interference, with the aim of establishing whether bilinguals, including interpreters, showed a distinct (less pronounced) pattern of cerebral asymmetry. Evidence of more right-hemisphere involvement during lan-guage processing in bilinguals and polyglots was subsequently followed up by Kurz (1995), who used EEG to study differential cerebral activation in simultaneous interpreters working into and out of their A language. With similar interest in DIRECTIONALITY, Rinne et al. (2000) report on the use of PET to visualize differential patterns of brain activation during SI and SHADOW-ING. These neuroimaging studies attempted first to isolate brain regions that were particularly solicited in SI as compared to general bilingual language behavior, and later to compare brain activation patterns in an EXPERT–NOVICE PARADIGM (Hervais-Adelman et al. 2014).

Given that the majority of neuroscience studies of the interpreting process focus on differ-ences between expert professionals and novices and/or experts and bilingual or multilingual controls, there appears to be an underlying assumption that controlled processing progressively gives way to more automated processing (Hill & Schneider 2006). As automation sets in with respect to newly acquired dimensions of the interpreting task, and performance becomes more reliable, the brain areas involved in controlled processing once again become available, leaving task-specific processing regions engaged to support task performance (Schneider & Chein 2003). Once the required new representations have been created and control routines have been modified and consolidated, these brain areas are likely to become less active. Changes in skill proficiency are thus accompanied by underlying changes in brain processing, with decreased/differential involvement of brain regions that are responsible for learning and control.

Investigations of the neural substrates of SI (Hervais-Adelman et al. 2011, 2014) found that these depend on a cortico-basal ganglia-cerebellar network, whose role during highly demanding multilingual processing is both executive and linguistic. While basal ganglia circuits are associated primarily with motor and general executive control, the caudate nucleus and the putamen have distinct roles during bilingual language management. Further executive regions, such as the pre-supplementary motor area and the anterior cingulate cortex, usually associated with conflict resolution and error monitoring, also appear to support performance of SI. These findings underline the similarity between general executive networks and bilingual language control networks.

Using ERP to study the neurophysiological basis of code-switching in simultaneous interpreters, Proverbio, Leoni and Zani (2004) found that both reaction times (RTs) and electrophysiological data from a semantic task indicated a lesser degree of hemispheric lateralization for linguistic function during L2 than during L1 processing in interpreters, and that the neuro-functional organization of L2 is dependent on the age of L2 acquisition.

Simultaneous interpreters' brains have been used as a model for investigating training-related reorganization in the domain of language processing. A study using an electrophysiological approach (EEG/N400) and a semantic decision task (Elmer et al. 2010) found functional adaptations in accessing lexical-semantic information.

Changes in grey matter volumes (i.e. structural change that occurs as a function of learning over both short and longer periods, and probably reflects alterations of the microstructure of grey matter) have been studied with voxel-based morphometry (VBM). Elmer, Hänggi and Jäncke (2014) found reduced grey matter volumes in professional simultaneous interpreters compared to multilingual control subjects in the left middle-anterior cingulate gyrus, bilateral pars triangularis, left pars opercularis, bilateral middle part of the insula and in the left supramarginal gyrus, with grey matter volume in the left pars triangularis, right pars opercularis, middle-anterior cingulate gyrus and bilateral caudate nucleus being negatively correlated with the cumulative number of interpreting hours of the professional subjects. This provides evidence of expertise-related changes in grey matter architecture, possibly reflecting a composite of brain characteristics that were present before training in interpreting commenced and training-related effects.

Cognitive neuroscience approaches have thus provided evidence of skill-acquisition-dependent changes in cognitive processing. At the same time, specific representational areas in the brain are also sensitive to skill-specific input and likely to change in response to the demands posed by skilled performance. Since SI is acquired during extensive training, changes in cognitive processing and resources required for skill execution may produce long-term functional and structural changes in the brain (Moser-Mercer 2010), both in general control areas and in domain-specific representational areas.

BARBARA MOSER-MERCER

NEUTRALITY

↑ ETHICS

→ ROLE

The neutrality or impartiality of the interpreter is stipulated as a key precept of professional practice in most published codes of ETHICS, especially in the legal or public service domain, but remains a controversial issue. Historical sources are full of examples of interpreters who served their own interests or those of one side (and the former through the latter), but also record earnest attempts to prescribe impartiality for interpreters, such as the provisions enacted in SPAIN for its colonial administration in the sixteenth century (Giambruno 2008). Neutrality has long been viewed as the hallmark of the professional interpreter. However, the notion has been challenged as impossible or undesirable on two fronts: for 'sceptics', the fact that understanding utterances depends on contextual disambiguation implies that interpreters cannot construe meaning in a vacuum and are therefore subject to the influence of their own background; 'activists', on the other hand, argue that the interpreter's ROLE should include advocacy.

The issue is complicated by the imprecise use of the terms 'neutrality' and 'impartiality' in the literature. According to the most commonly held position, maintaining impartiality (or neutrality) means not letting one's own views, prejudices or interests colour the interpretation; another widespread basic understanding of neutrality/impartiality is not taking sides or favouring one or another party to the exchange; yet another view defines neutrality as offering equal FIDELITY to all speakers, which Gile (2009) calls "rotating sender loyalty". Neutrality can also be construed as providing 'equal service' to all participants – for example, in providing cultural explanation and advice on negotiating, as well as drafting of minutes and communication facilitation of all kinds, though for others, it precludes offering such services to any party. In a more analytical distinction, impartiality is understood in relation to the interpreter's social role and function, whereas neutrality is discussed in terms of the discursive construction of realities in a given act of communication (see Prunč 2012a: 424). In situations of conflict, in particular (e.g. Baker 2010), neutrality in this sense would seem very difficult to attain.

Neutrality is a term less commonly found in codes than in the literature, where it is often discussed in terms of its theoretical converse, 'loyalty', and the wider issues of the interpreter's role and the appropriate scope and nature of MEDIATION to be provided. Impartiality is the preferred term in most codes for public service interpreting (COMMUNITY INTERPRETING), with some variance in scope. The ASTM (2007) Standard Guide for Language Interpretation Services merely specifies that interpreters should "maintain a neutral attitude", while some US codes for court interpreters (e.g. NAJIT) also warn against conduct that may give an appearance of bias. The UK NRPSI (2011) Code of Professional Conduct for public service interpreters both extends and limits the interpreter's responsibility, stipulating that "Practitioners shall at all times act impartially and shall not act in any way that might result in prejudice or preference on grounds of religion or belief, race, politics, gender, age, sexual orientation or disability otherwise than as obliged in order to faithfully translate, interpret or otherwise transfer meaning." In many codes, impartiality explicitly includes a commitment to avoid conflict of interest, and to derive no personal gain or advantage (other than a fee) from the performance of the interpreting task.

Conflicting demands on the interpreter's loyalty (or pressures against neutrality) may potentially come from many different quarters: the paying client, who may be a party to the exchange; some other external authority, such as national or corporate interest (in DIPLOMATIC

INTERPRETING and BUSINESS INTERPRETING), religion or ideology; required legal procedure (in COURTROOM INTERPRETING, where a different service may be provided for witnesses and defendants); political correctness; etiquette; a higher moral imperative, such as saving lives or protecting a patient's well-being (in HEALTHCARE INTERPRETING); and/or ethics and standards collectively defined by the PROFESSION.

Attitudes and NORMS vary significantly between SETTINGS or sub-branches of the profession. The strictest impartiality rules are found in codes governing LEGAL INTERPRETING: they extend explicitly to fidelity and exclude many mediating functions accepted elsewhere, such as clarifying or explaining vague or ambiguous statements or cultural references, and typically even forbid unnecessary contact with parties outside the proceedings. Beyond the courtroom, by contrast, interpreter neutrality is much more controversial, especially in healthcare and social service settings (see Metzger 1999), where several authors have argued for a proactive role for the interpreter, extending to advocacy, in order to redress POWER imbalances. Finally, in CONFERENCE INTERPRETING, neutrality is largely taken for granted, to the extent of being absent from codes of ethics (as in the case of AIIC). Neutrality is sometimes mentioned in the literature, but only in rather general terms: for Thiéry (1985), the interpreter's overriding duty is to 'the meeting'; for Viaggio (2006), his/her primary loyalty is due to 'the profession'. The classic position is that impartiality and neutrality in every sense are incumbent on the professional conference interpreter and can be applied unproblematically. Indeed, the inter-governmental organisations which form the core market of conference interpreting have written neutrality into their charters as a requirement for all personnel in their capacity as international civil servants, whether temporarily or permanently employed.

While there are notable differences in emphasis, the boundaries between the various professional domains are not clear-cut. Conference interpreters also work in business and diplomatic settings where each side in a negotiation typically employs its own interpreter(s), and where their clients may often ask them to tone down, summarise and even censor speakers (Setton & Guo 2011). Thus, two salient norms in which the interpreter's role is relatively well defined can be distinguished, alongside more ambivalent situations (Setton & Dawrant 2016). On the one hand, interpreters employed by international organisations are expected to observe complete neutrality and impartiality (including strict 'rotating sender loyalty'), to display equal fidelity and transparency to all participants, to perform no other service (consultancy, advocacy etc.), nor accept any instruction from any party on how to interpret (e.g. to omit, summarise, embellish, tone down, censor, or even summarise) that goes against their own professional judgment. On the other hand, when each party employs its own interpreter(s), as is common in diplomatic, business, in-house, military and other typically bilateral settings, interpreters may be considered 'attached' or affiliated to their clients. Interpreters (or teams) attached to one side will be accountable only to codes of conduct set by their employer, have privileged access to information and may be expected to perform various services (e.g. commentary, debriefing) for their side exclusively. In this case, therefore, neutrality in the sense of both equal fidelity and equal service to all parties does not apply.

Given these de facto variations in neutrality norms, some authors have sought to maintain ethical consistency by requiring interpreters to provide at least 'minimum fidelity' to all speakers. This has been defined as rendering the 'message' the speaker is trying to convey (Gile 2009: 62) or, more minimally, as fidelity to the communicative intent without misrepresentation (Setton & Dawrant 2016).

Drawing on Bourdieu's concept of shared HABITUS, Tipton (2008b) views the 'a priori neutral sites of (bureaucratic) practice' where public service interpreting takes place as naturally encouraging self-regulation and a commitment of all parties to 'baseline neutrality' – for example, using non-emotive language, refraining from offering (or asking the interpreter to offer) personal opinions, letting the interpreter interpret everything that is said, etc. This would accommodate different norms for different sites, such as courts and police stations, multilateral institutions, or bilateral settings subject to no superior external authority, such as business or diplomatic negotiations. In recognising that social practice is generated by structure (the site or institution) as well as by the agents involved, neutrality is not attributable to the interpreter alone. Baseline neutrality has to be established and perpetuated, but may also be threatened and re-established by any of the parties involved, including the interpreter. In this sense, the interpreter is not described as a 'neutral agent', neutrality being a fixed condition of the subject, but as an 'agent of neutrality', always leaving room for the interpreter's judgment and action.

Many authors recognise that both rigid codification and absolute, objective impartiality are impossible, since interpreters cannot abstract themselves entirely from their own background, beliefs and cultural biases. The requirement for neutrality is therefore widely understood as an attitude or disposition (Tipton 2008b), something that all translators should aim for in striving for excellence (Chesterman 2001). Others propose *transparency* as an ethical backstop, by ensuring that all parties are aware in advance of the interpreters' roles and functions (Tebble 1998; Setton & Dawrant 2016) or the 'premises and goals' of the translation process (Prunč 2008).

Neutrality and advocacy

Surveys have shown that, with the possible exception of healthcare, most existing standards (Bancroft 2005) speak against the interpreter acting as "an advocate, a counsellor, a gatekeeper or anything other than an interpreter" (Hale 2007: 126), and that interpreters typically do not see advocacy as part of their role. However, several authors in the field of community interpreting have asserted that, when personal and immediate medical, legal or humanitarian interests are at stake for a witness, a suspect, a defendant or an applicant for asylum who may not know the conventions, or who has much less information than their interlocutors, some degree of intervention and/or advocacy on the part of the interpreter may be ethically warranted as the best way of ensuring transparent, effective communication (Angelelli 2003; Barsky 1996).

On this argument, neutrality in the sense of providing 'equal loyalty' or identical fidelity to all parties may be overridden by a higher moral obligation, not just to correct misunderstandings and offer additional explanations, but also to compensate for inequalities and possible distortions – for example, by adjusting a lawyer's register for an illiterate asylum applicant, or a doctor's for a patient, or by supplying additional, perhaps life-saving information about a patient's symptoms, or an asylum applicant's situation, which the speaker may have forgotten or failed to express.

As Prunč (1997) points out, this entails a fourfold loyalty for the interpreter, in which his or her own ethical responsibility must be recognised as a criterion for decision-making alongside the traditional threesome of author, client and audience (Nord 1991). Noting that healthcare interpreting codes recognise the superior criterion of the patient's well-being, Prunč (2008, 2012a) argues for the empowerment of interpreters to 'be creative' in the face of cultural and other conflicts of interest, replacing neutrality with the responsibility to follow a 'value hierarchy' in which the first priorities are the safety of life and limb and respect for human rights and dignity, with the option to withdraw service or, in extreme cases such as totalitarianism, even subvert the message. A 'democratic translation culture' in which interpreters are entrusted to apply these criteria may seem utopian, especially in strictly adversarial situations such as military or even business interpreting; for more general civilian settings, its implementation would depend on an evolving understanding among all stakeholders of the interpreter's role and task.

ERICH PRUNČ AND ROBIN SETTON

NEWS INTERPRETING

↑ MEDIA INTERPRETING

News interpreting refers to SIMULTANEOUS INTERPRETING of TV broadcast news and is therefore a form of MEDIA INTERPRETING, alternatively called broadcast interpreting. News broadcasts are a special type of TV program, typically involving an anchorperson and prerecorded video clips. However, the boundaries are not clear when it comes to political messages, interviews or press conferences transmitted as part of news programming. Moreover, news interpreting can also be a part of special news programming for major news events such as warfare or natural disasters.

Spoken-language news interpreting is usually performed in interpreting booths at TV stations and broadcast in voice-over mode, with the interpreter's voice heard over the original. The interpreting may be from a foreign-language news program into the broadcaster's language, or from a domestic news program into another language. In news interpreting into signed languages, the interpreter is shown in a part of the screen.

Development

News interpreting began in the 1960s, and numerous major news events have led to increased demands on interpreters to convey the news in real time. Aside from news broadcast for the first time, news interpreting is also done for secondary use in repeat broadcasts or webcasts. In Japan, where news interpreting is particularly well established (Mizuno 1997; Tsuruta 2011), NHK-BS (Broadcast by Satellite) began broadcasting foreign news interpreted into Japanese in the late 1980s. Using spoken-language interpreters, this channel conveys news programs from overseas stations such as the BBC, Germany's ZDF and South Korea's KBS. BBC World first offered news interpreted into Japanese on cable TV in 1994, from London, and has been broadcasting from Tokyo since 2007. CNN news in Japanese has been broadcast on cable TV through interpreters since 1987, and several private networks in Japan employed interpreters to convey Japanese news in English from the 1980s until the practice was discontinued in 2009. The Franco-German channel ARTE employed simultaneous interpreters to provide interpreting for its regular news programs for 18 years, until the decision in early 2012 to produce separate news programs in French and German. In other countries, media interpreting of news into spoken languages is less common, and interpreters are used on an ad hoc basis rather than as part of a regular news interpreting service.

Japan is also prominent in the training of news interpreters: a subsidiary of NHK, the public broadcaster, started training English–Japanese interpreters in 1992, and private interpreter schools have offered classes in English, Korean and Chinese news interpreting.

Modes and language direction

The interpreting mode in news interpreting can be strictly simultaneous, with almost no time for PREPARATION, or 'prepared interpreting', where interpreters can view the material they will interpret in advance. This was the case at ARTE, and is also the mode mostly used at NHK.

The predominant language direction in Japan is from the foreign language into Japanese. However, NHK's two major TV news programs are interpreted into English, with partial use of interpreters (and pre-packaged parts presented by native-English newsreaders).

Aside from providing media access for the deaf and hard of hearing through subtitling, news is also conveyed in signed languages (e.g. Xiao & Li 2013). This may involve sign language interpreters working from spoken news in simultaneous mode (e.g. McKee 2014), as well as DEAF INTERPRETERS performing SIGHT TRANSLATION/INTERPRETING from a script.

Journalistic considerations

As in other forms of media interpreting, news interpreters are expected to have good VOICE QUALITY and INTONATION, with pronunciation close or nearly equivalent to the broadcast standard (Mizuno 1997). Smooth delivery is particularly important, since media audiences are not captive, as in the case of international conferences, but may switch channels at any time. Moreover, news interpreters are required to finish their rendition no later than the original or at least without lagging too far behind, and to synchronize their output with each of the speech segments in the source-language program.

An important consideration for news interpreters in Japan is to follow the journalistic norms of the national media. Thus, NHK needs to cut any commercials from the original programs and make sure that no product names are broadcast. By the same token, the interpreters will avoid using brand names like 'Barbie' or 'Lego' and will, instead, limit themselves to generic terms such as 'doll' or 'toy blocks'. They must also follow the custom of referring to criminals with honorifics and adding the Japanese word for 'suspect' or, after indictment, 'defendant' after the name.

In the case of 'prepared interpreting', news interpreters previewing the foreign-language material are asked to alert the news desk to the presence of material other than that from the original TV station, so as to avoid royalty claims, and also of images not conforming to broadcasting norms in Japan, such as minors in handcuffs or dead bodies lying in a field. In their preparation, interpreters will use the internet to check the accuracy of proper names and refer to domestic news material on the same topic to ensure consistent TERMINOLOGY. In addition, at NHK-BS interpreters are asked to view the foreign-language programs on the digital server and write down the main news items. The NHK-BS editors will then select the main news items of the day to be transmitted through 'prepared interpreting'.

CHIKAKO TSURUTA

NON-PROFESSIONAL INTERPRETING

→ NATURAL TRANSLATION/INTERPRETING
↓ CHILD LANGUAGE BROKERING

Non-professional interpreting refers to interpreting and linguistic mediation activities performed by people who have had no formal training and who are often not remunerated for their work as interpreters. The use of this term, however, is quite recent; other labels for this practice include ad hoc interpreting, family interpreting, informal interpreting, language brokering, lay interpreting, and NATURAL TRANSLATION/INTERPRETING.

Throughout history, untrained bilinguals have been interpreting (and translating) 'naturally' in a variety of situations and settings (colonization, war, trade, diplomacy, etc.). The first studies on non-professional interpreting date back to the 1970s, when Harris (1976) coined the term natural translation and theorized that the ability to translate and interpret was a natural aptitude and not the exclusive domain of professionals. Harris suggested that the empirical study of translation and interpreting should take as its point of departure the ability of bilingual children to perform translating activities without having received any special training. Other scholars have disputed the fact that translation competence is an aspect of bilingual competence, arguing that the development of translation competence is not coextensive with the degree of bilingualism (Toury 1995; Grosjean 2010) and that each individual differs in terms of the requisite knowledge and skills.

Akin to professional interpreting, non-professional interpreting can take place in events and interactions (often community-based) involving DIALOGUE INTERPRETING and in (international) conference settings. It is commonly practiced in contexts that include (but are not restricted to) business, religion, health, public and social services, the media, tourism, war and conflict. However, given the demographic changes triggered by mass migration in the past century and the contexts and settings in which foreigners and immigrants are more likely to require the services of an interpreter, namely when needing to access public services and to interact with representatives of mainstream institutions of the host country, non-professional interpreting tends to occur particularly as liaison and, more specifically, COMMUNITY INTERPRETING.

The ways in which individual countries deal with and address the need for these services vary enormously. In some places (e.g. Australia and California) there is a strict stance against the use of non-professional interpreters, particularly in healthcare and legal settings, including legislation that forbids the employment of untrained interpreters. Nonetheless, many countries tend to address problems related to increased linguistic diversity with ad hoc solutions (Ozolins 2010). The main consequence of this attitude is twofold: from a practical point of view it has made the use of non-professional interpreters a tolerated practice; from an academic point of view, it has meant a shift from the study of non-professional interpreting as a practice that bilinguals may engage in during the course of their lives to a more specific focus on non-professionals mediating for their immigrant language communities.

From its inception, research on non-professional interpreting has developed in two distinct, though at times overlapping, strands, depending on whether it is performed by children or by adults. In both cases, research is highly fragmented and widely dispersed across many disciplines, such as anthropology, sociology, psychology, educational studies, conversation analysis, linguistics, interpreting and translation studies.

Non-professional interpreting by children and adolescents, referred to as CHILD LANGUAGE BROKERING, has generated the bulk of academic production and research and has developed into a self-contained area of study (Orellana 2009). Within interpreting studies, the study of non-professional interpreting has only recently gained recognition and has focused mainly on its use in public service settings, particularly in healthcare. The negative impact of this practice on many aspects of communication within the medical setting has received considerable attention (e.g. Elderkin-Thompson et al. 2001; Schouten et al. 2012).

Relatively little attention has been given to non-professional interpreting in the media, in war, in conflict and disaster zones, in religious contexts, and in business and tourism, as well as to non-professional interpreting in signed languages. In the media context, there have been studies on non-professional TALK SHOW INTERPRETING (e.g. Chiaro 2002), but the practice is also found in many other media events (e.g. the Golden Globes and Academy Awards, news coverage and sports). Non-professional interpreting also comes up in the study of

FICTIONAL INTERPRETERS and the depiction of interpreting in film. In relation to war and CONFLICT ZONES, studies have focused on interpreting by prisoners in past conflicts (Kujamäki 2012) and in CONCENTRATION CAMPS. In this context, there is great potential for broader research efforts aimed at the activities of bilingual and multilingual individuals interpreting for foreign armed forces, international and humanitarian organizations, and journalists. Examples include work on volunteers engaging in DISASTER RELIEF INTERPRETING and on programmes devised to train such interpreters in the field (Moser-Mercer et al. 2012). Non-professional interpreting in RELIGIOUS SETTINGS is a recent strand of research which has focused on scripture interpreting and, to a much lesser extent, on non-professionals interpreting homilies and sermons. There is much uncharted territory in the provision and practice of non-professional interpreting by untrained sign language interpreters, with only a few studies on the interpreting activities of children of deaf adults (CODA) (Preston 1996). Likewise, non-professional interpreting in business settings (e.g. Traverso 2012) and in tourism are greatly neglected areas of research, and future work on interpreting in all these various settings would probably benefit from a move beyond the dichotomy of professional versus non-professional activities.

RACHELE ANTONINI

NON-RENDITION

↑ DISCOURSE MANAGEMENT

Non-rendition is an analytical concept that forms part of a classification system for utterances produced in interpreter-mediated encounters by dialogue interpreters in relation to utterances produced by other participants (primary participants) in another language. The taxonomy of interpreter utterances including 'non-rendition' was developed by Wadensjö (1992, 1998) to go beyond the traditional units of interest in translation studies – source text and target text – and better account for the complexity of naturally occurring interpreter-mediated face-to-face interaction, in which both the progression and the content of talk are continuously shaped by what participants add and what they take up. The aim of the typology of 'renditions' is to classify different ways in which the interpreter's talk relates to primary participants' immediately preceding talk (as target texts would relate to source texts).

The typology comprises categories of renditions that are based on a fairly straightforward ('close' or 'divergent') one-to-one correspondence with a prior utterance ('close', 'expanded', 'reduced', and 'substituted'), categories that correlate in more complex ways ('summarized', 'two-part', and 'multi-part' renditions), as well as utterances by primary parties that lack a corresponding utterance by the interpreter ('zero-renditions'). A non-rendition, by contrast, is "a 'text' which is analysable as an interpreter's initiative or response which does not correspond (as translation) to a prior 'original' utterance" (Wadensjö 1998: 108).

Interpreter utterances thus classified in the typology of renditions can be analysed in Wadensjö's parallel conceptual model, in which dialogue interpreters' turns at talk are perceived in terms of DISCOURSE MANAGEMENT, that is, as communicative activities answering to participants' current need for assistance in organizing and managing a shared discourse. This includes 'explicit coordinating moves', such as an interpreter's request for clarification, for time to interpret or for orderly TURN-TAKING. Such interpreter initiatives, analysed with regard to their contribution to the coordination of discourse and the progression of the interaction, are examples of what, in the typology of renditions, corresponds to non-renditions.

CECILIA WADENSJÖ

NONVERBAL COMMUNICATION

→ BODY LANGUAGE, → PROSODY

Nonverbal communication is the umbrella term used to designate a vast range of communicative phenomena that are not strictly linguistic: appearance (physical features and clothing), spatial behaviour (proxemics, posture, body orientation), body movements (gestures and adaptors), facial expressions and GAZE. In addition to these visually perceived phenomena, for which the term BODY LANGUAGE is also used, nonverbal communication comprises vocal elements (sometimes referred to as 'paralanguage') which include INTONATION, voice frequency, PAUSES and other features of PROSODY. The term gained currency after the publication of *Nonverbal Communication: Notes on the Visual Perception of Human Relations* by Ruesch and Kees (1956). Also in the 1950s, Paul Watzlawick and Gregory Bateson reinterpreted human communication in the light of the then newly proposed partition between analogical (iconic) and digital (linguistic) codes, and maintained that the two fulfilled completely different functions. Investigations in the domain of nonverbal communication in the 1950s and 1960s were thus marked by a sharp separation between the verbal channel, considered responsible for conveying referential content, and the nonverbal channel, responsible for communicating affective and social aspects. This dichotomy, however, has been overcome in the current cross-disciplinary perspectives on nonverbal communication, where verbal and nonverbal dimensions are viewed as forming complex interconnected wholes that create meaning and regulate social interaction (see Hall & Knapp 2013). The main impulse for this holistic, multimodal paradigm came from the study of GESTURE, especially in the 1980s and 1990s with the pioneering work of Adam Kendon and David McNeill, who regard speech and body movements as manifestations of the same underlying system (McNeill 1992; Kendon 2004). Thus, although the term nonverbal communication continues to be used, a new term has also emerged to stress that there is neither a division nor a hierarchical relationship among verbal, vocal and kinesic modalities: multimodality (Müller et al. 2013).

Multimodal sign systems in interpreting have been modeled most comprehensively by Fernando Poyatos (1997). His concept of speech as a "triple audiovisual reality made up of verbal language, paralanguage and kinesics" (1997: 249) has served to underpin current holistic views of 'text' in interpreting studies (e.g. Pöchhacker 1994c). With a focus on CONFERENCE INTERPRETING, Poyatos views the product of the interpreter's efforts as both verbal and nonverbal, as well as dependent on the speaker's verbal and nonverbal cues. Thus, he is probably the first scholar to include nonverbal communication in the very definition of interpreting. His is also the first attempt at systematizing into one single model the different communication channels and sign systems at work in interpreting (see Poyatos 1987/2002: 237, 1997: 251). This model, which includes the speaker's, the listener's and the interpreter's intentional and non-intentional audible and visible communication, accounts for the various basic situations stemming from (in)visibility conditions in both simultaneous and CONSECUTIVE INTERPRETING. As Poyatos's aim is mainly pedagogical, his contributions are enriched by practical examples of how interpreters should behave in situations where nonverbal communication plays an essential role, with special emphasis on cultural differences.

Bühler (1985) likewise viewed conference interpreting as a "multichannel communication phenomenon" and conducted two surveys among AIIC professionals on the importance of visual information in their work. The analysis of her data, collected by means of a questionnaire and interviews, indicated that visual signals by speakers, delegates, conference participants and other interpreters were considered very important by the majority of the respondents. Interpreters viewed facial expressions and co-verbal gestures as crucial elements for full COMPREHENSION of the message, for anticipating changes in speaking turns and languages used, and for monitoring the audience's reactions to the interpretation. Indeed, reciprocal VISUAL ACCESS between interpreters and delegates was considered vital by interpreters so as not to feel like "mere translation machines" working "in a vacuum" (Bühler 1985: 53) – an observation confirmed by recent studies on REMOTE INTERPRETING.

Other empirical contributions to the literature on nonverbal communication and interpreting reflect a strong focus on SIMULTANEOUS INTERPRETING (SI), and can be subsumed under two broad headings: (a) studies on the impact of visual input on performance in SI; and (b) studies on the importance of vocal/prosodic features (SPEECH RATE, intonation, pauses, etc.) in SI. For both (a) and (b), the preferred methodological approach has been EXPERIMENTAL RESEARCH.

Probably the very first study on the topic was the 1979 master's thesis by Linda Anderson (see Anderson 1994). This experimental study with professional interpreters assessed the effects of visual input on SI performance in a 'video on' and 'video off' condition, and concluded that there was no significant difference in performance QUALITY in the two conditions. Another experiment relating visual input to quality of performance (measured by ERROR ANALYSIS) was conducted with advanced interpreting students, who interpreted simultaneously an improvised and a read speech both with and without visual input (Balzani 1990). The main finding, partly contradicting Anderson, was that the interpreters' performance seemed to benefit from visual input, but only in the case of improvised speech. Further experimental studies with graduates and final-year students of interpreting (e.g. Alonso Bacigalupe 1999; Sineiro de Saa 2003; Rennert 2008) generally failed to find a significant positive or negative effect of the visual channel on simultaneous interpreters' performance, even though qualitative data from these studies strongly indicate that interpreters find visual cues helpful in understanding and processing the overall message.

Research on vocal behaviour and interpreting has focussed on different features of prosody (Ahrens 2005a), such as interpreters' unnatural intonation in SI and its effects on listeners' comprehension and recall (Shlesinger 1994), as well as monotonous intonation and its impact on SI quality assessment (Collados Aís 1998). The interpreter's VOICE QUALITY, FLUENCY, ACCENT and diction have been studied as QUALITY CRITERIA in SI from an interdisciplinary perspective (Collados Aís et al. 2007).

With few exceptions, nonverbal modalities in DIALOGUE INTERPRETING have only recently become an object of systematic study. The focus here is on nonverbal phenomena in relation to the interpreter's ROLE, and on their relevance to the interpreter's management of interaction and rapport (Iglesias Fernández 2010). Special attention has been given to gaze, as in Pasquandrea's (2011) study on the multimodal co-construction of TURN-TAKING in interpreter-mediated medical interaction.

ELENA ZAGAR GALVÃO AND ISABEL GALHANO RODRIGUES

NORMS

The notion of norms, utilized in interpreting research since the early 1990s, is borrowed from translation studies. First introduced by Gideon Toury in 1980 as a category for the descriptive analysis of translation phenomena, norms are defined as "the translation of general values or ideas shared by a community – as to what would count as right or wrong, adequate or inadequate – into performance 'instructions' appropriate for and applicable to concrete situations" (Toury 2012: 63). They are assimilated by novices in their training and socialization as professionals. In their operation, norms do not manifest themselves in any retrievable form, but are active in guiding decisions and determining "regularities of behaviour in recurrent situations" (Toury 2012: 64). Using such regularities as a clue, norms can thus be recovered from instances of behaviour, that is, extrapolated through generalization from interpreters' output – from what Toury calls 'textual sources'. They can also be inferred from 'extratextual sources', such as theoretical, evaluative and prescriptive statements made by interpreters/ translators, editors, trainers, etc., which help explain how regularities and conventions become normative. In the case of research on norms in interpreting, Gile (1999c) considers extratextual sources as possibly even more useful than textual ones.

The proposal to extend the concept of translational norms to interpreting, grounded in the conceptualization of interpreting as a specific form of translation, was originally made by SHLESINGER (1989a). She expressed some methodological reservations, however, regarding corpus collection and representativeness for the purposes of norm extrapolation, and with respect to the possibility of isolating meaningful general phenomena from individual idiosyncratic behaviour. She also noted that exposure of novices to actual interpreted text could be too limited to enable them to internalize norms through socialization. In subsequent research, these concerns have, on the whole, not been borne out (e.g. Gile 1999c; Garzone 2002b).

Instances of norms in professional interpreting are given by Harris (1990), in his response to Shlesinger (1989a). In particular, the 'true interpreter' norm, or norm of the 'honest spokesperson', hardly ever made explicit, establishes that interpreters reproduce the source speech accurately and completely, with no personal alterations. Furthermore, the interpreter speaks in the first person as if s/he were the orator; users accept the inevitable 'voice/personality dislocation' between interpreter and orator, together with the uncertainties, faults and infelicities which are tolerated in interpreted texts but would be less acceptable in written translation; and simultaneous interpreters translate only into their A language (Harris 1990: 118). This last precept, which is today applied only in international organizations (and no longer systematically, due to the high number of language combinations to be covered, e.g. in EU institutions), reflects the culturally determined character of norms.

According to Gile (1999c), recourse to norms in interpreting research may be useful to foster more empirical investigations and INTERDISCIPLINARITY. Far from being in contradiction with the traditional paradigm of cognitively oriented research, norms can be a tool for explaining the STRATEGIES interpreters deploy to address cognitive constraints and overload. Accordingly, Gile re-interprets some of the 'laws' described in connection with his EFFORT MODELS – 'maximizing information recovery', 'maximizing the impact of the speech', 'minimizing recovery interference' – as norms. He also discusses FIDELITY norms ('linguistic output norms') and behavioural norms, which are especially important in such domains of interpreting as BUSINESS INTERPRETING, COURTROOM INTERPRETING, and HEALTHCARE INTERPRETING.

The detailed categorization of translational norms, as conceived by Toury ('preliminary norms', 'initial norm', 'operational norms') and integrated by Chesterman (1993), is also applicable to interpreting. Preliminary norms encompass 'translation policy', that is, the decision to provide interpreting for a certain event or encounter, and the choice of the mode. Among the norms governing performance, the initial norm concerns the choice between an approach aiming at 'adequacy' (i.e. leaning heavily towards the original), and one aiming at 'acceptability', more concerned with the norms of the target language and culture. The latter choice has been formulated in interpreting studies in terms of the distinction between TRANSCODING and 'interpreting proper', or form-based and meaning-based interpreting (e.g. Dam 2001). Operational norms govern the relationship of the translated text with the source speech, in terms of OMISSIONS, additions and other manipulations ('matricial norms') and, above all, the actual formulation of the target text ('textual-linguistic norms').

Of the two categories of norms postulated by Chesterman (1993, 1997b), 'professional norms' are those constituted by competent professional behaviour, largely corresponding to Toury's initial and operational norms, while 'expectancy norms' essentially consist of USER EXPECTA-TIONS. The latter are relatively well established for interpreting, thanks to the immediate and shared situational context in which interpreter-mediated events are set (e.g. Moser 1996), and it appears evident that service users' beliefs about what a good interpretation ought to be like will contribute to shaping interpreters' professional norms. This introduces an element of social sanction which validates the normativity of the regularities identified, highlighting the socio-cultural nature of the act of interpreting, and of translation in general.

Various authors have taken up the notion of norms, to investigate it further and/or use it as a heuristic tool for research: Shlesinger (1999) discusses how norm-based strategies might be 'teased apart' from those dictated by COGNITIVE LOAD in SIMULTANEOUS INTERPRETING (SI); Schjoldager (1995) tests the validity of the notion of norms for application in SI research; Garzone (2002b) shows its usefulness in the investigation of QUALITY in SI; Marzocchi (2005) reviews its application in interpreting studies and its implications for professional ETHICS; Duflou (2007) discusses potential norms with reference to documentary sources in the EU institutions; Diriker (1999, 2004, 2008) uses the identification of norms to highlight the increasingly sociology-oriented approach to CONFERENCE INTERPRETING; while Straniero Sergio (2003) and Toledano Buendía (2010) propose to extend the application of a norm-based paradigm to MEDIA INTERPRETING and COMMUNITY INTERPRETING respectively.

The identification of norms may be more problematic in community interpreting than in conference interpreting, owing to the great diversity of SETTINGS and social contexts. Research must therefore focus on specific domains and institutions, as demonstrated by work on ASYLUM SETTINGS in the UK (Inghilleri 2003). An asset to the search for norms in community-based settings is the widespread codification of professional ethics and standards of practice in this domain (see Hale 2007), though empirical research has clearly shown that these extratextual sources do not necessarily reflect the norms governing actual interpreting practices. Another major obstacle to the identification of these norms is the uncertain professional STATUS of community interpreters and their frequent lack of recognition, making it difficult to identify a group of competent professionals whose interpreting behaviour is accepted as standard-setting and norm-setting, and a group of competent users whose expectations can be generalized as having norm-setting relevance.

GIULIANA GARZONE

NOTE-TAKING

↑ CONSECUTIVE INTERPRETING
→ MEMORY

CONSECUTIVE INTERPRETING of entire speeches presents major challenges to the interpreter's MEMORY. Faced with the need to render speeches lasting five to ten minutes or even longer, interpreters take notes to avoid overburdening their memory during the initial processing phase (COMPREHENSION) and to ensure the retrieval of content stored in memory during the second processing phase (production). However, notes do not replace memory; they are used by interpreters to aid their memory, which is achieved by jotting down the ideas, structure and some details of a speech, but not the source-language wording. Consecutive interpreters thus complement their cognitive memory with a 'material memory' (Kirchhoff 1979), that is, written cues taken down on their notepad. Kirchhoff (1979) talks of a 'parallel storage strategy', where the information to be remembered is stored simultaneously in two different but interdependent ways. While listening and simultaneously taking notes, interpreters are performing a continuous analysis of the speech which allows them to understand and remember its content and 'main thread' (Matyssek 1989). Aside from such items as unfamiliar names or NUMBERS, which are particularly difficult to remember, interpreters ideally note down only such units of the source text as they have successfully analysed and fully understood. The role of notes as merely an aid to memory is reflected in quantitative analysis of how much the interpreter actually commits to paper: according to Matyssek (1989), only 20 to 40 percent of the source text, at most, is represented by notes.

Principles and systems

Consecutive interpreting was the interpreting mode commonly used in the 1920s at conferences of the League of Nations and the International Labour Organization. Interpreters at that time had not gone through formal training, but developed their interpreting skills and techniques on the job (Herbert 1952). Note-taking strategies had to be developed individually in order to cope with long speeches; the introductory courses reportedly offered at the German Foreign Office from 1921 onwards (Schmidt 1949) were an exception. The note-taking systems developed individually and intuitively by interpreters in the course of their working experience were largely based on similar principles, such as writing down key idea units, logical links and marks of negation as well as dates, numbers and names, using different abbreviation procedures and arranging notes vertically. In the 1950s these practices came to be summarised by Herbert (1952) and, in particular, Rozan (1956), thus establishing the Geneva School's classic canon of note-taking. This approach, based on using mainly words and some 20 recommended symbols, was further developed by Ilg (1988; Ilg & Lambert 1996), integrating more symbols and also emoticons.

Unlike Rozan (1956), Minyar-Beloruchev (1969b) in the SOVIET SCHOOL opted for more symbols in order to avoid INTERFERENCE from source language notes during target text delivery. This 'language-independent' approach based on symbols to represent concepts was further developed in Heidelberg by Matyssek (1989), who proposed an elaborate system of combinatory symbols. Because of his emphasis on symbols, Matyssek has often been seen in opposition to Rozan, and criticized for his exhaustive collection of symbols. However, the various approaches do not differ that much with regard to basic principles (Ahrens 2005b). On the other hand, some disagreement exists over the choice of language in note-taking, with some favouring the target language (e.g. Herbert 1952), others the source language (e.g. Ilg 1988), and still others (e.g. Matyssek 1989) giving preference to the interpreter's A language.

Given the tradition of interpreter training in Europe, specialised literature on note-taking has a distinctly European focus, with publications mostly in French and German, and more recently Italian (e.g. Monacelli 1999); an English version of Rozan's 1956 classic became available only in 2002. With the notable exception of Gillies (2005), textbooks in English tend to focus on teaching consecutive interpreting more generally (e.g. Bowen & Bowen 1984). The same applies to publications in Asian languages, such as Chinese or Japanese (e.g. Liu 2008), where different writing systems and language combinations offer some additional note-taking options.

Empirical research

Although interpreters' notes attract curiosity and even admiration from those witnessing consecutive interpreting performances, note-taking has been the subject of only a limited number of empirical studies, often based on (quasi-)experimental designs.

The early study by Seleskovitch (1975), with thirteen professional interpreters working from English into French, was designed to provide evidence in support of the INTERPRETIVE THEORY, or *théorie du sens*. From the interpreters' comments on their notes and her own sense-based theoretical approach, Seleskovitch concluded that notes served as triggers for information retrieval from memory, and that note-taking needs to be 'automatic' so as to keep attention mainly on the conceptual processing of incoming information from the source text. Thus, her work clearly points to the cognitive dimension of the interpreting process.

The cognitive dimension is also at the heart of the study by Lambert (1989b), which links note-taking to memory and recall of source text information. In a sample of sixteen interpreters (eight professionals, eight students), she compared four different language-processing modalities: listening, consecutive interpreting (with notes), simultaneous interpreting and shadowing. Consecutive interpreting yielded better recall scores than simultaneous or shadowing, from which Lambert concluded that information is apparently processed more deeply in consecutive interpreting than in simultaneous, partly because the notes seem to enhance the information retention process.

In a study in the EXPERT–NOVICE PARADIGM, Andres (2002) compared the note-taking strategies of fourteen student interpreters and fourteen professional conference interpreters. Using an innovative video-recording method to analyse the real-time process of note-taking, Andres showed that this can be a discontinuous process, especially in the case of corrections or additions, and that the TIME LAG in writing down notes can have a considerable impact on note-taking and on subsequent target text production. Student interpreters were seen to fall behind the source text, which led to omissions in the notes as well as in the interpretation. Students focused more on specific problems at the 'micro' level, whereas professionals processed source text information on a more holistic 'macro' level and were better able to cope with micro-level problems without losing sight of the broader picture as a result.

A special line of research addresses the controversy over the form and language of notes. In a small-scale study with five professional interpreters working from Spanish into their A language, Danish, Dam (2004a) found that using symbols makes it possible to write down more, although no optimum word–symbol ratio can be suggested. With regard to the choice of language, Dam found a strong preference for note-taking in the target language, though with some use of source language notes in 'difficult' passages. She consequently hypothesised that note-taking patterns differed according to processing requirements. In a follow-up study with four student interpreters in the same language combination (Spanish/Danish), Dam (2004b) observed that the choice of language was strongly influenced by the status of the language in the interpreters' combination of working languages (A or B language): the interpreters' preference was for taking notes in their A language. Szabó (2006) tested Dam's findings in a group of eight student interpreters with Hungarian as their A and English as their B language, but was not able to confirm the predominance of A-language notes: her subjects preferred to take notes in English even when interpreting into their A language, Hungarian – a finding explained in part by the greater morphological complexity of Hungarian words. Thus, the language's status for the interpreter (A vs. B) and its role in the communication process (source vs. target) were both found to influence the choice of language for note-taking, and this choice also depends on actual processing requirements.

In a more theoretical contribution to the study of interpreters' notes, Albl-Mikasa (2008) analyses the notes of five trainee interpreters in the light of cognitive theories of language processing, in particular RELEVANCE THEORY. Notes are viewed not as a technique used to support memory, but as a 'notation text' to which processes of COHERENCE building and MENTAL REPRESENTATION at all text levels are applied. Albl-Mikasa makes reference to Allioni (1989), who had adopted a text-linguistic approach to notes and described these as a 'metalinguistic communicative code' governed by certain grammatical rules. In her analysis, Albl-Mikasa shows that interpreters' processing of the source speech, of their notes and of the target text relies on (micro-)propositions, and that processing conditions affect how explicitly the various items of meaning are noted.

Teaching

The status of systematic instruction in note-taking in the CURRICULUM for interpreter EDUCATION is unclear, but most programs introduce various note-taking systems and teach the general principles in order to provide trainees with some guidance and suggestions for developing their own technique. There are recommendations on how training should proceed in order to train the prerequisite text comprehension and memory skills (e.g. Alexieva 1994; Ilg & Lambert 1996), but there has been very little research on note-taking training as such. Gile (1991a) showed that student interpreters' note-taking often interferes with overall text comprehension, because too much effort is spent on writing instead of listening.

Recent advances in PEDAGOGY have come from new technologies that allow the note-taking process to be conveniently recorded. Orlando (2010) proposes the use of digital pen technology ('smart pens') for note-taking training. Thanks to their built-in audio-recording capability and digital note-recording on microchipped paper, these devices can capture the writing process in synchrony with the source text audio, making it possible to relate note-taking problems directly to the processing of the incoming source speech. The synchronised recordings, which can conveniently be played back on a computer screen, allow for new forms of analysis and assessment, directly relating the note-taking process to its product (the notes) as well as to target text delivery. Beyond its use in training, this new technology also offers new applications for research (Orlando 2014), both into note-taking and into new hybrid MODES of interpreting.

BARBARA AHRENS

NUMBERS

↑ INPUT VARIABLES

Numbers are among the source speech elements that are particularly vulnerable to incompleteness and inaccuracy in an interpretation. Strictly speaking, they are theoretical concepts (and arithmetical values). The symbols or words used to represent them (for example, '3', 'iii' or 'three') are referred to either by the specific term 'numerals', or simply 'numbers'.

Verbal expression of complex numerals is subject to syntactic rules which differ, sometimes considerably, from language to language (Wiese 2003). Irrespective of language combination, however, numerals have certain general features which help explain why they can create difficulties for interpreters. First, a numeral refers to the corresponding number as such, and therefore tends to be neither intrinsically associated with other extralinguistic referents nor predictable from context. Second, findings from neuroscience suggest that the neural representation of numbers in the brain (numerical cognition) is different from that of lexically expressed concepts (see Cheung 2009). These sources of difficulty in processing spoken (or signed) numerals are compounded by their lack of redundancy, as a result of which their accurate COMPREHENSION and storage in MEMORY requires much attention. Within the theoretical framework of the EFFORT MODELS (Gile 1997), numbers – like other low-redundancy speech elements such as proper names and acronyms – are therefore considered "problem triggers" for the interpreter, particularly in SIMULTANEOUS INTERPRETING. Where the interpreter needs to dedicate much of the available "processing capacity" to ensuring accuracy with these items, the resulting drain on the cognitive resources needed for production and overall coordination may disrupt the rendering not only of the numbers themselves, but of neighbouring speech segments as well.

The fact that numbers are generally unpredictable precludes any opportunity for 'top-down' comprehension or ANTICIPATION, except when the figures concerned can be readily associated with a familiar schema (e.g. *billions* and not *millions* as the correct order of magnitude for estimates of world population). When knowledge of the context offers no such clue and the processing of numerals is entirely 'bottom-up', a possible source of help to the interpreter is to write down numbers on the notepad in CONSECUTIVE INTERPRETING or in the booth; another is the inclusion of numbers in the speaker's presentation slides, making VISUAL ACCESS to the projection screen an important practical consideration.

Despite the ready identification of numbers as a source of difficulty for the interpreter, there has been relatively little systematic investigation of this topic. The subject has nevertheless generated an interesting line of EXPERIMENTAL RESEARCH, demonstrating that numbers and their context are reproduced with limited accuracy in simultaneous interpreting. In a pioneering study, Braun and Clarici (1996) found that about 70% of the numbers in the Italian and German source texts interpreted by their twelve student subjects were not rendered correctly, with OMISSIONS accounting for nearly 50% of all incorrect renditions. In the same experiment SHADOWING of numbers presented in lists proved more accurate than simultaneous interpreting of numbers in context, suggesting that part of the difficulty in interpreting lies in the need to alternate 'intelligent' listening to the context with 'literal' listening to numerical items (Braun & Clarici 1996). These findings were largely corroborated in follow-up studies by Mazza (2001) and Pinochi (2009), both of whom used broadly similar error classification systems adapted to their specific objectives and also explored the role of DIRECTIONALITY and NOTE-TAKING. On the whole, these studies suggest that ACCURACY in simultaneous interpreting of numbers does not differ greatly or consistently according to whether the interpreter takes notes. The language combination (with a focus here on interpreting between German or English and Italian) may make some difference, though language-specific difficulties need to be distinguished from the effects of DIRECTIONALITY. Interestingly, two specific features of numbers in a German source text seem to place additional strain on processing capacity: numerals in German are not only slightly lengthier than in Italian or English, but also place units before tens. These features appear to increase demands on the interpreter's WORKING MEMORY, requiring not only short-term storage but also a rearrangement of tens and units in the target language.

Such difficulties are even more pronounced in interpreting between Chinese and non-related languages. Troublesome features of the Chinese numerical system for the interpreter include the grouping of large numbers in multiples of 10,000 rather than thousands (this use of myriads also being found in Japanese and Korean), and the need to say 'zero' before the final digit in numbers like 1001. Experimental research by Cheung (2009), with student interpreters working from English into Chinese, indicates that special STRATEGIES are required to cope with these challenges. For students with limited experience, practising with numbers as part of a context seems to give better results than training with numbers in isolation, which lends further weight to the argument that processing numbers in interpreting requires flexible switching between 'intelligent' and 'literal' listening.

Given the inherent difficulty of number processing in interpreting, expedients like note-taking or enlisting a boothmate's help to write down figures offer only partial solutions (Mazza 2001). As so much hinges on the ability to switch attention between the bottom-up processing of numbers and the very different demands of interpreting the context they are part of, completeness and accuracy in rendering speech segments which contain numerical data are difficult to achieve and ultimately depend on the combined effect of the many other INPUT VARIABLES which affect the interpreter's performance.

PETER MEAD

NUREMBERG TRIAL

↑ HISTORY, ↑ TRIBUNAL INTERPRETING
→ SIMULTANEOUS INTERPRETING

The "Nuremberg Trial" refers to the trial of the major Nazi war criminals before the International Military Tribunal (IMT) held from November 1945 until October 1946 in the Palace of Justice in Nuremberg. It was a major event for international law (serving as an example for subsequent international tribunals) and one of the first ever major international media events. And it marked a turning point in the history of interpreting: under the gaze of a large international public, the first-time use of SIMULTANEOUS INTERPRETING in four languages for the entire proceedings laid the foundations for modern-day CONFERENCE INTERPRETING. Thanks to research based on INTERVIEWS and archival sources, in particular by Gaiba (1998), as well as some interpreters' MEMOIRS, there is now considerable knowledge about interpreting at the IMT.

The IMT Charter, signed by the Allies on 8 August 1945 as part of the London Agreement and establishing the Tribunal itself, postulated a fair trial, which included translation of all the documents used as well as interpretation of the proceedings into English, French, Russian and German. For reasons of cost and especially time, the traditional consecutive mode of interpreting did not seem suitable, and Colonel Léon DOSTERT came up with the idea of using the Filene–Finlay "International Translator System" by IBM for simultaneous interpretation of the trial. He convinced US Chief Prosecutor Robert H. Jackson, who, despite initial scepticism, helped persuade the other chief prosecutors and delegations of the need for the new system, and the IBM system was shipped to Nuremberg in late October 1945, a few weeks before the start of the trial.

Dostert masterminded a two-step recruitment process. Potential interpreters were first screened in their home countries for a near-native mastery of the required languages. Successful candidates were sent to Nuremberg, where they were also tested for general knowledge and vocabulary, especially in medical and legal TERMINOLOGY, and where they had to demonstrate stress resistance while interpreting in mock trials. The most important criterion, however, was linguistic agility enabling them to deal *immediately* with language input. Only about five per cent were selected, most of them between 35 and 45 years old and fluent in no more than two languages; roughly half of them were women. Quite a few of the interpreters had lost family members to Nazi brutality and/or had been detained in concentration camps; they were nevertheless expected, and apparently managed, to concentrate on their task despite a sense of personal involvement and the often shocking accounts they had to interpret in the courtroom.

The 36 simultaneous interpreters (in addition to 12 more who worked in consecutive mode during the pre-trial interrogations or consultations between the judges, as well as interpreters recruited to interpret witnesses testifying in languages such as Bulgarian, Polish or Yiddish) formed the Court Interpreting Branch of the IMT's Translation Division. The latter was in overall charge of all translation and interpreting and also comprised the Translating Branch, with about 180 translators, the Court Reporting Branch, with approximately 50 reporters, and the Transcript Reviewing Branch, with up to 100 people checking the protocols against the audio tapes of the original and the interpretations.

The work schedule of the so-called "linguists" providing simultaneous interpreting comprised a morning shift (10 am to 1 pm, with a ten-minute break) in the courtroom, and an afternoon shift (2 to 5 pm, with a ten-minute break) in the "ready-room", where they followed the proceedings, ready to replace a colleague if necessary. After two such days of work there was one day of rest.

There were four "booths", each with three interpreters – for example, for the English booth, one interpreter working from German, one from French and one from Russian. The WORKING CONDITIONS in the courtroom, from today's perspective, were rather poor. The IBM system was already 20 years old, the headphones were uncomfortable, and the single hand-held microphone had to be passed from one interpreter to the next. The so-called booths, which the interpreters called the "aquarium", were only glass partitions providing little sound insulation. They were installed in the corner of the courtroom, which did not allow direct and frontal VISUAL ACCESS to the speakers' rostrum or the judges. To ensure the ACCURACY of the interpretation (which was a major concern to sceptics of the simultaneous mode) a so-called monitor sitting next to the interpreters' booths checked the interpreters' renditions. He also watched over the technical functioning of the system (together with the technician) and provided the interpreters with written documents and their translations in advance. In order to ensure a SPEECH RATE that would allow the interpreters to keep up with the speaker, the monitor used a lamp signal (at the judges' table, the lectern and the witness stand) to remind the speaker to slow down (yellow bulb) or to ask for a short interruption (red light) (see Radisoglou 2008).

Since the audio recordings of the interpretations were destroyed at some point after the trial, little is known about how the interpreters performed their task. According to Ramler (2009), they intuitively applied many of the STRATEGIES for simultaneous interpreting that today are part of standard training: they rendered not only the words but the meaning of what was said – a task made particularly difficult by the intentional ambiguity of Nazi jargon – and dealt with complex syntax by using SEGMENTATION and ANTICIPATION, especially when working from German.

What little is known about the interpreters at Nuremberg comes mainly from several biographies of interpreters working into German and English (e.g. Ramler 2009; Sonnenfeldt 2006), whereas much less is known about their Soviet colleagues (e.g. Stupnikova 2003, 2013). Some of the interpreters' names sound familiar because they were well-established conference interpreters. Others, however, still remain virtually unknown, despite their pioneering work.

MARTINA BEHR

OMISSIONS

↑ ERROR ANALYSIS, ↑ STRATEGIES
→ ACCURACY

The concept of omission refers to translational source–target correspondence, or a lack thereof. Omissions in an interpreter's product or performance can be analysed with a view to assessing ACCURACY (as an aspect of QUALITY), as is done in ERROR ANALYSIS, or as one of the STRATEGIES used by interpreters to cope with the demands of the INTERPRETING process. The former perspective is typically found in earlier studies, which were based on a comparison of 'equivalent' sentences in source and target texts, whereas more recent studies attempt to place the production of omissions within the wider context of interpreting as a socially situated activity. There is a range of research studies that analyse omissions from these different perspectives, and key contributions are discussed here in more detail.

In his experimentally generated corpus, Barik (1975) studied the number and type of omissions made by professional and amateur interpreters in relation to text type and DIRECTIONALITY, and proposed a taxonomy that distinguishes between four types of omissions: skipping (of a single lexical item); COMPREHENSION (omission of a larger unit of meaning, as a result of an inability to comprehend the source language message); delay (omission of a larger unit of meaning, due to lagging too far behind the speaker); and compounding (conjoining elements from different clauses or sentences). Barik found that five out of his six subjects omitted approximately the same amount of material when working into their 'dominant' (native) language as they did when working into their second language. He also found that a greater TIME LAG resulted in a larger number of omissions.

Drawing on Barik's taxonomy, Kopczyński (1980) examined the performance of interpreting students working in consecutive and simultaneous mode, and made the distinction between 'obligatory' and 'optional' omissions according to whether they were triggered by structural differences between the two languages involved. He found that a higher proportion of omissions occurred in CONSECUTIVE INTERPRETING. Kopczyński clearly regarded omissions as errors of performance (e.g. due to MEMORY lapses, excessive time lag, time pressure and fatigue), but also asserted that they can be regarded as errors of receptive COMPETENCE when the interpreter fails to understand the source language message.

Cokely (1992a, 1992b) refined Barik's taxonomy for the purposes of analysing SIGNED LANGUAGE INTERPRETING, and defined morphological, lexical and cohesive omissions as 'miscue' types. In a specific study of the effects of time lag on interpreter errors, Cokely (1992b) applied his miscue taxonomy to the analysis of four videotaped conference interpretations. He found that lexical omissions were the most prevalent, followed by cohesive omissions and a much smaller number of morphological omissions, and that interpreters who had a shorter time lag made more omissions than those with a longer lag, with over twice as many total miscues, which contradicts Barik's earlier findings.

In the framework of his EFFORT MODELS, Gile (1995a, 1999a) has used omissions and other types of 'errors' to examine problems with FIDELITY as a result of interpreters working close to cognitive saturation. In a comparative study of MEDIA INTERPRETING performances, for instance, Gile (2011) found that the number of 'long omissions' was twice as high for simultaneous interpretations into Japanese as for interpretations of the same English speech into French and German, which is taken as an indication of language-pair-specific parameters in the interpreting process.

Further to this body of work, various authors suggest that omissions can be considered from a pragmatic perspective, whereby they are treated as conscious decisions made by the interpreter rather than mistakes resulting from miscomprehension. Bartłomiejczyk (2006) examines strategic omissions in relation to directionality, and Pym (2008), in a reanalysis of the study by Gile (1999a), suggests that omissions can be considered as 'low risk' or 'high risk', depending on their potential detrimental impact. Such conscious omissions have also been referred to as 'condensing strategies' (Sunnari 1995b), 'selective reductions' (Hatim & Mason 1990) and COMPRESSION strategies (Chernov 2004).

One of the most detailed examinations of the level of consciousness of omissions in SIMULTANEOUS INTERPRETING focused on the performances of ten professional interpreters working from English into Australian Sign Language (Napier 2002, 2004b). Through her analysis of the interpretations, and retrospective interviews with the interpreters to reflect on their reasons for producing omissions, Napier distinguished between five omission types depending on the level and the type of consciousness: (1) *Conscious strategic omissions:* made consciously by an interpreter, whereby a decision is made to omit information in order to enhance the effectiveness of the interpretation. The interpreter incorporates his or her linguistic and cultural knowledge to decide what information from the source language makes sense in the target language, what information is culturally relevant, and what is redundant; (2) *Conscious intentional omissions:* omissions which contribute to a loss of meaningful information. The interpreter is conscious of the omission and made it intentionally, either because s/he did not understand a particular lexical item or concept, or because s/he could not think of an appropriate target language equivalent; (3) *Conscious unintentional omissions:* omissions which contribute to a loss of meaningful information. The interpreter is conscious of the omission and made it unintentionally, meaning that s/he heard the lexical item(s) but decided to 'keep things on hold' and wait for more contextual information or greater depth of meaning. Further source language input and/or lag time then prevented completion of this processing, forcing the interpreter to omit the crucial lexical item(s) and move on; (4) *Conscious receptive omissions:* omissions that the interpreter is aware of, but for which s/he cannot properly decipher what was heard due to reported poor sound quality; and (5) *Unconscious omissions:* omissions which contribute to a loss of meaningful information. The interpreter is unconscious of the omission and does not recall hearing the particular lexical item (or items). Napier thus surmises that every interpretation has 'omission potential', and that interpreters can assess how likely they are to make appropriate or inappropriate omissions, based on their understanding of the situational context. Janzen and Korpinski (2005) support this claim, but state that strategic omissions can be successful only when interpreters deal critically with a text and give consideration to the needs of their audience and the intent of the source text speaker.

Whereas all the studies reported here analyse monologic interpretations in one language direction, Wadensjö's (1998) work gives an account of omissions in interpreter-mediated communication in dialogic contexts. While incorporating similar components to those of Barik and Cokely, she uses alternative TERMINOLOGY with more positive connotations.

In her taxonomy, Wadensjö defines three types of 'rendition' that could be considered as omissions: 'reduced renditions' (information expressed less explicitly than in the original), 'summarised renditions' (text corresponding to two or more prior originals) and 'zero renditions' (original utterance not translated). She stresses that the interpreter's renditions must be considered within the whole context of the dialogic interaction, as interpreters aim to produce contextually, linguistically and culturally appropriate utterances that meet the communicative goals of the original speakers.

Wadensjö's taxonomy has been applied by other researchers to studies of interpreting in dialogic or multiparty contexts. Examples from the field of HEALTHCARE INTERPRETING include Amato's (2007) examination of interpreters' zero- and non-renditions in multiparty medical encounters and Cirillo's (2012) analysis of the same categories to explore communication in doctor–patient talk.

JEMINA NAPIER

ORALITY

The term 'orality' can refer to oral culture or to oral communication. In both cases it is used in contrast to 'literate' culture or (written) communication. In the first sense, two kinds of orality can be distinguished: in 'primary orality', no writing exists on which to base the management and transmission of knowledge, whereas in the 'secondary orality' of present-day high-technology cultures, orality and literacy are in many ways intertwined (Ong 1982), and our perception of language, and in particular of spoken language, is deeply influenced by literate activities (Cronin 2002; Linell 2005).

INTERPRETING STUDIES is mainly concerned with orality in the sense of oral communication, as interpreting is typically associated with speech in the oral medium (as input and/or output). Much attention has focused on how spoken and written language differ, and on the implications of a move from one to the other for both processing and communication. On the one hand, there are differences inherent to the medium; on the other, many features viewed as characteristics of the language mode result from the communication situation. Accordingly, instead of a spoken–written dichotomy, an oral–literate continuum has been suggested, combining multiple dimensions (e.g. fragmentation vs. integration, involvement vs. detachment; Chafe 1982).

Spoken language is produced vocally, conveyed through sound waves and received by hearing. This means that speech is a dynamic process, a situated action, and as such ephemeral. While its acoustic manifestation can be captured using recording devices, it is practically impossible to document the entire speech event for analytical purposes. TRANSCRIPTION reflects mainly the verbal component, but not the rich set of paraverbal features included under the heading of PROSODY, which contribute significantly to meaning.

Temporal features such as SPEECH RATE, PAUSES and hesitation phenomena are central characteristics. In interpreting research they have been studied from various points of view, for example, comparing their occurrence and functions in source and target texts and examining their influence on the reception of input speech and on the interpreter's oral delivery. Hesitation phenomena (e.g. filled pauses, interruptions, restarts, REPAIRS) can be seen as indicators of cognitive processing and can shape the style of a speech and affect the impression made by the speaker (and, similarly, by the interpreter). Whereas in monologues hesitations appear as disfluencies, they also serve interactive functions in face-to-face communication.

Further medium-dependent features of spoken language are voice-related phenomena, such as INTONATION, tone, loudness and VOICE QUALITY, which are language- and speaker-specific. The role of intonation in meaning construction, text organization, COMPREHENSION and quality ASSESSMENT has been studied in particular with regard to SIMULTANEOUS INTERPRETING (SI) (e.g. Ahrens 2004; Collados Aís 1998, 1998/2002; Shlesinger 1994). Merlini and Favaron (2005), investigating 'voice' in HEALTHCARE INTERPRETING, found that interpreters use prosodic devices to create a sense of involvement.

The basic setting for oral communication is face-to-face conversation, in which speech is spontaneous, or 'impromptu' (Enkvist 1982), interaction is immediate (with interlocutors sharing the same time and place), and talk is jointly constructed in interaction. This is also the basic situation in DIALOGUE INTERPRETING. The interlocutors make use of multimodal resources (GESTURES, facial expressions, GAZE, postures, as well as objects), and the meaning of actions emerges in their interplay. Many intrinsic characteristics of spoken language, such as pronoun use, implicitness, loose syntax or redundancy, are related to the situatedness of speech and vary depending on the context and circumstances of production.

Speech and written texts are manifoldly intertwined in interpreting. The interpreter's input can be based on writing in various ways, as in the case of SIGHT INTERPRETING/TRANSLATION and SIMULTANEOUS WITH TEXT or a speech accompanied by a slide presentation (e.g. Power-Point). Speakers may use written notes or a manuscript drafted for delivery as a speech, or else read a text not originally intended for oral delivery. Orality is typically associated with spontaneity – whether production is spoken or signed – and thus with the immediacy assumed to be the defining characteristic of interpreting, whereas written text is designed for a reader who can look ahead and back. Since written texts can therefore display a much higher degree of complexity and lexical density, and reading aloud differs prosodically from speaking, scripted input has been widely recognized as posing a greater challenge for interpreting than impromptu speech, though features of the latter such as loose structure and REGISTER variation may pose obstacles. As demonstrated by SHLESINGER (1989b), interpreting is likely to induce shifts in the position of texts along the oral–literate continuum, rendering a literate source speech more oral in the interpretation.

Unlike the pervasive impact of literacy and written language on the orality of interpreting, changes in the opposite direction – from speech to the written medium – have received little attention (cf. Cronin 2002: 389). One example is SPEECH-TO-TEXT INTERPRETING, also known as print interpreting or captioning, which consists in the simultaneous rendering of speech into written text as a communication aid for people with hearing disability. To achieve the high production rate required by the need for simultaneity, RESPEAKING in combination with speech recognition software is increasingly used. Respeaking is used especially in intralingual live subtitling, but also in interlingual subtitling (e.g. from Welsh into English), where the respeaker produces an oral translation of the original speech. As this form of intermodal translation demonstrates, orality and literacy are closely intertwined, and translation activities cannot simply be divided into oral and written.

LIISA TIITTULA

OTTOMAN EMPIRE

see under DRAGOMANS

PARADIGMS

↑ INTERPRETING STUDIES
→ INTERDISCIPLINARITY, → METHODOLOGY

The term 'paradigm', as coined by Thomas Kuhn in 1962 to describe processes of change in the history of science, refers to a consensus within a scientific community regarding basic assumptions, models, values and standard methods. This consensus shapes the way things are done in a 'normal science', with the reigning paradigm representing a single 'truth' that is embraced by all members of the community at a given point in its historical development – until it is displaced by another paradigm. Although Kuhn's focus was on revolutionary changes in the natural sciences, spurred by the discovery of new materials, methods and types of measurement, his notion of *paradigm shift* has also been applied to the social sciences and the humanities, where different 'ways of seeing' could be expected to coexist rather than displace one another (Kuhn 1962/1996). Since the term 'paradigm' is also used in science in a much narrower sense, to refer to a specific methodological approach or design (such as the EXPERT-NOVICE PARADIGM), Kuhn subsequently proposed replacing it with the less ambiguous expression 'disciplinary matrix', which helpfully points to the level of the scientific community as the context in which the phenomenon is set.

It is therefore doubtful for several reasons whether the Kuhnian concept should be applied to a newly emerged field like INTERPRETING STUDIES, which is generally regarded as a subdiscipline within a wider, distinctly interdisciplinary domain in the arts and humanities.

Some have even argued that the field is too poorly established to claim a paradigm of its own, or that it is still in what Kuhn described as the 'pre-paradigmatic stage', in which multiple theories are put forward by competing schools of thought. Nevertheless, the idea of shifts, or 'turns', in the consensual assumptions shared within a scientific community can serve as a useful tool in describing a field's evolution (see Pöchhacker 2008b), even if the implications of change are not as radical as envisioned in Kuhn's account. Moreover, there was a phase in the development of interpreting studies that has been characterized with explicit reference to (incompatible) paradigms (Moser-Mercer 1994a), strengthening the rationale for an account of interpreting studies in terms of shifting or evolving paradigms.

As described in Pöchhacker (2004a, 2016), the establishment of an initial paradigm or 'single truth' in theorizing and researching interpreting was facilitated by the modest size of the community at the time. In the 1970s, there was no international community of scholars networking to forge a consensus. Rather, it was a close-knit group of professionals and educators of interpreters under the charismatic leadership of Danica SELESKOVITCH at ESIT in Paris that established the main theoretical assumptions and research approaches for the study of professional CONFERENCE INTERPRETING. This so-called PARIS SCHOOL, founded on Seleskovitch's INTERPRETIVE THEORY (IT), had few intellectual competitors, other than psychologists with an interest in interpreting, such as David GERVER, and a few interpreter-scholars in the Soviet Union, such as Ghelly CHERNOV. The IT paradigm established itself and held its ground until the late 1980s, when a new generation of interpreter-researchers with more scientific aspirations came to the fore, most visibly on the occasion of the TRIESTE SYMPOSIUM. These research-minded practitioners shared the dominant paradigm's focus on professional conference interpreting as well as its primary concern with the cognitive process of interpreting, but differed radically in their methodological orientation. Rather than introspection and the analysis of qualitative data, they took inspiration, among others, from Gerver's pioneering experimental work and model, and generally promoted an 'opening up' toward other scientific disciplines (Gile 1994). Among the fields regarded as holding the greatest promise was cognitive psychology, whose information processing paradigm informed the earliest MODELS of the interpreting process and had a lasting influence on subsequent research. It was the profound disagreement between the IT paradigm and the new cognitive information processing (CP) paradigm over fundamental issues of research METHODOLOGY and INTERDISCIPLINARITY that led Moser-Mercer (1994a) to describe the interpreting research community as divided into two distinct groups, or paradigms, and which also found expression in Daniel Gile's (1990) paper on 'scientific research vs. personal theories'.

A parallel development showcased at the Trieste Symposium was the investigation of interpreting processes at the neurophysiological and neuropsychological level, with a focus on the organization of languages in the bilingual brain. This neurolinguistic (NL) paradigm subsequently received a boost from the use of neuroimaging techniques for studying neuro-physiological activation patterns in the interpreter's brain (e.g. Tommola et al. 2000), with further progress made in more recent studies toward identifying the neural substrates of particular processing functions (e.g. Hervais-Adelman et al. 2011).

In the course of the 1990s, the study of interpreting became increasingly integrated into the wider disciplinary framework of translation studies (see Snell-Hornby et al. 1994). Nevertheless, the role of translation theory in informing research on interpreting remained relatively modest, a noteworthy exception being Miriam SHLESINGER's work on NORMS. While it is therefore difficult to identify a translation-theoretical (TT) paradigm as such, there has been a broader convergence between interpreting and translation research (e.g. Schäffner 2004), manifested, for example, by shared interest in CORPUS-BASED RESEARCH and by interpreting scholars readily joining translation scholars in their discipline's 'social turn' (Pöchhacker 2006c).

The ground for the adoption of insights and models from sociology and sociolinguistics was prepared by a more fundamental reorientation in interpreting studies in the course of the 1990s: following the First CRITICAL LINK Conference in 1995, COMMUNITY INTERPRETING increasingly attracted attention as a field of professional practice and academic research, and the work of Wadensjö (1998) and other discourse-based research approaches provided a new framework that proved particularly suitable to the analysis of DIALOGUE INTERPRETING as a process of social interaction and the co-construction of discourse. The resulting dialogic discourse-based interaction (DI) paradigm has since become established as one of the main ways of conceptualizing and investigating interpreting as situated (inter)action. Its focus on dialogue interpreting and authentic case studies of interpreter-mediated events using DISCOURSE ANALYTICAL APPROACHES places the DI paradigm in sharp contrast to the CP paradigm's alignment with COGNITIVE APPROACHES and reliance on EXPERIMENTAL RESEARCH for the study of simultaneous conference interpreting. Nevertheless, these two major paradigms in interpreting studies need not be viewed as competing for dominance in the Kuhnian sense; rather, the cognition-oriented and the interaction-oriented view seem perfectly complementary, and arguably indispensable for doing justice to the multifaceted nature of the concept of INTERPRETING.

FRANZ PÖCHHACKER

PARALANGUAGE

see under NONVERBAL COMMUNICATION

PARAPHRASING

see under PRE-INTERPRETING EXERCISES

PARIS SCHOOL

↑ INTERPRETING STUDIES
→ SELESKOVITCH
↓ INTERPRETIVE THEORY

The Paris School is a school of thought centred around the INTERPRETIVE THEORY (IT) of translation. It originated with Danica SELESKOVITCH in the 1960s and was further developed by her and her disciples. Its institutional base is the *École Supérieure d'Interprètes et de Traducteurs* (ESIT), a part of *Université Sorbonne Nouvelle – Paris 3*, where Seleskovitch started teaching interpreting in 1957, the year the school was founded.

Seleskovitch gradually developed IT to help fellow teachers of interpreting explain their instructional practices. Her basic tenet was that professional interpreters, with proper mastery of their languages and broad-based background knowledge, are able to build the sense of a speech from a combination of its words and their own relevant knowledge and re-express this sense in such a way as to make it understandable by those who do not master the source language and/or culture. This became the cornerstone of further research and also underpinned the training approach established at ESIT, with cross-fertilization between research and training.

Pedagogy

As early as 1965, at the first AIIC symposium on the teaching of interpreting, Seleskovitch proposed a structured and progressive teaching methodology (later published in Delisle 1981), for a course lasting two academic years. The program covered different speech types (narrative, argumentative, descriptive, rhetorical) and topics (concrete, abstract, affective), as well as the order in which the techniques should be taught (CONSECUTIVE INTERPRETING into A, SIMULTANEOUS INTERPRETING into A, consecutive into B). In the very first class, the now famous triangular model of interpreting was introduced, inviting the student interpreter to reduce words to nonverbal sense. This first general outline was slightly revised as IT research progressed, but the main pattern subsisted, with the later addition of courses in SIMULTANEOUS INTERPRETING WITH TEXT and conference PREPARATION, to accommodate changes in WORKING CONDITIONS.

Teaching at ESIT, based on IT principles, is always done by an A-language interpreter trainer: for example, a French-into-Russian interpreting class (whether into A or B) is always taught by an instructor with a Russian A.

During the 1970s, teachers' meetings were organized so as to reach methodological consensus among instructors. Gradually, former students who had become successful interpreters were recruited as instructors, ensuring that the same theoretical approach was applied to the teaching of interpreting in all language pairs. A few years later, the IT model was applied to the teaching of translation, with due adaptation to the written mode.

From 1974 and 1978 respectively, national postgraduate diplomas (*Maîtrise* and *Diplôme d'Études Supérieures Spécialisées* (DESS)) were awarded to interpreting and translation graduates, marking the recognition of interpreting and translation training at postgraduate level.

Doctoral studies

In the 1970s, academically minded professional interpreters and translators went on to earn a doctoral degree. Seleskovitch was the first to obtain a *Doctorat d'État* in 1973, with her groundbreaking study on NOTE-TAKING in CONSECUTIVE INTERPRETING (Seleskovitch 1975). Lederer (1981) followed suit with an empirical study of simultaneous interpreting. The year 1974 saw the beginning of a doctoral studies program at ESIT in *Science de l'interprétation et de la traduction*, a designation later replaced by *Traductologie*, which paved the way for more doctoral theses on interpreting: Thiéry (1975) studied the type of BILINGUALISM necessary for optimal 'bidirectional' interpreting, while a series of theses based on observational research addressed such topics as deliberate deviations from literality in CONFERENCE INTERPRETING (García-Landa 1978), the difference between interpreting impromptu speech and scripted texts (Déjean le Féal 1978), the specificities of court interpreting (Driesen 1985), and faithfulness in interpreting (Donovan-Cagigos 1990).

Aside from theoretical topics (e.g. Laplace 1994; Bodrova 2000), a number of doctoral theses have been devoted to the PEDAGOGY of interpreting, in different MODES, language pairs and language modalities. Examples include Liu (1996) and Ito-Bergerot (2006) for the teaching of consecutive, and Choi (1986) and Bomfim-Capellani (1987) for teaching consecutive and simultaneous interpreting in such (less common) language pairs as Korean/French and Portuguese/French. A thesis by Séro-Guillaume (1994) on interpreting between French and French Sign Language (LSF), demonstrated that IT methods could be applied to any pair of languages. Indeed, the Paris School recognized early on that the languages of the deaf were full-fledged languages: from 1993, first undergraduate and then postgraduate courses in SIGNED LANGUAGE INTERPRETING were offered at ESIT. Based on IT principles, such courses brought improved standards to this branch of the interpreting PROFESSION.

Application and dissemination

In 1984 the European Economic Community commissioned Seleskovitch and Lederer to provide an account of conference interpreter training both at ESIT and in their own Joint Interpreting and Conference Service (SCIC). The *Pédagogie raisonnée de l'interprétation* was published in 1989 and appeared in English in 1995 as *A Systematic Approach to Teaching Interpreting*. A second, updated edition (Seleskovitch & Lederer 2002) was requested by SCIC, to be used as a guide for the newly created interpreting schools in countries applying for accession to the EU. The European Parliament also commissioned ESIT to train Danish and Greek interpreters, in the run-up to EU (or EC, as it was then) accession.

Over the years, the ESIT doctoral studies program attracted more and more translators, both from France and abroad, who recognized that IT was equally applicable to written translation (both pragmatic and literary). A large number of dissertations in translation followed. Quite a number of these new PhDs were then appointed to positions in universities in Africa, Asia (China, Korea, Thailand), Europe (France, Norway, Spain, the UK) and South America, thus making IT the basis for translation teaching and research in some of those countries' universities.

The reputation of the Paris School is upheld the world over by the interpreters, translators and translation studies scholars trained in IT, who practice IT in their professional lives and further develop it in their teaching and research.

MARIANNE LEDERER

PARLIAMENTARY SETTINGS

↑ SETTINGS
→ CONFERENCE INTERPRETING, → SIMULTANEOUS INTERPRETING

The evolution of interpreting in parliamentary assemblies is closely linked with that of CONFERENCE INTERPRETING, and SIMULTANEOUS INTERPRETING (SI), in particular. Indeed, the French expression initially used to refer to the professional qualification that later came to be known as 'conference interpreter' was *interprète parlementaire* (e.g. Sanz 1930), but its link to 'parliamentary interpreting' is less direct than might appear. In French, one long-attested sense of the word *parlementaire* is that of an envoy who 'parleys' or negotiates with the enemy, or the context of such negotiations. Adopting the term *interprète parlementaire* at the dawn of the profession in the twentieth century may thus signal a shift away from well-established practices of MILITARY INTERPRETING and an early concern with a new, neutral role for the interpreter.

Interpreting in assemblies of a parliamentary type began at the League of Nations in the 1920s and 1930s, where various forms of consecutive and whispered interpreting were used. As new languages gained official status in the fledgling international organization of the 1930s, the need to reduce the time required for interpreting the proceedings spurred the development of SI (Baigorri-Jalón 2014).

SI quickly attracted the interest of national, multilingual parliaments (Keiser 2004); Belgium introduced it in 1936, Switzerland in 1948, and the Israeli *Knesset* used Arabic–Hebrew SI from the early 1950s until 1980. These developments, however, did not match the public exposure of SI (and the attention it received from the media) at the NUREMBERG TRIAL, which has imposed itself as the founding myth of the profession. The best documented exception to this in the Western world is CANADA, where parliamentary interpreting has a strong LANGUAGE POLICY significance (Delisle 2009).

Most multilingual parliaments in the Western world derive their multilingualism from a notion of equality between languages, and use symmetrical language combinations for SI at least in the most solemn settings (e.g. 23 languages into 23 in the European Parliament plenary). Elsewhere, asymmetrical combinations are more common, reflecting differences in prestige or domain extension of languages, and the role of former colonial languages. In the Indian federal parliament, SI has been provided since 1964 by default between Hindi and English, and on demand from other Indian languages into Hindi and English. In Malaysia, SI is from Malay into English and only occasionally in the other direction (Ibrahim 2009). In AFRICA, languages such as Zulu and Xhosa gained official status in South African national and regional legislatures from the late 1990s and are used in various asymmetrical combinations with English and Afrikaans (Wallmach 2000).

Interpreting in parliamentary settings is sometimes discussed in detail in works on the language policy of international organizations (Gazzola 2006). Within interpreting studies, the aspects of interpreting in parliamentary assemblies that have attracted scholarly interest make up three strands of research: (1) studies on organizational aspects and NORMS, (2) CORPUS-BASED RESEARCH, and (3) studies focusing on the issues of POWER and IDEOLOGY.

In the first strand, practitioners and scholars have explored the interplay between wider language policy issues, organizational arrangements and constraints on the interpreter's performance. Much of this research has centered on the European Parliament (EP), with Marzocchi (1998) as an initial analysis. Vuorikoski (2004) explores QUALITY in renditions of political RHETORIC in a multilingual corpus of EP interpreted speeches; Duflou (2007) extends the analysis to norms elicited from documentary sources; and Kent (2009) reports interpreters' views on patterns of language choice in the organization.

In the South African context, Wallmach (2000) describes determinants of interpreters' performance in the specific setting of a provincial legislature. Some of them, such as SPEECH RATE, technicality and organizational misconceptions of SI, are common to other parliamentary settings; others are peculiar to the language-policy landscape of South Africa and include code-mixing in original speeches, REGISTER limitations of the recent official languages and typological differences between languages (see also Lesch 2010).

Parliamentary assemblies are large-scale or at least authoritative employers of interpreters in their respective markets (although this can be said of institutional settings in general). As a result, they have been among the main arenas for the social organization of the profession (see Dam & Zethsen 2013 for a case study on perceptions of occupational STATUS). Similarly, they have been the testing grounds for changes in the profession's existential relationship with TECHNOLOGY, as in the case of REMOTE INTERPRETING (Roziner & Shlesinger 2010).

The legal or political requirements for openness of proceedings and the availability of audio streaming make parliamentary settings a welcome source of discourse data for corpus-based research, which makes up the second strand of inquiry. A variety of language combinations have been used to build parallel corpora, analyzed in many MA and PhD theses that often focus on language-pair-specific issues, sometimes complementing corpus analysis with contextual data from participants or documents. Research on parliamentary corpora, including the elaborate work on EPIC (European Parliament Interpreting Corpus), has explored issues such as the impact of DIRECTIONALITY (Monti et al. 2005), lexical patterns (Russo & Sandrelli 2006), INTONATION (Nafá Waasaf 2007), metaphors (Spinolo & Garwood 2010), disfluencies

(Bendazzoli et al. 2011) and ANTICIPATION (Liontou 2012, 2013). In a slightly different approach, García Becerra (2012) uses EP interpreted speeches to elicit and compare quality-related perceptions.

Finally, the research strand focusing on power and ideology reflects the prevalence of political speech in parliamentary settings. This has drawn the attention of scholars from beyond conference interpreting, or from translation studies in general, who use ETHNO-GRAPHIC METHODS and DISCOURSE ANALYTICAL APPROACHES (in particular Critical Discourse Analysis) to explore issues of power, ideology and agency on smaller corpora and case studies. Beaton (2007, 2013), for instance, finds that lexical and pragmatic features of inter-preted speech at the European Parliament reduce the inherent polyphony of political speech and reinforce institutional ideology.

CARLO MARZOCCHI

PARTICIPATION FRAMEWORK

↓ FOOTING

Participation framework is a concept used in interpreting studies in various senses, though authors discussing 'participation' in relation to interpreting or interpreter-mediated interaction do not always clarify how they understand this notion. Individuals' participation in interaction can be analysed in at least two rather different ways. Interestingly, in studies of interpreting and interpreter-mediated encounters, the same Goffmanian analytical models have served as a starting point both for authors applying a *cognitively* oriented approach to interpreting (in the sense of the individual interpreter's activities) and for researchers applying an *interactively* oriented approach to participation in interpreter-mediated interaction. The first approach focuses on the individual interpreter's (possible) states of mind, while an interactive approach focuses on how inter-preter-mediated encounters unfold and what participants' input, as hearers and speakers, reveals about their reading of the current combined 'participation status' (Goffman 1981) of people present. In both approaches, the content and form of utterances are used as indicators of a certain individual participant's state of mind, or of a negotiated, more or less shared meaning of manifest talk and social interaction (including gestures, gazes, and so forth).

In his book *Forms of Talk*, the sociologist Erving Goffman defines participation framework as the combined participation status of all participants in an encounter at a particular moment (Goffman 1981: 137). He suggests breaking down the notions of 'hearer' and 'speaker' into a 'participation framework' and a 'production format', respectively, and applies to these the rela-tional notion of FOOTING, that is, "the alignment we take up to ourselves and to others present as expressed in the way we manage the production or reception of an utterance" (Goffman 1981: 128). The notion of 'hearer' is decomposed into ratified and non-ratified participants, that is, the *addressed*, the *unaddressed* and the *bystander*, as opposed to *overhearers* and *eavesdroppers*. On the speaker side, three 'speaker roles' – *animator, author* and *principal* – are distinguished, ranging from mere vocalisation to composition to responsible ownership of an utterance.

Goffman never published any analyses of interpreter-mediated discourse data, and his dissection of 'hearer' and 'speaker' presupposes encounters in which participants are com-municating in a shared language. In other words, the inherent lack of mutual accessibility characteristic of interpreter-mediated encounters, implying that the interpreter plays a unique role in negotiating participants' continually evolving needs and assumptions, is not taken into account. Nevertheless, perhaps because interpreters' participation, involvement and alignment are key issues in studies of interpreting, Goffman's essays on participation have served as an influential source of inspiration, first and foremost in studies of DIALOGUE INTERPRETING (Wadensjö 1992; Mason 1999b, 2006, 2009b).

Cognitively oriented approaches

The linguist Stephen Levinson (1988) explicitly refers to interpreting in his exploration and development of Goffmanian concepts of participation. Levinson seems, however, to take the (conference) interpreter's listening and speaking for granted as a function of distinct mental states, rather than as a phenomenon in need of empirical study. He is thus a strong proponent of the cognitive approach to participation.

Levinson's (1988) critique of Goffman's categories as too vaguely defined and "empirically insufficient", and failing to take into account a distinction between 'utterance event' and 'speech event', must be understood in the light of his own programme – that of identifying a complete set of states of mind that humans can have as 'hearer' or as 'speaker', or what he calls 'production roles' and 'reception roles'. Without claiming the list to be complete, Levinson in his article suggests an extensive typology of such roles.

The cognitive approach is also evident in Edmondson's (1986) conceptual analysis, in which he compares the role of 'conversationalist' to that of 'interpreter'. Inspired by Goffman's analytical constructs, Edmondson outlines two new sets of conceptual tools, representing four mental stances, or 'roles', involved in the notion of 'speaker' and four 'roles' involved in the notion of 'hearer'. Edmondson does not apply his typologies to empirical data – unlike authors who later developed Goffman's concepts in various ways, like Wadensjö (1992, 1998), Merlini and Favaron (2005) and Pöchhacker (2012a).

Pöchhacker (2012a) explicitly argues for a more distinctly cognitive perspective on the sociolinguistic analysis of participation in discourse. Drawing particularly on Levinson (1988) and on his own previous study of SIMULTANEOUS INTERPRETING (e.g. Pöchhacker 1992, 1995c), he highlights the importance of separately studying the interpreter's participation at the 'utterance level' and at the 'communicative-event level', to which he also refers as the level of the HYPERTEXT. He also draws on the work of Merlini and Favaron (2005), who, in an article investigating interpreting practice in the setting of SPEECH PATHOLOGY, outline a typology of interpreters' alignment to the preceding primary speaker's utterance. Merlini and Favaron identify seven "categories of footing" that an interpreter may adopt – *principal, responder, direct recapitulator, indirect recapitulator, reporter, narrator,* and *pseudo-co-principal* (2005: 280). The categorization is based on how interpreters' speech production responds to primary parties' utterances. In this sense, the analysis can be said to be interactively oriented, yet the authors seem more interested in how interpreters think than in how people interact with interpreters, and it is not clear that the analytical resources they propose would be available to participants in interaction.

Interactively oriented approaches

Although Goffman, in both *Forms of Talk* and earlier work (e.g. Goffman 1967), under-scores that participants' (i.e. hearers' as well as speakers') behaviour in interaction, such as glances, gestures, and positionings, can transform the participation framework, Wadensjö's (1992, 1998) characterization of his models as designed to explore the dynamics of interaction is probably overstated. Goffman consistently talks about how participants shape each other's framing of events in face-to-face interaction, but his decomposition of 'hearer' and 'speaker' in his essay on "Footing" falls short of reflecting this. As Charles Goodwin points out, "in Footing, instead of collaborating together to build talk, speakers and hearers inhabit separate worlds, with quite different frameworks being used for the analysis of each" (2007: 28). Moreover, Goffman's main focus seems to be on the 'speaker'.

Understanding Goffman's notion of production format as comprising three *aspects of self* – animator, author, and principal – that participants can display and negotiate in interaction, Wadensjö (1992, 1998) suggests complementing this analytical cluster with another on the hearer's side, called the 'reception format'. The underlying idea is that interpreter-mediated discourse provides unique possibilities for studying how listeners (not least interpreters) align to the talk of others and to their own talk. By relating in different ways to others' utterances as and when they are exposed to them, participants can display and be ascribed a certain level of responsibility for content and for the progression of interaction. The reception format model comprises three modes of listening – as *reporter*, *recapitulator*, and *responder*. A *reporter* takes on (or is ascribed) minimal responsibility for the content and the progression of interaction; a *recapitulator* takes on (or is ascribed) greater responsibility, and a *responder* is prepared/expected to subsequently relate to his or her own talk as animator, author, and, technically, as principal, that is, without referring to someone else as the authority behind it. In Wadensjö's reading, participation framework and participation status are analytical resources available not only to researchers, but also to participants in interaction.

In an article exploring an interpreter-mediated talk show interview, Wadensjö (2008b) suggests integrating Goffman's notions of 'hearer' and 'speaker' by looking at participation in interpreter-mediated interaction as pertaining to three analytical levels. First, participation can be seen as an issue of the social identities of those taking part. In established, institutional forms of talk – police interrogations, medical interviews, journalistic interviews, and so forth – participants have more or less established rights and responsibilities to participate in one way or another, which partly define the situation. Their view of the interpreter's (professional) identity can be more or less shared, obvious or obscure. Second, referring to Goffman's notion of participation framework, Wadensjö places the interpreter in the flexible position of *non-person* (Goffman 1959/1990), "on the borderline between the dominant encounter and the off-stage region(s), with a potential of being included among the ratified *participants* [...] and the *bystanders* [...] as well as being excluded from both groups to end up among the *overhearers*" (Wadensjö 2008b: 188). The third analytical level refers to the production format and reception format of talk – aspects of the speaking and listening self that participants can display or that can be ascribed to participants in interaction.

Wadensjö's interactively oriented approach to studying participation in interpreter-mediated interaction is in agreement with empirical analyses of participation in monolingual situations as performed, for example, by C. Goodwin (e.g. 1996, 2007) and M. H. Goodwin (1990). Other researchers working with interpreter-mediated discourse data, and applying Goffman's models of participation framework (or frameworks) with a focus on exploring participants' interaction rather than interpreters' mental states, include Metzger (1999), who investigates encounters between Deaf and hearing persons involving SIGNED LANGUAGE INTERPRETING, and Straniero Sergio (1999, 2013), who studied the organization of talk and social interaction in TALK SHOW INTERPRETING on television.

CECILIA WADENSJÖ

PAUSES

↑ FLUENCY

Pauses are interruptions in the flow of speech. Their pattern of occurrence, along with other features of oral production like SPEECH RATE, contributes to perception of a speaker's (or an interpreter's) FLUENCY. A common tendency, in linguistic description, is to equate prominent pauses with a lack of fluency and to consider them, like false starts, as errors of performance accompanying inefficient speech planning (Goffman 1981). This view is reflected in early psycholinguistic research identifying pause distribution with the speaker's 'cognitive rhythm', an alternation of hesitant and fluent delivery which Goldman-Eisler (1967) attributes to the fluctuating demands of linguistic planning. Looking at pauses in this way, as disfluencies, has obvious implications for the interpreter: awkward pausing detracts from the fluency which studies of USER EXPECTATIONS identify as a hallmark of QUALITY in an interpreter's performance.

However, pauses are not necessarily signs of hesitation. Occupying a considerable amount of speaking time even in monologic production by native speakers, they may sometimes be 'punctuation marks' for the listener's benefit or, in some cases, simple breathing spaces. In SIMULTANEOUS INTERPRETING, another possible reason for pausing is the interpreter's need to wait for more source speech input. To a certain extent, the position of the interpreter's pauses (coinciding, or out of step, with breaks in syntax and intonation), their duration and the presence or absence of vocalisation can help the researcher understand whether they are (un)intentional; ultimately, though, these features often allow only a tentative explanation. Additional insight can be gained by using RETROSPECTIVE PROTOCOLS, to focus on the interpreter's perception of why s/he paused at certain points (e.g. Mead 2002a).

Examining pauses, in both interpreting and monolingual production, raises various questions of definition: whether to focus only on silences with no vocal signal (silent, or unfilled pauses), or also to include non-phonemic vocalisations like 'um' or 'ah' (non-silent, or filled pauses); how to distinguish between filled and unfilled pauses, given their often mixed status; how to separate filled pauses from neighbouring sounds like vowels; and whether to specify a minimum duration (often set at 0.25 seconds), thus excluding articulatory pauses which are not related to planning processes.

Research on pauses in interpreting has, until now, focused essentially on CONFERENCE INTERPRETING; in DIALOGUE INTERPRETING, the alternation of often overlapping turns obviously makes the identification and cataloguing of pauses even more complex. In some contexts, this complexity can be further increased by pragmatic nuances: in a study of pauses in interpreted interviews in POLICE SETTINGS, for example, Nakane (2011) demonstrates that silent pauses before and after the suspect's utterances can be used by the interpreter as openings for TURN-TAKING, and thus for co-management of the questioning.

In conference interpreting, research on pauses mostly focuses on one of two main subjects: (i) quantitative analysis of interpreters' pauses, in relation to speaking time and to the constraints of the interpreting process; and, to a lesser extent, (ii) listeners' perception of the interpreter's fluency, according to how much s/he pauses.

The first of these topics includes EXPERIMENTAL RESEARCH on both consecutive and simultaneous interpreting. In one study of simultaneous interpretations by students (Tissi 2000), silent and filled pauses were often associated with hesitation and sometimes also with REPAIRS. In another experiment, professional simultaneous interpreters paused less when the source text was faster (Cecot 2001), suggesting that the rhythm of target language production (at least in simultaneous) varies with source text speed. In terms of differences in pausing between the speaker and the interpreter, a study based on three professional simultaneous interpretations of a lecture found that the interpreters' pauses were less frequent – but longer – than the lecturer's and accounted for about a third of their speaking time (Ahrens 2004, 2005a, 2007). Many pauses in the interpretations were communicatively effective, accompanying changes in INTONATION and syntactic breaks. In addition, almost half the pauses in two of the interpretations, and about a third in the remaining interpretation, were short (up to 0.4 seconds); long pauses (over 1.3 seconds) were less frequent, accounting for about 15 to 20% of the total.

In CONSECUTIVE INTERPRETING, the interpreter's rhythm is not subject to the same time constraints as in the simultaneous mode. Research on consecutive interpreting by individuals at different stages of training and professional practice suggests that, while seasoned interpreters pause significantly less than beginner students, the decrease as a function of experience is neither constant nor particularly rapid (Mead 2002c). Beginners' filled pauses may take up more speaking time than silent pauses, and also tend to disrupt the flow of speech by not coinciding with syntactic breaks (Mead 2005). This probably reflects both linguistic problems and process-related difficulties with practical needs like reading notes or retrieving background knowledge. Pausing also seems to differ in relation to DIRECTIONALITY, occupying more time in interpreting into the B language than into the A language (Mead 2002b).

The second focus of research on interpreters' pauses is how they affect audience perception (Pradas Macías 2006; Rennert 2010). When pauses and other disfluencies are used as independent variables, listeners' judgments of fluency differ accordingly, and also seem to affect their assessment of other parameters like ACCURACY. In Pradas Macías' study, three groups of listeners each heard a different interpretation of a lecture, by the same interpreter: two of the interpretations contained additional silent pauses of varying length and frequency. Listeners rated the interpretation without extra pauses highest for fluency and content; however, overall quality and other parameters like reliability were rated higher in the interpretations with more pauses. The lack of a consistent correlation between added pauses and scores on the various criteria assessed might, in part, reflect differences in the listeners' previous exposure to interpreting.

These studies illustrate one of the methodological issues raised earlier: whether to focus only on pauses above a certain duration. Two authors do so, with a threshold value of 0.25 seconds (Tissi 2000; Cecot 2001); others set no such limit (though pauses of less than about 0.2 seconds are arguably of little relevance to COMMUNICATIVE EFFECT and fluency). In addition, most – but not all – of the studies take only silent pauses into account. Comparability of data across studies is obviously affected by such differences, which in turn limits the scope for systematic exploration of related parameters such as the length of continuous speech segments (or 'runs') between one pause and the next (Mead 2005).

Methodologically, the study of pauses poses fewer problems than in the past, in that specialist phonetics equipment is no longer needed: a digital audio signal can be visualised on a computer as an oscillogram, a continuous wave pattern on which any segment (including silences) can be matched with the corresponding sound sequence and measured in milliseconds. Admittedly, this can be a labour-intensive task, but at least the technology is readily available. There have even been attempts at using it to measure silent pauses automatically (though this still leaves problems like pinpointing exactly where a silence ends and a slow-onset speech sound begins). The audio editing software needed for measurement can also be used to create or manipulate silent pauses in recordings (e.g. Rennert 2010), considerably facilitating the control of pause duration as an independent variable in studies of perceived fluency.

PETER MEAD

PEDAGOGY

↑ EDUCATION
→ ASSESSMENT, → CURRICULUM
↓ E-LEARNING, ↓ PRE-INTERPRETING EXERCISES, ↓ ROLE PLAY

While the HISTORY of interpreting dates back several thousand years, very little is known about how the individuals performing that task in former ages acquired the necessary skills.

Indeed, the idea that preparing interpreters for their work requires systematic EDUCATION is relatively new. For most of history, the only requirement for an interpreter seems to have been proficiency in two (or more) languages, usually acquired by immersion – as when Columbus shipped captured natives from the Americas to SPAIN, or European powers sent JEUNES DE LANGUES to Constantinople to learn the language and subsequently serve as interpreters.

Major advances occurred only in the early twentieth century, when new demands on interpreters' abilities, such as rendering entire conference speeches or performing the newly invented mode of 'telephonic' (simultaneous) interpreting, required the acquisition of special skills. Even so, the first generation of interpreters working at the League of Nations was self-taught. Aside from the program established at a business college in Mannheim in 1930 (Wilss 1999), it was not until 1941 that the first school for the training of conference interpreters – the *École d'interprètes* in Geneva – was founded. Instruction was mainly in the hands of self-trained interpreters with considerable professional experience, which gave rise to an enduring master–apprentice approach to teaching and learning. Other pedagogical approaches, and more specific instructional techniques, emerged only over time, inspired in part by insights from research and also driven by new forms of practice and advances in TECHNOLOGY. Common to all these is the need to respond to the fundamental question of pedagogy, that is, how best to teach – or 'train'. For interpreting, this mainly refers to instructional practices in a group setting, as shaped by a given CURRICULUM and also including the complex issue of ASSESSMENT. Nevertheless, interpreting pedagogy embodies more than the sum of its parts – the skill components, course syllabi, exercises and learning materials; ideally, it represents the incorporation of a theoretical view of the skill to be trained into a learning model that offers the flexibility needed to accommodate different cognitive styles, variable degrees of aptitude, and preferences for specific forms of learning, such as master–apprentice models, collaborative learning, tutor support and peer tutoring.

Most of the pedagogical know-how to date has been developed for training in CONFERENCE INTERPRETING, but recent developments in the practice and study of DIALOGUE INTERPRETING have also led to significant advances in interpreter training for community-based SETTINGS, with educational practices in SIGNED LANGUAGE INTERPRETING situated to a certain extent within both these domains.

Evolution

There was little mention of training for interpreters before they attracted widespread public attention through the provision of SIMULTANEOUS INTERPRETING (SI) at the NUREM-BERG TRIAL. Still, the training methods used by the Court's Translation Division headed by Léon DOSTERT remain rather poorly documented: mock trials were organized for about two weeks to two months, where interpreters-to-be would read documents to each other and improvise speeches with their colleagues interpreting simultaneously. With the speed of speeches increasing gradually, feedback was provided on the interpreters' ACCURACY, VOICE QUALITY and overall performance (Moser-Mercer 2005b). Highly talented recruits were assigned to live courtroom proceedings without prior training (Skuncke 1989). But even prior to Nuremberg, the International Labour Organization had organized training for simultaneous interpreters using a system whereby speeches delivered at previous conferences were read at progressively faster speeds and interpreted using a telephone-like installation (Baigorri-Jalón 2014). At about the same time, Russian interpreters performed SI at the Sixth Congress of the Comintern in Moscow (Gofman 1963), but nothing is known about their training.

The publication of Jean HERBERT's (1952) *Manuel de l'Interprète/Interpreter's Handbook* ushered in the era of pedagogical reflection on interpreter training. His recommendations related mainly to CONSECUTIVE INTERPRETING, and to NOTE-TAKING in particular, but also covered simultaneous, including such issues as keeping an appropriate and variable TIME LAG and physical distance from the microphone, noting figures, giving preference to accuracy over style, and recording oneself regularly to catch mistakes and improve one's delivery. While he favored a structured training program, he believed that self-coaching was feasible, by listening to lectures, the radio or sermons and interpreting 'silently', and supplementing this with written translation work to improve style. Significantly, Herbert recommends progression in the acquisition of interpreting skills and advises against fast reading of speeches for training purposes unless the trainee has reached a higher level of proficiency.

The next set of pedagogical recommendations was published by Gérard Ilg in the form of articles in successive issues of *L'Interprète*. Ilg (1958, 1958) refines Herbert's advice on training by paying particular attention to production and to the quality of the interpreter's mother tongue, thereby foreshadowing the tenets of the PARIS SCHOOL (Seleskovitch & Lederer 1989). Some two decades later, Longley (1978) published her account of the London Polytechnic's approach to interpreter training, which had evolved from Teddy Pilley's working party at the Linguist Club in London, where scores of interpreters had been informally trained in the early 1960s. Longley's account of an integrated approach to conference interpreter training that included both consecutive and simultaneous interpreting can be considered the first comprehensive overview of how curriculum design supports efficient training methods, and how cognitive psychology could be leveraged to inform APTITUDE TESTING.

The need for improved training methods was recognized in a series of colloquia on the teaching of interpreting that began in 1965 and culminated in the TRIESTE SYMPOSIUM, organized by the School of Translators and Interpreters at the University of Trieste in late 1986. The year the proceedings of that event went to press (Gran & Dodds 1989), SELESKOVITCH and Lederer (1989) published their *Pédagogie Raisonnée de l'Interprétation* – a first systematic and detailed theory-driven treatment of interpreting pedagogy, based on their *théorie du sens*.

Beginning with the VENICE SYMPOSIUM in 1977, the cognitive sciences increasingly influenced the study of the interpreting process, and the evolving MODELS began to inform interpreter training (Gerver 1976; Moser 1978; Gile 1995a). The underlying premises were that: (i) the interpreting process can be decomposed into different phases; (ii) different component skills contribute to the successful execution of the overall task (Moser-Mercer et al. 1997); (iii) discourse characteristics impact on meaning assembly; and (iv) a variety of external and internal variables determine the amount of cognitive resources available at different stages of task execution. These theoretical insights began to shape didactic choices in interpreter training in many universities. At the same time, the holistic Paris School framework was implemented in the European Commission's short training program ('SCIC stage') until it was replaced in 2001 with the new initiative, driven by the European Language Council, DG SCIC and DG INTE, of the European Masters in Conference Interpreting (EMCI).

The launching of the EMCI ushered in an era of harmonized curricula across graduate and postgraduate interpreter training programs, with emphasis on skill progression (moving from consecutive to simultaneous interpreting), the importance of background knowledge, simulated practice and student self-practice to develop EXPERTISE. The study of skill acquisition and expertise began to emerge as a promising approach to understanding cognitive potential and constraints in interpreting (Ericsson 2000; Moser-Mercer et al. 2000; Liu et al. 2004), and as a relevant theory-driven pedagogical framework for the acquisition of a complex skill.

In response to the need for more qualified trainers, AIIC started offering 'training of trainers' seminars, and similar efforts were made by the EMCI consortium as part of its mandate to ensure compliance with its quality standards. By the same token, training needs in less widely used languages led to the creation of a certificate program at the University of Geneva. First offered in 1996, the course was transformed in 2004 into the Master of Advanced Studies (MAS) in Interpreter Training, which is offered virtually to professional interpreters wishing to become interpreter trainers at university level.

The Geneva MAS and the EMCI core curriculum embed the concept of learner progression, the expertise approach to skill acquisition, the concept of self-training to encourage self-regulation of learning and performance, and clearly defined curricular benchmarks to ensure efficiency and efficacy in admission, training and assessment.

Beyond the skills acquired in a postgraduate degree program, additional training for graduates to meet the specific needs of institutional employers has been offered through various pedagogical initiatives by international organizations. Examples include internship programs as part of the UN's Language Outreach initiative, and bilateral Virtual Classes offered by DG SCIC and DG INTE in the framework of the EMCI. These initiatives strengthen the relations of training institutions with prospective employers, provide feedback from professional interpreters to students during training, and help implement the notion of simulated practice.

Whereas pedagogical developments in conference interpreter training reflect a distinct focus on Europe, the evolution of teaching methods and standards in the education of sign language interpreters took place primarily in the US. Promoted by the Conference of Interpreter Trainers (founded in 1979), pedagogical innovation found expression in numerous publications, not least in the volumes of the Interpreter Education book series by Gallaudet University Press edited by Cynthia Roy (e.g. Roy 2000b, 2005, 2006). Systematic interest in how to teach signed language interpreting has since become more widespread elsewhere, as reflected for instance in the efforts of the European Forum of Sign Language Interpreters (efsli). As signed language interpreting is mostly provided in community-based institutional settings, this field has offered valuable insights also to educators of spoken-language community interpreters, who had initially looked to conference interpreter training for relevant know-how.

Diversification and technology

The growing recognition of COMMUNITY INTERPRETING as a field of professional practice and object of research since the 1990s (see e.g. Hale 2007; Wadensjö et al. 2004) has highlighted the need to train increasing numbers of interpreters qualified to work professionally in this diverse domain. With more explicit legal provisions and performance standards to be adhered to in the various areas of LEGAL INTERPRETING and HEALTHCARE INTERPRETING, professional bodies such as EULITA (European Legal Interpreters and Translators Association) and the Massachusetts-based IMIA (International Medical Interpreters Association, formerly MMIA) have promoted more formal training requirements, both for basic and continuing education at bachelor's or master's level. Training programs for these specialized domains of interpreting are of more recent origin and span the entire range from one-hour webinars and self-training packages to programs at the BA and MA levels teaching the professional skills required for CERTIFICATION. Given this diversity of educational products, pedagogical approaches vary greatly, from plainly practical basic memory exercises promising to enhance consecutive interpreting skills to full-fledged higher education curricula.

In the emerging literature on community interpreter training (e.g. Corsellis 2008; Hale 2007, Ch. 6; Rudvin & Tomassini 2011), special attention is given to the use of ROLE PLAY as a way of simulating the interactional dynamics of authentic settings in the teaching environment (see Wadensjö 2014). Another trend is to engage with, and reflect on, authentic interpreting performances on the basis of transcripts available from DISCOURSE ANALYTICAL APPROACHES to research (e.g. Davitti & Pasquandrea 2014).

Though its professionalization is of more recent origin compared to conference interpreting, community interpreting, broadly defined, appears to be leading the pedagogical way towards life-long learning as a prerequisite for maintaining high standards of QUALITY throughout an interpreter's career. The building-block approach that characterizes much community inter-preter training incorporates different models of apprenticeship, self-study, skill-specific exercises and tutoring and mentoring for interpreters to reach progressively higher levels of pro-fessional COMPETENCE. In addition, more attention than in conference interpreting has been devoted to defining reliable and valid assessment methods (see Angelelli & Jacobson 2009) to help regulate entry into the PROFESSION.

Across professional domains, the training of interpreters is increasingly mediated through TECHNOLOGY. This includes a wide range of resources for COMPUTER ASSISTED INTERPRETER TRAINING as well as various forms of E-LEARNING, and multipoint videoconferencing to create virtual classrooms. Working with new technologies of this type in interpreting requires a reassessment of cognitive potential and constraints, and therefore new approaches to training. Learners have to acquire the strategies needed for handling multiple input media as used in REMOTE INTERPRETING; manipulating different devices such as tablets, computers and smart-phones in the booth; and orienting themselves in virtual environments that may even be populated by avatars (see Braun & Slater 2014). Without guided exposure to working with (and through) different digital media during their studies, students are ill-equipped to enter the market, whether in conference, legal or healthcare interpreting.

Pedagogical models for working in technology-rich environments are still few and far between. Guidelines are slowly being developed, but it is difficult to keep up with the speed of technological development. Trainers must thus rely on 'learning by doing', while prioritizing the development of adaptive expertise in interpreter trainees rather than simply focusing on slavish adherence to specific exercises and drills as a means of developing routine interpreting skills (Moser-Mercer 2008). As professional practice evolves, the key task of pedagogy may well be to ensure that trainees learn how to keep perfecting their skills – and remain motivated to do so – throughout their professional career.

BARBARA MOSER-MERCER

PEDIATRIC SETTINGS

↑ HEALTHCARE INTERPRETING

Pediatric consultations are triadic in nature and do not focus solely on physical health. They may concern the psychosocial development and wellbeing of the child, hence implicating cultural representations and norms. Multiple individuals, such as the child, the parents, and the health professional, are present and interact, which leads to the creation of multiple alliances and to the need to adapt communication to children.

The situation becomes even more intricate when the pediatric patient (child or adolescent), the family or both do not speak the language of the practitioner (Leanza 2011). In such a scenario, it is recommended that a professional interpreter be called upon to take part in the consultation. The benefits of professional HEALTHCARE INTERPRETING in pediatric settings are similar to those for adult populations. Thus, the use of trained interpreters has been found to ensure shorter hospital stays (Grover et al. 2012), higher satisfaction with care (Crossman et al. 2010), a reduced likelihood of suffering from serious medical events when hospitalized

(Flores et al. 2002), and more rational resource utilization by pediatricians (Hampers & McNulty 2002).

Even though these benefits are well known, it is seldom the case that pediatricians resort to these professional services (Abbe et al. 2006; Thompson et al. 2013). As in other healthcare settings, utilization of ad hoc interpreters (e.g. family member, patient, bilingual staff) is frequent, even though research has shown that ad hoc interpreters may disrupt relations between individuals involved, as well as their roles and duties. A further complication of interpreted pediatric consultations is the need to develop triple alliances, as there are four parties involved (e.g. practitioner to patient, to interpreter, to family). Decisively, an interpreted pediatric consultation is complex and attention should be paid to two specific features: issues relating to practice, and psychosocial issues.

Practice-related issues

Practice-related issues specific to interpreted pediatric consultations are the need to adapt communication to children, and challenges regarding evaluation and diagnosis (Rousseau et al. 2011). First, language (i.e. word choice) needs to be tailored to the child both by the practitioner and by the interpreter. If the interpreter does not communicate in a manner the child understands, the child might become apprehensive and uncooperative. Adapting one's language can be even more imperative when the pediatric patient is acting as an interpreter for the parents. Medical jargon is rarely understood by children, whether or not they engage in CHILD LANGUAGE BROKERING, and may be complicated even for adults. Moreover, authors emphasize the active role the interpreter should play as a cultural informant (Leanza 2005). The need to accommodate one's language and to pay attention to cultural cues is essential: not only are emotions expressed differently by children than by adults from the very outset, but the expression of emotion is also tinted by culture.

It can be challenging for a practitioner to evaluate a child's general development and, more specifically, the child's language development, when cultural and linguistic barriers prevail (Leanza 2011). Evaluating development in the child's second language is strongly discouraged, as it is difficult to distinguish between developmental delays and poor knowledge of the second language (Rousseau et al. 2011). An interpreter should thus play an active role in a pediatric consultation, helping to evaluate development in the child's first language and acting as a cultural informant. Consequently, the interpreter should possess, at a minimum, training and knowledge with regard to normal developmental milestones both in the host country and in the migrant's country of origin.

Psychosocial issues

Specific psychosocial issues may emanate from an interpreted pediatric consultation: disruptions of roles, disturbances in family dynamics, and identity struggles. Concerning role disruptions, qualitative studies demonstrate that allophone migrant parents see their capacity to care for their child affected, and role reversals between parent and child may occur when the pediatric patient is used as an interpreter (Gulati et al. 2012). Parents feel it is harder to provide comfort and to protect their child from upsetting information, and report feeling infantilized, helpless, and inadequate in advocating for their child's health needs (as they can do so only through an intermediary). In order to prevent parents feeling excluded, especially when their child is proficient in the host language, researchers emphasize the importance of translating every utterance (Rousseau et al. 2011). On the other hand, migrant parents proficient in the host language may feel obliged to act as interpreters. Studies have shown that this added role further increases the already heavy burden of caring for one's child, since the presence of the parent who interprets is always requested (Gulati et al. 2012).

Family dynamics may influence an interpreted pediatric consultation and identity struggles may be at stake (Cohen et al. 1999; Rousseau et al. 2011). More precisely, intergenerational conflicts may influence the course of the consultation. The interpreter should be sensitive to such conflicts in order to avoid further aggravating the situation. For instance, as cautioned by Rousseau et al. (2011), the language-proficient child could perceive the interpreter to be siding with the parents, since they speak the same language. On the contrary, the interpreter may also play an active role of cultural mediator to alleviate parent–child tensions.

With respect to identity issues, an interpreted pediatric consultation may support the child in reconciling coexisting identities. By observing the interpreter speaking and integrating two languages, the child may learn that it is possible to coordinate both languages and identities, thus raising the child's self-esteem and solving identity struggles (Leanza et al. 2014).

Given the multiple specific issues that arise in interpreter-mediated pediatric consultations, it is crucial to recognize the profound complexity of the interpreter's roles (since s/he is at once an accurate translator, a cultural informant, a development professional and a mediator), and to offer training to practitioners and interpreters. Unfortunately, research, training and guidelines pertaining to interpreting in pediatric settings are lacking. What research is available has been conducted mostly in North America, and more specifically in the United States. This limits knowledge of distinctive characteristics linked to pediatric consultations, which may involve different settings and dynamics from one country to another.

YVAN LEANZA AND RHÉA ROCQUE

PERSONALITY

The psychological construct of personality broadly relates to values, temperament, motivation, and coping strategies. Efforts to categorize personality types, such as the five-factor or 'Big Five' model, divide traits into openness to experience, conscientiousness, extraversion, agreeableness, and neuroticism/emotional stability (McCrae & Costa 2003). Conscientiousness and emotional stability are consistently identified as predictive of occupational performance within the field of interpreting, with the personality factor of high self-esteem appearing as a primary predictor of interpreter COMPETENCE (Bontempo et al. 2014). Extraversion, in turn, was hypothesized to distinguish interpreters from translators, but without conclusive results. While characterizing the 'typical' (conference) interpreter as outgoing, assertive, and self-assured, Henderson (1980, 1987), who applied Cattell's 16 Personality Factors questionnaire to two samples of professionals, found little evidence to support the stereotypical assumption of the extravert interpreter as opposed to the introvert translator.

In one of the earliest studies exploring the link between personality and interpreter proficiency, Schein (1974) correlated the psychological test scores of twenty signed language interpreters with an assessment of their interpreting performance: successful interpreters emerged as individuals who wish to be the center of attention, value their independence, and are not overly anxious or rigid. Rudser and Strong (1986) likewise identified several personal factors influencing the quality of an interpreted message, including educational level, intelligence, and sociability. Moreover, the personality factors documented in the literature to date as contributing to an 'effective interpreter' profile include the ability to adapt to speakers, public-speaking skills, and professional distance. Good self-concept, diplomacy and teamwork are seen as important for spoken-language interpreters, while the personality factor of dominance, which is seen in high scores in assertive, resourceful, confident, task-oriented, responsible, and stress-resistant traits is emphasized for sign language interpreters (see López Gómez et al. 2007).

Resistance to and self-control of STRESS have been identified as necessary prerequisites for SIMULTANEOUS INTERPRETING (Kurz 1997b; López Gómez et al. 2007), and highly skilled interpreters have been shown to be less anxious about taking professional risks than their less proficient colleagues (Macnamara et al. 2011). In related research, Bontempo and Napier (2011) established emotional stability as a salient predictor of an interpreter's self-perceived COMPETENCE, whereas interpreters with higher levels of negative affectivity, such as neuroticism, anxiety and reactivity to stress, reported lower levels of perceived competence. This is in line with Schein's (1974) earlier finding that interpreters with higher rates of anxiety, rigidity, and perseverative concerns received poorer performance ratings. In another sample of sign language interpreters, maladaptive perfectionistic traits, defined by self-criticism, were positively associated with vulnerability to stress, fewer coping resources, and higher rates of BURNOUT (Schwenke et al. 2014).

Given the role of personality traits in successful vocational performance, interpreting researchers have devoted increasing attention to their impact on the way students of interpreting cope with educational demands (e.g. Shaw 2011a). Research indicates that psychological variation has broad implications for the acquisition of new skills and competencies (Bontempo et al. 2014). In a review of over forty years of research in the area of interpreter aptitude, Russo (2011) highlights the undisputed importance of cognitive abilities, such as language processing and MEMORY, while acknowledging the complementary role of 'soft skills' such as motivation, level of anxiety, and other personality traits. Timarová and Salaets (2011) found that successful interpreting students were those with effective coping skills who performed well with medium to high levels of reported anxiety. Conversely, anxious students learn at a slower pace and have greater difficulty with testing. Shaw and Hughes (2006) identified confidence and 'learning ability' as critical for student interpreters, who are expected to demonstrate skill, accept ongoing feedback, incorporate information, and enhance performance.

TOMINA SCHWENKE

POLICE SETTINGS

↑ LEGAL INTERPRETING

Research on LEGAL INTERPRETING has primarily been concerned with the study of courtroom settings, and the less 'public' police interview received little attention before the late 1990s. Building on Wadensjö's (1998) *Interpreting as Interaction*, which aimed at dispelling the myth of the invisible public service interpreter and was partly based on data collected in police stations, three factors have contributed to placing police interpreting firmly on the research agenda: first, a growing demand for translation, interpreting and communication support services in all legal settings; second, legislation and policies which predicate access to fair proceedings on the right to interact with judicial authorities in one's preferred language and, third, a growing awareness that the involvement of an interpreter makes the gathering of reliable evidence more complex in pre-trial stages, which are a crucial prerequisite to the success of any subsequent court proceedings.

In addition, growing interest in the interpreter-mediated police interview is undoubtedly linked to the largely negative media coverage in some countries of the challenges faced by police and interpreting professionals. These include accusations of institutional racism and the need to manage the shift from interrogation to investigative interviewing for police officers, as well as the lack of professionalisation and related QUALITY issues for interpreters.

From interrogation to investigative interviewing

In the 1980s, there was a shift from the coercive questioning of suspects in order to obtain a confession, towards a more cooperative style of interviewing. This led to the PEACE framework and its five stages of 'Preparation, Explain and Engage, Account, Closure and Evaluation', used in England and Wales as well as in other parts of the world (Schollum 2005). With more focus on training in interview techniques and on their effectiveness, monolingual investigative interviewing has developed as a field of investigation. Recent cross-disciplinary efforts (e.g. Böser 2013; Heydon & Lai 2013) show that some of the interviewing strategies employed, for example eliciting free recall, conflict with the linguistic strategies of those involved in the interpreter-mediated interview.

The administration of cautions throws some of the challenges into sharp focus. Several authors, including Russell (2000) and Nakane (2007), have sought to address these by making suggestions such as the use of standardised translations in police stations to improve the delivery of cautions through interpreters.

Drawing on interdisciplinary insights from related fields such as forensic linguistics is advocated as vital for further detailed exploration of what happens when an interpreter is involved in the investigative interview (see Kredens & Morris 2010). The ultimate aim is to work towards guidelines based on the investigative interviewing protocols in use, so as to professionalise the integration of interpreting into police settings and activities (e.g. Perez & Wilson 2007).

A few research studies have focused on the impact of interpreter MEDIATION on police practices, procedures and constraints in specific judicial systems (e.g. Chan 1997, for New South Wales), whilst others have explored the interpreter's ROLE and interventions (e.g. Krouglov 1999; Fowler 2003), in particular around politeness (Nakane 2008), FOOTING shifts, FACE-related issues and TURN-TAKING (Komter 2005).

Role and role perceptions

There is a mismatch between expectations of legal (including police) and interpreting professionals regarding the interpreter's role. Police officers may refer to codes/guidelines prescribing that the interpreter will adhere to the *verbatim* conduit model of interpreting (often justified on the grounds that hearsay evidence is not admissible in court) in fulfillment of a static role, whereas interpreters often consider their role to be that of a communication facilitator (e.g. Ortega Herráez & Foulquié Rubio 2008).

The dichotomy between codes of ETHICS and the reality of professional practice in legal settings is not readily recognized by the professions involved. Yet the INVISIBILITY of the interpreter in the mediated police interview has been questioned by interpreting scholars, as interpreters are often found to intervene in their own right or effect a number of pragmatic shifts which impact on the transfer of the interviewers' intentions or strategies.

Therefore, the focus of research has moved towards discussion of the POWER differential, the intimidating or even traumatic nature of exchanges in police settings, and the interpreting process as one of ongoing negotiation between all participants (Mason 2009b). The interpreter's role is no longer a fixed notion, as s/he adjusts his/her POSITIONING throughout the exchange along a spectrum from invisibility at one end to advocacy at the other. This approach leads to better understanding of what adjustments need to be agreed between the police and interpreting professionals, depending on whether a victim, witness or suspect is interviewed, in order to facilitate communication rather than rely on prejudices about 'what should happen' according to codes/guidelines. One recent study using a relevance theoretic analysis of discourse markers (Blakemore & Gallai 2014) has come full circle, to reveal the paradox that the interpreter's visible interventions reinforce the perception of the invisible interpreter favoured by police authorities.

Other areas of investigation

In addition to increased interest in the interpreter's, as well as the police professional's, roles, or positionings, within the interaction (including the latter positioning the former as co-interviewer), there have been calls to include the interviewee's perspective so as to determine his/her role in the co-construction of meaning and identification of adequate solutions. Nakane's study (2011) of silent PAUSES makes a contribution to this area.

Other relevant areas of investigation include TELEPHONE INTERPRETING (Wadensjö 2009) and forms of video-mediated interpreting such as REMOTE INTERPRETING and VIDEOCONFERENCE INTERPRETING, investigated in the AVIDICUS projects with regard to viability, reliability and QUALITY as well as its impact on the interpreting process (Braun & Taylor 2012a).

Further topics in need of systematic study are interpreting (and translation) in police wiretapping operations, which often involve hybrid working modes and role-related challenges, and the role of interpreters in various types of crisis negotiation.

A major concern in its own right is the professionalisation of interpreting in police settings. Scholars such as Berk-Seligson (e.g. 2009) have long questioned the use of unqualified interpreters, in particular 'bilingual' officers, in police investigative work, concluding that such practices breach the rights of interviewees. The experience of, and studies conducted by, interpreting and police communities of practice have led to increased awareness that training needs should be addressed jointly, that is, through reciprocal training arrangements based, for example, on a co-participative situated learning model (Perez & Wilson 2011).

A strong impetus in this regard comes from Directive 2010/64/EU on the right to interpretation and translation in criminal proceedings, implemented by October 2013. It motivated several EU-supported knowledge exchange projects dealing with police interpreting provision. One of these, on Improving Police and Legal Interpreting (IMPLI) (2011–12), was concerned with developing cooperation between police officers and interpreter trainers to enhance interpreter-mediated interviewing practices with suspects, victims, witnesses and experts.

ISABELLE PEREZ

POSITIONING

The term position or positioning is used in interpreting studies in at least two ways. In a more abstract sense, the term is used to describe the continuously changing nature of interaction among the participants in interpreter-mediated communication. In this sense it is conceived as a more flexible alternative to the notion of ROLE, and as close, but not identical, to the concept of 'FOOTING' in the PARTICIPATION FRAMEWORK of interpreted interaction (Wadensjö 1998). While footing describes the chosen position of an individual speaker, 'positioning' is the result of negotiation among the participants, which might be either accepted or rejected by other participants in interpreter-mediated encounters. In an illustration of different positioning behaviours, Mason (2009b) shows how participants in an interpreted immigration interview discursively position themselves and others, and how they are in turn affected by the positionings of the other participants. For example, the interpreter appears to show solidarity with the illegal immigrant by suggesting an appropriate response, whereas in the next instance she shifts her positioning, adding her own questions and eliciting responses from the interviewee, thus appearing to function as a co-investigator with the immigration officer (2009b: 62).

In a more concrete sense, the term can be used to describe the physical position of the interpreter in face-to-face encounters. This is particularly relevant in SIGNED LANGUAGE INTERPRETING, where the interpreter must be visible to the deaf client. Depending on the nature of the client's disability, the positioning of the interpreter must be adjusted, for instance when working for visually impaired deaf clients (close-vision interpreting) or INTERPRETING FOR DEAFBLIND PERSONS using tactile signing. Different types of positioning of sign language interpreters have also been discussed for THEATER INTERPRETING, where the interpreters can follow the actors on the stage ('shadowing'), place themselves in an assigned zone on the stage or on the platform before the stage (platform interpreting), or stand on the stage or on a platform at the back of the stage (sightline interpreting) (Kilpatrick & Andrews 2009).

The positioning of the interpreter in the sense of their physical position in face-to-face interaction has been problematized, particularly with reference to DIALOGUE INTERPRETING in public service SETTINGS. Whereas the interpreter's seating position in COURTROOM INTERPRETING may be constrained by the furniture and by judicial preferences, it is relatively undetermined for interview-type encounters in COMMUNITY INTERPRETING, and in particular in HEALTHCARE INTERPRETING. There is a widespread assumption that interpreting in a medical environment should make use of a triangular seating arrangement, allowing the patient, provider and interpreter to maintain eye contact and, in particular, ensuring unobstructed mutual GAZE, and thus direct interaction, between the health professional and the patient. Such an arrangement is believed to symbolize the equality of all three parties involved, and to ensure that the interpreter is in a neutral position while still being integrated into the communication process. Having the three parties seated in this way is advocated in particular by Wadensjö (2001a). She examined interpreter proxemics in PSYCHOTHERAPY sessions, where patients were prompted by the therapists to recount traumatic events from their recent past, and found that a triangular seating arrangement had a positive influence on the experience of all the participants and on the outcome of the treatment. Wadensjö argues that this positioning allows the interpreter to be included in the shared communicative radius and sight-lines with other participants in the interpreted interaction.

Thus, many codes of conduct and guidelines for public service interpreters, in particular in healthcare settings, promote this triangular seating arrangement which permits direct eye contact between the patient and the healthcare provider. However, they often insist on the avoidance of eye contact with the interpreter. For example, the *Medical Interpreting Standards of Practice* of the International Medical Interpreters Association (IMIA 2007) stress that the interpreter should arrange the spatial configuration to support direct communication between provider and patient, and should strive to ensure that patient and provider address each other directly. Similarly, the *Best Practice Guide* published by the British National Health Service advises a healthcare provider to "arrange the room setting in a triangle allowing you and your service user or carer to look directly at each other with the interpreter placed neutrally in between" (Soondar 2008: 8).

Aside from the triangle, some guidelines call for the so-called parallel seating arrangement (e.g. Wiener & Rivera 2004), where the interpreter is positioned just beside and slightly behind the patient, with the interpreter's eyes slightly downcast in order to ensure maximum eye contact between the physician and the patient (see e.g. NHANES 2006).

Though a triangular seating arrangement is undoubtedly appropriate for some interpreter-assisted therapeutic encounters (Wadensjö 2001a), there is little ground to insist on this positioning for all medical interpreting sessions: the physical environment in which the interaction takes place often does not allow the interpreter to adopt the recommended position, and this difficulty can be compounded by different factors, such as the space taken up by equipment, furniture or sources of light, the presence of a nurse or other members of the patient's family, the type of examination and the nature of the patient's illness. Very few guidelines take this into account. A notable exception is the *Guide to Interpreter Positioning in Health Care Settings*, developed by the US National Council on Interpreting in Health Care (NCIHC 2003), which suggests that the position of the interpreter should be defined primarily by the situation and the circumstances.

While little is known about how interpreters in different settings actually deal with the issue of positioning, surveys among practitioners (e.g. Pokorn et al. 2013) show that the preferred position is still the triangle, followed by parallel positioning. This preference may be related to persistent assumptions about the need for INVISIBILITY, that is, keeping the interpreter 'out of sight' and regarding him/her as a mere conduit. Clearly, questions related to appropriate positioning and gaze behaviour, as well as their actual effect on the interpreter-mediated interaction, await much further research.

NIKE K. POKORN

POWER

Since interpreting is a socially situated activity, relations of power and control are inevitably involved in all interpreting events, whether overtly (as in COURTROOM INTERPRETING) or less apparently (as in simultaneous CONFERENCE INTERPRETING). The interpreter, as a social actor, stands at the centre of such events and, consciously or not, may through his or her agency reinforce, weaken, or otherwise affect the institutionalized balance of power that characterizes the event. It is relatively rare that these power relations become an issue or are explicitly mentioned during the event, as long as all participants accept and act according to their pre-established role. From time to time, however, such relations may be challenged and at all times close analysis of interpreted encounters will reveal the interplay of power and control in and around the event. Three broad areas of power disparities affecting interpreting can be distinguished: power relations between languages, institutional power and interactional power.

Power relations between languages

While all languages are equally capable of serving as efficient and effective means of communication, it is a well-known fact that some languages enjoy greater power and prestige than others. There has always been a tendency for dominant powers to hold other languages in low esteem. For example, the ancient Greeks referred to languages of other nations as 'barbarian' (Delisle & Woodsworth 1995; Roland 1999). In colonial times, imperial powers often regarded the languages of conquered peoples as 'primitive', not through any proven linguistic deficiency but rather through belief in the superior nature of their own civilization. Moreover signed languages have, until recent times, suffered from low esteem in many parts of the world (see e.g. Grbić 2001). The current hegemony of ENGLISH AS A LINGUA FRANCA often results in speakers at international conferences, out of choice or obligation, using English instead of their native language, thereby limiting their expressive capabilities. In immigration hearings, claimants are often obliged to use English even though it is their second or third language, because no interpreter is available for their own tongue. These unequal relations, often determined by a certain LANGUAGE POLICY (or lack thereof), have a marked effect not only on what certain participants are able to say but also on the value attached to what someone says when it is interpreted into another language and cultural setting. Blommaert (2005) provides numerous examples of the ways in which persons using African styles of speech and writing lose their 'voice' (that is, their ability to make themselves heard and be taken seriously) when translated into powerful European languages and settings. (The interpreter's room for manoeuvre in handling such discourses is discussed below, in the context of interactional power.) Conversely, the prestige attached to English frequently results in the transfer, through interpreting, of Western, English-language concepts to other languages and cultures.

Institutional power

Histories of interpreting abound with attested cases in which interpreters enjoy very little prestige or authority within the institutions that employ them. The use by European powers of slaves or detainees as interpreters is well documented, for instance in colonial SPAIN. While this practice may be a thing of the remote past, the issue of interpreters' relatively low standing persists. In war and CONFLICT ZONES, for instance, interpreters are afforded little protection, both during hostilities and in the aftermath. In the case of courtroom interpreting, Pym (1999) relates that the EXPERTISE of interpreters at the trial of American football star O. J. Simpson was routinely challenged by attorneys and judge, who suggested consulting outside academic experts rather than the interpreter on problems of translation. Meanwhile, in comparison to conference interpreters affiliated with and represented by professional bodies like AIIC, the STATUS of interpreters working in COMMUNITY INTERPRETING (public service interpreting) is reflected in their less advantageous WORKING CONDITIONS: they receive relatively low pay, little professional recognition, and, in many countries, are seen as replaceable by any available bilingual. Yet conference interpreters too are subject to institutional power. Even where their bicultural expertise might be useful in resolving misunderstandings, they are expected not to intervene but simply to translate what is said and not hold up proceedings.

Virtually all interpreting events take place within an institutional context. In some cases, such as in BUSINESS INTERPRETING, DIPLOMATIC INTERPRETING and MILITARY INTERPRETING, institutions employ interpreters to represent their own interests and thus expect them to align themselves with one side only. More broadly, the requirement for strict NEUTRALITY may conflict with the interpreter's sense of ETHICS and morality, especially in war zones (see Inghilleri 2012, Ch. 5). Moreover, the institutional setting itself predetermines how power is distributed among participants: immigration officials have more power than asylum seekers, police than suspects, judges than witnesses, doctors than patients, and so on. Persuasive accounts of these power relations have been offered in terms of Pierre Bourdieu's theory of social practice: the distribution of economic, social and cultural capital within any particular field, and the HABITUS of each participant as determined by their own capital (Inghilleri 2003, 2005a; Valero Garcés & Gauthier Blasi 2010). These studies bring to light the tensions involved in the interpreter's negotiation of institutional power and the uncertainties of their own position within the field. In general, the institutional pressure to maintain an illusion of transparency exerts a constraining influence on the interpreter, who is then faced with on-the-job decisions regarding their own INVISIBILITY and the extent to which it can be maintained or resisted.

Interactional power

In an early insight, Anderson (1976: 218) wrote of the interpreter possessing "the advantage of power inherent in all positions which control scarce resources". Thus, other participants are dependent on the interpreter to the extent that they do not possess bilingual expertise, thus allowing interpreters some degree of control over both their own behaviour and that of others. In face-to-face interpreting, they act as gate-keeper and/or manager of the exchange. They have more control than others over the allocation of turns at talk, even when one of the participants (e.g. a doctor) is institutionally ratified as coordinator (of a consultation). Interpreters can: (1) assume the position of co-interlocutor, asking questions as a supplement to or even in place of those put forward by the institutionally more powerful party (immigration officer, doctor, lawyer, etc.) – see for example Bolden (2000); (2) adjust or adapt discourses in order to give them more voice (Barsky 1996; Hale 1997c; Angelelli 2004a); (3) control the attribution of turns at talk, to their own advantage or to that of another party (Wadensjö 1998; Roy 2000a); (4) by re-framing a question in a particular way, steer an interviewee towards a preferred answer (Wadensjö 1998); (5) by their own active participation, deflect attention from what is being said by primary participants (Pöchhacker 2012a); (6) through body posture, GAZE or kinesics, exhibit an attitude that may tacitly cast doubt on or lend authority to what is being said (Mason 2012). That such things happen is attested and corroborated in many studies, including those cited here.

It is not suggested that interpreters necessarily choose to adopt any of these procedures. Rather, the institutional and interactional pressures to which they are routinely subject may lead them, in the brief moment available for selecting their next move, unconsciously to align themselves and their co-participants in particular ways. In ASYLUM SETTINGS or HEALTHCARE INTERPRETING, for example, long-serving interpreters become habituated to interview routines and will often act in order to keep the interview on track, eliciting the required answers by fine-tuning questions or asking supplementary ones where an answer has not been sufficiently informative. Conversely, where they feel that a reply is inadequate or in some way incoherent, they may seek to fill in gaps or otherwise make good a communicative deficit. Less visibly, conference interpreters also seek to optimize communication and thus may spontaneously be more explicit or more articulate in their rendition than is warranted by the speech they are translating. In the courtroom, institutional constraints tend to over-ride any spontaneous behaviour of this kind and impose a requirement to translate all that is said and only what is said. Much depends therefore on the preliminary NORMS (Toury 1995) of the institution that commissions the interpreter and the degree of latitude that these afford.

The interactional power of the interpreter described above may appear to be local and inci-dental, depending as it does on individual moves he or she makes. Viewed thus, interactional power may seem to be of little consequence in comparison to that of social and institutional forces. However, the effect of each move on the subsequent moves of other participants in a triadic exchange – described by Wadensjö (1998: 10) as a "*pas de trois*" – has to be taken into account. The direction in which an interpreted event unfolds may be determined by parti-cular moves at particular junctures, and a small and seemingly insignificant addition by the interpreter to an interviewer's question may have lasting consequences.

In reality, all three kinds of power relations described here – interlingual, institutional and interactional – work together and exert a strong influence on communication rights in any interpreted speech event. Interpreters' agency, their room for interactional manoeuvre, and their ability to use their expertise to ensure fairness or correct imbalances, are involved in a constant interplay between a pre-existing network of power relations and the acquiescence or resistance of each participant.

IAN MASON

PRE-INTERPRETING EXERCISES

↑ PEDAGOGY
↓ SHADOWING

Training implies an understanding or model of the skill to be taught. Opinions are divided as to whether a complex task like interpreting should be understood holistically or in terms of component skills, but most authors recommend preliminary exercises before attempting the full task, either in the first few weeks of a course (or as a preparatory module) or to warm up at the beginning of a class. These may consist of a simpler version of the task, such as short CONSECUTIVE INTERPRETING without notes before full consecutive, or same-language paraphrase before SIGHT INTERPRETING/TRANSLATION or SIMULTANEOUS INTERPRETING (SI); or they may specifically be designed to target one of several theorized stages or components of the interpreting process, such as analysis and COMPREHENSION, MEMORY, attention management or expressional FLUENCY in the working languages.

Pre-interpreting exercises may aim to prepare for interpreting in a particular mode, such as (typically) SI, but also consecutive (e.g. Bowen & Bowen 1984; Ilg & Lambert 1996; Weber 1989). The teacher may also set specific tasks relating to particular challenges in the interpreting process, such as the need for ANTICIPATION or for COMPRESSION in the case of high SPEECH RATE, or for dealing with proper names and NUMBERS; but exercises to practice such STRATEGIES are not, strictly speaking, preliminary.

Exercises for *analysis and comprehension*, which are also used in foreign-language teaching, are designed to enhance listening and understanding. Students might listen to a text spoken in a foreign language with a predefined task in mind, such as answering multiple-choice questions; filling in a form or template; transcribing; or accurately rendering specific items such as numbers, proper names or dates, which would require taking a simple note, analysing the text and/or producing an outline of its structure (e.g. Ballester & Jiménez Hurtado 1992; Gillies 2013; Jiménez Ivars 2012, Ch. 6; Kautz 2000, Ch. 5; Setton & Dawrant 2016).

Exercises to enhance *active listening* focus on the basic process of ANTICIPATION through knowledge mobilization (INFERENCING) (Chernov 2004; Moser 1978). Students may be asked to write a script on the general ideas expected to be included in a speech prior to listening to it, or listen to a speech and continue the ideas expressed once the speech has been interrupted. On a more specific linguistic level, such anticipation exercises often take the form of CLOZE tasks (Gillies 2013; Jiménez Ivars 2012, Ch. 8; Kalina 1998, Ch. 5), which have also been used in APTITUDE TESTING.

Exercises aimed at enhancing *expression* in students' active working languages may target VOICE QUALITY and diction, and public-speaking skills more generally. Language enhancement drills may be designed to speed up vocabulary retrieval and improve FLUENCY (Nolan 2005, Ch. 7, 13). One option is that of choosing a speaker and imitating as closely as possible his/her INTONATION, use of PAUSES and modulation (Jiménez Ivars 2012, Ch. 6; Setton & Dawrant 2016). Language enhancement to improve expression and presentation may also include exercises with synonyms, parataxis, hyperonyms, antonyms, re-expression, paraphrasing, formulating definitions without using taboo words, making prepared or improvised speeches, 'oralising' written text, practising the use of idiomatic expressions and set phrases, or connective exercises (Ballester & Jiménez Hurtado 1992; Gillies 2013; Nolan 2005; Viaggio 1988).

Paraphrasing, in which the meaning of a message is re-expressed using different lexical and syntactic resources, is worth special attention, as it comes very close to interpreting itself (Le Ny 1978) and helps the interpreter to convey the message without being constrained by the linguistic form of the original speech (Kalina 1998, Ch. 5; Lambert 1988b; Moser 1978; Moser-Mercer 1994b). This can be taken further by requiring trainees to re-express the content of a linguistically complex original more concisely but also accurately, using appropriate SEGMENTATION and link words, without unnecessary adornment (Lambert 1988b). This helps students identify the shortest possible equivalent expression (e.g. acronyms or anaphoric markers) and eliminate redundancy (Nolan 2005; Pérez-Luzardo 2005, Ch. 3).

Exercises targeting MEMORY and attention management aim to help students use their WORKING MEMORY to memorize key concepts rather than words (e.g. Kautz 2000). Interpreter training often begins with memorization exercises (without notes), and Zhong (2003) suggests following these with the introduction of specific techniques of categorization, generalization, comparison and description. Other exercises that develop memory skills include written or spoken summaries and translations of a text that has been listened to, dictation-translations, and variations on these themes (Pérez-Luzardo 2005, Ch.3).

With a view to the skill of simultaneous listening and speaking, as required in SI, some authors propose 'dual-task' exercises that consist of listening to a text while carrying out a different cognitive task (e.g. counting from one to a hundred, forwards or backwards, or reading another text out loud), after which students are asked questions about the text they listened to (Kalina 1998, Ch. 5; Lambert 1988a, 1989b; Moser 1978; Seleskovitch & Lederer 2002; Shiryaev 1982a). However, there are doubts about the usefulness of combining such cognitively unrelated tasks. Criticism has also been voiced against the use of SHADOWING as an exercise to practise simultaneous listening and speaking, as it operates on the word level rather than focusing on message comprehension (see Kurz 1992).

Most preliminary exercises described in the literature are centered on the skill set required in the two basic MODES of CONFERENCE INTERPRETING and foreground cognitive processing. More recent proposals also include theatrical training for interpreters (e.g. Bahadır 2011; Bendazzoli 2009; Cho & Roger 2010) to help trainees grow in confidence, manage anxiety and develop situation-based problem-solving skills, which may be of particular relevance for DIALOGUE INTERPRETING.

JESSICA PÉREZ-LUZARDO

PREPARATION

→ COGNITIVE LOAD

↓ TERMINOLOGY

Preparation for an interpreting assignment is a crucial element of QUALITY in all types of interpreting. In simultaneous CONFERENCE INTERPRETING, where information load in technical meetings can be particularly high, thorough preparation includes in-depth study of the subject matter, conceptual, terminological and translational preparation, and the collection of information on speakers, their attitudes or affiliations as well as on the composition of the audience; a major effort also goes into the preparation of available manuscripts or presentation material (see Gile 2002). In LEGAL INTERPRETING, the interpreter will prepare for the case at hand (e.g. a violent crime or a patent litigation) with a focus on subject-related TERMINOLOGY and knowledge, and for the legal procedures and terms used in this setting (e.g. González et al. 1991/2012). Likewise, the dialogue interpreter in community-based settings has to prepare for the demands of a specific institutional context and be aware of his/her role and responsibility in the discourse and also of the linguistic and cultural challenges that might arise during the act of communication. Interpreters therefore need as much advance information as possible, above all about the purpose of the event, the subject and the participants, in the form of available documents, briefings and background material.

Different phases of preparation can be distinguished: advance, last-minute and in-conference preparation (Gile 1995a) or, in broader terms, pre-process, peri-process, in-process and post-process activities (Kalina 2005b). Advance or pre-process preparation is geared to the acquisition of subject knowledge, whereas last-minute preparation often takes the form of a terminology search or merely the marking of manuscripts or presentation slides where available. As interpreters may be called, or assigned, at short notice, they often have to rely on last-minute preparation. In-conference preparation is necessary when manuscripts are not made available before a meeting, but only just before the speech is delivered, which in practice limits opportunities for teamwork in the booth where the boothmate may be in need of help.

The methods of preparation have changed considerably with technological progress. Until the 1980s, preparation was sometimes characterized as cumbersome and time-consuming (e.g. Schweda Nicholson 1989); since the 1990s the World Wide Web has brought immense advances (Dawrant 2000), and documents can nowadays be shared and exchanged through online platforms, cloud computing, etc. (Drechsel 2013). Speeches, information material, audio and video recordings – even of entire conferences – are accessible on the Internet, with the concomitant risk of information overflow.

Despite this progress, many interpreters still find it difficult to get hold of the documents they need most – that is, scripts of speeches where they exist, written documents read at court, restricted information etc. Speakers, and users of interpreting services in general, often fail to understand why interpreters, who, in their view, are only concerned with the linguistic aspects of a speech or dialogue, would need such information, and are reluctant to provide it. Such problems are also encountered in MEDIA INTERPRETING, with political speeches that are broadcast and interpreted live on television (Straniero Sergio 2011). On the other hand, there are occasionally full rehearsals with interpretation for events on TV, press conferences and product rollouts. An even higher degree of preparation is possible in NEWS INTERPRETING, where interpreters can be given a chance to preview the video material before interpreting it (see Tsuruta 2011).

Little is known about how interpreters actually prepare when they do get access to documents. Most practitioners presumably develop their own individual method of preparation, which may include various text marking strategies and the creation of terminological glossaries (Rütten 2007; Stoll 2009; Jiang 2013). SIGHT TRANSLATION/INTERPRETING is sometimes recommended as an effective way of activating vocabulary, but this has not been systematically documented. As proposed by Stoll (2009), the goal of preparation more generally is to shift cognitive effort upstream in the interpreting workflow, reducing COGNITIVE LOAD during interpreting by finding equivalents and constructing semantic fields and mental maps in the pre-process phase. Targeted preparation of this type is part of a complex process of knowledge management (see Rütten 2007) that will enable the interpreter to resort to STRATEGIES such as ANTICIPATION and INFERENCING. Such effects have been demonstrated by Díaz Galaz (2011) for specialised technical texts. In a carefully designed experiment, both experienced interpreters and novices were found to achieve better quality in interpreting difficult segments of technical texts when they had received material for advance preparation (Díaz Galaz et al. 2015). This study also suggests that prior preparation tends to be associated with a shorter ear–voice span (EVS), a possible indication that the cognitive demands involved in the interpreting process are reduced when the interpreter has prepared beforehand.

In view of its importance for the quality of interpreting, especially of technical texts, efficient subject- and setting-related preparation is an important component of interpreter training. Ways of acquiring general knowledge of the subject, reading and annotating conference documents, preparation of glossaries, methods of advance and in-conference preparation (Gile 2002) are taught, and the use of search tools and terminology databases is practised.

SYLVIA KALINA

PRINCIPAL

see under FOOTING

PRISON SETTINGS

↑ COMMUNITY INTERPRETING
→ NON-PROFESSIONAL INTERPRETING

The myriad of communicative events that might take place inside correctional facilities makes the nature of interpreting in these settings inherently diverse. Communication needs of foreign-language-speaking inmates go beyond their interactions with the legal system – and thus beyond LEGAL INTERPRETING – and permeate every corner of their daily routines in their interactions with prison officers, including not only security staff, but also treatment staff and prison management board members.

The encounters in which allophone prisoners participate cover an array of communicative events that includes almost every setting subsumed under the umbrella term COMMUNITY INTERPRETING, and a few particular scenarios. Foreign-language-speaking inmates, just like national ones, are involved in verbal communication related to many different needs and circumstances: admission procedures; health care, mental health and legal consultations; training courses; job opportunities; internal hearings; security processes; treatment program sessions, etc.

Such exchanges, potentially posing a need for DIALOGUE INTERPRETING, vary greatly in terms of frequency, duration, complexity and formality. For spontaneous informal interactions, non-mediated communication tends to be favored. This usually takes the form of a combination of basic use of the mainstream language by the prisoner, use of a foreign language by the officer – either the prisoner's, or a LINGUA FRANCA known by both – and several methods of nonverbal communication. The need for a language broker arises either when these mechanisms still prove unsuccessful or, in any case, when more demanding instances of message transfer are involved.

The international reality of prison interpreting shows that it is mostly NON-PROFESSIONAL INTERPRETING (by prisoners or, in fewer cases, officers themselves) that is used to bridge the language and culture gap. Commonly, this strategy is resorted to on an ad hoc basis, if and when the need arises, allowing for no planning or structure. In an attempt at formalization, a few prison systems (Australia, England and Wales, USA) have developed initiatives to provide a framework from which these informal interpreters can work, and which includes training opportunities and small compensations for prisoners and pay differentials for staff (Martínez-Gómez 2014a).

Professional interpreters have timidly found their way into this setting in countries long committed to the professionalization of community interpreting. However, even in these cases, they tend to be considered a complementary measure to ad hoc solutions. Their involvement remains limited to particularly complex and confidential exchanges (e.g. induction and disciplinary procedures, medical treatment and legal advice), and their services are often provided through TELEPHONE INTERPRETING (Martínez-Gómez 2014a).

Professional interpreters are slightly more common in the case of interactions between inmates and outside individuals or organizations, when the prison system is not responsible for contracting the interpreting service. Attorney–client interviews are often conducted with the help of trained interpreters brought in by counsel, if and when their fees can be defrayed by the prisoners themselves. In recent years, prisoners' appearances before the courts while they remain in custody at the correctional facility have been made possible through VIDEOCONFERENCE INTERPRETING (Braun & Taylor 2012a; Fowler 2013).

Nevertheless, the extent to which professional interpreters are involved in prison work is still so limited that there is little incentive for training. The unique and commendable initiative of the Prison Service Add-on to the Diploma in Public Service Interpreting in the UK, a three-day training course focusing on this particular setting, was discontinued after one year.

A potential contributing factor to the slow professionalization of prison interpreting is the scarce support provided by relevant legal instruments. Although prisoners' communication rights are envisaged in most systems to a greater or lesser extent, provisions explicitly mentioning interpreting are not only rare but also phrased in such general terms that they fail to provide a clear definition of the profile of the interpreter, their tasks, rights, responsibilities, etc. Such provisions thus leave the door open to the perpetuation of non-professional interpreting in correctional facilities.

This language brokering approach, however, raises numerous questions and concerns – many of them common to those generally voiced in other community interpreting settings. Issues of ROLE, QUALITY and TRUST, the POWER invested in the interpreter, threats to CONFIDENTIALITY, etc., have stirred attention not only within the interpreting community but also in neighboring disciplines (e.g. van Kalmthout et al. 2007). Research in this area nevertheless remains scarce and isolated.

In INTERPRETING STUDIES, besides brief incidental references, only a few works have focused on prison interpreting itself. Descriptions of the state of the art (Colin & Morris 1996; Martínez-Gómez 2014a) have recently been complemented by works addressing thorny issues in greater depth. In this sense, Martínez-Gómez (2014b, 2015) engages in analyses of prisoners' interpretations from different perspectives, from NORMS to QUALITY, foregrounding the influence of interpersonal factors; and Baixauli-Olmos (2013) reflects on the contextual constraints imposed by the setting, including security procedures, physical surroundings and emotional burden, and analyzes them from a deontological perspective.

AÍDA MARTÍNEZ-GÓMEZ

PROBABILITY PREDICTION

see under ANTICIPATION

PROCESSING CAPACITY

see under EFFORT MODELS

PROFESSION

Interpreting as a profession has been a major topic of writings and research in INTERPRETING STUDIES. Handbooks on professional practice and applied research on a range of professional issues have contributed vitally to the construction and development of the profession. On the other hand, the interpreting profession has been an object of theorizing as well as empirical research.

Key concepts and approaches

In sociological research on occupations, the concepts of profession, professionalization and professionalism have been developed as central heuristic tools to explain the social position or development of occupational groups. In everyday language, the term 'profession' is used to refer to a type of occupation that requires special EDUCATION and skills, and consequently enjoys recognition and a certain STATUS in society. Although the term has been common in sociology since the early nineteenth century, its use is still controversial among social scientists. While some authors consider it an appropriate analytical concept for the study of archetypical occupational groups (e.g. in medicine or law), others refrain from using it in this general sense and treat it as a folk concept and an element of the subjective language of practitioners (Wrede 2012). As early as 1962, Becker (1976) pointed to the ambiguity of the term 'profession', with its descriptive as well as moral and evaluative sense, concluding that it should therefore be treated as a social symbol. Freidson (1988) argued, accordingly, that it makes sense to study professions only with reference to their specific historical and regional contexts, and not as a generalizable scientific concept with universally applicable traits.

The trait (or 'checklist') approach to distinguishing professions from occupations, which was prominent until the late 1960s, is a legacy of the Anglo-American functionalist school of thought. It focusses on functional and structural traits of an occupation, such as (a) a skill based on theoretical knowledge; (b) a skill requiring education and training; (c) demonstration of COMPETENCE by passing a test; (d) integrity by adherence to a code of ETHICS; (e) service for the public good; and (f) organization, none of which are universally acknowledged as essential (Millerson 1964).

In response to the criticism of the static concept of profession, the idea of a continuum has been introduced, which serves to defuse the controversy over how a profession is to be defined. According to this proposal, all occupations can be placed on a continuum extending from 'full professions' at one end, to 'semi-professions' in the middle and 'non-professions' at the other end. The process for achieving the status of a full profession is denoted as 'professionalization', while the reverse process is called 'de-professionalization' (Hermanowicz & Johnson 2014). This approach is in line with the idea that occupations are neither static nor monolithic, and do not necessarily fit into one single category. The idea of a continuum shifts attention from static conceptions of professions to social processes. Thus, Wilensky (1964) suggests a prototypical sequence of five stages of professionalization: (1) making the occupation full-time; (2) establishing formal training; (3) developing a professional association; (4) pushing for legalized protection; and (5) adopting a code of ethics. While Wilensky's model draws attention to the role of organizations and contexts, it still reflects the functional view of professional identity in terms of social prestige, foregrounding a limited number of professions as social elites.

Some authors therefore prefer to speak of a 'professional project' (Larson 1977), understood as a generalized course of collective action to forge a coherent IDEOLOGY. This line of thought has its roots in the early twentieth-century Chicago school of sociology, which is based on interactional social psychology and associated with such names as Elliot Freidson, Erving Goffman and Anselm Strauss. These scholars focussed on the 'social drama of work' (Wrede 2012: 1397) and sought to understand how face-to-face interactions are shaped by, and shape, social order. As a critical answer to the positivism of functionalist theorizing, the perspective on professional privilege and dominance, centred on the notion of power, became prominent in the 1970s through Freidson's (1970) study of the medical profession. Magali Sarfatti Larson's (1977) more system-based work views social mobility and market control not as reflections of expertise or ethical standards, but as the outcome of "an attempt to translate one order of scarce resources – special knowledge and skills – into another – social and economic rewards" (Larson 1977: xvii). Maintaining scarcity is seen as implying a tendency to monopoly, hence the need for a professional project to achieve this within recognized areas of EXPERTISE.

Unlike professionalization as a process, the concept of professionalism refers to the way practitioners define their collective social pursuits in terms of a 'work culture', including an ideology, value systems and ethics, as well as forms of (inter)action (Burkart 2006). Professionalism therefore comprises intrapersonal, interpersonal and public aspects. In sociology, professionalism was initially treated in a positive sense as a normative virtue, and subsequently, in a more pessimistic interpretation, as a successful ideology serving practitioners' occupational self-interest. In more recent approaches, professionalism is viewed as a discursive resource that has strong appeal for practitioners in their development of work identities and senses of self (Evetts 2014).

Most researchers now agree that there is no need to draw a clear-cut line between professions and other (expert) occupations. Evetts suggests a pragmatic operational definition, comprising "occupations which are predominantly service-sector and knowledge-based and achieved sometimes following years of higher/further education and specified years of vocational training and experience" (2014: 33). She adds that "sometimes professional groups are also elites with strong political links and connections, and some professional practitioners are licensed as a mechanism of market closure and the occupational control of the work".

Sociological theory and the interpreting profession(s)

The first handbooks on interpreting, focussing mainly on the tasks and abilities of conference interpreters, had a strong profession-building and status-raising effect. In his seminal *Handbook*, HERBERT (1952: 3) underscored the exceptional appeal of CONFERENCE INTERPRETING as a profession, describing it as "one of the fairest and loftiest occupations in the world of to-day". His rhetoric reflects the need to construct a positive image of what was then still a newly emerged field, and of an ideal practitioner as a model for those aspiring to join the profession, through a process of training and professional socialization.

Beyond profession-building publications, different scholars of interpreting as a profession have applied a number of SOCIOLOGICAL APPROACHES. The trait view of professions has been adopted especially in applied research motivated by professional policy issues in COMMUNITY INTERPRETING and SIGNED LANGUAGE INTERPRETING. Roberts (1994), for example, underlines the need for professionalization in terms of achieving 'objectives' or 'goals' that closely resemble the traits mentioned above. In a similar vein, Gentile, Ozolins and Vasilakakos (1996) list a set of elements central to professional socialization. More recently, Witter-Merithew and Johnson (2004) explicitly refer to 'trait theory' in their attempt to assess the degree of professionalization of signed language interpreting in the US with reference to nine traits.

Tseng (1992), in his unpublished master's thesis on the development of conference interpreting in Taiwan, took up the idea of a professionalization continuum consisting of successive phases. His model comprises four phases: (1) market disorder, (2) consensus and commitment, (3) publicity, and (4) professional autonomy (see Pöchhacker 2004a: 87). Tseng does not refer to Wilensky's five-stage model, and instead positions himself in the tradition of the 'power approach', acknowledging his interest in successful strategies to help achieve the status of a 'full-fledged profession' and acquire internal and external control.

Tseng's model has proved highly influential. Fenton (1993) and Mikkelson (1996) applied it to the emerging profession of community interpreting, and Grbić (1998) and Pollitt (1997) adapted it for accounts of professionalization in the field of signed language interpreting. On a broader conceptual level, Rudvin (2007) has taken up Freidson's idea of professionalism as ideology and discussed the cultural construction of professionalism and ethics with regard to differences between group-based and individualist identity-building processes.

Apart from the sociology of professions, Bourdieu's theory of practice, with its focus on the dynamics of power and the concepts of HABITUS, field and capital, has proved especially productive in the study of the interpreting profession(s). In (translation and) interpreting studies, the Bourdieusian framework has been not merely imported but also refined and complemented by other theoretical perspectives, drawing attention to intercultural and temporal aspects. Combining Bourdieu with the concept of NORMS, Inghilleri (2005a, 2006), in her work on interpreting in ASYLUM SETTINGS, demonstrates the impact of macro-social constraints on interpreting events and on the habitus of interpreters. She sees the interpreting profession as situated in contradictory spaces, which Bourdieu called 'zones of uncertainty'. Monzó (2005), studying the Spanish translation and interpreting professions in the legal field, combines Bourdieusian theory with Larson's notion of 'professional project'. She adopts an ACTION RESEARCH approach, with the aim of implementing actions to improve the socio-economic situation of the professions. With a similar focus on professional development and status, Prunč (2012b) uses Bourdieu's theory of symbolic forms to enrich his concept of 'translation culture', defined as "the set of norms, conventions, values and behavioural patterns used by all the partners involved in translation processes in a certain culture" (2012b: 2). Arguing that conference interpreters have managed to leverage all relevant forms of capital as 'symbolic capital' (and therefore status) in the social field of translation, he notes that the prevailing lack of recognition and status of community interpreters could be changed only through joint effort and solidarity in the translation culture concerned.

Starting from the assumption that professionalization implies processes of classification and typification, Grbić (2011) employs the concept of 'boundary work' as an explanatory framework in studying the construction of the sign language interpreting profession in Austria. Her special interest is in understanding the relational process of generating a shared sense of similarity and difference. Grbić (2014) extends the theoretical perspective to include the concept of habitus, so as to consider the enduring dispositions of the interpreters' differing biographical backgrounds. The relationship between micro-level experiences of community interpreters and macro-level structural factors is addressed by Guéry (2014), whose doctoral dissertation investigates the interplay of boundary work, 'ethics work' and 'emotional labour'.

Drawing on Giddens' theory of reflexivity and Schön's concept of reflective practice, Tipton (2008a, 2009) studies reflective practice in conference and community interpreting. Schön's idea of the 'reflective practitioner' was introduced in opposition to technical rationality: associating professional practice with complexity, uncertainty, instability and unpredictability, Schön challenged the role of standardized knowledge in developing problem solving and expertise, and emphasized the importance of reflection as a core element in professional growth.

Themes of research

Conceptualizing interpreting as a profession has involved classification in terms of MODES and SETTINGS, as well as an array of other typological parameters (e.g. Alexieva 1997). Special consideration has also been given to hybrid forms combining aspects of translation and interpreting, such as SIGHT TRANSLATION/INTERPRETING and signed language translation as well as FILM INTERPRETING and THEATER INTERPRETING. Rather than pursuing clear-cut definitions of such types and domains of work, preference has been given to a more fluid categorization (Pöchhacker 2004a). Nevertheless, some possible distinctions remain highly controversial and have a significant impact on efforts to promote professionalization. This concerns in particular the relationship between community interpreting and court interpreting. The latter has been construed as a domain within the broad area of interpreting in community-based settings (e.g. Hale 2007; Pöchhacker 2004a), but LEGAL INTERPRETING has been the focus of considerable boundary work underpinned by the existence of legal provisions and organizational structures. Similar trends can be discerned for HEALTHCARE INTERPRETING, as reflected in particular in efforts to establish CERTIFICATION.

Empirical research in the profession-oriented domain covers a wide variety of themes and approaches. While some studies take a holistic perspective on the profession as such, or on a given field of activity, others focus on particular aspects of the profession or professional practice. Topics range from the HISTORY and social status of the profession to the identity of interpreters and to actual workplace practices and constraints. While some authors draw on theoretical frameworks from the social sciences and/or use empirical research methods, it is not always easy to draw a clear line between 'professional writings' and 'academic research' (Pöchhacker 2004a).

Comprehensive accounts of the history of interpreting as a profession are rare (e.g. Baigorri-Jalón 2015), and most studies focus on practices in a particular region or country, such as CHINA, KOREA or SPAIN. Others address the recruitment, employment and practices of a specific group of interpreters, such as DRAGOMANS, or of interpreters at particular events, like the NUREMBERG TRIAL. Yet another type of study portrays individual professionals such as Paul MANTOUX or the first diplomatic interpreters in post-World War II JAPAN (Torikai 2009). Additionally, there has been some research on interpreters' MEMOIRS, turning attention to personal accounts and the subjective construction of a professional self-image.

The position and development of the profession in terms of professionalization processes has been an area of particular concern. The most common approach of applied research in this context has been functional, guided by professional policy issues as part of a more general effort to upgrade the profession. Sometimes building on trait theory or on Tseng's (1992) model, such studies identify a range of measures to put into practice. With a focus on the rather unexplored notion of control, Boéri (2015) discusses the role of 'internal players' (i.e. professional associations like AIIC, training institutions, practitioners, scholars and educators) in the development of the profession and control of the market. A complementary account by García-Beyaert (2015) presents case studies on the influence of 'external players' – made up of 'grantors', 'receivers' and 'providers' (including AGENCIES). Considering both professionalization and de-professionalization, García-Beyaert shows that the profession is far from monolithic, and is situated "within a complex social web of interests, powers, rights, and responsibilities" (2015: 45). Interprofessional relations have been of minor concern so far. Exceptions include a study by Tipton (2014) on the relations between interpreters and social workers, which draws on the Bourdieusian concepts of field, habitus and zones of uncertainty.

In a comprehensive theoretical account of parameters affecting the individual as well as the collective identity of interpreters, Rudvin (2015: 432) defines professional identity as "an aggregate set of beliefs, values, motives and experiences relating to work, shared by a definable group and leading to a professional role". Situated in a web of broader social, political and cultural contexts, professional identity is negotiated and often contested, resulting in multiple identity-building efforts at the social and individual levels. Professional identity has essentially been investigated with a focus on particular aspects such as status or ROLE, often by means of SURVEY RESEARCH on interpreters' attitudes and self-representation (e.g. Salaets & Van Gucht 2008; Setton & Guo 2011; Zwischenberger 2011).

The discursive construction of interpreters' identity has been investigated by Diriker (1999, 2004) in the meta-discourse of the profession as found in handbooks, codes of ethics, publications of professional organizations and the media. Other authors (e.g. Andres 2008; Kaindl & Spitzl 2014) have analyzed issues of professional role and identity in the depictions of FICTIONAL INTERPRETERS in literature and film.

Given the pivotal status of interpreting as a profession in the discipline of interpreting studies and its literature, there are few topics among those covered in this Encyclopedia that do not bear, directly or indirectly, on aspects of the profession and professional practice. A review of research on these numerous professional issues must therefore be accessed under the respective headings. For the purpose of the present overview, it will suffice to point to some of the main themes, such as the issues of occupational status, the interpreter's role and POWER, the significance of ethics and TRUST, standards of QUALITY, and the norms governing translation policy as well as strategic professional behaviour. Another set of relevant topics relates to the actual work and workplace of interpreters, including WORKING CONDITIONS and occupational STRESS, and their potential consequences for practitioners' health and well-being, as well as JOB SATISFACTION.

NADJA GRBIĆ

PROSODY

↑ NONVERBAL COMMUNICATION
→ FLUENCY
↓ INTONATION, ↓ PAUSES, ↓ SPEECH RATE

Prosody is a characteristic of oral language, and important in oral speech production, owing to the information it conveys. Since prosodic features go beyond isolatable phonological phenomena, they are also referred to as 'suprasegmentals' (Lehiste 1970).

Prosody comprises a series of individual suprasegmental phenomena of a tonal, dynamic and durational nature, which are linked to their respective acoustic parameters. Tonal phenomena are contingent upon the modification of fundamental frequency; they include INTONATION (pitch contour) and pitch range. Dynamic phenomena are based on the modulation of the acoustic parameter known as intensity, which results in the prosodic feature of loudness. Finally, durational phenomena are time-related, and their acoustic parameter is quantity. They include duration, speaking speed (SPEECH RATE and articulation rate), as well as PAUSES. There are also hybrid phenomena resulting from the interaction of tonal, dynamic and/or durational parameters. Prosodic stress ('accent') is a case in point, as is the more complex parameter of FLUENCY.

Prosody fulfills two main functions: it organizes the acoustic continuum (*structure*), and it emphasizes the contextually important elements of an utterance (*prominence*) (Ahrens 2005a). It thus helps listeners to process what is said, and in this way plays an important role in COMPREHENSION (Cutler 1983). In addition to organization and emphasis, prosody also has an indexical function, providing information about the speaker (GENDER, age, personality) and his or her emotional state (Scherer 1986). Moreover, there is a complementary-compensatory function: prosodic components can reinforce verbal elements or complete what was not said, and they may also compensate for the loss of certain elements of communication, for instance in whispering, where the tonal parameter of pitch is lost and where stress can be given only by varying intensity and duration.

In interpreting, prosody is of twofold importance. As professional speakers, interpreters must know how to make effective use of their voice and mode of speaking to ensure intelligibility in communicating the message. This requirement for an interpreter's vocal performance is repeatedly mentioned in the literature (e.g. Collados Aís 1998; Déjean le Féal 1990). No less important is the original speaker's prosody, as it provides the interpreter with signals that emphasize important elements and facilitate comprehension, particularly in cases such as irony. This was shown in an early empirical study by GERVER, who found that degraded source-speech prosody (i.e. flat intonation and the elimination of pauses in the experimental input material) significantly limited simultaneous interpreters' performance (Gerver 1976).

Most empirical research, however, has focused on the prosody of (simultaneous) interpreters. In her early psycholinguistic experiments, Goldman-Eisler (1968) investigated prosodic features such as pauses and hesitation as indicators of cognitive processes, in SIMULTANEOUS INTERPRETING and in spontaneous speech in general. More recent studies have focused on simultaneous interpreters' mode of speaking as such, which tends to be associated with certain anomalies. These include pauses in general, and hesitation pauses in particular; lack of consistent tempo; lengthening of syllables; anomalous stress; and conspicuous pitch movements, such as monotonous intonation or rising final pitch movements at the ends of sentences or units of meaning (e.g. Ahrens 2004, 2005a; Alexieva 1988; Collados Aís 1998; Lee 1999; Nafá Waasaf 2007; Shlesinger 1994; Williams 1995).

Studies on users' ASSESSMENT of QUALITY in simultaneous interpreting (e.g. Collados Aís 1998; Collados Aís et al. 2007; Rennert 2010) have shown that prosodic phenomena such as fluency, pauses and intonation can have a significant impact, as these are salient criteria by which listeners who do not speak the source language judge a simultaneous interpretation.

In CONSECUTIVE INTERPRETING, the interpreter's mode of speaking tends to be closer to what is typical of monolingual speech production, but may nevertheless be affected by the special processing requirements of memory retrieval and note-reading. Most studies on prosody in consecutive interpreters' output (e.g. Mead 2002a) consequently deal with hesitation and pausing phenomena.

BARBARA AHRENS

PSYCHIATRIC SETTINGS

see under MENTAL HEALTH SETTINGS

PSYCHOLINGUISTIC APPROACHES

↑ COGNITIVE APPROACHES

→ COMPREHENSION, → MEMORY, → WORKING MEMORY

Psycholinguistics is a subfield of cognitive psychology, concerned with how human language is acquired and used and what the underlying cognitive mechanisms are. Some of its main areas of study are language COMPREHENSION, WORKING MEMORY and speech production, all of which are central to interpreting. The insights gained from psycholinguistic research on these topics, as well as the experimental methods and tasks employed, can therefore be exploited in studying interpreting. In addition to the findings and methods of general psycholinguistics (with its traditional focus on monolingualism), those from the study of BILINGUALISM – an increasingly popular research domain in psycholinguistics – can also be used to learn about interpreting.

Though basic psycholinguistic processes must be assumed to be at work in all MODES of interpreting, psycholinguistic research on interpreting has focused primarily on SIMULTANEOUS

INTERPRETING (SI). A precedent was set in this respect by the pioneering work of Goldman-Eisler (e.g. 1967), on SEGMENTATION and PAUSES in SI. More recent psycholinguistic studies have tended to center on the assumed cognitive (sub)components of the full task. This is referred to as the 'basic skill', or 'component skill', approach to understanding SI.

In this approach, three research strategies can be distinguished. One is to examine whether performance on the (sub)component task in question (e.g. a comprehension task, or a task that measures working memory capacity) differs between simultaneous interpreters and other groups of participants and, if so, to explain why this is the case (e.g. Bajo et al. 2000; Christoffels et al. 2006; Padilla et al. 1995; Stavrakaki et al. 2012). The second strategy is to have the participants perform not only one or more tasks that are assumed to reflect the degree of proficiency in component skills of SI, but also full-fledged SI; performance on the isolated task(s) can then be directly related to SI as a whole (e.g. Christoffels et al. 2003; Tzou et al. 2012). The third path adopted is to find out whether executing the full task involves the modulation of one or more of its component parts, as compared to when these are performed in isolation. For instance, a researcher may try to find out whether the processes involved in source language comprehension during translation (and, by extension, also in interpreting) differ from those implicated when the same linguistic input is processed in normal speech comprehension (e.g. Macizo & Bajo 2006). As illustrated below, these three research strategies have been instrumental in identifying a number of the relevant subskills of SI.

Word recognition and word retrieval

Rapid, automatic word recognition and fluent word retrieval from MEMORY are important prerequisites for unobstructed language comprehension and production, respectively, even when a language user is involved in comprehension or production on its own rather than in both at the same time, as in SI. The more automatized word recognition and word retrieval, the more of the language user's limited attentional capacity can be dedicated to subcomponents of comprehension and production that defy automation. Automatic word processing is all the more important in interpreting, where the interpreter's resources must constantly be divided between comprehension and production and other subcomponents of SI (as illustrated in Daniel Gile's widely used EFFORT MODELS). The fact that professional interpreters can deal with the extremely demanding COGNITIVE LOAD imposed on them suggests that they may outperform other language users on tasks which reflect word-recognition and word-retrieval ability, and thus have more mental resources available for task components which cannot be automatized.

This hypothesis was given empirical support by Bajo et al. (2000), who found that in a self-paced reading task, professional interpreters read words faster than three other participant groups: bilinguals without any interpreting experience, but who are highly proficient in both their languages; second-year students in an interpreting program who had finished their training in translation but had yet to start their training in SI; and control participants, who were professionals in other fields holding university degrees. The professional interpreters were also faster than the other three groups in a semantic categorization task, in which they judged whether specific items (e.g. a chair) belong to a specific semantic category (e.g. furniture). These findings indicate that professional interpreters are relatively skilled in recognizing words and assigning meaning to them. A similar Dutch L1/English L2 study, focusing on word *retrieval*, showed that professional interpreters were better than a control group of bilingual university students untrained in SI at picture naming in English and at word translation from Dutch to English and vice versa (Christoffels et al. 2006). In contrast, the interpreters' performance on these tasks did not differ from that of a group of native Dutch speakers who were teachers of English. Similarly, a study with Greek L1 participants (Stavrakaki et al. 2012) showed only marginally higher semantic fluency scores for professional interpreters than for a group of foreign-language teachers, whereas the interpreters scored significantly higher than a control group of participants not professionally engaged in language use. These findings suggest that the superior word retrieval in interpreters may be due not to their experience with SI, the full task, but to specific training in lexical retrieval subskills. Plausibly, training programs for interpreters and foreign-language teachers both encompass the training of these subskills, which would explain why the two groups perform similarly on lexical retrieval tasks. But whatever the reason for their similar performance, the importance of fluent word retrieval as a subskill of SI is suggested by the high correlations between the interpreting performance of a group of bilingual participants without any prior interpreting experience and the response times observed for them on word-translation and picture-naming tasks (Christoffels et al. 2003): higher-quality SI output was associated with shorter response times on these tasks.

Memory

Several psycholinguistic studies have compared memory skills in interpreters and other participant groups (e.g. Bajo et al. 2000; Christoffels et al. 2006; Padilla et al. 1995; Tzou et al. 2012; Stavrakaki et al. 2012). The participants in these studies performed traditional short-term memory tasks, working memory tasks, or both. Short-term memory tasks, such as the 'word span' and 'digit span' tasks, are designed to test memory storage capacity, whereas working memory tasks such as the 'reading span' task (Daneman & Carpenter 1980) are devised to test the ability to simultaneously process and store information in memory. In all of these tasks, participants are presented with progressively larger series of input items (words, digits, sentences) and asked to recall these (or recall the sentence-final words). Testing stops the moment the participant fails to correctly recall all the items in the last series.

Interpreters usually do better on these tasks than other groups of language users. Padilla et al. (1995) and Bajo et al. (2000) showed that professional interpreters have higher recall scores on the digit span and reading span tasks than interpreting students and a control group of non-interpreters. Christoffels et al. (2006) found professional interpreters to have higher scores on the word span and reading span tasks than a control group of unbalanced bilingual university students without any SI training; the interpreters also performed better on the 'speaking span' task, an analogue of the reading span task designed to test the ability to produce sentences while simultaneously remembering language material, something that interpreters must clearly do. In Stavrakaki et al. (2012), a group of interpreters similarly outperformed a control group on the digit span and word span tasks. Interestingly, the interpreters in Christoffels et al. (2006) also scored better on all three memory measures than a group of teachers of L2 English. On the assumption that training programs for foreign-language teachers do not (at least to any appreciable degree) involve specific training in SI or memory training, whereas those for simultaneous interpreters do, these findings strongly suggest that the superior memory performance shown by the latter results from this specific training (including their on-the-job experience with SI). This view is supported by the results of a Mandarin/English study by Tzou et al. (2012), who found that interpreting students approaching the end of the second and final year in their graduate interpreter training program had higher digit spans and reading spans in both languages than graduate students in other fields of study. The participants in this study not only performed a set of memory span tasks but also actually interpreted a speech fragment. The same holds for an earlier study by Christoffels et al. (2003). In both studies, positive correlations between memory span measures and measures of SI QUALITY were observed. All these findings underscore the importance of superior memory skills for satisfactory SI, and indicate that the former develop from practicing the latter.

Modulation of subcomponents of SI

Having to execute all component processes of SI concurrently may well cause some or all of its separate components to be carried out differently from the way they are performed in isolation. Several studies support this idea, among them a number that examined the effect of 'articulatory suppression' (AS) on verbal recall in professional interpreters and other groups of language users (Bajo et al. 2000; Padilla et al. 1995; Yudes et al. 2012). The participants in these studies learn lists of stimuli, most often words. In a relatively simple AS condition, they are instructed to concurrently and uninterruptedly produce one and the same irrelevant syllable (e.g. 'bla' or 'pa'); in a complex AS condition, they must concurrently utter a small set of words (e.g. the word triad *'mesa, silla, sillón'* in Yudes et al. 2012). Performance in the AS condition(s) is compared to that in a non-AS condition, where participants can concentrate on the learning task in silence. AS is known to disrupt the rehearsal of the stimuli to be learned, and thus to adversely affect retention in common language users. Because interpreters must constantly memorize linguistic material while concurrently uttering language output, the question arises whether they might fare differently on this task.

Interestingly, concurrent AS did not negatively affect the interpreters' learning, except when in a complex (but not in a simple) AS condition, lists of pseudo-words instead of words had to be learned (Yudes et al. 2012). In contrast, both simple and complex AS adversely influenced word and pseudo-word learning in a group of monolinguals. This suggests that interpreting experience modulates memorization strategies. The recall scores for a group of student interpreters indicated that the changes involved already develop during initial SI training: this group's scores, while lower for both words and pseudo-words in the complex AS condition than in the silent condition, were not negatively affected by simple AS.

That performance on a complex task may involve modulated performance on component tasks, as compared with performing the latter on their own, also emerges from studies in which sentence reading was compared in two conditions: 'reading for repetition', where participants (translators and bilingual controls) had to repeat sentences after reading them; and 'reading for translation', where they had to translate them after reading (Macizo & Bajo 2006; Ruiz et al. 2008). Various manipulations of the stimulus materials, all devised to discover whether activation of the other language occurs *during* sentence reading, affected reading for translation but not reading for repetition. Importantly, the patterns of results always suggested that during reading for translation, but not during reading for repetition, words and grammatical structures in the input sentences *immediately* activated translation-equivalent structures in the output language. In other words, the results indicate that translation is not based (solely) on conceptual MEDIATION but also involves TRANSCODING (see e.g. Paradis 1994). Even though these studies did not include interpreters as participants, there is no obvious reason why the results would not also apply to interpreters.

ANNETTE M. B. DE GROOT AND INGRID K. CHRISTOFFELS

PSYCHOMETRIC TESTS

↑ ASSESSMENT
→ APTITUDE TESTING, → CERTIFICATION, → PERSONALITY, → STRESS

Psychometric tests are a class of tests which measure human abilities, attitudes and PERSONALITY. The measurement is quantitative (i.e. expressed by a numerical score) and the tests are standardized. Standardization means that the same test is administered, under the same conditions, to all test takers and that all tests are scored in the same way, often by computer. Standardized tests allow comparison of individual scores. For this information to be valid, test administration, scoring and interpretation must adhere to strict criteria defined as part of the standards.

Apart from standardization, a psychometric test may be normed, i.e. administered to a large sample of individuals in a predefined population whose scores then provide a norm against which future individual scores will be compared. Intelligence tests are a case in point. A more common approach is criterion-referenced testing, in which performance on a test is compared to a certain predefined level. This type of testing is widely used for measuring learning progress and achievement in educational settings, as well as for professional credentialing.

A test with good psychometric properties has to satisfy a number of criteria, including a sound theoretical or empirical rationale for the construct (ability, trait) to be tested (its relevance to the goal of testing), the relationship between the construct and the test (whether the test measures the intended construct), content validity of the test, reliability of the test score and fairness. There must be clear test administration specifications, rating and scoring instructions as well as detailed procedures for interpreting the results, and also a clearly stated purpose and a well-defined target population (see e.g. Kaplan & Saccuzzo 2012).

In interpreting studies, more specifically in interpreter EDUCATION and ASSESSMENT, psychometric principles of test development are not generally respected. Sawyer (2000) criticises current practices in interpreter assessment, claiming that evaluation is too intuitive and not sufficiently based on sound principles of measurement and testing. Such concerns are particularly relevant in contexts where high-stakes decisions are made, such as final examinations at the end of interpreter training and, especially, professional CERTIFICATION. With regard to the latter, Clifford (2005) discusses principles of psychometric test development in a study focusing on the validity of an existing Canadian certification test compared to a newly designed test.

Developing a psychometrically sound test requires specialist education and substantial resources. Some countries have highly developed interpreter certification programmes based on psychometric methods. Among the largest are the Federal Court Interpreter Certification Examination (FCICE) in the United States (e.g. FCICE 2014) and the certification scheme of the US Registry of Interpreters for the Deaf (RID). Both of these cater to a fairly large and homogenous population of interpreters. The FCICE, for example, offers certification only for the English/Spanish language combination, and the estimated cost of running the programme is several hundred thousand dollars annually.

Aside from their employment in determining levels of educational achievement and professional qualifications, psychometric tests have also been used in research on interpreters' psychological traits and mental faculties. In a rare example of using a norm-referenced test, Schweda Nicholson (2005) administered the Myers-Briggs Type Inventory, a well-established personality test, to a sample of 68 interpreting students in order to investigate whether there is a 'typical interpreter' personality profile. Her findings show that, while no single interpreter personality emerged, the sample included a substantially higher proportion of 'thinkers' (on the test's Thinking vs. Feeling scale) than is typical for the general population, especially considering the overrepresentation of women among interpreters (see also Bontempo & Napier 2009).

Other studies among interpreters have used existing tests for their psychometric properties, such as validity, reliability and a well-developed theoretical construct, in providing quantitative information about the sample, often without reference to the standard or norm. To investigate the role of STRESS in interpreting, for example, several researchers have employed the State-Trait Anxiety Inventory both in students (Jiménez Ivars & Pinazo Calatayud 2001; Chiang 2010) and in professional interpreters (Kurz 1997b). A number of studies have used psychometric instruments for testing specific personality traits, such as motivation (Shaw 2011a), affect and self-efficacy (Bontempo & Napier 2011), communication competence (Rosiers et al. 2011), foreign-language anxiety (Chiang 2009), dominance and self-strength (López Gómez et al. 2007), often with a view to finding traits which can be used as predictors of interpreter COMPETENCE and interpreting skill acquisition in the context of CURRICULUM design and APTITUDE TESTING.

Apart from using validated psychometric tests from outside interpreting studies, there is also a trend towards developing interpreter-specific instruments or adapting generic psychometric tests for use with interpreters (e.g. Angelelli 2004b; Lee 2014). Given the principles on which a valid psychometric test must be based, these efforts require access to substantial samples of individuals. As a consequence, new tests appear primarily in the US for sign language interpreters and students; they are also developed for large training programmes in Asia. Most of these tests tap personality traits and self-reported competences.

ŠÁRKA TIMAROVÁ

PSYCHOTHERAPY

↑ MENTAL HEALTH SETTINGS

Psychotherapy is a treatment method used in mental healthcare for psychic disorders and problems, in particular personality disorders. The patient can be an individual (child, adult or senior), a couple or a family, and treatment may be short or last several years. While there is a great variety of different schools and techniques, psychotherapy is essentially a 'talking cure': diagnosis and treatment, sometimes aided by psychological testing, are done through conversation ('sessions') between psychotherapist and patient. This crucial role of language poses special challenges when psychotherapist and client do not share a language, and an interpreter is required.

Interpreting in psychotherapy sessions has not been investigated very systematically to date. Most literature on interpreter-mediated psychotherapeutic interaction is based on anecdotal evidence, and often concerns the characteristics of therapeutic talk and the resulting challenges for interpreter behaviour. Research has been done from various disciplinary vantage points, by interpreters, linguists, communication specialists as well as therapists. Studies focus on the ROLE of the interpreter, specific difficulties in translation and the burden of dealing with emotionally charged material.

Publications dealing with *role* behaviour in this specific field have relied on anecdotal evidence or on a theoretical basis (Bot & Verrept 2013). Recommendations vary. Various authors (see Tribe & Raval 2002) advocate an extended role for the interpreter, in which there is room for 'cultural information' to be added, for 'cultural brokerage' or for the interpreter to act as a co-therapist. They argue that, without the addition of cultural information, mutual understanding will not take place. Thus, they favour a more target-language-oriented approach. Others promote a more restricted role, where the interpreter's main task is to translate, while recognising that the interpreter, through his/her presence (even if by telephone), has an impact both on the content and organisation of talk, through translation and coordination, and on the relationship between therapist and patient (e.g. Bot 2005; Bot &

Wadensjö 2004). This position emphasises the importance of source-oriented interpreting, which allows therapist and patient to perceive their misunderstandings and be aware of any differences. There is no evidence to show which role, under which circumstances, and for what kinds of patient, leads to the best results. Role behaviour thus still results from personal choices of the interpreter and the therapist involved.

There is very little research on the *translation* aspect of interpreting in psycho-therapeutic talk. Bot (2005) shows OMISSIONS of phatic tokens and referential phrases in six interpreter-mediated psychotherapy sessions, and concludes that problems in translation are mainly due to a target orientation and to interpreters' lack of knowledge about the aim of psychotherapeutic talk.

The position of the interpreter in the *therapeutic relationship* is another focus of attention. Bot (2005), for instance, mentions the importance for diagnostic purposes of therapists noticing patients' ability to deal with their dependence on the interpreter and with ambiguities in the translation process, and of taking into account how the patient treats the interpreter. In particular, personality problems may show in the patient–interpreter interaction. Transference and countertransference (i.e. the projection of feelings from patient to therapist and vice versa) occur between all three participants, with both positive and negative feelings having an impact on the session.

Much emphasis is also given to the burden for the interpreter of hearing and processing emotionally charged material, such as stories about atrocities and torture, and about patients in very difficult situations. Interpreters can come to suffer from BURNOUT and VICARIOUS TRAUMA.

Aside from dealing with victims of torture and traumatised refugees, special demands on interpreters have also been described for PEDIATRIC SETTINGS and for working with deaf persons. Recurrent topics include the organisation of the physical setting, issues of language and role, and especially the collaboration between therapist and interpreter (Cornes & Napier 2005; de Bruin & Brugmans 2006). Highlighting the multiple perspectives of cross-cultural therapy with deaf patients, the collective volume by Leigh (1999) describes mental health work with deaf patients from diverse social, cultural, ethnic and linguistic backgrounds, stressing the importance of the interplay between these characteristics and the deafness dimension.

Some work has also been published on *group therapy* with interpreters. Kennard, Roberts and Elliott (2002) describe group psychotherapy sessions in Russia with an English-speaking therapist and Russian-speaking therapists-in-training. The interpreter provided whispered SIMULTANEOUS INTERPRETING to the therapist, and some problems mentioned included omissions and misunderstandings of cultural significance.

HANNEKE BOT

PUBLIC SERVICE INTERPRETING

see COMMUNITY INTERPRETING

QUALITY

→ ETHICS, → NORMS, → ROLE, → WORKING CONDITIONS
↓ ASSESSMENT, ↓ COMMUNICATIVE EFFECT, ↓ ERROR ANALYSIS, ↓ QUALITY CRITERIA, ↓
USER EXPECTATIONS

Quality has been a crucial concern in all domains of the interpreting PROFESSION, and can be said to permeate most areas of INTERPRETING STUDIES, from the topic of individual qualifications to all aspects of task performance and to the way interpreting skills are acquired in training. On a superficial level, quality relates to something that is good or useful, or to behaviour that is sanctioned or expected. While quality has traditionally been viewed as a self-contained entity that can be achieved and controlled, it is now commonly regarded a complex and multifaceted concept that does not easily lend itself to empirical measurement. In what follows, the nature of this complex concept will be discussed, followed by a review of the state of the art in research on quality in interpreting in its textual, functional and institutional dimensions.

Conceptual complexity

Interpreting scholars do not have a single, universal and agreed definition of quality that could be applied to all interpreting events across historical, cultural and social contexts. Multiple, and sometimes even contradictory, definitions highlight different aspects of quality, depending on the object of study (i.e. interpreting in different SETTINGS or MODES) as well as on the aims of a given study, its underlying EPISTEMOLOGY and its theoretical approach.

In an analysis of how the concept of interpreting quality is constructed, Grbić (2008) discusses quality as *exception*, as *perfection*, and as *fitness for purpose*. While the idea of quality as exceptionally high performance has largely been displaced by the assumption that quality is a common feature that can (and must) be measured, fitness for purpose is reflected, for instance, in the ISO definition, which stipulates that a product or service must meet specified needs or requirements, but also in functionalist theoretical approaches to translation and interpreting.

The concept of quality can be applied to various dimensions: to material products, based on the recording (and possibly also TRANSCRIPTION) of an interpretation; to mental processes, for instance when an interpreter's output is analysed with regard to the use of certain STRATEGIES; or to social actions, as in the analysis of interpreter-mediated face-to-face interaction or of an entire conference event as HYPERTEXT.

The complexity of empirical research on quality in interpreting is related to the combination of three axiomatic features: (a) the variability of performance; (b) the relativity of judgements depending on the evaluators' perspective(s); and (c) the relativity of the evaluation process with reference to certain criteria.

Variability describes the relationship between the dimensions of immediacy and the choices made. Interpreting is a complex cognitive, linguistic, cultural and social process, with a range of different factors influencing any given performance. Thus, immediacy shapes the interpreting situation as well as the features of the utterance to be interpreted, forcing the interpreter to make cognitive, linguistic, ethical and other choices from the various options at his/her disposal. It has been shown that even in (quasi-)experimental studies, where the impact of external factors is kept to a minimum, there is considerable performance variability between subjects (Lamberger-Felber 2003), and also a high degree of variability in individual participants' interpretations of the same speech (Gile 1999a). The relativity of quality judgements is seen in the fact that evaluations vary not only between different groups of people (such as users, clients, peers, etc.), but also within a seemingly 'homogeneous' group (see Gile 1999b; Kurz 2001). Since judgements are always relative to certain QUALITY CRITERIA, there are bound to be expectations or requirements that can be fulfilled to a greater or lesser extent.

Measurement and evaluation

In early experimental research on SIMULTANEOUS INTERPRETING, quality was studied by measuring ACCURACY in terms of source–target correspondence. Early attempts at assessing output quality focussed on ERROR ANALYSIS, classifying and analysing various kinds of 'translation departures' (Barik 1975), such as OMISSIONS. More recent studies, based on authentic speeches, relate such phenomena to strategic choices by the interpreter (e.g. Napier 2002, 2004b) or use data to investigate difficulties specific to a given language pair (Gile 2011).

EXPERIMENTAL RESEARCH using output quality as the dependent variable has also been conducted to test the effect of INPUT VARIABLES, such as SPEECH RATE or ACCENT, on (simultaneous) interpreters' performance. A particular type of 'deviation', in this case from target-language norms, is INTERFERENCE, which has been studied in relation to processing constraints in different modes, including SIMULTANEOUS WITH TEXT. Constraints on interpreting quality have also been investigated with regard to WORKING CONDITIONS (sound, booth conditions, VISUAL ACCESS) and technological challenges in the realm of REMOTE INTERPRETING.

Research on quality in interpreting has also been conducted in the form of case studies, using authentic corpora. A noteworthy example is Cokely (1992a, 1992b), who analysed types and frequencies of 'miscues' in SIGNED LANGUAGE INTERPRETING in a conference setting. Pöchhacker (1994a) combined a text-based analysis with a comprehensive account of situational factors and contextual conditions in his study of spoken-language simultaneous interpreting at the level of an entire conference.

Quality measurement and evaluation are central concerns in interpreter EDUCATION and CERTIFICATION. Whether in admission tests, in the formative and summative ASSESSMENT of student interpreters' performance, or in certification procedures before a national board, the development of evaluation criteria and assessment instruments remains a substantial challenge (see Sawyer 2004).

In studies of EXPERTISE in interpreting, which often serve as a foundation for training and quality assessment, researchers have related quality assessment to the investigation of cognitive processes underlying the superior performance of expert practitioners. Within the EXPERT–NOVICE PARADIGM, developmental differences in interpreting COMPETENCE and skill have been studied by comparing the performance of experts to those of novices or non-interpreters (e.g. Moser-Mercer et al. 2000; Liu 2008).

Quality is a major concern in a much broader sense in COMMUNITY INTERPRETING, where a certain level of professional service delivery has yet to be assured. Discourse-based case studies therefore include examples of NON-PROFESSIONAL INTERPRETING, calling attention to the potential negative effects caused by untrained or inexperienced interpreters who lack awareness of issues such as accuracy or ROLE (Pöchhacker & Kadrić 1999).

Whereas quality measurement and evaluation were once limited to issues of source–target correspondence and target-text accuracy, often based on an abstract concept of 'optimum quality' (e.g. Moser-Mercer 1996), researchers have increasingly taken a broader view of the subject, including pragmatic, situational and cultural factors. This is particularly evident in the field of community interpreting. With this in mind, Pöchhacker (2001) proposes an 'onion' model of superimposed standards of quality, ranging from 'accurate rendition of source' and 'adequate target-language expression' to 'equivalent intended effect' and 'successful communicative interaction'.

Pragmatic and communicative effect

One branch of predominantly (quasi-)experimental studies of interpreting quality examines the effect of interpreters' performance on their listeners by manipulating features of output quality. In her research on COURTROOM INTERPRETING, Berk-Seligson (1988) presented mock jurors with two stylistically different versions of interpreted witness testimony. Her findings highlight the impact of REGISTER on mock jurors' perceptions of witnesses' intelligence and trustworthiness. Collados Aís (1998, 1998/2002) focussed on the role of NONVERBAL COMMU-NICATION in simultaneous interpreting and demonstrated the extent to which monotonous INTONATION may have a negative effect on the overall evaluation of an interpreting product.

Whereas these studies using manipulated target texts focus on judgements of the affective qualities of an interpretation, others have addressed the cognitive or COMMUNICATIVE EFFECT of the interpretation on the audience. In line with the axiom that an interpretation should produce the same effect and have the same cognitive content as the source speech (e.g. Déjean le Féal 1990), these studies use the degree of listener COMPREHENSION as an indicator of quality, and measure it with questionnaire-based comprehension tests in simulated communicative events (e.g. Marschark et al. 2004; Reithofer 2013).

Service quality and quality management

When interpreting is treated as a service to a customer, quality can be investigated externally in terms of USER EXPECTATIONS, or internally in terms of the quality culture of a given organization or institution. From the client-centred perspective, questionnaire-based SURVEY RESEARCH has been conducted to ask conference participants in hypothetical terms about the importance they attach to certain criteria. This amounts to the elicitation of what Chesterman (1993) calls 'expectancy norms' and implies that quality is construed as compliance with prevailing translational NORMS, defined as social notions of correctness and internalized models of behaviour. When interpreting is conceptualized as a norm-driven process, questions of responsibility and ethical behaviour come to the fore. With regard to ETHICS, the idea of a 'good' interpreter may be derived from values such as clarity (with regard to language), truth (with regard to source–target correspondence), TRUST (with regard to interpersonal qualities) and understanding (in the sense of responsibility to others) (Chesterman 1997a).

In community interpreting, expectations and perceptions of quality as well as the assessment of actual service provision have been studied among both clients and professional service providers, using quantitative as well as qualitative methods (see Hale 2006; Pöchhacker 2006b). It is hardly surprising that, in these settings, users' expectations may conflict, their understanding of 'good' interpreting often being linked to personal factors such as 'character' and interpersonal criteria such as trust (Edwards et al. 2005).

Kalina (2005b) has developed a framework for quality assurance in the area of CONFERENCE INTERPRETING, emphasizing that quality management must not be limited to the actual interpreting event but also encompass processes and conditions preceding and following it. In the fields of signed language interpreting and spoken-language community interpreting, a range of publications focussing on the development of the profession in terms of professionalization measures also addresses the broader theme of quality management, in relation to the more specific issue of gaining recognition and STATUS (e.g. Witter-Merithew & Johnson 2004).

Where the focus is on quality culture, quality is viewed as a collective mission (e.g. of an employer organization, public service institution or professional association) and as something that can be developed, controlled, assured and improved. Applied research in this domain focusses on professional policy measures aimed at the improvement of interpreting quality and service provision, including the optimization of working conditions. It encompasses the discussion and development of standards and best practice models; membership and certification procedures; standards established by national and international standardization agencies (e.g. ISO, EN, DIN); accreditation schemes to ensure the quality standards of training programmes and institutions; and provider training and consumer education.

NADJA GRBIĆ

QUALITY CRITERIA

↑ QUALITY
→ USER EXPECTATIONS
↓ ACCENT, ↓ ACCURACY, ↓ COHESION, ↓ FLUENCY, ↓ INTONATION, ↓ VOICE QUALITY

The lack of a universal definition of QUALITY in interpreting is one of the greatest obstacles to its measurement. While one may agree to view quality as a holistic concept that can be intuitively perceived, it is necessary to determine the criteria informing the ASSESSMENT of interpreting performances by researchers, professionals, teachers and trainees. The nature and number of quality criteria proposed to date, as well as their definitions and weighting, vary among different research methodologies, interdisciplinary approaches and interpreting domains, with most work focusing on quality assessment in CONFERENCE INTERPRETING.

In a first empirical attempt to study the construct of quality in operational terms, Bühler (1986) broke it down into more concrete components and proposed a set of sixteen items in a survey among professional conference interpreters (AIIC members) about the criteria they would apply in assessing fellow professionals' performance and behaviour (i.e. considering both the process and the product). Distinguishing between linguistic/semantic and extra-linguistic/pragmatic factors, her questionnaire comprised the following list: native accent, pleasant voice, FLUENCY of delivery, logical COHESION of utterance, sense consistency with original message, completeness of interpretation, correct grammatical usage, use of correct TERMINOLOGY, use of appropriate style, thorough PREPARATION of conference documents, endurance, poise, pleasant appearance, reliability, ability to work in a team, and positive feedback from delegates.

Research on USER EXPECTATIONS (e.g. Kurz 1993a; Moser 1996; Collados Aís et al. 2007) has adopted Bühler's proposal as a model focusing on the product perspective, with some items eliminated or added (e.g. INTONATION, synchronicity) and some combined into broader categories (e.g. 'easy to follow'). On the whole, these studies rely on a fairly stable set of criteria reflecting the traditional duality of 'content versus form'.

Research into the relative weight given to these criteria reflects differences in relation to factors such as setting (Kurz & Pöchhacker 1995), users' professional background (e.g. Kurz 1993a; Kopczyński 1994), GENDER, age and experience with interpreting, as well as type and size of event (e.g. Moser 1996). Nevertheless, findings suggest a steady overall pattern of preferences, with more importance given to content-related criteria than to aspects of delivery. However, these expectation patterns do not reflect the possible impact of 'less important' criteria on the way a given interpreting performance is perceived and assessed by the audience (e.g. Collados Aís 2002; Garzone 2003).

Conceptual analysis

Discrepancies between expectation patterns and the actual impact of certain criteria on assessment point to the need for more precise definitions. Aiming to ascertain the specific weight of individual parameters, researchers have therefore undertaken a 'vertical' analysis of quality criteria (e.g. Ahrens 2005a; Pradas Macías 2006), drawing on interdisciplinary insights from such fields as psychology, neuroscience, sociology, applied linguistics, language teaching, terminology and translation studies (Collados Aís et al. 2007). These efforts have also benefited from the development of new technologies for examining both verbal and nonverbal (temporal, acoustic) parameters, as studied in CORPUS-BASED RESEARCH.

Possible explanations for the differential weight of quality criteria in expectation and assessment studies include the impact of form-related (delivery) criteria on listeners' social

337

judgments, as nonverbal vocal features of speech condition assumptions about a speaker's personal traits, which then color the assessment. Experimental findings have also shown a number of interactions between different criteria (such as intonation and VOICE QUALITY, and ACCURACY and completeness), partly as a result of conceptual overlap (Collados Aís et al. 2007). Moreover, there is a clear link between nonverbal and verbal criteria, especially in terms of how intonation and cohesion may affect the perceived accuracy of rendition, which points to the difficulty, for most of the criteria, of separating form from substance.

Broader criteria

Beyond the focus on conference interpreting and a stable list of criteria, research into the components of quality has expanded to include other interpreting SETTINGS and domains (e.g. Hale et al. 2009). Pöchhacker (2001) suggests complementing the perspective on the interpreter's product in both conference and COMMUNITY INTERPRETING with a view of the service delivered, foregrounding functional criteria such as a speaker's intended COMMUNICATIVE EFFECT and the success of the communicative interaction as perceived by the participants. Along these lines, Reithofer (2013) uses audience COMPREHENSION as a yardstick for evaluating the quality of an interpretation, and related studies have investigated the impact of such criteria as fluency (Rennert 2010) and intonation (Holub 2010) on the achievement of comprehension. In DIALOGUE INTERPRETING, similar work could use as a criterion of quality whether interlocutors have understood, or feel understood, or whether they feel they have been heard and respected in the interpreter-mediated interaction.

The increasing attention given to the social dimension of quality assessment is reflected in research on elements such as first impressions of an interpreter (García Becerra 2012) or the activation of stereotypes (Stévaux 2011; Cheung 2013). This not only helps account for the complex relations between expectations and actual judgment, but also underscores the important idea that QUALITY is a dynamic concept which evolves in relation to a host of environmental variables and socially constituted NORMS.

ÁNGELA COLLADOS AÍS AND OLALLA GARCÍA BECERRA

RECAPITULATOR

see under PARTICIPATION FRAMEWORK

REGISTER

↑ SOCIOLINGUISTIC APPROACHES

The term 'register' is sometimes used synonymously with dialect, language variation, style, jargon, level of formality, level of education or a combination of all of the above. Holmes (2008) associates register with the language of groups of people with common interests or occupations, or the language used in situations involving such groups, and describes 'style' as referring to levels of formality. Hudson (1996: 46) distinguishes register from dialect by clarifying that "your dialect shows who (or what) you are, whilst your register shows what you are doing".

In translation studies, Hatim and Mason (1990), drawing on Halliday (1978), offer a similar distinction to Hudson's between dialect and register, by relating dialect to the 'user' and register to 'use'. The latter depends on the situation, participants, and purpose of the interaction. In the Hallidayan framework, a register is determined according to the 'field' (i.e. the situation and subject matter, such as a lecture, a courtroom or a medical consultation), the 'tenor' (i.e. the participants and the relationship between them, such as lawyers addressing the judge or a patient addressing the doctor) and the 'mode' of communication (written or spoken, prepared or spontaneous, or any other variation). Registers can be identified by the use of distinctive linguistic features at the lexical and syntactic levels. Quantitative studies using corpora (Biber 2012) as well as discourse analytical studies have been able to find patterns of use for different registers, such as 'policespeak' and 'lawyerspeak' (Coulthard & Johnson 2007). Nevertheless, such patterns are not strict or exhaustive. Only expert users of a language who master multiple registers have a choice of which register to use according to particular situations (Hale & Basides 2013). For others, their linguistic repertoire may be limited by age (generational dialect), exposure (geographical dialect) or educational level (social dialect). Interpreters, therefore, need to be expert users of at least two languages, in order to use the appropriate registers when interpreting.

The simplest way to view register in the context of interpreting is in terms of the distinction between 'what' is said (the propositional content) and 'how' the propositional content is presented (referred to as register, or often as style). How something is expressed can significantly influence the understanding of the utterance, as well as the way speakers are assessed by others, especially regarding character and credibility (e.g. O'Barr 1982). The register used by a speaker can also be chosen deliberately to achieve a certain effect, such as accommodating to the interlocutor(s) in order to facilitate mutual understanding. In this regard, interpreting scholars have argued that maintaining the registers of the original messages in the interpretation is an important part of ACCURACY, especially in COURTROOM INTERPRETING (e.g. Berk-Seligson 1990; González et al. 1991/2012; Hale 1997c). In several empirical studies, however, untrained interpreters working in court settings have been found to adjust the register to match the target language listener rather than the source language speaker (Berk-Seligson 1990; Hale 1997c, 2004). This practice is also quite common in HEALTHCARE INTERPRETING, where the gap in knowledge and expressive resources between physicians and patients leads interpreters to adopt a more active mediating role, among other things by listener-oriented changes in register (Tebble 1999).

Interpreting into an inappropriate register (for example, interpreting formal speech into colloquial speech, or specialised into general speech) can also cause unintended offence, misunderstanding between speakers or a misrepresentation of the original speaker's level of education, character or even age. This was exemplified for SIGNED LANGUAGE INTERPRETING in work by June Zimmer (1992), who showed how interpreters working from American Sign Language into English failed to match the deaf speaker's effective discourse style and consequently reduced the communicative impact of the message. There are situations, however, where there are register gaps across languages, and in particular across languages that are very different culturally or typologically, such as INDIGENOUS LANGUAGES. These situations, like many others in which interpreters face translational challenges, require the adoption of appropriate STRATEGIES, including various types of NON-RENDITION to help achieve the purpose of the interaction.

SANDRA B. HALE

RELAY INTERPRETING

↑ MODES
→ DIRECTIONALITY

Relay interpreting is a double or two-stage interpreting process, in which a source-language message is interpreted into a target language via a third language. This system is used when no interpreter is available to provide direct interpretation between the languages in question. For example, in the case of a speech in Khmer addressed to a Czech-speaking audience, a Cambodian speaker could first be interpreted into French by an interpreter in the visiting delegation, whose French rendering would then be interpreted into Czech by a local interpreter. Such indirect interpretation in relay mode has presumably been practiced when necessary throughout history, a famous example being the joint efforts of Spanish/Mayan interpreter Jerónimo de Aguilar and MALINCHE to enable communication between Spanish and Nahuatl in Hernán Cortéz's drive to conquer the Aztec Empire for SPAIN.

Relay interpreting is encountered in a great variety of SETTINGS, in the consecutive and simultaneous MODES, and spoken and signed languages alike. Given the additional time required for back-to-back CONSECUTIVE INTERPRETING (as used in the League of Nations for speeches in languages other than English or French), relay is much easier to accommodate with SIMULTANEOUS INTERPRETING (SI), where the extra cost in time is limited to the relay-taker's TIME LAG. This arrangement is indeed used on a large scale in multilingual meetings of international institutions such as the United Nations and the European Union (with interpreting from and into up to 24 languages). In these settings, the initial interpretation into the so-called *pivot* language (e.g. English) – for instance, from Chinese and Finnish respectively in the two organisations concerned – can be relayed into any number of other languages at the same time. This system was commonly used in the former Soviet Union and Eastern Bloc countries, with Russian serving as the pivot language.

The interpreter providing the relay (known as the *pivot* or relayer) may work into his or her A language, or else into a B language (known as 'doing a *retour*'). The latter is especially common with source languages of limited diffusion. In either scenario, regardless of the issue of DIRECTIONALITY, relay interpreting is generally viewed as problematic and as something to be avoided, by employers and interpreters alike. The rationale is that the added complexity resulting from the doubling of an already complex process makes relay doubly prone to errors or losses of message integrity. An additional inconvenience in SI is that the cumulative time lag deprives the relay-taker, and even more so his or her audience, of the full benefits of visual stimuli (such as GESTURES or slides) synchronised with the source speech. Paradoxically, considering its widespread use as an integral part of multilingual conferencing, there has been very little research investigating the alleged weaknesses of this 'second-best' practice.

The most substantial empirical study on relay interpreting in conference settings to date was reported in an unpublished Master's thesis by Jennifer Mackintosh (1983). With the aim of comparing message loss in direct SI versus relay interpreting (in the form of a reverse interpretation), Mackintosh generated an experimental corpus from the output of ten professional interpreters working in the French/English language pair and had a three-member jury perform a proposition-based ASSESSMENT of the interpretations. Though her quantitative results showed no significant difference in ACCURACY between the two conditions (with the exception of more frequent OMISSIONS and distortions of NUMBERS in the relay mode), Mackintosh concluded that changes in content were caused by different factors in the relay versus the direct mode, drawing particular attention to the 'pre-digested' nature of the *pivot*'s interpretation.

Subsequent publications, often of a didactic nature, mainly focus on recommendations for a 'good relay', often in connection with *retour* interpreting. Typical points of advice include maintaining FLUENCY, appropriate SEGMENTATION and INTONATION, and avoiding unusual stylistic choices (Jones 1998). Seleskovitch and Lederer (2002), while traditionally critical of the practice, confirm that working from relay can be easier than working from the original (see also Čeňková 2008; Harmer 2007; Jones 1998). At the same time they give expression to interpreters' main complaint about taking relay, which is the sense of being disconnected from the original, without access to the speaker's PROSODY and other nonverbal cues.

It is evident that serving as a *pivot* for other team members is likely to generate additional STRESS on the interpreter, but this issue, like many others, awaits systematic investigation.

There is a similar dearth of knowledge regarding relay interpreting in other settings, though its use in COMMUNITY INTERPRETING, including LEGAL INTERPRETING and HEALTHCARE INTERPRETING, has been mentioned by various authors (see Shlesinger 2010). As an example of a TECHNOLOGY-based solution, Braun (2015) cites a European initiative to create a remote-interpreter pool for 'rare' languages in ASYLUM SETTINGS, using a combination of remote and VIDEOCONFERENCE INTERPRETING. The arrangement in this case is for a remote interpreter to provide relay from the asylum seeker's language (for which no local interpreter is available) into a *pivot* language such as English; this is delivered via videoconference to a local interpreter co-present with the interviewer. In a much earlier initiative, Mikkelson (1999) had similarly drawn attention to the shortage of interpreters for INDIGENOUS LANGUAGES in the US court system, and described a course for 'indigenous relay interpreter training' which teaches Spanish speakers with a knowledge of indigenous languages spoken in Mexico and Guatemala to work in relay with certified Spanish/English interpreters.

Minority language situations with similar implications for relay interpreting needs also arise within Deaf communities. Thus, a DEAF INTERPRETER may be needed to perform relay INTERPRETING FOR DEAFBLIND PERSONS or to make a hearing sign language interpreter's rendering more accessible to socially isolated persons with limited sign language proficiency, or in situations requiring particular cultural sensitivity. More commonly, sign language interpreters working in international conference settings with more than one spoken language will take relay, via headphones, from a spoken-language simultaneous interpreter's output, and provide a relay into the spoken language when a Deaf client takes the floor. As Turner (2007) points out, SIGNED LANGUAGE INTERPRETING in conferences may also involve Deaf interpreters taking relay from an initial contact signing output (or 'feed') to work into International Sign, and vice versa, all of which is done in simultaneous mode.

IVANA ČEŇKOVÁ

RELEVANCE THEORY

↑ LINGUISTIC/PRAGMATIC APPROACHES

Relevance theory is a development of the inferential account of human communication proposed by Grice (1975) to replace the classic code model. Postulating the search for relevance as its driving principle, the theory offers an explicitly cognitive account of communication in which available context plays a key role in complementing the linguistic signal (Sperber & Wilson 1986/1995; Blakemore 1987; Carston 2002). Relevance theory has been applied to translation in particular by Gutt (1991/2000), and has also served as a framework for the study of interpreting alongside traditional LINGUISTIC/PRAGMATIC APPROACHES.

Origins and overview

In a code model of communication, meaning is assumed to be transmitted between Sender and Receiver by encoding and decoding, constrained only by the precision of the code, the degree of identity of Sender's and Receiver's 'codebooks' and the quality of the channel. In the 1950s and 1960s, however, 'ordinary language philosophers' like Austin (1962), Searle (1969) and the later Wittgenstein (1953) showed that, far from transparently and logically encoding propositional information, natural human languages vastly underdetermine speakers' meaning, leaving a large gap between what can be precisely encoded and what a speaker means to convey. Explaining how this gap is bridged became the goal of the new discipline of pragmatics.

According to Grice (1975), utterances merely provide evidence of a communicator's intended meaning, which listeners must then recover by inference: if the literal meaning of an utterance violated certain tacit and universally shared 'maxims' for cooperative communication, such as (literal) truthfulness, the speaker could be assumed to have spoken metaphorically, or ironically. However, the Gricean account did not explain *how* listeners arrived at the 'right' (and occasionally, wrong) non-literal meaning, and it seemed to require a two-step process, in which inference is applied only after a literal meaning is derived and rejected. Subsequent evidence has shown the underdeterminacy of natural language to be far more radical than at first believed, allowing a multitude of possible inferences, but also that people derive non-literal meanings just as fast as literal ones (e.g. Gibbs 2000).

For Sperber and Wilson (1986/1995) human communication is driven by the search for relevance (which Grice had proposed as a 'maxim', but without specifying how it might operate), and is 'ostensive-inferential': a speaker signals his communicative intent by an act of 'ostension', creating a presumption of relevance that justifies a hearer's effort in processing the stimulus to derive 'cognitive effects' that may enrich his cognitive environment. This effort involves decoding the linguistic signal to obtain semantic representations that (since the language code is underdetermined) must be disambiguated and otherwise enriched by inference in accessible contexts to yield plausible intended meanings, both explicit and implicit.

In relevance theory, in contrast with pre-cognitive pragmatic approaches, 'context' and 'relevance' have precise technical meanings: context is a psychological construct, an accessible subset of all the listener's current assumptions (knowledge, beliefs, perceptions); a 'relevant' interpretation is one that makes sense based on all the evidence provided by the semantic decoding of the utterance in these contexts. Cognitive effects can include any potential modification of the listener's knowledge, beliefs or perceptions (whether informative, persuasive, entertaining, etc.), and there is no guarantee that the 'correct' meaning is derived as intended by the speaker. In a world full of stimuli competing for attention, listeners stop at the first interpretation that yields satisfactory cognitive effects for the effort put in. Relevance is a trade-off, being optimal when it yields maximum effects for minimum effort.

Relevance theory distinguishes 'conceptual' elements in discourse that encode content, activating a MENTAL REPRESENTATION, from 'procedural' features (such as certain discourse markers, prosodic patterns or referential deictics) that activate computational processes and guide hearers to inferences. This account is consistent with the computational-representational model of mind in cognitive science and thus with the relevantists' aim of establishing a cognitive pragmatics.

Inferential accounts of interpreting

As listeners and speakers respectively, interpreters must derive and give access to meanings that are optimally relevant not to themselves but to the principal communicators, which entails acquiring and projecting their cognitive environments. This is achieved in part through PREPARATION, but in interpreting, unlike written translation, much of the immediately accessible context used by communicators comes from the live unfolding discourse and communicative situation. Research in a relevance-theoretic framework has shown, based on transcripts of discourse, how the inferential possibilities of co-presence are leveraged in SIMULTANEOUS INTERPRETING (Setton 1999, 2005, 2006a). Similarly, Schmitz (1997) suggests that in MACHINE INTERPRETING, albeit for restricted domains like appointment scheduling, references to a situation shared by both communicators can be left linguistically underspecified.

Relevance theory also provides a framework for analysing FIDELITY through the distinction between *explicatures*, which are a development of the logical form of the utterance, and *implicatures*, which are meanings communicated by implication in a given context with different strengths. Importantly, however, in contrast with the Gricean model, relevance theory shows how listeners must use inference not just to derive implicit meaning but also meaningful explicatures, via processes such as disambiguation and enrichment. Norms of fidelity in most SETTINGS require interpreters to aim to convey what was meant, but preserving the implicit–explicit profile as far as possible in the target text, that is, rendering explicatures explicitly, and providing the necessary communicative clues in TT for listeners to derive the implicatures at the same strengths. The distinction between the conceptual and procedural components of discourse has been used in interpreting studies to clarify the difference between EXPLICITATION, where the interpreter supplies additional content that listeners may need as context, notably to understand 'insider' jokes or culturally-marked references (e.g. Vianna 2005; Mason 2006; Gumul 2008), and the addition of 'procedural' (content-less) discourse markers (like 'well' or 'so') to help 'contribute to mutuality' and 'reflect the speaker's voice' (Blakemore & Gallai 2014). Both explicitation and the addition of procedural markers contribute to achieving optimal relevance.

Relevance theory has also served to discuss issues of COGNITIVE LOAD. Just as speakers and listeners represent their own and each other's meanings to themselves as they communicate, interpreters must *meta-represent* these meanings, adding one more order of meta-representation to the three or four routinely handled by the human mind (Sperber 1994). Bülow-Møller (1999) documented interpreting failure in the presence of multiple levels of attributed belief or quotation ('he said that they thought that … '), complex scope relations, and *irrealis* phenomena like counterfactuals, or irony, conditionals and certain types of negatives (see also Setton 2002b). Funayama (2004) suggests that cognitive load in simultaneous interpreting can be measured by the number of 'cognitive tags' that must be held by the interpreter to represent provisionally unresolved (not yet fully enriched) entities or relations in the unfolding discourse.

In a relevance-theoretic account of the CONSECUTIVE INTERPRETING process, Albl-Mikasa (2008) views NOTE-TAKING as the creation of an elliptical, restructured intermediate text from which the interpreter then formulates a full, extended target language utterance by supplying the missing details from context, as must be done with any body of coded evidence.

The definition of optimal relevance – maximum cognitive effects for minimum effort – also provides a good proxy for QUALITY in interpreting, subject to the additional requirement of fidelity to the speaker's message. The cognitive effects accessible to the interpreter's listeners will depend on his/her ability to minimise their processing effort. In an inferential account, superficial deletions or additions may not be errors, as implied by a code model, but a means of using listeners' inferential processes to convey meanings more effectively than TRANSCODING in the absence of one-to-one correspondences between languages. In this sense, Setton and Dawrant (2016) formulate the default goal of interpreting in relevance-theoretic terms as making accessible to the interpreter's audience the cognitive effects intended by the speaker as s/he understands them, at reasonable processing cost and risk, using whatever communicative devices available in the output language are appropriate and effective to do so in his or her projection of the listeners' available contexts.

Relevance theory has enjoyed increasing popularity in interpreting studies in Europe, but also in Japan and China. However, it has sometimes also been misapplied. This happens when it is presented as a method (to be taught to students) to correctly derive the intended message, or when the analysis fails to take into account the special situation of linguistic MEDIATION, where the interpreter, as both outsider and mediator, is not driven primarily by a personal search for relevance, as are the principals, but must artificially assume their cognitive environments and optimise relevance for them.

More generally, critics have pointed out that the mainstream exposition of the theory offers no examples in which the cognitive environments of communicators are significantly mismatched in terms of cultural background, identity or social status. This leaves relevance theory open to the charge of focusing on ideal communicators who are cognitively matched, or easily matchable, through purely 'logical' processes. In the second edition of their book, Sperber and Wilson (1986/1995) revise the definition of presumption of relevance to take into account the communicator's preferences and abilities. This may go some way towards modelling common interpreting situations involving non-native speakers and listeners and/or conflicting cognitive environments that must be bridged by the interpreter.

ROBIN SETTON

RELIGIOUS SETTINGS

→ JEWISH TRADITION, → NON-PROFESSIONAL INTERPRETING

Interpreting in a religious setting is one of the earliest documented types of interpreting, dating at least from the time of early Judaism around 500 BCE (Kaufmann 2005). This predates by several hundred years the translation of Judeo-Christian sacred texts; unlike Bible translation, however, with which it has a common lineage, interpreting in religious settings has emerged as a research topic only in the new millennium. This is not because the phenomenon as such is rare. Karlik (2010) suggests that across Africa interpreter mediation of scriptures might be more common than the reading aloud of written Bible translations; other religious communities, most notably Pentecostals and Mormons, have at their disposal state-of-the-art SIMULTANEOUS INTERPRETING facilities to provide interpreting of worship services in several languages. (The Church of the Latter Day Saints has a specialized office for interpreting; in its Central Temple, in situ and remote interpreting services cover 92 languages.)

The term 'interpreting in religious settings' has gained wide acceptance among scholars in the field and has come to replace 'church interpreting', which has been criticized for its narrow focus and lack of religious neutrality. Furthermore, a distinction is made between interpreting during religious functions (a special case of which is sermon interpreting) and interpreter mediation of sacred texts. The latter includes interpreting Bible passages in the oral and signed modalities; participatory study of scripture passages; and Bible 'storying', that is, the teaching and telling of biblical narratives.

Whereas in SIGNED LANGUAGE INTERPRETING, religious settings have been recognized as an area of professional practice (Frishberg 1990), spoken language interpreting in religious settings is primarily done as NON-PROFESSIONAL INTERPRETING, by untrained bi- or multi-linguals who are generally members of the worshipping community. Such volunteers learn 'on the job' and work primarily in the 'short consecutive' mode, which exhibits some setting-specific features such as discursive symmetry in the organization of TURN-TAKING and a high level of reciprocity (Giannoutsou 2014). Although the general tendency is to work in very short segments, their length and information density is actively negotiated between the interpreter and the preacher and is determined by factors such as the nature of the interactants' relationship and the interpreter's status in the community. Aside from the short consecutive and the simultaneous mode (including, to a lesser degree, whispered interpreting), SIGHT INTERPRETING/TRANSLATION is also used, mainly in scripture readings.

Interpreters in religious settings are exposed to a wide range of discourse types, such as speeches, debates, sermons, face-to-face prophecies, and songs, to mention but a few. This diversity of interpreting practices poses a challenge to existing classifications of interpreting domains, and Hokkanen (2012) argues that in religious settings a strict distinction between CONFERENCE INTERPRETING and COMMUNITY INTERPRETING becomes untenable.

In an early contribution, Kaufmann (2005) gives a historical overview of interpreting practices in early Judaism and highlights the fact that, at its inception, interpreting in religious settings in the JEWISH TRADITION was set up as a distinct practice with its own NORMS and performative structure. Her account also emphasizes the inherent link with theology, which remains true to the present day not only for the Judeo-Christian tradition. As a corollary of this link, interpreting in religious settings has been seen by its practitioners and, more recently, also by scholars, not as merely a linguistic act but as performance of a theological function.

The performative aspect of interpreting in religious settings has been explored in a number of studies, some of which were conducted by sociologists interested in the issue of ethnic interrelationships and POWER. For Vigouroux (2010) the performative aspect of interpreting in a church community in Canada bespeaks the community's efforts to legitimize its church. Rayman (2007), who studied interpreting into American Sign Language (ASL), suggests that the teleology of the interpreting performance was to give the Deaf community a voice and affirm its role in the congregation. Hild (2016) discusses the performative dimension of interpreting from the perspective of New Homiletics and Performance Studies, reviewing how consecutive church interpreters construct meaning by interweaving linguistic, vocal and kinesic gestures.

Jill Karlik's (2010) research is based on a number of corpora representing different types of church discourses in a non-literate community in the Gambia. She identifies different STRATEGIES (e.g. lexical simplification) used by the volunteer interpreters in her study. Alev Balcı (2008) argues that church interpreters in Turkey are encouraged to act as cultural mediators, introducing changes to the speech, mitigating culturally inappropriate references, and ensuring the acceptability of the target text. She also draws attention to the fact that preachers choose their interpreters not for their linguistic skills, but on the basis of their experience as worshippers. This is corroborated by Hild (2016), who emphasizes the importance to both interpreters and preachers of feeling personally connected. Karlik (2010) also asserts that church interpreters are expected to make additions and modifications to the text, so as to adapt it to the needs and expectations of the worshipping community. Interpreters are seen as co-creators of the worship event and consequently share responsibility for the success of the sermon, taking on the ROLE of co-preachers and co-constructors of charismatic meaning (Giannoutsou 2014; Hild 2016).

Scholarship on interpreting in religious settings is thus constructing a new interpreter profile that differs from the ones proffered by the professionalization literature or as outlined in studies of non-professional interpreters in other SETTINGS. The conduit model, which, in its strict sense, demands impartiality and, in a more relaxed construal, MEDIATION by the interpreter, is replaced by the partner model, which gives interpreters in religious settings more latitude as well as greater responsibility for the success of the performative activity they co-construct. Their performance is no longer judged primarily by the criterion of FIDELITY, but also with regard to performativity and functional adequacy. The norm of NEUTRALITY is thus superseded by the requirement of embodied experience and close involvement on an interpersonal level.

Research on interpreting in religious settings also challenges the methodological canon of interpreting research on account of its primarily endogenous character. It is conducted by researchers who are either interpreters and/or preachers, as well as members of their communities of practice. Discussing the auto-ethnographic method of her study of simultaneous church interpreting, Hokkanen (2012) highlights the need for reflexivity, and the difficulties in separating the roles of researcher, interpreter and devout Christian. While, understandably, such research rarely adopts an etic (i.e. non-participant) perspective, the subjectivity evidenced in most of the existing studies confronts researchers with the challenge of reconciling the inherent epistemological tensions and considering their implications for inquiries in this field.

ADELINA HILD

REMOTE INTERPRETING

↑ TECHNOLOGY
→ TELEPHONE INTERPRETING, → VIDEOCONFERENCE INTERPRETING, → VIDEO REMOTE INTERPRETING

The term 'remote interpreting' (RI) refers to the use of communication TECHNOLOGY for gaining access to an interpreter who is in another room, building, city or country and who is linked to the primary participants by telephone or videoconference. RI by telephone is nowadays often called TELEPHONE INTERPRETING or over-the-phone interpreting. RI by videoconference is often simply called remote interpreting when it refers to spoken-language interpreting. In SIGNED LANGUAGE INTERPRETING, the term VIDEO REMOTE INTERPRETING has become established. RI is best described as a modality or method of delivery. It has been used for SIMULTANEOUS INTERPRETING, CONSECUTIVE INTERPRETING and DIALOGUE INTERPRETING. This entry focuses on RI by videoconference in spoken-language interpreting.

The development of RI was originally driven by supranational multilingual institutions, which were interested in RI as a way of overcoming the linguistic and logistical challenges they faced. RI has sparked debate and raised questions regarding feasibility and interpreters' WORKING CONDITIONS, but it has also been linked to questions of efficiency and sustainability. Whilst uptake in supranational institutions has been relatively slow, there is a growing demand for RI in legal and healthcare settings.

RI in supranational institutions

The earliest documented experiment with RI was organised by UNESCO in 1976, to test the use of the Symphonie satellite. It linked the UNESCO headquarters in Paris with a conference centre in Nairobi, and actually involved three different modalities of interpreting: RI by telephone, RI by video link and interpreting in a videoconference between Paris and Nairobi, with the interpreters being situated in Paris. Similar experiments were organised by the UN in the 1970s and 1980s. When ISDN-based videoconferencing became available in the 1990s, feasibility studies were conducted in many supranational institutions, always in simultaneous mode (see Moser-Mercer 2003; Mouzourakis 2006; Roziner & Shlesinger 2010).

The studies used a variety of technical conditions. ISDN connections were incompatible with the ISO 2603 standard in terms of sound quality and were therefore considered to be unacceptable for simultaneous interpreting (AIIC 2000/2012). According to Mouzourakis (2006), however, the studies revealed physiological and psychological challenges which recurred in different technical conditions, making it difficult to attribute them to a particular technical setup.

Two studies in particular addressed physiological and psychological variables, as well as the quality of RI: the studies conducted by the International Telecommunications Union (ITU) in collaboration with the École de Traduction et d'Interprétation (ETI) (Moser-Mercer 2003), and by the European Parliament (EP) in 2004 (reported in Roziner & Shlesinger 2010). As well as investigating the performance of the participating interpreters, the studies also elicited the interpreters' emotional responses to RI, and measured STRESS indicators and aspects of the working environment. The outcomes of the two studies differ in several ways. For example, the ITU/ETI study revealed that the interpreters' performance in RI declined faster than their on-site performance, whilst the EP study found no significant differences in RI and on-site performance. What is common to both studies is a sense of discomfort with RI on the part of the interpreters which, as Roziner and Shlesinger (2010) point out, is hard to account for by objective measures. The most striking result of research on RI in this setting thus seems to be the discrepancy between objective findings and subjective perception.

RI in legal settings

In legal settings RI has been used to cope with a shortage of qualified interpreters, a lack of time and the short duration of many assignments, which make the interpreter's travel and physical presence particularly uneconomical.

The practice of RI in this field goes back to the 1980s, when RI by telephone was introduced in the US. Over time, this has gradually been replaced by video RI. A well-known example is the Ninth Judicial Circuit Court of Florida, which introduced a central video interpreting hub in 2007. The interpreters' workstations in the hub are configured to allow a combination of consecutive and simultaneous interpreting. The Metropolitan Police Service in London introduced RI in 2011, with interpreters working in consecutive mode from centralised hubs linked to London police stations. The European Directive on the right to interpretation and translation in criminal proceedings (2010/64/EU) explicitly refers to the possibility of using RI, which is likely to increase its use in legal proceedings in European countries.

The first studies to address RI in legal proceedings were conducted in the European AVI-DICUS projects. Based on the outcomes of a survey designed to identify problems and needs, AVIDICUS 1 (2008–2011) compared the quality of on-site interpreting and RI (and VIDEO-CONFERENCE INTERPRETING). The findings of these experiments reveal a significantly higher number of problems and, like Moser-Mercer's (2003) data, a faster decline of interpreting performance in RI (Braun 2013; Braun & Taylor 2012a). AVIDICUS 2 (2011–2013) replicated the experiments after providing the interpreters with short-term training, and using better equipment. The findings yield a complex picture, making it impossible to say without reservation that training, familiarisation and the use of better equipment led to a clear improvement in performance (Braun & Taylor 2015). AVIDICUS 3 (2014–2016) assesses videoconferencing facilities in legal institutions in Europe in terms of their fitness for interpreter-mediated communication.

RI in healthcare

In healthcare settings RI is used with similar motivations to those in legal settings, that is, optimising access to interpreters and achieving efficiency gains. RI in healthcare is often delivered by telephone, but this has been changing with the advent of mobile videoconferencing devices (Locatis et al. 2011).

A number of smaller, mostly survey-based studies of RI in medical encounters using telephone and video link have been carried out. However, their findings are difficult to compare due to highly variable conditions. In a review of nine studies conducted between 1996 and 2003, Azarmina and Wallace (2005) find evidence that RI is at least as acceptable as on-site interpreting to patients, doctors and (to a lesser extent) interpreters. Although none of these studies included an actual assessment of the interpreters' performance, the authors also conclude that RI "appears to be associated with levels of accuracy at least as good as those found in physically present interpretation" (2005: 144). They do, however, note that interpreters generally preferred on-site interpreting to RI, and video to telephone. This is corroborated by more recent studies comparing the three modalities (Locatis et al. 2010; Price et al. 2012).

Future directions

To date there is no consensus regarding the quality of interpreting that can be achieved in RI, nor on the nature and impact of the various contributing factors. Moreover, Moser-Mercer (2005a) and Mouzourakis (2006) suggest that the lack of a sense of 'presence' on the part of the interpreters may be the most likely common denominator for the difficulties associated with RI. The concept of 'presence' and its effects therefore require further research, as does the question of how interpreters adapt to RI.

SABINE BRAUN

REPAIRS

→ SLIPS

Repairs in language can be defined most broadly as attempts to resolve problems in speaking, hearing, or understanding. In conversation, they can be self- or other-initiated, and accomplished as self- or other-repairs (Schegloff et al. 1977). Thus, with respect to monologic production, the focus is essentially on self-initiated 'self-repairs'. The notion of repairs has been applied from a similar perspective in research on interpreting, though the topic has, on the whole, attracted relatively little attention. This might seem surprising, since interpreters, particularly in the simultaneous mode, are working under high COGNITIVE LOAD and are therefore particularly prone to disruptions reflected in their output. In this respect, GERVER (1976) was among the first who noticed that conference interpreters corrected themselves, and sought to accommodate this in his process model of SIMULTANEOUS INTERPRETING by positing a short-term buffer store for output monitoring.

Monitoring is not only crucial to repairing but also forms an integral part of language production in monolingual speech, and this is where it has been most thoroughly studied (e.g. Levelt 1983, 1989). The case of the interpreter is particularly interesting, however, given the requirement of correct target language expression and faithful reproduction of source language content. Repairs, often detectable as a result of false starts or other disruptions in the interpreter's speech flow (Kopczyński 1980; Pöchhacker 1995d), give a perceptible indication of how attentive this monitoring can be. However, it is important to understand that a repair does not necessarily follow what can be clearly identified as an error: in conversation, one might be present without the other (Schegloff et al. 1977) and, in interpreting, there is often no clear cause-and-effect sequence linking a repair to an evident problem. It is, in any case, inappropriate to think of a repair in interpreting as necessarily prompted by an error as such – hence the rationale for referring only to those which do rectify errors as 'corrections'.

A substantial contribution to the study of repairs in (simultaneous) interpreting was made in doctoral research by Petite (2005), who examined audio recordings of eight professional interpreters, mostly working from English into French or German as their 'A' language. Building on Levelt's (1983) theoretical account of the monitoring and repair process, Petite revisits the distinction between 'covert' and 'overt' (or pre- vs. post-articulatory) repairs in Levelt's model to fit the specificities of simultaneous interpreting. In particular, she differentiates between 'mid-articulatory' (i.e. within-word) repairs and the 'overt' category on which she mainly focuses. Petite's examples of overt repair often involve a sequence of an initial target language equivalent for a given lexical item or phrase, followed by a more satisfactory version in terms of wording or collocation. Kopczyński (1980: 85) also comments on such cases and, in a study of trainees interpreting simultaneously from Polish into English, reports the example "our common … eh … aims will come true … will be achieved". Petite (2005) points out that repairs of this kind are often more a question of fine-tuning, to maximise 'fitness for purpose', than of actual correction.

Classifying repairs according to what triggers them, Petite (2005) distinguishes between two broad categories: input-generated (prompted by concern with closer approximation to the source language input) and output-generated (when the interpreter reappraises target language expression entirely on its own merits – e.g. revisiting an inappropriate collocation, as illustrated in the previous paragraph). There are also different degrees of repair, according to whether the aim is to ensure greater appropriateness (disambiguation, precision, COHERENCE) or to correct various types of linguistic error. In addition, repairs can differ in terms of how 'seamlessly' they are incorporated into the interpretation: sometimes by simple juxtaposition, moving on without perceptible hesitation from the initial version in need of repair (the 'reparandum') to the corrected form (the 'reparatum'); sometimes judiciously covering the repair by rhythm and/or by a linking expression such as "in other words"; sometimes clearly 'signalling' that a change has been made (for example, by an accompanying apology).

Interestingly, Petite observes that many repairs in her sample occur in sequences. This suggests that, given the TIME LAG between the source-language and target-language speech segments managed at any given point in the interpretation, possible loss of balance among the various cognitive activities in the interpreting process is unlikely to be only a momentary difficulty affecting just one short segment. In addition, within a conceptual framework like that of Gile's EFFORT MODELS, the repair itself demands attention from the interpreter and therefore has to be factored into the far from constant equation which sets off available processing capacity against the competing demands of listening, short-term MEMORY and speech production. This means that the repair is actually likely to create, or to aggravate, problems of coordination – possibly precipitating further repairs in subsequent segments.

However, as underlined by Kopczyński (1980), keeping errors of linguistic performance like false starts to a minimum is not necessarily synonymous with QUALITY. FLUENCY achieved by avoiding repair may do communication a disservice if listener-friendliness is prioritised at the expense of FIDELITY. Moreover, repairs must be put in perspective with due regard for ORALITY: as an integral part of live situated language production, their communicative impact cannot be judged on the basis of transcripts and by the same linguistic standards as written translation.

PETER MEAD

REPORTER

see under PARTICIPATION FRAMEWORK

RESPEAKING

↑ MEDIA INTERPRETING, ↑ TECHNOLOGY

In broad terms, respeaking may be defined as the production of subtitles by means of speech recognition. A more thorough definition would present it as a technique in which a respeaker listens to the original sound of a live programme or event and respeaks it, including punctuation marks and some specific features for the deaf and hard-of-hearing audience, to speech recognition software, which turns the recognized utterances into subtitles displayed on the screen with the shortest possible delay (Romero-Fresco 2011). It is, in effect, a form of (usually intralingual) computer-aided SIMULTANEOUS INTERPRETING with the addition of punctuation marks and features such as the identification of the different speakers with colours or name tags. Although respeakers are usually encouraged to repeat the original soundtrack in order to produce verbatim subtitles, the high SPEECH RATES of some speakers and the need to dictate punctuation marks and abide by standard viewers' reading rates means that respeakers often end up paraphrasing rather than repeating (SHADOWING) the original soundtrack.

The origins of respeaking may be traced back to the experiments conducted by US court reporter Horace Webb in the early 1940s. Until then, court reporters used to take shorthand notes of the speech and then dictate their notes for transcription into typewritten form. Webb proposed to have the reporter repeat every word of the original speech into a microphone, using a stenomask to cancel the noise. The subsequent recording of the reporter's words would then be used for transcription. This was called *voice writing* and may thus be seen as the precursor of respeaking, or *realtime voice writing*, as it is called in the US. Respeaking involves the same technique but uses speech recognition software for the production of TV subtitles and transcriptions in courtrooms, classrooms, meetings and other settings. The very first use of respeaking or realtime voice writing dates back to 1999, when court reporter Chris Ales transcribed a session in the Circuit Court in Lapeer, Michigan, with the speech recognition software Dragon Naturally Speaking. Respeaking was introduced in Europe in 2001 by the Belgian public broadcaster VRT and by the BBC in the UK to replace less cost-effective live subtitling methods for TV, such as the use of keyboards or stenography.

Standard intralingual respeaking for live TV programmes and court reporting has since expanded to other applications and contexts. In many companies, subtitlers are using respeaking to subtitle pre-recorded programmes in order to increase productivity. This technique, known as *scripting*, allows respeakers to pause the original soundtrack if they wish, which brings this type of respeaking closer to CONSECUTIVE INTERPRETING than simultaneous interpreting. Respeaking is also being used for live public events (conferences, talks, religious ceremonies, university lectures, school classes, etc.) and business meetings, with respeakers working on site or remotely, sometimes (as in the case of telephone respeaking) with no VISUAL ACCESS to the speakers. Interlingual respeaking is also being used in these contexts, which highlights the resemblance between this technique and simultaneous CONFERENCE INTERPRETING.

Training in respeaking is usually focused on elements specific to this discipline (especially those related to the use of speech recognition software), and elements from both interpreting and subtitling for the deaf and hard of hearing (general subtitling skills, awareness of the needs of deaf and hard-of-hearing viewers). As far as interpreting is concerned, the emphasis is often placed on the skills required to listen, comprehend and synthesize the source text and to reformulate it and deliver it live as a target text. Multitasking is thus also involved in respeaking. As in simultaneous interpreting, respeakers must listen to the source text, translate it (or respeak it) and monitor their own voices. However, unlike interpreters, respeakers on TV often have to watch their output on the screen as they are respeaking and correct it live if there are any mistakes or if their subtitles are being obscured by on-screen text. Although more work is needed on this issue, research findings (Romero-Fresco 2012) suggest that interpreting students perform better in respeaking than those without prior training in this area, who seem to struggle to perform different tasks simultaneously. However, interpreting students find it difficult to dictate punctuation marks and must pay attention to their diction and INTONATION, which need to be more controlled than in interpreting.

Research on respeaking is still scarce, especially if compared to other modes of audiovisual translation and media accessibility. Early work focused on the process and the professional practice of respeaking as implemented in different countries (e.g. Eugeni 2009), which was followed by some contributions on respeaker training (e.g. Romero-Fresco 2012). Although there is widespread agreement that respeaking combines interpreting (as far as the process is concerned) and subtitling (especially regarding the product and the context), it was adopted from the beginning as a new modality of audiovisual translation. This may explain why, with few exceptions, it has been audiovisual translation scholars and not interpreting scholars who have conducted research in this area.

A more recent focus in research is on the reception and QUALITY of respoken subtitles. This includes the use of EYE-TRACKING (e.g. Rajendran et al. 2012) and SURVEY RESEARCH (Romero-Fresco 2013) on viewers' perception, comprehension and opinion of live subtitles. Moreover, studies analysing the ACCURACY of the respeakers' output have employed the so-called NER model – a formula calculating accuracy in terms of the number of words in the respoken text (N), editing errors (E) and recognition errors (R), which is used by regulators and broadcasters in different European countries.

On the whole, research on respeaking is still too limited to keep up with the industry, where TECHNOLOGY-based developments are constantly being introduced to make the production of subtitles more cost-effective. Further scholarly work in this field is needed, not least from the point of view of interpreting, in order to gain deeper insight into this practice and examine the effect of these new developments on the quality of live subtitling.

PABLO ROMERO-FRESCO

RESPONDER

see under PARTICIPATION FRAMEWORK

RETOUR INTERPRETING

see under DIRECTIONALITY

RETROSPECTIVE PROTOCOLS

↑ METHODOLOGY

Since it was first used for interpreting research in the mid-1990s, the retrospective method has been deployed in various types of research designs, most frequently as a secondary method for triangulating quantitative data. Its initial use reflected the burgeoning interest in new forms of inquiry that would recognise and value interpreters' personal experience. Translation process research, most notably by using TAPs (think-aloud protocols), served as a catalyst for adding this technique to the METHODOLOGY of interpreting studies (Kohn & Kalina 1996). Since the interpreting process does not allow for concurrent verbalisation, retrospective studies are based on verbal data gathered immediately after the interpreting task has been completed (Ivanova 2000). Such verbal data are thus based on information stored in long-term memory (Ericsson & Simon 1996).

Early methodological discourse revolved around specific problems arising from the adaptation of retrospection to interpreting, in particular the need for keeping data collection minimally invasive. There was a consensus that interrupting the task at regular intervals in order to collect verbal data would compromise the validity of the research findings (Ivanova 2000). This prompted researchers to devise effective memory cues to support recall of process-related information while at the same time ensuring that verbalisations were not post-process reconstructions, elaborations and speculations. Some researchers (e.g. Bartło-miejczyk 2006; Napier 2004b) provided interpreters with a recording of their own output; others (e.g. Ivanova 2000; Tiselius & Jenset 2011) have argued that using the transcript of the source text as a memory cue can increase the reliability of the procedure. This can be further supplemented by notes from the researcher's observation, including details on the interpreter's linguistic, kinesic and paralinguistic behaviour during task performance, to serve as probes for additional recall.

Another issue is the time delay between completion of the interpreting task and the beginning of retrospection. Apart from the ideal choice of immediate retrospection (Ivanova 2000), verbalisation has also been collected in cases where there is a considerable delay between the task and the initiation of recall, such as at the end of a working day (in naturalistic settings), but sometimes with delays of several days or even weeks. In these cases, the procedure cannot be assumed to collect data on the specific task-related processes, but it can be employed to provide information on hypothetical and general cognitive states (Ericsson & Simon 1996).

Retrospective questions and designs

Retrospective research to date has investigated four main questions, all in relation to SIMULTANEOUS INTERPRETING (SI): (1) expert–novice differences, (2) STRATEGIES, (3) DIRECTIONALITY and (4) NORMS.

(1) In classic TAP inquiries from education research, translation and expertise studies, the primary purpose of the analysis of the collected verbal reports is to develop models showing memory access, strategic inference and goal-directed reasoning that guide problem-solving behaviour (Hoffman & Militello 2009). Similarly, Ivanova (1999) analysed verbal protocols in an EXPERT–NOVICE PARADIGM to uncover problem-solving structures in the interpreting behaviour of experts and novices. The retrospective data indicated differences in processing along several strands: types of problem, and the complexity of how they were analysed; range and type of strategies, and how these relate to specific categories of problems; monitoring and metacognition. Similar differences were also uncovered by Tiselius and Jenset (2011), who adopted Ivanova's methodology. Vik-Tuovinen (2002), in a study using delayed retrospection, presented data showing skill-induced effects reminiscent of those in the two studies discussed above.

(2) In a summary report of the first naturalistic investigation of the 'strategic dimension' of interpreting, Kohn and Kalina (1996) offer a view of interpreting as "strategic discourse processing, geared to the interlingual transfer of mental world modelling from a source discourse to a target discourse" (1996: 132). They speculate that the complexity of the SI task necessitates appropriate strategic action in order for the interpreter to fulfil the function of 'mediating communicator'. The authors offer a text-based analysis of strategy use complemented by delayed retrospective comments from their interpreter-informants, and provide

an exhaustive list of strategies, which was subsequently adopted by Bartłomiejczyk (2006) in developing the coding scheme for her study. Focusing specifically on strategic OMISSIONS, Napier (2002, 2004b) analysed data from a recording-based 'task review' as well as retrospective interviews to establish whether the sign language interpreters in her experimental study had deliberately and/or consciously omitted parts of the source speech.

(3) Retrospection has also been used to study the effects of directionality on strategy use. Bartłomiejczyk (2006) found that the student interpreters in her study used different sets of strategies depending on the direction of processing: when working from their B into their A language, they employed strategies facilitating source text COMPREHENSION, while strategies used in A-to-B interpreting addressed translation problems. Chang and Schallert (2007) applied a grounded theory approach and focused on identifying strategies specific to any one direction of interpreting. They suggest that the effect of directionality on processing is best understood in terms of higher-order constraints: the professionals in their study were keenly aware of proficiency discrepancies between L1 and L2, and adjusted their strategies to preempt and compensate for them.

(4) The study by Chang and Schallert (2007) also highlights the potential of retrospection to provide evidence for norm-driven processing. They observe that the performance of the professional interpreter-subjects was constrained by expectancy norms (Chesterman 1993), and identify several other norms on the basis of their analysis.

Challenges

Retrospective studies on interpreting have used a variety of designs: some follow classic verbal protocol studies (e.g. Ivanova 1999); others employ grounded-theory approaches to data analysis (e.g. Chang & Schallert 2007); sometimes retrospection is the sole method of investigation (e.g. Bartłomiejczyk 2006), but more frequently it is nested in multi-method designs in combination with quantitative or other qualitative approaches, such as interviews and narratives (e.g. Chang & Schallert 2007; Vik-Touvinen 2002).

Several methodological challenges have to be addressed in order to enhance the credibility of retrospective research in interpreting studies. One is the effect of memory decay and the related issue of memory support for retrospection. Another is the interaction between researcher and participants in the data collection process. Some recent studies have sought to minimise this by instructing participants to conduct retrospection on their own in the interpreting booth, but the implications of these changes to the procedure have not been discussed. Yet another challenge arises from the fact that qualitative methods place a premium on understanding and valuing the subjective experience of the participants. The researcher is expected to provide solid descriptive data, on the basis of which the reader can come to an understanding of the meaning of the experience under study. This has to be balanced with the need to enhance validity by summarising the research findings by means of descriptive statistics. One way of addressing this methodological challenge is to use more 'lateral thinking' and experiment with different methods of data display. Mixing methods, for example by interspersing quotes among graphic summaries, can help elaborate on the findings and serve as a starting point for a more detailed and specific discussion. Hyperlinks to electronic repositories of verbal protocols offer another opportunity for privileged access to authentic data. On the other hand, designs which involve quantification of verbal data need to be explicit and transparent regarding data handling procedures, that is, how the coding schemes were derived, how the reliability of coding was ensured, and how the interpretation of the findings was reached.

The further successful application of retrospective methods in interpreting studies largely depends on how these challenges are resolved. Procedures for addressing these issues are available in the quantitative research paradigm (see Liu 2011). Hild (2007) examined the use of triangulation (methodological and data) as a strategy for ensuring the robustness of retrospective studies, and in a rare case of investigator triangulation, Tiselius and Jenset (2011) assessed the reliability of earlier expertise research by applying the same methodology for data collection and coding.

ADELINA HILD

RHETORIC

Rhetoric as the art of persuasive language use has been developed in the Western tradition since the fifth century BCE. Its original focus on spoken language use (ORALITY) would imply an immediate relevance to interpreting, but rather few authors in interpreting studies have engaged with the classic principles and ideas of rhetoric, as shaped by Aristotle, in their work.

Aristotle distinguished between three kinds of oratory – political, forensic, and ceremonial – and three modes of persuasion a speaker may resort to: *ethos* (the speaker's credibility); *pathos* (putting the audience into a certain frame of mind); and *logos* (the proof, or apparent proof, provided by the words of the speech). Most influential among his guidelines for successful communication in various rhetorical situations are the so-called canons of rhetoric – five stages reflecting how orators plan and execute their performance: *inventio* (ideation), *dispositio* (structuring), *elocutio* (verbal composition, including stylistic devices); *memoria* (memorizing) and *actio/pronuntiatio* (delivery).

As can be gleaned from this brief review of some central concepts, rhetoric is relevant to interpreting in multiple ways, with regard not only to original speakers and speeches as INPUT VARIABLES but also to interpreters and their own language production. Most obviously, much SIMULTANEOUS INTERPRETING in international conference settings is done in political fora. The study by Vuorikoski (2002, 2004) on interpreting in the European Parliament is an example of research drawing on principles of rhetoric and argumentation (New Rhetoric) in this setting. Examples of research incorporating rhetorical concepts can also be found in domains such as MEDIA INTERPRETING and COURTROOM INTERPRETING. Pöchhacker (2012b), for instance, investigated the fate of rhetorical devices in a corpus of six German simultaneous interpretations of President Barack Obama's inaugural address. Gallez and Reynders (2015), on the other hand, focus on ethos as the image a participant in court, in this case the prosecutor, wishes to convey of himself through the display of competence, and reveal how this can be altered through interpreting. Finally, research on QUALITY CRITERIA in simultaneous interpreting (e.g. Collados Aís et al. 2007) shows that, as in Aristotle's discussion of argumentation, the substance of the message takes priority, but listeners do appreciate good delivery.

The results of research on rhetorical aspects of communication in the contexts where interpreters are typically employed can serve to inform interpreter EDUCATION in two ways: (1) by supplying a more thorough understanding of the kind of language use interpreters are expected – and can expect – to deal with, including a speaker's 'personal touch' in addressing the audience (e.g. 'inclusive' language, phatic communication) and use of figures of speech, hedges and other rhetorical devices; (2) by foregrounding the oratorical skills that interpreters themselves, in their role as the speaker's alter ego, must possess. Indeed, many authors since Herbert (1952) have stressed public speaking skills as a *sine qua non* for professional interpreters, and consecutive interpreters in particular, but few institutions appear to have enshrined the teaching of classical rhetoric in their CURRICULUM.

ANNA-RIITTA VUORIKOSKI

ROLE

↑ SOCIOLOGICAL APPROACHES

→ ETHICS, → PARTICIPATION FRAMEWORK, → POSITIONING

The notion of role is one of the most central constructs in social science. Role theory, which became prominent in the 1950s and 1960s, serves as an umbrella term for work in different disciplines (sociology, social psychology, social anthropology) focusing on role construction and related concepts (social position, status, identity, expectations). The field is characterized by a confusing myriad of definitions and different concepts (see Biddle 1986).

The origins of role theory lie in a theatrical metaphor, borrowed from drama: writers have long described individuals slipping into different roles. Role theory attempts to funnel this everyday concept into a coherent theory. Metaphorically, a role is "the part each person is called on to play in the social drama" (Calhoun 2002). It can be viewed as a "script" for a particular behavior in a particular situation, staged in front of an audience. Less metaphorically, role can be defined as "a set of expectations society has of individuals in a given social position or status" (Baert 2006: 524).

Constructs such as role strain, role overload and role conflict are used to examine problematic roles. Top-down approaches see roles as associated primarily with stable positions within a larger social network. Bottom-up approaches focus more on interactive and dynamic aspects of role (Calhoun 2002). Biddle (1986) differentiates between five major theoretical perspectives within role theory: structural functionalism, symbolic interactionism, and structural, organizational and cognitive role theory. Role theories associated with the first two theoretical frameworks have found their way into interpreting studies.

The construct of role in interpreting studies

Prescriptive conceptualizations of the interpreter's role are consistent with structural functionalist role models, where roles are viewed as "fixed bundles of expectations" (Calhoun 2002), fulfilling a vital function within more-or-less stable social systems. Structural functionalism, prominent in social research up to the mid-1970s through the work of R. K. Merton, T. Parsons, and R. Linton, is characterized by a "neglect of agency" (Baert 2006: 525) and does not leave much room for negotiation of norms or creativity.

A symbolic interactionist perspective has been adopted in a number of micro-analyses of interpreted talk. In symbolic interactionism, which is derived from G. H. Mead's social behaviorism and represented by scholars such as R. Turner and E. Goffman, roles are seen as evolving through social interaction, with individuals not merely following scripted roles but creatively making, taking and managing them.

Throughout history, interpreters have been ascribed multiple roles, often appearing as Janus-faced intermediaries. With the regulation of interpreter behavior in codes of ETHICS and standards of professional conduct, the role of interpreters was restricted to that of mere conveyors of language, and, in less restrictive interpretations, of culture, though it soon became apparent that prescriptive, narrow role sets could frequently not be maintained in practice. This intrinsic contradiction has made the notion of role one of the most prominent topics in interpreting studies, one that has become increasingly complex and elusive. Mason (2009b), following Davies and Harré (1990), thus suggests substituting the static role construct with the more dynamic notion of POSITIONING.

The bulk of role-related publications have focused on COMMUNITY INTERPRETING and court interpreting, where asymmetrical power constellations and diverging social and cultural backgrounds make the interpreter's role particularly challenging. However, there are also publications on the topic of role in CONFERENCE INTERPRETING and MEDIA INTERPRETING. Role is a key concept in both spoken and SIGNED LANGUAGE INTERPRETING research, with seminal publications in both fields (e.g. Berk-Seligson 1990; Knapp-Potthoff & Knapp 1986; Metzger 1999; Roy 2000a; Wadensjö 1998).

Interpreter role constructions oscillate on a continuum between non-involvement and active agency (even intrusiveness). Narrow role constructs view interpreters as mechanistic conveyors of language: passive, neutral and invisible. Metaphorically, the role of interpreters is compared to that of a mere conduit, machine, telephone, transmission belt, robot, ghost or "non-person" (Roy 1993), to name but a few of the sometimes creative labels relating to the function of interpreters. The so-called 'conduit model' of interpreting, which has its roots in mechanistic communication models, continues to be maintained by ethical codes and has prevailed particularly in court interpreting. The myth of the interpreter's INVISIBILITY has been deconstructed by broader role constructs, which perceive interpreters as actively participating third parties (Knapp-Potthoff & Knapp 1986). Interpreters are portrayed as "communication facilitators", "helpers", "advocates", "bi-cultural experts" (Roy 1993), "culture brokers" (Kaufert & Koolage 1984), "intercultural agents" (Barsky 1996), "cultural mediators" (Straniero Sergio 1998) or even "conciliators" (Schneider 1992).

Research on interpreter role(s) has been conducted on both a conceptual (theoretical) and an empirical level, with scholars often discerning confusion as to what should or should not be considered part of an interpreter's role. At a macro-/meso-level, the role of interpreters has been addressed in interaction MODELS of prototypical interpreting constellations. Examples of such default constellations are Anderson's (1976) linear type case of three-party interaction, Pöchhacker's (1992, 2005) interactant model of the interpreting situation, Alexieva's (1997) multi-parameter typology of interpreting constellations, Gentile et al.'s (1996) model of "three-cornered interpreting" or, with a focus on NATURAL TRANSLATION/INTERPRETING, Knapp and Knapp-Potthoff's (1985) "normal format" of mediated interaction. Examples of a micro-level focus on role issues are fine-grained studies using ethnographic and DISCOURSE ANALYTICAL APPROACHES, as discussed further below.

Interpreter role from a conceptual perspective

At a conceptual level, there are publications leaning towards a structural functionalist perspective, often presenting a literature-based synopsis of role constructions and/or typologies of interpreter roles, and frequently advocating, in some cases even quite rigidly, one (or more) particular role type(s). Another strand of publications conceptualizes interpreter role constructions from an inter- or multi-disciplinary perspective, often trying to forge a more flexible or context-related understanding of interpreter roles.

Among the first to critically examine interpreter roles were Anderson (1976) and Brislin (1980). Anderson anticipated in the late 1970s what was later confirmed by others, namely that "the interpreter's role is always partially undefined" (1976: 216). He was also one of the first to systematically address role conflicts and issues of POWER inherent to the interpreter's role from a sociological perspective, specifically taking up Simmel's (1964) ideas on the triad. Brislin (1980), focusing on sources of misunderstanding in intercultural communication, made a case for expanding the role of interpreters to also include tasks such as advocacy.

Role metaphors and descriptions are at the center of a much-cited article by Roy (1993), which is based on a review of role issues in signed language interpreting by Witter-Merithew (1986). While Witter-Merithew (1986) described four major role constructs (interpreters as helpers, mechanistic conduits, communication facilitators, and bilingual, bicultural specialists), Roy contends that these may in fact be reduced to two major positions pivoting between "extreme personal interpreter involvement" and "extreme to not-so-extreme non-involvement" (1993/2002: 349). With a focus on signed language interpreting and from a practical and educational perspective, McIntire and Sanderson (1995) discuss issues of (dis)empowerment along the lines of the four interpreter roles outlined by Witter-Merithew (1986).

With regard to COURTROOM INTERPRETING and the widespread insistence on "verbatim translation" among judicial institutions, Morris (1995, 2010) discusses the inadequacy of the conduit model in court settings. Hale (2008), in a similar vein, presents a typology of five court interpreter roles, prioritizing, from a more prescriptive stance, the role of "faithful renderer of others' utterances".

Codified role prescriptions, and in particular central principles of ethical codes such as impartiality, NEUTRALITY and FIDELITY (or faithfulness), have been taken up in a number of predominantly theoretical publications on signed language, court and COMMUNITY INTERPRETING. These have called attention to the fact that codified role standards may not always be maintained, or even prove helpful, in ethically challenging situations (Hale 2007; Kaufert & Putsch 1997; Mikkelson 1998, 2008).

Interpreter agency has also been conceptualized on the basis of predominantly SOCIOLOGICAL APPROACHES. Wadensjö (1998) takes up Goffman's (1961) three-level role construct (normative role, typical role, and role performance), as well as his concepts of PARTICIPATION FRAMEWORK and FOOTING, and applies her theoretical framework to a corpus of authentic interpreter-mediated encounters. Llewellyn-Jones and Lee (2013, 2014) define a "role-space" for interpreters, based on Goffman's concept of self (1959). With respect to neutrality, Tipton (2008a) presents a theoretical perspective on interpreter agency based on Giddens' (1984) structuration theory. In a later paper she also takes up ideas from adult education, particularly Donald Schön's (1983) construct of reflective practice, to discuss the "de-centering of the self" among conference interpreters (Tipton 2009).

Drawing on Bourdieu's (1990) concepts of HABITUS and field, Bernstein's (1990) theory of pedagogic discourse and Toury's (1995) construct of translational NORMS, Inghilleri (2003, 2005a) focuses on interpreter agency and habitus in ASYLUM SETTINGS.

Interpreter role from an empirical perspective

Empirical research on interpreter role based on surveys, discourse-analytical, ethnographic and experimental approaches can be grouped into studies focusing on (a) the examination of role descriptions and expectations by interpreters or users, and (b) interpreters' role performance in authentic situations.

Research on role descriptions and expectations

Studies researching role descriptions and expectations use quantitative and/or qualitative data. They examine both interpreters' self-perceptions and their roles as perceived by others (users/clients). Most of these studies basically seek to examine the status quo in a specific setting, often (though not exclusively) with a focus on perceived role performance. They point to diverging views and inherent role conflicts. Based on their findings, a number of scholars have also attempted to develop new role typologies (e.g. Drennan & Swartz 1999; Leanza 2005; Bischoff et al. 2012) with sometimes very discrepant categories. The findings of many of these studies indicate that interpreters define their role along the lines of active intervention and cultural MEDIATION, often assuming a more active role than ascribed to them.

As an example of SURVEY RESEARCH on role expectations, Mesa's (2000) questionnaire-based study among service providers and community interpreters in Canada found that users have a different view of the confines of the interpreter's role, ranking the explanation of cultural terms lower than the interpreters themselves rank them. By contrast, Kadrić (2001), in a quantitative survey among Austrian judges, found surprising acceptance of interpreters explaining cultural concepts and simplifying legal language and terms. In one of the largest role-related quantitative studies across conference, court and healthcare settings, Angelelli (2004b) concludes on the basis of a questionnaire-based survey that interpreters assume the role of visible agents who, among other tasks, hold themselves responsible for building TRUST and bridging cultural gaps. Questionnaire-based surveys on the self-perception of interpreters in different community settings have also been conducted by the GRETI research group at the University of Granada (Martin & Abril Martí 2008; Martin & Ortega Herráez 2009; Ortega Herráez et al. 2009).

With reference to HEALTHCARE INTERPRETING, a quantitative questionnaire-based survey among Austrian doctors, nurses, therapists and social workers by Pöchhacker (2000b) points to widely varying views among respondents regarding interpreters' role profile, while Clifford (2004) has found a surprising degree of acceptance of a more active role of interpreters in qualitative in-depth INTERVIEWS with Canadian healthcare personnel and interpreters. Qualitative methods have been used in a growing number of studies in this domain (e.g. Hsieh et al. 2010; Bischoff et al. 2012), while Rudvin and Tomassini (2008) use both questionnaires and semi-structured interviews to highlight the over-burdened role of language mediators in healthcare and educational settings in Italy.

Focusing on PSYCHOTHERAPY, Bot (2005) conducted qualitative interviews with therapists, patients and interpreters to conclude that there is little communication and consensus as to the confines of the interpreter's role. Granger and Baker (2002) and Dabic (2010) present similar findings for MENTAL HEALTH INTERPRETING encounters.

Within conference interpreting research, issues related to the interpreter's role are featured in a smaller number of publications, all pointing to a preference for a less active role. Kopczyński (1994), in a questionnaire-based survey, points to a preference among conference participants for a "ghost role" of the interpreter over an "intruder role". Setton and Guo (2011) report on Chinese conference interpreters' dislike of a cultural mediator role, whereas Zwischenberger's (2011) large-scale web-based survey among AIIC members found that respondents mostly saw themselves as communication facilitators and mediators between two cultures.

The use of ETHNOGRAPHIC METHODS (such as participant observation, interviews and discourse-analytical corpus analysis) has been predominant in community interpreting research, with a strong focus on healthcare interpreting. Drennan and Swartz (1999) discuss interpreter roles (language specialist, culture specialist, patient advocate, institutional therapist), particularly addressing problems linked with the advocacy role. Based on a study of interpreter-mediated consultations in PEDIATRIC SETTINGS in Switzerland, Leanza (2005) presents a new role typology (system agent, integration agent, community agent and linguistic agent) adapted from a typology proposed by Jalbert (1998).

Research on role performance

The bulk of role-related publications focuses on interpreters' role performance, with qualitative discourse-analytical and ethnographic studies predominating. Among the theoretical frameworks that have been applied are interactional sociolinguistics, conversation analysis, ethnography of communication, critical discourse analysis, literary theory (dialogism) and norm theory. With few exceptions, data are mostly corpora of authentic interpreter-mediated encounters. Studies on role performance are often more descriptive, seeking to describe interpreter behavior in action and linking and explaining these findings with a particular theoretical framework or theoretical assumptions regarding role behavior.

Pioneering examples of qualitative discourse-analytical studies are Roy's (2000a) micro-analysis of a sign language interpreter's TURN-TAKING in an educational setting, Wadensjö's (1998) analysis of interpreter-mediated encounters in immigration and medical settings, Metzger's (1999) case study of a pediatric interview, and Barsky's (1994) study of Canadian asylum hearings. The core finding of all of these studies is that interpreters are not mere conduits and invisible non-persons, but often assume an active and even interventionist role.

Berk-Seligson's (1990) ground-breaking study of court interpreting draws attention to the fact that court interpreters are not "unobtrusive" but "intrusive elements" (1990: 96). She resorts to a wide range of methodological approaches, including fieldwork and an experimental research design. Focusing on linguistic politeness, she illustrates that interpreters' renditions may influence a juror's witness evaluation.

Often inspired by these seminal works, there are a number of discourse-analytical studies focusing on role issues in healthcare interpreting (e.g. Bolden 2000; Bot 2005; Pöchhacker 2000a), court interpreting (e.g. Angermeyer 2005; Berk-Seligson 2009; Kadrić 2001; Shlesinger 1991), police interpreting (e.g. Donk 1994) and asylum interpreting (e.g. Keselman et al. 2010; Mason 2009b; Merlini 2009a; Pöllabauer 2004).

Monacelli (2009) is one of the few authors to focus on the role of conference interpreters in a qualitative (and partly quantitative) study of an interpreted conference (English/Italian). She points to interpreters' instinct for self-preservation through distancing, de-personalization and mitigation, theoretically grounding her analysis in Goffman's (1967) participation framework. The only large-scale ethnographic study on the interpreter's role in simultaneous conference interpreting (English/Turkish) is Diriker's (2004) investigation of interpreters' (in)visibility, which proves that, in contrast to the idealized interpreter role prescriptions found in the meta-discourse on interpreting, interpreters are actively involved in the interactional dynamics.

The role of interpreters in media interpreting is taken up by Baker (1997), who analyzes instances of an interpreter-mediated TV interview with Saddam Hussein in which the interpreter opts for a literal rendition to avoid being accused of misrepresenting the speakers. Straniero Sergio (1999) focuses on TALK SHOW INTERPRETING and, based on conversation analysis and ethnomethodology, argues that the talk show format calls for stronger interpreter visibility.

Examples of quantitative discourse-analytical studies are Rosenberg's (2002) analysis of English/Spanish medical interviews in California and Hale's (2004) study of interpreted courtroom questions and discourse markers in Australian courts. Rosenberg (2002) points to the role of interpreters as "full-fledged" participants, while Hale (2004) calls attention to the power struggles interpreters may find themselves in.

From an ethnographic perspective, Angelelli (2004a) focuses on medical interpreting (English/Spanish) in a Californian hospital, pointing to a paradigmatic role shift from conduit to active participant. Likewise, Davidson (2000) discusses English/Spanish medical discourse, suggesting that interpreters are "gatekeepers" who keep the interview on track and speakers on schedule. Studies of interpreting in asylum hearings (e.g. Kolb & Pöchhacker 2008; Pöchhacker & Kolb 2009; Scheffer 2001) suggest that interpreters frequently take on a more active (co-interviewer) role, forging alliances with the institutional representatives. For the very specific setting of the Yehuda Military Court, Lipkin (2010) concludes that interpreters are assigned multiple duties and often assume tasks other than interpreting per se.

SONJA PÖLLABAUER

ROLE PLAY

↑ PEDAGOGY

Role play in the educational setting is a tool for promoting individual learning experiences that has received increasing attention in the PEDAGOGY of interpreting, and in particular, DIALOGUE INTERPRETING. The basic idea of role plays and simulations, as well as their practical application in different domains, have their foundation in psychology and can be traced back to psychodrama, as developed by Moreno (1946), which was at first used primarily in psychotherapy. Role plays give participants the opportunity to examine a situation from a variety of perspectives, thereby gaining a deeper understanding of it.

There is no single theoretical framework for role plays in interaction-related pedagogy. Different disciplines incorporate their specific points of interest and adapt the instrument of role play to their own requirements. This also applies to the use of role-playing in the EDU-CATION of interpreters. Irrespective of the context, however, role-playing always involves the human being with body and mind, including social and communicative needs. Combining intellect and feelings, role play requires the rational mind to operate in an emotional setting. More specifically, it allows students to practise the interplay between *emotions, identification* (with a role and certain personal attitudes) and *reflection* – to analyse and generate alternative views on a given situation.

Although role play has been applied to interpreter training for decades, there has been little systematic analysis of its use in this field. Recent innovative practices are mainly inspired by approaches from theatre pedagogy (e.g. Bahadır 2011; Kadrić 2011), with important contributions also from the fields of foreign language teaching (e.g. Okada 2010) and Conversation Analysis (Stokoe 2011).

As a pedagogical technique, role play is suitable for all interpreting SETTINGS, MODES and combinations of languages, whether spoken or signed (e.g. Metzger 2000). An important distinction is whether role plays are based on a (full or partial) *script* or on a *scenario* (a thorough description of the situation, the interactants and their goals and attitudes). While it can be useful and convenient to work with read-out scripts (e.g. Rudvin & Tomassini 2011), particularly when simulating conference-like interaction, reliance on fully scripted role plays foregrounds translational performance and deprives trainees of opportunities to 'live' the situation and assume responsibility for it, for instance by taking interactional initiatives (see Niemants 2013). By contrast, scenario-based role plays, especially in dialogue interpreting, promote authenticity, credibility and diversity of expression, and permit the co-constructed interaction to unfold as a unique interpersonal event. Enacted as a 'true situation', with emotion, identification and reflection, the role-play experience helps students prepare for similar situations in the future, rehearsing, as it were, a later 'performance' (Goffman 1959). Thus, the staged interaction in a role play allows interpreting students to discover and apply STRATEGIES for dealing with asymmetries of POWER and divergent expectations, while developing their communication skills and their awareness of linguistic and cultural differences (e.g. Kadrić 2014).

Aside from their use in training, role plays are also employed in ASSESSMENT (see Wadensjö 2014). In either context it is important to establish clear rules, including thoroughly described roles and well-defined criteria for evaluation. In training, this serves to create a safe space for teachers and students alike – an atmosphere that allows for openness and experimentation, with assessment carried out mainly in the reflection phase by the participants themselves.

Role plays emulate real-life situations, with students as participants. Simulations, as a special form of role play, involve one or more participants in their actual real-life roles, as when a medical interview is enacted with the help of a physician, thus bringing the role play even closer to professional reality.

MIRA KADRIĆ

ROME

↑ HISTORY

The Roman Empire was inhabited by speakers of many different languages (Adams 2003). As well as societal multilingualism, there was widespread individual multilingualism. Nevertheless, there were numerous language contact situations in which linguistic mediators were needed, whether in official dealings between the Roman authorities and subject populations, or in private dealings between individuals who did not speak one another's languages.

The Latin and Greek terminology for 'interpreter' brings certain problems in identifying and examining the roles of interpreters in ancient evidence. The Latin *interpres* (pl. *interpretes*) and Greek *hermēneus* (pl. *hermēneis*) are both also used in the more general sense of 'mediator' or 'middleman'. To identify an individual *interpres* or *hermēneus* as an interpreter in the linguistic sense requires gathering together whatever subsidiary evidence is available about that individual's language use, professional and social position, and precise role in the document in question.

There are comparatively few references to interpreters in contemporary written sources. An extensive, although not comprehensive, corpus of examples is collected in Wiotte-Franz (2001), whose discussion reviews the evidence but does not offer more in-depth analysis. Interesting insights can, however, be gleaned from the sources available, and the relative INVISIBILITY of interpreters in ancient sources in itself says something important about the contemporary perception of interpreters and their professional roles.

Evidence for interpreters and interpreting in the Roman Empire comes primarily from contemporary historical and literary works in Latin and Greek – the authors of which for the most part display no real insight into the actual process of interpreting and the ROLE of the interpreter as an active agent. In some cases, the position of the interpreter was stigmatised and associated with duplicitous or traitorous behaviour. Individuals involved in MILITARY INTERPRETING in the army of Julius Caesar in Gaul, for example, were mistrusted and vulnerable to attack for their perceived betrayal of both sides – a position similar to that of modern military interpreters in Iraq and Afghanistan (Mairs 2011). The interpreter might also be viewed as a lower class and low-status counterpart to elite literary translators, a group whose position has attracted dedicated studies in their own right (McElduff 2009).

Inscriptions and documentary texts on papyrus and wood offer an alternative body of source material for exploring the role and STATUS of interpreters in the Roman Empire. A document from Vindolanda, near Hadrian's Wall in Britain, contains the verb 'to interpret' (*interpretari*) in a more generic mediatory sense, although in a region where monolingual speakers of Latin will certainly have needed to call upon the services of bilingual middlemen (Mairs 2012b). In the Roman fortifications along the river Danube, there are several examples of tombstones belonging to *interpretes*, all of whom held positions within the Roman army and administration. One of these is described in addition as a *negotiator*, or trader, highlighting the role of interpreters in commercial activities (Kolnik 1978).

In the eastern Mediterranean and Black Sea region, where Greek, not Latin, was the LINGUA FRANCA, we find further references to interpreters. Examples from the Bosporan Kingdom, on the northern shore of the Black Sea, show interpreters in dealings with nomadic peoples of the steppe. In Syria, there is evidence of a local interpreter in the service of the Roman administration. Most sources, however, come from EGYPT and from the Greek papyrological record. Over a hundred references to interpreters and interpreting are preserved (Mairs 2012a). Some of these almost certainly refer to middlemen whose role was primarily commercial, although in the multilingual environment of Roman Egypt, knowledge of more than one language will have been an advantage to traders. In other examples, *hermēneus* appears as a professional title in connection with language MEDIATION.

Several key areas emerge in which the Roman authorities had recourse to interpreters to deal with non-Latin-speaking subjects of the empire (Eck 2004). The army is perhaps the most important of these. *Interpres* appears as a professional title on inscriptions almost exclusively in contexts associated with the army, such as those of the army officers who served as interpreters in the Danubian provinces. Interpreters were more frequently, however, denied any acknowledged professional role and status. The interpreters used by Julius Caesar in his campaigns in Gaul, for example, were recruited ad hoc from available bilinguals, and not considered as a professional corps. In the administration and in diplomacy, the role of interpreters is occasionally acknowledged.

The case of interpreters in the Roman Empire provides another example of the invisibility of the interpreter. In written sources, interpreters are seldom referred to. Only in certain specific contexts, such as the army, in specific provinces, was interpreter a recognised professional role. In the multilingual milieu of the Roman Empire, large numbers of individuals will nevertheless have acted as linguistic mediators on a daily basis.

RACHEL MAIRS

RUSSIA

↑ HISTORY

The history of interpreting in Russia can be broken down into periods consistent with the various stages in the development of the Russian language: the Old Rus' period (9th – 14th century); the Tsardom of Russia, or Muscovy (15th – 17th century); the age of Peter the Great and the subsequent formative period of modern Russian (18th – 19th century); and the Soviet period (20th century).

Old Rus' period

In 864 Cyril and Methodius, the two Greek monks known as the Apostles of the Slavs, were sent by the Byzantine Emperor to spread Christianity among Slavic peoples. They started by creating an alphabet, later to be called Cyrillic, and used it to translate several religious texts from Greek to Old Church Slavonic. It is then that Old Rus' is considered to have acquired a script and a literature, with a resulting need for translations.

Russian princes are known to have used interpreters' services in negotiations with Mongol khans who ruled over Rus' during the Tatar-Mongol 'Yoke' period (1243–1480). Prince Ivan

Kalita of Moscow, who conducted extensive trade with the Golden Horde, had a great need for interpreters. The word for 'interpreter' used then, *tolmach*, is of Tatar origin. Initially the *tolmaches* were Golden Horde soldiers who spoke Russian and lived among civilian Tatars in Tatar Sloboda, a settlement along the road leading from Moscow to the Golden Horde. The *tolmaches* acted exclusively as interpreters and were hired for ambassadorial missions, negotiations, feasts, and the like. Later on, interpreters of Tatar origin were joined by Russians who had learned the Tatar language (Semenets & Panasyev 1991).

Tsardom of Russia, or Muscovy

In the late fifteenth and early sixteenth centuries the Moscow district of Zamoskvorechye became home to Tolmatskaya Sloboda, a compact settlement of interpreters working from and into all the various languages needed at the royal court. The first documented mention of interpreting as an occupation was made in the sixteenth century, when several reports referred to payment for interpreters' services. Historical documents also mention the *dyaks* (high-ranking officials) Dmitry Gerasimov, Vlasy Viskovaty and Ivan Viskovaty, who were both fluent in several foreign languages and shone as diplomats under Tsar Ivan the Terrible. Their unique skills and activity contributed greatly to Russia's close relations with many nations.

Translators and interpreters in Muscovy formed a special category of civil servants on the staff of all the government agencies that were in contact with foreigners. A special role in the history of interpretation in Russia was played by *Posolsky Prikaz*, the government's central diplomatic office, which existed from 1549 to 1720 (see Kunenkov 2012). Its responsibilities included foreign affairs, ransom and exchange of prisoners, as well as the management of some south-eastern territories and certain categories of the 'service class' (persons bound by military obligations). Ivan Viskovaty was the first chief of Posolsky Prikaz, from 1549 to 1570. According to a report dated 1689, the agency's staff included 22 translators and 17 interpreters, working into and from Greek, Latin, Swedish, Dutch, English, Italian, Armenian, Tatar, Turkish, Kalmyk, Nogai, Khiva, Persian and Mongolian.

In the seventeenth century, as the Russian state attained a more prominent international status, the duties of Posolsky Prikaz and its staff were expanded considerably (Kunenkov 2012). The agency was now in charge of steering Russia's foreign policy and of everyday diplomatic functions, such as sending ambassadors abroad, receiving and taking leave of foreign missions, drafting diplomatic documents, correspondence, negotiations and, starting from the early eighteenth century, appointment and supervision of Russia's permanent diplomatic staff abroad.

Embassy staff interpreters often conducted negotiations on behalf of their ambassadors with the authorities of other countries. In addition, interpreters acted as couriers, delivering documents from Posolsky Prikaz to other agencies or cities. Before being taken on, translators and interpreters had to pass a language examination and swear loyalty to the monarch. Between 1645 and 1682, Posolsky Prikaz maintained positions for 84 translators and 185 interpreters. Each interpreter had to know at least two languages. The agency trained its own personnel, enrolling young men as apprentices to experienced employees who taught them languages and the intricacies of their job (see Voevoda 2009).

The translators and interpreters for Western languages were mostly European prisoners of war, whereas Oriental languages were handled by men of Eastern origin, including Tatars from Kazan, Astrakhan and other areas. Interpreters also included members of former noble families and boyars' sons rescued from Tatar, Turkish, Persian, Kalmyk or, less frequently, Polish or Swedish captivity. From 1646, all interpreters employed by Posolsky Prikaz had to be (or become) Orthodox Christians. Unlike translators, many interpreters worked with a combination of Western and Oriental languages.

Peter the Great and the formative period of modern Russian

In 1720 Posolsky Prikaz was disbanded and replaced with the College of Foreign Affairs (see Farafonova et al. 1998). Peter the Great's political reform broadened the country's economic and cultural ties with European nations, generating a demand for translation of texts on science and technology as well as fiction. The literary standard of Russian began to take shape at the time, enriched not least by translation.

As a result of Peter's reforms, the eighteenth century saw the emergence of an aristocratic class that spoke European languages as fluently as they spoke their mother tongue or, sometimes, even better. Whereas Peter the Great himself did not speak French, the principal language of eighteenth-century (and later nineteenth-century) diplomacy, and was accompanied by interpreters, international contacts were generally handled by members of the aristocracy serving in the diplomatic corps or in the military. As all of them spoke fluent French, they had no need for interpreters, which is probably why no names of outstanding interpreters in nineteenth-century Russia are known. Even so, it was then that the fundamental principles and rules of professional translation and interpreting were laid down.

Soviet period

In the 1920s and the 1930s, interpreting at official negotiations was done by employees of the People's Commissariat of Foreign Affairs, most of them former diplomats of tsarist Russia. Until the mid-twentieth century, consecutive interpreting remained the only option available for meetings and talks.

It is believed that the first experiment with SIMULTANEOUS INTERPRETING was carried out in the Soviet Union in 1928, during the Sixth Congress of the Communist International. The weekly *Krasnaya Niva* published photographs that year, in which interpreters are seen sitting in armchairs in front of the rostrum. Each of them has a bulky contraption around the neck to support a microphone, but no earphones. The interpreters listened directly to the speaker and translated simultaneously (see Gofman 1963).

The first specially equipped booths and earphones appeared at the thirteenth plenary meeting of the Communist International's Executive Committee, held in the USSR in 1933. The interpreters listened to the speakers through earphones. In Leningrad, simultaneous interpreting was first used at the International Congress of Physiology in 1935. Academician Ivan Pavlov's welcome address was interpreted simultaneously into French, English and German. After that, simultaneous interpreting was used occasionally at meetings of the Communist International's Executive Committee.

Interpreters played an enormous role in World War Two. Apart from interrogating prisoners and obtaining military intelligence, they were crucial to diplomatic negotiations among the Allies. After the war, a sizeable group of Soviet interpreters worked at the NUREMBERG TRIAL, where Russian was one of the working languages along with English, French and German (e.g. Stupnikova 2003). It was not until the Nuremberg and Tokyo trials that the term 'simultaneous interpreter' came into use in the USSR.

Congresses of the Communist Party of the Soviet Union opened up more opportunities to refine the practice and organization of simultaneous interpreting on a large scale, starting with the Nineteenth Congress in 1952. Fixed, ventilated, soundproof booths were installed in the Kremlin specially for the event. They were used to interpret speeches from Russian into other languages. However, interpreting of foreign speeches into Russian was consecutive, performed by an interpreter standing next to the speaker at the rostrum. The system was used in both directions at all subsequent Communist Party congresses and other conferences and forums with foreign participation. It was based on RELAY INTERPRETING, Russian being the pivot language.

Apart from foreign languages, simultaneous interpreting was also done into other languages of the Soviet Union at sessions of the USSR Supreme Soviet. The equipment installed in the Kremlin Palace of Congresses could accommodate up to 29 languages.

For many decades Soviet interpreter training developed in isolation behind the Iron Curtain. Students were not allowed to go abroad to practise their skills, and no native speakers from abroad were allowed to teach local students. There were few, if any, opportunities for direct communication with foreigners. Despite these limitations, a strong pedagogical tradition emerged, developing some unique teaching methods and producing numerous top-quality interpreters.

From the 1960s to the 1980s, the USSR gave massive support to developing countries in Asia, Africa and Latin America whose leaders had proclaimed plans to build socialist societies. Much of that support consisted in supplies of armaments and military hardware, followed by engineers and instructors. As few of these spoke foreign languages, they were accompanied by interpreters, most of them graduates of the Military Institute of Foreign Languages (now the Military University) or the Moscow Pedagogical Institute of Foreign Languages (now Moscow State Linguistic University), two of the Soviet Union's major training centres for translators and interpreters. The Military Institute was famous for having designed some very efficient methods of accelerated interpreter training, and for the great variety of languages it taught (up to 30), including some 'rare' languages like Khmer, Albanian and Amharic.

The Soviet educational approach aimed, as is still the case in Russia today, at training versatile professionals capable of both translation and interpreting. Moreover, students are taught foreign language skills in parallel with translation and interpreting, all in the framework of a single university curriculum. Simultaneous interpreting, however, has always been taught as an optional or postgraduate course.

Russian scholars teaching in these institutions have made considerable contributions to the theory of interpreting. The main representatives of what has been referred to as the SOVIET SCHOOL of interpreting studies are Ghelly CHERNOV, Anatoly Shiryaev (1979) and Rurik Minyar-Beloruchev (1969a, 1980).

With Soviet–US relations central to twentieth-century history, a number of English/Russian interpreters at the summit meetings of USSR and US leaders became media personalities known far beyond their professional circle, some of whom also published their MEMOIRS. Among them are Valentin Berezhkov and Oleg Troyanovsky, who worked with Iosif Stalin; Viktor Sukhodrev, who interpreted for Nikita Khrushchev and Leonid Brezhnev; and Pavel Palazhchenko, Mikhail Gorbachev's interpreter (see Palazchenko 1997).

By the early twenty-first century, some 150 Russian universities were enrolling students in interpreter training programmes, and the demand for professional interpreters in Russia continues to rise. Now as before, most degrees certify their holder's ability to both translate and interpret consecutively, from and into a foreign language.

SVETLANA BURLYAY, IGOR MATYUSHIN AND DMITRY YERMOLOVICH

SACAJAWEA

Sacajawea was a Shoshoni (also spelled Shoshone) woman associated with the Lewis and Clark Corps of Discovery expedition of 1804–6 from St. Louis, Missouri, to the mouth of the Columbia River on the Pacific Ocean and back. She was born in the late 1780s. The date of her death is controversial; it was either early December 1812, or April 9, 1884.

She joined the expedition at the beginning of 1805, when French Canadian Toussaint Charbonneau was hired as an interpreter. Charbonneau arrived at the expedition's encampment on the Missouri River with two adolescent Shoshoni girls who had previously been taken captive by the Hidatsas (called "Minnetaree" in the Lewis and Clark journals). Charbonneau had won or purchased them and impregnated both. The toddler of one of the girls would have been an inconvenience to the expedition, and that mother and child were left behind from the start.

The other, Sacajawea, gave birth to a son on February 11, 1805, and he was given the name Jean Baptiste Charbonneau. Soon thereafter the members of the expedition set out on the trek west, with Sacajawea's infant on a cradleboard strapped to her back.

Sacajawea performed four functions during the expedition. Daily, while breastfeeding her child, she located food resources to feed Lewis and Clark and their men. The mother and child accompanying the men signaled to groups they encountered along the way that theirs was not a war party. In negotiations with the Shoshonis, she was part of the interpreting chain from English to French to Hidatsa to Shoshoni and back. And when traveling through country familiar from her childhood, she directed Lewis and Clark to the best (or the only) routes.

During the westward journey, Sacajawea encountered her own people, the Lemhi Shoshonis, from whom she had been separated years before. Her reunion with her brother, the Shoshoni leader Cameahwait, was at first joyful, but relations between the two then cooled. Rather than rejoining the Shoshonis, she continued on in the service of Lewis and Clark.

At the conclusion of the expedition, Charbonneau was paid for his services, but Sacajawea was not. By that time, William Clark had bonded with Jean Baptiste, to whom he gave the pet name Pomp. He was determined to separate the boy from Sacajawea and Charbonneau in order to educate and mentor him. Clark succeeded in his intention, but in time Jean Baptiste returned to frontier life as a guide and interpreter.

A number of controversies have arisen concerning Sacajawea (McBeth 2003). One has to do with the etymology and pronunciation of her name. According to Meriwether Lewis, Charbonneau stated that her name meant "bird woman," which it would if the name she was known by at the time was Hidatsa rather than Shoshoni. In this case, the accepted spelling has been Sacagawea with a variant Sakakawea.

On the other hand, the common form Sacajawea is said to be derived from Shoshoni with the meaning "boat-puller" or "boat-launcher." This etymology is problematical on structural grounds, however.

Another controversy has to do with the extent to which Sacajawea served Lewis and Clark as a pathfinder. On a number of occasions, she did provide crucial directions, but it was not an everyday occurrence. She was not on the payroll of the expedition, although Clark, in retrospect, wrote that she deserved remuneration for her services. Lewis specifically remarked on her usefulness as an interpreter among the Shoshonis (Lewis & Clark 2005).

The strongest controversy has to do with the date and conditions of her death (Karttunen 1994b). On December 12, 1812, the clerk at Fort Manuel, a trading station on the Missouri River, recorded that Charbonneau's Shoshoni wife, a woman about twenty-five years old, had died there after giving birth to a daughter. Initially, the clerk was given guardianship of the baby and her ten-year-old brother, whose name was given as Toussaint, but the guardianship was transferred to William Clark.

In 1871 an elderly woman settled at Wind River in Wyoming, where she was known as "Bazil's mother." She told stories of having accompanied an expedition to the Pacific Ocean decades earlier, of having seen the skeleton of a whale there, and of having cooked dog meat to feed white men. These were Sacajawea's experiences, and the woman was, moreover, recognized as a skilled interpreter/negotiator. She possessed a Jefferson medal of the sort that Lewis and Clark distributed to Indians they met along the way, together with some paper documents. This led people to identify the woman as Sacajawea, returned to her people after leaving Charbonneau and living a transient life for many decades.

In 1925 Charles Eastman, a Dartmouth-educated Santee Sioux, was sent by the Bureau of Indian Affairs to Wind River to try to establish the facts. After conducting interviews and exhuming the packet of documents which had been interred with the woman's son Bazil, Eastman was inclined to accept that the aged woman had indeed been Sacajawea and that the woman who died in 1812 may have been one of the several other Indian women Charbonneau took as wives over the years (Eastman 1925). This view has been preferred by Shoshonis and women, whereas historical scholars and men seem more inclined to believe that the woman who died in 1884 was not the woman who traveled with Lewis and Clark.

By the beginning of the twentieth century Sacajawea was being promoted by American feminists as a patriotic heroine. An organization was formed to collect funds to commission a statue of her to be placed in a park in Portland, Oregon. The 1905 annual meeting of the Woman's Suffrage Association was held in Portland to coincide with the Lewis and Clark Centennial Exposition, and on this occasion, in one of the last public appearances of her life, Susan B. Anthony spoke of Sacajawea's contribution to American history.

Statues representing Sacajawea were erected throughout the twentieth century. In 1965 the Daughters of the American Revolution placed a marker in the cemetery on the Wind River Reservation in Wyoming, identifying the site as the grave of Sacajawea. In the year 2000 the United States Mint began issuing a "Sacagawea dollar", representing her as a young mother with her baby, and the following year the site of the federally funded Sacajawea Interpretive, Cultural, and Education Center was dedicated near the town of Salmon, in Lemhi County, Idaho.

FRANCES KARTTUNEN

SCIENTOMETRIC RESEARCH

see under BIBLIOMETRIC RESEARCH

SEGMENTATION

↑ STRATEGIES

The term 'segmentation' is used in relation to the interpreting process in different senses, with reference to the interpreter's processing of both input and output. The basic (and fairly obvious) meaning of the word relates to the decomposition of a speech, or written text, into processing-relevant units. As is evident from studies of discourse processing and language understanding, particularly in research on reading, some form of input segmentation (and concurrent analysis) takes place in any process of COMPREHENSION (e.g. van Dijk & Kintsch 1983), and the notion of parsing (i.e. the syntactic analysis of linguistic constituents) can be viewed as an example. Thus, segmentation also underlies the processing of perceptual input in the consecutive mode of interpreting, though it is difficult to observe, except for some reflection of it in NOTE-TAKING. By contrast, segmentation is more evident in SIMULTANEOUS

INTERPRETING (SI), which is based on segment-by-segment translational processing (Kirchhoff 1976/2002).

Early PSYCHOLINGUISTIC APPROACHES to the study of SI focused on the length of input in relation to output segments, or 'speech bursts' (Barik 1973), and on the nature of the input segment an interpreter processes before starting production. Rather than measuring segments as speech bursts, or word sequences ('chunks') between PAUSES, Goldman-Eisler (1972) proposed that input segmentation in SI – corresponding to the TIME LAG or ear–voice span – was largely based on propositions (i.e. complete predicative expressions). Comparing the temporal segmentation patterns (i.e. word sequences between pauses) in the input and the output, she observed that 'identity' obtained in only about ten percent of all cases, and that interpreters mostly imposed their own segmentation in delivering the output, fusing or splitting the pause-separated word sequences in the input.

Goldman-Eisler suggested that varying patterns of input segmentation in SI, shaped also by language- and message-related factors, might be a matter of the interpreter's capacity or preference; such a view points to the idea that segmentation is one of the STRATEGIES used in the interpreting process. Consistent with this idea, Kalina (1998) mentions segmentation, or 'chunking', as a comprehension-oriented strategy to facilitate memory storage. In a more specific sense, Gile (1995a), Setton (1999) and others have described segmentation in SI as a production strategy for coping with syntactic challenges in the input. Rather than wait for a complex input clause to be completed (and risk short-term memory overload), interpreters are advised to render a complex clause as a series of simple ones. This form of strategic chunking, or *saucissonnage*, roughly corresponds to what Seleskovitch and Lederer (1989) describe as 'working with sub-units of sense', and what Jones (1998) more popularly calls the 'salami technique'. Setton (1999) suggests, based on findings from CORPUS-BASED RESEARCH, that 'pre-emptive' segmentation may become a quasi-automatic, integral part of SI technique, regardless of language pair or local sentence structure.

In a rare example of an empirical study on professional interpreters' strategies for coping with syntactically challenging input, Meuleman and Van Besien (2009) had 16 professionals with Dutch as their A language interpret an impromptu French source speech containing a passage with an eight-layer-deep hypotactic construction. The authors found that nearly all participants opted for a segmentation strategy, and they also noted that, in most cases, segmenting (i.e. restructuring), rather than following the input-language syntax ('tailing'), led to renditions that were assessed as acceptable.

FRANZ PÖCHHACKER

SELESKOVITCH

When Danica Seleskovitch died on 17 April 2001 at the age of 79, she had supervised no fewer than 32 doctoral theses at the ESIT Research Center for Translation Studies at the University of Paris III – Sorbonne Nouvelle. Her own thesis (Seleskovitch 1975) – the first empirical study of consecutive note-taking – had broken new ground in translation studies with the INTERPRETIVE THEORY of interpreting and translation, which became the cornerstone of an influential school of thought sometimes referred to as the PARIS SCHOOL. For almost thirty years, her French, German, English, Lebanese, Egyptian, Russian, African, Spanish, Chinese and Korean disciples have followed her lead, covering a wide range of topics in the field of interpreting and translation studies, such as deliberate non-literal renditions in conference interpreting (Garcia-Landa 1978), the importance of the Hunayn Ibn Ishaq School for translation (Salama-Carr 1990) and the theories of language and translation of Kade,

Coseriu and Seleskovitch (Laplace 1994), to name but a few. They all found a keen and open-minded mentor in Danica Seleskovitch, and many, building on her legacy, continue her research today.

Born Nicole Danica Seleskovitch on 6 December 1921 in Paris, to an upper middle-class French mother and a Yugoslav father, a scholar and specialist on Kant, Seleskovitch grew up in a multicultural and multilingual environment. After her mother's tragic death when Seleskovitch was only four, she and her brother went to live with their French grandmother in Nice. It was only in 1931 that they were reunited with their father, who had remarried and begun lecturing at the Kaiser Wilhelm University in Berlin.

Seleskovitch did most of her secondary schooling in Germany. By the time she finished, in 1939, her command of German, non-existent eight years earlier, was close to that of her French mother-tongue and her almost native Serbo-Croat. Having acquired her languages naturally (the only language she learned at school was English), Seleskovitch remained skeptical all her life about interpreters acquiring their languages in the classroom.

At the outbreak of the Second World War, Seleskovitch left Germany to join her family in Yugoslavia. She stayed in Belgrade throughout the war, giving French lessons to support herself while studying medicine, until the German occupiers closed down the university.

In 1945, Seleskovitch, who was a French citizen, was awarded a scholarship by the French government, which enabled her to escape Marshal Tito's communist regime and continue her university education in France. She took an undergraduate degree in German and English at the Sorbonne, but had to abandon further studies for lack of financial support.

In 1949, she enrolled for a course in CONFERENCE INTERPRETING at the HEC business school in Paris and graduated in 1950. She was offered a contract with the United States Department of State under the Marshall Plan, to accompany groups of French economic and political leaders sent to the United States to explore the secrets of American productivity. After her three-year stay in Washington, Seleskovitch took up a position as an interpreter with the European Coal and Steel Community in Luxembourg.

Back in Paris in 1955, Seleskovitch set out on a long career as a freelance interpreter that lasted well into the 1980s. She joined the International Association of Conference Interpreters in 1956 and served as the Association's charismatic Executive Secretary from 1959 to 1963.

In 1957, she began her teaching career at the newly reorganized *Ecole Supérieure d'Interprètes et de Traducteurs* (ESIT) and served as the school's director from 1982 until her retirement in 1990. Over a period of nearly forty years, generations of students of conference interpreting benefitted from this outstanding pedagogue's unorthodox teaching methods.

As a teenager in Berlin, Seleskovitch would translate quite naturally for her visiting relatives and friends, without giving a thought to how she did it. As soon as she started her interpreting career, however, she began to ponder on the interpreting process, jotting down her thoughts on scraps of paper. By the mid-1960s, she had started writing seriously, mostly over the summer months in her house on the Sardinian coast. The Interpretive Theory of Translation, often referred to as the "*théorie du sens*," developed with Marianne Lederer, was born there (Seleskovitch 1968, 1975; Seleskovitch & Lederer 1984, 1989).

Seleskovitch's innovative method consisted in abandoning the linguistic approach that typified translation studies in the 1960s. Her ideas were simple and based on the conclusion she had reached in her own experience as a conference interpreter: in order to successfully achieve its objective, i.e., convey sense, a written or oral translation must focus on understanding the message, and not on TRANSCODING, or translating the words (Seleskovitch 1977).

At an early stage of her research, Seleskovitch had the intuition that her own findings were closer to those of psychological and cognitive studies of language than to those of linguistics as practiced at the time. In the late 1970s, she had the opportunity to work with scientists specialising in these fields, especially in neuro-psychology, at the University of Paris XII (e.g. Barbizet et al. 1981).

Danica Seleskovitch, whose life and work are the subject of an extensive biography (Widlund-Fantini 2007), published four books, translated into seven languages, and a large number of articles. She was a visiting professor at universities in Europe, North and South America, the Middle and the Far East. Her ideas are supported by scholars all over the world and remain the foundation of the work at the Research Center for Translation Studies in Paris.

ANNE-MARIE WIDLUND-FANTINI

SENSE

see under INTERPRETIVE THEORY

SETTINGS

Scholars and practitioners of interpreting make distinctions in terms of MODES, techniques, types or settings to differentiate between various forms of practice and help define their area of interest or activity. This is imperative in research, as terms and their underlying concepts create order and structure, and allow for systematic reflection and debate. However, such classifications do not exist independently of space and time, but always adjust to social and intellectual developments (Bowker & Star 2000). A good example of how broader trends can prompt changes of perspective in a field like interpreting studies is MILITARY INTERPRETING: viewed as one of the main types of interpreting work in the earlier part of the twentieth century (e.g. van Hoof 1962), it was largely eclipsed until international violent conflicts in the new millennium brought it (back) to widespread attention.

Whereas CONFERENCE INTERPRETING – itself a setting-based designation – has generally relied on a further subdivision by modes, SIGNED LANGUAGE INTERPRETING events have traditionally been categorized in terms of setting. This was later applied to COMMUNITY INTERPRETING, to refer to the social and/or institutional context in which an interpreter-mediated encounter takes place. In her comprehensive introduction to signed language interpreting, Frishberg (1990) identified eight settings (educational, legal, medical, mental health, rehabilitation and social service, business/industry and government, religious, performing arts), acknowledging that other researchers might prefer different ways of classification. At any rate, signed language interpreting comprises a broader range of settings than spoken-language interpreting, as it is needed in practically all walks of life, from EDUCATIONAL INTERPRETING to sports to THEATER INTERPRETING.

The term 'setting' is used either to refer to the particular place in which a given interpreting event occurs (e.g. a hospital or a police station), or in a more general and systematic way to denote subcategories of a broader domain, such as diplomatic and PARLIAMENTARY SETTINGS in conference interpreting, and healthcare setting(s) or legal setting(s) in community interpreting (Hale 2007). Thus, the healthcare 'setting' is conceptualized as a subtype of community interpreting, and the latter as a 'type' or 'domain' of interpreting in a broader, more abstract sense (see Grbić & Pöllabauer 2006). More broadly, scholars have traditionally distinguished two or three 'major types' of interpreting (conference vs. community; conference – court – community; or conference – community – BUSINESS INTERPRETING).

Settings are sometimes further subdivided into "quasi-specialized fields" (Gentile 1997), such as PEDIATRIC SETTINGS, PSYCHOTHERAPY and SPEECH PATHOLOGY for healthcare settings;

ASYLUM SETTINGS and PRISON SETTINGS for LEGAL INTERPRETING; or sermon interpreting and interpreting of sacred texts for RELIGIOUS SETTINGS. Some authors (e.g. Gentile 1997; Gentile et al. 1996; Mason 1999a; Wadensjö 2009) have also referred to settings as 'situations', 'environments', 'areas (of work)' and 'fields', but the term 'setting' has become widely established in academic as well as professional discourse.

In an attempt to provide a more fluid classification of interpreting events, with less clear-cut boundaries, Pöchhacker (2004a) proposes a model which uses eight dimensions to map the broad spectrum of interpreting phenomena, with setting representing one dimensional continuum extending from international to intra-social settings.

The term 'conference setting' is used mainly in opposition to other, non-conference settings (e.g. MEDIA INTERPRETING). Although 'setting' is generally not used to label subtypes of conference interpreting, there have been attempts to differentiate between various conference prototypes (e.g. Pöchhacker 1992, 1994a).

In summary, settings can be defined as the socio-spatial contexts of interaction in which interpreting events take place. A specific setting is therefore shaped by the interplay of the agents (including their mental, social and cultural dispositions) and the locations involved (including all physical, material structures), both of which are governed by institutional conditions as well as broader social forces. Although the various settings seem to involve customary patterns of action and are associated with specific NORMS and expectations regarding the interpreter's ROLE, they are in fact composed of habitualized and contingent actions and thus subject to historical change.

NADJA GRBIĆ

SHADOWING

Shadowing is a language-processing task, used since the 1960s both in research on SIMULTA-NEOUS INTERPRETING (SI) and in conference interpreter training. It consists in the repetition of a message presented over headphones, either with minimal lag (phonemic shadowing) or at longer latencies (phrase shadowing). The rationale is that this auditory-verbal task involves the same basic cognitive processes as simultaneous interpreting, that is, information processing and divided attention between listening and speaking. Shadowing is a monolingual task, however, whereas SI requires conveying the source message in a different language.

Shadowing in research

Shadowing was developed as a research tool in the early days of cognitive psychology by Colin Cherry (1953), to investigate selective attention and information processing in dichotic listening studies. Subjects were asked to repeat a target message as it was presented to one ear while a to-be-ignored message was presented to the other ear (see Broadbent 1958). Shadowing without a competing message was also used as a technique to study the production and perception of speech. In a series of experiments, psychologist William Marslen-Wilson (1985) demonstrated that the simultaneous decoding and encoding of messages not only involves auditory, articulatory and phonological processes, but also relies on syntactic and semantic analysis.

In one of the earliest psychological studies on interpreting, Treisman (1965) investigated SI as "a variation on the shadowing task". She found that the (untrained) subjects in her experimental study had a longer TIME LAG when translating than when shadowing, and attributed this to the higher "decision load" in the translation task. Subsequent studies comparing SI to shadowing as a way of investigating the underlying cognitive processes and components centered on attention sharing, information processing and MEMORY (e.g. Gerver 1974a, 1974b; Lambert 1989b; Darò & Fabbro 1994), as well as hemispheric lateralization of languages in the brain (Green et al. 1990). Most studies involved the shadowing of speeches, more rarely the shadowing of sentences or lists of words (Darò 1989). The findings from such research confirmed that the interpreting task imposes greater cognitive demands and is more easily disrupted than shadowing, which was thus characterized as a "rapidly automatized task with minimal attentional demands" (Green et al. 1990: 111).

Shadowing in testing and training

Seen as a simplified version of SI, shadowing has been used in APTITUDE TESTING or entrance exams for predicting candidates' ability to successfully complete a training course in CONFERENCE INTERPRETING (e.g. Moser-Mercer 1985; Lambert 1991). Based on its shared task demands, that is, the ability to speak and listen simultaneously, shadowing also found its way into the PEDAGOGY of interpreting. Many training institutions included shadowing among a set of PRE-INTERPRETING EXERCISES, and the shadowing task is widely used as an introductory exercise for learning to listen and speak at the same time before moving on to SI.

There has been considerable debate among trainers and researchers about the usefulness of shadowing and of other exercises meant to train subskills of SI, such as shadowing and recall, dual-task exercises, paraphrasing and processing NUMBERS, names and acronyms (Lambert 1992). Opponents have regarded shadowing, especially phonemic shadowing, as the exact opposite of what interpreting should be: repeating words verbatim, losing sight of meaningful context, is seen as alien to interpreting and hence as "a pointless and potentially harmful exercise" (Thiéry 1989: 4). In their opinion, the focus in any preparatory exercises for SI should therefore be on simultaneous listening and speaking along with COMPREHENSION and context (see Kurz 1992: 247).

Supporters, on the other hand, see shadowing as a useful introductory exercise for SI. They stress the importance of acquiring such a complex cognitive skill gradually, first learning to cope with single subskills that can be trained separately before bringing them together as a global ability (Moser-Mercer 1985; Lambert 1992). Other proposals combine shadowing with other tasks (e.g. delaying response, answering questions at the end of the exercise) or point to its usefulness in improving students' language proficiency, and particularly INTONATION and stress patterns (Schweda Nicholson 1990).

In recent years, shadowing in the A language appears to have lost some of its appeal as a training tool or as an introductory exercise for SI (Déjean le Féal 1997), while it is still used for enhancing and testing B-language proficiency and focusing on PROSODY. In this respect, it is considered an effective tool in foreign language learning much more than in interpreter training (Bovee & Stewart 2009).

There has been little recent research on shadowing in relation to interpreting. Among the few exceptions is a pilot study comparing shadowing proficiency in professionals and interpreting students (Moser-Mercer et al. 2000). The results of the shadowing task in the B language showed that professionals, contrary to what might be expected, performed less efficiently, with more errors and longer latencies than the students. This may suggest that professional interpreters' acquired and largely automatized interpreting STRATEGIES interfered with the task demands of (verbatim) shadowing. Shadowing has also been used in cognitive NEUROSCIENCE APPROACHES to the study of SI (e.g. Tommola et al. 2000), as well as in PSYCHOLINGUISTIC APPROACHES. In some cases (e.g. Christoffels & de Groot 2004), the choice of input for the shadowing task (c.g. sentences) and the use of unbalanced bilinguals without interpreting experience as subjects reaffirms the role of shadowing as a research tool for testing memory and processing conditions.

Shadowing in healthcare interpreter training

The term 'shadowing' has also been used in interpreter training in a very different sense. In the context of HEALTHCARE INTERPRETING, in particular, the term is used to refer to an opportunity for students to learn 'on the job' ('job shadowing'), usually towards the end of their training programme or upon its completion (e.g. Hasbún Avalos et al. 2013). It consists in observing and following an experienced healthcare interpreter at an actual interpreter-mediated event, to gain familiarity with the interpreting process and the institutional environment.

ALESSANDRA RICCARDI

SHLESINGER

Miriam Shlesinger (1947–2012) was an American-born Israeli translation and interpreting scholar and educator. Her wide-ranging and untiring commitment to the discipline came to epitomize the breadth and diversity of interpreting studies as a newly emerged field within translation studies in the new millennium.

Having spent part of her childhood in Israel and her teenage years in the US, her BILINGUALISM may have seemed a matter of course, and translation not worth special attention. Indeed, her fascination had been with medicine and music when she left Florida for Israel on her own at age 17, and she liked to explain her career choice very simply: "I went to Israel to study medicine, so I enrolled in musicology in order to become a translator" (Pöchhacker 2007: 5). Four years after completing her BA in linguistics and musicology, having taken a 'break' of three years to have three babies, she enrolled in the fledgling translation department at Bar-Ilan University, where she received her diploma in 1978. Three decades later, she was that university's first full Professor of Translation Studies, directing a program she had helped upgrade to a Master's degree in translation and interpreting studies.

Though it is one of the few topics to which she did not devote much further attention, Miriam Shlesinger's perfect bilingualism (and bicultural competence) was undoubtedly a cornerstone of her distinguished career in translation and interpreting – as a translator of plays, novels and short stories, and as a sought-after expert in LEGAL INTERPRETING, MEDIA INTERPRETING and DIPLOMATIC INTERPRETING at the highest levels.

From the late 1980s, her outstanding achievements as a professional came to be complemented, if not overshadowed, by her academic pursuits: her MA thesis (Shlesinger 1989b) on features of ORALITY and literacy in SIMULTANEOUS INTERPRETING (SI), under the supervision of Gideon Toury, was a first and influential milestone in her research career. Papers on the crucial issue of ROLE in court interpreting followed (e.g. Shlesinger 1991), as did ground-breaking experimental studies on INTONATION (Shlesinger 1994) and COHESION (1995a) in SI. In the late 1990s she pursued her interest in translational norms (e.g. Shlesinger 1989a), by endeavoring to investigate them on the methodological basis of corpus-linguistic studies (Shlesinger 1998), at the same time as taking on the difficult challenge of studying the role of WORKING MEMORY in SI. She spent several months at the Max Planck Institute for Psycholinguistics in Nijmegen, to prepare for and design the experiment for the PhD dissertation which she successfully defended in 2000 (Shlesinger 2003).

Beneath these many scholarly accomplishments was the almost secret life of Miriam Shlesinger the educator and editor. In education and course development, alongside her teaching at Bar-Ilan University, her efforts focused on two domains of interpreting in community-based settings. Having taught in the Israeli Sign Language interpreting program at Tel Aviv University as early as the mid-1990s, she managed, in the early 2000s, to launch a SIGNED LANGUAGE INTERPRETING course at Beit Berl College, where she had founded the translation program more than two decades earlier. In the area of healthcare interpreting, on the other hand, it took much more than course development to implement new training initiatives. After she had organized the first ever national conference on access to health care in 2005, years of determined networking in the unbroken tradition of Miriam the social activist were required to set up a training course and interpreting service, including TELEPHONE INTERPRETING, to facilitate access to medical care for Ethiopian, Chinese and other immigrants.

Barely more visible to the international academic community than such training initiatives to promote COMMUNITY INTERPRETING in Israel (Shlesinger 2007) was Miriam Shlesinger's dedicated work in editing publications by many translation and interpreting scholars – as style editor of *Target*, and of many a book-length manuscript for the Benjamins Translation Library series. Her appointment as editor of the journal *INTERPRETING*, from 2004, provided fuller recognition of her selfless devotion to helping others get their work published in impeccable style (see Shlesinger & Voinova 2013). Indeed, Miriam's standards of excellence as an author and editor convey the pleasure she took in language, whether spoken or written, in a courtroom or a classroom, for its essential role in human communication.

Well-deserved distinctions for Miriam Shlesinger included an honorary doctorate from the Copenhagen Business School in 2001 and the Danica Seleskovitch Prize in 2009, as well as her appointment as the 2007 CETRA Chair Professor in the Translation Research Summer School at KU Leuven, of which she remained an enthusiastic member of staff until shortly before the fatal recurrence of her lung cancer in late 2012.

FRANZ PÖCHHACKER

SIGHT INTERPRETING/TRANSLATION

↑ MODES
→ SIMULTANEOUS WITH TEXT

Sight interpreting/translation is one of the basic MODES of interpreting. It is a hybrid form, in that a written source text is turned into an oral – or signed – target text in another language in real time. The interpreter is expected to render the contents of the written text, often without time for even a cursory reading, at a consistent, fluent pace.

The term 'sight translation', generally used to identify this mode of interpreting in English as well as various other languages (e.g. *traduction à vue* in French, *traducción a la vista* in Spanish), is intrinsically inaccurate. Given the real-time processing demands, what is referred to as sight translation is more aptly defined as a form of interpreting and has indeed long been regarded as a form of SIMULTANEOUS INTERPRETING (e.g. Herbert 1952; Shiryaev 1979). Therefore, the term 'sight interpreting' is much better suited to convey the essence of this mode of interpreting (see also Čeňková 2010).

Sight interpreting is encountered in a wide range of SETTINGS and work situations. These include meetings, often of a bilateral nature, which are usually conducted in consecutive mode. Written documentation (e.g. annual reports, minutes) is then delivered in sight interpreting mode, either in full or in selected fragments. Sight interpreting is also frequently used at press conferences, where statements or press releases may be delivered by an interpreter in a language which the audience understands. Other documents which lend themselves to sight interpreting in conference settings include press reports which may be of interest to a meeting, letters of apology for absence, or congratulations. Sight interpreting may also be used for drafts prepared in one language to be submitted to a plenary or other body for completion.

In community-based institutional settings, sight interpreting may be required in back-translating the written record of an interpreter-mediated interview in POLICE SETTINGS and ASYLUM SETTINGS, for rendering expert witness statements in courtroom interpreting or for medical reports and patient files in HEALTHCARE INTERPRETING. Sight interpreting is similarly also used in SIGNED LANGUAGE INTERPRETING, a special example being that of a DEAF INTERPRETER working from a teleprompter in MEDIA INTERPRETING.

In terms of cognitive processing, the interpreter working at sight rather than from auditory input has the advantage of controlling his or her pace; on the other hand, sight interpreting makes additional cognitive demands as the text is constantly before the interpreter's eyes, which increases the risk of lexical and syntactic INTERFERENCE. Despite these constraints, the interpreter's delivery is expected to be natural and without unnecessary corrections and REPAIRS while maintaining eye contact with the listener(s) or user(s).

In interpreter EDUCATION, sight interpreting has been used in APTITUDE TESTING to determine whether candidates are able to quickly grasp the essentials of a text and render its meaning (see Russo 2011). Its use in interpreting PEDAGOGY, recommended and actual, varies in different schools. Training in sight interpreting often starts only once students master the basics of CONSECUTIVE INTERPRETING and are thus able to render the message, as opposed to words, based on their understanding and analysis of the source language text (e.g. Seleskovitch & Lederer 2002; Viaggio 1995; Weber 1990). Sight interpreting is generally considered a good exercise for working up speed and thus for preparing students to undertake simultaneous interpreting in the booth. When allowing for prior reading, sight interpreting is believed to improve students' ability to navigate in a text applying a non-linear approach and to identify core information. In this respect, it is essential preparation for the composite skill of SIMULTANEOUS WITH TEXT.

Sight interpreting has attracted relatively little research interest. Among the topics studied are the type of information processing in sight interpreting compared to other modes (Viezzi 1989, 1990; Lambert 2004), and output-related constraints, given the high probability of interference from the source text (e.g. Agrifoglio 2004; Gile 2009). In her PhD dissertation, Jiménez Ivars (1999) undertakes a comprehensive descriptive analysis of sight interpreting as a working mode and analyses the task in terms of the PACTE translation competence model.

More recent work has investigated 'sight translation' in the framework of translation process research. In a small-scale experimental study, Dragsted and Gorm Hansen (2007) compared the performance of translators and interpreters on a sight translation task and found differences in behaviour regarding temporal variables and translational approach. Translators paused more and took much longer to complete the task, and interpreters gave a 'freer' rendering, focusing less on individual words, as demonstrated by an EYE TRACKING analysis. Eye tracking data (pupil size, fixations and regressions) were also employed by Shreve, Lacruz and Angelone (2010) in an experimental study focusing on cognitive effort and visual interference in a sight-interpreting task. Their results were in line with earlier findings regarding interference from the continued visual presence of the source text, and confirmed the cognitive complexity of the task, resulting from the need to cope with the high lexical density and syntactic complexity of a written text under the demands of fluent oral production.

IVANA ČEŇKOVÁ

SIGN LANGUAGE INTERPRETING

see SIGNED LANGUAGE INTERPRETING

SIGNED LANGUAGE INTERPRETING

→ INTERPRETING FOR DEAFBLIND PERSONS
↓ DEAF INTERPRETER, ↓ FINGERSPELLING, ↓ TRANSLITERATION, ↓ VIDEO RELAY SERVICE, ↓
VIDEO REMOTE INTERPRETING

Signed language interpreting (SLI) prototypically means interpreting between a signed language and a spoken or another signed language, and is sometimes referred to as visual language interpreting, particularly in CANADA. (Since this may involve language modes other than sign languages proper, such as TRANSLITERATION, sign*ed* language interpreting is preferred as the broader term, whereas practitioners are commonly referred to as sign language interpreters.) Sign(ed) languages are different in every country; they are naturally occurring languages that are independent from, but related to, the spoken languages of the countries where they are used, and are used by deaf people as their first or preferred language of communication.

Spoken-language interpreters work between two linear languages, whereby one word is produced after another and the message is built up sequentially. Sign languages, however, are visual-spatial languages that can create meaning using space, location, referents and other visually descriptive elements. Therefore sign language interpreters are constantly transferring information between two alternate modalities, which requires the representation of information in very different ways. This is referred to as *bimodal*, as opposed to *unimodal*, interpreting (Nicodemus & Emmorey 2013).

Signed languages inherently encode 'real-world' visual information. When hearing certain abstract concepts or generic descriptions, it is necessary for sign language interpreters to visualize the information, and implicitly encode it in their interpretation. Brennan and Brown (1997) cite an example: In order to render 'X broke the window', the British Sign Language (BSL) interpreter ideally needs to know the shape of the window, and how it was broken, in order to give an accurate visual representation of the event. In the reverse direction, when 'voicing' for hearing people, interpreters need to distil visual information into idiomatic spoken-language usage. For example, a deaf person can immediately convey visually where a person they were having a conversation with was seated, but a hearing person would not expect to hear something like: 'I was chatting with John who was sitting on my right', unless this were relevant in a legal context. Thus, the bimodal nature of SLI creates additional COGNITIVE LOAD for interpreters (Padden 2000).

Profile of practitioners

Sign language interpreters are employed in any context where deaf signers and non-deaf, non-signing 'hearing' people need to interact. One of the unique aspects of SLI is that it is often described as a 'cradle to grave' profession: even if deaf people are bilingual in a signed and a written/spoken language, interpreters will still accompany them in all aspects of their lives in so far as they cannot hear the majority spoken language.

Only individuals who grow up with a sign language used in the home (because of parents, siblings or other family members) can claim to be native signers or to have acquired a sign language as their first language (L1). Many of these hearing people with deaf parents, referred to as Children of Deaf Adults (CODAs, or Codas), begin interpreting informally for their parents or family members as children, engaging in CHILD LANGUAGE BROKERING (Preston 1994).

As sign languages have increasingly gained legal recognition, they are now formally taught in tertiary institutions as second (L2) or 'foreign' languages. American Sign Language (ASL), for example, was the fourth most-commonly-studied language at college in the United States in 2009 (Quinto-Pozos 2011). This situation means that increasing numbers of non-Codas are able to enter the SLI profession after studying a signed language as an L2.

The challenge for teaching non-Codas to develop native-like FLUENCY in signed languages is how to replicate the language immersion experience that other foreign language students can access by going to live in the relevant country. There is no 'Deafland' for SLI students to go and live in, so students have to gain access to the Deaf community and signed language role models in other ways: by attending community events, developing friendships, and participating in 'service learning' projects for the community to develop cross-cultural competencies (Shaw 2011b).

Various surveys conducted over the years have confirmed that sign language interpreters are typically white females who work part-time. Studies carried out in the early 2000s among Australian Sign Language (Auslan) interpreters in Australia and BSL interpreters in the UK found that only a small minority (around 10%) were native signers, confirming that more people from 'outside' the Deaf community are being drawn to learn a signed language, and thus enter the SLI profession (Stone 2012).

There is a growing number of DEAF INTERPRETERS working unimodally between two different signed languages. Deaf interpreters may be employed in contexts where the (typically non-native signing) hearing interpreter feels the need for extra assistance to understand the signing of a deaf person or accurately convey a message to a deaf person. Deaf and hearing interpreters can be found working together in situations when the deaf client uses idiosyncratic signs or gestures that could be thought of as 'home signs', unique to a family; uses a foreign sign language; has minimal or limited communication skills; is deafblind, or deaf with limited vision (requiring tactile interpreting); uses signs particular to a given region, ethnic or age group; or has characteristics reflective of Deaf culture not familiar to hearing interpreters (see Napier et al. 2010).

Deaf interpreters may also be seen working as conference interpreters: either they work from a pivot interpreter – a hearing interpreter who listens to the spoken text and conveys the message to the deaf interpreter in one signed language, following which the deaf interpreter translates into another national signed language (or International Sign) – or they read from an auto-cue live transcription of the spoken source text. The deaf interpreter is on the platform facing the audience, and the hearing interpreter or auto-cue device is placed off-stage and within the direct eye-gaze of the interpreter who is deaf (see Adam et al. 2014).

Education and training

While some ad hoc sign language interpreter EDUCATION was available in short bursts from before the 1960s (Ball 2013), prior to the 1970s interpreting was seen as a charitable, voluntary activity, delivered by hearing people who had some degree of signed language proficiency. In the absence of external, objective ASSESSMENT of interpreting COMPETENCE, the Deaf community relied on the experience and judgment of its members in determining who could function effectively in the interpreting role (Cokely 2005b). Reflecting the collectivist view of the Deaf community (Mindess 2006), those who interpreted during this period tended to see interpreting as their contribution to the community, but didn't see themselves as 'interpreters'; their contribution did not define them professionally, as there was no expectation of payment for their work and interpreting was not considered to be a profession (Fant 1990). However, by 1972, the Registry of Interpreters for the Deaf (RID) had set up a CERTIFICATION system, testing and evaluating the qualifications of interpreters in the US (Cokely 2005b), and many other countries have followed suit.

In parallel with the development of assessment processes came the establishment of interpreter education. While opportunities for this vary significantly from country to country, in much of the Western world there is an expectation that interpreters undertake training, and some jurisdictions stipulate a bachelor's degree as a minimum requirement. Other regions have seen increased codification of expectations for graduates of interpreter education programmes (Leeson & Calle 2013). The idea of accrediting such programmes has also developed in some regions in line with protocols for many other practice professions. While master's degree programmes exist in some countries (Leeson & Vermeerbergen 2010), formal training is still not in place in many countries around the world and, instead, ad hoc training at community level remains the only route available for many practitioners (Napier 2009).

Moreover, even where there are established educational routes to practice, there are still cohorts of people who provide 'interpretation' without recourse to training (Leeson & Vermeerbergen 2010), including some deaf interpreters, some Codas, teachers of the deaf, chaplains, hearing people who have acquired some signed language, etc. Reasons for this include the simple fact that most countries are still experiencing problems in meeting the demand for professional interpreters.

While academicization brings benefits in terms of wider societal recognition of signed languages and interpreting, it has also functioned as a wedge between the interpreting community and the Deaf communities they serve. Cokely (2005b: 16) notes that interpreters have moved from being "service agents *of* the Community" to being "service providers *for* the Community", leading to a consumer-driven model of interpreting. This shift has also meant a move away from the process of selecting and training interpreters within the Deaf community, which has thus lost its gate-keeping role in this respect. One suggestion is that interpreter education programmes work to bridge the ensuing gap by ensuring that student activities in the community are seen by Deaf communities as beneficial to them (Monikowski & Peterson 2005), and that programmes are seen as being "of the community" even if individual would-be practitioners are not (Cokely 2005b). Further, in a growing number of countries, licensing bodies and interpreter associations, such as WASLI, the World Association of Sign Language Interpreters, and efsli, the European Forum of Sign Language Interpreters, are demanding that practitioners engage in continuous professional development, creating a demand for high quality post-qualification, in-service training.

Aspects of the profession

Three key movements strongly influenced legal responses to Deaf communities and impacted on the provision of sign language interpreting: (i) the disability rights movement, (ii) the linguistic rights framework, and (iii) the human rights agenda, leading to legislation at regional, national and pan-national levels (Wheatley & Pabsch 2010). Sometimes led by legal change, there have been moves away from traditional modes of educating deaf children in schools for the deaf, and in many countries the majority of deaf children are now educated in mainstream classrooms where they arrive at school with little or no sign language and sign language interpreters effectively serve as (typically non-native) language models. This has potential ramifications for cognitive, linguistic and educational achievement.

Ethics and role

In many ways, SLI has led the way in critical thinking about ethics and role in interpreting studies. Early SLI literature was dominated by discussions of 'models' of interpreting (Roy 1993), as practitioners and educators struggled to define the role of interpreters in relation to the Deaf community. For many years, deaf people had relied on individuals who had grown up in their community, typically people with deaf parents, who served as interpreters because they saw this as their duty. This was the era of the interpreter as 'helper', someone who would ask the deaf person what they wanted, and do it for them. Deaf people thus had little autonomy and – some would argue – were paternalistically oppressed (Ladd 2003). With the evolution of the profession, rehabilitation and disability anti-discrimination legislation provided for the right to access to information via interpreters in key life domains. Governments were prepared to pay for (some) interpreting services, and deaf welfare organizations recognized that the role of the interpreter should be separated from that of support worker. This heralded the professionalization of SLI, the establishment of professional SLI associations and the development of codes of ETHICS. Spoken-language conference interpreters were looked to for models of practice, which gave rise to the perpetuation of the 'conduit' model, a model that enabled interpreters to maintain a professional distance and avoid accusations of paternalism.

Practitioners and consumers subsequently expressed discomfort with the conduit model. People argued that by adopting certain 'professional' traits, sign language interpreters had lost their connection to community values, and that they needed to be allies of the Deaf community and provide not only bilingual, but also bicultural, MEDIATION.

Cynthia Roy's (2000a) seminal research provided further evidence that sign language interpreters are active participants in a dialogic communicative event, and thus cannot be neutral conduits that do not impact on the message and process of interaction. More recent proposals focus on how interpreters occupy a 'role space' and enact different roles according to contextual demands (Llewellyn Jones & Lee 2013), and on how interpreters need to respond to contextualization cues to account for communication requirements (Shaffer 2013).

Following from these shifts in conceptualizing role, the SLI literature has also led in analyzing interpreter ethics, with a strong push for ethical decision-making based on teleological morals, values and rights, rather than deontological duties and rigid codes of ethics (Cokely 2000; Hoza 2003; Tate & Turner 1997/2002). Dean and Pollard (2001, 2005, 2013) have been particularly influential in examining ethical decision-making with their DEMAND CONTROL SCHEMA, asserting that SLI is a 'practice profession' and that interpreters therefore need to be accountable for their decisions.

Modes

While sign language interpreters are taught and encouraged to use CONSECUTIVE INTERPRETING, and research has shown that it can actually be a more effective technique for ensuring ACCURACY, for example in court (Russell 2002), SLI is predominantly SIMULTANEOUS INTERPRETING, as sign language interpreters do not have to contend with acoustic overlap from the vocalization of two languages (Leeson 2005). Moreover, they cannot realistically take notes in order to interpret large consecutive chunks of information because they are using their hands to interpret, regardless of the setting in which they are interpreting. Given the bimodality of SLI, Padden (2000) argues that when working consecutively, sign language interpreters can operate more effectively in one mode at a time. They can also move between the two techniques within the same dialogic interaction, depending on the nature and complexity of the information.

The SLI literature often discusses two key interpreting methods or 'translation styles' (Napier 2002): interpreting and transliteration, which can be related to the distinction between free/dynamic and literal/formal translation. A free approach (a) focuses on conveying the message so that it is linguistically and culturally meaningful; and (b) gives consideration to the fact that discourse participants may bring different life experiences to an interaction, thus recognizing that interpreting takes place within a discourse process. This style allows for the use of a more creative lexicon, drawing on the visual parameters of signed languages. It is also recognized, however, that a literal approach is appropriate in some contexts – especially in higher education (Napier 2002) – for example, to provide access to academic language or subject-specific terminology in university lectures or tutorials by borrowing spoken-language words into the signed language through FINGERSPELLING or mouthing. In other words, it is acknowledged that interpreters can adopt strategies of language contact in their interpretations and can transfer features of a spoken language into the signed target text for specific purposes, particularly if required by the consumer (e.g. Leeson 2005; Napier & Barker 2004).

A more recent development, made possible by advances in technological capabilities for recording and editing signed languages on video, is signed language *translation*, that is, the rendering of a written text in recorded sign language, allowing for preparation and correction (Wurm 2010). Signed language translation provides opportunities for both deaf and hearing interpreters to work, and emerging practices include translations of website content, educational assessment tools, psychiatric assessment tools, information leaflets, conference reports, and children's books.

Technology

Far beyond video recording and editing, new technologies have engendered changes in SLI practice. Videoconference-based interpreting arrangements require interpreters to work in contexts that are less clearly specified than in face-to-face interpreting, with a more diverse and dispersed community and, in some countries, within a corporate culture. VIDEO REMOTE INTERPRETING (VRI) and VIDEO RELAY SERVICE place different demands on an interpreter than do face-to-face settings, and VRI may not be appropriate for situations involving high interactivity, complex dialogic exchange and sensitive information, or individuals with a secondary disability (e.g. low vision) that impedes their ability to utilize the technology.

Trends in research

Over the 35-year period from 1970 to 2005, some 900 research texts on SLI were produced (Grbić 2007), averaging 26 studies per year, and there has been enormous growth in recent years. Metzger (2006) analysed 97 published research papers sourced from two main databases, and tracked how the topics, methodologies and paradigms had shifted and expanded over the 40 years from the early 1970s to the late 2000s, from a narrower range of topics and methodologies in studies produced mainly by researchers in the United States, to a broader range on both counts by contributors from all over the world (see Roy & Napier 2015).

SLI research is interdisciplinary, drawing on a range of different theoretical frameworks. Four main approaches can be identified: (i) DISCOURSE ANALYTICAL APPROACHES (transcriptions of naturally occurring data); (ii) ETHNOGRAPHIC METHODS (focus groups, interviews, field observations); (iii) SURVEY RESEARCH (questionnaires), and (iv) EXPERIMENTAL RESEARCH. More SLI practitioners are becoming involved in conducting ACTION RESEARCH, engaging in reflective practice in what can be referred to as 'interpreter fieldwork research' (Napier 2011b).

Aside from the research already mentioned in this article concerning the role and ethics of SLI, a range of studies have undertaken linguistic, psycholinguistic and sociolinguistic analyses of interpreting output, focusing on: WORKING MEMORY and signed language; comparative text analyses of monologic interpretations into a signed language; sociolinguistic analyses of interpreter-mediated interactions; SLI and BILINGUALISM; analyses of evidence of language contact between spoken and signed languages in interpreting; and analyses of interpreters' teamwork strategies. Psychological studies have examined the relationship between PERSONALITY and interpreting aptitude; and several sociological studies have utilized surveys, interviews or focus groups to glean community or interpreter perspectives on notions of QUALITY, professionalism and practice in SLI. In line with the various domains of practice, research covers the analysis of interpreting in legal, medical, mental health, educational and conference contexts.

A growing trend in interpreting studies is the use of video recording for the capture of natural interpreting data. Given the inherent multimodality of signed languages, SLI researchers are pioneers in the use of video, despite the major challenges it presents (see Metzger & Roy 2011). In fact SLI educators and researchers are constantly pushing the boundaries in relation to using multimodal software, such as ELAN (Goswell 2012), to annotate and transcribe various layers of the SLI process.

JEMINA NAPIER AND LORRAINE LEESON

SIMULTANEOUS CONSECUTIVE

↑ MODES, ↑ TECHNOLOGY

Simultaneous consecutive, or SimConsec, is a TECHNOLOGY-assisted hybrid mode of interpreting in which a consecutive rendering is produced by the interpreter in simultaneous mode from the playback of a digital recording of the source speech. The invention of this new technique is generally credited to SCIC interpreter Michele Ferrari, who first used it at a press conference in Rome in early 2000. Two US court interpreters, Erik Camayd-Freixas and John Lombardi, have also laid claim to the idea, and written about it in professional bulletins.

Different terms have been proposed to label this working mode, including 'digital recorder assisted consecutive' and 'digitally (re)mastered consecutive'. The latter was suggested by Ferrari himself to allude to his use of accelerated playback of the recording for a time-saving rendition (Gomes 2002). Ferrari had initially spoken of 'consecutive simultaneous', but subsequently opted for the reverse. Both forms are equally meaningful: in terms of the interpreter's processing, the mode is clearly SIMULTANEOUS INTERPRETING, whereas from the perspective of the audience (and of the commissioning client) it is CONSECUTIVE INTERPRETING.

Although a number of practitioners have claimed to use this technique, and there are anecdotal reports of its use by blind interpreting students, very little is known as yet about its effectiveness other than from a number of trials and experiments. It appears to have gained little ground in professional conference interpreting circles, and established training institutions may be wary of introducing a tool that may steer students away from developing their NOTE-TAKING skills. However, the potential and limitations of simultaneous consecutive have been examined in a number of empirical studies. Aside from testing the claims made for it, these studies also address the fundamental question of the QUALITY achievable in the two basic MODES of interpreting, which remains surprisingly underresearched (e.g. Gile 2001b).

Claims and challenges

The basic claim for simultaneous consecutive as an improvement over traditional (note-based) consecutive centers on superior ACCURACY and completeness. Whereas reliance on note-taking and MEMORY is said to make consecutive interpreting prone to OMISSIONS or abridgments, rendering in simultaneous mode what one has heard once before is expected to allow both deeper under-standing of the source speech and greater FIDELITY in re-expressing it. In addition to content, the new technique is credited by its inventor as making the interpretation more faithful to the original speaker's PROSODY and style of delivery, including paralinguistic features such as tone and rhythm. Ferrari's initial expectation was also that, with little if any need to focus on the notepad, SimConsec would enhance the interpreter's eye contact – and rapport – with the audience (Gomes 2002).

Following informal tests conducted by Ferrari and colleagues within SCIC in the early 2000s, a small-scale independent study at the University of Vienna (Hamidi & Pöchhacker 2007) compared French–German interpretations by three experienced professionals working in conventional consecutive and SimConsec: the latter proved better in terms of FLUENCY and source–target correspondence. Similar findings emerged from a follow-up study with eight professionals working from English to German in front of an audience (Hawel 2010). However, a questionnaire-based comparison of audience response to the two modes yielded an overall preference for traditional consecutive, mainly due to interpreters' lack of eye contact in SimConsec (Sienkiewicz 2010). This finding echoed observations in Ferrari's initial trials, in which the SimConsec interpreter had managed very little visual engagement with the audience.

Given the crucial role of technology in this technique, the type of equipment used could be expected to be of primary concern. Indeed, this has evolved from what was then known as a handheld PC, palm-sized computer or personal digital assistant (PDA), to digital voice recorders (DVR) and mobile devices such as smartpens – pens that are in fact paper-based computers, capable of capturing both sound and writing in synchrony (Orlando 2014). Nevertheless, the basic technique of interpreting simultaneously via earphones what has been digitally recorded remains the same with any type of equipment. And though the method was intended to do away with the need for note-taking, the interpreter can still use the notepad for memory support.

While sound quality, usability and playback options all require consideration, one of the main challenges associated with simultaneous consecutive appears to be the lack of communicative rapport with the audience. Another limitation, inherent to the simultaneous mode, is that the interpreter has to follow the source speech segment by segment, even if the speaker is hesitant or repetitive. Accelerated playback of selected sections may offer a partial solution to this problem. An experimental study employing a smartpen (Hiebl 2011), in which participants were given the choice of producing their consecutive rendering of differ-ent source speeches from notes or from the recording, yielded a clear preference for Sim-Consec when the source speech was fast and dense, whereas a more redundant, impromptu-style input speech was preferably rendered on the basis of notes.

FRANZ PÖCHHACKER

SIMULTANEOUS INTERPRETING

↑ MODES
→ SIGHT INTERPRETING/TRANSLATION
↓ SIMULTANEOUS WITH TEXT

Broadly speaking, simultaneous interpreting (SI) is the mode of interpreting in which the interpreter renders the speech as it is being delivered by a speaker into another language with a minimal TIME LAG of a few seconds. When interpreting in simultaneous mode between spoken languages, interpreters generally work in soundproof booths with SI equipment that prevents acoustic overlap between the original speech, listened to via headphones, and its simultaneous interpretation spoken into a microphone. SI can also be practiced without a booth, as 'whispered interpreting' (*chuchotage*), for only a few listeners, or using a mobile system (*bidule*). Interpreters also work simultaneously between a spoken and a signed language (referred to as 'bimodal interpreting') or between two signed languages. Since these are expressed in a visual-gestural modality, there is no acoustic overlap, but visual contact between the interpreter and the deaf listener(s) or speaker is crucial.

In terms of processing, the simultaneous mode also includes SIGHT INTERPRETING/TRANSLATION, in which written texts are rendered into spoken or signed languages in real time. This is also done in the combined mode known as SIMULTANEOUS WITH TEXT, where the interpreter processes the speaker's speech at the same time as following the written text of that speech. Another hybrid form is SIMULTANEOUS CONSECUTIVE, where the interpreter, working consecutively, records the original speech with a digital device and then interprets the recording simultaneously rather than relying (only) on notes.

The widespread use of SI in international organizations in the post-war era, particularly following its initial public success at the NUREMBERG TRIAL, has led SI to be most closely associated with CONFERENCE INTERPRETING. Although this connection is undeniably present, interpreters had probably been rendering speeches simultaneously long before the institutionalization of simultaneous conference interpreting, both in the form of whispered interpreting and as the typical working mode in SIGNED LANGUAGE INTERPRETING. On the other hand, the close linkage established in the twentieth century between SI and TECHNOLOGY continues, paving the way for the new opportunities and challenges that have arisen with REMOTE INTERPRETING, and leading to new international standards for technical infrastructure.

From early on, researchers were interested in the element of simultaneity in SI, whereby a person listens to a speech as it is being delivered, processes it and (re)produces it in another language. As early as 1930, Sanz drew attention to the specific processes in SI, and since the 1970s psycholinguists have taken an interest in SI as a source of insights into aspects of bilingual human language processing. Despite the progress that has been achieved, the complexity of the task and the difficulty of isolating one single sensitive variable from the many which interact within the overall process continue to challenge PSYCHOLINGUISTIC APPROACHES and, more generally, COGNITIVE APPROACHES to research on SI. The main areas of investigation to date include MODELS of the cognitive process; the function of key components such as WORKING MEMORY; the neural correlates of bilingual processing in SI; the dynamics of INPUT VARIABLES and output features in professional performance; and the STRATEGIES used by interpreters to cope with cognitive and linguistic challenges.

Modeling the interpreting process has been a major concern of research on SI. Some of the models developed have attempted to sequence and explain the interconnections between micro-level cognitive processes (e.g. Gerver 1976; Moser 1978), while others have focused on the interplay of the main operational tasks (Kirchhoff 1976a, 1976/2002; Lederer 1981; Darò & Fabbro 1994; Gile 1995a). The 'pragmatic' dimension, which was initially neglected, was also incorporated into a number of the later models, acknowledging the importance of input-related factors as well as situational and psychological dimensions (Cokely 1992a; Setton 1999).

Working memory and the allocation of attentional resources have figured centrally in process models and have also been studied separately. Although good working memory has been considered an essential requirement for SI, research to date has not offered much conclusive evidence of the posited connection (see Timarová et al. 2014). There is some evidence that it is not superior working memory capacity per se which leads to expert performance, but rather an acquired ability to manage competing demands on limited cognitive resources in SI (Liu et al. 2004); other studies emphasize that experts distinguish themselves from novices by the more meaningful relations they have formed between items in MEMORY (Köpke & Signorelli 2012). In addition to the storage function, researchers are increasingly interested in exploring the executive functions of working memory, such as 'controlled attention' (Timarová et al. 2014) or the management of COGNITIVE LOAD.

The cognitive mechanisms of INTERFERENCE and suppression have also received attention due to their relevance in SI, where various resources need to be shared. Based on studies exploring both unimodal and bimodal SI, researchers have attempted to examine the impact of phonological interference and the interplay between SI and suppression in lexical access, metaphor comprehension and syntactic parsing (e.g. Gernsbacher & Shlesinger 1997; Isham 2000).

In a move beyond cognitive constructs, the neural correlates of SI were studied in the 1990s, first using neuropsychological techniques, such as dichotic listening and verbal–manual interference tasks (Darò & Fabbro 1994), and then with more direct methods like electroencephalography (EEG) and advanced imaging techniques such as positron emission tomography (PET) and functional magnetic resonance imaging (fMRI) (Tommola et al. 2000). Following an earlier focus on brain lateralization in bilinguals, NEUROSCIENCE APPROACHES to the study of SI have come to target language control and experience-related changes in the interpreting brain.

At the interface of cognitive and linguistic aspects of SI, important elements of both the input and the output in SI have been studied, in original speeches as well as interpreters' renditions. These include determinants of source speech difficulty like lexical choice, density and mode of presentation (read vs. extemporaneous), and in particular prosodic features, such as ACCENT, INTONATION, SPEECH RATE and PAUSES (e.g. Ahrens 2005a). In addition to their impact on cognitive processes and SI performance, prosodic aspects of the interpreter's delivery have been found to play a role in the way users perceive and assess the simultaneous interpreter's output. PROSODY has, therefore, also featured prominently in research focusing on USER EXPECTATIONS and ASSESSMENT in SI (e.g. Collados Aís et al. 2007, 2011).

Understanding how interpreters cope with the challenges of SI has triggered considerable research on strategies and coping skills. ANTICIPATION has been seen as a critical aspect, with a particularly prominent role in interpreting between structurally different languages. Studies have also highlighted the use of a range of compensatory strategies, such as OMISSIONS and COMPRESSION. In addition to using these to cope with the challenges of the task, it seems that interpreters may deliberately omit, add, explicitate or compress in instances where this does not seem required. In one illuminating case, professional interpreters omitted most of the adjectives the experimenter had included in her experimental design because they considered them repetitive and senseless (Shlesinger 2003). This finding highlights the fact that decision-making processes in SI are shaped not only by cognitive constraints but also by professional norms, aside from pointing to the issue of ecological validity in the design of EXPERIMENTAL RESEARCH, which has been the methodological approach of choice in many studies on SI.

Yet another cross-cutting concern in SI has been DIRECTIONALITY. While there is evidence that working from one's mother tongue into a foreign language ('into B') is associated with higher mental load and a different pattern of brain lateralization (e.g. Rinne et al. 2000), there are also findings pointing to an advantage of this language direction when it comes to anticipation (e.g. Jörg 1997) and coping with sources of COMPREHENSION difficulties like accents and noise, as well as 'problem triggers' like proper names and NUMBERS.

Given the demand for professionals capable of performing this specialized task, the PEDAGOGY of SI has long been an area of great interest (e.g. Seleskovitch 1999; Moser-Mercer 2005b). While most writings on training methods continue to be based on personal reflection rather than empirical findings, there is a growing body of knowledge on skill acquisition, progression, testing and assessment (e.g. Angelelli & Jacobson 2009), including the long-standing issue of screening for aptitude in interpreting.

EBRU DIRIKER

SIMULTANEOUS WITH TEXT

↑ SIMULTANEOUS INTERPRETING
→ SIGHT INTERPRETING/TRANSLATION

'Simultaneous with text' (SI with text) refers to SIMULTANEOUS INTERPRETING (SI) of a speech read from a source text that is available to the interpreter, who uses it as part of the input to follow the speaker. This dual input (auditory and visual) makes SI with text a cognitive task distinct from SI done from speech alone, and from SIGHT INTERPRETING/TRANSLATION (done from written text), whether or not the interpreter has seen the text before interpreting. For this reason, 'SI with text' is a more accurate label for this task than other terms found in the literature such as 'sight interpreting', 'oral sight translation' or 'simultaneous sight translation'. Although SI with text can in theory be performed as a mixture of SI and sight translation, going from 'pure' SI without any reference to the text to 'pure' sight translation without any reference to the sound (Gile 1997), it is best classified as a form of SI, since the oral input has priority: the interpreter must 'check against delivery' and, in the event of deviation, follow the speaker's actual words rather than the text which has been provided.

Interpreting a speaker reading from a prepared text that has not been supplied to the interpreter is widely recognized as stressful and unsatisfactory (Mackintosh 2002); indeed, contracts initially exempted conference interpreters from this task, though this is now hardly applicable in practice. SI with text is considered more acceptable, but nevertheless highly complex. Written text tends to be more informationally and linguistically dense than impromptu or semi-prepared speech, and may be presented at a high speed and/or without the natural PROSODY that facilitates oral communication. The interpreter's auditory input may thus be too fast to manage without the written text; yet relying only on the latter poses the risk of falling behind and missing the speaker's deviations. Like sight translation, SI with text is also assumed to involve a higher risk of linguistic INTERFERENCE – one of the few aspects of this mode that have been the object of empirical research (Lamberger-Felber & Schneider 2008).

In an experimental study with twelve experienced professionals interpreting three authentic English conference speeches either with or without the written text available in the booth, Lamberger-Felber (2001, 2003) sought to compare SI and SI with text (either with or without time to prepare) with regard to target-text ACCURACY and completeness, in particular OMISSIONS. Though complicated by high individual variability of performance and perceptions of task difficulty, the results showed that the percentage of correctly rendered proper names and NUMBERS was distinctly higher for SI with text (98% with time to prepare, 92% without) than when the interpreters did not have the written text.

In a similar vein, Coverlizza (2004) compared interpreters' SI performance on certain items in read-out presentations, either without text or with the text provided ten minutes in advance, and found that participants performed better with the text on strings of adjectives, numbers, long lists and an anecdote, but were more fluent when working without a text. Lambert (2004) found significantly improved SI-with-text performance in student interpreters when the text was available with ten minutes to prepare.

In addition to the difficulty of the written text, the time available for PREPARATION stands out as a key factor determining the effectiveness of SI with text. Acceptable QUALITY can be achieved for all but the most 'written' material, if provided to the interpreter with sufficient time for advance preparation. This may include reading and annotating it in various ways to direct the eye, for example by underlining or highlighting numbers or unfamiliar names, or to guide restructuring (especially for typologically contrasting language pairs), noting idiomatic target-language expressions to combat the risk of interference, or making notes in the margin to capture the gist of a dense paragraph and facilitate COMPRESSION (see Seleskovitch & Lederer 2002; Setton 2006b).

STRATEGIES for using the written text while interpreting from auditory input may thus vary with the time available for preparation, but also depend on individual preferences linked to the interpreter's abilities in fast reading, text scanning and eye–ear coordination (or the availability of help from a boothmate). If the text arrives too late to prepare, the interpreter may prefer to set it aside and work purely by ear. However, such preferences and strategic decision-making and their effects have yet to be investigated.

Based on available research findings as well as professional experience, a strong case can be made for the inclusion of SI with text in interpreter training programs, with the focus on preparation techniques and training eye–ear coordination (Setton & Dawrant 2016). Moreover, the skills acquired for SI with text can also be applied to 'mixed-media' presentations (e.g. PowerPoint) and, most recently, to speeches delivered with real-time captioning on a screen. Even more so than SI with text, however, such dual-input modes are still relatively unresearched.

ROBIN SETTON

SLIPS

→ REPAIRS

A slip, also referred to as slip of the tongue or speech error, is defined as "an involuntary deviation from the speaker's current phonological, grammatical, or lexical intention" (Boomer & Laver 1973: 123). In Chomskyan terms, slips are errors of performance, not of competence, and occur naturally in spontaneous speech. In psycholinguistics, research on slips provided the foundation of error-based speech production models (e.g. Fromkin 1980; Levelt 1989), and slips remain an important area of psycholinguistic study, especially with the advent of modern speech analysis tools.

In the broadest sense, speech errors include grammar errors (linked to performance, not competence), blends, false word activation, 'tip of the tongue' and ordering problems (anticipation, perseveration), as well as simple slips (addition, omission, exchange) and Freudian slips (Levelt 1989). However, there seems to be little agreement regarding a unified taxonomy, which makes it difficult to compare research results. In addition, slips are often investigated together with other disfluency phenomena, such as hesitations, PAUSES and REPAIRS.

As a special form of spontaneous speech produced under time pressure and other cognitive constraints, interpreting can be assumed to be particularly prone to speech errors. Even so, research on the topic in interpreting studies is scant, and limited to such issues as the occurrence of slips in the output of interpreters as well as original speakers, and the perception and strategic handling of slips in the source speech.

Slips in the output of simultaneous interpreters and conference speakers were first investigated by Pöchhacker (1995d). Distinguishing between corrected and uncorrected slips and 'structure shifts' (false starts, lexical blends and syntactic blends), he found more simple slips and false starts in the output of speakers, while interpretations contained a higher percentage of lexical and structural blends.

Concerning the perception of slips in the source language during SHADOWING, Tonelli and Riccardi (1995) found that phonological errors were detected less readily than morphological or lexical ones. This suggests that, during simultaneous listening and speaking, errors at deeper linguistic levels are more easily detected. The STRATEGIES used by interpreters to deal with speakers' errors and repairs were investigated by Van Besien and Meuleman (2004), who found that interpreters corrected speakers' unrepaired errors and interpreted repairs without rendering the original utterance.

Further studies on the production of slips in SIMULTANEOUS INTERPRETING (SI) have shown that speech errors in the target texts (in this case in Hungarian) signal malfunctions related to lexical activation and grammatical planning (Bakti 2009; Tóth 2011). Although there is some evidence that the slips occurring in the target-language output of interpreters show a different, SI-specific pattern compared to slips in their own extemporaneous speech, language-specific factors are also likely to influence the pattern of slips in simultaneously interpreted speech.

MÁRIA BAKTI

SOCIOLINGUISTIC APPROACHES

→ DISCOURSE ANALYTICAL APPROACHES, → LINGUISTIC/PRAGMATIC APPROACHES
↓ BILINGUALISM, ↓ GENDER, ↓ LANGUAGE POLICY, ↓ REGISTER

Sociolinguistics examines the interplay of language and society, with a focus on how aspects of the latter affect the way language is used. It studies how language varieties differ depending on certain social variables, such as ethnicity, GENDER and status, and how individuals and groups select among the possibilities for expressing meaning in their everyday lives. This vast field of inquiry requires and combines insights from a number of disciplines, including linguistics, sociology, anthropology, and social psychology.

Sociolinguistic processes are inherent in the practice of interpreting. Each interpreted interaction is situated within communities that harbor their own multilingual and language contact phenomena; within a setting that represents a snapshot of what may be a long history of language policies and planning; and in a social environment beset with language attitudes about one or both of the languages involved. Sociolinguistic studies of interpreting begin with the underlying assumption that interpreting itself constitutes a sociolinguistic activity from the moment an assignment is accepted, including the products and processes inherent to the task, variously reflecting issues of BILINGUALISM or multilingualism, language contact, variation, REGISTER, LANGUAGE POLICY and planning, and language attitudes.

Interactional sociolinguistics, a term coined by US linguist John Gumperz (1982), takes into account both the macro-level social meanings of talk (group differences) and the micro-level meanings (what any one individual says and does at any one moment in time) embedded within a communicative situation (Schiffrin 1994). Methodologically, this means drawing upon naturally occurring interactions between speakers of different cultural backgrounds, often in institutional settings. This involves recording such events, via audio or video recordings, transcribing these and often coding for linguistic evidence of how people mean what they say or sign. Researchers may also replay these events for the participants, asking about their perceptions.

Sociolinguistic studies of interpreting first appeared in the mid-eighties in the area of SIGNED LANGUAGE INTERPRETING. Cokely (1992a), in his miscue analysis to account for a cognitive processing model, drew attention to the sociolinguistic factors that could impact such a model. Roy (2000a) studied an interpreter's TURN-TAKING behavior in a meeting between a professor and a graduate student, and Metzger (1999) described multiple linguistic features of interpreter participation, both in relaying the message and managing the process, in a doctor's office.

Overall, relatively few studies are explicitly presented as sociolinguistic. Examples can be found in LEGAL INTERPRETING settings (e.g. Angermeyer 2010; Berk-Seligson 2011; Maryns 2013a) and in HEALTHCARE INTERPRETING (Davidson 2000; Aranguri et al. 2006). Most research, however, particularly on DIALOGUE INTERPRETING (e.g. Wadensjö 1998), mirrors the methodology of (interactional) sociolinguistic approaches – studying authentic interactions in institutional contexts, recording natural language use, and interviewing the participants. Such research, typically under the heading of 'discourse and interaction', also shares many issues of sociolinguistic concern.

There is also a growing body of interpreting research in which sociolinguistic concerns relating to bilingualism, multilingualism, language contact, language variation, language policy and planning, and language attitudes all constitute aspects of the processes and products of interpreting. Both professional and lay interpreters, whether native speakers/signers or second language speakers/signers, are by the very nature of their task bilinguals or multilinguals using languages within a language contact situation, which gives rise to such phenomena as INTERFERENCE (e.g. Davis 1990). In the context of geographical and/or political boundaries, interpreters are faced with understanding the linguistic variation of multiple minority groups (e.g. Hlavac 2010, 2013b; Ramsey & Peña 2010), whose choices reflect social factors as well as linguistic constraints.

CYNTHIA B. ROY

SOCIOLOGICAL APPROACHES

→ PROFESSION
↓ HABITUS, ↓ ROLE, ↓ STATUS

Unlike such disciplines as psychology and linguistics, sociology, as the scientific study of human social behavior and institutions, became a source of theoretical insights (and new methodological approaches) rather late in the development of interpreting studies. It was not until the 1990s that an explicit or implicit recognition of interpreters' visibility gained ground, and with it an increased awareness of the significant relationship between interpreters' agency and the social and institutional structures within which they work.

The earliest known published research to draw attention to interpreting as a socially situated activity was by sociologist R. Bruce W. Anderson (1976), though his work was not taken up by interpreting scholars until over a decade later. SHLESINGER's (1989b) efforts to apply Toury's notion of NORMS to interpreting activity paved the way for research that analyzed interpreting practices as social acts, not merely linguistic ones, equally influenced and constrained by normative rules as acts of translation (see Garzone 2002b). However, it was not until

Cecilia Wadensjö (e.g. 1998) highlighted the triadic nature of interpreter-mediated interaction, drawing on the work of Erving Goffman (e.g. 1981), that sociological models came to be explicitly applied to the empirical study of interpreting. This social interactionist approach, based on the micro-sociological study of discourse-based interpersonal interaction, has become a strong current in interpreting studies. At the same time, broader, macro-sociological approaches have come to the fore, drawing on social theory to account for interpreters' agency in social fields.

Social interactionist approaches

In social interactionist approaches to interpreting research, discourse analysis has been widely used as a method, particularly since the groundbreaking work of Wadensjö (1998). Major contributions were also made by Ian Mason (1999a, 2001) and, in SIGNED LANGUAGE INTERPRETING, Melanie Metzger (1999) and Cynthia Roy (2000a), all of which called attention to the triadic nature of DIALOGUE INTERPRETING. Within these DISCOURSE ANALYTICAL APPROACHES, Wadensjö's work introduced the concept of PARTICIPATION FRAMEWORK into the micro-analysis of the interpreted event – what Goffman (1983) referred to as the 'interaction order', to characterize social encounters as partially bounded domains whose communicative structures involve shifts in 'footing' that are determined principally by the demands of the situation. The emphasis on the shifting ROLE of the interpreter in interaction highlights how agency, despite being culturally or socially inscribed, is achieved in and through local communicative practices, even in situations of institutionalized POWER asymmetry between interlocutors. The focus on the interactional dimension emphasizes the role that interpreters play in the negotiation, maintenance, or manipulation of structures of participation as they, with other members of different or the same cultures, enter into some previously uncharted social and linguistic relationship. Relevant work in this area also includes Pöllabauer's (2004) and Bot's (2005) use of conversation analysis to examine the function of discursive interpreter interventions and their impact on meaning construction in ASYLUM SETTINGS and PSYCHOTHERAPY sessions with refugees and asylum seekers, respectively. The findings of research centered on the micro-analysis of participation frameworks across diverse contexts have made significant contributions to challenging the view of the interpreter's INVISIBILITY in the interaction. Generally speaking, this research has tended to emphasize specific realizations of discourse processes within interpreted interactions, and has advocated a continued restrictive role for interpreters in the interpreted encounter, albeit with a firm recognition of the undeniable active presence of the interpreter.

Mason's research draws on different theoretical and methodological traditions, including Halliday's (1978) social semiotics, Hodge and Kress's (1993) focus on language and ideology, and Fairclough's (1995) development of critical discourse analysis. Research stemming from these traditions has tended to focus more explicitly on the social and discursive issues within specific interpreting contexts that are linked to language, power and IDEOLOGY. Interpreters are theorized as active social agents within broader communicative, social and political processes. Beaton's (2007) focus on the interface of interpreting, ideology and institutional discourse, in her textual analysis of interpreter mediation and agency during political debates in the European Parliament, is a good example of this broader perspective.

Narrative approaches

Narrative theory, its concepts and methodological tools, have also been used in interpreting research to demonstrate the potential for symbolic violence to occur when sociolinguistic repertoires and resources, mediated by bureaucratic processing and geopolitical agendas, are interpreted across social and linguistic borders. Barsky's (1996) pioneering work on ASYLUM SETTINGS showed how institutional and discursive constraints impacted on applicants' narrative accounts in Canadian refugee hearings. Baker (2006) applies narrative theory to consider the public narratives that precede and accompany military combat in which interpreters are narrated by other participants in the war zone as either one of 'us' or one of 'them'. She also considers how public narratives can serve to conceal the variety of ways in which military interpreters participate in the narratives concerning a particular conflict. Boéri (2008) and Baker (2009) also apply narrative theory to study the emergence and construction of communities adopting an ACTIVIST APPROACH to interpreting – a phenomenon which, like sociological approaches more generally, directly challenges the notion of interpreters as subservient and non-interventionist. This recent focus on interpreting and social activism (Boéri & Maier 2010) merges with the increasing attention that has been given in recent interpreting research – highlighted in sociological approaches – to the ideological, ethical and political dimensions of interpreting activity (Cronin 2006; Inghilleri 2012).

Interpreters as agents in social fields

Adopting a distinctly macro-sociological approach, Inghilleri engages with Bourdieu's theory of social construction and reproduction (2005b), emphasizing the relationship between socially, culturally and linguistically constituted norms and the way different forms of knowledge and power are constituted in interpreting activity in the asylum system (2003, 2005a, 2014) and in the military (2008). Bourdieu's social theory has since been considered in relation to interpreters and the multiple fields in which they work by a number of interpreting scholars. In some of this research, there is a tendency to apply the theory, and especially the concept of HABITUS, rather loosely and without sufficient attention to Bourdieu's wider theoretical framework, of which habitus is but one component. From a Bourdieusian perspective, acts of interpreting are examined in relation to the social practices and relevant fields in which they are embedded. Taking this more macro-sociological approach helps to highlight the extent to which interpreters are implicated in – but may also assist in challenging – practices promoting inequality, discrimination and other forms of injustice, in settings where local and global relations of power are associated with specific institutions. Research incorporating habitus within this broader view has been done in relation to the legal/political field, the medical field, the military field (Torikai 2009, 2014), and with reference to specific areas of interpreting, for example, COMMUNITY INTERPRETING and signed language interpreting (Grbić 2014).

In the field of interpreting studies, Bourdieu's work stands out as having introduced an important theoretical and methodological framework originating in the social sciences. However, the emergence of sociologically oriented perspectives in interpreting research has given rise to additional theories and methodologies for investigating interpreting activity as a social and political phenomenon, at both the macro- and micro-sociological levels. There is a significant body of research which identifies itself as sociological or sociocultural and which draws on a more eclectic range of explanatory frameworks (see Pym et al. 2006; Wolf & Fukari 2007). These include ethnography and social interactionism, discourse analysis (particularly conversation analysis and critical discourse analysis) and narratology. Relevant work that adopts ETHNOGRAPHIC METHODS includes Diriker's (2004) examination of the social positioning and relationships that are constructed between speakers and interpreters in the context of an academic conference. Diriker's research challenges long-held assumptions about conference interpreters as seemingly passive 'subjects', and instead reveals them to be powerful agents of communication. Angelelli's (2004a) research on interpreting in the medical field draws on data from observations of medical encounters and INTERVIEWS with interpreters, challenging the characterization of interpreters as conduits by highlighting their active role in interpreted interactions.

Taken together, the body of work emanating from sociological approaches highlights the crucial role of interpreters in both the process and products of interpreting activity. It suggests ways for interpreters to embrace both their visibility and their accountability, and affords a conceptual framework in which to view interpreting studies and the interpreting profession as forces working toward ensuring universal access to social and political justice.

MOIRA INGHILLERI

SOVIET SCHOOL

↑ INTERPRETING STUDIES

→ RUSSIA

↓ CHERNOV

Educational institutions for the training of professional interpreters started to form in the Soviet Union in the 1940s, but interpreting, above all SIMULTANEOUS INTERPRETING, became a subject of research only after the Second World War, as the need for interpreters in international communication continued to rise.

The Soviet tradition of scholarship in interpreting, as well as the Russian school of thought which inherited its main tenets, have a number of specific features distinguishing them from the Western tradition of interpreter training and research. Most fundamentally, the Soviet tradition is strongly shaped by the fact that there is a single concept for translation and interpreting as a cognitive-linguistic activity, expressed by the Russian term '*perevod*'. *Perevod* thus encompasses interpreting as well as translation, without any distinction regarding the modes of perception and production involved. In order to make this distinction, the adjective '*ustnyi*' is added to denote 'oral translation' (i.e. interpreting), while the adjective '*pismennyi*' is used to refer to 'written translation'. By the same token, 'simultaneous interpreting' is expressed by qualifying *perevod* with the adjective '*sinkhronnyi*'.

Based on this conceptual unity, the functions of translator and interpreter in the USSR and, partly, in modern RUSSIA are not always clearly distinguished. Evgeny Gofman (1963) emphasized that at the NUREMBERG TRIAL, unlike the interpreters from other countries, simultaneous interpreters from the Soviet Union were involved in the translation of documents as well as the editing and proofreading of verbatim reports.

The uniform conceptual foundation provided in the Russian language by the term *perevod* also predetermined Soviet and Russian scientific thinking about interpreting and translation, the central branch of which developed primarily as the 'general theory of interpreting and translation'. It was in this general theoretical framework that problems common to all types of translational activity (e.g. equivalence, unit of translation) were studied, and models, built on an exclusively linguistic basis, were developed. Interpreting as a particular form of mental and linguistic activity was only a secondary concern. This asymmetry was already apparent in the first book on the theory of translation and interpreting, by Andrei Fedorov (1953), which established a linguistic approach to Soviet translation scholarship and made very little mention of interpreting. Fedorov devoted only ten pages to a brief analysis of interpreting public speeches, and was mainly concerned with the linguistic features of oral statements to be interpreted. Similarly, throughout the twentieth century, few works written by Soviet and Russian scholars focused on interpreting.

The general theoretical approach, encompassing translation as well as interpreting, was also reflected in the CURRICULUM and in didactic concepts for the training of translators/ interpreters. In 1959, Rurik K. Minyar-Beloruchev, a graduate of the Military Institute of Foreign Languages and interpreter for the leaders of the USSR, published a book on the teaching of interpreting or, more specifically, of translating auditorily perceived source texts. Based on insights by Soviet psychologists (e.g. Artemov, A. A. Leontiev, A. N. Leontiev, Vygotsky) into speech activity, the author distinguished three main aspects of an interpreter's mental activity: listening, comprehension, and retention of a source text that is heard only once. Based on his personal experience as an interpreter, Minyar-Beloruchev (1959) offered a first theoretical account of consecutive and simultaneous interpreting and proposed systematic exercises for the training of interpreting skills at different stages of the learning process.

The didactic orientation was also dominant in subsequent publications on interpreting by Soviet scholars, which often took the form of textbooks for interpreter training. The 1960s to the 1980s can be considered the heyday of the Soviet School of interpreting studies. Conference interpreters like Mikhail Zwilling, Ghelly CHERNOV and Anatoly Shiryaev undertook studies of simultaneous interpreting and built theoretical models of this activity. Much of their work was published in the annual journal *Tetradi Perevodchika* [The Translator's/Interpreter's Notebooks], which first appeared in 1963 and ceased publication in the late 1980s (e.g. Zwilling 1966; Chernov 1971, 1975; Shiryaev 1982b); Shiryaev also published articles, in the early 1970s, in *Inistrannye Yazyki*, the 'Yearbook' of the Military Institute of Foreign Languages. Monographs on interpreting were published in this period by Minyar-Beloruchev (1969a, 1969b, 1980), Chernov (1978) and Shiryaev (1979, 1982a).

Minyar-Beloruchev focused on CONSECUTIVE INTERPRETING. Based on Shannon's mathematical theory of communication, he viewed interpreting as a means of information transmission and elaborated a theory of text informativity that enabled him to develop a system of NOTE-TAKING for consecutive interpreting. He also suggested the notion of 'non-equivalence' as a basis for quality ASSESSMENT.

Chernov and Shiryaev studied simultaneous interpreting from the standpoint of Soviet psycholinguistics. With a focus on the structure of the activity, Shiryaev analyzed the parallelism of source text perception and target text production; the mechanisms ensuring source text comprehension while pronouncing a text in the target language; quantitative characteristics of the interpreting process; and techniques of speech COMPRESSION. He designed and conducted an experimental study and, based on its findings, defined a 'unit of orientation' in simultaneous interpreting as "a segment of a source text, the semantic perception of which allows an interpreter to start the search for or selection of an interpretation solution" (Shiryaev 1979: 19; my translation). Around this fundamental concept Shiryaev built a comprehensive model, highlighting both the continuous and the discrete nature of the simultaneous interpreting process. Chernov, in turn, conceived a probabilistic and predictive model of simultaneous interpreting based on the redundancy that is part of all speech at the phonetic, syntactic and semantic levels. Exploiting this redundancy in its various forms, the simultaneous interpreter forms anticipatory hypotheses that must be checked against the continuing source speech input, as demonstrated in an innovative interdisciplinary experiment (see also Chernov 2004).

Minyar-Beloruchev, Shiryaev and Chernov were the pioneers and main representatives of the Soviet School of interpreting studies. Their experimental research and models of the interpreting process served as the underpinning for didactic approaches that are still successfully used for interpreter training in modern Russia.

NIKOLAY GARBOVSKIY

SPAIN

Spain is understood here as a geographical and historical entity, based on the current political map, which has served throughout history as a crossroads of migrations from and to various continents. This implies that peoples from different cultures and languages have coexisted in this territory since prehistoric times, and interacted through the mediation of bilingual individuals. Using a slightly modified Western periodization, reference is made in this entry to four historical stages: ancient history, from the first millennium BCE to the seventh century CE, with emphasis on the Romanization process; the Middle Ages, from the Muslim conquest in 711 until 1492; the period of the Spanish Empire, under the Habsburgs and the Bourbons (1492–1808); and modern Spain, from the nineteenth century until the present day.

Ancient history

Phoenicians, Greeks, Carthaginians and Romans created settlements in various areas, and the territory of present-day Spain became an arena of geopolitical competition to exploit agricultural and mineral resources. Eventually, after the Punic wars, the Roman Empire was able to secure control of the Western Mediterranean, including the Iberian Peninsula and the Balearic Islands (around 20 BCE). The Romanization process spread over those territories, with differing degrees of intensity, for more than four centuries. It entailed the influence of Latin as a LINGUA FRANCA and of Roman culture as the backbone of civilization, particularly in urban centers, from where a language shift into Latin started. Bilinguals must have been required throughout the whole process of acculturation, particularly during the military campaigns, where interpreters were recruited among local individuals, in many cases slaves or freedmen, who learned Latin through contacts with native or near-native speakers. In the mostly illiterate societies of those days, only educated elites would have mastered Latin (Gehman 1914), speaking it with regional accents, local loan words, language mixing or cross-language imitation, while the majority of the local inhabitants, including army veterans who were given land after retirement, would have spoken various languages and the 'Latin of the camp'. Mixed and evolving linguistic identities would continue to develop until local languages of Iberian and Celtic origin, not without resistance, were superseded by Latin and eventually died (Adams 2003, 2007), the only exception being Basque. After the fall of the (Western) Roman Empire, regional varieties of Latin would evolve into Romance vernaculars (mainly Galician, Castilian and Catalan), creating diglossic societies. This also applied to the period of Visigoth domination (the sixth to seventh centuries CE), with Latin as the official language of administration and the Church, particularly after Catholicism became the official religion of the monarchs. A very influential role was thus played by a powerful Latin-speaking Church, a situation that persisted through the Middle Ages in all the Iberian Christian kingdoms.

The Middle Ages

The arrival of Muslim troops under Tariq and Musa in the Iberian Peninsula in 711 ushered in an eight-century-long period of confrontation with numerous political, military and social consequences, including a state of accelerated shift and tension in the relations between languages and cultures. Conflict along changing frontiers was a defining feature of the societies that developed in these territories, marked by the coexistence of the three mono-theistic religions (Judaism, Christianity and Islam), each with its own ritual language: Hebrew, Latin and Arabic respectively (Martinell Gifré et al. 2000). Contacts among them generated various interlingual and intercultural phenomena, such as the presence of 'alfaqueques' and the tradition of oral translation.

Captives from the Muslim or the Christian side were a common feature in the medieval period, as were their rescuers, who on the Christian side acquired an administrative status recognized in municipal and 'national' laws in all peninsular Christian kingdoms. As the agent of this brokered frontier, the rescuer – known as an *alfaqueque* in Castile and Leon and as an *exea* in Aragon – was charged with the task of negotiating with the Muslim authorities the ransom that Christian authorities or families were ready to pay. Negotiations in Arabic required language proficiency, as mandated in the *Partidas* code enacted by Alfonso X the Wise to regulate the activity of *alfaqueques* (López de Coca Castañer 1989; Pym 1996; Brodman 2011).

Compared with the mostly rural and culturally backward Christian kingdoms, the Muslim kingdoms showed a high level of sophistication, commanding the legacy of the Greek, Roman and Byzantine classics that had been translated into Arabic by Muslim scholars, who also added their own classic traditions from Persia and the Middle East. That body of knowledge trickled down to the Christian monarchies through translation in places such as Tarazona or Toledo (Pym 1994; Foz 1998). The translation process was carried out by Christian scholars and, typically, educated Jews familiar with Semitic languages, who would perform SIGHT INTERPRETING/TRANSLATION to render the Arabic text into Castilian while copyists noted down their words in vernacular for further translation into Latin.

In addition, the use of Latin as the official language of public administration and all transactions involving the omnipresent Church created a need for intracultural pragmatic translation into the vernacular. Thus, public clerks or priests and monks orally translated documents that concerned the lives of the illiterate vernacular-speaking populations (Santoyo 1999).

The colonial empire (1492–1808)

Events in 1492 under the 'Catholic Monarchs' (Isabella of Castile and Ferdinand of Aragon), namely the conquest of the Muslim kingdom of Granada, the expulsion of the Jews, and the 'discovery' of America, ushered in an era characterized by the consolidation of an incipient modern state, the exclusion of the two other religions that had coexisted with Christianity for centuries, and the beginning of the Spanish overseas colonial endeavor across the Atlantic and beyond.

The two mainstays of the early modern state's foreign policy were diplomacy and war. The former involved the creation by Emperor Charles V of the *Oficina de Lenguas* in the then embryonic Ministry of Foreign Affairs, which has survived through the centuries until today (Cáceres Würsig 2004, 2012). Wars served the preservation of the Habsburgs' heritage rights in Europe and the defense of Roman Catholic Christendom against potential enemies – so-called infidels, represented broadly by the Ottoman Empire, as well as Christians who had broken with Catholic orthodoxy on the European continent and in the colonies. Latin continued to be the diplomatic language in Europe, although other languages were also used, including Spanish, whose influence was concomitant with increasing political power. The armies that fought in Europe were made up of multilingual troops, with mercenaries from various countries, and the presence of interpreters was necessary to make communication possible.

Interpreters were also needed as a result of the exclusion of other religions and the persecution of non-Catholic Christians. They mediated in land use controversies in formerly Muslim territories and in the conversion of *moriscos*, who stayed in Spain despite the expulsion orders, forming pockets of Arabic-speaking communities (Vincent 1994).

Religious reformation movements in Europe made their influence felt (albeit to only a limited extent) in ultra-orthodox Spain, and Inquisition tribunals, first established in 1478, were held to suppress any divergence from Catholic doctrine. Although their proceedings were mostly conducted only in the vernacular, while Latin was the official language of the ecclesiastical administration, many documents attest to the presence of interpreters in cases in which heretics who did not speak Spanish were prosecuted, both in Spain itself and in the colonial empire (Sarmiento Pérez 2016).

The overseas colonial undertaking, preceded by the (interpreter-mediated) colonization of North African enclaves and the conquest of the Canary Islands (Sarmiento Pérez 2011), combined the Christian medieval crusade in the Iberian Peninsula (evangelization) with the exploration of an alternative spice route after the Ottoman Empire had severed Asian land routes. On his first voyage to the New World, Columbus took with him an interpreter whose language combination was, in the event, useless for interaction with the Caribbean peoples actually encountered by the explorers (Alonso Araguás 2005). The use of signs and the seizing of young natives to teach them the language of the European voyagers, as was commonly practiced by the Portuguese along the West African coast, were initial solutions, which more often than not failed. A mixture of what Cronin (2002) calls autonomous and heteronomous systems of interpreting was used in order to cope with communication problems caused by the myriad languages spoken in the islands and in the two subcontinents of the New World. Missionaries tried to preach the gospel in the natives' languages; conquistadors resorted to local interpreters, such as MALINCHE in Mexico (Karttunen 1994a; Valdeón 2013) or Felipillo in Peru (Valdeón 2014).

The Spanish Crown took the issue of communication with the locals very seriously and enacted a series of laws on interpreters. The 14 laws, included in Book Two, Title 29, of a compilation dating from 1681 (Ayala 1946), emphasize strict observance of basic principles of ETHICS so as to safeguard indigenous peoples' rights in their contact with the Spanish administration at the *Audiencias* (Alonso & Payàs 2008; Giambruno 2008; Alonso-Araguás 2016).

Although Spanish was used for several centuries as the language of administration, with Latin serving religious purposes, many INDIGENOUS LANGUAGES survived colonial rule (Yannakakis 2008).

Expeditions of exploration and conquest that required the use of interpreters continued until the end of the eighteenth century, reaching as far afield as remote areas of the Pacific Ocean. So when the crisis of the *Ancien régime* erupted in metropolitan Spain at the beginning of the nineteenth century, and independent republics were established in most of the former Spanish colonial territories, the new states faced the need to use language mediators to manage large regions. Throughout the colonial period, and even beyond, 'maritime interpreters' were appointed at Spanish ports to facilitate trade with foreign partners (Santoyo 2008).

Modern Spain

At the start of the nineteenth century, the Bourbon dynasty was replaced by Napoleon Bonaparte's brother, Joseph, who addressed people in Italian through an interpreter during his initial journey from France to Madrid. The subsequent war against French occupation, which involved British and Portuguese troops, also required the use of military interpreters.

In 1898 the loss of the last vestiges of the Spanish overseas empire (Cuba, Puerto Rico and the Philippines) was negotiated with the United States at a conference in Paris. Rather than resort to French as the lingua franca, the proceedings were held in English and Spanish, with Arthur Ferguson, a member of the US delegation, serving as the only interpreter (Bowen 1994).

In the domain of LEGAL INTERPRETING, the sworn interpreters' corps, as a group distinct from the maritime interpreters or those who acted overseas, was established through legislation enacted at various points in time (Peñarroja 2000; Cáceres Würsig 2004), and exists to this day.

The consolidation of the Spanish presence in North Africa, which had started in the fifteenth century, involved diplomatic and military actions carried out through interpreters, from the 1767 Treaty of Friendship and Commerce between Spain and Morocco (Feria García 2005, 2007) to Spain's larger intervention in the area in 1859, which lasted until Spanish Morocco's independence in the late 1950s (Zarrouk 2009; Arias Torres & Feria García 2013).

The Spanish Civil War (1936–1939) was an international conflict which required the participation, on both sides, of many interpreters. Most of them were recruited spontaneously among the combatants (e.g. in the International Brigades), and others were brought from Germany with the Condor Legion or from the Soviet Union with their military and political experts (Baigorri-Jalón 2012). The regime established by Franco in 1939 in turn sent the 250th Infantry Division to support the *Wehrmacht*'s efforts against the Soviet Union, and interpreters were needed for liaison in the general staff of the respective armies (Ackermann Hanisch 1993).

The thirty thousand Spanish children sent abroad by their parents during the Civil War were repatriated relatively easily from Western countries, but not from the Soviet Union, which had no diplomatic relations with Franco. Initially educated in Spanish by tutors who traveled with them, the roughly 3000 children hosted there later went through the Soviet educational system in Russian. Their bilingualism was a great asset for the Soviet authorities to facilitate communication between their civil and military experts and Cuban authorities after Castro's revolution in 1959 (Baigorri-Jalón 2003).

The Franco government's economic stabilization plan of 1959 sparked off large-scale labor migration, with hundreds of thousands of Spaniards emigrating in search of employment, mainly to European countries. Some of their children, born and schooled abroad between the early 1960s and mid-1970s, later enrolled in the translation and interpreting schools that mushroomed in Spain after its accession to the European Communities (now European Union) in 1986. In 1991 education authorities authorized the establishment of some twenty university degree programs in translation and interpreting (in addition to previously existing schools in Barcelona, Granada and Las Palmas), most of which focused on CONFERENCE INTERPRETING.

In Spanish regions with an additional official language other than Spanish (Galicia, the Basque country, Navarre, Catalonia, Valencia and the Balearic Islands), interpreting services are also required in public institutions, for instance in regional parliaments. On a much broader scale, the need for trained – but also untrained – community interpreters has been increasingly felt in public services, given the arrival of millions of immigrants since the early 1990s (Valero Garcés 2006) and the language requirements of over 50 million tourists per year, mostly from European countries. Both immigrants and tourists, particularly retirees, have changed traditionally homogeneous communities into multilingual and multicultural neighborhoods in need of regular interpreting services, mostly in the form of DIALOGUE INTERPRETING and by sworn interpreters where required.

JESÚS BAIGORRI-JALÓN

SPEECH PATHOLOGY

↑ HEALTHCARE INTERPRETING

Speech pathologists, also referred to as speech and language therapists, have aspects of communication as their central area of professional interest. Beyond the body structures and functions relevant to speech, language and swallowing, their concern extends to communication in the activities and social roles a person wants to participate in. The six main areas of speech pathology practice include (1) the production of speech sounds, (2) the effective functioning of the voice, (3) using spoken and written forms of language for learning and everyday interaction, (4) stuttering, (5) using multi-modal systems of communication, and (6) swallowing.

When speech pathologists do not share the same language background as their clients, a professional interpreter is one of the most effective resources, yet this can involve significant challenges to both professionals (Gentile et al. 1996; Guiberson & Atkins 2012; Isaac 2002).

Interpreters are most likely to be called upon by speech pathologists during the diagnostic process, when the speech pathologist is trying to determine the presence and/or nature of a communication or swallowing impairment. In the assessment of any aspect of communicative competence, interpreters will require highly developed syntactic, semantic, pragmatic and phonological knowledge of both languages involved so as to attend to nuances in the patient's comprehension and style of expression. The interpreter must then convey any hesitations, self-repairs or false starts that may be part of the client's verbal output. In addition, the interpreter must appreciate the specific discourse of assessment practices that apply in this professional domain, including interviewing and the administration of formal diagnostic tests. Moreover, the interpreter will inevitably face situations where it is difficult to understand what the client is saying.

These general challenges can be further compounded by the fact that a speech pathologist may ask an interpreter to become involved in some type of analysis of the client's responses. This comparison to community and cultural norms is central to determining the extent to which any deviations from the language norms of the patient's community might indicate some kind of communication impairment. Interpreters are rightly hesitant about being asked their opinion, as this brings them into conflict with their own professional code of ETHICS.

Thus, in order to be most productive for the client, the working relationship between the speech pathologist and the interpreter should be understood as a 'professional collaboration'. Since training programs do not currently prepare novice professionals for managing the complexities of this professional relationship, individual practitioners must take responsibility and allocate sufficient time to both preparation and debriefing phases of any assessment.

LIBBY CLARK

SPEECH RATE

↑ INPUT VARIABLES, ↑ PROSODY

Speech rate is a temporal feature and a component of the PROSODY of speech that is often decomposed into two separate but related measures – speaking rate and articulation rate. Speaking rate, also referred to as speech tempo or speed, measures the words (or syllables) per minute (or second) of a speaker's actual output, including PAUSES. On the other hand, articulation rate is the speed of articulatory movements and refers to speech uninterrupted by pauses above a certain threshold, usually between 150 and 250 milliseconds, which are excluded from the measurement (Kendall 2013). As the number of words expressed per time unit depends on factors such as the language involved (mean word length) and the type and genre of discourse, syllables have been suggested as a more reliable unit of measurement for interlingual comparisons.

The rate of speech production may vary between speakers and for individual speakers depending on a range of cognitive, linguistic and social constraints as well as the mode of delivery, that is, whether speech is produced spontaneously (impromptu) or on the basis of a previously scripted text (i.e. read). As pointed out by Goldman-Eisler (1968), perception of speech rate is greatly influenced by the duration and number of pauses in the speech stream. She suggested that, in a read speech, pauses amount to 30% of total speaking time, while in an ad-lib speech they may represent up to 50%. Studies on the impact of speech rate on listening COMPREHENSION have shown a gradual decline, beginning at around 150 words per minute, until a threshold level is reached at about 250 words per minute, beyond which comprehension drops off sharply (Carver 1973).

In interpreting, speech rate, more often referred to as input rate, presentation rate or input speed, has long been considered as one of the key INPUT VARIABLES in the interpreting process, especially in relation to SIMULTANEOUS INTERPRETING (SI). As early as 1965, during an AIIC symposium on training, 100 to 120 words per minute was indicated as a comfortable speech rate for SI. Lederer (1981) reported 100 words per minute as the ideal rate for a read text, while indicating 150 to 170 words per minute as the threshold beyond which SI cannot be performed. Generally speaking, a rate between 100 and 130 words per minute is considered reasonably comfortable for ad-lib speeches, depending on the source language, while 135 to 180 words per minute is considered a fast input rate.

In his classic study on speech rate in SI, GERVER (1969) aimed to ascertain the possible impact of variations in speech rate during SI in comparison with SHADOWING. Ten professional interpreters with English as their A language were divided into two groups and were asked to either simultaneously interpret or shadow a French text (550 words). The speech rate was augmented every 110 words, giving rates of 95, 112, 120, 142 and 164 words per minute for successive sections of the text. Results indicated that interpreters can only keep up with the source speech tempo to a certain extent. More errors and OMISSIONS were found in SI at an input rate above 120 words per minute, while performance deterioration during shadowing began only at the highest input rate. Given the experimental nature of the study, results could not be generalized, but they largely confirmed what had been suggested by professionals.

In an experimental study of German–Italian SI inspired by Gerver's seminal work, Pio (2003) examined the impact of a high input rate on QUALITY in an EXPERT–NOVICE PARADIGM. Drawing on Barik's (1971) approach to ERROR ANALYSIS, she found that the number of errors, in particular omissions, was higher at the fast input rate (302 syllables per minute) than at the slow rate (196 syllables per minute) for both groups of participants, with students experiencing greater problems in coping with the high input rate.

Beyond objectively measureable input rates, Déjean le Féal (1978, 1980) pointed to the subjective nature of speech rate, the perception of which is determined by a number of variables. One crucial factor is the relative proportion of new or previously known information: the listener (i.e. the interpreter) will perceive a speech as more or less rapid depending on the cognitive processing effort required for comprehension (and in subsequent production in the target language). Déjean le Féal's work focuses on the role of impromptu versus read speech in SI, highlighting a number of interrelated variables. She argues that the characteristics of impromptu speech, including hesitations, repetitions, false starts, redundancy and syntactic coordination, help the interpreter follow the speaker's line of thought; a written text, by contrast, is informationally dense and features elaborate lexical choices and ample use of syntactic subordination, so that, even at the same speech rate, the read text will require more processing effort than the spontaneous one (see Déjean le Féal 1982). Moreover, orally presented written texts are assumed to require higher concentration than spontaneous speech delivered at the same rate because pauses tend to be shorter and less frequent in reading. She found that the length of segments between pauses measured in her corpus was one to nine words in impromptu speech and three to twenty-three words in read speeches. The mean values were below seven words in spontaneous speech and more than seven in read speeches (Déjean le Féal 1980). In addition, speech rate is interrelated with INTONATION: higher rates tend to be associated with flattened intonation contours, which in turn affects the comprehension process and increases cognitive strain. Thus, a high speech rate, typically encountered in combination with read texts, has been reported as one of the main stress-inducing factors in surveys on occupational STRESS in interpreting.

ALESSANDRA RICCARDI

SPEECH-TO-TEXT INTERPRETING

Speech-to-text interpreting, which is also known as captioning or as real-time speech-to-text services, is increasingly being used in some countries, such as the United States, to provide communication access for individuals who are deaf or hard of hearing (D/HH), mostly in educational settings. In speech-to-text interpreting, the provider of the service, who is often in the classroom or meeting next to the D/HH individual(s), produces text as it is being spoken by a speaker, such as a teacher, and displays it on a portable device so that the individual can understand what is happening. The process is typically intra-lingual – that is, the text interpreter listens to the spoken words and produces the text display in the same language. Speech-to-text interpreting services are occasionally provided to individuals with other needs, such as a hearing student with a learning disability.

In the two common speech-to-text interpreting service options, the text interpreter uses either (a) a standard typing (QWERTY) keyboard or (b) a stenographic machine. A little used option is (c) automatic speech recognition (Steinfeld 1998; Stinson et al. 2008).

These services may be provided in the classroom or meeting location, or remotely. If remotely, the speaker typically wears a bluetooth microphone and the spoken message is delivered using either a cellular phone or Voice over Internet Protocol (VoIP) via a cellular or broadband Internet connection (i.e. Skype, Google Hangout). These services also support display of text on a variety of devices (standard laptops, smartphones, etc.). The text interpreter may produce copies, typically electronic, of the saved text (Stinson et al. 2014).

Typing-based services (C-Print, Typewell) use a standard QWERTY keyboard (Stinson et al. 2008). A trained service provider uses the word-abbreviation feature in the system's software to speed up typing. The software transforms abbreviations into full words on the computer screen. In addition, text interpreters learn strategies for identifying important points and for condensing information. These systems cannot provide word-for-word transcription, because they cannot keep up with the speed of speech; however, the systems do capture almost all of the meaning of what is being said (Elliot et al. 2001).

Research has compared comprehension and retention of information after viewing a lecture with C-Print speech-to-text support and after viewing a comparable lecture with interpreter support. Students retained more or an equal amount of information with C-Print as with interpreter support (Marschark et al. 2006; Stinson et al. 2009).

With a steno-based system, a trained stenographer uses a 24-key machine to encode spoken words phonetically into a computer that converts them into the written characters of the language concerned (often English) and displays the resulting text in real time. The stenographer depresses several keys simultaneously, instead of sequentially as in conventional typing. Equipment includes special software that translates entries into complete words, as well as a laptop. Generally the text is produced verbatim.

Research has found that D/HH students demonstrated significantly better comprehension of a spoken message with this technology than when only following the video and audio of the message (Steinfeld 1998). A study that compared student lecture comprehension with steno-, C-Print, and interpreting services did not find significant differences in comprehension for the three methods (Marschark et al. 2006).

MICHAEL S. STINSON

SPEED

see under SPEECH RATE

STATUS

↑ PROFESSION

The term 'status' has a wide variety of meanings and usages, but is conceived here more specifically as *occupational status*, that is, the social position an occupation or PROFESSION, in this case interpreting, affords its members, interpreters, on an (imaginary) prestige scale. Alternative and near-synonymous terms are 'job status', 'job prestige' and, especially, 'occupational prestige', the term of choice in sociology, where the concept has its disciplinary roots.

Professionalization

From a sociological viewpoint, occupational status or prestige is mainly achieved through *professionalization*, the process that turns a mere occupation into a full-fledged profession. The sociology of professions has seen some disagreement about which factors constitute professionalization, but in a recent review of the field, Weiss-Gal and Welbourne (2008) propose to reconcile the different positions and list the following eight criteria as indicative of a profession: (1) public recognition of professional status, (2) professional monopoly over specific types of work, (3) professional autonomy of action, (4) possession of a distinctive knowledge base, (5) professional education, (6) an effective professional organization, (7) codified ethical standards and (8) remuneration reflecting professional standing.

Although attempts to professionalize the field of interpreting have been partially successful in some areas and in some national contexts, there is probably no sub-branch of interpreting anywhere in the world that meets all eight criteria. In COMMUNITY INTERPRETING in particular, the degree of professionalization appears to be low. As described by Hale (2011b: 345), community interpreting is "relegated in most instances to unprofessional, unpaid or poorly paid, ad hoc language assistance, with its status, levels of recognition, education and remuneration varying greatly from country to country". Community interpreting scholars also lament the lack of uniformity in requirements for entry to the profession, and the absence of a standard-setting professional body. In the small and elitist area of CONFERENCE INTERPRETING, the situation is radically different. The launch of university-level training programs in the 1940s and 1950s and the establishment of AIIC in 1953 have been key factors in securing almost full professional status for conference interpreters at international level (Dam & Zethsen 2013). Only criterion number 2 – professional monopoly – has yet to be achieved.

Research

The topic of occupational status is not new in the interpreting literature, but it has only started to attract sustained scholarly attention in recent years. The subject has mainly been addressed indirectly or partially in research with a broader thematic focus, most of which has been conducted as SURVEY RESEARCH aimed at eliciting interpreters' attitudes, opinions and perceptions of their professional selves, their jobs and WORKING CONDITIONS. Ozolins (2004), for example, conducted a comprehensive survey of 150 Australia-based interpreters of all kinds (trained and untrained, conference as well as community interpreters, but with a focus on the latter group) and, among many interesting findings, noted clear evidence of discontent especially among trained interpreters. The main source of dissatisfaction was identified as inadequate remuneration, but the interpreters also persistently voiced concerns over poor working conditions and lack of respect, recognition and status. Many respondents were particularly troubled by non-interpreters' lack of understanding of the complexities of inter-preting and the skills required to perform it. Converging evidence was obtained in a survey conducted by Hale (2007) among 23 community interpreters in Australia: poor remuneration and lack of recognition of community interpreting as a skilled profession were salient find-ings in this study too. Largely the same issues came to the fore in a survey by Salaets and Van Gucht (2008), who investigated 19 Belgium-based community interpreters' perceptions of their profession and found that these interpreters, though aware of the fact that they have an important role in the community, lacked appreciation and adequate remuneration.

In a study capturing the user perspective, Hale (2007) surveyed 41 medical and legal practitioners in Australia about their perceptions and expectations of (community) interpreters' work and concluded that interpreting was mostly thought of as an unskilled occupation, requiring no training and therefore not meriting professional remuneration.

A slightly different line of research investigates and compares the situation of translators and interpreters, with less of a focus on community interpreters. Based on a survey among 890 translators, interpreters, teachers and students worldwide, Katan (2009) studied the perceptions of the work and role of translators and interpreters (of all kinds) and found that interpreters are generally perceived as having higher status than translators. A survey on translators' and interpreters' attitudes to their role, status and professional identity conducted among 62 practitioners by Setton and Guo (2011) points to a similar pattern of status differentials among interpreters and translators in Shanghai and Taipei. Finally, Dam and Zethsen (2013) investigated the occupational status of the presumed "stars" of the interpreting (and translation) profession – that is, conference interpreters – by means of questionnaires admi-nistered to 23 Danish staff interpreters employed at the EU and, for comparison, 63 Danish EU-employed staff translators. The status of the respondents was assessed by means of questions modeled on five indicators of status: (1) remuneration, (2) education/expertise, (3) visibility, (4) POWER/influence and (5) importance/value to society. The main conclusions were that these interpreters were highly paid and highly trained professionals, that they saw themselves as highly skilled experts and that this view was shared by non-interpreters. Responses regarding professional visibility were less clear: the interpreters generally indicated that they worked at the very center of events but still assessed their work as only moderately visible to others; their assessment of their influence as interpreters was extremely low (below two on a five-point scale), but they generally regarded their job as important. In addition, the interpreters were asked to rate their occupational status on a five-point scale, and they positioned themselves higher than the translators (3.39 vs 2.56) but clearly not at the very top of the prestige scale. This relatively modest result for the branch generally considered the most prestigious among interpreters (and translators) suggests that the occupational status of translators in general, including interpreters, is hampered by structural factors.

Research that can shed light on the reasons for, and implications of, interpreters' relatively low occupational status is, by and large, still pending. A particularly promising avenue has been suggested by Sela-Sheffy and Shlesinger (2008), in the context of a comprehensive project on translators and interpreters in Israel. In contrast with the bulk of research on the interpreting (and translation) profession, this project advances a distinctly qualitative approach to inquiry, based on a constructivist EPISTEMOLOGY and narrative INTERVIEWS as the method of choice. This approach has proved useful in elucidating important aspects of the situation of literary translators in Israel (e.g. Sela-Sheffy 2010) and should prove equally illuminating for a better understanding of the complexities of interpreters' occupational status.

HELLE V. DAM

STRATEGIES

↑ COGNITIVE APPROACHES
→ INPUT VARIABLES
↓ ANTICIPATION, ↓ COMPRESSION, ↓ INFERENCING, ↓ SEGMENTATION

Strategic processes in communication have been the subject of research in monolingual discourse analysis, L2 acquisition and translation (e.g. Færch & Kasper 1984; Lörscher 1991), and research into interpreting strategies is derived from these approaches. Interest has traditionally centered on SIMULTANEOUS INTERPRETING (SI), whereas interpreters' behaviour in COMMUNITY INTERPRETING settings, with their typically asymmetric POWER relations in dialogic interaction, has been dealt with under such headings as DISCOURSE MANAGEMENT, TURN-TAKING, and intercultural MEDIATION (e.g. Englund Dimitrova 1997; Mason & Stewart 2001; Roy 2000a; Wadensjö 2001b). There is very little research that explicitly addresses strategies in LEGAL INTERPRETING, HEALTHCARE INTERPRETING, or DIALOGUE INTERPRETING in general. However, many strategies used in conference settings may also be identified in dialogic settings (Wadensjö 1998).

Concept and classification

With reference to scholarship in applied linguistics, strategies can be defined as "potentially conscious plans for solving what to an individual presents itself as a problem in reaching a particular communicative goal" (Færch & Kasper 1984: 47). In translation, they are defined as "procedures which the subjects employ in order to solve translation problems" (Lörscher 1991: 76). Whereas the conceptual focus on goal-oriented (intentional) problem-solving is generally accepted, the degree to which strategies are conscious has been a matter of debate.

While the notion of strategy has become widely adopted in COGNITIVE APPROACHES to the study of the interpreting process, the concept was given little importance in the INTERPRETIVE THEORY of the PARIS SCHOOL. On the assumption that COMPREHENSION and production processes in interpreting were much the same as in monolingual communication, interpreters would apply their linguistic and world knowledge to grasp the 'sense' of the original speech in a process of 'deverbalization' and then render it naturally in the target language (Seleskovitch 1978b). Kohn and Kalina (1996), on the other hand, argue that the discourse strategies of monolingual communication are not sufficient to solve all interpreting problems; since interpreting takes place under 'adverse conditions' (involving great time pressure and high COGNITIVE LOAD), discourse strategies have to be adapted, complemented and used far more efficiently.

Various terms have been used by authors conceiving of interpreting as involving strategic behaviour. What is here defined as a strategy is also referred to as a 'tactic' (Gile 1995a), 'technique' (Jones 1998) or 'skill' (Setton 1999). Pöchhacker (2004a) distinguishes between process-oriented strategies for coping with high-load-inducing input ('coping strategies') and product-oriented strategies for achieving effective communication. Other classifications relate to the mode of interpreting (consecutive vs. simultaneous) and the phases in the interpreting process. For Kirchhoff, strategies are decisions taken in a given situation or in view of certain probabilities; they include the SEGMENTATION of input, ANTICIPATION, phase shifting, keeping data available for subsequent processing, selecting or deleting, reducing or generalizing information, and monitoring output, possibly followed by repair operations (1976/2002: 114). Kalina (1998) distinguishes between comprehension-enhancing strategies, which include PREPA-RATION, segmentation of input, and INFERENCING, and production-oriented strategies. The latter may be conditioned by the characteristics of the source text but are mainly user-oriented, that is, designed to produce a target text that functions in the target culture. They include stylistic strategies (e.g. the choice of an appropriate REGISTER), REPAIRS (i.e. different types of self-correction as well as the conscious decision not to correct an error detected) and the use of nonverbal features of ORALITY (INTONATION, PROSODY) for delivery management (e.g. Ahrens 2007). Addition (or elaboration) is a strategic decision whereby the interpreter chooses to be more explicit than the speaker when rendering a given segment (e.g. Shlesinger 1995a; Kalina 1998; Gumul 2006b). Such EXPLICITATION may serve the purpose of explaining something that is otherwise incomprehensible to the target audience or which has no equivalent in the target culture (Bartłomiejczyk 2006).

Strategies may be used for different purposes. TRANSCODING (Lederer 1978; Gile 1995a; Kalina 1998; Bartłomiejczyk 2006) is a strategy which involves word-for-word translation, and is advisable especially for rendering NUMBERS, names, and lists of items. It is an emergency strategy if the interpreter fails to fully understand the source text and relies on its surface structure rather than semantic content. Gile (1995a) also mentions 'reproduction' or 'calque', whereby a source-text word or phrase is uttered in the target language (cf. 'phonetic shift'; Lederer 1978). Text-surface-based strategies are, however, prone to result in INTERFERENCE. The strategy of restructuring or syntactic transformation refers to the use of different word order in the target language even where this is not required by linguistic norms (Kalina 1998). This may help avoid interference from the source language in target text production (e.g. Riccardi 1996, 1998; Bartłomiejczyk 2006). According to the Interpretive Theory, linguistic surface structures have disappeared when sense is conveyed in the target language (deverbalization); there is therefore no language-pair specificity or need for strategic processing (Seleskovitch 1978b). By contrast, Riccardi (1996) and Bartłomiejczyk (2006) regard the use of strategies as potentially depending on DIRECTIONALITY (i.e. on whether the interpreter works into his or her A or B language). Other source-text-related strategies are paraphrasing and sentence splitting (*saucissonage*), based on successful segmentation or chunking.

When interpreters adopt the strategy of COMPRESSION (Alexieva 1983; Gile 1995a; Kalina 1998; Bartłomiejczyk 2006), longer speech segments are summarized and rendered in more concise wording, often by means of generalization and deletion operations. Compression is a production-oriented or coping strategy in SI, when the elements deleted have been chosen deliberately; this is akin to strategic OMISSIONS, as identified by Napier (2004b) in the output of sign language interpreters. In CONSECUTIVE INTERPRETING, compression is a general text production strategy, as the interpreter is often expected by users to be more concise than the speaker.

Some strategies are specific to the simultaneous mode, and these have attracted most attention in empirical research. Thus, early interest focused on the TIME LAG or 'ear–voice span' (EVS) in SI, and Kade (1967) suggested that a strategy of prolonged EVS was an advantage to the simultaneous interpreter. EVS, a defining property of all SI, is strategic insofar as its variability depends on differences in syntactic structure, source text delivery characteristics and interpreters' MEMORY capacity. Likewise, the segmentation or chunking of incoming text in SI (Goldman-Eisler 1972) is strategic in nature. Most typical, though, among strategies of SI is anticipation, which has been the subject of a considerable number of empirical studies over the years (e.g. Wilss 1978; Liontou 2012) and lies at the heart of CHERNOV's (2004) theoretical model for SI.

Coping strategies

Generally speaking, interpreters have to allocate attention among different activities that they have to manage at the same time, especially if they work in the simultaneous mode. In the framework of his EFFORT MODELS, Gile (1995a) assumes that simultaneous interpreters usually work close to the limit of their processing capacity, and that source-text features triggering a sudden increase in capacity requirements may disrupt the smooth functioning of the process. In order to cope with such 'problem triggers', Gile notes that interpreters tend to use a number of 'tactics'. These include comprehension tactics, such as 'stalling' or delaying response, reconstructing a segment from context (i.e. inferencing), relying on help from the booth mate, and consulting documents; preventive tactics (noting down figures or names, adjusting EVS, segmenting, changing the order of elements); and reformulation tactics (replacing an element by a more general one, paraphrasing, calque, transcoding). In extreme situations, omitting segments or even switching off the microphone are tactics of last resort.

Most authors agree that interpreters may have to resort to coping or emergency strategies, or compensatory strategies (Al-Khanji et al. 2000), which are needed when they fail to render all dimensions of a source text and simply strive to maintain some degree of communication which enables their listeners to respond. Such textual production strategies are compression (when it serves to render the main points), paraphrasing, deletion, generalization and mitigation (toning down when in doubt) or simplification of linguistic structure or of content. If the most appropriate term or expression cannot be retrieved immediately, the closest available equivalent is chosen by approximation, sometimes in several steps (e.g. Kalina 1998; Al-Khanji et al. 2000; Bartłomiejczyk 2006).

Gaining time to find a solution, if the meaning of a message has not yet been understood, can take different forms. Delaying response is a strategy described by several authors (e.g. Gile 1995a; Setton 1999; Bartłomiejczyk 2006); it may take the form of waiting (pausing) or stalling (slowing down delivery and filling in silences with general remarks). When the interpreter fails to reconstruct the meaning of a segment by inferencing, s/he may resort to 'parallel reformulation' (Gile 1995a). In this case, the interpreter is aware of the problem and tries to produce a message that is more or less plausible in the context so as not to pause or leave a sentence unfinished (Bartłomiejczyk 2006). Compensatory strategies may also be necessary when paralinguistic means of communication or graphic source material used by a speaker have to be rendered in the interpretation (Pöchhacker 1994c).

Interpreting problems are often caused by high SPEECH RATE. If source text delivery is extremely fast, and/or the speaker reads from a written text, there is a risk of information loss (Meuleman & Van Besien 2009). The interpreter either speaks faster, which may impact on comprehension processes, or resorts to compression.

Strategic decision-making in the interpreting process is essential, and the interpreter may have to choose between several competing strategies. Observational studies on the use of individual strategies are sparse, which is partly due to the difficulty in observing, measuring or counting the processes involved. Setton (2003) proposes individual strategic profiles that would need to be further studied. A combination of CORPUS-BASED RESEARCH and RETRO-SPECTIVE PROTOCOLS has been used to gain insight into the use of strategies by interpreters (Kalina 1998; Ivanova 2000; Vik-Tuovinen 2002; Gumul 2006b; Wang 2012), but there is room for much more research to unravel the complexity of strategic processes in interpreting.

To a certain extent, interpreting strategies may become automated in the course of time if they are trained appropriately, thus leaving enough capacity for the cognitive operations to be performed (Kohn & Kalina 1996; Kalina 2000; Riccardi 2005). There is therefore widespread agreement among interpreter trainers (e.g. Sunnari 1995a; Kalina 2000; Pöchhacker 2010a) that strategic processing needs to be taught to students, in theory as well as in practice.

SYLVIA KALINA

STRESS

→ COGNITIVE LOAD, → WORKING CONDITIONS

The intrinsic complexity of interpreting, both from the cognitive point of view and as a social activity in which the interpreter bears responsibility towards clients in many different SETTINGS, represents a likely stimulus condition for (occupational) stress. Stress, a term 'coined' by Hans Selye in the 1930s in a biomedical context (Selye 1956), is generally defined as a psychological reaction experienced when an individual feels an imbalance between task requirements and the resources available for coping with them (Lazarus 1966). The require-ments may be external (environmental) and/or internal (set by the individual), and the acti-vating response may be perceived as positive ('eustress') or negative ('distress'). The level of stress, typically understood in the negative sense, depends on the subjective cognitive eva-luation of a given stimulus as threatening or challenging, and on the perceived consequences of failure to cope with requirements. Thus, the PERSONALITY traits of a person will determine, and to some extent predict, what is experienced as stressful.

Job-related stress in interpreting has been investigated with particular reference to CONFERENCE INTERPRETING, and especially SIMULTANEOUS INTERPRETING (SI). Stress endurance (Longley 1989), including ability to cope with speed stress (Gerver et al. 1989), was con-sidered a crucial aspect of the interpreter's task and included among the features to be taken into account in APTITUDE TESTING.

Sources of occupational stress among (conference) interpreters were first investigated on a large scale in a study commissioned by AIIC (Cooper et al. 1982). The researchers first ana-lyzed data from 33 interviews and stress logs kept by AIIC interpreters during five working days, and identified four categories of stress factors (stressors): physical-environmental con-ditions (in the booth); task-related factors (concentration, SPEECH RATE, PREPARATION, work organization, evaluation); interpersonal relations; and home/work interface. On this basis they developed a questionnaire for a worldwide survey among AIIC members, with items concerning physical health, JOB SATISFACTION, personality characteristics, perceived stress and coping mechanisms. The 826 respondents (mainly freelance interpreters) indicated that the main sources of stress were environmental, followed by task-related factors and organizational aspects.

Some two decades later, another AIIC-commissioned study on occupational stress – the so-called Workload Study (AIIC 2002) – focused on interpreter stress and BURNOUT, investigating psychological, physiological, physical and performance aspects. A postal survey was developed for the psychological aspects, yielding 607 responses. Blood pressure, heart rate and salivary cortisol levels in a sample of 48 interpreters were collected for the physiological values, and 47 booths (permanent and mobile) in which the subjects were working were examined. Performance data (recordings) were collected for 42 interpreters, in 23 different booths, 6 times during the working day. While results indicated a high level of overall job satisfaction, the most frequently mentioned stress-inducing factors had to do with source texts and their delivery (e.g. speed, read texts, strong accents, lack of material and time to prepare) as well as booth discomfort.

In further studies on the physiological effects of stress in SI, Klonowicz (1994) investigated adjustments in resource mobilization using measures of cardiovascular activity (blood pressure, heart rate), while Kurz (2002a) assessed pulse rate and skin conductance to examine differences in stress response according to the setting (conference vs. MEDIA INTERPRETING). The latter method was also used to compare physiological stress levels in experts and novices (Kurz 2003). Moser-Mercer et al. (1998) combined measures of physiological stress (cortisol and immunoglobulin A concentrations) with questionnaires for psychological stress as well as output QUALITY data, to examine the effects of prolonged turns in SI, and found evidence of negative effects associated with turns lasting longer than 30 minutes.

The new challenges arising from REMOTE INTERPRETING led to a growing number of studies to identify any effects it might have on interpreters' WORKING CONDITIONS and health. For simultaneous conference interpreting in international settings, there is considerable evidence that the lack of direct VISUAL ACCESS to the speaker and setting, and the lack of feedback from the audience, lead to greater fatigue and a more rapid decline in performance quality (Moser-Mercer 2005a). In a large-scale experimental study on stress and performance in remote interpreting carried out in the European Parliament, results pointed to the sense of alienation and isolation felt by interpreters working in the remote condition, but showed no significant negative impact on performance quality and health (Roziner & Shlesinger 2010).

In SIGNED LANGUAGE INTERPRETING, where VIDEO REMOTE INTERPRETING is increasingly common, occupational stress is a prominent topic. Coping strategies and training-related suggestions are often discussed in the framework of the DEMAND CONTROL SCHEMA, a job analysis method used in studies of occupational stress (Dean & Pollard 2001). Given the high risk of stress-related illness, injury and burnout associated with signed language interpreting, an extended period of supervised practice in the final stage of training is suggested to guard against repetitive strain injury and other trauma disorders. In MENTAL HEALTH SETTINGS, in particular, the risk of VICARIOUS TRAUMA or secondary traumatic stress and burnout is very high (Bontempo & Malcolm 2012). Aside from the job's considerable emotional and psychological impact, Hetherington (2011), in a phenomenological study involving six sign language interpreters in England, identified lack of recognition as a major source of occupational stress: clients' unachievably high expectations were felt to be greatly at odds with interpreters' sense of the complexity of their ROLE and the responsibility they feel to ensure effective communication.

Lack of recognition is also likely to apply to spoken-language COMMUNITY INTERPRETING, though research on job stress in this domain is still scarce. Among the few exceptions is a study by the British National Union of Professional Interpreters and Translators (NUPIT

2001), based on survey responses from some 150 public service interpreters and translators. More than half the respondents reported a considerable level of emotional stress, and many pointed to poor working conditions and remuneration and a lack of professional appreciation as obstacles to a high level of performance.

ALESSANDRA RICCARDI

SUBSTITUTION

see under ERROR ANALYSIS

SURVEY RESEARCH

↑ METHODOLOGY

A survey, according to the American Statistical Association, is a method of gathering information from a sample of people, the sample usually being only a fraction of the population being studied (Scheuren 2004). Surveys are a widely used way of collecting empirical data in the social sciences, and have also become prominent in the METHODOLOGY of interpreting studies (Liu 2011).

There are basically four modes of conducting a survey: by post, over the telephone, face-to-face, and online (using the internet). Online data collection, using files sent via email or, much more frequently now, a document made available on the web, has become particularly popular. Web-based surveying saves time and money and is convenient to use, thanks to questionnaire generator software supporting the automatic processing of data. Even so, careful attention must be given to the cornerstones of surveying – coverage, response, sampling and measurement (de Leeuw et al. 2008; Couper 2000). Above all, coverage implies the clear specification of the target population, for which a 'sampling frame' needs to be constructed that can be used to generate a 'random' (or probabilistic) sample (Czaja & Blair 2005; Groves et al. 2004).

Surveys are typically associated with quantitative research relying on numerical and/or quantifiable data for statistical processing (Fowler 2014), but they may equally be of a qualitative nature, generating text (as in INTERVIEWS) that is interpreted by the researcher. These two approaches to surveying can also be combined, as done in so-called MIXED METHODS RESEARCH (Creswell 2003).

The very first survey on interpreters and their work was conducted by Sanz (1930), a Spanish educator who conducted interviews with some twenty professional conference interpreters in Geneva. Apart from this exception, survey research on interpreting generally dates back to the late 1970s. Several survey-based papers were presented at the VENICE SYMPOSIUM, including Anderson's (1978) early work on ROLE in different interpreting situations, the survey by Thiéry (1978) on 'true' BILINGUALISM among AIIC members, and the small-scale study by Parsons (1978) on STRESS factors among UN interpreters. Stress was also the topic of a large-scale survey commissioned by AIIC (Cooper et al. 1982), with 826 respondents.

In the late 1980s, survey research gathered momentum in the wake of Bühler's (1986) seminal study on QUALITY CRITERIA in CONFERENCE INTERPRETING, which generated a series of (quantitative) surveys on USER EXPECTATIONS, mostly in the form of self-administered paper-and-pencil questionnaires. Revisiting Bühler's study, the very first web-based survey – not only in interpreting studies but also in the broader field of translation studies – was reported by Chiaro and Nocella (2004), and this technique has since then been used for a growing number of surveys on various aspects of interpreting.

Until early in the new millennium, most survey research in interpreting studies centered on conference interpreters, and conference interpreting. In a review of 40 survey studies published up to 2008, Pöchhacker (2011d) noted that these were predominantly (85%) quantitative (questionnaire-based) but mostly involved fewer than 100 respondents. While the problem of sample size seems to have become less of an obstacle with the advent of web-based surveying, the issue of coverage remains difficult to resolve. Beyond established professional organizations on a national or international level, most notably AIIC, the population of interpreters is often difficult to identify, and even more difficult to access with a systematic sampling approach. This applies in particular to less professionalized domains of interpreting, even though the use of survey research in such fields as HEALTHCARE INTERPRETING and LEGAL INTERPRETING is now widespread, often targeting clients and users of interpreting services as much as interpreters themselves (e.g. Hale 2007; Hsieh 2008; Hsieh & Hong 2010).

Irrespective of domain, or research topic, web-based questionnaires have largely become the surveying mode of choice in interpreting studies. Examples include the survey on QUALITY and role by Zwischenberger (2013, 2015) and the study on interpreters' glossaries by Jiang (2013): both of these were designed as full-population surveys of AIIC members, achieving response rates of 28.5 and 21 percent respectively. A more restricted population – Danish staff interpreters in the European Commission and European Parliament – was targeted by Dam and Zethsen (2013), in an investigation of the self-perceived STATUS of interpreters vs. translators in the EU institutions.

Even if the use of email for questionnaire distribution in online research has now become rare (e.g. Martínez-Gómez 2014a), it sometimes serves as a complement to traditional postal surveys and/or onsite distribution (e.g. Lee 2009a; Bontempo & Napier 2011). The telephone mode seems to be almost non-existent. A singular example is the quantitative survey by Lee (2007) on TELEPHONE INTERPRETING in AUSTRALIA (Lee 2007), in which the very topic may have influenced the choice of data collection mode.

CORNELIA ZWISCHENBERGER

SYNTACTIC COMPLEXITY

see under INPUT VARIABLES

TACTILE INTERPRETING

see under INTERPRETING FOR DEAFBLIND PERSONS

TALK SHOW INTERPRETING

↑ DIALOGUE INTERPRETING, ↑ MEDIA INTERPRETING

TALK SHOW INTERPRETING is a form of MEDIA INTERPRETING, performed within the genre of the TV talk show. In a typical scenario, the interpreter is on the set, sitting next to the guest(s), rendering the host's statements or questions in whispered simultaneous mode and using CONSECUTIVE INTERPRETING to translate the guest's turns aloud. Alternatively, talk shows may use SIMULTANEOUS INTERPRETING (SI) from a booth off-screen (and off-stage), with the interpreter's voice audible to the public in 'voice-over' mode only when rendering the guest's turns into the audience's language. Whereas the use of SI in remote mode allows great efficiency with very limited 'visibility' of the interpreter, it is the presence of the interpreter on the set that gives rise to the unique features of talk show interpreting discussed below.

With regard to such characteristics as the constellation of participants, power distribution, discourse type and interaction structure, talk show interpreting is similar to other forms of DIALOGUE INTERPRETING. What makes it different, however, is that it is performed on television and involves a specific kind of television discourse, namely talk show interaction. The TV setting, with its institutional and technological specificities, implies a certain degree of formality and unique constraints on task performance, including asymmetry in terms of knowledge distribution, access to conversational resources, and the organization of participation in the interaction (Heritage & Greatbatch 1991; Drew & Heritage 1992). Talk show participants' task-based orientation is guided, first and foremost, by the principle of entertainment (Katan & Straniero Sergio 2003). Thus, participants are required to maintain a constant flow of talk throughout the show, since, as a general rule, silence on entertainment programmes is to be avoided (Linell 1998). On the other hand, participants' talk does not follow a rigid agenda, as conversation within the programme is expected to mimic real-life talk. Consequently, the interaction is heavily dependent on the situation and on the relational dynamics that develop between the interacting parties during their conversation. Most importantly, the primary recipients of the talk exchange are not the on-screen participants but viewers in front of the TV screen. Talk shows, particularly on commercial television, address an audience expecting to enjoy the comfort of their own environment while being entertained by the show. Therefore, the staging and framing of the discussion (*mise en scène*) generally prevail over what is actually being said (Straniero Sergio 2007). The *mise en scène* is the responsibility of the talk show host, who dominates the interaction by controlling topics and TURN-TAKING, acting as *report elicitor* rather than *report recipient* of participants' utterances (Atkinson & Heritage 1984; Heritage 1985; Linell & Luckmann 1991) in accordance with the broadcast director's aims and designs. This input includes the choice of interpreting mode, as well as any instructions regarding the interpreter's behaviour on stage.

Given these characteristics of the genre, talk show interpreters are very much in the spotlight – both during the show and afterwards, in comments by the press. The INVISIBILITY taken for granted as an imperative in most interpreting SETTINGS is of no concern in entertainment television (but see Wadensjö 2008b), which has significant implications for the interpreter's interactional ROLE and identity. Talk show interpreters enjoy great flexibility in producing their renditions, which are expected first and foremost to be applause-relevant, regardless of pragmatic repercussions due to almost unavoidable information loss (Linell et al. 1992; Katan & Straniero Sergio 2001). Additions, OMISSIONS and elaboration of the original utterances, as well as REPAIRS, tend to be perceived not so much as indicators of processing difficulties, but more as signs of the interpreter's involvement and participation. Changes of FOOTING are frequent, as the interpreter often alternates between relaying the other interlocutors' talk and speaking for him/herself as a ratified participant in the conversation. Talk show interpreters are expected to serve the logic and dynamics of entertainment with their every action, playing along as seasoned performers and responding with professional aplomb while at the same time performing their actual task of interpreting.

As a result, the tendency is for the interpreter's twofold role (both as interpreter and as a ratified interlocutor) not to be fully and consistently respected by the other participants – whether in conversational (turn allocation) or in ethical terms (professionalism). A case in point is what Straniero Sergio (2007) describes as 'negotiated translation management', which occurs when the host knows the guest's language. Translation turns in this constellation often do not fit into a clear-cut host–interpreter–guest structure, but are co-produced by interpreter and host in a kind of translational turn-sharing. This may be collaborative in nature, but it may also turn competitive, to the point of becoming antagonistic. Aside from encroaching on the interpreter's communicative space, the host may delegitimize the interpreter's professional role for entertainment purposes, leveraging the privileged status of his/her own turns to single out the interpreter's translational choices and difficulties for unscripted humorous comment.

EUGENIA DAL FOVO

TEACHING

see under PEDAGOGY

TECHNOLOGY

↓ COMPUTER ASSISTED INTERPRETER TRAINING, ↓ E-LEARNING, ↓ MACHINE INTERPRETING, ↓ REMOTE INTERPRETING, ↓ SIMULTANEOUS CONSECUTIVE, ↓TELEPHONE INTERPRETING, ↓ VIDEOCONFERENCE INTERPRETING

Ever since the emergence of professional interpreting in the twentieth century, TECHNOLOGY has been important for different interpreting SETTINGS and MODES. While SIMULTANEOUS INTERPRETING in conference settings was only made possible by progress in electro-technical communication equipment, and the development of CONFERENCE INTERPRETING as a PROFESSION was closely linked to that technology, it is only in the last decades that the use of technology has spread in COMMUNITY INTERPRETING (or public service interpreting) settings, particularly in LEGAL INTERPRETING and HEALTHCARE INTERPRETING. Recent advances in information and communication technology (ICT) are even reshaping interpreting practices in a way that eliminates the need for an interpreter's physical presence at a given communicative event, if not doing away with human interpreters altogether (see Svoboda 2014; Władyka 2014). This manifests itself in the growing use of videoconference technology and REMOTE INTERPRETING, and considerable research efforts are geared towards fully automatic speech-to-speech translation, or MACHINE INTERPRETING.

The use of technology in (human) interpreting has been studied in three different dimensions: (1) technology for rendering interpreting services; (2) technology for interpreter training; and (3) technology to aid an interpreter's performance. Moreover, as in other fields of science, digital technologies have become widely used and indeed indispensable in research on interpreting, whatever the choice of METHODOLOGY and empirical approach.

Technology for rendering interpreting services

Simultaneous interpreting, or 'telephonic interpreting' as it was initially called, was developed in the mid-1920s at the initiative of Edward Filene at the International Labour Organization (ILO), an affiliate body of the League of Nations. As described in detail by Baigorri-Jalón (2014), it took several years and the engineering solutions of Gordon Finlay before the system, later patented as the Filene-Finlay Speech Translator and taken over by IBM, came into broader (though still limited) use at ILO conferences and beyond. However, it was only when Léon DOSTERT decided to use the IBM system for interpreting arrangements at the NUREMBERG TRIAL (Gaiba 1998) that it gained worldwide attention, and it was soon adopted by the United Nations (see Baigorri-Jalón 2004).

Despite the significance of these developments, interest in the strictly technological aspects remained rather limited in the field of interpreting. Thanks to efforts led by the Technical Committee of AIIC, international standards for fixed and mobile interpreting booths (ISO 2603 and ISO 4043, respectively, last modified 1998) as well as electrical and audio requirements for conference systems (IEC 60914) were established by the 1980s (see Jumpelt 1985).

The advent of videoconferencing technology soon impacted on interpreting (see Mouzourakis 1996). Initially, individual speakers who were not present at the conference venue were interpreted via a videoconference link made possible by satellite technology; advances in ICT then made VIDEOCONFERENCE INTERPRETING and remote interpreting more feasible, and they came to be increasingly employed in legal and healthcare settings. Researchers in these various domains have studied the implications of the technology-based delivery of interpreting services, with special attention to the effects of remote interpreting on performance, initially in the simultaneous mode and then also in non-conference settings (Moser-Mercer 2005a; Roziner & Shlesinger 2010; Braun 2013). The advantages and drawbacks of videoconference interpreting in different settings are described in Mouzourakis (2006) and Braun & Taylor (2012a).

By contrast, rather marginal interest has been devoted to technological improvements in portable equipment for ('whispered') simultaneous interpreting, also known as the *bidule* system, possibly because conference interpreters are wary of its use in place of booths as a cost-saving exercise when mobility is not a requirement. There has also been little technological change in the practice of on-site CONSECUTIVE INTERPRETING. Despite various efforts at developing technology for NOTE-TAKING in an electronic format, or for storing source text information and related details in some other way, interpreters continue to take notes with pen and notepad. There have been some trials of recorder-based SIMULTANEOUS CONSECUTIVE interpreting, a hybrid mode combining the advantages of simultaneous and consecutive interpreting (Hamidi & Pöchhacker 2007), but this has not yet found its way into practice on any larger scale.

A technology with potentially much greater impact on interpreting services is voice recognition, or automatic speech recognition, used as a key component of machine interpreting and applied in SPEECH-TO-TEXT INTERPRETING for deaf or hard-of-hearing audiences. In combination with RESPEAKING, voice recognition software is employed particularly in live subtitling, mainly in intra-lingual form, but with potential for inter-lingual application.

Technology for interpreter training

Training in the field of CONFERENCE INTERPRETING, both simultaneous and consecutive, has been revolutionized by new media and new technology such as web-based video platforms (e.g. YouTube), and by the huge supply of videos of original speeches on official websites. Tailored specifically to conference interpreter training, a Speech Repository was set up at the initiative of the DG Interpretation (SCIC) of the European Commission, combined with a tutorial platform (SCICRec). A number of other such speech banks have since become available. Underlying and accompanying these developments are digital recording technologies used to capture authentic speech material and also record student output in the classroom in dual-track mode, with easy access to particular passages and even precise measurement of temporal phenomena.

Technologies such as these are vital to COMPUTER ASSISTED INTERPRETER TRAINING, which has evolved from pre-established speech banks and training packages, such as Melissi *Black Box* (Sandrelli 2007), to flexible online platforms for a host of E-LEARNING activities. The use of ICT in interpreter EDUCATION was advocated long before the widespread availability of digital online technologies (e.g. Kurz 2002b), triggering research into its impact on teaching and learning in the (real or virtual) interpreting classroom (see Sandrelli & de Manuel Jerez 2007; Class & Moser-Mercer 2013). Other examples include the ACTION RESEARCH study by de Manuel Jerez (2006) on the introduction of authentic video material throughout all stages of the skill acquisition process, and the analysis by Gorm Hansen and Shlesinger (2007) of new tools to help achieve a balanced combination of face-to-face training and technology-assisted self-study in dialogue and consecutive interpreting.

An interesting new technology for the latter is the digital pen (Smartpen), a writing instrument capable of audio recording, with an infrared camera for the capture and subsequent synchronized replay of handwritten notes on micro-chipped paper. This offers great possibilities for recording, displaying and exchanging notes taken in consecutive interpreting exercises (Orlando 2010). Moreover, the digital pen can be employed in SIMULTANEOUS CONSECUTIVE interpreting, allowing for note-taking and audio recording at the same time.

Yet another, highly complex technology that has been tested for use in interpreter training is available in the shape of virtual reality systems, in which students can interact as avatars in virtual environments simulating specific settings of professional practice (Braun et al. 2013).

Technology to aid an interpreter's performance

Beyond their use in enabling and delivering interpreting services and in training, digital technologies have also permeated all phases in the interpreter's workflow. There is a broad range of applications in what one might thus refer to as computer-aided interpreting. Apart from non-specific communication and office tools, these include, in particular, software and electronic tools used in advance PREPARATION for an interpreting assignment. Most attention in this regard has been given to the documentation and management of TERMINOLOGY, with research conducted to identify interpreters' specific needs and practices (e.g. Stoll 2009; Jiang 2013) and a number of software tools developed with leading input from professional conference interpreters. These have progressed from a first generation of database tools in the 1990s to more comprehensive 'workbench' systems such as Interplex and InterpretBank (Fantinuoli 2013), which may also incorporate term extraction capabilities (e.g. Fantinuoli 2006).

The use of advanced and specialized software by conference interpreters in the booth, for terminology management in particular, and document and knowledge management in general (Rütten 2007), is evidently associated with the availability of appropriate hardware. Here, the PC has given way to notebook and tablet computers connected to the Web, and these mobile devices have become an essential part of interpreters' working environment.

Beyond their role in augmenting the individual interpreter's performance, web-based technologies such as cloud computing also offer enhanced possibilities for teamwork.

SYLVIA KALINA AND KLAUS ZIEGLER

TELEPHONE INTERPRETING

↑ REMOTE INTERPRETING
↓ VIDEO RELAY SERVICE

The term 'telephone interpreting' refers to the use of TECHNOLOGY to give one or more participants in interaction access to an interpreter, via a telephone or teleconference call. Telephone interpreting, also known as over-the-phone interpreting, is a form of REMOTE INTERPRETING, with the interpreter located in a different place from the communicating parties. Since remote interpreting is now commonly associated with interpreting by videoconference as a special form of teleconferencing (Mouzourakis 1996), Braun (2015) proposes the term 'telephone-based interpreting' to refer to interpreter-mediated telephone calls and remote interpreting via telephone, as distinct from 'videoconference-based interpreting', which subsumes remote interpreting via videoconference and interpreter-mediated videoconferencing.

Telephone interpreting is mostly used for DIALOGUE INTERPRETING in consecutive mode, especially in COMMUNITY INTERPRETING settings. Due to the limitations of the technology used, telephone interpreting between spoken languages is not possible in the simultaneous mode. Where a signed language is involved, however, SIMULTANEOUS INTERPRETING is possible, and this form of telephone interpreting, involving an audio-visual link, is known as VIDEO RELAY SERVICE.

Development

As the oldest among modern telecommunication systems, the telephone was the first to be used in interpreter-mediated communication. Unlike the technology used for SIMULTANEOUS INTERPRETING, which was initially referred to as 'telephonic interpreting' (Baigorri-Jalón 2014), telephone lines were proposed as early as the 1950s as a medium for the delivery of interpreting services (Nestler 1957). However, it was not until the 1970s that large-scale implementation began to take shape. Driven by the need to provide interpreting for individuals seeking services in locations where in-person interpreters were not readily available for the languages required due to distance and other logistical factors, an Emergency Telephone Interpreter Service was set up by the Department of Immigration of AUSTRALIA in 1973. As described by Ozolins (1998), the service originally offered telephone interpreting in eight languages; two decades later, it handled calls using 2.500 interpreters covering more than 100 languages and dialects, and by 2010 was providing close to a million over-the-phone assignments per year (Ozolins 2011).

In the United States, telephone interpreting became popular after the introduction of Language Line in 1982. Founded in Monterey, California by a policeman and a refugee advocate to help police officers communicate with speakers of Vietnamese and other languages, the service grew into a successful business successively owned by the AT&T corporation and private equity investment firms. With its commercialization throughout the US from the 1990s, telephone interpreting was extended into a variety of other fields such as healthcare, legal services, social services, education, and the nation's network of jails and federal prisons. Eventually, telephone interpreting also became popular for businesses seeking to sell their services and products to immigrants, refugees, and tourists, and became commonly used in insurance companies, travel agencies, banks, call centers, and retail locations (Kelly 2008).

Telephone interpreting has become a global billion-dollar business and is available in numerous countries throughout the world. But while commercial providers have played an important part in this development, telephone-interpreting services may also be managed by public-sector institutions or community-based organizations, and operated on a smaller scale. As pointed out by Ozolins (2011), the most significant drivers of change in the field of telephone interpreting in recent decades have been the declining cost of fixed-line telephony, the rise of mobile telephony, and the spread of internet-based voice communication; all of this creates opportunities for both (inter)national corporate providers (see Kelly 2008) and local AGENCIES in countries without the economies of scale achieved in large (often English-based) markets (e.g. Legreve 1999; Schuster 2013). At the same time, videoconference-based services over the internet have emerged as a viable alternative, fueling the controversy over the suitability of audio-only communication in certain SETTINGS. Indeed, this is one of the few issues that have been investigated in empirical studies, in a field that is otherwise characterized by untested assumptions and a surprising lack of research by interpreting scholars.

Critical issues

One of the basic issues surrounding telephone interpreting is the extent to which it is suitable for interpreter-mediated communication that goes beyond simple inquiries and requests for information. Recalling the origins of the service in response to health and security emergencies, the raison d'être of telephone interpreting as the fastest and most widely available method of accessing an interpreter is uncontested. It is moot, however, what kinds of interpersonal interaction, particularly in medical settings and in COURTROOM INTERPRETING, lend themselves to MEDIATION via an interpreter who is not present and has no VISUAL ACCESS to the speakers.

In a review of seven studies on telephone interpreting and two on videoconference-based interpreting, Azarmina and Wallace (2005) concluded that satisfaction by patients and doctors alike was as good with remote interpreting as with face-to-face interpreting, though interpreters preferred the latter. Similar findings regarding feasibility and acceptability emerged from a comparative pilot study covering 35 interpreter-mediated consultations with Turkish-speaking patients (Jones et al. 2003). A study in the US with a much larger sample (241 Spanish postpartum patients, 24 healthcare providers and 7 interpreters) compared encounter-quality ratings and interview comments in 80 cases each of in-person and telephone interpreting (as well as a video-interpreting condition); results indicated the perceived superiority of on-site face-to-face interpreting over remote modes (Locatis et al. 2010). Telephone interpreting was the least-liked option, dispreferred by six out of the seven interpreters because of the lack of visual communication. This was echoed by the results of a survey among 52 interpreters at 3 medical centers, who were asked to assess the adequacy of interpreting arrangements (in person, over the phone, video remote) for 21 common clinical scenarios (Price et al. 2012). While all modalities were found equally satisfactory for information exchange, respondents significantly preferred in-person over telephone interpreting for interpersonal aspects of communication, such as establishing rapport and facilitating intercultural understanding, particularly in scenarios with substantial educational and psychosocial components. Beyond the medical setting, a case-based comparison of face-to-face versus over-the-phone interpreting in a police interview (Wadensjö 1999) identified a lack of FLUENCY and smooth coordination in the tele-interpreted encounter. Wadensjö concludes that the two types of interaction differ in the possibilities they provide for the participants to coordinate and synchronize their joint activity.

An important factor in assessing the adequacy of interpreting service delivery via telephone is the technical set-up used. In a rare systematic analysis of authentic telephone interpreting assignments, Rosenberg (2007) categorized 1876 interpreter-mediated calls he had handled in the course of two years, some two-thirds of which related to healthcare settings and the remaining third to business calls. More than half were three-way telephone conversations, with three speakers on the phone in different locations, and close to 40 percent were assignments in which face-to-face conversations were interpreted remotely using a speakerphone. It was these calls via a speakerphone that were most frequently affected by poor sound quality, with instances of ambiguity due to the lack of visual access. The most problematic set-up for telephone interpreting in Rosenberg's experience is 'telephone passing', used for 70 of the calls in his sample.

Aside from the technical set-up and its implications for the quality of the interaction, the study by Rosenberg (2007) also points to the way the technology impacts on the interpreter's technique. Thus, the practitioner-researcher found himself using reported speech rather than first-person interpreting most of the time, the main reason being that clients mostly (or, in the case of telephone passing, always) addressed each other in the third person. Whereas this deviation from the norm of first-person interpreting is not unique to telephone interpreting (see e.g. Bot 2005), Rosenberg sees the specific challenge of telephone interpreting in the extra-linguistic, situational demands resulting from "the interpreter's physical distance and lack of a shared frame of reference" (2007: 75). The author also alludes to the difficult process of adaptation from in-person work to interpreting over the telephone, a subject which was investigated in a long-term study by Ko (2006b). The author asked six interpreters without prior experience of telephone interpreting to participate in a total of eight training sessions over a period of four weeks. Participants used ROLE PLAY and kept a diary to record their impressions regarding concentration span and fatigue, technical set-ups, and coping with the lack of visual information. Based on his observations and analysis of qualitative data, Ko (2006b) concludes that the constraints of telephone interpreting can be overcome after a period of practice, though little is known about specialized training approaches as such.

Given the difference in WORKING CONDITIONS for telephone interpreting, which range from full-time employment in call-center-like operations of well-equipped corporate providers to the use of mobile phones by interpreters on standby, the need to broaden the base of research findings is evident. As Rosenberg (2007) points out, systematic studies should investigate in particular whether the lack of visual cues results in more frequent OMISSIONS and NON-RENDITIONS, and whether this affects the efficacy and ACCURACY of the interpreter-mediated communicative exchange. In addition to examining the dialogue interpreter's core activities of translation and coordination (Wadensjö 1998), research also needs to engage with the ethical dimension of telephone interpreting. Although remote interpreting via telephone has often been thought to safeguard confidentiality, Ozolins (2011) raises tricky issues of role and ETHICS, for example in connection with a call being put on hold and the interpreter being drawn into a conversation with the client.

Among the broader professional issues surrounding telephone interpreting is its relatively low STATUS, which is presumably linked with often poor remuneration and concerns about inferior quality, compared to in-person interpreting. In a small-scale survey by Lee (2007), Korean interpreters in Australia voiced frustration with their telephone interpreting work as a result of low remuneration and task-related challenges. Noting that fees were not related to levels of NAATI accreditation, the author finds particular dissatisfaction among the more highly qualified subgroup in her sample (Professional Interpreters in the NAATI system) and argues that the lack of financial incentive for pursuing higher levels of CERTIFICATION may make it difficult to retain interpreters with superior COMPETENCE in this domain. As noted above, however, systematic research on quality in telephone interpreting is still lacking, and claims and opinions will continue to vary. Whereas Ozolins (2011: 46) expects interpreting over the phone to remain "the most likely medium for remote spoken language interpreting", Kelly (2008), while challenging the view of telephone interpreting as "an inferior but necessary alternative to on-site interpreting" (2008: 83), notes that the growing trend toward videoconference-based interpreting over the internet may see telephone interpreters replaced by video remote interpreters.

NATALY KELLY AND FRANZ PÖCHHACKER

TEMPO

see under SPEECH RATE

TERMINOLOGY

↑ INPUT VARIABLES, ↑ QUALITY CRITERIA
→ PREPARATION

Terminology, generally speaking, is the vocabulary of special language, or language for special purposes. The underlying theoretical model of terminology is the semiotic triangle made up of a concept, a term and an object (i.e. anything perceivable or conceivable being talked about). As defined in ISO Standard 1087, a concept is a "unit of knowledge created by a unique combination of characteristics", and a term is a "verbal designation of a general concept in a specific subject field" (ISO 2000).

Unlike translation or terminology work, interpreting is set in an immediate and unique situational context involving a defined group of participants. Thus, for interpreters, any term may be legitimate to use as long as the participants in a given communicative situation know what is being referred to. The more technical an interpreter-mediated encounter, the greater the importance of terminology among the INPUT VARIABLES in the interpreting process and as a feature of the interpreter's output. As studies on USER EXPECTATIONS among conference participants have shown, use of correct terminology is consistently among the highest-ranking QUALITY CRITERIA for the evaluation of a conference interpreter's performance, although the importance attached to terminology varies according to respondent group and type of assignment.

While terminology work in CONFERENCE INTERPRETING and COMMUNITY INTERPRETING has much in common, there are also some differences. When the interpreter has to stand or move around (as may be the case in CONSECUTIVE INTERPRETING or DIALOGUE INTERPRETING), the chance to make terminological queries may be reduced to consulting a notepad or small mobile computer, so the interpreter must rely much more on MEMORY. Furthermore, community interpreters tend to work in asymmetric communication situations, involving experts (lawyers, health professionals etc.) on the one hand and laypersons on the other. This makes shifts in REGISTER and explanations of technical terms more relevant than in typical conference settings.

The importance of terminology work in any type of interpreting also varies depending on the different phases of an interpreter's workflow – pre-, peri-, in- and post-process (Kalina 2005b). Due to situational constraints and the high COGNITIVE LOAD, opportunities for in-process terminology work are mostly limited to the occasional search for a specific term. It is therefore all the more essential that in-depth PREPARATION, taking into account the conceptual background and specific context, takes place pre-process as well as peri- and post-process in order to ensure correct understanding and efficient retrieval and production (see Stoll 2009). This involves studying terms from texts pertaining directly to an event ("texterms"), checking them against corresponding terms from independent background texts ("systerms") and, ideally, assigning them a place within a holistically structured knowledge system (Will 2007). On the other hand, interpreters do not need complete documentation of a given subject. They merely need to check the relevant information against their personal knowledge and fill the gaps.

Therefore, terminology management must always be considered in the broader context of an interpreter's information and knowledge management (see Rütten 2007). Like the latter, the workflow of an interpreter's terminology management involves different levels of 'enrichment', from data to information to knowledge. The first level involves the rather mechanical retrieval of all sorts of data (manuscripts, presentations, glossaries and the like). The second level consists in extracting from this 'raw material' the elements which are potentially relevant for the assignment at hand (terms, definitions, context), thus turning data into information, and organising it to ensure that it is visible or retrievable when needed. The third level involves the interpreter's personal knowledge. It consists in checking which relevant items of information are already actively known by the interpreter (i.e. retrievable from memory even under cognitive load) and memorising the most relevant previously unknown information before the conference; any gaps remaining should be identified and filled post-process for future assignments on the same subject. These levels are of course not strictly sequential, but interwoven: new data comes in during the process, and knowledge is already activated at the beginning of the preparation phase.

When it comes to terminology documentation, many interpreters tend to rely on fairly traditional resources, preparing glossaries as handwritten lists or with nothing more than a basic word-processing programme (Jiang 2013). Nevertheless, database software tailored to the needs of (conference) interpreters is increasingly becoming available, as are other tools for computer-aided interpreting. In particular, interpreters need to document situation-related information (speaker, conference, customer, etc.) so that they can reuse terms in the appropriate context. For preparation purposes, automatic terminology extraction may save time, and classification and filtering helps interpreters memorise the key terms. In the booth, intuitive quick-searching, different ways of sorting items (e.g. by order of appearance in a speech), parallel text display, and the display of key terms (through a 'post-it' function) are of interest in this regard. For follow-up, a well-organised database allows the entry of new information quickly (see Rütten 2004).

With the increasing use of computers in simultaneous conference interpreting, follow-up tends to move from desk to booth, that is, it merges into peri-process instead of taking place post-process. Preparation (both pre- and peri-process), on the other hand, becomes more demanding, with interpreting assignments becoming more and more specialised while preparation time is increasingly limited. The availability of cloud computing technology makes it possible to address this challenge through teamwork, increasing the efficiency of preparation and overall output quality.

ANJA RÜTTEN

TEXT INTERPRETING

see SPEECH-TO-TEXT INTERPRETING

THEATER INTERPRETING

→ SIGNED LANGUAGE INTERPRETING, → FILM INTERPRETING

Interpreting in the theater is used to make live performances accessible in another language. Spoken-language interpreters may interpret at theater festivals or for visiting performances (Bondas 2013); more typically, theater interpreting involves interpreting into signed languages for the benefit of Deaf audience members, and this constitutes the focus of this article.

Although a small number of theater companies integrate the sign language interpreter into the production, in the vast majority of cases, the interpreter is situated outside the performance area. For Deaf audience members, the linguistic element is dislocated from the rest of the performance, and they must look away from the stage activity to see the rendered dialogue.

While theater interpreting is relatively common, there is no standardized approach to this form of translation for the stage. Gebron (2000) proposes translating in rehearsal with the performing company, while Turner and Pollitt position themselves with the literary translator, translating the text "in anticipation of its instantiation on stage" (2002: 37), and Llewellyn-Jones (2004) advocates the working method of analyzing the finished stage performance to determine the intended effect of the production upon the audience before interpreting the text.

The main challenges result from multimodality and simultaneity. Theater is a gestalt multimodal art form. Theater dialogue often mimics everyday talk, but lacks redundancy, and is crafted to contain very specific information about situation, character and plot. Meaning is constructed through the interaction of audible and visual information in the context of the performance.

Since interpreting is done live and in simultaneous mode, the transfer is both interlingual and cross-modal, and is critically shaped by constraints of time and space. The interpreter must synchronize her rendition with the performance, timing the rendered utterances so that they coincide with those of the speakers on stage, while also allowing time for the audience to look back to the stage to witness salient mimetic activity.

Since signed languages use space, location and movement for COHESION and reference, and to demonstrate the actual and metaphorical relationships between the entities in a discourse, the theater interpreter constructs a rendition based not only on the source dialogue, but also on the three-dimensional construction of the world of the drama. The interpreter maintains distinct character voices through role shift (also referred to as perspective shift or referential shift), which not only depicts the speech and affect of the character, but also requires the interpreter to match, as far as possible, the actor's physical orientation in space, and direction of address. In addition, the objects the characters interact with on stage and their spatial relationships to each other influence the interpreter's placement of referents in her signing space, which should replicate the spatial arrangement of entities on stage.

Because the Deaf audience is unable to hear the original dialogue, the interpreter's rendition must not only contain linguistic information, but also reflect paralinguistic elements such as tone, loudness, tempo and pitch fluctuation that are part of spoken language but have visual equivalents in signed language. Moreover, the interdependent relationship between the verbal and the visual in the theatrical context means that the visual channels of the performance text function not only as part of the source text for the interpreter, but also as part of the target text for the receiving audience (see Rocks 2011).

Thus, the overall challenge for theater interpreting into signed languages is to assist the Deaf spectator in reconstructing the sense of the performance from deconstructed mimetic and linguistic elements.

SIOBHÁN ROCKS

THÉORIE DU SENS

see under INTERPRETIVE THEORY

TIME LAG

↑ COGNITIVE APPROACHES, ↑ SIMULTANEOUS INTERPRETING
→ COGNITIVE LOAD, → SEGMENTATION

Time lag, also referred to by the French term *décalage*, is the delay between the speaker's delivery and the interpreter's output in SIMULTANEOUS INTERPRETING (hence the alternative term 'ear–voice span' (EVS), referring to the interval between the interpreter's hearing of what the speaker says and his or her vocal articulation of the interpretation). Though usually applied to spoken-language SI, time lag is also a relevant phenomenon in SIGNED LANGUAGE INTERPRETING as well as in SIGHT INTERPRETING/TRANSLATION and in NOTE-TAKING for CONSECUTIVE INTERPRETING. The delay has traditionally been measured in units of time, but other measures are possible, notably the number of (content) words. Invariably, time lag raises intriguing questions about what exactly happens during this interval and whether there are patterns and limits.

Time lag measurements were undertaken in the very first academic studies of simultaneous interpreting, both by interpreters (Paneth 1957/2002) and by psychologists (Barik 1973; Oléron & Nanpon 1965/2002; Treisman 1965). Most commonly, average time lag measured across a number of measurement points is between two and four seconds, but at individual points it can be longer than ten seconds, and even negative, where true ANTICIPATION occurs. While there is an observed average time lag, it is not always the same for all interpreters and all types of speeches. Early studies compared time lag in interpreting and in simpler tasks. Oléron and Nanpon (1965/2002) refer to an experiment comparing the delay in repeating a word in the same language and in translating it, for which they had found that the average time lag for word translation was approximately 1.5 times longer than for repetition. Treisman (1965), who compared simultaneous interpreting to SHADOWING (i.e. verbatim simultaneous repetition) of prose passages, similarly found longer lag times for interpreting (2.8 seconds) than for shadowing (1.3 seconds), though her study tested non-interpreters. Such comparisons show that even simple repetition does not happen instantly, and in this respect Oléron and Nanpon (1965/2002) note that the added delay for translation is actually quite small compared to the delay for repetition only. These pioneering studies show that time lag reflects cognitive processing, with even simple tasks requiring a certain amount of time for completion. By this logic, the more complex the task, the longer it should take and the more delay would be expected. However, the simultaneous interpreter is constrained in the amount of time available by the continuous input of new information which needs to be processed. Information awaiting processing must be stored in WORKING MEMORY, which itself has a limited capacity and can only hold the information for several seconds. To keep up with the flow of information, the interpreter must either process very fast and/or selectively, or risk loss of information in the upcoming segment (as explained, for instance, by Gile's EFFORT MODELS). In fact, research indicates that a time lag longer than approximately four seconds leads to reduced ACCURACY (Lee 2002; Timarová et al. 2014), especially if the input currently being processed and the information stored in memory come from different sentences (Lee 2003).

Relatively little is known about time lag in signed language interpreting, where the visual language modality also makes the delay more difficult to measure, but descriptive research indicates it is broadly similar to time lag in spoken-language interpreting (Cokely 1992a, 1992b). It therefore seems that the observed average time lag of two to three seconds is at least partly determined by human cognitive limitations.

Since there are substantial individual differences in time lag, as well as differences between measurement points within the same speech, cognitive limitations may explain only the minimum lag (determined by the speed of processing) and the maximum lag an interpreter can keep (subject to available memory resources), with room for variation between these limits. One of the determinants of individual time lag is professional experience and EXPERTISE. More experienced interpreters have been found to have shorter time lag, suggesting that they are able to process the input faster (Timarová et al. 2014), whether this is due to the use of STRATEGIES or automatism (Gile 1997). It has also been suggested that experienced interpreters have differently organised knowledge, which allows them to process input in larger chunks, resulting in longer EVS compared to students and novices (Moser-Mercer et al. 2000). Moreover, there is evidence of individual differences in EVS among interpreters, which perhaps reflects their individual cognitive constraints. Lamberger-Felber (2001) noted great variability in the average EVS of different individuals, and GERVER (1976) found that interpreters maintained a constant EVS independently of environmental (normal versus noisy) conditions.

Language has also been found to play a role. Goldman-Eisler (1972) focused on the linguistic structure of input segments, and evidence of SEGMENTATION: interpreters wait until they have heard a constitutive speech segment, typically a complete predicative expression, before they proceed with production of their output. Since languages differ in their structure, so does the size of a segment an interpreter will wait for, and hence the time lag. Other determining factors are input SPEECH RATE (higher rates being associated with longer time lag; Gerver 1969/2002), source text difficulty (the greater the difficulty, the longer the time lag), as well as prior knowledge and PREPARATION (leading to shorter time lag; Díaz Galaz et al. 2015).

The various effects observed and associated with ear–voice span suggest that time lag is linked to a number of relevant aspects of the interpreting process (Timarová et al. 2011) and can thus serve as a sensitive measure reflecting the speed of underlying processing in COGNITIVE APPROACHES to research on interpreting.

ŠÁRKA TIMAROVÁ

TOKYO TRIBUNAL

see under TRIBUNAL INTERPRETING

TRAINING

see under Education

TRANSCODING

↑ INTERPRETIVE THEORY

Although the controversy between 'literal' and 'free' approaches to translation is age-old, a new terminological distinction – 'transcoding' vs. 'interpretive' – appeared in the mid-twentieth century. The word 'transcoding' took its cue from the communication engineers who saw the transmission of information as the encoding of a message by a sender and its decoding by the receiver. It did not take long for this intralingual view of information transmission to be applied to oral and written translation – and for scholars (and practitioners) of translation and interpreting to reject this as a narrow and distorted view of these operations.

Nida noted that translation "has often been regarded only as a more complicated form of talking or writing, in which one decodes from one language and encodes into another" (1969: 48), while SELESKOVITCH, in her 1968 book on CONFERENCE INTERPRETING, deplored the fact that interpreting was often seen as 'transcoding': "To the conference delegate, interpretation thus appears to be a series of encoding and decoding operations. The message that he emits in his own code to the interpreter is converted into another code to which he does not have the key" (1978a: 4).

Taking issue with prevailing linguistic and psychological views, Seleskovitch proposed a narrower view of 'transcoding' that inspired the definition given in Delisle et al.'s *Translation*

Terminology as "[a]n operation where the translator establishes correspondences between two languages on the lexical or phraseological level" (1999: 188). Seleskovitch asserted that translation at language level was TRANSCODING, and the products of transcoding 'correspondences'. Listing both the ways in which transcoding can be put to good use and its limitations, she wrote: "Transcoding may produce correct entries in bilingual dictionaries, excellent comparative grammars, usable machine translation, but it cannot generate technical or literary translations that would be acceptable equivalents of the original texts such as good human translators are apt to produce" (1988: 86). Her INTERPRETIVE THEORY thus posited an important distinction between correspondences, which obtain between words or set phrases, and equivalent texts (oral or written) or segments thereof.

The interpretive theory stresses that successful interpreting (and translating) requires analysis and COMPREHENSION of the sense of the message in context, which entails 'deverbalization' and reformulation. However, transcoding is not rejected altogether. From her empirical study of NOTE-TAKING in CONSECUTIVE INTERPRETING, Seleskovitch (1975) concluded that some lexical items (names, NUMBERS, technical terms) lend themselves to transcoding, while the rest of the speech is usually rendered interpretively. In addition, words describing universal phenomena, such as physical and psychological attributes of human beings and phenomena of the natural world, are present in all languages and may best be rendered by correspondences (Lederer 2003). It is not surprising, therefore, that word correspondences can be found between languages. However, no text, no speech can ever be properly translated by transcoding alone. As Seleskovitch (1976) put it: no translation, however literal, is ever entirely devoid of interpretation; no interpretation, however freed from the constraints of the original linguistic system, is ever entirely devoid of transcoding.

MARIANNE LEDERER

TRANSCRIPTION

↑ CORPUS-BASED RESEARCH, ↑ DISCOURSE ANALYTICAL APPROACHES, ↑ INTERVIEWS

Transcription is a multidisciplinary concern which can be broadly described as the transfer of communication data from one medium to another. In the case of spoken languages, this transfer is generally from speech to writing, while in the case of signed languages it is mainly from signing to a written format. Transcription essentially serves to create a record of past communicative events, such as INTERVIEWS, speeches or other forms of talk, including interpreted discourse. In DISCOURSE ANALYTICAL APPROACHES and CORPUS-BASED RESEARCH, transcripts facilitate analysis and dissemination as well as the verification and replication of discourse-based work.

Transcription is always theory-laden (Ochs 1979), being the result of interpretive choices (i.e. what to transcribe) and representational ones (i.e. how to transcribe), depending on the research objectives (Niemants 2012). For qualitative analysis, transcripts need to be reader-friendly, highlighting those features that are relevant given the theoretical assumptions. For quantitative corpus-based research, transcripts need to be machine-friendly, allowing the automatic extraction, counting and combination of relevant linguistic and/or functional units. In both cases, transcription is part of a wider research 'cycle' whose real object of analysis is a past event. The audio/video of the event is the primary source of data, and the transcript a secondary source. Just as recording selects elements from the observable event, transcription selects elements from the recording.

Transcribing is never easy and always time-consuming, and requires a number of decisions. In the case of interpreted discourse, in particular, transcribing is complicated by the need to represent overlap, when two distinct floors of talk are simultaneously engaged.

Choices and methods

The literature in INTERPRETING STUDIES offers little guidance on transcribing, as researchers have only recently turned their attention to this aspect of METHODOLOGY, seeking inspiration in that branch of (socio)linguistics most concerned with the study of talk: conversation analysis (CA). The transcription conventions developed within CA (e.g. Jefferson 2004) aim to account for *all* aspects of oral communicative behavior that can cast light on what participants are constructing with their talk-in-interaction, and hence at completeness. But completeness in transcribing communicative events is an illusory goal, and various degrees and levels of representation ('granularity') have been proposed. Levels of granularity depend on the research aims, and may range from narrative accounts of the communicative event to (para)linguistic, interactional, prosodic, and multimodal features (Jenks 2011). Linguistic and paralinguistic features concern *what* is uttered, i.e. the words pronounced by different participants, as well as non-verbal vocalizations – laughter, coughs, audible inhalations, exhalations and the like. Interactional features concern *when* and *by whom* things are uttered, i.e. PAUSES and TURN-TAKING: turns-at-talk may be produced one after the other or they may overlap, there may be pauses between (or within) turns, or a turn may be latched onto the end of a previous one, etc. Prosodic features describe *how* things are uttered, i.e. tempo (faster/slower), volume (louder/softer), pitch (higher/lower), duration (lengthening/truncation), and INTONATION (rising/falling). Lastly, multimodality subsumes kinesic elements such as GAZE, GESTURE and BODY LANGUAGE, which may be largely ancillary to utterances in speech, but are primary in signed languages, where signers make simultaneous use of a number of articulators, such as hands, head, face and body (Frishberg et al. 2012).

A first decision is whether to use a phonetic or an orthographic transcription. The choice generally falls on the latter, as one needs trained phoneticians to produce and decode the International Phonetic Alphabet, and it may be easier to vernacularize standard orthography to account for pronunciation differences. Next, one has to decide what should constitute the basic units (e.g. syllables, words, tone groups, turns at talk or exchanges of turns) and how to indicate the beginning, the end, the language, and the speaker of each unit. These decisions are also linked to the choice of spatial arrangement for data display: either a vertical format as in playscripts, where time unfolds line by line; or a multi-tier format like a musical score, where entities contained in the different staves refer to a shared timeline. While vertical formats have probably been the most widely used in orthographic transcriptions of audio data over the past decades, multi-tier formats seem better equipped to represent video-recorded interpreted discourse in spoken and especially signed languages, where multiple tiers can be used to capture the simultaneous dimensions of communication (Antinoro Pizzuto et al. 2010).

Not surprisingly, there is no single or commonly adopted approach to transcription in interpreting studies. However, various groups of researchers have agreed on some sets of conventions to standardize their analyses and share their results. The most widely used systems of transcription conventions were developed by the Santa Barbara School (Du Bois et al. 1993) and by two groups of German analysts (see Ehlich 1993, for HIAT; and Selting et al. 2011, for GAT). Proposals focusing on specific corpora include those developed for the CLAPI corpus of French language spoken in interaction (Groupe ICOR 2006), the CorIT corpus of Italian television interpreting (Falbo 2012) and the European Parliament Interpreting Corpus (EPIC), made up of speeches and their corresponding simultaneous interpretations (Russo et al. 2012).

Tools

Transcripts have long been produced as typescript or using a word processor. More recently, specially developed transcription tools have become available that allow the transcript to be linked to the (digital) recording, giving instant access from the secondary to the primary data source, and vice versa. These tools include CLAN, ELAN, EXMARaLDA, syncWRITER, Transcriber, Transana and WinPitch. Although many transcribers still prefer to rely on separate software tools to manage the recordings and produce transcripts (if nothing else because learning to use such alignment tools takes time), there is a case for working in a single interface where the transcript acts as a dynamic index to the recording, and is displayed in synchrony with the audio/video data. This facilitates editing, which may involve adding or subtracting details for the purposes of specific analyses or presentations, where the type of audience, the language spoken, and the consent obtained from recorded participants will be crucial in determining the form in which to present data.

NATACHA S. A. NIEMANTS

TRANSLITERATION

↑ SIGNED LANGUAGE INTERPRETING

→ FINGERSPELLING

Interpreting is generally understood as a process between two natural languages, whether spoken or signed. Within SIGNED LANGUAGE INTERPRETING there is the additional dimension of transliteration, where the interpreter works between a spoken language and a form of signed language called contact sign – which incorporates features of the spoken and signed language in use and may include phenomena such as loan translation, FINGERSPELLING and mouthing (Lucas & Valli 1989). Contact sign does not exist in a standardized form, but varies depending on the language users, the setting and a number of other sociolinguistic factors. Thus, Deaf persons with much prior exposure to the spoken language may prefer to use a form of contact sign that represents the structure of the spoken language. Deaf people working in technical and professional roles involving specialized vocabulary and terminology may also prefer transliteration.

The term 'transliterating' continues to elude a standardized, unambiguous definition, although it is used as if one were commonly understood. Humphrey and Alcorn (2001) define transliterating as "the process of taking a message and expressing it in a different form of the *same* language", and other authors similarly view it as simply a change in mode. However, studies that analyze actual transliterating samples point to the fact that the transliterator incorporates features of both signed and spoken language, and is constantly deciding which combination of features will most readily convey the speaker's intended meaning to the Deaf consumer (Siple 1993; Winston 1989).

Several researchers have investigated Deaf students' COMPREHENSION of college-level material when presented via interpreting or transliterating. In a carefully controlled set of studies, Marschark et al. (2004) failed to find a significant effect of interpreting vs. transliterating on overall student comprehension. To date, no studies have been conducted that contrast the effectiveness of interpreting and transliterating in medical, mental health, legal and other COMMUNITY INTERPRETING settings.

KAREN MALCOLM

TRIBUNAL INTERPRETING

↑ COURTROOM INTERPRETING
↓ NUREMBERG TRIAL

The term 'tribunal' in this context refers to an ad hoc court established for a specific purpose. Those dealt with in INTERPRETING STUDIES include multilingual tribunals in both international and domestic settings, but are primarily international tribunals involving war criminals. The most prominent examples are the International Military Tribunal, or NUREMBERG TRIAL (1945–46); the International Military Tribunal for the Far East, or Tokyo Trial (1946–48); and the International Criminal Tribunal for the Former Yugoslavia (ICTY), set up in 1993. In these tribunals interpreters play a vital part in enabling court proceedings and assuring the defendants' right to a fair trial through the provision of the necessary language services.

There are two main approaches in studies of tribunal interpreting: one draws on archival and historical materials to examine tribunals in the past, and the other focuses on contemporary tribunals to address various issues of COURTROOM INTERPRETING.

Historical research

The prime subjects of historical research on tribunal interpreting have been the Nuremberg and Tokyo trials. Interpreting at the Nuremberg Trial is generally recognized as the 'coming of age' of SIMULTANEOUS INTERPRETING, which led to the widespread adoption of this interpreting mode by international organizations. In addition to personal accounts by some Nuremberg interpreters (e.g. Ramler 1988; Skinner & Carson 1990; Sonnenfeldt 2006), there have been scholarly inquiries into this milestone event in the evolution of CONFERENCE INTERPRETING. Among them, Gaiba (1998) is the most extensive work in English so far. Based on a close examination of transcripts and archival documents, and personal communication with several interpreters who worked during the trial, the study describes the preparation stage, the interpreting system, the impact of interpreting on the proceedings, and interpreter profiles. The rich information it offers can be used for further theory-based research on such topics as interpreter aptitude and training, as well as procedural issues of courtroom interpreting.

For the Tokyo Trial, following the pioneering work by Watanabe (2009), Takeda (2010a) provides a detailed description of the trial's interpreting arrangements through archival research and INTERVIEWS, examining salient features of the interpreting system in sociopolitical terms such as POWER, TRUST, control and race. Particular attention is paid to the hierarchical structure in which Japanese nationals interpreted the proceedings, *Kibei* (second-generation Japanese Americans who had some schooling in Japan) checked the ACCURACY of interpretation as monitors, and Caucasian US military officers ruled language disputes as language arbiters. Takeda discusses why this three-tier system was devised, how the complex standing of *Kibei* linguists is relevant to current discussions of interpreters in CONFLICT ZONES, and how the interpreting procedures were developed through trial and error during the first stage of the court proceedings. In addition, the behavior of the interpreters, monitors and arbiters is examined in relation to their position in the power constellations of the tribunal.

Recent tribunals

Studies on interpreting at tribunals that have taken place in recent decades focus on the description of interpreting arrangements and on specific issues of courtroom interpreting. Early investigations include research on the Demjanjuk trial in Jerusalem in the late 1980s. Morris (1990, 1998) discusses its highly complex interpreting arrangements and refers to institutional constraints and courtroom dynamics as major factors in the behavior of interpreters, while SHLESINGER (1991) examines the 'latitude' shown by interpreters during the trial and issues a far-sighted call for further discussion on the definition of court interpreters' ROLE.

While TRUTH AND RECONCILIATION COMMISSIONS can be considered as a separate setting, they share some important features with tribunal interpreting. A case in point is interpreting at the Truth and Reconciliation Commission (TRC) in South Africa (1996–98), which has generated further reflections on the interpreter's role. Describing the interpreting arrangements at the hearings, Du Plessis and Wiegand (1998) draw parallels between interpreting at the TRC and interpreting at the Nuremberg Trial. Wallmach (2002) examines the gaps between the prescribed role of interpreters as neutral intermediaries and the reality of interpreters who experienced difficulties and VICARIOUS TRAUMA while interpreting about atrocities.

As a prolonged, large-scale tribunal with open access to most of the transcripts and court proceedings, the ICTY in The Hague has attracted considerable attention from scholars of interpreting. Schweda Nicholson (2010) provides an overview of the interpreting practices, interpreter STRESS and training courses on interpreting issues for attorneys. More focused analysis of linguistic challenges interpreters face can be found in Stern (2004) and Elias-Bursać (2012): the former deals with the difficulties of, and STRATEGIES for, interpreting particular legal terms; the latter focuses on courtroom discussions about how to translate and interpret a specific military term in BCS (Bosnian/Croatian/Serbian), and their impact on the related proceedings.

Tribunal interpreting has also been the subject of some comparative studies. Stern (2012) discusses the WORKING CONDITIONS of interpreters at the ICTY and other international courts, such as the International Criminal Tribunal for Rwanda and the International Criminal Court, in contrast with those in domestic courts, and calls for improvement in domestic practices. Inspired by discussions among legal scholars and historians on the links between Tokyo, Nuremberg and the ICTY as regards the development of international humanitarian law and international criminal court systems, Takeda (2013) identifies links in certain interpreting phenomena between these tribunals and national courts. Shared features discussed include the use of simultaneous interpreting in court proceedings, the psychological burden on interpreters who work in trials against their former leaders, and the professional code of ETHICS observed by court interpreters.

KAYOKO TAKEDA

TRIESTE SYMPOSIUM

↑ INTERPRETING STUDIES

The International Symposium on "The Theoretical and Practical Aspects of Teaching Conference Interpretation" was an interdisciplinary conference, held at the University of Trieste from 27 to 29 November 1986, which proved a turning point for studies on CONFERENCE INTERPRETING. Research in this field had previously been characterized by two opposing approaches: experimental studies conducted by psychologists and psycholinguists, often with insufficient regard for specific features of professional practice; and theories and MODELS proposed mainly by the PARIS SCHOOL, the dominant school of thought in interpreting during the 1970s and 1980s.

Against this backdrop, the conference at the SSLMIT (*Scuola Superiore di Lingue Moderne per Interpreti e Traduttori*) in Trieste was held with the objective of fostering discussion and research related to the training of conference interpreters, not only among professionals and trainers, but also opening up to cooperation with researchers from other disciplines. This INTERDISCIPLINARITY was expected to contribute to a better understanding of the interpreting process, which in turn would have an impact on training, and ultimately on the PROFESSION.

Thus, professional interpreters, teachers of interpreting and representatives from the fields of psychology, neurophysiology, audiology and linguistics met to discuss themes related to language learning, COMPREHENSION and interpreting in the light of recent theories and experimental studies.

Some 350 participants from Europe, the United States and CANADA, as well as AUSTRALIA and JAPAN, compared their teaching methods with those adopted in the USSR and other Eastern European countries, reflecting an opening up which also extended to the 'East'. In addition, representatives of AIIC and international institutions such as the Commission of the EC, the European Parliament, the European Court of Justice and NATO also took part, indicating the potential and need for reconciling academic work and professional requirements.

Topics included MEMORY and recall in conference interpreters, consecutive and liaison interpreting, APTITUDE TESTING, discourse analysis and STRATEGIES of SIMULTANEOUS INTERPRETING, with a special focus on the then new neurophysiological research paradigm (Gran & Dodds 1989). This paradigm, in particular, offers an example of very fruitful cooperation between interpreters and experts from other disciplines: Laura Gran, a professional interpreter and trainer, collaborated closely with neurophysiologist Franco Fabbro in a number of studies on language representation in the brain, cerebral asymmetries, and shifts in language competence between the cerebral hemispheres during interpreter training (Gran & Fabbro 1988; Fabbro et al. 1990).

Notwithstanding different viewpoints, a considerable degree of convergence emerged at the Trieste Symposium regarding the need for a scientific, interdisciplinary approach in studies of conference interpreting. This resulted in a diversification of methods and research areas, which is now seen as a defining characteristic of INTERPRETING STUDIES.

ALESSANDRA RICCARDI

TRUE BILINGUALISM

see under BILINGUALISM

TRUST

→ PROFESSION, → USER EXPECTATIONS

Trust, and the related concept of trustworthiness, may be understood as a belief that a person or organisation will act in a particular way (Edwards et al. 2006) and as a means to making social cooperation 'easier and even possible' (Hardin 2006). Although its precise constitution remains debated, trust is often viewed as a process involving risk and therefore as contingent and evolutive. Research on trust commonly distinguishes between 'general' (abstract) and 'specific' (personal) levels, which help to frame investigations into trust *in* the interpreting PROFESSION and trust as a *feature* of interpreting activity respectively.

Inghilleri (2010) draws attention to the 'contradictory esteem' in which interpreters are often held, being at once objects of 'necessary trust' and 'deep suspicion', evidence of which is found, for instance, in colonial history, not least in the figure of MALINCHE, in CONFLICT ZONES where military interpreters provide intelligence to insurgents, and in institutional contexts where (mis)perceptions of interpreters' alignment with the authorities that employ them are common. By contrast, the NUREMBERG TRIAL helped to establish interpreters as trustworthy experts, a STATUS which has been fostered through the development of professional bodies such as AIIC and accredited programmes for the training and EDUCATION of professional interpreters. Indeed, in the more established domain of CONFERENCE INTERPRET-ING, the notion of trust (in the profession) appears to have been taken for granted and has been investigated, if at all, only indirectly, with reference to issues of QUALITY and the discursive construction of interpreters' professional identity (e.g. Diriker 2004).

The special sensitivities of interpreting in community settings highlight the importance of specific trust at the interpersonal level and draw attention to the interpreter's ROLE. Interpreter NEUTRALITY – often construed as a form of non-participation and an unspoken NORM – is a common, though not unproblematic, tenet of interpreters' ETHICS that provides no guarantee of trust in either the interpreter or the interpreting process. Specific trust, therefore, must be understood primarily as an interactional achievement that is subject to (re-)negotiation between interlocutors and in which interpreters play an active part.

Difficulties in operationalising and measuring trust have led researchers to employ a range of methodologies and proxy measures. In COMMUNITY INTERPRETING, for example, Edwards et al. (2005, 2006) explore trust as praxis through INTERVIEWS with users of a range of health, welfare and other services from five different ethnic-minority groups. Their findings demonstrate how personal character and trust are important in people's understanding of good interpreting, which often leads service users to favour interpreters from their own informal networks of friends and family.

Hale (2007) reports on a small survey study involving medical and legal practitioners in Sydney, in which both groups indicated that mistrust emerges when interpreters take on a 'gatekeeper' role, lose their impartiality and edit utterances. The findings are supported by Tipton's (2010) focus group research on relationships of trust in interpreter-mediated social work, which also shows that greater negotiation at the interstices of interaction can enhance mutual trust through better expectation management. Davidson's (2000) ethnographic work in a California hospital, by contrast, shows how institutional pressures can oblige personnel – often against their professional judgement – to place high levels of trust in interpreters as informational gatekeepers in order to expedite service delivery, suggesting that a comprehensive understanding of trust in interpreter MEDIATION presupposes insight into factors other than interpreter COMPETENCE alone.

REBECCA TIPTON

TRUTH AND RECONCILIATION COMMISSIONS

↑ SETTINGS
→ TRIBUNAL INTERPRETING, → VICARIOUS TRAUMA

Truth commissions have come to play a pivotal role in post-conflict reconciliation processes as mechanisms of transitional justice around the world. A common claim is that truth-telling is healing and will lead to reconciliation (Brounéus 2010). Truth commissions have been established in Argentina, Brazil, Chad, Chile, East Germany, East Timor, Ghana, Nigeria, Peru, the Philippines, Poland, Sierra Leone and the Solomon Islands, amongst other countries. Sixteen truth commissions predate the South African Truth and Reconciliation Commission (TRC), but the TRC was the first to take place in the public eye. Established in 1996, after the ending of apartheid, by President Nelson Mandela and chaired by Archbishop Desmond Tutu, the TRC is undoubtedly the most widely discussed, and possibly one of the most effective commissions any country has yet produced.

Just as the multilingual NUREMBERG TRIAL at the end of World War II marked the beginning of the use of SIMULTANEOUS INTERPRETING with electronic equipment worldwide, the

TRC hearings marked the first opportunity for many South Africans to become acquainted with the marvels of simultaneous interpreting in their own languages. Training suitable interpreters for the TRC was a huge task, given the time constraints (Lotriet 2002) as well as the fact that there were no conference-interpreting programmes for local languages in South Africa at the time. From April 1996 to October 1998, interpreters produced 28,412 hours or 3,551 days of interpreting (Du Plessis & Wiegand 1998). In fact, the Truth Commission, being a multilingual process, could not have operated at all without simultaneous interpreting and the use of RELAY INTERPRETING from English, the pivot language of the proceedings (Wallmach 2002). Equally important was the ideological underpinning of the use of simultaneous interpreting. Just as the testimonies of thousands of victims of human rights violations were framed within the wider discourse of nation-building and reconciliation, so each of South Africa's eleven official languages was granted equal respect during the TRC for the first time. This represented an IDEOLOGY of linguistic pluralism consistent with the concept of nation-building (Verdoolaege 2008), in contrast to the bilingual and exclusionary LANGUAGE POLICY during the apartheid years prior to 1994, which recognised only Afrikaans and English.

Despite their important function in this process, interpreters have remained largely 'invisible' in relation to this setting. Many researchers have questioned the justification of the idea of a truth commission, and what constitutes 'truth' and reparation in such a context, but very few critics take into account that most testimonies are recounted originally in other languages, and that the interpreter's voice might have influenced the 'truth' of these testimonies. Notable exceptions are Verdoolaege (2008) and Krog, Mpolweni and Ratele (2009), who explore the gaps between original and interpretation, translation and TRANSCRIPTION. There are few references to the interpreters in the TRC transcripts. Commissioners spoke of "translation devices" and the mechanics of the process, but it is only in the foreword to the final report that chairperson Archbishop Tutu recognises the interpreters' traumatisation in recounting the atrocities in the first person, as either a victim or the perpetrator. In a partly fictionalised account based on her work as a reporter during this period, Krog (1998) is one of the few authors to accord prominence to the role of the TRC interpreters and the enormous difficulty of attempting to remain neutral under conditions of extreme emotion (see FICTIONAL INTERPRETERS). Similar issues were encountered by the interpreters for the International Criminal Tribunal for Rwanda (ICTR) in Arusha, Tanzania and in other instances of TRIBUNAL INTERPRETING. Apart from the challenges of establishing new training programmes for interpreters in INDIGENOUS LANGUAGES within a short time-frame, an important aspect of the training of the first cohort of Kinyarwanda-speaking interpreters in Arusha was dealing with trauma, as many of the interpreters had families who had suffered directly during the genocide and, despite efforts to keep the identities of the interpreters secret, several of the interpreters and their families had received threats. Thus, the gap between the metadiscourse of interpreting as expressed in codes of ETHICS (ACCURACY, impartiality, confidentiality, accountability), and the actual practices and processes of interpreting, poses a constant challenge in this setting.

KIM WALLMACH

TURN-TAKING

↑ DISCOURSE ANALYTICAL APPROACHES
→ DIALOGUE INTERPRETING↓ GAZE

Theories of interaction share the idea that interactive communication systems are based on forms of coordinated action. The notion of turn-taking was first developed in Conversation

Analysis (CA), in order to describe participants' contributions to talk in different settings of ordinary life (Sacks 1995). According to CA, the turn-taking system is an ordered, regulated system in which participants systematically intervene in reference to each other's contributions (Sacks et al. 1974). Participants in talk shape their actions as relevant to the ongoing talk and, in so doing, they make sense of their own and the other participants' actions. When asking a question, for instance, participants not only accomplish the function of asking, but they also project relevant actions that will come next. For example, a question normally projects an answer. In replying to a question, though, the next participant-in-turn not only provides the answer (or evidence that s/he cannot do so) but also displays understanding (or non-understanding) that what was uttered was in fact a question (and not, for instance, a comment), and that s/he can (or cannot) provide the answer. This coordinated mechanism constructs the interaction and orients the interlocutors' participation in it (see Heritage & Clayman 2010).

DIALOGUE INTERPRETING, including interpreter-mediated encounters in business, public service and media settings, is explicitly interactional, since it cannot take place with less than three participants overtly contributing to a process of communication. These participants' contributions can thus be looked at as 'turns', and their organization can be analysed as a 'turn-taking system'. From this perspective, the construction of communication and interpreters' contributions can be looked at as relevant actions in relation to the other actions produced through talk.

The most systematic account of the turn-taking system in interpreter-mediated interaction is provided in Davidson's (2002) work on HEALTHCARE INTERPRETING. He shows that, within the system of turn-taking, (1) participants, while speaking or listening, are equally engaged in the ongoing process of constructing conversational meaning; and (2) in order to negotiate and capture the meaning of the various utterances produced within an ongoing discourse, one must be party to it. Since interpreters can provide no rendition without understanding (and, of course, interpreting) the communication process, interpreters 'cannot not participate' in talk (Pöchhacker 2012a: 50). It is their participation which allows them to produce meaningful utterances that elicit the intended response from, or have the intended COMMUNICATIVE EFFECT upon, the interlocutors.

Interpreters' critical engagement in turn-taking was first addressed in the literature on interpreter-mediated interaction through Wadensjö's notion of coordination (1998). Wadensjö notes that, within the turn-taking system, interpreters' renditions make sense of what is said by (i) providing an 'interaction-orientated' translation and (ii) managing turns at talk. To ensure the former, interpreters translate according to contextual information which is generated not only by the situation in which the interaction takes place, including the communicative system it is part of (e.g. the medical or the legal system), but also by the sequence of turns a contribution is embedded in (e.g. before or after another turn). For purposes of turn management, interpreters coordinate either by translating (in that selecting a language inevitably selects one of the speakers or parties) or by other means, such as asking participants to repeat, to clarify or to stop for translation.

The system of turn-taking gives meaning to the participants' contributions, including those of the interpreters. In applying the notion of 'underdeterminacy' to dialogue interpreting, Mason (2006) notes that, taken singularly, turns at talk are often incomplete, redundant and vague. Their significance is subject to (i) their being in a particular position in the sequence, and (ii) a series of contextual assumptions which are negotiated by participants as relevant to the interaction. In order to make the rendition of turns meaningful in conversation, interpreters need to 'determine' their meaning by addressing not only what is said in the utterance, but also the contextual assumptions that are clear to those participating in the interaction. In other words, personal pronouns, deictics, acronyms, nods of the head, hesitations, backchanneling and even more complex talk sequences such as story-telling acquire meaning on the basis of the participants' local assumptions in that particular conversation, and need to be addressed in translation in order to make their meaning and function accessible to the interlocutors.

The turn-taking system explains the need for interpreters to deviate from the conduit model (Roy 1993/2002). A system where each turn is systematically followed by an interpreter's rendition is not necessarily optimal for purposes of effective communication. Metzger (1999), for instance, shows that, in order to avoid interactional problems, sign language interpreters often provide procedural information on the ongoing conversation. This may involve various forms of NON-RENDITION, such as responses or longer explanations.

A number of studies have looked at the regulatory function of interpreters' contributions to turn-taking. Minimal responses are transparent to interlocutors in most languages, and can be used to overtly manage turn-taking. For instance, 'mhm' can be a way of encouraging hesitant patients to say more and to express their worries, while 'okay' can be used to mark a turn shift by indicating that the interpreter now intends to provide a rendition for the benefit of the next interlocutor (Englund Dimitrova 1997; Gavioli 2012). Similarly, GAZE serves to involve interlocutors and encourage them to go on speaking, or to convey the interpreter's disengagement (Mason 2012; Davitti 2013). Shifts from triadic (participant A – interpreter – participant B) to dyadic (interpreter – participant A or B) organizations of turn sequences have been seen as relevant to achieving particular goals, such as explaining (Pasquandrea 2011), clarifying technical procedures (Angelelli 2012) and promoting weak participants' (e.g. migrant patients') contribution to talk (Baraldi 2012).

Studies of turn-taking organization and its functions in relation to specific interactional goals are now considered fundamental, both for the training of dialogue interpreters and for enabling public service providers to cope more efficiently with the increasing demand for multilingual communication in their institutions.

LAURA GAVIOLI

TV INTERPRETING

see under MEDIA INTERPRETING

USER EXPECTATIONS

↑ QUALITY
→ ROLE
↓ QUALITY CRITERIA

Interpreters as service providers – enabling two parties to communicate – will seek to fulfill the expectations of those using that service. These users are, first and foremost, the individuals engaged in (interpreter-mediated) communication, but in a broader sense may also include the person or institution requesting (and paying for) the service (also referred to as 'client'). Expectations, understood as beliefs about what one is likely to get, or would like to get, are crucial to assessing the QUALITY of service provision, and will depend on a given user's perspective on the interpreter-mediated event. Hence the need for research to ascertain USER EXPECTATIONS, which got under way in the domain of CONFERENCE INTERPRETING in the late 1980s and has also been an important concern more recently in COMMUNITY

INTERPRETING, where asymmetrical constellations of interaction imply highly dissimilar needs and perspectives on the event – and differing expectations with regard to the interpreter. In the latter (public-service) SETTINGS, however, interpreters and researchers often speak of 'clients' rather than 'users', and such client expectations regarding interpreting services mostly relate to interpreters' qualifications, role and behavior rather than their linguistic production (see Hale 2007, Ch. 5).

User expectation surveys

The method of choice for finding out about users' expectations has been to ask them – through INTERVIEWS and questionnaires. Such SURVEY RESEARCH on user expectations in conference interpreting was sparked off indirectly by Bühler (1986), who had asked 47 members of AIIC to rate the importance of 16 criteria for assessing the quality of interpreters and interpretation, and had concluded that the priorities expressed by her sample of conference interpreters also reflected the requirements of users. This was put to the test by Kurz (1993a), who used eight of Bühler's criteria to survey participants at three technical conferences with simultaneous interpretation, asking them to rate, on a four-point scale, the importance of QUALITY CRITERIA such as logical COHESION, completeness, correct TERMINOLOGY, FLUENCY of delivery and native accent. Kurz (1993a) found that conference participants were, on the whole, less demanding than the professional interpreters surveyed by Bühler, while sharing their top priorities: both interpreters and users attached the greatest importance to the criteria "sense consistency with original message" and "logical cohesion of utterance", followed by "use of correct terminology" and "fluency of delivery". Similar agreement was found for "pleasant voice" and "native accent", which received the lowest ratings of importance.

The surveys by Kurz (1993a) prompted several other interpreters to conduct similar studies on user expectations in various countries and domains, often adopting the eight output-related criteria used by Kurz and Bühler and focusing on the listener perspective in the simultaneous mode (see Kurz 2001). In particular, Collados Aís et al. (2007) conducted several replications among nearly 200 law professors in Spain, with largely consistent results. On the other hand, Kurz (1993a) had found some divergences in the expectation patterns of different user groups (doctors, engineers and delegates at a Council of Europe conference on education), suggesting that domain-related preferences may play a role. This was brought out most clearly for SIMULTANEOUS INTERPRETING in media settings, where a sample of German-speaking TV anchors and program heads gave priority to fluent delivery and pleasant voice over completeness (Kurz & Pöchhacker 1995; see also FILM INTERPRETING). The variability of user preferences was confirmed on a broader scale in a study commissioned by AIIC (Moser 1996). Led by a social scientist, 94 interpreters conducted 201 interviews with participants at 84 different events in various countries. User expectations for some aspects of performance quality were found to vary with the size and type of meeting (large/small, general/technical) and in relation to factors such as age, GENDER and conference-going experience. Aside from essential demands such as faithfulness (FIDELITY) to meaning, it is thus difficult to identify a fixed pattern of user expectations to which conference interpreters might orient their performance. What is more, users' hypothetical expectations regarding a certain feature of quality may not correspond to the impact of that feature on user judgments of an actual interpreting performance, as shown, for example, by Collados Aís (1998) for monotonous INTONATION and by Cheung (2013) for non-native ACCENT. Moreover, user expectation surveys suffer from methodological limitations, as criteria like completeness, correct grammar or pleasant VOICE may mean different things to different respondents. This conceptual uncertainty had been indicated already by Bühler (1986), and was thoroughly investigated through interviews by Collados Aís et al. (2007).

On the whole, research into user expectations in conference settings has yielded a stable order of preferences, with aspects of content such as sense consistency and logical cohesion, complemented by fluency and correct terminology, dominating over features of delivery such as lively intonation, pleasant voice and native accent. In the light of methodological limitations and considerable variability, however, current knowledge about user expectations provides little specific guidance to (conference) interpreters' decision-making in a given situation. This applies with a vengeance to community-based settings, where the expectations in particular of institutional service providers may vary from one domain and country (and indeed organization) to another. Documents designed to codify what clients may expect, in the form of codes of ETHICS or professional conduct, remain necessarily vague, often relying on such key criteria as ACCURACY, completeness and impartial behavior. On the other hand, (community) interpreters who develop a close working relationship with a particular service provider or individual client (e.g. a Deaf person) can develop a sense for much more specific task-related expectations.

FRANZ PÖCHHACKER

VELLEMAN

Antoine Velleman (1875–1962), a polyglot with a background in economic and social science, was one of the first freelance conference interpreters in Geneva, where he taught at the university and founded the *École d'interprètes de Genève* in 1941.

Velleman was born in Vienna, where his father, a Belgian architect, was working on the new parliament building. He spent the first years of his life between Vienna and Paris, obtained his *Abitur* in Cologne (1894), and studied political and economic science in London, Bonn, Zurich and Halle-Wittenberg, obtaining his PhD in 1898 with a dissertation on "Luxury in its relations with social economy". He began his teaching career in Switzerland in 1899, first in Neuchâtel and subsequently in Zuoz (Grisons), where he learnt Romansh, the local language, moved by the beauty of its sounds and the richness of its vocabulary (Caflisch 1964). In 1917 he started teaching at the University of Geneva, in the faculties of arts and economic and social sciences, while working as a freelance interpreter for the League of Nations and the International Labour Organization (ILO). After holding an associate professorship for Romansh, he was appointed Professor of Spanish Studies in 1937.

Noting the multilingual potential of the many displaced persons in Switzerland during World War II, Velleman managed to persuade university authorities to establish a program for interpreter training, and the *École d'interprètes* was founded in 1941. Originally set up outside regular faculty structures, the 'school', according to Velleman (1943), aimed at training interpreters in three languages – 'as currently spoken' – and in thematic subjects they would follow in other institutions. Translation was considered as a prerequisite for interpreters, and scribbled rather than stenographic notes were seen as the ideal tool for CONSECUTIVE INTERPRETING. Velleman coordinated the school until 1951, the year simultaneous interpreting became part of the official CURRICULUM. In 1952, already in his mid-seventies, Velleman was appointed first Director of the Institute for Languages and Interpreting (*Sprachen- und Dolmetscherinstitut*) in Munich. He resigned a few months later for health reasons and was succeeded by Paul Otto Schmidt, formerly Hitler's interpreter (SDI 2013).

Velleman is said to have spoken eight languages fluently, with the deep knowledge of a true linguist; his grammar and dictionary of Romansh (Velleman 1929) were steps towards the standardisation of that language. At the same time he was an active political and economic scientist, and a man with entrepreneurial vision.

As early as the inter-war period, Velleman contributed to the consolidation of interpreting as a PROFESSION by striving to secure better WORKING CONDITIONS, among other things by insisting on a professional rate of remuneration for work at international conferences, including the time interpreters spent on PREPARATION as well as any 'free' days in the conference schedule, and by giving beginners the opportunity to be trained by veteran interpreters (see Baigorri-Jalón 1998). Those points, which he made clear in different documents (kept at the archives of the League of Nations), were based on his experience as a freelance interpreter in international conferences starting from the first ILO conference in 1919 (Baigorri-Jalón 2005). Velleman can thus be seen as a key figure in the establishment of interpreting not just as a professional practice but also as an institutionalized career that would allow future generations of interpreters to be trained. In this connection he was consulted by Dr Gutkind, the academic director of the first twentieth-century interpreter training program, set up in 1930 in Mannheim (Wilss 1999). A decade later, as the war continued to escalate, Velleman was to succeed in founding the Geneva school, later known as ETI (*École de Traduction et d'Interprétation*) until it was given its status as a Faculty of Translation and Interpreting (FTI) in 2011. The Interpreter School in Geneva was the breeding ground for some of the interpreters recruited for the NUREMBERG TRIAL and, in particular, for the early generation of interpreters at the United Nations.

JESÚS BAIGORRI-JALÓN

VENETIAN INTERPRETERS

see under DRAGOMANS

VENICE SYMPOSIUM

↑ INTERPRETING STUDIES
→ GERVER, → INTERDISCIPLINARITY

The symposium "Language Interpretation and Communication", organized as part of the NATO Human Factors Conference and Symposium Series, brought together some 100 participants from 16 countries and 6 international organizations at the Giorgio Cini Foundation in Venice, from 26 September to 1 October 1977. It was hailed as the first interdisciplinary forum on practical and theoretical aspects of CONFERENCE INTERPRETING, with participants drawn from the fields of psychology, linguistics, translation, anthropology, sociology and psychiatry, as well as conference and SIGNED LANGUAGE INTERPRETING. Up to that time, interpreter training programs had hardly been influenced by educational research, or by psycholinguistic research into language COMPREHENSION and production; Symposium conveners David GERVER and H. Wallace Sinaiko therefore felt that integrating knowledge from different areas, and in particular the methodological approaches used in cognitive psychology, held considerable promise for advancing the development of a theory of interpreting and for interpreter training.

The Symposium's stated objectives were to disseminate and exchange theory and research findings in the fields of psychology, linguistics, translation and sociology as they relate to interpreting, and to create synergies in terms of research collaboration (Gerver & Sinaiko 1978). For the first time, professional interpreters and behavioral scientists were attempting to create a framework for the study of the skill of interpreting. In light of the heterogeneity of the participants' scientific and professional backgrounds, this proved to be a challenge. Behavioral scientists had to confront important issues of research methodology and begin to reconsider the typical approach of studying perception, comprehension and memory of words and sentences in isolation if they were to contribute fruitfully to an improved understanding of the interpreting process. Professional interpreters in turn needed to revisit their claim that only studies set in real-life conditions could yield insights into the interpreting process. The Symposium advocated careful integration of results from basic and applied research, encouraging efforts to conduct well-designed research projects in all areas related to interpreting.

In the two decades that followed the Symposium, progress in INTERDISCIPLINARITY of the kind advocated in Venice was slow to evolve, in part because of the almost complete absence of researchers with dual qualifications in cognitive psychology and interpreting. The goal of developing a good scientific theory of interpreting – one that would be accurate, internally and externally consistent with available data from related disciplines, simple and yet sufficiently broad in scope to accommodate the different phenomena observed in interpreting – thus became somewhat caught up in competitive arguments about which approach would be best suited to meeting these requirements (Moser-Mercer 1994a). Over time, though, interpreter training has become more firmly established in academic departments, and SIMULTANEOUS INTERPRETING has evolved into a challenging research paradigm in cognitive psychology (e.g. Shreve & Angelone 2010) which is now also being explored through cognitive NEUROSCIENCE APPROACHES. These developments reflect progress towards fulfilling the promise, held out at the Venice Symposium, of increased interdisciplinary research on interpreting.

BARBARA MOSER-MERCER

VERBMOBIL

see under MACHINE INTERPRETING

VICARIOUS TRAUMA

Vicarious traumatization (VT) refers to a transformation in the self that results from a professional helper's empathic engagement with survivors of traumatic experiences. The helper may display symptoms parallel to those of trauma survivors and experience changes in different areas of the self, including worldview, identity, sense of self, psychological needs, memory and perception (Pearlman & Saakvitne 1995). Empathic engagement with the survivor and the desire to help create the emotional vulnerability to VT, which is commonly explained with reference to constructivist self-development theory.

Most research into VT focuses on doctors, nurses, therapists, and crisis counselors – in other words, individuals who are on the front lines of caring and helping professions. More recent studies, however, show that features of VT are commonly seen in all professionals who engage in empathic listening with trauma survivors, including interpreters (Y. Shlesinger 2007).

There is scant data on the emotional toll of interpreting, most likely as a result of the traditional view of the interpreter as a neutral part of the interpreted interaction. In truth, any traumatic material told through an interpreter may challenge the interpreter's beliefs and cognitive schemas. Given that the interpreter is supposed to recognize and convey the speaker's affect, s/he must listen empathically. It is therefore inevitable that the interpreter will be affected by the experience of interpreting about violence, abuse, loss and the like (Harvey 2003). The use of the first person when delivering this information amplifies the effect on the interpreter and significantly increases the risk of VT (Bontempo & Malcolm

2012). Interpreters who undertake stressful assignments, especially those that conflict with their personal goals, values or beliefs, are even more susceptible to traumatization.

VT can be addressed and minimized through the use of a variety of strategies, whether at the organizational or personal level. According to Pross (2006), the most important strategy to minimize the effect of VT is self-awareness. If this is lacking during training, it should at least be provided on the job. Additionally, regular self-examination with collegial or external supervision is crucial. It is important that during supervision the helper feels open to talk about any difficulties s/he experiences at work. This should help in assessing whether the interpreter has overidentified with any clients, particularly in cases where the interpreter and the client are from a similar background or the interpreter is a survivor of trauma. Anderson (2012) suggests the use of a peer-support model for interpreters, to increase positive perception of being part of a professional network and to develop self-care and self-management strategies.

Aside from supportive resources provided at an organizational level, it is important for the individual professional to be able to identify his or her own reactions to stress (somatic and psychological) and to be educated about VT, including its early signs and the factors contributing to its occurrence.

YAEL SHLESINGER

VIDEO RELAY SERVICE

↑ SIGNED LANGUAGE INTERPRETING, ↑ TELEPHONE INTERPRETING

Until the late twentieth century, deaf people in many countries who wanted to communicate over the phone with another person would call through a teletypewriter, or TTY. Telephone communication through text became available in the 1970s and required both parties to have a TTY for direct communication or to use a relay service whereby a third person, known as a communication assistant, read the typed TTY message to the non-TTY user and then typed the response to the TTY user. In the 1990s broadband technologies and video equipment replaced TTYs, and Sweden, followed by other countries such as New Zealand, Norway, Germany, and the US, began providing video relay service (VRS) to deaf and hard-of-hearing citizens. Signed language interpreters working as 'video interpreters' replaced communication assistants, allowing consumers to communicate over the phone in a signed language with videophones, smartphones, or computers with video communication capabilities. Though VRS shares many features with VIDEO REMOTE INTERPRETING, in which two parties may be in the same location but unable to communicate without an interpreter (e.g. in medical settings), VRS is provided for two parties in separate locations.

In the US, where government mandates and funds telecommunication access for deaf people's business and personal use, private companies provide VRS around the clock. Other countries may limit VRS availability to business hours and often find it difficult to sustain the service, especially for personal communication, without legislative support and financing (CSMG 2012).

Signed language interpreters, who traditionally worked face-to-face with consumers, underwent dramatic change in their work options with the advent of VRS. Research indicates that, while VRS interpreting provides dependable and steady income, the rapidity with which calls are processed and the difficulty of obtaining contextual and linguistic cues prior to interpreting a call affect the interpreter's ability to manage emotional extremes and avoid VICARIOUS TRAUMA experienced on the job (Brunson 2011; Wessling & Shaw 2014). In addition to the inherent complexities of interpreting between two people who do not see one another (Warnicke & Plejert, 2012), interpreters in VRS are likely to interpret for people outside their own community or region of the country due to random call assignment. This introduces a layer of unfamiliarity with local language nuances and cultural influences. Many interpreters find these challenges stimulating, while others report the need to maintain balance between community interpreting and VRS work in order to cope with the emotional impact of being first responders, particularly in the case of emergency calls (Bower 2015).

The working conditions of signed language interpreters in VRS are likely to reflect corporate policy and procedures. When VRS is regulated by government or industry, the evaluation process for interpreters is based less on whether the interpretation is effective and more on a numeric formula that tracks call connection time and the billable hours in a given shift (Brunson 2011; Peterson 2011). Thus, the corporate model of VRS provision turns interpreters who are accustomed to autonomous work in community settings into employees.

Many countries have implemented trial periods to identify efficient ways of expanding telecommunication access to persons who are deaf or hard-of-hearing, as researchers continue to focus on collaboration between VRS providers, governments, organized labor, consumers and individual interpreters to develop a better understanding of this practice and its implications.

JEREMY L. BRUNSON

VIDEO REMOTE INTERPRETING

↑ REMOTE INTERPRETING, ↑ SIGNED LANGUAGE INTERPRETING

In areas where qualified interpreters are scarce or unavailable, or where the cost and logistics of obtaining an onsite interpreter are prohibitive, video remote interpreting can be a useful alternative. The term 'video remote interpreting' (VRI) is used in reference to SIGNED LANGUAGE INTERPRETING and falls under the general term REMOTE INTERPRETING, commonly used to refer to spoken-language interpreting provided via a videoconference link by an interpreter in a remote location (Braun & Taylor 2012). VRI allows the interpreter to provide services to deaf and hearing individuals who are together in a different place from the interpreter. It is distinct from video relay service interpreting, which provides access to telephone communication for deaf persons through video calls when the two parties are in separate locations.

In the US, VRI is used in multiple settings with deaf consumers (e.g. educational, legal, employment), but most frequently in healthcare-related scenarios, where the primary benefit is medical triage before an interpreter can arrive. Most practitioners and consumers agree that VRI is less suitable in situations where having a personal connection between the interacting parties is paramount; deaf consumers report that VRI is not an acceptable substitute for a qualified onsite interpreter (Simon et al. 2010). In some countries, where VRI services are billed on a per-minute basis, costs may be lower than for onsite interpreting, thereby increasing the appeal of VRI to contractors.

Conditions for interpreting in VRI settings differ from onsite conditions due to fundamental difficulties of working in a two-dimensional environment where interpreters may not have full VISUAL ACCESS to the remote location. Interpreters are therefore prone to miss interactions off-camera, visual materials such as models or charts, or TURN-TAKING cues of participants located outside of camera range. Technological considerations such as video and audio quality, connection stability and hardware usability as well as lighting contribute to the complexity of effective VRI services (Simon et al. 2010). Napier (2012) concludes that VRI can be effective for COURTROOM INTERPRETING, but deaf participants and interpreters are concerned about screen and image sizes, visibility (lighting, camera angles) and restrictions in turn-taking.

Factors and conditions that impact the QUALITY of VRI include the interpreter's background and familiarity with consumers and subject matter, cultural and linguistic fluency, prior access to materials, and technology training (Simon et al. 2010). Performance quality is central to evaluating VRI as a feasible substitute for a 'present' interpreter, and although research has documented increased STRESS, anxiety, and BURNOUT in remote interpreting, there is no evidence that quality suffers from using VRI, especially when team interpreter turns are shortened to allow for optimal performance (Moser-Mercer 2003; Roziner & Shlesinger 2010). Thus, despite the inherent challenges to the interpreter's performance and the need for physical and psychological adjustment to working in isolation, VRI is considered a viable option in certain multilingual settings subject to proper controls.

JEREMY L. BRUNSON

VIDEOCONFERENCE INTERPRETING

↑ TECHNOLOGY
→ REMOTE INTERPRETING

The evolution of videoconference technologies has led to two new modalities of interpreting. On the one hand, videoconferences are used to link remotely located interpreters to the primary participants. This is generally referred to as REMOTE INTERPRETING (RI). On the other hand, interpreters are used in videoconferences between parties who do not share the same language. This is termed videoconference interpreting (VCI) and comprises different configurations: the interpreter can be either co-located with one of the parties, or work from a separate site. The latter configuration leads to a multi-point videoconference between three (or more) sites. Similar configurations occur in TELEPHONE INTERPRETING. VCI has similarities with RI, and the modalities overlap to a certain extent, for example in three-way videoconferences. However, they have different motivations and are not interchangeable. Historically, the demand for both RI and VCI came from the language service needs of supranational organisations; today VCI is mostly required in legal settings.

VCI in supranational institutions

The earliest documented experiment with videoconferencing and interpreting took place in UNESCO in 1976. It linked the UNESCO headquarters in Paris with a conference centre in Nairobi via satellite, and included tests of both RI and VCI. In the VCI tests, the interpreters were situated in Paris and interpreted for delegates at both sites. Similar experiments were organised by the United Nations in the 1970s and 1980s (see Mouzourakis 1996). At the UNISPACE conference in Vienna in 1982, communication from the Soviet cosmonauts on board the MIR space station was transmitted to the Vienna delegates by video link and interpreted for them by interpreters in the Vienna conference room. Although reports about these early tests do not always make a clear distinction between RI and VCI, they suggest that RI was perceived to be challenging or unacceptable, whilst VCI seemed less problematic. This overall trend was not reflected in VCI tests using ISDN-based videoconferences, e.g. in the European Commission in 1995 (see Mouzourakis 2006), where sound quality was found to be insufficient for simultaneous interpreting. However, the view that VCI is acceptable under defined circumstances, whilst RI is not, is also reflected in the AIIC guidance on the use of technologies in interpreting (AIIC 2000/2012). Subsequent research into videoconference-based interpreting in supranational institutions has focused on RI, mainly to identify the exact sources of the problems associated with it.

VCI in legal settings

Legal institutions have turned to videoconferencing to make legal proceedings more efficient, minimise security concerns arising from prisoner transport, and support cross-border judicial co-operation. This has led to a growing demand for VCI in legal proceedings, normally conducted in consecutive mode. In many English-speaking countries, ISDN-based videoconference facilities were installed in the 1990s to link courts to other courts (e.g. to hear remote witnesses) and to prisons (e.g. for bail hearings). A worldwide spread of videoconference technology in legal proceedings began in the 2000s, following the availability of broadband technology. In some countries, notably the Netherlands, the same equipment and layout were used in all courtrooms to facilitate the work of all involved, including the interpreter. Such approaches are likely to have contributed to relatively positive attitudes towards VCI among interpreters in these countries, whilst scepticism prevails in countries such as the UK, where videoconference equipment often still dates from the ISDN era (Braun & Taylor 2012a). Fowler (2013) notes problems with the interpreter's POSITIONING and access to the microphone, and with the quality of the video image, in English magistrates' courts. She argues that these problems, together with the absence of specific protocols on VCI in court, lead to frequent disruptions, requests for repetition and misunderstanding.

One question arising, regardless of such issues, concerns the location of the interpreter in VCI. This was also one of the questions addressed by a comprehensive survey of VCI in Canadian immigration proceedings (Ellis 2004). In the setting examined, the immigration judge, the refugee protection officer and the interpreter sat in the immigration office, whilst the refugee and his/her lawyer were in another city. The fact that the interpreter was not co-located with the refugee was thought to have weakened the personal rapport between the two. It also caused interactional difficulties and precluded whispered interpreting. Judges felt that consecutive interpreting was disruptive. The hearings by video link also tended to be longer and were considered to be more fatiguing than comparable face-to-face hearings.

These findings were corroborated by the European AVIDICUS projects, which have focused on the viability of VCI and RI in legal proceedings. In addition, experimental studies conducted in AVIDICUS 1 (2008–11) showed that VCI (and RI) affected the QUALITY of interpreting and caused more interaction problems than onsite interpreting. Overlapping speech proved difficult to resolve and led to information loss (Braun & Taylor 2012a). Furthermore, qualitative analyses of the communicative dynamics in interpreter-mediated videoconference-based investigative interviews, court hearings and cross-border settlement cases, carried out in AVIDICUS 2 (2011–13), suggest that VCI entails not only a reduction in the quality of the relations between the participants but also a greater fragmentation of the discourse (Braun & Taylor 2015). AVIDICUS 3 (2014–16) assesses the implementation of videoconferencing facilities in legal institutions across Europe in terms of their fitness for VCI.

Other settings

The use of VCI in other settings is not very well documented, but some reports and interpreting service provider websites suggest that VCI is used across different segments of the interpreting market and that solutions in the commercial sector tend to be custom-made. They may also combine the use of the telephone and of videoconferencing to integrate interpreters into meetings.

One configuration that is likely to gain momentum is three-way videoconferencing, whereby the primary participants and the interpreter are each in a different location. In the late 1990s, the ViKiS project in Germany assessed this configuration (Braun 2004). Using a prototype system, problems as well as adaptation strategies developed by the participating interpreters in this (then) novel working condition were identified. As in other studies, participants found the communication fatiguing and had difficulty establishing a rapport with the other participants. The sound quality in the ISDN-based prototype was insufficient. The one aspect to which interpreters were able to adapt was the interaction. The strategies evolved from reactive to more proactive strategies. However, the interpreters felt that they had to moderate the interaction, which posed ethical problems and increased the coordination effort (Braun 2004, 2007).

With regard to cognitive processing, Moser-Mercer (2005a) outlines problems with multi-sensory integration in videoconferences, which she believes make it more difficult for interpreters to process information and build MENTAL REPRESENTATIONS of the situation.

SABINE BRAUN

VISUAL ACCESS

↑ WORKING CONDITIONS
→ POSITIONING, → REMOTE INTERPRETING

According to Poyatos (1997), the triple structure of communication is made up of language, paralanguage (including PROSODY) and kinesics (GESTURE, GAZE, facial expressions and other BODY LANGUAGE). Of these, language is verbal information, paralanguage is vocal NONVERBAL COMMUNICATION, and kinesics is visual nonverbal communication. Since kinesic expression can add information, support, repeat, emphasize, de-emphasize or contradict what is being said verbally, and may even be used instead of words, visual access to the speaker is considered vital in interpreting in order to ensure COMPREHENSION.

In DIALOGUE INTERPRETING in face-to-face interaction, this is usually not too difficult to achieve, though the interpreter's physical POSITIONING may in some cases not allow for full visual access (e.g. when s/he is behind a speaker for whom whispered or sign-to-voice interpreting is provided). In SIMULTANEOUS INTERPRETING from a booth, however, a view of the speaker, the screen and the conference room (e.g. for visual feedback from the audience) has long been a strict demand when it comes to defining conference interpreters' WORKING CONDITIONS (Bühler 1985). Indeed, the need for an 'unobstructed view' is also enshrined in the ISO standards for simultaneous interpreting booths. Even so, there is little conclusive empirical evidence to date of a direct link between visual access and the QUALITY of interpreters' performance. Whereas Anderson (1994) found no significant benefit when the interpreters in her experiment had access to a video image rather than working from the audio only, the results of a small-scale qualitative study by Rennert (2008) suggest that kinesics may be helpful in particular for ANTICIPATION of the speaker's message.

In multi-party interaction, kinesics can also indicate who will take the floor next. Such 'speech-preparatory movements' or TURN-TAKING cues are a valuable source of information for interpreters (Bühler 1985).

There is clearly a strong theoretical case for multichannel processing in interpreting. Auditory and visual stimuli are processed in parallel, making them complementary sources of information that deliver a clearer message in conjunction than they do separately (Jesse et al. 2000; Moser-Mercer 2005a). As nonverbal signals are usually decoded without conscious effort, they are by and large unlikely to increase the interpreter's COGNITIVE LOAD, and can actually provide information that s/he may have missed in the acoustic input. Given the widespread use of visual information in conference presentations (e.g. Power-Point slides), having a good view of speakers is also an increasingly relevant prerequisite for full access to their verbal message, as much of it may be presented on the screen. This can be important for many types of information, including items like NUMBERS or proper names.

Direct vs. mediated visual access

Visual access can be provided in different ways, either in a live situation where the interpreter is in the same room as the speakers or can see them directly from the booth, or via a video screen, as is the case in VIDEOCONFERENCE INTERPRETING and frequently in TV interpreting and other types of REMOTE INTERPRETING. Not all forms of visual access are of equal quality. The guidelines of professional organisations such as AIIC include the demand for good visibility of the speaker, the audience and any visual material. AIIC's guidelines for remote interpreting require a high-quality, uninterrupted colour display of 'the speaker in close-up, the audience, the chairman and conference officers', and any visual material shown to the audience (AIIC 2000).

A joint code (AIIC 2000/2012) developed by conference interpreters of several international and professional organisations states that, however good the picture and sound, if interpreters follow a debate on screen, 'they are deprived of the general nonverbal context required to fulfil their task'. It also makes reference to eye strain, absence of daylight, the need for extra concentration and the additional stress caused by videoconferencing. Moreover, when visual access is mediated via a screen, interpreters report a lack of 'presence' and a sense of being alienated from the proceedings (Moser-Mercer 2005a; Mouzourakis 2003), which may also add to their psychological stress.

SYLVI RENNERT

VISUAL LANGUAGE INTERPRETING

see SIGNED LANGUAGE INTERPRETING

VOICE QUALITY

↑ NONVERBAL COMMUNICATION, ↑ QUALITY CRITERIA
→ INTONATION

Voice is a central aspect of human communication, and evidently fundamental to interpreters working into spoken languages. The nature and quality of the human voice is an object of study in various disciplines, from medical specialties (phoniatrics, speech-language pathology) and psychology (social psychology, cognitive psychology) to linguistics (phonetics, forensic linguistics), language technology (voice recognition), and media and communication studies. The term 'voice quality' has therefore been variously defined. In strict phonetic terms, it is determined by the laryngeal muscles involved in phonation and the supralaryngeal features related to the setting of the vocal tract. In this narrow sense, voice quality is one of the quasi-permanent features of the human voice, alongside pitch, loudness and timbre – that is, a particular phonation type that can be described, for instance, as creaky, breathy, or harsh. In a broader sense, voice quality can refer to the total 'vocal image' of a speaker, including the prosodic features arising from the way the voice is handled (Laver 1980).

In the literature on interpreting, voice quality has generally been understood very broadly as all the vocal aspects of an interpreter's delivery. In keeping with findings from social psychology on the central role of vocal expression in interpersonal interaction and social influence (e.g. Scherer 1979), interpreting scholars have stressed the role of voice quality in inspiring credibility and TRUST, to the extent that an interpreter's pleasant voice could have a more persuasive COMMUNICATIVE EFFECT than what is actually said (e.g. Namy 1978; Shlesinger 1997). The contrary effect was also observed, namely when an unpleasant voice undermined good content (Gile 1991b). Consequently, voice quality has long been considered as part of an interpreter's professional COMPETENCE (e.g. Herbert 1952; Gerver et al. 1989; Feldweg 1996).

The voice quality of original speakers may be relevant as an INPUT VARIABLE in the interpreting process, but the focus in the research carried out to date has been on voice quality as a feature of an interpreter's performance (Iglesias Fernández 2007), and hence one of the QUALITY CRITERIA for its ASSESSMENT

'Pleasant voice'

In the line of research on quality criteria launched by Bühler (1986), the item relating to vocal characteristics of an interpreter's output was labeled 'pleasant voice', and consistently received some of the lowest ratings in surveys among interpreters as well as users on the relative importance of quality criteria (see also Collados Aís et al. 2007; Zwischenberger 2010; Iglesias Fernández 2013a). In contrast with such low expectations, the experimental study by Iglesias Fernández (2007) showed how an accurate interpretation received less favorable quality judgments when it was delivered with an unpleasant voice. A high pitch and a nasal timbre seemed to be perceived as indicators of the speaker's (i.e. interpreter's) immaturity and lack of competence, whereas vocal attributes such as a lower pitch, wider pitch range and higher resonance typically combine to give an impression of credibility and reliability.

Another interesting finding emerging from that study was that the interpreter's unpleasant voice negatively impacted the perception and assessment of other prosodic features, including INTONATION and FLUENCY (Iglesias Fernández 2007). The perception of voice seems to defy the atomistic approach to the study of QUALITY, which breaks delivery components down into separate criteria. When listeners are asked to judge the various aspects of an interpreter's delivery, they seem to find it difficult to make the necessary distinctions. Further evidence for this comes from a concept-mapping study aimed at eliciting users' definitions of 'pleasant voice'. These invariably crossed the strict conceptual boundary of voice and extended to prosodic features, in particular pitch, intonation and fluency, whereas timbre and voice quality were not mentioned (Iglesias Fernández 2013b). In future research, the impact of voice quality on judgments of overall performance quality may therefore best be examined more holistically as a cluster of voice and prosodic features.

EMILIA IGLESIAS FERNÁNDEZ

WHISPERED INTERPRETING

see under SIMULTANEOUS INTERPRETING

WORKING CONDITIONS

↑ PROFESSION
→ QUALITY, → STRESS

INTERPRETING as a situated activity is always performed in a social context, and the interpreter's work is therefore influenced by a wide range of physical and psycho-social conditions as well as mental demands in the work environment. From the broadest to the most specific level, these factors can be characterized as employment-related, assignment-related, and task-related, though categorization along these lines is by no means clear-cut and involves

441

considerable overlap. To varying degrees, these three sets of factors are related to a number of issues in an interpreter's exercise of the PROFESSION, from the QUALITY of the service rendered to occupational STRESS and JOB SATISFACTION.

With regard to *employment*, conditions differ considerably between interpreters hired on a freelance basis for a given assignment, and those permanently employed as members of staff. In the field of CONFERENCE INTERPRETING, employment conditions for staff interpreters in international organizations were shaped significantly in the formative decades of the profession by the efforts of AIIC, the International Association of Conference Interpreters. The vast majority of its members being freelance interpreters, AIIC negotiates collective agreements for interpreters on 'short-term' contracts with major institutional employers. These agreements for 'conference interpreters paid by the day' cover a range of issues, from remuneration and provision for retirement and insurance, to details of recruitment and working conditions. These include the definition of a working day (two sessions of three hours each), team strength, and allowances for travel and subsistence for assignments away from the interpreter's professional domicile. Such bargaining power is rare in the domain of COMMUNITY INTERPRETING, though conditions vary greatly across the fields of work subsumed under this broad heading. In some areas, such as LEGAL INTERPRETING, remuneration levels and working conditions may be set by public authorities, with or without negotiated agreements. This also applies to SIGNED LANGUAGE INTERPRETING in many countries. Statistics are sparse; a study on remuneration of US sign language interpreters employed in EDUCATIONAL INTERPRETING found wage discrepancies, but no correlation between compensation and interpreters' level of education (K. Hale 2010). For many community-based SETTINGS, employment conditions may be controlled by AGENCIES that have secured an overall contract for service provision, or else, such aspects of work as hours and breaks may be left to the discretion of the interpreter's institutional client or professional service provider, who may also be involved in rehiring decisions. On the other hand, agencies and institutional employers may be in a position to offer continuing education or professional support services, such as supervision. This is especially relevant for interpreters exposed to a high risk of BURNOUT or VICARIOUS TRAUMA, as reported for sign language interpreters in general, and interpreters working in MENTAL HEALTH SETTINGS, in particular. While little is known about their specific impact, general employment conditions, not least with regard to job (in)security, clearly play a major role for such psycho-social issues as work–home interface and work–life balance in the exercise of interpreting as a profession. A study among community interpreters in Sweden (Norström et al. 2012) is among the few attempts at addressing the occupational situation in a comprehensive manner, with regard to employment issues as well as the challenges of individual assignments.

At the level of the *assignment*, working conditions come into play in various ways and at different stages. In terms of Kalina's (2005b) comprehensive scheme of the conference interpreting assignment, this applies particularly to the pre-process and peri-process stages, whereas some of her in-process factors correspond to what is described as task-related conditions below. In one-off assignments, the pre-process stage includes the contractual specification of the various factors mentioned above in relation to short-term employment conditions, with special attention to collaboration with the commissioning client and such aspects of PREPARATION as the provision of documents, access to TERMINOLOGY resources, and the scheduling of a briefing. Many other important aspects of the interpreter's working conditions, including the technical equipment and media used and specific language needs (including the need for RELAY INTERPRETING), are ideally determined at the level of the assignment but, in actual practice, are often first encountered and addressed, for better or worse, by the interpreter on site: it is a vital component of professional ETHICS for the interpreter, across working MODES, to negotiate adequate conditions directly at the venue of the assignment, with special regard to such aspects as POSITIONING and VISUAL ACCESS – and visibility, in the case of signed language interpreting. In a longitudinal, questionnaire-based survey of all interpreting assignments in the Austrian province of Styria over a period of two years, Grbić (2006) asked sign language interpreters to report on such factors as booking, preparation, type of assignment, time and place, clients and payment, as well as task-oriented challenges. Although respondents judged nearly 50% of their jobs as 'difficult', for various reasons (including extensive preparation, unfavorable lighting, poor ventilation, crowded surroundings, difficult input, chaotic discussions, hostility, psychological stress, physical strain, etc.), they felt content with almost 90% of their assignments.

For interpreters in various community settings, issues of health and safety may loom large. Examples include the risk of infection in HEALTHCARE INTERPRETING and aggressive behavior by individuals in POLICE SETTINGS. In conference settings, on the other hand, it is the protected workspace of the interpreter's booth that constitutes the main work environment and impacts on specific working conditions, including light and sound, ventilation, and a view of the proceedings. These have been specified by the International Organization for Standardization (ISO), in collaboration with AIIC, and laid down in ISO 2603 for built-in (permanent) booths and ISO 4043 for mobile booths. These international standards, as well as IEC 60914 for sound systems equipment, were first adopted in the 1970s (see Jumpelt 1985) and have undergone several updates. However, as demonstrated in the AIIC Workload Study (AIIC 2002), actual conditions often fall considerably short of what is mandated by these standards. Such gaps between the ideal and the actual situation are also likely to characterize the next frontier in the definition and implementation of appropriate working conditions for interpreters – that is, the various forms of REMOTE INTERPRETING as used in conference as well as community settings. A milestone study on remote conference interpreting and its impact on output quality in the simultaneous mode is reported by Roziner and Shlesinger (2010), and similar analyses of the relationship between remote interpreting mode and quality were performed in the context of the AVIDICUS projects (Braun 2013; Braun & Taylor 2012a, 2015).

For conference interpreters, in particular, the dimension of working conditions that is associated most closely with occupational stress and performance quality is at the level of the *task* as such (see Moser-Mercer 1996). As listed by Kalina (2005b) under in-process factors, this includes the difficulty of the input material (e.g. density, technicality) and features of the speaker's delivery such as a non-native ACCENT and high SPEECH RATE. All of these can be subsumed under the heading of INPUT VARIABLES, which play a key role in conference interpreters' perception of their working conditions as stressful and detrimental to quality. Some of these task-related challenges, such as accents and idiosyncratic forms of expression, also apply in DIALOGUE INTERPRETING in institutional settings. In general, though, community interpreters are more likely to encounter difficult task demands arising from the interaction situation, such as overlapping speech and other issues of TURN-TAKING, as well as dilemmas pertaining to role behavior and professional ethics.

NADJA GRBIĆ AND FRANZ PÖCHHACKER

WORKING MEMORY

↑ MEMORY→ COGNITIVE LOAD

Working memory is a cognitive mechanism responsible for short-term storage, maintenance, and processing of information, and for executive control of cognitive processes. Storage refers to simple retention of information for a few moments (such as reading a price tag and noting down the amount without looking at the tag again). Maintenance is a process of active refreshing of the information so that it is not forgotten. Processing refers to manipulation of information, such as hearing the word 'dog' and mentally translating it into another language. Finally, executive control is a collection of processes which include attention management.

Working memory can be distinguished from short-term and long-term MEMORY. Short- and long-term memory serve for storage only, for different periods of time as their names suggest: short-term memory is limited to a matter of seconds, while long-term memory can store information for a lifetime. Working memory, on the other hand, is characterised by an element of manipulation of information and/or sharing attention between several tasks. Working memory is therefore often described as the workspace of the mind. A textbook example of working memory in action is mental arithmetic, which involves storing the input, performing the calculation (typically in several steps), storing the intermediate results, and dividing attention between the calculations and the storage of input and intermediate results until the final result is reached.

Another important feature of working memory is its limited capacity, measured either temporally or in terms of the number of discrete items which can be stored and manipulated at the same time. The latter has been famously set at 7 ± 2 items by Miller (1956), suggesting that normal individuals can usually remember around seven discrete units, such as letters, digits or words. When the items are not discrete and can be combined into meaningful chunks, capacity is increased: people can remember about seven unrelated words, but when the stimulus is a meaningful sentence, the capacity increases to about 16 words (but not 7 ± 2 verbatim sentences; Baddeley 2000). Working memory also has a temporal limitation. Without maintenance, information will decay in about two seconds. Maintaining information in working memory for a longer period of time is possible, but it is an effortful process and requires attention, which in turn is difficult to maintain for extended periods of time and assumes that no other information will make demands on working memory resources.

A number of models of working memory have been developed. The first was proposed by Baddeley and Hitch (1974). It consisted of several structurally independent units, corresponding to stores for different types of stimuli (verbal, visual), and a central executive responsible for processing control. More recent models focus less on structure and more on function. Cowan's (1988) model considers working memory to be an activated part of long-term memory, with a few of the activated items being available to consciousness through focused attention. Cowan's model highlights the role of attention in working memory. A third approach is illustrated by the long-term working memory model suggested by Ericsson and Kintsch (1995). Their model is based on observations of better memory performance in areas in which an individual is skilled, and thus emphasises the role of EXPERTISE in working memory performance. These three models are representative of working memory research in cognitive psychology, and have also been applied to research on interpreting. For example, work by Bajo and colleagues (e.g. Padilla et al. 1995) is based on Baddeley's model, as is the study by SHLESINGER (2003); Mizuno (2005) proposed the use of Cowan's model as an explanatory framework for interpreting; and the Ericsson and Kintsch model has been used to underpin expertise studies (e.g. Hild 2011).

Working memory has come to the fore as a major topic in interpreting studies, in theory and in empirical research. Most interest has focused on SIMULTANEOUS INTERPRETING, which requires a mixture of fast manipulation and attention management. Working memory has been suggested as a crucial mechanism underlying (simultaneous) interpreting, and continues to receive attention in empirical research, which addresses two main questions: (1) Do interpreters have better working memory than non-interpreters? (2) How is working memory involved in interpreting?

Interpreters and working memory

A number of studies have compared working memory in interpreters and non-interpreters. The basic rationale is that, if working memory is indeed crucial for interpreting, its intensive use will lead to better working memory performance in interpreters compared to non-interpreters. Additionally, if professional interpreters were found to have better working memory than interpreting students, there would be further evidence that working memory is enhanced with interpreting practice, rather than superior working memory being a component of interpreting aptitude. Research results are mixed, however, and also appear to depend on how working memory performance is measured. Most studies to date have used tests targeting storage and maintenance components of working memory, rather than executive control, or their combination. There is currently little evidence of interpreters having a larger memory capacity (remembering more items) as measured by tests such as the digit span task (presentation of series of digits and their subsequent recall). The strongest evidence for the hypothesis of superior working memory in interpreters comes from studies employing complex tasks which combine storage and processing functions. A classic example is the reading span task, in which participants are presented with a series of sentences and asked to read each sentence aloud (processing) and remember the last word (storage and maintenance). At the end of each series of sentences, participants have to recall the last word of each sentence. The longest series correctly recalled determines the size of the memory span. Studies using the reading span task typically found that interpreters outperformed non-interpreters (e.g. Christoffels et al. 2006; Padilla et al. 1995; Signorelli et al. 2012; Tzou et al. 2012). Other studies used a variant of the reading span task – its auditory version called the listening span task – as it seems that listening, rather than reading, is closer to what interpreters actually do during interpreting. Intriguingly, results with this task do not corroborate the findings achieved with the reading span task (e.g. Liu et al. 2004; Köpke & Nespoulous 2006).

A somewhat different approach to working memory capacity testing is taken by researchers in SIGNED LANGUAGE INTERPRETING. While spoken language interpreting focuses on differences between interpreters and non-interpreters, sign language interpreting research has focused on the issue of BILINGUALISM, or differences in working memory capacity for the two languages – one spoken and one signed. Several studies (e.g. Rudner et al. 2007; van Dijk et al. 2012) compared interpreters' spans, but found no language effect, nor was there evidence of any difference between interpreters who were native signers and non-native signers (Wang 2013). The issue of bilingual proficiency with regard to working memory capacity has not been investigated in detail in spoken language interpreters, although one study found that interpreters outperformed non-interpreters in both a native and a non-native language, despite the two groups being considered equal in knowledge of the non-native language (Christoffels et al. 2006).

One area where interpreters are consistently superior to non-interpreters is what is known as articulatory suppression. In general, working memory performance is affected when participants are required to speak while trying to remember, which suggests that short-term remembering is partly dependent on (silent) rehearsal of the information to be stored. Interpreters, however, have been found to be less affected by inhibition of this subvocal rehearsal as a result of speech production (Padilla et al. 2005), and the same can also be said of interpreting students (Chincotta & Underwood 1998; Yudes et al. 2012).

Working memory in interpreting

A second major strand of research addresses the question of how working memory supports interpreting. Several MODELS of the interpreting process include an explicit and significant working memory component (e.g. Gerver 1975; Moser 1978; Darò & Fabbro 1994), but these modeling efforts were not followed up empirically, and the models were not further refined. Nevertheless, they are important in that they provide a complete conceptual framework of the interaction of various processes underlying interpreting and propose specific roles for working memory.

Empirical work, on the other hand, has taken a simpler route and compared interpreters' performance on working memory tasks with their performance on a (simultaneous) interpreting task (e.g. Christoffels 2004; Liu et al. 2004; Timarová et al. 2014; Tzou et al. 2012). These studies used different working memory tasks, ranging from simple span tasks (storage and maintenance without processing, such as the digit span task), through complex working memory capacity tasks (memory and processing, such as the reading span task) to pure executive control tasks (such as attention shifting). Broadly speaking, a relationship between working memory and simultaneous interpreting has indeed been found. Among untrained bilinguals (Christoffels 2004) and interpreting students (Tzou et al. 2012), better working memory performance was related to better performance in interpreting. In professional interpreters, no relationship between working memory capacity (i.e. the storage component of working memory) and interpreting was found (Liu et al. 2004), but other evidence suggests involvement of executive control (attention management) in superior simultaneous interpreting performance by professionals (Timarová et al. 2014). Importantly, one aspect of attention, namely the ability to ignore distractors, was found to improve with interpreting experience, which suggests that it is an integral part of professional interpreting skill. This finding is in line with research into articulatory suppression, and the finding that interpreters are less affected in their performance of working memory tasks by speaking at the same time.

Review

Working memory research in interpreting is an example of advances in INTERDISCIPLINARITY. Interpreting research has been informed both theoretically (models) and empirically (working memory task design) by more general working memory research in cognitive psychology, and much of the working memory research with interpreters was carried out by cognitive psychologists (e.g. Bajo, Christoffels, Köpke, Signorelli).

Some of the discrepant results, especially in the research strand related to the potentially better working memory of interpreters, create the need for meta-research and review papers that consider various methodological differences as possible explanations behind the divergent findings. Refinements in research designs and methods are an essential requirement for consolidation, allowing the collection of a larger body of comparable evidence, which is immensely important in a research area where participant samples remain very small. For example, the work of Köpke and Signorelli (2012), who explored possible reasons for the discrepant findings achieved with the listening and reading span tasks, including differences in scoring methods and participant selection, highlights the need for careful methodological choices and detailed reporting if further progress in understanding the intricacies of working memory is to be made.

ŠÁRKA TIMAROVÁ

ZERO RENDITION

see under OMISSIONS

BIBLIOGRAPHY

Abbe, Marisa, Simon, Christian, Angiolillo, Anne, Ruccione, Kathy & Kodish, Eric D. (2006) A survey of language barriers from the perspective of pediatric oncologists, interpreters, and parents. *Pediatric Blood & Cancer* 47 (6), 819–824.

Abel, Laura (2009) *Language Access in State Courts*. New York: Brennan Center for Justice, New York University School of Law. www.brennancenter.org/publication/language-access-state-courts (accessed 16 December 2014).

Abuín González, Marta (2007) *El Proceso de Interpretación Consecutiva: Un Estudio del Binomio Problema/estrategia*. Granada: Editorial Comares.

Abuín González, Marta (2012) The language of consecutive interpreters' notes: Differences across levels of expertise. *Interpreting* 14 (1), 55–72.

Abutalebi, Jubin & Green, David (2007) Bilingual language production: The neurocognition of language representation and control. *Journal of Neurolinguistics* 20 (3), 242–275.

Abutalebi, Jubin, Miozzo, Antonio & Cappa, Stefano F. (2000) Do subcortical structures control 'language selection' in polyglots? Evidence from pathological language mixing. *Neurocase* 6 (1), 51–56.

Ackermann Hanisch, Juan (1993) *A las Órdenes de Vuecencia. Autobiografía del Intérprete de los Generales Muñoz Grandes y Esteban-Infantes*. Madrid: Barbarroja.

Ács, Pál (2000) Tarjumans Mahmud and Murad: Austrian and Hungarian renegades as sultan's interpreters. In B. Guthmüller (ed.) *Europa und die Türken in der Renaissance*. Tübingen: Max Niemeyer, 307–316.

Adam, Carolin & Castro, Ginette (2013) Schlaggesten beim Simultandolmetschen – Auftreten und Funktionen. *Lebende Sprachen* 58 (1), 71–82.

Adam, Robert, Carty, Breda & Stone, Christopher (2011) Ghost writing: Deaf translators within the Deaf community. *Babel* 57 (4), 375–393.

Adam, Robert, Stone, Christopher, Collins, Steven D. & Metzger, Melanie (eds) (2014) *Deaf Interpreters at Work: International Insights*. Washington, DC: Gallaudet University Press.

Adams, James N. (2003) *Bilingualism and the Latin Language*. Cambridge: Cambridge University Press.

Adams, James N. (2007) *The Regional Diversification of Latin 200 BC–AD 600*. Cambridge: Cambridge University Press.

AERA, APA & NCME (1999) *Standards for Educational and Psychological Testing*. Washington, DC: American Educational Research Association.

Agrifoglio, Marjorie (2004) Sight translation and interpreting: A comparative analysis of constraints and failures. *Interpreting* 6 (1), 43–67.

Ahamer, Vera S. (2013) *Unsichtbare Spracharbeit: Jugendliche Migranten als Laiendolmetscher. Integration durch "Community Interpreting"*. Bielefeld: Transcript-Verlag.

Ahrens, Barbara (2004) *Prosodie beim Simultandolmetschen*. Frankfurt: Peter Lang.

Ahrens, Barbara (2005a) Prosodic phenomena in simultaneous interpreting: A conceptual approach and its practical application. *Interpreting* 7 (1), 51–76.

Ahrens, Barbara (2005b) Rozan and Matyssek: Are they really that different? A comparative synopsis of two classic note-taking schools. *Forum* 3 (2), 1–15.

Ahrens, Barbara (2007) Pauses (and other prosodic features) in simultaneous interpreting. *Forum* 5 (1), 1–18.

AIIC (1984) Random selection from reports and notes on the Brussels seminar. *AIIC Bulletin* 12 (1), 21.

AIIC (2000) Guidelines for remote conferencing. http://aiic.net/page/143/ (accessed 31 October 2013).

AIIC (2000/2012) Guidelines for the use of new technologies in conference interpreting. *Communicate!* March–April 2000. www.aiic.net/ViewPage.cfm?page_id=120 (accessed 24 January 2014).

AIIC (2002) *Interpreter Workload Study – Full Report.* http://aiic.net/page/657 (accessed 10 January 2014).

AIIC (2012) *Code of professional ethics.* http://aiic.net/code-of-ethics (accessed 24 February 2015).

AIIC History Group (2013) *Naissance d'une Profession: Les Soixante Premières Années de l'Association Internationale des Interprètes de Conférence (AIIC).* Geneva: AIIC.

Alam, Muzaffar & Subrahmanyam, Sanjay (2004) The making of a Munshi. *Forms of Knowledge in Early Modern South Asia.* Special Issue of *Comparative Studies of South Asia, Africa and the Middle East* 24 (2), 61–72.

Alam, Muzaffar & Subrahmanyam, Sanjay (2010) Witnesses and agents of empire: Eighteenth-Century historiography and the world of the Mughal Munshi. *Journal of the Economic and Social History of the Orient* 53 (1/2), 393–423.

Albl-Mikasa, Michaela (2006) Reduction and expansion in notation texts. In C. Heine, K. Schubert & H. Gerzymisch-Arbogast (eds) *Text and Translation: Theory and Methodology of Translation.* Tübingen: Gunter Narr, 195–214.

Albl-Mikasa, Michaela (2008) (Non-)Sense in note-taking for consecutive interpreting. *Interpreting* 10 (2), 197–231.

Albl-Mikasa, Michaela (2010) Global English and English as a lingua franca (ELF): Implications for the interpreting profession. *Trans-kom* 3 (2), 126–148.

Albl-Mikasa, Michaela (2013a) Developing and cultivating expert interpreter competence. *The Interpreters' Newsletter* 18, 17–34.

Albl-Mikasa, Michaela (2013b) ELF speakers' restricted power of expression – implications for interpreters' processing. *Translation and Interpreting Studies* 8 (2), 191–210.

Alexander, Philip S. (1976) The rabbinic lists of forbidden Targumim. *Journal of Jewish Studies* 27 (2), 177–191.

Alexieva, Bistra (1983) Compression as a means of realisation of the communicative act in simultaneous interpreting. *Fremdsprachen* 27 (4), 233–239.

Alexieva, Bistra (1985) Semantic analysis of the text in simultaneous interpreting. In H. Bühler (ed.) *Translators and their Position in Society: Proceedings of the Xth World Congress of FIT.* Vienna: Wilhelm Braumüller, 195–198.

Alexieva, Bistra (1988) Analysis of the simultaneous interpreter's output. In P. Nekeman (ed.) *Translation, our Future: Proceedings, XIth World Congress of FIT.* Maastricht: Euroterm, 484–488.

Alexieva, Bistra (1994) On teaching note-taking in consecutive interpreting. In C. Dollerup & A. Lindegaard (eds) *Teaching Translation and Interpreting 2: Insights, Aims, Visions. Selected Papers from the Second Language International Conference, Elsinore, Denmark, 4–6 June 1993.* Amsterdam: John Benjamins, 199–206.

Alexieva, Bistra (1997) A typology of interpreter-mediated events. *The Translator* 3 (2), 153–174.

Alexieva, Bistra (1999) Understanding the source language text in simultaneous interpreting. *The Interpreters' Newsletter* 9, 45–59.

Alexieva, Bistra (2001) Interpreter-mediated TV live interviews. In Y. Gambier & H. Gottlieb (eds) *(Multi) Media Translation: Concepts, Practices and Research.* Amsterdam: John Benjamins, 113–124.

Al-Khanji, Rajai, El-Shiyab, Said & Hussein, Riyadh (2000) On the use of compensatory strategies in simultaneous interpretation. *Meta* 45 (3), 548–557.

Allioni, Sergio (1989) Towards a grammar of consecutive interpreting. In L. Gran & J. Dodds (eds) *The Theoretical and Practical Aspects of Teaching Conference Interpretation.* Udine: Campanotto, 191–197.

Allsop, Lorna & Kyle, Jim (2008) Translating the news: A Deaf translator's experience. In C. J. Kellett Bidoli & E. Ochse (eds) *English in International Deaf Communication.* Bern: Peter Lang, 383–401.

Alonso Araguás, Icíar (2005) *Intérpretes de Indias. La Mediación Lingüística y Cultural en los Viajes de Exploración y Conquista: Antillas, Caribe y Golfo de México (1492–1540).* PhD dissertation, Universidad de Salamanca.

Alonso Araguás, Icíar (2012) Negociar en tiempos de guerra: Viajes de ida y vuelta entre España y América (ss. XV–XVII). In G. Payàs & J. M. Zavala (eds) *La Mediación Lingüístico-cultural en Tiempos de Guerra: Cruce de Miradas desde España y América*. Temuco: Universidad Católica de Temuco, 37–64.

Alonso-Araguás, Icíar (2016) Interpreting practices in the Age of Discovery: The early stages of the Spanish Empire in the Americas. In K. Takeda & J. Baigorri-Jalón (eds) *New Insights in the History of Interpreting*. Amsterdam: John Benjamins.

Alonso, Icíar & Payàs, Gertrudis (2008) Sobre alfaqueques y nahuatlatos: Nuevas aportaciones a la historia de la interpretación. In C. Valero-Garcés (ed.) *Investigación y Práctica en Traducción e Interpretación en los Servicios Públicos. Desafíos y Alianzas*. Alcalá de Henares: Universidad de Alcalá, CD-ROM, 39–52.

Alonso Bacigalupe, Luis (1999) Visual contact in simultaneous interpreting: Results of an experimental study. In A. Álvarez Lugrís & A. Fernández Ocampo (eds) *Anovar/Anosar Estudios de Traducción e Interpretación*. Vol. 1. Vigo: Servicio de Publicacións da Universidade de Vigo, 123–137.

Al-Salman, Saleh & Al-Khanji, Rajai (2002) The native language factor in simultaneous interpretation in an Arabic/English context. *Meta* 47 (4), 233–239.

Altman, Janet (1994) Error analysis in the teaching of simultaneous interpreting: A pilot study. In S. Lambert & B. Moser-Mercer (eds) *Bridging the Gap: Empirical Research in Simultaneous Interpretation*. Amsterdam/Philaelphia: John Benjamins, 25–38.

Alvstad, Cecilia, Hild, Adelina & Tiselius, Elisabet (2011) Methods and strategies of process research: Integrative approaches in translation studies. In C. Alvstad, A. Hild & E. Tiselius (eds) *Methods and Strategies of Process Research: Integrative Approaches in Translation Studies*. Amsterdam: John Benajmins, 1–12.

Amato, Amalia (2002) Interpreting legal discourse on TV: Clinton's deposition with the Grand Jury. In G. Garzone & M. Viezzi (eds) *Perspectives on Interpreting*. Bologna: CLUEB, 269–290.

Amato, Amalia (2007) The interpreter in multi-party medical encounters. In C. Wadensjö, B. Englund Dimitrova & A.-L. Nilsson (eds) *The Critical Link 4: Professionalisation of Interpreting in the Community*. Amsterdam: John Benjamins, 27–38.

Anaya Dávila Garibi, Graciela & Lopez Islas, Javier (1990) Oral cloze: A backup exercise for interpreting. *Meta* 35 (3), 647–651.

Anderson, Arlyn (2012) Peer support and consultation project for interpreters: A model for supporting the well-being of interpreters who practice in mental health settings. *Journal of Interpretation* 21 (1), 2–12.

Anderson, Laurie (2012) Code-switching and coordination in interpreter-mediated interaction. In C. Baraldi & L. Gavioli (eds) *Coordinating Participation in Dialogue Interpreting*. Amsterdam: John Benjamins, 115–148.

Anderson, Linda (1994) Simultaneous interpretation: Contextual and translation aspects. In S. Lambert & B. Moser-Mercer (eds) *Bridging the Gap: Empirical Research in Simultaneous Interpretation*. Amsterdam: John Benjamins, 101–120.

Anderson, R. Bruce W. (1976) Perspectives on the role of interpreter. In R. W. Brislin (ed.) *Translation: Applications and Research*. New York: Gardner Press, 208–228.

Anderson, R. Bruce W. (1978) Interpreter roles and interpretation situations: Cross-cutting typologies. In D. Gerver & H. W. Sinaiko (eds) *Language Interpretation and Communication*. New York: Plenum Press, 217–229.

Andres, Dörte (2002) *Konsekutivdolmetschen und Notation*. Frankfurt: Peter Lang.

Andres, Dörte (2008) *Dolmetscher als literarische Figuren. Von Identitätsverlust, Dilettantismus und Verrat*. München: Meidenbauer.

Andres, Dörte (2012) Erwin Weit: Gratwanderung eines Dolmetschers. In: A. Kelletat & A. Meger (eds) *Worte und Wendungen. Texte für Erika Worbs mit Dank für zwei Jahrzehnte Germersheim*. Berlin: Saxa, 11–19.

Andres, Dörte (2013) History of interpreting. In C. A. Chapelle (ed.) *The Encyclopedia of Applied Linguistics*. Oxford: Blackwell, 2512–2521.

Andres, Dörte (2014) The apocalyptical interpreter and the end of Europe: Alain Fleischer's *Prolongations*. In K. Kaindl & K. Spitzl (eds) *Transfiction: Research into the Realities of Translation Fiction*. Amsterdam: John Benjamins, 271–284.

Andres, Dörte & Fünfer, Sarah (2011) TV interpreting in Germany: the television broadcasting company ARTE in comparison to public broadcasting companies. *The Interpreters' Newsletter* 16, 99–114.

Andres, Dörte, Behr, Martina & Dingfelder Stone, Maren (eds) (2013) *Dolmetschmodelle – erfasst, erläutert, erweitert.* Frankfurt: Peter Lang.

Angelelli, Claudia (2003) The visible co-participant: The interpreter's role in doctor–patient encounters. In M. Metzger, S. Collins, V. Dively & R. Shaw (eds) *From Topic Boundaries to Omission: New Research on Interpretation.* Washington, DC: Gallaudet University Press, 3–26.

Angelelli, Claudia V. (2004a) *Medical Interpreting and Cross-cultural Communication.* Cambridge: Cambridge University Press.

Angelelli, Claudia V. (2004b) *Revisiting the Interpreter's Role: A Study of Conference, Court, and Medical Interpreters in Canada, Mexico, and the United States.* Amsterdam: John Benjamins.

Angelelli, Claudia V. (2007) Validating professional standards and codes: Challenges and opportunities. *Interpreting* 8 (2), 175–193.

Angelelli, Claudia V. (2010) A professional ideology in the making: Bilingual youngsters interpreting for their communities and the notion of (no) choice. *Translation and Interpreting Studies* 5 (1), 94–108.

Angelelli, Claudia (2011a) "Can you ask her about chronic illnesses, diabetes and all that?" In C. Alvstad, A. Hild & E. Tiselius (eds) *Methods and Strategies of Process Research: Integrative Approaches in Translation Studies.* Amsterdam: John Benjamins, 231–246.

Angelelli, Claudia V. (2011b) Expanding the abilities of bilingual youngsters: Can translation and interpreting help? In M. J. Blasco Mayor & M. A. Jiménez Ivars (eds) *Interpreting Naturally: A Tribute to Brian Harris.* Frankfurt: Peter Lang, 103–120.

Angelelli, Claudia V. (2012) Challenges in interpreters' coordination of the construction of pain. In C. Baraldi & L. Gavioli (eds) *Coordinating Participation in Dialogue Interpreting.* Amsterdam: John Benjamins, 251–268.

Angelelli, Claudia V. & Baer, Brian James (eds) (2015) *Researching Translation and Interpreting.* London/New York: Routledge.

Angelelli, Claudia V. & Jacobson, Holly E. (eds) (2009) *Testing and Assessment in Translation and Interpreting Studies.* Amsterdam: John Benjamins.

Angelelli, Claudia V., Agger-Gupta, Niels, Green, Carola E. & Okahara, Linda (2007) The California Standards for Healthcare Interpreters: Ethical principles, protocols and guidance on roles and intervention. In C. Wadensjö, B. Englund Dimitrova & A.-L. Nilsson (eds) *The Critical Link 4: The Professionalisation of Interpreting in the Community.* Amsterdam: John Benjamins, 167–177.

Angermeyer, Philipp S. (2005) Who is "you"? Polite forms of address and ambiguous participant roles in court interpreting. *Target* 17 (2), 203–226.

Angermeyer, Philipp Sebastian (2010) Interpreter-mediated interaction as bilingual speech: Bridging macro- and micro-sociolinguistics in codeswitching research. *International Journal of Bilingualism* 14 (4), 466–489.

Angermeyer, Philipp S. (2013) Multilingual speakers and language choice in the legal sphere. *Applied Linguistics Review* 4 (1), 105–126.

Angermeyer, Philipp Sebastian, Meyer, Bernd & Schmidt, Thomas (2012) Sharing community interpreting corpora: A pilot study. In T. Schmidt & K. Wörner (eds) *Multilingual Corpora and Multilingual Corpus Analysis.* Amsterdam: John Benjamins, 275–294.

Antinoro Pizzuto, Elena, Chiari, Isabella & Rossini, Paolo (2010) Representing signed languages: Theoretical, methodological and practical issues. In M. Pettorino, A. Giannini, I. Chiari & F. Dovetto (eds) *Spoken Communication.* Cambridge: Cambridge Scholars Publishing, 205–240.

Antonini, Rachele (2010) The study of child language brokering: Past, current and emerging research. In R. Antonini (ed.) *Child Language Brokering: Trends and Patterns in Current Research.* Special Issue of *mediAzioni* 10, 1–23. http://mediazioni.sitlec.unibo.it (accessed 30 January 2015).

Apfelbaum, Birgit (2004) *Gesprächsdynamik in Dolmetsch-Interaktionen.* Radolfzell: Verlag für Gesprächsforschung.

Apostolou, Fotini (2011) Introduction: Interpreting and translation in the European Union. *Gramma: Journal of Theory and Criticism* 19, 95–110. www.enl.auth.gr/gramma/gramma11/apostolou2.pdf (accessed 31 July 2014).

Aranguri, Cesar, Davidson, Brad & Ramirez, Robert (2006) Patterns of communication through interpreters: A detailed sociolinguistic analysis. *Journal of General Internal Medicine* 21 (6), 623–629.

Argyle, Michael (1988) *Bodily Communication*. 2nd edn. London: Methuen.

Argyle, Michael & Cook, Mark (1976) *Gaze and Mutual Gaze*. Cambridge: Cambridge University Press.

Arias Torres, Juan Pablo & Feria García, Manuel C. (2013) *Los Traductores de Árabe del Estado Español. Del Protectorado a nuestros Días*. Barcelona: Bellaterra.

Arjona, Etilvia (1984) Issues in the design of curricula for the professional education of translators and interpreters. In M. L. McIntire (ed.) *New Dialogues in Interpreter Education. Proceedings of the Fourth National Conference of Interpreter Trainers Convention*. Silver Spring, MD: Registry of Interpreters for the Deaf, 1–35.

ASTM (2007) *ASTM F2089-01, Standard Guide for Language Interpretation Services*. ASTM International, West Conshohocken, PA: ASTM International.

Atkinson, J. Maxwell & Heritage, John (1984) *Structures of Social Action: Studies in Conversation Analysis*. Cambridge: Cambridge University Press.

Atkinson, Richard C. & Shiffrin, Richard M. (1968) Human memory: A proposed system and its control processes. In K. W. Spence & J. T. Spence (eds) *The Psychology of Learning and Motivation: Advances in Research and Theory*. Vol. 2. New York: Academic Press, 89–195.

Austin, John (1962) *How to Do Things with Words*. Oxford: Clarendon Press.

AVLIC (2000) *Code of Ethics and Guidelines for Professional Conduct*. www.avlic.ca/ethics-and-guidlines/english (accessed 25 February 2015).

Ayala, Manuel José de (1946) *Notas a la Recopilación de Indias: Origen e Historia Ilustrada de las Leyes de Indias*. Vol. I. Madrid: Ediciones Cultura Hispánica.

Azarmina, Pejman & Wallace, Paul (2005) Remote interpretation in medical encounters: A systematic review. *Journal of Telemedicine and Telecare* 11, 140–145.

Bâ, Amadou Hampâté (1973) *L'étrange Destin de Wangrin ou Les Roueries d'un Interprète Africain*. Paris: Union Générale d' Editions.

Bachman, Lyle F. (2004) *Statistical Analyses for Language Assessment*. Cambridge: Cambridge University Press.

Baddeley, Alan (2000) The episodic buffer: A new component of working memory? *Trends in Cognitive Sciences* 4 (11), 417–423.

Baddeley, Alan (2003) Working memory: Looking back and looking forward. *Nature Reviews Neuroscience* 4, 829–839.

Baddeley, Alan D. & Hitch, Graham J. (1974) Working memory. In G. Bower (ed.) *The Psychology of Learning and Motivation: Advances in Research and Theory*. Vol. 8. New York: Academic Press, 47–89.

Baek, Ok-kyung (2003) Chosŏn jŏngi yŏkkwanŭi ch'ungwŏne daehan goch'al. [A Study on the Recruitment of Translators in the Earlier Choson Dynasty]. *Chosŏnshidaesahakpo* [*The Society of the History of the Chosŏn Era*] 26, 76–114.

Baert, Patrick (2006) Role. In A. Harrington, B. I. Marshall & H.-P. Müller (eds) *Encyclopedia of Social Theory*. London/New York: Routledge, 524–526.

Bahadır, Şebnem (2011) Interpreting enactments: A new path for interpreting pedagogy. In C. Kainz, E. Prunč & R. Schögler (eds) *Modelling the Field of Community Interpreting: Questions of Methodology in Research and Training*. Wien/Berlin: LIT-Verlag, 177–210.

Baigorri-Jalón, Jesús (1998) En torno a Antoine Velleman, fundador de la Escuela de Ginebra. *Parallèles* 20, 9–30.

Baigorri Jalón, Jesús (2003) Guerras, extremos, intérpretes. In R. Muñoz Martín (ed.) *I AIETI: Actas del I Congreso Internacional de la Asociación Ibérica de Estudios de Traducción e Interpretación, Granada, 12–14 de febrero de 2003*. Vol. II. Granada: AIETI, 159–176.

Baigorri-Jalón, Jesús (2004) *Interpreters at the United Nations: A History* (Trans. Anne Barr). Salamanca: Ediciones Universidad de Salamanca.

Baigorri-Jalón, Jesús (2005) Conference interpreting in the First International Labor Conference (Washington, D. C., 1919). *Meta* 50 (3), 987–996.

Baigorri-Jalón, Jesús (2006) Perspectives on the history of interpretation: Research proposals. In G. Bastin & P. Bandia (eds) *Charting the Future of Translation History*. Ottawa: University of Ottawa Press, 101–110.

Baigorri Jalón, Jesús (2012) La lengua como arma: Intérpretes en la Guerra Civil Española o la enmarañada madeja de la geografía y la historia. In G. Payàs & J. M. Zavala (eds) *La Mediación Lingüístico-cultural en Tiempos de Guerra: Cruce de Miradas desde España y América*. Temuco: Universidad Católica de Temuco, 85–108.

Baigorri-Jalón, Jesús (2014) *From Paris to Nuremberg: The Birth of Conference Interpreting* (Trans. Holly Mikkelson & Barry S. Olsen). Amsterdam: John Benjamins.

Baigorri-Jalón, Jesus (2015) The history of the interpreting profession. In H. Mikkelson & R. Jourdenais (eds) *The Routledge Handbook of Interpreting*. London/New York: Routledge, 11–28.

Baixauli-Olmos, Lluis (2013) A description of interpreting in prisons: Mapping the setting through an ethical lens. In C. Schäffner, K. Kredens & Y. Fowler (eds) *Interpreting in a Changing Landscape: Selected Papers from Critical Link 6*. Amsterdam: John Benjamins, 45–60.

Bajo, María Teresa, Padilla, Francisca & Padilla, Presentación (2000) Comprehension processes in simultaneous interpreting. In A. Chesterman, N. Gallardo San Salvador & Y. Gambier (eds) *Translation in Context: Selected Papers from the EST Congress, Granada 1998*. Amsterdam: John Benjamins, 127–142.

Bajo, M. Teresa, Padilla, Presentación, Muñoz, Ricardo, Padilla, Francisca, Gómez, Carlos, Puerta, M. Carmen, Gonzalvo, Pilar & Macizo, Pedro (2001) Comprehension and memory processes in translation and interpreting. *Quaderns. Revista de traducció* 6, 27–31.

Baker, Catherine (2010) The care and feeding of linguists: The working environment of interpreters, translators and linguists during peacekeeping in Bosnia-Herzegovina. *War and Society* 29 (2), 154–175.

Baker, Mona (1993) Corpus linguistics and translation studies: Implications and applications. In M. Baker, G. Francis & E. Tognini-Bonelli (eds) *Text and Technology: In Honour of John Sinclair*. Amsterdam: John Benjamins, 233–250.

Baker, Mona (1997) Non-cognitive constraints and interpreter strategies in political interviews. In K. Simms (ed.) *Translating Sensitive Texts: Linguistic Aspects*. Amsterdam/Atlanta: Rodopi, 111–129.

Baker, Mona (ed.) (1998) *Routledge Encyclopedia of Translation Studies*. London/New York: Routledge.

Baker, Mona (2006) *Translation and Conflict: A Narrative Account*. London/New York: Routledge.

Baker, Mona (2009) Resisting state terror: Theorizing communities of activist translators and interpreters. In E. Bielsa & C. Hughes (eds) *Globalisation, Political Violence and Translation*. Basingstoke: Palgrave Macmillan, 222–242.

Baker, Mona (2010) Interpreters and translators in the war zone: Narrated and narrators. *The Translator* 16 (2), 197–222.

Baker, Mona (2013) Translation as an alternative space for political action. *Social Movement Studies: Journal of Social, Cultural and Political Protest* 12 (1), 23–47.

Baker, Mona & Saldanha, Gabriela (eds) (2009) *Routledge Encyclopedia of Translation Studies*. 2nd edn. London/New York: Routledge.

Baker-Shenk, Charlotte (ed.) (1990) *A Model Curriculum for Teachers of American Sign Language and Teachers of ASL/English Interpreting*. Silver Spring, MD: RID Publications.

Baker-Shenk, Charlotte, Bienvenu, M. J., Colonomos, Betty, Cokely, Dennis R., Kanda, Janice, Neumann-Solow, Sharon & Witter-Marithew, Anna (1988). *Sign Language Interpreter Training Curriculum*. Fredericton: University of New Brunswick.

Bakhtin, Mikhail (1981) *The Dialogic Imagination: Four Essays by M. Bakhtin* (Ed. Michael Holquist). Austin: University of Texas Press.

Bakti, Mária (2009) Speech disfluencies in simultaneous interpretation. In D. De Crom (ed.) *Translation and the (Trans)formation of Identities. Selected Papers of the CETRA Research Seminar in Translation Studies 2008*. www.arts.kuleuven.be/cetra/papers/files/bakti.pdf (accessed 20 July 2014).

Bakti, Mária & Bóna, Judit (2014) Source language-related erroneous stress placement in the target language output of simultaneous interpreters. *Interpreting* 16 (1), 34–48.

Balcı, Alev (2008) *Interpreter Involvement in Sermon Interpreting*. Minor dissertation, Universitat Rovira i Virgili.

Balcı, Sezai (2013) *Babıâli tercüme odası*. Istanbul: Libra Kitapçılık ve Yayıncılık.

Bale, Richard (2013) Undergraduate consecutive interpreting and lexical knowledge: The role of spoken corpora. *The Interpreter and Translator Trainer* 7 (1), 27–50.

Ball, Carolyn (2013) *Legacies and Legends: History of Interpreter Education from 1800 to the 21st Century.* Edmonton: Interpreting Consolidated.

Ballester, Ana & Jiménez Hurtado, Catalina (1992) Approaches to the teaching of interpreting: Mnemonic and analytic strategies. In C. Dollerup & A. Loddegaard (eds) *Teaching Translation and Interpreting: Training, Talent and Experience.* Amsterdam: John Benjamins, 237–243.

Balliu, Christian (2005) *Les Confidents du Sérail. Les Interprètes Français du Levant à l'Époque Classique.* Beyrouth: Université St. Joseph.

Balliu, Christian (2008) *Christopher Thiéry. Interprète de la République.* Bruxelles: Les Éditions du Hazard.

Balzani, Maurizio (1990) Le contact visuel en interprétation simultanée: resultats d'une expérience (Français–Italien). In L. Gran & C. Taylor (eds) *Aspects of Applied and Experimental Research on Conference Interpretation.* Udine: Campanotto, 93–100.

Bancroft, Marjory (2005) *The Interpreter's World Tour: An Environmental Scan of Standards of Practice for Interpreters.* Washington, DC: National Council on Interpreting in Health Care.

Bancroft, Marjory A., Bendana, Lola, Bruggeman, Jean & Feuerle, Lois (2013) Interpreting in the gray zone: Where community and legal interpreting intersect. *Translation & Interpreting* 5 (1), 94–113.

Bandia, Paul (2009) African tradition. In M. Baker & G. Saldanha (eds) *Routledge Encyclopedia of Translation Studies.* 2nd edn. London/New York: Routledge, 313–320.

Bandia, Paul (2010) Translation. In F. A. Irele & B. Jeyifo (eds) *The Oxford Encyclopedia of African Thought.* Vol. 2. Oxford/New York: Oxford University Press, 386–390.

Baraldi, Claudio (2012) Interpreting as dialogic mediation: The relevance of expansions. In C. Baraldi & L. Gavioli (eds) *Coordinating Participation in Dialogue Interpreting.* Amsterdam: John Benjamins, 297–326.

Baraldi, Claudio & Gavioli, Laura (2007) Dialogue interpreting as intercultural mediation: An analysis in healthcare multicultural settings. In M. Grein & E. Weigand (eds) *Dialogue and Culture.* Amsterdam: John Benjamins, 155–175.

Baraldi, Claudio & Gavioli, Laura (eds) (2012a) *Coordinating Participation in Dialogue Interpreting.* Amsterdam: John Benjamins.

Baraldi, Claudio & Gavioli, Laura (2012b) Understanding coordination in interpreter-mediated interaction. In C. Baraldi & L. Gavioli (eds) *Coordinating Participation in Dialogue Interpreting.* Amsterdam: John Benjamins, 1–22.

Barbizet, Jacques (1968) Les bases neuro-anatomiques de la genèse de la signification dans le langage oral. In R. Husson, J. Barbizet, J. Cauhépé, P. Debray, P. Laget & A. Sauvageot (eds) *Mécanismes Cérébraux du Langage Oral et Structure des Langues.* Paris: Masson, 51–61.

Barbizet, Jacques, Pergnier, Maurice & Seleskovitch, Danica (eds) (1981) *Comprendre le Langage. Actes du Colloque de Créteil 25–27 Septembre 1980.* Paris: Didier Erudition.

Barik, Henri C. (1971) A description of various types of omissions, additions and errors of translation encountered in simultaneous interpretation. *Meta* 16 (4), 199–210.

Barik, Henri C. (1973) Simultaneous interpretation: Temporal and quantitative data. *Language and Speech* 16 (3), 237–270.

Barik, Henri C. (1975) Simultaneous interpretation: Qualitative and linguistic data. *Language and Speech* 18 (3), 272–297.

Barik, Henri C. (1975/2002) Simultaneous interpretation: Qualitative and linguistic data. In F. Pöchhacker & M. Shlesinger (eds) *The Interpreting Studies Reader.* London/New York: Routledge, 79–91.

Barsky, Robert F. (1994) *Constructing a Productive Other: Discourse Theory and the Convention Refugee Hearing.* Amsterdam: John Benjamins.

Barsky, Robert F. (1996) The interpreter as intercultural agent in Convention refugee hearings. *The Translator* 2 (1), 45–63.

Bartłomiejczyk, Magdalena (2004) Simultaneous interpreting AB vs. BA from the interpreters' standpoint. In G. Hansen, K. Malmkjær & D. Gile (eds) *Claims, Changes and Challenges in Translation Studies.* Amsterdam: John Benjamins, 239–250.

Bartłomiejczyk, Magdalena (2006) Strategies of simultaneous interpreting and directionality. *Interpreting* 8 (2), 149–174.

Bartolini, Giulio (2009) General principles of International Humanitarian Law and their application to interpreters serving in conflict situations. http://aiic.net/page/3396/general-principles-of-international-humanitarian-law/lang/1 (accessed 10 April 2014).

Bashan, Eliezer (1993) Jewish interpreters in British Consular Service in the Middle East, 1581–1825 [in Hebrew]. *Sfunot* 6 (21), 41–69.

Beaton, Morven (2007) Interpreted ideologies in institutional discourse: The case of the European Parliament. *The Translator* 13 (2), 271–296.

Beaton-Thome, Morven (2010) Negotiating identities in the European Parliament: The role of simultaneous interpreting. In M. Baker, M. Olohan & M. Calzada Perez (eds) *Text and Context: Essays on Translation and Interpreting in Honour of Ian Mason*. Manchester: St. Jerome, 117–138.

Beaton-Thome, Morven (2013) What's in a word? Your *enemy combatant* is my *refugee*: The role of simultaneous interpreters in negotiating the lexis of Guantánamo in the European Parliament. *Journal of Language and Politics* 12 (3), 378–399.

Beaugrande, Robert-Alain de & Dressler, Wolfgang U. (1981) *Introduction to Text Linguistics*. London/New York: Longman.

Bechtel, William & Abrahamsen, Adele (2002) *Connectionism and the Mind: Parallel Processing, Dynamics, and Evolution in Networks*. Malden/Oxford: Blackwell.

Becker, Howard S. (1962/1976) The nature of a profession. In: H. S. Becker, *Sociological Work: Method and Substance*. New Brunswick, NJ: Transaction Publishers, 87–103.

Beeby, Allison, Rodríguez Inés, Patricia & Sánchez-Gijón, Pilar (eds) (2009) *Corpus Use and Translating: Corpus Use for Learning to Translate and Learning Corpus Use to Translate*. Amsterdam: John Benjamins.

Bell, Lanny (1973) Once more the *a.w*: "Interpreters"or "foreigners"? *Newsletter of the American Research Center in Egypt* 87, 33.

Bell, Lanny (1976) *Interpreters and Egyptianized Nubians in Ancient Egyptian Foreign Policy: Aspects of the History of Egypt and Nubia*. PhD thesis, University of Pennsylvania.

Bendazzoli, Claudio (2009) Theatre and creativity in interpreter training. In M. I. Fernández García, M.-L. Zucchiatti & M. G. Biscu (eds) *L'Esperienza Teatrale nella Formazione dei Mediatori Linguistici e Culturali*. Bologna: Bononia University Press, 153–164.

Bendazzoli, Claudio (2010a) *Corpora e Interpretazione Simultanea*. Bologna: Asterisco. http://amsacta.unibo.it/2897/ (accessed 5 December 2013).

Bendazzoli, Claudio (2010b) The European Parliament as a source of material for research into simultaneous interpreting: Advantages and limitations. In L. N. Zybatow (ed.) *Translationswissenschaft – Stand und Perspektiven. Innsbrucker Ringvorlesungen zur Translationswissenschaft VI*. Frankfurt: Peter Lang, 51–68.

Bendazzoli, Claudio (2012) From international conferences to machine-readable corpora and back: An ethnographic approach to simultaneous interpreter-mediated communicative events. In F. Straniero Sergio & C. Falbo (eds) *Breaking Ground in Corpus-Based Interpreting Studies*. Frankfurt: Peter Lang, 91–117.

Bendazzoli, Claudio, Sandrelli, Annalisa & Russo, Mariachiara (2011) Disfluencies in simultaneous interpreting: A corpus-based analysis. In A. Kruger, K. Wallmach & J. Munday (eds) *Corpus-based Translation Studies: Research and Applications*. London/New York: Continuum, 282–306.

Benmaman, Virginia (1997) Legal interpreting by any other name is still legal interpreting. In S. E. Carr, R. Roberts, A. Dufour & D. Steyn (eds) *The Critical Link: Interpreters in the Community*. Amsterdam: John Benjamins, 179–190.

Bentley-Sassaman, Jessica (2009) The experiential learning theory and interpreter education. *International Journal of Interpreter Education* 1, 62–67.

Berezhkov, Valentin M. (1993) *Kak ja stal perevodtschikom Stalina*. Moskva: DEM.

Berezhkov, Valentin M. (1994) *At Stalin's Side: His Interpreter's Memoirs from the October Revolution to the Fall of the Dictator's Empire* (Trans. S. V. Mikheyev). New York: Carol Publishing Group.

Berge, Sigrid Slettebakk (2014) Social and private speech in an interpreted meeting of deafblind persons. *Interpreting* 16 (1), 82–106.

Berge, Sigrid Slettebakk & Raanes, Eli (2013) Coordinating the chain of utterances: An analysis of communicative flow and turn taking in an interpreted group dialogue for Deaf-Blind persons. *Sign Language Studies* 13 (3), 350–371.

Berk-Seligson, Susan (1988) The impact of politeness in witness testimony: The influence of the court interpreter. *Multilingua* 7 (4), 411–439.

Berk-Seligson, Susan (1990) *The Bilingual Courtroom: Court Interpreters in the Judicial Process.* Chicago: University of Chicago Press.

Berk-Seligson, Susan (1999) The impact of court interpreting on the coerciveness of leading questions. *Forensic Linguistics* 6 (1), 30–56.

Berk-Seligson, Susan (2008) Judicial systems in contact: Access to justice and the right to interpreting/translating services among the Quichua of Ecuador. *Interpreting* 10 (1), 9–33.

Berk-Seligson, Susan (2009) *Coerced confessions: The Discourse of Bilingual Police Interrogations.* Berlin/New York: Mouton de Gruyter.

Berk-Seligson, Susan (2011) Negotiation and communicative accommodation in bilingual police interrogations: A critical interactional sociolinguistic perspective. *International Journal of the Sociology of Language* 207, 29–58.

Bernardini, Silvia & Castagnoli, Sara (2008) Corpora for translator education and translation practice. In E. Yuste (ed.) *Topics in Language Resources for Translation and Localisation.* Amsterdam: John Benjamins, 39–55.

Bernstein, Basil (1990) *The Structuring of Pedagogic Discourse: Class, Codes and Control.* London: Routledge.

Berridge, Geoff R. (2004) Notes on the origins of the diplomatic corps: Constantinople in the 1620s (Clingendael Discussion Paper in Diplomacy 92). www.clingendael.nl/publications/2004/20040500_cli_paper_dip_issue92.pdf (accessed 29 September 2014).

Berthier, Annie (1997) Turquerie ou turcologie? L'effort de traduction des langues au XVIIe siècle, d'après la collection des manuscrits conservée à la Bibliotheque nationale de France. In F. Hitzel (ed.) *Istanbul et les Langues Orientales.* Istanbul: Isis, 283–317.

Bevilacqua, Lorenzo (2009) The position of the verb in Germanic languages and simultaneous interpretation. *The Interpreters' Newsletter* 14, 1–31.

Bialystok, Ellen (2009) Bilingualism: The good, the bad, and the indifferent. *Bilingualism: Language and Cognition* 12 (1), 3–11.

Biber, Douglas (1993) Representativeness in corpus design. *Literary and Linguistic Computing* 8 (4), 243–257.

Biber, Douglas (2012) Register and discourse analysis. In J. P. Gee & M. Handford (eds) *The Routledge Handbook of Discourse Analysis.* London/New York: Routledge, 191–208.

Bickman, Leonard & Rog, Debra J. (2009) Applied research design: A practical approach. In L. Bickman & D. J. Rog (eds) *Handbook of Applied Social Research Methods.* 2nd edn. Thousand Oaks/London/New Delhi: Sage, 3–43.

Biddle, Bruce J. (1986) Recent developments in role theory. *Annual Review of Sociology* 12, 67–92.

Bienvenu, M. J. & Colonomos, Betty (1992) Relay interpreting in the 90s. In L. Swabey (ed.) *The Challenge of the 90s: New Standards in Interpreter Education. Proceedings of the Eighth National Convention, Conference of Interpreter Trainers, October 5–7, 1990, Pomona, California.* Northridge, CA: Conference of Interpreter Trainers, 69–80.

Binder, Pauline, Borné, Yan, Johnsdotter, Sara & Essén, Birgitta (2012) Shared language is essential: Communication in a multiethnic obstetric care setting. *Journal of Health Communication* 17 (10), 1171–1186.

Birdwhistell, Ray L. (1970) *Kinesics and Context: Essays on Body Motion Communication.* Philadelphia: University of Pennsylvania Press.

Bischoff, Alexander (2012) Do language barriers increase inequalities? Do interpreters decrease inequalities? In D. Ingleby, A. Chiarenza, W. Devillé & I. Kotsioni (eds) *COST Series on Health and Diversity. Volume 2: Inequalities in Health Care for Migrants and Ethnic Minorities.* Philadelphia, PA: Garant, 128–143.

Bischoff, Alexander, Kurth, Elisabeth & Henley, Alix (2012) Staying in the middle: A qualitative study of health care interpreters' perception of their work. *Interpreting* 14 (1), 1–22.

Bischoff, Alexander, Bovier, Patrick A., Rrustemi, Isah, Gariazzo, Françoise, Eytan, Ariel & Loutan, Louis (2003) Language barriers between nurses and asylum seekers: Their impact on symptom reporting and referral. *Social Science & Medicine* 57 (3), 503–512.

Björk Brämberg, Elisabeth & Dahlberg, Karin (2013) Interpreters in cross-cultural interviews: A three-way co-construction of data. *Qualitative Health Research* 23, 241–247.

Blakemore, Diane (1987) *Semantic Constraints on Relevance*. Oxford: Blackwell.

Blakemore, Diane & Gallai, Fabrizio (2014) Discourse markers in free indirect style and interpreting. *Journal of Pragmatics* 60, 106–120.

Blasco Mayor, María J. & Jiménez Ivars, Amparo (2007) E-Learning for interpreting. *Babel* 53 (4), 292–302.

Blom, Frans (1928) Gaspar Antonio Chi, Interpreter. *American Anthropologist* 30 (2), 250–262.

Blommaert, Jan (2001) Investigating narrative inequality: African asylum seekers' stories in Belgium. *Discourse & Society* 12 (4), 413–449.

Blommaert, Jan (2005) *Discourse: A Critical Introduction*. Cambridge: Cambridge University Press.

Blommaert, Jan (2009) Language, asylum and the national order. *Current Anthropology* 50 (4), 415–441.

Blum-Kulka, Shoshana (1986) Shifts of cohesion and coherence in translation. In J. House & S. Blum-Kulka (eds) *Interlingual and Intercultural Communication: Discourse and Cognition in Translation and Second Language Acquisition Studies*. Tübingen: Gunter Narr, 17–35.

Bodrova, Tatiana (2000) *La Traductologie Russe (Théorie, Pratique et Enseignement) – ses Apports, ses Limites*. Villeneuve d'Ascq: Presses Universitaires du Septentrion.

Boéri, Julie (2008) A narrative account of the Babels vs. Naumann controversy: Competing perspectives on activism in conference interpreting. *The Translator* 14 (1), 21–50.

Boéri, Julie (2012) Translation/interpreting politics and praxis: The impact of political principles on Babels' interpreting practice. In Ş. Susam-Sarajeva & L. Pérez-González (eds) *Non-Professionals Translating and Interpreting: Participatory and Engaged Perspectives*. Special Issue of *The Translator* 18 (2), 269–290.

Boéri, Julie (2015) Key internal players in the development of the interpreting profession. In H. Mikkelson & R. Jourdenais (eds) *The Routledge Handbook of Interpreting*. London/New York: Routledge, 29–44.

Boéri, Julie & de Manuel Jerez, Jesús (2011) From training skilled conference interpreters to educating reflective citizens: A case study of the Marius action research project. In C. Maier & M. Baker (eds) *Ethics and the Curriculum: Critical perspectives*. Special Issue of *The Interpreter and Translator Trainer* 5 (1), 41–64.

Boéri, Julie & Maier, Carol (eds) (2010) *Compromiso Social y Traducción/Interpretación – Translation/Interpreting and Social Activism*. Granada: ECOS.

Bögner, Diana, Brewin, Chris & Herlihy, Jane (2010) Refugees' experiences of Home Office interviews: A qualitative study on the disclosure of sensitive personal information. *Journal of Ethnic and Migration Studies* 36 (3), 519–535.

Bolden, Galina (2000) Toward understanding practices of medical interpreting: Interpreters' involvement in history taking. *Discourse Studies* 2 (4), 387–419.

Bomfim-Capellani, Amelia (1987) *Apprendre l'Interprétation de Conférence – La Compréhension et l'Intelligibilité des Discours comme Guides et Garants de l'Apprentissage*. Thèse de doctorat, Université Sorbonne Nouvelle – Paris 3.

Bondas, Irina (2013) *Theaterdolmetschen: Phänomen, Funktionen, Perspektiven*. Berlin: Frank & Timme.

Bontempo, Karen & Malcolm, Karen (2012) An ounce of prevention is worth a pound of cure: Educating interpreters about the risk of vicarious trauma in healthcare settings. In L. Swabey & K. Malcolm (eds) *In our Hands: Educating Healthcare Interpreters*. Washington, DC: Gallaudet University Press, 105–130.

Bontempo, Karen & Napier, Jemina (2009) Getting it right from the start: Program admission testing of signed language interpreters. In C. V. Angelelli & H. E. Jacobson (eds) *Testing and Assessment in Translation and Interpreting Studies*. Amsterdam: John Benjamins, 247–295.

Bontempo, Karen & Napier, Jemina (2011) Evaluating emotional stability as a predictor of interpreter competence and aptitude for interpreting. *Interpreting* 13 (1), 85–105.

Bontempo, Karen, Napier, Jemina, Hayes, Laurence & Brashear, Vicki (2014) Does personality matter? An international study of sign language interpreter disposition. *Translation & Interpreting* 6 (1), 23–46.

Boomer, Donald S. & Laver, John D. (1973) Slips of the tongue. In V. Fromkin (ed.) *Speech Errors as Linguistic Evidence*. The Hague: Mouton, 120–131.

Borromeo, Elisabetta (2007) *Voyageurs Occidentaux dans l'Empire Ottoman, 1600–1644: Inventaire des Récits et Études sur les Itinéraires, les Monuments Remarqués et les Populations Rencontrées (Roumélie, Cyclades, Crimée)*. Paris/Istanbul: Maisonneuve & Larose.

Böser, Ursula (2013) "So tell me what happened!": Interpreting the free recall segment of the investigative interview. *Translation and Interpreting Studies* 8 (1), 112–136.

Bosworth, Clifford Edmund (2000) Tarjuman. In P. J. Bearman, T. Bianquis, C. E. Bosworth, E. van Donzel & W. P. Heinrichs (eds) *Encyclopaedia of Islam*. Vol. 10. Leiden: Brill, 236–238.

Bot, Hanneke (2005) *Dialogue Interpreting in Mental Health*. Amsterdam/New York: Rodopi.

Bot, Hanneke & Verrept, Hans (2013) Role issues in the Low Countries: Interpreting in mental healthcare in the Netherlands and Belgium. In C. Schäffner, K. Kredens & Y. Fowler (eds) *Interpreting in a Changing Landscape: Selected Papers from Critical Link 6*. Amsterdam: John Benjamins, 117–131.

Bot, Hanneke & Wadensjö, Cecilia (2004) The presence of a third party: A dialogical view on interpreter-assisted treatment. In B. Drosdek & J. Wilson (eds) *Broken Spirits: The Treatment of Traumatized Asylum Seekers, Refugees, War and Torture Victims*. New York: Brunner-Routledge, 355–378.

Boudreault, Patrick (2005) Deaf interpreters. In T. Janzen (ed.) *Topics in Signed Language Interpreting*. Amsterdam: John Benjamins, 323–356.

Bourdieu, Pierre (1977) *Outline of a Theory of Practice* (Trans. Richard Nice). Cambridge: Cambridge University Press.

Bourdieu, Pierre (1990) *The Logic of Practice* (Trans. Richard Nice). London: Polity Press.

Bourlard, Hervé, Dines, John, Magimai-Doss, Mathew, Garner, Philip N., Imseng, David, Motlicek, Petr, Liang, Hui, Saheer, Lakshmi & Valente, Fabio (2011) Current trends in multilingual speech processing. *Sādhanā* 36 (5), 885–915.

Bovee, Nicholas & Stewart, Jeff (2009) The utility of shadowing. In A. M. Stoke (ed.) *JALT2008 Conference Proceedings*. Tokyo: Japan Association for Language Teaching, 888–900. http://jalt-publications.org/recentpdf/proceedings/2008/E158.pdf (accessed 7 January 2014).

Bowen, David & Bowen, Margareta (1984) *Steps to Consecutive Interpretation*. Washington, DC: Pen & Booth.

Bowen, Margareta (1994) Negotiations to end the Spanish–American War. In M. Snell-Hornby, F. Pöchhacker & K. Kaindl (eds) *Translation Studies: An Interdiscipline*. Amsterdam: John Benjamins, 73–81.

Bowen, Margareta [with D. Bowen, F. Kaufmann & I. Kurz] (1995) Interpreters and the making of history. In J. Delisle & J. Woodsworth (eds) *Translators through History*. Amsterdam: John Benjamins, 245–273.

Bowen, Margareta (2012) Interpreters and the making of history. In J. Delisle & J. Woodsworth (eds) *Translators through History*. Rev. edn. Amsterdam: John Benjamins, 247–282.

Bower, Kathryn (2013) Stress and burnout in video relay service interpreting. *RID Views* 30, 18–19.

Bower, Kathryn (2015) Stress and burnout in VRS interpreting. *Journal of Interpretation* 24 (1), Art. 2.

Bowker, Geoffrey C. & Star, Susan Leigh (2000) *Sorting Things Out: Classification and its Consequences*. Cambridge, MA/London: MIT Press.

Bowker, Lynne & Pearson, Jennifer (2002) *Working with Specialized Language: A Practical Guide to Using Corpora*. London/New York: Routledge.

Braun, Sabine (2004) *Kommunikation unter widrigen Umständen? Fallstudien zu einsprachigen und gedolmetschten Videokonferenzen*. Tübingen: Gunter Narr.

Braun, Sabine (2007) Interpreting in small-group bilingual videoconferences: Challenges and adaptation. *Interpreting* 9 (1), 21–46.

Braun, Sabine (2013) Keep your distance? Remote interpreting in legal proceedings: A critical assessment of a growing practice. *Interpreting* 15 (2), 200–228.

Braun, Sabine (2015) Remote interpreting. In H. Mikkelson & R. Jourdenais (eds) *The Routledge Handbook of Interpreting*. London/New York: Routledge, 352–367.

Braun, Sabine & Slater, Catherine (2014) Populating a 3D virtual learning environment for interpreting students with bilingual dialogues to support situated learning in an institutional context. *The Interpreter and Translator Trainer* 8 (3), 469–485.

Braun, Sabine & Taylor, Judith L. (eds) (2012a) *Videoconference and Remote Interpreting in Criminal Proceedings*. Cambridge/Antwerp: Intersentia.

Braun, Sabine & Taylor, Judith L. (2012b) Video-mediated interpreting in criminal proceedings: Two European surveys. In S. Braun & J. Taylor (eds) *Videoconference and Remote Interpreting in Criminal Proceedings*. Cambridge/Antwerp: Intersentia, 69–98.

Braun, Sabine & Taylor, Judith L. (eds) (2015) *Advances in Videoconferencing and Interpreting in Legal Proceedings*. Cambridge/Antwerp: Intersentia.

Braun, Sabine, Slater, Catherine, Gittins, Robert, Ritsos, Panagiotis D. & Roberts, Jonathan C. (2013) Interpreting in Virtual Reality: designing and developing a 3D virtual world to prepare interpreters and their clients for professional practice. In D. Kiraly, S. Hansen-Schirra & K. Maksymski (eds) *New Prospects and Perspectives for Educating Language Mediators*. Tübingen: Gunter Narr, 93–120.

Braun, Susanne & Clarici, Andrea (1996) Inaccuracy for numerals in simultaneous interpretation: Neurolinguistic and neuropsychological perspectives. *The Interpreters' Newsletter* 7, 85–102.

Bregman, Marc (1982) The Darshan: Preacher and teacher of Talmudic times. *The Melton Journal* 14, 3–48.

Brennan, Mary (1999) Signs of injustice. *The Translator* 5 (2), 221–246.

Brennan, Mary & Brown, Richard (1997) *Equality before the Law: Deaf People's Access to Justice*. Durham: Deaf Studies Research Unit, University of Durham.

Brislin, Richard W. (ed.) (1976) *Translation: Applications and Research*. New York: Gardner Press.

Brislin, Richard W. (1980) Expanding the role of the interpreter to include multiple facets of intercultural communication. *International Journal of Intercultural Relations* 4, 137–148.

Brisset, Camille, Leanza, Yvan & Laforest, Karine (2013) Working with interpreters in health care: A systematic review and meta-ethnography of qualitative studies. *Patient Education and Counseling* 91 (2), 131–140.

Broadbent, Donald E. (1958) *Perception and Communication*. London: Pergamon Press.

Brodman, James W. (2011) Captives or prisoners: Society and obligation in medieval Iberia. *Anuario de Historia de la Iglesia* 20, 201–219.

Brounéus, Karen (2010) The trauma of truth telling: Effects of witnessing in the Rwandan *gacaca* courts on psychological health. *Journal of Conflict Resolution* 54, 408–437.

Brown, Gillian & Yule, George (1983) *Discourse Analysis*. Cambridge: Cambridge University Press.

Brown, Penelope & Levinson, Stephen C. (1987) *Politeness: Some Universals of Language Usage*. Cambridge: Cambridge University Press.

Brown Kurz, Kim & Caldwell Langer, E. (2004) Student perspectives on educational interpreting: Twenty deaf and hard of hearing students offer insights and suggestions. In E. A. Winston (ed.) *Educational Interpreting: How It Can Succeed*. Washington, DC: Gallaudet University Press, 9–47.

Browning, Anne H., Bugbee, Alan C. Jr. & Mullins, Meredith A. (eds) (1996) *Certification: A NOCA Handbook*. Washington, DC: National Organization for Competency Assurance.

Brunson, Jeremy L. (2011) *Video Relay Service Interpreting: The Intricacies of Sign Language Access*. Washington, DC: Gallaudet University Press.

Buck, Vincent (2002) One world, one language? http://aiic.net/page/732/one-world-one-language (accessed 24 February 2015).

Bühler, Hildegund (1985) Conference interpreting: A multichannel communication phenomenon. *Meta* 30 (1), 49–54.

Bühler, Hildegund (1986) Linguistic (semantic) and extra-linguistic (pragmatic) criteria for the evaluation of conference interpretation and interpreters. *Multilingua* 5 (4), 231–235.

Bührig, Kristin, Kliche, Ortrun, Meyer, Bernd & Pawlack, Birte (2012) The corpus "Interpreting in Hospitals": Possible applications for research and communication training. In T. Schmidt & K. Wörner (eds) *Multilingual Corpora and Multilingual Corpus Analysis*. Amsterdam: John Benjamins, 305–315.

Bülow-Møller, Anne Marie (1999) Existential problems: On the processing of irrealis in simultaneous interpreting. *Interpreting* 4 (2), 145–167.

Bulut, Alev & Kurultay, Turgay (2001) Interpreters-in-aid at disasters: Community interpreting in the process of disaster management *The Translator* 7 (2), 249–263.

Burkart, Günter (2006) Professions and professionalization. In A. Harrington, B. I. Marshall & H.-P. Müller (eds) *Encyclopedia of Social Theory*. London/New York: Routledge, 470–471.

Butler, Yuko Goto (2013) Bilingualism/multilingualism and second-language acquisition. In T. K. Bhatia & W. C. Ritchie (eds) *The Handbook of Bilingualism and Multilingualism*. 2nd edn. Oxford/Malden, MA: Blackwell, 109–136.

Butow, Phyllis N., Goldstein, David, Bell, Melaine L., Sze, Ming, Aldridge, Lynley J., Abdo, Sarah, Tanious, Michelle, Dong, Skye, Iedema, Rick, Vardy, Janette, Ashgari, Ray, Hui, Rina & Eisenbruch, Maurice (2011) Interpretation in consultations with immigrant patients with cancer: How accurate is it? *Journal of Clinical Oncology* 29 (20), 2801–2807.

Cáceres Würsig, Ingrid (2004) Breve historia de la secretaría de interpretación de lenguas. *Meta* 49 (3), 609–628.

Cáceres Würsig, Ingrid (2012) The jeunes de langues in the eighteenth century: Spain's first diplomatic interpreters on the European model. *Interpreting* 14 (2), 127–144.

Caflisch, Artur (1964) *Le professeur Antoine Velleman: 1875–1962* (Transl. from Romansh by Gabriel Mützenberg). Geneva: La Sirène.

Calhoun, Craig (2002) *Dictionary of the Social Sciences*. New York: Oxford University Press.

Caminade, Monique & Pym, Anthony (1998) Translator-training institutions. In M. Baker (ed.) *Encyclopedia of Translation Studies*, London/New York: Routledge, 280–285.

Carabelli, Angela (1999) Multimedia technologies for the use of interpreters and translators. *The Interpreters' Newsletter* 9, 149–155.

Carr, Silvana E., Roberts, Roda P., Dufour, Aideen & Steyn, Dini (eds) (1997) *The Critical Link: Interpreters in the Community. Papers from the 1st International Conference on Interpreting in Legal, Health and Social Service Settings, Geneva Park, Canada, 1–4 June 1995*. Amsterdam: John Benjamins.

Carroll, John B. (1966) An experiment in evaluating the quality of translations. *Mechanical Translation* 9, 55–66.

Carroll, John B. (1978) Linguistic abilities in translators and interpreters. In D. Gerver & H. W. Sinaiko (eds) *Language Interpretation and Communication*. New York/London: Plenum Press, 119–129.

Carston, Robyn (2002) *Thoughts and Utterances: The Pragmatics of Explicit Communication*. Oxford: Blackwell.

Carver, Ronald P. (1973) Effects of increasing the rate of speech presentation upon comprehension. *Journal of Educational Psychology* 65 (1), 118–126.

Castiglione, Frank (2014) 'Levantine' dragomans in nineteenth century Istanbul: The Pisanis, the British, and issues of subjecthood. *Journal of Ottoman Studies* 54, 169–195.

Castillo, Pedro (2015) Interpreting for the mass media. In H. Mikkelson & R. Jourdenais (eds) *The Routledge Handbook of Interpreting*. London/New York: Routledge, 280–301.

Cattaneo, Elena (2004) *Idiomatic Expressions in Conference Interpreting*. Graduation thesis, SSLMIT, Università degli Studi di Bologna, Sede di Forlì.

Cazden, Courtney B. (2001) *Classroom Discourse: The Language of Teaching and Learning*. Portsmouth, NH: Heinemann.

Cecot, Michela (2001) Pauses in simultaneous interpreting: A contrastive analysis of professional interpreters' performances. *The Interpreters' Newsletter* 11, 63–85.

Cencini, Marco (2002) On the importance of an encoding standard for corpus-based interpreting studies: Extending the TEI scheme. *CULT2K*. Special Issue of *InTRALinea*. www.intralinea. org/specials/article/1678 (accessed 26 November 2012).

Cencini, Marco & Aston, Guy (2002) Resurrecting the corp(us/se): Towards an encoding standard for interpreting data. In G. Garzone & M. Viezzi (eds) *Interpreting in the 21st Century: Challenges and Opportunities*. Amsterdam: John Benjamins, 47–62.

Čeňková, Ivana (2008) Retour et relais – un défi et une réalité quotidienne pour les interprètes de conférence au sein des institutions Européennes. *Forum* 6 (2), 1–21.

Čeňková, Ivana (2010) Sight translation: Prima vista. In Y. Gambier & L. van Doorslaer (eds) *Handbook of Translation Studies*. Vol. 1. Amsterdam: John Benjamins, 320–323.

Cervato, Emanuela & de Ferra, Donatella (1995) Interpr-It: A computerised self-access course for beginners in interpreting. *Perspectives: Studies in Translatology* 2, 191–204.

Chabasse, Catherine & Kader, Stephanie (2014) Putting interpreting admissions exams to the test. The MA KD Germersheim Project. *Interpreting* 16 (1), 19–33.

Chafe, Wallace L. (1982) Integration and involvement in speaking, writing, and oral literature. In D. Tannen (ed.) S*poken and Written Language: Exploring Orality and Literacy*. Norwood: Ablex, 35–53.

Chan, Janet (1997) *Changing Police Culture: Policing in a Multicultural Society*. Cambridge/New York: Cambridge University Press.

Chan, Sin-wai (ed.) (2015) *Routledge Encyclopedia of Translation Technology*. London/New York: Routledge.

Chang, Chia-chien & Schallert, Diane L. (2007) The impact of directionality on Chinese/English simultaneous interpreting. *Interpreting* 9 (2), 137–176.

Chang, Chia-chien & Wu, Michelle Min-chia (2014) Non-native English at international conferences: Perspectives from Chinese–English conference interpreters in Taiwan. *Interpreting* 16 (2), 169–190.

Chang, Feng-lan (2009) Do interpreters need to sound like broadcasters? *Compilation and Translation Review* 2 (1), 101–150.

Chapelle, Carol A. (ed.) (2013) *The Encyclopedia of Applied Linguistics*. 10 vols. Oxford: Wiley-Blackwell.

Chen, Nian-Shing & Ko, Leong (2010) An online synchronous test for professional interpreters. *Journal of Educational Technology & Society* 13 (2), 153–165.

Chen, Yan (2010) *The Effects of Note-taking Language Choice in Consecutive Interpreting* [in Chinese]. Unpublished master's thesis, Shanghai International Studies University.

Chernov, Ghelly V. (1969) Sinhronnyj perevod: recevaja kompressija – lingvisticeskaja problema [Simultaneous interpreting: Linguistic problems of speech compression]. *Tetradi Perevodchika* 6, 52–65.

Chernov, Ghelly V. (1971) Eksperimentalnaya proverka odnoi modeli [Experimental testing of a model]. *Tetradi Perevodchika* 8, 55–61.

Chernov, Ghelly V. (1975) Kommunikativnaya situatsiya sinkhronnogo perevoda i izbytochnost soobshcheniya [The communicative situation of simultaneous interpreting and redundant messages]. *Tetradi Perevodchika* 12, 83–100.

Chernov, Ghelly V. (1978) *Teoriya i Praktika Sinkhronnogo Perevoda* [*Theory and Practice of Simultaneous Interpretation*]. Moscow: Mezhdunarodnye otnosheniya.

Chernov, Ghelly V. (1979/2002) Semantic aspects of psycholinguistic research in simultaneous interpretation. In F. Pöchhacker & M. Shlesinger (eds) *The Interpreting Studies Reader*. London/New York: Routledge, 98–109.

Chernov, Ghelly V. (1987) *Osnovy Sinkhronnogo Perevoda* [*Fundamentals of Simultaneous Interpreting*]. Moscow: Vysshaya shkola.

Chernov, Ghelly V. (1994) Message redundancy and message anticipation in simultaneous interpreting. In S. Lambert & B. Moser-Mercer (eds) *Bridging the Gap: Empirical Research in Simultaneous Interpretation*. Amsterdam: John Benjamins, 139–153.

Chernov, Ghelly V. (2004) *Inference and Anticipation in Simultaneous Interpreting: A Probability-Prediction Model* (Ed. Robin Setton & Adelina Hild). Amsterdam: John Benjamins.

Cherry, Colin (1953) Some experiments on the recognition of speech with one and two ears. *Journal of the Acoustic Society of America* 25 (5), 975–979.

Chesterman, Andrew (1993) From "is"to "ought": Laws, norms and strategies in translation studies. *Target* 5 (1), 1–20.

Chesterman, Andrew (1997a) Ethics of translation. In M. Snell-Hornby, Z. Jettmarová & K. Kaindl (eds) *Translation and Intercultural Communication. Selected Papers from the EST Congress, Prague 1995*. Amsterdam: John Benjamins, 147–157.

Chesterman, Andrew (1997b) *Memes of Translation: The Spread of Ideas in Translation Theory*. Amsterdam: John Benjamins.

Chesterman, Andrew (2001) Proposal for a Hieronymic Oath. *The Translator* 7 (2), 139–154.

Chesterman, Andrew & Arrojo, Rosemary (2000) Shared ground in translation studies. *Target* 12 (1) 99–127.

Cheung, Andrew K. F. (2003) Does accent matter? The impact of accent in simultaneous interpretation into Mandarin and Cantonese on perceived performance quality and listener satisfaction level. In A. Collados Aís, M. M. Fernández Sánchez & D. Gile (eds) *La Evaluación de la Calidad en Interpretación: Investigación*. Granada: Comares, 85–96.

Cheung, Andrew Kay-Fan (2007) The effectiveness of summary training in consecutive interpreting delivery. *Forum* 5 (2), 1–22.

Cheung, Andrew Kay-fan (2009) Numbers in simultaneous interpreting: An experimental study. *Forum* 7 (2), 61–88.

Cheung, Andrew K. F. (2012) The use of reported speech by court interpreters in Hong Kong. *Interpreting* 14 (1), 72–90.

Cheung, Andrew K. F. (2013) Non-native accents and simultaneous interpreting quality perceptions. *Interpreting* 15 (1), 25–47.

Cheung, Martha (2005) "To translate" means "to exchange"? A new interpretation of the earliest Chinese attempts to define translation ("*fanyi*"). *Target* 17 (1), 27–48.

Chi, Michelene T. H. (2006) Two approaches to the study of experts' characteristics. In K. A. Ericsson, N. Charness, P. J. Feltovich & R. R. Hoffman (eds) *The Cambridge Handbook of Expertise and Expert Performance*. Cambridge: Cambridge University Press, 21–30.

CHIA (2002) *California Standards for Healthcare Interpreters: Ethical Principles, Protocols, and Guidance on Roles and Interventions*. Sacramento, CA: California Healthcare Interpreters Association.

Chiang, Yung-nan (2009) Foreign language anxiety in Taiwanese student interpreters. *Meta* 54 (3), 605–621.

Chiang, Yung-nan (2010) Foreign language anxiety and student interpreters' learning outcomes: Implications for the theory and measurement of interpretation learning anxiety. *Meta* 55 (3), 589–601.

Chiaro, Delia (2002) Linguistic mediation on Italian television: When the interpreter is not an interpreter. A case study. In G. Garzone & M. Viezzi (eds) *Interpreting in the 21st Century: Challenges and Opportunities*. Amsterdam: John Benjamins, 215–225.

Chiaro, Delia & Nocella, Giuseppe (2004) Interpreters' perception of linguistic and non-linguistic factors affecting quality: A survey through the World Wide Web. *Meta* 49 (2), 278–293.

Chincotta, Dino & Underwood, Geoffrey (1998) Simultaneous interpreters and the effect of concurrent articulation on immediate memory: A bilingual digit span study. *Interpreting* 3 (1), 1–20.

Cho, Jinhyun & Roger, Peter (2010) Improving interpreting performance through theatrical training. *The Interpreter and Translator Trainer* 4 (2), 151–171.

Choi, Jungwha (1986) *L'Interprétation Consécutive Coréen-français du Point de Vue de son Enseignement*. Thèse de doctorat, Université Sorbonne Nouvelle – Paris 3.

Choi, Jungwha (2007) Study on job satisfaction and directions for the training of conference interpreters. *Forum* 5 (2), 23–38.

Chŏng, Ok-cha (1993) *Chosŏnhugi yŏksaŭi ihae* [*Understanding History during the Second Half of Chosŏn*]. Seoul: Iljisa.

Chŏng, Ok-cha (2003) *Chosŏnhugi junginmunhwa yeongu* [*Study on the Jungin Culture during the Second Half of Chosŏn*]. Seoul: Ilchisa.

Christoffels, Ingrid K. (2004) *Cognitive Studies in Simultaneous Interpreting*. Ipskamp/Enschede: PrintPartners.

Christoffels, Ingrid K. (2006) Listening while talking: The retention of prose under articulatory suppression in relation to simultaneous interpreting. *European Journal of Cognitive Psychology* 18 (2), 206–220.

Christoffels, Ingrid K. & de Groot, Annette M. B. (2004) Components of simultaneous interpreting: Comparing interpreting with shadowing and paraphrasing. *Bilingualism: Language and Cognition* 7 (3), 227–240.

Christoffels, Ingrid K. & de Groot, Annette M. B. (2005) Simultaneous interpreting: A cognitive perspective. In J. F. Kroll & A. M. B. de Groot (eds) *Handbook of Bilingualism: Psycholinguistic Approaches*. New York: Oxford University Press, 454–479.

Christoffels, Ingrid K., de Groot, Annette M. B. & Kroll, Judith F. (2006) Memory and language skills in simultaneous interpreters: The role of expertise and language proficiency. *Journal of Memory and Language* 54 (3), 324–345.

Christoffels, Ingrid K., De Groot, Annette M. B. & Waldorp, Lourens J. (2003) Basic skills in a complex task: A graphical model relating memory and lexical retrieval to simultaneous interpreting. *Bilingualism: Language and Cognition* 6 (3), 201–211.

Çiçek, Kemal (2002) Interpreters of the Court in the Ottoman Empire as seen from the Sharia Court Records of Cyprus. *Islamic Law and Society* 9 (1), 1–15.

Cirillo, Letizia (2012) Managing affective communication in triadic exchanges: Interpreters' zero-renditions and non-renditions in doctor–patient talk. In C. J. Kellett Bidoli (ed.) *Interpreting across Genres: Multiple Research Perspectives.* Trieste: Edizioni Università di Trieste, 102–124.

Class, Barbara & Moser-Mercer, Barbara (2013) Training conference interpreter trainers with technology – a virtual reality. In O. García Becerra, E. M. Pradas Macías & R. Barranco-Droege (eds) *Quality in Interpreting: Widening the Scope.* Vol. 1. Granada: Editorial Comares, 293–313.

Classroom Interpreting (2014) Educational Interpreting Performance Assessment: EIPA rating system. www.classroominterpreting.org/EIPA/performance/rating.asp (accessed 5 August 2014).

Clifford, Andrew (2004) Is fidelity ethical? The social role of the healthcare interpreter. *TTR* 17 (2), 89–114.

Clifford, Andrew (2005) Putting the exam to the test: Psychometric validation and interpreter certification. *Interpreting* 7 (1), 97–131.

Cohen, Raymond & Westbrook, Raymond (eds) (2000) *Amarna Diplomacy: The Beginnings of International Relations.* Baltimore: The Johns Hopkins University Press.

Cohen, Suzanne, Moran-Ellis, Jo & Smaje, Chris (1999) Children as informal interpreters in GP consultations: Pragmatics and ideology. *Sociology of Health & Illness* 21 (2), 163–186.

Cokely, Dennis (1992a) *Interpretation: A Sociolinguistic Model.* Burtonsville, MD: Linstok Press.

Cokely, Dennis (1992b) The effects of lag time on interpreter errors. In D. Cokely (ed.) *Sign Language Interpreters and Interpreting.* Burtonsville, MD: Linstok Press, 39–69.

Cokely, Dennis (2000) Exploring ethics: A case for revising the code of ethics. *Journal of Interpretation* 2000, 25–57.

Cokely, Dennis (2005a) Curriculum revision in the twenty-first century: Northeastern's experience. In C. B. Roy (ed.) *Advances in Teaching Sign Language Interpreters.* Washington, DC: Gallaudet University Press, 1–21.

Cokely, Dennis (2005b) Shifting positionality: A critical examination of the turning point in the relationship of interpreters and the Deaf community. In M. Marschark, R. Peterson & E. A. Winston (eds) *Interpreting and Interpreter Education: Directions for Research and Practice.* New York: Oxford University Press, 3–28.

Colin, Joan & Morris, Ruth (1996) *Interpreters and the Legal Process.* Winchester: Waterside Press.

Collados Aís, Ángela (1998) *La Evaluación de la Calidad en Interpretación Simultánea: La Importancia de la Comunicación no Verbal.* Granada: Comares.

Collados Aís, Ángela (1998/2002) Quality assessment in simultaneous interpreting: The importance of nonverbal communication. In F. Pöchhacker & M. Shlesinger (eds) *The Interpreting Studies Reader.* London/New York: Routledge, 327–336.

Collados Aís, Ángela, Iglesias Fernández, Emilia, Pradas Macías, E. Macarena & Stévaux, Elisabeth (eds) (2011) *Qualitätsparameter beim Simultandolmetschen: Interdisziplinäre Perspektiven.* Tübingen: Gunter Narr.

Collados Aís, Ángela, Pradas Macías, E. Macarena, Stévaux, Elisabeth & García Becerra, Olalla (eds) (2007) *La Evaluación de la Calidad en Interpretación Simultánea: Parámetros de Incidencia.* Granada: Comares.

Colonomos, Betty M. (1992) Pedagogical model of the interpreting process. www.interpreter-guild.com/Forrest/Home_files/Colonomos%20Model-Pedagogical%20Perspective.pdf (accessed 17 September 2014).

Commission on Education of the Deaf (1988) *Toward Equality: Education of the Deaf.* Washington, DC: US Government Printing Office.

Conley, Thomas (2002) The speech of Ibrahim at the coronation of Maximilian II. *Rhetorica* 20 (3), 263–273.

Cooke, Michael (1996) A different story: Narrative versus "question and answer" in Aboriginal evidence. *Forensic Linguistics* 3, 273–288.

Cooke, Michael (2009a) Anglo/Aboriginal communication in the criminal justice process: A collective responsibility. *Journal of Judicial Administration* 19 (1), 26–35.

Cooke, Michael S. (2009b) Interpreter ethics versus customary law: Quality and compromise in Aboriginal languages interpreting. In S. B. Hale, U. Ozolins & L. Stern (eds) *The Critical Link 5: Quality in Interpreting – a Shared Responsibility*. Amsterdam: John Benjamins, 85–97.

Cooper, Cary L., Davies, Rachel & Tung, Rosalie L. (1982) Interpreting stress: Sources of job stress among conference interpreters. *Multilingua* 1 (2), 97–107.

Corbett, Vincent E. H. (1927) *Reminiscences: Autobiographical and Diplomatic*. London: Hodder and Stoughton.

Cornes, Andy & Napier, Jemina (2005) Challenges of mental health interpreting when working with deaf patients. *Australasian Psychiatry* 13 (4), 403–407.

Corsellis, Ann (2008) *Public Service Interpreting: The First Steps*. Basingstoke: Palgrave Macmillan.

Cortés, Hernán (1986) *Hernán Cortés: Letters from Mexico* (Trans. & ed. Anthony Pagden, with an Introduction by J. H. Elliot). New Haven/London: Yale University Press.

Cotterill, Janet (2002) "Just one more time.": Aspects of intertextuality in the trials of O. J. Simpson. In J. Cotterill (ed.) *Language in the Legal Process*. Basingstoke: Palgrave Macmillan, 147–161.

Cotterill, Janet (2003) *Language and Power in Court: A Linguistic Analysis of the O. J. Simpson Trial*. Basingstoke: Palgrave Macmillan.

Coulthard, Malcolm & Johnson, Alison (2007) *An Introduction to Forensic Linguistics: Language in Evidence*. London/New York: Routledge.

Coulthard, Malcolm & Johnson, Alison (eds) (2010) *The Routledge Handbook of Forensic Linguistics*. London/New York: Routledge.

Couper, Mick P. (2000) Web surveys: A review of issues and approaches. *The Public Opinion Quarterly* 64 (4), 464–494.

Coverlizza, Laura (2004) *L'interpretazione Simultanea con e senza il Testo Scritto del Discorso di Partenza: uno Studio Sperimentale* [Simultaneous interpreting with and without the written source text: an experimental study]. Graduation thesis, SSLMIT, Università degli Studi di Bologna, Sede di Forlì.

Cowan, Nelson (1988) Evolving conceptions of memory storage, selective attention, and their mutual constraints within the human information-processing system. *Psychological Bulletin* 104 (2), 163–191.

Craik, Fergus I. M. & Tulving, Endel (1975) Depth of processing and the retention of words in episodic memory. *Journal of Experimental Psychology: General* 104 (3), 268–294.

Cranston, James H. (1969) *Étienne Brûlé, Immortal Scoundrel*. Toronto: Ryerson Press.

Creswell, John W. (2003) *Research Design: Qualitative, Quantitative, and Mixed Methods Approaches*. 2nd edn. Thousand Oaks/London/New Delhi: Sage.

Cronin, Michael (2002) The Empire talks back: Orality, heteronomy and the cultural turn in interpreting studies. In F. Pöchhacker & M. Shlesinger (eds) *The Interpreting Studies Reader*. London/New York: Routledge, 387–397.

Cronin, Michael (2006) *Translation and Identity*. London/New York: Routledge.

Cronin, Michael (2009) *Translation Goes to the Movies*. London/New York: Routledge.

Crossman, Kristen L., Wiener, Ethan, Roosevelt, Genie, Bajaj, Lalit & Hampers, Louis C. (2010) Interpreters: Telephonic, in-person interpretation and bilingual providers. *Pediatrics* 125 (3), 631–638.

Cruttenden, Alan (1997) *Intonation*. Cambridge/New York: Cambridge University Press.

Crystal, David (2003) *English as a Global Language*. Cambridge: Cambridge University Press.

CSMG (2012) International deployments of video relay services. http://stakeholders.ofcom.org.uk/binaries/research/telecoms-research/video-relay-services-2012.pdf (accessed 11 November 2014).

Cutler, Anne (1983) Speakers' conception of the function of prosody. In A. Cutler & D. R. Ladd (eds) *Prosody: Models and Measurements*. Berlin: Springer, 79–91.

Czaja, Ronald & Blair, Johnny (2005) *Designing Surveys: A Guide to Decisions and Procedures*. 2nd edn. Thousand Oaks/London/New Delhi: Pine Forge Press.

D'Hayer, Danielle (2012) Public service interpreting and translation: Moving towards a (virtual) community of practice. *Meta* 57 (1), 235–247.

D'hulst, Lieven (2010) Translation history. In Y. Gambier & L. van Doorslaer (eds) *Handbook of Translation Studies*. Vol. 1. Amsterdam: John Benjamins, 397–405.

Dabic, Mascha (2010) The role of the interpreter in intercultural psychotherapy. *CTIS Occasional Papers* 5, 65–80.

Dakhlia, Jocelyne (2008) *Lingua Franca*. Arles: Actes Sud.

Dal Fovo, Eugenia (2011) Through the CorIT looking-glass and what MA students found there. *The Interpreters' Newsletter* 16, 1–20.

Dal Fovo, Eugenia (2012) Topical coherence in television interpreting: Question/answer rendition. In F. Straniero Sergio & C. Falbo (eds) *Breaking Ground in Corpus-Based Interpreting Studies*. Bern: Peter Lang, 187–209.

Dal Fovo, Eugenia (2013) Quality as coherence maintenance: A corpus-based pilot study on topical coherence in simultaneous interpretation on television. The question/answer group. In O. García Becerra, E. M. Pradas Macías & R. Barranco-Droege (eds) *Quality in Interpreting: Widening the Scope*. Vol. 1. Granada: Comares, 149–174.

Daly, Albert (1985) Interpreting for international satellite television. *Meta* 30 (1), 91–96.

Dam, Helle Vrønning (1993) Text condensing in consecutive interpreting. In Y. Gambier & J. Tommola (eds) *Translation and Knowledge: SSOTT IV.* Turku: University of Turku, Centre for Translation and Interpreting, 297–313.

Dam, Helle V. (2001) On the option between form-based and meaning-based interpreting: The effect of source text difficulty on lexical target text form in simultaneous interpreting. *The Interpreters' Newsletter* 11, 27–55.

Dam, Helle V. (2004a) Interpreters' notes: On the choice of form and language. In G. Hansen, K. Malmkjær & D. Gile (eds) *Claims, Changes and Challenges in Translation Studies. Selected Contributions from the EST Congress, Copenhagen 2001*. Amsterdam: John Benjamins, 251–261.

Dam, Helle V. (2004b) Interpreters' notes: On the choice of language. *Interpreting* 6 (1), 3–17.

Dam, Helle V. & Zethsen, Karen Korning (2013) Conference interpreters – the stars of the translation profession? A study of the professional status of Danish EU interpreters as compared to Danish EU translators. *Interpreting* 15 (2), 229–259.

Daneman, Meredyth & Carpenter, Patricia A. (1980) Individual differences in working memory and reading. *Journal of Verbal Learning and Verbal Behavior* 19 (4), 450–466.

Danks, Joseph H. & Griffin, Jennifer (1997) Reading and translation: A pycholinguistic perspective. In J. H. Danks, G. M. Shreve, S. B. Fountain & M. K. McBeath (eds) *Cognitive Processes in Translation and Interpreting*. Thousand Oaks/London/New Delhi: Sage, 161–175.

Danks, Joseph H., Shreve, Gregory M., Fountain, Stephen B. & McBeath, Michael K. (eds) (1997) *Cognitive Processes in Translation and Interpreting*. Thousand Oaks/London/New Delhi: Sage.

Danquah, Joseph Boakye (1928) *Gold Coast: Akan Laws and Customs and the Akim Abuakwa Constitution*. London: George Routledge & Sons.

Dark, Eleanor (1966) Bennelong. *Australian Dictionary of Biography*. Vol. 1. Melbourne: Melbourne University Press. http://adb.anu.edu.au/biography/bennelong-1769 (accessed 11 December 2014).

Darò, Valeria (1989) The role of memory and attention in simultaneous interpretation: A neurolinguistic approach. *The Interpreters' Newsletter* 2, 50–56.

Darò, Valeria & Fabbro, Franco (1994) Verbal memory during simultaneous interpretation: Effects of phonological interference. *Applied Linguistics* 15 (4), 365–381.

DARPA (2008) *DARPA: 50 Years of Bridging the Gap*. Tampa, FL: Faircount.

Davidson, Brad (2000) The interpreter as institutional gatekeeper: The social-linguistic role of interpreters in Spanish–English medical discourse. *Journal of Sociolinguistics* 4 (3), 379–405.

Davidson, Brad (2001) Questions in cross-linguistic medical encounters: The role of the hospital interpreter. *Anthropological Quarterly* 74 (4), 170–178.

Davidson, Brad (2002) A model for the construction of conversational common ground in interpreted discourse. *Journal of Pragmatics* 34, 1273–1300.

Davies, Bronwyn & Harré, Rom (1990) Positioning: The discursive production of selves. *Journal for the Theory of Social Behaviour* 20 (1), 43–63.

Davis, Jeffrey (1990) Linguistic transference and interference: Interpreting between English and ASL. In C. Lucas (ed.) *Sign Language Research: Theoretical Issues*. Washington, DC: Gallaudet University Press, 308–321.

Davitti, Elena (2013) Dialogue interpreting as intercultural mediation: Interpreters' use of upgrading moves in parent–teacher meetings. *Interpreting* 15 (2), 168–199.

Davitti, Elena & Pasquandrea, Sergio (2014) Enhancing research-led interpreter education: An exploratory study in Applied Conversation Analysis. *The Interpreter and Translator Trainer* 8 (3), 374–398.

Dawrant, Andrew C. (2000) Using the web for conference preparation. *Communicate!* (September 2000) http://aiic.net/page/223/lang/1 (accessed 4 February 2014).

De Bot, Kees (2000) Simultaneous interpreting as language production. In B. Englund Dimitrova & K. Hyltenstam (eds) *Language Processing and Simultaneous Interpreting: Interdisciplinary Perspectives*. Amsterdam: John Benjamins, 65–88.

De Bruin, Ed & Brugmans, Petra (2006) The psychotherapist and the sign language interpreter. *Journal of Deaf Studies and Deaf Education* 11 (3), 360–368.

De Groot, Alexander H. (1978) *The Ottoman Empire and the Dutch Republic: A History of the Earliest Diplomatic Relations, 1610–1630*. Leiden: Nederlands Historisch-Archaeologisch Instituut.

De Groot, Alexander H. (1997) Protection and nationality: The decline of the dragomans. In F. Hitzel (ed.) *Istanbul et les Langues Orientales*. Istanbul: Isis, 235–255.

De Groot, Annette M. B. (2000) A complex-skill approach to translation and interpreting. In S. Tirkkonen-Condit & R. Jääskeläinen (eds) *Tapping and Mapping the Processes of Translation and Interpreting: Outlooks on Empirical Research*. Amsterdam: John Benjamins, 53–68.

De Groot, Annette M. B. (2011) *Language and Cognition in Bilinguals and Multilinguals: An Introduction*. NewYork/Hove: Psychology Press.

De Jongh, Elena M. (2012) *From the Classroom to the Courtroom: A Guide to Interpreting in the U.S. Court System*. Amsterdam: John Benjamins.

De Leeuw, Edith D., Hox, Joop J. & Dillman, Don A. (2008) The cornerstones of survey research. In E. D. de Leeuw, J. J. Hox & D. A. Dillman (eds) *International Handbook of Survey Methodology*. New York: Psychology Press, 1–17.

De Manuel Jerez, Jesús (ed.) (2003) *Nuevas Tecnologías y Formación de Intérpretes*. Granada: Atrio.

De Manuel Jerez, Jesús (2006) *La Incorporación de la Realidad Professional a la Formación de Intérpretes de Conferencias Mediante las Nuevas Tecnologías y la Investigación-acción*. Tesis doctoral, Universidad de Granada.

De Manuel Jerez, Jesús (2010) From ethics to politics: Toward a new generation of citizen interpreters (Trans. Maria Constanza Guzmán & Rosalind M. Gill). In J. Boéri & C. Maier (eds) *Compromiso Social y Traducción/Interpretación – Translation/Interpreting and Social Activism*. Granada: ECOS, 134–145.

De Quadros, Ronice M. & Stumpf, Marianne R. (2009) Brazilian Sign Language interpreter education in Brazil: From voluntary work to formal distance learning. In J. Napier (ed.) *International Perspectives on Sign Language Interpreter Education*. Washington, DC: Gallaudet University Press, 221–247.

Dean, Robyn K. & Pollard, Robert Q. (2001) Application of demand–control theory to sign language interpreting: Implications for stress and interpreter training. *Journal of Deaf Studies and Deaf Education* 6 (1), 1–14.

Dean, Robyn K. & Pollard, Robert Q. (2005) Consumers and service effectiveness in interpreting work: A practice profession perspective. In M. Marschark, R. Peterson & E. A. Winston (eds) *Interpreting and Interpreter Education: Directions for Research and Practice*. New York: Oxford University Press, 259–282.

Dean, Robyn K. & Pollard, Robert Q. (2011) Context-based ethical reasoning in interpreting: A demand control schema perspective. *The Interpreter and Translator Trainer* 5 (1), 155–182.

Dean, Robyn K. & Pollard, Robert Q (2013) *The Demand Control Schema: Interpreting as a Practice Profession*. North Charleston, SC: CreateSpace.

Degros, Maurice (1984) Les jeunes de langues sous la revolution et l'empire. *Revue d'Histoire Diplomatique* 98 (1/2), 77–107.

Déjean le Féal, Karla (1978) *Lectures et Improvisations: Incidences de la Forme de l'Énonciation sur la Traduction Simultanée Français–Allemand*. Thèse de doctorat, Université Sorbonne Nouvelle – Paris 3.

Déjean le Féal, Karla (1980) Die Satzsegmentierung beim freien Vortrag bzw. beim Verlesen von Texten und ihr Einfluß auf das Sprachverstehen. In W. Kühlwein & A. Raasch (eds) *Sprache und Verstehen*. Tübingen: Gunter Narr, 161–168.

Déjean le Féal, Karla (1982) Why impromptu speech is easy to understand. In N. E. Enkvist (ed.) *Impromptu Speech: A Symposium*. Åbo: Åbo Akademi, 221–239.

Déjean le Féal, Karla (1990) Some thoughts on the evaluation of simultaneous interpretation. In D. Bowen & M. Bowen (eds) *Interpreting: Yesterday, Today, and Tomorrow*. Binghamton, NY: SUNY, 154–160.

Déjean le Féal, Karla (1997) Simultaneous interpretation with "training wheels". *Meta* 42 (4), 616–621.

Déjean le Féal, Karla (2003) Impact of the international status of the interpreting student's mother tongues on training. *Forum* 1 (1), 53–76.

Delabastita, Dirk & Grutman, Rainier (eds) (2005) *Fictionalising Translation and Multilingualism. Linguistica Antverpiensia – New Series* 4. Antwerp: Hoger Instituut voor Vertalers en Tolken.

Delisle, Jean (ed.) (1981) *L'enseignement de l'Interprétation et de la Traduction: De la Théorie à la Pédagogie*. Ottawa: University of Ottawa Press.

Delisle, Jean (1984) *Bridging the Language Solitudes*. Ottawa: Minister of Supply and Services Canada.

Delisle, Jean (1990) *The Language Alchemists*. Ottawa: University of Ottawa Press.

Delisle, Jean (2009) Fifty years of parliamentary interpretation. *Canadian Parliamentary Review* 32 (2), 27–32. www.revparl.ca/english/issue.asp?param=193& art = 1333 (accessed 28 February 2015).

Delisle, Jean (2012) Jean L'Heureux: Interpreter, false priest and Robin Hood. *Language Update* 9 (2), 11–16. www.publications.gc.ca/site/eng/431640/publication.html (accessed 28 February 2015).

Delisle, Jean & Woodsworth, Judith (eds) (1995) *Translators through History*. Amsterdam: John Benjamins.

Delisle, Jean, Lee-Jahnke, Hannelore & Cormier, Monique (eds) (1999) *Translation Terminology*. Amsterdam: John Benjamins.

Denissenko, Jurij (1989) Communicative and interpretative linguistics. In L. Gran & J. Dodds (eds) *The Theoretical and Practical Aspects of Teaching Conference Interpretation*. Udine: Campanotto, 155–158.

Denzin, Norman K. & Lincoln, Yvonna S. (eds) (2011) *The SAGE Handbook of Qualitative Research*. 4th edn. Thousand Oaks, CA: Sage.

DeVito, Joseph A. (1997) *Human Communication: The Basic Course*. 7th edn. New York: Longman.

Dew, Nicholas (2009) *Orientalism in Louis XIV's France*. Oxford/New York: Oxford University Press.

Diamond, Lisa C., Tuot, Delphine & Karliner, Leah (2012) The use of Spanish language skills by physicians and nurses: Policy implications for teaching and testing. *Journal of General Internal Medicine* 27 (1), 117–123.

Diamond, Lisa C., Schenker, Yael, Curry, Leslie, Bradley, Elizabeth H. & Fernandez, Alicia (2009) Getting by: Underuse of interpreters by resident physicians. *Journal of General Internal Medicine* 24 (2), 256–262.

Díaz del Castillo, Bernal (2012) *The True History of the Conquest of New Spain* (Trans. Janet Burke & Ted Humphrey). Cambridge, MA: Hackett Publishing Company.

Díaz Galaz, Stephanie (2011) The effect of previous preparation in simultaneous interpreting: Preliminary results. *Across Languages and Cultures* 12 (2), 173–191.

Díaz Galaz, Stephanie, Padilla, Presentación & Bajo, María Teresa (2015) The role of advance preparation in simultaneous interpreting: A comparison of professional interpreters and interpreting students. *Interpreting* 17 (1), 1–25.

Dien, Albert E. (1965) The glories of Sogdiana. www.silk-road.com/artl/sogdian.shuml (accessed 18 December 2013).

Dillinger, Mike (1990) Comprehension during interpreting: What do interpreters know that bilinguals don't? *The Interpreters' Newsletter* 3, 41–58.

Dillinger, Mike (1994) Comprehension during interpreting: What do interpreters know that bilinguals don't? In S. Lambert & B. Moser-Mercer (eds) *Bridging the Gap: Empirical Research in Simultaneous Interpretation*. Amsterdam: John Benjamins, 155–189.

Dingman, Roger (2009) *Deciphering the Rising Sun: Navy and Marine Corps Codebreakers Translators and Interpreters in the Pacific War*. Annapolis, MD: Naval Institute Press.

Diriker, Ebru (1999) Problematizing the discourse on interpreting: A quest for norms in simultaneous interpreting. *TextconText* 13 (2), 73–90.

Diriker, Ebru (2004) *De-/Re-Contextualizing Conference Interpreting: Interpreters in the Ivory Tower?* Amsterdam: John Benjamins.

Diriker, Ebru (2008) Exploring conference interpreting as a social practice: An area for intra-disciplinary cooperation. In A. Pym, M. Shlesinger & D. Simeoni (eds) *Beyond Descriptive Translation Studies: Investigations in Homage to Gideon Toury.* Amsterdam: John Benjamins, 209–221.

Diriker, Ebru (2011) Agency in conference interpreting: Still a myth? *Gramma: Journal of Theory and Criticism* 19, 27–36. www.enl.auth.gr/gramma/gramma11/apostolou2.pdf (accessed 31 July 2014).

Doğan, Aymil (2012) A study on the volunteers of Emergency and Disaster Interpreting Initiative (ARÇ) in Turkey. *Hacettepe University Journal of Faculty of Letters* 29 (2), 45–58.

Doğan, Aymil & Kahraman, Rana (2011) Emergency and disaster interpreting in Turkey: Ten years of a unique endeavour *Hacettepe University Journal of Faculty of Letters* 28 (2), 61–77.

Dollerup, Cay & Ceelen, Leo (1996) *A Corpus of Consecutive Interpreting, Comprising Danish, Dutch, English, French and Italian.* Copenhagen: University of Copenhagen.

Donato, Valentina (2003) Strategies adopted by student interpreters in SI: A comparison between the English–Italian and the German–Italian language-pairs. *The Interpreters' Newsletter* 12, 101–134.

Donk, Ute (1994) Der Dolmetscher als Hilfspolizist. *Zeitschrift für Rechtssoziologie* 15 (1), 37–57.

Donovan, Clare (2004) European Masters Project Group: Teaching simultaneous interpretation into a B language. *Interpreting* 6 (2), 205–216.

Donovan-Cagigos, Claire (1990) *La Fidélité en Interprétation.* Thèse de doctorat, Université Sorbonne Nouvelle – Paris 3.

Dostert, Léon (1953) The Georgetown Institute language program. *PMLA* 68 (2), 3–12.

Dragovic-Drouet, Mila (2007) The practice of translation and interpreting during the conflicts in the former Yugoslavia (1991–1999). In M. Salama-Carr (ed.) *Translating and Interpreting Conflict.* Amsterdam/New York: Rodopi, 29–40.

Dragsted, Barbara & Gorm Hansen, Inge (2007) Speaking your translation: Exploiting synergies between translation and interpreting. In F. Pöchhacker, A. L. Jakobsen & I. M. Mees (eds) *Interpreting Studies and Beyond: A Tribute to Miriam Shlesinger.* Copenhagen: Samfundslitteratur Press, 251–274.

Drechsel, Alexander (2013) Translation versus Technik? Überlegungen zum Verhältnis von Dolmetscher und Technologie. In A.-K. Ende, S. Herold & A. Weilandt (eds) *Alles hängt mit allem zusammen. Translatologische Interdependenzen. Festschrift für Peter A. Schmitt.* Berlin: Frank & Timme, 123–136.

Drennan, Gerard & Swartz, Leslie (1999) A concept over-burdened: Institutional roles for psychiatric interpreters in post-apartheid South Africa. *Interpreting* 4 (2), 169–198.

Drew, Paul & Heritage, John (1992) Analyzing talk at work: An introduction. In P. Drew & J. Heritage (eds) *Talk at Work.* Cambridge: Cambridge University Press, 3–65.

Drew, Paul & Heritage, John (eds) (1992) *Talk at Work: Interaction in Institutional Settings.* Cambridge/New York: Cambridge University Press.

Driesen, Christiane (1985) *L'Interprétation dans les Cours Pénales en R.F.A.* Thèse de doctorat, Université Sorbonne Nouvelle – Paris 3.

Du Bois, John W., Schuetze-Coburn, Stephan, Cumming, Susanna & Paolino, Danae (1993) Outline of discourse transcription. In J. A. Edwards & M. D. Lampert (eds) *Talking Data: Transcription and Coding in Discourse Research.* Hillsdale, NJ: Lawrence Erlbaum, 45–89.

Du Plessis, Theodorus & Wiegand, Chriss (1998) Interpreting at the hearings of the Truth and Reconciliation Commission: April 1996 to February 1997. In A. Kruger, K. Wallmach & M. Boers (eds) *Language Facilitation and Development in Southern Africa.* Pretoria: South African Translators' Institute, 25–30.

Dubslaff, Friedel & Martinsen, Bodil (2007) Interpreter's use of direct vs. indirect speech. *Interpreting* 7 (2), 211–236.

Duflou, Veerle (2007) Norm research in conference interpreting: Some methodological aspects. In P. A. Schmitt & H. E. Jüngst (eds) *Translationsqualität.* Frankfurt: Peter Lang, 91–99.

Durand, Claude (2005) La relève – the next generation: The results of the AIIC project. http://aiic.net/page/2076/ViewPage.cfm/page1954.htm (accessed 10 February 2014).

Eastman, Charles (1925) Report to the United States Department of the Interior, Office of Indian Affairs. March 2, 1925. Washington, DC: National Archives. Reprinted in *Sacajawea: Her True Story* by Rich Haney, Xlibris 1999, 141–154. Also reprinted as Charles Eastman's Report on Sacajawea in *Annals of Wyoming* 13 (July, 1941) 187–194.

Eck, Matthias, Lane, Ian, Zhang, Ying & Waibel, Alex (2010) Jibbigo: Speech-to-speech translation on mobile devices. In *Spoken Language Technology Workshop (SLT), 2010 IEEE*, 165–166.

Eck, Werner (2004) Lateinisch, Griechisch, Germanisch. … ? Wie sprach Rom mit seinen Unter-tanen? In L. de Ligt, E. A. Hemelrijk & H. W. Singor (eds) *Roman Rule and Civic Life: Local and Regional Perspectives*. Amsterdam: J. C. Gieben, 3–19.

Edmondson, Willis J. (1986) Cognition, conversing and interpreting. In J. House & S. Blum-Kulka (eds) *Interlingual and Intercultural Communication*. Tübingen: Gunter Narr, 129–138.

Edwards, Rosalind (1998) A critical examination of the use of interpreters in the qualitative research process. *Journal of Ethnic and Migration Studies* 24, 197–208.

Edwards, Rosalind (2013) Power and trust: An academic researcher's perspective on working with interpreters as gatekeepers. *International Journal of Social Research Methodology* 16, 503–514.

Edwards, Rosalind & Alexander, Claire (2011) Researching with peer/community researchers – ambivalences and tensions. In M. Williams & W. P. Vogt (eds) *The SAGE Handbook of Innovation in Social Research Methods*. London: Sage, 260–292.

Edwards, Rosalind & Holland, Janet (2013) *What Is Qualitative Interviewing?* London: Bloomsbury Academic.

Edwards, Rosalind, Alexander, Claire & Temple, Bogusia (2006) Interpreting trust: Abstract and personal trust for people who need interpreters to access services. *Sociological Research Online* 11 (1). www.socresonline.org.uk/11/1/edwards.html (accessed 30 October 2013).

Edwards, Rosalind, Temple, Bogusia & Alexander, Claire (2005) Users' experiences of interpreters: The critical role of trust. *Interpreting* 7 (1), 77–95.

Egner, Tobias & Hirsch, Joy (2005) Cognitive control mechanisms resolve conflict through cortical amplification of task-relevant information. *Nature Neuroscience* 8 (12), 1784–1790.

Ehlich, Konrad (1993) HIAT: A transcription system for discourse data. In J. A. Edwards & M. D. Lampert (eds) *Talking Data: Transcription and Coding in Discourse Research*. Hillsdale, NJ: Lawrence Erlbaum, 123–148.

Ekman, Paul & Friesen, Wallace V. (1969) The repertoire of nonverbal behavior: Categories, origins, usage, and coding. *Semiotica* 1 (1), 49–98.

Ekvall, Robert (1960) *Faithful Echo*. New York: Twayne.

Elderkin-Thompson, Virginia, Cohen Silver, Roxane & Waitzkin, Howard (2001) When nurses double as interpreters: A study of Spanish-speaking patients in a US primary care setting. *Social Science & Medicine* 52, 1343–1358.

Elgohary, Baher Mohamed (1979) *Joseph Freiherr von Hammer-Purgstall (1774–1856): Ein Dichter und Vermittler orientalischer Literatur*. Stuttgart: Akademischer Verlag Hans-Dieter Heinz.

Elias-Bursać, Ellen (2012) Shaping international justice: The role of translation and interpreting at the ICTY in The Hague. *Translation and Interpreting Studies* 7 (1), 34–53.

Elliot, Lisa B., Stinson, Michael S., McKee, Barbara G., Everhart, Victoria S. & Francis, Pamela J. (2001) College students' perceptions of the C-Print speech-to-text transcription system. *Journal of Deaf Studies and Deaf Education* 6 (4), 285–298.

Ellis, Ronald (2004) *Videoconferencing in Refugee Hearings*. Ellis Report to the Immigration and Refugee Board Audit and Evaluation Committee. www.irb-cisr.gc.ca/Eng/transp/ReviewEval/Pages/Video.aspx (accessed 24 January 2014).

Elmer, Stefan, Hänggi, Jürgen & Jäncke, Lutz (2014) Processing demands upon cognitive, linguistic, and articulatory functions promote grey matter plasticity in the adult multilingual brain: Insights from simultaneous interpreters. *Cortex* 54, 159–189.

Elmer, Stefan, Meyer, Martin & Jäncke, Lutz (2010) Simultaneous interpreters as a model for neuronal adaptation in the domain of language processing. *Brain Research* 1317, 147–156.

EMCI (2002) *Teaching Simultaneous Interpretation into a 'B' Language: EMCI Workshop Paris 2002*. Paris: ESIT. www.emcinterpreting.org/?q=projects (accessed 05 October 2013).

EMT (2009) Competences for professional translators, experts in multilingual and multimedia communication. http://ec.europa.eu/dgs/translation/programmes/emt/key_documents/emt_com petences_translators_en.pdf (accessed 24 February 2015).

Englund Dimitrova, Birgitta (1997) Degree of interpreter responsibility in the interaction process in community interpreting. In S. E. Carr, R. Roberts, A. Dufour & D. Steyn (eds) *The Critical Link: Interpreters in the Community*. Amsterdam: John Benjamins, 147–164.

Englund Dimitrova, Birgitta (2005) *Expertise and Explicitation in the Translation Process*. Amsterdam: John Benjamins.

Englund Dimitrova, Birgitta & Hyltenstam, Kenneth (eds) (2000) *Language Processing and Simultaneous Interpreting: Interdisciplinary Perspectives*. Amsterdam: John Benjamins.

Enkvist, Nils (ed.) (1982) *Impromptu Speech: A Symposium*. Åbo: Åbo Akademi.

Erasmus, Mabel, Mathibela, Lebohang, Hertog, Erik & Antonissen, Hugo (eds) (1999) *Liaison Interpreting in the Community*. Hatfield: Van Schaik.

Erasmus, Peter (1976) *Buffalo Days and Nights*. Calgary: Glenbow-Alberta Institute.

Ergene, Boğaç A. (2004) Evidence in Ottoman courts: Oral and written documentation in early-modern courts of Islamic law. *Journal of the American Oriental Society* 124 (3), 471–491.

Ericsson, K. Anders (2000) Expertise in interpreting: An expert-performance perspective. *Interpreting* 5 (2), 187–220.

Ericsson, K. Anders (2006) An introduction to the *Cambridge Handbook of Expertise and Expert Performance*: Its development, organization, and content. In K. A. Ericsson, N. Charness, P. J. Feltovich & R. R. Hoffman (eds) (2006) *The Cambridge Handbook of Expertise and Expert Performance*. Cambridge: Cambridge University Press, 3–20.

Ericsson, K. Anders & Kintsch, Walter (1995) Long-term working memory. *Psychological Review* 102 (2), 211–245.

Ericsson, K. Anders & Simon, Herbert A. (1996) *Protocol Analysis: Verbal Reports as Data*. Cambridge, MA/London: MIT Press.

Ericsson, K. Anders, Charness, Neil, Feltovich, Paul J. & Hoffman, Robert R. (eds) (2006) *The Cambridge Handbook of Expertise and Expert Performance*. Cambridge: Cambridge University Press.

Ersöz Demirdağ, Hande (2013) *L'Enseignement de l'Interprétation Consécutive: une Étude de Cas Turc-Français*. Doctoral dissertation, Université Sorbonne Nouvelle – Paris 3.

Ertl, Anita & Pöllabauer, Sonja (2010) Training (medical) interpreters – the key to good practice. MedInt: A joint European training perspective. *JoSTrans: The Journal of Specialised Translation* 14. www.jostrans.org/issue14/art_ertl.php (accessed 30 July 2014).

Eufe, Rembert (2003) Politica linguistica della Serenissima: Luca Tron, Antonio Condulmer, Marin Sanudo e il volgare nell'amministrazione veneziana a Creta. *Philologie im Netz* 23, 15–43. http://web.fu-berlin.de/phin/phin23/p23t2.htm (accessed 29 September 2014).

Eugeni, Carlo (2009) Respeaking the BBC news: A strategic analysis of respeaking on the BBC. *The Sign Language Translator and Interpreter* 3 (1), 29–68.

Evetts, Julia (2014) The concept of professionalism: Professional work, professional practice, and learning. In S. Billet, C. Harteis & H. Gruber (eds) *International Handbook of Research in Professional and Practice-based Learning*. Dordrecht: Springer, 29–56.

Eyckmans, June, Anckaert, Philippe & Segers, Winibert (2009) The perks of norm-referenced translation evaluation. In C. V. Angelelli & H. E. Jacobson (eds) *Testing and Assessment in Translation and Interpreting Studies*. Amsterdam: John Benjamins, 73–93.

Fabbro, Franco, Gran, Bruno & Gran, Laura (1991) Hemispheric specialization for semantic and syntactic components of language in simultaneous interpreters. *Brain and Language* 41 (1), 1–42.

Fabbro, Franco, Skrap, Miran & Aglioti, Salvatore (2000) Pathological switching between languages after frontal lesions in a bilingual patient. *Journal of Neurology, Neurosurgery and Psychiatry* 68 (5), 650–652.

Fabbro, Franco, Gran, Laura, Basso, Gianpaolo & Bava, Antonio (1990) Cerebral lateralization in simultaneous interpretation. *Brain and Language* 39 (1), 69–89.

Færch, Claus & Kasper, Gabriele (1984) Two ways of defining communication strategies. *Language Learning* 3 (1), 45–63.

Fairclough, Norman (1995) *Critical Discourse Analysis: The Critical Study of Language*. London: Longman.

Falbo, Caterina (2002) Error analysis: A research tool. In G. Garzone, P. Mead & M. Viezzi (eds) *Perspectives on Interpreting*. Bologna: CLUEB, 111–127.

Falbo, Caterina (2012) CorIT (Italian Television Interpreting Corpus): Classification criteria. In F. Straniero Sergio & C. Falbo (eds) *Breaking Ground in Corpus-based Interpreting Studies.* Bern: Peter Lang, 155–185.

Fant, Louie J. (1990) *Silver Threads: A Personal Look at the First Twenty-Five Years of the Registry of Interpreters for the Deaf.* Silver Spring, MD: RID Publications.

Fantinuoli, Claudio (2006) Specialized corpora from the Web and term extraction for simultaneous interpreters. In M. Baroni & S. Bernardini (eds) *Wacky! Working Papers on the Web as Corpus.* Bologna: Gedit, 173–190.

Fantinuoli, Claudio (2013) *InterpretBank: Design and Implementation of a Terminology and Knowledge Management Software for Conference Interpreters.* Berlin: epubli.

Farafonova, Larisa G., Sorokina, Anna V. & Sikorsky, Vilen V. (1998) Istorija jazykovoj podgotovki diplomatov v ministerstve inostrannyh del Rossii (k 175-letiju služby jazykovoj podgotovki v MID Rossii) [A history of diplomats' linguistic training at the Ministry of Foreign Affairs of Russia (in commemoration of the 175th anniversary of the linguistic service at the Russian Ministry of Foreign Affairs)]. *Diplomatičeskij Vestnik* 5, 67–70.

Fardy, Bernard D. (1984) *Jerry Potts, Paladin of the Plains.* Langley: Mr. Paperback.

Farooq, Saeed & Fear, Chris (2003) Working through Interpreters. *Advances in Psychiatric Treatment* 9, 104–109.

FCICE (2014) *Examinee Handbook.* www.ncsc.org/sitecore/content/microsites/fcice/home/About-the-program/Examinee-Handbook/4-The-oral-examination.aspx#4.3 (accessed 13 February 2014).

Federman, Mark (2006) On the media effects of immigration and refugee board hearings via videoconference. *Journal of Refugee Studies* 19 (4), 433–452.

Fedorov, Andrei (1953) *Vvedenie v teoriyu perevoda [Introduction to the Theory of Translation and Interpreting].* Moscow: Izdatelstvo literatury na inostrannyh yazykah.

Feldweg, Erich (1996) *Der Konferendolmetscher im Internationalen Kommunikationsprozess.* Heidelberg: Julius Groos.

Feldweg, Erich (2003) Seit dreißig Jahren erfolgreich: Einsprachige Dolmetscherlehrgänge. *Lebende Sprachen* 48 (1), 1–5.

Fenton, Sabine (1993) Interpreting in New Zealand: An emerging profession. *Journal of Interpretation* 6 (1), 155–166.

Feria García, Manuel C. (2005) El Tratado Hispano-Marroquí de Amistad y Comercio de 1767 en el punto de mira del traductor (I). Contextualización histórica: encuentro y desencuentros. *Sendebar* 16, 3–26.

Feria García, Manuel C. (2007) El Tratado Hispano-Marroquí de Amistad y Comercio de 1767 en el punto de mira del traductor (II). Daguerrotipo de la trujamanería dieciochesca. *Sendebar* 18, 5–44.

Fernández-Ocampo, Anxo & Wolf, Michaela (eds) (2014) *Framing the Interpreter: Towards a Visual Perspective.* London/New York: Routledge.

Fernández Sánchez, María Manuela (2012) A bilingual officer remembers Korea: A closer look at untrained interpreters in the Korean War. In H. Footitt & M. Kelly (eds) *Languages and the Military: Alliances, Occupation and Peace Building.* Basingstoke: Palgrave Macmillan, 115–130.

Fetterman, David M. (1998) *Ethnography: Step by Step.* 2nd edn. Thousand Oaks, CA: Sage.

Feuerle, Lois Marie (2013) Testing interpreters: Developing, administering, and scoring court interpreter certification exams. *Translation & Interpreting* 5 (1), 79–93.

Figley, Charles R. (ed.) (1995) *Compassion Fatigue: Coping with Secondary Traumatic Stress Disorder in those who Treat the Traumatized.* New York: Brunner-Routledge.

Findley, Carter V. (2003) *Presenting the Ottomans to Europe: Mouradgea d'Ohsson and His Tableau Général de L'Empire Othoman.* Stockholm: Swedish Research Institute in Istanbul.

Fischer, Steven L. & Woodcock, Kathryn (2012) A cross-sectional survey of reported musculoskeletal pain, disorders, work volume and employment situation among sign language interpreters. *International Journal of Industrial Ergonomics* 42 (4), 335–340.

Fishman, Joshua A. (1967) Bilingualism with and without diglossia; diglossia with and without bilingualism. *Journal of Social Issues* 23 (2), 29–38.

Flores, Glenn, Rabke-Verani, Jennifer, Pine, Whitney & Sabharwal, Ashu (2002) The importance of cultural and linguistic issues in the emergency care of children. *Pediatric Emergency Care* 18 (4), 271–284.

Flores, Glenn, Laws, M. Barton, Mayo, Sandra J., Zuckerman, Barry, Abreu, Milagros, Medina, Leonardo & Hardt, Eric J. (2003) Errors in medical interpretation and their potential clinical consequences in pediatric encounters. *Pediatrics* 111 (1), 6–14.

Flynn, Priscilla M., Ridgeway, Jennifer L., Wieland, Mark L., Williams, Mark D., Haas, Lindsey R., Kremers, Walter K. & Radecki Breitkopf, Carmen (2013) Primary care utilization and mental health diagnoses among adult patients requiring interpreters: A retrospective cohort study. *Journal of General Internal Medicine* 28 (3), 386–391.

Fodor, Jerry A. (1975) *The Language of Thought*. Cambridge, MA: Harvard University Press.

Foley, Tony (2006) Lawyers and legal interpreters: Different clients, different culture. *Interpreting* 8 (1), 97–104.

Footitt, Hilary & Kelly, Michael (eds) (2012a) *Languages and the Military: Alliances, Occupation and Peace Building*. Basingstoke: Palgrave Macmillan.

Footitt, Hilary & Kelly, Michael (eds) (2012b) *Languages at War: Policies and Practices of Language Contacts in Conflict*. London: Palgrave Macmillan.

Footitt, Hilary & Tobia, Simona (2013) *War Talk: Foreign Languages and the British War Effort in Europe, 1940–1947*. London: Palgrave Macmillan.

Forrest, Alan (1998) The politics of language in the European Union. *European Review* 6 (3), 299–319.

Fowler, Floyd J. Jr. (2014) *Survey Research Methods*. 5th edn. Thousand Oaks/London/New Delhi: Sage.

Fowler, Yvonne (1997) The courtroom interpreter: Paragon and intruder. In S. E. Carr, R Roberts, A. Dufour & D. Steyn (eds) *The Critical Link: Interpreters in the Community*. Amsterdam: John Benjamins, 191–200.

Fowler, Yvonne (2003) Taking an interpreted witness statement at the police station: What did the witness actually say? In L. Brunette, G. Bastin, I. Hemlin & H. Clarke (eds) *The Critical Link 3: Interpreters in the Community*. Amsterdam: John Benjamins, 195–209.

Fowler, Yvonne (2013) Business as usual? Prison video link in the multilingual courtroom. In C. Schäffner, K. Kredens & Y. Fowler (eds) *Interpreting in a Changing Landscape: Selected Papers from Critical Link 6*. Amsterdam: John Benjamins, 225–248.

Foz, Clara (1998) *Le Traducteur, l'Église et le Roi (Espagne, XIIe et XIIIe siècle)*. Ottawa: Presses de l'Université d'Ottawa/Artois Presses Université.

Franco Aixelá, Javier (2013) Who's who and what is what in Translation Studies: A preliminary approach. In C. Way, S. Vandepitte, R. Meylaerts & M. Bartłomiejczyk (eds) *Tracks and Treks in Translation Studies*. Amsterdam: John Benjamins, 7–28.

Frankel, Mindy A. (2002) Deaf-blind interpreting: Interpreters' use of negation in tactile American Sign Language. *Sign Language Studies* 2 (2), 169–181.

Fraser, Elisabeth (2010) "Dressing Turks in the French manner": Mouradgea d'Ohsson's panorama of the Ottoman Empire. *Ars Orientalis* 39, 198–230.

Freidson, Eliot (1970) *Profession of Medicine. A Study of the Sociology of Applied Knowledge*. New York: Harper & Row.

Freidson, Eliot (1988) *Professional Powers: A Study of the Institutionalization of Formal Knowledge*. Chicago: The University of Chicago Press.

Freihoff, Roland (1995) Das Curriculum als Orientierungsrahmen. *TextconText* 10, 149–178.

Frishberg, Nancy (1990) *Interpreting: An Introduction*. Rev. edn. Silver Spring, MD: RID Publications.

Frishberg, Nancy, Hoiting, Nini & Slobin, Dan I. (2012) Transcription. In R. Pfau, M. Steinbach & B. Woll (eds) *Sign Language: An International Handbook*. Berlin/Boston: De Gruyter, 1045–1074.

Fromkin, Victoria (ed.) (1980) *Errors in Linguistic Performance: Slips of the Tongue, Ear, Pen and Hand*. New York: Academic Press.

Fukui, Naohiro & Asano, Tasuku (1961) *Eigo tsuyaku no jissai* [*Practice of English interpreters*]. Tokyo: Kenkyusha.

Funayama, Chuta (2004) Conceptualization processes in simultaneous interpretation. *Tsuuyaku-kenkyuu* [*Interpretation Studies*] 4, 1–13.

Gaechter, Paul (1936) Die Dolmetscher der Apostel. *Zeitschrift für Katholische Theologie* 60, 61–87.

Gaiba, Francesca (1998) *The Origins of Simultaneous Interpretation: The Nuremberg Trial.* Ottawa: University of Ottawa Press.

Galhano Rodrigues, Isabel (2007) Body in interpretation: Nonverbal communication of speaker and interpreter and its relation to words and prosody. In P. A. Schmitt & H. Jüngst (eds) *Translationsqualität.* Frankfurt: Peter Lang, 739–753.

Gall, Meredith D., Borg, Walter R. & Gall, Joyce P. (1996) *Educational Research: An Introduction.* 6th edn. White Plains, NY: Longman.

Gallez, Emmanuelle & Maryns, Katrijn (2014) Orality and authenticity in an interpreter-mediated defendant's examination: A case study from the Belgian Assize Court. *Interpreting* 16 (1), 49–80.

Gallez, Emmanuelle & Reynders, Anne (2015) Court interpreting and classical rhetoric: Ethos in interpreter-mediated monological discourse. *Interpreting* 17 (1), 64–90.

Gallina, Sandra (1992) Cohesion and the systemic-functional approach to text: Applications to political speeches and significance for simultaneous interpretation. *The Interpreters' Newsletter* 4, 62–71.

Gambier, Yves (2007) Réseaux de traducteurs/interprètes bénévoles. *Meta* 52 (4), 658–672.

Gambier, Yves & van Doorslaer, Luc (eds) (2010) *Handbook of Translation Studies.* Vol. 1. Amsterdam/Philadelphia: John Benjamins.

Gambier, Yves & van Doorslaer, Luc (eds) (2011) *Handbook of Translation Studies.* Vol. 2. Amsterdam/Philadelphia: John Benjamins.

Gambier, Yves & van Doorslaer, Luc (eds) (2012) *Handbook of Translation Studies.* Vol. 3. Amsterdam/Philadelphia: John Benjamins.

Gambier, Yves & van Doorslaer, Luc (eds) (2013) *Handbook of Translation Studies.* Vol. 4. Amsterdam/Philadelphia: John Benjamins.

Gambier, Yves & van Doorslaer, Luc (eds) (2014) *Handbook of Translation Studies* (4 vols). Amsterdam: John Benjamins.

Gambier, Yves, Gile, Daniel & Taylor, Christopher (eds) (1997) *Conference Interpreting: Current Trends in Research.* Amsterdam: John Benjamins.

Gany, Francesca, Kapelusznik, Luciano, Prakash, Kavitha, Gonzalez, Javier, Orta, Lurmag Y., Tseng, Chi-Hong & Changrani, Jyotsna (2007) The impact of medical interpretation method on time and errors. *Journal of General Internal Medicine* 22 (Suppl. 2), 319–323.

García Becerra, Olalla (2012) First impressions in interpreting quality assessment: The incidence of nonverbal communication. In A. Jiménez Ivars & M. J. Blasco Mayor (eds) *Interpreting Brian Harris: Recent Developments in Translatology.* Bern: Peter Lang, 173–192.

García-Beyaert, Sofía (2015) Key external players in the development of the interpreting profession. In H. Mikkelson & R. Jourdenais (eds) *The Routledge Handbook of Interpreting.* London/New York: Routledge, 45–61.

García-Landa, Mariano (1978) *Les Déviations Délibérées de la Littéralité en Interprétation de Conférence.* Thèse de doctorat, Université Sorbonne Nouvelle – Paris 3.

García-Landa, Mariano (1981) La "théorie du sens", théorie de la traduction et base de son enseignement. In J. Delisle (ed.) *L'Enseignement de l'Interprétation et de la Traduction: De la Théorie à la Pédagogie.* Ottawa: University of Ottawa Press, 113–134.

García-Landa, Mariano (1995) Notes on the epistemology of translation theory. *Meta* 40 (3), 388–405.Gardiner, Alan H. (1915) The Egyptian word for 'dragoman'. *Proceedings of the Society of Biblical Archaeology* 37, 117–125.

Garzone, Giuliana (2002a) Conflict in linguistically asymmetric business negotiations: The case of interpreter-mediated encounters. In M. Gotti, D. Heller & M. Dossena (eds) *Conflict and Negotiation in Specialised Texts. Selected Papers of the 2nd CERLIS Conference.* Bern: Peter Lang, 249–271.

Garzone, Giuliana (2002b) Quality and norms in interpretation. In G. Garzone & M. Viezzi (eds) *Interpreting in the 21st Century: Challenges and Opportunities.* Amsterdam: John Benjamins, 107–119.

Garzone, Giuliana (2003) Reliability of quality criteria evaluation in survey research. In A. Collados Aís, M. M. Fernández Sánchez & D. Gile (eds) *La Evaluación de la Calidad en Interpretación: Investigación.* Granada: Comares, 23–30.

Gavioli, Laura (2012) Minimal responses in interpreter-mediated medical talk. In C. Baraldi & L. Gavioli (eds) *Coordinating Participation in Dialogue Interpreting.* Amsterdam: John Benjamins, 201–228.

Gavioli, Laura & Baraldi, Claudio (2011) Interpreter-mediated interaction in healthcare and legal settings: Talk organization, context and the achievement of intercultural communication. *Interpreting* 13 (2), 205–233.

Gazzola, Michele (2006) Managing multilingualism in the European Union: Language policy evaluation for the European Parliament. *Language Policy* 5, 393–417.

Gebron, Julie (2000) *Sign the Speech: An Introduction to Theatrical Interpreting.* Hillsboro, OR: Butte Publications Inc.

Gehman, Henry S. (1914) *The Interpreters of Foreign Languages among the Ancients: A Study Based on Greek and Latin Sources.* PhD dissertation,University of Pennsylvania.

Gelb, Ignaz J. (1968) The word for dragoman in the Ancient Near East. *Glossa* 2, 93–104.

Gentile, Adolfo (1997) Community interpreting or not? Practices, standards and accreditation. In S. E. Carr, R. Roberts, A. Dufour & D. Steyn (eds) *The Critical Link: Interpreters in the Community.* Amsterdam: John Benjamins, 109–118.

Gentile, Adolfo, Ozolins, Uldis & Vasilakakos, Mary (1996) *Liaison Interpreting: A Handbook.* Melbourne: Melbourne University Press.

Gernsbacher, Morton Ann (1990) *Language Comprehension as Structure Building.* Hillsdale, NJ: Lawrence Erlbaum.

Gernsbacher, Morton Ann & Givón, Talmy (eds) (1995) *Coherence in Spontaneous Text.* Amsterdam: John Benjamins.

Gernsbacher, Morton Ann & Shlesinger, Miriam (1997) The proposed role of suppression in simultaneous interpretation. *Interpreting* 2 (1), 119–140.

Gerver, David (1969) The effects of source language presentation rate on the performance of simultaneous conference interpreters. In E. Foulke (ed) *Proceedings of the 2nd Louisville Conference on Rate and/or Frequency Controlled Speech.* Louisville, KY: University of Louisville, 162–184.

Gerver, David (1969/2002) The effects of source language presentation rate on the performance of simultaneous interpreters. In F. Pöchhacker & M. Shlesinger (eds) *The Interpreting Studies Reader.* London/New York: Routledge, 53–66.

Gerver, David (1974a) The effects of noise on the performance of simultaneous interpreters: Accuracy of performance. *Acta Psychologica* 38 (3), 159–167.

Gerver, David (1974b) Simultaneous listening and speaking and retention of prose. *Quarterly Journal of Experimental Psychology* 26 (3), 337–341.

Gerver, David (1975) A psychological approach to simultaneous interpreting. *Meta* 20 (2), 119–128.

Gerver, David (1976) Empirical studies of simultaneous interpretation: A review and a model. In R. W. Brislin (ed.) *Translation: Applications and Research.* New York: Gardner Press, 165–207.

Gerver, David (1981) Frames for interpreting. In A. Kopczyński [et al.] (ed.) *Proceedings of the IXth World Congress of FIT.* Warsaw: Interpress, 371–380.

Gerver, David & Dineley, G. (1972) ASPA: Automatic speech-pause analyzer. *Behavior Research Methods & Instrumentation* 4 (5), 265–270.

Gerver, David & Sinaiko, H. Wallace (eds) (1978) *Language Interpretation and Communication. Proceedings of the NATO Symposium, Venice, Italy, September 26–October 1, 1977.* New York/London: Plenum Press.

Gerver, David, Longley, Patricia, Long, John & Lambert, Sylvie (1984) Selecting trainee conference interpreters: A preliminary study. *Journal of Occupational Psychology* 57 (1), 17–31.

Gerver, David, Longley, Patricia E., Long, John & Lambert, Sylvie (1989) Selection tests for trainee conference interpreters. *Meta* 34 (4), 724–735.

Ghobrial, John-Paul A. (2014) *The Whispers of Cities: Information Flows in Istanbul, London, and Paris in the Age of William Trumbull.* Oxford: Oxford University Press.

Giambruno (Miguélez), Cynthia (2008) The role of the interpreter in the governance of sixteenth- and seventeenth-century Spanish colonies in the "New World": Lessons from the past for the present. In C. Valero-Garcés & A. Martin (eds) *Crossing Borders in Community Interpreting: Definitions and Dilemmas.* Amsterdam: John Benjamins, 27–49.

Giannoutsou, Margarita Zoe (2014) *Kirchendolmetschen: Interpretieren oder Transformieren?* Berlin: Frank & Timme.

Gibbs, Raymond (2000) Metarepresentations in staged commmunicative acts. In D. Sperber (ed.) *Metarepresentations: A Multidisciplinary Perspective.* Oxford: Oxford University Press, 389–410.

Giddens, Anthony (1984) *The Constitution of Society: Outline of the Theory of Structuration.* Berkeley: University of California Press.

Gile, Daniel (1983) Des difficultés de langue en interprétation simultanée. *Traduire* 117, Octobre, 2–8.

Gile, Daniel (1985) Le modèle d'efforts et l'équilibre d'interprétation en interprétation simultanée. *Meta* 30 (1), 44–48.

Gile, Daniel (1989) Les flux d'information dans les réunions interlinguistiques et l'interprétation de conférence: premières observations. *Meta* 34 (4), 649–660.

Gile, Daniel (1990) Scientific research vs. personal theories in the investigation of interpretation. In L. Gran & C. Taylor (eds) *Aspects of Applied and Experimental Research on Conference Interpretation.* Udine: Campanotto, 28–41.

Gile, Daniel (1991a) Prise de notes et attention en début d'apprentissage de l'interprétation consécutive – une expérience – démonstration de sensibilisation. *Meta* 36 (2–3), 431–439.

Gile, Daniel (1991b) A communication-oriented analysis of quality in nonliterary translation and interpretation. In M. L. Larson (ed.) *Translation: Theory and Practice. Tension and Interdependence.* Binghamton, NY: SUNY, 188–200.

Gile, Daniel (1992) Predictable sentence endings in Japanese and conference interpretation. *The Interpreters' Newsletter*, Special Issue 1, 12–23.

Gile, Daniel (1994) Opening up in interpretation studies. In M. Snell-Hornby, F. Pöchhacker & K. Kaindl (eds) *Translation Studies: An Interdiscipline. Selected Papers from the Translation Studies Congress, Vienna, 9–12 Sept. 1992.* Amsterdam: John Benjamins, 149–158.

Gile, Daniel (1995a) *Basic Concepts and Models for Interpreter and Translator Training.* Amsterdam: John Benjamins.

Gile, Daniel (1995b) *Regards sur la Recherche en Interprétation de Conférence.* Lille: Presses Universitaires de Lille.

Gile, Daniel (1995c) Fidelity assessment in consecutive interpretation. *Target* 7 (1), 151–164.

Gile, Daniel (1997) Conference interpreting as a cognitive management problem. In J. E. Danks, G. M. Shreve, S. B. Fountain & M. K. McBeath (eds) *Cognitive Processes in Translation and Interpreting.* Thousand Oaks/London/New Delhi: Sage, 196–214.

Gile, Daniel (1999a) Testing the Effort Models' tightrope hypothesis in simultaneous interpreting – a contribution. *Hermes: Journal of Linguistics* 23, 153–172.

Gile, Daniel (1999b) Variability in the perception of fidelity in simultaneous interpretation. *Hermes* 22, 51–79.

Gile, Daniel (1999c) Norms in research on conference interpreting: A response to Theo Hermans and Gideon Toury. In C. Schäffner (ed.) *Translation and Norms.* Clevedon: Multilingual Matters, 98–105.

Gile, Daniel (2000) The history of research into conference interpreting: A scientometric approach. *Target* 12 (2), 297–321.

Gile, Daniel (2001a) The role of consecutive in interpreter training: A cognitive view. http://aiic. net/page/377/the-role-of-consecutive-in-interpreter-training-a-cognitive-view/lang/1 (accessed 7 October 2014).

Gile, Daniel (2001b) Consecutive vs. simultaneous: Which is more accurate? *Tsuuyakukenkyuu* [*Interpretation Studies*] 1 (1), 8–20.

Gile, Daniel (2001c) Being constructive about shared ground. *Target* 13 (1), 149–153.

Gile, Daniel (2002) The interpreter's preparation for technical conferences: Methodological questions in investigating the topic. *Conference Interpretation and Translation* 4 (2), 7–27.

Gile, Daniel (2003) Quality assessment in conference interpreting: Methodological issues. In A. Collados Aís, M. M. Fernández Sánchez & D. Gile (eds) *La Evaluación de la Calidad en Interpretación: Investigacíon.* Granada: Comares, 109–123.

Gile, Daniel (2005a) Citation patterns in the T& i didactics literature. *Forum* 3 (2), 85–103.

Gile, Daniel (2005b) Directionality in conference interpreting: A cognitive view. In R. Godijns & M. Hinderdael (eds) *Directionality in Interpreting: The "Retour" or the Native?* Ghent: Communication and Cognition, 9–26.

Gile, Daniel (2006) L'interdisciplinarité en traductologie: une optique scientométrique. In S. Öztürk Kasar (ed.) *Interdisciplinarité en Traduction.* Vol. 2. Istanbul: Isis, 23–37.

Gile, Daniel (2009) *Basic Concepts and Models for Interpreter and Translator Training.* Rev. edn. Amsterdam: John Benjamins.

Gile, Daniel (2011) Errors, omissions and infelicities in broadcast interpreting: Preliminary findings from a case study. In C. Alvstad, A. Hild & E. Tiselius (eds) *Methods and Strategies of Process Research: Integrative Approaches in Translation Studies.* Amsterdam: John Benjamins, 201–218.

Gile, Daniel (2012) Institutionalization of translation studies. In Y. Gambier & L. van Doorslaer (eds) *Handbook of Translation Studies.* Vol. 3. Amsterdam: John Benjamins, 73–80.

Gile, Daniel, Dam, Helle V., Dubslaff, Friedel, Martinsen, Bodil & Schjoldager, Anne (eds) (2001) *Getting Started in Interpreting Research: Methodological Reflections, Personal Accounts and Advice for Beginners.* Amsterdam: John Benjamins.

Gillies, Andrew (2005) *Note-Taking for Consecutive Interpreting: A Short Course.* Manchester: St. Jerome.

Gillies, Andrew (2013) *Conference Interpreting: A Student's Practice Book.* London/New York: Routledge.

Godijns, Rita & Hinderdael, Michael (eds) (2005) *Directionality in Interpreting: The "Retour"or the Native?* Ghent: Communication & Cognition.

Goedicke, Hans (1966) An additional note on 'ꜣ 'foreigner'. *Journal of Egyptian Archaeology* 52, 172–174.

Goffman, Erving (1959/1990) *The Presentation of Self in Everyday Life.* Harmondsworth: Penguin.

Goffman, Erving (1961) *Encounters: Two Studies in the Sociology of Interaction.* Indianapolis/New York: Bobby-Merrill Company.

Goffman, Erving (1967) *Interaction Ritual: Essays on Face-to-Face Behavior.* New York: Pantheon.

Goffman, Erving (1974) *Frame Analysis.* New York: Harper and Row.

Goffman, Erving (1981) *Forms of Talk.* Philadelphia: University of Pennsylvania Press.

Goffman, Erving (1983) The interaction order. *American Sociological Review* 48, 1–17.

Gofman, Evgeny (1963) K istorii sinhronnogo perevoda [On the history of simultaneous interpreting]. *Tetradi Perevodchika* 1, 20–26.

Goldflam, Russell (1997) "Silence in court!" Problems and prospects in Aboriginal legal interpreting. *Australian Journal of Law and Society* 13, 17–53.

Goldman-Eisler, Frieda (1967) Sequential temporal patterns and cognitive processes in speech. *Language and Speech* 10 (2), 122–132.

Goldman-Eisler, Frieda (1968) *Psycholinguistics: Experiments in Spontaneous Speech.* London/New York: Academic Press.

Goldman-Eisler, Frieda (1972) Segmentation of input in simultaneous translation. *Journal of Psycholinguistic Research* 1 (2), 127–140.

Gomes, Miguel (2002) Digitally mastered consecutive: An interview with Michele Ferrari. *Lingua Franca: Le Bulletin de l'Interprétation au Parlement Européen* 5 (6), 6–10.

Gómez Díez, Isabel (2010) The role of the interpreter in constructing asylum seekers' credibility: A hearing at the Spanish Asylum and Refugee Office. *Sociolinguistic Studies* 4 (2), 333–370.

González, Roseann D., Vasquez, Victoria F. & Mikkelson, Holly (1991/2012) *Fundamentals of Court Interpretation: Theory, Policy and Practice.* 2nd edn. Durham, NC: Carolina Academic Press.

Goodwin, Charles (1981) *Conversational Organization: Interaction between Speakers and Hearers.* New York: Academic Press.

Goodwin, Charles (1996) Transparent vision. In E. Ochs, E. A. Schegloff & S. A. Thompson (eds) *Interaction and Grammar.* Cambridge: Cambridge University Press, 370–404.

Goodwin, Charles (2007) Interactive footing. In E. Holt & R. Clift (eds) *Reporting Talk.* Cambridge: Cambridge University Press, 16–46.

Goodwin, Marjorie H. (1990) *He-said-she-said: Talk as Social Organization among Black Children.* Bloomington, IN: Indiana University Press.

Göpferich, Susanne, Jakobsen, Arnt Lykke & Mees, Inger M. (eds) (2008) *Looking at Eyes: Eye-Tracking Studies of Reading and Translation Processing.* Copenhagen: Samfundslitteratur.

Gorm Hansen, Inge & Shlesinger, Miriam (2007) The silver lining: Technology and self-study in the interpreting classroom. *Interpreting* 9 (1), 95–118.

Goswell, Della (2012) Do you see what I see? Using ELAN for self-analysis and reflection. *International Journal of Interpreter Education* 4 (1), 73–82.

Graesser, Arthur C., Singer, Murray & Trabasso, Tom (1994) Constructing inferences during comprehension. *Psychological Review* 101 (3), 371–395.

Graesser, Arthur C., Louwerse, Max M., McNamara, Danielle S., Olney, Andrew, Cai, Zhiqiang & Mitchell, Heather H. (2007) Inference generation and cohesion in the construction of situation models: Some connections with computational linguistics. In F. Schmalhofer & C. A. Perfetti (eds) *Higher Level Language Processes in the Brain: Inference and Comprehension Processes*. Mahwah, NJ: Lawrence Erlbaum Associates, 289–310.

Grainger, Jonathan & Dijkstra, Ton (1992) On the representation and use of language information in bilinguals. In R. J. Harris (ed.) *Cognitive Processing in Bilinguals*. Amsterdam: Elsevier, 207–220.

Gran, Laura & Dodds, John (1988) From the editors. *The Interpreters' Newsletter* 1, 2–3.

Gran, Laura & Dodds, John (eds) (1989) *The Theoretical and Practical Aspects of Teaching Conference Interpretation*. Udine: Campanotto.

Gran, Laura & Fabbro, Franco (1988) The role of neuroscience in the teaching of interpretation. *The Interpreters' Newsletter* 1, 23–41.

Gran Tarabocchia, Laura, Carabelli, Angela & Merlini, Raffaela (2002) Computer-assisted interpreter training. In G. Garzone & M. Viezzi (eds) *Interpreting in the 21st Century: Challenges and Opportunities*. Amsterdam: John Benjamins, 277–294.

Granger, Emily & Baker, Martyn (2002) The role and experience of interpreters. In R. Tribe, & H. Raval (eds) *Working with Interpreters in Mental Health*. New York: Brunner-Routledge, 99–121.

Grbić, Nadja (1998) Professionalisierung. Ein soziologisches Modell und ein Beispiel aus der Praxis des Gebärdensprachdolmetschens in Österreich. *Das Zeichen* 12 (46), 612–623.

Grbić, Nadja (2001) First steps on firmer ground: A project for the further training of sign language interpreters in Austria. In I. Mason (ed.) *Triadic Exchanges: Studies in Dialogue Interpreting*. Manchester/Northampton, MA: St Jerome Publishing, 149–171.

Grbić, Nadja (2006) From 10-minute wedding ceremonies to three-week spa treatment programs: Reconstructing the system of sign language interpreting in Styria. In A. Pym, Z. Jettmarová & M. Shlesinger (eds) *Sociocultural Aspects of Translating and Interpreting*. Amsterdam: John Benjamins, 202–214.

Grbić, Nadja (2007) Where do we come from? What are we? Where are we going? A bibliometrical analysis of writings and research on sign language interpreting. *The Sign Language Translator and Interpreter* 1 (1), 15–51.

Grbić, Nadja (2008) Constructing interpreting quality. *Interpreting* 10 (2), 232–257.

Grbić, Nadja (2009) Sign language interpreter training in Austria: An integrated approach. In J. Napier (ed.) *International Perspectives on Sign Language Interpreter Education*. Washington, DC: Gallaudet University Press, 3–14.

Grbić, Nadja (2011) "Boundary work" as a concept for studying professionalization processes in the interpreting field. In R. Sela-Sheffy & M. Shlesinger (eds) *Identity and Status in the Translational Professions*. Amsterdam: John Benjamins, 247–262.

Grbić, Nadja (2013) Bibliometrics. In Y. Gambier & L. van Doorslaer (eds) *Handbook of Translation Studies*. Vol. 4. Amsterdam: John Benjamins, 20–24.

Grbić, Nadja (2014) Interpreters in the making: Habitus as a conceptual enhancement of boundary theory? In G. M. Vorderobermeier (ed.) *Remapping Habitus in Translation Studies*. Amsterdam: Rodopi, 91–109.

Grbić, Nadja & Pöllabauer, Sonja (2006) Community interpreting: Signed or spoken? Types, modes, and methods. In E. Hertog & B. van der Veer (eds) *Taking Stock: Research and Methodology in Community Interpreting. Linguistica Antverpiensia – New Series* 5, 247–261.

Grbić, Nadja & Pöllabauer, Sonja (2008a) Counting what counts: Research on community interpreting in German-speaking countries – a scientometric study. *Target* 20 (2), 297–332.

Grbić, Nadja & Pöllabauer, Sonja (2008b) To count or not to count: Scientometrics as a methodological tool for investigating research on translation and interpreting. *Translation and Interpreting Studies* 3 (1/2), 87–146.

Grbić, Nadja & Pöllabauer, Sonja (2009) An author-centred scientometric analysis of Daniel Gile's *oeuvre*. In G. Hansen, A. Chesterman & H. Gerzymisch-Argobast (eds) *Efforts and Models in Interpreting and Translation Research*. Amsterdam: John Benjamins, 3–24.

Green, Adele, Schweda Nicholson, Nancy, Vaid, Jyotsna, White, Nancy & Steiner, Richard (1990) Hemispheric involvement in shadowing vs. interpretation: A time-sharing study of simultaneous interpreters with matched bilingual and monolingual controls. *Brain and Language* 39 (1), 107–133.

Grenet, Mathieu (2013) Alexis Gierra, "interprète juré de langues orientales" à Marseille: une carrière entre marchands, frères et refugiés (fin XVIIIe-premier tiers du XIXe siècle). In G. Buti, M. Janin-Thivos & O. Raveux (eds) *Langues et Langages du Commerce en Méditerranée et en Europe à l'Époque Moderne*. Aix-en-Provence: Presses Universitaires de Provence, 51–64.

Grice, H. Paul (1975) Logic and conversation. In P. Cole & J. L. Morgan (eds) *Syntax and Semantics Vol. 3: Speech Acts*. New York: Academic Press, 41–58.

Gringiani, Angela (1990) Reliability of aptitude testing: A preliminary study. In L. Gran & C. Taylor (eds) *Aspects of Applied and Experimental Research on Conference Interpretation*. Udine: Campanotto, 42–53.

Grosjean, François (1997) Processing mixed language: Issues, findings, and models. In A. M. B. de Groot & J. F. Kroll (eds) *Tutorials in Bilingualism: Psycholinguistic Perspectives*. Mahwah, NJ: Lawrence Erlbaum, 225–254.

Grosjean, François (2001) The bilingual's language modes. In J. L. Nicol (ed.) *One Mind, Two Languages: Bilingual Language Processing*. Oxford/Malden, MA: Blackwell, 1–22.

Grosjean, François (2010) *Bilingual: Life and Reality*. Cambridge, MA/London: Harvard University Press.

Groupe ICOR (2006) CORINTE: Corpus d'interactions. http://icar.univ-lyon2.fr/projets/corinte/ (accessed 17 February 2014).

Grover, Amy, Deakyne, Sara, Bajaj, Lalit & Roosevelt, Genie E. (2012) Comparison of throughput times for limited English proficiency patient visits in the emergency department between different interpreter modalities. *Journal of Immigrant & Minority Health* 14 (4), 602–607.

Groves, Robert M., Fowler, Floyd J.,Couper, Mick P., Lepkowski, James M., Singer, Eleanor & Tourangeau, Roger (2004) *Survey Methodology*. Hoboken, NJ: John Wiley & Sons.

Grucza, Sambor, Płużyczka, Monika & Zajac, Justyna (eds) (2013) *Translation Studies and Eye-Tracking Analysis*. Frankfurt: Peter Lang.

Guardini, Paola (2000) La traduzione simultanea del film: produzione e percezione. In C. Taylor (ed.) *Tradurre il Cinema*. Trieste: Dipartimento di scienze del linguaggio dell'interpretazione e della traduzione, Università degli Studi di Trieste, 117–126.

Guéry, Fréderique (2014) *Learning to Be a Public Service Interpreter: Boundaries, Ethics and Emotion in a Marginal Profession*. PhD dissertation, Manchester Metropolitan University.

Guiberson, Mark & Atkins, Jenny (2012) Speech-language pathologists' preparation, practices, and perspectives on serving culturally and linguistically diverse children. *Communication Disorders Quarterly* 33 (3), 169–180.

Gulati, Sonia, Watt, Lisa, Shaw, Nicola, Sung, Lillian, Poureslami, Iraj M., Klaassen, Robert, Dix, David & Klassen, Anne F. (2012) Communication and language challenges experienced by Chinese and South Asian immigrant parents of children with cancer in Canada: Implications for health services delivery. *Pediatric Blood & Cancer* 58 (4), 572–578.

Gumperz, John (1982) *Discourse Strategies*. Cambridge: Cambridge University Press.

Gumul, Ewa (2006a) Conjunctive cohesion and the length of ear–voice span in simultaneous interpreting: A case of interpreting students. *Linguistica Silesiana* 27, 93–103.

Gumul, Ewa (2006b) Explicitation in simultaneous interpreting: A strategy or a by-product of language mediation? *Across Languages and Cultures* 7 (2), 171–190.

Gumul, Ewa (2007) Explicitation in conference interpreting. In M. Thelen & B. Lewandowska-Tomaszczyk (eds) *Translation and Meaning. Part 7*. Maastricht: Department of Translation and Interpreting, Maastricht School of International Communication, Zuyd University, 449–456.

Gumul, Ewa (2008) Explicitation in simultaneous interpreting – the quest for optimal relevance. In E. Walaszewska, M. Kisielewska-Krysiuk, A. Korzeniowska & M. Grzegorzewska (eds) *Relevant Worlds: Current Perspectives on Language, Translation and Relevance Theory*. Newcastle: Cambridge Scholars Publishing, 188–205.

Gumul, Ewa (2012) Variability of cohesive patterns: Personal reference markers in simultaneous and consecutive interpreting. *Linguistica Silesiana* 33, 147–172.

Günergun, Feza (2007) Ottoman encounters with European science: Sixteenth- and seventeenth-century translations into Turkish. In P. Burke (ed.) *Cultural Translation in Early Modern Europe*. Cambridge: Cambridge University Press, 192–211.

Guo, Ting (2015) Interpreting for the enemy: Chinese interpreters in the Second Sino-Japanese War (1931–1945). *Translation Studies* 8 (1), 1–15.

Gürçağlar, Aykut (2004) Representation of Ottoman interpreters by Western painters. *Acta Orientalia Academiae Scientiarum Hungaricae* 57 (2), 231–252.

Gürkan, Emrah Safa (2012) *Espionage in the 16th Century Mediterranean: Secret Diplomacy, Mediterranean Go-Betweens and the Ottoman-Habsburg Rivalry*. PhD dissertation, Georgetown University.

Gutt, Ernst-August (1991/2000) *Translation and Relevance: Cognition and Context*. Manchester: St Jerome.

Hadziabdic, Emina & Hjelm, Katarina (2013) Working with interpreters: Practical advice for use of an interpreter in healthcare. *International Journal of Evidence-Based Healthcare* 11 (1), 69–76.

Hagemann, Susanne (2004) *Translation and Interpreting Studies Programmes and the Bologna Process*. www.fask.uni-mainz.de/user/hagemann/publ/texte.html (accessed 10 February 2014).

Hagen, Gottfried (2003) Translations and translators in a multilingual society: A case study of Persian-Ottoman translations, late 15th to early 17th century. *Eurasian Studies* 2 (1), 95–134.

Haiber, Udo (2004) Spracherkennungssysteme. In K.-U. Carstensen, Ch. Ebert, C. Ebert, S. Jekat, R. Klabunde & H. Langer (eds) *Computerlinguistik und Sprachtechnologie: Eine Einführung*. 2nd rev. ext. edn. Heidelberg: Spektrum, 524–531.

Hale, Adrian & Basides, Helen (2013) *The Keys to Academic English*. South Yarra: Palgrave Macmillan.

Hale, Kimberly J. (2010) Educational interpreters' salaries: Correlations with demographic and employment characteristics. *Journal of Interpretation* 20 (1), 9–30.

Hale, Sandra (1997a) The interpreter on trial: Pragmatics in court interpreting. In S. E. Carr, R. Roberts, A. Dufour & D. Steyn (eds) *The Critical Link: Interpreters in the Community. Papers from the First International Conference on Interpreting in Legal, Health and Social Service Settings*. Amsterdam: John Benjamins, 201–211.

Hale, Sandra (1997b) Interpreting politeness in court: A study of Spanish–English interpreted proceedings. In S. Campbell & S. Hale (eds) *Proceedings of the 2nd Annual Macarthur Interpreting and Translation Conference "Research, Training and Practice"*. Milperra: UWS Macarthur/LARC, 37–45.

Hale, Sandra (1997c) The treatment of register variation in court interpreting. *The Translator* 3 (1), 39–54.

Hale, Sandra, B. (1999) Interpreters' treatment of discourse markers in courtroom questions. *Forensic Linguistics* 6 (1), 57–82.

Hale, Sandra (2001) How are courtroom questions interpreted? An analysis of Spanish interpreters' practices. In I. Mason (ed.) *Triadic Exchanges: Studies in Dialogue Interpreting*. Manchester: St Jerome, 21–50.

Hale, Sandra Beatriz (2004) *The Discourse of Court Interpreting: Discourse Practices of the Law, the Witness and the Interpreter*. Amsterdam: John Benjamins.

Hale, Sandra (2005) The interpreter's identity crisis. In J. House, M. R. Martin Ruano & N. Baumgarten (eds) *Translation and the Construction of Identity*. Seoul: IATIS, 14–29.

Hale, Sandra (2006) Themes and methodological issues in court interpreting research. In E. Hertog & B. van der Veer (eds) *Taking Stock: Research and Methodology in Community Interpreting. Linguistica Antverpiensia – New Series* 5, 205–228.

Hale, Sandra Beatriz (2007) *Community Interpreting*. Basingstoke: Palgrave Macmillan.

Hale, Sandra (2008) Controversies over the role of the court interpreter. In C. Valero-Garcés & A. Martin (eds) *Crossing Borders in Community Interpreting: Definitions and Dilemmas*. Amsterdam: John Benjamins 99–121.

Hale, Sandra B. (2010) The need to raise the bar: Court interpreters as specialized experts. In M. Coulthard & A. Johnson (eds) *The Routledge Handbook of Forensic Linguistics*. London/New York: Routledge, 440–454.

Hale, Sandra (2011a) *Interpreter Policies, Practices and Protocols in Australian Courts and Tribunals: A National Survey*. Melbourne: The Australasian Institute of Judicial Administration Incorporated. www.aija.org.au/online/Pub%20no89.pdf (accessed 11 December 2014).

Hale, Sandra (2011b) Public service interpreting. In K. Malmkjær & K. Windle (eds) *The Oxford Handbook of Translation Studies*. Oxford: Oxford University Press, 343–356.

Hale, Sandra (2013) Interpreting culture: Dealing with cross-cultural issues in court interpreting. *Perspectives: Studies in Translatology* 22 (3), 321–331.

Hale, Sandra B. & Gibbons, John (1999) Varying realities: Patterned changes in the interpreter's representation of courtroom and external realities. *Applied Linguistics* 20 (2), 203–220.

Hale, Sandra B. & Luzardo, César (1997) What am I expected to do? The interpreter's ethical dilemma: A study of Arabic, Spanish and Vietnamese speakers' perceptions and expectations of interpreters. *Antipodean. The Australian Translation Journal* 1, 10–16.

Hale, Sandra & Napier, Jemina (2013) *Research Methods in Interpreting: A Practical Resource*. London: Bloomsbury.

Hale, Sandra & Stern, Ludmila (2011) Interpreter quality and working conditions: Comparing Australian and international courts of justice. *Judicial Officers' Bulletin* 23 (9), 75–78.

Hale, Sandra B., Bond, Nigel & Sutton, Jeanna (2011) Interpreting accent in the courtroom. *Target* 23 (1), 48–61.

Hale, Sandra B, Ozolins, Uldis & Stern, Ludmila (eds) (2009) *Quality in Interpreting – a Shared Responsibility*. Amsterdam: John Benjamins.

Hall, Judith A. & Knapp, Mark L. (2013) *Nonverbal Communication*. Berlin/Boston: De Gruyter Mouton.

Hall, Nigel & Sham, Sylvia (2007) Language brokering as young people's work: Evidence from Chinese adolescents in England. *Language and Education* 21 (1), 16–30.

Halliday, Michael A. K. (1966) Intonation systems in English. In A. McIntosh & M. A. K. Halliday (eds) *Patterns of Language: Papers in General, Descriptive and Applied Linguistics*. London: Longmans, 111–133.

Halliday, Michael A. K. (1978) *Language as Social Semiotic: The Social Interpretation of Language and Meaning*. London: Edward Arnold.

Halliday, Michael A.K. & Hasan, Ruqaiya (1976) *Cohesion in English*. London/New York: Longman.

Halverson, Sandra (1998) Translation studies and representative corpora: Establishing links between translation corpora, theoretical/descriptive categories and a conception of the object of study. *Meta* 43 (4), 494–514.

Hamidi, Miriam & Pöchhacker, Franz (2007) Simultaneous consecutive interpreting: A new technique put to the test. *Meta* 52 (2), 276–289.

Hamilton, Alastair & Richard, Francis (2004) *André Du Ryer and Oriental Studies in Seventeenth-Century France*. London: Arcadian Library in association with Oxford University Press.

Hampers, Louis C. & McNulty, Jennifer E. (2002) Professional interpreters and bilingual physicians in a pediatric emergency department: Effect on resource utilization. *Archives of Pediatrics & Adolescent Medicine* 156 (11), 1108–1113.

Hardin, Russell (2006) *Trust*. Cambridge/Malden, MA: Polity Press.

Hari, Daoud (2008) *The Translator – a Tribesman's Memoir of Darfur*. New York: Random House.

Harmer, Jacolyn (2007) Relay interpretation: A preliminary study. In F. Pöchhacker, A. L. Jakobsen & I. M. Mees (eds) *Interpreting Studies and Beyond: A Tribute to Miriam Shlesinger*. Copenhagen: Samfundslitteratur, 73–88.

Harris, Brian (1977) The importance of natural translation. *Working Papers in Bilingualism* 12, 96–114.

Harris, Brian (1990) Norms in interpretation. *Target* 2 (1), 115–119.

Harris, Brian & Sherwood, Bianca (1978) Translating as an innate skill. In D. Gerver & H. W. Sinaiko (eds) *Language Interpretation and Communication*. New York/London: Plenum Press, 155–170.

Harvey, Michael A. (2003) Shielding yourself from the perils of empathy: The case of sign language interpreters. *Journal of Deaf Studies and Deaf Education* 8 (2), 207–213.

Hasbún Avalos, Oswaldo, Pennington, Kaylin & Osterberg, Lars (2013) Revolutionizing volunteer interpreter services: An evaluation of an innovative medical interpreter education program. *Journal of General Internal Medicine* 28 (12), 1589–1595.

Hatim, Basil & Mason, Ian (1990) *Discourse and the Translator.* London/New York: Longman.

Hatim, Basil & Mason, Ian (1997) *The Translator as Communicator.* London: Routledge.

Haviland, John B. (2003) Ideologies of language: Some reflections on language and U.S. Law. *American Anthropologist* 105 (4), 764–774.

Hawel, Kirsten (2010) *Simultanes versus klassisches Konsekutivdolmetschen: Eine vergleichende textuelle Analyse.* MA thesis, University of Vienna.

Haworth, Kate (2013) Language of police interviews. In C. A. Chapelle (ed.) *The Encyclopedia of Applied Linguistics.* Oxford: Wiley-Blackwell, 3079–3084.

Heffer, Chris (2010) Narrative in the trial. Constructing crime stories in court. In M. Coulthard & A. Johnson (eds) *The Routledge Handbook of Forensic Linguistics.* London/NewYork: Routledge, 199–217.

Heimburger, Franziska (2012a) Fighting together: Language issues in the military coordination of First World War Allied Coalition warfare. In H. Footitt & M. Kelly (eds) *Languages and the Military: Alliances, Occupation and Peace Building.* Basingstoke: Palgrave Macmillan, 47–57.

Heimburger, Franziska (2012b) Of go-betweens and gatekeepers: Considering disciplinary biases in interpreting history through exemplary metaphors. Military interpreters in the Allied Coalition during the First World War. In B. Fischer & M. Nisbeth Jensen (eds) *Translation and the Reconfiguration of Power Relations.* Berlin: LIT, 21–34.

Henderson, John A. (1980) Siblings observed. *Babel* 26 (4), 217–225.

Henderson, John A. (1987) *Personality and the Linguist.* Bradford: Bradford University Press.

Herbert, Jean (1952) *The Interpreter's Handbook: How to Become a Conference Interpreter.* Geneva: Georg.

Herbert, Jean (1976) *Conference Terminology: A Manual for Conference Members and Interpreters.* Amsterdam/New York: Elsevier.

Herbert, Jean (1978) How conference interpretation grew. In D. Gerver & H. W. Sinaiko (eds) *Language Interpretation and Communication.* New York/London: Plenum Press, 5–10.

Heritage, John (1985) Analyzing news interviews: Aspects of the production of talk for an overhearing audience. In T. A. van Dijk (ed.) *Handbook of Discourse Analysis, Vol. III: Discourse and Dialogue.* London: Academic Press, 95–117.

Heritage, John & Clayman, Steven (2010) *Talk in Action: Interactions, Identities and Institutions.* Oxford: Wiley-Blackwell.

Heritage, John & Greatbatch, David (1991) On the institutional character of institutional talk: The case of news interviews. In D. Boden & D. H. Zimmerman (eds) *Talk and Social Structure: Studies in Ethnomethodology and Conversational Analysis.* Cambridge: Blackwell, 93–137.

Hermann, Alfred (1956/2002) Interpreting in Antiquity. In F. Pöchhacker & M. Shlesinger (eds) *The Interpreting Studies Reader.* London/New York: Routledge, 15–22.

Hermanowicz, Joseph C. & Johnson, David R. (2014) Professions. In S. Masamichi, J. Goldstone & E. Zimmermann (eds) *Concise Encyclopedia of Comparative Sociology.* Leiden/Boston: Brill, 209–216.

Hermans, Daan, Bongaerts, Theo, de Bot, Kees & Schreuder, Robert (1998) Producing words in a foreign language: Can speakers prevent interference from their first language? *Bilingualism: Language and Cognition* 1 (3), 213–229.

Hertog, Erik (2013) Legal interpreting. In C. A. Chapelle (ed.) *The Encyclopedia of Applied Linguistics.* Oxford: Wiley-Blackwell, 3274–3281.

Hertog, Erik & van der Veer, Bart (eds) (2006) *Taking Stock: Research and Methodology in Community Interpreting. Linguistica Antverpiensia – New Series* 5. Ghent: Communication & Cognition.

Hervais-Adelman, Alexis G., Moser-Mercer, Barbara & Golestani, Narly (2011) Executive control of language in the bilingual brain: Integrating the evidence from neuroimaging to neuropsychology. *Frontiers in Psychology* 2 (15 September), Art. 234, 1–8.

Hervais-Adelman, Alexis, Moser-Mercer, Barbara, Michel, Christoph M. & Golestani, Narly (2014) fMRI of simultaneous interpretation reveals the neural basis of extreme language control. *Cerebral Cortex.* First published online July 17, 2014. doi: 10.1093/cercor/bhu158.

Hetherington, Ali (2011) A magical profession? Causes and management of occupational stress in the sign language interpreting profession. In L. Leeson, S. Wurm & M. Vermeerbergen (eds) *Signed Language Interpreting: Preparation, Practice and Performance.* Manchester: St. Jerome, 138–159.

Heydon, Georgina & Lai, Miranda (2013) Police interviews mediated by interpreters: An exercise in diminishment? *Investigative Interviewing Research and Practice* 5 (2), 82–98.

Heywood, Colin (2000) A *Buyuruldu* of AH 1100 / AD 1689 for the dragomans of the English Embassy at Istanbul. In Ç. Balim-Harding & C. Imber (eds) *The Balance of Truth: Essays in Honour of Professor Geoffrey Lewis.* Istanbul: Isis Press, 125–144.

Hiebl, Bettina (2011) *Simultanes Konsekutivdolmetschen mit dem Livescribe Echo Smartpen.* MA thesis, University of Vienna.

Hild, Adelina (2007) Establishing rigour in a between-method investigation of SI expertise. In Y. Gambier, M. Shlesinger & R. Stolze (eds) *Doubts and Directions in Translation Studies.* Amsterdam: John Benjamins, 99–112.

Hild, Adelina (2011) Effects of linguistic complexity on expert processing during simultaneous interpreting. In C. Alvstad, A. Hild & E. Tiselius (eds) *Methods and Strategies of Process Research: Integrative Approaches in Translation Studies.* Amsterdam: John Benjamins, 249–267.

Hild, Adelina (2016) Constructing the profile of voluntary interpreters in religious settings. In R. Antonini, L. Cirillo, L. Rossato & I. Torresi (eds) *Non-Professional Interpreting and Translating in Institutional Settings.* Amsterdam: John Benjamins.

Hill, Nicole M. & Schneider, Walter (2006) Brain changes in the development of expertise: Neuroanatomical and neurophysiological evidence about skill-based adaptations. In K. A. Ericsson, N. Charness, P. J. Feltovich & R. R. Hoffman (eds) *The Cambridge Handbook of Expertise and Expert Performance.* Cambridge: Cambridge University Press, 653–682.

HIN (2007) *National Standard Guide for Community Interpreting Services.* Toronto: Healthcare Interpretation Network. http://healthcareinterpretationnetwork.ca/publications/standards/ (accessed 6 September 2013).

Hitzel, Frédéric (ed.) (1995) *Enfants de Langue et Drogmans.* Istanbul: Yapı Kredi Yayınları.

Hlavac, Jim (2010) Shifts in the language of interpretation with bi- or multi-lingual clients: Circumstances and implications for interpreters. *Interpreting* 12 (2), 186–213.

Hlavac, Jim (2013a) A cross-national overview of translator and interpreter certification procedures. *Translation & Interpreting* 5 (1), 32–65.

Hlavac, Jim (2013b) Interpreting in one's own and in closely related languages: Negotiation of linguistic varieties amongst interpreters of the Bosnian, Croatian and Serbian languages. *Interpreting* 15 (1), 94–125.

Hodge, Robert & Kress, Gunther (1993) *Language as Ideology.* 2nd edn. London: Routledge.

Hodzik, Ena (2013) Anticipation during simultaneous interpreting from German into English: An experimental approach. In R. Barranco-Droege, O. García Becerra & M. Pradas Macías (eds) *Quality in Interpreting: Widening the Scope.* Vol. 2. Granada: Editorial Comares, 87–110.

Höfert, Almut (2003) *Den Feind beschreiben: "Türkengefahr" und europäisches Wissen über das Osmanische Reich 1450–1600.* Frankfurt: Campus Verlag.

Hoen, Beth, Nielsen, Kristofer & Sasso, Angela (2006) *Health Care Interpreter Services: Strengthening Access to Primary Health Care. National Report: An overview of the accomplishments, outcomes and learnings of the SAPHC project.* www.criticallink.org/publications-and-links/resources (accessed 6 September 2013).

Hoffman, Robert R. (1997) The cognitive psychology of expertise and the domain of interpreting. *Interpreting* 2 (1/2), 189–230.

Hoffman, Robert R. & Militello, Laura G. (2009) *Perspectives on Cognitive Task Analysis: Historical Origins and Modern Communities of Practice.* New York: Psychology Press.

Hoffman, Robert R., Shadbolt, Nigel R., Burton, Mike A. & Klein, Gary (1995) Eliciting knowledge from experts: A methodological analysis. *Organizational Behavior and Human Decision Processes* 62, 129–158.

Hokkanen, Sari (2012) Simultaneous church interpreting as service. *The Translator* 18 (2), 291–309.

Holmes, James S. (1972/2000) The name and nature of translation studies. In L. Venuti (ed.) *The Translation Studies Reader.* London/New York: Routledge, 172–185.

Holmes, Janet (2008) *An Introduction to Sociolinguistics.* 3rd edn. Harlow: Pearson Longman.

Holmqvist, Kenneth, Nyström, Marcus, Andersson, Richard, Dewhurst, Richard, Jarodzka, Halszka & van de Weijer, Joost (2011) *Eye Tracking: A Comprehensive Guide to Methods and Measures.* New York: Oxford University Press.

Holt, Elizabeth & Johnson, Alison (2010) Legal talk: Socio-pragmatic aspects of legal talk. Police interviews and trial discourse. In M. Coulthard & A. Johnson (eds) *The Routledge Handbook of Forensic Linguistics*. London: Routledge, 21–36.

Holub, Elisabeth (2010) Does intonation matter? The impact of monotony on listener comprehension. *The Interpreters' Newsletter* 15, 117–126.

Horváth, Ildikó (2010) Creativity in interpreting. *Interpreting* 12 (2), 148–158.

Hossain, Mary (1993) The training of interpreters in Arabic and Turkish under Louis XIV: The Ottoman Empire. *Seventeenth-Century French Studies* 15 (1), 279–295.

House, Juliane, Meyer, Bernd & Schmidt, Thomas (2012) CoSi – A corpus of consecutive and simultaneous interpreting. In T. Schmidt & K. Wörner (eds) *Multilingual Corpora and Multilingual Corpus Analysis*. Amsterdam: John Benjamins, 295–304.

Hoza, Jack (1999) Saving face: The interpreter and politeness. *Journal of Interpretation* 1999, 39–70.

Hoza, Jack (2003) Toward an interpreter sensibility: Three levels of ethical analysis and a comprehensive model of ethical decision-making for interpreters. *Journal of Interpretation* 2003, 1–48.

Hsieh, Elaine (2006a) Understanding medical interpreters: Reconceptualizing bilingual health communication. *Health Communication* 20 (2), 177–186.

Hsieh, Elaine (2006b) Conflicts in how interpreters manage their roles in provider–patient interactions. *Social Science & Medicine* 62, 721–730.

Hsieh, Elaine (2007) Interpreters as co-diagnosticians: Overlapping roles and services between providers and interpreters. *Social Science & Medicine* 64, 924–937.

Hsieh, Elaine (2008) "I am not a robot!" Interpreters' views of their roles in health care settings. *Qualitative Health Research* 18 (10), 1367–1383.

Hsieh, Elaine & Hong, Soo Jung (2010) Not all are desired: Providers' views on interpreters' emotional support for patients. *Patient Education and Counseling* 81 (2), 192–197.

Hsieh, Elaine & Kramer, Eric M. (2012) Medical interpreters as tools: Dangers and challenges in the utilitarian approach to interpreters' roles and functions. *Patient Education & Counseling* 89 (1), 158–162.

Hsieh, Elaine, Ju, Hyejung & Kong, Haiying (2010) Dimensions of trust: The tensions and challenges in provider–interpreter trust. *Qualitative Health Research* 20 (2), 170–181.

Hsieh, Elaine, Pitaloka, Dyah & Johnson, Amy J. (2013) Bilingual health communication: Distinctive needs of providers from five specialties. *Health Communication* 28 (6), 557–567.

Hu, Yi & Ericsson, K. Anders (2012) Memorization and recall of very long lists accounted for within long-term working memory framework. *Cognitive Psychology* 64 (4), 235–266.

Huang, Chih-Chieh (2011) *Tracking Eye Movements in Sight Translation – the Comprehension Process in Interpreting*. MA thesis, Graduate Institute of Translation and Interpretation, National Taiwan Normal University.

Hudson, Richard A. (1996) *Sociolinguistics*. 2nd edn. Cambridge: Cambridge University Press.

Humphrey, Janice H. & Alcorn, Bob J. (2001) *So You Want to Be an Interpreter? An Introduction to Sign Language Interpreting*. 3rd edn. Amarillo, TX: H & H Publishing.

Hung, Eva 孔慧怡 (2005) 重寫翻譯史 [*Rewriting Chinese Translation History*]. Hong Kong: Chinese University of Hong Kong.

Hung, Eva & Pollard, David (1998) Chinese tradition. In M. Baker (ed.) *Routledge Encyclopedia of Translation Studies*. London/New York: Routledge, 365–374.

Hurtado Albir, Amparo (2010) Competence. In Y. Gambier & L. van Doorslaer (eds) *Handbook of Translation Studies*. Vol. 1. Amsterdam: John Benjamins, 55–59.

Hymes, Dell (1968) The ethnography of speaking. In J. Fishman (ed.) *Readings in the Sociology of Language*. The Hague: Mouton, 99–138.

Hyönä, Jukka, Tommola, Jorma & Alaja, Anna-Mari (1995) Pupil dilation as a measure of processing load in simultaneous interpretation and other language tasks. *Quarterly Journal of Experimental Psychology Section A* 48 (3), 598–612.

Ibrahim, Noraini (2009) Parliamentary interpreting in Malaysia: A case study. *Meta* 54 (2), 357–369.

Ibrahim, Zubaidah (2007) The interpreter as advocate: Malaysian court interpreting as a case in point. In C. Wadensjö, B. Englund Dimitrova & A.-L. Nilsson (eds) *The Critical Link 4: Professionalisation of Interpreting in the Community*. Amsterdam: John Benjamins, 205–214.

Iglesias Fernández, Emilia (2007) La incidencia del parámetro "agradabilidad de la voz". In A. Collados Aís, E. M. Pradas Macías, E. Stévaux & O. García Becerra (eds) *La Evaluación de la Calidad en Interpretación Simultánea: Parámetros de Incidencia.* Granada: Comares, 37–51.

Iglesias Fernández, Emilia (2010) Verbal and nonverbal concomitants of rapport in health care encounters: Implications for interpreters. *JoSTrans: The Journal of Specialised Translation* 14, 216–228.

Iglesias Fernández, Emilia (2013a) Understanding variability in interpreting quality assessment: Users' sex and judgments for pleasant voice. In C. Way, S. Vandepitte & M. Bartłomiejczyk (eds) *Tracks and Treks in Translation Studies.* Amsterdam: John Benjamins, 103–125.

Iglesias Fernández, Emilia (2013b) Unpacking delivery criteria in interpreting quality assessment. In D. Tsagari & R. van Deemter (eds) *Assessment Issues in Language Translation and Interpreting.* Frankfurt: Peter Lang, 51–66.

Ilg, Gérard (1958) L'interprétation consécutive. *L'Interprète* 13 (3), 10–13.

Ilg, Gérard (1959) L'enseignement de l'interprétation simultanée à l'École d'interprètes de l'Université de Genève. *L'Interprète* 14 (1), 4–11.

Ilg, Gérard (1988) La prise de notes en interprétation consécutive. Une orientation générale. *Parallèles* 9, 9–13.

Ilg, Gérard & Lambert, Sylvie (1996) Teaching consecutive interpreting. *Interpreting* 1 (1), 69–99.

IMIA (2007) *Medical Interpreting Standards of Practice.* www.imiaweb.org/uploads/pages/102.pdf (accessed 12 June 2014).

Inghilleri, Moira (2003) Habitus, field and discourse: Interpreting as a socially situated activity. *Target* 15 (2), 243–268.

Inghilleri, Moira (2005a) Mediating zones of uncertainty: Interpreter agency, the interpreting habitus and political asylum adjudication. *The Translator* 11 (1), 69–85.

Inghilleri, Moira (2005b) The sociology of Bourdieu and the construction of the "object" in translation and interpreting studies. *The Translator* 11 (2), 125–145.

Inghilleri, Moira (2006) Macro-social theory, linguistic ethnography and interpreting research. In E. Hertog & B. van der Veer (eds) *Taking Stock: Research and Methodology in Community Interpreting. Linguistica Antverpiensia – New Series* 5, 57–68.

Inghilleri, Moira (2007) National sovereignty versus universal rights: Interpreting justice in a global context. *Social Semiotics* 17 (2), 195–212.

Inghilleri, Moira (2008) The ethical task of the translator in the geo-political arena: From Iraq to Guantánamo Bay. *Translation Studies* 1 (2), 212–223.

Inghilleri, Moira (2009) Translators in war zones: Ethics under fire in Iraq. In E. Bielsa & C. Hughes (eds) *Globalization, Political Violence and Translation.* Basingstoke: Palgrave Macmillan, 207–221.

Inghilleri, Moira (2010) Afterword: Exploring the task of the activist translator. In J. Boéri & C. Maier (eds) *Compromiso Social y Traducción/Interpretación / Translation/Interpreting and Social Activism.* ECOS: Granada, 152–155.

Inghilleri, Moira (2012) *Interpreting Justice: Ethics, Politics and Language.* London/New York: Routledge.

Inghilleri, Moira (2014) Bourdieu's habitus and Dewey's habits: Complementary views of the social? In G. M. Vorderobermeier (ed.) *Remapping Habitus in Translation Studies.* Amsterdam: Rodopi, 183–199.

Inghilleri, Moira & Harding, Sue-Ann (eds) (2010) *Translation and Violent Conflict.* Special Issue of *The Translator* 16 (2).

Ingram, Robert M. (1985) Simultaneous interpretation of sign languages: Semiotic and psycholinguistic perspectives. *Multilingua* 4 (2), 91–102.

Insana, Lina N. (2009) *Arduous Tasks: Primo Levi, Translation, and the Transmission of Holocaust Testimony.* Toronto: University of Toronto Press.

IoLET (2010) Chartered Institute of Linguists Educational Trust. *Diploma in Public Service Interpreting: Handbook for Candidates.* https://www.ciol.org.uk/images/Qualifications/DPSI/DPSIHandbook.pdf (accessed 13 February 2014).

Isaac, Kim (2002) *Speech Pathology in Cultural and Linguistic Diversity.* London: Whurr.

Isham, William P. (1995) On the relevance of signed languages to research in interpretation. *Target* 7 (1), 135–149.

Isham, William P. (2000) Phonological interference in interpreters of spoken languages: An issue of storage or process? In B. Englund Dimitrova & K. Hyltenstam (eds) *Language Processing and Simultaneous Interpreting: Interdisciplinary Perspectives*. Amsterdam: John Benjamins, 133–149.

Isham, William & Lane, Harlan (1994) A common conceptual code in bilinguals: Evidence from simultaneous interpretation. *Sign Language Studies* 23, 291–317.

ISO (1974/1998) *ISO 2603:1998 Booths for Simultaneous Interpretation: General Characteristics and Equipment*. Geneva: International Organization for Standardization.

ISO (1998) *ISO 4043:1998 Mobile Booths for Simultaneous Interpretation: General Characteristics and Equipment*. Geneva: International Organization for Standardization.

ISO (2000) *ISO 1087-1:2000 Terminology work – Vocabulary – Part 1: Theory and Application*. Geneva: International Organization for Standardization.

Israël, Fortunato (2005) Une théorie en mouvement – Bilan (provisoire) des acquis de la Théorie Interprétative de la Traduction. In F. Israël & M. Lederer (eds) *La Théorie Interprétative de la Traduction – Genèse et Développement*. Caen: Minard lettres modernes, 67–88.

ITI (2014) Professional Interpreters for Justice. www.iti.org.uk/about-us/our-partners/266-professional-interpreters-for-justice (accessed 14 May 2014).

Ito-Bergerot, Hiromi (2006) *Le Processus Cognitif de la Compréhension en Interprétation Consécutive: Acquisition des Compétences chez les Étudiants de la Section Japonaise*. Thèse de doctorat, Université Sorbonne Nouvelle – Paris 3.

Ivanova, Adelina (1999) *Discourse Processing during Simultaneous Interpreting: An Expertise Approach*. PhD dissertation, University of Cambridge.

Ivanova, Adelina (2000) The use of retrospection in research on simultaneous interpretation. In S. Tirkkonen-Condit & R. Jääskeläinen (eds) *Tapping and Mapping the Processes of Translation and Interpretation*. Amsterdam: John Benjamins, 27–52.

Jackson, Philip W. (1992) Conceptions of curriculum and curriculum specialists. In P. W. Jackson (ed.) *Handbook of Research on Curriculum: A Project of the American Educational Research Association*. New York: Macmillan, 3–40.

Jacob, Hans (1962) *Kind meiner Zeit. Lebenserinnerungen*. Köln: Kiepenheuer und Witsch.

Jacobs, Elizabeth A., Diamond, Lisa C. & Stevak, Lisa (2010) The importance of teaching clinicians when and how to work with interpreters. *Patient Education and Counseling* 78 (2), 149–153.

Jacobs, Elizabeth A., Chen, Alice Hm, Karliner, Leah S., Agger-Gupta, Niels & Mutha, Sunita (2006) The need for more research on language barriers in health care: A proposed research agenda. *Milbank Quarterly* 84 (1), 111–133.

Jacobsen, Bente (2003) Pragmatics in court interpreting: Additions. In L. Brunette, G. Bastin, I. Hemlin & H. Clarke (eds) *The Critical Link 3: Interpreters in the Community*. Amsterdam: John Benjamins, 223–238.

Jacobsen, Bente (2008a) Interactional pragmatics and court interpreting: An analysis of face. *Interpreting* 10 (1), 128–158.

Jacobsen, Bente (2008b) Court interpreting and face: An analysis of a court interpreter's strategies for conveying threats to own face. In D. Russell & S. B. Hale (eds) *Interpreting in Legal Settings*. Washington, DC: Gallaudet University Press, 51–71.

Jacobsen, Bente (2012) The significance of interpreting modes for question–answer dialogues in court interpreting. *Interpreting* 14 (2), 217–241.

Jacobson, Holly E. (2009) Moving beyond words in assessing mediated interaction: Measuring interactional competence in healthcare settings. In C. Angelelli & H. Jacobson (eds) *Testing and Assessment in Translation and Interpreting Studies: A Call for Dialogue between Research and Practice*. Amsterdam: John Benjamins, 49–70.

Jacquemet, Marco (2010) The registration interview: Restricting refugees' narrative performances. In M. Baker (ed.) *Critical Readings in Translation Studies*. London: Routledge, 133–151.

Jacquemet, Marco (2011) Crosstalk 2.0: Asylum and communicative breakdowns. *Text & Talk* 31 (4), 475–497.

Jalbert, Maya (1998) Travailler avec un interprète en consultation psychiatrique. *P.R.I.S.M.E.* 8 (3), 94–111.

Janos, Damien (2006) Panaiotis Nicousios and Alexander Mavrocordatos: The rise of the Phanariots and the Office of Grand Dragoman in the Ottoman administration in the second half of the seventeenth century. *Archivum Ottomanicum* 23, 177–196.

Janzen, Terry & Korpinski, Donna (2005) Ethics and professionalism in interpreting. In T. Janzen (ed.) *Topics in Signed Language Interpreting*. Amsterdam: John Benjamins, 165–199.

Jefferson, Gail (2004) Glossary of transcript symbols with an introduction. In G. H. Lerner (ed.) *Conversation Analysis: Studies from the First Generation*. Amsterdam: John Benjamins, 13–31.

Jekat, Susanne & v. Hahn, Walther (2000) Multilingual Verbmobil-dialogs: Experiments, data collection and data analysis. In W. Wahlster (ed.) *Verbmobil: Foundations of Speech-to-Speech Translation*. Berlin: Springer, 577–584.

Jekat, Susanne & Volk, Martin (2010) Maschinelle und computergestützte Übersetzung. In K.-U. Carstensen, Ch. Ebert, C. Ebert, S. Jekat, R. Klabunde & H. Langer (eds) *Computerlinguistik und Sprachtechnologie. Eine Einführung*. 3rd rev. ext. edn. Heidelberg: Spektrum, 642–658.

Jenks, Christopher J. (2011) *Transcribing Talk and Interaction*. Amsterdam: John Benjamins.

Jesse, Alexandra, Vrignaud, Nick, Cohen, Michael M. & Massaro, Dominic W. (2000) The processing of information from multiple sources in simultaneous interpreting. *Interpreting* 5 (2), 95–115.

Jewitt, Carey (ed.) (2009) *The Routledge Handbook of Multimodal Analysis*. London: Routledge.

Ji, Chaozhu (2008) *The Man on Mao's Right: From Harvard Yard to Tiananmen Square, my Life inside China's Foreign Ministry*. New York: Random House.

Jiang, Hong (2013) The interpreter's glossary in simultaneous interpreting: A survey. *Interpreting* 15 (1), 74–93.

Jiménez Ivars, Amparo (1999) *La Traducción a la Vista. Un Análisis Descriptivo*. PhD dissertation, Universitat Jaume I. http://repositori.uji.es/xmlui/bitstream/handle/10234/29703/jimenez-tdx.pdf?sequence=1 (accessed 14 January 2014).

Jiménez Ivars, M. Amparo (2012) *Primeros Pasos hacia la Interpretación Inglés–Español* [*First Steps towards Interpreting English/Spanish*]. Madrid: Edelsa.

Jiménez Ivars, Amparo & Pinazo Calatayud, Daniel (2001) "I failed because I got very nervous". Anxiety and performance in interpreting trainees: An empirical study. *The Interpreters' Newsletter* 11, 105–118.

Jin, Jae-kyo (2011) 18 19 segi tongashiawa chishik chŏngboŭi meshinjŏ, yŏkkwan [The messengers of knowledge/information in eighteenth- and nineteenth-century East Asia: Translating officials]. *Hanguk Hanmunhak Yŏn'gu* [*Research on Korean Literature*] 47, 105–137.

Jörg, Udo (1997) Bridging the gap: Verb anticipation in German–English simultaneous interpreting. In M. Snell-Hornby, Z. Jettmarová & K. Kaindl (eds) *Translation as Intercultural Communication*. Amsterdam: John Benjamins, 217–228.

Johnson, R. Burke & Onwuegbuzie, Anthony J. (2004) Mixed method research: A research paradigm whose time has come. *Educational Researcher* 33 (7), 14–26.

Johnston, Trevor & Schembri, Adam (2007) *Australian Sign Language*. New York: Cambridge University Press.

Jones, Bernhardt E. (2004) Competencies of K–12 educational interpreters: What we need versus what we have. In E. A. Winston (ed.) *Educational Interpreting: How It Can Succeed*. Washington, DC: Gallaudet University Press, 113–131.

Jones, David, Gill, Paramjit, Harrison, Robert, Meakin, Richard & Wallace, Paul (2003) An exploratory study of language interpretation services provided by videoconferencing. *Journal of Telemedicine and Telecare* 9 (1), 51–56.

Jones, Kelly (1996) African languages – a project manager's perspective. *The ATA Chronicle* 25 (5), 23–24.

Jones, Roderick (1998) *Conference Interpreting Explained*. Manchester: St Jerome.

Joukova, Alexandra (2004) "Ein Glück für jeden fremden Mann, der selbst mit Türken sprechen kann". Zur Sprachausbildung vor und kurz nach Etablierung der Orientalischen Akademie. In O. Rathkolb (ed.) *250 Jahre: Von der Orientalischen zur Diplomatischen Akademie in Wien*. Innsbruck: StudienVerlag, 29–46.

Jumpelt, R. Walter (1985) The conference interpreter's working environment under the new ISO and IEC standards. *Meta* 30 (1), 82–90.

Jüngst, Heike E. (2012) Simultaneous film interpreting for children. In M. B. Fischer & M. Wirf Naro (eds) *Translating Fictional Dialogue for Children and Young People*. Berlin: Frank & Timme, 287–300.

Jupp, James (1998) *Immigration*. Melbourne: Oxford University Press.

Just, Marcel A. & Carpenter, Patricia A. (1980) A theory of reading: From eye fixations to comprehension. *Psychological Review* 87 (4), 329–354.

Kaan, Edith (2007) Event-related potentials and language processing: A brief overview. *Language and Linguistics Compass* 1 (6), 571–591.

Kaczmarek, Łukasz (2010) *Modelling Competence in Community Interpreting: Expectancies, Impressions and Implications for Accreditation*. PhD thesis, University of Manchester. https://www.escholar.manchester.ac.uk/item/?pid=uk-ac-man-scw:86535 (accessed 24 February 2015).

Kade, Otto (1963) Der Dolmetschvorgang und die Notation. Bedeutung und Aufgaben der Notiertechnik und des Notiersystems beim konsekutiven Dolmetschen. *Fremdsprachen* 7 (1), 12–20.

Kade, Otto (1967) Zu einigen Besonderheiten des Simultandolmetschens. *Fremdsprachen* 11 (1), 8–17.

Kade, Otto (1968) *Zufall und Gesetzmäßigkeit in der Übersetzung*. Leipzig: Verlag Enzyklopädie.

Kade, Otto & Cartellieri, Claus (1971) Some methodological aspects of simultaneous interpreting. *Babel* 17 (2), 12–16.

Kadric, Mira (2000) Interpreting in the Austrian courtroom. In R. P. Roberts, S. E. Carr, D. Abraham & A. Dufour (eds) *The Critical Link 2: Interpreters in the Community. Selected Papers from the Second International Conference on Interpreting in Legal, Health and Social Service Settings, Vancouver, BC, Canada, 19–23 May 1998*, 153–164.

Kadrić, Mira (2001) *Dolmetschen bei Gericht. Erwartungen, Anforderungen, Kompetenzen*. Wien: WUV-Universitätsverlag.

Kadrić, Mira (2011) *Dialog als Prinzip. Für eine emanzipatorische Praxis und Didaktik des Dolmetschens*. Tübingen: Gunter Narr.

Kadrić, Mira (2014) Giving interpreters a voice: Interpreting studies meets theatre studies. *The Interpreter and Translator Trainer* 8 (3), 452–468.

Kahane, Eduardo (2008) Interpreters in conflict zones: What are the real issues? (Transl. from Spanish by Phil Smith). *Communicate!* www.aiic.net/ViewPage.cfm/page3038.htm (accessed 29 November 2013).

Kaindl, Klaus & Kurz, Ingrid (eds) (2008) *Helfer, Verräter, Gaukler? Das Rollenbild von TranslatorInnen im Spiegel der Literatur*. Wien: LIT-Verlag.

Kaindl, Klaus & Kurz, Ingrid (eds) (2010) *Machtlos, selbstlos, meinungslos? Interdisziplinäre Analysen von ÜbersetzerInnen und DolmetscherInnen in belletristischen Werken*. Wien: LIT-Verlag.

Kaindl, Klaus & Spitzl, Karlheinz (eds) (2014) *Transfiction: Research into the Realities of Translation Fiction*. Amsterdam: John Benjamins.

Kajzer-Wietrzny, Marta (2013) Idiosyncratic features of interpreting style. *New Voices in Translation Studies* 9, 38–52. www.iatis.org/index.php/publications/item/730-current-issue9-2013 (accessed 20 December 2013).

Kälin, Walter (1986) Troubled communication: Cross-cultural misunderstandings in the asylum-hearing. *International Migration Review* 20 (2), 230–241.

Kalina, Sylvia (1998) *Strategische Prozesse beim Dolmetschen. Theoretische Grundlagen, empirische Fallstudien, didaktische Konsequenzen*. Tübingen: Gunter Narr.

Kalina, Sylvia (2000) Interpreting competence and how it is acquired. *The Interpreters' Newsletter* 10, 3–32.

Kalina, Sylvia (2002) Quality in interpreting and its prerequisites – a framework for a comprehensive view. In G. Garzone & M. Viezzi (eds) *Interpreting in the 21st Century: Challenges and Opportunities*. Amsterdam: John Benjamins, 121–130.

Kalina, Sylvia (2005a) Quality in the interpreting process: What can be measured and how? In R. Godijns & M. Hinderdael (eds) *Directionality in Interpreting: The 'Retour' or the Native?* Ghent: Communication and Cognition, 27–46.

Kalina, Sylvia (2005b) Quality assurance for interpreting processes. *Meta* 50 (2), 769–784.

Kammarkollegiet (2014) *Förklaring till bedömningsschema för rollspel, AT-prov* [*Roleplay Evaluation Form Key*]. www.kammarkollegiet.se/sites/default/files/rollspelsbedomning.pdf (accessed 13 February 2014).

Kamwangamalu, Nkonko M. (2013) *Multilingualism in Southern Africa* (Eds. T. K. Bhatia & W. C. Ritchie). Oxford/Malden, MA: Blackwell, 791–812.

Kang, Sinhang (1966) Ijoch'ogi yŏk'akchae taehan koch'al [Research on foreign language scholars during the early Chosŏn Period]. *Chindanhakpo* [*Jindan Journal*] 29/30, 324–338.

Kaplan, Robert M. & Saccuzzo, Dennis P. (2012) *Psychological Testing: Principles, Applications, and Issues*. Belmont, CA: Wadsworth.

Kappler, Matthias (1999) Eine griechische Übersetzung (1664) von Giovanni Molinos "Brevi rudimenti del parlar turchesco". *Archivum Ottomanicum*, no. 17, 271–295.

Karasek, Robert (1979) Job demands, job decision latitude, and mental strain: Implications for job redesign. *Administrative Science Quarterly* 24, 285–307.

Karasek, Robert & Theorell, Töres (1990) *Healthy Work*. New York: Basic Books.

Karlik, Jill (2010) Interpreter-mediated scriptures: Expectation and performance. *Interpreting* 12 (2), 160–185.

Karttunen, Frances (1994a) To the Valley of Mexico: Doña Marina, "La Malinche" (ca. 1500–1527). In F. Karttunen *Between Worlds: Interpreters, Guides, and Survivors*. New Brunswick, NJ: Rutgers University Press, 1–23.

Karttunen, Frances (1994b) Over the Continental Divide: Sacajawea (ca. 1790–1812 or 1884). In F. Karttunen *Between Worlds: Interpreters, Guides, and Survivors*. New Brunswick, NJ: Rutgers University Press, 23–45.

Karttunen, Frances (1997) Rethinking Malinche. In S. Schroeder, S. Wood & R. Haskett (eds) *Indian Women of Early Mexico*. Norman, OK: University of Oklahoma Press, 291–312.

Kaschula, Russell H. (1999) Imbongi and griot: Toward a comparative analysis of oral poetics in Southern and West Africa. *Journal of African Cultural Studies* 12 (1), 55–76.

Katan, David (2009) Translation theory and professional practice: A global survey of the great divide. *Hermes* 42, 111–153.

Katan, David & Straniero Sergio, Francesco (2001) Look who's talking: The ethics of entertainment and talkshow interpreting. *The Translator* 7 (2), 213–237.

Katan, David & Straniero Sergio, Francesco (2003) Submerged ideologies in media interpreting. In M. Calzada Pérez (ed.) *Apropos of Ideology*. Manchester: St. Jerome, 131–144.

Kaufert, Joseph M. & Koolage, William W. (1984) Role conflict among 'culture brokers': The experience of native Canadian medical interpreters. *Social Science & Medicine* 18 (3), 283–286.

Kaufert, Joseph M. & Putsch, Robert W. (1997) Communication through interpreters in healthcare: Ethical dilemmas arising from differences in class, culture, language, and power. *Journal of Clinical Ethics* 8 (1), 71–87.

Kaufmann, Francine (2005) Contribution à l'histoire de l'interprétation consécutive: le *metourguemane* dans les synagogues de l'Antiquité. *Meta* 50 (3), 972–986.

Kautz, Ulrich (2000) *Handbuch Didaktik des Übersetzens und Dolmetschens* [*Translation and Interpreting Teaching Handbook*]. Munich: Iudicium.

Keenan, Edward L. (1967) Muscovy and Kazan: Some introductory remarks on the patterns of steppe diplomacy. *Slavic Review* 26 (4), 548–558.

Keiser, Walter (2004) L'interprétation de conférence en tant que profession et les précurseurs de l'Association Internationale des Interprètes de Conférence (AIIC) 1918–1953. *Meta* 49 (3), 576–608.

Keiser, Walter (2005) When to quit, how to quit: Should AIIC do something about it? www.aiic. net/page/1789/ (accessed 16 July 2014).

Keith, Hugh A. (1984) Liaison interpreting – an exercise in linguistic interaction. In W. Wilss & G. Thome (eds) *Die Theorie des Übersetzens und ihr Aufschlusswert für die Übersetzungs- und Dolmetschdidaktik / Translation Theory and its Implementation in the Teaching of Translation and Interpreting*. Tübingen: Gunter Narr, 308–317.

Kellett Bidoli, Cynthia Jane (2004) Intercultural features of English-to-Italian sign language conference interpretation: A preliminary study for multimodal corpus analysis. *Textus* 17, 127–142.

Kelly, Dorothy & Martin, Anne (2008) Training and education. In M. Baker & G. Saldanha (eds) *Routledge Encyclopedia of Translation Studies*. 2nd edn. London/New York: Routledge, 294–299.

Kelly, Dorothy, Martin, Anne, Nobs, Marie-Luise, Sanchez, Dolores & Way, Catherine (eds) (2003) *La Direccionalidad en Traducción e Interpretación. Perspectivas Teoréticas, Profesionales y Didacticas*. Granada: Atrio.

Kelly, Michael & Baker, Catherine (2013) *Interpreting the Peace: Peace Operations, Conflict and Language in Bosnia-Herzegovina*. London: Palgrave Macmillan.

Kelly, Nataly (2008) *Telephone Interpreting: A Comprehensive Guide to the Profession*. Victoria, BC: Trafford Publishing.

Kemmis, Stephen & McTaggart, Robin (eds) (1988) *The Action Research Reader*. 3rd edn. Deakin: Deakin University Press.

Kemmis, Stephen, McTaggart, Robin & Nixon, Rhonda (2014) *The Action Research Planner: Doing Critical, Participatory Action Research*. Singapore: Springer.

Kendall, Tyler (2013) *Speech Rate, Pause and Sociolinguistic Variation: Studies in Corpus Sociophonetics*. Basingstoke: Palgrave Macmillan.

Kendon, Adam (1967) Some functions of gaze direction in social interaction. *Acta Psychologica* 26, 22–63.

Kendon, Adam (2004) *Gesture: Visible Action as Utterance*. Cambridge: Cambridge University Press.

Kennard, David, Roberts, Jeff & Elliott, Barbara (2002) Group-analytic training conducted through a language interpreter: Are we understanding each other? *Group Analysis* 35 (2), 209–235.

Kennedy, Declan, Hyland, Áine & Ryan, Norma (2009) Learning outcomes and competences. In E. Froment, J. Kohler, L. Purser & L. Wilson (eds) *EUA Bologna Handbook: Making Bologna Work*. Berlin: Raabe, B 2.3-3.

Kent, Stephanie Jo (2009) A discourse of danger and loss: Interpreters on interpreting for the European Parliament. In S. Hale, U. Ozolins & L. Stern (eds) *The Critical Link 5: Quality in Interpreting – a Shared Responsibility*. Amsterdam: John Benjamins, 55–70.

Keselman, Olga, Cederborg, Ann-Christin & Linell, Per (2010) "That is not necessary for you to know!" Negotiation of participation status of unaccompanied children in interpreter-mediated asylum hearings. *Interpreting* 12 (1), 83–104.

Kida, Parvin (2013) Attitudes towards intra-lingual and inter-lingual translation in courtrooms in Japan: Implications for court interpreters. *Ritsumeikan Journal of Asia Pacific Studies* 32, 62–74.

Kilpatrick, Brian R. & Andrews, Jean (2009) Accessibility to theater for deaf and deaf-blind people: Legal, language and artistic considerations. *International Journal of Interpreter Education* 1, 77–94.

Kim, Yang-soo (2003) Chosŏn hugi kyohoeyŏkkwan kyohoech'ŏngsŏnsaenganŭi punsŏgŭl chungshimŭ-ro [The training group among the official interpreters during the late Chosŏn dynasty: On the analysis of Gyohoecheong-seonsaengan]. *Chosŏn shidaesahakpo* [*Journal of History of the Chosŏn Period*] 26, 79–143.

Kintsch, Walter (1988) The role of knowledge in discourse comprehension: A construction-integration model. *Psychological Review* 95 (2), 163–182.

Kintsch, Walter (2004) The construction-integration model of text comprehension and its implications for instruction. In R. B. Ruddell & N. Unrau (eds) *Theoretical Models and Processes of Reading*. 5th edn. Newark, DE: International Reading Association, 1270–1329.

Kirchhoff, Helene (1976a) Das Simultandolmetschen: Interdependenz der Variablen im Dolmetschprozess, Dolmetschmodelle und Dolmetschstrategien. In H. W. Drescher & S. Scheffzek (eds) *Theorie und Praxis des Übersetzens und Dolmetschens*. Bern: Peter Lang, 59–71.

Kirchhoff, Hella (1976b) Das dreigliedrige, zweisprachige Kommunikationssystem Dolmetschen. *Le langage et l'homme* 31, 21–27.

Kirchhoff, Hella (1976/2002) Simultaneous interpreting: Interdependence of variables in the interpreting process, interpreting models and interpreting strategies. In F. Pöchhacker & M. Shlesinger (eds) *The Interpreting Studies Reader*. London/New York: Routledge, 110–119.

Kirchhoff, Helene (1979) Die Notationssprache als Hilfsmittel des Konferenzdolmetschers im Konsekutivvorgang. In W. Mair & E. Sallager (eds) *Sprachtheorie und Sprachenpraxis. Festschrift für Henri Vernay zu seinem 60. Geburtstag*. Tübingen: Gunter Narr, 121–133.

Kishino, Hisashi (2001) *Xavier no dohansha Anjiro* [*Anjiro Accompanying Xavier*]. Tokyo: Yoshikawa-kobun-kan.

Klonowicz, Tatiana (1994) Putting one's heart into simultaneous interpretation. In S. Lambert & B. Moser-Mercer (eds) *Bridging the Gap: Empirical Research in Simultaneous Interpretation*. Amsterdam: John Benjamins, 213–224.

Knapp, Karlfried & Knapp-Potthoff, Annelie (1985) Sprachmittlertätigkeit in interkultureller Kommunikation. In J. Rehbein (ed.) *Interkulturelle Kommunikation*. Tübingen: Gunter Narr, 450–463.

Knapp-Potthoff, Annelie & Knapp, Karlfried (1986) Interweaving two discourses: The difficult task of the non-professional interpreter. In J. House & S. Blum-Kulka (eds) *Interlingual and Intercultural Communication*. Tübingen: Gunter Narr, 151–168.

Knapp-Potthoff, Annelie & Knapp, Karlfried (1987) The man (or woman) in the middle: Discoursal aspects of non-professional interpreting. In K. Knapp, W. Enninger & A. Knapp-Potthoff (eds) *Analyzing Intercultural Communication*. The Hague: Mouton, 181–211.

Ko, Leong (1996) Business setting. In A. Gentile, U. Ozolins & M. Vasilakakos, *Liaison Interpreting: A Handbook*. Melbourne: Melbourne University Press, 116–124.

Ko, Leong (2006a) Teaching interpreting by distance mode: Possibilities and constraints. *Interpreting* 8 (1), 67–96.

Ko, Leong (2006b) The need for long-term empirical studies in remote interpreting research: A case study of telephone interpreting. In E. Hertog & B. van der Veer (eds) *Taking Stock: Research and Methodology in Community Interpreting. Linguistica Antverpiensia – New Series* 5. Antwerp: Hoger Instituut voor Vertalers en Tolken, 325–340.

Ko, Leong (2008) Teaching interpreting by distance mode: An empirical study. *Meta* 53 (4), 814–840.

Ko, Leong & Chen, Nian-Shing (2011) Online interpreting in synchronous cyber classrooms. *Babel* 57 (2), 123–143.

Köpke, Barbara & Nespoulous, Jean Luc (2006) Working memory performance in expert and novice interpreters. *Interpreting* 8 (1), 1–23.

Köpke, Barbara & Signorelli, Teresa M. (2012) Methodological aspects of working memory assessment in simultaneous interpreters. *International Journal of Bilingualism* 16 (2), 183–197.

Kohn, Kurt & Kalina, Sylvia (1996) The strategic dimension of interpreting. *Meta* 41 (1), 118–138.

Kolb, Waltraud & Pöchhacker, Franz (2008) Interpreting in asylum appeal hearings: Roles and norms revisited. In D. Russell & S. Hale (eds) *Interpreting in Legal Settings*. Washington, DC: Gallaudet University Press, 26–50.

Kolnik, Titus (1978) Q. Atilius Primus – Interprex Centurio und Negotiator. *Acta Archaeologica Academiae Scientiarum Hungaricae* 30, 61–75.

Kołodziejczyk, Dariusz (2011) *The Crimean Khanate and Poland-Lithuania: International Diplomacy on the European Periphery (15th–18th Century). A Study of Peace Treaties Followed by Annotated Documents*. Leiden: Brill.

Komter, Martha L. (2002) The suspect's own words: The treatment of written statements in Dutch courtrooms. *International Journal of Speech, Language and the Law* 9 (2), 168–192.

Komter, Martha (2005) Understanding problems in an interpreter-mediated police interrogation. In S. Lee Burns (ed.) *Ethnographies of Law and Social Control*. Bingley: Emerald Group Publishing, 203–224.

Komter, Martha L. (2006) From talk to text: The interactional construction of a police record. *Research on Language and Social Interaction* 39 (3), 201–228.

Kondo, Masaomi (1990) What conference interpreters should not be expected to do. *The Interpreters' Newsletter* 3, 59–65.

Kondo, Masaomi (2003) 3-party 2-language model of interpreting revisited. *Forum* 1 (1), 77–96.

Kondo, Masaomi (2009) Genesis of the Japan Association for Interpretation Studies. http://aiic. net/page/3263 (accessed 31 January 2014).

Kopczyński, Andrzej (1980) *Conference interpreting: Some Linguistic and Communicative Problems*. Poznań: Adam Mickiewicz University Press.

Kopczyński, Andrzej (1982) Effects of some characteristics of impromptu speech on conference interpreting. In N. E. Enkvist (ed.) *Impromptu Speech: A Symposium*. Åbo: Åbo Akademi, 255–266.

Kopczyński, Andrzej (1994) Quality in conference interpreting: Some pragmatic problems. In M. Snell-Hornby, F. Pöchhacker & K. Kaindl (eds) *Translation Studies: An Interdiscipline*. Amsterdam: John Benjamins, 189–198.

Korchilov, Igor (1999) *Translating History: Thirty Years on the Front Lines of Diplomacy with a Top Russian Interpreter*. New York: Scribner.

Koutzakiotis, Georgios (2011) Αναμένοντας Το Τέλος Του Κόσμου Τον 17ο Αιώνα. Ο Εβραίος Μεσσίας Και Ο Μέγας Διερμηνέας [*Awaiting the End of the World in the 17th Century. The Jewish Messiah and the Grand Dragoman*]. Athens: Institute for Neohellenic Research / National Hellenic Research Foundation.

Kredens, Krzysztof & Morris, Ruth (2010) "A shattered mirror?" Interpreting in legal contexts outside the courtroom. In M. Coulthard & A. Johnson (eds) *The Routledge Handbook of Forensic Linguistics*. London/New York: Routledge, 455–469.

Krings, Hans P. (1986) *Was in den Köpfen von Übersetzern vorgeht. Eine empirische Untersuchung zur Struktur des Übersetzungsprozesses an fortgeschrittenen Französischlernern*. Tübingen: Gunter Narr.

Krog, Antjie (1998) *Country of My Skull*. Johannesburg: Random House.

Krog, Antjie, Mpolweni, Nosisi & Ratele, Kopano (2009) *There was this Goat: Investigating the Truth Commission Testimony of Notrose Nobomvu Konile*. Durban: University of KwaZulu-Natal Press.

Krouglov, Alexander (1999) Police interpreting: Politeness and sociocultural context. *The Translator* 5 (2), 285–302.

Krouse, Lauri (2010) Cooperative learning applied to interpreting education. *International Journal of Interpreter Education* 2, 180–200.

Krstić, Tijana (2009) Illuminated by the light of Islam and the glory of the Ottoman Sultanate: Self-narratives of conversion to Islam in the age of confessionalization. *Comparative Studies in Society and History* 51 (1): 35–63.

Krstić, Tijana (2011) Of translation and Empire: Sixteenth-century Ottoman imperial interpreters as Renaissance go-betweens. In C. Woodhead (ed.) *The Ottoman World*. London: Routledge, 130–142.

Krystallidou, Demi (2012) On mediating agents' moves and how they might affect patient-centredness in mediated medical consultations. *Linguistica Antverpiensia – New Series* 11, 75–94.

Kuhiwczak, Piotr (2011) Mediating trauma: How do we read the Holocaust memoirs? In J. Parker & T. Mathew (eds) *Tradition, Translation, Trauma*. Oxford: Oxford University Press, 283–297.

Kuhn, Thomas S. (1962/1996) *The Structure of Scientific Revolutions*. 3rd edn. Chicago/London: The University of Chicago Press.

Kujamäki, Pekka (2012) Mediating for the Third Reich: On military translation cultures in World War II in Northern Finland. In H. Footitt & M. Kelly (eds) *Languages and the Military: Alliances, Occupation and Peace Building*. Basingstoke: Palgrave Macmillan, 86–99.

Kumcu, Alper (2011) *Visual Focal Loci in Simultaneous Interpreting*. Master's thesis, Department of Translation and Interpreting, Hacettepe University Graduate School of Social Sciences.

Kunenkov, Boris A. (2012) Perevodčiki i tolmači Posolskogo prikaza vo vtoroj četverti XVII v.: funkcii, čislennost', porjadok priema [Posolsky Prikaz translators and interpreters in the second quarter of the 17th century: Functions, numbers, enrolment procedures]. http://mkonf.iriran.ru/papers.php?id=50 (accessed 07 May 2014).

Kurz, Ingrid (1985) The rock tombs of the Princes of Elephantine: Earliest references to interpretation in Pharaonic Egypt. *Babel* 31, 213–218.

Kurz, Ingrid (1990) Overcoming language barriers in European television. In D. Bowen & M. Bowen (eds) *Interpreting – Yesterday, Today and Tomorrow*. New York: SUNY, 168–175.

Kurz, Ingrid (1991) Conference interpreting: Job satisfaction, occupational prestige and desirability. In M. Jovanović (ed.) *XIIth World Congress of FIT – Belgrade 1990. Proceedings*. Belgrade: Prevodilac, 363–376.

Kurz, Ingrid (1992) "Shadowing" exercises in interpreter training. In C. Dollerup & A. Loddegaard (eds) *Teaching Translation and Interpreting: Training, Talent and Experience*. Amsterdam: John Benjamins, 245–250.

Kurz, Ingrid (1993a) Conference interpretation: Expectations of different user groups. *The Interpreters' Newsletter* 5, 13–21.

Kurz, Ingrid (1993b) The 1992 U.S. presidential elections: Interpreting the American debathon for Austrian television. In C. Picken (ed.) *Translation – The Vital Link. 13th World Congress of FIT*. Vol. 1. London: Institute of Translation and Interpreting, 441–445.

Kurz, Ingrid (1995) Watching the brain at work – an exploratory study of EEG changes during simultaneous interpreting (SI). *The Interpreters' Newsletter* 6, 3–16.

Kurz, Ingrid (1997a) Getting the message across – simultaneous interpreting for the media. In M. Snell-Hornby, Z. Jettmarová & K. Kaindl (eds) *Translation as Intercultural Communication*. Amsterdam: John Benjamins, 195–205.

Kurz, Ingrid (1997b) Interpreters: Stress and situation-dependent control of anxiety. In K. Klaudy & J. Kohn (eds) *Transferre Necesse est: Proceedings of the 2nd International Conference on Current Trends in Studies in Translation and Interpreting.* Budapest: Scholastica, 201–206.

Kurz, Ingrid (2001) Conference interpreting: Quality in the ears of the user. *Meta* 46 (2), 394–409.

Kurz, Ingrid (2002a) Physiological stress responses during media and conference interpreting. In G. Garzone & M. Viezzi (eds) *Interpreting in the 21st Century: Challenges and Opportunities.* Amsterdam, John Benjamins, 195–202.

Kurz, Ingrid (2002b) Interpreting training programmes: The benefits of coordination, cooperation, and modern technology. In E. Hung (ed.) *Teaching Translation and Interpreting 4: Building Bridges.* Amsterdam: John Benjamins, 65–72.

Kurz, Ingrid (2003) Physiological stress during simultaneous interpreting: A comparison of experts and novices. *The Interpreters' Newsletter* 12, 51–67.

Kurz, Ingrid (2007) The fictional interpreter. In F. Pöchhacker, A. Lykke Jakobsen & I. M. Mees (eds) *Interpreting Studies and Beyond. A Tribute to Miriam Shlesinger.* Copenhagen: Samfund-slitteratur Press.

Kurz, Ingrid (2008) The impact of non-native English on students' interpreting performance. In G. Hansen, A. Chesterman & H. Gerzymisch-Arbogast (eds) *Efforts and Models in Interpreting and Translation Research: A Tribute to Daniel Gile.* Amsterdam: John Benjamins, 179–192.

Kurz, Ingrid & Färber, Birgit (2003) Anticipation in German–English simultaneous interpreting. *Forum* 1 (2), 123–150.

Kurz, Ingrid & Kaindl, Klaus (eds) (2005) *Wortklauber, Sinnverdreher, Brückenbauer? Dolmetscher-Innen und ÜbersetzerInnen als literarische Geschöpfe.* Wien: LIT.

Kurz, Ingrid & Pöchhacker, Franz (1995) Quality in TV interpreting. *Translatio. Nouvelles de la FIT – FIT Newsletter* N.s. 14 (3/4), 350–358.

Kurz, Marlene, Scheutz, Martin, Vocelka, Karl & Winkelbauer, Thomas (2005) The Ottoman Empire and the Habsburg Monarchy. In M. Kurz, M. Scheutz, K. Vocelka & T. Winkelbauer (eds) *Das Osmanische Reich und die Habsburgermonarchie.* Vienna: R. Oldenbourg, 24–33.

Kussmaul, Paul (1995) *Training the Translator.* Amsterdam: John Benjamins.

Kusterer, Hermann (1995) *Der Kanzler und der General.* Stuttgart: Neske.

Kutz, Wladimir (1997) Gut für wen? Zur Bewertung von Konsekutivdolmetschleistungen. In E. Fleischmann, W. Kutz & P. Schmitt (eds) *Translationsdidaktik – Grundfragen der Übersetzungswissenschaft.* Tübingen: Gunter Narr, 243–253.

Kutz, Wladimir (2010) *Dolmetschkompetenz: Was muss der Dolmetscher wissen und können?* Munich: Europäischer Universitätsverlag.

Kvale, Steinar (1996) *InterViews: An Introduction to Qualitative Research Interviewing.* London: Sage.

Ladd, Paddy (2003) *Understanding Deaf Culture: In Search of Deafhood.* Clevedon: Multilingual Matters.

Lamberger-Felber, Heike (2001) Text-oriented research on interpreting: Examples from a case study. *Hermes: Journal of Linguistics* 26, 29–64.

Lamberger-Felber, Heike (2003) Performance variability among conference interpreters: Examples from a case study. In Á. Collados Aís, M. M. Fernández Sánchez & D. Gile (eds) *La evaluación de la calidad en interpretación: Investigación.* Granada: Comares, 147–168.

Lamberger-Felber, Heike & Schneider, Julia (2008) Linguistic interference in simultaneous interpreting with text: A case study. In G. Hansen, A. Chesterman & H. Gerzymisch-Arbogast (eds) *Efforts and Models in Interpreting and Translation Research: A Tribute to Daniel Gile.* Amsterdam: John Benjamins, 215–236.

Lambert, Silvie (1988a) Information processing among conference interpreters: A test of the depth-of-processing hypothesis. *Meta* 33 (3), 377–387.

Lambert, Sylvie (1988b) A human information processing and cognitive approach to the training of simultaneous interpreters. In D. L. Hammond (ed.) *Languages at Crossroads: Proceedings of the 29th Annual Conference of the American Translator Association.* Medford, NJ: Learned Information, 379–387.

Lambert, Sylvie (1989a) La formation d'interprètes: la méthode cognitive. *Meta* 34 (4), 736–744.

Lambert, Sylvie (1989b) Information processing among conference interpreters: A test of the depth-of-processing hypothesis. In L. Gran & J. Dodds (eds) *The Theoretical and Practical Aspects of Teaching Conference Interpretation.* Udine: Campanotto, 83–91.

Lambert, Sylvie (1991) Aptitude testing for simultaneous interpretation at the University of Ottawa. *Meta* 36 (4), 586–594.

Lambert, Sylvie (1992) Shadowing. *The Interpreters' Newsletter* 4, 15–24.

Lambert, Sylvie (2004) Shared attention during sight translation, sight interpretation and simultaneous interpretation. *Meta* 49 (2), 294–306.

Lampropoulou, Anastasia (2010) Babels' interpreting policy in the Athens European Social Forum: A socio-political approach to interpreting. In J. Boéri & C. Maier (eds) *Compromiso Social y Traducción/Interpretación – Translation/Interpreting and Social Activism*. Granada: ECOS, 28–37.

Lan, Shi-chi Mike (2016) Crime *of* interpreting: Taiwanese interpreters as war criminals of the Second World War. In K. Takeda & J. Baigorri-Jalón (eds) *New Insights in the History of Interpreting*. Amsterdam: John Benjamins.

Lang, Ranier (1976) Interpreters in local courts in Papua New Giunea. In W. M. O. Barr & J. F. O. Barr (eds) *Language and Politics*. The Hague: Mouton, 327–365.

Lang, Ranier (1978) Behavioural aspects of liaison interpreters in Papua New Guinea: Some preliminary observations. In D. Gerver & H. W. Sinaiko (eds) *Language Interpretation and Communication*. New York/London: Plenum Press, 231–244.

Lansing, Robert (1921) *The Big Four and Others of the Peace Conference*. Boston/New York: Houghton Mifflin.

Laplace, Colette (1994) *Théorie du Langage et Théorie de la Traduction. Les Concepts-clés de Trois Auteurs: Kade (Leipzig), Coseriu (Tübingen), Seleskovitch (Paris)*. Paris: Didier Érudition.

Laplace, Colette (2005) La genèse de la Théorie Interprétative de la Traduction. In F. Israël & M. Lederer (eds) *La Théorie Interprétative de la Traduction – Genèse et Développement*. Caen: Minard lettres modernes, 21–66.

Larson, Magali Sarfatti (1977) *The Rise of Professionalism: A Sociological Analysis*. Berkeley/Los Angeles/London: University of California Press.

Laster, Kathy & Taylor, Veronica (1994) *Interpreters and the Legal System*. Sydney: Federation Press.

Lauterbach, Eike (2009) *Sprechfehler und Interferenzprozesse beim Dolmetschen [Speech Errors and Interference Processes in Interpreting]*. Frankfurt: Peter Lang.

Laver, John (1980) *The Phonetic Description of Voice Quality*. Cambridge: Cambridge University Press.

Laviosa, Sara (2003) Corpora and translation studies. In S. Granger, J. Lerot & S. Petch-Tyson (eds) *Corpus-based Approaches to Contrastive Linguistics and Translation Studies*. Amsterdam/New York: Rodopi, 45–54.

Lavric, Eva (2007) Traduttore, traditore? Javier Marías' interpreting scene. *Perspectives. Studies in Translatology* 15 (2), 73–91.

Lawrance, Benjamin N., Osborn, Emily Lynn & Roberts, Richard L. (eds) (2006) *Intermediaries, Interpreters and Clerks: African Employees in the Making of Colonial Africa*. Madison, WI: The University of Wisconsin Press.

Lazarus, Richard S. (1966) *Psychological Stress and the Coping Process*. New York: McGraw-Hill.

Le Ny, Jean François (1978) Psychosemantics and simultaneous interpretation. In D. Gerver & H. W. Sinaiko (eds) *Language Interpretation and Communication*. New York/London: Plenum Press, 289–298.

Leanza, Yvan (2005) Roles of community interpreters in pediatrics as seen by interpreters, physicians and researchers. *Interpreting* 7 (2), 167–192.

Leanza, Yvan (2011) *Exercer la Pédiatrie en Contexte Multiculturel. Une Approche Complémentariste du Rapport Institutionnalisé à l'Autre*. Genève: Georg.

Leanza, Yvan, Boivin, Isabelle, Moro, Marie-Rose, Rousseau, Cécile, Brisset, Camille, Rosenberg, Ellen & Hassan, Ghayda (2014). Integration of interpreters in mental health interventions with children and adolescents: The need for a framework. *Transcultural Psychiatry*. First published online 11 December 2014.

Lebese, Samuel (2011) A pilot study on the undefined role of court interpreters in South Africa. *Southern African Linguistics and Applied Language Studies* 29 (3), 343–357.

LeCompte, Margaret D. & Schensul, Jean J. (1999) *Analyzing and Interpreting Ethnographic Data (The Ethnographer's Toolkit Vol. 5)*. Walnut Creek, CA: Altamira Press.

Lederer, Marianne (1976/2014) Synecdoque et traduction. *Etudes de Linguistique Appliquée* 24, 13–41. Repr. in D. Seleskovitch & M. Lederer (2014) *Interpréter pour Traduire* (5th edn) as "Implicite et explicite". Paris: Les Belles Lettres, 86–9.

Lederer, Marianne (1978) Simultaneous interpretation – units of meaning and other features. In D. Gerver & H. W. Sinaiko (eds) *Language Interpretation and Communication*. New York/London: Plenum Press, 323–332.

Lederer, Marianne (1981) *La Traduction Simultanée – Expérience et Théorie*. Paris: Minard Lettres Modernes.

Lederer, Marianne (1990) The role of cognitive complements in interpreting. In D. Bowen & M. Bowen (eds) *Interpreting – Yesterday, Today, and Tomorrow*. Binghamton, NY: SUNY, 53–60.

Lederer, Marianne (2002) Correspondances et équivalences – faits de langue et faits de discours en traduction. In F. Israël (ed.) *Identité, Altérité, Équivalence: La Traduction comme Relation*. Paris: Minard lettres modernes, 17–34.

Lederer, Marianne (2003) *Translation – the Interpretive Model* (Trans. Ninon Larché). Manchester: St Jerome.

Lederer, Marianne (2008) Des méthodes de recherche en traductologie. In C. Balliu (ed.) *Traduire: un Métier d'Avenir*. Bruxelles: Les Éditions du Hazard, Vol. 1, 127–154.

Lee, Jieun (2007) Telephone interpreting – seen from the interpreter's perspective. *Interpreting* 9 (2), 231–252.

Lee, Jieun (2009a) Conflicting views on court interpreting examined through surveys of legal professionals and court interpreters. *Interpreting* 11 (1), 35–56.

Lee, Jieun (2009b) Interpreting inexplicit language during courtroom examination. *Applied Linguistics* 30 (1), 93–114.

Lee, Jieun (2010) Interpreting reported speech in witnesses' evidence. *Interpreting* 12 (1), 60–82.

Lee, Jieun (2013) A study of facework in interpreter-mediated courtroom examination. *Perspectives: Studies in Translatology* 21 (1), 82–99.

Lee, Jin-hee (1986) Chosŏnwangjohuban'giŭi t'ongshinsa [Tongsinsa during the second half of the Chosŏn Dynasty]. In National Museum of Korea (ed.) *Chosŏnshidaet'ongshinsa* [*Delegations to Japan during the Chosŏn Dynasty*]. Seoul: Samhwa, 98–117.

Lee, Mi-sook (2006) Won ganseobgi yeoggwanui hwaldong [The activities of interpreters during the Mongolian intervention period]. *Sangmyeongsahak* [*The Sangmyeong History*] Vols 10–12, 171–200.

Lee, Mi-sook (2009) Koryŏ shidaeŭi yŏkkwan yŏn-gu [A study of Yuk-kwan of the Koryo period]. *Han'guksasanggwa munhwa* [*Korean Ideology and Culture*] 46, 201–234.

Lee, Sang-Bin (2014) An interpreting self-efficacy (ISE) scale for undergraduate students majoring in consecutive interpreting: Construction and preliminary validation. *The Interpreter and Translator Trainer* 8 (2), 183–203.

Lee, Tae-Hyung (1999) Speech proportion and accuracy in simultaneous interpretation from English into Korean. *Meta* 44 (2), 260–267.

Lee, Tae-Hyung (2002) Ear voice span in English into Korean simultaneous interpretation. *Meta* 47 (4), 596–606.

Lee, Tae-Hyung (2003) Tail-to-tail span: A new variable in conference interpreting research. *Forum* 1 (1), 41–62.

Leeson, Lorraine (2005) Making the effort in simultaneous interpreting: Some considerations for signed language interpreters. In T. Janzen (ed.) *Topics in Signed Language Interpreting*. Amsterdam: John Benjamins, 51–68.

Leeson, Lorraine (2008) Quantum leap: Leveraging the Signs of Ireland digital corpus in Irish Sign Language/English interpreter training. *The Sign Language Translator and Interpreter* 2 (2), 149–176.

Leeson, Lorraine & Vermeerbergen, Myriam (2010) Sign language interpreting and translating. In Y. Gambier & L. van Doorslaer (eds) *Handbook of Translation Studies*. Vol. 1. Amsterdam: John Benjamins, 324–328.

Leeson, Lorraine & Calle, Lourdes (2013) *Learning Outcomes for Graduates of a Three Year Sign Language Interpreting Programme*. Brussels: European Forum of Sign Language Interpreters.

Legreve, Robert (1999) Telephone interpreting in Belgium and the Netherlands. In M. Erasmus, L. Mathibela, E. Hertog & H. Antonissen (eds) *Liaison Interpreting in the Community*. Hatfield: Van Schaik, 190–196.

Lehiste, Ilse (1970) *Suprasegmentals*. Cambridge, MA/London: MIT Press.

Leigh, Irene W. (ed.) (1999) *Psychotherapy with Deaf Clients from Diverse Groups*. Washington, DC: Gallaudet University Press.

Lesch, Harold (2010) A descriptive overview of the interpreting service in parliament. *Acta Academica* 42 (3), 38–60.

Lesznyák, Márta (2007) Conceptualizing translation competence. *Across Languages and Cultures* 8 (2), 167–194.

Levelt, Willem J. M. (1983) Monitoring and self-repair in speech. *Cognition* 14 (1), 41–104.

Levelt, Willem J. M. (1989) *Speaking: From Intention to Articulation*. Cambridge, MA: MIT Press.

Levelt, Willem J. M. & Florès d'Arcais, Giovanni B. (1978) *Studies in the Perception of Language*. New York/Toronto: John Wiley and Sons.

Levi, Primo (1988) *The Drowned and the Saved* (Trans. Raymond Rosenthal). London: Abacus.

Levin, Michael E. (2006) Language as a barrier to care for Xhosa-speaking patients at a South African paediatric teaching hospital. *South African Medical Journal* 96 (10), 1076–1079.

Levinson, Stephen C. (1988) Putting linguistics on a proper footing: Explorations in Goffman's concepts of participation. In P. Drew & A. Wootton (eds) *Erving Goffman: Exploring the Interaction Order*. Cambridge: Polity Press, 160–227.

Levy, Isaac (1963) *The Synagogue: Its History and Function*. London: Vallentine Mitchell.

Lewin, Kurt (1947) Frontiers in group dynamics: Concept, method and reality in social science: social equilibria and social change. *Human Relations* 1 (1), 5–41.

Lewis & Clark (2005) *The Journals of the Lewis and Clark Expedition*. University of Nebraska–Lincoln Libraries–Electronic Text Center. http://lewisandclarkjournals.unl.edu/namesindex (accessed 9 October 2013).

Li, Nanqiu 黎難秋 (2002) 中國口譯史 [*A Chinese History of Interpreting*]. Qingdao: Qingdao chubanshe.

Li, Nanqiu (2006) 中國科學翻譯史 [*The History of Science Translation in China*]. Hefei: University of Science and Technology of China Press.

Lichtheim, Miriam (1973–1980) *Ancient Egyptian Literature: A Book of Readings*. 3 Vols. Berkeley: University of California Press.

Licoppe, Christian & Vernier, Maud (2013) Interpreting, video communication and the sequential reshaping of institutional talk in the bilingual and distributed courtroom. *International Journal of Speech, Language and the Law* 20 (2), 247–275.

Lin, I-hsin Iris, Chang, Feng-lan Ann & Kuo, Feng-lan (2013) The impact of non-native accented English on rendition accuracy in simultaneous interpreting. *Translation & Interpreting* 5 (2), 30–44.

Lin, Yuru, Lei, Tianfang, Lonergan, Jack, Chen, Jing, Xiao, Xiaoyan & Zhang, Youping (1999) *Interpreting for Tomorrow (Teachers' Book)* [*Xinbian yingyu kouyi jiaocheng (jiaoshi yong shu)*]. Shanghai: Shanghai Foreign Language Education Press.

Linell, Per (1998) *Approaching Dialogue: Talk, Interaction and Contexts in Dialogical Perspectives*. Amsterdam, John Benjamins.

Linell, Per (2005) *The Written Language Bias in Linguistics: Its Nature, Origins and Transformations*. London: Routledge.

Linell, Per & Luckmann, Thomas (1991) Asymmetries in dialogue: Some conceptual preliminaries. In I. Marková & K. Foppa (eds) *Asymmetries in Dialogue*. Hemel Hempstead: Harvester Wheatsheaf, 1–20.

Linell, Per, Wadensjö, Cecilia & Jönsson, Linda (1992) Establishing communicative contact through a dialogue interpreter. In A. Grindsted & J. Wagner (eds) *Communication for Specific Purposes / Fachsprachliche Kommunikation*. Tübingen: Gunter Narr, 125–142.

Liontou, Konstantina (2011) Strategies in German-to-Greek simultaneous interpreting: A corpus-based approach. *Gramma* 19, 37–56. www.enl.auth.gr/gramma/gramma11/Liontou.pdf (accessed 25 December 2013).

Liontou, Konstantina (2012) *Anticipation in German to Greek Simultaneous Interpreting: A Corpus-Based Approach*. PhD dissertation, University of Vienna.

Liontou, Konstantina (2013) Anticipation in German-to-Greek simultaneous interpreting: Does (erroneous) anticipation influence interpreting quality? In O. García Becerra, E. M. Pradas Macías & R. Barranco-Droege (eds) *Quality in Interpreting: Widening the Scope*. Granada: Comares. Vol. 1, 221–244.

Lipkin, Shira L. (2010) Norms, ethics and role among military court interpreters: The unique case of the Yehuda Court. In M. Shlesinger & F. Pöchhacker (eds) *Doing Justice to Court Interpreting*. Amsterdam: John Benjamins, 85–100.

Liu, Heping (1996) *Enseignement de la Consécutive en fin de Cursus d'Enseignement d'Études Universitaires de Langues: Application aux Combinaisons Français-Chinois et Chinois-Français.* Thèse de doctorat, Université Sorbonne Nouvelle – Paris 3.

Liu, Minhua (1993/2008) 逐步口譯與筆記 [*Consecutive Interpreting and Note-taking*]. Taipei: Bookman.

Liu, Minhua (2008) How do experts interpret? Implications from research in interpreting studies and cognitive science. In G. Hansen, A. Chesterman & H. Gerzymisch-Arbogast (eds) *Efforts and Models in Interpreting and Translation Research: A Tribute to Daniel Gile*. Amsterdam: John Benjamins, 159–177.

Liu, Minhua (2011) Methodology in interpreting studies: A methodological review of evidence-based research. In B. Nicodemus & L. Swabey (eds) *Advances in Interpreting Research: Inquiry in Action*. Amsterdam: John Benjamins, 85–119.

Liu, Minhua (2013) Design and analysis of Taiwan's interpretation certification examination. In D. Tsagari & R. van Deemter (eds) *Assessment Issues in Language Translation and Interpreting*. Frankfurt: Peter Lang, 163–178.

Liu, Minhua & Chiu, Yu-Hsien (2009) Assessing source material difficulty for consecutive interpreting: Quantifiable measures and holistic judgment. *Interpreting* 11 (2), 244–266.

Liu, Minhua, Chang, Chia-chien & Wu, Shao-chuan (2008) 口譯訓練學校之評估作法：臺灣與中英美十一校之比較 [Interpretation evaluation practices: Comparison of eleven schools in Taiwan, China, Britain, and the USA]. *Compilation and Translation Review* 1 (1), 1–42.

Liu, Minhua, Schallert, Diane L. & Carroll, Patrick J. (2004) Working memory and expertise in simultaneous interpreting. *Interpreting* 6 (1), 19–42.

Livingston, Sue, Singer, Bonnie & Abramson, Theodore (1994) Effectiveness compared: ASL interpretation vs. transliteration. *Sign Language Studies* 82 (1), 1–54.

Llewellyn-Jones, Peter (2004) Interpreting Shakespeare's plays into British Sign Language. In A. J. Hoenselaars (ed.) *The Arden Companion: Shakespeare and the Language of Translation*. London: Thomson Publishing, 199–213.

Llewellyn Jones, Peter & Lee, Robert G. (2013) Getting to the core of role: Defining interpreters' role-space. *International Journal of Interpreter Education* 5 (2), 54–72.

Llewellyn-Jones, Peter & Lee, Robert G. (2014) *Redefining the Role of the Community Interpreter: The Concept of Role-Space*. Lincoln, UK: SLI Press.

Locatis, Craig, Williamson, Deborah, Sterrett, James, Detzler, Isabel & Ackerman, Michael (2011) Video medical interpretation over 3G cellular networks: A feasibility study. *Telemedicine and e-Health* 17 (10), 809–813.

Locatis, Craig, Williamson, Deborah, Gould-Kabler, Carrie, Zone-Smith, Laurie, Detzler, Isabel, Roberson, Jason, Maisiak, Richard & Ackerman, Michael (2010) Comparing in-person, video, and telephonic medical interpretation. *Journal of General Internal Medicine* 25 (4) 345–350.

Locke, Edwin A. (1976) The nature and causes of job satisfaction. In M. D. Dunnette (ed.) *Handbook of Industrial and Organizational Psychology*. Chicago, IL: Rand McNally, 1297–1349.

Longley, Patricia (1978) An integrated programme for training interpreters. In D. Gerver & H. W. Sinaiko (eds) *Language Interpretation and Communication*. New York/London: Plenum Press, 45–56.

Longley, Patricia (1989) The use of aptitude testing in the selection of students for conference interpretation training. In L. Gran & J. Dodds (eds) *The Theoretical and Practical Aspects of Teaching Conference Interpretation*. Udine: Campanotto, 105–108.

Lonni, Ada (2009) Tradurre parole o tradurre culture? Identità nazionale e percezione di sé nella figura del dragomanno gerosolimitano del XIX secolo. In P. de Gennaro (ed.) *Per le Vie del Mondo*. Turin: Università degli studi di Torino, 300–309.

Lonsdale, Deryle (1997) Modeling SI: A cognitive approach. *Interpreting* 1 (2), 235–260.

López de Coca Castañer, José Enrique (1989) Institutions on the Castilian–Granadan Frontier 1369–1482. In R. Bartlett & A. MacKay (eds) *Medieval Frontier Societies*. Oxford: Clarendon Press, 127–150.

López de Gómara, Francisco (1964) *Cortes: The Life of the Conqueror by his Secretary* (Trans. Leslie Byrd Simpson). Berkeley, CA: University of California Press.

López Gómez, María José, Bajo Molina, Teresa, Padilla Benítez, Presentación & Santiago de Torres, Julio (2007) Predicting proficiency in signed language interpreting: A preliminary study. *Interpreting* 9 (1), 71–93.

Lörscher, Wolfgang (1991) *Translation Performance, Translation Process and Translation Strategies: A Psycholinguistic Investigation.* Tübingen: Gunter Narr.

Lotriet, Annelie (2002) Can short interpreter training be effective? In E. Hung (ed.) *Teaching Translation and Interpreting 4: Building Bridges.* Amsterdam: John Benjamins, 83–98.

Luca, Cristian (2003) Alcuni "confidenti"del bailaggio veneto di Costantinopoli nel seicento. *Annuario dell' Istituto Romeno di Cultura e Ricerca Umanistica* 5, 299–310.

Lucas, Ceil (ed.) (2003) *Language and the Law in Deaf Communities.* Washington, DC: Gallaudet University Press.

Lucas, Ceil & Valli, Clayton (1989) Language contact in the American deaf community. In C. Lucas (ed.) *The Sociolinguistics of the Deaf Community.* San Diego: Academic Press, 11–40.

Lucchetta, Francesca (1989) La scuola dei "giovani di lingua" veneti nei secoli XVI e XVII. *Quaderni di Studi Arabi* 7, 19–40.

Lung, Rachel (2008a) Translation officials of the Tang central government in medieval China. *Interpreting* 10 (2), 175–196.

Lung, Rachel (2008b) Translation and historiography: How an interpreter shaped historical records in Latter Han China. *TTR* 19 (2), 225–252.

Lung, Rachel (2009a) Interpreters and the writing of histories in China. *Meta* 54 (2), 201–217.

Lung, Rachel (2009b) Perceptions of translating/interpreting in first-century China. *Interpreting* 11 (2), 119–136.

Lung, Rachel (2011) *Interpreters in Early Imperial China.* Amsterdam: John Benjamins.

MacDonald, Ross R. (1967) Léon Dostert. In W. M. Austin (ed.) *Papers in Linguistics in Honor of Léon Dostert.* The Hague: Mouton, 9–14.

Macizo, Pedro & Bajo, M. Teresa (2006) Reading for repetition and reading for translation: Do they involve the same processes? *Cognition* 99 (1), 1–34.

Macizo, Pedro & Bajo, Maria Teresa (2007) Comprehension processes in translation. In D. Alamargot, P. Terrier & J.-M. Cellier (eds) *Written Documents in the Workplace.* Oxford: Elsevier, 193–204.

Macizo, Pedro & Bajo, M. Teresa (2009) Schema activation in translation and reading: A paradoxical effect. *Psicológica* 30 (1), 59–89.

Mack, Gabriele (2001) Conference interpreters on the air: Live simultaneous interpreting on Italian television. In Y. Gambier & H. Gottlieb (eds) *(Multi) Media Translation: Concepts, Practices and Research.* Amsterdam: John Benjamins, 125–132.

Mack, Gabriele & Cattaruzza, Lorella (1995) User surveys in SI: A means of learning about quality and/or raising some reasonable doubt. In J. Tommola (ed.) *Topics in Interpreting Research.* Turku: University of Turku, Centre for Translation and Interpreting, 37–49.

Mackintosh, Jennifer (1983) *Relay Interpretation: An Exploloratory Study.* MA dissertation, Birkbeck College, University of London.

Mackintosh, Jennifer (1985) The Kintsch and van Dijk model of discourse comprehension applied to the interpretation process. *Meta* 30 (1), 37–43.

Mackintosh, Jennifer (1995) A review of conference interpretation: Practice and training. *Target* 7 (1), 119–133.

Mackintosh, Jennifer (1999) Interpreters are made not born. *Interpreting* 4 (1), 67–80.

Mackintosh, Jennifer (2002) The AIIC workload study – executive summary. www.aiic.net/page/888/ (accessed 26 March 2014).

Mackridge, Peter (2010) *Language and National Identity in Greece, 1766–1976.* Oxford: Oxford University Press.

Macnamara, Brooke N., Moore, Adam B., Kegl, Judy A. & Conway, Andrew R. A. (2011) Domain-general cognitive abilities and simultaneous interpreting skill. *Interpreting* 13 (1), 121–142.

MacRae, Sheila M. (1989) Information-crunching and other aspects of interpretation: Technique or creative process? In D. L. Hammond (ed.) *Coming of Age: Proceedings of the 30th Annual*

Conference of the American Translators Association, October 11–15, 1989, Washington, DC. Medford, NJ: Learned Information, 149–153.

Madariaga, Salvador de (1974) *Morning without Noon: Memoirs.* Farnborough: Saxon House.

Mairs, Rachel (2011) *Translator, Traditor*: The interpreter as traitor in classical tradition. *Greece & Rome* 58, 64–81.

Mairs, Rachel (2012a) Interpreters and translators in Hellenistic and Roman Egypt. In P. Schubert (ed.) *Actes du 26e Congrès International de Papyrologie, Genève 16–21 Août 2010.* Geneva: Droz, 457–462.

Mairs, Rachel (2012b) "Interpreting" at Vindolanda. *Britannia* 43, 1–2.

Major, George & Napier, Jemina (2012) Interpreting and knowledge mediation in the healthcare setting: What do we really mean by "accuracy"? In V. Montalt & M. Shuttleworth (eds) *Translation and Knowledge Mediation in Medical and Health Settings. Linguistica Antverpiensia – New Series* 11, 207–225.

Makarová, Viera (1995) The interpreter as an intercultural mediator. In J. Tommola (ed.) *Topics in Interpreting Research.* Turku: University of Turku, Centre for Translation and Interpreting, 51–59.

Malakoff, Marguerite E. (1992) Translation ability: A natural bilingual and metalinguistic skill. In R. J. Harris (ed.) *Cognitive Processing in Bilinguals.* Amsterdam: North-Holland, 515–530.

Malmkjær, Kirsten & Windle, Kevin (eds) (2011) *The Oxford Handbook of Translation Studies.* Oxford/New York: Oxford University Press.

Mantoux, Paul J. (1955) *Les Délibérations du Conseil des Quatre (24 Mars – 28 Juin 1919). Notes de l'Officier Interprète Paul Mantoux.* Vol. 1. Paris: CNRS Éditions.

Marcos, Luis R. (1979) Effects of interpreters on the evaluation of psychopathology in non-English-speaking patients. *American Journal of Psychiatry* 136 (2), 171–174.

Marković, Savo (2005) Barski patricijski rod Borisi u prošlosti: Jadran, Evropa, Mediteran. *Povizesni Prilozi/Historical Contributions* 28, 71–105.

Marrone, Stefano (1993) Quality: A shared objective. *The Interpreters' Newsletter* 5, 35–41.

Marschark, Marc & Spencer, Patricia E. (2009) *Evidence of Best Practice Models and Outcomes in the Education of Deaf and Hard-of-Hearing Children: An International Review.* Trim (Ireland): National Council for Special Education. www.ncse.ie/uploads/1/1_NCSE_Deaf.pdf (accessed 5 August 2014).

Marschark, Marc, Lang, Harry G. & Albertini, John A. (2002) *Educating Deaf Students: From Research to Practice.* New York: Oxford University Press.

Marschark, Marc, Sapere, Patricia, Convertino, Carol, Seewagen, Rose-Marie & Maltzen, Heather (2004) Comprehension of sign language interpreting: Deciphering a complex task situation. *Sign Language Studies* 4 (4), 345–368.

Marschark, Marc, Leigh, Greg, Sapere, Patricia, Burnham, Denis, Convertino, Carol, Stinson, Michael, Knoors, Harry, Vervloed, Mathijs P. J. & Noble, William (2006) Benefits of sign language interpreting and text alternatives for deaf students' classroom learning. *Journal of Deaf Studies and Deaf Education* 11 (4), 421–437.

Marslen-Wilson, William D. (1985) Speech shadowing and speech comprehension. *Speech Communication* 4 (1–3), 55–73.

Martin, Anne (2005). Interpreting from A to B: A Spanish case study. In R. Godijns & M. Hinderdael (eds) *Directionality in Interpreting: The 'Retour' or the Native?* Ghent: Communication & Cognition, 83–100.

Martin, Anne & Abril Martí, Isabel (2008) Community interpreter self-perception: A Spanish case study. In C. Valero-Garcés & A. Martin (eds) *Crossing Borders in Community Interpreting: Definitions and Dilemmas.* Amsterdam: John Benjamins, 203–230.

Martin, Anne & Ortega Herráez, Juan Miguel (2009) Court interpreters' self perception: A Spanish case study. In R. de Pedro Ricoy, C. Wilson & I. Perez (eds) *Interpreting and Translating in Public Service Settings: Policy, Practice, Pedagogy.* Manchester: St Jerome, 139–155.

Martin, Anne & Ortega Herráez, Juan Miguel (2013) From invisible machines to visible experts: Views on interpreter role and performance during the Madrid train bomb trial. In C. Schäffner, K. Kredens & Y. Fowler (eds) *Interpreting in a Changing Landscape: Selected Papers from Critical Link 6.* Amsterdam: John Benjamins, 101–114.

Martin, Jean (1978) *The Migrant Presence.* Hornsby: George Allen and Unwin.

Martinell Gifré, Emma, Cruz Piñol, Mar & Ribas, Rosa (eds) (2000) *Corpus de Testimonios de Convivencia Lingüística (ss. XII–XVIII)*. Kassel: Reichenberger.

Martinez, Liza B. (2007) Initial observations on code-switching in the voice interpretations of two Filipino interpreters. In M. Metzger & E. Fleetwood (eds) *Translation, Sociolinguistic, and Consumer Issues in Interpreting*. Washington, DC: Gallaudet University Press, 71–102.

Martínez-Gómez, Aída (2014a) Interpreting in prison settings: An international overview. *Interpreting* 16 (2), 233–259.

Martínez-Gómez, Aída (2014b) Criminals interpreting for criminals: Breaking or shaping norms? *JoSTrans: The Journal of Specialized Translation* 22, 174–193. www.jostrans.org/issue22/art_martinez.php (accessed 4 November 2014).

Martínez-Gómez, Aída (2015) Interpreting quality in prison settings: A proposal for an assessment tool. In C. Zwischenberger & M. Behr (eds) *Interpreting Quality: A Look Around and Ahead*. Berlin: Frank & Timme, 205–230.

Maryns, Katrijn (2006) *The Asylum Speaker: Language in the Belgian Asylum Procedure*. Manchester: St. Jerome.

Maryns, Katrijn (2013a) Disclosure and (re)performance of gender-based evidence in an interpreter-mediated asylum interview. *Journal of Sociolinguistics* 17 (5), 661–686.

Maryns, Katrijn (2013b) "Theatricks" in the courtroom: The intertextual construction of legal cases. In J. Conley, C. Heffer & F. Rock (eds) *Legal–Lay Communication: Textual Travel in the Legal Process*. Oxford: Oxford University Press, 107–125.

Marzocchi, Carlo (1998) The case for an institution-specific component in interpreting research. *The Interpreters' Newsletter* 8, 51–74.

Marzocchi, Carlo (2005) On norms and ethics in the discourse on interpreting. *The Interpreters' Newsletter* 13, 87–107.

Maslach, Christina (1982) *Burnout: The Cost of Caring*. Englewood Cliffs, NJ: Prentice-Hall.

Maslach, Christina & Jackson, Susan E. (1981) The measurement of experienced burnout. *Journal of Occupational Behaviour* 2, 99–113.

Mason, Ian (1999a) Introduction. *The Translator* 5 (2), 147–160.

Mason, Ian (ed.) (1999b) *Dialogue Interpreting*. Special Issue of *The Translator* 5 (2).

Mason, Ian (ed.) (2001) *Triadic Exchanges: Studies in Dialogue Interpreting*. Manchester: St Jerome.

Mason, Ian (2005a) Ostension, inference and response: Analyzing participant moves in community interpreting dialogues. In E. Hertog & B. van der Veer (eds) *Taking Stock: Research and Methodology in Community Interpreting. Linguistica Antverpiensia – New Series* 5. Antwerp: Hoger Instituut voor Vertalers en Tolken, 103–120.

Mason, Ian (2005b) Projected and perceived identities in dialogue interpreting. In J. House, R. M. Martin Ruano & N. Baumgarten (eds) *Translation and the Construction of Identity*. Seoul: IATIS, 30–52.

Mason, Ian (2006) On mutual accessibility of contextual assumptions in dialogue interpreting. *Journal of Pragmatics* 38 (3), 359–373.

Mason, Ian (2009a) Dialogue interpreting. In M. Baker & G. Saldanha (eds) *Routledge Encyclopedia of Translation Studies*. 2nd edn. London/New York: Routledge, 81–84.

Mason, Ian (2009b) Role, positioning and discourse in face-to-face interpreting. In R. de Pedro Ricoy, I. Perez & C. Wilson (eds) *Interpreting and Translating in Public Service Settings: Policy, Practice, Pedagogy*, 52–73.

Mason, Ian (2012) Gaze, positioning and identity in interpreter-mediated dialogues. In C. Baraldi & L. Gavioli (eds) *Coordinating Participation in Dialogue Interpreting*. Amsterdam: John Benjamins, 177–200.

Mason, Ian & Stewart, Miranda (2001) Interactional pragmatics, face and the dialogue interpreter. In I. Mason (ed.) *Triadic Exchanges: Studies in Dialogue Interpreting*. Manchester: St. Jerome, 51–70.

Mason, Ian & Ren, Wen (2012) Power in face-to-face interpreting events. *Translation and Interpreting Studies* 7 (2), 233–252.

Massaro, Dominic & Shlesinger, Miriam (1997) Information processing and a computational approach to the study of simultaneous interpretation. *Interpreting* 2 (1/2), 13–53.

Matoesian, Gregory (2001) *Law and the Language of Identity. Discourse in the William Kennedy Smith Rape Trial*. Oxford: Oxford University Press.

Matsubara, Shigeki, Takagi, Akira, Kawaguchi, Nobuo & Inagaki, Yasuyoshi (2002) Bilingual spoken monologue corpus for simultaneous machine interpretation research. In M. González Rodríguez & C. P. Suárez Araujo (eds) *LREC 2002: Proceedings of the Third International Conference on Language Resources and Evaluation, 29th, 30th & 31st May 2002, Las Palmas de Gran Canaria*. Vol. 1. Paris: ELRA, 153–159.

Mattern, Nanza (1974) *Anticipation in German–English Simultaneous Interpreting*. MA thesis, Universität des Saarlandes.

Matthews, Gerald (1997) Intelligence, personality and information-processing: An adaptiveperspective. In W. Tomic & J. Kingma (eds) *Advances in Cognition and Educational Practice. Vol. 4: Reflections on the Concept of Intelligence*. Greenwich, CT: JAI Press, 174–198.

Matyssek, Heinz (1989) *Handbuch der Notizentechnik für Dolmetscher. Ein Weg zur sprachunabhängigen Notation*. 2 vols. Heidelberg: Julius Groos.

Mauranen, Anna (2004) Corpora, universals and interference. In A. Mauranen & P. Kujamäki (eds) *Translation Universals: Do They Exist?* Amsterdam: John Benjamins, 65–82.

Mauranen, Anna (2012) *Exploring ELF: Academic English Shaped by Non-native Speakers*. Cambridge: Cambridge University Press.

Mazza, Cristina (2001) Numbers in simultaneous interpretation. *The Interpreters' Newsletter* 11, 87–104.

Mazzetti, Andrea (1999) The influence of segmental and prosodic deviations on source-text comprehension in simultaneous interpretation. *The Interpreters' Newsletter* 9, 125–147.

McAllister, Robert (2000) Perceptual foreign accent and its relevance for simultaneous interpreting. In B. Englund Dimitrova & K. Hyltenstam (eds) *Language Processing and Simultaneous Interpreting: Interdisciplinary Perspectives*. Amsterdam: John Benjamnis, 45–63.

McBeth, Sally (2003) Memory, history,and contested pasts: Reimagining Sacagawea/Sacajawea. *American Indian Culture and Research Journal* 27 (1), 1–32.

McCrae, Robert R. & Costa, Paul T. Jr. (2003) *Personality in Adulthood: A Five-Factor Theory Perspective*. 2nd edn. New York: Guilford Press.

McDermid, Campbell (2009) The ontological beliefs and curriculum design of Canadian interpreter and ASL educators. *International Journal of Interpreter Education* 1, 7–32.

McDermid, Campbell (2014) Cohesion in English to ASL simultaneous interpreting. *Translation & Interpreting* 6 (1), 76–101.

McElduff, Siobhán (2009) Living at the level of the word: Cicero's rejection of the interpreter as translator. *Translation Studies* 2, 133–146.

McIntire, Marina & Sanderson, Gary (1995) Who's in charge here? Perceptions of empowerment and role in the interpreting setting. *Journal of Interpretation* 7 (1), 99–113.

McKee, Rachel (2014) Breaking news: Sign language interpreters on television during natural disasters. *Interpreting* 16 (1), 107–130.

McNamara, Danielle S. & O'Reilly, Tenaha (2010) Theories of comprehension skill: Knowledge and strategies versus capacity and suppression. In A. M. Columbus (ed.) *Advances in Psychology Research*. Vol. 62. Hauppage, NY: Nova Science, 113–136.

McNamara, Danielle S., O'Reilly, Tenaha & de Vega, Manuel (2007) Comprehension skill, inference making, and the role of knowledge. In F. Schmalhofer & C. A. Perfetti (eds), *Higher Level Language Processes in the Brain: Inference and Comprehension Processes*. Mahwah, NJ: Erlbaum, 233–251.

McNeill, David (1992) *Hand and Mind: What Gestures Reveal about Thought*. Chicago: University of Chicago Press.

Mead, Peter (2002a) Exploring hesitation in consecutive interpreting. In G. Garzone & M. Viezzi (eds) *Interpreting in the 21st Century: Challenges and Opportunities*. Amsterdam: John Benjamins, 73–82.

Mead, Peter (2002b) *Evolution des Pauses dans l'Apprentissage de l'Interprétation Consécutive*. Doctoral dissertation, Université Lumière Lyon 2.

Mead, Peter (2002c) Pauses as an index of fluency in consecutive interpreting. In *Proceedings of the XVI FIT World Congress, Vancouver, B.C., Canada, 7–10 August 2002*, 207–210.

Mead, Peter (2005) Methodological issues in the study of interpreters' fluency. *The Interpreters' Newsletter* 13, 39–63.

Meehl, Gerald A. (2012) *One Marine's War: A Combat Interpreter's Quest for Humanity in the Pacific*. Annapolis: Naval Institute Press.

Ménage, Victor L. (1971) Another text of Uruc's Ottoman Chronicle. *Islam* 47, 273–277.

Merlini, Raffaela (1996) Interprit – Consecutive interpretation module. *The Interpreters' Newsletter* 7, 31–41.

Merlini, Raffaela (2007) Teaching dialogue interpreting in higher education: A research-driven, professionally oriented curriculum design. In M. T. Musacchio & G. Henrot Sostero (eds) *Tradurre: Formazione e Professione*. Bologna: CLEUP, 278–306.

Merlini, Raffaela (2009a) Seeking asylum and seeking identity in a mediated encounter: The projection of selves through discursive practices. *Interpreting* 11 (1), 57–93.

Merlini, Raffaela (2009b) Interpreters in emergency wards: An empirical study of doctor–interpreter–patient interaction. In R. de Pedro Ricoy, I. Perez & C. Wilson (eds) *Interpreting and Translating in Public Service Settings: Policy, Practice, Pedagogy*. Manchester, St Jerome, 89–114.

Merlini, Raffaela (2013) Changing perspectives: Politeness in cooperative multi-party interpreted talk. In C. Schäffner, K. Kredens & Y. Fowler (eds) *Interpreting in a Changing Landscape: Selected Papers from Critical Link 6*. Amsterdam: John Benjamins, 267–283.

Merlini, Raffaela & Falbo, Caterina (2011) *Faccia* a *faccia* con l'interprete: strategie di cortesia nelle interazioni mediche bilingui. In G. Held & U. Helfrich (eds) *Cortesia – Politesse – Cortesía*. Frankfurt: Peter Lang, 193–209.

Merlini, Raffaela & Favaron, Roberta (2005) Examining the "voice of interpreting" in speech pathology. *Interpreting* 7 (2), 263–302.

Merlino, Sara (2009) La mitigazione nell'attività dell'interprete. Il caso di una trattativa d'affari. In L. Gavioli (ed.) *La Mediazione Linguistico-culturale: una Prospettiva Interazionista*. Perugia: Guerra Edizioni, 231–257.

Mesa, Anne-Marie (2000) The cultural interpreter: An appreciated professional. Results of a study on interpreting services: Client, health care worker and interpreter points of view. In R. P. Roberts, S. E. Carr, D. Abraham & A. Dufour (eds) *The Critical Link 2: Interpreters in the Community*. Amsterdam: John Benjamins, 67–82.

Messina, Alessandro (2000) The reading aloud of English language texts in simultaneously interpreted conferences. *Interpreting* 3 (2), 147–161.

Metzger, Melanie (1995) Constructed dialogue and constructed action in American Sign Language. In C. Lucas (ed.) *Sociolinguistics in Deaf Communities*. Washington, DC: Gallaudet University Press, 255–271.

Metzger, Melanie (1999) *Sign Language Interpreting: Deconstructing the Myth of Neutrality*. Washington, DC: Gallaudet University Press.

Metzger, Melanie (2000) Interactive role-plays as a teaching strategy. In C. B. Roy (ed.) *Innovative Practices for Teaching Sign Language Interpreters*. Washington, DC: Gallaudet University Press, 83–108.

Metzger, Melanie (2006) Salient studies of signed language interpreting in the context of community interpreting scholarship. *Linguistica Antverpiensia – New Series* 5, 263–291.

Metzger, Melanie & Roy, Cynthia (2011) The first three years of a three-year grant: When a research plan doesn't go as planned. In B. Nicodemus & L. Swabey (eds) *Advances in Interpreting Research: Inquiry in Action*. Amsterdam: John Benjamins, 59–84.

Metzger, Melanie, Fleetwood, Earl & Collins, Steven D. (2004) Discourse genre and linguistic mode: Interpreter influences in visual and tactile interpreted interaction. *Sign Language Studies* 4 (2), 118–137.

Meuleman, Chris & Van Besien, Fred (2009) Coping with extreme speech conditions in simultaneous interpreting. *Interpreting* 11 (1), 20–34.

Meuter, Renata F. I. & Allport, Alan (1999) Bilingual language switching in naming: Asymmetrical costs of language selection. *Journal of Memory and Language* 40, 25–40.

Meyer, Bernd (2012) Ad hoc interpreting for partially language-proficient patients: Participation in multilingual constellations. In C. Baraldi & L. Gavioli (eds) *Coordinating Participation in Dialogue Interpreting*. Amsterdam: John Benjamins, 99–113.

Michael, Awoii P. (2011) A glimpse at the development of sign language interpretation in Uganda. In B. Costello, M. Thumann & R. Shaw (eds) *Proceedings of the 4th Conference of the World Association of Sign Language Interpreters, Durban, South Africa, July 14–16, 2011*. WASLI, 24–35.

Mikkelson, Holly (1996) The professionalization of community interpreting. In M. M. Jerôme-O'Keeffe (ed.) *Global Vision: Proceedings of the 37th Annual Conference of the American Translators Association. October 30–November 2, 1996, Colorado Springs, Colorado.* Alexandria, VA: American Translators Association, 77–89.

Mikkelson, Holly (1998) Towards a redefinition of the role of the court interpreter. *Interpreting* 3 (1), 21–45.

Mikkelson, Holly (1999) Relay interpreting: A viable solution for languages of limited diffusion? *The Translator* 5 (2), 361–380.

Mikkelson, Holly (2000) *Introduction to Court Interpreting.* Manchester: St Jerome.

Mikkelson, Holly (2008) Evolving views of the court interpreter's role: Between Scylla and Charybdis. In C. Valero-Garcés & A. Martin (eds) *Crossing Borders in Community Interpreting: Definitions and Dilemmas.* Amsterdam/Philadelphia: John Benjamins, 81–97.

Mikkelson, Holly & Jourdenais, Renée (eds) (2015) *The Routledge Handbook of Interpreting.* London/New York: Routledge.

Mildner, Vesna (2008) *The Cognitive Neuroscience of Human Communication.* New York: Lawrence Erlbaum Associates.

Millán, Carmen & Bartrina, Francesca (eds) (2013) *The Routledge Handbook of Translation Studies.* London/New York: Routledge.

Miller, George A. (1956) The magical number seven plus or minus two: Some limits on our capacity for processing information. *Psychological Review* 63, 81–97.

Miller, Kenneth E., Martell, Zoe L., Pazdirek, Linda, Caruth, Melissa & Lopez, Diana (2005) The role of interpreters in psychotherapy with refugees: An exploratory study. *American Journal of Orthopsychiatry* 75 (1), 27–39.

Millerson, Geoffrey (1964) *The Qualifying Associations: A Study in Professionalization.* London: Routledge & Kegan Paul/New York: The Humanities Press.

Mindess, Anna (2006) *Reading between the Signs: Intercultural Communication for Sign Language Interpreters.* 2nd edn. Boston, MA: Intercultural Press.

Minyar-Beloruchev, Rurik K. (1959) *Metodika obucheniya perevodu na slukh* [*Method of Teaching Auditory Translation*]. Moscow: Izdatelstvo Instituta mezhdunarodnykh otnoshenii.

Minyar-Beloruchev, Rurik K. (1969a) *Posledovatelnyi perevod* [*Consecutive Interpreting*]. Moscow: Voenizdat.

Minyar-Beloruchev, Rurik K. (1969b) *Posobie po ustnomu perevodu (Zapisi v posledovatelnom perevode)* [*Textbook of Interpreting (Notes in Consecutive Interpreting)*]. Moscow: Vysshaya shkola.

Minyar-Beloruchev, Rurik K. (1980) *Obshchaya teoriya perevoda i ustnyi perevod* [*General Theory of Translation and Oral Translation*]. Moscow: Voenizdat.

Miović, Vesna (2001) Dragomans of the Dubrovnik Republic: Their training and career. *Dubrovnik Annals* 5, 81–94.

Miović, Vesna (2002) Miho Zarini – Dragoman (Interpreter for the Turkish Language) of Republic of Dubrovnik. In F. Ferluga-Petronio (ed.) *Plurilingvizem v Evropi 18. Stoletja.* Ljubljana: Slavisticno drustvo Maribor, 303–318.

Miović, Vesna (2013) Diplomatic relations between the Ottoman Empire and the Republic of Dubrovnik. In G. Karman & L. Kunčević (eds) *The European Tributary States of the Ottoman Empire in the Sixteenth and Seventeenth Centuries.* Leiden: Brill, 187–208.

Mishler, Elliot G. (1984) *The Discourse of Medicine: The Dialectics of Medical Interviews.* Norwood, NJ: Ablex.

Mizuno, Akira (1997) Broadcast interpreting in Japan: Some theoretical and practical aspects. In Y. Gambier, D. Gile & C. Taylor (eds) *Conference Interpreting: Current Trends in Research.* Amsterdam: John Benjamins, 192–194.

Mizuno, Akira (1999) Shifts of cohesion and coherence in simultaneous interpretation from English into Japanese. *Interpreting Research: Journal of the Interpreting Research Association of Japan* 8 (2), 31–41.

Mizuno, Akira (2005) Process model for simultaneous interpreting and working memory. *Meta* 50 (2), 739–752.

Mizuno, Makiko (2012) Community interpreting in Japan: Present state and challenges. In N. Sato-Rossberg & J. Wakabayashi (eds) *Translation and Translation Studies in the Japanese Context.* London/New York: Continuum, 202–221.

Mizuno, Makiko & Nakamura, Sachiko (2010) Fatigue and stress of court interpreters in lay judge trials. *Kinjō Gakuin Daigaku ronshū. Shakai kagaku hen.* [*Studies in Social Sciences*] 7 (1), 71–80.

Mizuno, Makiko, Nakamura, Sachiko & Kawahara, Kiyoshi (2013) Observations on how the lexical choices of court interpreters influence the impression formation of lay judges. *Kinjo Gakuin Daigaku Ronshu, Studies in Social Science* 9 (2), 1–11.

Möbius, Bernd & Haiber, Udo (2010) Verarbeitung gesprochener Sprache. In K.-U. Carstensen, Ch. Ebert, C. Ebert, S. Jekat, R. Klabunde & H. Langer (eds) *Computerlinguistik und Sprachtechnologie: Eine Einführung.* 3rd rev. ext. edn. Heidelberg: Spektrum, 214–235.

Moeketsi, Rosemary & Wallmach, Kim (2005) From *sphaza* to *makoya*!: A BA degree for court interpreters in South Africa. *International Journal of Speech, Language and the Law* 12 (1), 77–108.

Monacelli, Claudia (1999) *Messaggi in Codice. Analisi del Discorso e Strategie per Prendere Appunti.* Milan: FrancoAngeli.

Monacelli, Claudia (2000) Mediating castles in the air: Epistemological issues in interpreting studies. In M. Olohan (ed.) *Intercultural Faultlines.* Manchester: St. Jerome, 193–214.

Monacelli, Claudia (2006) Implications of translational shifts in interpreter-mediated texts. *Pragmatics* 16 (4), 457–473.

Monacelli, Claudia (2009) *Self-Preservation in Simultaneous Interpreting: Surviving the Role.* Amsterdam: John Benjamins.

Monacelli, Claudia & Punzo, Roberto (2001) Ethics in the fuzzy domain of interpreting: A "military" perspective. *The Translator* 7 (2), 265–282.

Monikowski, Christine (2004) Language myths in interpreted education: First language, second language, what language? In E. A. Winston (ed.) *Educational Interpreting: How It Can Succeed.* Washington, DC: Gallaudet University Press, 48–60.

Monikowski, Christine & Peterson, Rico (2005) Service learning in interpreting education: Living and learning. In M. Marschark, R. Peterson & E. Winston (eds) *Interpreting and Interpreter Education: Directions for Research and Practice.* New York: Oxford University Press, 188–206.

Monnier, Michel A. (1995) The hidden part of asylum seekers' interviews in Geneva, Switzerland: Some observations about the socio-political construction of interviews between gatekeepers and the powerless. *Journal of Refugee Studies* 8 (3), 305–325.

Monti, Cristina, Bendazzoli, Claudio, Sandrelli, Annalisa & Russo, Mariachiara (2005) Studying directionality in simultaneous interpreting through an electronic corpus: EPIC (European Parliament Interpreting Corpus). *Meta* 50 (4). www.erudit.org/revue/meta/2005/v50/n4/019850ar. pdf (accessed 30 June 2014).

Monzó, Esther (2005) Being ACTIVE in legal translation and interpreting: Researching and acting on the Spanish field. *Meta* 50 (4). www.erudit.org/revue/meta/2005/v50/n4/019922ar.pdf (accessed 28 February 2015).

Moran, Joe (2010) *Interdisciplinarity.* 2nd edn. London/New York: Routledge.

Moran, William L. (1992) *The Amarna Letters.* Baltimore: The Johns Hopkins University Press.

Moreno, Jacob L. (1946) Psychodrama and group psychotherapy. *Sociometry* 9 (2/3), 249–253.

Morgan, Pamela & Adam, Robert (2013) Deaf interpreters in mental health settings: Some reflections on and thoughts about Deaf interpreter education. In K. Malcolm & L. Swabey (eds) *In Our Hands: Educating Healthcare Interpreters.* Washington, DC: Gallaudet University Press, 190–208.

Mori, Kimiyuki (1998) *Kodai Nihon no taigai-ninshiki to tsuko* [*International Consciousness and Trade in Classical Japan*]. Tokyo: Yoshikawa-kobun-do.

Morris, Ruth (1990) Interpretation at the Demjanjuk Trial. In D. Bowen & M. Bowen (eds) *Interpreting – Yesterday, Today, and Tomorrow.* Binghamton, NY: SUNY, 101–107.

Morris, Ruth (1995) The moral dilemmas of court interpreting. *The Translator* 1 (1), 25–46.

Morris, Ruth (1998) Justice in Jerusalem – interpreting in Israeli legal proceedings. *Meta* 43 (1), 110–118.

Morris, Ruth (1999a) The gum syndrome: Predicaments in court interpreting. *Forensic Linguistics* 6 (1), 6–29.

Morris, Ruth (1999b) The face of justice: Historical aspects of court interpreting. *Interpreting* 4 (1), 97–123.

Morris, Ruth (2007) Dies, Attard or Lockerbie? Enlightened and unenlightened judicial views of interpreters in English-speaking legal systems. In F. Pöchhacker, A. L. Jakobsen & I. M. Mees (eds) *Interpreting Studies and Beyond: A Tribute to Miriam Shlesinger*. Copenhagen: Samfundslitteratur Press, 103–119.

Morris, Ruth (2008) Missing stitches: An overview of judicial attitudes to interlingual interpreting in the criminal justice systems of Canada and Israel. *Interpreting* 10 (1), 34–64.

Morris, Ruth (2010) Images of the court interpreter: Professional identity, role definition and self-image. *Translation and Interpreting Studies* 5 (1), 20–40.

Moser, Barbara (1978) Simultaneous interpretation: A hypothetical model and its practical application. In D. Gerver & H. W. Sinaiko (eds) *Language Interpretation and Communication*. New York/London: Plenum Press, 353–368.

Moser-Mercer, Barbara (1985) Screening potential interpreters. *Meta* 30 (1), 97–100.

Moser-Mercer, Barbara (1994a) Paradigms gained or the art of productive disagreement. In S. Lambert & B. Moser-Mercer (eds) *Bridging the Gap: Empirical Research in Simultaneous Interpretation*. Amsterdam: John Benjamins, 17–23.

Moser-Mercer, Barbara (1994b) Aptitude testing for conference interpreting: Why, when and how. In S. Lambert & B. Moser-Mercer (eds) *Bridging the Gap: Empirical Research in Simultaneous Interpretation*. Amsterdam: John Benjamins, 57–68.

Moser-Mercer, Barbara (1996) Quality in interpreting: Some methodological issues. *The Interpreters' Newsletter* 7, 43–55.

Moser-Mercer, Barbara (1997) Methodological issues in interpreting research: An introduction to the Ascona workshops. *Interpreting* 2 (1/2), 1–11.

Moser-Mercer, Barbara (2000a) The rocky road to expertise in interpreting: Eliciting knowledge from learners. In M. Kadric, K. Kaindl & F. Pöchhacker (eds) *Translationswissenschaft: Festschrift für Mary Snell-Hornby zum 60. Geburtstag*. Tübingen: Stauffenburg, 339–352.

Moser-Mercer, Barbara (2000b) Simultaneous interpreting: Cognitive potential and limitations. *Interpreting* 5 (1), 83–94.

Moser-Mercer, Barbara (2003) Remote interpreting: Assessment of human factors and performance parameters. http://aiic.net/page/1125/ (accessed 11 November 2014).

Moser-Mercer, Barbara (2005a) Remote interpreting: Issues of multi-sensory integration in a multilingual task. *Meta* 50 (2), 727–738.

Moser-Mercer, Barbara (2005b) The teaching of simultaneous interpreting: The first 60 years (1929–1989). *Forum* 3 (1), 205–225.

Moser-Mercer, Barbara (2008) Skill acquisition in interpreting: A human performance perspective. *The Interpreter and Translator Trainer* 2 (1), 1–28.

Moser-Mercer, Barbara (2010) The search for neuro-physiological correlates of expertise in interpreting. In G. M. Shreve & E. Angelone (eds) *Translation and Cognition*. Amsterdam: John Benjamins, 263–287.

Moser-Mercer, Barbara (2015) Interpreting in conflict zones. In R. Jourdenais & H. Mikkelson (eds) *Handbook of Interpreting*. London/New York: Routledge, 302–316.

Moser-Mercer, Barbara, Class, Barbara & Seeber, Kilian S. (2005) Leveraging virtual learning environments for training interpreter trainers. *Meta* 50 (4). www.erudit.org/revue/meta/2005/v50/n4/019872ar.pdf (accessed 28 February 2015).

Moser-Mercer, Barbara, Delgado Luchner, Carmen & Kherbiche, Leila (2012) Uncharted training territory: Reaching interpreters in the field. In H. Lee-Jahnke & M. Forstner (eds) *CIUTI-Forum 2012: Translators and Interpreters as Key Actors in Global Networking*. Bern: Peter Lang, 403–422.

Moser-Mercer, Barbara, Kherbiche, Leïla & Class, Barbara (2014) Interpreting conflict: Training challenges in humanitarian field interpreting. *Journal of Human Rights Practice* 6 (1), 140–158 doi:10.1093/jhuman/hut025.

Moser Mercer, Barbara, Künzli, Alexander & Korac, Marina (1998) Prolonged turns in interpreting: Effects on quality, physiological and psychological stress (Pilot study). *Interpreting*, 3(1), 47–64.

Moser-Mercer, Barbara, Frauenfelder, Uli H., Casado, Beatriz & Künzli, Alexander (2000) Searching to define expertise in interpreting. In B. Englund Dimitrova & K. Hyltenstam (eds)

Language Processing and Simultaneous Interpreting: Interdisciplinary Perspectives. Amsterdam/ Phildelphia: John Benjamins, 107–132.

Moser-Mercer, Barbara, Lambert, Sylvie, Darò, Valeria & Williams, Sarah (1997) Skill components in simultaneous interpreting. In Y. Gambier, D. Gile & C. Taylor (eds) *Conference Interpreting: Current Trends in Research.* Amsterdam: John Benjamins, 133–148.

Moser, Peter (1996) Expectations of users of conference interpretation. *Interpreting* 1 (2), 145–178.

Moskal, Barbara M. (2000) Scoring rubrics: What, when and how? *Practical Assessment, Research & Evaluation* 7 (3). http://PAREonline.net/getvn.asp?v=7&n=3 (accessed 5 February 2015).

Mouzourakis, Panagiotis (1996) Videoconferencing: Techniques and challenges. *Interpreting* 1 (1), 21–38.

Mouzourakis, Takis (2003) That feeling of being there: Vision and presence in remote interpreting. *Communicate!* Summer 2003. http://aiic.net/page/1173/ (accessed 31 October 2013).

Mouzourakis, Panagiotis (2006) Remote interpreting: A technical perspective on recent experiments. *Interpreting* 8 (1), 45–66.

Mühlhäusler, Peter & Harré, Rom (1990) *Pronouns and People: The Linguistic Construction of Social and Personal Identity.* Oxford: Blackwell.

Müller, Cornelia, Cienki, Alan, Fricke, Ellen, Ladewig, Silva, McNeill, David & Tessendorf, Sedinha (eds) (2013) *Body – Language – Communication: An International Handbook on Multimodality in Human Interaction.* Berlin/Boston: De Gruyter Mouton.

Müller, Frank (1989) Translation in bilingual conversation: Pragmatic aspects of translatory interaction. *Journal of Pragmatics* 13 (5), 713–739.

Müller, Frank E. (1998) Verblümte Kritik – "Face-work" im interkulturellen Diskurs und seine Übersetzung beim Simultandolmetschen. In B. Apfelbaum & H. Müller (eds) *Fremde im Gespräch. Gesprächsanalytische Untersuchungen zu Dolmetschinteraktionen, interkultureller Kommunikation und instituionalisierten Interaktionsformen.* Frankfurt: IKO, 145–162.

Munday, Jeremy (2001) *Introducing Translation Studies: Theories and Applications.* London/New York: Routledge.

Muñoz Martín, Ricardo (2011) Nomen mihi Legio est: A cognitive approach to natural translation. In M. J. Blasco Mayor & M. A. Jiménez Ivars (eds) *Interpreting Naturally: A Tribute to Brian Harris.* Frankfurt: Peter Lang, 35–66.

Muñoz Martín, Ricardo (2014) Situating translation expertise: A review with a sketch of a construct. In J. Schwieter & A. Ferreira (eds) *The Development of Translation Competence: Theories and Methodologies from Psycholinguistics and Cognitive Science.* Cambridge: Cambridge Scholars Publishing, 2–56.

NAATI (2010) Outlines of NAATI credentials. www.naati.com.au/PDF/Misc/Outliness%20of% 20NAATI%20Credentials.pdf (accessed 7 February 2015).

Nafá Waasaf, María Lourdes (2007) Intonation and the structural organization of texts in simultaneous interpreting. *Interpreting* 9 (2), 177–198.

Nakamura, Satoshi (2009) Overcoming the language barrier with speech translation technology. *Science & Technology Trends – Quarterly Review* 31, 35–48.

Nakane, Ikuko (2007) Problems in communicating the suspect's rights in interpreted police interviews. *Applied Linguistics* 28 (1), 87–112.

Nakane, Ikuko (2008) Politeness and gender in interpreted police interviews. *Monash University Linguistics Papers* 6 (1), 29–40.

Nakane, Ikuko (2011) The role of silence in interpreted police interviews. *Journal of Pragmatics* 43 (9), 2317–2330.

Namy, Claude (1978) Reflections on the training of simultaneous interpreters: A metalinguistic approach. In D. Gerver & H. W. Sinaiko (eds) *Language Interpretation and Communication.* New York/London: Plenum Press, 25–34.

Napier, Jemina (2002) *Sign Language Interpreting: Linguistic Coping Strategies.* Coleford, UK: Douglas McLean.

Napier, Jemina (2004a) Sign language interpreter training, testing, and accreditation: An international comparison. *American Annals of the Deaf* 149 (4), 350–359.

Napier, Jemina (2004b) Interpreting omissions: A new perspective. *Interpreting* 6 (2), 117–142.

Napier, Jemina (2005a) Making learning accessible for sign language interpreters: A process of change. *Educational Action Research* 13 (4), 505–523.

Napier, Jemina (2005b) Training sign language interpreters in Australia. *Babel* 51 (3), 207–223.

Napier, Jemina (2008) Exploring linguistic and cultural identity: My personal experience. In M. Bishop & S. L. Hicks (eds) *Hearing, Mother Father Deaf: Hearing People in Deaf Families*. Washington, DC: Gallaudet University Press, 219–243.

Napier, Jemina (ed.) (2009) *International Perspectives on Sign Language Interpreter Education*. Washington, DC: Gallaudet University Press.

Napier, Jemina (2011a) "It's not what they say but the way they say it." A content analysis of interpreter and consumer perceptions of signed language interpreting in Australia. *Translators and Interpreters: Geographic Displacement and Linguistic Consequences*. Special Issue of *The International Journal of the Sociology of Language* 207, 59–87.

Napier, Jemina (2011b) If a tree falls in the forest and no one is there to hear it, does it make a noise? The merits of publishing interpreting research. In B. Nicodemus & L. Swabey (eds) *Advances in Interpreting Research: Inquiry in Action*. Amsterdam: John Benjamins, 121–152.

Napier, Jemina (2012) Here or there? An assessment of video remote signed language interpreter-mediated interaction in court. In S. Braun & J. L. Taylor (eds) *Videoconference and Remote Interpreting in Criminal Proceedings*. Cambridge: Intersentia, 167–214.

Napier, Jemina (2014) The evolution of interpreter education research and dissemination. *International Journal of Interpreter Education* 6 (1), 1–2.

Napier, Jemina & Barker, Roz (2004) Accessing university education: Perceptions, preferences, and expectations for interpreting by deaf students. *Journal of Deaf Studies and Deaf Education* 9 (2), 228–238.

Napier, Jemina & Leneham, Marcel (2011) "It was difficult to manage the communication": Testing the feasibility of video remote signed language interpreting in court. *Journal of Interpretation* 21 (1), 52–63.

Napier, Jemina & Spencer, David (2008) Guilty or not guilty? An investigation of deaf jurors' access to court proceedings via sign language interpreting. In D. Russell & S. Hale (eds) *Interpreting in Legal Settings*. Washington, DC: Gallaudet University Press, 72–122.

Napier, Jemina, McKee, Rachel & Goswell, Della (2010) *Sign Language Interpreting: Theory & Practice in Australia and New Zealand*. 2nd edn. Sydney: Federation Press.

Napier, Jemina, Song, Zhongwei & Ye, Shiyi (2013) Innovative and collaborative use of iPads in interpreter education. *International Journal of Interpreter Education* 5 (2), 13–42.

NCCC (2001) *The National Curriculum: An Introduction to Working and Socializing with People who are Deaf-Blind*. San Diego, CA: DawnSignPress.

NCIHC (2003) *Guide to Interpreter Positioning in Health Care Settings*. Washington, DC: National Council on Interpreting in Health Care.

Neisser, Ulric (1967) *Cognitive Psychology*. New York: Appleton Century Crofts.

Nestler, Fredo (1957) Tel-Interpret. Begründung und Grundlagen eines deutschen Telefon-Dolmetschdienstes. *Lebende Sprachen* 2 (1), 21–23.

Neudecker, Hannah (2005) From Istanbul to London? Albertus Bobovius' appeal to Isaac Basire. In A. Hamilton (ed.) *The Republic of Letters and the Levant*. Leiden, Boston: Brill, 173–196.

Ng, Eva N. S. (2013) Who is speaking? Interpreting the voice of the speaker in court. In C. Schäffner, K. Kredens & Y. Fowler (eds) *Interpreting in a Changing Landscape: Selected Papers from Critical Link 6*. Amsterdam: John Benjamins, 249–266.

NHANES (2006) National Health and Nutrition Examination Survey: Interpretation guidelines. www.cdc.gov/nchs/data/nhanes/nhanes_07_08/Interpretation_Guidelines.pdf (accessed 8 April 2014).

Niang, Anna (1990) History and role of interpreting in Africa. In D. Bowen & M. Bowen (eds) *Interpreting – Yesterday, Today, and Tomorrow*. Binghamton, NY: SUNY, 34–36.

Nicodemus, Brenda & Emmorey, Karen (2013) Direction asymmetries in spoken and signed language interpreting. *Bilingualism: Language and Cognition* 16 (3), 624–636.

Nida, Eugene A. (1964) *Toward a Science of Translating*. Leiden: E. J. Brill.

Nida, Eugene A. (1969) Science of translation. *Language* 45 (3), 483–498.

Niemants, Natacha S. A. (2012) The transcription of interpreting data. *Interpreting* 14 (2), 165–191.

Niemants, Natacha S. A. (2013) From role-playing to role-taking: Interpreter role(s) in healthcare. In C. Schäffner, K. Kredens & Y. Fowler (eds) *Interpreting in a Changing Landscape: Selected Papers from Critical Link 6*. Amsterdam: John Benjamins, 305–319.

Niño-Murcia, Mercedes & Rothman, Jason (eds) (2009) *Bilingualism and Identity: Spanish at the Crossroads with other Languages*. Amsterdam: John Benjamins.

Nishiyama, Sen (1988) Simultaneous interpreting in Japan and the role of television: A personal narration. *Meta* 33 (1), 64–69.

Nocella, Paola (1995) Business interpreting. In U. Ozolins & D. Egan (eds) *Interpreters and Translators: A Practitioner's Perspective: Proceedings of the Victorian Interpreter Awareness Day Conference (December 1994, Melbourne)*. Malvern/Hawker: NLLIA-Centre for Research and Development in Interpreting and Translating, Deakin University/NAATI, 28–33.

Nolan, James (2005) *Interpretation: Techniques and Exercises*. Clevedon: Multilingual Matters.

Nord, Christiane (1991) Scopos, loyalty, and translational conventions. *Target* 3 (1), 91–109.

Norris, Sigrid (2004) *Analyzing Multimodal Interaction*. London: Routledge.

Norström, Eva, Fioretus, Ingrid & Gustafsson, Kristina (2012) Working conditions of community interpreters in Sweden. *Interpreting* 14 (2), 242–260.

NRPSI (2011) *Code of Professional Conduct*. London: National Register of Public Service Interpreters. www.nrpsi.org.uk/for-clients-of-interpreters/code-of-professional-conduct.html (accessed 20 January 2015).

Ntuli, Deuteronomy Bhekinkosi & Swanepoel, Christiaan F. (1993) *Southern African Literature in African Languages: A Concise Historical Perspective*. Pretoria: Acacia Books.

NUPIT (2001) *What Do Interpreters and Translators Talk about among Themselves? A Survey of Employment Conditions among Interpreters and Translators*. London: NUPIT/MSF.

O'Barr, William M. (1982) *Linguistic Evidence: Language, Power, and Strategy in the Courtroom*. New York: Academic Press.

Obst, Harry (2010) *White House Interpreter: The Art of Interpretation*. Bloomington: Author House.

Ochs, Elinor (1979) Transcription as theory. In E. Ochs & B. B. Schieffelin (eds) *Developmental Pragmatics*. New York: Academic Press, 43–72.

Okada, Yusuke (2010) Role-play in oral proficiency interviews: Interactive footing and interactional competencies. *Journal of Pragmatics* 42 (6), 1647–1668.

Okombo, Okoth, Mweri, Jefwa & Akaranga, Washington (2009) Sign language interpreter training in Kenya. In J. Napier (ed.) *International Perspectives on Sign Language Interpreter Education*. Washington, DC: Gallaudet University Press, 295–300.

Oléron, Pierre & Nanpon, Hubert (1965) Recherches sur la traduction simultanée. *Journal de Psychologie Normale et Pathologique* 62, 73–94.

Oléron, Pierre & Nanpon, Hubert (1965/2002) Research into simultaneous translation. In F. Pöchhacker & M. Shlesinger (eds) *The Interpreting Studies Reader*. London/New York: Routledge, 42–50.

Oliva, Gina (2004) *Alone in the Mainstream*. Washington, DC: Gallaudet University Press.

Oliva, Gina A. & Lytle, Linda R. (2014) *Making Life Better for Deaf and Hard of Hearing Schoolchildren*. Washington, DC: Gallaudet University Press.

Oller, John W. & Conrad, Christine A. (1971) The cloze technique and ESL proficiency. *Language Learning*, 21 (2), 183–194.

Ong, Walter J. (1982) *Orality and Literacy: The Technologizing of the Word*. London: Routledge.

Ono, Naoko, Kiuchi, Takahiro & Ishikawa, Hirono (2013) Development and pilot testing of a novel education method for training medical interpreters. *Patient Education and Counseling* 93 (3), 604–611.

Ono, Takahiro, Tohyama, Hitomi & Matsubara, Shigeki (2008) Construction and analysis of word-level time-aligned simultaneous interpretation corpus. In N. Calzolari, K. Choukri, B. Maegaard, J. Mariani, J. Odjik, S. Piperidis & D. Tapias (eds) *Proceedings of the Sixth International Conference on Language Resources and Evaluation (LREC '08)*. ELRA. www.lrec-conf.org/proceedings/lrec2008/ (accessed 13 January 2014).

Opdenhoff, Jan-Hendrik (2012) Directionality and working memory in conference interpreting – an experimental study. In B. Harris, B. Mayor, M. Jesus, J. Ivars & M. Amparo (eds) *Interpreting Brian Harris: Recent Developments in Translatology*. Bern: Peter Lang, 161–171.

Orellana, Marjorie F. (2009) *Translating Childhoods: Immigrant Youth, Language, and Culture.* New Brunswick, NJ: Rutgers University Press.

Orellana, Marjorie F. (2010) From here to there: On the process of an ethnography of language brokering. In R. Antonini (ed.) *Child Language Brokering: Trends and Patterns in Current Research.* Special Issue of *mediAzioni* 10, 47–67. http://mediazioni.sitlec.unibo.it (accessed 18 February 2014).

Orlando, Marc (2010) Digital pen technology and consecutive interpreting: Another dimension in note-taking training and assessment. *The Interpreters' Newsletter* 15, 71–86.

Orlando, Marc (2014) A study on the amenability of digital pen technology in a hybrid mode of interpreting: *Consec-simul with notes. Translation & Interpreting* 6 (2), 39–54.

Ortega Herráez, Juan M. & Foulquié Rubio, Ana I. (2008) Interpreting in police settings in Spain: Service providers' and interpreters' perspectives. In C. Valero-Garcés & A. Martin (eds) *Crossing Borders in Community Interpreting: Definitions and Dilemmas.* Amsterdam: John Benjamins, 123–146.

Ortega Herráez, Juan M., Abril Martí, María Isabel & Martin, Anne (2009) Community interpreting in Spain: A comparative study of interpreters' self perception of role in different settings. In S. Hale, U. Ozolins & L. Stern (eds) *The Critical Link 5: Quality in Interpreting – a Shared Responsibility.* Amsterdam/Philadephia: John Benjamins, 149–167.

Oyung, Guu-a 烏雲高娃 (2001) 東亞譯語考—兼論元明與朝鮮時代譯語之演變 [Examining '*yiyu*' in East Asia: The transformation of '*yiyu*' during the Yuan and Ming dynasties and in the Chosen era]. 元史及北方民族史研究集刊 [*Studies on Yuan and Northern Nationalities History*] 14, 166–179.

Ozolins, Uldis (1998) *Interpreting and Translating in Australia: Current Issues and International Comparisons.* Melbourne: Language Australia.

Ozolins, Uldis (2000) Communication needs and interpreting in multilingual settings: The international spectrum of response. In R. P. Roberts, S. E. Carr, D. Abraham & A. Dufour (eds) *The Critical Link 2: Interpreters in the Community.* Amsterdam: John Benjamins, 21–33.

Ozolins, Uldis (2004) *Survey of Interpreting Practitioners.* Melbourne: VITS Language Link.

Ozolins, Uldis (2007) The interpreter's "third client": Interpreters, professionalism and interpreting agencies. In C. Wadensjö, B. Englund Dimitrova & A.-L. Nilsson (eds) *The Critical Link 4: Professionalisation of Interpreting in the Community.* Amsterdam: John Benjamins, 121–131.

Ozolins, Uldis (2010) Factors that determine the provision of Public Service Interpreting: Comparative perspectives on government motivation and language service implementation. *JoSTrans: The Journal of Specialised Translation* 14, 194–215. www.jostrans.org/issue14/art_ozolins.php (accessed 14 May 2014).

Ozolins, Uldis (2011) Telephone interpreting: Understanding practice and identifying research needs. *Translation & Interpreting* 3 (2), 33–47.

Ozolins, Uldis & Bridge, Marianne (1999) *Sign Language Interpreting in Australia.* Melbourne: Language Australia.

Ozuru, Yasuhiro, Dempsey, Kyle & McNamara, Danielle S. (2009) Prior knowledge, reading skill, and text cohesion in the comprehension of science texts. *Learning and Instruction* 19 (3), 228–242.

Paas, Fred G. W. C. & van Merriënboer, Jeroen J. G. (1993) The efficiency of instructional conditions: An approach to combine mental effort and performance measures. *Human Factors* 35 (4), 737–743.

Padden, Carol A. (1998) The ASL lexicon. *Sign Language and Linguistics* 1 (1), 39–60.

Padden, Carol A. (2000) Simultaneous interpreting across modalities. *Interpreting* 5 (2), 169–186.

Padden, Carol A. (2006) Learning to fingerspell twice: Young signing children's acquisition of fingerspelling. In B. Schick, M. Marschark & P. E. Spencer (eds) *Advances in the Sign Language Development of Deaf Children.* New York: Oxford University Press, 189–201.

Padilla, Francisca, Bajo, M. Teresa & Macizo, Pedro (2005) Articulatory suppression in language interpretation: Working memory capacity, dual tasking and word knowledge. *Bilingualism: Language and Cognition* 8 (3), 207–219.

Padilla, Presentación, Bajo, Maria Teresa & Padilla, Francisca (1999) Proposal for a cognitive theory of translation and interpreting: A methodology for future empirical research. *The Interpreters' Newsletter* 9, 61–78.

Padilla Benítez, Presentación, Macizo Soria, Pedro & Bajo Molina, M. Teresa (2007) *Tareas de Traducción e Interpretación desde una Perspectiva Cognitiva: Una Propuesta Integradora.* Granada: Atrio.

Padilla, Presentación, Bajo, M. Teresa, Cañas, José J. & Padilla, Francisca (1995) Cognitive processes of memory in simultaneous interpretation. In J. Tommola (ed.) *Topics in Interpreting Research.* Turku: University of Turku, Centre for Translation and Interpreting, 61–71.

Pakenham, Thomas (1991) *The Scramble for Africa: White Man's Conquest of the Dark Continent from 1876 to 1912.* London: Weidenfeld & Nicolson.

Paker, Saliha (2011) Translation, the pursuit of inventiveness and Ottoman poetics: A systemic approach. In R. Sela-Sheffy & G. Toury (eds.) *Culture Contacts and the Making of Cultures.* Tel Aviv: Tel Aviv University, Unit of Culture Research, 459–474.

Palazchenko, Pavel R. (1997) *My Years with Gorbachev and Shevardnadze: The Memoir of a Soviet Interpreter.* University Park, PA: Pennsylvania State University Press.

Palmer, Russ & Lahtinen, Riitta (2005) Social-haptic communication for acquired deafblind people and family: Incorporating touch and environmental information through holistic communication. *DbI Review* 35, 6–8.

Palumbo Fossati Casa, Isabella (1997) L'école vénitienne des "giovani di lingua". In F. Hitzel (ed.) *Istanbul et les Langues Orientales.* Istanbul: Isis, 109–122.

Paneth, Eva (1957/2002) An investigation into conference interpreting. In F. Pöchhacker & M. Shlesinger (eds) *The Interpreting Studies Reader.* London/New York: Routledge, 31–40.

Paradis, Michel (1994) Toward a neurolinguistic theory of simultaneous interpreting: The framework. *International Journal of Psycholinguistics* 10 (3), 319–335.

Paradis, Michel (2004) *A Neurolinguistic Theory of Bilingualism.* Amsterdam: John Benjamins.

Park, Sung-rae (2003) Han'gukkŭndaeŭi sŏyangŏ t'ongyŏksa (2) - 1883nyŏnbut'ŏ 1886nyŏnkkaji [The interpreters of Western languages in modern times in Korea (2) – from 1883 until 1886]. *Kukchejiyŏngnyŏngu [International Area Studies]* 7 (1), 353–382.

Park, William M. (1998) *Translating and Interpreting Programs in North America: A Survey.* Alexandria, VA: American Translators Association.

Parsons, H. McIlvaine (1978) Human factors approach to simultaneous interpretation. In D. Gerver & H. W. Sinaiko (eds) *Language Interpretation and Communication.* New York/London: Plenum Press, 315–321.

Pasquandrea, Sergio (2011) Managing multiple actions through multimodality: Doctors' involvement in interpreter-mediated interactions. *Language in Society* 40 (4), 455–481.

Patel, Vimla L. & Groen, Gerbrand J. (1991) The general and specific nature of medical expertise: A critical look. In K. A. Ericsson & J. Smith (eds) *Towards a General Theory of Expertise: Prospects and Limits.* New York: Cambridge University Press, 93–125.

Patrie, Carol J. & Johnson, Robert E. (2011) *Fingerspelled Word Recognition through Rapid Serial Visual Presentation.* San Diego, CA: DawnSignPress.

Patrinelis, Christos G. (2001) The Phanariots before 1821. *Balkan Studies* 42 (1/2), 177–198.

Patton, Michael Q. (2002) *Qualitative Research & Evaluation Methods.* 3rd edn. Thousand Oaks, CA: Sage.

Păun, Radu G. (2008) Réseaux de livres et réseaux de pouvoirs dans le sud-est de l'Europe: le monde des drogmans (XVIIe-XVIIIe siècles). In F. Barbier & I. Monok (eds.) *L'Europe en Réseaux: Contribution a l'Histoire Intellectuelle de l'Europe. Réseaux du Livre, Réseaux des Lecteurs.* Leipzig: Leipziger Universitätsverlag, 63–107.

Pearlman, Laurie A. & Saakvitne, Karen W. (1995) Treating therapists with vicarious traumatization and secondary traumatic stress disorders. In C. R. Figley (ed.) *Compassion Fatigue: Coping with Secondary Traumatic Stress Disorder in those who Treat the Traumatized.* New York: Brunner-Routledge, 150–177.

Pedani, Maria Pia (1994) *In Nome del Gran Signore: Inviati Ottomani a Venezia dalla Caduta di Costantinopoli alla Guerra di Candia.* Venice: Deputazione editrice.

Peirce, Leslie (2010) Polyglottism in the Ottoman Empire: A reconsideration. In G. Piterberg, T. F. Ruiz & G. Symcox (eds) *Braudel Revisited: The Mediterranean World, 1600–1800.* Toronto: University of Toronto Press, 76–98.

Peñarroja Fa, Josep (2000) Historia de los intérpretes jurados. *Traducción & Comunicación* 1, 69–88.

Peng, Gracie (2011) Using Rhetorical Structure Theory (RST) to describe the development of coherence in interpreting trainees. In R. Setton (ed.) *Interpreting Chinese, Interpreting China.* Amsterdam: John Benjamins, 106–133.

Penn, Claire & Watermeyer, Jennifer (2012) Cultural brokerage and overcoming communication barriers: A case study from aphasia. In C. Baraldi & L. Gavioli (eds) *Coordinating Participation in Dialogue Interpreting.* Amsterdam: John Benjamins, 269–298.

Penn, Claire, Watermeyer, Jennifer & Evans, Melanie (2011) Why don't patients take their drugs? The role of communication, context and culture in patient adherence and the work of the pharmacist in HIV/AIDS. *Patient Education and Counseling* 83 (3), 310–318.

Perez, Isabelle A. & Wilson, Christine W. L. (2007) Interpreter-mediated police interviews: Working as a professional team. In C. Wadensjö, B. Englund Dimitrova & A.-L. Nilsson (eds) *The Critical Link 4: Professionalisation of Interpreting in the Community.* Amsterdam: John Benjamins, 79–93.

Perez, Isabelle & Wilson, Christine (2011) The interlinked approach to training for interpreter mediated police settings. In C. Kainz, E. Prunč & R. Schögler (eds) *Modelling the Field of Community Interpreting: Questions of Methodology in Research and Training.* Wien: LIT Verlag, 242–262.

Pérez Fernández, José Manuel (2011) Linguistic rights of indigenous peoples in the states of Latin America. *Intercultural Human Rights Law Review* 6, 379–425.

Pérez-Luzardo, Jessica (2005) *Didáctica de la Interpretación Simultánea/Simultaneous Interpreting Didactics.* Michigan: UMI Dissertation Services.

Perocco, Daria (2010) Tra cinquecento e seicento: Incomprensione, ambiguità, reticenza davanti al sovrano straniero. In A. Ghersetti (ed.) *Il Potere della Parola-la Parola del Potere. Tra Europa e Mondo Arabo-Ottomano, tra Medioevo ed Età Moderna.* Venice: Filippi, 59–74.

Peterson, Rico (2011) Profession in pentimento: A narrative inquiry into interpreting in video settings. In B. Nicodemus & L. Swabey (eds) *Advances in Interpreting Research: Inquiry in Action.* Amsterdam: John Benjamins, 199–223.

Petite, Christelle (2005) Evidence of repair mechanisms in simultaneous interpreting: A corpus-based analysis. *Interpreting* 7 (1), 27–49.

Petritsch, Ernst Dieter (1987) Die Wiener Turkologie vom 16. bis zum 18. Jahrhundert. In K. Kreiser (ed.) *Germano-Turcica: Zur Geschichte des Türkisch-Lernens in den deutschsprachigen Ländern.* Bamberg: Universitätsbibliothek Bamberg, 25–39.

Petritsch, Ernst Dieter (2004) Die Anfänge der Orientalischen Akademie. In O. Rathkolb (ed.) *250 Jahre: Von der Orientalischen zur Diplomatischen Akademie in Wien.* Innsbruck: StudienVerlag, 47–64.

Petritsch, Ernst Dieter (2005) Erziehung in *guten Sitten, Andacht und Gehorsam*: Die 1754 gegründete Orientalische Akademie in Wien. In M. Kurz, M. Scheutz, K. Vocelka & T. Winkelbauer (eds) *Das Osmanische Reich und die Habsburgermonarchie.* Vienna: R. Oldenbourg, 491–501.

Petsche, Hellmuth, Etlinger, Susan C. & Filz, Oliver (1993) Brain electrical mechanisms of bilingual speech management: An initial investigation. *Electroencephalography and Clinical Neurophysiology* 86, 385–394.

Pfau, Roland, Steinbach, Markus & Woll, Bencie (eds) (2012) *Sign Language: An International Handbook.* Berlin/Boston: De Gruyter Mouton.

Phelan, Mary (2011) Legal interpreters in the news in Ireland. *Translation & Interpreting* 3 (1), 76–105.

Phelan, Mary (2012) Medical interpreting and the law in the European Union. *European Journal of Health Law* 19 (4), 333–353.

Philliou, Christine (2001) Mischief in the Old Regime: Provincial dragomans and social change at the turn of the nineteenth century. *New Perspectives on Turkey* 25, 103–121.

Philliou, Christine (2011) *Biography of an Empire: Governing Ottomans in an Age of Revolution.* Berkeley: University of California Press.

Piaget, Jean (1967) *La Psychologie de l'Intelligence.* Paris: Armand Colin.

Pierce, Tamara & Napier, Jemina (2010) Mentoring: A vital learning tool for interpreter graduates. *International Journal of Interpreter Education* 2, 58–75.

Piller, Ingrid (2012) Intercultural communication: an overview. In C. B. Paulston, S. Kiesling & E. Rangel (eds) *The Handbook of Intercultural Discourse and Communication.* Oxford: Blackwell, 3–18.

Pinochi, Diletta (2009) Simultaneous interpretation of numbers: Comparing German and English to Italian. An experimental study. *The Interpreters' Newsletter* 14, 33–57.

Pio, Sonia (2003) The relation between ST delivery rate and quality in simultaneous interpretation. *The Interpreters' Newsletter* 12, 69–100.

Pippidi, Andrei (2006) Tre antiche casate dell'Istria: Caratteri e sviluppo di un gruppo professionale: I dragomanni di Venezia a Costantinopoli. *Quaderni della Casa Romena di Venezia* 4, 61–76.

Pittarello, Sara (2009) *Interpreter mediated* medical encounters in North Italy: Expectations, perceptions and practice. *The Interpreters' Newsletter* 14, 59–90.

Podruchny, Carolyn (2006) *Making the Voyageur World: Travelers and Traders in the North American Fur Trade.* Lincoln, NE: University of Nebraska Press.

Pöchhacker, Franz (1992) The role of theory in simultaneous interpreting. In C. Dollerup & A. Loddegaard (eds) *Teaching Translation and Interpreting: Training, Talent and Experience. Papers from the First Language International Conference, Elsinore, Denmark, 31 May–2 June 1991.* Amsterdam: John Benjamins, 211–220.

Pöchhacker, Franz (1994a) *Simultandolmetschen als komplexes Handeln.* Tübingen: Gunter Narr.

Pöchhacker, Franz (1994b) Quality assurance in simultaneous interpreting. In C. Dollerup & A. Lindegaard (eds) *Teaching Translation and Interpreting: Aims, Insights, Visions.* Amsterdam: John Benjamins, 233–242.

Pöchhacker, Franz (1994c) Simultaneous interpretation: "Cultural transfer" or "voice-over-text"? In M. Snell-Hornby, F. Pöchhacker & K. Kaindl (eds) *Translation Studies: An Interdiscipline. Selected Papers from the Translation Studies Congress, Vienna, 9–12 Sept. 1992.* Amsterdam: John Benjamins, 169–178.

Pöchhacker, Franz (1995a) "Those who do … ": A profile of research(ers) in interpreting. *Target* 7 (1), 47–64.

Pöchhacker, Franz (1995b) Writings and research in interpreting: A bibliographic analysis. *The Interpreters' Newsletter* 6, 17–31.

Pöchhacker, Franz (1995c) Simultaneous interpreting: A functionalist perspective. *Hermes. Journal of Linguistics* 14, 31–53.

Pöchhacker, Franz (1995d) Slifts and shifts in simultaneous interpreting. In J. Tommola (ed.) *Topics in Interpreting Research.* Turku: University of Turku, Centre for Translation and Interpreting, 73–90.

Pöchhacker, Franz (1997) Clinton speaks German: A case study of live broadcast simultaneous interpreting. In M. Snell-Hornby, Z. Jettmarovà & K. Kaindl (eds) *Translation as Intercultural Communication.* Amsterdam: John Benjamins, 207–216.

Pöchhacker, Franz (2000a) *Dolmetschen: Konzeptuelle Grundlagen und deskriptive Untersuchungen.* Tübingen: Stauffenburg.

Pöchhacker, Franz (2000b) The community interpreter's task: Self-perception and provider views. In R. P. Roberts, S. E. Carr, D. Abraham & A. Dufour (eds) *The Critical Link 2: Interpreters in the Community.* Amsterdam: John Benjamins, 49–65.

Pöchhacker, Franz (2001) Quality assessment in conference and community interpreting. *Meta* 46 (2), 410–425.

Pöchhacker, Franz (2004a) *Introducing Interpreting Studies.* London/New York: Routledge.

Pöchhacker, Franz (2004b) I in TS: On partnership in Translation Studies. In C. Schaffner (ed.) *Translation Research and Interpreting Research: Traditions, Gaps and Synergies.* Clevedon/Buffalo/Toronto: Multilingual Matters, 104–115.

Pöchhacker, Franz (2005) From operation to action: Process-orientation in interpreting studies. *Meta* 50 (2), 682–695.

Pöchhacker, Franz (2006a) Interpreters and ideology: From "between" to "within". *Across Languages and Cultures* 7 (2), 191–207.

Pöchhacker, Franz (2006b) Research and methodology in healthcare interpreting. In E. Hertog & B. van der Veer (eds) *Taking Stock: Research and Methodology in Community Interpreting. Linguistica Antverpiensia – New Series* 5, 135–159.

Pöchhacker, Franz (2006c) "Going social?" On pathways and paradigms in interpreting studies. In A. Pym, M. Shlesinger & Z. Jettmarová (eds) *Sociocultural Aspects of Translating and Interpreting.* Amsterdam: John Benjamins, 215–232.

Pöchhacker, Franz (2007) Coping with culture in Media Interpreting. *Perspectives: Studies in Translatology* 15 (2), 123–142.

Pöchhacker, Franz (2007) Interpreter translator teaching research: Miriam Shlesinger – translation scholar. In F. Pöchhacker, A. L. Jakobsen & I. M. Mees (eds) *Interpreting Studies and Beyond: A Tribute to Miriam Shlesinger.* Copenhagen: Samfundslitteratur Press, 5–16.

Pöchhacker, Franz (2008a) Interpreting as mediation. In C. Valero-Garcés & A. Martin (eds) *Crossing Borders in Community Interpreting: Definitions and Dilemmas.* Amsterdam: John Benjamins, 9–26.

Pöchhacker, Franz (2008b) The turns of interpreting studies. In G. Hansen, A. Chesterman & H. Gerzymisch-Arbogast (eds) *Efforts and Models in Interpreting and Translation Research: A Tribute to Daniel Gile.* Amsterdam: John Benjamins, 25–46.

Pöchhacker, Franz (2010a) The role of research in interpreter education. *Translation & Interpreting* 2 (1), 1–10.

Pöchhacker, Franz (2010b) Media interpreting. In Y. Gambier & L. van Doorslaer (eds) *Handbook of Translation Studies.* Vol. 1. Amsterdam: John Benjamins, 224–226.

Pöchhacker, Franz (2011a) Assessing aptitude for interpreting: The SynCloze test. *Interpreting* 13 (1), 106–120.

Pöchhacker, Franz (2011b) Researching interpreting: Approaches to inquiry. In B. Nicodemus & L. Swabey (eds) *Advances in Interpreting Research: Inquiry in Action.* Amsterdam: John Benjamins, 5–25.

Pöchhacker, Franz (2011c) Researching TV interpreting: Selected studies of US presidential material. *The Interpreters' Newsletter* 16, 21–36.

Pöchhacker, Franz (2011d) Conference interpreting: Surveying the profession. In R. Sela-Sheffy & M. Shlesinger (eds) *Identity and Status in the Translational Professions.* Amsterdam: John Benjamins, 49–64.

Pöchhacker, Franz (2012a) Interpreting participation: Conceptual analysis and illustration of the interpreter's role in interaction. In C. Baraldi & L. Gavioli (eds) *Coordinating Participation in Dialogue Interpreting.* Amsterdam: John Benjamins, 45–69.

Pöchhacker, Franz (2012b) Obama's rhetoric in German: A case study of the inaugural address. In B. Adab, P. A. Schmitt & G. Shreve (eds) *Discourses of Translation. Festschrift in Honour of Christina Schäffner.* Frankfurt: Peter Lang, 123–137.

Pöchhacker, Franz (2013a) Conference interpreting. In K. Malmkjaer & K. Windle (eds) *The Oxford Handbook of Translation Studies.* Oxford: Oxford University Press, 307–325.

Pöchhacker, Franz (2013b) The position of interpreting studies. In C. Millán & F. Bartrina (eds) *The Routledge Handbook of Translation Studies.* London/New York: Routledge, 60–72.

Pöchhacker, Franz (2016) *Introducing Interpreting Studies.* 2nd edn, London/New York: Routledge.

Pöchhacker, Franz & Kadrić, Mira (1999) The hospital cleaner as healthcare interpreter. *The Translator* 5 (2), 161–178.

Pöchhacker, Franz & Kolb, Waltraud (2009) Interpreting for the record: A case study of asylum review hearings. In S. Hale, U. Ozolins & L. Stern (eds) *The Critical Link 5: Quality in Interpreting – a Shared Responsibility.* Amsterdam: John Benjamins, 119–134.

Pöchhacker, Franz & Liu, Minhua (eds) (2014) *Aptitude for Interpreting.* Amsterdam: John Benjamins.

Pöchhacker, Franz & Shlesinger, Miriam (eds) (2002) *The Interpreting Studies Reader.* London/New York: Routledge.

Pöchhacker, Franz & Shlesinger, Miriam (eds) (2007) *Healthcare Interpreting: Discourse and Interaction.* Amsterdam: John Benjamins.

Pöllabauer, Sonja (2004) Interpreting in asylum hearings: Issues of role, responsibility and power. *Interpreting* 6 (2), 143–180.

Pöllabauer, Sonja (2007) Interpreting in asylum hearings: Issues of saving face. In C. Wadensjö, B. Englund Dimitrova & A.-L. Nilsson (eds) *The Critical Link 4: Professionalisation of Interpreting in the Community*. Amsterdam: John Benjamins, 39–52.

Pointurier-Pournin, Sophie (2014) *L'interprétation en Langue des Signes Française: Contraintes, Tactiques, Efforts*. Doctoral dissertation, Université Sorbonne Nouvelle – Paris 3.

Pokorn, Nike K., Felgner, Lars, Pokorn, Marko, Kores Plesničar, Blanka & Ahčan, Uroš (2013) Položaj tolmača in usmerjenost njegovega pogleda v medicinskem okolju. In V. Gorjanc (ed.) *Slovensko tolmačeslovje*. Ljubljana: Znanstvena založba Filozofske fakultete, 154–183.

Pollitt, Kyra (1997) The state we're in: Some thoughts on professionalisation, professionalism and practice among the UK's sign language interpreters. *Deaf Worlds* 13 (3), 21–26.

Powell, Clydette & Pagliara-Miller, Claire (2012) The use of volunteer interpreters during the 2010 Haiti earthquake: Lessons learned from the USNS COMFORT Operation Unified Response Haiti. *American Journal of Disaster Medicine* 7 (1), 37–47.

Power, Michael J. (1986) A technique for measuring processing load during speech production. *Journal of Psycholinguistic Research* 15 (5), 371–382.

Poyatos, Fernando (1987/2002) Nonverbal communication in simultaneous and consecutive interpretation: A theoretical model and new perspectives. In F. Pöchhacker & M. Shlesinger (eds) *The Interpreting Studies Reader*. London/New York: Routledge, 235–246.

Poyatos, Fernando (1997) The reality of multichannel verbal-nonverbal communication in simultaneous and consecutive interpretation. In F. Poyatos (ed.) *Nonverbal Communication and Translation: New Perspectives and Challenges in Literature, Interpretation and the Media*. Amsterdam: John Benjamins, 249–282.

Poyatos, Fernando (2002) *Nonverbal Communication across Disciplines*. 3 Vols. Amsterdam: John Benjamins.

Pradas Macías, E. Macarena (2006) Probing quality criteria in simultaneous interpreting: The role of silent pauses in fluency. *Interpreting* 8 (1), 25–43.

Preston, Paul (1994) *Mother Father Deaf: Living Between Sound and Silence*. Cambridge, MA: Harvard University Press.

Preston, Paul (1996) Chameleon voices: Interpreting for deaf parents. *Social Science & Medicine* 42, 1681–1690.

Price, Erika L., Pérez-Stable, Eliseo J., Nickleach, Dana, López, Monica & Karliner, Leah S. (2012) Interpreter perspectives of in-person, telephonic, and videoconferencing medical interpretation in clinical encounters. *Patient Education and Counseling* 87 (2), 226–232.

Price, John (1975) Foreign language interpreting in psychiatric practice. *Australian and New Zealand Journal of Psychiatry* 9 (4), 263–267.

Pross, Christian (2006) Burnout, vicarious traumatization and its prevention. *Torture* 16 (1), 1–9.

Proverbio, Alice M., Leoni, Giuliana C. & Zani, Alberto (2004) Language switching mechanisms in simultaneous interpreters: An ERP study. *Neuropsychologia* 42, 1636–1656.

Prunč, Erich (1997) Translationskultur (Versuch einer konstruktiven Kritik des translatorischen Handelns). *TextconText* 11 (2), 99–127.

Prunč, Erich (2008) Zur Konstruktion von Translationskulturen. In L. Schippel (ed.) *Translationskultur – ein innovatives und produktives Konzept*. Berlin: Frank & Timme, 19–41.

Prunč, Erich (2012a) *Entwicklungslinien der Translationswissenschaft. Von den Asymmetrien der Sprachen zu den Asymmetrien der Macht*. 3rd edn. Berlin: Frank & Timme.

Prunč, Erich (2012b) Rights, realities and responsibilities in community interpreting. *The Interpreters' Newsletter* 17, 1–12.

Puková, Zdeňka (2006) *Daniel Gile's Effort Model and Its Application to Simultaneous Interpreting of Texts with a High Concentration of Numerical Data and Enumerations*. Master's thesis, Charles University in Prague.

Pym, Anthony (1994) Twelfth-century Toledo and strategies of the literalist Trojan horse. *Target* 6 (1), 43–66.

Pym, Anthony (1996) The price of Alfonso's wisdom: Nationalist translation policy in thirteenth-century Castile. In R. Ellis & R. Tixier (eds) *The Medieval Translator / Traduire au Moyen Age* 5. Turnhout: Brepols, 448–467.

Pym, Anthony (1999) "Nicole slapped Michelle": Interpreters and theories of interpreting at the O. J. Simpson trial. *The Translator* 5 (2), 265–283.

Pym, Anthony (2000) *Negotiating the Frontier: Translators and Intercultures in Hispanic History.* Manchester: St Jerome.

Pym, Anthony (2008) On omission in simultaneous interpreting: Risk analysis of a hidden effort. In G. Hansen, A. Chesterman & H. Gerzymisch-Arbogast (eds) *Efforts and Models in Interpreting and Translation Research: A Tribute to Daniel Gile.* Amsterdam: John Benjamins, 83–105.

Pym, Anthony, Shlesinger, Miriam & Jettmarová, Zuzana (eds) (2006) *Sociocultural Aspects of Translating and Interpreting.* Amsterdam: John Benjamins.

Pym, Anthony, Grin, François, Sfreddo, Claudio & Chan, Andy L. J. (2012) *The Status of the Translation Profession in the European Union.* http://ec.europa.eu/dgs/translation/publications/studies/translation_profession_en.pdf (accessed 31 January 2015).

Qin, Jin, Marshall, Matthew, Mozrall, Jacqueline & Marschark, Marc (2008) Effects of pace and stress on upper extremity kinematic responses in sign language interpreters. *Ergonomics* 51 (3), 274–289. doi:10.1080/00140130701617025.

Quigley, Stephen P. (1972) *Interpreting for Deaf People: A Report of a Workshop on Interpreting. Governor Baxter State School for the Deaf, Portland, Maine, July 7–27, 1965.* Washington, DC: U.S. Department of Health, Education, and Welfare, Vocational Rehabilitation Administration.

Quinto-Pozos, David (2011) Teaching American Sign Language to hearing adult learners. *Annual Review of Applied Linguistics* 31, 137–158.

Radisoglou, Theodoros (2008) Kommentierte fotographische Dokumentation. Dolmetscher und Übersetzer, ihre Arbeit und Arbeitsbedingungen beim Nürnberger Prozess. In H. Kalverkämper & L. Schippel (eds) *Simultandolmetschen in Erstbewährung.* Berlin: Frank & Timme, 33–149.

Rafael, Vicente (2007) Translation in wartime. *Public Culture* 19 (2), 239–246.

Rafael, Vicente (2012) Translation and the US Empire. *The Translator* 18 (1), 1–22.

Rajendran, Dhevi J., Duchowski, Andrew T., Orero, Pilar, Martínez, Juan & Romero-Fresco, Pablo (2012) Effects of text chunking on subtitling: A quantitative and qualitative examination. *Perspectives: Studies in Translatology* 21 (1), 5–21.

Ramler, Siegfried (1988) Origins and challenges of simultaneous interpretation: The Nuremberg trials experience. In D. Lindberg Hammond (ed.) *Languages at Crossroads: Proceedings of the 29th Annual Conference of the American Translators Association, Seattle, WA, October 12–16, 1988.* Medford: Learned Information, 437–440.

Ramler, Siegfried (2009) *Nuremberg and beyond.* Honolulu: Ahuna Press.

Ramsey, Claire L. (1997) *Deaf Children in Public Schools: Placement, Context, and Consequences.* Washington, DC: Gallaudet University Press.

Ramsey, Claire L. (2004) Theoretical tools for educational interpreters. In E. A. Winston (ed.) *Educational Interpreting: How It Can Succeed.* Washington, DC: Gallaudet University Press, 206–226.

Ramsey, Claire & Peña, Sergio (2010) Sign language interpreting at the border of the two Californias. In R. Locker McKee & J. Davis (eds) *Interpreting in Multilingual, Multicultural Contexts.* Washington, DC: Gallaudet University Press, 3–27.

Rathkolb, Oliver (ed.) (2004) *250 Jahre: Von der Orientalischen zur Diplomatischen Akademie in Wien.* Innsbruck: Studien Verlag.

Raupach, Manfred (1980) Temporal variables in first and second language speech production. In H. W. Dechert & M. Raupach (eds) *Temporal Variables in Speech: Studies in Honour of Frieda Goldman-Eisler.* The Hague: Mouton, 263–270.

Rayman, Jennifer (2007) Visions of equality: Translating power in a deaf sermonette. *The Sign Language Translator and Interpreter* 1 (1), 73–114.

Rayner, Keith (1998) Eye movements in reading and information processing: 20 years of research. *Psychological Bulletin* 124 (3), 372–422.

Reason, Peter & Bradbury, Hilary (2008) *The SAGE Handbook of Action Research: Participative Inquiry and Practice.* 2nd edn. London: Sage.

Red T (2012) *The Conflict Zone Field Guide for Civilian Translators/Interpreters and Users of their Services.* http://red-t.org/documents/T-I_Field_Guide_2012.pdf (accessed 10 April 2014).

Reiter, Clara (2013a) " … wo der Dollmetsch allzeit interpretirt". Das Hofdolmetscheramt am Wiener Hof: Vom Karrieresprungbrett zum Abstellgleis. *Lebende Sprachen* 58 (1), 197–220.

Reiter, Clara (2013b) Vermittler zwischen West und Ost: Hofdolmetscher am Habsburger Hof (1650–1800). In G. Barth-Scalmani, H. Rudolph & C. Steppan (eds) *Politische Kommunikation zwischen Imperien*. Innsbruck: StudienVerlag, 257–273.

Reithofer, Karin (2010) English as a lingua franca vs. interpreting: Battleground or peaceful co-existence? *The Interpreters' Newsletter* 15, 143–157.

Reithofer, Karin (2013) Comparing modes of communication: The effect of English as a lingua franca vs. interpreting. *Interpreting* 15 (1), 48–73.

Renfer, Christoph (1992) Translator and interpreter training: A case for a two-tier system. In C. Dollerup & A. Loddegaard (eds) *Teaching Translation and Interpreting: Training, Talent and Experience*. Amsterdam: John Benjamins, 173–184.

Rennert, Sylvi (2008) Visual input in simultaneous interpreting. *Meta* 53 (1), 204–207.

Rennert, Sylvi (2010) The impact of fluency on the subjective assessment of interpreting quality. *The Interpreters' Newsletter* 15, 101–115.

Repko, Allen F. (2012) *Interdisciplinary Research: Process and Theory*. 2nd edn. Thousand Oaks/London/New Delhi: Sage.

Riccardi, Alessandra (1996) Language-specific strategies in simultaneous interpreting. In C. Dollerup & V. Appel (eds) *Teaching Translation and Interpreting 3: New Horizons. Papers from the Third Language International Conference, Elsinore, Denmark 9–11 June 1995*. Amsterdam: John Benjamins, 213–222.

Riccardi, Alessandra (1998) Interpreting strategies and creativity. In A. Beylard-Ozeroff, J. Kralova & B. Moser-Mercer (eds) *Translators' Strategies and Creativity. Selected Papers from the 9th International Conference on Translation and Interpreting, Prague, September 1995*. Amsterdam: John Benjamins, 171–179.

Riccardi, Alessandra (2005) On the evolution of interpreting strategies in simultaneous interpreting. *Meta* 50 (2), 753–767.

Richardson, Daniel C. & Spivey, Michael J. (2004) Eye-tracking: Characteristics and methods. In G. E. Wnek & G. L. Bowlin (eds) *Encyclopedia of Biomaterials and Biomedical Engineering*. New York: Marcel Dekker, 568–572.

Rico, Celia (2010) Translator training in the European Higher Education Area: Curriculum design for the Bologna Process. A case study. *The Interpreter and Translator Trainer* 4 (1), 89–114.

RID (2005) *NAD-RID Code of professional conduct*. www.rid.org/UserFiles/File/NAD_RID_ETHICS.pdf (accessed 24 February 2015).

RID (2007) Interpreting for individuals who are deaf-blind. Standard practice paper. Alexandria, VA: RID Publications. www.rid.org/UserFiles/File/pdfs/Standard_Practice_Papers/Drafts_June_2006/Deaf-Blind_SPP%281%29.pdf (accessed 25 July 2014).

RID (2014) *JOI*. www.rid.org/publications/joi/index.cfm/AID/112 (accessed 17 January 2014).

RID-EIC (2009) The educational interpreter's niche in RID from the practitioner's perspective: Survey results. www.rid.org/UserFiles/File/pdfs/About_RID/For_Educational_Interpreters/EDTERP_SURVEY_RESULTS.pdf (accessed 5 August 2014).

Rigney, Azucena C. (1999) Questioning in interpreted testimony. *Forensic Linguistics* 6 (1), 83–108.

Rinne, Juha O., Tommola, Jorma, Laine, Matti, Krause, Bernd J., Schmidt, Daniela, Kaasinen, Valtteri, Teräs, Mika, Sipilä, Hannu & Sunnari, Marianna (2000) The translating brain: Cerebral activation patterns during simultaneous interpreting. *Neuroscience Letters* 294 (2), 85–88.

Risku, Hanna (2013) Cognitive approaches to translation. In C. A. Chapelle (ed.) *Encyclopedia of Applied Linguistics*. Oxford: Wiley-Blackwell, 675–684.

Roat, Cynthia E. (1996) *Bridging the Gap: A Basic Training for Medical Interpreters*. Seattle, WA: Cross Cultural Health Care Program.

Roberson, Len, Russell, Debra & Shaw, Risa (2011) American Sign Language/English interpreting in legal settings: Current practices in North America. *Journal of Interpretation* 21 (1), 65–79.

Roberts, Roda P. (1994) Community interpreting today and tomorrow. In P. W. Krawutschke (ed.) *Vistas: Proceedings of the 35th Annual Conference of the American Translators Association, October 12–16, 1994*. Medford, NJ: Learned Information, 127–138.

Roberts-Smith, Len (2009) Forensic interpreting: Trial and error. In S. B. Hale, U. Ozolins & L. Stern (eds) *The Critical Link 5: Quality in Interpreting – a Shared Responsibility*. Amsterdam: John Benjamins, 13–35.

Rocks, Siobhán (2011) The theatre sign language interpreter and the competing visual narrative: The translation and interpretation of theatrical texts into British Sign Language. In R. Baines, C. Marinetti & M. Perteghella (eds) *Staging and Performing Translation: Text and Theatre Practice*. London: Palgrave Macmillan, 72–86.

Roland, Ruth A. (1999) *Interpreters as Diplomats: A Diplomatic History of the Role of Interpreters in World Politics*. Ottawa: University of Ottawa Press.

Romero-Fresco, Pablo (2011) *Subtitling through Speech Recognition: Respeaking*. Manchester: St Jerome.

Romero-Fresco, Pablo (2012) Respeaking in translator training curricula: Present and future prospects. *The Interpreter and Translator Trainer* 6 (1), 91–112.

Romero-Fresco, Pablo (2013) Quality in live subtitling: The reception of respoken subtitles in the UK. In A. Remael, P. Orero & M. Carroll (eds) *Audiovisual Translation and Media Accessibility at the Crossroads. Media for All 3*. Amsterdam/New York: Rodopi, 111–133.

Rosenberg, Brett A. (2002) A quantitative discourse analysis of community interpreting. In *Translation: New Ideas for a New Century. Proceedings of the XVI FIT Congress*. Paris: FIT, 222–226.

Rosenberg, Brett Allen (2007) A data driven analysis of telephone interpreting. In C. Wadensjö, B. Englund Dimitrova & A.-L. Nilsson (eds) *The Critical Link 4: Professionalisation of Interpreting in the Community*. Amsterdam: John Benjamins, 65–76.

Rosenberg, Ellen, Seller, Robbyn & Leanza, Yvan (2008) Through interpreters' eyes: Comparing roles of professional and family interpreters. *Patient Education and Counseling* 70 (1), 87–93.

Rosiers, Alexandra, Eyckmans, June & Bauwens, Daniel (2011) A story of attitudes and aptitudes? Investigating individual difference variables within the context of interpreting. *Interpreting* 13 (1), 53–69.

Rossano, Federico (2012) Gaze in conversation. In J. Sidnell & T. Stivers (eds) *The Handbook of Conversation Analysis*. Malden, MA: Wiley-Blackwell, 308–329.

Rothman, E. Natalie (2009a) Interpreting dragomans: Boundaries and crossings in the early modern Mediterranean. *Comparative Studies in Society and History* 51 (4), 771–800.

Rothman, E. Natalie (2009b) Self-fashioning in the Mediterranean contact zone: Giovanni Battista Salvago and his *Africa Overo Barbaria* (1625). In K. Eisenbichler (ed.) *Renaissance Medievalisms*. Toronto: Centre for Reformation and Renaissance Studies, 123–143.

Rothman, E. Natalie (2011a) *Brokering Empire: Trans-Imperial Subjects between Venice and Istanbul*. Ithaca: Cornell University Press.

Rothman, E. Natalie (2011b) Conversion and convergence in the Venetian–Ottoman borderlands. *Journal of Medieval and Early Modern Studies* 41 (3), 601–633.

Rothman, E. Natalie (2012) Visualizing a space of encounter: Intimacy, alterity, and trans-imperial perspective in an Ottoman–Venetian miniature album. *Osmanlı Araştırmaları / Journal of Ottoman Studies* 40, 39–80.

Rothman, E. Natalie (2013) Dragomans and "Turkish Literature": The making of a field of inquiry. *Oriente Moderno* 93 (2), 390–421.

Rousseau, Cécile, Measham, Toby & Moro, Marie-Rose (2011) Working with interpreters in child mental health. *Child & Adolescent Mental Health* 16 (1), 55–59.

Roy, Cynthia B. (1993) The problem with definitions, descriptions and the role metaphors of interpreters. *Journal of Interpretation* 6, 127–154.

Roy, Cynthia (1993/2002) The problem with definitions, descriptions and the role metaphors of interpreters. In F. Pöchhacker & M. Shlesinger (eds) *The Interpreting Studies Reader*. London/New York: Routledge, 345–353.

Roy, Cynthia B. (1996) An interactional sociolinguistic analysis of turn-taking in an interpreted event. *Interpreting* 1 (1), 39–67.

Roy, Cynthia B. (2000a) *Interpreting as a Discourse Process*. New York/Oxford: Oxford University Press.

Roy, Cynthia B. (ed.) (2000b) *Innovative Practices for Teaching Sign Language Interpreters*. Washington, DC: Gallaudet University Press.

Roy, Cynthia B. (ed.) (2005) *Advances in Teaching Sign Language Interpreters.* Washington, DC: Gallaudet University Press.

Roy, Cynthia B. (ed.) (2006) *New Approaches to Interpreter Education.* Washington, DC: Gallaudet University Press.

Roy, Cynthia B. & Napier, Jemina (eds) (2015) *The Sign Language Interpreting Studies Reader.* Amsterdam: John Benjamins.

Rozan, Jean-François (1956) *La prise de Notes en Interprétation Consécutive.* Geneva: Georg.

Roziner, Ilan & Shlesinger, Miriam (2010) Much ado about something remote: Stress and performance in remote interpreting. *Interpreting* 12 (2), 214–247.

Rudner, Mary, Fransson, Peter, Ingvar, Martin, Nyberg, Llars & Rönnberg, Jerker (2007) Neural representation of binding lexical signs and words in the episodic buffer of working memory. *Neuropsychologia* 45 (10), 2258–2276.

Rudser, Steven F. & Strong, Michael (1986) An examination of some personal characteristics and abilities of sign language interpreters. *Sign Language Studies* 53, 315–331.

Rudvin, Mette (2006) The cultural turn in community interpreting: A brief analysis of epistemological developments in community interpreting literature in the light of paradigm changes in the humanities. In E. Hertog & B. van der Veer (eds) *Taking Stock: Research and Methodology in Community Interpreting. Linguistica Antverpiensia – New Series* 5, 21–41.

Rudvin, Mette (2007) Professionalism and ethics in community interpreting: The impact of individualist versus collective group identity. *Interpreting* 9 (1), 47–69.

Rudvin, Mette (2015) Interpreting and professional identity. In H. Mikkelson & R. Jourdenais (eds) *The Routledge Handbook of Interpreting.* London/New York: Routledge, 432–446.

Rudvin, Mette & Tomassini, Elena (2008) Migration, ideology and the interpreter–mediator: The role of the language mediator in education and medical settings in Italy. In C. Valero-Garcés & A. Martin (eds) *Crossing Borders in Community Interpreting: Definitions and Dilemmas.* Amsterdam: John Benjamins, 245–266.

Rudvin, Mette & Tomassini, Elena (2011) *Interpreting in the Community and Workplace: A Practical Teaching Guide.* Basingstoke: Palgrave Macmillan.

Ruesch, Jurgen & Kees, Weldon (1956) *Nonverbal Communication: Notes on the Visual Perception of Human Relations.* Berkeley/Los Angeles, CA: University of California Press.

Ruiz, Carmen, Paredes, Natalia, Macizo, Pedro & Bajo, M. Teresa (2008) Activation of lexical and syntactic target language properties in translation. *Acta Psychologica* 128, 490–500.

Rumelhart, David E. & McClelland, James L. (1986) *Parallel Distributed Processing: Explorations in the Microstructure of Cognition. Vol. 1: Foundations.* Cambridge, MA: MIT Press.

Russell, Debra L. (2002) *Interpreting in Legal Contexts: Consecutive and Simultaneous Interpretation.* Burtonsville, MD: Linstok Press.

Russell, Debra (2012) Court/legal interpreting. In L. van Doorslaer & Y. Gambier (eds) *Handbook of Translation Studies.* Vol. 3. Amsterdam: John Benjamins, 17–20.

Russell, Debra & Hale, Sandra B. (eds) (2008) *Interpreting in Legal Settings.* Washington, DC: Gallaudet University Press.

Russell, Debra L., Shaw, Risa & Malcolm, Karen (2010) Effective teaching strategies for consecutive interpreting. *International Journal of Interpreter Education* 2, 111–119.

Russell, Sonia (2000) "Let me put it simply.": The case for a standard translation of the police caution and its explanation. *International Journal of Speech Language and the Law* 7 (1), 26–48.

Russell, Sonia (2002) "Three's a crowd": Shifting dynamics in the interpreted interview. In J. Cotterill (ed.) *Language in the Legal Process.* Basingstoke: Palgrave Macmillan, 111–126.

Russo, Mariachiara (1997) Film interpreting: Challenges and constraints of a semiotic practice. In Y. Gambier, D. Gile & C. Taylor (eds) *Conference Interpreting: Current Trends in Research.* Amsterdam: John Benjamins, 188–192.

Russo, Mariachiara (2005) Simultaneous film interpreting and users' feedback. *Interpreting* 7 (1), 1–26.

Russo, Mariachiara (2010) Reflecting on interpreting practice: Graduation theses based on the European Parliament Interpreting Corpus (EPIC). In L. N. Zybatow (ed.) *Translationswissenschaft – Stand und Perspektiven. Innsbrucker Ringvorlesungen zur Translationswissenschaft VI.* Frankfurt: Peter Lang, 35–50.

Russo, Mariachiara (2011) Aptitude testing over the years. *Interpreting* 13 (1), 5–30.

Russo, Mariachiara (2014) Testing aptitude for interpreting: The predictive value of oral paraphrasing, with synonyms and coherence as assessment parameters. *Interpreting* 16 (1), 1–18.

Russo, Mariachiara & Pippa, Salvador (2004) Aptitude to interpreting: Preliminary results of a testing methodology based on paraphrase. *Meta* 49 (2), 409–432.

Russo, Mariachiara & Sandrelli, Annalisa (2006) Looking for lexical patterns in a trilingual corpus of source and interpreted speeches: Extended analysis of EPIC (European Parliament Interpreting Corpus). *Forum* 4 (1), 221–255.

Russo, Mariachiara, Bendazzoli, Claudio & Sandrelli, Annalisa (2006) Looking for lexical patterns in a trilingual corpus of source and interpreted speeches: Extended analysis of EPIC (European Parliament Interpreting Corpus). *Forum* 4 (1), 221–254.

Russo, Mariachiara, Bendazzoli, Claudio, Sandrelli, Annalisa & Spinolo, Nicoletta (2012) The European Parliament Interpreting Corpus (EPIC): Implementation and developments. In F. Straniero Sergio & C. Falbo (eds) *Breaking Ground in Corpus-Based Interpreting Studies.* Frankfurt: Peter Lang, 53–90.

Rütten, Anja (2004) Why and in which sense do conference interpreters need special software? In R. Temmerman & U. Knops (eds) *The Translation of Domain Specific Languages and Multilingual Terminology Management. Linguistica Antverpiensia – New Series* 3, 167–177.

Rütten, Anja (2007) *Informations- und Wissensmanagement beim Konferenzdolmetschen.* Frankfurt: Peter Lang.

Saar, Erik & Novak, Viveca (2005) *Inside the Wire: A Military Intelligence Soldier's Eyewitness Account of Life at Guantánamo.* New York: The Penguin Press.

Sabatini, Elisabetta (2000) Listening comprehension, shadowing and simultaneous interpreting of two "non-standard" English speeches. *Interpreting* 5 (1), 25–48.

Sacks, Harvey (1995 [1964–72]) *Lectures on Conversation* (Ed. Gail Jefferson). Oxford: Blackwell.

Sacks, Harvey, Schegloff, Emanuel & Jefferson, Gail (1974) A simplest systematics for the organization of turn-taking in conversation. *Language* 50, 696–736.

Sadava, Mike (2010) Misinterpretation: Crisis in Canadian court interpreting. *The Lawyers Weekly*, December 3, 27. www.lawyersweekly-digital.com/lawyersweekly/3029?folio=27#pg28 (accessed 15 December 2014).

Sahagún, Bernardino de (1577) *General History of the Things of New Spain by Fray Bernardino de Sahagún: The Florentine Codex.* World Digital Library (www.wdl.org/en/item/10096) Volume 3, 823–997.

Salaets, Heidi & Van Gucht, Jan (2008) Perceptions of a profession. In C. Valero-Garcés & A. Martin (eds) *Crossing Borders in Community Interpreting: Definitions and Dilemmas.* Amsterdam: John Benjamins, 267–287.

Salama-Carr, Myriam (1990) *L'école de Hunayn Ibn Ishaq et son Importance pour la Traduction.* Paris: Didier Erudition.

Salama-Carr, Myriam (ed.) (2007) *Translating and Interpreting Conflict.* Amsterdam/New York: Rodopi.

Salevsky, Heidemarie (1993) The distinctive nature of interpreting studies. *Target* 5 (2), 149–167.

Salevsky, Heidemarie (1994) Möglichkeiten und Grenzen eines Interaktionmodells des Dolmetschens [Potential and limitations of an interaction model of interpreting]. In M. Snell-Hornby, F. Pöchhacker & K. Kaindl (eds) *Translation Studies: An Interdiscipline.* Amsterdam: John Benjamins, 159–168.

Salomon, Jean-Jacques (1993) Paul Mantoux et la Révolution industrielle. *Les Cahiers du CNAM* [Conservatoire National des Arts et Métiers] 2, 119–154.

Sánchez Balsalobre, Leticia, Monteoliva García, Eloisa, Romero Gutiérrez, Esther & de Manuel Jerez, Jesús (2010) ECOS: 12 years breaking down the barriers of silence and languages (Transl. from Spanish by Anne Martin). In J. Boéri & C. Maier (eds) *Compromiso Social y Traducción/ Interpretación – Translation/Interpreting and Social Activism.* Granada: ECOS, 7–18.

Sandrelli, Annalisa (2007) Designing CAIT (Computer-Assisted Interpreter Training) tools: Black Box. In H. Gerzymisch-Arbogast & S. Nauert (eds) *Challenges of Multidimensional Translation. Proceedings of the Marie Curie Euroconferences Saarbrücken 2–6 May 2005.* www.euroconferences.info/proceedings/2005_Proceedings/2005_Sandrelli_Annalisa.pdf (accessed 29 May 2014).

Sandrelli, Annalisa (2010) Corpus-based interpreting studies and interpreter training: A modest proposal. In L. N. Zybatow (ed.) *Translationswissenschaft – Stand und Perspektiven. Innsbrucker Ringvorlesungen zur Translationswissenschaft VI.* Frankfurt: Peter Lang, 69–90.

Sandrelli, Annalisa (2011a) Computer assisted interpreter training (CAIT) for legal interpreters and translators (LITs). In B. Townsley (ed.) *Building Mutual Trust: A Framework Project for Implementing EU Common Standards in Legal Interpreting and Translation.* London: Middlesex University, 234–268. www.lr.mdx.ac.uk/mutual-trust/mtdocs/BMT%20Report.pdf (accessed 12 December 2014).

Sandrelli, Annalisa (2011b) Training in business interpreting and the role of technology. In J. F. Medina Montero & S. Tripepi Winteringham (eds) *Interpretazione e Mediazione. Un'Opposizione Inconciliabile?* Rome: Aracne, 209–233.

Sandrelli, Annalisa (2012) Introducing FOOTIE (Football in Europe): Simultaneous interpreting in football press conferences. In F. Straniero Sergio & C. Falbo (eds) *Breaking Ground in Corpus-Based Interpreting Studies.* Frankfurt: Peter Lang, 119–153.

Sandrelli, Annalisa (2015) Becoming an interpreter: The role of computer technology. In C. Iliescu Gheorghiu & J. M. Ortega Herráez (eds) *Interpreting: Insights in Interpreting. Status and Developments.* Special Issue of *MonTI* 2, 118–138.

Sandrelli, Annalisa & de Manuel Jerez, Jesús (2007) The impact of information and communication technology (ICT) on interpreter training: State-of-the-art and future prospects. *The Interpreter and Translator Trainer* 1 (2), 269–303.

Sandrelli, Annalisa, Bendazzoli, Claudio & Russo, Mariachiara (2010) European Parliament Interpreting Corpus (EPIC): Methodological issues and preliminary results on lexical patterns in simultaneous interpreting. *International Journal of Translation* 22 (1/2), 165–203.

Santoyo, Julio César (1999) *Historia de la Traducción: Quince Apuntes.* León: Universidad de León.

Santoyo, Julio César (2008) *Historia de la Traducción: Viejos y Nuevos Apuntes.* León: Universidad de León.

Sanz, Jesús (1930) Le travail et les aptitudes des interprètes parlementaires. *Anals d'Orientació Professional* 4, 303–318.

Sarmiento Pérez, Marcos (2011) The role of interpreters in the conquest and acculturation of the Canary Archipelago. *Interpreting* 13 (2), 155–175.

Sarmiento Pérez, Marcos (2016) Interpreting for the Inquisition. In K. Takeda & J. Baigorri-Jalón (eds) *New Insights in the History of Interpreting.* Amsterdam: John Benjamins.

Saville-Troike, Muriel (2003) *The Ethnography of Communication: An Introduction.* 3rd edn. Malden, MA/Oxford: Blackwell.

Savvalidou, Flora (2011) Interpreting (im)politeness strategies in a media political setting: A case study from the Greek prime ministerial TV debate as interpreted into Greek Sign Language. In L. Leeson, S. Wurm & M. Vermeerbergen (eds) *Signed Language Interpreting: Preparation, Practice and Performance.* Manchester: St. Jerome, 87–109.

Sawyer, David B. (2000) Towards meaningful, appropriate, and useful assessment: How the false dichotomy between theory and practice undermines interpreter education. *ATA Chronicle* 29 (2), 32–40.

Sawyer, David B. (2004) *Fundamental Aspects of Interpreter Education: Curriculum and Assessment.* Amsterdam: John Benjamins.

Sawyer, David B. (2008) Interpreter training and education at the U.S. Department of State: Origins, developments, and current practices. *Interpreting and Translation Studies: The Journal of the Japan Association for Interpreting and Translation Studies* 8, 267–277.

Schacter, Daniel L., Wagner, Anthony D. & Buckner, Randy L. (2000) Memory systems of 1999. In E. Tulving & F. I. M. Craik (eds) *The Oxford Handbook of Memory.* New York: Oxford University Press, 627–643.

Schäffner, Christina (ed.) (2004) *Translation Research and Interpreting Research: Traditions, Gaps and Synergies.* Clevedon: Multilingual Matters.

Schäffner, Christina, Kredens, Krzysztof & Fowler, Yvonne (eds) (2013) *Interpreting in a Changing Landscape: Selected Papers from Critical Link 6.* Amsterdam: John Benjamins.

Scheffer, Thomas (2001) *Asylgewährung. Eine ethnographische Verfahrensanalyse.* Stuttgart: Lucius & Lucius.

Schegloff, Emanuel (1992) On talk and its institutional occasions. In P. Drew & J. Heritage (eds) *Talk at Work: Interaction in Institutional Settings.* Cambridge: Cambridge University Press, 101–134.

Schegloff, Emanuel (1997) Whose text? Whose context? *Discourse and Society* 8, 165–187.

Schegloff, Emanuel A., Jefferson, Gail & Sacks, Harvey (1977) The preference for self-correction in the organization of repair in conversation. *Language* 53 (2), 361–382.

Schein, Jerome D. (1974) Personality characteristics associated with interpreter proficiency. *Journal of Rehabilitation of the Deaf* 7, 33–43.

Schembri, Adam, Fenlon, Jordan, Rentelis, Ramas, Reynolds, Sally & Cormier, Kearsy (2013) Building the British Sign Language Corpus. *Language Documentation and Conservation* 7, 136–154.

Schenker, Yael, Pérez-Stable, Eliseo J., Nickleach, Dana & Karliner, Leah S. (2011) Patterns of interpreter use for hospitalized patients with limited English proficiency. *Journal of General Internal Medicine* 26 (7), 712–717.

Scherer, Klaus R. (1979) Voice and speech correlates of perceived social influence. In H. Giles & R. N. St. Clair (eds) *Language and Social Psychology*. London: Arnold, 88–120.

Scherer, Klaus R. (1986) Vocal affect expression: A review and a model for future research. *Psychological Bulletin* 99 (2), 143–165.

Scheuren, Fritz (2004) What is a survey? www.amstat.org/sections/srms/pamphlet.pdf (accessed 10 July 2014).

Schick, Brenda (2003) The development of American Sign Language and manually coded English systems. In M. Marschark & P. E. Spencer (eds) *Oxford Handbook of Deaf Studies, Language, and Education*. New York: Oxford University Press, 219–231.

Schiffrin, Deborah (1994) *Approaches to Discourse*. Malden, MA: Blackwell.

Schjoldager, Anne (1995) An exploratory study of translational norms in simultaneous interpreting: Methodological reflections. *Hermes: Journal of Linguistics* 14, 65–87. Repr. in F. Pöchhacker & M. Shlesinger (eds) (2002) *The Interpreting Studies Reader*. London/New York: Routledge, 301–311.

Schlemmer, Arina & Mash, Bob (2006) The effects of a language barrier in a South African district hospital. *South African Medical Journal* 96 (10), 1084–1087.

Schmidt, Jan (2000) Franz von Dombay, Austrian Dragoman at the Bosnian Border 1792–1800. *Wiener Zeitschrift für die Kunde des Morgenlandes* 90, 75–168.

Schmidt, Paul (1949) *Statist auf diplomatischer Bühne 1923–45. Erlebnisse des Chefdolmetschers im Auswärtigen Amt mit den Staatsmännern Europas* [*An Extra on the Diplomatic Stage, 1923–45: Experiences of the Chief Interpreter in the Foreign Office in Dealing with Europe's Statesmen*]. Bonn: Athenäum.

Schmitz, Birte (1997) The translation objective in automatic dialogue interpreting. In C. Hauenschild & S. Heizmann (eds) *Machine Translation and Translation Theory*. Berlin: Mouton de Gruyter, 193–210.

Schmitz, Birte & Jekat-Rommel, Susanne (1994) *Eine zyklische Approximation an Sprechhandlungstypen – zur Annotierung von Äusserungen in Dialogen*. Verbmobil-Report 28. Hamburg: TU Berlin/Universität Hamburg.

Schneider, P. Diane (1992) Interpreter/conciliator, an evolving function. In E. F. Losa (ed.) *Frontiers. Proceedings of the 33rd Annual Conference of the American Translators Association, November 4–8, 1992, San Diego, California*. Medford, NJ: Learned Information, 57–64.

Schneider, Walter & Chein, Jason M. (2003) Controlled and automatic processing: Behavior, theory, and biological mechanisms. *Cognitive Science* 27 (3), 525–559.

Schollum, Mary (2005) *Investigative interviewing: The literature*. Wellington: Office of the Commissioner of Police.

Schön, Donald A. (1983) *The Reflective Practitioner: How Professionals Think in Action*. New York: Basic Books.

Schott, Björn H., Wüstenberg, Torsten, Wimber, Maria, Fenker, Daniela B., Zierhut, Kathrin C., Seidenbecher, Constanze I., Heinze, Hans-Jochen, Walter, Henrik, Düzel, Emrah & Richardson-Klavehn, Alan (2013) The relationship between level of processing and hippocampal-cortical functional connectivity during episodic memory formation in humans. *Human Brain Mapping* 34 (2), 407–424.

Schouten, Barbara, Ross, Jonathan, Zendedel, Rena & Meeuwesen, Ludwien (2012) Informal interpreters in medical settings: A comparative socio-cultural study of the Netherlands and Turkey. *The Translator* 18 (2), 311–338.

Schultz, Tanja (2006) Multilingual acoustical modeling. In T. Schultz & K. Kirchoff (eds) *Multilingual Speech Processing*. Burlington, MA: Elsevier, 71–122.

Schuster, Michal (2013) From chaos to cultural competence: Analyzing language access to public institutions. In C. Schäffner, K. Kredens & Y. Fowler (eds) *Interpreting in a Changing Landscape: Selected Papers from Critical Link 6*. Amsterdam: John Benjamins, 61–82.

Schweda Nicholson, Nancy (1986) Language planning and policy development for court interpretation services in the United States. *Language Problems and Language Planning* 10 (2), 140–157.

Schweda Nicholson, Nancy (1989) Documentation and text preparation for simultaneous interpretation. In D. L. Hammond (ed.) *Coming of Age. Proceedings of the 30th Annual Conference of the American Translators Association*. Medford, NJ: Learned Information, 163–181.

Schweda Nicholson, Nancy (1990) The role of shadowing in interpreter training. *The Interpreters' Newsletter* 3, 33–37.

Schweda Nicholson, Nancy (1994) Professional ethics for court and community interpreters. In D. L. Hammond (ed.) *Professional Issues for Translators and Interpreters*. Amsterdam: John Benjamins, 79–97.

Schweda Nicholson, Nancy (2005) Personality characteristics of interpreter trainees: The Myers-Briggs Type Indicator (MBTI). *The Interpreters' Newsletter* 13, 109–142.

Schweda Nicholson, Nancy (2010) Interpreting at the International Criminal Court for the Former Yugoslavia (ICTY): Its linguistic and cultural challenges. In H. Tonkin & M. E. Frank (eds) *The Translator as Mediator of Cultures*. Amsterdam: John Benjamins, 37–52.

Schwenke, Tomina J., Ashby, Jeffrey S. & Gnilka, Philip B. (2014) Sign language interpreters and burnout: The effects of perfectionism, perceived stress, and coping resources. *Interpreting* 16 (2), 209–232.

Scollon, Ron & Scollon, Suzanne Wong (1995) *Intercultural Communication: A Discourse Approach*. Oxford: Blackwell.

SDI (2013) Direktorengalerie: Prof. Dr. Antoine Velleman (1875–1962). www.sdi-muenchen.de/home/profil/kurzchronik/prof-dr-antoine-velleman/ (accessed 12 October 2014).

Searle, John (1969) *Speech Acts*. Cambridge: Cambridge University Press.

Seeber, Kilian G. (2001) Intonation and anticipation in simultaneous interpreting. *Cahiers de Linguistique Française* 23, 61–97.

Seeber, Kilian G. (2011) Cognitive load in simultaneous interpreting: Existing theories – new models. *Interpreting* 13 (2), 176–204.

Seeber, Kilian G. (2012) Multimodal input in simultaneous interpreting: An eye-tracking experiment. In L. N. Zybatow, A. Petrova & M. Ustaszewski (eds) *Translation Studies: Old and New Types of Translation in Theory and Practice. Proceedings of the 1st International Conference TRANSLATA "Translation & Interpreting Research: yesterday – today – tomorrow", Innsbruck, May 12–14, 2011*. Frankfurt: Peter Lang, 341–347.

Seeber, Kilian G. (2013) Cognitive load in simultaneous interpreting: Measures and methods. *Target* 25 (1), 18–32.

Seeber, Kilian G. & Kerzel, Dirk (2012) Cognitive load in simultaneous interpreting: Model meets data. *International Journal of Bilingualism* 16 (2), 228–242.

Seidlhofer, Barbara (2011) *Understanding English as a Lingua Franca*. Oxford: Oxford University Press.

Sela-Sheffy, Rakefet (2010) "Stars" or "professionals": The imagined vocation and exclusive knowledge of translators in Israel. In O. Diaz Fouces & E. Monzó (eds) *MonTI 2: Applied Sociology in Translation Studies/Sociología Aplicada a la Traducción*. Alicante: Publicaciones de la Universidad de Alicante, 131–152.

Sela-Sheffy, Rakefet & Shlesinger, Miriam (2008) Strategies of image-making and status advancement of translators and interpreters as a marginal occupational group. A research project in progress. In A. Pym, M. Shlesinger & D. Simeoni (eds) *Beyond Descriptive Translation Studies: Investigations in Homage to Gideon Toury*. Amsterdam: John Benjamins, 79–90.

Seleskovitch, Danica (1968) *L'Interprète dans les Conférences Internationales – Problèmes de Langage et de Communication*. Paris: Minard lettres modernes.

Seleskovitch, Danica (1975) *Langage, Langues et Mémoire – Étude de la Prise de Notes en Interprétation Consécutive*. Préface de Jean Monnet. Paris: Minard lettres modernes.

Seleskovitch, Danica (1976/2014) Traduire: de l'expérience aux concepts. *Etudes de Linguistique Appliquée* 24, 64–91. Repr. in D. Seleskovitch & M. Lederer (2014) *Interpréter pour Traduire* (5th edn) as "De l'expérience aux concepts". Paris: Les Belles Lettres, 87–123.

Seleskovitch, Danica (1976) Interpretation, a psychological approach to translation. In R. W. Brislin (ed.) *Translation: Applications and Research*. New York: Gardner Press, 92–116.

Seleskovitch, Danica (1977) Take care of the sense and the sounds will take care of themselves or Why interpreting is not tantamount to translating languages. *The Incorporated Linguist* 16, 27–33.

Seleskovitch, Danica (1978a) *Interpreting for International Conferences: Problems of Language and Communication* (Trans. Stephanie Dailey & Eric N. McMillan). Washington: Pen & Booth.

Seleskovitch, Danica (1978b) Language and cognition. In D. Gerver & H. W. Sinaiko (eds) *Language Interpretation and Communication*. New York: Plenum Press, 333–341.

Seleskovitch, Danica (1988) Technical and literary translation: A unifying view. In C. Picken (ed.) *Translators and Interpreters Mean Business*. London: Aslib, 83–88.

Seleskovitch, Danica (1999) The teaching of conference interpretation in the course of the last 50 years. *Interpreting* 4 (1), 55–66.

Seleskovitch, Danica & Lederer, Marianne (1984) *Interpréter pour Traduire*. Paris: Didier Érudition.

Seleskovitch, Danica & Lederer, Marianne (1989) *Pédagogie Raisonnée de l'Interprétation*. Paris: Didier Érudition. Trans. J. Harmer (1995) as *A Systematic Approach to Teaching Interpretation*. Silver Springs, MD: RID Publications.

Seleskovitch, Danica & Lederer, Marianne (2002) *Pédagogie Raisonnée de l'Interprétation*. 2nd edn. Luxembourg/Paris: OPOCE/Didier Érudition.

Selting, Margret et al. (2011) A system for transcribing talk-in-interaction: GAT 2 (Trans. E. Couper-Kuhlen & D. Barth-Weingarten). *Gesprächsforschung* 12, 1–51.

Selye, Hans (1956) *The Stress of Life*. New York: McGraw-Hill.

Semenets, Oleg E. & Panasyev, Aleksandr N. (1991) *Istorija perevoda (Srednevekovaja Azija, Vostočnaja Evropa XV-XVIII vekov)* [*History of Translation (Medieval Asia, Eastern Europe in the 15th to 18th Centuries)*]. Kiev: Lybid.

Séro-Guillaume, Philippe (1994) *L'Interprétation en Langue des Signes Française (L.S.F.)*. Thèse de doctorat, Université Sorbonne Nouvelle – Paris 3.

Şeşen, Ramazan (1992) The translator of the Belgrade Council Osman b. Abdülmennân and his place in the translation activities. In E. İhsanoğlu (ed.) *Transfer of Modern Science & Technology to the Muslim World*. Istanbul: Research Centre for Islamic History, Art and Culture, 371–383.

Setton, Robin (1998) Meaning assembly in simultaneous interpretation. *Interpreting* 3 (2), 163–200.

Setton, Robin (1999) *Simultaneous Interpretation: A Cognitive-Pragmatic Analysis*. Amsterdam: John Benjamins.

Setton, Robin (2002a) Seleskovitch: A radical pragmatist before her time. *The Translator* 8 (1), 117–124.

Setton, Robin (2002b) A methodology for the analysis of interpretation corpora. In G. Garzone & M. Viezzi (eds) *Interpreting in the 21st Century: Challenges and Opportunities. Selected Papers from the 1st Forlì Conference on Interpreting Studies, 9–11 November 2000*. Amsterdam: John Benjamins, 29–45.

Setton, Robin (2003) Models of the interpreting process. In A. Collados Aís & J. A. Sabio Pinilla (eds) *Avances en la Investigación Sobre la Interpretación*. Granada: Comares, 29–91.

Setton, Robin (2005) Pointing to contexts: A relevance-theoretic approach to assessing quality and difficulty in interpreting. In H. V. Dam, J. Engberg & H. Gerzymisch-Arbogast (eds) *Knowledge Systems and Translation*. Berlin/New York: Walter de Gruyter, 275–312.

Setton, Robin (2006a) Context in simultaneous interpretation. *Journal of Pragmatics* 38 (3), 374–389.

Setton, Robin (2006b) New demands on interpreting and the learning curve in interpreter training. In M. Chai & J. Zhang (eds) *Professionalization in Interpreting: International Experience and Developments in China*. Shanghai: Shanghai Foreign Language Education Press, 36–71.

Setton, Robin (2011) Corpus-based Interpreting Studies (CIS): Overview and prospects. In A. Kruger, K. Wallmach & J. Munday (eds) *Corpus-based Translation Studies: Research and Applications*. London/New York: Continuum, 33–75.

Setton, Robin & Dawrant, Andrew (2016) *Conference Interpreting: A Complete Course and Trainer's Guide* (2 vols). Amsterdam: John Benjamins.

Setton, Robin & Guo, Alice Liangliang (2011) Attitudes to role, status and professional identity in interpreters and translators with Chinese in Shanghai and Taipei. In R. Sela-Sheffy & M. Shlesinger (eds) *Identity and Status in the Translational Professions*. Amsterdam: John Benjamins, 89–117.

Setton, Robin & Motta, Manuela (2007) Syntacrobatics: Quality and reformulation in simultaneous-with-text. *Interpreting* 9 (2), 199–230.

Shaffer, Barbara (2013) Evolution of theory, evolution of role: How interpreting theory shapes interpreter role. In E. A. Winston & C. Monikowski (eds) *Evolving Paradigms in Interpreter Education*. Washington, DC: Gallaudet University Press, 128–150.

Shanahan, Timothy, Meehan, Maureen & Mogge, Stephen (1994) *The Professionalization of the Teacher in Adult Literacy Education*. Philadelphia: National Center on Adult Literacy.

Shannon, Claude E. & Weaver, Waren (1949) *The Mathematical Theory of Communication*. Urbana, IL: University of Illinois Press.

Shannon, Sheila M. (1990) English in the barrio: The quality of contact among immigrant children. *Hispanic Journal of Behavioral Sciences* 12 (3), 256–276.

Shaw, Risa, Collins, Steven D. & Metzger, Melanie (2006) MA to BA: A quest for distinguishing between undergraduate and graduate interpreter education, Bachelor of Arts in Interpretation curriculum at Gallaudet University. In C. B. Roy (ed.) *New Approaches to Interpreter Education*. Washington, DC: Gallaudet University Press, 1–21.

Shaw, Sherry (2011a) Cognitive and motivational contributors to aptitude: A study of spoken and signed language interpreting students. *Interpreting* 13 (1), 70–84.

Shaw, Sherry (2011b) *Service Learning in Interpreter Education*. Washington, DC: Gallaudet University Press.

Shaw, Sherry & Hughes, Gail (2006) Essential characteristics of sign language interpreting students: Perspectives of students and faculty. *Interpreting* 8 (2), 195–221.

Shaw, Sherry, Grbić, Nadja & Franklin, Kathy (2004) Applying language skills to interpretation: Student perspectives from signed and spoken language programs. *Interpreting* 6 (1), 69–100.

Shaw, Sherry, Timarová, Šárka & Salaets, Heidi (2008) Measurement of cognitive and personality traits in determining aptitude of spoken and signed language interpreting students. In L. Roberson & S. Shaw (eds) *Proceedings of the 16th National Convention of the Conference of Interpreter Trainers: Putting the Pieces Together: A Collaborative Approach to Educational Excellence*. Conference of Interpreter Trainers, 91–109.

Shimizu, Tohru, Ashikari, Yutaka, Sumita, Eiichiro, Zhang, Jinsong & Nakamura, Satoshi (2008) NICT/ATR Chinese-Japanese-English Speech-to-Speech Translation System. *Tsinghua Science & Technology* 13 (4), 540–544.

Shiryaev, Anatoly F. (1979) *Sinkhronnyi perevod. Deyatelnost sinkhronnogo perevodchika i metodika prepodavaniya sinkhronnogo perevoda* [*Simultaneous Interpreting: The Simultaneous Interpreter's Work and Methodology of Teaching Simultaneous Interpreting*]. Moscow: Voenizdat.

Shiryaev, Anatoly F. (1982a) *Posobie po sinkhronnomu perevodu. Frantsuzskij yazyk* [*Textbook of Simultaneous Interpreting: French*]. Moscow: Vysshaya shkola.

Shiryaev, Anatoly F. (1982b) O nekotorykh lingvisticheskikh osobennostyakh funktsionalnoi sistemy sinkhronnogo perevoda [On some linguistic features of the simultaneous interpreting functional system]. *Tetradi Perevodchika* 18, 73–84.

Shlesinger, Miriam (1989a) Extending the theory of translation to interpretation: Norms as a case in point. *Target* 1 (1), 111–115.

Shlesinger, Miriam (1989b) *Simultaneous Interpretation as a Factor in Effecting Shifts in the Position of Texts on the Oral–Literate Continuum*. MA thesis, Tel Aviv University.

Shlesinger, Miriam (1991) Interpreter latitude vs. due process: Simultaneous and consecutive interpretation in multilingual trials. In S. Tirkkonen-Condit (ed.) *Empirical Research in Translation and Intercultural Studies*. Tübingen: Gunter Narr, 147–155.

Shlesinger, Miriam (1994) Intonation in the production and perception of simultaneous interpretation. In S. Lambert & B. Moser-Mercer (eds) *Bridging the Gap: Empirical Research in Simultaneous Interpretation*. Amsterdam: John Benjamins, 225–236.

Shlesinger, Miriam (1995a) Shifts in cohesion in simultaneous interpreting. *The Translator* 1 (2), 193–214.

Shlesinger, Miriam (1995b) Stranger in paradigms: What lies ahead for simultaneous interpreting research? *Target* 7 (1), 7–28.

Shlesinger, Miriam (1997) Quality in simultaneous interpreting. In Y. Gambier, D. Gile & C. Taylor (eds) *Conference Interpreting: Current Trends in Research. Proceedings of the International Conference on Interpreting: What Do We Know and How?* Amsterdam: John Benjamins, 123–131.

Shlesinger, Miriam (1998) Corpus-based interpreting studies as an offshoot of corpus-based translation studies. *Meta* 43 (4), 486–493.

Shlesinger, Miriam (1999) Norms, strategies and constraints: How do we tell them apart? In A. Álvarez Lugrís & A. Fernández Ocampo (eds) *Anovar/Anosar Estudios de Traducción e Interpretación*. Vigo: Universidade de Vigo, 65–77.

Shlesinger, Miriam (2001) Shared ground in interpreting studies too. *Target* 13 (1), 99–127.

Shlesinger, Miriam (2003) Effects of presentation rate on working memory in simultaneous interpreting. *The Interpreters' Newsletter* 12, 37–49.

Shlesinger, Miriam (2004) Doorstep inter-subdisciplinarity and beyond. In C. Schäffner (ed.) *Translation Research and Interpreting Research: Traditions, Gaps and Synergies*. Clevedon: Multilingual Matters, 116–123.

Shlesinger, Miriam (2007) Making the most of settling for less. *Forum* 5 (2), 147–170.

Shlesinger, Miriam (2008) Towards a definition of Interpretese: An intermodal, corpus-based study. In G. Hansen, A. Chesterman & H. Gerzymisch-Arbogast (eds) *Efforts and Models in Interpreting and Translation Research: A Tribute to Daniel Gile*. Amsterdam: John Benjamins, 237–253.

Shlesinger, Miriam (2010) Relay interpreting. In Y. Gambier & L. van Doorslaer (eds) *Handbook of Translation Studies*. Vol. 1. Amsterdam: John Benjamins, 276–278.

Shlesinger, Miriam (2011) The "true interpreter" revisited: On (im)partiality and (in)consistency in court interpreting. In M. J. Blasco Mayor & M. A. Jiménez Ivars (eds) *Interpreting Naturally: A Tribute to Brian Harris*. Bern: Peter Lang, 195–214.

Shlesinger, Miriam & Ordan, Noam (2012) More spoken or more translated? Exploring a known unknown of simultaneous interpreting. *Target* 24 (1), 43–60.

Shlesinger, Miriam & Pöchhacker, Franz (eds) (2010) *Doing Justice to Court Interpreting*. Amsterdam: John Benjamins.

Shlesinger, Miriam & Voinova, Tanya (2012) Self-perception of female translators and interpreters in Israel. In B. Adab, P. A. Schmitt & G. Shreve (eds) *Discourses of Translation: Festschrift in Honour of Christina Schäffner*. Frankfurt: Peter Lang, 191–211.

Shlesinger, Miriam & Voinova, Tanya (2013) From editing to editing – via professional practice, teaching and research. *Interpreting* 15 (1), 11–23.

Shlesinger, Yael (2007) Vicarious traumatization among interpreters who work with torture survivors and their therapists. In F. Pöchhacker, A. L. Jakobsen & I. M. Mees (eds) *Interpreting Studies and Beyond: A Tribute to Miriam Shlesinger*. Copenhagen: Samfundslitteratur Press, 153–172.

Shreve, Gregory M. (2012) Bilingualism and translation. In Y. Gambier & L. van Doorslaer (eds) *Handbook of Translation Studies, Vol. 3*. Amsterdam: John Benjamins, 1–6.

Shreve, Gregory M. & Angelone, Erik (eds) (2010) *Translation and Cognition*. Amsterdam: John Benjamins.

Shreve, Gregory & Diamond, Bruce (1997) Cognitive processes in translation and interpreting: Critical issues. In J. H. Danks, G. M. Shreve, S. B. Fountain & M. K. McBeath (eds) *Cognitive Processes in Translation and Interpreting*. Thousand Oaks/London/New Delhi: Sage, 233–252.

Shreve, Gregory M., Lacruz, Isabel & Angelone, Erik (2010) Cognitive effort, syntactic disruption and visual interference in a sight translation task. In G. M. Shreve & E. Angelone (eds) *Translation and Cognition*. Amsterdam: John Benjamins, 63–84.

Sienell, Stefan (2001) Die Wiener Hofstaate zur Zeit Leopolds I. In K. Malettke, C. Grell & P. Holz (eds) *Hofgesellschaft und Höflinge an europäischen Fürstenhöfen in der Frühen Neuzeit (15.–18.Jh.)*. Münster: LIT-Verlag, 89–110.

Sienkiewicz, Birgit (2010) *Das Konsekutivdolmetschen der Zukunft: Mit Notizblock oder Aufnahmegerät?* MA thesis, University of Vienna.

Signorelli, Teresa M., Haarmann, Henk J. & Obler, Loraine K. (2012) Working memory in simultaneous interpreters: Effects of task and age. *International Journal of Bilingualism* 16 (2), 198–212.

Simeoni, Daniel (1998) The pivotal status of the translator's habitus. *Target* 10 (1), 1–39.

Simmel, George (1964) *The Sociology of George Simmel.* Trans. & ed. K. H. Wolff. New York: The Free Press.

Simon, Julie, Hollrah, Beverly, Lightfoot, Mary, Laurion, Richard & Johnson, Leilani (2010) *Steps toward Identifying Effective Practices in Video Remote Interpreting. 2010 Report.* National Consortium of Interpreter Education Centers. www.interpretereducation.org/wp-content/uploads/2011/06/VRIStepsReportApril2010_FINAL1.pdf (accessed 11 November 2014).

Simonetto, Francesca (2002) Interference between cognate languages: Simultaneous interpreting from Spanish into Italian. In G. Garzone, P. Mead & M. Viezzi (eds) *Perspectives on Interpreting.* Bologna: CLUEB, 129–146.

Simpson, Stewart (1991) A stimulus to learning, a measure of ability. In S. Gregory & G. Hartley (eds) *Constructing Deafness.* London: Pinter in association with the Open University, 217–226.

Sineiro de Saa, Marta (2003) Linguaxe corporal e interpretación simultânea: ¿Son os intérpretes un reflexo do orador? In L. Alonso Bacigalupe (ed.) *Investigación Experimental en Interpretación de Linguas: Primeiros Passos.* Vigo: Servicio de Publicacións da Universidade de Vigo, 39–59.

Singy, Pascal & Guex, Patrice (2005) The interpreter's role with immigrant patients: Contrasted points of view. *Communication & Medicine* 2, 45–52.

Siple, Linda (1993) Interpreters' use of pausing in voice to sign transliteration. *Sign Language Studies* 79, 147–180.

Skaaden, Hanne & Wattne, Maria (2009) Teaching interpreting in cyberspace: The answer to all our prayers? In R. De Pedro Ricoy, I. Perez & C. Wilson (eds) *Interpreting and Translating in Public Service Settings: Policy, Practice, Pedagogy.* Manchester: St Jerome, 74–88.

Skarsten, Malvin O. (1964) *George Drouillard: Hunter and Interpreter for Lewis and Clark and Fur Trader, 1807–1810.* Glendale, CA: Arthur H. Clark.

Skinner, William & Carson, Thomas F. (1990) Working conditions at the Nuremberg trials. In D. Bowen & M. Bowen (eds) *Interpreting – Yesterday, Today, and Tomorrow.* Binghamton, NY: SUNY, 14–22.

Skuncke, Marie-France (1989) Tout a commencé à Nuremberg. *Parallèles* 11, 5–8. Repr. in http://aiic.net/page/984/ (accessed 27 January 2015).

Slatyer, Helen (2006) Researching curriculum innovation in interpreter education: The case of initial training for novice interpreters in languages of limited diffusion. In C. B. Roy (ed.) *New Approaches to Interpreter Education.* Washington, DC: Gallaudet University Press, 47–66.

Sleigh, Dan (2004) *Islands* (Trans. André Brink). London: Secker & Warburg.

Smelik, Willem (2003) Orality, manuscript reproduction, and the Targums. In A. A. den Hollander, U. Schmid & W. F. Smelik (eds) *Paratext and Megatext as Channels of Jewish and Christian Traditions.* Leiden/Boston: Brill, 49–81.

Smirnov, Stanislav (1997) An overview of liaison interpreting. *Perspectives: Studies in Translatology* 5 (2), 211–226.

Snell-Hornby, Mary (2006) *The Turns of Translation Studies: New Paradigms or Shifting Viewpoints?* Amsterdam: John Benjamins.

Snell-Hornby, Mary, Pöchhacker, Franz & Kaindl, Klaus (eds) (1994) *Translation Studies: An Interdiscipline.* Amsterdam: John Benjamins.

Snelling, David (1989) A typology of interpretation for teaching purposes. In L. Gran & J. Dodds (eds) *The Theoretical and Practical Aspects of Teaching Conference Interpretation.* Udine: Campanotto, 141–142.

Snelling, David (1990) Upon the simultaneous translation of films. *The Interpreters' Newsletter* 3, 14–16.

Soler Caamaño, Emma (2006) *La Calidad en Formación Especializada en Interpretación: Análisis de los Criterios de Evaluación de un Jurado en un Posgrado de Interpretación de Conferencia Médica.* Doctoral dissertation, Universitat Pompeu Fabra, Barcelona.

Somers, Harold (2003) Machine translation: Latest developments. In R. Mitkov (ed.) *The Oxford Handbook of Computational Linguistics.* Oxford: Oxford University Press, 512–528.

Someya, Yasumasa, Saito, Miwako, Tsuruta, Chikako, Tanaka, Miyuki & Ino, Kinuyo Yoshida (2005) Wagakuni no daigaku daigakuin ni okeru tsuyaku-kyoiku no jittaichosa [A survey on the current state of interpreting education at Japanese universities and graduate schools]. *Interpretation Studies* 5, 285–310.

Song, Ki-joong (2001) *The Study of Foreign Languages in the Chosŏn Dynasty (1392–1910)*. Seoul: Somerset Jipoongdang.

Sonnenfeldt, Richard W. (2006) *Witness to Nuremberg*. New York: Arcade.

Soondar, Jordan (2008) The Best Practice Guide: When Using Interpreters. East London: NHS Foundation Trust. www.eastlondon.nhs.uk/About-Us/Our-Staff/Interpreting,-Translating–Sign-Language/Trust-Best-Practice-Guide-When-Using-Interpreters.pdf (accessed 8 April 2014).

Spector, Paul E. (1997) *Job Satisfaction: Applications, Assessment, Causes and Consequences*. Thousand Oaks, CA: Sage.

Spencer-Oatey, Helen (2008) Face, (im)politeness and rapport. In H. Spencer-Oatey (ed.) *Culturally Speaking: Culture, Communication and Politeness Theory*. London/New York: Continuum, 11–47.

Sperber, Dan (1994) Understanding verbal understanding. In J. Khalfa (ed.) *What Is Intelligence?* Cambridge: Cambridge University Press, 179–198.

Sperber, Dan & Wilson, Deirdre (1986/1995) *Relevance: Communication and Cognition*. Oxford: Blackwell.

Spinolo, Nicoletta & Garwood, Christopher John (2010) To kill or not to kill: Metaphors in simultaneous interpreting. *Forum* 8 (1), 181–211.

Splevins, Katie A., Cohen, Keren, Joseph, Stephen, Murray, Craig & Bowley, Jake (2010) Vicarious posttraumatic growth among interpreters. *Qualitative Health Research* 20 (12), 1705–1716.

Springer, Pamela J., Black, Mikal, Martz, Kim, Deckys, Cathy & Soelberg, Terri (2010) Somali Bantu refugees in Southwest Idaho: assessment using participatory research. *Advances in Nursing Science* 33, 170–181.

Stahuljak, Zrinka (1999) The violence of neutrality: Translators in and of the war (Croatia, 1991–92). *College Literature* 26 (1), 34–51.

Stahuljak, Zrinka (2000) Violent distortions: Bearing witness to the task of wartime translators. *TTR* 13 (1), 37–51.

Stavrakaki, Stavroula, Megari, Kalliopi, Kosmidis, Mary H., Apostolidou, Maria & Takou, Eleni (2012) Working memory and verbal fluency in simultaneous interpreters. *Journal of Clinical and Experimental Neuropsychology* 34 (6), 624–633.

Steiner, Ben (1998) Signs from the void: The comprehension and production of sign language on television. *Interpreting* 3 (2), 99–146.

Steinfeld, Aaron (1998) The benefit of real-time captioning in a mainstream classroom as measured by working memory. *Volta Review* 100 (1), 29–44.

Stenzl, Catherine (1983) *Simultaneous Interpretation: Groundwork towards a Comprehensive Model*. MA thesis, Birkbeck College, University of London.

Stern, Ludmila (2004) Interpreting legal language at the International Criminal Tribunal for the Former Yugoslavia: Overcoming the lack of lexical equivalents. *JoSTrans: The Journal of Specialised Translation* 2, 63–75.

Stern, Ludmila (2011) Courtroom interpreting. In K. Malmkjaer & K. Windle (eds) *The Oxford Handbook of Translation Studies*. Oxford: Oxford University Press, 325–342.

Stern, Ludmila (2012) What can domestic courts learn from international courts and tribunals in good practice in interpreting? *T&I Review* 2, 7–30.

Sternberg, Martin L. A., Tipton, Carol C. & Schein, Jerome D. (1973) *Curriculum Guide for Interpreter Training*. New York: Deafness Research and Training Center, School of Education, New York University.

Sternberg, Robert J. (ed.) (1988) *The Nature of Creativity: Contemporary Psychological Perspectives*. Cambridge: Cambridge University Press.

Sternberg, Robert J. (2005) Intelligence, competence, and expertise. In A. J. Elliot & C. S. Dweck (eds) *Handbook of Competence and Motivation*. New York: Guilford Press, 15–30.

Stévaux, Elisabeth (2007) La incidencia del parámetro acento. In A. Collados Aís, E. M. Pradas Macías, E. Stévaux & O. García Becerra (eds) *La Evaluación de la Calidad en Interpretación Simultánea: Parámetros de Incidencia*. Granada: Comares, 17–35.

Stévaux, Elisabeth (2011) Akzent. In A. Collados Aís, E. Iglesias Fernández, E. M. Pradas Macías & E. Stévaux (eds) *Qualitätsparameter beim Simultandolmetschen. Interdisziplinäre Perspektiven*. Tübingen: Gunter Narr, 141–172.

Stewart, David A. & Kluwin, Thomas N. (1996) The gap between guidelines, practice, and knowledge in interpreting services for deaf students. *Journal of Deaf Studies and Deaf Education* 1 (1), 29–39.

Stinson, Michael S., Elliot, Lisa B. & Easton, Donna (2014) Deaf/hard of hearing and other postsecondary learners' retention of STEM content with tablet computer-based notes. *Journal of Deaf Studies and Deaf Education* 19 (2), 251–269.

Stinson, Michael, Elliot, Lisa & Francis, Pamela (2008) The C-Print system: Using captions to support classroom communication access and learning by deaf and hard of hearing students. In C. Schlenker-Schulte & A. Weber (eds) *Barrieren überwinden – Teilhabe ist möglich!* Villingen-Schwenningen: Neckar-Verlag, 102–122.

Stinson, Michael S., Elliot, Lisa B., Kelly, Ronald R. & Liu, Yufang (2009) Deaf and hard-of-hearing students' memory of lectures with speech-to-text and interpreting/note taking services. *Journal of Special Education* 43 (1), 52–64.

Stivers, Tanya & Jack Sidnell (2005) Introduction: Multimodal interaction. *Semiotica* 156, 1–20.

Stokoe, Elizabeth (2011) Simulated interaction and communication skills training: The "Conversation Analytic Role-play Method". In C. Antaki (ed.) *Applied Conversation Analysis*. New York: Palgrave Macmillan, 119–139.

Stokoe, William C., Casterline, Dorothy C. & Croneberg, Carl G. (1965) *A Dictionary of American Sign Language on Linguistic Principles*. Washington, DC: Gallaudet University Press.

Stoll, Christoph (2009) *Jenseits simultanfähiger Terminologiesysteme. Methoden der Vorverlagerung und Fixierung von Kognition im Arbeitsablauf professioneller Konferenzdolmetscher*. Trier: Wissenschaftlicher Verlag Trier.

Stone, Christopher (2009) *Towards a Deaf Translation Norm*. Washington, DC: Gallaudet University Press.

Stone, Christopher (2012) Interpreting. In R. Pfau, M. Steinbach & B. Woll (eds) *Sign Language: An International Handbook*. Berlin: De Gruyter, 980–998.

Stone, Christopher & Russell, Debra (2014) Conference interpreting and interpreting teams. In R. Adam, S. D. Collins, C. Stone & M. Metzger (eds) *Deaf Interpreters at Work: International Insights*. Washington, DC: Gallaudet University Press, 140–156.

Straniero Sergio, Francesco (1998) Notes on cultural mediation. *The Interpreters' Newsletter* 8, 151–168.

Straniero Sergio, Francesco (1999) The interpreter on the (talk) show: Interaction and participation frameworks. *The Translator* 5 (2), 303–326.

Straniero Sergio, Francesco (2003) Norms and quality in media interpreting: The case of Formula One press-conferences. *The Interpreters' Newsletter* 12, 135–174.

Straniero Sergio, Francesco (2007) *Talkshow Interpreting: La Mediazione Linguistica nella Conversazione Spettacolo*. Trieste: Edizioni Università di Trieste.

Straniero Sergio, Francesco (2011) Language mediation in news making: From simultaneous interpreting to other (hybrid) transfer modes. *The Interpreters' Newsletter* 16, 175–198.

Straniero Sergio, Francesco (2013) "You are not too funny": Challenging the role of the interpreter on Italian talkshows. In C. Baraldi & L. Gavioli (eds) *Coordinating Participation in Dialogue Interpreting*. Amsterdam: John Benjamins, 71–98.

Straniero Sergio, Francesco & Falbo, Caterina (eds) (2012) *Breaking Ground in Corpus-Based Interpreting Studies*. Frankfurt: Peter Lang.

Straw, Barry M. & Ross, Jerry (1985) Stability in the midst of change: A dispositional approach to job attitudes. *Journal of Applied Psychology* 70 (3), 469–480.

Stuart, James (1968) *Izibingo: Zulu Praise Poems*. Oxford: Clarendon Press.

Stüker, Sebastian, Herrmann, Teresa, Kolss, Muntsin, Niehues, Jan & Wölfel, Matthias (2012) Research opportunities in automatic speech-to-speech translation. *IEEE Potentials* 31 (3), 26–33.

Stupnikova, Tatjana (2003) *Ničego krome pravdy: Njurnbergskij process. Vospominanija perevo-dčika* [*Nothing but the Truth: The Nuremberg Trial. Memories of an Interpreter*]. Moscow: Vozvraščenie.

Stupnikova, Tatjana (2013) *Die Wahrheit, die reine Wahrheit und nichts als die Wahrheit. Erinnerungen der russischen Dolmetscherin Tatjana Stupnikova an den Nürnberger Prozess.* (Ed. Dörte Andres & Martina Behr). Berlin: Frank & Timme.

Sunnari, Marianna (1995a) Processing strategies in simultaneous interpreting: Experts vs. novices. In P. Krawutschke (ed.) *Connections: Proceedings of the 36th Annual Conference of the American Translators Association, November 8–12 (1995).* Medford, NJ: Information Today, 157–164.

Sunnari, Marianna (1995b) Processing strategies in simultaneous interpreting: "Saying it all" versus synthesis. In J. Tommola (ed.) *Topics in Interpreting.* Turku: University of Turku, Centre for Translation & Interpreting, 109–119.

Svoboda, Tomáš (2014) Man and machine: Translation in the era of augmented reality. In W. Baur, B. Eichner, S. Kalina, N. Keßler, F. Mayer & J. Ørsted (eds) *Im Spannungsfeld zwischen Mensch und Maschine. Die Zukunft von Übersetzern, Dolmetschern und Terminologen. Band I. Tagungsband des 20. FIT-Weltkongresses.* Berlin: BDÜ Weiterbildungs- und Fachverlagsgesellschaft, 93–99.

Swartz, Daniel B. (1999) *Job Satisfaction of Interpreters for the Deaf.* PhD dissertation, Capella University.

Swartz, Daniel B. (2006) Job satisfaction among interpreters for the deaf. *Journal of Interpretation* 2006, 47–78.

Święcicka, Elżbieta (2000) Interpreter Yovhannēs Ankiwrac'i also called Giovanni Molino. *Folia Orientalia*, no. 36, 329–342.

Szabó, Csilla (2006) Language choice in note-taking for consecutive interpreting: A topic revisited. *Interpreting* 8 (2), 129–147.

TAC (2015) CATTI. www.tac-online.org.cn/en/node_515764.htm (accessed 7 February 2015).

Takada, Eiichi & Koide, Shin'ichi (2009) Training of sign language interpreters in Japan: Achievements and challenges. In J. Napier (ed.) *International Perspectives on Sign Language Interpreter Education.* Washington, DC: Gallaudet University Press, 190–199.

Takeda, Kayoko (2010a) *Interpreting at the Tokyo War Crimes Tribunal.* Ottawa: University of Ottawa Press.

Takeda, Kayoko (2010b) Interpreting at the Tokyo War Crimes Tribunal. In M. Shlesinger & F. Pöchhacker (eds) *Doing Justice to Court Interpreting.* Amsterdam: John Benjamins, 9–28.

Takeda, Kayoko (2012) The emergence of translation studies as a discipline in Japan. In N. Sato-Rossberg & J. Wakabayashi (eds) *Translation and Translation Studies in the Japanese Context.* London/New York: Continuum, 9–32.

Takeda, Kayoko (2013) Nuremberg, Tokyo, soshite The Hague: kokusai-senpan-hotei ni okeru tsuyaku system no hatten [Nuremberg, Tokyo, and The Hague: The development of interpreting systems at international war crimes trials]. In F. Gaiba (Trans. K. Takeda) *Nuremberg saiban no tsuyaku [The Origins of Simultaneous Interpretation: The Nuremberg Trial].* Tokyo: Misuzu Shobo, 215–233.

Takeda, Kayoko (2016) Guilt, survival, opportunities and stigma: Japanese interpreters in the post-war occupation period (1945–1952). In K. Takeda & J. Baigorri-Jalón (eds) *New Insights in the History of Interpreting.* Amsterdam: John Benjamins.

Takimoto, Masato (2006) Interpreters' role perceptions in business dialogue interpreting situations. *Monash University Linguistics Papers* 5 (1), 47–57.

Takimoto, Masato (2008) *"Keeping an Eye on All Balls": Interpreters' Functions in Multi-party Business Interpreting Situations.* PhD dissertation, Monash University.

Talbot, Mary (2010) *Language and Gender.* 2nd edn. Cambridge: Polity Press.

Tang, Fang (2010) A bibliometric analysis of the empirical research on interpreting in China – based on the experimental research papers on interpreting. *Foreign Language World* 2010 (2), 39–46.

Tashakkori, Abbas & Creswell, John W. (2007) Editorial: The new area of mixed methods. *Journal of Mixed Methods Research* 1 (1), 3–7.

Tate, Granville & Turner, Graham H. (1997/2002) The code and the culture: Sign language interpreting – in search of the new breed's ethics. In F. Pöchhacker & M. Shlesinger (eds) *The Interpreting Studies Reader.* London: Routledge, 372–385.

Taylor, Christopher (1999) The translation of film dialogue. *Textus* 12 (2), 443–458.

Tebble, Helen (1993) A discourse model for dialogue interpreting. In *AUSIT Proceedings of the First Practitioners' Seminar*. Canberra: Australian Institute of Interpreters and Translators, 1–26.

Tebble, Helen (1998) *Medical Interpreting: Improving Communication with Your Patients*. Melbourne: Deakin University/Language Australia.

Tebble, Helen (1999) The tenor of consultant physicians: Implications for medical interpreting. *The Translator* 5 (2), 179–199.

Tebble, Helen (2012) Interpreting or interfering? In C. Baraldi & L. Gavioli (eds) *Coordinating Participation in Dialogue Interpreting*. Amsterdam: John Benjamins, 23–44.

Tebble, Helen (2013) Researching medical interpreting: An applied linguistics perspective. In E. Winston & C. Monikowski (eds) *Evolving Paradigms in Interpreter Education*. Washington, DC: Gallaudet University Press, 42–75.

Teddlie, Charles & Tashakkori, Abbas (2009) *Foundations of Mixed Methods Research: Integrating Quantitative and Qualitative Approaches in the Social and Behavioral Sciences*. Thousand Oaks, CA: Sage.

Testa, Marie de & Gautier, Antoine (2003) *Drogmans et Diplomates Européens auprès de la Porte Ottomane*. Istanbul: Isis.

Thagard, Paul (2005) *Mind: An Introduction to Cognitive Science*. 2nd edn. Cambridge, MA: MIT Press.

Theunissen, Hans (1998) Ottoman-Venetian diplomatics: The Ahd-names. The historical background and the development of a category of political-commercial instruments together with an annotated edition of a corpus of relevant documents. *EJOS: Electronic Journal of Oriental Studies* 1 (2), 1–698.

Thiéry, Christopher (1975) *Le Bilinguisme chez les Interprètes de Conférence Professionnels*. Thèse de doctorat, Université Sorbonne Nouvelle – Paris 3.

Thiéry, Christopher (1978) True bilingualism and second language learning. In D. Gerver & H. W. Sinaiko (eds) *Language Interpretation and Communication*. New York/London: Plenum Press, 145–153.

Thiéry, Christopher (1985) La responsabilité de l'interprète de conférence professionnel ou pourquoi nous ne pouvons pas écrire nos mémoires. *Meta* 30 (1), 78–81.

Thiéry, Christopher (1989) Letters to the Editors. *The Interpreters' Newsletter* 2, 2–5.

Thompson, Darcy A., Hernandez, Raquel G., Cowden, John D., Sisson, Stephen D. & Moon, Margaret (2013) Caring for patients with limited English proficiency: Are residents prepared to use medical interpreters? *Academic Medicine* 88 (10), 1–8.

Thompson, Paul (2004) Spoken language corpora. In M. Wynne (ed.) *Developing Linguistic Corpora: A Guide to Good Practice*. Oxford: Oxbow Books, 59–70. www.ahds.ac.uk/creating/guides/linguistic-corpora/chapter5.htm (accessed 26 November 2013).

Ticca, Anna Claudia (2008) *L'interprete ad hoc nel Dialogo Mediato Medico-paziente: Processi Interazionali in una Clinica dello Yucatán Indigeno* [*The ad hoc Interpreter in Mediated Doctor-patient Dialogue: Interactional Processes in a Hospital in Yucatán*]. PhD dissertation, University of Pisa.

Ticca, Anna C. (2013) The use of laughter in bilingual doctor-patient interactions: Displaying resistance to doctor's talk in a Mexican village. In P. Glenn & E. Holt (eds) *Studies of Laughter in Interaction*. London/New York: Bloomsbury Academic, 107–129.

Timarová, Šárka & Salaets, Heidi (2011) Learning styles, motivation and cognitive flexibility in interpreter training: Self-selection and aptitude. *Interpreting* 13 (1), 31–52.

Timarová, Šárka & Ungoed-Thomas, Harry (2008) Admission testing for interpreting courses. *The Interpreter and Translator Trainer* 2 (1), 29–46.

Timarová, Šarka & Ungoed-Thomas, Harry (2009) The predictive value of admission tests for conference interpreting courses in Europe: A case study. In C. V. Angelelli & H. E. Jacobson (eds) *Assessment in Translation and Interpreting Studies*. Amsterdam: John Benjamins, 225–246.

Timarová, Šárka, Dragsted, Barbara & Hansen, Inge G. (2011) Time lag in translation and interpreting: A methodological exploration. In C. Alvstad, A. Hild & E. Tiselius (eds) *Methods and Strategies of Process Research: Integrative Approaches in Translation Studies*. Amsterdam: John Benjamins, 121–146.

Timarová, Šárka, Čeňková, Ivana, Meylaerts, Reine, Hertog, Erik, Szmalec, Arnaud & Duyck, Wouter (2014) Simultaneous interpreting and working memory executive control. *Interpreting* 16 (2), 139–168.

Ting-Toomey, Stella & Cocroft, Beth-Ann (1994) Face and facework: Theoretical and research issues. In S. Ting-Toomey (ed.) *The Challenge of Facework: Cross-Cultural and Interpersonal Issues*. Albany: State University of New York, 307–340.

Tipton, Rebecca (2008a) Reflexivity and the social construction of identity in interpreter-mediated asylum interviews. *The Translator* 14 (1), 1–19.

Tipton, Rebecca (2008b) Interpreter neutrality and the structure/agency distinction. In C. Valero-Garcés (ed.) *Investigación y Práctica en Traducción e Interpretación en los Servicios Públicos – Desafíos y Alianzas. Research and Practice in Public Service Interpreting and Translation – Challenges and Alliances*. Alcalá: Universidad de Alcalá de Henares [CD]. www2.uah.es/traduccion//Actas/2008/TRADUCCION.pdf (accessed 20 November 2014).

Tipton, Rebecca (2009) The simultaneous interpreter and the self: What role for reflective practice? *CTIS Occasional Papers* 4, 53–70.

Tipton, Rebecca (2010) On trust: Relationships of trust in interpreter-mediated social work encounters. In M. Baker, M. Olohan & M. Calzada Perez (eds) *Text and Context: Essays on Translation and Interpreting in Honour of Ian Mason*. Manchester: St Jerome, 188–208.

Tipton, Rebecca (2014) Perceptions of the "occupational Other": Interpreters, social workers and intercultures. *The British Journal of Social Work*. First published online 23 November 2014. doi:10.1093/bjsw/bcu136.

Tiselius, Elisabet (2009) Revisiting Carroll's scales. In C. V. Angelelli & H. E. Jacobson (eds) *Testing and Assessment in Translation and Interpreting Studies*. Amsterdam: John Benjamins, 95–121.

Tiselius, Elisabet (2010) A sociological perspective on expertise in conference interpreting: A case study on Swedish conference interpreters. In O. Azadibougar (ed.) *Translation Effects: Selected Papers of the CETRA Research Seminar in Translation Studies 2009*. Leuven: KU Leuven. www.arts.kuleuven.be/cetra/papers/files/elisabet-tiselius-a-sociologicalperspective-on.pdf (accessed 13 February 2014).

Tiselius, Elisabet (2013) *Experience and Expertise in Conference Interpreting: An Investigation of Swedish Conference Interpreters*. PhD dissertation, University of Bergen.

Tiselius, Elisabet & Jenset, Gard B. (2011) Process and product in simultaneous interpreting: What they tell us about experience and expertise. In C. Alvstad, A. Hild & E. Tiselius (eds) *Methods and Strategies of Process Research: Integrative Approaches in Translation Studies*. Amsterdam: John Benjamins, 269–300.

Tissi, Benedetta (2000) Silent pauses and disfluencies in simultaneous interpretation: A descriptive analysis. *The Interpreters' Newsletter* 10, 103–127.

TMGJ (1998) *T'ongmun'gwanji* [*The Handbook of Interpreting Officials*] (1720–) Korean edition, edited by G. Kim & H. Lee. 2 vols. Seoul: The Memorial Organization of King Sejong the Great.

Tohyama, Hitomi & Matsubara, Shigeki (2006) Development of web-based teaching material for simultaneous interpreting learners using bilingual speech corpus. In E. Pearson & P. Bohman (eds) *Proceedings of ED-MEDIA 2006: World Conference on Educational Multimedia and Hypermedia, Orlando, Florida, USA, June 26–30*. Chesapeake, VA: AACE, 2906–2911. www.editlib.org/p/23420 (accessed 9 January 2014).

Tohyama, Hitomi, Matsubara, Shigeki, Kawaguchi, Nobuo & Inagaki, Yasuyoshi (2005) Construction and utilization of bilingual speech corpus for simultaneous machine interpretation research. *Proceedings of 9th European Conference on Speech Communication and Technology (Eurospeech-2005)*, 1585–1588. http://slp.itc.nagoya-u.ac.jp/web/papers/2005/eurospeech2005_tohyama_final.pdf (accessed 13 January 2014).

Toledano Buendía, Carmen (2010) Community interpreting: Breaking with the "norm" through normalisation. *JoSTrans: The Journal of Specialised Translation* 14. www.jostrans.org/issue14/art_toledano.php (accessed 31 October 2013).

Tommola, Jorma & Niemi, Pekka (1986) Mental load in simultaneous interpreting: An online pilot study. In L. S. Evensen (ed.) *Nordic Research in Text Linguistics and Discourse Analysis*. Trondheim: Tapir, 171–184.

Tommola, Jorma, Laine, Matti, Sunnari, Marianna & Rinne, Juha O. (2000) Images of shadowing and interpreting. *Interpreting* 5 (2), 147–169.

Tonelli, Livia & Riccardi, Alessandra (1995) Speech errors, shadowing and simultaneous interpretation. *The Interpreters' Newsletter* 6, 67–74.

Torikai, Kumiko (2009) *Voices of the Invisible Presence: Diplomatic Interpreters in post-World War II Japan.* Amsterdam: John Benjamins.

Torikai, Kumiko (2014) Oral history as a research method to study interpreters' habitus. In G. M. Vorderobermeier (ed.) *Remapping Habitus in Translation Studies.* Amsterdam: Rodopi, 133–146.

Tóth, Andrea (2011) Speech disfluencies in simultaneous interpreting: A mirror on cognitive processes. *SKASE Journal of Translation and Interpreting* 5 (2), 23–31. www.skase.sk/Volumes/ JTI06/ pdf_doc/03.pdf (accessed 20 June 2013).

Toury, Gideon (1995) *Descriptive Translation Studies – and beyond.* Amsterdam: John Benjamins.

Toury, Gideon (2012) *Descriptive Translation Studies – and beyond.* Rev. edn. Amsterdam: John Benjamins.

Touzard, Anne-Marie (2005) *Le Drogman Padery: Émissaire de France en Perse, 1719–1725.* Paris: Geuthner, Société d'histoire de l'orient.

Townsend, Camilla (2006) *Malintzin's Choices: An Indian Woman in the Conquest of Mexico.* Albuquerque, NM: University of New Mexico Press.

Townsley, Brooke (2007). Interpreting in the UK community: Some reflections on public service interpreting in the UK. *Language and Intercultural Communication* 7 (2), 163–170.

Traverso, Véronique (2012) *Ad hoc*-interpreting in multilingual work meetings: Who translates for whom? In C. Baraldi & L. Gavioli (eds) *Coordinating Participation in Dialogue Interpreting.* Amsterdam: John Benjamins, 149–176.

Treisman, Anne M. (1965) The effects of redundancy and familiarity on translating and repeating back a foreign and a native language. *British Journal of Psychology* 56 (4), 369–379.

Tribe, Rachel & Lane, Pauline (2009) Working with interpreters across language and culture in mental health. *Journal of Mental Health* 18 (3), 233–241.

Tribe, Rachel & Raval, Hitesh (eds) (2003) *Working with Interpreters in Mental Health.* Hove/ New York: Brunner Routledge.

Tribe, Rachel & Thompson, Kate (2015) *Working with Interpreters in Health Settings: Guide for Psychologists.* Leicester: The British Psychological Society.

Trudgill, Peter (2000) *Sociolinguistics: An Introduction to Language and Society.* 4th edn. Harmondsworth: Penguin.

Truschke, Audrey Angeline (2012) *Cosmopolitan Encounters: Sanskrit and Persian at the Mughal Court.* PhD dissertation, Columbia University.

Tryuk, Małgorzata (2010) Interpreting in Nazi concentration camps during World War II. *Interpreting* 12 (2), 125–145.

Tse, Lucy (1995) Language brokering among Latino adolescents: Prevalence, attitudes, and school performance. *Hispanic Journal of Behavioral Sciences* 17 (2), 180–193.

Tseng, Joseph (1992) *Interpreting as an Emerging Profession in Taiwan – a Sociological Model.* Master's thesis, Fu Jen Catholic University.

Tsuruta, Chikako (2011) Broadcast interpreters in Japan: Bringing news to and from the world. *The Interpreters' Newsletter* 16, 157–173.

Tucker, G. Richard & Zarechnak, Michael (1989) Appendix: Three historical notes. In J. E. Alatis (ed.) *Georgetown University Round Table on Languages and Linguistics 1989. Language Teaching, Testing, and Technology: Lessons from the Past with a View toward the Future.* Washington, DC: Georgetown University Press, 408–411.

Tulving, Endel (2002). Episodic memory: From mind to brain. *Annual Review of Psychology*, 53, 1–25.

Turner, Barry, Lai, Miranda & Huang, Neng (2010) Error deduction and descriptors: A comparison of two methods of translation test assessment. *Translation & Interpreting* (2) 1, 11–23.

Turner, Graham H. (2005) Toward real interpreting. In M. Marschark, R. Peterson & E. Winston (eds) *Interpreting and Interpreter Education: Directions for Research and Practice.* New York: Oxford University Press, 29–56.

Turner, Graham H. (2007) Exploring inter-subdisciplinary alignment in interpreting studies: Sign language interpreting at conferences. In F. Pöchhacker, A. L. Jakobsen & I. M. Mees (eds) *Interpreting Studies and Beyond: A Tribute to Miriam Shlesinger.* Copenhagen: Samfundslitteratur, 191–216.

Turner, Graham & Brown, Richard (2001) Interaction and the role of the interpreter in court. In F. J. Harrington & G. H. Turner (eds) *Interpreting Interpreting: Studies and Reflections on Sign Language Interpreting.* Coleford: Douglas McLean, 152–167.

Turner, Graham & Pollitt, Kyra (2002) Community interpreting meets literary translation: English–British Sign Language interpreting in the theatre. *The Translator* 8 (1), 25–48.

Tymoczko, Maria (2003) Ideology and the position of the translator: In what sense is a translator "in between"? In M. Calzada Pérez (ed.) *Apropos of Ideology: Translation Studies on Ideology – Ideologies in Translation Studies.* Manchester: St Jerome, 181–201.

Tzou, Yeh-Zu, Eslami, Zohreh R., Chen, Hsin-Chin & Vaid, Jyotsna (2012) Effect of language proficiency and degree of formal training in simultaneous interpreting on working memory and interpreting performance: Evidence from Mandarin–English speakers. *International Journal of Bilingualism* 16 (2), 213–227.

UNHCR (2005) *Refugee Status Determination: Identifying Who Is a Refugee. Self-Study Module 2.* Geneva: UNHCR.

UNHCR (2009) *Interpreting in a Refugee Context. Self-Study Module 3.* Geneva: UNHCR.

UNHCR (2010) *Improving Asylum Procedures: Comparative Analysis and Recommendations for Law and Practice.* Brussels: UNHCR.

Vaissière, Jacqueline (1983) Language-independent prosodic features. In A. Cutler & D. R. Ladd (eds) *Prosody: Models and Measurements.* Berlin: Springer, 53–66.

Valdeón, Roberto A. (2013) Doña Marina/La Malinche: A historiographical approach to the interpreter/traitor. *Target* 25 (2), 157–179.

Valdeón, Roberto A. (2014) *Translation and the Spanish Empire in the Americas.* Amsterdam: John Benjamins.

Valdés, Guadalupe & Angelelli, Claudia (2003) Interpreters, interpreting, and the study of bilingualism. *Annual Review of Applied Linguistics* 23, 58–78.

Valdés, Guadalupe & Figueroa, Richard A. (1994) *Bilingualism and Testing: A Special Case of Bias.* Norwood, NJ: Ablex.

Valdés, Guadalupe, Chávez, Christina, Angelelli, Claudia, Enright, Kerry, González, Marisela, García, Dania & Wyman, Leisy (2000) Bilingualism from another perspective: The case of young interpreters from immigrant communities. In A. Roca (ed.) *Research on Spanish in the United States: Linguistic Issues and Challenges.* Somerville, MA: Cascadilla Press, 42–81.

Valero-Garcés, Carmen (2003) Responding to communication needs: Current issues and challenges in community interpreting and translating in Spain. In L. Brunette, G. Bastin, I. Hemlin & H. Clarke (eds) *The Critical Link 3: Interpreters in the Community.* Amsterdam: John Benjamins, 177–194.

Valero-Garcés, Carmen (2005) Doctor–patient consultations in dyadic and triadic exchanges. *Interpreting* 7 (2), 193–210.

Valero Garcés, Carmen (2006) *Formas de Mediación Intercultural: Traducción e Interpretación en los Servicios Públicos. Conceptos, Datos, Situaciones y Práctica.* Granada: Comares.

Valero Garcés, Carmen (2010) The difficult task of gathering information on PSI&t. *Babel* 56 (3), 199–218.

Valero Garcés, Carmen & Gauthier Blasi, Laura (2010) Bourdieu y la traducción e interpretación en los servicios públicos. Hacia una teoría social. In O. Diaz Fouces & E. Monzó (eds) *MonTI 2: Applied Sociology in Translation Studies/Sociología Aplicada a la Traducción.* Alicante: Publicaciones de la Universidad de Alicante, 97–117.

Valero-Garcés, Carmen & Martin, Anne (eds) (2008) *Crossing Borders in Community Interpreting: Definitions and Dilemmas.* Amsterdam: John Benjamins.

Van Besien, Fred (1999) Anticipation in simultaneous interpretation. *Meta* 44 (2), 250–259.

Van Besien, Fred & Meuleman, Chris (2004) Dealing with speakers' errors and speakers' repairs in simultaneous interpretation: A corpus-based study. *The Translator* 10 (1), 59–81.

Van De Mieroop, Dorien, Bevilacqua, Giovanni & van Hove, Lotte (2012) Negotiating discursive norms: Community interpreting in a Belgian rest home. *Interpreting* 14 (1), 23–54.

Van den Boogert, Maurits H. (2005) *The Capitulations and the Ottoman Legal System: Qadis, Consuls, and Beraths in the 18th Century*. Leiden/Boston: Brill.

Van den Boogert, Maurits H. (2009) Intermediaries par excellence? Ottoman dragomans in the eighteenth century. In B. Heyberger (ed.) *Hommes de l'Entre-deux. Parcours Individuels et Portraits de Groupes sur la Frontière de la Méditerranée (XVIe–XXe siècle)*. Paris: Les Indes Savantes, 95–115.

Van den Broek, Paul, Rapp, David N. & Kendeou, Panayiota (2005) Integrating memory-based and constructionist processes in accounts of reading comprehension. *Discourse Processes* 39 (2/3), 299–316.

Van den Broek, Paul, Young, Michael, Tzeng, Yuhtsuen & Linderholm, Tracy (1999) The Landscape Model of reading: Inferences and the online construction of memory representation. In H. van Oostendorp & S. R. Goldman (eds) *The Construction of Mental Representations during Reading*. Mahwah, NJ: Lawrence Erlbaum, 71–98.

Van Dijk, Rick, Boers, Eveline, Christoffels, Ingrid K. & Hermans, Daan (2011) Directionality effects in simultaneous language interpreting: The case of sign language interpreters in the Netherlands. *American Annals of the Deaf* 156 (1), 47–55.

Van Dijk, Rick, Christoffels, Ingrid K., Postma, Albert & Hermans, Daan (2012) The relation between the working memory skills of sign language interpreters and the quality of their interpretations. *Bilingualism: Language and Cognition* 15 (2), 340–350.

Van Dijk, Teun A. & Kintsch, Walter (1983) *Strategies of Discourse Comprehension*. New York: Academic Press.

Van Doorslaer, Luc (2009) Risking conceptual maps: Mapping as a keywords-related tool underlying the online *Translation Studies Bibliography*. In Y. Gambier & L. van Doorslaer (eds) *The Metalanguage of Translation*. Amsterdam/Philadelphia: John Benjamins, 27–43.

Van Doorslaer, Luc (2011) Bibliographies of translation studies. In Y. Gambier & L. van Doorslaer (eds) *Handbook of Translation Studies*. Vol. 2. Amsterdam: John Benjamins, 13–16.

Van Hoof, Henri (1962) *Théorie et Pratique de l'Interprétation*. Munich: Max Hueber.

Van Kalmthout, Anton M., Hofstee-van der Meulen, Femke B. A. M. & Dünkel, Frieder (eds) (2007) *Foreigners in European Prisons*. Nijmegen: Wolf Legal Publishers.

Van Maanen, John (2011) *Tales of the Field: On Writing Ethnography*. 2nd edn. Chicago: The University of Chicago Press.

Vasconcellos, Muriel (2000) The Georgetown Project and Léon Dostert: Recollections of a young assistant. In W. J. Hutchins (ed.) *Early Years in Machine Translation: Memoirs and Biographies of Pioneers*. Amsterdam: John Benjamins, 87–96.

Veinstein, Gilles (2000) The Ottoman administration and the problem of interpreters. In K. Çiçek (ed.) *The Great Ottoman Turkish Civilization Vol. 3: Philosophy, Science and Institutions*. Ankara: Yeni Turkiye, 607–615.

Velleman, Antoine (1929) *Dicziunari scurznieu da la lingua ladina: cun traducziun tudais-cha, francesa ed inglaisa e numerusas indicaziuns topograficas e demograficas*. Samedan: Engadin Press.

Velleman, Antoine (1943) L'École d'interprètes de l'Université de Genève. *Die Friedens-Warte. Blätter für Internationale Verständigung und zwischenstaatliche Organisation* 1943 (3/4), 167–176.

Venuti, Lawrence (1995) *The Translator's Invisibility: A History of Translation*. New York: Routledge.

Verdoolaege, Annelies (2008) *Reconciliation Discourse: The Case of the Truth and Reconciliation Commission*. Amsterdam: John Benjamins.

Verhoef, Marlene & du Plessis, Theo (eds) (2008) *Multilingualism and Educational Interpreting: Innovation and Delivery*. Hatfield: Van Schaik.

Vermeer, Hans J. (1992) *Skizzen zu einer Geschichte der Translation, Bd. 1: Anfänge: von Mesopotamien bis Griechenland; Rom und das frühe Christentum bis Hieronymus*. Frankfurt: Verlag für Interkulturelle Kommunikation.

Viaggio, Sergio (1988) Teaching interpretation to beginners, or how not to scare them to death. In D. L. Hammond (ed.) *Languages at Crossroads: Proceedings of the 29th Annual Conference of the American Translators Association*. Medford, NJ: Learned Information, 399–406.

Viaggio, Sergio (1989) Teaching beginners the blessings of compressing (and how to save a few lives in the process). In D. L. Hammond (ed.) *Coming of Age: Proceedings of the 30th Annual Conference of the American Translators Association*. Medford, NJ: Learned Information, 189–203.

Viaggio, Sergio (1995) The praise of sight translation (and squeezing the last drop thereout of). *The Interpreters' Newsletter* 6, 33–42.

Viaggio, Sergio (1997) Kinesics and the simultaneous interpreter: The advantages of listening with one's eyes and speaking with one's body. In F. Poyatos (ed.) *Nonverbal Communication and Translation.* Amsterdam: John Benjamins, 283–293.

Viaggio, Sergio (2001) Simultaneous interpreting for television and other media: Translation doubly constrained. In Y. Gambier & H. Gottlieb (eds) *(Multi) Media Translation: Concepts, Practices and Research.* Amsterdam: John Benjamins, 23–33.

Viaggio, Sergio (2006) *A General Theory of Interlingual Mediation.* Berlin: Frank & Timme.

Vianna, Branca (2005) Simultaneous interpreting: A relevance-theoretic approach. *Intercultural Pragmatics* 2 (2), 169–190.

Viezzi, Maurizio (1989) Information retention as a parameter for the comparison of sight translation and simultaneous interpretation: An experimental study. *The Interpreters' Newsletter* 2, 65–69.

Viezzi, Maurizio (1990) Sight translation, simultaneous interpretation and information retention. In L. Gran & C. Taylor (eds) *Aspects of Applied and Experimental Research on Conference Interpretation.* Udine: Campanotto, 54–60.

Viezzi, Maurizio (1992) The translation of film subtitles from English into Italian. *The Interpreters' Newsletter* 4, 84–86.

Viezzi, Maurizio (1993) Considerations on interpretation quality assessment. In C. Picken (ed.) *Translation – the Vital Link: Proceedings of the XIIIth World Congress of FIT.* Vol. 1. London: Institute of Translation and Interpreting, 389–397.

Vigouroux, Cécile B. (2010) Double-mouthed discourse: Interpreting, framing, and participant roles. *Journal of Sociolinguistics* 14 (3), 314–369.

Vikør, Lars (2004) Lingua franca and international language / Verkehrssprache und Internationale Sprache. In U. Ammon, N. Dittmar, K. J. Mattheier & P. Trudgill (eds) *Sociolinguistics / Soziolinguistik: An International Handbook of the Science of Language and Society. Ein internationales Handbuch zur Wissenschaft von Sprache und Gesellschaft.* 2nd edn. Berlin: de Gruyter, 328–335.

Vik-Tuovinen, Gun-Viol (2000) Retrospection as a method of studying the process of simultaneous interpreting. In S. Tirkkonen-Condit & R. Jääskeläinen (eds) *Tapping and Mapping the Processes of Translation and Interpreting.* Amsterdam: John Benjamins, 63–71.

Vik-Tuovinen, Gun-Viol (2002) Retrospection as a method of studying the process of simultaneous interpreting. In G. Garzone & M. Viezzi (eds) *Interpreting in the 21st Century: Challenges and Opportunities.* Amsterdam: John Benjamins, 63–71.

Vik-Tuovinen, Gun-Viol (2006) *Tolkning på olika nivåer av professionalitet.* Vaasa: University of Vaasa.

Vilela Biasi, Edith (2003) Court interpreters as social actors: Venezuela, a case study. In L. Brunette, G. Bastin, I. Hemlin & H. Clarke (eds) *The Critical Link 3: Interpreters in the Community.* Amsterdam: John Benjamins, 239–245.

Vinay, Jean-Paul & Darbelnet, Jean (1958) *Stylistique Comparée du Français et de l'Anglais. Méthode de Traduction.* Paris: Didier.

Vincens, Simone (2011) *Madame Montour and the Fur Trade (1667–1752).* Trans. & ed. Ruth Bernstein. Bloomington, IN: Xlibris.

Vincent, Bernard (1994) Reflexión documentada sobre el uso del árabe y las lenguas románicas en la España de los moriscos (ss. XVI–XVII). *Sharq Al-Andalus* 10–11, 731–748.

Voevoda, Elena V. (2009) Yazykovaja podgotovka diplomatov i perevodčikov dlja Posol'skogo prikaza v XVII veke [Language training of diplomats, translators and interpreters for the Posolsky Prikaz in the 17th century]. *Vestnik Moskovskogo Gosudarstvennogo Oblastnogo Universiteta. Serija Pedagogika* No. 3, 20–23.

Volansky, Vered, Ordan, Noam & Wintner, Shuly (2013) On the features of translationese. *Literary and Linguistic Computing.* First published online July 3, 2013. doi:10.1093/llc/fqt031.

Vuorikoski, Anna-Riitta (1998) User responses to simultaneous interpreting. In L. Bowker, M. Cronin, D. Kenny & J. Pearson (eds) *Unity in Diversity? Current Trends in Translation Studies.* Manchester: St Jerome, 184–197.

Vuorikoski, Anna-Riitta (2002) Rhetoric as an opportunity for interpreting studies. In G. Garzone, P. Mead & M. Viezzi (eds) *Perspectives on Interpreting.* Bologna: CLUEB, 21–35.

Vuorikoski, Anna-Riitta (2004) *A Voice of Its Citizens or a Modern Tower of Babel? The Quality of Interpreting as a Function of Political Rhetoric in the European Parliament*. Tampere: Tampere University Press. http://tampub.uta.fi/handle/10024/67348 (accessed 16 December 2013).

Wadensjö, Cecilia (1992) *Interpreting as Interaction: On Dialogue Interpreting in Immigration Hearings and Medical Encounters*. Linköping: Linköping University, Department of Communication Studies.

Wadensjö, Cecilia (1993) Dialogue interpreting and shared knowledge. In Y. Gambier & J. Tommola (eds) *Translation and Knowledge*. Turku: Centre for Translation and Interpreting, University of Turku, 101–113.

Wadensjö, Cecilia (1998) *Interpreting as Interaction*. London/New York: Longman.

Wadensjö, Cecilia (1999) Telephone interpreting and the synchronization of talk in social interaction. *The Translator* 5 (2), 247–264.

Wadensjö, Cecilia (2001a) Interpreting in crisis: The interpreter's position in therapeutic encounters. In I. Mason (ed.) *Triadic Exchanges: Studies in Dialogue Interpreting*. Manchester: St Jerome, 71–85.

Wadensjö, Cecilia (2001b) Approaching interpreting through discourse analysis. In D. Gile, H. V. Dam, F. Dubslaff, B. Martinsen & A. Schjoldager (eds) *Getting Started in Interpreting Research*. Amsterdam: John Benjamins, 185–198.

Wadensjö, Cecilia (2004) Dialogue interpreting: A monologising practice in a dialogically organised world. *Target* 16 (1), 105–124.

Wadensjö, Cecilia (2008a) The shaping of Gorbachev: On framing in an interpreter-mediated talk-show interview. *Text & Talk* 28 (1), 119–146.

Wadensjö, Cecilia (2008b) In and off the show: Co-constructing "invisibility" in an interpreter-mediated talk show interview. *Meta* 53 (1), 184–203.

Wadensjö, Cecilia (2009) Community interpreting. In M. Baker & G. Saldanha (eds) *Routledge Encyclopedia of Translation Studies*. 2nd edn. London/New York: Routledge, 43–48.

Wadensjö, Cecilia (2010) Expanded and minimal answers to yes/no questions in interpreter-mediated trials. In M. Baker, M. Olohan & M. C. Perez (eds) *Text and Context: Essays on Translation and Interpreting in Honour of Ian Mason*. Manchester: St Jerome, 9–26.

Wadensjö, Cecilia (2014) Perspectives on role play: Analysis, training and assessments. *The Interpreter and Translator Trainer* 8 (3), 437–451.

Wadensjö, Cecilia, Englund Dimitrova, Birgitta & Nilsson, Anna-Lena (eds) (2004) *The Critical Link 4: Professionalisation of Interpreting in the Community. Selected Papers from the 4th International Conference on Interpreting in Legal, Health and Social Service Settings, Stockholm, Sweden, 20–23 May 2004*. Amsterdam: John Benjamins.

Wahab, Saima (2012) *In My Father's Country: An Afghan Woman Defies Her Fate*. New York: Crown.

Wahlster, Wolfgang (ed.) (2000) *Verbmobil: Foundations of Speech-to-Speech Translation*. Berlin: Springer.

Wakabayashi, Judy (2011) The first Aboriginal intermediaries: Interpreting and interpreted. *Across Languages and Cultures* 12 (1), 49–69.

Wallensteen, Peter (2007) *Understanding Conflict Resolution*. London: Sage.

Wallmach, Kim (2000) Examining simultaneous interpreting norms and strategies in a South African legislative context: A pilot corpus analysis. *Language Matters* 31 (1), 198–221.

Wallmach, Kim (2002) "Seizing the surge of language by its soft, bare skull": Simultaneous interpreting, the Truth Commission and *Country of my skull*. *Translation and Power*. Special Issue of *Current Writing* 14 (2), 64–82.

Wallmach, Kim (2013) Providing truly patient-centred care: Harnessing the pragmatic power of interpreters. *Stellenbosch Papers in Linguistics* 42, 1–16.

Wallmach, Kim (2014) Recognising the little perpetrator in each of us: Complicity, responsibility and translation in institutional contexts in multilingual South Africa. *Perspectives: Studies in Translatology* 22 (4), 566–580.

Wang, Binhua (2012) Interpreting strategies in real-life interpreting: Corpus-based description of seven professional interpreters' performance. *Translation Journal* 16 (2). http://translationjournal.net/journal/60interpreting.htm (accessed 9 January 2014).

Wang, Binhua & Mu, Lei (2009) Interpreter training and research in mainland China: Recent developments. *Interpreting* 11 (2), 267–283.

Wang, Jihong (2013) Bilingual working memory capacity of professional Auslan/English interpreters. *Interpreting* 15 (2), 139–167.

Wansbrough, John E. (1996) *Lingua Franca in the Mediterranean*. Richmond: Curzon Press.

Warchal, Krystyna, Łyda, Andrzej & Jackiewicz, Alina (2011) Whose face? Us and them in English–Polish consecutive interpreting. *Meta* 56 (4), 775–795.

Warnicke, Camilla & Plejert, Charlotta (2012) Turn-organisation in mediated phone interaction using Video Relay Service (VRS). *Journal of Pragmatics* 44, 1313–1334.

Watanabe, Tomie (2009) Interpretation at the Tokyo War Crimes Tribunal: An overview of Tojo's cross-examination. *TTR: Traduction, Terminologie, Rédaction* 22 (1), 57–91.

Watts, Richard J. (2003) *Politeness*. Cambridge: Cambridge University Press.

Weale, Edna (1997) From Babel to Brussels: Conference interpreting and the art of the impossible. In F. Poyatos (ed.) *Nonverbal Communication and Translation*. Amsterdam: John Benjamins, 295–312.

Weber, Orest, Singy, Pascal & Guex, Patrice (2005) Gender and interpreting in the medical sphere: What is at stake? In J. Santaemilia (ed.) *Gender, Sex and Translation: The Manipulation of Identities*. Manchester: St. Jerome, 137–147.

Weber, Wilhelm K. (1989) Improved ways of teaching consecutive interpretation. In L. Gran & J. Dodds (eds) *The Theoretical and Practical Aspects of Teaching Conference Interpretation*. Udine: Campanotto, 161–166.

Weber, Wilhelm K. (1990) The importance of sight translation in an interpreter training program. In D. Bowen & M. Bowen (eds) *Interpreting – Yesterday, Today, and Tomorrow*. Binghamton, NY: SUNY, 44–52.

Wehrmeyer, Jennifer (2014) Eye-tracking Deaf and hearing viewing of sign language interpreted news broadcasts. *Journal of Eye Movement Research* 7 (1), 3:1–16.

Wehrmeyer, Ella (2015) Comprehension of television news sign language interpreters – a South African perspective. *Interpreting* 17 (2).

Wei, Li (ed.) (2007) *The Bilingualism Reader*. London/New York: Routledge.

Weiss-Gal, Idit & Welbourne, Penelope (2008) The professionalisation of social work: A cross-national exploration. *International Journal of Social Welfare* 17, 281–290.

Weisskirch, Robert S. (2007) Feelings about language brokering and family relations among Mexican American early adolescents. *Journal of Early Adolescence* 27 (4), 545–561.

Weit, Erwin (1973) *Eyewitness: The Autobiography of Gomulka's Interpreter*. London: Deutsch.

Wenger, Etienne (1998) *Communities of Practice*. Cambridge: Cambridge University Press.

Wessling, D. M. & Shaw, S. (2014) Persistent emotional extremes and video relay service interpreters. *Journal of Interpretation* 23 (1), Article 6. http://digital.commons.unf.edu/joi/vol23/iss1/6 (accessed 20 October 2014).

Westermeyer, Joseph (1990) Working with an interpreter in psychiatric assessment and treatment. *Journal of Nervous and Mental Disease* 178 (12), 745–749.

Wheatley, Mark & Pabsch, Annika (2010) *Sign Language Legislation in the European Union*. Brussels: European Union of the Deaf.

Widdowson, Henry (2004) *Text, Context, Pretext: Critical Issues in Discourse Analysis*. Malden, MA/Oxford: Blackwell.

Widlund-Fantini, Anne-Marie (2007) *Danica Seleskovitch. Interprète et Témoin du XXe Siècle*. Lausanne: L'Age d'Homme.

Wiener, Ethan S. & Rivera, Maria I. (2004) Bridging language barriers: How to work with an interpreter. *Clinical Pediatric Emergency Medicine* 5 (2), 93–101.

Wiese, Heike (2003) *Numbers, Language and the Human Mind*. Cambridge: Cambridge University Press.

Wilbur, Ronnie B. (2003) Modality and the structure of language: Signed languages versus signed systems. In M. Marschark & P. E. Spencer (eds) *Oxford Handbook of Deaf Studies, Language, and Education*. New York: Oxford University Press, 219–231.

Wilensky, Harold L. (1964) The professionalization of everyone? *The Americal Journal of Sociology* 70 (2), 137–158.

Will, Martin (2007) Terminology work for simultaneous interpreters in LSP conferences: Model and method. In H. Gerzymisch-Arbogast & G. Budin (eds) *LSP Translation Scenarios:*

Proceedings of the Marie Curie Euroconference, Vienna, 30 April to 4 May 2007. www.euro conferences.info/proceedings/2007_Proceedings/2007_proceedings.html (accessed 4 April 2014).

Williams, Kayla & Staub, Michael E. (2005) *Love My Rifle More than You: Young and Female in the U.S. Army*. New York: Norton.

Williams, Lucy (2005) Interpreting services for refugees: Hearing voices? *International Journal of Migration, Health and Social Care* 1 (1), 37–49.

Williams, Sarah (1995) Observations on anomalous stress in interpreting. *The Translator* 1 (1), 47–64.

Williams, Wes (2002) The diplomat, the trucheman and the mystagogue: Forms of belonging in early modern Jerusalem. In S. Coleman (ed.) *Pilgrim Voices: Narrative and Authorship in Christian Pilgrimage*. New York: Berghahn Books, 17–39.

Wilss, Wolfram (1978) Syntactic anticipation in German–English simultaneous interpretation. In D. Gerver & H. W. Sinaiko (eds) *Language Interpretation and Communication*. New York/London: Plenum Press, 335–343.

Wilss, Wolfram (1999) *Translation and Interpreting in the 20th Century: Focus on German*. Amsterdam: John Benjamins.

Winston, Elizabeth A. (1989) Transliteration: What's the message? In C. Lucas (ed.) *The Sociolinguistics of the Deaf Community*. San Diego: Academic Press, 147–164.

Winston, Elizabeth A. (1992) Mainstream interpreting: An analysis of the task. In L. Swabey (ed.) *The Challenge of the 90s: New Standards in Interpreter Education. Proceedings of the Eighth National Convention, Conference of Interpreter Trainers, October 5–7, 1990, Pomona, California*. Northridge, CA: Conference of Interpreter Trainers, 51–67.

Winston, Elizabeth A. (2004) Interpretability and accessibility of mainstream classrooms. In E. A. Winston (ed.) *Educational Interpreting: How It Can Succeed*. Washington, DC: Gallaudet University Press, 132–168.

Winston, Elizabeth A. (2005) Designing a curriculum for American Sign Language/English interpreting educators. In M. Marschark, R. Peterson & E. A. Winston (eds) *Sign Language Interpreting and Interpreter Education: Directions for Research and Practice*. New York: Oxford University Press, 208–233.

Winston, Elizabeth A. & Monikowski, Christine (eds) (2013) *Evolving Paradigms in Interpreter Education*. Washington, DC: Gallaudet University Press.

Wiotte-Franz, Claudia (2001) *Hermeneus und Interpres: Zum Dolmetscherwesen in der Antike*. Saarbrücken: Saarbrücker Druckerei und Verlag.

Witter-Merithew, Anna (1986) Claiming our destiny. *RID Views: Newsletter of the Registry of Interpreters for the Deaf* (October 1986), 12.

Witter-Merithew, Anna & Johnson, Leilani (2004) Market disorder within the field of sign language interpreting: Professionalization implications. *Journal of Interpretation* 2004, 19–55.

Wittgenstein, Ludwig (1953) *Philosophical Investigations* (Trans. G. E. M. Anscombe). New York: Macmillan.

Władyka, Anna Maria (2014) Translating and interpreting for the future: When do computers fail and humans succeed? In W. Baur, B. Eichner, S. Kalina, N. Keßler, F. Mayer & J. Ørsted (eds) *Im Spannungsfeld zwischen Mensch und Maschine. Die Zukunft von Übersetzern, Dolmetschern und Terminologen. Band I. Tagungsband des 20. FIT-Weltkongresses*. Berlin: BDÜ Weiterbildungs- und Fachverlagsgesellschaft, 222–229.

Wolf, Michaela (2005) "Diplomatenlehrbuben" oder angehende "Dragomane"? Zur Rekonstruktion des sozialen "Dolmetschfeldes" in der Habsburgermonarchie. In M. Kurz, M. Scheutz, K. Vocelka & T. Winkelbauer (eds) *Das Osmanische Reich und die Habsburgermonarchie*. Vienna: R. Oldenbourg, 503–513.

Wolf, Michaela (2013a) "German speakers, step forward!" Surviving through interpreting in Nazi concentration camps. *Translation and Interpreting Studies* 8 (1), 1–22.

Wolf, Michaela (2013b) "Prompt, at any time of the day.": The emerging translatorial *habitus* in the late Habsburg Monarchy. *Meta* 58 (3), 504–521.

Wolf, Michaela (2015) *The Habsburg Monarchy's Many-Languaged Soul: Translating and Interpreting, 1848–1918* (Trans. Kate Sturge). Amsterdam: John Benjamins.

Wolf, Michaela & Fukari, Alexandra (eds) (2007) *Constructing a Sociology of Translation.* Amsterdam: John Benjamins.

Woodsworth, Judith (1998) History of translation. In M. Baker (ed.) *Routledge Encyclopedia of Translation Studies.* London: Routledge, 100–105.

Wrede, Sirpa (2012) Professions. In H. K. Anheier & M. Juergensmeyer (eds) *Encyclopedia of Global Studies.* Los Angeles/London/New Delhi/Singapore/Washington, DC: Sage, 1396–1400.

Wright, Richard D. & Ward, Lawrence M. (2008) *Orienting of Attention.* New York: Oxford University Press.

Wu, Fred S. (2013) How do we assess students in the interpretation examinations? In D. Tsagari & R. van Deemter (eds) *Assessment Issues in Language Translation and Interpreting.* Frankfurt: Peter Lang, 15–33.

Wu, Jessica, Liu, Minhua & Liao, Cecilia (2013) Analytic scoring in an interpretation test: Construct validity and the halo effect. In H.-H. Liao, T.-E. Kao & Y. Lin (eds) *The Making of a Translator: Multiple Perspectives.* Taipei: Language Training & Testing Center, 277–292.

Wurm, Svenja (2010) *Translation across Modalities: The Practice of Translating Written Text into Recorded Signed Language – An Ethnographic Case Study.* PhD dissertation, Heriot-Watt University.

Xiao, Xiaoyan & Li, Feiyan (2013) Sign language interpreting on Chinese TV: A survey on user perspectives. *Perspectives: Studies in Translatology* 21 (1), 100–116.

Xiao, Xiaoyan, Chen, Xiaoyan & Palmer, Jeffrey Levi (2015) Chinese Deaf viewers' comprehension of sign language interpreting: An experimental study. *Interpreting* 17 (1), 91–117.

Xie, Bin & Salvendy, Gavriel (2000) Prediction of mental workload in single and multiple tasks environments. *International Journal of Cognitive Ergonomics* 4 (3), 213–242.

Yannakakis, Yanna (2008) *The Art of Being In-between: Native Intermediaries, Indian Identity, and Local Rule in Colonial Oaxaca.* Durham, NC/London: Duke University Press.

Yeh, Shu-Pai & Liu, Minhua (2008) 口譯評分客觀化初探：採用量表的可能 [A more objective approach to translation evaluation: Evaluation scales and evaluation units]. *Journal of the National Institute for Compilation and Translation* 35 (3), 55–72.

Yin, Bo, Chen, Fang, Ruiz, Natalie & Ambikairajah, Eliathamby (2008) Speech-based cognitive load monitoring system. In *Proceedings of the 2008 IEEE International Conference on Acoustics, Speech and Signal Processing.* Las Vegas, NV: ICASSP, 2041–2044.

Yin, Kexiu (2011) Disfluencies in consecutive interpreting among undergraduates in the language lab environment. In *PACLIC 25: 25th Pacific Asia Conference on Language, Information and Computation, 16–18 December 2011,* 459–466. www.aclweb.org/anthology/Y11-1048 (accessed 24 November 2014).

York, Anthony D. (1979) The Targum in the synagogue and in the school. *Journal for the Study of Judaism* 10 (1), 74–86.

Youdelman, Mara K. (2008) The medical tongue: U.S. laws and policies on language access. *Health Affairs* 27 (2), 424–433.

Youdelman, Mara (2015) The development of certification for healthcare interpreters in the United States. *Translation & Interpreting* 5 (1), 114–126.

Yu, Jung-hwa (2011) *19segi Han, Chung, Il t'ongbŏnyŏk kyoyukchedo pigyoyŏn-gu [Comparative Study of Translator Training Institutions of Korea, China, Japan in the 19th Century].* PhD dissertation, Hankuk University of Foreign Studies.

Yudes, Carolina, Macizo, Pedro & Bajo, Teresa (2010) Cognate effects in bilingual language comprehension tasks. *Neuroreport* 21 (7), 507–512.

Yudes, Carolina, Macizo, Pedro & Bajo, Teresa (2011) The influence of expertise in simultaneous interpreting on non-verbal executive processes. *Frontiers in Psychology* 2 (28 October), Art. 309. doi:10.3389/fpsyg.2011.00309.

Yudes, Carolina, Macizo, Pedro & Bajo, Teresa (2012) Coordinating comprehension and production in simultaneous interpreters: Evidence from the articulatory suppression effect. *Bilingualism: Language and Cognition* 15 (2), 329–339.

Yudes, Carolina, Macizo, Pedro, Morales, Luis & Bajo, M. Teresa (2013) Comprehension and error monitoring in simultaneous interpreters. Applied Psycholinguistics 34 (5), 1039–1057.

Yuzawa, Tadayuki (2010) *Kodai Nihonjin to gaikokugo [Japanese and Foreign Languages in Classical Japan].* Tokyo: Bensei Shuppan.

Zagar Galvão, Elena (2009) Speech and gesture in the booth – a descriptive approach to multi-modality in simultaneous interpreting. In D. De Crom (ed.) *Translation and the (Trans)formation of Identities. Selected Papers of the CETRA Research Seminar in Translation Studies 2008.* Leuven: CETRA. www.arts.kuleuven.be/cetra/papers/files/galvao.pdf (accessed 4 September 2014).

Zagar Galvão, Elena (2013) Hand gestures and speech production in the booth: Do simultaneous interpreters imitate the speaker? In C. Carapinha & I. A. Santos (eds) *Estudos de Linguística.* Vol. II. Coimbra: Coimbra University Press, 115–130.

Zanettin, Federico, Bernardini, Silvia & Stewart, Dominic (eds) (2003) *Corpora in Translator Education.* Manchester/Northampton: St Jerome.

Zarrouk, Mourad (2009) *Los Traductores de España en Marruecos (1859–1939).* Barcelona: Bellaterra.

Zavala, José-Manuel (2000) *Les Indiens Mapuche du Chili. Dynamiques Inter-éthniques et Stratégies de Résistance, XVIII siècle.* Paris: L'Harmattan.

Zele, Walter (1990) Alî Bey, un interprete della Porta nella Venezia dell'500. *Studi Veneziani* 19, 187–224.

Zhan, Cheng 詹成 (2010) 中國口譯教學三十年：發展及現狀 [Thirty years of the teaching of interpreting in China: Evolution and status quo]. 廣東外語外貿大學學 [*Journal of Guangdong University of Foreign Studies*] 21 (6), 89–92.

Zhong, Weihe (2003) Memory training in interpreting. *Translation Journal* 7 (3). http://translationjournal.net/journal/25interpret.htm (accessed 12 November 2013).

Zhou, Jing (2010) *Strategies for Short-term Memory in Interpreting Based on Gile's Effort Models* [in Chinese]. Master's thesis, Central South University.

Zimmer, June (1992) Appropriateness and naturalness in ASL/English interpreting. In J. Plant-Moeller (ed.) *Expanding Horizons: Proceedings of the Twelfth National Convention of the Registry of Interpreters for the Deaf.* Silver Spring, MD: RID Publications, 81–92.

Zimnyaya, Irina A. (1973) *Psikhologiya slushaniya i govoreniya* [*The Psychology of Listening and Speaking*]. Postdoctoral dissertation, Lomonosov Moscow State University.

Żmudzki, Jerzy (2008) Ein holistisches Modell des Konsekutivdolmetschens [A holistic model of consecutive interpreting]. In B. Lewandowska-Tomaszczyk & M. Thelen (eds) *Translation and Meaning, Part 8. Proceedings of the Łódź Session of the 2005 Maastricht-Łódź Duo Colloquium on "Translation and Meaning", Łódź, Poland, 23–25 September 2005.* Maastricht: School of International Communication, Department of Translation and Interpreting, 175–183.

Zwaan, Rolf A. & Radvansky, Gabriel A.(1998) Situation models in language comprehension and memory. *Psychological Bulletin* 123 (2), 162–185.

Zwilling, Mikhail (1966) Sinhronnyi perevod kak ob'ekt eksperimentalnogo issledovaniya [Simultaneous interpreting as a subject of experimental research]. *Tetradi Perevodchika* 3, 87–93.

Zwischenberger, Cornelia (2010) Quality criteria in simultaneous interpreting: An international vs. a national view. *The Interpreters' Newsletter* 15, 127–142.

Zwischenberger, Cornelia (2011) Conference interpreters and their self-representation: A worldwide web-based survey. In R. Sela-Sheffy & M. Shlesinger (eds) *Identity and Status in the Translational Professions.* Amsterdam: John Benjamins, 119–133.

Zwischenberger, Cornelia (2013) *Qualität und Rollenbilder beim simultanen Konferenzdolmetschen.* Berlin: Frank & Timme.

Zwischenberger, Cornelia (2015) Simultaneous conference interpreting and a supernorm that governs it all. *Meta* 60 (1), 90–111.

AUTHOR INDEX

SUBJECT INDEX

*For Product Safety Concerns and Information please contact
our EU representative GPSR@taylorandfrancis.com Taylor & Francis
Verlag GmbH, Kaufingerstraße 24, 80331 München, Germany*

T - #0099 - 230425 - C0 - 246/174/33 - PB - 9780367867263 - Gloss Lamination